Modern Money and Banking

Modern Money and Banking

Third Edition

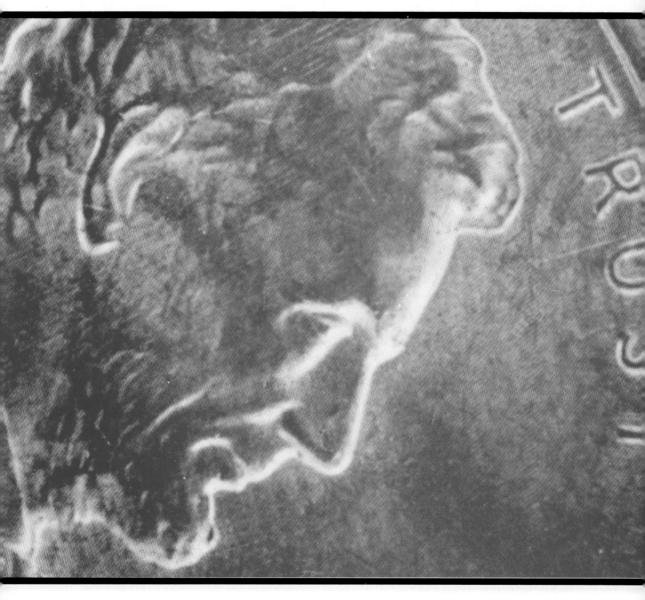

McGraw-Hill, Inc.

New York   St. Louis   San Francisco   Auckland
Bogotá   Caracas   Lisbon   London   Madrid
Mexico   Milan   Montreal   New Delhi   Paris
San Juan   Singapore   Sydney   Tokyo   Toronto

Roger LeRoy Miller
Center for Policy Studies
Clemson University

David D. VanHoose
University of Alabama

MODERN MONEY AND BANKING

1 2 3 4 5 6 7 8 9 0 DOC DOC 9 0 9 8 7 6 5 4 3 2

ISBN 0-07-042335-0

This book was set in Times Roman by Ruttle Shaw & Wetherill, Inc.
The editors were James A. Bittker and Peggy Rehberger;
the design was done by Circa '86.
New drawings were done by Fine Line Illustrations, Inc.
R. R. Donnelley & Sons Company was printer and binder.

Photo Credits:

Unit 1   The Stock Market, Inc./Gerald Zanetti
Unit 2   The Stock Market, Inc./Dave Wilhelm
Units 3, 4, 5, 6   Index Stock Photography, Inc./Peter Gregoire
Unit 7   Comstock

Library of Congress Cataloging-in-Publication Data

Miller, Roger LeRoy.
    Modern money and banking / Roger LeRoy Miller, David D. VanHoose.
    —3rd ed.
        p.   cm.
    Includes bibliographical references and index.
    ISBN 0-07-042335-0
    1. Money.   2. Banks and banking.   3. Finance.   I. VanHoose, David
D. II. Title.
HG221.M646   1993
332.1—dc20   92-12189

ABOUT THE AUTHORS

Roger LeRoy Miller is presently at the Center for Policy Studies at Clemson University. He has also taught at the University of Washington (Seattle) and the University of Miami, where he co-founded the Law and Economics Center and was its associate director and director. He has authored and co-authored numerous books, including *Applied Econometrics, Intermediate Microeconomics, The Economics of Public Issues,* and *Economics Today,* as well as professional articles in *The American Economic Review, The Review of Economic Studies,* and has written for the *Wall Street Journal* and the *Senior Economist.* He has reviewed for *The American Economic Review, Economic Inquiry, The Journal of the American Statistical Association,* and *The Journal of Political Economy.*

David D. VanHoose received his Ph.D. in economics from the University of North Carolina in 1984 and presently is associate professor of economics at the University of Alabama. He has authored or coauthored over twenty articles on topics in money, banking, and macroeconomics in several leading academic journals, such as the *Journal of Money, Credit, and Banking,* the *Journal of Banking and Finance,* the *Quarterly Journal of Economics,* the *International Economic Review, Economic Inquiry,* and the *Southern Economic Journal.* Professor VanHoose served as a staff economist with the Board of Governors of the Federal Reserve System in 1988, and he was a visiting scholar at the Federal Reserve Bank of Kansas City in 1989. He received the 1991 Iddo Sarnat award for the outstanding article of the year published in the *Journal of Banking and Finance.* In his spare time, he enjoys astronomy and history. He and his wife Carol reside in Tuscaloosa, Alabama.

To Shawn G. Miller,
Whose successes have not gone unnoticed

R.L.M.

To Elmus Wicker,
a true scholar and friend

D.D.V.

Contents in Brief

Contents

U N I T

1

UNIT 2
FINANCIAL INSTRUMENTS, MARKETS, AND INSTITUTIONS   65

U N I T

3

DEPOSITORY INSTITUTIONS AND THEIR ENVIRONMENTS 169

UNIT 4

CENTRAL BANKING, MONETARY POLICY, AND THE FEDERAL RESERVE SYSTEM   327

U N I T

6

MONETARY STABILIZATION POLICY   **621**

List of International Perspectives

List of Current Controversies

Preface

This third edition of *Modern Money and Banking* essentially is a new textbook. While we have sought to retain the broad organizational structure and specific strengths of the earlier editions, we have largely *rewritten* this text. We have taken on this task for two reasons.

PRESENTATION OF MAJOR RECENT INSTITUTIONAL AND THEORETICAL DEVELOPMENTS

First, much has happened in the area of money and banking in recent years. A nonexhaustive listing of recent institutional and theoretical developments that we have discussed in this edition follows.

1. The wave of deregulation of depository institutions, while beneficial to the economy in some ways, led to the near-collapse of the savings and loan industry. Simultaneously, commercial bank failures reached new heights. These events have led to more regulatory concern with establishing risk-based capital requirements and initiating deposit insurance reform.

2. Efforts to alter the foundations of depository institution regulation took place with passage of the Financial Institutions Reform, Recovery, and Enforcement Act (FIRREA) of 1989. This act hastened the recognition of possible need for further regulatory reform, yet it has failed to be a panacea for the underlying problems that confront the American financial services industry.

3. A wave of banking mergers has begun and continues.

4. Payments system innovations have continued unabated, giving rise to a host of new regulatory issues.

5. In recent years the Federal Reserve has continued to reevaluate its monetary policy targets and procedures. Yet, many observers continue to question the Fed's management of monetary policy.

6. New classical macroeconomics has lost its intellectual monopoly on the concept of rational expectations. The hypothesis of rational expectations now is central to a variety of theories of the macroeconomic transmission of monetary policy.

7. There has been a redoubled effort by economists to explore the controversy over rules versus discretion in monetary policy.

8. The magnitudes of international trade flows relative to output in the United States have increased since the 1970s, and the United States and the rest of the world have witnessed a continuing integration of financial markets.

INCREASED THEORY

Second, we felt that the text needed to be updated *and* upgraded, particularly in its theoretical content. While we feel strongly that history and institutions are important, we also want students to finish their money and banking coursework in possession of a firm theoretical background that they can draw upon in future years as monetary and banking institutions continue to evolve. Money and banking texts that exclusively emphasize institutions become outdated all too soon; we want this edition of our text to be an indispensable resource for making sense of developments in the field for more than a year or two after publication.

AN EMPHASIS ON THE INTEGRATION OF ECONOMIC THEORY, INSTITUTIONS, AND HISTORY

Money and banking by nature is a broad and diverse field. Its natural subjects are economic theory and policy, current banking and monetary institutions, and the historical development of monetary and financial policies and institutions. A key task we set out for ourselves in revising this text has been to bring its theoretical and current institutional content as up-to-date as we could. Toward this end, however, we have made a strong effort wherever possible to *integrate and expand* the discussions of theory, institutions, *and* history throughout the book. This change is noticeable from the outset. In Unit 1, for instance, we provide theoretical models of the historical evolution of money and of the competitive and monopolistic provision of money, and in Unit 2 we now provide a full exposition of the role of the interest rate as a measure of terms of trade between present and future.

Models of Competitive and Monopoly Banking   Our renewed emphasis on theoretical foundations perhaps stands out most in Unit 3. There we now provide a common framework of analysis via economic models of competitive and monopolistic banking. We apply these models to such past and present topics as economies of scale and scope in banking, bank market structure and performance, and the effects of recent changes in deposit insurance premiums. Furthermore, in Unit 4 we have expanded the discussion of the money multiplier model and have provided more complete accounts of the manner in which Federal Reserve policy instruments affect the quantities of money and credit.

Extension of Basic Macro Model   Our efforts to update the theory content of the book are also particularly evident in Unit 5, which we also have rewritten entirely. Although we have not abandoned the *IS–LM* model or the basics of aggregate demand–aggregate supply analysis, we have sought in this unit to bring the student fully up to date on recent macroeconomic developments and their implications for the effectiveness of monetary policy. Included in this new material is a full discussion of the monetarist natural rate of unemployment, rational expectations and the new classical macroeconomics, modern Keynesian contracting theory, and the recent contributions of the new Keynesian and real business cycle theories.

Modernization of Monetary Stabilization Policy Materials   Unit 6 on monetary stabilization policy is completely reorganized and rewritten. We have expanded the discussion of ultimate goals and targets of monetary policy and have included a chapter on the implementation of Federal Reserve monetary policy operating procedures since the 1970s. We also have provided a complete chapter addressing time inconsistency and commitment versus discretion in monetary policy.

International Financial Markets Examined in Detail   Finally, we have expanded the material on international money and finance in Unit 7 by discussing international financial markets and instruments in much more detail and by adding a concluding chapter on international policy coordination. Appearances to the contrary, however, we have not relegated international topics to this concluding unit of the text. Throughout the text, we have included highlight sections entitled *International Perspectives.* Each of these places topics that other texts traditionally treat as purely domestic issues into worldwide contexts.

History and Institutions Examined Throughout   In our effort to upgrade the theory in the text, we have not disregarded the importance of history and institutions. Indeed, in Unit 3 we have expanded the historical and institutional background behind banking regulation, deposit insurance, and the savings and loan debacle of the 1980s and 1990s. Our discussions of the Federal Reserve System and payments systems in Unit 4 contain significantly broadened historical foundations, our survey of Federal Reserve operating procedures in Unit 6 explores in detail more than two decades of Fed policy making, and our analysis and historical evaluation of international monetary and banking arrangements in Unit 7 is both expanded and strengthened.

A FLEXIBLE STRUCTURE

We believe that there is more in this text than an instructor typically will be able to cover in a single semester. This is not an accident; we want this book to be one from which a money and banking instructor may choose particular units and chapters to suit the needs of her or his own course. In our view, there are at least three separate types of money and banking courses that one could teach using this text:

1. *A Macro/Money-Oriented Course:* After surveying most of the material in Units 1 and 2, this type of money and banking course would cover the essential aspects of banking markets and regulations in Chapters 8, 10, and 11 in Unit 3. It would include Chapters 14 and 17 in detail and spend less time on Chapters 15 and 16 in Unit 4. All parts of Units 5, 6, and 7 then could be covered.

2. *A Banking/Financial-Markets-Oriented Course:* After covering the subjects in Unit 1, this course would include all of the material in Units 2, 3, and 4 in detail. Much of the material in Chapters 18 through 22 would be covered, but little or no time would be devoted to the remaining chapters in Unit 5. Chapters 24 and 25 in Unit 6 on Fed goals, targets, and procedures then would be covered, followed by coverage of the first two chapters of Unit 7.

3. *A Middle-of-the-Road Course:* This course would attempt to strike a balance between extremes. It would cover both Units 1 and 2 and a more equalized (in terms of micro or macro content) sampling of selected chapters from remaining units of the text, depending on the specific objectives of the instructor.

A HOST OF STUDENT LEARNING TOOLS

A previous strength of this text was its student learning aids. Nevertheless, in this edition we have redoubled our efforts to simplify the teaching and learning of money and banking.

- **Chapter Preview**   Each chapter begins with a listing of questions that make clear to the student the learning objectives of the chapter.

- **Glossary of Key Terms**   We introduced every key term in **boldface** within the text and provide a full glossary at the end of each chapter. In addition, an alphabetized glossary is included at the end of the book.

- **Current Controversies**   Nearly every chapter contains a *Current Controversy* feature that is set off from the rest of the text. Each of these has been designed to generate student and instructor interest in real-world and research topics of monetary economists. Almost all the *Current Controversies* in this edition are new, and they are as up-to-date as possible.

- **International Perspectives**   A new feature in this edition is the additon of *International Perspectives* highlights that are set off from the rest of the text. These also appear in nearly every chapter. We have designed the *International Perspectives* to fit naturally into the flow of each chapter, yet to broaden the horizon of the text beyond American experiences in the money and banking area. This approach brings home to the student the applicability of the study of money and banking to issues that truly are global in nature—and also emphasizes to the student that we can learn by looking beyond our own borders.

- **Chapter Summaries**   There is a point-by-point summary at the conclusion of every chapter. This reinforces the student's reading comprehension and serves as a student checklist for review and study prior to class lectures and examinations.

- **Self-Test Questions**   A new feature of this edition is the inclusion of several self-test questions at the conclusion of each chapter. These are intended to help the student test his or her comprehension of the chapter material and to induce the student to think about the chapter content from a slightly different slant, thereby reinforcing the concepts.

- **Problems**   We have expanded the number of problems in this edition considerably. The problems require specific calculations, thereby giving the student an applications-oriented view of text material. Fully explained answers now are provided in the instructor's manual.

- **Selected References**   Each chapter concludes with many appropriately selected references from which the student or instructor may consult for additional reading about the chapter content.

THE BEST AVAILABLE TEACHING-LEARNING PACKAGE

We believe that we have compiled the most complete package of teaching-learning supplements available in the field of money and banking.

Student Guide The *Study Guide to Accompany Modern Money and Banking* has been competely revised by J. Michael Morgan, Professor at the College of Charleston. For each corresponding chapter of the text, the *Guide* includes:

- A chapter review summarizing the major ideas contained within the chapter
- A detailed chapter outline
- A vocabulary drill and at least one exercise problem
- A set of fill-in questions, true-false questions and multiple-choice questions
- A set of learning objectives entitled, ''AT THIS POINT YOU SHOULD BE ABLE TO . . .''
- Answers to all the problems, exercises, and questions contained in the *Guide.*

Test Bank The *Test Bank to Accompany Modern Money and Banking,* also written by J. Michael Morgan, consists of over one thousand questions and problems. Most of the questions are new for this edition or have been completely reworked. The questions are presented at three different levels of difficulty and measure different cognitive learning skills. The *Test Bank* is available in both hard copy and computerized formats.

Instructor's Manual David VanHoose, one of the coauthors, composed the *Instructor's Manual* for this edition. For each chapter of the text, the instructor's manual includes:

- Detailed outlines to assist the instructor in putting together lecture notes
- Discussions of the key concepts and objectives
- Tips for the classroom
- Additional questions to help promote class discussion
- Answers to the chapter preview questions
- *Fully-worked-out* answers to the chapter problems.

Also included for the majority of chapters are *Lecture Enrichment Packages* consisting of extra readings that extend theories, cover current policy or institutional issues, or expand on historical topics that were covered in less detail in the text. For several chapters, extra problems relevant to the *Lecture Enrichment Packages* are included.

Instructional Software: Money and Banking Tools *Money and Banking Tools* is a menu-driven computer program to accompany *Modern Money and Banking* by Roger Miller and David VanHoose. The software is designed primarily for student use although professors may find certain exercises useful in classroom settings. Explicit attention is given to making the program as user friendly as possible. The goal is to minimize the startup time required to run the program. Only the most fundamental understanding of computer operating systems is required to work through the program.

Money and Banking Tools consists of three separate programs: (1) the Microeconomic Foundations of Money and Banking, (2) the Macroeconomics of Money and Banking, and (3) a Financial Calculator. The programs contain a number of ''what-if'' exercises which allow the student to explore the models under development. While fundamentals are emphasized, the exercises contain sufficient flexibility to address more sophisticated concepts.

Fed Reader and Customized Publishing This is a special supplement of articles from Federal Reserve publications such as the *Federal Reserve Bulletin* and economic research reviews of Federal Reserve banks. David VanHoose has selected these articles on the basis of their complementarity to the subjects covered in the text, and he has provided advice in the *Instructor's Manual* on how to integrate each reading into the content of the course.

Each instructor can have a customized *Fed Reader* made available for her or his students. This unique feature, available with no other competing text, allows every instructor to determine what best set of readings will work for her or his students. McGraw-Hill will print and bind customized versions of the *Fed Reader,* complete with table of contents and sequential paging. Instructors interested in this customized supplement should contact their local McGraw-Hill representative.

ACKNOWLEDGMENTS

Because we largely rewrote this edition of *Modern Money and Banking,* we are very grateful to the critical and helpful comments we received from a variety of individuals, most notably Robert Pulsinelli, who served as master reviewer of every draft of the manuscript. With profound appreciation we thank: Paul Altieri, Central Connecticut State University; Harjit Arora, Le Moyne College; Ronald Ayers, University of Texas at San Antonio; Elizabeth Dickhaus, University of Missouri at Columbia; Donald Dutkowsky, Syracuse University; Paul Estenson, Gustavus Adolphus; David Findlay, Colby College; Daniel Fuller, Weber State University; Peter Frevert, University of Kansas; Lance Girton, University of Utah; Beverly Hadaway, University of Texas at Austin; Jack Haney, Oral Roberts University; Arthur James, Texas A & M University; Richard Keehn, University of Wisconsin–Parkside; Elaine Koppana, College of William and Mary; Thomas Mc-Gahagan, University of Pittsburgh at Johnstown; J. Michael Morgan, College of Charleston; Theodore Muzio, St. John's University; Cynthia Salzman, Widener University; Donald Schilling, University of Missouri at Columbia; Larry Sechrest, University of Texas at Arlington; and Duane Stock, University of Oklahoma.

We are also grateful to the good people at McGraw-Hill who worked with us on this major revision. For contributing to the quality and attractiveness of *Modern Money and Banking,* we wish to thank Jim Bittker, Economics Editor, Lori Ambacher, Assistant Editor, Peggy Rehberger, Editing Supervisor, Anita Kahn, Production Supervisor, and Karen Jackson, Senior Marketing Manager.

We, of course, are fully responsible for any errors in the book. We very much welcome feedback from users of this text. While we believe that we have written a money and banking textbook that offers more than any other text, we recognize that we can learn much from the criticisms of users. Only through the comments and suggestions of the text's readers will we be able to improve the book even more in future editions.

Roger LeRoy Miller
David D. VanHoose

Acknowledgments

Chapter 1: Adaptation partly from W. A. Bomberger and G. E. Makinen, "Indexation, Inflationary Finance, and Hyperinflation: The 1945–1946 Hungarian Experience," *Journal of Political Economy,* 88 (June 3, 1980), pp. 550–560, reprinted by permission of *Journal of Political Economy* and the authors; and partly from Everett G. Martin, "Precarious Pesos: Amid Wild Inflation, Bolivians Concentrate on Swapping Currency," *The Wall Street Journal,* Aug. 13, 1985, p. 5. © 1985 Dow Jones & Company, Inc., reprinted by persmission of The Wall Street Journal. All rights reserved worldwide.

Chapter 2: Table "Average Inflation and Estimates of Seigniorage . . ." adapted in part from Brian Cody, "Seigniorage and European Monetary Union," *Contemporary Policy Issues* (published by Western Economic Association International), 9 (Apr. 2, 1991), pp. 72–80, by permission; and adapted in part from Daniel Gros, "Seigniorage in the EC: The Implications of the European Monetary System and Financial Market Integration," *International Monetary Fund Working Paper No. WP/89/7,* Jan. 23, 1989, by permission of the International Monetary Fund.

Chapter 3: Adaptation from Dallas S. Batten, Michael P. Blackwell, In-Su Kim, Simon E. Nocera, and Yuzuru Ozeld, "The Conduct of Monetary Policy in the Major Industrial Countries: Instruments and Operating Procedures," *International Monetary Fund Occasional Paper No. 70,* July 1990, by permission of the International Monetary Fund, Washington, DC.

Adaptation from Tony Horwitz and Craig Forman, "Buying Breakfast in Kuwait Can Be a Dinar Adventure," *The Wall Street Journal,* March 14, 1991, p. A1, © 1991 Dow Jones & Company, Inc., reprinted by permission of The Wall Street Journal. All rights reserved worldwide.

Table "Volumes of Nonelectronic and Electronic Payments . . ." and "Dollar Values of Nonelectronic and Electronic Payments . . ." adapted in part from Allen N. Berger and David B. Humphrey, "Market Failure and Resource Use: Economic Incentives to Use Different Payment Instruments," in *The U.S. Payments System: Efficiency, Risk, and the Role of the Federal Reserve,* ed. David B. Humphrey, 1989, by permission of Kluwer Academic Publishers.

Chapter 5: Partial adaptation from John P. Caskey, "Pawnbroking in America: The Economics of a Forgotten Credit Market," *Journal of Money, Credit and Banking,* 23 (Feb. 1, 1991), pp. 85–99, by permission of Ohio State University Press.

Table "Futures Prices for Treasury Bills . . ." adapted from *The Wall Street Journal,* Feb. 10, 1988, © 1988 Dow Jones & Company, Inc., by permission of The Wall Street Journal. All rights reserved worldwide.

Chapter 6: Table "Numbers of Banks and Note-Deposit Ratios, 1803–1818" from J. Van Fenstermake, "The Statistics of American Commercial Banking: 1782–1818," *Journal of Economic History,* 1965, pp. 400–413. Reprinted by permission of Cambridge University Press and the author.

Chapter 9: Adaptations from Duane Graddy, Austin Spencer, and William Brunsen, *Commercial Banking and the Financial Services Industry* (Reston, 1985), by permission of Prentice Hall, Inc.

Adaptation from H. G. Moulton, "Commercial Banking and Capital Formation," *Journal of Political Economy,* May-June-July 1978, by permission of Journal of Political Economy.

Adaptation from Herbert Prochnow, *Term Loans and Theories of Bank Liquidity* (Englewood Cliffs, 1949), by permission of Prentice Hall, Inc.

Figure "The Credit Card Interest Spread . . ." by permission of *Bank Rate Monitor,* North Palm Beach, Florida 33408.

Adaptation from Craig Smith, "Banks' Internal Turf Battles Are Costly: Branches Need to Feed Most Profitable Divisions," *The Wall Street Journal,* p. B7B, © 1990 Dow Jones & Company, Inc., by permission of The Wall Street Journal. All rights reserved.

Quote from Ron Chernow, *The House of Morgan* (1990), p. xiii, © 1990 by Ron Chernow, by permission of Atlantic Monthly Press, Simon & Schuster Ltd., and Melanie Jackson Agency for the author.

Chapter 10: Adaptation partly from Jean Dermine (ed.), *European Banking in the 1990s* (1990), by permission of Basil Blackwell Ltd.; and partly from Philip Revzin, Terence Roth, and Margaret Studer, "Universal Banks in Europe Win Plaudits for One-Stop Shopping," *The Wall Street Journal* (Feb. 26, 1991), p. C1, © 1991 Dow Jones & Company, Inc., by permission of The Wall Street Journal. All rights reserved worldwide.

Adaptation partly from Maureen O'Hara, "From Too Big to Fail to Too Sick to Save," *The Wall Street*

Journal (Feb. 19, 1991), p. A21, © 1991 Dow Jones & Company, Inc., by permission of The Wall Street Journal. All rights reserved worldwide. And partly from Maureen O'Hara and Wayne Shaw," "Deposit Insurance and Wealth Effects: The Value of Being Too Big to Fail," *Journal of Finance,* 45 (Dec. 5, 1990), pp. 1587–1600, by permission of American Finance Association.

Chapter 12: Adaptation from Ron Chernow, *The House of Morgan* (1990), chapter 7, © 1990 by Ron Chernow, by permission of Atlantic Monthly Press, Simon & Schuster Ltd., and Melanie Jackson Agency for the author.

Adaptation from Anita Raghavan, "Banks Pass Along U.S. Insurance Costs," *The Wall Street Journal,* May 13, 1991, p. B5B, © 1991 Dow Jones & Company, Inc., by permission of The Wall Street Journal. All rights reserved worldwide.

Chapter 13: Figure "Functional Relationships Etablished by the . . ." from Lawrence J. White, *The S&L Debacle: Public Policy Lessons for Bank and Thrift Regulation,* pp. 190–191. Copyright © by Oxford University Press, Inc. Reprinted by permission.

Chapter 15: Adaptation from Hugh Rockoff, " 'The Wizard of Oz' as a Monetary Allegory," *Journal of Political Economy,* 98 (August 1990), pp. 739–760, by permission of Journal of Political Economy and the author.

Table from A. J. Rolnick and W. E. Weber, "Inherent Instability in Banking: The Free Banking Experience," *Cato Journal,* 5:3 (Winter 1986), based on Hugh Rockoff, *The Free Banking Era: A Re-Examination* (Salem, New Hampshire: Arno Press, 1975), by permission of Hugh Rockoff.

Figure "Prices and the Money Stock . . ." from Hugh Rockoff, "Money, Prices, and Banks in the Jacksonian Era," in R. W. Fogel and S. L. Engerman (eds.), *The Reinterpretation of American Economic History,* Table 1, p. 451. Copyright © 1971 by Harper & Row, Publishers, Inc. Reprinted by permission of HarperCollins Publishers.

Chapter 18: Adaptation based on Keith Crane, "How Not to Cure a Monetary 'Hangover,' " *The Wall Street Journal,* Jan. 28, 1991, p. A10, © 1991 Dow Jones & Company, Inc., by permission of The Wall Street Journal. All rights reserved worldwide.

Chapter 19: Adaptation from John Maynard Keynes, *The General Theory of Employment, Interest, and Money,* by permission of Cambridge University Press; Harcourt Brace Jovanovich, Inc.; the Provost and Fellows of King's College, Cambridge; and the Royal Economic Society.

Adaptation from David Alan Aschauer, "Is Government Spending Stimulative?" *Contemporary Policy Issues,* 8 (October 1990), pp. 30–46, by permission of Western Economic Association International.

Chapter 21: Quote from Robert Gordon (ed.), *Milton Friedman's Monetary Framework: A Debate With His Critics* (1974), p. 134, by permission of University of Chicago Press.

Chapter 23: Adaptation from N. Gregory Mankiw, "Commentary," in *Monetary Policy on the 75th Anniversary of the Federal Reserve System,* ed. Michael T. Belongia (1991), pp. 275–276, by permission of Kluwer Academic Publishers.

Tables "Measures of Annual Inertia . . . ," "Measures of . . . to Changes in Real Output Growth for Five Nations," "Measures of . . . to Deviations of Output Growth from Trend Growth for Five Nations"; and figure [Fig. 23-1] from Robert J. Gordon, "What Is New-Keynesian Economics?" *Journal of Economic Literture,* 28 (Sept. 3, 1990), p. 1131 and p. 1146, by permission of Journal of Economic Literature and the author.

Chapter 24: Results from William Poole, "Optimal Choice of Monetary Policy Instruments in a Simple Stochastic Macro Model," *Quarterly Journal of Economics,* 84 (May 2, 1970), pp. 197–216. Copyright © 1970. By permission of The MIT Press, Cambridge, Massachusetts.

Chapter 25: Adaptation from Milton Friedman, "The Fed Hasn't Changed Its Ways," *The Wall Street Journal,* Aug. 20, 1985, Editorial Page, © 1985 Dow Jones & Company, Inc., by permission of The Wall Street Journal. All rights reserved worldwide.

Chapter 27: Adaptation from Jeffrey A. Frieden, *Banking on the World: The Politics of International Finance.* Copyright © 1987 by Jeffrey Frieden. Reprinted by permission of HarperCollins Publishers.

Figures "U.S. Trade Deficits" and "The Dollar's Value" adapted in part from Morgan Guaranty Trust Co. Source: J. P. Morgan. Used by permission.

Chapter 28: Adaptation from Paul Krugman, *The Age of Diminished Expectations* (1990), Chapter 4, by permission of The MIT Press.

Quote and adaptation from Michael D. Bordo and Anna J. Schwartz, "What Has Foreign Exchange Market Intervention Since the Plaza Agreement Accomplished?" *Open Economies Review,* 2 (1991), pp. 39–64, by permission of Kluwer Academic Publishers.

Figure "The European Monetary System (EMS)" from *IMF Survey,* Mar. 21, 1988, p. 96, by permission of the International Monetary Fund.

Chapter 29: Figure "Year-to-Year Changes in World CPI . . ." from John Mueller, "The World's Real Money Supply," *The Wall Street Journal,* Mar. 5, 1991, Editorial Page, © 1991 Dow Jones & Company, Inc., by permission of The Wall Street Journal. All rights reserved worldwide.

Unit 1

Introduction

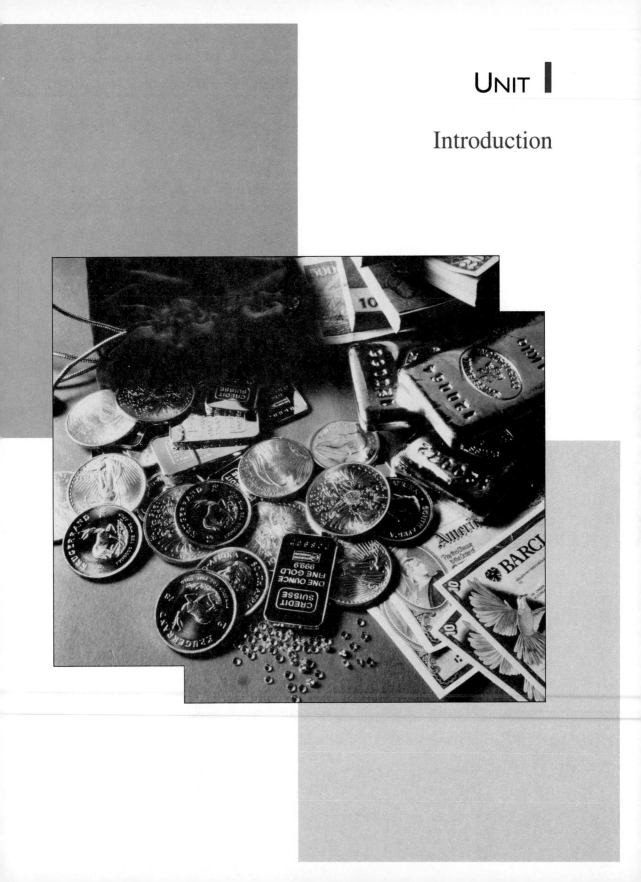

Functions and Forms of Money

CHAPTER PREVIEW

1. What is money, and what are its functions?
2. Is money related to economic activity?
3. Societies have used different items as money. How do these items differ? What are their similarities?
4. What properties are necessary for something to be considered money?
5. What are various types of monetary and nonmonetary economies?

Together, money and banking constitute one of the most fascinating and important topic areas in economics. The study of money and banking is *fascinating* because our day-to-day routine entails—and, indeed, requires—making monetary payments and undertaking banking transactions. Hence, even though most of us often take our society's monetary and banking arrangements for granted, it does not take much intellectual effort for us to recognize that there is something special about money. This gives the field of money and banking immediate and obvious relevance.

Indeed, as we shall discuss in this chapter, economists agree that money is a very special kind of **economic good,** or scarce commodity. We use money to make purchases of other goods and services, and this function of money makes it valuable to us, even though money often takes forms that otherwise might seem intrinsically ''valueless,'' such as pieces of paper, bookkeeping entries in accounting ledgers, or even bits of information transferred between computers via fiber-optic cables. We use money every day, and so we typically take for granted the fact that money has value. Yet, understanding exactly why this is so requires that we consider very interesting questions about the broader role that money plays in our society.

Money and banking is an *important* area of study because there are so many ways that money and banking issues affect us, individually and collectively. For instance, rarely a day passes without a story in the American media concerning recent actions or decisions by the Federal Reserve System. Hence, it is difficult for any of us not to recognize that money and banking issues must be of broad importance to us. More narrowly, in recent years each of us has been affected by a money and banking issue in a place that really counts—our pocketbooks. As taxpayers, we collectively have financed literally hundreds of billions of dollars of payments to rescue savings and loan institutions and their depositors from financial disaster, and events in recent years have forced us to contemplate the all-too-real possibility of facing similar resource losses in other parts of our nation's financial system.

In this text, we hope to help you understand both broad and narrow issues in the field of money and banking. Our desire is that when you have finished reading this text, you will understand such topics as the important role that money performs in human societies, the reasons that participants in financial markets so carefully scrutinize actions of the

Federal Reserve System, and the causes and consequences of recent crises in the banking system of the United States. In addition, our hope is that reading this book will make you even more fascinated by money and banking than you might be now, at the outset of your study of this topic area in economics.

WHY STUDY MONEY?

Imagine the following headline of a future newspaper: COMPUTERS FINALLY ELIMINATE A NEED FOR MONEY. Is such a headline conceivable? Well, just a quarter of a century ago, in the late 1960s, some economists viewed the dawning of the computer age, with its mini-transistors, computer punch cards, and mammoth IBM computers, as the beginning of the twilight for the use of money. They wrote of the coming ''cashless society'' in which money would be unnecessary. People would abandon money, they predicted, because the ability to transmit payments instantaneously across telephone lines and to tabulate them automatically via computer processors would eliminate the usefulness of cash or any other form of money.

Now, almost a generation later, we still use money despite the development of microchips, personal computers, supercomputers, and fiber-optic cables—technology that many in the 1960s never even imagined. The way people make exchanges certainly has changed (see Chapter 3), but money is remarkably durable.

Also in existence, as we near the start of the next millennium, are courses and textbooks in money and banking. The fact that you are reading these words indicates that you or your college's faculty believe that understanding money and banking issues is important, even in today's age of nearly instantaneous communication and information processing. Indeed, some might argue that studying money and banking is more important in today's world than ever before.

There are many reasons that some people, such as the authors of this text, may find themselves fascinated by the study of money. In the 1980s there was a popular television situation comedy called *Family Ties*. The main character in the television show was a college economics major who loved the study of money simply because he loved money. The character's favorite daydream was of having a roomful of money and of being able, whenever he wanted, to roll around in the cash. Indeed, a few students who take a college money and banking course surely have visions of dollar signs dancing in their heads when they arrive for the first day of class.

Certainly, there may be selfish motives for studying money. For instance, if one understands money and related concepts, one may have an advantage over others in earning a higher income and accumulating greater wealth. Nevertheless, a person may also study money for purely unselfish reasons. Most economists agree that the quantity of money in a nation's economy can have an important influence on the aggregate performance of the nation's economy and thereby can affect, for better or for worse, the welfare of all its citizens. Hence, a good reason to study money is that money is important to all of us, whether or not we would like to be able to roll around in rooms full of cash.

MONEY AND NATIONAL INCOME AND PRODUCT

Money may influence the performance of a nation's economy by affecting the aggregate level of economic activity. There are many ways to analyze overall economic activity. The most common measure of overall economic activity is the **gross domestic product (GDP),** defined as the dollar value of all *final* goods and services produced with only

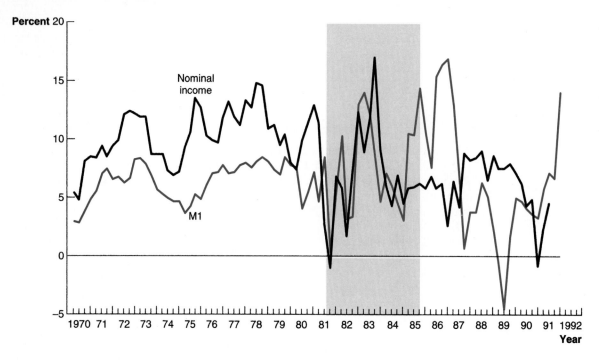

Figure 1-1
**The Relationship between the Rate of Growth of Nominal National Income and the
Rate of Growth of the Money Supply.**   The two time-series lines show a rough correspondence between the rate of change in the money supply, M1, and the rate of change in nominal
national income two quarters (six months) later. Note, however, that the correspondence is much
closer between 1981 and 1985 (the shaded area) than for other periods shown in the graph.
(*Source:* Federal Reserve Board of Governors.)

home-country factors of production in one year in the domestic economy. Consider Figure
1-1, which shows the historic relationship between money and nominal national income.
Nominal national income refers to the dollar amount of gross output expressed in the
prices that prevail each year. It is not adjusted for changes in the level of prices.

An examination of Figure 1-1 reveals a loose but consistent relationship between growth
rates of the quantity of money (defined in Chapter 3 in detail) and nominal income. Some
economists use this evidence to argue that money is an important determinant of the level
of economic activity in the economy; others disagree. Whether money supply changes
affect real (inflation-adjusted) income and output is an issue to which we return in later
chapters. Nonetheless, because of the relationship between money and overall economic
activity, most economists agree that money demands serious study.

MONEY AND PRICES

Another key economic variable in our economy is the price level and its rate of change.
Economists have linked **inflation,** defined as a sustained rise in the (weighted) average of
all prices, to a variety of causes. We shall discuss the measurement of inflation in Chapter

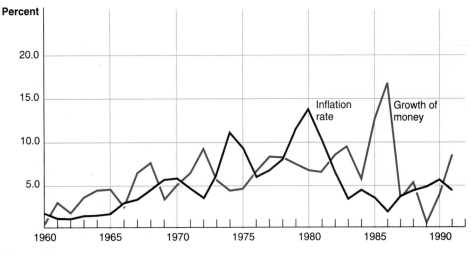

Figure 1-2
The Relationship Between the Rate of Growth of the Money Supply and the Inflation Rate. These times-series lines indicate a loose correspondence between money supply growth and the inflation rate. Actually, closer inspection reveals a direct relationship between changes in the growth rate of money and changes in the inflation rate *in a later period.* Increases in the rate of growth of money seem to lead to later-period increases in the inflation rate; decreases in the rate of money growth seem to lead to subsequent reductions in the inflation rate. (*Source:* Economic Report of the President, 1992, and various *Federal Reserve Bulletins.*)

21. One theory attributes inflation to changes in the amount of money in circulation. Figure 1-2 shows the relationship between the rate of change of the money supply (its growth rate) and the inflation rate. Again, as with money and economic activity, there is a loose, albeit consistent, direct relationship between changes in the money supply and changes in the rate of inflation; increases in the growth of the money supply seem to lead to an increase in the inflation rate—after a time lag.

THE ROLES OF MONEY

According to the ancient Greek philosopher Aristotle (384–322 B.C.), "Everything . . . must be assessed in money; for this enables men always to exchange their services, and so makes society possible." Following Aristotle, and the many social, political, and economic philosophers who succeeded him, we shall use the term **money** to mean any good that people generally accept in exchange for goods and services. People most often think of money as the paper bills and coins that they carry in their wallets or purses. But the concept of money today is normally more inclusive. For example, the quantity of money in the United States includes a variety of items in addition to paper bills and coins (currency). One of the most important elements of any measure of the amount of money in circulation is checkable (checking account) balances. A **checkable account** is a medium of exchange because, like currency, it can be exchanged immediately for the goods and services that people wish to buy.

MONEY AS AN ASSET

We can consider money to be an asset, or something of value. As such, it is a part of our **wealth**—our net worth, or assets minus debts. Wealth in the form of money has a unique characteristic; we can exchange money directly for other assets, goods, or services. Although it is not the only form of wealth that is exchangeable for goods and services, money is the one most widely accepted. Economists call this attribute of money **liquidity.** An asset is liquid when we can exchange it easily for a good or service without high transactions costs and with relative certainty of its nominal (non-inflation-adjusted) value; there is a minimum probability of capital loss for money holding.

By definition, money is the most liquid of all assets. Compare it, for example, with a stock listed on the New York Stock Exchange. To sell that stock, you must call a stockbroker to place a sell order for you. This must be done during normal business hours, and you must pay a percentage commission to the broker. Moreover, there is a distinct probability that you will receive more or less for the shares of stock than you originally paid for them. This is not the case with money. We can easily convert money into other asset forms, and money always has the same *nominal* value. Most individuals, therefore, hold at least part of their wealth in this most liquid of assets.

THE FUNCTIONS OF MONEY

Money has four basic functions:

1. Medium of exchange
2. Store of value
3. Unit of account (standard of value)
4. Standard of deferred payment

Money As a Medium of Exchange To say that money serves as a **medium of exchange** means that market participants will accept it as payment. Individuals can sell their output for money and use that money to buy goods and services in the future. In the process, money makes specialization possible. Specialization is essential to any efficient economy; it allows individuals to purchase most products rather than produce the products themselves. Individuals will specialize in areas in which they have the greatest talents and skills, and they will receive money payments for the fruits of their labor. Individuals then can exchange these money payments for the fruits of other people's labor. As the volume of trade and the range of available goods and services increase, money assumes a more significant role in the economy. As a medium of exchange, then, money is critical to modern economies.

Money As a Store of Value To see how money is a **store of value,** consider this simple example. A fisherman comes into port after several days of fishing. At the going price of fish that day he has $1,000 worth of fish. Those fish are not a good store of value, because if the fisherman keeps them too long, they will rot. If he tries to exchange them with other tradespeople, some of the fish may rot before he can exchange the entire catch for the goods and services he desires. In contrast, if the fisherman sells the entire catch for money, he can store the value of his catch in the money that he receives. (Of course, he can freeze the fish, but that's costly; it's also not a very precise way to store the value of fresh fish.)

Under certain conditions, holding money as a store of value may cause the holder to incur a cost. Particularly in the past (when bank regulators prohibited banks from paying interest on transaction accounts), holders of currency and transaction account balances paid an **opportunity cost** (what must be given up) for any benefits obtained from holding money as a store of value. The opportunity cost is the interest income that one can earn if one holds the money in another form, such as a savings account. In other words, we can measure the cost of holding money—its opportunity cost—by the highest alternative interest yield obtainable by holding some other asset.

This analysis applies to all currency held as a store of value. Today, however, it has only a limited application to those transaction accounts held in various financial institutions that now pay interest on such balances. Nevertheless, often the interest rate paid is less than the interest rate an individual can earn if the individual were to transfer the money to an alternative asset form. In this case we can measure the incurred opportunity cost by the interest-income differential that one could earn if that same amount of money were stored (saved) in a higher-interest income-earning asset.

Money As a Unit of Account (Standard of Value)   A unit of account is a means of placing a specific value on economic goods and services. Thus, as a unit of account, we can use the monetary unit to measure the value of goods and services relative to other goods and services. The unit of account is the common denominator or measure. The dollar, for example, is the monetary unit in the United States. It is the yardstick that allows individuals to compare easily the relative value of goods and services. Accountants at the Department of Commerce use dollar prices to measure national income and national product; a firm uses dollar prices to calculate profits and losses; a typical household budgets daily and regular expenses using dollar prices as its unit of account.

Another way of describing money as a unit of account is to say that it is a *standard of value* that allows economic transactors to compare the relative worth of various goods and services.

Money As a Standard of Deferred Payment   The fourth function of the monetary unit is as a **standard of deferred payment.** This function simultaneously involves the use of money as a medium of exchange and as a unit of account. We typically state debts in terms of a unit of account; we pay these debts with a monetary medium of exchange. That is to say, we specify a debt in a dollar amount and repay the debt in currency or by check. A corporate bond, for example, has a face value (the value printed on it, which is paid upon maturity) stated in terms of dollars. The bond contract specifies the periodic interest payments on that corporate bond. When the bond comes due (at maturity), the corporation pays the face value to the holder of the bond in dollars.

Not all countries nor the firms and individuals in those countries will specify debts owed to be repaid in their own national monetary unit. For example, individuals, private corporations, and governments in other countries have been known to incur debts in terms of the U.S. dollar, even though the dollar is neither the medium of exchange nor the monetary unit in those countries. Additionally, contracts for some debts may specify repayment in gold rather than in a nation's currency.

THE DISTINCTION BETWEEN MONEY AND CREDIT

You must be clear about the distinction between money and credit. Money is the most liquid asset in which people choose to hold part of their wealth. Credit, in contrast, consists of purchasing power lent or made available to borrowers. The credit market makes it

DIVIDING THE FUNCTIONS OF MONEY AMONG DIFFERENT NATIONAL MONIES

Do individual national monetary units always perform all four of the functions we attribute to money? The answer to this question is no. Indeed, there have been many recent examples in which people in a nation may use their own nation's monetary unit to perform some of money's functions while using the monetary unit of another nation for the other functions of money.

Dollars and Shekels in Israel

For example, in the early 1980s in Israel, inflation of prices denominated in terms of the Israeli currency, the shekel, became so great that managers of grocery stores and other retail outlets found it too costly to change the shekel prices of goods as often as required in light of their own cost changes. Therefore, they began listing their prices in terms of U.S. dollars, and at various places around their stores they posted the most up-to-date dollar-shekel conversion rates. Shoppers literally would carry calculators with them in stores so that they could convert the posted dollar prices into the actual shekel prices they would pay at the checkout counters. Effectively, the shekel continued to function as the medium of exchange in Israel, but the dollar was the unit of account.

Dollars Versus Pesos in Bolivia

Throughout the 1980s and into the 1990s, Bolivia was beset by inflation that, at some points, seemed unimaginable. In one 6-month period in the early 1980s, prices soared at an annual rate of *38,000 percent!* This inflation experience by far dwarfed the inflation problems of Israel (which averaged around 300 percent inflation per year in the mid-1980s), or even of Bolivia's inflation-prone southern neighbor, Argentina, whose annual inflation rate ran in the neighborhood of 1,000 percent in the 1980s, or of its equally inflation-prone northeastern neighbor, Brazil, whose annual inflation rate passed 1,200 percent in 1991.

The response to inflation in Bolivia was even more complicated than in Israel. The Bolivian government

continued to collect taxes in pesos, and it paid government employees in pesos. Yet, some private firms began to pay their employees in dollars. Many store owners and managers continued pricing their goods and services in pesos, but others, like those in Israel, started quoting dollar prices for their products. Before long, it was unclear which monetary unit people should hold. Dollars held their value better than pesos, but the exchange value of the peso was falling so rapidly that it began to pay for people to swap the two currencies continually. Soon, even children and housewives were engaged in wild currency speculations. The *Wall Street Journal* reported, for instance, an eyewitness account of a housewife on a shopping trip who slowed down in traffic on a city street in Santa Cruz, rolled down her window, and shouted to a group of youths on the curb, "What's your price?" Within seconds, her car was surrounded by youths shouting offers for dollar-peso exchanges.

In the 1990s, however, Bolivia and neighboring Argentina both found ways to reduce their inflation problems. By 1991, Argentina's inflation rate had fallen below 50 percent per year. In Bolivia, inflation fell even further, to an annual rate below 25 percent. The Bolivian monetary chaos ended.

Two Monetary Units in Postwar Hungary

Perhaps the most chaotic experience in this century, however, is that of Hungary from August 1945 to July 1946. During this period, Hungary experienced the largest documented rate of inflation ever recorded, at one point reaching a rate of 4.2×10^{16} percent (that is, *42,000,000,000,000,000 percent) per month!* The average inflation rate for the period was 19,800 percent per month. The Hungarian government, desperate to protect tax revenues held in banks from the ravages of inflation, responded by creating two separate Hungarian monetary units. One unit, the Hungarian *pengo,* circulated as normal money. The other, the *tax pengo,* was a unit used to denominate bank deposit accounts. While the nominal value of the pengo was constant, the value of the tax pengo was indexed continuously to changes in the level of prices; for instance, if prices rose by 40 percent from one day to the next, the amount of a tax pengo deposit account automatically increased by 40 percent as well. In this way, government deposits of collected taxes held in banks did not lose value from one day to the next.

Naturally, this made the tax pengo a much better store of value than the regular pengo. Furthermore, the Hungarian government permitted banks to denominate loans in tax pengo units, and so the tax pengo became a standard of deferred payment as well. Yet the regular pengo continued to be used as the medium of exchange and the unit of account for most transactions.

While this was a fascinating system, Hungary's inflation eventually got so out of hand that the Hungarian government ultimately had to start the nation's monetary system over from scratch in August 1946. The Hungarian experiment with two monetary units ended.

Source: Adapted in part from Everett G. Martin, "Precarious Pesos: Amid Wild Inflation, Bolivians Concentrate on Swapping Currency," *Wall Street Journal,* August 13, 1985, p. 5, and from W. A. Bomberger and G. E. Makinen, "Indexation, Inflationary Finance, and Hyperinflation: The 1945–1946 Hungarian Experience," *Journal of Political Economy,* 88 (3, June 1980), pp. 550–560.

possible for those individuals who are unwilling to wait for goods—or purchasing power—to have more goods or purchasing power now. Of course, this impatience has a price—the interest rate.

To demonstrate further the distinction between money and credit, consider a society in which no money exists, but where, nonetheless, credit can indeed exist. In such an economy, Mr. Jones could lend Mrs. Smith one of his machines for a year. Mrs. Smith could promise to return the machine to Jones at the end of one year and pay him 5 units of the output she produces as interest for the credit that he extended to her. In this situation, the amount of credit clearly does not depend on the existence of or the amount of money in society.

THE DESIRABLE PROPERTIES OF MONEY

At a minimum, money has five requisite properties. They are:

1. *Portability:* Money must be easy to carry around and easy to transfer in order to make purchases in different locations. If money is not portable, people will not widely use it.

2. *Durability:* Money that does not have the quality of physical durability will lose its value as money. For example, popcorn could be money, but it would be difficult to keep it in its current form. It would become stale and soggy, wear out, flake apart, and so on. Money has not always been characterized by durability, however. The Roman government paid its soldiers in salt (hence the origin of the word "salary"), which is not particularly durable in a humid or wet climate.

3. *Divisibility:* We must be able to divide money easily into equal parts to allow for purchases of smaller units. Some monies, however, have been indivisible. Historically, people in some parts of the world have at various times used cows as money, although a fraction of a cow is a much different entity than a whole cow.

4. *Standardizability:* We must be able to standardize money if money is to be useful; its units should be of equal quality and physically indistinguishable. Only if we can standardize money can individuals be certain of what they are receiving when they make economic exchanges. Counterexamples do nonetheless exist. The American colonists used tobacco as money, but they could never standardize tobacco. Equal quantities by weight were not available to represent equal value because of the different *qualities* of tobacco; humidity also caused problems on occasion.

5. *Recognizability:* Money must be easily recognized. If people cannot easily recognize money, they will find it difficult to determine whether they are dealing with money or some inferior asset (a counterfeit).

In modern nations, money typically consists of coins, paper currency, and checking account balances (on which individuals can write checks). All these types of money have the five desirable properties previously discussed.

In the past, societies have most often chosen a precious metal or coin as money. Silver and gold, for example, have proved to be durable, portable, divisible, standardizable, and recognizable. Societies have designated precious metals as money more often in the past than virtually any other commodity.

Societies typically go through trial-and-error procedures before adopting a common medium of exchange. Eventually, individuals will choose the commodity that offers the least costly benefits of a common medium of exchange. Hence, what serves as money in an economy will change as the costs of production of the alternative monies change. Whenever a government chooses an ''appropriate'' money, that money will continue to serve as a medium of exchange only if it is generally worthwhile for individuals to use it. A case in point is the Susan B. Anthony dollar, designed to replace the discontinued Eisenhower dollar in the United States. In 1979, the U.S. Treasury issued the Anthony dollar and believed that it would come into widespread use. Unfortunately for the Treasury, individuals did not take too keenly to the new dollar because of its similarity to the quarter. In spite of its eleven-sided border, it still looked and felt very much like a quarter. Given the availability of dollar bills, few people chose to use the Anthony dollar; it is now an unimportant part of our circulating coins.

TYPES OF MONETARY AND NONMONETARY ECONOMIES

History shows that economies have functioned with and without money. There are two basic types of economic trading systems: barter economies and monetary economies. Each type of system, in turn, can take different forms, as we shall see.

BARTER ECONOMIES

Pure Barter Economies   **Barter** is the direct exchange of goods and services for other goods and services. In **pure barter economies,** an individual who wishes to obtain goods and services must search for a second individual who is willing to provide those goods and services in exchange for goods and services that the first individual happens to be able to provide. That is, there must be what William Stanley Jevons (1835–1882) called a **double coincidence of wants.** Two individuals must, by coincidence, own, and desire to trade, goods and services.

Consider the following example. Suppose that Ms. Hanford wishes to acquire bread but has only shoes for exchange. Then she must seek someone else (say, Mr. Terry) who is a baker seeking shoes. The search for Mr. Terry involves a use of time; there is an opportunity cost of that time spent searching for a trading partner. It is virtually impossible to find someone in an economy at all times who simultaneously wants the good or service that another individual at that time wants to exchange. In other words, the double coincidence of wants rarely occurs in a complex modern society. Consequently, the absence of a double coincidence of wants requires individuals either to hold goods and services for long periods or to make many costly intermediary exchanges to get the goods and services they want to have.

Suppose that Mr. Terry has just produced 10 loaves of bread by working all day. In exchange for 8 of those loaves of bread, he wishes to acquire a pair of shoes for his daughter. There may be someone out there—Ms. Hanford—who has a pair of girl's shoes and who needs bread for her large family. Unless Terry knows about Hanford's situation, he will have to seek her out, which entails the use of his time. If he fails to do so rather quickly, his bread will become stale. He may decide, therefore, to exchange 8 loaves of bread for 3 pots, even though he has enough pots. Then he might find a trading partner who will take the 3 pots in exchange for 10 pounds of apples. Finally, he might find someone willing to take the 10 pounds of apples in exchange for the pair of girl's shoes. All of which amounts to a complicated, time-consuming, and costly process, to be sure.

This does not mean that barter has always been inefficient. Some societies produce a limited range of goods and services, and little trade transpires. In such societies, barter may have worked well and may continue to do so. But when the array of goods and services expands and frequent trading with other societies occurs, the cost of barter will greatly exceed its benefits. A new payment mechanism will gradually replace barter, even though limited barter may continue in a fully developed monetary system. For example, barter still occurs in the United States today.

The shortcomings of a pure barter economy   A pure barter economy has several shortcomings. Consider the following.

1. *Absence of a method of storing generalized purchasing power:* With money, individuals and businesses have a store of generalized purchasing power (as opposed to specific purchasing power in the form of, say, shoes, pots, pans, and so on). Barter provides only a specific store of purchasing power. It allows individuals to store only specific goods, which may decrease in value due to physical deterioration or a change in tastes.

2. *Absence of a common unit of measure and value:* Under a barter system, we must express the price of every good or service in terms of every other good and service. Barter therefore leads to the absence of a standardized way to state the price of commodities. Consider the number of prices that would exist if there were only 1,000 goods in the economy but no money or monetary unit of accounting. People could exchange every good for the remaining 999 goods. That means that people could exchange shoes for haircuts, symphony orchestra tickets, oranges, milk, or other items. Without a monetary unit, it would be possible to express the price of shoes in terms of the remaining 999 commodities. What is true for shoes would be true for every one of the other 999 commodities. We could determine the number of unique exchange rates, or prices, by the formula

$$\text{Exchange rates (prices)} = N(N - 1)/2$$

where N signifies the number of goods and services exchanged. In the simple example used here, N equals 1,000; therefore:

$$\text{Exchange rates (prices)} = 1,000(999)/2 = 499,500$$

Each time a person in this 1,000-good economy tried to make a purchase, he or she would need to know almost one-half million potential rates of exchange. Switching to a monetary unit of accounting greatly simplifies matters. With one monetary unit of accounting, such as the dollar, the individual in this economy would contend with only $N - 1$ rates of exchange, or, in this case, 999. Thus, the use of a monetary unit would reduce the number of rates of exchange in this example to one five-hundredths of what they would be without such a system. Clearly, this reduction in the number of relative prices would make economic life less costly and facilitate trade.

Typically, the monetary unit used as a unit of account is the same as the medium of exchange. There are exceptions, however. Until recently, in Britain people expressed the values of many commodities in guineas. A guinea was a gold coin worth 21 shillings, but guineas had not circulated for most of the time during which people used that common term of value.

3. *Absence of a designated unit to use in writing contracts requiring future payments:* Many contracts deal with future activities and future exchanges. In a barter system, it is difficult to write contracts for future payments in a unit that is readily acceptable to both parties. It is still possible to make such contracts for the future payment of goods or services, but the market value of those agreed-upon goods or services may change drastically by the time the future payment is due.

Trading-Post Economies Because of the shortcomings of pure barter, individuals usually seek to organize exchanges of goods and services. Members of a society accomplish this by establishing **trading-post economies,** or systems of organized barter. In this type of economy, individuals continue to trade goods and services directly for other goods and services. They organize specific trading arrangements, however, to lessen the problem of double coincidence of wants. A common trading arrangement is the establishment of physical locations, or trading posts, at which people see specific types of goods or services. For instance, people might designate a certain location on a town square for a farmers' market, while they might set aside another spot as a location for sidewalk sales of clothing and linen goods.

Setting up trading posts provides information to potential buyers of goods about where sellers of specific goods will be located. This benefits the buyers, who save the transaction costs of searching out producers of goods they desire. It also benefits the sellers, who then will not have to carry their goods in search of potential buyers.

Although establishing trading posts reduces the double-coincidence problem arising from barter, it does not eliminate entirely this problem nor the costs it imposes on individuals. While a person knows what will be available at a particular trading post, he or she does not necessarily know what good or service the seller at that trading post would like in exchange.

A way of resolving this problem is for members of society to settle on the widespread acceptance of a single good at all trading posts. This good then is the medium of exchange, or money good. In an organized trading-post system, it is a relatively simple matter to make this step. Once it is taken, the economy has made the switch from barter to money.

MONETARY ECONOMIES

Historically, money has existed in diverse forms. Table 1-1 lists some of the different types of money that have existed throughout history. As the table shows, the types of monies that societies have used are indicative of the broad range of human imagination and ingenuity. The type of money used by a society reflects to a large extent the technical capabilities of the society. It also reflects choices the society has made about its trading system.

T A B L E 1-1 Different Types of Money		
Iron	Red woodpecker scalps	Leather
Copper	Feathers	Gold
Brass	Glass	Silver
Wine	Polished beads (wampum)	Knives
Corn	Rum	Pots
Salt	Molasses	Boats
Horses	Tobacco	Pitch
Sheep	Agricultural implements	Rice
Goats	Round stones with centers	Cows
Tortoise shells	removed	Slaves
Porpoise teeth	Crystal salt bars	Paper
Whale teeth	Snail shells	Cigarettes
Boar tusk	Playing cards	

Commodity Money Economies   Most types of money people have used are **commodity monies:** They are physical commodities. Early commodity monies, such as wool, boats, sheep, and corn, had equivalent monetary and nonmonetary values.

More advanced societies that were able to mine and process scarce metals like gold and silver found that these metals possessed in abundance the key properties of a satisfactory money good. Gold and silver are recognizable and durable metals. While heavy, they nonetheless are portable. It is possible to measure their purities as metals, so that individuals can standardize them by both weight and degree of purity. Heating, chemical, and physical processes can make gold and silver completely divisible. For this reason, gold and silver have been predominant types of commodity monies, particularly since the onset of the industrial revolution in the 1800s.

Commodity Standards   As nations progressed in their use of money, they minted coins whose metallic content had a value in nonmonetary uses (e.g., in jewelry) equal to their exchange value as money. Governments typically issued gold or silver coins as **full-bodied money** whose face value is equal to its market value. Citizens could legally melt the coins for nonmonetary uses.

The fact that full-bodied coins have money value (purchasing power) equivalent to their nonmonetary uses does not mean that they have a constant value. The purchasing power of a full-bodied coin will change in terms of other commodities. As the prices of all other goods and services change, so, too, does the purchasing power of a full-bodied money. Thus, the use of full-bodied coins does not prevent inflation or **deflation** (a decline in the weighted average of all prices through time) from occurring.

Consider an example. A country using full-bodied gold coins could still experience inflation if a new discovery of large amounts of gold occurred or if the costs of mining gold fell dramatically. With the same amount of goods and services available, but, say, twice the supply of gold money available, the prices of available goods and services in terms of gold would have to rise; the relative price of gold would fall. This means that it would take more units of gold to buy the same quantities of other goods and services. In short, inflation results. We shall discuss this process more thoroughly in Chapter 2.

The use of coins, and of paper currency, bank notes, or other token forms of money, represents a significant step in the evolution of an economy. When people widely use tokens, rather than actual physical commodities, in exchange for goods and services, an economy has adopted a **commodity standard.** Under a commodity standard, individuals use tokens whose values are fully or partially related to, or *backed* by, the value of a physical commodity, such as gold or silver. Full-bodied money such as gold coins is a form of a commodity standard in which people transform the actual physical commodity, gold, into standardized tokens to use in exchange. Because individuals can melt the gold coins for use in other purposes, their inherent value depends on the value of the underlying commodity, gold; the value of gold *fully backs* the value of the coins.

People may use alternative tokens other than coins, such as pieces of paper, alongside or in place of gold or silver coins. These are examples of **representative full-bodied money.** This is a type of money that is of negligible intrinsic value, but that is backed by (can be converted into) a commodity such as gold or silver. In other words, a paper currency in a representative full-bodied monetary system is the equivalent of full-bodied coins. The paper itself is representative and has no value as a commodity. But it does represent the total amount of full-bodied money in existence.

Before 1933, for example, in the United States gold certificates were widely circulated. These certificates represented the equivalent amount of gold coin, or bullion, held by the Treasury. Hence, the gold certificates were fully backed by the actual commodity. A $50 gold certificate was a claim to $50 worth of gold (at the official, or governmentally guaranteed, exchange price of $20 per ounce of gold) usually stored by the U.S. government at Fort Knox, Kentucky.

Another example is the silver certificates that formerly existed in the United States. They were fully redeemable in silver at the official exchange rate. In the mid-1960s, the price of silver on the world market rose dramatically. Individuals started exchanging their silver certificates for silver at the official price (the rate at which the government promised to exchange dollars and silver) of $1.29 an ounce of silver. The U.S. Treasury honored its commitment at this exchange rate until June 24, 1968.

Representative full-bodied money saves transaction costs because the transfer of large sums of money in gold or silver is unwieldy. Paper claims on the physical commodity are much easier and cheaper to use.

Fiat Money   An economy uses **fiat money** when all the money it uses has a commodity value much less than its value as money. In a fiat money system, then, money has little worth other than as money. For example, a copper coin whose copper value when melted down is, say, one-tenth of a cent, but whose monetary value is one cent, is fiat money. Fiat money can be broken down into two major subclassifications: fiat money issued by governments and central banks and that issued by depository institutions.

Governments and central banks issue much of the fiat money that exists in the world today. The U.S. government issued the copper coin mentioned above. It was a token coin—money whose metal value was worth less than its money value. In the United States, the U.S. Treasury issues all token coins. In other countries, central banks (we call our central bank the Federal Reserve System, or the Fed) also issue token coins.

Governments and central banks also issue paper fiat money. Today, the only fiat paper of the federal government is the U.S. notes (''greenbacks'') that the government used to finance the Civil War. About $350 million worth of these promissory notes are still in circulation. The remainder of the paper fiat money used today is in the form of Federal Reserve notes, issued by the Federal Reserve System. Chances are that all the paper currency in your wallet or handbag consists of Federal Reserve notes that the Fed issued.

Many financial institutions in this country have the legal right to issue fiat money in the form of transactions accounts; we call such financial institutions depository institutions.

Banks, savings and loan associations, credit unions, and the like all offer some form of transactions account to their customers. Depositors can write a check to pay for their purchases of goods and services. All these depository institutions are private, that is, not owned by the government.

In the distant past, private banks also issued paper currency. These were promissory notes (the banks "promised" to redeem them for a precious metal) of the private banks, and they played an important role in our monetary system. The First and Second Banks of the United States, chartered by the federal government, as well as national banks (also chartered by the federal government), have at times issued paper notes. So, too, have state-chartered banks.

WHAT BACKS FIAT MONEY?

Today in the United States, all of us accept coins, Federal Reserve notes, and transactions balances in exchange for items sold, including labor services. The question remains: Why are we willing to accept for payment something that has no intrinsic value? The reason is that in this country the payments arise from a **fiduciary monetary standard.** This means that the value of the payments rests on people's confidence that they can exchange money for goods and services. "Fiduciary" comes from the Latin *fiducia,* which means "trust" or "confidence." In other words, under our fiduciary monetary standard, money, whether in the form of currency or checkable accounts, is not convertible into a fixed quantity of gold or silver or into some other precious commodity. People cannot exchange the paper money that they hold in their wallets or purses or checkable account balances for a specified quantity of some specific commodity; pieces of paper money are, by themselves, just pieces of paper. Coins have a value stamped on them that is normally greater than the market value of the metal in them. Nevertheless, currency and checkable accounts are money because of their acceptability and their predictability of value.

ACCEPTABILITY

Checkable accounts and currency are money because individuals widely accept them in exchange for goods and services. Individuals accept checks and currency because they have confidence that they will be able to exchange these checks and currency for other goods and services. This confidence lies in the knowledge that such exchanges have occurred in the past without problems.

PREDICTABILITY OF VALUE

For money to have a predictable value, the relationship between the quantity of money supplied and the quantity of money demanded must not change frequently, abruptly, or in great magnitude. In this sense, the value of money is like the economic value of other goods and services. Supply and demand determine what the dollar "sells" for. What is the selling price of a dollar? It is what has to be given up in order to "purchase" a dollar. It is the value of the goods and services that could have been obtained instead of the dollar. In other words, in order to own one dollar, an individual must give up the **purchasing power** inherent in that dollar. That purchasing power might be equal to a used paperback book or a bag of french fries.

The purchasing power of the dollar (that is, its value) therefore varies inversely with the price level. Thus, the more rapid the rate of increase of the price level, the more rapid

STONE CURRENCY

INTERNATIONAL

PERSPECTIVE

People on the island of Uap (one of the Caroline Islands) called their medium of exchange "fei." This currency consisted of large, solid, thick stone wheels ranging in diameter from 1 foot to 12 feet. In the center of each wheel was a hole varying in size with the diameter of the stone, which permitted natives to sling the currency on poles to be carried. The stones were not found on Uap itself, but were quarried in Babelthuap, some 400 miles away to the south. Size was the most important factor, but also the fei had to be of a certain fine, white, close-grained limestone. A traveler on Uap described the fei as follows:

A feature of this stone currency, which is also an equally noteworthy tribute to Uap honesty, is that it is not necessary for its owner to reduce it to possession. After concluding a bargain which involves the price of a fei too large to be conveniently moved, its new owner is quite content to accept the bare acknowledgment of ownership; and without so much as a mark to indicate the exchange, the coin remains undisturbed on the former owner's premises.

My faithful old friend Fatumak assured me that there was in a village nearby a family whose wealth was unquestioned—acknowledged by every one, and yet no one, not even the family itself, had ever laid eye or hand on this wealth; it consisted of an enormous fei, whereof the size is known only by tradition: for the past two or three generations it had been, and at that very time it was lying at the bottom of the sea! Many years ago an ancestor of this family, on an expedition after fei, secured this remarkably valuable stone, which was placed on a raft to be towed homeward. A violent storm arose and the party, to save their lives, were obliged to cut the raft adrift, and the stone sank out of sight. When they reached home they all testified that the fei was of magnificent proportions and of extraordinary quality, and that it was lost through no fault of the owners. Thereupon it was universally considered in their simple faith that the mere accident of its loss overboard was too trifling to mention, and that a few hundred feet of water off shore ought not to affect its marketable value, since it was all chipped out in proper form. The purchasing power of that stone remained, therefore, as valid as if it were leaning visibly against the side of its owner's house.

When the German government purchased the Caroline Islands from Spain in 1898, no wheeled vehicles existed on Uap, and hence there were no roads. The paths, too, were in poor shape, and the government ordered the natives to put them into better condition. Somehow or other the natives were quite happy with the paths as they were; the job did not get done. The government was in a dilemma. It would be rather difficult to fine the natives and carry off the fei to Germany. In the first place, German shopkeepers might have been a little doubtful about exchanging their wares for fei, and then in the second place, it would have taken the labors of every available native to get the fei off the island, and the repairing of the paths would have had to wait while the natives paid up. Finally the government hit on a sound scheme. It simply sent a man around to mark some of the most valuable stones with a cross in black paint to show the government claim. The impoverished natives immediately fell to work, and the paths were soon in good order. Then a second man went round for the government to remove the crosses; and there was great rejoicing on the island of Uap.

Source: Quoted entirely from Norman Angell, *The Story of Money* (New York: Garden City Publishing Co., 1929), pp. 88–89, as reprinted on the back cover of the *Journal of Political Economy,* 90 (4, August 1982).

the decrease in the value, or purchasing power, of the dollar. Money retains its usefulness even if its value—its purchasing power—declines every year. Money can still be used and accepted during periods of inflation if it retains the characteristic of predictability of value. If individuals believe that the rate of inflation is going to be 10 percent next year, then they expect that a dollar received a year hence will have approximately 10 percent less purchasing power than the same dollar this year. Individuals will not necessarily refuse to use money or accept it in exchange simply because they know that its value will decline approximately 10 percent over the next year. As will be discussed later, the expectation of a declining value of money will change the amounts and types of financial assets that people want to hold—including the desired amount of money.

CHAPTER SUMMARY

1. Money is that which is accepted as such. People use it as a medium of exchange, a store of value, a unit of accounting, and a standard of deferred payment. By definition, money is the most liquid of all assets.

2. Economists study money because they believe it affects other economic variables. Changes in the money stock are highly correlated with changes in the price level, nominal interest rates, and nominal GDP.

3. Money and credit are not the same thing; credit is the extension of purchasing power to others for a future payment. Credit and interest rates can exist even in a barter economy.

4. In order for something to be useful as money, it must be portable, durable, divisible, standardizable, and recognizable; but we can find exceptions to each of these desirable properties in history. Gold and silver have these properties and have been very popular money forms throughout the ages. In theory and in practice, what is acceptable as money is subject to change.

5. There are two basic types of money: commodity-based money and fiat money. In a commodity money system, individuals use an actual commodity as money. In a commodity-based system that uses a commodity standard, people use full-bodied money and representative full-bodied money. The basis of fiat money, in contrast, is a fiduciary arrangement in which trust in the acceptability of money is what gives money value. Fiat money is issued by governments and central banks and/or by depository institutions.

6. The United States is presently on a fiduciary monetary standard; our money is not backed by anything other than the public's faith that it will be accepted as payment for goods and services. As long as money has acceptability and its value is reasonably predictable, a fiduciary monetary standard can operate. Under a gold standard, a nation's currency is defined in terms of a fixed quantity of gold; the government promises to convert this currency into gold at an established rate ''on demand.''

GLOSSARY

Barter: Trading a good or service for another without the use of money.

Checkable account: A bank deposit that can be exchanged immediately for the goods or services that an individual wishes to buy.

Commodity monies: Physical commodities such as wool, corn, or livestock that have equivalent monetary and nonmonetary values.

Commodity standard: The use of standardized tokens as money whose value is backed by the value of a physical commodity such as gold or silver.

Deflation: A decline in the weighted average of all prices through time.

Double coincidence of wants: A situation in which a person who has good A to trade and wants good B finds someone who has good B to trade and wants good A.

Economic good: A scarce commodity.

Fiat money: Money whose face value is more than its market value; paper money not backed by anything but faith in its universal acceptance, e.g., paper bills and transaction account balances.

Fiduciary monetary standard: A monetary standard under which the currency is not backed by anything except the public's confidence, or faith, that the currency can be exchanged for goods and services.

Full-bodied money: Money whose face value is equal to its market value, such as pure gold or silver coins.

Gross domestic product (GDP):   The market value of all final goods and services produced over a period of time (usually a year) using home-country factors of production.

Inflation: A sustained rise in the weighted average of all prices over time.

Liquidity: The degree to which an asset can be sold for cash at a low transaction cost and without a loss in nominal value. Money, by definition, is the most liquid of all assets.

Medium of exchange: Whatever is accepted as payment for purchases of goods or services; a necessary property of money.

Money: Medium that is universally acceptable in an economy both by sellers of goods and services as payment for the goods and services and by creditors as payment for debts.

Opportunity cost: The economic cost of any activity, measured by the highest-valued alternative activity.

Purchasing power of money: A measure of the amount of goods and services that a unit of money can be used to purchase.

Pure barter economy: An economy in which an individual who wishes to obtain goods and services must search for a second individual who is willing to provide those goods and services in exchange for goods and services that the first individual is able to provide.

Representative full-bodied money: Money that is of negligible value as a commodity but is ''backed by'' (can be converted into, at a fixed nominal price) a valuable commodity, such as gold or silver.

Standard of deferred payment: A property of an asset that makes it desirable for use as a means of settling debts maturing in the future; an essential property of money.

Store of value: The ability of an item to hold value over time; a necessary property of money.

Trading-post economy: A system of organized barter in which individuals continue to trade goods and services directly for other goods and services.

Unit of account: A measure by which prices and values are expressed; the common denominator of the price system; an essential property of money.

Wealth: Net worth; the value of assets minus liabilities (debt), at a given moment in time.

SELF-TEST QUESTIONS

1. Explain, in your own words, the functions of money.
2. Why is it that times of high inflation induce people to find alternative monetary units, as in the cases discussed in the International Perspective on page 8?
3. Explain the meaning of the term ''double coincidence of wants.''
4. Is there any substantive difference between barter and trading-post economies? Support your answer.
5. Explain the distinctions among the following terms: full-bodied money, representative full-bodied money, and fiduciary monetary standard.

PROBLEMS

1-1. Consider a barter economy in which ten goods and services are produced and exchanged. How many exchange rates exist in that economy?

1-2. Assume that there are seven different goods in a hypothetical economy. In how many different ways can the price of a particular good be expressed under barter? Because the price of each particular good can be expressed in that many ways, it may at first seem that there would be seven times that many prices that would exist at a particular point in time. Some of those prices, however, would be redundant. What is the actual total number of *different* prices?

SELECTED REFERENCES

Alchian, Armen, "Why Money?" *Journal of Money, Credit, and Banking,* 9 (1, February 1977), pp. 133–141.

Angell, Norman, *The Story of Money* (New York: Frederick A. Stokes Co., 1929).

Brunner, Karl, and Allan A. Meltzer, "The Uses of Money: Money in the Theory of an Exchange Economy," *American Economic Review,* 61 (5, December 1971), pp. 784–805.

Einzig, Paul, *Primitive Money,* 2d ed. (New York: Oxford University Press, 1966).

Nussbaum, Arthur, *A History of the Dollar* (New York: Columbia University Press, 1957).

The Evolution of Money

CHAPTER PREVIEW

1. Why do barter economies typically evolve into monetary economies?

2. What is the purchasing power of money, and how is it determined in a commodity money economy? How is the level of prices of goods and services in such an economy determined?

3. How does a commodity standard, such as a gold standard, function? How are the purchasing power of money and the level of prices of goods and services determined under a gold standard?

4. What is seigniorage? Why is it possible for seigniorage to be earned by a government that produces money monopolistically?

5. How can an economy produce the socially optimal quantity of money at the socially optimal price?

In the last chapter, we introduced fundamental concepts concerning money, barter, and the types of monetary and nonmonetary economies that have existed in human societies. We provided only a broad overview of these concepts, however. Therefore, in this chapter we shall explain concretely the economic reasons that societies have evolved from using barter exchange to trading in the complex monetary and financial systems we observe today.

In addition, in Chapter 1 we introduced the ideas of commodity monies and commodity standards, but we did not really explain how these systems functioned in the past. We provide these explanations in the present chapter. You may wonder why we should even spend any time thinking about such monetary systems. There are two very good reasons. First, the fiat money system we use today really has been a recent *experiment;* it still remains to be seen whether that experiment ultimately will succeed or fail. Second, many important lessons are to be learned from an understanding of the functioning of commodity-based monetary systems. As you will learn, issues that arise in such systems remain with us today.

THE EVOLUTION OF MONEY[1]

The history of money has been a movement away from barter to commodity monies such as gold and silver coins, and then from commodity monies to commodity standards, and

---

[1] This section draws from Robert Clower, ''Introduction,'' in *Monetary Theory: Selected Readings* (New York: Penguin Books, 1969).

then to fiat money. What accounts for this historical progression? The answer has to do with the costs society incurs in using different types of exchange systems.

EXCHANGE COSTS

Trading goods and services entails costs. To obtain food items, for instance, you must wait for the best time to purchase the groceries in light of your own schedule. Then you must make your way through traffic to a grocery store, walk up and down the aisles of the grocery, make difficult choices about different brands that may or may not be on sale that day, get through the checkout line, and, finally, make payment for the goods you have purchased. Only at this point do the food items you desired become yours to consume.

Waiting Costs   The example of purchasing food at a grocery store illustrates the types of costs that individuals must incur as part of an effort they make to undertake an exchange. We can divide these costs into two separate categories. One type of cost we shall term **waiting costs.** In the example of grocery shopping, many of us find ourselves waiting until the best moment to make the trip to the grocery store, despite the fact that we might be yearning to consume a good, such as a chocolate bar. Although we find ourselves desiring a chocolate bar, we must wait to purchase that item, and the *time we spend waiting* imposes a *cost* on us.

Furthermore, this waiting cost increases as time passes. If we really feel that we need the "sugar fix" and associated calories we will derive from consumption of a chocolate bar, then the longer we must wait, the higher are the costs we perceive from waiting to exchange some of our accumulated wealth for the chocolate bar.

Figure 2-1 depicts this relationship between waiting costs and time. Measured vertically in the figure are real costs (the psychic loss we experience because of our desire for chocolate) incurred; time is measured horizontally. The *waiting cost schedule* (C_W) slopes upward to indicate that waiting costs rise as time passes.

Figure 2-1

Waiting Costs.   Waiting costs are the costs an individual must incur as time passes before a desired good is obtained. The longer the wait, the higher the cost that the individual incurs.

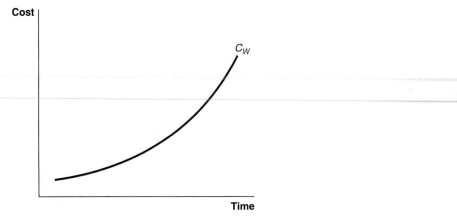

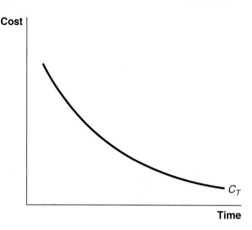

Figure 2-2
Transaction Costs.   Transaction costs are the explicit costs an individual must incur to make a trade. Making a trade in a short time interval requires that an individual incur a higher cost than if the individual takes a longer time to make the trade.

Transaction Costs   To obtain our chocolate bar, we must make a trip to the grocery store and exert ourselves to shop for and purchase the chocolate bar. These tasks require energy and effort and thereby force us to incur explicit costs, which economists lump together as **transaction costs.**

Suppose that we rush to the grocery store. Indeed, suppose that we drive fast and somewhat recklessly to save time. In addition, suppose that we dodge our way past other shoppers, arguing with them as we shove and bump our way down the aisles, push our way into a line at the counter, throw a few coins to the grocery clerk, and rush back home. We would be able to get our chocolate bar quickly, but at a high cost—especially if we have an accident along the way or get into a fight with another shopper or the clerk.

Alternatively, we could shop for our chocolate bar in a more leisurely—and less costly—manner. This would take more time but would reduce the explicit transaction costs that we would incur in shopping for, and purchasing, our chocolate bar.

Therefore, transaction costs we incur in an exchange fall with the amount of time spent in making an exchange. Figure 2-2 depicts the relationship between transaction costs and time. The downward-sloping *transaction cost schedule* (C_T) shows that if we make an exchange quickly, we must incur higher transaction costs than if we make our exchange at a slower pace.

Total Exchange Costs and the Minimum-Cost Exchange   To make any exchange for a good or service, an individual must incur both waiting and transaction costs. Therefore, *total exchange costs* are the sum of waiting costs, C_W, and transaction costs, C_T. Figure 2-3 shows that we can add these costs by summing vertically the C_W and C_T schedules; that is, we sum together vertically the waiting and transaction costs for any given time interval. This produces a new schedule that measures the total exchange costs (C_E) incurred by an individual. Because the total exchange cost schedule is the sum of downward-sloping and upward-sloping schedules, it is U-shaped.

The goal of an individual is to undertake an exchange at the least possible total cost. Cost minimization then requires that the individual spend the time interval that we have

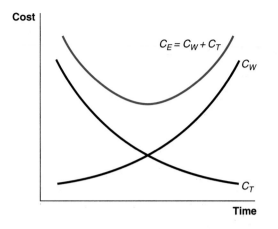

Figure 2-3
Total Exchange Costs.   Total exchange costs are the sum of waiting and transaction costs. Therefore, the total exchange cost schedule is obtained by summing waiting and transaction costs together at each possible time interval.

labeled T^* in Figure 2-4 making an exchange. At this interval of time, he incurs the minimum possible level of exchange costs, C_E^*.

EXCHANGE COSTS AND THE EVOLUTION OF MONEY

Waiting costs are unrelated to the type of trading system an economy uses. For instance, consider again our desire to obtain a chocolate bar. The cost we incur by waiting to buy

Figure 2-4
The Minimum Cost Exchange.   The goal of an individual who seeks to make an exchange is to minimize the total exchange cost that he or she incurs. This is shown as the point of minimum cost, C_E^*, on the total exchange cost schedule. At this point, the individual spends the optimal amount of time, T^*, making an exchange.

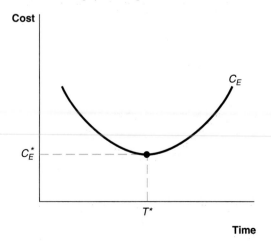

our chocolate bar will be the same whether we plan to purchase it by trading some vanilla ice cream for the chocolate bar in a barter agreement, by using gold nuggets as an exchange medium, by offering silver coins, or by handing over some Federal Reserve notes and copper coins. For a given individual and desired good or service, the position of the waiting cost schedule is invariant to the form of the economy's trading system.

Transaction Costs and Trading Systems   In contrast, the explicit transaction costs that individuals incur in making exchanges vary considerably with the type of trading system they use. Under pure barter, with its need for a double coincidence of wants, these transaction costs are very high for any given time interval. As shown in Figure 2-5, establishment of a trading-post system lowers transaction costs by providing buyers more information about the locations of sellers.

Traders can realize a further transaction cost saving by using a commodity money in exchanges at trading posts, as shown in Figure 2-5. Individuals can gain more cost savings by substituting tokens for money, and so transaction costs typically are smaller, for any given time interval, under a commodity standard. Finally, switching to a fiat money system eliminates the need to hold stocks of a commodity to back the value of the token money units, yielding a further transaction cost saving, as shown in Figure 2-5.

Cost Savings and Monetary Evolution   Figure 2-6 shows what happens to the total exchange cost schedule as an economy gradually evolves from pure barter to a fiat money system. Because waiting costs are unchanged during this evolution while transaction costs fall, the minimum exchange cost falls. So does the time interval that corresponds to the minimum exchange cost. In general, evolution to a fiat money system leads to both less costly exchange and less time allocated to that task. Each individual gains, and so society gains. This cost saving explains why economies historically have evolved toward the fiat money systems that we see today.

Figure 2-5
Transaction Costs in Different Trading Systems.   As an economy evolves from barter systems to more sophisticated monetary systems, the transaction cost associated with making an exchange falls for any given exchange time interval.

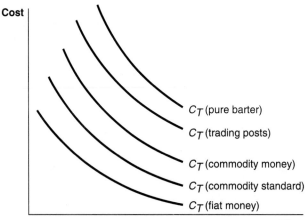

Cost

C_T (pure barter)

C_T (trading posts)

C_T (commodity money)

C_T (commodity standard)

C_T (fiat money)

Time

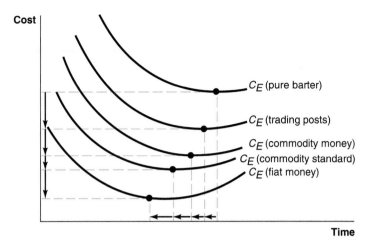

Figure 2-6
Exchange Costs and the Evolution of Trading Systems and Money.   As an economy evolves from barter systems to more sophisticated monetary systems, transaction costs fall, and so total exchange costs fall. Hence, the minimum cost of exchange is reduced, and the time spent making exchanges decreases.

LESSONS OF THE PAST: COMMODITY MONEY AND COMMODITY STANDARDS

We presently use a fiat money system. This does not mean, however, that we should not study other types of monetary systems. This is true for two reasons. First, it is within the realm of possibility that we could return to a commodity-based system at some future time. Indeed, there have been consistent calls for a return to a gold standard ever since the United States dropped formal ties to gold over two decades ago. It is important to understand how commodity-based systems function if we are to evaluate claims that we should return to a gold standard.

Second, the economics of commodity-based monetary systems can tell us much about the relationships between the quantity of money and other economic variables, such as prices. In fact, we shall see that there are many lessons we can learn from the economics of commodity-based monetary systems.

THE ECONOMICS OF A COMMODITY MONEY SYSTEM[2]

In a commodity money system, a specific commodity functions as money. As we discussed above, individuals and societies throughout history have used many commodities as money. The most frequently used commodity, however, has been gold. Thus, we shall assume throughout our discussion of the economics of a commodity money system that gold is the commodity money. It is important to recognize, nonetheless, that the economic

---

[2] This discussion of the workings of a commodity money system parallels the presentation in James Pierce, *Monetary and Financial Economics* (New York: John Wiley and Sons, 1984), Chapter 2.

theory would be the same no matter what commodity money individuals might agree to use.

The Demand for Gold   An interesting feature of commodity money systems is that the commodity used as money often may have other uses as well. Gold is a good example. Historically, people have used gold dust, nuggets, or bars as money, but individuals also can melt and form gold for use in a variety of ways. People commonly use gold for jewelry or other types of ornamentation. It also has industrial uses; a modern use of gold, for instance, is in electrical connections in devices such as computer equipment and expensive stereo components.

Whether used for monetary or other purposes, gold has a price, which is the other goods and services that individuals must give up in exchange for gold. We denote this price as P_G, which is measured in terms of units of goods and services per unit of gold. (Keep in mind that in a true gold commodity money system, there are no dollars, francs, yen, etc., to use as units of account for pricing gold or any other goods and services.) We also assume that the law of demand holds for gold just as it does for any other good: As the price of gold rises, other things constant, the quantity of gold demanded for any purpose declines.

Figure 2-7 shows demand schedules for gold both for monetary and for alternative, nonmonetary purposes. Panel (a) shows the demand for gold for monetary purposes, labeled G_M^d. As shown in panel (a), the quantity of gold demanded for monetary purposes, G_M, falls as the price of gold, P_G, rises. At the gold price P_G^0, for instance, the total

Figure 2-7
Gold Demand Schedules.   Gold has two separate uses: It may be used as money, or it may be used for other (for instance, industrial or ornamental) purposes. In either case, the demand for gold is negatively related to the price of gold, measured in units of goods and services per unit of gold. Therefore, the demand for gold for monetary purposes, G_M^d, slopes downward against the price of gold in panel (a); likewise, the demand for gold for nonmonetary purposes, G_N^d, is downward-sloping in panel (b).

At the gold price P_G^0, the quantity of gold demanded for monetary purposes [panel (a)] is G_M^0, and the quantity of gold demanded for nonmonetary use [panel (b)] is G_N^0. When the price of gold increases to P_G^1, the quantity of gold demanded for monetary purposes falls to G_M^1 [panel (a)], and the quantity of gold demanded for nonmonetary purposes declines to G_N^1 [panel (b)].

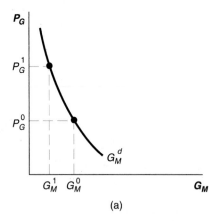

(a)

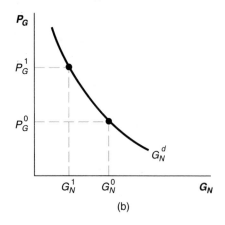

(b)

quantity of gold demanded for monetary purposes is G_M^0. When the price of gold rises to P_G^1, the quantity of gold demanded for monetary purposes falls to G_M^1.

Likewise, panel (b) of Figure 2-7 shows the demand for gold for nonmonetary purposes, labeled G_N^d. This schedule indicates that the quantity of gold demanded for nonmonetary purposes, G_N, also declines as the price of gold, P_G, increases. For example, at the gold price P_G^0, the quantity of gold demanded for ornamental, industrial, or other purposes is equal to G_N^0. A rise in the price of gold to P_G^1 lowers the quantity of gold demanded for these purposes to G_N^1.

Figure 2-8 shows the construction of the total gold demand schedule. This schedule is the horizontal sum of the G_M^d and G_N^d schedules. That is, at the gold price P_G^0, the total quantity of gold demanded is $G^0 = G_M^0 + G_N^0$. Likewise, at the gold price P_G^1, the total quantity of gold demanded falls to $G^1 = G_M^1 + G_N^1$. Hence, the total gold demand schedule, $G^d = G_M^d + G_N^d$, tells us the total quantity of gold demanded for both monetary and nonmonetary purposes at any given price of gold, measured in goods and services that must be given up in exchange for a unit of gold.

The Supply of Gold   The supply of gold, labeled G^s, slopes upward, as shown in Figure 2-9. That is because the price of gold must increase in order for people to mine, transport, and refine more gold for use as money or for ornamental, industrial, or other uses. That is, the amount of goods and services that gold producers receive for each unit of gold must rise if these producers are to increase their production and sale of gold.

Equilibrium in the Market for Gold   Figure 2-10 shows equilibrium in the market for gold. Equilibrium in this market occurs when the total quantity of gold demanded is

Figure 2-8
The Total Demand for Gold.   The total demand schedule for gold, G^d, is constructed by summing horizontally the demand schedules for monetary and nonmonetary uses of gold. For instance, at the gold price P_G^0, the total quantity of gold demanded is G^0. This total quantity of gold demanded is the sum of G_M^0, the amount of gold demanded for monetary use at that gold price, and G_N^0, the amount of gold demanded for nonmonetary purposes at that gold price. Likewise, at the gold price P_G^1, the total quantity of gold demanded, G^1, is equal to the total of G_M^1 and G_N^1, the quantities of gold demanded for monetary and nonmonetary purposes, respectively, at that higher gold price. An increase in the price of gold reduces the total quantity of gold demanded.

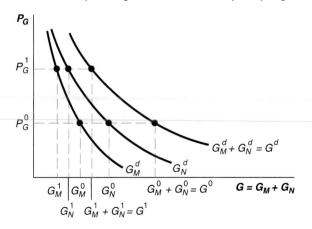

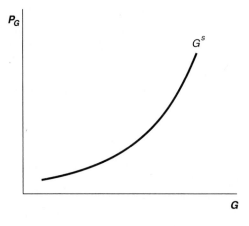

Figure 2-9
The Supply of Gold.   The supply of gold, G^s, slopes upward against the price of gold, measured in units of goods and services per unit of gold. As the amount of goods and services that gold producers receive, in exchange for each unit of gold they produce, increases, the producers supply a larger amount of gold.

equal to the total quantity of gold supplied. This occurs where the total gold demand schedule, G^d, crosses the gold supply schedule, G^s, at the amount G^0 in the diagram. The price of gold adjusts to achieve this equality between the quantities of gold supplied and demanded; this occurs at the equilibrium gold price P_G^0 in the diagram.

We measure the equilibrium price of gold, P_G^0, in terms of units of goods and services

Figure 2-10
Equilibrium in the Market for Gold.   Equilibrium in the market for gold occurs at the point at which the total demand schedule for gold, G^d, intersects the gold supply schedule, G^s. The equilibrium quantity of gold supplied and demanded is G^0, at the equilibrium price of gold, P_G^0.

At this gold price, the quantity of gold demanded for monetary use is G_M^0, and the amount demanded for nonmonetary purposes is $G^0 - G_M^0 = G_N^0$. Because the level of prices of goods and services is the reciprocal of the price of gold, the equilibrium level of prices for this economy is $1/P_G^0$.

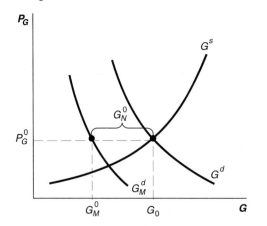

per unit of gold. Therefore, this equilibrium price tells us how many units of goods and services a unit of gold can buy. For this reason, the price of gold is a measure of the *equilibrium purchasing power of gold money,* which is the value, in goods and services, of a unit of gold money.

Also depicted in Figure 2-10 is the demand schedule for gold used for monetary purposes. At the equilibrium price of gold for which the *total* quantity of gold demanded is equal to the total quantity of gold supplied, P_G^0, the quantity of gold demanded for use as money is G_M^0. The equilibrium total quantity of gold demanded is G^0, and so the quantity of gold demanded for nonmonetary uses is the difference, $G^0 - G_M^0 = G_N^0$.

Gold Money and the Price Level   In a pure gold commodity money system, there are no dollars or other measures of money; gold functions as the medium of exchange, store of value, standard of deferred payment, and unit of account. Because gold is the unit of account, we measure all prices of goods and services in terms of gold. That is, the units of measurement of prices of goods and services are units of gold per unit of goods and services.

Recall that the price, or purchasing power, of gold, P_G, is measured in units of goods and services per unit of gold. The reciprocal of the price of gold, $1/P_G$, then, is measured in units of gold per unit of goods and services. This reciprocal is a measure of the aggregate level of prices of goods and services in the economy. Therefore, if the gold market is in equilibrium at the gold price (or gold purchasing power) P_G^0 in Figure 2-10, the level of prices of goods and services is the reciprocal of this gold price, which is $1/P_G^0$. As an example, if the value of P_G^0 were equal to 0.5 unit of goods and services per unit of gold, then the price level would be $1/P_G^0 = 1/(0.5$ units of goods and services per unit of gold) $= 2$ units of gold per unit of goods and services. That is, on average it would take 2 units of gold to purchase a standardized unit of a good or service in the economy.

The effect of a gold discovery on the price of gold and the level of prices of goods and services   Suppose that a major gold discovery occurs. More gold will be supplied at any given price of gold. Therefore, the gold supply schedule shifts to the right, as shown in Figure 2-11. There will be an excess quantity of gold supplied at the initial equilibrium gold price P_G^0. As a result, the equilibrium price of gold falls to P_G^1. The equilibrium total quantity of gold supplied and demanded rises, on net, from G_0 to G_1.

As a result of the gold discovery, the equilibrium price of gold, P_G, which is measured in terms of units of goods and services that must be given up for a unit of gold, has decreased. This means that the level of aggregate prices of goods and services, $1/P_G$, which is measured in units of gold that must be given up for a unit of a good or service, must increase. That is, the aggregate price level of goods and services in the economy rises. We may conclude that a gold discovery causes inflation in a gold commodity money system. Inflation, in turn, is accompanied by a fall in the price of gold, or a reduction in the purchasing power of gold money. In other words, it takes more units of gold to purchase the same quantity of nongold goods and services.

History is replete with examples in which gold discoveries caused inflation. For instance, when sixteenth-century Spanish explorers plundered native civilizations in the Americas and transported gold from the Americas back to Europe, there was significant inflation. Furthermore, there is a broader lesson we can glean from this example: An increase in the supply of any money (not just in the supply of the *gold* commodity money) causes higher nominal prices. As we shall see, this typically is true for any type of monetary system.

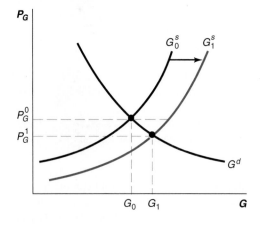

Figure 2-11
The Effects of a Gold Discovery. If more gold deposits are discovered by gold producers, there is more gold supplied at any given price of gold; the gold supply schedule shifts rightward. At the original equilibrium gold price, P_G^0, there is now an excess quantity of gold supplied. Gold producers will bid down the price of gold until it reaches the new equilibrium price, P_G^1, at which the quantity of gold demanded, G_1, again is equal to the quantity supplied. Because the level of prices of goods and services is the reciprocal of the price of gold, the fall in the price of gold implies that there is a rise in the level of prices of other goods and services. The gold discovery causes inflation, because it takes more units of gold to purchase a unit of a nongold good or service.

The effects of an increase in the demand for gold on the price of gold and the level of prices of goods and services Now consider what happens in a gold commodity money system when there is an increase in the demand for gold. Specifically, suppose that people discover a new industrial use for gold. As shown in Figure 2-12, this would cause an increase in the total demand for gold. At the initial equilibrium gold price P_G^0, there will be an excess quantity of gold demanded following the rise in gold demand. As a result, the equilibrium price of gold will rise to P_G^1; that is, the quantity of goods and services that must be given up in exchange for a unit of gold will increase. In turn, this implies that the amount of gold required to obtain a unit of goods and services will fall; the level of prices of goods and services must fall. Hence, an increase in the demand for gold reduces the aggregate level of prices of goods and services, which means that the economy experiences deflation. This deflation is accompanied, in turn, by a rise in the price of gold, or an increase in the purchasing power of gold money.

This example further illustrates how the price level in the economy is subject to conditions in the market for the commodity—gold—that people use as money. Even though the rise in the demand for gold resulted from an increased demand for gold for nonmonetary uses, gold still is the commodity money, and so there are effects on the prices of goods and services measured in terms of gold units.

A COMMODITY STANDARD SYSTEM

For much of the financial history of the United States, gold was the centerpiece of the nation's monetary system. Indeed, an international gold standard functioned effectively

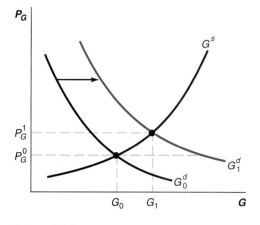

Figure 2-12

The Effects of an Increase in the Demand for Gold.   If a new industrial use for gold is developed, there will be an increase in the total quantity of gold demanded at any given price of gold; the gold demand schedule shifts rightward. At the initial equilibrium price of gold, P_G^0, there is, as a result, an excess quantity of gold demanded. Buyers of gold bid up the price to the point at which the quantity of gold demanded, G_1, again is equal to the quantity of gold supplied, but at the new, higher equilibrium gold price, P_G^1. Because the level of prices of goods and services is the reciprocal of the price of gold, this increase in the equilibrium price of gold implies that the level of prices of other goods and services falls. An increase in the demand for gold, other things constant, causes deflation in the economy.

off and on from the early 1800s until World War I, and the United States remained on a gold standard until 1933, just a couple of years beyond the abandonment of the gold standard by Great Britain. The reason that the gold standard was so durable was that mechanisms existed that could prevent gold discoveries or sudden changes in the demand for gold from affecting the aggregate level of prices of goods and services.

The Monetary Base   Under a gold standard, the primary foundation of a nation's monetary system is the quantity of gold. As in a gold commodity system, people may use the total amount of gold for monetary and nonmonetary purposes. Economists call the quantity of gold used as a basis for the commodity standard system **gold bullion.**

In a system in which gold fully backs money, the amount of gold bullion is the nation's **monetary base.** The monetary base is what its name implies; it is a "base" amount of money that serves as a foundation for the entire nation's monetary system.

Under a commodity standard, individuals no longer measure prices of goods and services in terms of units of gold. Instead, they measure prices in *currency units* such as dollars per unit of goods and services. That is, currency functions as the medium of exchange, unit of account, store of value, and standard of deferred payment. A currency's value, however, is linked to gold. This is done by establishing a *rate of exchange* between the nation's currency and gold.

In most instances in history a "central bank," such as a private bank like the Bank of England (which was privately owned and operated from 1694 until 1946) or a government agency such as the Federal Reserve System, has "pegged" the exchange rate of currency (pounds or dollars) for gold. Central banks did this by standing ready to buy or sell any quantity of gold at the fixed currency exchange. This would ensure that no one else would be able to buy gold for less or sell gold for more than that "pegged" currency price of gold.

For example, suppose that there are 100,000 ounces of gold bullion and that the fixed dollar-gold exchange rate established by the government is $30 per ounce of gold. Then the total *dollar value* of gold bullion would be $30 per ounce of gold times 100,000 ounces of gold bullion, which equals $3 million.

The Quantity of Money and the Price Level   The quantity of money under a commodity standard has at least two components. One is the amount of gold bullion, usually in the form of gold coins or precisely measured and marked bars of gold, which can function as a medium of exchange and therefore is money. Another is the amount of gold-backed tokens used as media of exchange. These could take several possible forms: coins backed by gold, currency notes issued by a private banking system, or currency notes issued by the government. Historically, societies have used all these types of monies under gold standards.

What does society gain from using a commodity standard? As previously discussed, one advantage is lower transaction costs. Private or governmental currency notes are much easier to use as means of payment than a heavy metal such as gold.

There is another *potential* benefit, however. Under a gold standard, the government can undertake policies that influence the quantity of money. For instance, in a system in which private bank notes circulate as currency, the government (or a central bank) can regulate the ratio of notes that the private banks issue relative to the amounts of gold they hold as assets, or the **gold reserve ratio.** Through such regulation, the government can influence the quantities of both notes and gold bullion; that is, it can influence the quantity of money in the economy.

Governmental policies also can affect the level of prices of goods and services under a gold standard. Because the government fixes the value of currency or coins in terms of gold, equilibrium in the market for gold continues to determine the equilibrium price level for goods and services in terms of gold. Even though prices in stores would be quoted in dollars, the dollar's gold value is fixed, and so a dollar price essentially is the same as a gold price. For example, if a dress were priced at $60 and the dollar-gold exchange rate were fixed at $30 per ounce of gold, then the gold price of the dress would be 2 ounces of gold ($60/$30 per ounce = 2 ounces).

Hence, under a gold standard, the price level in gold units remains the inverse of the price of gold in terms of goods and services, as in our model of the gold commodity system (recall Figure 2-10). The price level of goods and services measured in dollar terms then may be calculated by dividing by the dollar-gold exchange rate.

This does not mean, however, that the gold standard is identical to a gold commodity system. Under the gold standard, the government could influence the position of the gold demand schedule. It could do so by varying the gold reserve ratio: To increase the demand for gold, the government could require banks to hold more gold relative to the currency notes and coins they issue; to cause the demand for gold to decrease, the government could reduce the required bank gold reserve ratio. This means that the government could, in principle, vary the gold reserve ratio as needed to *stabilize the price of gold* in the face of gold discoveries or changes in the demand for gold for industrial uses. By stabilizing the price of gold, the government thereby could stabilize the level of prices of goods and services.

THE MONOPOLISTIC PROVISION OF MONEY

Because centralized policymaking can stabilize prices under a commodity standard such as a gold standard, governments historically have assumed responsibility for the supervision of nations' monetary systems. Indeed, in the past many governments have required that their citizens use only government-produced money as the single, legal medium of exchange. If a government assumes this power and enforces its control over the production of money, it becomes the *monopoly producer* of money. It is the only entity from which citizens of a nation can obtain a legally recognized, widely accepted medium of exchange.

A MONOPOLY MODEL OF MONEY

Suppose that a government were to declare that only gold coins that bear an official seal (that depicts, perhaps, a likeness of the leader of the government) are *legal* money for transactions in goods and services. Also, suppose that the government effectively enforces this rule through a system of severe penalties. (As we shall see below, there may be a reason that the government imposes severe penalties upon violators.) Let us consider how the market for gold coin money would function.

Figure 2-13 depicts the market for gold coins (GC) when the government is the sole producer of the coins. GC^d is the demand schedule for gold coins. Because the government is the sole producer of gold coins, it faces this demand schedule with no other competition.

Because the government is the sole producer of gold coins, it is able to choose the price of the gold coins, P_{GC}, measured in terms of units of goods and services per gold coin. Therefore, the **marginal revenue** that the government obtains from producing gold coins, which is the revenue gained from each coin produced, varies with the quantity of gold coins produced, along the marginal revenue schedule MR in Figure 2-13.

Suppose that the **marginal cost** of producing gold coins, which is the additional cost incurred in producing the next coin, is constant. In this case, the marginal cost schedule, MC, is horizontal, as shown in Figure 2-13. Under this assumption, the government incurs the same cost of producing each additional gold coin. This means that the average total cost (ATC) of producing gold coins, which is the total cost of gold coin production averaged over all units produced, is constant and equal to marginal cost, MC.

Seigniorage   In Figure 2-13, how many coins will the government produce, and what will be the price of gold coins? As we shall see, this depends on the aims of the government. For now, let us suppose that the government's goal is to maximize its own profit from producing gold coins as a medium of exchange for its citizens. If this is the government's goal, then it will produce gold coins to the point at which the marginal revenue it obtains from gold coin production is just equal to the marginal cost of producing gold coins, at the quantity GC_0. If it produced fewer coins than GC_0, the marginal revenue obtained from producing more coins would exceed the marginal cost of producing the coins, and so the government would increase its production. If it produced more coins than GC_0, the marginal cost of producing more coins would exceed the marginal revenue obtained, and so the government would cut back its production.

The government will charge a price for gold coins equal to the price that citizens are willing to pay for the quantity of gold coins produced. This price is equal to P_{GC}^0. By definition, revenue the government obtains at this price is equal to this price of gold coins, measured in terms of units of goods and services per gold coin, times the number of gold coins produced, or P_{GC}^0 times GC_0. For instance, if the price of gold coins is equal to 0.75

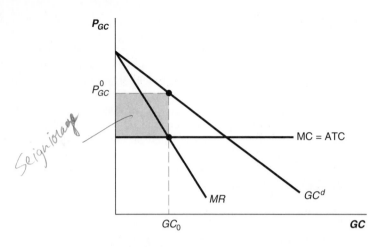

Figure 2-13
The Monopolistic Provision of Gold Coin Money. If the government is the sole supplier of gold coins, it alone faces the demand schedule for gold coin money of its citizens, GC^d, and the corresponding marginal revenue schedule, MR. If we assume that the government's marginal cost of producing gold coins is constant, then its marginal cost schedule is horizontal, and marginal cost is equal to average total cost of producing each gold coin.

If the government's goal is to maximize seigniorage from money production, it produces gold coins to the point at which marginal revenue is equal to marginal cost for the last gold coin produced, and GC_0 gold coins are produced. The government charges the price that its citizens are willing and able to pay for this quantity of gold coins, which is P_{GC}^0, measured in units of goods and services per gold coin. Its maximized seigniorage then is equal to $(P_{GC}^0 - ATC)$ times GC_0, which is the shaded rectangle in the diagram. The price level for the economy is equal to the reciprocal of the price of gold coins, or $1/P_{GC}^0$, and is measured in gold coins per unit of goods and services.

unit of commodities per unit of gold coins and the quantity of gold coins produced is 20 million, the total revenue the government obtains from producing gold coins is 15 million units of commodities. That is, in order to obtain the government-supplied medium of exchange, gold coins, the citizens of the country would have to sacrifice 15 million units of real goods and services.

The government's total cost of producing gold coins would be equal to the average total cost of production, ATC, times the number of gold coins produced. For instance, if ATC is equal to 0.50 unit of goods and services per gold coin and the quantity of gold coins produced by the government is equal to 20 million, then the total cost the government incurs in producing these coins is 10 million units of goods and services.

The difference between the total revenue and total cost in this example would be 5 million units of goods and services. This amount would be the maximum amount of profit obtained by the government as a result of its monopoly power over the production of gold coin money in this economy. Economists call the monopoly profit from money production **seigniorage.** Note that we measure seigniorage in terms of real goods and services. This means that seigniorage amounts to a real resource transfer from the citizens of the nation to the government that monopolisitically produces the gold coins. Hence, seigniorage really amounts to a tax that the government imposes on its citizens.

Note that we computed the amount of seigniorage by subtracting the government's total cost, ATC times GC_0 in Figure 2-13, from the government's total revenue, P_{GC}^0 times

GC_0. The difference between these quantities is the shaded rectangle in the figure. This area, then, is the maximum amount of seigniorage, measured in terms of goods and services, that the government can earn from producing gold coins monopolistically.

Note that seigniorage exists whenever the price, or market value, of the gold coin exceeds the average cost, or value of the underlying materials (such as gold) used to produce the coins. Seigniorage, then, is a charge levied by the government for the conversion of the metal into a bona fide, legal coin.

We assumed at the outset of our example that the government imposed stiff penalties for violating its laws concerning the use and treatment of gold coins. Why would the government do this? The reason is to keep the demand up. If the government permitted its citizens to use other types of money, then the demand for the coins it produces would fall. This would reduce the government's total revenues and, hence, the amount of seigniorage it would earn. If seigniorage is an important source of revenue for the government, it might view severe penalties for using other forms of money as a rational policy.

Debasement and Inflation Suppose that the government found a way to reduce the marginal cost of producing gold coins. A simple way to do this, for example, would be to put less gold into each coin. For instance, the government might start making its coins from an alloy of 10 percent gold and 90 percent brass. The coin would still be gold-colored but would be much cheaper to produce. Economists call the practice of reducing the gold base of coins, which historically was a commonplace action by governments that produced gold coins, **debasement.**

Figure 2-14 shows the effect of debasement. By lowering the marginal and average cost of producing coins, this action makes it profitable for the government to produce more coins; the amount of coins produced increases from GC_0 to GC_1. The government

Figure 2-14
The Effects of Debasement of Gold Coins. If the government debases gold coins by lowering the gold content in the coins, this action lowers the marginal cost of gold coin production. The seigniorage-maximizing quantity of gold coins produced increases to GC_1, and the seigniorage-maximizing price charged by the government falls to P_{GC}^1. The area of the seigniorage rectangle increases in the figure, and so seigniorage is larger as a result of debasement. Because the reciprocal of the price of gold coins is the level of prices of goods and services, the fall in the price of gold coins implies a rise in the price level, or inflation.

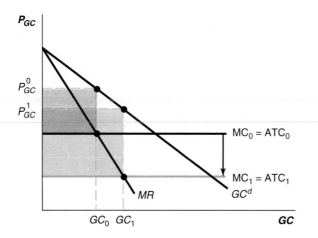

SEIGNIORAGE IN THE EUROPEAN COMMUNITY

INTERNATIONAL PERSPECTIVE

As we shall discuss in more detail in Chapter 30, several nations in Western Europe have formed a grouping of policy-cooperating and policy-coordinating nations called the European Community, or EC. One commonly expressed goal of the EC is to nearly equalize, at low levels, the inflation rates of the member nations. As the first column in the table below indicates, average annual inflation varied considerably across many EC nations for the period 1979–1988. Of the nations in the table, the average annual inflation rate over this period ranged from a low of 3 percent for Germany to a high of 18 percent for Portugal. Nevertheless, there has been a gradual movement toward inflation convergence for many nations in Europe, at least as compared with times past.

Complicating achievement of this goal, however, is the fact that several European governments traditionally have relied on seigniorage rather than direct taxation to finance government expenditures. Recent estimates of

seigniorage relative to national gross domestic product for the years range from a high of 4.6 percent for Portugal in 1983 to a low of 0.3 percent for Britain in 1987. That is, relative to national gross domestic product, seigniorage was over fifteen times greater in Portugal in 1983 than in Britain in 1987. Portugal, Greece, and, until recently, Italy (and, to a lesser extent, Spain) traditionally have experienced higher levels of seigniorage.

As the table indicates, those nations with the higher seigniorage levels also have been those with the higher average inflation rates. This, of course, accords with the theory developed earlier in the chapter. High seigniorage and high inflation go together. In contrast, reduction of inflation rates throughout Europe, which is a key goal of the EC, has also tended to reduce the amounts of seigniorage earned by countries such as Portugal and, in particular, Italy; as the table indicates, seigniorage in these nations fell over time. Indeed, with some exceptions the gradual overall trend across nations, including the United States, has been a decline in seigniorage. This has caused problems for those nations, such as Portugal

Average Inflation and Estimates of Seigniorage Relative to Gross Domestic Product

Country	Average Inflation Rate (%)* (1981-1991)	Seigniorage as a Percentage of Gross Domestic Product (%)[†]										
		1982	1983	1984	1985	1986	1987	1988	1989	1990	1991	1992
Portugal	17.1	4.4	4.6	4.3	3.5	2.7	2.4	2.0	1.6	1.3	0.9	0.6
Italy	9.8	2.6	2.2	1.7	1.5	1.1	0.9	0.9	0.8	0.7	0.6	0.5
Spain	9.4	1.8	2.4	1.5	0.9	0.8	1.4	1.2	1.1	0.9	0.8	0.6
Greece	19.0	2.4	2.3	2.1	2.1	1.9	2.4	2.0	1.7	1.4	1.0	0.7
France	6.4	1.1	1.0	0.9	0.8	0.5	0.6	0.6	0.6	0.5	0.5	0.5
Britain	6.4	0.6	0.5	0.4	0.4	0.4	0.3	0.4	0.4	0.4	0.4	0.4
Belgium	2.7	1.3	1.1	1.1	0.9	0.6	0.6	0.6	0.6	0.6	0.6	0.6
Germany	4.7	0.9	0.8	0.7	0.7	0.6	0.6	0.6	0.6	0.5	0.5	0.5
For comparison:												
U.S.	4.7	0.8	0.6	0.7	0.6	0.5	0.5	0.5	0.5	0.5	0.5	0.5

*Source: IMF International Financial Statistics, various issues.

[†]Source: Daniel Gros, "Seigniorage in the EC: The Implications of the European Monetary System and Financial Market Integration," International Monetary Fund Working Paper No. WP/89/7, Jan. 23, 1989. Ratios rounded to the nearest tenth. Ratios after 1988 are projected estimates of Gros.

and Italy, that in the past have depended heavily on seigniorage to help fund public expenditures. These nations have been forced to consider cutting back on spending or enacting direct tax increases.

A future problem the EC may have to address is what to do if the member nations create a single European central bank. Although that is unlikely to happen soon, the creation of a common "EuroFed" is an ex-pressed goal of many EC members. Such a EuroFed would earn seigniorage income from supplying money to the member nations of the EC; the big issue is, how would the seigniorage be divided up "fairly" among the member nations' governments? This problem complicates the task of creating a EuroFed. We shall see in the near future if the task is so complicated by the seigniorage issue that the idea of a EuroFed is abandoned.

also charges a lower price for gold coins, P^1_{GC} rather than the initial price of P^0_{GC}. As can be seen in Figure 2-14, debasement produces a larger amount of seigniorage, which is why governments have often debased their coins.

Note that the price of gold coins is measured in units of goods and services per gold coin. This price tells us the amount of goods and services that a gold coin can buy, or its purchasing power. Therefore, debasement lowers the purchasing power of the gold coin money that the government monopolistically produces. The reciprocal of the price of gold coins is measured in units of gold coins per unit of good or service, which is a measure of the prices of goods and services. As the price of gold coins, or their purchasing power, falls, the level of prices of goods and services rises. Although debasement increases seigniorage, it also causes inflation.

The Socially Optimal Provision of Money   Economists say that the economy achieves **allocative efficiency** in the production of a good or service when the price that members of society pay for the good or service is just equal to the additional cost incurred in producing that good or service, which is its marginal cost. When the good in question is money (say, gold coins), the economy achieves allocative efficiency if the price of gold coin money is equal to the marginal production cost of gold coin money.

There are two ways that the economy might achieve allocative efficiency in the production of gold coin money. One way would be for private firms to produce gold coins competitively. Consider our example in which the marginal cost of producing gold coins is constant and, as a result, equal to average total cost, as shown in Figure 2-15. Suppose that many firms are able to produce gold coins that individuals may use as money, that all firms are able to use the same technology for producing gold coins and therefore have to incur the same costs, that marginal cost is constant for each firm, and that both the firms and the coins they produce are indistinguishable. In this case, the industry would be perfectly competitive, and the constant marginal cost schedule in Figure 2-15 would be the supply schedule for the gold coin industry. This would be true because each firm's supply schedule would be the same marginal cost schedule. Summing these schedules horizontally then would produce the same horizontal schedule.

The competitive market equilibrium price of gold coins would be the point at which this horizontal industry supply schedule crosses the gold coin demand schedule, GC^d. The equilibrium quantity of gold coins would be equal to GC*, and the equilibrium price of a gold coin would be P^*_{GC} units of goods and services per gold coin. This price would be equal to the marginal cost of gold coin production. Therefore, competition among gold coin–producing firms would be allocatively efficient. For this reason, economists would call GC* the socially optimal quantity of money for this economy.

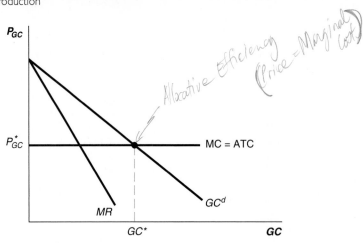

Figure 2-15
The Socially Optimal Provision of Gold Coin Money.   Allocative efficiency is achieved when the price of gold coins, P^*_{GC}, is equal to the marginal cost of the last gold coin produced. At this price of gold coins, the socially optimal quantity of gold coin money produced and supplied in the economy is equal to GC*.

There is another way that the economy could achieve allocative efficiency in the production of gold coin money. Rather than permitting many private firms to produce gold coins, the government could again take sole control of this process. Instead of maximizing its seigniorage, however, the government could itself choose to produce gold coins to the point at which the price it charges is equal to the marginal cost it incurs to produce the coins. The socially optimal quantity of gold coins produced again would be equal to GC* in Figure 2-15. At this price, given our assumption that the marginal cost of producing gold coins is constant and equal to average total cost, the government earns zero seigniorage.

Economists disagree about which approach to the socially optimal provision of money is most likely to succeed. On the one hand, some argue that we cannot trust governments to forego seigniorage in the interests of their citizens. On the other hand, other economists believe that a free, competitive market in the production of money may, for a variety of reasons, also fail to produce allocative efficiency. Leaving the production of money in the hands of private firms also prevents the government from controlling the gold reserve ratio, which limits its ability to stabilize the level of prices of goods and services.

As we shall see in subsequent chapters, governments historically have opted for a mix of governmental and private production of money. Typically, governments monopolisitically control the monetary base (for instance, the amount of gold bullion) and earn some seigniorage income; however, they typically permit private firms—banks—to produce other media of exchange. Indeed, this is the fundamental reason that money and banking are topics that naturally go together in a single textbook.

CHAPTER SUMMARY

1. Societies historically have adopted monetary systems rather than systems involving barter, because total exchange costs under barter typically are much higher. It is differences in exchange costs under different trading systems that largely account for an economy's monetary evolution.

2. Under a pure commodity money system, the demand for and supply of the commodity used as money determine the equilibrium purchasing power of that money commodity, and the reciprocal of the purchasing power of the money commodity is a measure of the level of prices of goods and services. Therefore, the purchasing power of the commodity money and the price level can vary with changes in the supply of and demand for the money commodity.

3. Under a commodity standard, a private or governmental central bank can influence the gold reserve ratio, which is the ratio of the monetary base (gold bullion under a gold standard) to the total quantity of money used in the economy. Therefore, a central bank can vary the total demand for gold in the economy, which permits it to attempt to stabilize the purchasing power of money and the level of prices of goods and services.

4. When governments produce the amount of money monopolistically, they are able to determine both the quantity of money and its purchasing power. As a result, they can earn profits from producing money by charging a higher price than the underlying marginal and average cost of producing money. We call the profits earned in this way monetary seigniorage.

5. The economy produces the socially optimal amount of money when the price of money, its purchasing power, is equal to the marginal cost of producing money, which economists call allocative efficiency.

6. Allowing competitive firms to produce money is one way that the economy can achieve allocative efficiency. Another way is for the government to produce money and charge a price equal to marginal cost, which reduces the government's seigniorage.

GLOSSARY

Allocative efficiency: A situation in which the price that members of society pay to purchase a good or service is just equal to the marginal cost of producing the last unit of that good or service.

Debasement: A reduction in the quantity of precious metal in a metal coin that the government issues as money.

Gold bullion: In a gold standard, the amount of gold used as money.

Gold reserve ratio: In a gold standard, the ratio of gold bullion to the total quantity of money, including bullion and other media of exchange such as currency notes.

Marginal cost: The increase in total production cost resulting from a 1-unit increase in production of a good or service.

Marginal revenue: The gain in total revenues resulting from a 1-unit increase in production of a good or service.

Monetary base: A ''base'' amount of money that serves as the foundation for a nation's monetary system. Under a gold standard, this is the amount of gold bullion.

Seigniorage: The process whereby governments gain ''profit'' by placing a face value on a coin or other monetary token that exceeds its inherent market value.

Transaction costs: The explicit costs an individual incurs in making a trade for a good or service.

Waiting costs: The costs that an individual incurs while waiting to make an exchange for a desired good or service.

SELF-TEST QUESTIONS

1. Can paper money be more valuable than the market, or intrinsic, value of the paper itself? Explain.

2. Why is the total exchange cost schedule U-shaped?

3. Why is it that the position of an individual's waiting cost schedule is unaffected by a switch from the use of barter to the use of money, while the position of the transaction cost schedule is altered?

4. During Poland's transformation from a command economy to a more market-oriented economy in the 1980s, there was a large amount of price inflation. In addition, inflation was very unpredictable during that period. As a result, many individuals began using cigarettes as money rather than the official Polish currency. Explain why this may have occurred.

5. A nation has a gold standard economy. Industries within this nation discover that they can use a newly developed metal alloy to produce goods and services that previously required gold. What can you predict will happen to the purchasing power of this nation's money, which includes both gold bullion and paper notes? What will happen to the level of prices of goods and services? How might a central bank that can control the nation's gold reserve ratio attempt to stabilize the purchasing power of money and the price level? Use a diagram to explain your answer.

6. A recent development in trading systems is computer trading, through which funds are transferred electronically by telephone lines or wire networks. Such exchanges have very low transaction costs and take place almost instantaneously. Explain why the development of computer trading might be expected to continue.

PROBLEMS

2-1. In a gold commodity money system, the purchasing power of money recently fell from 2 units of goods and services per unit of gold to 1 unit of goods and services per unit of gold.
   a. What has happened to the price of gold?
   b. What has happened to the level of prices of goods and services?

2-2. It is star date 2248.9. Captain Kirk and the crew of the starship *Enterprise* are involved in their continuing exploration of the galaxy under the direction of the governing body of the United Federation of Planets. The Federation has chosen to use gold as a free-market commodity money, partly because gold has been viewed as relatively scarce throughout the galaxy. Recently, however, Mr. Spock and a party of science officers discovered that an uninhabited sector of space is rich in massive gold deposits. What can Mr. Spock predict will happen to the purchasing power of money in the Federation? What can he predict will happen to the level of prices of goods and services throughout the galaxy? Explain.

2-3. Despite some undesirable properties, chocolate-covered cherry chewies are used as a commodity money in a free-market economy. The individuals in this economy recently have become caught up in a diet craze and have dramatically reduced their candy consumption of chocolate-covered cherry chewies. Nevertheless, they continue to use this commodity as money as before. What can you predict will happen to the purchasing power of money as a result of this diet craze? What will happen to the level of prices of other goods and services?

2-4. Suppose that a queen produces money monopolistically and maximizes the seigniorage that she earns. If the queen incurs a constant marginal cost of producing money of 0.25 unit of goods and services per unit of money produced and produces 100 million units of money, what price must she charge if she earns the maximum amount of seigniorage of 5 million units of goods and services at this level of money production? Explain, and show your work.

2-5. Presently, a king is producing gold coins to maximize his seigniorage from being the sole supplier of money. His present total revenue from producing gold coins is equal to 150 million units of goods and services, and this total cost of producing the coins is equal to 100 million units of goods and services. The marginal cost of gold coin production is constant, and the profit-maximizing quantity of gold coins produced is 50 million. If the king decided to set the price of gold at a level optimal for the citizens of his kingdom, what price should he set? Explain, and show your work.

2-6. Presently, a queen who wishes to maximize her seigniorage from money production observes that if she sells 10 million gold coins, her total revenue from gold coin production is 300 million units of goods, and the amount of seigniorage she earns is 200 million units of goods. The marginal cost of gold coin production is constant, and the ten-millionth gold coin sold increased the queen's revenues by 7 units of goods and services.

    a. Should the queen increase, decrease, or leave unchanged her production of gold coins, if her goal is to maximize her seigniorage?

    b. What is the average total cost of producing gold coins?

2-7. An explosion of the matter-antimatter engines of the starship *Enterprise* has stranded Captain Picard, First Officer Riker, Commander Data, and other members of the next generation of the *Star Trek* crew on an uninhabited planet. Starfleet regulations specify that, in such an event, the officers of the ship are to implement a monopolistic commodity standard as the monetary system for the starship's economy, using coins minted from dilithium crystals as money. Commander Data conducts a complete analysis of the desires of the crew and reports the following information to Captain Picard. If Captain Picard impounds all dilithium crystals and mints them into coins to be used as the only legal money, a price of 10 units of goods and services would result in no use of the money by the crew. If Captain Picard charged a price that maximized the seigniorage earned by the ship's officers, the appropriate price would be 6 units of goods and services per coin, and the crew would use 200 units. Commander Data also determined that the marginal cost of producing the coins is constant and equal to 2 units of goods and services per coin produced. Finally, sophisticated computer analysis has demonstrated that the crew's demand for dilithium crystal coins is a straight line. Draw a diagram of the market for dilithium crystal coins. Answer the following questions. Show all work, explain your answers, and express all answers in appropriate units of measurement.

    a. What is the maximum amount of seigniorage that can be earned by Captain Picard and his fellow officers?

    b. What is the socially optimal price of dilithium crystal coins?

    c. What would be the amount of dilithium crystal coins sold at the socially optimal price?

    d. What would be the amount of seigniorage earned by officers of the *Enterprise* at the socially optimal price of coins?

SELECTED REFERENCES

Barro, Robert J., "Money and the Price Level under the Gold Standard," *The Economic Journal,* 89 (353, March 1979), pp. 13–33.

Clower, Robert, "Introduction," in *Monetary Theory: Selected Readings* (New York: Penguin Books, 1969).

Pierce, James, *Monetary and Financial Economics* (New York: John Wiley and Sons, 1984).

CHAPTER 3

Money: Present and Future

1. Why is the quantity of money so difficult to measure?

2. What are the transactions and liquidity approaches to measuring money?

3. How is money officially defined in the United States?

4. What is the best definition of money?

5. Does money have a future? What is it likely to be?

Money is important. Changes in the total quantity of money and changes in the rate at which the quantity of money grows affect important economic variables, such as the rate of inflation, interest rates, employment, national income, the exchange value of a nation's money relative to the money of another nation, and national output. Although there is widespread agreement among economists that money is important, they have never agreed on how to define and how to measure money. In this chapter we will:

1. Discuss why it is important to define and measure money.

2. Analyze the two basic approaches to defining and measuring money.

3. Show how the Federal Reserve officially defines money and relate the official definitions to the basic approaches analyzed in item 2 above.

4. Explore how recent financial innovations have compounded the problems of defining and measuring money.

WHY IT IS IMPORTANT TO DEFINE AND MEASURE MONEY

Because changes in the total amount of money and in the growth rate of the quantity of money affect important economic variables, they can also affect the attainment of ultimate national economic goals. High employment, price stability (a situation in which neither significant inflation nor significant deflation exists), economic growth, and an equilibrium in international payments are all, directly or indirectly, related to changes in the total supply of money and to changes in the growth of money. The optimal quantity and optimal growth of money, therefore, are whatever quantity and growth rate that enable the nation to achieve these goals. Later chapters show how elusive these concepts of an ''optimal'' quantity and growth rate of money actually are. United States monetary policy—the determination of actions that change the quantity of money supplied by the Federal Reserve (the **Fed**) to achieve national economic goals—requires a meaningful definition of money. In particular, monetary policy requires the following:

1. A close correspondence must exist between the theoretical definition of money and the empirical (or measurable) definition of money. The real world doesn't allow scientists to measure their theoretical constructs perfectly; this problem is particularly important for monetary policy.

2. The Fed must be able to control the empirically defined quantity of money and to meet the targets that it sets for the growth of money with the tools at its disposal. The Fed cannot achieve ultimate national goals directly; what it can do is use its powers to alter some "moneylike" variables. We shall discuss the problem of setting monetary targets (or goals for the growth rate of money) in Chapter 25; we shall analyze the tools that the Fed can use to alter the quantity of money in Chapter 17.

3. The empirical definition of money must be closely and predictably related to ultimate national goals. It is not very useful to the nation if the Fed achieves its monetary growth-rate targets unless such achievement alters economic variables in a desired direction.

In short, a successful monetary policy requires that the Fed properly measure money and effectively control its growth rate.

TWO APPROACHES TO DEFINING AND MEASURING MONEY

There is honest disagreement about the proper definition of money and the "best" measure of money. The two basic approaches to measuring money are the **transactions approach,** which stresses the role of money as a medium of exchange, and the **liquidity approach,** which stresses the role of money as a temporary store of value.

THE TRANSACTIONS APPROACH

The transactions approach to measuring money emphasizes money's function as a medium of exchange. Proponents of this approach claim that the essence of money is that people accept it (and only it) as a means of payment for other goods and services. They stress that this is an important difference between money and other assets; a qualitative difference exists between those assets that perform as a medium of exchange and all other assets. All assets serve as a store of value; people accept only a few as a medium of exchange.

Given this theoretical preference for the definition of money, the transactions approach suggests that we should include only assets that serve as media of exchange in the empirical measurement of money. Such assets would include the coins and paper currency that people generally accept as a means of payment. Also included would be checkable accounts, on which people can write checks.

Regarding the second criterion for monetary policy, proponents of the transactions approach assert that the Fed can control the supply of money that people use to make transactions. Finally, many economists (some dating back to the nineteenth century, as Chapter 18 discusses) believe that money thus defined shows a reliable and predictable relationship to national economic goals. Households and businesses hold money to finance anticipated (and regular) expenditures in the near future; people hold "spending money." Economists refer to this as the *transactions motive* for holding money (Chapter 19). This should not be confused with holding money due to uncertainty about expenditures that may be incurred at some unknown time. Economists call this latter reason for holding money to meet emergencies the *precautionary motive* (also discussed in Chapter 19).

Traditionally, assets held in such forms (coins, currency, checkable accounts) have not earned interest and therefore have been subject to an opportunity cost of forgone interest. For that reason, we should expect that people are likely to minimize the money they hold as a medium of exchange. If the total supply of money were to increase (as a result of monetary authorities' actions or, in former times, new discoveries of those metals used as money), then we would expect that society as a whole would increase its spending. In turn, this increase in spending might well increase national output, national income, employment, and the price level. A decrease in the quantity of money would lead to a predictable reduction in community spending, with predictable effects on the variables associated with national economic goals.

THE LIQUIDITY APPROACH

The liquidity approach to measuring money stresses that the essential distinguishing property of money is that it is the most liquid of all assets. The **liquidity** attribute of an asset refers to the ease with which an individual can sell (or redeem) the asset at an unknown future time at a known nominal dollar price on short notice and with minimum costs.[1]

The Liquidity Continuum   This approach emphasizes the function of money as a store of value, and plays down the medium-of-exchange role that money plays. In effect, this approach implies that money is not qualitatively different from other assets; liquidity is a property of all assets, to some degree. We can rank assets along a continuum, ranging from money to financial assets such as stocks and bonds or real (nonfinancial) assets such as cars, stereos, and houses. Each of these assets serves as a store of value, but each possesses a different degree of liquidity.

Money is the most liquid of all assets; an individual does not need to convert money into something else before purchasing a good or service. Moreover, because the dollar is the unit of account (the specific measure in which people express prices and values), it can neither gain nor lose nominal value. The nominal (but not real) value of a dollar bill is always $1. By contrast, a house is not a very liquid asset. Real estate prices fluctuate in value; the dollar price of a house in the future is very likely to be different from the dollar price of that house at present. A house, furthermore, may take a long time to sell, and the eventual sale may entail substantial brokerage fees in converting that asset called a house into a spendable asset called money.

Liquidity and "Moneyness" of Money Assets   Using a liquidity definition of money to explain the role of money in the economy leads one to broaden the definition of money beyond the transactions approach. The liquidity approach includes in the measurement of money those assets that are highly liquid, that is, those assets that people can convert to money quickly, without loss of nominal dollar value and without much cost.

In general, any asset that guarantees to the holder a fixed nominal dollar value in the future is a candidate for inclusion in the liquidity measure of money. Another way to state this is that any asset for which no nominal capital gain or loss is possible qualifies as a perfectly liquid asset and is therefore money. Clearly, those assets that serve as media of exchange—coins, paper currency, and checkable accounts—meet this requirement. Economists call those highly liquid assets for which only slight capital gains or losses are

---

[1] John R. Hicks, "Liquidity," *Economic Journal,* 72 (288, December 1962), p. 787. Note that for ease of exposition we are equating money with the U.S. dollar—which holds true only in the United States.

How Does a Country Measure Money After a War?

INTERNATIONAL PERSPECTIVE

From August 1990 to February 1991, the army of Iraq occupied the neighboring country of Kuwait. During this occupation, Iraq declared the Kuwaiti *dinar*, the Kuwaiti fiduciary money, to be worthless. The Iraqis announced that Kuwait was an Iraqi province and forced the Kuwaiti people to use only the *Iraqi* dinar as their money during the time of occupation, and some Kuwaitis complied with this restriction. (Taking advantage of this restriction, some clever debtors paid off their Kuwaiti debts in Iraqi dinars during the occupation, because one Iraqi dinar actually was worth one-fifteenth of one Kuwaiti dinar.) Nevertheless, many Kuwaiti citizens buried their holdings of Kuwaiti dinars in their backyards or behind their businesses in anticipation of liberation by United States' and other allied forces. Others used Saudi Arabian riyals (the Saudi currency unit) and United States dollars as media of exchange and as stores of value, although the Iraqi occupiers required that the Iraqi dinar be used as the unit of account by all businesses.

By March 1991, U.S. and allied forces had liberated Kuwait, and the Kuwaiti people and their government began to pick up the pieces of their economy. One of the most pressing problems was figuring out what constituted money following the end of the war, given that Iraqi dinars, Saudi riyals, U.S. dollars, and, once again, Kuwaiti dinars all were circulating as money. As a further complication, following the war some people accepted Iraqi dinars in exchange while others rejected that currency.

Naturally, if people in a country do not agree on their media of exchange, it is very difficult to define and measure money in that country using the transactions approach. After all, this approach to measuring money counts only those financial assets that are used as exchange media. For this reason, the liquidity approach, which counts both monies and near monies, might seem a more useful definition of money for a country, such as Kuwait, after it has been through a war.

Needless to say, the Kuwaiti government faced a monetary nightmare after the war ended. It immediately sought to restore the Kuwaiti dinar–denominated accounts of all Kuwaitis to their preinvasion balances, regardless of what had subsequently been deposited or withdrawn. In anticipation of a return to a purely Kuwaiti dinar monetary system, many individuals and businesses rushed to use the Iraqi dinar while it still retained some purchasing power within Kuwait.

Estimates in early 1991 were that the real cost of the Kuwait government's "bailout" of the Kuwaiti monetary system, measured in 1991 U.S. dollars, would likely be about $20 billion—a significant cost for such a small country. Another estimate at the time, which surely was exaggerated, was that it would take about 200 years for accountants to sort out the assets and liabilities of Kuwaiti citizens. The Kuwaiti monetary recovery is not over yet.

Source: Adapted from Tony Horwitz and Craig Forman, "Buying Breakfast in Kuwait Can Be a Dinar Adventure," *Wall Street Journal,* March 14, 1991, p. A1.

possible **near monies.** Because they are highly liquid, they become candidates for inclusion as money, following the liquidity approach. As we shall see shortly, it is not clear where the cutoff point along the asset-liquidity continuum should be when categorizing assets into ''money'' and ''nonmoney.''

HOW THE FED MEASURES MONEY

The Fed incorporates both the transactions approach and the liquidity approach when it measures the quantity of money. As a result, it considers a variety of measures of money in the United States.

THE MONETARY BASE: THE NARROWEST MEASURE OF "MONEY"

We learned in the last chapter that under a gold standard the monetary base is the amount of gold bullion. In our fiat money system, however, gold does not play a direct role. Nonetheless, there is a **monetary base,** which is the quantity of government-produced money. In the United States, this money is equal to currency plus the reserves of depository institutions.

Consider Table 3-1, which shows specific amounts of the components of the monetary base as of January 1992. The $267.9 billion figure in the table represents the value of coins and paper currency outside the U.S. Treasury, the Federal Reserve banks, and the vaults of commercial banks. The paper currency consists of $1, $2, $5, $10, $20, $50, and $100 denominations; $500, $1,000, $5,000, and $10,000 bills were all discontinued in 1945. If high inflation rates return, we might see them again. Indeed, it is an interesting phenomenon that we continue to use bills of the same low denomination even as it takes more of them to buy goods and services: Between 1960 and 1990 there was nearly 425 percent inflation, so a $20 bill today buys less than a $5 bill did in 1960.

Currency   The following assets (owned by the nonfinancial institution public) compose the amount of **currency:**

1. *Coins minted by the U.S. Treasury:* The value of the metal in each coin is normally less than the face value of the coin. From time to time, the market value of the metal used in coins has risen so high that the coins have disappeared from circulation. Individuals have held the coins or melted them down and sold the metal, although this practice was and still is illegal. For example, in 1950 the market value of the silver in a dime was 7 cents. By 1962 the market value had risen to more than 10 cents. Dimes minted with a 90 percent silver content disappeared from circulation. People melted many for the silver content; they kept many more as collectors' items. When silver was selling for $2 per ounce, a bag of silver coins with a face value of $1,000 had a market value of $1,550.

2. *Federal Reserve notes issued by the Federal Reserve banks and U.S. notes issued by the U.S. Treasury:* Until 1960, the U.S. Treasury issued all $1 bills. These bills were called silver certificates. There are several hundred million dollars' worth of silver certificates still in circulation. The remainder of the paper bills in circulation are Federal Reserve notes. The Bureau of Engraving and Printing prints Federal Reserve notes under contract to the various Federal Reserve banks. As we shall discuss in Chapter 15, the Federal Reserve System consists of twelve separate banks. Each of these banks issues its own currency.

Reserves of Depository Institutions   Reserves of depository institutions are funds that these institutions—financial firms such as commercial banks, savings and loan associations, savings banks, and credit unions, that issue highly liquid liabilities called "deposits"—hold with the Federal Reserve System, plus the vault cash these institutions hold to meet the Fed's reserve requirements. As we shall see in some detail in Chapter 14, actions of the Fed ultimately determine the amount of reserves of depository institutions. Hence, these funds, like currency, directly represent government-supplied money.

Because the monetary base consists of money provided directly through actions of governmental institutions, it is the foundation of the fiduciary monetary system of the United States. People and firms generally accept currency and bank reserves in all trans-

TABLE 3-1
The Monetary Base, January 1992 (in billions)

Monetary Base Component	Amount
Currency	$267.9
Total reserves of depository institutions*	59.8
Total monetary base	$327.7

*Includes Federal Reserve cash items in process of collection less deferred cash items, and reserve clearing balances.
Source: Federal Reserve Bulletin.

actions (although some businesses, from fear of robbery, have become less accepting of currency in recent years). Hence, the monetary base satisfies the minimum requirements of the transactions approach to measuring money. In addition, however, the government guarantees that each unit of currency and bank reserves has a nominal value of $1. Therefore, these are unambiguously the most liquid of possible measures of money. Thus, the monetary base also satisfies the requirements of the liquidity approach to monetary measurement.

M1: THE TRANSACTIONS APPROACH

A broader measure of money than the monetary base includes both currency issued by the Federal Reserve and checking deposit money produced by private depository institutions. As we shall see in Chapter 14, the amounts of these deposits, in turn, depend on the amount of reserves supplied by the Fed. This measure of money, known as **M1,** is tabulated in Table 3-2.

All of us use currency in numerous transactions—in vending machines or for miscellaneous small purchases. Indeed, an estimate (see more detailed figures discussed later in this chapter) is that in 1993 Americans made more than 80 percent of all transactions in the United States using currency.

The Increased Importance of Currency as a Component of M1 in the United States   Both on a per capita basis and as a percentage of M1, currency has increased in significance in the United States. In 1973, for example, the amount of currency in circulation per American was about $325. By 1993 it had risen to about $1,050. As a percentage of M1, it has risen from 20.5 percent at the end of 1960 to more than 30 percent at the end of 1992.

Why has there been such a large expansion of the use of currency during recent decades? We're not sure, but one major reason is the increased size of the so-called underground economy.

The Growth in the Underground Economy   The **underground, or subterranean, economy** consists of cash transactions that individuals do not report to the Internal Revenue Service as income. Such cash transactions occur for several reasons, which include but are not limited to illicit drug sales, tax evasion, and payments of wages to illegal immigrants.

Putting illegal activities (such as drug dealing and prostitution) aside, the major increase

TABLE 3-2
The Fed's Measure of Money as a Medium of Exchange: M1, January 1992 (in billions)

M1 Component	Amount
Currency	$267.9
Transactions deposits:	
Demand deposits	300.0
Other checkable deposits	342.5
Traveler's checks	7.9
Total M1	$918.3

Source: Federal Reserve Bulletin. Figures rounded to nearest tenth of a billion.

in the underground economy has been due to individuals' attempts to avoid taxation by the federal and state governments. Tax rates in the United States had been rising until the Reagan administration reduced them significantly in the early 1980s. As more and more individuals were driven into higher and higher tax brackets, the incentive to engage in unreported economic exchange increased. For example, many professional home repair workers want to receive payments in cash so that there will be no record of their having received income.

Economists have made various estimates of the size of the underground economy. The lowest is around 2 percent of the reported gross national product, and the highest reaches 30 percent—a wide spread, to be sure.

Transactions Accounts Although people use currency for most transactions, because they use it mainly for small transactions, it accounts for a very small portion of the total dollar value of exchanges in the economy. For instance, in 1993 currency transactions only accounted for less than one-half of one percent of the dollar amounts in these transactions. (See the last section of this chapter for more details.) For larger transactions, individuals typically transfer funds from their transactions accounts. **Transactions accounts** include demand deposits and other checkable deposits (OCDs).

Demand deposits owned by the nonfinancial institution public Older money-and-banking texts emphasized the distinction between commercial banks and all other depository institutions. The distinction was crucial then because commercial banks were the only type of financial (depository) institution allowed by law to accept **demand deposits** (checking accounts). This was a reasonable definition until 1981. As we shall discuss in detail in Chapters 6 and 13, savings banks, savings and loan associations, and credit unions (which together commonly are called **thrift institutions**) now offer demand deposit accounts. Demand deposits nevertheless are the largest component of the M1 measure of money.

Economists use the term ''demand deposit'' because people can convert such a deposit to currency on demand (immediately) or use a check drawn on the deposit to make a payment to a third party. The checking account deposit itself does not have legal-tender status. Nonetheless, demand deposits are clearly a medium of exchange in this economy. The physical check itself is not money, however; rather, it is the *account balance* that is money. That is why one refers to demand deposits, or transaction account balances, rather than checks, as part of the quantity of money.

Other checkable deposits   Of growing importance in all definitions of the money supply are other checkable deposits in commercial banks and thrift institutions. These consist of the following:

1. *Negotiable orders of withdrawal (NOW) accounts:* **NOW accounts** are interest-bearing savings accounts on which people may write checks. Until 1981, NOW accounts were authorized only in New England, New York, and New Jersey. Since 1981, all states have allowed NOW accounts or their equivalent. Business corporations may not use NOW accounts.

2. *Automatic-transfer-system (ATS) accounts at commercial banks:* An **ATS account** is a combination of a savings account on which depository institutions pay interest on the outstanding balance and a regular checking account on which these institutions pay no interest. Usually, the account holder keeps a relatively small balance in the checking account but writes checks freely. Whenever there is a negative balance in the checking account, the depository institution makes an automatic transfer from the interest-earning savings account.

Traveler's Checks   A purchaser pays for traveler's checks at the time of transfer. The total quantity of traveler's checks outstanding issued by institutions other than banks is part of the M1 measure of money.[2] American Express, Citibank, Cooks, and other institutions issue traveler's checks.

M2: THE LIQUIDITY APPROACH

The narrowest definition of the money supply, M1, does not include the so-called near monies, which are slightly less liquid assets. To the extent that an individual's willingness to spend depends on his or her total liquidity, the inclusion of near monies in the measure of money provides a ''better'' definition of the money supply for the purpose of explaining changes in economic activity. The Fed calls this somewhat broader definition of the money supply **M2.** Table 3-3 details the composition of M2. M2 consists of M1 plus the following:

1. Savings and small-denomination time deposits at all depository institutions
2. Overnight repurchase agreements (RPs) at commercial banks
3. Overnight Eurodollars held by U.S. residents (other than banks) at Caribbean branches of Fed member banks
4. Balances in money market mutual funds
5. Money market deposit accounts

Savings Deposits   Savings deposits in all depository institutions (e.g., commercial banks, mutual savings banks, savings and loan associations, and credit unions) are part of the M2 money supply. Savings deposits—in contrast to time deposits, discussed below—have no set maturities. Savings deposits also include the money market deposit account (introduced on December 14, 1982), which allows limited checking privileges (six checks per month) and unceilinged interest rates. Savings deposits can be of two kinds: statement or passbook.

---

[2] Banks place the funds they use to redeem traveler's checks in a special deposit account. Therefore, traveler's checks at banking institutions already are counted as transactions deposits. Nonbank issuers, however, do not place these funds in transactions accounts. Improvements in data collection made it possible to begin including traveler's checks in M1 beginning in June 1981.

T A B L E   3-3
A Fed Measure of Money as a Temporary Store of Value: M2, January 1992 (in billions)

M2 Component	Amount
MI	$ 918.3
Savings deposits and money market deposit accounts	1,055.7
Small-denomination time deposits	1,048.1
Overnight RPs and Eurodollars	77.8
Money market mutual funds	360.2
Total M2*	$3,460.1

* M2 is not exactly equal to the sum of its components for a technical reason. See any H-6 series, a Federal Reserve statistical release.
Source: Federal Reserve Bulletin. Figures rounded to nearest tenth of a billion.

Statement savings deposits   With a **statement savings account,** the depositor receives a monthly statement or record of deposits and withdrawals and the interest earned during the month. The holder can make deposits and withdrawals by mail.

Passbook savings deposits   A **passbook savings account** requires that the owner physically present a paper passbook each time he or she makes a deposit or a withdrawal. The depository institution or deposit holder marks the passbook to record the deposits and withdrawals. In the United States, passbook savings deposits are more popular than statement savings deposits.

Small-Denomination Time Deposits   Time deposits include savings certificates and small certificates of deposit. These deposits have set maturities. The Fed includes only time deposits with denominations less than $100,000 in the M2 definition of money—hence the name small-denomination time deposits. The owner of a savings certificate, or a certificate of deposit (CD), is given a receipt indicating the amount deposited, the interest rate the owner will receive, and the maturity date. A CD is an actual certificate that indicates the date of issue, its maturity date, and other relevant contractual matters. Like other time deposits, the CD cannot be withdrawn before its maturity date without being subject to an interest rate penalty for early withdrawal.

A variety of small-denomination time deposits are available. They include six-month money market certificates as well as floating-rate (varying with market rates) certificates of 2 to 4 years' maturity or more.

Overnight Repurchase Agreements at Commercial Banks   A **repurchase agreement at a commercial bank (REPO, or RP)** allows a bank to sell Treasury or federal agency securities to its customers and then to repurchase them at a higher price that includes accumulated interest. An *overnight* repurchase agreement permits the bank to sell Treasury or federal agency securities to its customers, coupled with an agreement to repurchase them at a higher price the following day. RPs help to fill a gap because existing laws do not allow businesses to use NOW accounts; RPs are a financial innovation that bypasses regulation. We shall discuss them in more detail in Chapter 5.

Overnight Eurodollars   Overnight Eurodollars are dollar-denominated, one-day-term deposits in foreign commercial banks and in foreign branches of U.S. banks. The phrase ''dollar-denominated'' means simply that although an individual or firm might hold the deposit at (say) a Caribbean commercial bank, it is valued in U.S. dollars rather than in the local currency. The term ''Eurodollar'' is inaccurate, because banks outside continental Europe participate in the so-called Eurodollar market, and also because banks in some countries issue deposits denominated in German marks, Swiss marks, British sterling, and Dutch guilders.

Money Market Mutual Fund Balances   Many individuals and institutions keep part of their assets in the form of shares in **money market mutual funds.**[3] These mutual funds hold only short-term debt instruments. Most of these money market funds allow check-writing privileges, provided that the size of the check exceeds some minimum, such as $500 or $1,000. It is important to realize that federal deposit insurance does *not* apply to these funds; note also that they are not subject to interest rate ceilings or reserve requirements.

Money Market Deposit Accounts   These are accounts issued by banks and thrift institutions. They have no minimum maturity, allow limited checking privileges, and pay an interest rate comparable to the money market mutual fund rate. Federal deposit insurance, which we discuss in Chapter 12, covers these accounts. After depository institutions introduced these accounts in 1982, they grew explosively, to $350 billion within a year.

M3: AN EVEN BROADER DEFINITION OF MONEY

An even broader definition of money officially tabulated by the Federal Reserve System is M3. **M3** consists of M2 plus the following:

1. Large-denomination time deposits at all depository institutions
2. Term repurchase agreements at commercial banks and savings and loan associations
3. Term Eurodollars
4. Institution-only money market mutual fund balances

Large-Denomination Time Deposits   Time deposits that have face values of $100,000 or more are **large-denominaton time deposits.** A major difference between large-denomination and small-denomination time deposits is that the former are negotiable; people can buy and sell these deposits with little difficulty and with no interest penalty. A small-denomination time deposit is not negotiable. The most common name for a large-denomination time deposit is a **jumbo certificate of deposit,** or **jumbo CD.** Business firms own most large-denomination CDs. Firms use the CDs as a means to save idle funds for short periods of time.

Term Repurchase Agreements at Commercial Banks, Savings Banks, and Savings and Loan Associations   Term RPs are similar to the overnight RPs described previously, but they are for longer than overnight. Maturities may range from a week to a month.

---

[3] First introduced by Bruce Brent's Reserve Fund in 1972, they are pools of funds contributed by savers. The institution, or ''fund,'' uses the pooled funds to purchase short-term instruments such as Treasury bills, bank certificates of deposit, and commercial paper (all discussed in Chapter 5).

Term Eurodollars   Term Eurodollars are similar to the overnight Eurodollars discussed earlier, but they mature after a week or a month.

Institution-only money market mutual fund balances   These are accounts held at money market mutual funds by institutions rather than individuals.

What distinguishes items in M3 from those included in M2? The difference is liquidity. Term RPs and term Eurodollars are less liquid than overnight RPs and overnight Eurodollars because they have longer terms to maturity. Likewise, large time deposits are less liquid than small time deposits. The Fed separates institution-only money market accounts from those held by individuals for exclusion from M2 because, after detailed studies, the Fed determined that these accounts had rates of turnover—a rough measure of liquidity—lower than those of money market mutual fund accounts held by individuals.

A MEASURE OF LIQUIDITY: L

The Federal Reserve System uses a broad definition of liquidity and labels it L. **L** consists of M3 plus other liquid assets such as term Eurodollars held by U.S. residents other than banks, banker's acceptances, commercial paper, Treasury bills and other liquid Treasury securities, and U.S. savings bonds. Although the Fed publishes data for L, it really does not concern itself with controlling L.

WHAT IS THE "BEST" DEFINITION OF MONEY?

Which, then, is the best definition of money: M1, M2, or M3? To answer this question, recall that we began this chapter by noting that monetary policy requires (1) a close correspondence between the theoretical definition and the empirical (measurable) definition of money, (2) an ability on the part of the monetary authorities to control the empirically defined money supply, and (3) a close and predictable relationship between changes in the empirically defined money supply and ultimate national economic goals.

The determination of which of the three monetary aggregates, M1, M2, or M3, most closely meets these three criteria is not an easy job. For one thing, economic theory suggests two theoretical approaches: the transactions approach and the liquidity approach. Which of these two is superior depends ultimately on which is easier to control and which relates more closely to economic goals.

FINANCIAL DEREGULATION AND MONEY

One problem in determining the "best" measure of money is that, even though the dust generated from the financial services revolution is settling, we can't be sure which monetary aggregate is most controllable by the Fed. In October 1979 the Fed announced that it would place more emphasis on targeting the growth rates of monetary aggregates. Because M1 related closely to the transactions concept, many people believed that it was the "best definition of money." One of the important early effects of the 1980s deregulation, however, involved the flow of funds into newly authorized types of accounts. That is, households moved their funds, in search of higher interest rates, whenever depository institutions or new legal regulations created a new financial instrument—or whenever individuals or firms found a new loophole in existing financial regulations. This funds transfer distorted the data, and in 1982 the Fed decided to deemphasize the M1 target temporarily and concentrate on the broader monetary aggregates.

Since 1981, no other regulatory efforts have had such distortive effects. After a short period the Fed again set M1 targets, but in 1987 the Fed once more abandoned the M1 targets, amid much controversy, in favor of M2 and M3. We shall have much more to say about financial deregulation in Chapters 10 and 11, and we shall return to the issue of which targets to set in Chapter 25.

MONEY AND OTHER ECONOMIC VARIABLES

A significant problem for choosing the best measure of money is that there is mixed evidence about which aggregate is most closely and predictably related to national economic goals. In some periods M1 seems to relate more closely; in other periods a narrower or broader monetary aggregate seems to predict better. Figure 3-1 shows that the monetary aggregates grow at different rates—and, at times, even in different directions. Because they do not change in tandem, policy makers must eventually choose one over the others as being ''best.'' Also, because the monetary aggregates grow at different rates, outside observers often come to very different conclusions about what kind of monetary policy the Fed is actually pursuing.

In recent years, the one point on which most economists have agreed is that M1 has not been a very good indicator of other economic variables. Beyond this point, however, there is sharp disagreement. Some economists and policy makers, for instance, promote the use of the monetary base as the measure of money most closely related to economic activity. Others, in contrast, claim that a broader aggregate such as M2 or M3 is preferable.

ALTERNATIVES TO SIMPLE-SUM MONETARY AGGREGATES

Because the monetary base, M1, M2, M3, and L are sums of different components, economists call them **simple-sum monetary aggregates.** In recent years economists have experimented with construction of alternative monetary aggregates, called **divisia aggregates.** These are constructed by converting conventional monetary aggregates such as M1 into weighted averages of their components. This approach tries to separate the individual components of M1 and weight them by their transactions, not savings, component. This method assigns the highest weights to assets such as currency, which yield the greatest flow of monetary services, and assigns a lower weight to such assets as NOW accounts, which yield a flow of store-of-value services as well as monetary services.

According to proponents of divisia aggregates, monetary economists and policy makers have a lot to learn from the theory of constructing *statistical index numbers,* such as price or wage indexes. Indeed, they argue that the simple-sum measures of money are very poor statistical measures of money. They further argue that measures such as M1, M2, and M3 have a very weak, if any, logical basis, as viewed from either a transactions or a liquidity perspective.

This view has enjoyed some success in recent years. The Fed now tabulates divisia monetary aggregates on a regular basis, and it continues to evaluate their relationship to other economic variables like output, employment, and inflation. Nevertheless, the simple-sum aggregates continue to dominate policy discussions. How best to calculate the weights used in divisia indexes is debatable, and the simple-sum aggregates are, by definition, simple to work with.

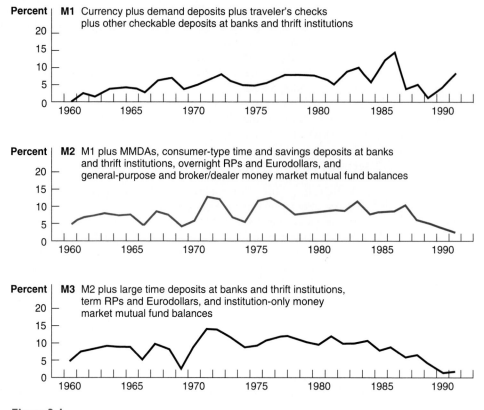

Figure 3-1
Growth of the Monetary Aggregates.   A close inspection of these three graphs shows that the three monetary aggregates, M1, M2, and M3, grow at different rates and even in different directions. This presents the possibility that one could be the "best" empirically defined money supply. (*Source:* Federal Reserve Board of Governors.)

CONTROLLABILITY OF MONETARY AGGREGATES

One reason that a simple-sum measure of money such as M1 or M2 continues to receive the most attention from the Fed is that experience with these measures has taught the Fed how policy actions influence them. After working so long with simple-sum measures of money, it would be a lengthy and costly process for the Fed to switch to index-number measures of money, because it would have to learn how to control such a new measure of money. Any measure of money, whatever its logical foundations, must be controllable if it is to be of practical use for monetary policy. For this reason, Fed pragmatism has led to continued use of simple-sum measures of money, which are thought to be more controllable at present.

Nevertheless, some economists recently have explored the possibility that properly constructed divisia aggregates may relate more closely to other economic variables. Some have even concluded that it may be possible that these aggregates also may be more controllable than simple-sum measures. Research on this issue is likely to continue.

MONETARY AGGREGATES IN OTHER COUNTRIES

INTERNATIONAL PERSPECTIVE

The central banks of other nations use their own special monetary aggregates. The Bank of France, for instance, focuses on its own M2, measured in francs. The French M2 consists of currency, checking accounts, and "savings accounts available at sight," which are analogous to passbook savings accounts in the United States. Germany's central bank, the Deutsche Bundesbank, follows most closely the behavior of its own, deutschemark, version of M3, which is composed of currency, "savings accounts available at sight," time deposits with maturities under 4 years, and "savings deposits at statutory notice," which are similar to statement savings deposits in the United States. The Bank of Japan recently has monitored most closely the "broadly defined money stock," measured in yen. This measure of money is the Japanese M2 (currency plus all demand, savings, and time deposits) plus certificates of deposit. Finally, the Bank of England pays closest attention to its M3, which consists of currency and *all* sterling deposits, including certificates of deposit, held at banks in the United Kingdom.

There are some clear similarities among the measures of money in these nations and the M2 and M3 measures used by the Federal Reserve System in the United States. Indeed, an interesting development over the past two decades has been the convergence in the ways that central banks in different countries measure their nation's money stocks.

Another type of convergence has been a trend toward the use of broad aggregates such as the various "M2s" and "M3s," rather than the monetary base or an M1-type measure, as the main indicators or targets of monetary policy. The United Kingdom may be an exception, because the Bank of England recently began adopting fairly narrow growth targets for what it calls "M0," which is the British monetary base. There also have been discussions about the possibility of paying more attention to growth of the monetary base in the United States. Nonetheless, most central banks in recent years have focused their attention and efforts on broad, rather than narrow, monetary aggregates. The liquidity approach appears to be winning out over the transactions approach in most parts of the world.

Source: Dallas S. Batten, Michael P. Blackwell, In-Su Kim, Simon E. Nocera, and Yuzuru Ozeld, The Conduct of Monetary Policy in the Major Industrial Countries: Instruments and Operating Procedures, International Monetary Fund Occasional Paper No. 70, Washington, D.C., July 1990.

We return to the issue of monetary control in Chapter 25. Right now you need only be aware of the seeds of the problem—the difficulty of separating the transactions definition of money from the liquidity definition, or distinguishing between the function of money as a medium of exchange and its function as a temporary store of value.

THE FUTURE OF MONEY

According to the theory of the evolution of money that we developed in Chapter 2, a natural progression for any economy is to use trading systems with lowest total exchange costs. When the technology for making transactions improves, society tends to adopt more "high-tech" means of trading goods and services, lowering the minimum possible exchange cost. As a result, the time people spend making exchanges falls. We like to think that we live in a high-tech or "information" age; it is natural to expect that our society has found imaginative ways to lower exchange costs and the amount of time spent making exchanges. We also might expect that our efforts to achieve these goals would have implications for the use of money in our high-tech world.

Traditionally, coin and currency (cash), checks, and traveler's checks have represented the media of exchange most used for transactions for goods and services, as shown in Table 3-4. According to these estimates, individuals and firms used currency and checks in about 97.5 percent of all transactions made in the United States in the years shown. These and other nonelectronic means of payment—including traveler's checks, **credit cards,** and **money orders**—accounted for almost (but not quite) 100 percent of all transactions. Electronic means of payment—payments made through transmitting electronic impulses, instead of pieces of paper or coins, over wires between people and their computers—accounted for less than one-half of one percent of transactions in the U.S. economy.

There are a variety of means of payment besides cash and checks. Other nonelectronic means of payment are traveler's checks (discussed earlier in this chapter), credit cards—with which many of us are acquainted—and money orders. The total numbers of transactions for these types of payments are listed in the "other" category in Table 3-4. Credit card purchases amount to immediate loans from a firm or financial institution to a customer. The customer signs a receipt for, say, a Sears credit card or VISA transaction, receives the merchandise or service on the spot, and the firm (Sears) or financial institution (say, Citibank) honors payment or extends credit to the customer. Because the customer receives the good or service, she has purchased it without immediately using cash or checks. (Hence, credit cards do not appear in the money definitions; they *defer* rather than complete transactions.) In a money order transaction, individuals exchange cash or a check for a title (the money order) to those funds, which some firms prefer to either cash or a private check.

T A B L E   3-4
Volume of Nonelectronic and Electronic Payments
Estimates and Projections for the United States

Means of Payment	Number of Transactions (millions)			Percent of Total Transactions		
	1978	1987	1993*	1978	1987	1993*
Cash	250,000	278,600	299,500	86.87	83.42	80.55
Checks	30,000	47,000	63,400	10.42	14.07	17.05
Other	7,000	7,300	7,500	2.43	2.17	2.02
Total non-electronic	287,000	332,900	370,400	99.72	99.66	99.62
Wire transfers	29	84	171	0.01	0.03	0.05
Other	750	1,020	1,250	0.27	0.30	0.33
Total electronic	779	1,104	1,421	0.28	0.33	0.38
Total	287,779	334,004	371,821	100.00	100.00	100.00

*Authors' projections; simple growth extrapolations.

Sources: 1978 estimates: Ralph C. Kimball, "Wire Transfer and the Demand for Money," *New England Economic Review,* Federal Reserve Bank of Boston, March/April 1980.

1987 estimates: Allen N. Berger and David B. Humphrey, "Market Failure and Resource Use: Economic Incentives to Use Different Payment Instruments," in *The U.S. Payments System: Efficiency, Risk, and the Role of the Federal Reserve,* ed. David B. Humphrey (Boston: Kluwer Academic Publishers, 1989).

Because people accomplish credit card or money order transactions on paper, these, similar to cash or checks, are nonelectronic means of payment. There are four main ways that individuals or firms can make payments electronically. They can use the services of **automated clearing houses,** which are electronic-processing intermediaries between senders of funds and ultimate receivers. Alternatively, they can bypass these intermediaries by sending funds directly, via **wire transfers** (for instance, over telephone lines).

The technology also exists (and has existed since the 1960s) to transmit funds directly from a bank account to a firm when a customer purchases a good or service. This is called a **point-of-sale transfer.** A person and firm could accomplish this by using a plastic card with an account number magnetically encoded. The clerk could insert the card into the point-of-sale cash register at the firm's retail outlet when the customer purchases a good or service, and a computer-guided electronic system would send funds, by wire, automatically from the customer's bank account to the firm. Such systems exist, but people and firms presently do not widely use them. Some people also arrange for their depository institutions to pay some of their bills from their deposit account; **automated teller machine bill payment** is one way to do this. People also do not widely use this type of electronic means of payment at present. In Table 3-4, automated-clearing house, point-of-sale, and automated-teller-machine transactions are included together in the ''other'' category, and wire transfer transactions are listed separately.

Table 3-4 makes clear that most of our transactions are done nonelectronically. It would be tempting to conclude that we are not so high-tech after all. But this would be a mistaken conclusion.

Rather than concentrating on the *numbers* of transactions accomplished using various means of payment, Table 3-5 depicts the *dollar values* of those transactions. That is, it emphasizes the dollar amounts exchanged using different means of payment, rather than the numbers of payments made.

Viewed from this perspective, it is apparent that electronic means of payment are very important. By far, most dollar exchanges in the United States are electronic. Wire transfers alone are estimated to account for more than 83 percent of the dollar amounts of exchanges in 1993. In contrast, people probably used cash and private and traveler's checks to make no more than 16 percent of their dollar payments in that year.

When we compare Tables 3-4 and 3-5, we can conclude that cash and checks are primarily used for smaller dollar transfers, while wire tranfers represent much larger dollar transfers. From Table 3-5, we see for 1993 an estimated 299,500 million cash transactions probably will account for about $3,400 billion dollars' worth of transfers, or a little over $11 per cash transaction. In contrast, about 63,400 million check transactions are estimated to account for about $134,000 billion dollars' worth of transfers in 1993, or about $2,114 per check transaction (keep in mind that many checks, such as paychecks, are made out in large dollar amounts, and so the average is higher than you might otherwise have expected). In the case of wire transfers, about 171 million transactions are estimated to account for about $738,300 billion in exchanges in 1993, or about $4,317,544 per transfer! People—usually firms or financial institutions—clearly use wire transfers when they exchange very large sums.

THE CASHLESS SOCIETY

A couple of decades ago, one would commonly encounter speculation that by the end of the twentieth century people would no longer use cash and checks—nor any other forms of paper or coin—as media of exchange. All ''money,'' pundits speculated, would ultimately be ''electric money,'' or computer impulses transmitted across copper wires—or,

TABLE 3-5
Dollar Values of Nonelectronic and Electronic Payments
Estimates and Projections for the United States

Means of Payment	Total Dollar Value (billions)			Percent of Total Dollar Payments		
	1978	1987	1993*	1978	1987	1993*
Cash	$ 375	$ 1,400	$ 3,400	0.45	0.41	0.38
Checks	15,000	55,800	134,000	18.13	16.37	15.16
Other	125	434	995	0.15	0.12	0.11
Total non-electronic	$15,500	$ 56,234	$138,395	18.73	16.49	16.65
Wire transfers	$65,983	$281,000	$738,300	79.75	82.45	83.52
Other	1,250	3,601	7,290	1.51	1.05	0.82
Total electronic	$67,233	$284,601	$745,590	81.26	83.51	84.34
Total	$82,733	$340,835	$883,985	100.00	100.00	100.00

*Authors' projections; simple growth extrapolations.

Sources: 1978 estimates: Ralph C. Kimball, "Wire Transfer and the Demand for Money," *New England Economic Review,* Federal Reserve Bank of Boston, March/April 1980.

1987 estimates: Allen N. Berger and David B. Humphrey, "Market Failure and Resource Use: Economic Incentives to Use Different Payments Instruments," in *The U.S. Payments System: Efficiency, Risk, and the Role of the Federal Reserve,* ed. David B. Humphrey (Boston: Kluwer Academic Publishers, 1989).

using more recent technology, via fiber-optic cables. Were these guesses correct? It depends upon how one chooses to measure money.

The Transactions Approach   From a transactions perspective, an M1 definition of money is not perilously out-of-date. As Table 3-4 indicates, people make a very large percentage of all their transactions using cash or checks. If what really counts is what media people use to make exchanges, these media of exchange are what really matter in our economy, and measuring these items as money is appropriate.

Consequently, some current observers argue that the evidence demonstrates that those who have claimed that we are becoming a cashless (and, eventually, checkless) society are wrong. According to these observers, who use the transactions approach to measuring money, M1 (or, perhaps, a divisia monetary aggregate) remains a perfectly legitimate measure of money, irrespective of all the technological developments of the past couple of decades.

The Liquidity Approach   Those who continue to believe that new payments-system technologies are making us more and more a cashless society adopt the liquidity approach to measuring money. These observers find the data in Table 3-5 most indicative of what really matters, which is the dollar amounts of liquidity available for use in purchasing goods and services. They conclude that cash and checks—the M1 measure of money—represent a small fraction of the available liquidity in our "high-tech" economy. Consequently, they view M1 as an overly narrow measure of money in a nearly cashless society. These advocates of the liquidity approach argue that continuing improvements in payments-system technology require that the Federal Reserve use broader measures of money, such as M2, M3, or even L.

THE FUTURE OF MONEY

What should be clear is that how one forecasts the future of money depends on the approach one takes to measuring what money is. The history of projections of a "cashless society" by the year 2000 demonstrates that this is the conclusion we must reach. Those economists who adopt the transactions approach to measuring money likely will remain convinced that narrow measures of money such as the monetary base or M1 will remain useful concepts into the far future. In contrast, those economists who use a liquidity approach to measuring money are likely to reach the conclusion that broader monetary aggregates are appropriate.

We should expect, then, that this divergence in views will widen as time passes. Technology surely holds much more in store for us—after all, scientists speculate today about someday having the ability to store information on individual molecules instead of today's "bulky" microchips. Trading systems will grow ever more sophisticated, and people may trade more and more dollars using media besides cash or checks. Money's future in all these developments may not significantly change, or it eventually may disappear, depending upon how one views money.

CHAPTER SUMMARY

1. Because money is what people accept as money, in practice money assumes different forms. Also, technological changes in the banking industry lead to changes in the form of money. For these reasons, money is difficult to define and measure.

2. There are two basic approaches to measuring money: the transactions approach and the liquidity approach. The transactions approach stresses that money is a medium of exchange. This approach excludes asset forms that cannot be used directly to make transactions; the Fed excludes U.S. government securities and savings deposits from such a strict definition of money because individuals must first convert them before making purchases. The liquidity approach stresses that people can, by definition, easily convert very liquid assets into money without loss of nominal value; any capital gains or losses are very small. As such, they represent an asset form that measures potential transactions. Hence, the liquidity approach includes near monies in the definition of money.

3. Today there are several official definitions of money: M1, M2, and M3. These range from narrow to broad measures of money. The broader measures include less liquid assets.

4. An effective monetary policy requires (a) a close correspondence between the theoretical definition and the empirical definition of money, (b) an ability to control the empirically defined money supply, and (c) a close and predictable relationship between changes in the money supply and ultimate national economic goals.

5. In practice, neither M1, M2, nor M3 best satisfies the three criteria described in item 4 above.

6. Because of the revolution in money and banking financial services, divergences in views about what constitutes money are likely to widen with time.

GLOSSARY

Automated clearing houses: Electronic processing intermediaries between senders of funds and ultimate receivers.

Automated teller machine bill payment: Transfer of funds from an individual's account at a depository institution to another individual or firm, initiated at an automated teller machine, which is commonly known as a ''bank machine.''

ATS accounts: Automatic-transfer-system accounts; a combination of interest-bearing savings accounts and non-interest-bearing checking accounts, in which funds are automatically transferred from savings accounts to checking accounts when the latter are overdrawn.

Credit cards: Cards used to initiate automatic loans to a customer, enabling the customer to purchase a good or service from a firm without need for cash or check.

Demand deposits: Deposits placed in a depository institution, payable on demand and transferable by check.

Depository institutions: Financial institutions that accept deposits for savers and lend those deposits out at interest.

Divisia aggregate: A monetary aggregate that is constructed by converting a conventional monetary aggregate into a weighted average of its individual components; those components that mostly provide a transactions service are weighted more heavily than those components that provide more of a store-of-value service.

Fed: The Federal Reserve System; the central banking system of the United States.

Jumbo certificate of deposit (jumbo CD): A large (face value over $100,000) time deposit, usually issued to businesses, that matures at a specific date; the interest rate depends on market conditions at the time of issuance.

L: M3 plus other liquid assets (such as Treasury bills and U.S. savings bonds).

Large-denomination time deposits: Savings deposits with set maturities that have denominations greater than or equal to $100,000.

Liquidity: The ease with which an individual can, at an unknown future time, sell an asset, at a known nominal dollar price, on short notice, and with minimum costs.

Liquidity approach: An approach to measuring money that stresses the role of money as a temporary store of value.

M1: The value of currency and transactions deposits owned by the nonfinancial institution public.

M2: M1 plus (1) savings and small-denomination time deposits at all depository institutions, (2) overnight repurchase agreements at commercial banks, (3) overnight Eurodollars held by U.S. residents (other than banks) at Caribbean branches of member banks, and (4) balances of money market mutual funds.

M3: M2 plus (1) large-denomination (over $100,000) time deposits at all depository institutions, (2) term repurchase agreements at commercial banks and savings and loan associations, and (3) institution-only money market mutual fund balances.

Monetary base: Currency held by the public and in vaults of depository institutions, plus reserves of depository institutions.

Money market mutual funds: Funds from the public that an investment company accepts and uses to acquire credit instruments. The funds can usually be withdrawn by checks written on the fund.

Money orders: Titles to currency that sometimes are used in exchange for goods and services.

Near monies: Assets that are highly liquid but are not considered M1 money, such as U.S. Treasury bills and savings deposits in banks and in savings and loan associations; only slight capital gains or losses are likely on near monies.

NOW accounts: Negotiable order of withdrawal accounts; interest-bearing savings accounts on which checks can be written.

Passbook savings accounts: Savings accounts in which a ''passbook'' contains all records of account balances and activity; the accounts have no set maturities, and the passbook must be presented for withdrawals and deposits.

Point-of-sale transfers: Transfers of funds made directly, using wire networks, from an individual's account to the firm from which a good or service is purchased at the location where the sale is made.

Repurchase agreement at a commercial bank (REPO, or RP):   An agreement made by a bank to sell Treasury or federal agency securities to its customers, coupled with an agreement to repurchase them at a price that includes accumulated interest.

Simple-sum monetary aggregates: Measures of money that are constructed by directly summing together different components.

Small-denomination time deposits: Savings deposits with set maturities for which the amount of the deposit is less than $100,000.

Statement savings accounts: Savings accounts in which the holder receives periodic written statements of balances and account activity; accounts have no set maturities, and withdrawals and deposits may be made by mail.

Thrift institutions: Mutual savings banks, savings and loan associations, and credit unions.

Transactions accounts: NOW accounts, ATS accounts, CUSD accounts, and demand deposits at mutual savings banks.

Transaction approach: An approach to measuring money that stresses the role of money as a medium of exchange.

Underground, or subterranean, economy: That economy which consists of illegal activities and otherwise legal activities that are unreported to the Internal Revenue Service.

Wire transfers: Transfers of funds between individuals or firms accomplished through electronic transmissions over wire or cable networks or telephone lines.

SELF-TEST QUESTIONS

1. What are the main distinctions between the liquidity and transactions approaches to measuring money?
2. What are the three largest components of M1 in the United States?
3. What are the primary components of M2 in the United States?
4. What are the main components of M3 in the United States?
5. What, *conceptually,* is L?
6. What means of payment in the United States account for most physical transfers of funds? What means of payment account for the largest dollar values of transfers?
7. Why is it that recent technological developments in means of payment are likely to further divide the transactions and liquidity approaches to measuring money?

PROBLEMS

3-1.   What are the components of M1?

3-2.   What are the components of M2?

3-3.   Consider the following data, and compute M1, M2, M3, and L:

Currency outside of the Treasury, Federal Reserve banks, and vaults of depository institutions	$ 193.2
Demand deposits other than those owned by depository institutions, the U.S. government, foreign banks, and foreign institutions	296.4
Large time deposits, term RP liabilities, and term Eurodollars	743.4
Nonbank public holdings of U.S. savings bonds	643.0
Other checkable deposits	254.5
Overnight RPs and Eurodollars, noninstitution money market fund balances, MMDAs, and savings deposits	2,111.1
Nondepository institution traveler's checks	6.9

3-4. Suppose that we wish to construct a simple divisia monetary aggregate. A way to do this would be to construct weights based on the rate of turnover of different components of the monetary aggregate. Each of these weights would be multiplied by the component to which it corresponds, and then each of the resulting products of weights multiplied by respective components would be summed. Suppose that we are interested in computing a divisia aggregate we shall call D1. The components of D1 are currency ($100 billion), demand deposits and other checkable deposits ($200 billion), and traveler's checks ($10 billion). The turnover weight for currency is 0.6, for demand deposits and other checkable deposits it is 0.4, and for traveler's checks it is 1.0. What is the value, in dollar terms, of D1?

3-5. Cash and currency account for nearly 98 percent of the number of all payments in the United States. Wire transfers account for over 82 percent of the dollar value of all payments in the United States. Explain why this is possible and why these figures make it difficult to decide what money really is.

SELECTED REFERENCES

Barnett, William A., Melvin Hinich, and Piyu Yue, "Monitoring Monetary Aggregates under Risk Aversion," in *Monetary Policy on the 75th Anniversary of the Federal Reserve System,* ed. Michael T. Belongia (Boston: Kluwer Academic Publishers, 1991).

Batten, Dallas S., Michael P. Blackwell, In-Su Kim, Simon E. Nocera, and Yuzuru Ozeld, *The Conduct of Monetary Policy in the Major Industrial Countries: Instruments and Operating Procedures,* International Monetary Fund Occasional Paper No. 70, Washington, D.C., July 1990.

Berger, Allen N., and David B. Humphrey, "Market Failures and Resource Use: Economic Incentives to Use Different Payment Instruments," in *The U.S. Payments System: Efficiency, Risk, and the Role of the Federal Reserve,* ed. David B. Humphrey (Boston: Kluwer Academic Publishers, 1989).

Broaddus, Alfred, "Financial Innovation in the United States: Background, Current Status and Prospects," *Economic Review,* Federal Reserve Bank of Richmond, 71 (1, January/February 1985), pp. 2–22.

Darby, Michael R., Angelo R. Mascaro, and Michael L. Marlow, "The Empirical Reliability of Monetary Aggregates as Indicators: 1983–1986," Research Paper No. 8701, U.S. Department of the Treasury, 1987.

Flannery, Mark S., and Dwight J. Jaffee, *The Economic Implications of an Electronic Monetary Transfer System* (Lexington, MA, 1973).

Gavin, William T., and Michael R. Pakko, *Economic Commentary,* Federal Reserve Bank of Cleveland, July 1, 1987.

Higgins, Bryan, and Jon Faust, ''NOWs and Super NOWs: Implications for Defining and Measuring Money,'' *Economic Review,* Federal Reserve Bank of Kansas City, January 1983, pp. 3–18.

Porter, Richard D., Thomas D. Simpson, and Eileen Manskopf, ''Financial Innovation and the Monetary Aggregates,'' *Brookings Papers on Economic Activity,* 1, 1979.

Richardson, Dennis W., *Electric Money: Evolution of an Electronic Funds-Transfer System* (Cambridge, MA, 1970).

Sprenkle, Case, Stephen Turnovsky, and Roger Fujihara, ''Assets, Aggregates, and Monetary Control,'' *Journal of Banking and Finance,* 14 (March 1990), 155–177.

Walter, John R., ''Monetary Aggregates: A User's Guide,'' *Economic Review,* Federal Reserve Bank of Richmond, 75 (1, January/February 1989), pp. 20–28.

Financial Instruments, Markets, and Institutions

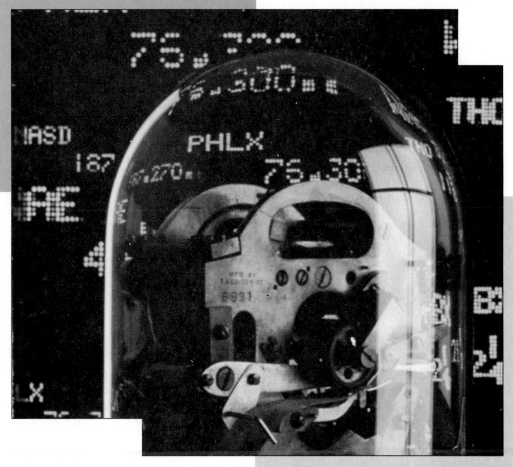

CHAPTER 4

The Foundations of Saving, Investment, and Credit Markets

CHAPTER PREVIEW

1. What are consumption and production opportunities sets? What do their slopes tell us about the rate of exchange across time?

2. What is an indifference curve? How are indifference curves used to tell us the optimal consumption choice of an individual who must decide how much to consume in two time periods?

3. What is saving? What is investment? In a one-person economy, how are consumption, saving, and investment related?

4. What is the rate of return from saving? How does it permit us to measure a per-

son's perception of the present value of a future quantity?

5. What is the marginal product of capital? How is it related to the rate of return from saving in a one-person economy?

6. What is credit? What are assets and liabilities?

7. What is the loan principal? What is interest? How do we compute an interest rate?

8. What are producer surplus and consumer surplus? How do these concepts help explain the existence of credit markets?

AN OLD ECONOMICS JOKE

There are a lot of old jokes about economists. For instance, consider the following listing of short ones:

1. President Herbert Hoover (1874–1964) supposedly said that he would give anything to have a one-armed economic adviser—so that he wouldn't always have to hear, ''On the one hand . . . , but on the other hand. . . .''

2. Another is in question-answer form: ''*Question*—What is an economist, anyway? *Answer*—It is an expert who will know tomorrow why the things he predicted yesterday didn't happen today.''

3. Yet another is now an old saying: ''If the nation's economists were laid end-to-end, they would point in all directions.''

4. A play on that old saying is, ''If the nation's economists were laid end-to-end, we would all be better off.''

A much longer joke is helpful for setting the stage for this chapter. It has to do with an economist who recently won the Nobel Prize. This economist is world renowned. He has been an adviser to presidents, dictators, kings, and queens. He has appeared on national morning news programs and major television talk shows. He has published theories of economic activity more widely than nearly any other living economist and is revered by his peers in the profession, and yet he also is known as a top economic expert by the average person on the street.

By chance, on the flight back to the United States the economist is seated adjacent to two other Nobel recipients—a biochemist and a physicist. The flight attendants fuss over the famous economist during the flight but largely ignore the two physical scientists. The physical scientists are very understanding, however. After all, they also have seen the economist's exploits on television and in the newspapers. They realize that they are in the company of a true leader in his field.

Suddenly, the side of the plane rips open—an undetected structural fault in the plane's fuselage has given way. The plane's flight crew and passengers are horrified when the commotion dies down. The seats containing the three Nobel winners have disappeared.

The economist, physicist, and biochemist find themselves floating in their seats in the waters of the mid-Atlantic. Fortunately, the ocean is calm, and a current has carried them toward a small grouping of deserted islands. They wash ashore on the largest of these. Quickly, they take stock of their surroundings, which are meager. There appears to be little to eat. Luckily, however, they discover that a single, very large can of beans—one large enough to have fed two servings to all of the plane's passengers—was blown out of the plane and has floated along with them to the shore of the island. The issue, of course, is how to open the can.

The physicist is the first to propose a hypothetical means of opening the can of beans. She points out that the thermal expansion coefficient for the water content of the can of beans is likely to exceed the thermal expansion coefficient for the aluminum that composes the can. Therefore, she theorizes, building a fire under the can will result in a pressure increase that should break open the can, permitting the three scientists to eat the beans.

The economist immediately points out that there is a severe defect in the physicist's plan, which is that the beans will be blown out of the can and into the sand; he announces that he would be unwilling to eat sand-contaminated beans. The biochemist answers the economist's criticism with a different theory for opening the can of beans. This is to squeeze juice from some rotted pineapples nearby onto the ground and combine that with some palm leaves and sea water to produce a strong acid. This acid, he argues, could eat through the can, permitting the three scientists to get to the beans.

The economist quickly decries this suggestion. ''After all,'' he points out, ''who wants to eat acidic beans?'' At this, the physicist and biochemist finally lose their tempers with this world-famous economist. ''What,'' they ask, ''do *you* suggest be done to get to the beans?'' ''Elementary,'' answers the economist. ''Let's begin by *assuming* that we have a *can opener*. We can construct our plan from there.''

Like many old jokes, there are several different endings to this one. The most popular ending is that the physicist and biochemist eat the economist instead of the beans. Another is the one that we'll adopt, which is that they banish the economist to another island with instructions never to return until he has more constructive theories to offer.

A One-Person, Island Economy[1]

Let us consider the predicament faced by the banished economist alone on his own island. He finds that the only available food is 100 pineapples that he has scrounged up in a search through the island. Like the Nobel economist, let us make some rather outlandish

---

[1] While one-person models are very standard in economics, the one used here owes much to the approach used by James Pierce in Chapter 3 of *Monetary and Financial Economics* (New York: John Wiley & Sons, 1984).

assumptions. The first is that the pineapples are of a previously unknown nonspoiling variety (we could account for some spoilage over time, but our theory of the economist's predicament would be made much more complicated). The second is that the economist can subsist on nothing but pineapples for an extended period of time. Finally, we shall assume that the economist knows from previous study he did of the economics of ocean transportation that a ship will be along to rescue him at the end of exactly 2 months.

Given these conditions, the economist must make decisions on how to allocate his accumulated wealth, which consists of the 100 pineapples, over the 2-month period. He anticipates no further incoming food during the 2 months, and the physicist and biochemist are not speaking to him and therefore are unlikely to trade any of their beans for his pineapples. He is on his own and must put his economics training to work.

CONSUMPTION POSSIBILITIES

The economist first must face the hard, harsh facts. He has only 100—albeit nonspoiling—pineapples. He recalls an old saying that when two or three economists get together, there are always seven or eight options to consider, and he reasons immediately that there are three simple options he might think of considering. One extreme option would be to eat all 100 pineapples in the first month on the island and then to subsist on (acidic, according to the biochemist) palm tree leaves the second month. Another extreme possibility would be to subsist on palm tree leaves the first month and eat all 100 pineapples the second month on the island. Finally, he could immediately envision the less extreme, middle-of-the-road course of consuming 50 pineapples in his first month and 50 in the second month.

The economist has a pen and paper with him. On the first day on the island he draws Figure 4-1, which measures current-month consumption of pineapples vertically and next-month pineapple consumption horizontally. The figure shows that, in fact, he has many possible pineapple consumption possibilities, including the three cases that first occurred to him. These all lie on a straight line that is his **consumption opportunities set,** which contains all possible consumption opportunities available to him during his 2-month stay on the island.

The straight-line consumption opportunities set in Figure 4-1 has a slope equal to the ratio of the "rise" relative to the "run," which is $\frac{-100}{100} = -1$ pineapple this month per pineapple next month. This means that the economist must give up consuming one pineapple in the first month in order to consume an additional pineapple the next month. Hence, the **opportunity cost** of one pineapple consumed this month is equal to one pineapple forgone in the next month. The absolute value of the slope of the consumption opportunities set is equal to the opportunity cost of consuming a pineapple this month.

The opportunity cost of consuming pineapples is also a measure of the **rate of exchange** of current pineapples for future pineapples. That is, it tells the economist how many pineapples he implicitly must exchange this month for pineapples next month. Even though the economist does not trade with the physicist and biochemist on the other island, he effectively must exchange pineapples *across time.* The reason is that consumption of a pineapple this month leaves less pineapples to consume the next month.

UTILITY AND INDIFFERENCE CURVES

Our intrepid economist realizes that he cannot consume more than 100 pineapples during the next 2 months. This means that he cannot possibly consume more than his consumption opportunities set; he cannot be at a point in Figure 4-1 that lies above and to the right of the straight-line opportunities set. He could consume less than 100 pineapples over the

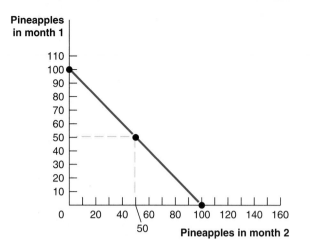

Figure 4-1

The Consumption Opportunities Set.   The marooned economist has 100 nonspoiling pineapples as he begins his 2-month stay on the deserted island. One 2-month consumption possibility
would be to eat all 100 the first month on the island, leaving zero to consume the second month.
Another would be to eat zero in the first month, leaving 100 to consume in the second month. Yet
another consumption possibility would be to eat 50 in the first month and 50 in the second month.
A straight line containing these possibilities illustrates these and all other consumption choices he
might make during his 2 months on the island.

   The slope of the consumption opportunities set is equal to the "rise" divided by the "run," or
$-100/100 = -1$. The absolute value of this slope is equal to 1, meaning that 1 pineapple must
always be given up in the first month to consume 1 additional pineapple in the second month.

course of the next 2 months, but he knows that he will be rescued at that time, so he
decides he probably would be happier if he consumed all 100 pineapples. He can be as
happy as possible by choosing a consumption point somewhere *on* his consumption
opportunities set.

   The economist has been trained to think of measuring his happiness in terms of **utility,**
which is a measure of his satisfaction. He decides that his next task should be to contemplate on how much utility he is likely to get from consuming pineapples over the next 2
months. The place to start, he determines, is to think about this problem in the abstract,
without reference to the consumption opportunities set he actually faces.

The Indifference Curve   Indeed, the economist daydreams about an island with unlimited numbers of pineapples. Suppose, he says to himself, it were possible to consume 70
pineapples this coming month and 40 pineapples the next month. He plots this combination
as point *A* in a new figure, Figure 4-2. Now he supposes that an alternative first-month
consumption level was 40 pineapples. How many pineapples would have to be available
for consumption in the second month to stay equally satisfied? After some contemplation,
the economist decides that it would take 60 pineapples in the second month to be as happy
as he would be consuming 70 in the first month and 40 in the second month. He labels
this new combination point *B*.

   As another possibility to consider—after all, there is little else to do all alone on the
island—the economist thinks about how many pineapples he would need in the second
month to keep himself equally happy, as compared with the 2-month consumption com-

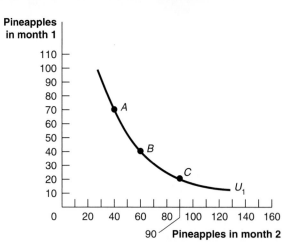

Figure 4-2
An Indifference Curve.   Along an indifference curve, the marooned economist is equally satisfied with any consumption point. That is, he derives equal utility from any consumption combination along the indifference curve. Hence, even though consumption levels are different at points A,
B, and C, the economist is just as happy with any one of those three consumption choices; he is
indifferent between any of them.

binations plotted as points *A* and *B*, if he could consume only 20 pineapples the first
period, instead of 70 or 40. After some introspection, he decides that he would need to
consume 90 pineapples in the second month to be equally satisfied. He graphs this combination as point *C* in Figure 4-2.

By construction, points *A*, *B*, and *C* all are points of equal utility for the economist.
This means that he is *indifferent* among consuming any of the three consumption combinations. These three points, along with others the economist could construct, lie on an
indifference curve, which is a schedule of consumption combinations among which the
economist is completely indifferent. He is just as happy consuming at any point along the
indifference curve. If he could somehow measure his level of utility, or satisfaction, he
would call it U_1, which is the level of utility all along the indifference curve.

The Law of Diminishing Marginal Utility   The economist's indifference curve is
bowed, or convex with respect to the origin. The reason is the **law of diminishing
marginal utility.** According to the law of diminishing marginal utility, the gain in utility,
or satisfaction, that a person obtains from consuming an additional unit of a good tends
to fall as the amount consumed increases. The fact that the economist's indifference curve
becomes more shallow as his second-month consumption increases, for instance, means
that he requires progressively smaller decreases in his first-month consumption to stay
equally happy. He experiences progressively smaller increases in second-period happiness
from second-month pineapple consumption that would need to be offset by decreases in
first-month consumption to keep him indifferent. The economist's additional utility from
second-month consumption therefore is decreasing as second-month consumption increases, which satisfies the law of diminishing marginal utility.

Utility Levels and Indifference Curves   The economist also thinks about what would
happen if he redrew his indifference curve in Figure 4-3 and then envisioned what would

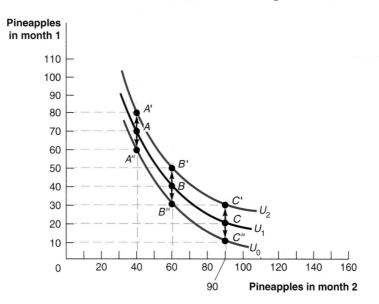

Figure 4-3

Higher and Lower Utility Levels.   If the marooned economist were to receive 10 extra pineapples to consume without being required to give up any pineapples in the second month, the resulting points A', B', and C' all would lie on a new indifference curve above and to the right of the original indifference curve containing points A, B, and C. Because the economist gets to consume more in the first month without losing any second-month consumption, his utility level along the new indifference curve, denoted U_2, would exceed his original level of utility, U_1.

In contrast, if the economist had to give up 10 pineapples in his first month on the island without being compensated in the second month, the result would be points like A'', B'', and C'' that are 10 units below points A, B, and C. Because the economist in this case consumes less in the first month with no additional consumption in the second month, his utility level along the indifference curve containing A'', B'', and C'' denoted U_0, would be less than his original utility level, U_1.

happen if 10 extra pineapples could be consumed in the first month with no need to give up pineapples in the second month. He determines that this would mean that his points of indifference, A, B, and C, would all be shifted upward by 10 units. He would be equally happy at any of the new points such as A', B', and C', and so these points would lie on a new indifference curve. Nonetheless, he also would be *happier* at any of these new points than he would be at the original points A, B, or C, because his first-month consumption would be higher with no loss of second-month consumption. Hence, his utility level along this new indifference curve, which we shall denote U_2, is higher than along the original indifference curve with utility level U_1.

Our intrepid economist immediately (after all, he won a Nobel Prize) reasons that he could in principle construct an infinite number of indifference curves from the first one by imagining adding to or subtracting from his first-month consumption levels, holding second-month consumption equal. Additions would produce indifference curves such as U_2 but at positions successively higher and to the right on the graph, and so utility would rise with rightward and upward shifts of the indifference curve. Subtractions, in contrast, would yield indifference curves at positions lower and to the left that would correspond to lower utility levels. For example, if the economist had to give up 10 units of first-month pineapple consumption at points A, B, and C in Figure 4-3 without any compensating increases in second-month consumption, he would be at points such as A'', B'', or C'' on a lower indifference curve with a lower utility level (compared with both U_1 and U_2), U_0.

THE OPTIMAL CONSUMPTION CHOICE

After a few minutes, the island-bound economist snaps out of his daydream about unbounded utility and theoretically limitless numbers of indifference curves. He cannot simply choose any given indifference curve, he knows, because in fact he has only 100 nonspoiling pineapples. He has real, not imaginary, choices to make.

Nevertheless, his daydreaming has helped him figure out how to decide. He thinks about how this will work by drawing Figure 4-4. On the figure, he draws his consumption opportunities set from Figure 4-1 together with the three indifference curves from Figure 4-3.

The economist can see that, on the one hand, the utility level U_2 would be nice to obtain but simply is not possible in light of his consumption opportunities set. Points A', B', and C', and any other point on the highest indifference curve, all lie above the consumption opportunities set. On the other hand, the utility level U_0 is obtainable, because points where it intersects the consumption opportunities set, plus all points along the lowest indifference curve that are inside the opportunities set, such as point B'', are consistent with consuming 100 or fewer pineapples.

The economist also can see in Figure 4-4, however, that he can achieve a higher utility level than U_0 along the higher indifference curve U_1. In addition, there is one single point on that higher indifference curve that is tangent to the consumption opportunities set and therefore consistent both with the economist's desires *and* with his consumption opportunities. This is point B. If the economist tried to get to a higher utility level, he would be outside his consumption opportunities set, and so the utility level U_1 at point B is the highest possible level of utility he can obtain. At point B, the economist will consume 40 pineapples during his first month on the island and 60 pineapples in the second month. This will be his *optimal consumption choice*.

The economist notes that at point B his indifference curve is exactly tangent to his consumption opportunities set. This means that at this point the slope of his indifference curve is equal to the slope of the opportunities set, which, as we discussed previously, is -1 unit of first-month consumption per unit of second-month consumption. (Note that the slope is negative because the opportunities set slopes downward; the economist must *give up*—subtract—one pineapple in the first month to obtain an additional pineapple in the second month.) Hence, in making his optimal decision the economist must make a choice that is consistent with the rate of exchange between present and future pineapple consumption.

PRODUCTION AND CONSUMPTION IN A ONE-PERSON, ISLAND ECONOMY

Before our intrepid economist has a chance to implement his decision, however, he sees a bottle wash up on the shore of his island. In it is a lengthy note from the physicist and biochemist indicating their pity for his plight—but not necessarily their forgiveness. Because they pity the economist, they have decided to let him know that they have recognized the species of pineapples as one in which, for every two pineapples that are not eaten but

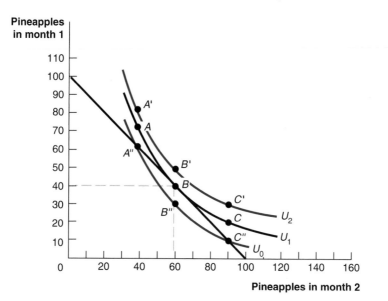

Figure 4-4

The Optimal Consumption Choice. Given his consumption opportunities, the marooned economist cannot obtain the utility level U_2; points such as A', B', and C' are outside his consumption opportunities set. Utility level U_0 is *obtainable*; nonetheless, it is *less desirable* than the utility level U_1, which is the highest possible level of utility that can be obtained given the consumption opportunities set. The utility level U_1 can be obtained at point B, which corresponds to the consumption of 40 pineapples in the first month and 60 pineapples in the second month. Point B, then, is the *optimal consumption choice.*

instead are replanted, three trees will grow that will each produce a pineapple within a single month.

The economist quickly deduces that, for every pineapple he plants this month, he will have $1\frac{1}{2}$ pineapples next month. He immediately realizes that he must recompute his optimal pineapple consumption decision, because he can now potentially *produce* pineapples, which would allow him to consume more than 100 pineapples during his 2 months on the island.

PRODUCTION OPPORTUNITIES, CAPITAL, SAVING, AND INVESTMENT

To prove this to himself, the economist gets out another sheet of paper. He begins in Figure 4-5 by redrawing his previous optimal consumption decision. He now sees that there are at least a couple of new possibilities he faces now that he can produce more pineapples. He could, for instance, consume all 100 pineapples the first month on the island. In this case, he again would have no pineapples left to consume the second month. At the other extreme, he could consume none of the pineapples the first month. He could then plant all 100 of the pineapples and grow trees that would yield him 150 pineapples next month, which he could then consume.

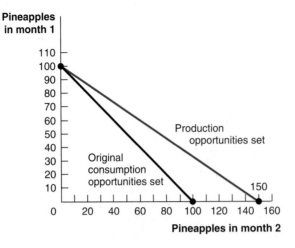

Figure 4-5
The Production Possibilities Set.   The economist learns that he can plant pineapples in the first month and receive a second-month pineapple yield of 1 ½ pineapples for each pineapple planted. As before, if he consumes all 100 pineapples in the first month, he will have none to consume in the second month. Now, however, if he does not consume any pineapples in his first month on the island, he can plant the 100 pineapples to produce a yield of 150 pineapples to consume in the second month. These and all possibilities in between represent the economist's production possibilities set. Because the economist is the only consumer on the island, this is also his new consumption opportunities set.

Except for the one point that they share in common, the economist's new production/consumption opportunities set lies above and to the right of his original consumption opportunities set. The slope of the production/consumption opportunities set is equal to $-100/150 = -2/3$. Therefore, the economist must give up $^2/_3$ of a pineapple in the first month to obtain 1 pineapple to consume in the second month. The absolute value of the reciprocal of this slope is $1/(2/3) = {}^3/_2 = 1\,{}^1/_2$, which tells us that the economist receives 1 ½ pineapples in the second month for each pineapple planted in the first month, which is the marginal product of capital.

The Production Possibilities Set   These extreme points, and all points lying on a straight line in between, represent the economist's **production possibilities set.** It *also* represents an expanded consumption opportunities set for the economist, because there is no one on the island to consume the pineapples except a single producer/consumer, the economist. The slope of this consumption/production opportunities set is equal to the "rise" divided by the "run," or -100 pineapples in the first month divided by 150 pineapples in the second month, or $-\frac{2}{3}$ pineapple in the first month per pineapple in the second month. Because this schedule is the economist's consumption opportunities set, the slope again is a measure of the rate of exchange ($-\frac{2}{3}$ pineapple in the first month per pineapple in the second month) of first-month pineapple consumption for second-month pineapple consumption. This means that the reciprocal of this rate of exchange, $\frac{3}{2} = 1\frac{1}{2}$ pineapples in the second month per pineapple in the first month, is a measure of the rate of exchange of second-month pineapple consumption for first-month pineapple consumption.

Capital and Its Marginal Product   Now, however, the schedule also is the economist's *production* opportunities set, and so the slope also provides the economist with information about his productive capabilities. He can now use pineapples to *create* (with the aid of the soil, rain, and sunlight) more pineapples in the future. Economists call goods that are used to produce more goods in the future **capital goods**. Therefore, the marooned economist recognizes that his pineapples function as both consumption *and* capital goods. Furthermore, planting 2 pineapples (that is, using 2 units of capital goods) this month yields 3 pineapples (3 units of consumption goods) in the future. This means that the gain in production of pineapples (consumption goods) for each pineapple planted is 3 pineapples gained for every 2 pineapples he plants (for every 2 units of capital goods he uses), or, alternatively, $1\frac{1}{2}$ pineapples produced for each single pineapple planted. Economists refer to this amount of output yielded by a unit of capital—$1\frac{1}{2}$ pineapples in the future for every 1 pineapple used as capital goods today—as the **marginal product of capital.** In general, the marginal product of capital is the additional output of goods and services obtained from each additional unit of capital used in production. For our economist, then, the marginal product of capital has a value of $1\frac{1}{2}$.

Our intrepid economist realizes that because he can use some of this month's pineapples as capital goods to produce additional pineapple consumption goods, he can improve on his original optimal consumption choice in Figure 4-4. To deduce this, he draws Figure 4-6, which shows both his old consumption opportunities set, complete with his original optimal choice, and his new consumption/production opportunities set. Upon contemplation, the economist recognizes that because his new opportunities set lies to the right of his original opportunities set, he can now move to a higher indifference curve (labeled U^*) tangent to the new opportunities set; the economist can increase his utility!

Figure 4-6
The New Optimal Consumption Choice.   Because the economist now can produce additional pineapples in the second month on the island using pineapples planted in the first month, he is able to attain a utility level, U^*, that is greater than the level U_1 that previously could have been attained. To do so, the economist chooses a new optimal consumption point, B^*, that is above and to the right of his original optimal consumption choice, B.

At B^*, the economist will consume only 50 pineapples in the first month. He saves the remaining 50 pineapples. In addition, he plants these, using them as capital goods. Because the marginal product of capital is $1\frac{1}{2} = \frac{3}{2}$, in the second month he will have produced $50 \times \frac{3}{2} = 75$ pineapples that he can then consume.

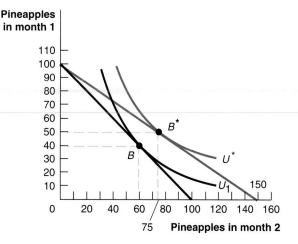

Saving and Investment   The economist discovers that, at this point of tangency, labeled B^*, his optimal choice is to consume 50 pineapples in the first month and 75 pineapples in the second month. That is, he will consume only 50 of his original 100 pineapples in the first month, leaving 50 pineapples that are not consumed. These pineapples will be *saved* by the economist; the 50 pineapples represent the economist's first month's **saving,** which by definition is forgone consumption.

The economist will save the pineapples for a purpose; he will plant them to produce the 75 pineapples for consumption in the second month (each pineapple planted yields $1\frac{1}{2}$, or $\frac{3}{2}$, pineapples in the second month, and so the 50 pineapples planted in the first month yield $\frac{3}{2} \times 50 = 75$ pineapples in the second month). Recall that pineapples used to produce future pineapples are, by definition, *capital goods.* Therefore, by setting aside the 50 pineapples in the first month as capital goods, the economist will undertake what he and other economists call *capital investment,* or more simply, **investment.** Investment is defined to be an addition to the stock of capital goods, and the 50 pineapples set aside for use in planting represents the amount of investment by the economist.

Note that the amount of saving is 50 pineapples and that the amount of investment is 50 pineapples. That is, saving is equal to investment. To produce additional pineapples— above and beyond the amount he could obtain by not planting pineapples—in the future, the economist must make a capital investment, but this requires that he forgo some current consumption. He must save if he is to gain from investing, or adding to his productive capital. As we shall see in Chapter 18, an equality of saving and investment is an important outcome in economies much more complicated than our economist's single-person economy.

The Marginal Product of Capital and the Rate of Return from Saving   By saving 50 pineapples in the first month, the economist will be able to use the 50 pineapples to produce and consume 75 pineapples in the second month on the island. In contrast, if he were to choose *not* to plant the 50 pineapples, he would only have 50 pineapples to consume in the second month. Clearly, the economist will reap a return from saving pineapples and using them as capital goods, rather than just allowing them to sit idle until the following month. His total return from saving is the additional 25 pineapples (the 75 he gets by planting minus the 50 he would have if he did not plant). This means that the **rate of return from saving** is the total return from saving (25 pineapples) divided by the total number of pineapples saved (50 pineapples), which is equal to $\frac{1}{2}$, or 0.5. In percentage terms, then, the rate of return from saving is 50 percent.

Our economist recalls that the marginal product of capital is equal to $\frac{3}{2}$, or $1\frac{1}{2}$. He notes that the following relationship holds:

$$1 + \frac{\text{rate of return}}{\text{from saving}} = 1\frac{1}{2} = \frac{\text{marginal product}}{\text{of capital}} \qquad \textbf{(4-1)}$$

Therefore, there is, for the economist, a relationship that links his desired saving and capital investment. Specifically, the relationship in equation (4-1) says that the rate of return from saving, $\frac{1}{2}$ pineapple per 1 pineapple saved, plus the 1 pineapple saved, is equal to the $1\frac{1}{2}$ pineapples that he can produce with each single pineapple used as a capital good, which is the marginal product of capital. As long as this relationship holds, the amount of desired saving is equal to the amount of desired investment for the economist; that is, the economist is at his optimal consumption point in Figure 4-6.

Present Value of Future Pineapples   The economist also recalls from his previous calculation that the slope of his consumption/production opportunities set is equal to

$$\text{Slope} = \frac{\text{rise}}{\text{run}} = -\tfrac{2}{3} = -1/(\tfrac{3}{2}) = -1/(1 + \tfrac{1}{2}) \tag{4-2}$$

But the denominator of this slope is the marginal product of capital and is equal to $1\tfrac{1}{2}$, and, according to equation (4-1), the marginal product of capital is equal to 1 plus the rate of return from saving. Therefore, if the rate of return from saving is denoted by the shorthand notation r_s, another way to express the slope of the consumption/production opportunities set is

$$\text{Slope} = -1/(1 + r_s) \tag{4-3}$$

Because the absolute value of the slope of the consumption opportunities set by definition is the rate of exchange of first-month pineapple consumption for second-month pineapple consumption, it follows that, if Q_2 is a quantity of pineapples consumed in the second month, it must be true that

$$Q_1 = [1/(1 + r_s)]Q_2 \tag{4-4}$$

where Q_1 is the value of Q_2 pineapples consumed in the second month in terms of an amount of pineapples consumed in the first month. If we think of the first month as the present and the second month as the future, then Q_1 is a measure of the **present value** of Q_2 pineapples received in the future.

Consider the situation faced by our marooned economist. The rate of return from saving, r_s, is equal to $\tfrac{1}{2}$, and so $1/(1 + r_s)$ is equal to $1/\tfrac{3}{2} = \tfrac{2}{3}$. If the economist knows that he will receive $Q_2 = 75$ pineapples in the second (future) month (as is true at point B^* in Figure 4-6), then the value of those pineapples from the perspective of the first (present) month is, from equation (4-4), equal to

$$Q_1 = [1/(1 + \tfrac{1}{2})] \times 75 = \tfrac{2}{3} \times 75 = 50$$

That is, the present value of the 75 pineapples to be received in the second month is equal to 50 pineapples in the first month. This makes sense, because this is the number of pineapples he saves in the first place, upon which he earns the return of 25 pineapples, to yield the 75 pineapples in the second month. Therefore, when the rate of return on saving is equal to $\tfrac{1}{2}$, or 50 percent, 75 pineapples in the next month is equal to 50 pineapples in the first month, and vice versa.

As you shall learn in Chapter 7, the concept of present value has many useful applications. It is what allows us to value future quantities of goods and services, or quantities of money, from the point of view of the present. Because many decisions that households and firms make concern decisions about wealth allocations between present and future (through a procedure that is called *discounting,* which we shall discuss in Chapter 7), this concept is very important.

WHAT ACCOUNTS FOR VARIATION IN SAVING, AND THE GENERAL DECLINE IN SAVING, ACROSS COUNTRIES?

INTERNATIONAL PERSPECTIVE

The story of our marooned economist is, of course, fictitious and oversimplified. Yet it captures the essential elements of consumption and saving decisions across time. These decisions vary across individuals. In addition, it turns out, these decisions also typically differ across countries. Individuals in some countries seem to save more than individuals in other countries, as is reflected by international variations in rates of saving relative to a nation's income.

Saving Rates

The table below shows international comparisons of *gross saving rates*. The gross saving rate is defined as the ratio of a nation's total gross saving to its gross do-

Average Annual Saving Rates in Various Countries

Gross domestic saving as a percentage of gross domestic product

Country	Average Annual Saving Rate	
	1960–1974	1980–1992
Australia	24.5	20.6
Austria	28.7	24.6
Belgium	23.2	17.1
Canada	21.8	20.4
Denmark	22.0	16.4
Finland	28.8	24.9
France	25.1	19.8
Germany	27.0	22.3
Greece	22.2	18.1
Ireland	19.7	16.8
Italy	23.7	20.0
Japan	36.6	31.5
Netherlands	28.4	22.3
New Zealand	23.0	21.4
Sweden	24.3	18.0
United Kingdom	28.9	17.2
United States	28.8	14.4

mestic product. Gross saving includes the amount of saving that ultimately is used toward depreciation of a nation's capital stock, and gross domestic product is the amount of output produced using factors of production only within a nation. The figures in the table are national averages for the periods 1960–1974 and 1980–1992.

Two interesting facts become apparent from a review of the data. First, the United States consistently has experienced the lowest gross saving rate. Second, average annual gross saving rates have declined for every single country listed. There appears to be a worldwide decline in rates of saving.

Explaining Recent Saving Behavior across Countries

What accounts for differences in national saving rates? What accounts for the downward trend in saving across nations? There are no easy answers, but there are several *possible* reasons, which, taken together, could explain the saving data. One is that some nations, such as the United States and the United Kingdom, have governmental social security programs that tax the incomes of their citizens, leaving less left over to *count* as saving, while other nations, such as Japan, have little if any social security system. Second, insurance programs have improved in the economies listed, albeit at different rates in different nations, improving the ability of their citizens to guard against uncertainty and thereby reducing the need for excess precautionary saving.

Third, in some nations, such as the United States, the population distribution may be "bulged" in such a way that one generation—in the United States, the "baby-boom" generation—may be very large relative to other age groups. People save differentially based on their age—up to a point older people tend to save more—and so differences in countries' age distributions could account for differences in saving rates. Fourth, the rate of return from saving is taxed in some countries, such as the United States, but is not taxed in others, such as Japan (see the Current Controversy later in this chapter). Fifth, it is possible that high government borrowing to finance its deficits may reduce saving, as we shall see in later chapters, and governments have borrowed much more in recent years than in the past.

Finally, productivity is now lower in many nations of the world than it was in past years. That is, the marginal product of capital has declined in these nations. Our theory of consumption and saving, of course, predicts that a fall in the marginal product of capital will lower the return from saving, causing actual saving to decline. That is exactly what we appear to see in the real world.

Another Possible Explanation

There is one other interesting, though perhaps somewhat depressing, potential explanation for differences in saving rates across countries, and perhaps for the gradual decline in saving worldwide. A recent study found, using surveys of citizens of different countries about their perceptions of the chance of nuclear war, that saving rates were lower in nations whose citizens most firmly believed in a high probability of nuclear war. Leading the list of nations whose citizens thought the chances of nuclear war were "high" was the United States, the nation with the lowest saving rate. Near the bottom in concern about the chance of nuclear war were citizens of Japan, Germany, Finland, and the Netherlands, nations with high saving rates. Naturally, the basic idea is that people who think nuclear war is likely are less likely to save for the future (for instance, if our fictitious economist expected that his island would be hit by a nuclear missile in his second month there, it is unlikely he would save any pineapples during the first month), while those who believe nuclear war is unlikely will undertake greater saving. In addition, a general worldwide increase in the perceived threat of nuclear war would tend to lower saving in all nations.

Since 1989 saving rates have increased somewhat in most nations. Does this change reflect a diminished threat of nuclear war since the breakup of the communist bloc? This is an interesting question for an enterprising researcher to consider in future years.

Sources: Roger S. Smith, "Factors Affecting Saving, Policy Tools and Tax Reform," *International Monetary Fund Staff Papers,* 37 (1, March 1990), pp. 1–70; *OECD National Accounts*; and author estimates. Also adapted from Joel Slemrod, "Fear of Nuclear War and Intercountry Differences in the Rate of Saving," *Economic Inquiry,* 28 (4, October 1990), pp. 647–657.

CREDIT AND THE RATE OF INTEREST

Of course, the most important thing to the economist is that he now has made his consumption, saving, and investment decision. At B^*, he will consume 50 of his initial 100 pineapples in the first month and will save the remaining 50 pineapples. These pineapples will be invested to yield 75 pineapples in the second month. The economist is now ready to begin planting his 50 pineapples.

CREDIT, PRINCIPAL, AND INTEREST

Just as he prepares to do so, however, he sees on the horizon a makeshift raft containing, of all people, the biochemist and physicist. After exchanging greetings, they explain to the economist the reason they have come to visit his island. It is that they are bored. Aside from eating their can of beans and consuming and planting their own pineapples, they have nothing to stimulate them intellectually. They have worked out a plan, they explain, to conduct a series of experiments on increasing the nutritional value of the species of pineapples indigenous to the islands. The problem is that they presently do not have enough pineapples to make their experiments statistically valid.

For this reason, the biochemist and physicist explain, they would like to borrow as many pineapples from the economist this month as he is willing to lend, with the understanding that they will return those pineapples to him the following month plus an additional payment to compensate him for the loan. They point out that there are two issues that must be resolved. First, after the way they have treated the economist, is he willing to trust them with a loan? Second, if so, how much should the additional payment be to compensate the economist for the loan?

Because the economist is not a vindictive person, he indicates that he is, in principle, willing to lend pineapples to the biochemist and the physicist. By doing so, he points out, he will be extending them **credit,** a term derived from the Latin word *credo,* which means "I believe." Credit, he explains, is the ability to obtain title to and receive goods for use in the present, with payment for those goods deferred to a future date. Consequently, by extending credit to the biochemist and physicist, the economist will be transferring pineapples to them in exchange for a *promise,* which he believes they will keep, to repay him the next month, when total repayment will be due.

In addition, the economist explains, the amount of the loan itself will be the **principal.** The additional payment that the two physical scientists are offering to make in compensation for the receipt of credit by definition is the amount of **interest** that they will pay on the loan. Under the terms of the loan they are discussing, the full amount of principal and interest will be due in a month. Therefore, the **maturity,** or duration of the loan, will be 1 month.

ASSETS AND LIABILITIES

On the one hand, points out the economist, because the biochemist and the physicist will be in debt to the economist during that 1-month period, for that period of time the amount of indebtedness will be a **liability** for the biochemist and physicist; that is, it will be an obligation on their part to transfer goods to the economist in the following month. On the other hand, from the economist's perspective the loan will be an **asset** during that month, because it represents the title to receipt of principal and interest payments at the maturity date 1 month hence.

The physicist and biochemist indicate that they understand the obligations that they would be shouldering by borrowing pineapples from the economist. The remaining issue, all parties then agree, is the amount of principal and interest. The economist indicates that, based on his own situation, he potentially can lend the physicist and biochemist as many as 50 pineapples. The two physical scientists are delighted, because that is just the number they need to make their nutritional experiments statistically valid. All that remains, then, is to settle on the amount of interest that they will repay, along with the principal of 50 pineapples, at the end of a month's time.

THE MARKET RATE OF INTEREST

After some private discussion, the physicist and biochemist offer to pay the economist an amount of interest next month of 20 pineapples. The economist quickly does some mental calculations. As he computed earlier, in equation (4-1), the rate of return he could earn by saving pineapples on his own is equal to $1/2$ pineapple in the second month per pineapple saved in the first month, or a rate of return from saving of 50 percent. As a result, he would have 75 pineapples in the second month after saving 50 pineapples for investment this month. His return from saving, if he does not make the loan, would be 25 pineapples. Clearly, he cannot accept the terms of the physical scientists' offer of interest. The **interest rate,** which is the percentage return he would receive from the loan, would be $20/50 = 0.4$ (40 percent) under the terms he has been offered. This is less than the rate of return on saving, 50 percent, that he could otherwise earn on his own.

Therefore, the economist makes a counteroffer. He is willing to make the loan, he indicates, if he is paid an amount of interest at maturity equal to 30 pineapples, or an interest rate of $^{30}/_{50} = 0.6$ (60 percent). Of course, the economist recognizes that this is more than is really needed to compensate him for the rate of return he could otherwise have earned from his own saving. Nevertheless, he would like to earn what he and other economists call **producer surplus.** In general, producer surplus is an amount that a producer of any good, including credit, earns over and above the minimum amount needed to justify supplying it in exchange. The minimum rate of return the economist requires to justify making the loan is an interest rate of 50 percent. If he can get the physicist and biochemist to agree to an interest rate of 60 percent, he therefore will earn producer surplus. In percentage terms the amount of producer surplus would be the difference between 60 percent and 50 percent, or 10 percent; in terms of total interest, it would be 30 pineapples less the minimum amount of 25 pineapples needed to induce the economist to make the loan, or 5 pineapples.

To the economist's delight, the biochemist and physicist immediately accept the economist's counteroffer; all three shake hands on the agreement. They have agreed to a **market rate of interest,** the rate of interest at which a loan actually is extended between parties to the agreement, of 60 percent. (As we shall see in Chapter 7, normally market rates of interest are determined by the interaction of *numerous* buyers and *numerous* sellers of credit, but in our island market there is only one pair of buyers and one seller.) The biochemist and physicist load the 50 pineapples onto their raft to transport them back to their own island, where they can now conduct their nutrition experiments. As they float back to their island, they discuss their own good fortune; unbeknownst to the economist the two physical scientists were so desperate to obtain pineapples for their experiments that they would have been willing to borrow at an interest rate of 100 percent. Consequently, by agreeing to a market interest rate of 60 percent *they* have earned **consumer surplus,** in percentage terms, of 40 percent. Consumer surplus is the amount by which the market price of a good (in our case, credit) exceeds the price (the interest rate) that consumers would have been willing to pay for the good. In terms of total interest, then, the consumer surplus the physical scientists have earned is equal to 40 percent of the principal amount of 50 pineapples they have borrowed, or 20 pineapples.

Therefore, both the economist and the physical scientists have gained from this loan agreement. Both the lender and the borrowers gain from the existence of a market for credit in their island economy.

SOME REAL-WORLD IMPLICATIONS OF THE ISLAND ECONOMY

Obviously, we have taken an unlikely situation described in a rather old economics joke and extended it to construct an even less realistic environment. Nevertheless, we have done so because it has allowed us to illustrate some very important concepts in money and banking and, indeed, in the field of economics in general. All these concepts will resurface at various points throughout this text. Nonetheless, let us consider briefly some of the important implications of the topics we have discussed in this chapter.

IMPLICATIONS FOR REAL-WORLD CONSUMPTION, SAVING, AND INVESTMENT

In the simple island economy, our intrepid economist determines his optimal consumption for each month on the island based on his initial and future incomes of pineapples.

Therefore, one key determinant of his consumption in the current and future months is his flow of income from one period to the next. As we shall see in Unit 5, this basic fact—that individuals' consumption of goods and services depends primarily on the amount of income they earn—is a feature of any economic model of a real-world economy.

The Relationship between Income, Consumption, and Saving   Also true in our story was the fact that the marooned economist, in the first month, found it optimal to consume only 50 of his initial 100 pineapples. In the absence of an opportunity to extend credit, he found it optimal to forgo consuming the other 50 pineapples. This amount of consumption forgone represented saving.

For *any* individual or economy, therefore, saving by definition is equal to forgone consumption. Furthermore, it is true that available income during a given time period is divided into two components: saving and consumption. Just as the 50 pineapples consumed and the 50 pineapples saved during the first month by our fictitious economist summed to his first-month income of 100 pineapples, in any real-world economy saving and consumption must sum to total net income receipts.

The Relationship between Saving and Investment   In the absence of an opportunity to extend credit, the island economist found that, in equilibrium, saving was equal to capital investment. The amount saved, in turn, was determined by the relationship between the rate of return from saving and the marginal product of capital—the gain in future goods and services yielded by use of another unit of capital—in equation (4-1). Specifically, 1 plus the rate of return from saving was equal to the marginal product of capital in equilibrium. Hence, the rate of return from saving needed to adjust so that saving and investment could be equated.

These same basic relationships hold in a real-world economy, as we shall discuss in Unit 5. In the absence of a government that taxes and spends some of the incomes of its citizens, equilibrium requires that saving and investment are equalized. Furthermore, when this is true, the rate of return from saving must adjust relative to the marginal product of the economy's stock of productive capital goods—although in the real world the relationship between the two is more complex than was true in our island economy.

The Relationship between Investment and the Interest Rate   When our island economist was given the opportunity to earn interest on a loan that exceeded the equilibrium rate of return from saving and investing, he decided to make the loan. This loan represented an alternative way to save his 50 pineapples, and so the total amount of saving by the economist remained unchanged. Because he agreed to lend the 50 pineapples to the physical scientists, however, by implication he decided to forgo his earlier plans to plant the pineapples—that is, he decided to forgo a capital investment. He did so because he could earn a higher interest return by making the loan. The higher market interest rate (of 60 percent) induced the economist to reduce his planned investment.

The fact that a rise in the market interest rate brings about a fall in planned capital investment is another implication of our simple island model that carries over to the real world. Indeed, as we shall see in Unit 5, this inverse relationship between desired investment and the rate of interest is a very important relationship in economics.

Calculating the Present Value of a Future Sum   The rate of exchange between current and future consumption in the two-period situation faced by our fictitious economist was equal to the absolute value of the slope of his consumption/production opportunities set. In turn, this was equal to $1/(1 + r_s)$. Multiplication of this factor by an amount to be consumed in the future period automatically converts it into present-period units; that is, it permits us to calculate the present value of the amount to be consumed in the future period.

Whenever any of us makes a decision about the future, such as choices about mortgage or auto loans, annuities, retirement plans, or bond holdings, we need to be able to value future amounts that we will have to pay into present-valued quantities. This permits us to compare these amounts to quantities of income or wealth we have to work with in the present. Hence, the very simple expression for present value that we developed in our simple model, equation (4-4), has very important applications, especially in financial markets, as we shall discuss in more detail in Chapter 7.

IMPLICATIONS FOR REAL-WORLD CREDIT MARKETS

In the subsequent chapters of this unit of the text, we shall devote ourselves to issues related to markets and institutions that deal in money and credit. What does our simple island economy tell us about these issues?

The Distinction between Money and Credit   The first important implication of the story told in this chapter is that money and credit are "different animals." Nowhere in this chapter was the word "money" ever used until the last paragraph, and yet we were able to discuss the full determination of a credit contract. According to the contract, the economist extended a loan principal of 50 pineapples to the physical scientists at a market loan interest rate of 60 percent, which meant that he would receive a total interest payment of 30 pineapples. There was no underlying need for the agreement to be made in money terms—although it could have been if the parties had desired. Instead, the contract was specified in terms of delivery and exchange of real goods—the pineapples.

Credit, then, represents title, or claim, to a real resource. Although it is commonplace for people to talk about "borrowing and lending money," money and credit are *not* the same. In real-world economies, as we discussed in Chapter 2, money usually functions as a *standard of deferred payment,* meaning that most credit contracts typically are specified in terms of a common unit of measurement, money. Nonetheless, by its nature credit amounts to a transfer of title to real goods and services. Money is used to *value* this title in a modern economy, but credit *is* the title.

Credit as an Asset and a Liability   Another important implication of our island example is that credit contracts have two parties, each of whom perceives credit from a different viewpoint. From the perspective of the borrower, credit is a *liability,* or future obligation. Nonetheless, the borrower's credit liability represents an *asset,* or future receipt, from the perspective of the lender. This basic fact of life is just as true for the real world as it was for the economist and the physical scientists in their fictitious island credit market.

Societal Gains from the Existence of Markets for Credit   The example discussed in this chapter also illustrates another important fact. A society usually stands to gain from the existence of markets for credit. The island society composed of the economist, bio-chemist, and physicist, for instance, unambiguously gained from the existence of a market for credit. All earned returns in excess of the minimum amount necessary to induce each party to enter into the credit contract. The economist, as producer of the loan, earned a producer surplus of 10 percent, and the physical scientists, as loan consumers, earned a consumer surplus of 40 percent.

CURRENT

CONTROVERSY

IS SAVING TOO LOW IN THE UNITED STATES?

From the 1970s until the present there has been considerable concern about the slowing down of the economic growth rate of the United States and the slowing down of its labor productivity growth rate. The economic growth rate is measured by the annual percentage change in real (inflation-adjusted) national output, or real GDP. Labor productivity is measured by the ratio of real GDP to the quantity of labor required to produce that output. One important determinant of both economic growth and labor productivity growth is the rate of capital-goods expansion—that is, investment. As this chapter indicated, saving must take place before investment is possible.

The International Perspective presented in this chapter indicated that, relative to other developed nations, the United States has low gross saving rates. Two important questions come to mind:

1. Why are U.S. saving and investment ratios relatively low?

2. Are low saving and investment ratios necessarily bad?

Why are U.S. saving rates particularly low? Experts offer different reasons, such as those we discussed in the International Perspective. Here we consider specifically whether high U.S. tax rates adversely affected saving.

It is alleged that higher tax rates reduce saving in the following manner. Interest earnings that correspond to the return from saving are taxed. You know from the

discussion in this chapter that when people decide how to divide their income between present consumption and saving (for future consumption), they are concerned with the rate of return from saving. In a country such as the United States, in which the returns from savings are taxed, however, people must consider the *after-tax* rate of return from saving. At any given pretax rate of return, the higher the tax rate, the lower the after-tax rate of return. The lower the after-tax rate of return from saving, the more people are likely to substitute present consumption for future consumption and the less they are likely to save from a given income level. Higher tax rates, therefore, provide disincentives to save.

Is lower saving—and, by implication, lower investment—necessarily bad? At first blush, this would seem to be the case, because reduced investment slows down a nation's rate of economic growth. As indicated in earlier chapters, economic growth is one of our national economic goals.

Let's now assume away the tax issue. It is important to realize that a trade-off exists between present consumption and future consumption. In order to consume more in the future, society must save more now—and convert those saving funds into capital expansion. It can't be true that it is always better for a nation to increase its growth rate at the expense of present consumption; an optimal growth rate must reflect the community's preferences for present versus future consumption. In short, it is possible that the U.S. growth rate has slowed because its residents want it to. People may be inclined to save less now, relative to the past, because they are not as willing to wait to consume in the future.

There does seem to be some glimmer of hope for the U.S. saving rate, as shown in the table below, which

Gross and Net Saving Rates, United States, 1981–1991											
	1981	1982	1983	1984	1985	1986	1987	1988	1989	1990	1991
Gross saving rate (ratio of gross saving to GDP)	18.4	16.2	14.7	17.0	15.1	13.5	13.6	14.4	14.2	12.9	12.7
Net saving rate (ratio of net saving to NDP)	6.9	3.6	2.8	6.3	4.0	2.6	2.9	3.6	3.6	2.4	1.9

displays two different measures of saving rates for the years 1980–1991. The first is the ratio of gross saving relative to gross domestic product (GDP, or total output produced by a nation irrespective of ownership of factors of production) and an alternative gross saving rate, as compared with that discussed in the International Perspective. The second is the *net* saving rate, which is the ratio of *net* (of depreciation of capital) saving to *net* (of depreciation of capital) domestic product (NDP).

Although there was some year-to-year variation in both measures of saving rates for the United States, the table indicates that the general downward trend of saving rates in the 1980s showed some signs of reversal in the last two years of the decade. U.S. saving could yet rebound from its lowest levels of 1990–1991.

A real-world credit market typically has many lenders (producers) and borrowers (consumers). Nevertheless, parties on both sides of credit transactions often gain from participation in these markets, just as in our island credit market example. It is this fact that leads to the existence of real-world credit markets.

Furthermore, the total gain to society from the existence of credit markets can be measured in terms of the total consumer and producer surpluses gained by all borrowers and lenders. Indeed, as we shall discuss in more detail in Chapter 11, economists use these measures as a means of judging the *performance* of credit markets. Credit markets are most efficient when the combination of total consumer surplus and total producer surplus across all market participants is as large as possible under prevailing market conditions. If this does not occur, there may be a justification for governmental involvement in credit markets aimed at improving their performance.

The Theoretical Nonnecessity of Banks and Other Financial Institutions   Our island example illustrates another interesting fact. From a theoretical standpoint, there is no fundamental reason why people need banks and other financial institutions. In principle, they could borrow and lend directly, without any need for a third party like a bank.

Nevertheless, financial institutions such as banks are an important feature of real-world economies. The next several chapters focus on why "third-party" institutions exist, how they behave, and what crucial roles they play in the markets for money and credit.

CHAPTER SUMMARY

1. People must allocate their consumption of goods and services across time. They do so in light of their consumption opportunities set, which tells them how much they can potentially consume in each period of time. Hence, the consumption opportunities set constrains an individual's consumption choices. The absolute value of the slope of this set tells the individual how much present consumption must be given up to consume more in the future.

2. An indifference curve tells us combinations of consumption choices that keep a person equally satisfied. That is, all along an indifference curve a person's utility is constant.

3. The optimal consumption choice for an individual occurs when the individual attains the highest possible level of utility, given his consumption opportunities set. This is at the point at which an indifference curve is tangent to the consumption opportunities set.

4. The production opportunities set tells an individual how many goods or services can be produced in different periods of time. In a one-person economy the production possibilities set and consumption opportunities set are the same.

5. Saving is forgone consumption. To save, an individual must consume less than current income.

6. Capital goods are goods that may be used in production of other goods and services in the future. The marginal product of capital is the addition to the output of future goods or services achieved from a 1-unit addition to the quantity of capital goods.

7. Investment is an addition to the stock of capital goods. Investment cannot take place unless there is saving by individuals in the economy. For an economy with no government, saving and investment are equal in equilibrium.

8. The rate of return from saving may be derived from the slope of the consumption/production opportunities set for an individual. Because the absolute value of the slope measures the rate of exchange of present for future consumption, multiplying this value times any given amount of goods to be consumed in the future tells us the value of that amount of goods as viewed from the perspective of the present, or the present value of those goods.

9. Interest is the amount of payment made on a loan. The interest rate is the rate of return the borrower pays on the loan and is equal to the ratio of interest to the loan principal, which is the amount borrowed. The equilibrium interest rate is the rate at which borrowers and lenders are satisfied with the amount of credit extended via a loan.

10. When a person extends credit to an individual or a firm, that person provides the individual or firm with goods, services, or funds in the present in exchange for a promise that he or she will be repaid in the future.

11. The reason that credit markets exist is that both borrowers and lenders potentially can gain from credit transactions. Although borrowers must pay a market rate of interest to receive a loan, they may pay a lower rate for a loan than they otherwise would have been willing to pay; as consumers of loans, they thereby would earn consumer surplus. Likewise, lenders may receive a market interest rate that exceeds the rate at which they would have been willing to extend credit to borrowers; as producers of loans, lenders thereby would earn producer surplus.

GLOSSARY

Asset: Title to receipt of a payment at some future date.

Capital good: A good that may be used in the present to produce other goods or services for future consumption.

Consumer surplus: The amount by which the interest an individual would have been willing to pay for a loan exceeds the market interest that the individual actually has to pay.

Consumption opportunities set: All possible consumption possibilities an individual faces over a given time interval.

Credit: Provision of goods, services, or funds in exchange for a promise of repayment in the future.

Indifference curve: A schedule of combinations of consumption alternatives that yield the same level of utility.

Interest: A payment for obtaining credit.

Interest rate: The percentage rate of return received from lending or saving funds.

Investment: An addition to the amount of capital goods.

Law of diminishing marginal utility: As more of a good or service is consumed, utility rises, and so marginal utility—the gain in utility—is positive; nevertheless, as more is consumed, the gain in utility for each extra unit declines, so that marginal utility diminishes.

Liability: An obligation to make a payment at some future date.

Marginal product of capital: The gain in production of goods and services that may be consumed in the future yielded by the use of an additional unit of a capital good in the present.

Market rate of interest: The actual interest rate at which parties agree to exchange a loan for a promise to repay the loan in the future.

Maturity: The termination or due date of a debt.

Opportunity cost: The cost of a forgone alternative.

Present value: The value of a future quantity from the perspective of the present.

Principal: The amount of a loan.

Producer surplus: The amount by which the interest that a lender receives for a loan exceeds the market interest that the lender would have been willing to accept for making the loan.

Production possibilities set: All possible production possibilities that an individual or firm faces over a given time interval.

Rate of exchange: The amount of one good or service that must be given up to obtain another good or service.

Rate of return from saving: The ratio of a total return from saving to the initial amount saved.

Saving: Forgone consumption.

Utility: Satisfaction derived from consuming a good or service.

SELF-TEST QUESTIONS

1. Redraw a rough version of Figure 4-5. Now suppose that the marooned economist has 25 of his pineapples wash away during a storm on his first day on the island, so that he really begins his 2 months on the deserted island with 75 pineapples that have a marginal product of capital of $1 \frac{1}{2}$. Show what would happen to his consumption/production opportunities set and to his optimal consumption choice. Does he experience an income effect or a substitution effect?

2. Why is the economist's indifference curve always downward-sloping?

3. Saving and investment are equal in equilibrium. But are they equivalent concepts? (*Hint:* The answer is no. Explain why.)

4. Can you think of a situation in which you earned consumer surplus? Producer surplus? Explain.

5. Does an economy need to have money for credit markets to exist? Why or why not?

PROBLEMS

4-1.   Our fictitious, marooned economist faces the following situation. Presently, his optimal consumption choice of pineapples is 80 pineapples in the first month and 120 pineapples in the second. The marginal product of capital is 1.5.

a. Draw a rough, but neat, diagram of the economist's consumption/production possibilities set, with his first-month consumption/production of pineapples on the vertical axis and his second-month consumption/production of pineapples on the horizontal axis. Draw the point where the economist's indifference curve is tangent to his opportunities set, and label the appropriate quantities on the axis, using the data given above. On the basis of the data, calculate the maximum quantity of pineapples that the economist could possibly have consumed in his first month, and label this quantity at the appropriate location on your diagram. In addition, calculate the maximum quantity of pineapples that he could possibly consume in his second month, and label this quantity at the appropriate location on your diagram.

b. What is the rate of exchange of pineapples this month for pineapples next month?

c. Based on your answer to part b, how many pineapples does the economist save in the first month? What is the rate of return on saving? What is the minimum monthly rate of interest at which the economist would lend to someone else the amount of pineapples that he saves?

4-2. Consider the following diagram for our fictitious, island-bound economist. Shown on the diagram are alternative consumption/production opportunities sets (I and II), alternative indifference curves (U_I and U_{II}), and alternative decision points (X and Y).

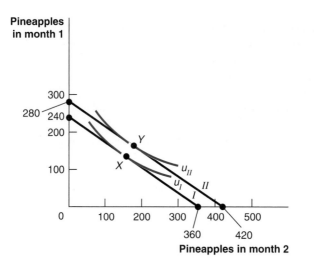

Answer the following questions and show your work on any computations.

a. What are the rates of exchange for consumption opportunities lines I and II? (Be careful to express your answers in terms of units of second-month consumption per unit of first-month consumption or vice versa.)

b. If the consumption good is also a capital good, what is the marginal product of capital for each of the opportunities sets I and II? (Again, be sure to express your answer in appropriate units.)

c. What is the minimum rate of interest at which this individual will make a loan if schedule I is applicable? If schedule II is applicable?

4-3. Our fictitious economist faces the following situation. The marginal product of capital is 1.25. He chooses an optimal consumption/production combination of 100 pineapples in his first month on his island and 125 in his second month. Draw a diagram illustrating his consumption/production opportunities set and his optimal combination, complete with an indifference curve appropriately drawn, and answer the following questions.

a. What is the maximum number of pineapples the economist could possibly have consumed in his first month? Explain.

b. What is the maximum number of pineapples he could possibly have consumed in his second month? Explain.

c. At what minimum rate of interest would the economist be willing to make a pineapple loan?

4-4. Suppose that an individual is thinking about entering into a contract that guarantees her 1,100 units of a good to consume in the future. From the perspective of today, she values the 1,100 units in the future as equivalent to 1,000 units today. What does she perceive to be her rate of return on saving?

4-5. Our marooned economist begins his 2-month island stay with 100 pineapples. Suppose now that a disease infects his pineapples and makes half of them inedible and unplantable. If the marginal product of capital remains at $1 \frac{1}{2}$, what is the maximum number of pineapples he could have available for consumption next month?

4-6. If the rate of return from saving for our marooned economist is equal to 0.25, what is the marginal product of capital on his island?

SELECTED REFERENCES

Bovenberg, A. Lans, and Owen Evans, ''National and Personal Saving in the United States,'' *International Monetary Fund Staff Papers,* 37 (3, September 1990), pp. 636–669.

Hirshleifer, Jack, *Investment, Interest, and Capital* (Englewood Cliffs, N.J.: Prentice-Hall, 1970).

Pierce, James, *Monetary and Financial Economics* (New York: John Wiley & Sons, 1984), chap. 3.

Slemrod, Joel, ''Fear of Nuclear War and Intercountry Differences in the Rate of Saving,'' *Economic Inquiry,* 28 (4, October 1990), pp. 647–657.

Smith, Roger S., ''Factors Affecting Saving, Policy Tools, and Tax Reform,'' *International Monetary Fund Staff Papers,* 37 (1, March 1990), pp. 1–70.

Financial Instruments and Markets

FINANCIAL INTERMEDIATION

Chapter 2 indicated that barter provides only a specific store of purchasing power; people must save by acquiring real goods directly. When people save in a barter economy, they do so by ''nonconsuming'' (or by not selling) some of the goods they produce or some that they earned by offering their services to an employer. Saving also is nonconsumption of income in a money economy; saving equals income minus consumption. In a money economy, however, saving takes the form of a generalized purchasing power—money. People can acquire money instead of goods.

In a barter economy, investment—the purchase of productive equipment, such as physical structures, machines, and inventories—can be undertaken through personal saving. Would-be investors who want to expand their business operations or start a business do so by consuming less than their income and then trading the real goods that they thereby acquire for investment goods.

When an economy evolves from a barter to a money standard, it becomes easier for people to separate the act of saving from the act of investment. Investors don't have to save personally; they can obtain generalized purchasing power (money) from savers. This is beneficial to savers because they gain a generalized store of value and because they can earn interest on this extension of credit. Savers would not voluntarily make such an exchange unless they perceived a benefit from doing so. Part of the gain is that interest earnings allow them to consume more in the future. Investors perceive a gain because they can start a new business or expand their existing one. If everything works out well, investors can pay savers interest out of the profits they earn from their investments. (Chapter 7 indicates how the market interest rate is determined by the interaction of household saving and business investment.) Because society can now more easily separate the acts of saving and investment, it too is better off: Those who save need not be the ones who seek to recognize a business opportunity and capitalize on it.

In short, a money economy encourages saving and investment, and it facilitates the transfer of purchasing power from savers to investors. These advantages promote economic growth and a rising living standard for the community.

As economies moved from barter to money, the stage was set for a new business: banking. By connecting savers (ultimate lenders) with investors (ultimate borrowers), banks could facilitate the transferal of purchasing power. Banks provided a "middleperson" service—for a fee, of course. The origins of commercial banks and other depository institutions are discussed in the following chapter.

As the economy and the financial system developed, other financial institutions (or financial intermediaries) emerged. Today, governments, commercial banks, savings and loan associations, mutual savings banks, credit unions, insurance companies, pension funds, and mutual funds are all in the business of transferring funds from savers to investors. This process has come to be known as **financial intermediation.** The process of financial intermediation has spawned a variety of financial assets, or **financial instruments,** such as stocks, bonds, mortgages, mutual funds, and repurchase agreements. These financial assets are traded in specific markets; our financial system has evolved into a complex web wherein various types of financial institutions trade a wide variety of financial assets in many different financial markets.

CHANNELING SAVING TO BORROWING

Financial markets perform the function of channeling saving funds to borrowing. Two basic economic groups are households and businesses. Those specific households or businesses that spend more than their incomes are net borrowers; those specific households or businesses that spend less than their incomes are net savers. Specific households or businesses can be net savers or net borrowers. As a group, however, households are net savers; and as a group, businesses are net borrowers. For ease of exposition, we ignore household borrowing and business saving.

DIRECT FINANCING

Businesses can start up or expand by obtaining funds directly from households. One way to do so is by selling common stock to the public. Common stock is evidence of part ownership in a corporation; it entitles the owner to vote on certain corporate decisions and to share in any profits. A share of common stock is a financial asset to the owner and a financial liability to the issuer, or corporation. A business can also obtain funds by issuing (selling) bonds. A **bond** is evidence that a promise has been made by a corporation to pay a specified amount of money in recognition of a loan to the business. The bond is a financial asset to the lender-owner and a financial liability (debt) to the borrower-corporation.

In both these examples, direct financing has occurred; businesses have borrowed directly from households. In turn, businesses use these saving funds to make purchases of plant, equipment, and inventory. Figure 5-1 shows the process of direct financing. Markets have evolved to facilitate direct financing. Stocks and bonds are originally sold in primary

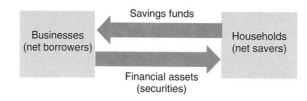

Figure 5-1
Direct Financing.   This figure shows the process of direct financing. Borrowers borrow directly from households by selling them securities such as stocks and bonds. No financial intermediaries are used to channel saving into borrowing.

markets; often they are resold (many times), through transactions taking place in secondary markets. Primary and secondary markets are analyzed below.

INDIRECT FINANCING

Indirect financing occurs as a result of financial intermediation. Financial institutions, acting as intermediaries, perform the function of channeling saving funds from households (ultimate lenders) to businesses (ultimate borrowers). For example, commercial banks and other depository institutions accept monetary liabilities, such as demand deposits and savings deposits, and insurance companies accept monetary liabilities, such as payments of premiums that obligate the insurance companies to reimburse expected losses. In turn, financial institutions purchase assets (relend the funds). For example, commercial banks purchase IOUs from businesses, and thrift institutions purchase mortgages from home buyers (this latter transaction implies a relending back to households).

INTERMEDIATION AND PORTFOLIO DIVERSIFICATION

Financial intermediaries do more than play the role of intermediaries between ultimate lenders (savers) and ultimate borrowers. They also perform a valuable role by offering savers an asset that is really a well-diversified portfolio of assets. For example, if a small saver were required to deal directly with ultimate borrowers, such as perhaps a home buyer seeking mortgage money, the small saver essentially would be ''putting all his or her eggs in one basket.'' The small saver would end up with only one asset—a mortgage contract on one piece of property. Having such a limited number of assets increases the risk of default and of losing the entire asset portfolio. The financial intermediary, such as a savings and loan association, can offer the small saver a reduction in risk through diversification. This is accomplished by pooling the excess funds of numerous small savers in order to purchase a large variety of assets from numerous ultimate borrowers. As a result, the small saver might end up with, say, $20,000 in a savings deposit, but implicitly the saver has ''purchased'' a small fraction of each of thousands of mortgage contracts. Looked at another way, financial intermediaries allow savers to purchase assets that are relatively safe and more liquid and that also earn interest. For example, when a saver deposits money in his or her account at the local credit union, that saver is implicitly purchasing shares in the credit union. The financial intermediaries in turn purchase assets, such as mortgages and land, which are sold by the ultimate borrowers.

Consider Figure 5-2, which shows the process of intermediation. Note that the ultimate lenders comprise the same economic units as the ultimate borrowers; financial institutions clearly play the role of intermediaries.

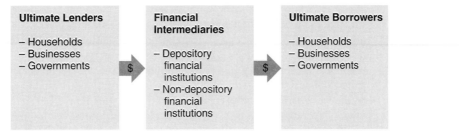

Figure 5-2

The Process of Financial Intermediation.   The process of financial intermediation is depicted here; the different types of financial intermediaries—depository and nondepository financial institutions—are described later on in this chapter. Note that ultimate lenders and ultimate borrowers are the same economic units—households, businesses, and governments—but not necessarily the same individuals. Whereas individual households can be net lenders or borrowers, households as an economic unit are net lenders. Specific businesses or governments, similarly, can be net lenders or borrowers; both, as economic units, are net borrowers.

FINANCIAL DISINTERMEDIATION

The reverse of the financial intermediation process is **financial disintermediation.** Savers take funds out of deposit accounts and invest directly in, say, a bond issued by the U.S. government. In other words, rather than allowing the financial intermediary to use the saver's deposited funds to purchase U.S. Treasury bonds, the saver does it directly.

Why Disintermediation Occurs   Individuals remove their savings from financial institutions when the direct purchase of financial claims issued by households, corporations, and governments will bring a higher rate of return than a savings account in a financial intermediary. If, for example, a savings account in a thrift institution offers 5.25 percent interest, while securities issued by the U.S. government offer 12 percent interest, some savers will reduce the funds they maintain in thrifts or commercial bank saving deposits and increase their holdings of U.S. government securities.

Not surprisingly, the amount of disintermediation that occurs depends, in large part, on differences between interest rates offered by financial intermediaries and those offered by such ultimate borrowers as corporations and governments. The most rapid rate of disintermediation in the United States has occurred when nominal rates of interest have risen rapidly because of high rates of inflation (and therefore high anticipated future rates of inflation). This was possible because the regulations of the federal government prevented financial intermediaries from offering higher interest rates on normal savings-type accounts. Other interest rates were unregulated and rose with the rate of inflation.

Conditions for disintermediation existed in 1969, 1973, and 1974. During those periods, people predictably withdrew their savings deposits from thrifts and financial institutions and purchased financial assets directly; the rate of savings deposit growth fell dramatically during these episodes.

In 1975, as a reaction to the process of disintermediation, a new financial intermediary sprang up—money market mutual funds. These institutions were unregulated, and they offered interest rates on savings that were competitive with market interest rates. Although this financial innovation helped to stem the tide of disintermediation, it didn't help the thrifts.

By the end of 1977, yields on U.S. Treasury bills (short-term bonds issued by the U.S.

Treasury) again rose above the maximum interest rates that commercial banks and thrift institutions were legally permitted to pay on passbook savings deposits. In order to forestall another loss of savings deposits to the disintermediation process and to the mutual funds—an event that would have threatened the very existence of thrift institutions—federal regulators of depository institutions authorized a new category of 6-month time deposits called *money market certificates.* Commercial banks, savings and loans, and mutual savings banks were permitted to offer these certificates after June 1, 1978. This new liability and others have made the thrift institutions more competitive in the market for saving funds. Of special importance in reversing the intra-intermediary movement of funds from thrifts to money market mutual fund accounts is the *money market deposit account,* an instrument that competes directly with money market mutual funds.

FINANCIAL INSTRUMENTS

A variety of financial instruments are available to individuals and firms in today's world. Most financial instruments take the form of **securities.** Securities are printed documents proving ownership or creditorship in a business organization or public body such as local, state, or federal government.

SECURITIES

As you learned in Chapter 4, when lenders and borrowers transact voluntarily, both parties perceive gains. Otherwise, they would not make the transaction. Of course, in the final analysis, one party may gain more than the other. It is possible, and it is usually the case, for both parties to be better off as a result of a loan. A loan is an extension of credit, and a security is written evidence of the extension of a loan. Securities are exchanged in credit markets, and such markets facilitate economic growth. In fact, variations in the amount of credit in an economy may affect economic activity as much as variations in the money supply.

An extension of credit allows the borrower to make expenditures sooner than otherwise; it also allows the lender to earn interest and to purchase more goods in the future. This transferal of purchasing power is an element that is common to all securities. Because all securities can substitute for each other, interest rates earned on the various securities will move up and down together as market conditions change.

If Mr. Smith wanted to borrow a sizable amount for a very long period of time, in principle he could find someone to make him a large loan. It is likely, however, that he would find few willing to make such a loan. Those few that would be willing to extend credit would insist on a very high interest rate, because a good deal of uncertainty would exist.

Suppose, however, that it were possible for original lenders to sell *individual parts* of Mr. Smith's total debt obligation—to transfer the extension of credit—to a third party, such as Ms. Johnson. Indeed, suppose further that Johnson could resell an individual part of Mr. Smith's debt obligation—a security—to someone else, and so on. The net result of such sales and resales of the original securities issued to cover Mr. Smith's original total debt would be that many people would be extending smaller amounts of credit to Smith for shorter periods of time. The ability to resell securities, therefore, lowers the risk of credit extension and increases the liquidity of the security. By increasing the liquidity of securities, the ability to resell debt (or transfer credit extension) permits greater quantities of credit extension, facilitates trade, and lowers interest rates to borrowers.

TYPES OF SECURITIES

All securities convey the same basic information: the identity of the borrower, the amount to be paid when the instrument matures, and the amount of interest and when it is to be paid. Nevertheless, there are a wide variety of securities used in our economy. These may be subdivided into basic groupings, which enables us to discuss them in a relatively organized manner.

Equity Instruments   Shares of ownership in a firm are **equity instruments,** or shares of *stock* in the company. These ownership shares may be **preferred stock** or **common stock** shares. Of those who own shares in a company, those with preferred stock have first claim upon assets and dividends of the company, while those holding common stock have last claim and, therefore, the greatest risk of loss. Hence, common stock holders generally have greatest voting control over the firm's management.

Debt Instruments   Direct debt obligations of individuals or firms that borrow are **debt instruments.** A loan that a bank makes to you, for instance, is a debt instrument; it is a direct obligation from you to the bank. There are a variety of debt instruments; we highlight only a few:

1. *Commercial paper* From a legal standpoint, **commercial paper** is a term that applies to all classes of short-term negotiable (that is, sellable by the holder) instruments that arise from commercial transactions. In the narrower sense commonly used in financial markets, however, commercial paper refers to short-term (usually with maturities less than nine months) debt obligations issued by companies that need to raise funds for use for a relatively short period of time. Commercial paper may be issued directly by the borrowing firm or through brokers, but either way the firm has a direct debt obligation to the holder of the commercial paper.

2. *Corporate bonds* These are intermediate- to long-term debt obligations issued by companies. Again, these instruments may be issued directly by the specific company or may be issued through a broker.

3. *Convertible bonds* **Convertible bonds** are debt instruments that are convertible into stock at a specified price at the discretion of the holder.

4. *''Junk bonds''* These are corporate bonds that possess both high yields and high risk. They are issued by firms that are not regarded as low-risk borrowers in the bond markets but that wish to obtain long-term financing in national credit markets. Originally developed as a substitute for short-term bank loans, junk bonds were a major vehicle for financing corporate takeovers—''leveraged buyouts''—in the 1980s; indeed, in 1988 over 75 percent of the junk bonds issued were used for this purpose. By the early 1990s the use of junk bonds had declined somewhat, but they remain an important debt instrument for many companies.

5. *United States government securities* The U.S. government issues three types of debt instruments:
   a. *Treasury bills* The shortest-term U.S. Treasury securities are **Treasury bills** issued for periods of 15 days to 1 year. The most often issued are 3- and 6-month bills. The minimum face value on these bills is $10,000. There is no stated interest; rather, bills are sold at a discount. A $10,000, 3-month Treasury bill might sell, for example, for $9,700. The discount is $300; the buyer earns interest by purchasing the bill for $9,700 and redeeming it for $10,000 on the maturity date.
   b. *Treasury notes* **Treasury notes** have a stated coupon rate of interest, and the inter-

est is most often paid every 6 months. The minimum face value of Treasury notes is $1,000. They are issued for periods of 1 to 10 years.

    c. *Treasury bonds* **Treasury bonds** usually have a maturity of 10 years or more. They, too, have a coupon rate of interest that is usually paid semiannually. The coupon rate is set by law at a maximum of $4\frac{1}{4}$ percent, although the Tax Equity and Fiscal Responsibility Act of 1982 increased the allowable exceptions to this rate to $110 billion. That is, the Treasury is permitted to have $110 billion of debt issued at a stated coupon rate above $4\frac{1}{4}$ percent. All of this is irrelevant, however, because the $4\frac{1}{4}$ percent coupon bonds can be sold at discount; their yields, therefore, will reflect market (not coupon) rates.

       Since January 1983, all Treasury notes and bonds are issued in registered form; only bills are issued in bearer form. This means that, for notes and bonds, the name and address of the current owner are registered with the Treasury, and any ownership change therefore must be recorded with the Treasury. The maturity payment on bills, in contrast, is made to the current holder of the bills.

6. *State and local government securities* State and local governments issue debt (borrow) in the form of state and local bonds called municipal bonds, or simply "munies." Their chief characteristic is that they are tax-exempt; that is, interest income earned on munies is exempt from federal income taxes.

       There are two types of municipal bonds: **general-obligation bonds** and **revenue bonds.** General-obligation bonds are secured by the taxing power of the issuing municipality. Revenue bonds are secured by the revenues to be obtained from the specific project that the bonds are used to finance (e.g., a toll bridge).

Asset-Backed Securities Securities that represent shares of the market value of a pooled grouping of assets are known as **asset-backed securities.** An important type of asset-backed security is the **mortgage-backed security,** which is a share in the value of a group of home mortgages. Mortgage-backed securities commonly are issued by federal government agencies (see the discussion of governmental involvement in financial intermediation later in this chapter) but are privately issued as well.

Hedging Instruments An instrument that permits an individual or firm to ensure against asset price fluctuations is a **hedging instrument.** These instruments include **options** and **futures.** Options are financial contracts that grant the holder the right to buy and/or sell specified securities or goods in specific amounts and at specific prices for a specific period of time. Futures are financial contracts under which a person or firm agrees to provide a specific quantity of a security or a commodity at a specific price at some future time. By using options and futures contracts, a person or firm can smooth out the risk of price fluctuation for purchase or sale of some other financial instrument, such as an exchange of another nation's currency in the foreign exchange market. We shall have more to say about futures contracts later in this chapter. Both options and futures are used extensively in foreign currency transactions, which we discuss in much more detail in Chapter 27.

FINANCIAL INSTITUTIONS

Among those who trade all the instruments mentioned above are individuals like you and the authors. In reality, however, many of us, such as the authors of this text, aren't wealthy enough to hold many of these instruments. In principle, all of us could purchase debt instruments, such as corporate bonds or U.S. Treasury bills, directly from a company or from the U.S. government. Most of us, however, do not do so. Instead, we hold debt instruments issued by **financial institutions,** which intermediate between us and other borrowers, including other households and business firms.

There are a variety of financial institutions. These commonly are separated into three basic groups: **depository institutions,** nondepository institutions, and the federal government financial institutions. Depository institutions are financial intermediaries that issue debt instruments they call *deposits.* Among these deposits are checking deposits such as demand deposits or NOW account deposits (see Chapter 3), which function as money. Therefore, a particularly important feature of depository institutions is that they issue debt instruments that function as media of exchange and are included in common measures of money such as M1. Depository institutions also issue deposits denominated in foreign currencies, commonly called *Eurocurrencies,* which we discuss in detail in Chapter 27. Nondepository institutions, in contrast, are private financial institutions that do not issue deposits. Most of us do not think of the government as a financial institution, but in fact it has become a very important financial intermediary, as we shall see.

DEPOSITORY INSTITUTIONS

There are two basic types of depository institutions: commercial banks and thrift institutions, which include savings and loan associations, savings banks, and credit unions. All these institutions have the legal privilege of issuing checking, savings, and time deposits. The following chapter and much of the next two units of the text are devoted to these institutions, and so we shall not say too much more about them at present.

NONDEPOSITORY INSTITUTIONS

There are a variety of nondepository institutions. We concentrate on a few of the most important of these.

Insurance Companies   These include life insurance and property and casualty insurance companies. Life insurance companies, which rank third in asset size, receive funds (premiums) that insure people against the financial consequences of death. Actuarial tables permit the companies to predict with great accuracy the annual number of deaths (and therefore the amount of money they must pay to policy beneficiaries) for long periods of time. They consequently purchase longer-term assets, such as long-term corporate bonds and long-term commercial (nonresidential) mortgages. Property and casualty insurance companies insure car owners against theft and collision and homeowners against fire and burglary. They are not as certain of what their annual payments to policyholders will be; consequently, they purchase highly liquid, short-term assets and low-risk bonds.

Pension and Retirement Funds   These institutions are akin to life insurance companies; they can predict with high accuracy what their annual payouts (pension annuities) will be for long periods into the future. They invest in long-term corporate bonds, high-grade common stocks, large-denomination time deposits, and long-term mortgages.

Mutual Funds   These are investment companies that issue redeemable securities that are shares in assets held by the funds, which typically include stocks, bonds, government securities, and asset-backed securities such as mortgage-backed securities. These funds

CURRENT
CONTROVERSY

PAWNSHOPS—LENDERS TO THOSE WITHOUT ACCESS TO MAINSTREAM CREDIT MARKETS

Pawnshops, or *pawnbrokers,* are financial institutions that extend very small loans (in the range of $50 to $75 in the early 1990s) with very short maturities. These loans are collateralized by personal property of the borrower (such as watches, jewelry, televisions, stereos, musical instruments, cameras, and firearms), and such loans typically are made at rates of interest *significantly* higher than those charged by mainstream financial institutions such as depository financial institutions—annual percentage interest rates anywhere from 30 to 240 percent!

Pawnshops have been in existence for centuries. They take their name from the old term "pawn," meaning a pledge for the payment of a debt. (In England, this term is still applied to the deposit of collateral as security for a bank loan.) A famous frequenter of pawnshops was the great nineteenth-century Russian author of *Crime and Punishment, The Idiot, The Possessed,* and *The Brothers Karamozov,* Fyodor Dostoyevsky, who got ideas for some of his more down-and-out characters from his visits to the shops. Dostoyevsky himself frequented pawnshops to raise funds to pay debts accumulated during his nearly life-long addiction to gambling—he, like many other pawnshop borrowers past and present, could find no other individuals or institutions that would extend him credit because of his propensity not to repay loans.

In most developed nations, the pawnshop industry has been in decline. For instance, in Great Britain, there were about 3,000 pawnshops in 1900, but by the late 1980s there were less than 175. In stark contrast, the pawnshop business has *grown* in the United States during this past century, from under 2,000 in 1911 (one pawnshop for about 47,000 citizens) to just under 7,000 (one pawnshop for about 36,000 citizens) today. By 1992, all pawnshops probably made between 35 million and 40 million loans, and the aggregate dollar amount of loans ranged from $700 million to $750 million.

Most pawnshops in the United States are located in the southeastern and central mountain areas of the nation. Pawnshop regulations vary from state to state,

because states license pawnshops. Typically, state regulations require that, when a customer pawns a personal item, terms of the loan contract must be specified by the pawnshop on a *pawn ticket.* The customer retains a copy of the ticket, which states the customer's name, address, and means of identification; a detailed description of the pawned item with a serial number if available; the amount lent; the maturity of the loan; the interest rate; and the total amount (principal plus interest) that must be repaid to redeem the pawned item. If the customer defaults on the loan (as Dostoyevsky often did, and as between 14 and 22 percent of current-day borrowers do), the pawned item becomes the property of the pawnshop following a specified delinquency date. Typically, the amount lent by the pawnshop is around 50 to 60 percent of the resale value of the pawned item, and so pawnshops nearly always profit from defaults. Nevertheless, most pawnbrokers prefer that customers repay the loan because such customers often become repeat customers, who account for 70 to 80 percent of pawnshops' business.

What accounts for the growth of pawnbroking in the United States? One is the improvement in transportation during this century, because pawnbrokers need a large number of customers to maintain their profitability. Another is that many states—notably in the southeastern and mountain regions where pawnbroking has grown the most—have relaxed some of their *usury laws* that place upper legal limits on loan interest rates. Therefore, pawnshops can now legally charge the high rates that most of them need to receive to remain profitable. Recent growth, however, may be due primarily to two other factors: the increased imposition of fees on basic services by banks and other financial institutions and the simultaneous increase in the proportion of United States citizens classified as "low income" individuals. For these people, mainstream financial institutions and markets may not be viable options; pawnshops are their "lenders of last resort."

Are the typically low-income pawnshop borrowers "cheated" by the fact that they cannot get loans from mainstream financial institutions? This is a normative issue, and so we shall not take a stand on a single answer. Like most economic issues, this one exhibits trade-offs. On the one hand, pawnshop borrowers obtain loans only at very high rates of interest that those of us with access to mainstream markets are tempted to view as excessive. On the other hand, these high rates compensate pawnshop owners for the high risk that low-income borrowers will not repay loans. Further, the fact that pawnshop borrowers are willing to pay such high rates of interest could be interpreted as implying that borrowers would be worse off if pawnshop loans were unavailable, because they cannot get mainstream bank loans at lower interest rates.

Adapted from John P. Caskey and Brian J. Zikmund, "Pawnshops: The Consumer's Lender of Last Resort," Federal Reserve Bank of Kansas City *Economic Review*, 75 (2, March/April 1990), pp. 5–18; and John P. Caskey, "Pawnbroking in America: The Economics of a Forgotten Credit Market," *Journal of Money, Credit, and Banking*, 23 (1, February 1991), pp. 85–99.

permit relatively small individual savers to hold shares that are diversified among such a variety of financial instruments rather than holding just one or two instruments.

Finance Companies   These, in effect, are small loan companies. They issue a variety of debt instruments of their own to finance small loans, most often to individuals or to small businesses.

THE FEDERAL GOVERNMENT

In its 1992 fiscal year the U.S. federal government spent over $400 billion more than it received in revenues; in 1991 the deficit figure was $320.9 billion. Those deficits presumably represented the amount of credit demanded by the federal government in those years. Currently the federal government borrows over 40 percent of all the funds borrowed on U.S. capital markets. Actually, however, the impact of federal government activity on the financial markets is even greater. The federal government's presence in the financial markets has three other sources: (1) activities of ''off-budget'' agencies, (2) operation of government-sponsored enterprises, and (3) provision of federally guaranteed loans.

The Federal Financing Bank   The most important off-budget agency is the Federal Financing Bank (FFB), which began operation in 1974. Today it provides most of the financing for off-budget agencies and also for certain on-budget agencies. The FFB lends by three methods:

1. Purchasing agency debt (bonds)
2. Purchasing loans and loan assets
3. Purchasing loan guarantees

All these purchases are financed with funds borrowed directly from the Treasury. The original purpose of the FFB was to coordinate and to consolidate the borrowing of a number of federal agencies. The FFB was designed to act as an intermediary—buying securities issued by off-budget agencies and paying for them with funds borrowed from the Treasury. Funds lent by the FFB to off-budget agencies do not show up in the budget totals voted and authorized by Congress.

   Federal agencies often guarantee loans to insure the lender against any loss resulting from default by the borrower. Some of the most famous cases of loan guarantees involved the City of New York, Chrysler, and Lockheed. When the FFB purchases a guaranteed loan at the request of a federal agency, that purchase is ultimately paid for by the Treasury, which will probably sell securities to cover the expense. Such an action is an indirect loan from the Treasury to the private-sector borrower, but it is a "loan" that will not show up anywhere in the federal budget or deficit. Nonetheless, total borrowing by the Treasury has increased to finance the purchase.

Government-Sponsored Enterprises   Another way the federal government affects credit markets without it showing up in the federal budget is by lending to government-sponsored enterprises that were originally established to perform specific credit functions but are now privately owned. Although the transactions of these enterprises are not included in the federal budget, they are subject to government supervision. Three of these agencies operate under the watchful eye of the Farm Credit Administration; they are Banks for Cooperatives, Federal Intermediate Credit Banks, and Federal Land Banks. These banks issue securities and then use the proceeds to lend to farmers. Four other agencies support the housing market: the Federal National Mortgage Association (FNMA or Fannie Mae), the General National Mortgage Association (GNMA or Ginnie Mae), the Federal Home Loan Banks (FHLBs), and the Federal Home Loan Mortgage Corporation (FHLMC or Freddie Mac). These agencies provide funds to the mortgage market by selling mortgage-backed securities and using the proceeds to buy mortgages.

Guaranteed Loans or Mortgage Pools   The third category of federal government activities that affects the credit markets but doesn't contemporaneously affect the federal budget is the guaranteed mortgage pool. Guaranteed mortgage pools are loans that the federal government insures wholly or partly, or guarantees the payment of principal or interest, or both. Like the off-budget agencies and federally sponsored agencies, federal loan guarantees do not show up in the federal budget. The bulk of loan guarantees has been used to support housing. In recent years, however, guarantees have been used increasingly for other purposes, such as the loan guarantees involving Chrysler and the City of New York.   .

FINANCIAL MARKETS

Financial instruments are traded both by individual households and firms and by financial institutions in a wide variety of *financial markets,* or markets for financial instruments. Financial markets are categorized in different ways, as we discuss below.

PRIMARY AND SECONDARY FINANCIAL MARKETS

Financial transactions occur in both primary and secondary financial markets. A **primary market** is one in which a new security is bought and sold. A **secondary market** is one in which existing securities are exchanged; secondary markets are important to primary markets because they make the instruments traded in the latter markets more liquid. A primary financial market exists for U.S. government securities, corporate bonds, and corporate stocks. Newly issued securities constitute additions to the supply of credit. When the U.S. Treasury sells $1 billion of newly created bonds, they are purchased in what is called the primary securities market. Primary markets also exist for newly issued stocks and bonds of nongovernment corporations.

Primary Markets   The issuance of stocks and bonds in the primary securities market is aided by so-called investment bankers (who often also act as brokers and dealers in secondary markets). An investment banker undertakes what is called an underwriting of a new issue. Underwriting means that the investment banker normally guarantees to the issuing corporations and governments a fixed price and (in the case of a bond) a fixed yield. The underwriting investment banker publicly announces the upcoming new issue in financial publications and elsewhere.

Underwriters will attempt to sell the underwritten stocks or bonds within a day or so of the date of issuance. The investment bankers underwriting the new issues in the primary securities market earn their profit by attempting to ''buy cheap and sell dear.'' They attempt to sell the new issues at a price higher than the price they have guaranteed to the issuer. Note, however, that investment bankers are not true bankers, and they do not carry out investment spending. Rather, they are simply market makers in the sense that they make sure a market exists for about-to-be-issued new securities. Investment bankers do not accept deposits, nor do they make commercial or consumer loans. In fact, commercial bankers were prohibited from underwriting corporate securities by the Glass-Steagall Act of 1933, which separated commercial banking and investment banking. (We update this in Chapters 10 and 11.) Commercial banks can and do participate in underwriting the bonds of state and municipal governments, because their securities are presumed to be relatively safe—even though at times the governments of New York City, Cleveland, Boston, and the state of Michigan were more or less teetering on the brink of bankruptcy. Virtually all types of individuals, households, and businesses buy new issues. Some of the assets owned by financial intermediaries, for example, will have been purchased in the primary securities market.

The actual marketplace for the underwriting of new securities is the conference suites of investment banking firms, which are linked by telephone with each other and with the corporations or governments that are issuing the new securities. The investors (for example, large insurance companies and pension plans) will also be in communication via telephone with the underwriting investment banking firms. By far the most important commodity sold by investment banking firms is information about the yield required to sell an issue and the identity of prospective buyers.

Investment bankers are able to underwrite new issues not because they have acquired funds from deposits, but rather because they have enough of their own capital to buy up what is not sold to buyers at the guaranteed price. Consider an example: The Big Investment Banking Firm underwrites XYZ Corporation's issuance of 1,000 bonds with a face value of $10,000, offering a coupon rate of 10 percent per year for 10 years. The Big Investment Banking Firm guarantees that the bonds will sell for at least their face value of $10,000 apiece. As it turns out, the bonds can only be sold at a discount. The average price is $9,000. The Big Investment Banking Firm will incur a loss of $1,000 on each bond, for a total loss of $1,000,000.

Secondary Markets   In the past, an active secondary market existed only for U.S. government securities and stocks listed on major exchanges. Smaller secondary markets did exist for corporate, state, and local bonds, but they were inactive most of the time. During the last decade, the secondary markets for corporate, state, and local bonds have expanded. Additionally, secondary markets have developed for consumer credit and bank business loans.

While many primary markets are the province of investment bankers, brokers intermediate many secondary market transactions. A broker is an intermediary who brings together buyers and sellers of the same financial instrument. Brokers typically specialize in particular types of markets, for which they become specialists in demand, supply, and price conditions. In return for the broker's services, which include executing market exchanges for buyers and sellers, the broker receives a commission, or "brokerage fee."

CAPITAL MARKETS

Capital market transactions include the purchase and sale of securities with a maturity of one year or more—that is, long-term securities. The stock market is arbitrarily included as part of the capital market. In a sense, a share of stock is a long-term security because it has no maturity date. As long as the corporation exists, the share of stock can remain in existence.

The stock market is by far the largest capital market in terms of the dollar value of the securities outstanding. About 35 percent of all stocks outstanding are owned by individuals; the remainder are owned indirectly by individuals through their pension plans, insurance companies, and corporations.

The second largest component of the capital market by dollar value is the mortgage market. There are two categories of mortgages:

1. Residential, for from one- to four-family homes

2. Agricultural and commercial

Table 5-1 shows the dollar value of mortgages owned by commercial banks, savings and loan associations, mutual savings banks, and life insurance companies. Only recently have commercial banks expanded into the home and commercial mortgage market.

The third largest component of the capital market is the market for corporate bonds. Life insurance companies are the main owners of corporate bonds; they own slightly more than one-third of all corporate bonds.

Finally, long-term U.S. government securities and those issued by federal government agencies, as well as state and local governments, are purchased by a broad spectrum of institutions and individuals. The attractiveness of U.S. government notes and bonds to the private investor lies in their insulation from default risk.

THE MONEY MARKETS

Capital markets consist of securities issued in principal for 1 year or more. The term **money market** typically applies to the trading of credit instruments issued for less than 1 year. Money market instruments are highly liquid and readily marketable. The largest sector of the money market is the market for U.S. Treasury bills of less than 1-year maturity (T-bills).

Large-denomination certificates of deposit (CDs), defined in Chapter 3, were "invented" simultaneously by several aggressive U.S. commercial banks in 1961. All negotiable CDs are of $100,000 denominations or more. They are deposits in the issuing institution. A commercial bank carries a CD on its accounting books as a liability. Purchasers of CDs, of course, consider them assets.

CDs may be negotiable, meaning that holders may sell them in secondary markets. Negotiable CDs play an increasingly important role in money market transactions. They constitute an important source of funds for medium- and large-sized banks. Corporate treasurers purchase negotiable CDs because they provide earnings with a high degree of liquidity and because there is an active resale (secondary) market.

T A B L E   5-1
Dollar Volume of Mortgages Owned by Commercial Banks, Savings Associations,
Finance Companies, and Life Insurance Companies, 1991
(Millions of dollars)

Commercial banks	$ 870,797
Savings institutions	754,834
Finance companies	48,972
Life insurance companies	259,218
Total, major financial institutions	$1,933,821

Source: Board of Governors of the Federal Reserve System, *Federal Reserve Bulletin.*

In addition to the CDs and T-bills discussed above, the markets for commercial paper and banker's acceptances are other important parts of the money market.

Repurchase agreements, defined in Chapter 3, make up an important part of today's money market. RPs enable a holder of securities to acquire funds by selling the securities and simultaneously agreeing to repurchase them at a later date. They are a means of facilitating borrowing and lending for short periods of time and for providing the lender with liquidity. RPs typically involve a commercial bank and a corporation. The bank sells securities (often U.S. Treasury bills) to a corporate treasurer and promises to buy them back (often the next day) at a predetermined price. The difference between today's selling price and tomorrow's repurchase price is the implicit interest payment.

Another form of money market trading is in the **federal funds market,** in which banks borrow from and lend to each other the deposits (reserves) they have at the Fed. Most banks use the federal funds market to meet reserve requirements or earn interest over short accounting periods. Chapter 6 discusses federal funds in more detail.

RECENT INNOVATIONS IN FINANCIAL MARKETS

In recent years dramatic developments have occurred in the securities markets and mortgage markets. New financial instruments and entire new markets have emerged, and changes in existing financial instruments and financial markets have also occurred. The common theme in all these innovations is the desire to reduce (or at least shift to others) the risks associated with fluctuations in interest rates (which themselves are often due to fluctuations in expected inflation rates).

Mortgage Markets   A majority of newly issued residential mortgages in the United States are **adjustable-rate mortgages (ARMs).** ARMs allow the lender to vary the interest rate during the period of the loan—on specified dates and subject to well-defined restrictions. Also, a large market for new securities backed by pools of mortgages has developed. Many of these mortgage-backed securities are guaranteed by the Government National Mortgage Association, but private firms have become important participants in this market. Most of these mortgage-backed securities are purchased by insurance companies and pension funds. In effect, some troubled thrifts have been able to transfer their risk to the government and thereby increase their liquidity; as a consequence the mortgage market has become somewhat insulated from a depressed thrift industry, and the residential housing industry was able to rebound from the 1981–1982 recession.

On balance these two innovations seem to have benefited both home buyers and the residential construction industry. Still, one wonders if a large stock of variable-rate mortgage debt has greatly increased default risk; will defaults rise precipitously in the future if renewed inflation turns interest rates upward?

Bond Markets[1]   An increasing proportion of new corporate bonds issued in the United States are floating-interest-rate bonds—and the remaining fixed-rate issues often have early sell or buy provisions. Also, since the early 1980s there has been an increase in the volume of **zero-coupon bonds,** which pay their return in the form of price appreciation rather than coupon interest payments and therefore eliminate reinvestment risk.

An interesting development in the bond market appeared in the mid-1980s. Inspired by mortgage-backed securities, a new type of asset-backed debt instrument emerged: the **collateralized mortgage obligation (CMO).** CMOs are similar to the real estate mortgage-backed securities described above, except that they are backed by something other than residential structures. The whole process of pooling similar loans to produce a stable and predictable cash flow is called **securitization.**

In effect, a pool of accounts receivable is segregated into a specifically created subsidiary or trust, and investors buy shares of the pooled assets. In return for their shares, investors receive principal and interest (minus service fees and other costs, of course) as the receivables, or loans, are paid off by the original borrowers. The biggest buyers are pension funds, S&Ls, money managers, and bank trust departments.

There are three major reasons for the increased popularity of CMOs. First, these securities are liquid and tradable—unlike most loans. Second, debt securities have well-defined risks that can be assessed and rated by debt-rating agencies, which makes them enticing to many investors such as pension funds, insurance companies, and S&Ls. Finally, debt securities often have lower transactions costs than loans.

There now is little doubt that securitized debt is the wave of the future. Given today's regulatory structure (analyzed in Chapter 10), it may be that in 10 or 15 years commercial banks and thrifts will become, in essence, only loan originators. Their assets will be mostly structured, rated, placed, traded, and invested by other financial institutions. This scenario augurs well for the investment banking industry, but not for banks and S&Ls, which will play a minor role in the intermediation process. We consider this issue again in Chapter 9.

Forward Contracts and Futures Markets   Under the terms of a **forward contract,** buyers and sellers agree to trade a certain quantity of a commodity for a specific price at a specified date in the future. Many people engage in such common future delivery contracts as ordering next year's model of a Chevrolet from the local Chevrolet dealer two months before the car is scheduled to arrive, or ordering a book from the bookstore that will not be delivered for three weeks. As another example, a farmer may make a contract to deliver 1 million bushels of grain to the operator of a grain elevator at a specific month in the future at a price agreed upon by both parties today. All these contracts are called forward contracts.

A forward contract is not, strictly speaking, the same as a futures contract; the latter applies only to those contracts executed in formal commodities exchange markets. Until

---

[1] Some of the material in this section is derived from Alfred Broaddus, ''Financial Innovation in the United States—Background, Current Status, and Prospects,'' Federal Reserve Bank of Richmond *Economic Review,* 71 (1, January/February 1985), pp. 2–22.

THE PRICE-LEVEL-ADJUSTED MORTGAGE

INTERNATIONAL

PERSPECTIVE

A financial instrument becoming increasingly common in many nations of the world—such as Australia, Brazil, Canada, Colombia, Finland, Paraguay, and Peru—is the *price-level-adjusted* mortgage, or PLAM. Unlike fixed-rate mortgages, for which nominal monthy payments are fixed, and adjustable-rate mortgages, for which nominal monthly payments are fixed for specified intervals until interest rates vary sufficiently for interest payments to be adjusted, under a PLAM the *real* monthly payments are constant over the life of the loan. That is, nominal monthly payments are adjusted automatically to variations in the price level so that the real value of each month's payment is the same.

The common justification for a PLAM is that, in times of inflation, such as those that have existed throughout much of the world since World War II, fixed-nominal-payment mortgage loans have the characteristic that, early in the loan's life, real payments are high. Later in the loan's life, as prices rise with steady inflation, the real values of payments on the loan decline. For example, suppose that the annual rate of inflation is constant at 5 percent. If an individual finances the purchase of a house priced at $111,111 with a down payment of $11,111 and a fixed-rate, 30-year mortgage loan of $100,000 at an annual rate of interest of 10 percent, the nominal monthly payment on the loan stays constant at $884 over the 30 years. The average *real* monthly payment in the first year of the loan, however, is $842; by the thirtieth year the average real monthly payment falls, as a result of continual 5 percent annual inflation, to $205.

The problem that arises from use of a standard fixed-nominal-payment mortgage is that first-time home buyers—typically young individuals or couples just getting started—often are those who can least afford the high real payments they will have to make early in the lifetime of a mortgage loan. This forces many of them to save for higher down payments—or to forget the idea of purchasing a home.

A PLAM overcomes this problem, because the real value of mortgage loan payments is fixed during the life of the loan. For the same numerical example considered above, the average nominal monthly payment for the first year under a PLAM would be $569; by the thirtieth year it would be $2,343. But the *real* payment would remain constant at $542, in price-level-adjusted dollars. This real payment of $542 is over 35 percent less—in terms of required real purchasing power typically in short supply for a first-time home buyer—than the first-year real monthly payment of $842 for a fixed-rate mortgage.

PLAMs are the only mortgage in Israel. Furthermore, efforts by the World Bank have added Argentina, Chile, Ecuador, Ghana, Mexico, and Turkey to the list of nations where PLAMs are becoming commonplace financial instruments. Eastern European nations such as Hungary may be next.

Why is it that PLAMs are uncommon in the United States and other nations not among the PLAM countries? One reason is that PLAMs are most clearly desirable to citizens of nations with particularly high inflation rates, and several of the nations with PLAMs meet this criterion. A commonly cited reason that PLAMs are not common in the United States is that in the past there has been uncertainty about whether and how tax laws, interest rate ceilings, and loan disclosure rules and related legal regulations would apply to PLAMs. Recently, however, federal government agencies have issued tax rulings and have clarified how regulations affect PLAMs, clearing away many of these obstacles to their use. PLAMs have "arrived" in many points on the globe; the United States may be next.

Adapted from Joe Peek and James A. Wilcox, "A Real, Affordable Mortgage," Federal Reserve Bank of Boston *New England Economic Review*, (January/February 1991), pp. 51–66.

recently, agricultural commodities were the most well-known goods for which futures contracts were traded. These were traded on the Chicago Board of Trade, the Chicago Mercantile Exchange, and other exchanges. Now, however, there are futures contracts for T-bills, T-bonds, and government-insured mortgages. These financial futures are traded primarily on the Chicago Board of Trade, the International Monetary Market of the

Chicago Mercantile Exchange, the New York Futures Exchange, and the New York Commodity Exchange. The bulk of financial futures is traded on the two Chicago exchanges.

Trading in interest rate futures in the United States first opened in 1975. These markets have grown rapidly in volume and breadth. There are, at present, interest rate futures markets for six instruments: U.S. Treasury bills, U.S. Treasury notes, U.S. Treasury bonds, mortgage-backed securities issued by GNMA, domestic bank CDs, and Eurodollars.

The difference between a forward and a futures contract is more complicated than this simple explanation has indicated. In a futures market, the dealings are strictly impersonal; buyers and sellers know nothing but the price, a few characteristics of the product, and the date and the place of delivery. Unlike forward contracts, futures contracts rarely result in actual delivery. Buyers usually settle their contracts by purchasing offsetting contracts before the last day of trading. For example, a contract to deliver can be settled (or closed) by purchasing an offsetting contract (in effect, promising to receive delivery).

A purchaser of a futures contract today in effect agrees to accept delivery of, say, $1 million of T-bills at a specific date in the future at a specific price (or implicit coupon yield). The price specified in the futures contract is called the **futures price.** Table 5-2 gives some futures prices and other information on T-bills for February 24, 1992. A **spot price** is the price for which the commodity can be purchased today, or ''on the spot.'' It is also called today's cash price. The futures settlement discount rate on the March 1992 contract is 3.98+ percent, as shown in Table 5-2.

On the other side of the exchange, it is possible to sell a futures contract. When an investor sells a futures contract, he or she in effect agrees to deliver a specified amount of a commodity at a specified date and price. Those who have agreed to deliver commod-

---

T A B L E 5-2
Futures Prices for Treasury Bills as of February 24, 1992

This table shows the implicit discount rate at which different contracts of 91-day Treasury bills traded.* Column (1) shows the month in which the contract matures; column (2), the implicit rate at which the contract opened; column (3), the high for the day; column (4), the low for the day; and column (5), the change from the preceding day. Columns (6) and (7) show the settlement and change in discount rates directly (so that they need not be implied from the index); column (8) shows the open interest (or number of contracts that have not been closed by offsetting contracts).

Treasury bills (IMM)—$1 mil.; pts. of 100%

(1)	Open (2)	High (3)	Low (4)	Settle	Chg (5)	Discount Settle (6)	Discount Chg (7)	Open interest (8)
Mar 92	96.02	96.04	95.99	96.02 −	0.05	3.98 +	0.05	20,762
June	95.93	95.94	95.78	95.80 −	0.18	4.22 +	0.18	20,948
Sept	95.64	95.64	95.47	95.48 −	0.21	4.52 +	0.21	4,684
Dec	95.01	95.01	94.95	94.95 −	0.21	5.05 +	0.21	1,566

* The International Monetary Market (IMM) developed a method of quoting T-bill discount rates for futures that conforms to the conventional methods of trading in stocks and commodities futures. The IMM system is an index based on the difference between the actual T-bill discount rate and 100. A T-bill discount rate of 6.00 percent would be quoted as 94.00 on the IMM in terms of the index. (Note 94.00 is *not* the price; the price of a 90-day T-bill is $985.00.)

Source: Adapted from *The Wall Street Journal,* Feb. 24, 1992.

ities in the future at a stated price are said to have a **short position,** or *to be short,* or *to have gone short;* they have sold futures contracts. Those who agree to buy a certain quantity at a stated price in the future are said to have a **long position,** or *to have gone long.*

The Why of Securities Futures   Financial futures provide an opportunity for bond purchasers to protect themselves against rises in the market rate of interest that reduce the market price of bonds. Bond purchasers guarantee themselves an interest rate (bond price) in the future, thereby reducing the interest rate risk—and potential profit—of purchasing bonds. The risk is placed on speculators who accept it voluntarily (by guaranteeing the future bond price to the futures seller), hoping to earn large profits.

This risk transfer is akin to the situation in which farmers sell their growing products for a guaranteed price in the future (because they fear that market prices will fall by the time the crops are ready for market) to speculators who are betting on a future price rise. The farmer is guaranteed a modest profit, and the speculator is liable for big gains or losses.

It is interesting that a T-bill, which is already quite liquid because it is of short maturity and because it is traded in secondary markets, can be made simultaneously more liquid (to hedgers) and less liquid (to speculators) due to the emergence of a T-bill futures market.

The T-Bill Futures Market   One of the most active financial futures markets is that for 3-month (91-day) T-bills. An investor could buy a contract today to take delivery of (and pay for) $1 million of 3-month T-bills 91 days from today. After a seller of a contract to make delivery has been located in the trading pits by open outcry (quite unlike the sedate telephone conversations in the markets for the T-bills themselves), the trade is concluded with an agreement on the price. At this point, a clearing house interposes itself in the transaction in the following way: The buyer's contract and the seller's contract are now with the clearing house and not with the other party in the transaction.

The key role of the clearing house is to administer the different requirements imposed on the transactors in futures contracts. For example, certain **margin requirements** are created by the exchanges, such as the Chicago Board of Trade or the Chicago Mercantile Exchange. A specified margin requirement of, say, 20 percent means that the purchaser must ''put up'' 20 percent of the purchasing price—in effect, the purchaser can borrow only 80 percent of the purchase price. Higher margin requirements presumably reduce the degree of risk in such transactions.

Generally, margin requirements are not that high. For instance, an initial margin of, say, 0.0012 percent, or $1,200, per $1 million contract in T-bills may be imposed on the buyer. This margin may be posted in the form of cash, eligible securities, or bank letters of credit.

For as long as the contract is outstanding, it will be *marked to market.* That is, a buyer of a contract to take delivery in 91 days will have his or her margin account credited with the profit if the market price of the contract rises, or debited with a loss if its price declines. Profits in the margin account may be withdrawn immediately; but when sufficient losses occur to reduce the margin below $1,200 per contract, the buyer must pay the difference in cash into his or her account before trading opens the next day.

When the customer wishes to get out of the contract before maturity, he or she must take an offsetting position. That is, in order for a buyer to get out of the futures contract to take delivery of $1 million of T-bills on some day in the future, he or she must sell a futures contract for delivery of $1 million of T-bills on that same date. The order is sent to the trading pit, and a sales contract is executed (not with the party who sold it in the first place). Once again, the clearing house interposes itself between the two parties, and the latest sale is offset against the original purchase. If the prices of T-bill futures contracts go up after the customer purchases a futures contract, the customer obtains a profit; and conversely, a loss occurs if T-bill futures prices fall.

We conclude our description of our evolving financial markets with the observation that their existence allows both individuals and institutions to avoid risk of interest rate variability more cheaply than otherwise, but such markets also encourage speculation. Whether the existence of futures markets, as well as the new mortgage and bond markets, has reduced the overall risk in financial markets is not yet known. We return to this issue in Chapters 11, 12, and 13.

CHAPTER SUMMARY

1. People save in a barter economy by nonconsuming some of the goods they receive for their work efforts; they thereby acquire real goods. Investment also requires some nonconsumption of real-goods income, which then must be traded for plant and equipment.

2. Money makes it easier for people to separate the acts of saving and investment. Saving represents a nonexpenditure out of money income; when people save, they accumulate wealth, or a generalized store of purchasing power. This generalized store of purchasing power, or saving funds, can be turned over to an investor—who need not engage personally in the act of saving. This transfer of purchasing power from savers to investors benefits savers—who benefit by earning interest paid willingly by profit-seeking investors. The transfer also benefits investors, who can now earn profits from which interest payments can be made, because they are not forced to save.

3. The transfer of funds from savers to investors can be made directly, through direct financing. Businesses can sell stocks or bonds directly to the public in primary markets. These assets are made more liquid for the public when secondary markets permit the public to resell them.

4. Financial institutions have evolved as financial intermediaries that channel saving funds from savers to businesses that use the funds to make investments. This process is referred to as financial intermediation, and it is beneficial to society because it allows smaller businesses (for whom stock and bond issuance is impractical) access to saving funds. Financial intermediation also benefits smaller savers because financial institutions can pool their funds and diversify their investments, thereby reducing risk to small savers. Moreover, saving deposits are insured by regulatory agencies.

5. Governments also affect the process of financial intermediation. Through the Federal Financing Bank, three mortgage associations provide funds to the housing mortgage market by selling bonds and using the funds to purchase mortgages; and three federal government agency banks issue securities and use the proceeds to make loans to farmers.

6. Financial intermediaries are financial institutions that borrow funds (accept deposits) from people who willingly surrender current purchasing power. Financial intermediaries then lend these funds to (or buy securities from) those who wish to use the funds for current expenditures. In effect, financial intermediaries act as middlepersons who accept household saving and lend it to businesses that use the saving for investment purposes.

7. Securities are written promises to pay the holder a specified amount at a specified time. Financial institutions, corporations, and governments issue a variety of securities. These typically take the form of debt instruments, asset-backed securities, and hedging instruments.

8. A primary market is one in which a new issue is bought and sold. Secondary markets are those in which previously issued securities are bought and sold.

9. The market in which long-term securities (those that mature in one year or more) are traded is called the capital market. The capital market includes the stock market, the mortgage market, the corporate bond market, and the market for long-term U.S. government securities.

10. The market in which short-term securities (those that mature in less than one year) are traded is called the money market. The money market includes the markets for U.S. Treasury bills, negotiable CDs, commercial paper, banker's acceptances, federal funds, and money market mutual funds.

11. A primary market exists for Treasury bills; every week an auction for T-bills is conducted.

12. Recent innovations in financial markets include adjustable-rate mortgages, mortgage-backed securities, collateralized mortgage obligations, securitization, and zero-coupon bonds.

13. A futures market for securities provides lenders with an opportunity to protect themselves (hedge) against changes in the market rate of interest. Of course, decreased interest rate risk is obtained only by sacrificing potential capital gains. In effect, traders who wish to avoid risk are able to earn modest returns, while others are allowed to speculate and try for higher returns.

GLOSSARY

Adjustable-rate mortgages (ARMs):   Mortgages that permit the lender to vary the interest rate during the period of the loan.

Asset-backed securities: Securities that represent shares of the market value of a pooled grouping of assets.

Bond: Evidence that a corporation has received a loan and has promised to pay the lender a specific amount of money at specific future dates.

Capital market: A market in which securities with a maturity of one year or more (long-term) are exchanged.

Collateralized mortgage obligations (CMOs):   Structured debt financing secured by an asset such as car loans, commercial mortgages, credit card debt, and lease receivables.

Commercial paper: Unsecured short-term promissory notes issued by banks, corporations, and finance companies.

Common stock: A certificate of part ownership in a corporation that entitles the owner to certain voting privileges and to a share in any profits.

Convertible bonds: Bonds that firms issue that may be converted to shares of stock ownership at a specified price after a specified period of time.

Debt instrument: Direct debt obligations of the issuing individual or firm.

Depository institutions: Financial institutions that issue deposits, such as checking accounts, as debt instruments.

Equity instruments: Shares of ownership, such as stock, in a company.

Federal funds market: A market in which very short-term (usually overnight) funds are exchanged between financial institutions; the funds borrowed and lent are usually reserves on deposit with a Federal Reserve district bank.

Financial disintermediation: The process by which ultimate lenders remove funds from financial intermediaries and lend funds directly to ultimate borrowers.

Financial institutions: Institutions, such as commercial banks, savings and loan associations, insurance companies, pension funds, and so on, that receive funds from households and lend them to businesses and others.

Financial instruments: Financial assets such as money and securities.

Financial intermediation: The process by which financial institutions accept savings from households and lend these savings to businesses.

Forward contract: A financial contract in which people agree to exchange a specific commodity for a specified price on some specific future date.

Futures contract: A forward contract executed in a formal commodities exchange contract.

Futures price: The price specified in a futures contract.

General-obligation bonds: Municipal bonds that are secured by the taxing power of the issuing municipality.

Hedging instrument: A financial instrument that permits an individual or firm to ensure against asset price fluctuations.

Long position: An agreement to buy a specific quantity of some commodity in the future at a stated price.

Margin requirement: The percentage of the purchase price of stocks or bonds that a customer must pay when funds are borrowed to finance the purchase.

Money market: A market in which securities with a maturity of less than one year (short-term) are exchanged.

Mortgage-backed securities: Mortgages that are collateralized by pools of real estate mortgages.

Options: Financial contracts that grant the holder the right to buy and/or sell specified securities or goods in specific amounts and at specific prices for a specific period of time.

Preferred stock: A share of ownership in a firm that entitles the holder to first claim on the assets of the firm but less control over the firm's direction and management.

Primary market: A market in which the purchases and sales of a newly issued security are made.

Revenue bonds: Municipal bonds that are secured by the earnings of the project financed by the bond sales.

Secondary market: A market in which previously issued securities are bought and sold.

Securities: Printed documents attesting to ownership or creditorship in a business organization or public body such as local, state, or federal government.

Securitization: The process of pooling similar loans and selling the loan package as a tradable security, an asset-backed obligation, or a form of CMO.

Short position: An agreement to deliver a specific quantity of some commodity in the future at a stated price.

Spot price: The price at which a commodity can be purchased right now; today's cash price.

Subscription: An offering of new issues of U.S. Treasury notes or bonds at announced coupon rates.

Treasury bill: A short-term (15 days to 1 year) promissory note issued by the U.S. Treasury and secured by the ''full faith and credit of the United States.''

Treasury bond: A long-term (10 years or more) promissory note issued by the U.S. Treasury and secured by the ''full faith and credit of the United States.''

Treasury note: A medium-term (1- to 10-year) promissory note issued by the U.S. Treasury and secured by the ''full faith and credit of the United States.''

Zero-coupon bonds: A security that pays interest in the form of an agreed-upon price appreciation, rather than through regular coupon payments.

SELECTED REFERENCES

Broaddus, Alfred, ''Financial Innovation in the United States—Background, Current Status, and Prospects,'' Federal Reserve Bank of Richmond *Economic Review,* 71 (1, January/February 1985), pp. 2–22.

Cook, Timothy R., and Bruce J. Summers (eds.), *Instruments of the Money Market* (Richmond, Va.: Federal Reserve Bank of Richmond, 1981).

First Boston Corporation, *Handbook of Securities of the United States Government and Federal Agencies,* published every second year.

Goldsmith, Raymond W., *Financial Intermediaries in the American Economy since 1900* (Princeton, N.J.: Princeton University Press, 1958).

Jefferis, Richard H., Jr., ''The High-Yield Debt Market: 1980–1990,'' Federal Reserve Bank of Cleveland *Economic Commentary* (April 1, 1990), pp. 1–6.

Morris, Charles S., ''Managing Interest Rate Risk with Stock Index Futures,'' Federal Reserve Bank of Kansas City *Economic Review,* 74 (3, March 1989), pp. 3–20.

———, ''Managing Stock Market Risk with Stock Index Futures,'' Federal Reserve Bank of Kansas City *Economic Review,* 74 (6, June 1989), pp. 3–16.

Munn, Glenn G., F. L. Garcia, and Charles J. Woelfel, *Encyclopedia of Banking and Finance,* 9th ed. (Rolling Meadows, Ill.: Bankers Publishing Company, 1991).

Polakoff, Murray E., and Thomas Durkin et al., *Financial Institutions and Markets,* 2d ed. (Boston: Houghton Mifflin, 1981).

Robbins, Sidney, *The Securities Markets: Operations and Issues* (New York: The Free Press, 1966).

Rosengren, Eric S., ''The Case for Junk Bonds,'' Federal Reserve Bank of Boston *New England Economic Review* (May/June 1990), pp. 40–49.

Stigum, Marcia, *The Money Market,* 2nd ed. (Homewood, Ill.: Dow Jones-Irwin, 1983).

CHAPTER 6

Depository Financial Institutions

CHAPTER PREVIEW

1. How did the dual banking system in the United States originate?

2. What are thrift institutions? What were the beginnings of the thrift industry in the United States?

3. What are the primary assets and liabilities of commercial banks?

4. What are the primary assets and liabilities of thrift institutions?

5. Why is the distinction between commercial banks and thrift institutions becoming narrower?

THE ORIGINS OF BANKING AND DEPOSITORY INSTITUTIONS

Historically, societies have recognized the inconvenience of barter. Initially, people instead used uncoined metals (bullion) as money. Bullion, however, has serious disadvantages as a medium of exchange. Weighing and assaying apparatus to assure quality was not always available at the site of exchange, and short-weighting and adulteration came to represent an implicit transactions cost.

Coinage, however, represented a solution to the problems of using bullion as money. A seal imprinted upon a lump of metal certified a specific weight of metal of a given purity. The names of many present-day monetary units (pounds, lira, and shekels) were originally units of weight. Nevertheless, although coinage represented an important advancement in the development of money, certain disadvantages remained. Among the more significant were the possibility of the theft of money that was being transported or stored, transportation costs, and the absence of an interest return on the coins.

THE GOLDSMITH

Largely as a result of the danger of theft, the practice arose of leaving precious bullion and coins in the custody of goldsmiths. Because goldsmiths worked with those precious metals, they, of necessity, had established the means to protect them. This made goldsmiths the natural choice to receive and store monetary gold and silver (for a fee) for wary owners.

At this early stage in the history of banking, a depositor who wanted to make a payment for a transaction would go to the custodian, redeem some of his coins, and use them to make the payment. To simplify things, however, people began using warehouse receipts (papers documenting the precious metal coins in storage) signed by the goldsmith custodians as payment. These early "goldsmith notes" were acceptable to the payee for one reason—the payee believed that the notes could be exchanged for gold coins at the goldsmith's place of business. A vital step in the evolution of money had occurred. People began to use paper claims (instead of the precious metal coins, or specie, themselves) as a medium of exchange.

THE GOLDSMITH BECOMES A BANKER

The next step in the development of banking was the goldsmiths' discovery that they need not hold in their vaults all the coins deposited with them. They found that daily withdrawals typically were about equal to daily deposits. Nevertheless, there were days when withdrawals exceeded deposits. If goldsmiths could predict the amount by which withdrawals were likely to exceed deposits, then they could hold a contingency coin **reserve.**

The goldsmiths wrote warehouse receipts for a much larger value than the value of the precious metal coins they were safeguarding. Thus, the value of ''money'' (or reserves) the goldsmiths had on hand to meet withdrawals in gold and silver coins represented only a fraction of the value of all the warehouse receipts they had issued. The concept of **fractional reserve banking** was born, and goldsmiths were transformed from mere custodians of specie into bankers. If the practice originated surreptitiously (as it doubtless did), the secret was soon out. The public could be convinced, however, that a mutual advantage existed in the fractional reserve system. The banker provided safety, convenience, ease of transfer, and bookkeeping services at little or no charge to the public. In exchange, the banker was allowed to use the public's deposits as reserves against lending activity. As is the case in most communities of interest, a way to achieve their mutual advantages was found. Any moral or ethical implications of holding less than 100 percent reserves in order to increase profits have long since been rationalized; the only problem is the possibility of a sporadic failure of confidence and a ''run'' on the bank (when people rush to get their money out of the bank before reserves are depleted). Sound, conservative practices by banks and a stodgy demeanor by bankers helped to alleviate the fears of the public—and fractional reserve banking had arrived.

We now skip several centuries and describe the early stages of the evolution of banking in the United States.

EARLY BANKING IN THE UNITED STATES

No other country has a banking system as extensive and complex as the system in the United States. Other countries typically have a central bank and only ten to twenty commercial banks (each with many branches). The United States, in contrast, has a dual banking system, which includes both state-chartered banks and federally chartered banks. This two-tiered chartering arrangement accounts for the relatively large number of banks in this country. The best way to understand this dual banking system is through a historical review of the separate forces that have molded our financial world.

The Revolutionary War   In American history classes we learn that one thing the American colonists agreed on was that they wanted independence and were willing to fight for it. They disagreed on just about everything else. Two major controversies arose concerning governmental power (whether to have a strong central government or strong state governments framed within a federal system) and financial power (whether to have a strong central bank concentrating financial power or many independent banks, none more financially powerful than the others).

During the War of Independence, the Continental Congress confronted these controversies. It also faced the problem of financing the War of Independence. It confronted these challenges in the face of severe financial handicaps. Nearly all commercial banking ties of the colonies had been with banks of Great Britain, and the act of revolution had severed these ties. Although there were some "finance companies" owned and operated by colonists, there were no true, stand-alone banks in the rebellious colonies. Hence, the Continental Congress faced the daunting task of financing a war with no home-grown banking system.

Financing the War of Independence   Even though the total cost of the war to the United States was only $100 million and probably less than 10 percent of national income per year from 1775 to 1783, the Continental Congress had difficulty raising this sum. The Articles of Confederation were quite weak and did not authorize the Continental Congress to tax citizens. Congress, however, was able to borrow almost $8 million in gold from abroad; more than three-fourths of it came from France, the rest from Holland and Spain. About $2 million was raised by borrowing from individuals and businesses. Requests from the Congress for state contributions brought only $6 million. From the viewpoint of any particular state, it often seemed wise to hold back and let the other states pay. This was a good example of what economists call the "free rider problem"—each state attempted to let the other states shoulder the war's financial burden. When each state acted this way, little revenue was raised.

Continental Dollars   The Continental Congress authorized an issue of almost $200 million in paper currency during the four-year period commencing in 1775. During that period this paper money was actually worth little more than $40 million in gold. Few individuals had confidence that this paper currency, called "Continentals," would be redeemed in specie (gold or silver) after the Revolution. Given a lack of faith in the future exchange value of Continentals, their current exchange value in terms of gold declined steadily. Congress did not have the power at that time to declare Continentals to be legal tender (currency that, by law, must be accepted as payment for debt obligations). Instead, Congress asked the states to penalize persons who refused to take them in exchange for goods and services.

By 1781, Continentals were worth one five-hundredth of their face value. There were two reasons for this extremely low exchange value: (1) the public's lack of faith in the government and (2) the tremendous increase in the number of Continentals issued. The relationship between the supply of money in circulation and its price (purchasing power) became quite clear during this period with the expression "not worth a Continental." As with all commodities, when the supply expands more rapidly than the demand, the equilibrium, or market-clearing, price falls. Because the "price" of a dollar is its purchasing power, the rapid increase in the supply of Continentals led to a decline in their purchasing power. This is otherwise known as an inflationary situation: It takes more units of money to buy the same units of goods and services.

The Early Years of the Republic   Following the ratification of the U.S. Constitution in 1789, the new federal government was empowered to "coin money, regulate the value thereof, and mint coins, in addition to fixing the standard of weights and measures." Implicit in this section of the Constitution was the ability of the federal government to create a national currency. This was important for the future development of commercial activities and capital markets (markets in which the buying and selling of debts and shares in companies take place). The Constitution also allowed the federal government to redeem the debts of the "several" (individual) states. This further aided the development of capital markets.

The Views of Hamilton   A key provision of the Constitution is that the federal government is empowered to regulate (control the size of) the money supply. Initial efforts to regulate the money supply were lacking, but some important attempts to provide a stable monetary system were made in the early years of the republic. Alexander Hamilton was appointed secretary of the treasury in 1791. The powers granted to him by this office were second only to those of the president. Hamilton's financial program reflected his belief in a powerful national government (as opposed to powerful separate state governments). Hamilton was adamant about the establishment of a basic unit of value in the monetary system, as evidenced by his famous statement in *The Federalist Paper No. 30:*

> Money is, with propriety, considered as the vital principle of the body politic; as that which sustains its life and motion and enables it to perform its most essential functions.

At Hamilton's prodding, the Mint Act of 1792 was passed. The dollar was to be the basic unit of value, and the decimal system was to replace the British system of pounds, shillings, and pence.

Consistent with his view that the national government should be powerful, Hamilton was in favor of a national bank; as he stated in a 1781 letter to Robert Morris, then the superintendent of finance for the Continental Congress:

> The tendency of a national bank is to increase public and private credit. Industries increase, commodities will multiply, agriculture and manufacturing flourishes, and herein consists the true wealth and prosperity of a state.

An Alternative View   While Alexander Hamilton was an ardent proponent of a strong commercial banking sector, Thomas Jefferson, the first secretary of state, wanted the United States to remain a largely agricultural country. Jefferson was thus generally opposed to the interests of bankers, because he believed they were associated mainly with industrial and commercial activities.

Nevertheless, Jefferson was actively interested in monetary issues; in 1776 he drafted a report entitled "Notes on the Establishment of a Money Unit, and of Coinage for the United States." In this report, he advocated modeling the American currency on the Spanish silver dollar, which was of a convenient size and already was widely used. Jefferson also was one of the first advocates of a decimal system for the nation's monetary unit; he recommended dividing the currency into units of tenths (the dime), along the lines of the Spanish bit, and hundredths (the cent), which was similar to the existing "copper" coin unit of the time.

Robert Morris and members of the Continental Congress were much influenced by Jefferson's report. The Continental Congress adopted his suggestions, and Alexander Hamilton himself later adopted most of Jefferson's suggestions in his own proposals for the currency of the new republic. Later, when he was secretary of state and thus operation of the federal mint was under his purview (along with a hodge-podge of other responsibilities, including supervision of the U.S. Patent Office), Jefferson drew on his earlier thinking in his report to the first U.S. Congress, entitled "Plan for Establishing Uniformity in the Coinage, Weights, and Measures of the United States."

Clash of Titans and the Birth of National Banking   Alexander Hamilton belonged to the Federalists, who favored centralization of political power in the federal government. This included the ability to control, charter, and supervise banks. Indeed, the Federalists did not believe that the Constitution allowed state regulation of banking. The Antifederalists, led by Jefferson, championed states' rights. Not only did they argue for state chartering and supervision of banks, but they also fought for laws that would prevent the involvement of the federal government in any of these activities. Indeed, Jefferson, along with the first attorney general, Edmund Randolph, and Virginia representative and constitutional authority James Madison, recommended to President George Washington in 1791 that he veto a bill authorizing a national bank. Jefferson wrote:

> I consider the foundation of the Constitution as laid on this ground: That ''all powers not delegated to the United States, by the Constitution, nor prohibited by it to the States, are reserved to the States or to the People'' [XIIth amendment]. To take a single step beyond the boundaries thus specially drawn around the powers of Congress, is to take possession of a boundless field of power, no longer susceptible of any definition.
>
> The incorporation of a bank, and the powers assumed by this bill, have not, in my opinion, been delegated to the United States, by the Constitution.[1]

Hamilton and the Federalists had rested their argument in favor of the power of the federal government to charter banks on the ''implied powers clause'' of the Constitution granting Congress the power to pass laws ''. . . necessary and proper for carrying into effect the foregoing powers and all powers invested by this Constitution in the government of the United States.'' To this argument, Jefferson responded in his opinion to Washington, ''But they can all be carried into execution without a bank. A bank therefore is not *necessary,* and consequently not authorized by this phrase.'' Washington wavered on whether or not he should veto the national bank bill, but on the day before a veto deadline, he received Hamilton's classic reply to Jefferson and Randolph:

> Now, it appears to the Secretary of the Treasury, that this *general principle* is *inherent* in the very definition of government, and *essential* to every step of the progress to be made by that of the United States; namely that every power vested in a government, is, in its nature, SOVEREIGN, and included, by *force* of the *term*, a right to employ all the means requisite, and fairly applicable, to the attainment of the *ends* of such power, and which are not precluded by restrictions and exceptions specified in the constitution, or not immoral, or not contrary to the essential ends of political society.

In direct reference to Jefferson's emphasis on the necessity of a national bank, Hamilton replied,

> The degree in which a measure is necessary, can never be a test of the *legal right* to adopt it. That must be a matter of opinion, and can only be a test of expediency. The relation between the *measure* and the *end;* between the *nature* of the *mean* employed towards the execution of that power, and the *object* of that power; must be the criterion of constitutionality; not the more or less of necessity or utility.[2]

Persuaded by Hamilton's reasoning, President Washington permitted the bill to become law. It must be recognized, nonetheless, that the power of the federal government to nationally charter banks was at that time a real issue of weight; the matter could have, without the persistence of Hamilton, been decided in the opposite direction, in which case we might today only have state banks.

---

[1] Thomas Jefferson, ''Opinion on the Constitutionality of a National Bank, February 15, 1791,'' in *Jefferson: Public and Private Papers* (New York: Vintage Library of America, 1990), p. 90.
[2] Alexander Hamilton, ''Opinion on the Constitutionality of a National Bank,'' in M. St. Clair Clarke and D. A. Hall, eds., *Legislative and Documentary History of the Bank of the United States* (Washington: Gales and Seaton, 1832), pp. 95 and 98.

The important thing to realize is that during this period (from the beginning of the republic to the end of the 1780s), a main function of a bank was to issue **bank notes.** Bank notes were pieces of paper representing a liability on the part of the issuing bank; these notes were easily transferred from one person to another. The feature distinguishing a bank note from a bank deposit was that the bank note did not require the payer to specify the payee. Bank notes, then, were similar to coins; but the notes were more portable because, in principle, any amount of money could be specified and printed on a bank note.

As a means of payment, bank notes were much more important than demand deposits. Checking accounts were used only in cities from the period 1781 to 1811, during which time the number of banks grew from two to more than one hundred. During this period, few towns existed, travel was slow, and communication was difficult.

By 1789, the year the U.S. Constitution was ratified, the United States had three incorporated banks. These were the Bank of North America and Philadelphia, established in 1782; the Bank of New York, established in 1784; and the Bank of Massachusetts, established in 1784. A number of unincorporated, or private, banks had also been formed. At that time, common law provided that individuals could engage in any business of their choice, including banking. Not until the 1800s did the states attempt to limit banking by these private, unincorporated firms.

BANKING SINCE 1791

We will continue a full historical account of the evolution of the U.S. banking system in Chapter 15. Nevertheless, we can complete a very brief, albeit sweeping, history of banking and depository institutions in the United States. From 1791 until 1836, with a brief interlude from 1811 to 1815, the United States had a dual banking system composed of numerous state-chartered banks and a single, semiprivate, semipublic national bank that maintained branches throughout the states. (As we shall discuss in greater detail in Chapter 15, the "national bank" also functioned as a central bank for the federal government, as envisioned by Hamilton.)

Rapid Growth of Banking in the New Republic   Somewhat ironically, banking grew considerably in the United States during the presidencies of Thomas Jefferson and James Madison, the traditional political foes of banking interests. Table 6-1 shows the numbers of banks that existed from 1803 to 1818. The table indicates that the number of banks grew by between six and seven times within this sixteen-year period. In addition, the ratios of bank notes to deposits for these years are tabulated to show how important bank notes were during this period. There were always at least half as many bank notes as deposits and often more notes than deposits.

The Free Banking Era and the Civil War   National banking ended in 1836 with Andrew Jackson's veto of a bill extending the charter of the nation's national bank of the time, the Second Bank of the United States. The period ranging roughly from 1837 to 1860 in the United States is often called the "Free-Banking Era." During this period, all banks were again state-chartered. In addition, many states had relatively simple requirements for obtaining a bank charter; thus banking was a relatively competitive industry in many states, complete with freedom of banks to enter the industry and freedom of banks to fail.

Naturally, the advent of the Civil War in 1861 complicated considerably the nation's financial affairs; there was a "dual" banking system in the fullest meaning of the term—the Confederate rebellion against the Union led to an unavoidable geographic separation

TABLE 6-1

Numbers of Banks and Note-Deposit Ratios, 1803–1818

Year	Number of Banks	Note-Deposit Ratio	Year	Number of Banks	Note-Deposit Ratio
1803	53	1.41	1811	117	1.22
1804	64	0.56	1812	143	1.16
1805	71	0.56	1813	147	1.30
1806	78	0.79	1814	202	1.20
1807	83	0.78	1815	212	1.12
1808	86	0.79	1816	232	0.70
1809	92	0.78	1817	262	0.88
1810	102	1.08	1818	338	0.87

Source: J. Van Fenstermake, "The Statistics of American Commercial Banking: 1782–1818," *Journal of Economic History* (1965), pp. 400–413.

of the nation's financial system. Toward the conclusion of the Civil War, in 1863, the Union Congress made this separation unalterable by passing a law (the National Banking Act) constructing a national banking system and imposing a 10 percent tax on the notes of state-chartered banks (designed, naturally, to punish Confederate bank note-holders). Earlier, in 1862, Congress also had created a national currency called ''greenbacks,'' which functioned as money alongside private bank notes.

National Banks, Greenbacks, and the Fed During the five decades following the Civil War, the nation's financial structure evolved back toward a dual state/national banking system. In the first decade after the war, Congress perpetuated the greenbacks, experimented with a bimetallic standard in which the currency was backed by both gold and silver, and ultimately, through the Resumption Act of 1875, returned to a gold standard in 1879. Agitation for reforms of money and banking continued unabated into the 1890s and were stimulated by large numbers of bank failures during that decade. The Panic of 1907 induced Theodore Roosevelt to form a commission to make recommendations for reform, and these ultimately led to the formation of the Federal Reserve System in 1913 (we shall have much more to say about this development in Chapter 15). Thereafter, the United States had a banking system composed of a single, semigovernmental, central bank; federally chartered, privately owned, ''national'' banks; and state-chartered, privately owned, ''state'' banks.

Regulated Banking Nonetheless, until 1933, banking remained largely unregulated; and although checking accounts had become widespread, some bank notes still circulated. Congressional passage of laws in 1933 (the Glass-Steagall Act and the FDIC Act) and in 1935 (the Banking Act of 1935) completely changed the face of banking. Banks found themselves subject to a large number of legal restrictions. As you will learn in Chapter 10, many of these restrictions remain today, although banks discovered several ways to avoid regulations in the 1950s, 1960s, and 1970s. Furthermore, legislation passed since 1980 and subsequent Federal Reserve and court decisions have relaxed or removed many banking regulations. Nevertheless, the period since 1933 commonly is called the time of ''regulated banking.''

THE ORIGINS OF THRIFT INSTITUTIONS

Aside from commercial banks, the other main category of depository institutions are **thrift institutions.** These include **savings banks, savings and loan associations,** and **credit unions.** Like commercial banks, these institutions issue checkable deposits that are part of the nominal quantity of money. It is this feature of their operations that makes them, along with commercial banks, of special significance for the field of money and banking.

Below, we trace the beginnings of the thrift industry. We provide a more thorough and recent history of the development of these depository institutions in Chapter 13.

History of Savings Banks   Savings banks were first organized as institutions intended to encourage thrift among people of limited means through payment of dividends (interest) on saving ''shares'' (deposits). Daniel Defoe, the British author of *Robinson Crusoe* and other books, is credited with a 1697 suggestion to organize ''Friendly Societies for the Provident Habits in General,'' but the first of these proposed ''Friendly Societies'' for provident saving was not organized until 1765. The name ''savings bank'' was first used in Scotland in 1810, and the first United States savings bank, sponsored by a wealthy businessman in Philadelphia, was formed in 1816.

After an initial period of slow growth, savings banks grew quickly, especially in the northeastern states of the union, before and after the Civil War. By 1900, there were 492 savings banks in the United States. Many savings banks were formed with ''mutual'' charters under which depositors were general creditors of the institutions, which did not issue stock shares of ownership. This meant that the depositors shared proportionately in the mutual savings banks' earnings, much as stockholders would share in a company's earnings.

Beginnings of Savings and Loan Associations   Similarly to savings banks, most savings and loan associations, or ''S&Ls,'' typically have been mutually owned by depositors. In addition, the first savings and loan association also was formed in Philadelphia, in 1831; it was a closed society that had 40 members who agreed to save a specified amount every week and to pool their funds for home loans for members. This organizational structure was modeled after ''building societies'' in England and reflected the primary aims of the associations: to encourage thrift and to pool funds for loans to finance home construction and ownership.

By 1850, most S&Ls had opened their operations to any member of the general public who wished to make deposits. This led to rapid expansion of the industry, and by 1890 there were savings and loan associations in every state in the United States. Geographic diversity of S&Ls then bred organizational diversity as well. While most remained mutual institutions, many converted to stock-issuing corporations controlled by the stockholders. Indeed, a gradual trend toward stock ownership of savings and loan associations that began early in the twentieth century has accelerated in recent years as this industry has faced considerable difficulties.

Origins of Credit Unions   Credit unions, like the early savings and loan associations, are a type of ''closed'' financial association; they are organized as cooperatives for members who share a common interest—such as employees of a company, unions, a fraternal order, or a church. Members buy shares that make them eligible to borrow from the credit union.

The idea of credit unions arose in Germany in 1848 and spread to Italy, where it enjoyed particular success. The first North American credit unions appeared in Canada in 1900, and the first United States credit union was formed in 1909. Most growth of credit unions in the United States has occurred since 1930. In 1934, the Federal Credit Union Act was passed; it established national charters for credit unions.

THE COMMERCIAL BANKING INDUSTRY

Commercial banks and thrift institutions together compose a large and well-developed depository financial services industry in the United States. As we discuss below, the distinctions between these two groups of institutions have narrowed in recent years. Nevertheless, enough differences remain that we can—and should—discuss each group separately. We begin with commercial banks.

Commercial banks are the most important of all the depository financial institutions. They are ranked number one in asset size, and they are the most diversified with respect to both assets and liabilities. Traditionally, their main sources of funds have been demand deposits. As we shall see, this situation has changed over the past thirty years; savings and time deposits (including certificates of deposit, called CDs) have become an even more important source of funds for commercial banks.

DEFINING A COMMERCIAL BANK

An interesting development in recent years has been controversy over how to define a commercial bank. Until the 1970s and the passage of important banking legislation in 1980, it was easy to distinguish commercial banks from other financial institutions because they were the only institutions that legally could issue checking accounts as liabilities. That distinction, however, became defunct following the legalization of S&L and savings bank NOW accounts and credit union share draft accounts.

Current definitions of commercial banking, therefore, focus on commercial banks' assets as well as their liabilities. Although this distinction too is blurring, as we shall see, commercial banks remain the only financial institutions that face very few legal restrictions on holdings of commercial (business-related) loans *and* simultaneously offer checking deposits as liabilities. Therefore, we shall follow current practice by defining a **commercial bank** to be a *depository institution that is relatively unrestricted in its ability to make commercial loans and that is legally permitted to issue checking accounts.*

COMMERCIAL BANK ASSETS AND LIABILITIES

Table 6-2 lists the total assets and liabilities of domestically chartered commercial banks in the United States as of the last Wednesday in January 1992. There are five important categories of bank assets. We discuss each of these in turn.

Cash Assets   The first grouping of commercial bank assets is **cash assets.** These are assets that function as media of exchange, and they include the following:

1. *Vault cash* **Vault cash** is currency that commercial banks hold on location to meet the needs of their depositors for cash withdrawals from their accounts. Recall from Chapter 3 that, because it is not in circulation in payment for goods and services, vault cash is not counted as part of the M1 measure of money. Since 1959, vault cash has been counted toward the amount of cash assets that commercial banks are required to hold

T A B L E   6-2
Assets and Liabilities and Net Worth of Domestic Commercial Banks,
United States, as of January 1992 ($ billions)

Assets			Liabilities and Net Worth		
Vault cash	$ 31.1	(1%)	Transactions deposits	$ 634.1	(21%)
Reserve deposits	23.3	(1%)	Savings deposits	663.6	(22%)
Correspondent balances	26.2	(1%)	Time deposits	994.3	(33%)
Cash items in process of			Total deposits	$2,292.0	(76%)
collection	71.0	(2%)			
Other cash assets	24.7	(1%)			
Total cash assets	$ 176.3	(6%)	Borrowings	367.9	(12%)
U.S. government securities	$ 508.5	(17%)	Other liabilities	145.3	(5%)
Other securities	143.8	(5%)	Equity capital*	227.0	(7%)
Total securities	$ 652.3	(22%)	**Total Liabilities and Net Worth**	$3,032.2	
Commmercial/industrial					
loans	$ 454.9	(15%)			
Real estate loans	815.7	(27%)			
Consumer loans	367.5	(12%)			
Other loans	203.4	(7%)			
Total loans	$1,841.5	(61%)			
Other assets	$ 362.1	(11%)			
Total Assets	$3,032.2				

Source: Federal Reserve Bulletin (April 1992), p. A1.
*Author estimate.

to meet *legal reserve requirements,* which we shall discuss more thoroughly in Chapters 14 and 17. Vault cash typically accounts for around 1 percent of all commercial bank assets.

2. *Reserve deposits held with the Federal Reserve System* Commercial banks hold accounts at Federal Reserve Banks, and the deposits—called **reserve deposits**—in these accounts make up about 1 percent of total commercial bank assets. Commercial banks use these accounts for two reasons. First, holding reserve deposits is another way, besides holding vault cash, that commercial banks may meet *legal reserve requirements.* Second, commercial banks use reserve deposit accounts at the Fed to exchange funds in their lending and borrowing activities; these accounts are the commercial banks' checking accounts with the "bankers' bank," the Federal Reserve System.

3. *Correspondent balances* **Correspondent balances,** which account for another 1 percent of commercial bank assets, are deposits that are held with other private banks, known as "correspondents." Many banks, especially in smaller towns or rural areas, find it convenient to hold accounts with a regional center bank in a larger town or city. For instance, a bank in Clanton, Alabama, might hold a correspondent balance with a

C   U   R   R   E   N   T
CONTROVERSY

THE GROWTH OF OFF-BALANCE-SHEET BANKING

One of the most interesting banking developments of the past two decades has been the growth of bank **loan commitments.** Loan commitments are promises by a bank to make a loan to a borrower, at the borrower's discretion, during a specified time interval, up to some prenegotiated, maximum amount (known as the "commitment cap"), and under contracted interest terms. Most growth in the volume of loans made under commitment occurred between the late 1970s and the middle 1980s. In late 1978 the share of total bank commercial and industrial loans with maturities less than 1 year was less than 40 percent. By 1986, that share had leveled off at around 80 percent. It has remained at about that level in the 1990s.

Reasons for and Types of Commitments

By precommitting themselves to making loans at the discretion of the borrower, banks engage in *off-balance-sheet banking.* This simply means that by granting a commitment they effectively increase the amount of lending that they are likely to do in the future without these expected future loans actually being booked as assets on their balance sheets. Why do banks agree to do this? Standard in the terms of most loan commitment agreements is a clause that requires the banks' customers to pay the banks fees for any unborrowed portion of the loan commitment. For instance, if the commitment cap granted by a bank to a customer is $1 million but the customer borrows only $200,000, the customer would have to pay a fee on the unused $800,000. This fee income reimburses the bank for the risk it incurs by letting the customer decide when to borrow the funds. In addition, banks usually protect themselves by imposing "material adverse change" clauses on borrowers, which state that if the borrowers' creditworthiness declines beyond some critical threshold, the bank can revoke the commitment.

Most loan commitments are **revolving credit commitments** that permit the borrower to borrow and repay repeatedly, much like personal credit card accounts. Some commitments are in the form of **confirmed lines of credit,** which are less formal in their terms and typically have relatively short maturities. The

interest rate charged on commitment loans may be predetermined in the contract, in which case the loan commitment is a *fixed-rate commitment.* Alternatively, it may be tied to some other market interest rate, such as the prime loan rate (discussed in the next chapter) or the interest rate on negotiable certificates of deposit; if so, the commitment is a *floating-rate commitment.* Although the proportion varies from year to year, typically the large majority of loan commitments are floating-rate commitments.

The Implications of Loan Commitments

The growth of loan commitments has raised a host of important questions. One is whether or not loan commitments protect bank borrowers from "credit crunches" that can result from economic contractions or from Federal Reserve efforts to reduce the flow of credit through contractionary monetary policy actions. When loan commitments first became prevalent, many observers speculated that such commitments would protect firms from such credit contractions. Indeed, some speculated that the growth of commitment lending would, because commitments are legal contracts that banks must honor, cause the Fed to lose the ability to contract the economy without seriously damaging the banking industry.

Although there are still some disagreements on this issue, most economists have concluded that loan commitments do not protect borrowers from the effects of credit contractions. For one thing, small businesses as a whole often are the least creditworthy—because, by definition, many small businesses are new firms that may or may not have solid long-term prospects—and these borrowers typically are not the ones that banks agree to offer loan commitments. Instead, the larger, safer borrowers—those who normally get credit from banks whether or not it is in short supply—are the ones who receive loan commitments. Consequently, in a credit crunch, experience has shown that it is the same smaller, riskier firms that are denied credit, as was the case in past years before the advent of loan commitments.

In addition, "material adverse change" clauses give banks the flexibility to deny committed loans if the economy really goes into a tailspin. Indeed, during the so-called credit crunch of 1990–1991 many large retailers, including Bloomingdale's, Jordan Marsh, Burdines, Paul

Harris, Abraham & Strauss, and Lazarus, were forced to declare bankruptcy when their banks used these clauses to end their revolving credit agreements.

This does not mean that the growth of loan commitments has no policy implications. Bank regulators have expressed concern in recent years that banks have made commitments to too many risky borrowers, thereby threatening the safety and soundness of the offending banks and, perhaps, of the banking system as a whole. In addition, changes in the aggregate amount of floating-rate commitments can affect the responsiveness of economic activity to interest rate variations. Now that there are many floating-rate commitments in which loan rates automatically adjust to other market interest rates, reductions in market interest rates— caused perhaps by monetary policy actions—could automatically result in much larger and quicker increases in bank credit extensions to borrowers than in the past. This can complicate the Fed's monetary policy task; it now has to take this fact into account when deciding on the appropriate monetary policy.

bank in Montgomery, or a bank in upstate New York might hold a correspondent balance with a bank in New York City. In return for these balances, the larger banks typically provide check-clearing and computer services and assist the smaller banks in making bond and federal funds transactions. In addition, even large commercial banks often have correspondent relationships with banks in other nations; they assist each other in clearing checks in different currencies and in transferring funds in foreign exchange transactions. Note that, unlike vault cash and reserve deposits held at the Fed, correspondent balances do *not* legally count toward meeting reserve requirements.

4. *Cash items in the process of collection* Often called ''cash items'' for short, **cash items in the process of collection** are checks or other types of cash drafts that are deposited with a bank for immediate credit but that are subject to cancellation of credit if they are not paid after the fact. Any item other than currency that is deposited at a teller's window, such as a personal or payroll check, is a cash item until the check ''clears''—that is, until the check actually is honored by a payment through the issuer's financial institution. At any point in time, some portion of checks and other cash drafts have not cleared; Table 6-2 indicates that, as of January 1992, about 2 percent of total commercial bank assets fell into this category.

Securities As discussed in Chapter 5, securities are printed documents providing proof of ownership or creditorship. In general, then, securities are a wide category of financial instruments that include both U.S. government and state and municipal securities as well as corporate bonds and stocks. Under the terms of the Glass-Steagall Act of 1933, however, commercial banks have not been permitted to hold securities (stocks) issued by private companies. This law is under reevaluation, but it is still binding on commercial banks at present. Hence, security holdings of commercial banks fall under two categories:

1. *U.S. government securities* Holdings of these securities, which include both Treasury bills and bonds, accounted for about 17 percent of commercial bank assets at January 1992.

2. *State and municipal securities* Approximately 5 percent of commercial bank assets are allocated to holdings of these securities, which are listed as ''other securities'' in Table 6-2.

Although the United States government and many cities run significant deficits, rates of default on these securities are very low; consequently, state and municipal securities are relatively low-risk assets for a commercial bank.

Loans   Traditionally, one of the main businesses of banking is lending, and this remains the case. There are three basic categories of commercial bank loans:

1. *Commercial and industrial (C&I) loans* **Commercial and industrial (C&I) loans,** which accounted for about 15 percent of total commercial bank assets as of January 1992, are loans to business firms. They have varying degrees of default risk. Unlike securities, which can be sold in a variety of secondary markets, C&I loans generally are illiquid assets. One exception is a loan instrument called a **bank acceptance,** which is a loan typically used to finance shipments or storage of goods by a firm. Bank acceptances may be sold by the original lending bank to other banks. Another exception is shares in bank **loan participations,** in which commercial banks together share in large loans to a business. These shares also can in many circumstances be sold to other banks.

2. *Real estate loans* **Real estate loans,** which constituted about 27 percent of commercial bank assets as of January 1992, are made primarily to businesses to finance construction or purchase of new buildings.

3. *Consumer loans* **Consumer loans** are extended to individuals for use in purchasing a variety of consumer goods. As of January 1992, these loans accounted for about 12 percent of all commercial bank assets. Traditionally, at least 30 percent of consumer loans issued by banks are used to finance purchases of automobiles. Other major categories are revolving credit loans, such as those associated with bank credit cards, and loans for mobile home purchases, which are counted as consumer loans rather than real estate loans.

Purchases of Repurchase Agreements   These and other assets discussed below typically are not separated out in aggregate balance sheet data. As we discussed in Chapter 3, repurchase agreements (RPs) are contracts to sell securities under agreement to buy the securities back at a given date. Banks commonly are the buyers that agree to resell securities in these transactions. They are willing to do this because the contracts call for the seller of the securities to repurchase them at the original face value plus interest.

By buying an RP, a commercial bank therefore makes an interest-earning loan. RP purchases, however, are not counted as loans because they have very different characteristics, the most important of these being their very short maturities, which range from hours to days.

Sales of Federal Funds   **Federal funds** is a term applied to a loan of reserve deposits by one depository institution to another. All depository institutions are eligible to participate in the federal funds market, which is a well-organized market for trading reserves between the institutions, and commercial banks traditionally are the most active participants.

To understand what a federal funds loan is, consider the following example. Suppose that a bank anticipates that the principal and remaining interest from an outstanding 3-month loan to a business will be repaid tomorrow, but it has an opportunity today to make another high-yield 3-month loan of a similar size. Its problem is that it presently does not have enough cash assets on hand to make the loan. To raise the cash, the bank could borrow enough reserve deposits from another bank to make the loan today, and it could use the proceeds from the loan repayment tomorrow to repay the borrowed reserve deposits, plus interest on the borrowed deposits, to the lending bank. The reserve deposits borrowed from the lending bank for 1 day are the federal funds. The name "federal funds" comes from the fact that these loans between banks typically involve transfer of title of funds held on deposit at the Federal Reserve System. The name commonly is a source of confusion, because it conjures up the notion that the funds come from the federal goverment. Don't let this confuse you. Federal funds are private, interbank loans.

Commercial bank sales of federal funds, therefore, are loans to other depository institutions. These loans, which account for about 5 percent of all commercial bank assets, typically are made in very large denominations. Indeed, among larger banks these loans are made in blocks of $1 million units, while for smaller banks the blocks commonly are measured in $200,000 units. The maturity of federal funds loans most often is 1 day, although *term federal funds* are lent for periods exceeding a day.

Unlike RP transactions, in which securities sold by the initial holder represent collateral in the loan agreement, federal funds loans typically are *unsecured*, or noncollateralized, loans. Oftentimes, however, smaller banks insist on security collateralization of federal funds loans, in which case the loan is a *secured federal funds transaction* and is little different from a repurchase agreement. Although large banks both borrow and lend federal funds, smaller banks predominately are federal funds sellers (lenders).

Figure 6-1 shows the shares of bank assets held as cash assets, securities, and all other assets (including loans, RPs, and federal funds) since 1961. As the figure indicates, there has been a trend during the last three decades for assets and securities to occupy smaller relative portions of total commercial bank assets as compared with total loans. We shall discuss some reasons for this trend in Chapter 9.

As Table 6-2 indicates, commercial banks issue several liabilities. Bankers commonly subdivide liabilities into two categories. They call the first category by the somewhat misleading name of **noncontrollable liabilities.** This term is rather misleading because, in fact, a bank *could* choose not to issue any one of these liabilities. Nevertheless, the name gets at the idea that once a bank issues one of these liabilities to a customer, the customer has significant control over when the liabilities may increase or decrease in size. Among these "noncontrollable" liabilities are the following types of deposits:

1. *Transactions (checking) deposits* These deposits were discussed in some detail in Chapter 3. Recall that checking deposits come in two basic types: demand deposits upon which banks pay no interest and "other checkable deposits" including NOW and Super-NOW accounts upon which interest payments are made. As of January 1992, these deposits represented 21 percent of total commercial bank liabilities and net worth.

2. *Savings deposits* As discussed in Chapter 3, these deposits, which constituted 22 percent of total commercial bank liabilities and net worth as of January 1992, consist of passbook savings accounts, statement savings deposits, and money market deposit accounts. These deposits have no set maturities.

3. *Small-denomination time deposits* These are deposits with fixed maturities and denominations below $100,000.

Bankers refer to the second main category of liabilities as **controllable** (or *managed*) **liabilities.** These are liabilities over whose quantities bankers can exercise much more week-to-week or day-to-day control. They include:

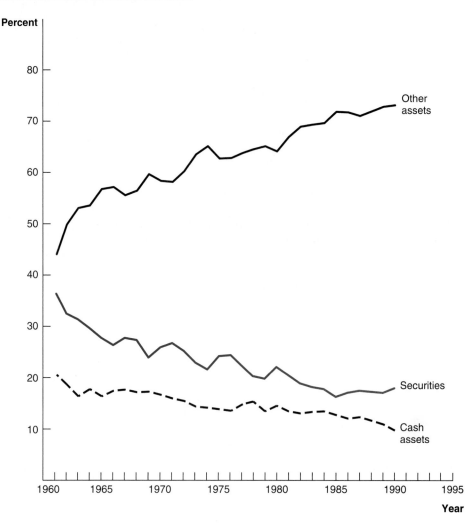

Figure 6-1
Commercial Bank Asset Shares, December 31, 1961–1991.   (*Source: Federal Reserve Bulletin,* various issues.)

1. *Large-denomination time deposits* These accounts have denominations of $100,000 or more and, together with small time deposits, accounted for 33 percent of total commercial bank liabilities and net worth at January 1992. Bankers include large-denomination time deposits among managed liabilities because they typically have maturities less than 6 months, so that banks can issue them in lots of different sizes over staggered time periods. The bank also is able to choose the denominations that it wishes to issue.

2. *Eurodollar liabilities* As discussed in Chapter 3, Eurodollar liabilities are dollar-denominated liabilities that commercial banks issue outside the United States. These liabilities are included in both the deposit and borrowings categories in Table 6-2, because some Eurodollar liabilities are deposits and others are borrowed funds.

3. *Sales of repurchase agreements* When a bank sells securities with the agreement to repurchase them at a later date and to pay interest on the transaction, it effectively borrows funds for the length of the RP agreement from the buyer of the securities. Therefore, sales of RPs represent liabilities of the selling bank. These and the other liabilities listed below are included in the borrowings category in Table 6-2.

4. *Purchases of federal funds* Larger banks are the primary purchasers (borrowers) of federal funds.

5. *Federal Reserve discount window borrowings* All depository institutions, including commercial banks, have the right to apply for loans from the Federal Reserve System. As we shall discuss in more detail in Chapter 17, banks may borrow from the Federal Reserve to help in dampening fluctuations in other liabilities resulting from seasonal variations (for example, rural banks typically lose deposits when farmers need to purchase seed and fertilizer in the early spring), to assist them in times of acute distress that has made the bank illiquid but not insolvent (loans known as ''extended credit'' from the Fed), or simply to enable the bank to ride out a temporary rough spot in its liquidity (loans known as ''adjustment credit'' from the Fed).

6. *Subordinated debt* Often in the form of financial instruments known as **subordinated debentures,** subordinated debt is liability claims issued by commercial banks in which the owner of the claim purchases it with the agreement that, if the bank should fail, the owner's claim will be subordinate, or junior, to the claims of other bank liability holders, such as depositors. As we shall see in Chapter 10, bank regulators view this type of liability as a depositor *cushion* that protects bank depositors' interests (and those of the Federal Deposit Insurance system) in the event of failure.

7. *Equity capital* **Equity capital** is the owners' share in the bank. It is the value of all bank assets less the value of all liabilities, or the *net worth* of the banking firm. Bank regulators also regard this as an important cushion protecting the interests of depositors in the event of bank failure, as we shall discuss in Chapter 11.

Figure 6-2 plots the shares, relative to total liabilities and net worth, of deposits, equity capital, and other liabilities (federal funds, RPs, Eurodollars, etc.) from 1961 to 1991. Clearly, equity capital has declined considerably in the last several decades, and banks have also come to rely more and more on nondeposit sources of funds. As we shall see in later chapters, these developments have had important consequences for the commercial banking industry.

THE THRIFT INDUSTRY

Thrift institutions—savings banks, savings and loan associations, and credit unions—really represent two groupings of institutions, even though they commonly are lumped together. All these institutions are similar to each other—and to commercial banks—in that they issue checking and other deposits as liabilities and hold securities and make loans. Nevertheless, as we shall see below, they differ markedly in the compositions of their assets. Savings banks and S&Ls traditionally have allocated significant fractions of their total assets to mortgage loans and to holdings of mortgage-related financial instruments. In contrast, credit unions specialize in consumer loans to their members.

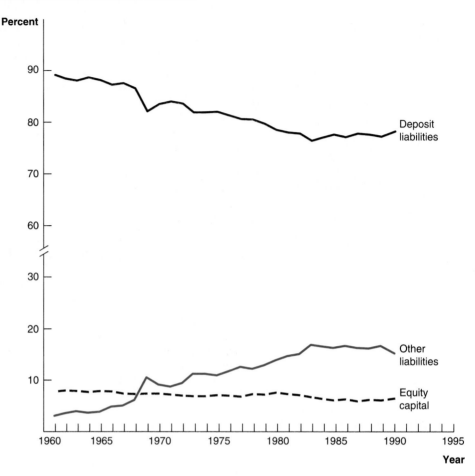

Figure 6-2
Commercial Bank Liability and Equity Capital Shares, December 31, 1961–1991.
(*Source: Federal Reserve Bulletin,* various issues.)

DEFINING A THRIFT INSTITUTION

So, what exactly is a thrift institution? What is it that distinguishes it from commercial banks? The answer is legal regulation. Under the law, thrift institutions are limited in their ability to allocate their assets to differing uses. Indeed, for years savings banks and S&Ls were prohibited (or severely restricted) from making consumer and commercial loans. Likewise, credit unions are limited to lending to individual members, which must be private citizens and not business firms.

The diverging histories of savings banks and S&Ls as compared with credit unions have made the common practice of lumping them into the same "thrift institution" category less relevant than once was the case. Practically speaking, even though thrift institutions can be very distinct from each other, the term is applied to *any depository institution* (that is, *any institution with the legal right to issue liabilities with unrestricted checking privileges) that is not a commercial bank.* Hence, it is easier to define a thrift

AMERICAN BANKING IN DECLINE?

INTERNATIONAL PERSPECTIVE

The table below shows the shares of assets of the top 300 banks of seven major industrialized nations as of 1969, 1975, 1981, and 1986. The asset figures for non-U.S. banks, whose assets would be denominated in different currencies, have been made comparable by applying the 1969 U.S. dollar exchange rates for the various currencies.

Evident from the table is the relative decline of United States banks and the relative growth of banks in Japan, Italy, and France. Indeed, current prognosticators argue that this trend will continue and, further, that European banks have the edge. Of the twelve banks that banking experts predicted in 1991 to be among the global banking "powerhouses" by the year 2000, six were based in European nations. Only three of these twelve—Bankers Trust, Citicorp, and JP Morgan—were based in the United States, and three others were headquartered in Japan.

What accounts for the relative decline in American banking? Most observers agree that the key is differences in regulations. Relative to the United States, banking in the rest of the world is subject to significantly fewer legal restrictions. For instance, as discussed earlier, U.S. banks legally cannot hold stocks and bonds issued by corporations in the United States; in contrast, banks abroad either are subject to fewer restrictions on these asset holdings or are almost unregulated. U.S. banks have not been able to underwrite investment securities since 1933, but most foreign banks are not subjected to this restriction. U.S. banks also are subject to higher "capital requirements" than most overseas banks, meaning that they are legally required to possess higher levels of equity capital in proportion to their total assets. (We shall see more on these regulatory issues in Chapter 10.)

The International Banking Act of 1987 requires the Federal Reserve to review regulations of U.S. bank operations abroad. In March 1991 the Fed took advantage of this feature of the law to lessen some of the restrictions on *foreign* securities underwriting by U.S. banks (which is not illegal). Changes in capital requirements for U.S. commercial banks enacted in 1989 and 1990 also were intended to improve the competitive position of U.S. banks.

Another likely reason for the decline in the relative size of banks headquartered in the United States is that the U.S. economy as a whole is not as important, in relation to the rest of the world, as it once was. Many observers feel that the world only recently has readjusted from the destruction of World War II and that the predominance of the United States in the postwar period could not last. According to these observers, the predominance of American banking likewise could not continue; they see the data in the table as an indication of greater worldwide competition in banking that is likely to be good for everyone.

Other observers disagree. They fear a growing concentration of financial power in banks in Europe and Asia ultimately will create serious problems for the United States, both economically and politically. One thing is certain: This issue likely will be an important one as we approach the next century.

Exchange-Rate-Adjusted Share of Assets (%) Top 300 Banks in Seven Major Countries: 1969–1986				
Country	**1969**	**1975**	**1981**	**1986**
Canada	4.6	4.3	5.2	2.7
France	4.2	7.6	10.2	10.7
Germany	7.7	9.2	6.9	6.5
Italy	8.0	9.3	11.6	13.8
Japan	16.0	17.8	14.6	19.8
United Kingdom	7.1	7.0	8.3	7.3
United States	35.8	27.0	17.8	13.1

Source: Lawrence G. Goldberg and Gerald A. Hanweck, "The Growth of the World's 300 Largest Banking Organizations by Country," *Journal of Banking and Finance,* 15 (1, February 1991), pp. 207–223. Also drawn from Michael R. Sesit, Craig Forman, Terence Roth, and Marcus W. Brauchli, "Free-for-All: As Competition Rises in Global Banking, Europeans Have Edge," *Wall Street Journal* (Monday, March 25, 1991), p. A1, and "Experts Pick Banks They Expect to Be Global Elite by 2000," *Wall Street Journal* (Monday, March 25, 1991), p. A4.

institution by what it isn't than what it is. We may predict that this term will become less descriptive with the passage of time, but for now we are stuck with it.

THE STATUS OF THRIFT INSTITUTIONS

As a whole, thrift institutions are not in good shape. The reason is that the bulk of thrift institutions are S&Ls and savings banks, and many of these institutions have faced severe crises in recent years. Indeed, Chapter 13 is devoted specifically to a discussion of the history of, reasons for, and attempts to address these ongoing crises. For now, we concentrate on laying out the basic facts about this set of institutions and postpone the bulk of our discussion about their problems to that chapter.

Savings and Loan Associations and Savings Banks   Savings and loan associations are incorporated, and their deposits can be insured by federal or state governments (although the latter is becoming less prevalent in recent years). They are either state or federally chartered. The source of funds for the approximately 2,100 savings and loan associations has traditionally been savings deposits; traditionally, S&Ls purchased mortgage loans with those funds. While they still perform this function, deregulation in the 1980s (discussed in Chapter 11) allowed S&Ls to broaden both their liabilities (they can offer NOW accounts and money market certificates—a form of time deposits) and their assets (they can make some consumer and business loans).

Table 6-3 lists the assets and liabilities of federally insured savings and loan associations and savings banks as of January 1, 1992. As shown in the table, rough similarities exist between the assets and liabilities of these thrift institutions and those of banks; what differs is the composition of the assets and liabilities.

Consider first the asset side of the consolidated balance sheet for these institutions, which is where the major differences lie. Cash and regular government security holdings together accounted for only 13 percent of total assets of federally insured S&Ls and savings banks in January 1992 as compared with 25 percent for commercial banks in January 1992 (see Table 6-2). Consumer and commercial loans together composed only 7 percent of total assets, as compared with nearly 30 percent for commercial banks.

TABLE 6-3
Assets and Liabilities and Net Worth of Federally Insured
Savings Institutions, as of January 1, 1992 ($ billions)

Assets			Liabilities and Net Worth		
Cash and securities	$ 112	(13%)	Deposits	$ 695	(79%)
Mortgage-backed securities	126	(14%)	Government borrowings	64	(7%)
Mortgage loans	409	(47%)	Other borrowings	49	(6%)
Commercial loans	17	(2%)	Other liabilities	18	(2%)
Consumer loans	40	(5%)	Net worth	50	(6%)
Other assets	172	(19%)			
Total Assets	$ 876		**Total Liabilities and Net Worth**	$ 876	

Source: Office of Thrift Supervision.

As of January 1992, S&Ls and savings banks held 47 percent of their assets in the form of mortgage loans. In addition, they held 14 percent of their assets as mortgage-backed (FNMA, GNMA, etc.—see Chapter 5) securities. Clearly, despite 1980s deregulation permitting these institutions to expand beyond housing-related finance, they have continued to specialize in that area (a total of 61 percent of their assets). On the one hand, this makes good sense, because this is the endeavor in which managers of these institutions have the greatest expertise. On the other hand, this specialization has been a continuing source of problems for S&Ls and savings banks, as we shall discuss in great detail in Chapter 13.

On the liability side of the consolidated balance sheet, we can see that, like commercial banks, the main source of funds for S&Ls and savings banks is deposits of various types, which accounted for over 79 percent of total liabilities and net worth of federally insured S&Ls and savings banks in January 1992. About 10 percent of total liabilities of S&Ls and savings banks are borrowings from various sources, including about 7 percent from the government through the Federal Home Loan Bank system. The aggregate net worth of S&Ls and savings banks as of January 1992 officially was listed as 0 percent of the sum of total liabilities and net worth. This figure, which probably is an overstatement (that is, the aggregate net worth of these institutions in 1992 really is less than this), reflects the troubles that the S&L industry has experienced. (Keep in mind, however, that many individual S&Ls are in fine shape; it is the industry as a whole that has low net worth.)

Credit Unions   There are roughly 12,000 credit unions in the United States. As the consolidated balance sheet displayed in Table 6-4 indicates, credit unions have rather simple balance sheets, as compared to other depository institutions. Over 90 percent of liabilities and net worth arises from member shares (deposits), and 59 percent of all assets are loans to members. Remaining assets primarily are cash and securities.

Until the early 1980s, credit unions were only able to offer savings deposits and to purchase consumer debt. Deregulation since then has permitted them to offer transactions accounts and to make long-term mortgage loans to their members.

THE BLURRING DISTINCTION BETWEEN DEPOSITORY INSTITUTIONS

Many of the traditional distinctions between banks and thrift institutions are blurring. Thrift institutions can borrow from the Fed, and they are subject to liquidity ratios (comparable to the reserve ratios imposed on commercial banks) that range from 3 to 10

T A B L E   6-4
Assets and Liabilities and Net Worth of Credit Unions, as of January 1, 1992

Assets			Liabilities and Net Worth		
Loans to members	$133	(59%)	Share deposits	$206	(91%)
Other assets	94	(41%)	Other liabilities and net worth	21	(9%)
Total Assets	**$227**		**Total Liabilities and Net Worth**	**$227**	

Source: National Credit Union Administration.

percent. S&Ls and savings banks offer NOW accounts, and credit unions offer share draft accounts; these accounts, as you will recall, are equivalent to interest-earning checking accounts. Converging from the other direction, commercial banks have become important lenders in the real estate market, traditionally the province of S&Ls. Thus, in the past one could distinguish easily among financial institutions merely by examining the structure of their assets and liabilities. This distinction remains important but likely will become less so with the passage of time.

Finally, in recent years commercial banks have been permitted to purchase failing S&Ls. Indeed, commercial banks have been permitted to purchase healthy savings associations, and healthy savings institutions also have sought to switch to commercial banking charters—amid much controversy, as we shall see in Chapter 13.

CHAPTER SUMMARY

1. Uncoined metals were probably the first monies to pass the test of time. Short-weighting and adulteration problems, however, made the transactions costs high for such money. A king's seal imprinted on a specific quantity of metal—coinage—was an improvement over the use of uncoined metal as money. Still, coinage did not eliminate the problems of (a) the danger of theft, (b) high transportation costs, or (c) an absence of an interest return on the coin.

2. Because coins can easily be stolen, people started leaving them (and their other valuable assets) with goldsmiths, who had safe vaults. Before long, people left coins with goldsmiths in return for warehouse receipts, or claims against the deposits. Eventually, these warehouse receipts became a medium of exchange; this was a vital step in the evolution of money, because people became accustomed to using paper claims (instead of gold coins) as a medium of exchange.

3. Eventually, goldsmiths came to realize that it was not necessary to hold 100 percent of the specie deposited in reserve. Most withdrawal requests were met out of current deposits; only a contingency reserve was necessary for the periods when withdrawals exceeded new deposits. Goldsmiths loaned out money not necessary for reserves at interest, and depositors kept their wealth where it was safe. Thus was born the system of fractional reserve banking. The system worked well—except during bank runs.

4. The United States has a dual banking system: Banks are chartered either by the federal government or by a state. This dual system exists partly because of the long controversy regarding states' rights versus the federal government's rights and partly because of a desire to keep financial power diffused.

5. Because wars must be financed and because people have always been reluctant to pay taxes, it has often been politic for governments to increase the money supply during wartime. During the Revolutionary War, the Continental Congress was not empowered to tax; the War of Independence was financed partly by borrowing gold from abroad and partly by borrowing from the states. It was financed mostly by issuing paper currency called ''Continentals.'' Predictably, a rapid increase in the supply of Continentals led to inflation.

6. The U.S. Constitution, ratified in 1789, empowered the federal government to issue a national currency and to redeem the debts of state governments. This allowed capital markets to develop. Alexander Hamilton used his considerable powers to advance the course of a strong central government in general, and a national bank with important powers in particular. Thomas Jefferson was a powerful foe of Hamilton on both these issues.

7. An important link in the evolution of banking was the development of the bank note, which is a piece of paper that represents a liability on the part of the issuing bank to the holder, and not a specific payee. A key function of banks during the early years of our republic was to issue bank notes.

8. Today, commercial banks are depository institutions that are permitted unlimited issue of transactions (checking) deposit liabilities and that are relatively unrestricted in their ability to extend commercial (business) loans. The term ''thrift institutions'' applies to all non-commercial-banking depository institutions, which include savings banks, savings and loans associations, and credit unions.

9. Commercial banks hold a variety of assets, including cash assets, securities, loans, sales of RPs, and purchases of federal funds. There has been a general trend toward less holdings of cash and securities by commercial banks. They issue a variety of liabilities, including transactions (checking), savings, and time deposits; purchases of RPs; sales of federal funds; borrowings from the Federal Reserve System; and subordinated debt. There has been a general trend toward more use of nondeposit liabilities by commercial banks.

10. Savings and loan associations and savings banks originated in the early 1800s in the United States. Until the early 1980s, these depository institutions faced legal restrictions on their powers to make commercial and consumer loans. For this reason they traditionally have specialized in mortgage finance and largely continue this pattern today. Much of the savings bank and savings and loan portion of the thrift industry has faced severe difficulties in recent years as reflected in the very low aggregate net worth of these institutions.

11. Credit unions, which first arose early in this century, specialize in pooling deposit ''shares'' of their members for use in lending to their members. Although these institutions commonly are classified as thrift institutions alongside S&Ls and savings banks, they actually specialize in consumer lending and borrow less heavily than these other thrift institutions.

Glossary

Bank acceptance: A bank loan that is usually used by a firm to finance shipments or storage of goods and which may be sold by the original lending bank to other banks.

Bank note: A piece of paper that represents a liability on the part of the issuing bank to the holder—and not to a specific payee.

Cash asset: An asset that functions as a medium of exchange.

Cash items in the process of collection: Checks or other types of cash drafts that are deposited with a bank for immediate credit but that are subject to cancellation of credit if they are not subsequently honored by the issuer.

Commercial bank: A depository institution that is relatively unrestricted in its ability to make commercial loans and that is legally permitted to issue checking accounts.

Commercial and industrial (C&I) loans: Bank loans to businesses.

Confirmed line of credit: An informal type of bank loan commitment in which not all terms of the loan are fully worked out and in which either party has significant latitude to cancel the agreement before a loan actually is extended.

Consumer loans: Bank loans to individuals.

Controllable liabilities: Liabilities whose quantities a bank can determine in the near term.

Correspondent balances: Bank deposits held with other banks, called correspondents.

Credit union: Depository institution that accepts deposits from and makes loans to only a closed group of members.

Equity capital: Owners' share in a depository institution.

Federal funds: Loans of reserve deposits from one depository institution to another.

Fractional reserve banking: A system in which depository institutions hold reserves equal to less than 100 percent of total deposits.

Loan commitment: A bank promise to make a loan, up to some specified maximum limit, within a given period at predetermined interest rate terms.

Loan participations: Lending arrangements in which banks own shares in large loans to businesses and may in some circumstances sell these loan shares to other banks.

Noncontrollable liabilities: Liabilities whose quantities primarily are controlled by bank customers instead of the bank.

Note issuance: The creation of paper money by a government or a central or commercial bank.

Real estate loans: Bank loans for construction and purchases of buildings.

Reserve deposits: Deposits that depository institutions hold at the Federal Reserve System.

Reserves: The portion of total deposits held by depository institutions that is not lent; instead these funds are held to meet day-to-day withdrawals.

Revolving credit commitment: A bank loan commitment in which the borrower may borrow and/or repay repeatedly, much like a credit card account.

Savings and loan association: An institution that traditionally has specialized in mortgage-related activities.

Savings bank: An institution that originally was intended to be primarily a savings institution for small savers; like savings and loan associations, these institutions have tended to specialize in mortgage financing.

Subordinated debt: A bank liability issued with the provision that all other liability holders have priority in the event of failure of the institution; often issued in the form of subordinated debentures.

Thrift institution: At present, any depository institution that is not a commercial bank, including savings and loan associations, savings banks, and credit unions.

Vault cash: Currency held by a depository institution.

SELF-TEST QUESTIONS

1. Why was it so natural for goldsmiths to become bankers in the past?

2. What were the main issues separating the views of Alexander Hamilton and Thomas Jefferson concerning the chartering of national banks?

3. How did the United States find itself with the dual banking system it has today?

4. What are the rough allocations of commercial bank assets between cash assets, securities, and loans at present in the United States, in percentage terms?

5. What are the rough allocations of commercial bank liabilities between deposits and other liabilities and net worth at present in the United States, in percentage terms?

6. What key features presently distinguish S&Ls and savings banks from commercial banks? From credit unions?

PROBLEMS

6-1.   Consider the following balance sheet for a goldsmith:

Assets		Liabilities	
Gold	$500	Deposits	$500
Loans	0		

Suppose that the goldsmith typically used about 20 percent of gold deposits to handle short-term withdrawals and to make transfers to its other customers that are then redeposited.

Although that amount varies, assume that the goldsmith never would need more than 25 percent of gold deposit reserves. Determine the maximum value for loans from which withdrawals, and transfers that are redeposited, can be made with assurance that any short-term withdrawal or transfer could be handled.

6-2. Suppose that the consolidated balance sheet of commercial banks is given by the example below:

Assets		Liabilities	
Reserves	$ 500	Deposits	$2,000
Loans	1,500		

Construct the new account balances if monetary authorities required reserves to be 40 percent of deposits.

6-3. Consider the following balance sheet of a commercial bank subject to a 10 percent legal reserve requirement against its deposit liabilities:

Assets		Liabilities	
Vault cash	$ 300	Deposits	$4,000
Correspondent balances	100		
Loans	3,600		

Is this bank meeting its legal reserve requirement? Explain.

6-4. Consider the following balance sheet for a commercial bank:

Assets		Liabilities	
Cash assets	$ 250	Deposits	$3,500
Securities	750	Subordinated debentures	300
Loans	4,000	Equity capital	200

a. Suppose that regulators require that the ratio of equity capital to loans must at least be equal to 6 percent and that the ratio of equity capital to total assets must at least be equal to 4 percent. Is the bank presently meeting both of these standards?

b. Suppose that the bank makes an argument to its regulators that equity capital is not the only cushion it has available to protect depositors from loss in the event the bank fails. Irrespective of whether or not the regulators agree, do you believe that the bank has a legitimate argument? Explain why or why not.

6-5. Compare Tables 6-2, 6-3, and 6-4 to assist in answering the following questions.

a. In terms of total assets, about how much larger (in percentage terms) is the commercial banking industry relative to the thrift industry, given the data in the tables?

b. In terms of total assets, about how much larger (in percentage terms) are federally insured savings institutions (S&Ls and savings banks) relative to credit unions?

SELECTED REFERENCES

Allen, Linda, Stavros Peristiani, and Anthony Saunders, ''Bank Size, Collateral, and Net Purchase Behavior in the Federal Funds Market,'' *Journal of Business,* 62 (4, October 1989), pp. 501–515.

Angell, Norman, *The Story of Money* (New York: Frederick J. Stokes Co., 1929).

Clarke, M. St. Clair, and D. A. Hall, eds., *Legislative and Documentary History of the Bank of the United States* (Washington: Gales and Seaton, 1832; reprinted New York: Augustus M. Kelley, 1967).

Duca, John V., and David D. VanHoose, ''Loan Commitments and Optimal Monetary Policy,'' *Journal of Money, Credit, and Banking,* 22 (2, May 1990), pp. 178–194.

Friedman, Milton, and Anna J. Schwartz, *A Monetary History of the United States, 1867–1960* (Princeton, N.J.: Princeton University Press, 1963).

Goldberg, Lawrence G., and Gerald A. Hanweck, ''The Growth of the World's 300 Largest Banking Organizations by Country,'' *Journal of Banking and Finance,* 15 (1, February 1991), pp. 207–223.

Hamilton, Alexander, James Madison, and John Jay, *The Federalist Papers* (New York: Mentor, 1961).

Jefferson, Thomas, *Public and Private Papers* (New York: Vintage Library of America, 1990), pp. 67–89.

Malone, Dumas, *Jefferson and His Time,* vols. 1 and 2 (Boston: Little, Brown, 1948 and 1951).

McDonald, Forrest, *Alexander Hamilton: A Biography* (New York: W. W. Norton, 1979).

Morgan, Donald P., ''Bank Credit Commitments: Protection from a Credit Crunch?'' Federal Reserve Bank of Kansas City *Economic Review,* 75 (5, September/October 1990), pp. 51–59.

Munn, Glenn, F. L. Garcia, and Charles Woelfel, *Encyclopedia of Banking and Finance,* 9th ed. (Rowling Meadows, Ill.: Bankers Publishing Company, 1991).

Robertson, D. H., *Money,* 6th ed. (New York: Pitman Publishing Corp., 1948).

Sofianos, George, Paul Wachtel, and Arie Melnik, ''Loan Commitments and Monetary Policy,'' *Journal of Banking and Finance,* 14 (4, October 1990), pp. 677–689.

Tracy, James D., *A Financial Revolution in the Habsburg Netherlands: Renten and Renteniers in the Country of Holland, 1515–1565* (Los Angeles and London: University of California Press, 1985).

Interest Rates

CHAPTER PREVIEW

1. How is the market rate of interest determined?

2. What is the economic function of the interest rate?

3. What is the difference between real and nominal interest rates?

4. What is the relationship between bond prices and the market rate of interest?

5. How are short-term and long-term interest rates related?

6. How are interest rates and risk related?

In Chapter 4 we considered an economy in which no money existed, and yet there was the possibility of the existence of a market for credit. It also is instructive to consider a money economy in which no credit markets exist. Under a creditless system, income recipients have two options. They can exchange their money income for goods and services (consume), or they can save some of their income and hold money, a generalized store of purchasing power. The money they hold can be spent at a later date, and it can buy, assuming no inflation and no change in the relative prices of goods and services, the same bundle of goods and services at any time in the future.

If credit markets emerge in an economy, income recipients now have a third option—they can lend some of their savings and earn interest. In short, income recipients can consume and save as before, but now they can save by lending their savings to others. As you learned in Chapter 4, credit markets allow people to hold their savings in a nonmoney form—credit instruments.

INTEREST AND THE INTEREST RATE

In a real-world economy in which money exists, interest is the amount of funds, valued in terms of money, that lenders receive when they extend credit; the interest rate is the ratio of interest to the amount lent. For example, suppose that $100 is lent, and, at the end of 1 year, $110 must be paid back. The loan principal then is $100, the interest paid is $10, and the interest rate is 10 percent (because $10/$100 = 0.10). All these quantities are valued in monetary units, because money is used as a standard of deferred payment.

As we saw in Chapter 4, credit markets typically will arise whether or not money exists. The reason is that both lenders and borrowers can gain from credit transactions. In a modern, diverse economy in which households specialize in consumption and firms specialize in production, there are further reasons that credit markets arise: (1) different households have different personalities—they have different preferences for present versus future consumption, and (2) businesses can make investments in plant, equipment, and/or inventory that are profitable enough to enable them to pay back interest.

In this chapter, we seek to explain the determination of market interest rates (taking into account inflation in measuring interest rates) and the relationship between interest rates and bond prices. We also consider the computation of interest rate yields and the relationships among interest rates on assets with different risks and maturities.

DETERMINATION OF THE MARKET RATE OF INTEREST

Net savers, or net lenders, will supply funds to the credit market. Net borrowers will demand funds from the credit market.

THE SUPPLY OF CREDIT

The supply-of-credit schedule is positively sloped; it rises from left to right. At higher interest rates more households and businesses will become net lenders. As the rate of interest increases, more households observe a market rate of interest that exceeds their personal trade-off between present and future consumptions. At some very high interest rate, even extremely present-oriented, ''live-for-today'' individuals will find it worthwhile to save more of their incomes. Similarly, at some very high interest rate, even very profitable businesses will find that they cannot repay interest out of earnings; they can earn a better rate of return by becoming net savers. Figure 7-1 shows the probable shape of an economy's supply-of-credit curve.

In the United States, domestic households and firms are not the only suppliers of credit. Indeed, foreigners are major suppliers of credit to Americans. We shall have more to say about this in Chapter 28.

THE DEMAND FOR CREDIT

The economy's demand-for-credit schedule will be negatively sloped; it falls from left to right. As the rate of interest falls, more people prefer to become net borrowers. As the

Figure 7-1
The Supply of Credit.   This schedule indicates that at higher interest rates more households and businesses prefer to become net lenders.

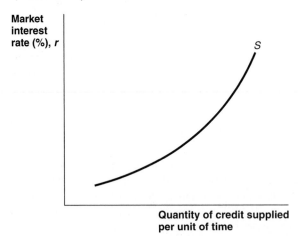

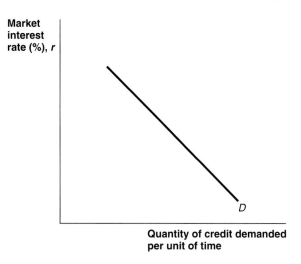

Market interest rate (%), *r*

Quantity of credit demanded per unit of time

Figure 7-2
The Demand for Credit.   The demand-for-credit schedule is negatively sloped, indicating that as the rate of interest falls, the quantity demanded for credit rises. This is because at lower interest rates more investment projects are profitable than at higher rates. In short, as the rate of interest falls, more households and businesses find it worthwhile to become net borrowers.

interest rate decreases, more households discover that the market rate of interest is below their personal rate of interest. They decide to reduce their saving rate. At some very low rate of interest (for some it may be negative), even future-oriented people find that they prefer to consume more in the present and save less. For businesses, lower interest rates mean that more investment projects exist for which they can borrow funds, pay the interest, and keep some net profit. In short, as the rate of interest falls, other things constant, the quantity demanded for credit rises. The probable shape of a demand-for-credit curve is depicted in Figure 7-2.

A nation's households and firms need not be the only demanders of credit. In fact, local, state, and federal governments in the United States make up a very large part of the demand side of the U.S. credit market.

THE MARKET RATE OF INTEREST

Figure 7-3 indicates how the economy's supply of and demand for credit determine the market rate of interest. For the economy depicted, the market rate of interest will be 10 percent. At a rate of interest above 10 percent (at 12 percent, for example), the quantity of credit supplied exceeds the quantity demanded for credit; a surplus of credit exists. Lenders, competing with each other for interest earnings, will force the interest rate down toward 10 percent.

On the other hand, at 8 percent a shortage of credit exists; the quantity demanded for credit exceeds the quantity supplied at that interest rate. Borrowers, competing with each other for credit, will drive the interest rate up toward 10 percent. Eventually, the market rate of interest will be established at 10 percent, at which point the quantity of credit supplied and the quantity demanded for credit are both equal to $100,000. Equilibrium is said to exist, because neither suppliers nor demanders of credit have any incentive to change their behavior.

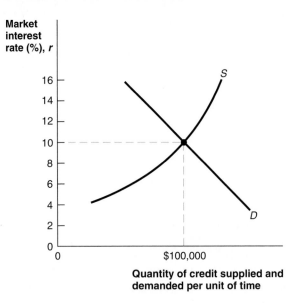

Figure 7-3

The Supply of and Demand for Credit.   Given the supply and demand schedules above, the market rate of interest will be established at 10 percent, where the curves intersect. At a 12 percent market rate of interest, the quantity of credit supplied exceeds the quantity of credit demanded, and a surplus of credit exists. Some net lenders will not be able to earn any interest and will offer to accept less than 12 percent interest for their savings. Their competition for interest earnings causes the market rate of interest to fall toward 10 percent. At an 8 percent interest rate, the quantity demanded exceeds the quantity of credit supplied; therefore a shortage of credit exists. Some borrowers will be unable to obtain funds; competition among borrowers for credit will drive interest rates toward 10 percent.

THE ALLOCATIVE ROLE OF INTEREST

Any study of a market system involves the realization that prices allocate resources in the economy. Interest is the price that allocates loanable funds (credit) to consumers and to businesses. Businesses compete with each other for loanable funds, and the interest rate allocates loanable funds to different firms and therefore to the investment projects of those firms. Those investment, or capital, projects whose rates of return are higher than the market rate of interest in the credit market will be undertaken, given an unrestricted, or free, market for loanable funds. For example, if the expected rate of return on the purchase of a new factory in an industry is 20 percent and loanable funds can be acquired for 15 percent, then that investment project—the new factory—will be purchased. If, by contrast, that same project has an expected rate of return of 9 percent, it will not be undertaken. The funds will go to the highest bidders—those who are willing and able to pay the highest interest rates. In practice, the funds will go to those firms that are the most profitable. By this method, profitable firms are allowed to expand and unprofitable firms are forced to contract or go bankrupt.

This allocation of credit among businesses can be considered efficient if efficiency is defined in terms of consumer sovereignty. If it is ''good'' for consumers to influence output by their dollar votes in the marketplace, then it is ''good'' to allow profitable businesses to expand and force unprofitable (or less profitable) businesses to contract.

Consumers also compete with each other for credit. By allowing credit to go to the highest bidder, the interest rate allocates consumption through time. It allows present-oriented people, who are willing to pay high interest rates, to consume more now and less later. Allowing credit to go to the highest bidder also allows future-oriented people to substitute more future consumption for less present consumption. If it is ''good'' to allow people to choose their rate of consumption through time, then it is ''good'' to allow the rate of interest to allocate credit among competing households.

NOMINAL VERSUS REAL INTEREST RATES

A **nominal interest rate** is defined as the rate of exchange between a dollar today and a dollar at some future time. For example, if the market, or nominal, rate of interest is 10 percent per year, then a dollar today can be exchanged for $1.10 one year from now.

The **real interest rate,** on the other hand, is the rate of exchange between goods and services (real things) today and goods and services at some future date. In a world of no inflation or deflation, the nominal rate of interest is equal to the real rate of interest. A 10 percent annual rate of interest with no inflation guarantees a rate of exchange of $1.00 in money terms with $1.10 in money terms a year from now, and vice versa. Because, in our hypothetical example, there is no inflation in real terms (purchasing-power terms), the rate of exchange is between $1.00 of real goods and services today and $1.10 of real goods and services a year from now.

But what about a world in which inflation (or deflation) is anticipated? Assume that everyone anticipates a 10 percent annual rate of inflation, and leave aside the complications of taxes. A nominal rate of interest of 10 percent per year will still mean that the rate of exchange between dollars today and dollars a year from now is 1 to 1.1. But $1.10 in dollar terms a year from now will buy only $1.00 worth of the goods and services that can be purchased today. If everyone anticipates a 10 percent annual inflation rate, then in real terms the 10 percent annual nominal rate of interest effectively means a zero real rate of interest.

AN EQUATION RELATING REAL AND NOMINAL INTEREST RATES

The relationship between the nominal rate of interest and the real rate of interest can be shown as an equation, given by

$$\begin{array}{c}\text{Nominal rate}\\\text{of interest}\end{array} = \begin{array}{c}\text{real rate}\\\text{of interest}\end{array} + \begin{array}{c}\text{expected rate}\\\text{of inflation}\end{array} + \left(\begin{array}{c}\text{real rate}\\\text{of interest}\end{array} \times \begin{array}{c}\text{expected rate}\\\text{of inflation}\end{array}\right)$$

In normal times, the product in the parentheses is small enough to be ignored (for instance, if the real interest rate is 0.03 and the expected rate of inflation is 0.06, the value of the term would be equal to 0.0018, which is less than one-fourth of 1 percent). It cannot, of course, be ignored in times of high inflation such as hyperinflations.

Assuming that interest rates and inflation rates are relatively small, however, it is safe to simplify by abstracting from the product in parentheses, in which the equation for the nominal interest rate is

$$\text{Nominal rate of interest} = \text{real rate of interest} + \text{expected rate of inflation}$$

This equation can be rearranged to show that

$$\text{Real rate of interest} = \text{nominal rate of interest} - \text{expected rate of inflation}$$

Note that it is the expected rate of inflation, rather than the actual rate of inflation, that matters for calculating the real interest rate. The reason is that credit contracts by definition are *forward-looking*. The real interest rate applicable to a loan or a bond issued today is measured from the present forward to the maturity date of the credit agreement. It is impossible to know exactly what the inflation rate from now until that date will turn out to be, and so the parties to the transaction must *forecast* the rate of inflation to compute the real interest rate.

Needless to say, the real rate of interest is impossible to measure exactly, because the expected rate of inflation can only be estimated. Only nominal rates of interest are published. Some economists have attempted to estimate the expected rate of inflation by looking at past rates of inflation. These attempts have been unsuccessful, however, because there is no way of knowing people's actual expectations. In fact, the St. Louis Federal Reserve used to publish an estimated real rate of interest, but it stopped doing so when it realized how inaccurate these estimates turned out to be. Nonetheless, the distinction between nominal and real rates of interest, which was first clarified by the American economist Irving Fisher (1867–1947), is crucial in a world of inflation and expected inflation when trying to predict household and business behavior, as later chapters will emphasize.

THE DEMAND FOR AND SUPPLY OF CREDIT, OR LOANABLE FUNDS, REVISITED

Earlier in this chapter, demand and supply curves for loanable funds were given in Figure 7-3. This diagram is now redone. Remember, it was originally drawn under the implicit assumption that there were no inflationary expectations. Those same demand and supply curves are shown in Figure 7-4 as D and S. Now assume that demanders have inflationary expectations of 10 percent per year. The demand curve will shift upward by that amount to D'. Assume further that the suppliers of credit have the same expectations. The supply curve will also shift up by 10 percent to S'. If (as is assumed) the expectations of demanders and suppliers of credit are the same, the nominal rate of interest, denoted r_n, will rise by that expected rate of inflation to $r_r + 10$ percent.

The historical evidence of the relationship between the actual rates of inflation and nominal rates of interest is compelling. Figure 7-5 indicates what has happened to long-term nominal rates of interest in the United States since 1955 and what has happened to the actual rate of inflation over the same period. As the rate of inflation began to rise in

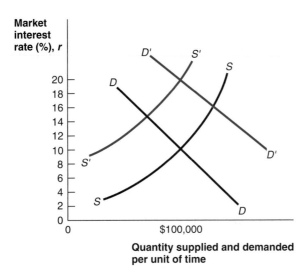

Figure 7-4
Inflationary Expectations and the Interest Rate.   This figure shows the result of inflationary expectations. If both lenders (suppliers) and borrowers (demanders) of loanable funds expect an annual rate of inflation of 10 percent, the demand schedule curve will shift to the right (from *D* to *D'*, an increase) and the supply curve will shift to the left (from *S* to *S'*, a decrease). The new nominal interest rate will rise by about 10 percentage points, from 10 percent to 20 percent.

1965, so, too, did nominal interest rates. The relationship is not exact, however, because the nominal rate of interest consists of a nonobserved variable—the anticipated rate of inflation. Data exist, unfortunately, only for the actual rate of inflation. Nonetheless, it can

Figure 7-5
Inflation and Long-Term Interest Rates.   This figure illustrates the relation between long-term interest rates (as measured by the interest rate on 10-year government securities) and the rate of inflation (as measured by year-to-year changes in the consumer price index) from 1955 to early 1992.

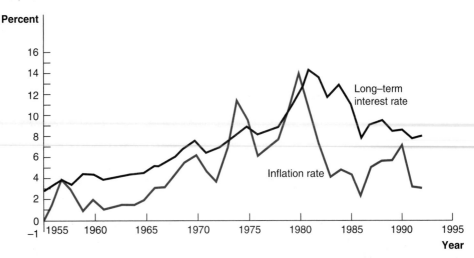

be said that during periods of inflation, nominal interest rates tend to be higher than during periods of zero inflation, because individuals expect prices to continue to rise in the future. It takes time for people to adjust to rates of inflation that are higher than those experienced in the past. Thus, when rates of inflation rise relatively rapidly compared with the past, nominal rates will not rise so rapidly. Only after individuals fully expect the new higher rate of inflation to continue will nominal interest rates fully compensate for the inflation.

DIFFERENT TYPES OF NOMINAL INTEREST RATES

Every lending market has its own interest rate. There is a mortgage market, a short-term business loan market, and a government securities market. For every type of market lending instrument—such as a government bond or a mortgage—there is a particular interest rate. In the sections that follow, some of the most important interest rates are discussed.

THE PRIME RATE

Perhaps the most frequently quoted interest rate is the **prime rate.** This is the rate that banks charge on short-term loans made to large corporations with impeccable financial credentials—their "most creditworthy customers," as the newspapers refer to them. The published prime rate is typically the lowest interest rate that such creditworthy businesses pay for short-term loans. Such business transactions are characterized by relatively little default or credit risk. Fewer expenses are incurred by the lending bank to investigate the creditworthiness of the borrowing company. In Figure 7-6 the prime rate is shown for a

Figure 7-6
Prime Rate of Interest since 1929.   (*Source:* Board of Governors of the Federal Reserve System.)

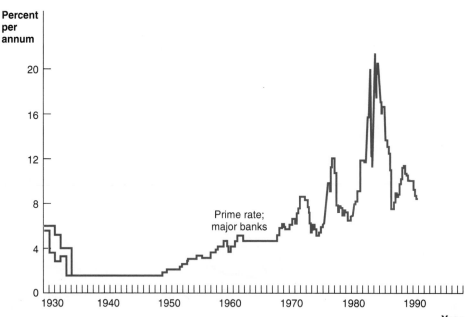

HOW IS THE PRIME RATE DETERMINED?

Interestingly, although many interest rates that we shall discuss in this chapter seem very flexible, a distinguishing feature of the prime rate is its rigidity. It changes, on average, only about once each month, even though most interest rates change from day to day, if not from hour to hour. Unlike most other interest rates, which change immediately in response to the forces of demand and supply, the prime rate is a *posted rate,* meaning that it is altered by discretionary announcements by large money center (typically based in New York City) banks.

Some Background

This "prime rate convention," as economists call it, emerged in 1934 following the onset of the Great Depression when the demand for loans was very low and many market interest rates were below one-half of 1 percent. At that time, the prime rate convention was initiated when banks agreed to set a loan rate of $1\frac{1}{2}$ percent for their best customers as the minimum rate then consistent with profitable operations. This convention of posting the prime rate and keeping it fixed for weeks on end proceeded to outlive the slack loan-demand period of the Great Depression, much to the consternation of economists, whose theories indicate that the convention in fact should not have prevailed against variations in demand and supply that are observed in normal economic times.

Explaining the Stickiness of the Prime Rate

Why is the prime rate so rigid? One hypothesis is that banking is such a regulated industry that the perfect competition model, which assumes a large number of firms free to enter or exit the industry, may not be applicable (we shall have more to say about this hypothesis in Chapter 11). According to this view, a few large banks dominate the industry and act as "price leaders." Their leadership is manifested by their ability to post the prime interest rate with little fear that any individual smaller, rival bank will undercut their posted rate and steal away their customers. These leading banks lower the prime rate, according to this hypothesis, only when other market interest rates have fallen so much that all rivals together might be induced to undercut the lead-

ers. Therefore, the prime rate will stay rigid for prolonged periods of time even as other interest rates vary.

An alternative hypothesis is that prime rate loan customers—the so-called most creditworthy customers—actually constitute a very heterogeneous group. This makes it difficult for banks to evaluate the group as a whole when economic conditions improve or worsen. Because it takes time for banks to process information about changes in these customers' aggregate creditworthiness in response to altered conditions, banks are hesitant to raise or lower the prime rate. They do so only when they are certain that the general creditworthiness of their "prime" customers has changed in one direction or the other.

A third theory is that the prime rate is not the true interest rate that "prime" customers pay for loans from banks. According to this view, the prime rate really is a *benchmark* interest rate that serves as a guidepost for banks and borrowers. As credit market conditions change, banks adjust other loan terms, such as borrowing limits or compensating deposit balance requirements that borrowers must meet to get a loan. For instance, if economic conditions worsen, banks might lower the cap on the amount that a customer can borrow at the prime rate, or they might require the borrower to hold more deposits with the bank to compensate it for making the loan. Effectively, the interest rate paid by the borrower would then be greater than the officially posted prime rate. Furthermore, although there is little hard evidence to support this stand, some observers have claimed that when economic conditions are good, it is not unusual for the most creditworthy of banks' prime customers to get loans at interest rates below the officially posted prime rate. At the same time, others on the list of prime customers that are deemed slightly less creditworthy pay rates higher than the prime rate. Under this third interpretation, then, the market for loans to prime customers really functions much like the theory of competition would predict—except for the anachronistic use of the "prime rate" as a benchmark.

There is some strong evidence that, whatever theory is closest to the mark with respect to the short-run determination of the prime rate, this interest rate ultimately is subject to market forces. Before 1979, other interest rates were not particularly volatile, and neither was the prime rate. Beginning in late 1979, however, for reasons we shall discuss in Chapter 26, most interest rates become highly variable (see Figure 7-6). Although the prime rate was still more rigid than these other rates—it still changed only about once a month during the period of greatest variability that stretched until late 1982—the magnitudes of the adjustment in the prime rate were much larger than before. Furthermore, banks varied the rate in opposite directions much more often than they had in previous years in which they preferred not to enact alternating, back-to-back decreases and increases in the rate. Ultimately, then, it appears that the prime rate must bend under the forces of supply and demand, even if superficially it appears immune from such forces over short intervals.

60-year period. Notice that it changes in discrete jumps. It is usually a fixed rate posted by the majority of lending banks.

Before 1972, the prime rate had been constant for a long period of time. After that year, the prime rate began to change more often and became known as a variable prime rate. The interest rate actually paid by borrowing corporations is sometimes much higher than the published prime rate. The banks require borrowers to leave a **compensating balance** to obtain a loan. The compensating balance is a checking account balance of some specified amount earning zero interest.

Consider an example: General Motors desires to borrow $10 million from the ABC Bank. ABC agrees to make the loan at the published 10 percent annual prime rate but requires that General Motors leave $2.5 million in a non-interest-bearing corporate checking account. General Motors is really not getting its $10 million loan at a 10 percent interest rate, because it can withdraw only $7.5 million from the bank. What, then, is the true interest payment for borrowing the $10 million? General Motors pays 10 percent on $10 million (or $1 million per year), but it gets the use of only $7.5 million. It is therefore actually paying $1 million on a yearly basis to borrow $7.5 million. General Motors ends up paying, not a 10 percent annual rate, but a $13\frac{1}{3}$ percent annual rate. Thus, unless the compensating balance is publicly known, the actual interest rate paid cannot be determined by anyone but the parties involved.

There is another method used by banks to get borrowers to pay interest rates above the apparent prime rate. Sometimes banks switch their most creditworthy borrowers into a less creditworthy category, requiring them to pay a higher interest rate. Banks do this to raise the actual rates paid without raising their posted, or published, interest rate schedule.

THE CORPORATE BOND RATE

Another important interest rate is the one paid on high-grade (low-risk) corporate bonds. Suppose that a corporation such as International Chemical Corporation (ICC) wants to expand its production facilities and must borrow money to do this. One way to raise that money is to borrow it by issuing IOUs in the form of ICC corporate bonds. ICC sells these bonds for, say, $1,000 apiece and agrees to pay back the principal to the lenders at the end of 10 years. During those years, ICC also promises to pay annual interest on the loan. That annual interest payment, divided by the price of the bond, is the corporate bond rate. Different corporations borrow at different bond rates, depending on the financial soundness (creditworthiness) of the institution backing the rate.

Bond Rating Services   Risk ratings for corporate (and state and local government) bonds are provided by Moody's Investors Service and Standard & Poor's Corporation. The Moody's ratings consist of nine different classes or grades, ranging from Aaa (best quality), to Baa (lower-medium quality), to Caa (poor standing), to C (extremely poor prospect). The ratings are based on detailed studies designed to assess the financial soundness of a particular corporation (or government) to determine how risky its bonds are for investors. More precisely, the studies are designed to assess the ability of a government or corporation to make its interest and principal payments on schedule. Each corporate issue is given a particular rating.

Published corporate bond rates are usually given only for the highest-grade bonds—those that are rated Aaa by Moody's (or AAA by Standard & Poor's). Look at Figure 7-7, which indicates that average corporate bond rates moved up and down until about the 1950s. Since the 1950s, there seems to have been an upward trend in nominal corporate bond rates.

THE FEDERAL FUNDS RATE

The federal funds rate is the rate at which depository institutions borrow and lend reserves in the federal funds market, the market for interbank lending we touched on in Chapters 5 and 6. In fact, there is no single "federal funds rate"; the federal funds rate reported daily in the *Wall Street Journal* and other news sources really is an average of rates across institutions. Different depository institutions typically pay different rates to borrow or lend federal funds, a phenomenon known as *tiering* of the federal funds rate.

Figure 7-7
History of Corporate Bond Rates.   (*Source:* Board of Governors of the Federal Reserve System.)

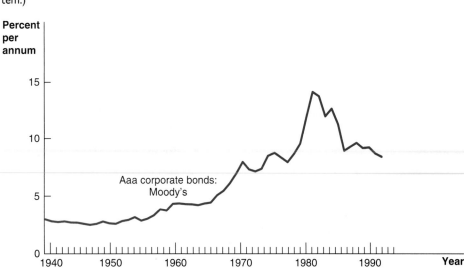

This tiering results, in part, from the fact that the federal funds market is somewhat segmented. That is, there are different parts of the federal funds market that are interlinked but function differently, leading to differentials between the federal funds rates paid by different financial institutions. A large segment of market transactions on any given day are ''brokered'' trades in which depository institutions make bids to buy or sell funds through intermediating federal funds brokers who process information and assist in matching borrowers and lenders of federal funds.

Another segment of the federal funds market is dominated by large depository institutions that function as major *dealers* of federal funds. These dealers stand ready both to borrow from and to lend to other depository institutions that are said to constitute the *retail* portion of this segment of the market. These dealing banks then profit from differentials between the rates at which they lend and borrow federal funds.

Another reason for tiering in the federal funds rate is that some depository institutions are regarded as better risks than others. Those that are widely regarded poorer risks often must pay a **risk premium** to borrow federal funds. This means that they must pay a higher interest rate than those depository institutions that lenders believe are much safer borrowers.

The federal funds rate is important not only to the depository institutions that trade federal funds. It also has been an important variable in the conduct of monetary policy. Indeed, at various times it has represented the most important gauge of the intent of monetary policy actions by the Federal Reserve System, as we shall learn in Chapter 26.

An interesting development in recent years has been the very gradual unfolding of an *intraday* federal funds market—a market for federal funds loans with maturities of a few hours during the day. There are two key reasons that depository institutions have begun to make such trades. One is that computer and communications technology of modern payments systems has made such exchanges easier and safer to conduct. The second is that, for a variety of reasons, some depository institutions are finding that funds of such short maturities have intraday value for which they are willing to pay interest. We shall discuss both of these features of our modern payments system, and their implications for intraday trading, more thoroughly in Chapter 16.

THE CALCULATION OF INTEREST YIELDS

NOMINAL YIELD

If a bond is issued for $1,000 with an agreement to pay, say, $100 in interest every year, then it has an annual coupon rate of interest of 10 percent. This is also called its **nominal yield** (''yield'' is synonymous with interest rate). The nominal yield is defined as

$$r_n = C/F$$

where r_n = nominal yield

C = annual coupon interest payment

F = face amount of the bond

There are two other measures of return to a bond—its current yield and its yield to maturity (or effective yield).

CURRENT YIELD

Current yield is the dollar annual interest expressed as a percentage of the current market price of the bond. Bonds are often issued (and resold) at a price different from their face value. Thus, a 6 percent bond currently selling at $900 would have a nominal yield of 6 percent ($60 divided by $1,000) but a current yield of 6.67 percent ($60 divided by $900). Thus,

$$r_c = C/P$$

where r_c stands for the current yield and P stands for the price of the bond.

YIELD TO MATURITY (OR EFFECTIVE YIELD) ON LONG-TERM BONDS

The **yield to maturity** on a long-term bond is more difficult to calculate. The difficulty stems from the fact that such bonds typically are sold at a discount—at a price less than their face value—and are redeemed at maturity for their face value. The interest rate, or yield, therefore requires taking into account the value of the automatic capital gain and the coupon interest payments. For example, consider a 3-year bond that has a face value of $1,000, pays $50 per year in coupon interest, and is currently selling for $875.65. What is the effective yield on that 3-year bond?

Discounted Present Value In order to answer that question, it is helpful to understand the concept of **discounted present value,** or the value today of dollars in the future. We have already indicated that the rate of interest provides a means of translating the value of future purchasing power into present purchasing power; the market interest rate reflects the trade-off between present and future consumption. In Chapter 4, we saw that if there are only two periods and the relevant interest rate is the rate of return from saving, r_s, then there is a direct relationship between a future value of a good, a service, or an amount of funds and the value as perceived in the present.

This value was given by equation (4-4) in Chapter 4, which we restate below:

$$Q_1 = [1/(1 + r_s)]Q_2$$

where Q_2 is the value of a good, a service, or an amount of funds in the second period and Q_1 is the present value of that future amount Q_2. Because the present value of future funds in a two-period setting depends on a rate of interest, it should come as no surprise that computing discounted present value across several time periods also is intimately related to the interest rate.

The value today of any amount of funds in the future is given by the equation

$$P = R_1/(1 + r) + R_2/(1 + r)^2 + R_3/(1 + r)^3 + \cdots + R_n/(1 + r)^n \qquad \text{(7-1)}$$

where P = discounted present value—the value today, or the market price of the asset (today's market price of an asset will reflect the asset's present value)

R_1 = the amount of funds to be received 1 year hence

R_2 = the amount of funds to be received 2 years hence

R_3 = the amount of funds to be received 3 years hence

R_n = the amount of funds to be received n years hence

r = the market rate of interest

The first thing to note is that there is a direct relationship between P and a given future stream of revenues, R. Other things constant, the higher the coupon interest, the higher will be the selling price of the bond, P. Next, notice that an inverse relationship exists between the price of the bond and the market interest rate. For a given R stream (R_1, R_2, . . . , R_n), the higher the market rate of interest, the less the bond will sell for today; the lower the interest rate, the higher the value today of a given future R stream.

Suppose that a bond with a face value of $1,000 pays $50 per annum and matures in 3 years. If the market rate of interest is 10 percent, what will be the selling price of that bond today? According to our equation (remembering that in the third year the bond owner receives $50 coupon interest and the face value of the bond and ignoring the common real-world complication of semiannual payments of coupon interest),

$$P = \$50/(1.1) + \$50/(1.1)^2 + \$1,050/(1.1)^3$$
$$= \$45.45 + \$41.32 + \$788.88$$
$$= \$875.65 \hspace{3cm} \textbf{(7-2)}$$

Because the discounted present value of that bond is $875.65, a competitive market will price that bond precisely at its economic value.

It might be helpful to interpret what the value $875.65 means in this context. If someone were to place $875.65 today in an investment program that earns 10 percent per annum coupon interest, she could draw out $50 in year 1, $50 in year 2, and $1,050 in year 3, and then there would be nothing left in the investment account. For that reason, a bond that gives $50 per year for 3 years and pays a $1,000 face value at the end of 3 years has a present value of $875.65 when the market rate of interest is 10 percent.

Yield to Maturity and Discounting   We are now ready to return to our original question. What is the yield to maturity of a 3-year bond that has a face value of $1,000, pays $50 per annum in coupon interest (has a nominal yield of 5 percent), and is currently selling for $875.65? We can use equation (7-1) to help us calculate the yield to maturity of this bond. Note that $P = \$875.65$, $R_1 = R_2 = \$50$, $R_3 = \$1,050$, and r is the unknown. Thus,

$$\$875.65 = \$50/(1 + r) + \$50/(1 + r)^2 + \$1,050/(1 + r)^3$$

Solving for r will give

$$r = r_m \, 0.10 \hspace{1cm} (10 \text{ percent})$$

where r_m stands for the yield to maturity. Because r_m calculations are so complicated, yield to maturity is best determined by using a bond table or a programmed calculator. Table 7-1, a portion of an actual bond table, shows the yield to maturity of bonds with different maturities, given a face value of $1,000 and a nominal yield of 6 percent.

The Market for Long-Term Bonds   Bonds are credit instruments, and buyers and sellers of bonds exchange in bond markets. As is usually the case, supply and demand determine price; the price of a bond is determined at the intersection of the supply and demand curves. Consider Figure 7-8, which indicates the supply of and demand for 3-year bonds that have a nominal yield of 5 percent.

The demand for bonds reflects the intentions of suppliers of credit; bond purchasers are lenders, and they will purchase more bonds at a lower price than they will at a higher

TABLE 7-1
Portion of Bond Table for 6% Nominal Yield

Assume that a bond with a face value of $1,000, a nominal yield of 6 percent, and a maturity date of $7\frac{1}{2}$ years can be purchased for approximately $900. The owner is paid $1,000 at the end of that period. To find the yield to maturity, or total effective yield, look for the number closest to 90.00 under the years to maturity column of $7\frac{1}{2}$. That number is 89.92, or $899.20, which is closest to $900. In the extreme left-hand column, the yield to maturity is 7.8 percent for a 6 percent coupon, or nominal, yield on a bond with a face value of $1,000.

Yield to Maturity, % (6% annual yield)	Years to Maturity				
	6	$6\frac{1}{2}$	7	$7\frac{1}{2}$	8
7.00	95.17	94.85	94.54	94.24	93.95
7.20	94.24	93.86	93.49	93.14	92.80
7.40	93.31	92.88	92.46	92.05	91.66
7.60	92.40	91.91	91.44	90.98	90.54
7.80	91.50	90.96	90.43	89.92	89.44
8.00	90.61	90.01	89.44	88.88	88.35

price. This is because bonds yield a fixed and determined R stream. The lower the price of a bond, the higher the yield to maturity; the higher the yield to maturity, the more people are willing to lend. Note that this demand-for-bonds curve is equivalent to the supply-of-credit curve illustrated in Figures 7-1 and 7-3.

The supply-of-bonds curve reflects the intentions of demanders of credit; bond sellers

Figure 7-8

The Supply of and Demand for 3-Year Bonds with a 5 Percent Nominal Yield. This figure indicates that the equilibrium price will be established at $875.65 when the market rate of interest is 10 percent. At a higher price, say, $922.69, a surplus of bonds exists. This bond price is equivalent to an 8 percent yield to maturity, and so this situation corresponds to a shortage in Figure 7-3. A surplus of bonds means that a shortage of funds exists for borrowers. At a lower price, say, $831.87, a shortage of bonds exists. At that bond price, the yield to maturity is 12 percent, and as Figure 7-3 indicates, a surplus of credit exists. A shortage of bonds implies that lenders cannot find a sufficient quantity of borrowers at the going bond price.

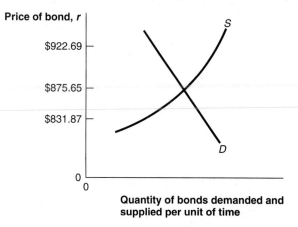

are borrowers, and they will offer more bonds at a higher price than at a lower price. As implied in the paragraph above, because the *R* stream of bonds is constant, higher bond prices mean lower yields to maturity. Bond suppliers are willing to supply more bonds (borrow more) at lower interest rates than at higher interest rates.

Consider Figure 7-8 and compare it with Figure 7-3. A bond price of $922.69 is equivalent to a yield to maturity of 8 percent (for a 3-year bond with a nominal yield of 5 percent). Such a situation implies a surplus of bonds in Figure 7-8 and a shortage of credit in Figure 7-3. A surplus of bonds implies that bond sellers (borrowers) cannot find sufficient buyers (lenders). Hence, a shortage of credit exists and interest rates will rise— bond prices will fall.

At a price of $831.87, which is equivalent to a yield to maturity of 12 percent, a shortage of bonds exists in Figure 7-8 and a surplus of credit exists in Figure 7-3. A shortage of bonds implies that bond buyers (lenders) cannot find enough sellers (borrowers). If lenders cannot find enough borrowers at the going interest rate, a surplus of credit exists and interest rates will fall—bond prices will rise.

THE YIELD ON NONMATURING BONDS, OR CONSOLS

Consider an economy in which there is only one interest rate, which fluctuates over time depending on the supply of and the demand for credit, or loanable funds. Also assume that only one bond exists. It is issued by the government every January 1 with a face value of $1,000. The coupon rate of interest (yield) is whatever the market rate of interest is on that date. Also, the bond has an infinite lifetime; it can never be turned in for $1,000. Actually, this type of nonmaturing bond exists; it is called a **consol** and is issued by the British government.

Now suppose that on January 1 the market rate of interest in the economy is 10 percent. The consol issued to you, if you give the government $1,000, has a large (infinite!) number of coupons, one of which you can turn in at the end of each year to obtain $100 in interest payments. In other words, you send in the coupon at the end of each year, and a short time later you receive $100 in the mail. The nominal yield on the bond is 10 percent per year. Suppose that by the beginning of the following year, the market rate of interest in the economy rises from 10 percent to 20 percent. Let's say that you decide to sell your consol on January 1 of the following year. Would anyone be willing to pay you $1,000 for that bond with its coupon rate of 10 percent? Probably not. After all, anyone could purchase a newly issued government consol with a coupon rate of 20 percent a year since, by assumption, the government issues each bond at the market rate of interest. What is the highest price you could get for your bond? You would have to give the buyer a deal comparable to the one he or she would receive on a new bond. Thus, with a coupon rate giving only $100 a year in an economy with a 20 percent interest rate, you would be able to obtain only $500 if you sold your consol ($100 is equal to 20 percent of $500).

This simple example illustrates a key point that will be used throughout the rest of this book:

> **The market value or price of existing (old) bonds is inversely related to the market rate of interest in the economy.**

There is a simple formula for consols (bonds) with an infinite lifetime (no maturity date). The value of $1 in interest payments per year forever is equal to $1 divided by *r*, where *r* is the market (nominal) rate of interest (in decimal form). Otherwise stated:

$$\text{Value of \$1 in interest payments forever} = \$1/r$$

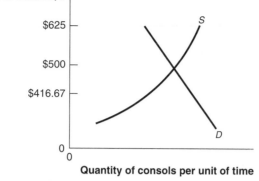

Figure 7-9
The Supply of and Demand for Consols.   This figure shows the supply of, and demand for, consols that pay $50 per annum. Equilibrium exists at a price of $500, which is equivalent to a market yield of 10 percent. At a consol price of $625, which is equivalent to a yield of 8 percent, a surplus of consols and a shortage of credit exist. At a conso! price of $416.67, a shortage of consols and a surplus of credit exist. After surpluses and shortages are eliminated in competitive markets, the consol price will be established at $500, where equilibrium exists.

In general, if R is the annual coupon interest paid and r is the rate of interest, the value of a consol is equal to R/r. In our example, then, $R = \$1$.

In the above example, the amount of dollars paid out per year was $100. With a market rate of interest of 10 percent, the formula indicates that the market price of the bond would be $1,000 divided by 0.10, or $1,000. With a market rate of interest of 20 percent, the formula indicates that the market price of the existing consols would equal $100 divided by 0.20, or $500. Thus, even in the absence of risk of interest payment (or principal with a bond that does have a specified life, or maturity), one can never be certain that the market price of an existing bond will remain the same as it was when the bond was purchased. Whenever interest rates in the economy rise, the price of existing bonds will fall because bonds, by definition, are assets whose income consists of a fixed quantity of nominal dollars per year. Conversely, if interest rates fall, the market price of existing bonds will rise. In other words, owners of bonds can incur capital losses or obtain capital gains due to the changing market value of such assets.

Figure 7-9 shows the supply of and demand for consols; like Figure 7-8, it is equivalent to Figure 7-3. Figure 7-9 shows the price of consols that pay $50 per annum, forever, to the consol owners. At a price of $500, which is equivalent to a yield of 10 percent, equilibrium exists. At any lower price, a shortage of consols (and a surplus of credit in Figure 7-3) exists, which causes consol prices to rise and interest rates to fall. At any price above $500 for consols, a surplus of consols and a shortage of credit exist, causing consol prices to fall and interest rates to rise.

INTEREST RATE CHANGES AND BOND PRICE CHANGES

You can understand why an inverse relationship exists between bond prices and interest rates (given fixed coupon interest payments) by recalling equation (7-1):

$$P = R_1/(1 + r) + R_2/(1 + r)^2 + R_3/(1 + r)^3 + \cdots + R_n/(1 + r)^n$$

For a bond the Rs are given. If r rises, P must fall; if r falls, P must rise.

Throughout this chapter we have made calculations on yields and bond prices. Consider Table 7-2, which shows various market interest rates and the corresponding bond prices for bonds of differing maturities. For both the 3-year bonds and the consols, the coupon interest is $50 per annum. Note that a given change in the rate of interest generates a much less dramatic change in the price of the bonds with a 3-year maturity.

In the next section, when we discuss the yields on short-term bonds, or bills, we will again have occasion to note that the shorter the term to maturity of a bond, the smaller will be the price change of the bond, for a given change in the market rate of interest.

Bonds are capable of bestowing capital gains and losses on their owners. Furthermore, longer-term bonds bestow greater capital gains or losses than do short-term bonds, for given interest rate changes. This important conclusion implies that long-term bonds are less liquid than short-term bonds, an implication that will loom large in later chapters.

CALCULATING PUBLISHED TREASURY BILL RATES

Published Treasury bill rates are discount rates based on a 360-day year. (The 360-day year is used for ease of calculation.) Consider the following example: A $10,000, 91-day T-bill is sold at auction for $9,685. The T-bill rate is calculated from the following equation:

$$r_B = [(F - P)/F] \times (360/n) \tag{7-3}$$

where r_B = the T-bill rate
$\quad F$ = the face value of the T-bill
$\quad P$ = the price paid for the T-bill
$\quad n$ = the number of days to maturity

In our example,

$$r_B = [(\$10,000 - \$9,685)/\$10,000] \times (360/91) \tag{7-4}$$

The Treasury would therefore list the T-bill rate for this auction at 12.462 percent.

T A B L E   7-2

Market Interest Rate, %	Price of 3-Year Bond	Price of Consol
12	$831.87	$416.67
10	$875.65	$500.00
8	$922.69	$625.00

Calculating a Treasury Bill Equivalent Coupon Yield   Published Treasury bill rates are based on a 360-day year and the face value of the investment. **Coupon yield equivalents** are based on a 365-day year and the market price of the bill. To obtain a coupon yield equivalent, or an approximation to the true annual yield, substitute a 365-day year and the actual purchase price of the T-bill at the beginning of the period in equation (7-3). The formula for an approximate coupon yield equivalent is

$$r_Y = \left|(F - P)/P\right| \times (365/n) \tag{7-5}$$

Here, r_Y equals the approximate coupon yield, P equals the price paid for the T-bill, and n is the number of days to maturity. The term $(F - P)/P$ gives the interest rate *per period,* and $365/n$ gives the number of periods per year. By multiplying the former by the latter, an annualized interest rate results, and so the rate can be made comparable to annual yields on longer-term securities—hence the term "equivalent" yield. This calculated rate is considered to be an "approximate" annual rate because it assumes that the market conditions do not change over the periods—an unlikely happenstance.

Using the above example for a 91-day, $10,000 T-bill sold at auction for $9,685, the simplified formula becomes

$$r_Y = [(100 - 96.850)/96.850] \times (365/91) = 0.13046 \tag{7-6}$$

The coupon yield on this T-bill is 13.046 percent. It is higher than the published T-bill rate because it takes into account: (1) the actual number of days in a year and (2) the fact that the interest is earned on the price paid for the T-bill rather than its face value.

THE SECONDARY MARKET FOR TREASURY BILLS

Treasury bills are traded actively in a secondary market, because some buyers (households, businesses, banks, the Fed) prefer to sell their 91-day (or other) Treasury bills before the maturity date. The existence of a large secondary market in T-bills allows for their transfer before maturity. This secondary market makes T-bills the most liquid, next to money itself, of all financial assets. There are specialized dealers in government securities who are ready to buy and sell existing T-bills to ultimate lenders at all times.

These dealers compile information about the bid and asked T-bill (discount) rates for currently outstanding T-bills. These discount rates are not the same as the already indicated approximate coupon yields, which give the rates in the primary market. Rather they are a means of determining the prices at which existing T-bills will be traded in the secondary market. For example, consider a T-bill due to mature in 73 days. The asked price for this security is 96.785. This means that, if purchased, the buyer must give the dealer $9,678.50. In turn, the buyer will receive a $10,000 T-bill that will mature in 73 days. The formula for calculating the approximate coupon yield is

$$r_Y = [(F - P)/P] \times (365/n) \tag{7-7}$$

where, as before, P represents the asked price and n represents the number of days remaining before the T-bill matures. Note that now, because we are not dealing with the primary market, n need not be just 91 or 282; it represents the *remaining* days to maturity for the bill in question.

The yield to maturity for this T-bill is computed to be

$$r_Y = [(\$10,000 - \$9,678.50)/\$9,678.50] \times (365/73)$$
$$= 0.16608 \tag{7-8}$$

The approximate coupon yield is therefore 16.608 percent per year. This figure represents the approximate annual return to a buyer who purchases this existing bill and holds it to maturity (73 days later) and then redeems it with the U.S. Treasury for $10,000. On the other side of the coin, the seller forgoes a rate of return of 16.608 percent per year by selling the bill.

Liquidity and T-Bills Note that the approximate equivalent coupon yields for T-bills in the secondary market bear no necessary relationship to either the published T-bill rate when the T-bills were sold at auction or the approximate equivalent coupon rate on that auction day. If demand and supply conditions for the new T-bills sold on the market change abruptly, the equivalent coupon rates in the secondary market can differ signficantly from the rate on the date of issue. The shorter the length of the T-bill, however, the less the actual price of that bill will change in the secondary market for any given interest rate change in the economy. After all, once sold at auction, a 91-day T-bill has only 90 days to maturity. Even if general interest rates in the economy were to rise dramatically, say, 10 days after the T-bill was sold, its value in the secondary market would not fall significantly because owners would merely have to wait 81 days to exchange the proceeds of the T-bill for higher-interest-earning assets.

To make this clear, consider an extreme example: Suppose that one day after a large number of T-bills were sold at auction at a coupon yield equivalent of 10 percent, all interest rates in the economy doubled. Remember that in this situation the market value of outstanding consols would fall to half their original value on the day after they were issued. What would happen to the market price of T-bills that had, say, 90 days left to run? Let's first determine their price on the day of issue and then their price on the next day. If these T-bills were earning a 10 percent effective coupon yield on the day they were issued, their price on that day could be found by using the formula

$$r_Y = [(F - P)/P] \times (365/n) \tag{7-9}$$

Solving for P gives

$$P = F/[(r_Y \times n/365) + 1] \tag{7-10}$$

Therefore,

$$P = \$10,000/[0.10(91/365) + 1] \tag{7-11}$$

So,

$$P = \$9,756.75$$

In other words, when sold, the $10,000, 91-day T-bill will command a market price of $9,756.75.

If interest rates everywhere double overnight, yesterday's new issue of T-bills would now sell on the secondary market at a price that reflects the new market conditions. The equivalent coupon yield would now be 20 percent. Let's calculate the value of those T-bills that were sold yesterday and have 90 days to maturity. Substituting the new values into equation (7-10) gives

$$P = \$10,000/[0.20(90/365) + 1] \qquad \textbf{(7-12)}$$

Therefore,

$$P = \$9,530.03$$

The market value of the T-bill would fall from its issue price of $9,756.75 to $9,530.03 on the next day. That represents a reduction in value of only 2.3 percent, *even though interest rates have doubled.*

Now calculate the change in the market price of a 5-year bond when interest rates double. Recalling equation (7-1), which indicates the value of long-term bonds, we know that, at issue, if interest rates are 10 percent, 5-year bonds that have a nominal yield of 5 percent and a face value of $10,000 will be priced at

$$P = \$500/1.1 + \$500/(1.1)^2 + \$500/(1.1)^3 + \$500/(1.1)^4 \\ + \$10,500/(1.1)^5 \qquad \textbf{(7-13)}$$

Therefore,

$$P = \$454.55 + \$413.22 + \$375.66 + \$341.51 + \$6,519.67 \\ = \$8,104.61$$

If interest rates were to double to 20 percent, that bond now will sell for

$$P = \$500/1.2 + \$500/(1.2)^2 + \$500/(1.2)^3 + \$500/(1.2)^4 \\ + \$10,500/(1.2)^5 \\ = \$416.67 + \$347.22 + \$289.35 + \$241.12 + \$4,219.71 \\ = \$5,514.07$$

The price of this bond would fall from $8,104.61 to $5,514.07. If you bought a newly issued 5-year bond with a 5 percent nominal yield, and the next day interest rates doubled, your bond would be worth $2,590.59 less than the day before—a drop in value of 31.96 percent.

This result confirms our earlier conclusion. The shorter the term to maturity of a bond or bill, the less its price will fluctuate for a given change in market interest rates. T-bills are extremely liquid because they are of short duration and hence their market values are relatively insensitive to changes in the interest rate. Also they can be easily traded in secondary markets.

ACCOUNTING FOR DIFFERENT INTEREST RATES

By now you are aware that there are many different kinds of bonds and that their interest rates often differ significantly. In this section we explain that such differences are caused by the fact that bonds have:

1. Different default, or credit, risks
2. Different degrees of liquidity
3. Different tax treatment
4. Different terms to maturity

To simplify the discussion, economists analyze different interest rate patterns by:

1. Holding the term to maturity constant and determining how interest rates differ from bonds with different (a) default risks, (b) liquidity, and (c) tax treatment. This general approach is referred to as the **risk structure of interest rates.**
2. Holding default risk, degree of liquidity, and tax treatment constant and determining why bonds with different terms to maturity earn different interest rates. This is called the **term structure of interest rates.**

RISK STRUCTURE OF INTEREST RATES

For a given term to maturity, different bonds will earn different interest rates if, as we have already indicated, they are subject to different default risk, different degrees of liquidity, or different tax treatment.

Differential Default Risk   Consider two bonds, A and B, for which everything is the same; they have the same degree of liquidity, have the same term to maturity, have the same default risk, are subject to the same tax treatment, and so on. Given this situation, the bonds will have the same market value, P; and because they have the same coupon payment, they will yield the same interest rate. Now suppose that corporation B, which issued bond B, experiences some financial or economic woes and the bond rating services lower corporation B's ratings. Because the default risk is now relatively higher for bond B than for bond A, the demand for bond B will fall—causing its price to fall and its interest rate yield to rise. At the same time there will be an increase in the demand for bond A, causing its price to rise and its interest rate to fall. In short, there will now be an interest rate spread (difference) between bond A and bond B that reflects a risk premium.

Note that the interest rate on bond B will exceed the interest rate on bond A because each bond generates the same coupon payments but the price of bond A is higher than the price of bond B. Another way to view this is to note that because the default risk is higher on bond B, investors require a higher interest yield on B. The prices of such bonds will adjust until the interest rate spread reflects their differential default risks. We conclude that different bonds yield different interest rates, in part because they are subject to different default risks.

Differential Liquidity   Again consider two bonds for which the circumstances are identical in all respects, bond C and bond D. Suppose now that bond D becomes more liquid, perhaps because it is more widely traded. Following our previous analysis, we conclude that the demand for bond D rises while the demand for bond C falls, that the price of bond D rises while the price of bond C falls, and that the interest rate on bond D falls while the interest rate on bond C rises. (Remember, if both bonds pay the same coupon value and their prices differ, they now yield different interest rates.)

We conclude that if different bonds are subject to different degrees of liquidity, they will earn different interest rates. Specifically, those bonds that are more liquid, other things constant, will earn lower interest rates than those bonds that are less liquid. Stated differently, investors will require a lower interest rate on bonds that are more liquid, other things constant.

This analysis explains why U.S. government securities, which are more liquid than corporation bonds (the market for an individual corporation's bonds is much thinner than the market for government securities), pay relatively low interest rates. Of course, U.S. government securities also sell at a low interest rate because of their extremely low default risk.

Differential Tax Treatment   Tax-exempt securities are available for purchase. The value of the tax-exempt status of the income from bonds issued by municipal governments is directly proportional to one's marginal tax bracket. As of 1991 there were only three brackets for federal personal income tax purposes: 15 percent, 28 percent, and 31 percent, although because of a variety of phaseouts of deductions and exemptions the actual marginal tax rate can be as high as 35 percent for certain individuals. The value of nontaxable income is less for someone in the 15 percent bracket than in the 31 percent bracket.

In the marketplace, individuals in higher marginal tax brackets bid up the price of tax-free municipal bonds so that their yields fall below yields on equivalent taxable bonds. On the margin, actual yields of tax-exempts will reflect the marginal tax bracket of the marginal buyer of such bonds. That is why, on any given day, tax-exempt yields are less than taxable yields. Thus everyone who buys tax-exempts implicitly pays a tax, which is the difference between the interest yield on a municipal bond and the interest yield on an equivalent corporate bond. The purchase of tax-exempts only allows investors to escape explicit taxation.

TERM STRUCTURE OF INTEREST RATES

Even if we hold constant default risk, liquidity, and tax treatment differences among bonds, it is very often the case that bonds with different terms to maturity earn different rates. For example, often Treasury securities of different maturities (which are default-free, equally liquid, and subject to the same tax treatment) tend to have higher yields as the time to maturity rises. Figure 7-10, which appeared in the *Wall Street Journal* on March 12, 1992, shows a typical **yield curve** for Treasury securities; a yield curve illustrates the relationship that exists on a specific date between bonds that are similar in all respects except term to maturity. Note that this curve is positively sloped, indicating that as the term to maturity rises, so too does the yield. (Note that this is the usual, but not necessary, shape of the yield curve for U.S. government bonds.)

There are two major hypotheses concerning the term structure of interest rates: the segmented markets hypothesis and the pure expectations hypothesis. We analyze each in turn.

Segmented Markets Hypothesis   The segmented markets hypothesis maintains that the various markets for bonds of different maturities are completely separated and segmented. Accordingly, buyers and sellers of bonds specialize in different term maturities. To these specialists, bonds of different maturities are not substitutes. Commercial banks tend to have short-term liabilities and therefore tend to acquire short-term assets. Life insurance companies have very predictable, long-term liabilities (policy payments) and therefore tend to purchase long-term bonds. Because bonds of differing terms to maturity are traded in segmented markets, the yield curve can take any shape.

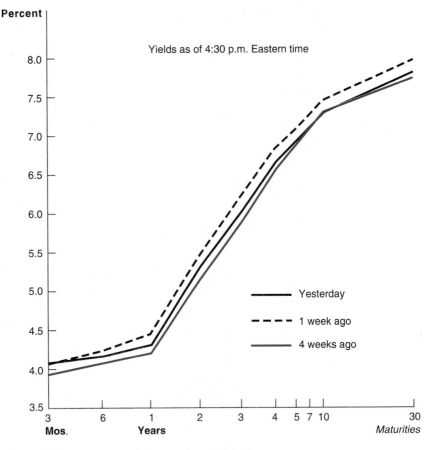

Figure 7-10
A Treasury Yield Curve. This is a typically shaped Treasury yield curve. It indicates that as the term to maturity rises, other things constant, Treasury interest rates rise. Treasury yield curves, however, are not always positively sloped. At times they are flat or even slightly negatively sloped. (*Source:* Federal Reserve and U.S. Department of Commerce.)

Thus, the segmented markets theory can help explain why, at different times, yield curves for various bonds are positively sloped, flat, or negatively sloped. The differing curves are accounted for by the different supply and demand conditions in each (separated) market as they happen to exist at any given moment in time.

Three problems exist for the segmented markets hypothesis. First, the theory cannot explain the empirical fact that interest rates on bonds of different maturities tend to rise and fall together. Second, at least for T-bills, it is usually the case that the yield curve is positively sloped. It would seem unlikely that the supply of long-term bonds relative to the demand for such bonds would normally be greater than the supply of short-term bonds relative to their demand. Finally, as the next section will argue, there will be some investors who are indifferent between buying and/or selling in markets that trade bonds with different maturities. These marginal investors can earn profits by trading in the markets for bonds of different maturities, and ultimately the market price of bonds (and therefore the market interest rates on bonds) will reflect the behavior of the marginal investors who are not wedded to a specific market—and not of average investors who are. In short, interest rates on bonds of different maturities will be determined by people who view those bonds as perfect substitutes, not by those who view them as nonsubstitutes. This brings us to our next hypothesis concerning the term structure of interest rates.

Pure Expectations Hypothesis[1]   The pure expectations hypothesis assumes that there will be a sufficient quantity of bond market buyers and sellers who find bonds of different maturities to be perfect substitutes. The insight you need to understand is straightforward: The interest rate on a long-term bond will equal an average of short-term interest rates that people expect to occur over the life of the long-term bond. Let's consider a simple example.

Assume that there is a market for a 1-year discount bond in which the current yield is 9 percent, and another market for a 2-year discount bond in which the current annualized yield is 10 percent. Assume that all other particulars concerning these bonds are identical. We are viewing, of course, a yield curve that is positively sloped. How should we interpret this yield curve? Well, if the marginal investors are indifferent between the purchases and sales of these bonds, then each bond must be equally profitable to them. Otherwise they would start buying and selling, and bond prices (and interest rates) would change to equate the return on each bond. Stated differently, the rate of return on buying the 1-year coupon bond and using the proceeds 1 year hence to purchase another 1-year coupon bond (strategy 1) must equal the rate of return on purchasing a 2-year bond right now (strategy 2).

Suppose that an investor follows the second strategy and buys the 2-year coupon bond; she earns 10 percent per year. If, in contrast, she follows the first strategy, she will earn 9 percent in the first year; but how much must she earn in the second year, on a 1-year bond, in order to earn the 10 percent average rate of return realized on the second strategy? The answer is 11 percent, because the average of 9 percent and 11 percent is 10 percent. In this example, the positively sloped curve implies that marginal investors expect future 1-year interest rates to rise (from 9 percent to 11 percent). The approximate equation for determining this implied future interest rate is

$$F_r = 2r_2 - r_1 \qquad (7\text{-}14)$$

where F_r = implied future short-term rate, or forward rate

r_2 = annualized yield on the 2-year coupon bond

r_1 = annual yield on the 1-year coupon bond

Suppose that expectations suddenly change, so that now marginal investors expect future short-term interest rates to be unchanged—in our example, 1-year coupon rates are now expected to continue earning 9 percent in the future. Now our marginal investors believe they can earn profits by taking advantage of a positively sloped yield curve that currently exists—and in the process, flatten the yield curve. For example, consider the quick-witted investor who expects the future 1-year coupon rate still to equal 9 percent 1 year hence (that is, the expected yield on the 1-year bond, or r_1^e, 1 year hence equals r_1, and this is less than the implied interest rate; or $r_1 = r_1^e < F_r$). Such an investor can (1) borrow at 9 percent this year by selling a 1-year bond at 9 percent right now; (2) lend

[1] This section is based on Timothy D. Rowe, Thomas A. Lawler, and Timothy Q. Cook, ''Treasury Bill versus Private Money Market Yield Curves,'' Federal Reserve Bank of Richmond *Economic Review,* 72 (4, July/August 1986), pp. 3–12.

at 10 percent for 2 years by buying a 2-year coupon now; and (3) borrow at 9 percent 1 year hence, by buying a 1-year coupon bond next year—if she is right!

Thus, by borrowing short at 9 percent and lending long at 10 percent, an investor can earn a spread of 1 percent (minus transactions costs).

Note that if many investors expect that the future short-term interest rate will remain unchanged, then there will be an increase in the demand for long-term bonds, forcing their price up and their interest rate down. This process will continue as long as $r_1 = r_1^e < F_r$; eventually the implied interest rate on future short-term bonds will equal the expected rate, and the short-term bond yield and the long-term bond yield will be equated. Thus, if marginal investors expect future short-term rates to equal current short-term rates (no change is expected), then their profit-maximizing activities will generate a flat yield curve. As already indicated, if they expect short-term rates to rise, the yield curve will be positively sloped. We leave it to you to convince yourself that if they believe that short-term rates will fall in the future, the yield curve will be negatively sloped. (Is your answer consistent with the fact that negatively sloped yield curves usually exist during recessions?)

Note that the pure expectations hypothesis can also explain why interest rates on bonds of different maturity move together over time. If events transpire that cause short-term rates to rise, people will expect future short-term rates to rise also; and if they expect future short-term rates to rise, then rates on longer-term bonds will rise to reflect this higher implied interest rate.

The Term Premium   Empirical studies of yield curves typically concentrate on T-bills, and they usually find that the T-bill yield curve is positively sloped. This is troublesome because it implies that marginal investors usually expect short-term interest rates to rise; in fact, however, they are just as likely to fall as they are to rise. Another way to state this is that investors can earn a higher rate of return by investing in T-bills of longer maturity than they can by buying short-term bills and continually reinvesting them. This clearly contradicts the pure expectations hypothesis.

In light of prevailing empirical evidence against the pure expectations hypothesis, revisions to that hypothesis typically include a role for a **term premium,** which is a yield differential that investors demand for holding a security of one maturity rather than another and that issuers are willing to pay to issue a security of that maturity. If the term premium increases with the maturity of the security, its existence provides an explanation of the upward slope of the yield curve while preserving the essential elements of the expectations hypothesis. One complication, however, is that empirical evidence does not support the assumption that the term premium for a given maturity is constant—term premiums appear to vary over time as well as across differing maturities. In general, they seem to be lower in periods of economic expansion and higher in periods of economic contraction. Most recent theories indicate that this pattern of the term premium is sensible if the behaviors of securities investors and issuers are sensitive to interest rate levels and variabilities, which change over the course of the business cycle.

Why the Term Structure of Interest Rates Is Important   Understanding the term structure of interest rates is important not only from an intellectual but also from a practical point of view. Corporate treasurers must make decisions at all times about what to do with available cash and about how to finance expansion. In both instances, a decision about the purchase or sale of short-term versus long-term securities is crucial. The U.S. Treasury also must decide how to manage the sizable debt of the U.S. government. When some of those bonds mature, should the Treasury refund them by selling new short-term bonds or new long-term bonds? In principle, when armed with an understanding of the term structure of interest rates, a policy maker can make a reasonably sound decision in such circumstances.

Can the yield curve aid in financial decision making? The answer to this question hinges on the answer to another: Does the slope of the yield curve assist in forecasting future interest rate movements? According to the expectations theory of the term structure of interest rates, the answer to this latter question should be yes, implying that attention to the yield curve should help individuals, firms, and policy makers in their decision making.

An interesting implication of recent research on this issue, however, is that some parts of the yield curve have been useful in forecasting future interest rates while other parts have not. This is not consistent with the basic expectations theory of the term structure, with or without inclusion of a term premium.

A last note will close this section. Any explanation of the term structure of interest rates describes a pattern of interest rates only at a given moment in time. Do not get the impression that the term structure of interest rates can explain why interest rates in general either rise or fall through time. As we shall see later on, the Federal Reserve has something to say about that; indeed, possible explanations for the failure of theories of the term structure to account for all aspects of the behavior of the yield curve focus on the Fed's role in influencing actual and expected security yields. We shall have much more to say about the Fed's role in the determination of interest rates in later chapters.

CHAPTER SUMMARY

1. In the simplest model, the market rate of interest is established at the intersection of the supply of and the demand for credit, or loanable funds. The demand for loanable funds consists of the demand for consumer loans (consumption) and business loans (investment); each varies inversely as the rate of interest rises or falls. The supply of loanable funds consists mostly of household saving; it varies directly with the rate of interest.

2. The rate of interest is the price of credit. As such, it performs the allocative function that all prices do. It allocates scarce loanable funds to the highest bidders. By doing so, it allocates physical capital to the most profitable businesses and durable consumer goods to those households that are more present-oriented.

3. The nominal interest rate is the market rate of interest. It is the rate of exchange between a dollar today and a dollar in the future. The real rate of interest is adjusted for expected future changes in the price level; it is the rate of exchange between goods and services today and goods and services in the future.

4. Various yields can be calculated for a given bond. The nominal yield is equal to the coupon interest divided by the face amount of the bond. The current yield equals the coupon interest divided by the market price of the bond. The yield to maturity of the same bond is also expressed as a percentage, and it is the effective annual rate of return that would be earned by holding the bond to maturity; it reflects the bond price, its coupon interest earnings, and any capital gain or loss resulting from holding the bond to maturity.

5. The nature of a bond is such that it offers a fixed nominal coupon payment to the holder at specific future dates. However, its selling price can differ from its face value. When market interest rates change, the prices of bonds will change. More specifically, if interest rates rise, the prices of bonds will fall; if interest rates fall, the prices of bonds will rise. Hence, rises in the general level of interest rates generate capital losses

for bond owners; reductions in the rate of interest create capital gains for bond owners. The longer the term to maturity of the bond, the greater the possibility of capital gain or loss, other things constant.

6. Interest rates on different securities vary considerably. Causes of interest rate differences include differences in default or credit risk, liquidity, tax treatment, and term to maturity.

7. The risk structure of interest rates considers bonds with the same term to maturity. Such bonds will have lower interest rate returns if they have a lower default risk, are more liquid, or receive preferential tax treatment.

8. The term structure of interest rates considers bonds that are similar in all respects except term to maturity. The yield curves of such bonds can be positively sloped, negatively sloped, or flat.

9. The segmented markets theory explains yield curves by assuming that bond markets of different maturities are completely separate; different investors are wedded only to short-term, intermediate-term, or long-term lending or borrowing. This theory has difficulty explaining why interest rates on bonds of different maturities rise and fall together. It also implies that investors who do find short-term and long-term bonds to be good substitutes would refuse to earn profits by simultaneously trading in both markets.

10. The pure expectations hypothesis explains various yield curves based on the expectations of marginal, not average, investors, who find bonds of different maturities to be good substitutes.

11. No single theory of the term structure of interest rates explains all aspects of the behavior of the yield curve. One feature that helps salvage existing theories is the existence of a term premium for securities of different maturities. Nonetheless, most empirical evidence indicates that the term premium is not constant but instead varies over time, possibly in response to Federal Reserve policies.

GLOSSARY

Compensating balance: Funds that a borrower agrees to maintain in a checking account (earning no interest) as a condition for obtaining a loan; a way to charge a rate of interest higher than the apparent rate.

Consol: A nonmaturing bond, issued (usually) by the British government, that pays coupon interest but is not redeemable.

Coupon yield equivalent: The yield on a T-bill when it is adjusted for a 365-day year, using the bond's market price instead of its face value.

Current yield: The annual coupon interest divided by the current market price of a bond.

Discounted present value: The value today of funds to be received in the future.

Federal funds rate: The interest rate at which federal funds, or interbank loans of reserves, are traded.

Nominal interest rate: The rate of exchange between a dollar today and a dollar at some future date.

Nominal yield: The annual coupon interest divided by the face amount of a bond.

Prime rate: The interest rate charged by banks on short-term loans to the most creditworthy corporations.

Real interest rate: The rate of exchange between real things (goods and services) today and real things at some future period; an interest rate that has been adjusted for expected changes in the price level.

Risk premium: A differential between interest rates on different securities with the same maturity that arises from perceptions of lenders that the securities have differing risks of default.

Risk structure of interest rates: The relationship among yields for bonds that have the same term to maturity but have differing default risks, liquidity, and tax treatment.

Term premium: A yield differential that securities investors and issuers demand for differing maturities.

Term structure of interest rates: The relationship on a specific date between short-term and long-term interest rates for credit instruments that have similar risks.

Treasury bill rate: The percentage discounted from the par value of a T-bill, calculated on a 360-day year.

Yield curve: The relationship that exists on a specific date between nominal interest rates earned by different bonds with similar characteristics but with different maturities.

Yield to maturity: The rate of return that would be earned by holding a bond to maturity. It reflects the bond price, coupon interest earnings, and any capital gain or loss resulting from holding the bond to maturity.

SELF-TEST QUESTIONS

1. Explain, in your own words, what discounting is all about.
2. Explain, in your own words, why the credit supply schedule slopes upward and why the credit demand schedule slopes downward. Also, explain why the market rate of interest is determined at the point at which these two schedules intersect.
3. Compare and contrast alternative theories of the term structure of interest rates.
4. Suppose that a yield curve slopes downward. What would this tell us about expectations of short-term interest rates, according to different theories of the term structure?
5. What is the key distinction between the risk structure of interest rates and the term structure of interest rates?
6. Why is it that the yield to maturity for the same bond differs depending on how long it is until the bond matures? Explain this in words, rather than with formulas.

PROBLEMS

7-1.   What is the value of a consol that promises to pay $100 per year to the holder forever if the rate of interest is (a) 5 percent, (b) 10 percent, (c) 20 percent?

7-2.   Turn to Table 7-1 and estimate the yield to maturity of a bond that has a face value of $1,000, matures in 6 years, has a nominal yield of 6 percent, and is currently selling for $906.10.

7-3.   A 4-year bond has a face value of $1,000 and a nominal yield of 7 percent. If the market rate of interest is currently 10 percent, what is the percent value (or market price) of that bond?

7-4.   Calculate the published T-bill rate for a $10,000, 91-day bill that is sold at auction for $9,700.

7-5.   Calculate the approximate coupon yield equivalent of the T-bill indicated in problem 7-4.

7-6. Calculate the approximate coupon yield equivalent of a 91-day T-bill purchased in a secondary market for $9,700 that matures in 79 days.

7-7. Assume a 10 percent effective coupon yield on the date of issuance of a 91-day T-bill that has a face value of $10,000.
  a. What is its selling price?
  b. What is its selling price 10 days later if interest rates rise to 25 percent?

7-8. Assume that the demand for and supply of funds with no anticipation of inflation is indicated by the functions $r = 15 - q$ and $r = 5 + q$, where r is the interest rate and q is the quantity of funds.
  a. Determine the equilibrium values for q and r.
  b. If usury laws limit the interest rate to 8 percent, what condition would result?
  c. What would be the magnitude of the excess?

7-9. How could one rationally claim (as has been done) that the volume of loans would be expected to increase as a result of the elimination of usury laws (and the subsequent increase in the interest rate)?

7-10. Suppose that the real and nominal interest rates on 1-year contracts are both 4 percent (with no anticipation of inflation).
  a. If the prices of goods are expected to increase by 6 percent over the next year, determine the expected new nominal interest rate.
  b. If the prices of goods are expected to decrease by 6 percent, determine the expected new nominal interest rate.

7-11. Suppose that a nonmaturing bond pays $500 annually.
  a. Determine the expected market price of such a bond if the return on other assets of the same risk is 8 percent.
  b. If the return on other assets increased to 10 percent, would the market price of that bond increase or decrease, and to what amount?

SELECTED REFERENCES

Clayton, Gary E., and Christopher B. Spivey, *The Time Value of Money* (Philadelphia: W. B. Saunders, 1978).

Cook, Timothy, and Thomas Hahn, ''Interest Rate Expectations and the Slope of the Money Market Yield Curve,'' Federal Reserve Bank of Richmond *Economic Review,* 76 (5, September/October 1990), pp. 3–26.

Cuthbertson, Keith, *The Supply and the Demand for Money* (Oxford and New York: Basil Blackwell, 1985).

Fischer, Irving, *The Theory of Interest* (New York: Augustus M. Kelley, 1965).

Forbes, Shawn M., and Lucille S. Mayne, ''A Friction Model of the Prime,'' *Journal of Banking and Finance,* 13 (1, March 1989), pp. 127–135.

Goldberg, Michael A., ''The Pricing of the Prime Rate,'' *Journal of Banking and Finance,* 6 (2, June 1982), pp. 277–296.

———, ''The Sensitivity of the Prime Rate to Money Market Conditions,'' *Journal of Financial Research,* 7 (4, Winter 1984), pp. 269–280.

Gurley, John G., ''Financial Institutions in the Saving-Investment Process,'' *Proceedings of the 1959 Conference on Saving and Residential Financing,* 1959.

Humphrey, Thomas M., ''The Early History of the Real-Nominal Interest Rate Relationship,'' Federal Reserve Bank of Richmond *Economic Review,* 69 (3, May/June 1983), pp. 2–10.

————, ''Can the Central Bank Peg Real Interest Rates? A Survey of Classical and Neoclassical Opinion,'' Federal Reserve Bank of Richmond *Economic Review,* 69 (5, September/October 1983), pp. 12–21.

Malkiel, Burton G., *The Term Structure of Interest Rates: Theory, Empirical Evidence and Application* (Silver Burdett Co., 1970). Reprinted in Thomas M. Havrilesky and J. T. Boorman (eds.), *Current Issues in Monetary Theory and Policy,* 2d ed. (Arlington Heights, Ill.: AHM Publishing Corp., 1980), pp. 395–418.

————, *A Random Walk down Wall Street,* 4th ed. (New York: W. W. Norton, 1985).

Munn, Glenn G., F. L. Garcia, and Charles J. Woelfel, *Encyclopedia of Banking and Finance,* 9th ed. (Rolling Meadows, Ill.: Bankers Publishing Company, 1991).

Rowe, Timothy D., Thomas A. Lawler, and Timothy Q. Cook, ''Treasury Bill versus Private Money Market Yield Curves,'' Federal Reserve Bank of Richmond *Economic Review,* 72 (4, July/August 1986), pp. 3–12.

Simmons, Richard D., ''Would Banks Buy Daytime Fed Funds?'' Federal Reserve Bank of Chicago *Economic Perspectives,* 11 (3, May/June 1987), pp. 36-43.

Spindt, Paul A., and J. Ronald Hoffmeister, ''The Micromechanics of the Federal Funds Market: Implications for Day-of-the-Week Effects in Funds Rate Volatility,'' *Journal of Financial and Quantitative Analysis,* 23 (4, December 1988), pp. 401–416.

Stigum, Marcia, *The Money Market,* 2d ed. (Homewood, Ill.: Dow Jones-Irwin, 1983).

VanHoose, David D., ''Bank Behavior, Interest Rate Determination, and Monetary Policy in a Financial System with an Intraday Federal Funds Market,'' *Journal of Banking and Finance,* 15 (2, April 1991), pp. 343–365.

UNIT 3

Depository Institutions
and Their
Environments

The Economic Behavior
of Depository Institutions

CHAPTER PREVIEW

1. In a simple model of bank behavior with only loans and deposits, what is a bank's balance sheet constraint? What are its sources of revenues and costs?

2. How is the loan supply schedule for an individual bank determined? How do we derive the loan market supply schedule and analyze loan market equilibrium?

3. How is the deposit demand schedule for an individual bank determined? How do we derive the deposit market demand schedule and analyze deposit market equilibrium?

4. Why are bank loan and deposit markets interdependent? Why is this interdependence important?

5. How do we analyze bank behavior in monopolistic markets?

To understand issues concerning the banking industry and its regulation, it is necessary for us to construct a theory of how banks make decisions and of how they interact in markets for financial instruments that they hold as assets and issue as liabilities. This chapter is devoted to this task.

Banks and other depository institutions are businesses. Economists assume that banks, like any other business, seek to maximize their profits. In this chapter, our goal is to explain the economic theory of the behavior of depository institutions in markets for loans and deposits. To do this, we shall apply concepts from principles of microeconomics concerning theories of firm behavior, perfect competition, and monopoly.

As we shall see in later chapters, the theories we develop in this chapter will be useful to us in a variety of contexts. Therefore, we encourage you to persevere as you read the material in this chapter. This material represents straightforward applications of the theories of markets that you learned in your introductory economics course to the issue of banking markets. The key to understanding these theories is to *practice* using them, and so we particularly encourage you to work through the Self-Test Questions and Problems at the end as you read the chapter.

A MODEL DEPOSITORY INSTITUTION

As you learned in Chapter 6, depository institutions typically have numerous assets and liabilities. In this chapter, however, our goal is to understand the basic economics of bank decision making. For this reason, we shall simplify a great deal by considering a very simple depository institution. We shall also simplify our terminology a little by referring to this depository institution as a ''bank.'' Keep in mind, though, that the economic model we shall develop can also be used to describe the behavior of thrift institutions.

THE BANK BALANCE SHEET

Our simple ''bank'' specializes in two tasks. First, it issues checking deposits to customers. The bank pays interest to all its depositors. Hence, all the deposits it issues are identical NOW-account-type deposits; the bank issues no demand deposits subject to a zero interest restriction. Furthermore, these checking deposits are the only source of funds for this bank, which, for the sake of simplicity, issues no shares of stock. This is perhaps the most unrealistic assumption we shall make, but it makes our model much simpler and, therefore, easier to understand. Another assumption we make is that the deposits issued by the bank are not subject to legal reserve requirements, and so the bank can lend out all deposits it receives, if it so chooses.

The bank uses deposit funds for its second task, which is making a specific type of loan, such as commercial loans. All the loans the bank makes are of this type, and the bank's loan customers are similar; for instance, no one customer exhibits particularly more or less risk of default. Furthermore, all the loans have the same maturity, which we shall just think of as a ''period'' in length. In return for making these one-period loans, the bank receives interest payments from its borrowers.

Under these assumptions, this clearly is a very simple bank to think about. It has one category of liabilities, checking deposits, and one category of assets, commercial loans.

Shortly, we shall think about the interactions of this particular bank with other banks in markets for loans and deposits. For this reason, we shall find it helpful to have some special notation to denote our specific bank. Our bank might have a long and fancy name, such as National City Federal Bank and Trust Company, but we would find it cumbersome to carry along such a long name for our model bank, and so we shall just think of it as ''bank j.''

Let us suppose that, at a point in time, the total dollar amount of interest-bearing checking deposits at bank j is equal to the quantity D_j. This amount might, for instance, be equal to $100 million. Likewise, let us denote bank j's lending as the dollar quantity L_j. Because our simple bank only issues deposits and makes loans, the entire amount of lending by bank j must be equal to the total amount of deposit funds it has obtained from its deposit customers. That is, if the amount of checking deposits held at the bank is equal to $100 million, that is the amount that the bank can lend. This means that, in general, if the bank has received a dollar amount of deposits D_j and makes a dollar amount of loans L_j, it must be the case that these two quantities are equal:

$$L_j = D_j \qquad\qquad (8\text{-}1)$$

Equation (8-1) is the bank's **balance sheet constraint;** it says that our bank cannot issue more loans than deposits. Indeed, assets and liabilities must be equal at bank j, and so loans must equal deposits.

BANK REVENUES, COSTS, AND PROFITS

The owners of bank j are in the banking business for a purpose: They wish to earn income in the form of **economic profits.** The economic profits of any business firm, of course, are revenues less economic costs. (Recall that *accounting profits* are the difference between revenues and *explicit costs* incurred by a firm, while economic profits are the difference between revenues and *economic costs,* which include both explicit costs and *implicit opportunity costs* a firm incurs by being in its chosen line of business instead of an alternative line of business.) Let us consider the revenues and economic costs of bank j.

Bank Revenues

Bank Revenues   For bank j, there is a single source of revenues: the interest it receives from its commercial and industrial lending activities. Suppose that the one-period interest rate on loans made by the bank is equal to a rate r_L. Then the total interest return earned by the bank on its total quantity of one-period loans must be equal to $r_L \times L_j$.

For instance, if the bank extends $100 million in commercial and industrial loans and the one-period loan interest rate it receives per dollar lent is $0.10 in interest per $1.00 in loans, or 0.10 (10 percent), then the bank's total interest earned for the period is equal to $0.10 \times \$100$ million, which equals $10 million. This amount would represent the total revenues received by the bank for that period.

Consequently, for bank j, total revenues earned during a given time period, denoted TR_j, are equal to

$$TR_j = r_L \times L_j \tag{8-2}$$

Equation (8-2) says that, for our model bank, total revenues during a given period are equal to the interest earnings received on the commercial and industrial loans it makes to its loan customers.

Bank Costs

Bank Costs   Any bank incurs three basic types of expenses, or costs. One is explicit **interest expenses.** To raise funds to use in its lending activities—that is, to have any hope of earning any revenues from making loans—the bank must issue checking deposits, and it must, if the deposits are NOW-account-type deposits, compensate its depositors by paying them interest. If the one-period interest rate that bank j pays is equal to r_D, then the total deposit interest expense that the bank incurs during a given period is equal to $r_D \times D_j$. For example, if the one-period deposit interest rate is $0.07 per $1.00 in deposits, or 0.07 (7 percent), and the amount of checking deposits it issues during a period is $100 million, then the bank's interest expense for that period is equal to $0.07 \times \$100$ million, or $7 million.

Banks cannot take in deposits and make loans without using real resources, however. People must be involved: The bank must hire tellers to take in deposits and credit managers to make and process loans. These people require office supplies, equipment, and furniture to accomplish these tasks. Hence, in addition to deposit interest expenses, banks also incur **real resource expenses.** Real resource expenses include *explicit costs* that the bank must incur in its day-to-day operations. Employees must be paid wages and salaries, and other factors of production must be purchased or leased if the bank is to perform its operations effectively and maximize profits. In addition, however, the bank incurs *opportunity costs;* it could be devoting its factors of production to alternative uses, and so it incurs an implicit real opportunity cost. Real resource costs for any firm include both explicit and opportunity costs—economists call these **economic costs**—and the same is true for banking.

Let us denote the total dollar amount of the economic costs of real resources devoted to the bank's efforts to obtain deposits (for instance, expenses on advertising its deposit services) and to service its depositors' accounts (for example, costs incurred in clearing the checks written by its depositors) as RC_D. The total real resource cost associated with the bank's deposit activities is a *function* of the total amount of deposits issued by the bank, because as the amount of deposits issued increases, the bank's total real deposit

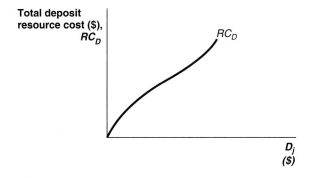

Figure 8-1
The Total Resource Cost of Deposits.   As the amount of deposits issued increases, the bank's total real deposit resource expenses incurred also increase. The reason is that when the bank issues more deposits, it must clear more checks, hire more tellers, and so on. As a result, its expenses on factors of production in servicing its deposit accounts, such as wages and salaries paid to bank employees, must increase. Hence, the total real resource cost associated with the bank's deposit activities is a *function* of the total amount of deposits issued by the bank.

resource expenses incurred also increase; when the bank issues more deposits, it must clear more checks, hire more tellers, and so on, and so its expenses on factors of production in servicing its deposit accounts must increase, as shown in Figure 8-1.

Making loans also requires that the bank incur economic costs through expenses on real resources. We denote the total dollar amount of the real resource cost incurred by bank j in its lending activities as RC_L. As shown in Figure 8-2, the total real resource cost of making loans must rise with the amount of loans made by the bank; when the bank makes more loans, it must, for example, hire more credit analysts and loan managers. Therefore, the bank's total real resource expenses must increase as its dollar amount of lending rises.

The *total economic costs of bank operations* for bank j, then, must be equal to

$$TC_j = (r_D \times D_j) + RC_D + RC_L \qquad (8\text{-}3)$$

Equation (8-3) says that the total cost incurred by the bank is the sum of three components: total deposit interest expense, total real resource costs incurred in servicing its customers' deposit accounts, and total real resource expenses incurred in making and processing loans.

Bank Profits   As for any business firm, a bank's economic profits are equal to total revenues less total economic costs. For bank j, the amount of profit earned during a period, then, is equal to $TR_j - TC_j$. Bank j's economic profits, then, are determined by subtracting equation (8-3) from equation (8-2):

$$TR_j - TC_j = (r_L \times L_j) - (r_D \times D_j) - RC_D - RC_L \qquad (8\text{-}4)$$

Equation (8-4) tells us that the profits earned by the bank are loan interest revenues less deposit expenses, real deposit resource costs, and real loan resource costs. Therefore, it tells us some very important facts about depository institution behavior. First of all, interest rates are very important to banks, because they affect both the banks' revenues

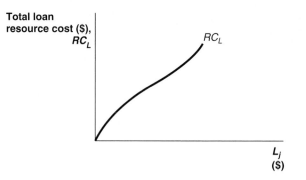

Figure 8-2
The Total Resource Cost of Loans.   As the amount of bank lending increases, the bank's total real loan resource expenses incurred also increase. The reason is that when the bank makes more loans, it must hire more loan managers and credit analysts, gather more information on prospective borrowers, and so on. As a result, its expenses on factors of production used in its loan function must increase. Hence, the total real resource cost associated with the bank's lending activities is a *function* of the total amount of lending by the bank.

and their expenses. A commonplace view is that banks benefit from higher interest rates. Equation (8-4) tells us, however, that if both the interest rate earned on loans and the interest rate paid on deposits increase, then a bank's revenues and its costs both increase, and the bank's economic profits may rise or fall; in theory, then, banks may either gain or lose profits when there is a general rise in interest rates. Holding all other things constant, a bank's profits rise from a general increase in interest rates only if loan rates rise more than deposit rates.

Equation (8-4) also tells us that a very important issue to banks must be their expenditures on real resources. Banking is not just a business of making loans at "high" interest rates and taking in deposit funds at "low" interest rates to earn the highest possible profit—though this certainly is part of the main goal of banking. Loans must be made by people (bank employees) using other factors of production, and deposits must be issued and services provided by people (other bank employees) using other factors of production, and expenses on all these resources have a major bearing on the profitability of banks.

DEPOSITORY INSTITUTIONS IN COMPETITIVE MARKETS

Banks and other depository institutions seek, naturally, to maximize their economic profits. How they go about doing this depends crucially on the market environment in which they find themselves. In most of this chapter, we shall assume that banking markets are *perfectly competitive*. This means that bank j is one of *many* banks issuing checking deposits and making commercial and industrial loans. In addition, its customers view it as no better or worse than any of the other banks in the markets for its deposits and loans; the deposits bank j and other banks issue, therefore, are perceived as *homogeneous,* as are the loans made by it and other banks. Finally, bank j and other banks have access to the same technologies for employing people and other factors of production in their banking tasks; no single bank has better access to banking technologies or to factors of bank deposit and loan production than any other bank.

MARGINAL REVENUE, MARGINAL COST, AND BANK PROFIT MAXIMIZATION

Any bank, whether or not it is a participant in perfectly competitive loan and deposit markets, must decide the dollar volume of deposits to issue and how much lending to do. It does so with an aim to maximize its economic profits. In turn, a bank's profits are maximized when the bank lends to the point at which the last dollar of deposits raised by the bank and lent to a loan customer yields zero economic profit to the bank. The reason is that if the economic profit earned on the last dollar lent were positive, it would pay—in terms of profitability—for the bank to lend another dollar of deposit funds. If the economic profit earned on the last dollar lent were negative—meaning that lending that last dollar would reduce the bank's total profits—then the bank's total profits could be increased by lending one less dollar of deposit funds.

The Marginal Revenue Schedule   Therefore, bank profit maximization requires that the bank make loans to the point at which the additional revenues earned on the last dollar of loans made to its customers is just equal to the additional costs incurred on that last dollar it lends. The additional revenue earned on the last additional dollar of loans is a bank's *marginal revenue* (MR). For a bank, whose revenues and loans are measured in dollar terms, units of measurement for marginal revenue are dollars per dollar ($/$). Hence, marginal revenue for a bank is measured as fractions, which we can convert to percentages.

Under perfect competition, the amount of lending by an individual bank is so small relative to the total amount of lending by all banks that an individual bank cannot affect the market loan rate. Hence, for a given bank, such as bank j, marginal revenue is equal to the interest rate earned on the next dollar lent, which is the market loan interest rate, r_L. Hence, $MR_j = r_L$ for bank j. As shown in Figure 8-3, this means that the bank's *marginal revenue* (MR_j) *schedule*, which is a set of all combinations of marginal revenue and dollar amounts of lending, is horizontal; that is, the bank's marginal revenue is constant and equal to r_L no matter how much lending the bank does.

The Marginal Cost Schedule   Recall that a bank's total cost is the sum of three components: total deposit interest expense, total deposit resource costs, and total loan resource costs. It follows that a bank's *marginal cost*, which is the addition to the bank's total cost from obtaining an additional dollar of deposits to lend in the market for loans, must also be the sum of three types of marginal costs: marginal deposit interest expense, marginal deposit resource costs, and marginal loan resource costs.

The marginal deposit interest expense incurred by a bank is the additional interest it must pay per dollar of deposits. As long as the deposit market is perfectly competitive, so that the actions by the individual bank cannot influence the market deposit interest rate, r_D, this market interest rate is the marginal interest expense that the bank must incur per dollar of deposits it uses to make loans. For example, Figure 8-4 plots a marginal interest expense schedule for bank j if the market deposit rate is 7 percent; it is horizontal at $r_D = \$0.07/\$1.00 = 0.07$, meaning that no matter how many dollars in deposits are issued by bank j, the marginal interest expense the bank incurs is constant and equal to this market deposit rate.

We assume that, as is true for most firms, the short-run marginal deposit resource cost schedule for bank j, labeled MC_D, generally slopes upward against the total quantity of deposits issued by the bank, as shown in Figure 8-5. This means that as the bank issues more deposits, the additional dollar cost, per dollar of deposits, of servicing deposits (providing teller services and clearing checks) rises in the short run (a period short enough

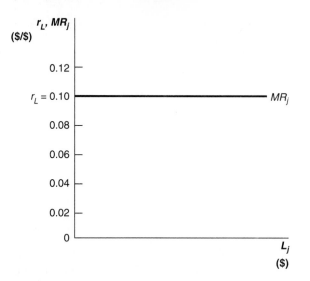

Figure 8-3
A Perfectly Competitive Bank's Marginal Revenue Schedule.   The additional revenue earned on the last additional dollar of loans made by a bank is the bank's marginal revenue. Under perfect competition, the amount of lending by an individual bank is so small relative to the total amount of lending by all banks that an individual bank cannot affect the market loan rate. Hence, for a given bank, such as bank j, marginal revenue is equal to the interest rate earned on the next dollar lent, which is the market loan interest rate r_L. Hence, $MR_j = r_L$ for bank j, and the marginal revenue schedule is horizontal; that is, the bank's marginal revenue is constant and equal to r_L no matter how much lending the bank does.

Figure 8-4
A Competitive Bank's Marginal Interest Expense Schedule.   The marginal deposit interest expense incurred by a bank is the additional interest it must pay per dollar of deposits. In a perfectly competitive deposit market, in which actions by an individual bank cannot influence the market deposit interest rate, this market interest rate, $r_D = \$0.07/\$1.00 = 0.07$, is the marginal interest expense that the bank must incur per dollar of deposits it uses to make loans. Hence, the marginal interest expense the bank incurs is constant and equal to this market deposit rate.

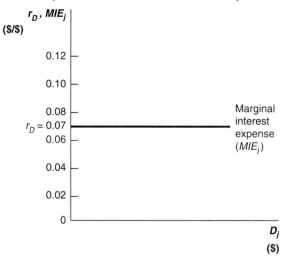

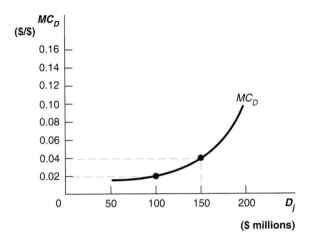

Figure 8-5
A Bank's Marginal Deposit Resource Cost Schedule.   As a bank issues more deposits, the additional dollar cost, per dollar of deposits, of servicing deposits increases. For bank j, it is the case that the real resource cost incurred on the 100 millionth dollar of deposits is equal to $0.02 of real resource expenses per $1.00 of deposits, or 0.02 (2 percent), while for the 150 millionth dollar it is $0.04 per $1.00, or 0.04 (4 percent). Hence, the marginal deposit resource cost schedule for bank j, labeled MC_D, slopes upward against the total quantity of deposits issued by the bank.

that some of the bank's factors of production are fixed). For example, Figure 8-5 indicates that for bank j it is the case that the real resource cost incurred on the 100 millionth dollar of deposits is equal to $0.02 of real resource expenses per $1.00 of deposits, or 0.02 (2 percent), while for the 150 millionth dollar it is $0.04 per $1.00, or 0.04 (4 percent).

Likewise, the marginal loan resource cost schedule, MC_L, slopes upward against the quantity of loans made by the bank. For instance, Figure 8-6 shows that, for bank j, the 100 millionth dollar of loans costs the bank $0.01 worth of real resource expenses per $1.00 of loans, or 0.01 (1 percent), while the 150 millionth dollar of loans costs the bank $0.02 per $1.00 of loans, or 0.02 (2 percent).

Figure 8-7 shows the construction of the bank's marginal cost schedule. By definition, marginal cost for the bank is given by

$$MC_j = r_D + MC_D + MC_L \tag{8-4}$$

That is, marginal cost is the sum of marginal interest expense, marginal deposit resource cost, and marginal loan resource cost. Therefore, the bank's marginal cost schedule is the sum of the schedules in Figures 8-4, 8-5, and 8-6. For the 100 millionth dollar of deposits, marginal deposit interest expense is, from Figure 8-4, equal to the market deposit rate, $r_D = \$0.07/\$1.00 = 0.07$, and marginal deposit resource cost is, as shown in Figure 8-5, equal to $0.02/$1.00 = 0.02. From the bank's balance sheet constraint, equation (8-1), we know that if the bank has $100 million in deposits, it also has $100 million in loans. Therefore, we also know, from Figure 8-6, that the bank incurs a marginal loan resource cost of $0.01/$1.00 = 0.01. Adding these three marginal expense components together, we deduce that, for the 100 millionth dollar of lending done by bank j, its marginal cost is equal to ($0.07 + $0.02 + $0.01) per $1.00, or $0.10/$1.00 = 0.10 (10 percent).

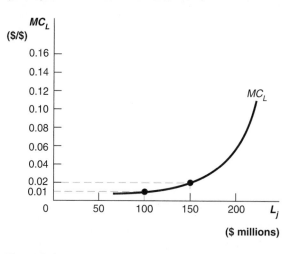

Figure 8-6
A Bank's Marginal Real Loan Resource Cost Schedule.   For bank j, the 100 millionth dollar of loans costs the bank $0.01 worth of real resource expenses per $1.00 of loans, or 0.01 (1 percent), while the 150 millionth dollar of loans costs the bank $0.02 per $1.00 of loans, or 0.02 (2 percent). For bank j or any other typical bank, the marginal loan resource cost schedule, MC_L, slopes upward against the quantity of loans made by the bank.

By similar reasoning, we can determine that for the 150 millionth dollar lent by the bank, the marginal cost is equal to ($0.07 + $0.04 + $0.02) per $1.00, or $0.13/$1.00 = 0.13 (13 percent). Hence, we have determined two combinations of marginal cost and total lending by bank j that lie on the bank's *marginal cost* (MC_j) *schedule* shown in Figure 8-7.

The Profit-Maximizing Quantity of Loans and the Bank's Loan Supply Schedule   We can now determine how many dollars in loans that bank j will desire to make if its goal is to maximize its profits. Figure 8-8 shows the determination of the profit-maximizing quantity of lending by bank j. As we discussed earlier, to maximize its total profits the bank extends loans to the point at which marginal revenue ($MR_j = r_L = 0.10$) is equal to marginal cost ($MC_j = r_D + MC_D + MC_L$), or, in equation form,

$$r_L = r_D + MC_D + MC_L \tag{8-5}$$

where $r_L = 0.10$ in this case. This equality occurs at the point at which the bank's marginal revenue schedule intersects its marginal cost schedule, which is the single point at which $MR_j = MC_j = 0.10$, at $100 million. Hence, the profit-maximizing amount of lending by bank j is $100 million when the market loan interest rate is equal to 0.10 (10 percent).

What will bank j do if the market loan interest rate changes, holding all other things (including the market deposit rate) constant? Specifically, let us consider in Figure 8-9 what happens if the market loan rate rises to $r_L = 0.13$ (13 percent). Before the rise in the loan rate, when the loan rate was equal to 0.10 (10 percent), the profit-maximizing quantity of lending was $100 million. The rise in the loan rate to a new level of 0.13, however, results in a higher marginal revenue for any given amount of lending the bank might undertake; that is, the marginal revenue schedule shifts upward, as shown in Figure

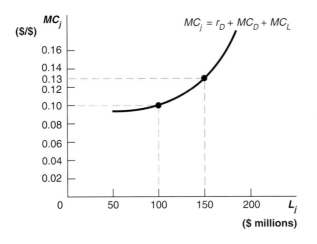

Figure 8-7
A Bank's Marginal Cost Schedule. For a bank, marginal cost is the sum of marginal interest expense, marginal deposit resource cost, and marginal loan resource cost. From Figure 8-4, the 100 millionth dollar of deposits requires the marginal deposit interest equal to the market deposit rate, r_D = $0.07/$1.00 = 0.07. From Figure 8-5 the bank's marginal deposit resource cost for the 100 millionth deposit dollar is equal to $0.02/$1.00 = 0.02. We know from the bank's balance sheet constraint that if the bank has $100 million in deposits, it also has $100 million in loans; therefore, we also know, from Figure 8-6, that the bank incurs a marginal loan resource cost of $0.01/$1.00 = 0.01. Adding these three marginal expense components together, we deduce that, for the 100 millionth dollar of lending done by bank j, its marginal cost is equal to ($0.07 + $0.02 + $0.01) per $1.00, or $0.10/$1.00 = 0.10 (10 percent).

Likewise, we can determine from Figures 8-4, 8-5, and 8-6 that for the 150 millionth dollar lent by the bank, the marginal cost is equal to ($0.07 + $0.04 + $0.02) per $1.00, or $0.13/$1.00 = 0.13 (13 percent).

This yields two combinations of marginal cost and total lending by bank j that lie on bank j's marginal cost (MC_j) schedule.

8-9. This means that the profit-maximizing level of lending must rise to a higher level corresponding to a new point at which marginal revenue equals marginal cost, or where MR_j = MC_j = 0.13. At this new point, as Figure 8-9 indicates, the profit-maximizing quantity of loans for bank j is equal to $150 million.

Note that, in Figure 8-9, a rise in the market loan rate (from 0.10 to 0.13) caused bank j to move along its marginal cost schedule from one initial profit-maximizing loan quantity ($100 million) to another ($150 million). Points along the marginal cost schedule tell us combinations of loan rates and loan quantities that maximize bank j's profits. In other words, the bank's marginal cost schedule tells us the profit-maximizing quantities of loans that bank j will *supply* at different loan interest rates. This means that over most of its length the marginal cost schedule is bank j's *loan supply schedule*. (Of course, if the loan rate falls to a level at which the bank is unable to cover its variable costs of banking operations, it will shut down, so that not all of the lower part of the marginal cost schedule is part of the bank's supply schedule; as a simplification, however, we assume that the loan rate never falls below the *shut-down point* for the bank.) A rise in the market loan rate induces the bank to supply more loans along this schedule; if the market loan rate were to fall again, the bank would choose to supply fewer loans.

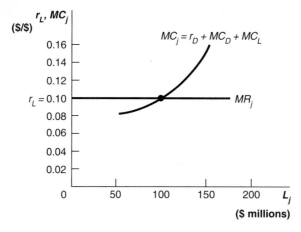

Figure 8-8

A Competitive Bank's Profit-Maximizing Lending Level.   To maximize its total profits the bank makes loans to the point at which marginal revenue ($MR_j = r_L = 0.10$) is equal to marginal cost ($MC_j = r_D + MC_D + MC_L$). This equality occurs at the point at which the bank's marginal revenue schedule intersects its marginal cost schedule, which, for bank j, is the single point at which $MR_j = MC_j = 0.10$, at $100 million. Therefore, the profit-maximizing amount of lending by bank j is $100 million when the market loan interest rate is equal to 0.10 (10 percent).

Figure 8-9

A Competitive Bank's Loan Supply Schedule.   A rise in the loan rate, from an initial value of 0.10 to a new level of 0.13, results in a higher marginal revenue for any given amount of lending the bank might undertake. Therefore, the marginal revenue schedule shifts upward. This means that the profit-maximizing level of lending must rise from the initial level of $100 million to a higher level of $150 million. Thus, the rise in the market loan rate (from 0.10 to 0.13) causes bank j to move along its marginal cost schedule from one initial profit-maximizing loan quantity ($100 million) to another ($150 million). This means the bank's marginal cost schedule gives us combinations of loan rates and loan quantities that maximize bank j's profits; that is, it tells us the profit-maximizing quantities of loans that bank j will *supply* at different loan interest rates. The marginal cost schedule is bank j's loan supply schedule. A rise in the market loan rate induces the bank to supply more loans along this schedule; a fall in the market loan rate would induce the bank to supply fewer loans.

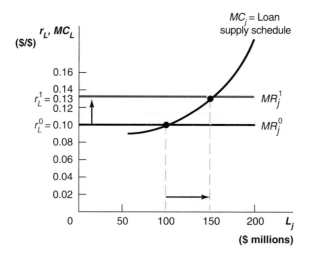

The Profit-Maximizing Quantity of Deposits and the Bank's Deposit Demand Schedule   Now that we have determined that the profit-maximizing quantity of loans at a loan rate of 10 percent is $100 million, it is tempting to look at the balance sheet constraint in equation (8-1) and conclude that, obviously, this must also be the profit-maximizing quantity of deposits at this loan rate. Likewise, because the profit-maximizing amount of lending at a loan rate of 13 percent is $150 million, that amount must be the profit-maximizing quantity of deposits at that higher loan rate. Indeed, these are the correct answers, as we shall see. It turns out, however, that we can say much more than this based on the theory we have developed.

We know that, from equation (8-5), bank j's profits are maximized when $r_L = r_D + MC_D + MC_L$. If we subtract MC_D and MC_L from both sides of this equation, we get $r_L - (MC_D + MC_L) = r_D$, or

$$r_D = r_L - (MC_D + MC_L) \tag{8-6}$$

This equation says that when bank j's profits are maximized, it must be true that the interest rate bank j pays on its deposits is equal to the interest rate it earns on loans less the sum of the marginal deposit and loan resource costs. Recall that the left-hand side of equation (8-6), the interest rate on deposits, is the marginal interest expense incurred by the bank. The difference on the right-hand side of this equation is the loan rate, or the bank's constant marginal revenue, less the combination of marginal loan and deposit resource costs. We call the difference on the right-hand side of equation (8-6) the *net marginal revenue* the bank earns on an additional dollar of deposits it issues. Hence, equation (8-6) says that a bank maximizes profits by issuing deposits up to the point at which marginal deposit interest expense (the deposit interest rate) is equal to the net marginal revenue the bank earns by using the last dollar of deposits issued to make a loan.

Figure 8-10 shows the bank's profit-maximizing deposit choice. As in Figure 8-4, we have drawn it under the assumption that the market deposit rate r_D is equal to 0.07 (7 percent). Because the deposit rate is determined in a perfectly competitive deposit market, bank j's *marginal interest expense* (MIE$_j$) *schedule* is horizontal at $r_D = 0.07$.

Also drawn in Figure 8-10 is a downward-sloping schedule depicting the net marginal revenue from deposits for bank j, or the bank's *net marginal revenue* (NMR$_j$) *schedule*. To derive this schedule, we have assumed that, as in our initial example, the market loan rate is 0.10 (10 percent), and we have subtracted from this constant loan rate the marginal loan and deposit resource costs at each possible level of deposits issued by the bank. For example, as we saw in Figure 8-5, bank j's marginal deposit resource cost was 0.02 for the 100 millionth dollar of deposits, and its marginal loan resource cost was, as shown in Figure 8-6, 0.01 for the 100 millionth dollar of loans, which, from the bank's balance sheet constraint in equation (8-1), would correspond to the 100 millionth dollar of deposits. Subtracting $(0.02 + 0.01)$ from the loan rate of 0.10, we have 0.07 as the bank's net marginal revenue from deposits, as depicted in Figure 8-10. Likewise, for the 150 millionth dollar of deposits, its marginal deposit and loan costs are 0.04 and 0.02, respectively, and so its net marginal revenue from deposits for the 150 millionth dollar of deposits is equal to $0.10 - (0.04 + 0.02) = 0.04$, as shown in Figure 8-10.

Figure 8-10 shows us that, for bank j, the profit-maximizing quantity of deposits for a market loan rate of 0.10 and a market deposit rate of 0.07 is equal to $100 million. At this quantity of deposits, the marginal interest expense schedule intersects the net marginal revenue schedule in Figure 8-10, so that equation (8-6) is satisfied, meaning that bank j's profits are maximized. This answer is reassuring, because that is the profit-maximizing quantity of loans that Figure 8-8 indicated the bank would choose at these two market

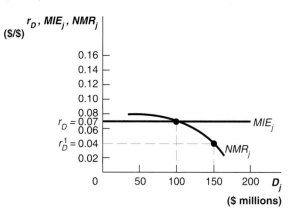

Figure 8-10
A Competitive Bank's Profit-Maximizing Deposit Choice.   If the market deposit rate, r_D, is equal to 0.07 (7 percent), bank j's marginal interest expense (MIE$_j$) schedule is horizontal at $r_D = 0.07$. The bank's net marginal revenue (NMR$_j$) schedule is derived by subtracting from the market loan rate of 0.10 (10 percent) the marginal loan and deposit resource costs at each possible level of deposits issued by the bank. For example, in Figure 8-5, bank j's marginal deposit resource cost is 0.02 for the 100 millionth dollar of deposits, and its marginal loan resource cost is, from Figure 8-6, equal to 0.01 for the 100 millionth dollar of loans. Subtracting (0.02 + 0.01) from the loan rate of 0.10, we have 0.07 as the bank's net marginal revenue from deposits, as shown. Likewise, for the 150 millionth dollar of deposits, the bank's marginal deposit and loan costs are 0.04 and 0.02, respectively, and so its net marginal revenue from deposits for the 150 millionth dollar of deposits is equal to 0.10 − (0.04 + 0.02) = 0.04. As indicated, for bank j the profit-maximizing quantity of deposits for a market loan rate of 0.10 and a market deposit rate of 0.07 is equal to $100 million.

interest rates. Note that this answer also makes *sense*, because equation (8-6) is just a rearrangement of equation (8-5), and so the intersection point in Figure 8-10, which corresponds to equation (8-6), must give us the same dollar quantity—given the bank's balance sheet constraint that loans must equal deposits—as the intersection point in Figure 8-8, which corresponds to equation (8-5).

Why have we gone to all the additional trouble to put together Figure 8-10, given that we could have just looked at Figure 8-8 to reach the conclusion that the bank makes $100 million in loans—and therefore issues $100 million in deposits—given a loan rate of 0.10 and a deposit rate of 0.07? The answer is that Figure 8-10 does give us some additional, and important, information. To see this, suppose that the market interest rate on deposits, r_D falls from 0.07 to 0.04, holding all other factors including the loan rate constant, as shown in Figure 8-11.

If the deposit rate falls to 0.04, then the bank's marginal interest expense schedule shifts downward. As a result, marginal interest expense equals net deposit marginal revenue at a higher quantity of deposits. Specifically, as indicated in Figure 8-11, the bank's new profit-maximizing quantity of deposits at this lower deposit rate of 0.04 is equal to $150 million. The fall in the deposit rate has caused the bank to increase the quantity of deposits *demanded*. This means that, over most of its range, the bank's net deposit marginal revenue schedule is the bank's *deposit demand schedule*. As the market deposit rate falls, the bank demands more deposits along this schedule; if the market deposit rate were to rise again, the bank would decrease the quantity of deposits demanded.

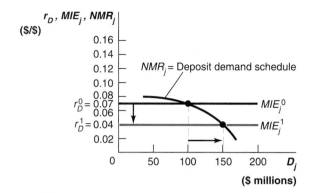

Figure 8-11

A Competitive Bank's Deposit Demand Schedule.   If the market interest rate on deposits falls from 0.07 to 0.04, holding all other factors including the loan rate constant, then the bank's marginal interest expense schedule shifts downward, and the marginal interest expense equals net deposit marginal revenue at a higher quantity of deposits. Hence, the bank's profit-maximizing quantity of deposits rises from $100 million to $150 million. Because the fall in the deposit rate has caused the bank to increase the quantity of deposits *demanded* along the bank's net deposit marginal revenue schedule, this schedule is the bank's deposit demand schedule.

As the market deposit rate falls, the bank demands more deposits along this schedule; if the market deposit rate were to rise, the bank would decrease the quantity of deposits demanded.

THE MARKETS FOR LOANS AND DEPOSITS

Now that we have analyzed an individual bank's loan supply and deposit demand decisions, we shall next turn our attention to how the ''market'' interest rates on loans and deposits that banks take as given actually get determined. In a competitive market, as we shall explain, they are determined by the interaction of the forces of demand and supply.

THE MARKET FOR BANK LOANS

Market exchanges are made by buyers and sellers of goods and services. In the market for bank loans, the sellers of loans are banks. Hence, banks *supply* loans. The borrowers of loans are their customers who *demand* loans. Let us consider the supply and demand sides of the loan market in turn.

The Market Loan Supply Schedule   In a competitive market for any good or service, the market supply schedule is simply the horizontal summation of the supply schedules for all producers of that good or service. That is, we can sum the quantities producers desire to supply at each possible price to obtain a set of price-quantity combinations that constitute a total market supply schedule.

We can do the same thing using our model of bank behavior, in which banks are loan producers. As we discussed above and showed in Figure 8-9, an individual bank j's marginal cost schedule is its loan supply schedule. We reproduce bank j's loan supply schedule, for the case in which the market deposit rate is equal to 0.07, in panel (*a*) of Figure 8-12. In addition, we show the supply schedule for another bank, bank k, in panel (*b*). The total demand for loans by banks j and k is constructed in panel (*c*) of Figure

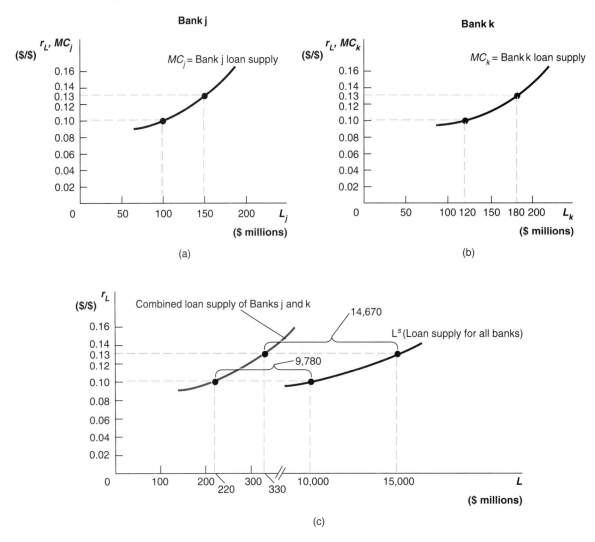

Figure 8-12

The Market Loan Supply Schedule.   When the interest rate on loans is equal to 0.10, bank j desires to supply $100 million in loans [panel (a)], while bank k wishes to lend $120 million [panel (b)]. Consequently, in panel (c), the total amount of desired lending by the two banks is equal to $220 million when the loan interest rate is 0.10. Likewise, if the loan rate rises to 0.13, bank j desires to supply $150 million in loans [panel (a)], and bank k desires to supply $180 million in loans [panel (b)], and so the total desired lending by the two banks is equal to $330 million at this higher loan interest rate [panel (c)]. The schedule in panel (c) containing the loan rate–loan quantity combinations for these two banks—0.10 and $220 million, and 0.13 and $330 million—is the total loan supply schedule for the two banks.

The remaining banks in the loan market desire to supply $9,780 million in loans at a loan rate of 0.10 and $14,670 million in loans at a loan rate of 0.13. Hence, the total quantity of loans supplied by all banks—including bank j and bank k—at a loan rate of 0.10 is equal to $10,000 million, or $10 billion. The total quantity of loans supplied by all banks at a loan rate of 0.13 is equal to $15,000 million, or $15 billion. The final schedule labeled L^s in panel (c), then, is the market loan supply schedule.

8-12. When the interest rate on loans is equal to 0.10, bank j desires to supply $100 million in loans [panel (*a*)], while bank k wishes to lend $120 million [panel (*b*)]. Consequently, in panel (*c*), the total amount of lending by the two banks is equal to $220 million when the loan interest rate is 0.10. Likewise, if the loan rate rises to 0.13, bank j desires to supply $150 million in loans [panel (*a*)], and bank k desires to supply $180 million in loans [panel (*b*)], and so the total lending by the two banks is equal to $330 million at this higher loan interest rate [panel (*c*)]. The schedule in panel (*c*) of Figure 8-12 containing the loan rate–loan quantity combinations for these two banks—0.10 and $220 million, and 0.13 and $330 million—is the total loan supply schedule for the two banks.

In a competitive market, numerous banks supply loans in addition to bank j and bank k. Consequently, the total *market loan supply schedule* (L^s) is the sum of the total quantities of lending by all banks in the loan market at every possible loan interest rate. As shown in panel (*c*) of Figure 8-12, the remaining banks in the loan market desire to supply $9,780 million in loans at a loan rate of 0.10 and $14,670 million in loans at a loan rate of 0.13. Hence, the total quantity of loans supplied by all banks—including bank j and bank k— at a loan rate of 0.10 is equal to $10,000 million, or $10 billion. The total quantity of loans supplied by all banks at a loan rate of 0.13 is equal to $15,000 million, or $15 billion. The final schedule constructed in panel (*c*) of Figure 8-12, then, is the market loan supply schedule and is labeled L^s.

The Demand for Loans by the Nonbank Public   Banks make loans to individual households and firms, which economists refer to collectively as the **nonbank public.** Each household and firm has its own loan demand schedule, which, via the law of demand, slopes downward. We can sum the quantities of loans demanded by the nonbank public at any given loan interest rate to construct the *market loan demand schedule* (L^d). A possible market loan demand schedule is shown in panel (*a*) of Figure 8-13.

Loan Market Equilibrium   Also shown in panel (*a*) of Figure 8-13 is a situation of loan market equilibrium. In equilibrium, the quantity of loans demanded by the nonbank public is equal to the quantity of loans supplied by banks; in panel (*a*) of Figure 8-13 the equilibrium quantity of loans demanded and supplied is $10 billion. The loan interest rate adjusts until this condition is satisfied. For instance, if the interest rate were equal to 0.12, there would be an excess quantity of loans supplied—which we could alternatively call surplus lending—by banks. The loan rate would be bid downward until this loan surplus was eliminated. In contrast, if the loan rate were equal to 0.08, there would be an excess quantity of loans demanded—a shortage of loans; if this were to occur, the loan rate would be bid upward until the shortage of loans was eliminated. The equilibrium interest rate on loans—0.10 in panel (*a*) of Figure 8-13—is the single loan interest rate at which the equilibrium quantity of lending is attained.

Panel (*b*) of Figure 8-13 shows bank j's lending decision. As discussed previously, if the market loan rate is 0.10, bank j desires to make $100 million in loans. Why does bank j take the market loan rate of 0.10 as "given"? Perhaps the best way to visualize why this is so is to imagine what would happen if bank j made no loans at all: If so, the amount of lending would be reduced by only $100 million, which, in relation to the total amount of lending of $10 *billion*, is a proverbial "drop in the bucket." The loss of bank j's presence from the banking system would scarcely be noticeable; therefore, by itself bank j cannot influence the market loan rate. It takes the market loan rate as given and beyond its own control.

This does not mean that bank j could not charge a loan rate above or below the market

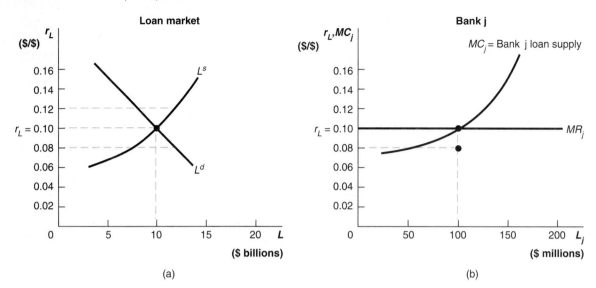

Figure 8-13

Loan Market Equilibrium. In equilibrium, the quantity of loans demanded by the nonbank public is equal to the quantity of loans supplied by banks, at $10 billion [panel (*a*)]. If the interest rate were equal to 0.12, there would be an excess quantity of loans supplied, and the loan rate would be bid downward until this loan surplus was eliminated; if the loan rate were equal to 0.08, there would be an excess quantity of loans demanded, and the loan rate would be bid upward until the shortage of loans was eliminated. This occurs at the equilibrium loan rate of 0.10.

At the market loan rate of 0.10, bank j desires to make $100 million in loans [panel (*b*)]. If bank j were to charge a loan rate above the market loan rate, such as 0.12, then no one would borrow from bank j. If bank j were to charge a loan rate below the market loan rate, such as 0.08, then marginal revenue would be below marginal cost at $100 million in lending, as shown in panel (*b*), and the net profit on the last dollar of lending would be negative; so the bank could earn more profits by charging the market loan rate of 0.10. Hence, bank j earns maximum profits by supplying $100 million in loans at the market loan rate of 0.10.

loan rate if it wished to do so. It will not want to do this, however, because doing so would be inconsistent with profit maximization. On the one hand, if it were to charge a loan rate above the market loan rate, such as 0.12, then no customers would borrow from bank j, because they could get a loan from any other bank at the lower market interest rate of 0.10. Bank j would lose all its loan customers.

On the other hand, if bank j were to charge a loan rate below the market loan rate, such as 0.08, then marginal revenue would be below marginal cost at $100 million in lending, as shown in panel (*b*) of Figure 8-13. The net profit on the last dollar of lending would be *negative*, and so the bank could earn more profits by charging the market loan rate of 0.10. Indeed, it earns maximum profits by supplying $100 million in loans at this market loan rate.

The Effect of an Increase in the Demand for Loans   Figure 8-14 traces through the effects of an increase in the demand for loans by the nonbank public. An increase in the demand for loans means that, at any given loan interest rate, including the initial equilibrium loan rate, there is a rise in the quantity of loans demanded by the nonbank public.

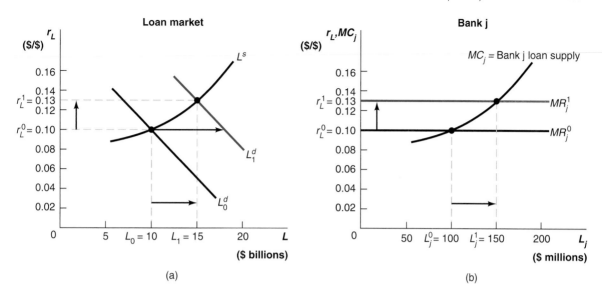

Figure 8-14

The Effect of an Increase in the Nonbank Public's Demand for Loans.   An increase in the demand for loans causes a rightward shift of the market loan demand schedule, from L_0^d to L_1^d [panel (a)]. Following the increase in loan demand, there is now an excess quantity of loans demanded at the old equilibrium loan rate, 0.10. To obtain more loans, competing bank customers must make higher loan rate bids; as the loan rate is bid upward, the shortage of loans is eliminated, and the quantity of loans demanded now is equal to the quantity of loans supplied at a new equilibrium loan interest rate of 0.13.

As the loan interest rate is bid upward, each bank, including bank j, supplies a larger quantity of loans [panel (b)]. For instance, as the market loan rate rises from 0.10 to 0.13, bank j increases its quantity of loans supplied from $100 million to $150 million. Ultimately, a new market equilibrium is attained at a total quantity of loans supplied of $15 billion [panel (a)].

(For instance, households and firms could become convinced that a general economic upturn is in the offing and that now is a good time for households to buy new homes and for firms to invest in new machinery and plants—because they feel confident they will be able to repay the loans when their incomes rise during the coming economic upturn.) Hence, an increase in the demand for loans is shown in panel (a) of Figure 8-14 as a *rightward shift* of the market loan demand schedule, from L_0^d to L_1^d.

Following the increase in loan demand shown in panel (a) of Figure 8-14, there is now an excess quantity of loans demanded at the old equilibrium loan rate, 0.10. Consequently, the original equilibrium quantity of loans demanded and supplied, $10 billion, is no longer the equilibrium amount of lending. To obtain more loans, competing bank customers must make higher loan rate bids; as the loan rate is bid upward, the shortage of loans is eliminated, and the quantity of loans demanded now is equal to the quantity of loans supplied at a new equilibrium loan interest rate of 0.13.

As the loan interest rate is bid upward, each bank, including bank j, is willing to supply a larger quantity of loans, as shown in panel (b) of Figure 8-14. As the market loan rate rises from 0.10 to 0.13, bank j increases its quantity of loans supplied from $100 million to $150 million. This movement along bank j's loan supply schedule in panel (b) mirrors the *movement along* the market loan supply schedule in panel (a) of Figure 8-14, as bank j and all other banks in the market increase the quantity of loans supplied until a new market equilibrium is attained at a total quantity of loans supplied of $15 billion.

THE MARKET FOR BANK DEPOSITS

In the loan market, banks are sellers, and borrowers are buyers. Hence, banks supply loans, and borrowers demand loans. In contrast, in the deposit market, banks are the buyers; they *demand* deposit funds for use in making loans. Their deposit customers are the sellers of deposits who *supply* their funds to banks.

The Market Deposit Demand Schedule　In the market for any particular good or service, the market demand schedule is the horizontal summation of the demand schedule of all agents that wish to purchase the good or service in question. This basic relationship also extends to the market for bank deposits, in which banks are the agents that demand deposit funds from their customers.

As we saw in Figure 8-11, an individual bank j's net marginal revenue schedule, $NMR_j = r_L - (MC_D + MC_L)$, is that bank's deposit demand schedule, for a given market loan rate. We reproduce bank j's deposit demand schedule from Figure 8-11, which was derived given a market loan rate of 0.10, in panel (*a*) of Figure 8-15. If the market deposit rate is equal to 0.07, bank j demands $100 million in deposits; if the deposit rate falls to 0.04, the bank demands $150 million in deposits.

In panel (*b*) of Figure 8-15, we display the deposit demand schedule for bank k. Bank k would like to obtain $80 million in deposits if the market deposit rate is equal to 0.07, but if the market deposit rate falls to 0.04, this bank demands $110 million in deposits. Panel (*c*) shows the horizontal summation of both banks' demands for deposits; at the deposit rate of 0.07 the two banks' combined quantity of deposits demanded is equal to $180 million, and at the deposit rate of 0.04 both banks together wish to obtain $260 million in deposits.

To derive the total market deposit demand schedule, we must include the quantities of deposits demanded by all other banks. This also is done in panel (*c*) of Figure 8-15. If the market deposit rate is equal to 0.07, all banks other than bank j and bank k desire $9,820 million in deposits. Together with banks j and k, therefore, the total quantity of deposits demanded at a deposit rate of 0.07 is equal to $10,000 million, or $10 billion. If the deposit rate declines to 0.04, however, all other banks demand a total of $13,740 million in deposits, and so the total amount of deposits demanded by all banks including bank j and bank k is equal to $14,000 million, or $14 billion. The final schedule constructed in panel (*c*) of Figure 8-15, then, is the *market deposit demand schedule* (D^d).

The Supply of Deposits by the Nonbank Public　Households and firms are willing to supply more deposits to banks as the market deposit interest rate paid by banks increases. Hence, the *market deposit supply schedule* (D^s) of the nonbank public slopes upward. A possible market deposit supply schedule is depicted in panel (*a*) of Figure 8-16.

Deposit Market Equilibrium　Figure 8-16 displays a possible equilibrium situation in the market for bank deposits. This occurs at the point at which the quantity of deposits demanded by banks equals the quantity of deposits supplied by the nonbank public. In panel (*a*) of Figure 8-16, the equilibrium quantity of deposits demanded and supplied is $10 billion. The interest rate on deposits adjusts until deposit market equilibrium is attained. On the one hand, if the deposit interest rate were equal to 0.09, there would be an excess quantity of deposits supplied by the nonbank public, or a surplus of deposits.

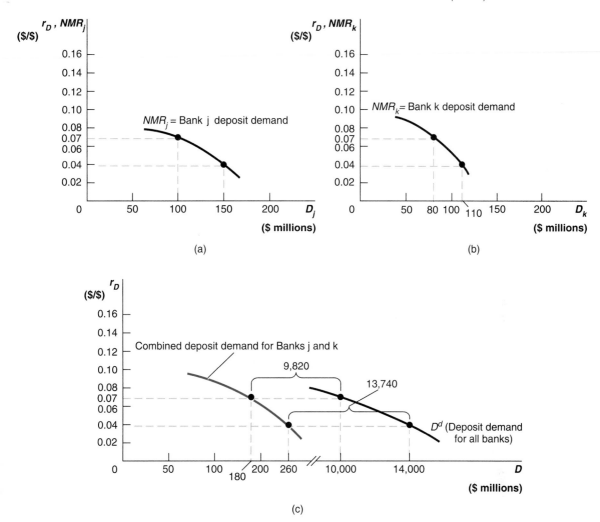

Figure 8-15
The Market Deposit Demand Schedule.   If the market deposit rate is equal to 0.07, bank j demands $100 million in deposits; if the deposit rate falls to 0.04, the bank demands $150 million in deposits [panel (a)]. If the market deposit rate is equal to 0.07, bank k wishes to obtain $80 million in deposits, but if the market deposit rate falls to 0.04, bank k demands $110 million in deposits [panel (b)]. At the deposit rate of 0.07 the two banks' combined quantity of deposits demanded is equal to $180 million, and at the deposit rate of 0.04 both banks together wish to obtain $260 million in deposits [panel (c)].

If the market deposit rate is equal to 0.07, all banks other than bank j and bank k desire $9,820 million in deposits, and so the total quantity of deposits demanded by all banks at a deposit rate of 0.07 is equal to $10,000 million, or $10 billion [panel (c)]. If the deposit rate declines to 0.04, however, all other banks demand a total of $13,740 million in deposits, and so the total amount of deposits demanded by all banks including bank j and bank k is equal to $14,000 million, or $14 billion. The final schedule containing these points, then, is the market deposit demand schedule (D^d).

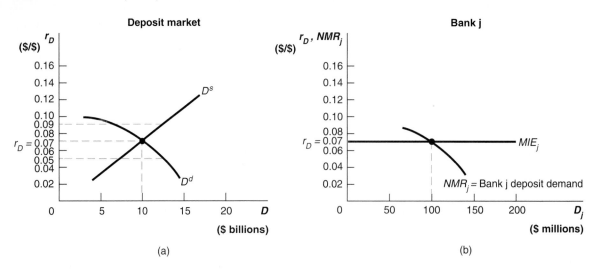

Figure 8-16

Deposit Market Equilibrium.   Equilibrium in the deposit market occurs at the point at which the quantity of deposits demanded by banks equals the quantity of deposits supplied by the nonbank public, which is $10 billion [panel (a)]. If the deposit interest rate were equal to 0.09, there would be an excess quantity of deposits supplied by the nonbank public, and the deposit rate woud be bid downward to the point at which this surplus was eliminated. If the deposit rate were equal to 0.05, there would be an excess quantity of deposits demanded by banks, and the deposit rate would be bid upward until there was no longer a shortage of deposits. The equilibrium interest rate on deposits, at which there is no surplus or shortage of deposits, is equal to 0.07.

   Bank j takes the market deposit rate of 0.07 as given [panel (b)]. If bank j were to pay a deposit rate below the market loan rate, such as 0.05, then no one would hold their funds on deposit with bank j. If bank j were to pay a deposit rate above the market loan rate, such as 0.09, then its net marginal interest expense would be above its net deposit marginal revenue at $100 million in deposits, and the net profit derived from the last dollar of deposits obtained by the bank would be negative. Hence, the bank could earn more profits by paying the market deposit rate of 0.07. At this deposit rate, bank j demands $100 million in deposits.

Depositors competing for interest earnings would bid the deposit rate downward to the point at which this surplus was eliminated. On the other hand, if the deposit rate were equal to 0.05, there would be an excess quantity of deposits demanded by banks, or a shortage of deposits. In this event, the competing banks would bid the deposit rate upward until there was no longer a shortage of deposits. The equilibrium interest rate on deposits— 0.07 in panel (a) of Figure 8-16—is the single interest rate at which there is no surplus or shortage of deposits, given the positions of the deposit demand and supply schedules.

   Panel (b) of Figure 8-16 shows bank j's decision about how many dollars in deposits it should obtain. Bank j recognizes that it is an insignificant part of the total demand for deposits, and so it takes the market deposit rate of 0.07 as given and beyond its control. Although bank j could pay a deposit rate above or below the market deposit rate if it wished to do so, it will not do so if it wishes to maximize its profits. If it were to pay a deposit rate below the market loan rate, such as 0.05, then virtually no households or firms would hold their funds on deposit with bank j, because they could keep their funds at any other bank at the higher market interest rate of 0.07. Bank j would lose all its depositors.

   Furthermore, if bank j were to pay a deposit rate above the market loan rate, such as

0.09, then its net marginal interest expense would be above its net deposit marginal revenue at $100 million in deposits, as shown in panel (b) of Figure 8-16. The net profit derived from the last dollar of deposits obtained by the bank would be *negative*, and so the bank could earn more profits by paying the market deposit rate of 0.07. Indeed, it earns maximum profits by demanding $100 million in deposits at this market deposit rate.

The Effects of an Increase in Deposit Supply   Figure 8-17 traces through the effects of an increase in the supply of deposits by the nonbank public. An increase in the supply of deposits means that, at any given deposit interest rate, including the initial equilibrium deposit rate, there is a rise in the quantity of deposits supplied by the nonbank public. (For instance, interest rates on government securities or yields on corporate bonds could fall, inducing households and firms to hold more deposit funds at banks rather than continue to hold these alternative financial instruments.) Therefore, an increase in the supply of deposits is shown in panel (a) of Figure 8-17 as a *rightward shift* of the market deposit supply schedule, from D_0^s to D_1^s.

Following the increase in deposit supply shown in panel (a) of Figure 8-17, there is now an excess quantity of deposits supplied at the old equilibrium deposit rate, 0.07. As a result, the original equilibrium quantity of deposits demanded and supplied, $10 billion, is no longer the equilibrium amount of deposits. As the interest rate on deposits is bid downward, the surplus of deposits is eliminated, and the quantity of deposits supplied

Figure 8-17
The Effects of an Increase in the Nonbank Public's Supply of Deposits.   An increase in the supply of deposits by the nonbank public causes a rightward shift of the market deposit supply schedule, from D_0^s to D_1^s [panel (a)]. At the initial equilibrium deposit rate, 0.07, there now is an excess quantity of deposit supplied, and the interest rate on deposits is bid downward toward a new equilibrium deposit interest rate of 0.04.

As the deposit interest rate is bid downward, each bank, including bank j, demands a larger quantity of deposits [panel (b)]. For instance, when the market deposit rate declines from 0.07 to 0.04, bank j increases its quantity of deposits demanded from $100 million to $150 million. Across all banks, similar increases in the quantity of deposits demanded occur, and a new market equilibrium is attained at a total quantity of loans supplied of $14 billion [panel (a)].

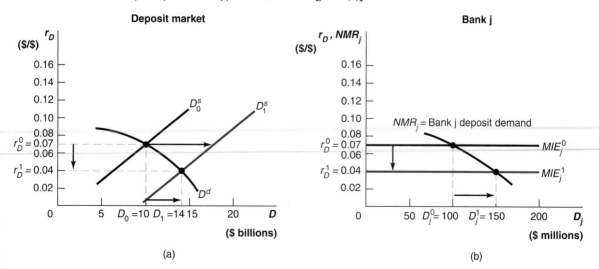

(a)   (b)

now is equal to the quantity of deposits demanded at a new equilibrium deposit interest rate of 0.04.

As the deposit interest rate is bid downward, each bank, including bank j, demands a larger quantity of deposits, as shown in panel (*b*) of Figure 8-17. As the market deposit rate declines from 0.07 to 0.04, bank j increases its quantity of deposits demanded from $100 million to $150 million. This movement along bank j's deposit demand schedule in panel (*b*) mirrors the *movement along* the market deposit demand schedule in panel (*a*) of Figure 8-17, as bank j and all other banks in the market increase the quantity of deposits demanded until a new market equilibrium is attained at a total quantity of deposits supplied of $14 billion.

THE INTERDEPENDENCE OF BANK LOAN AND DEPOSIT MARKETS

Our above discussion has considered the markets for loans and deposits in isolation from one another. For instance, our analysis of the loan market was predicated on the assumption that the deposit rate was equal to 0.07, even though we saw in our discussion of the deposit market that the equilibrium deposit rate can vary with changes in deposit market conditions. Likewise, our analysis of the deposit market assumed throughout that the loan rate was equal to 0.10, even though we saw in our discussion of the loan market that variations in loan market conditions can cause the equilibrium loan rate to change.

In fact, events that take place in the loan market influence events in the deposit market, and vice versa. It turns out that this *interdependence* between events in the loan and deposit markets helps explain why loan and deposit interest rates commonly (though not always) move in the same general direction over time.

Why Loan and Deposit Interest Rates Often Move Together Why is this so? To see why, first take a look back at Figure 8-14, which showed the effect of a rise in the public's demand for loans. As we discussed in this example, the effects of the rise in loan demand are increases in both the total equilibrium quantity of lending and the equilibrium loan interest rate.

But what happens if the loan interest rate rises? Recall that a bank's net marginal return from deposits is equal to $r_L - (MC_D + MC_L)$. If the equilibrium loan interest rate rises, it follows that the net marginal return from deposits for each bank increases—meaning that each bank's demand for deposits will rise. Therefore, in the market for deposits the demand for deposits will rise, which will cause an increase in the equilibrium deposit rate. As a result, the market interest rate on deposits tends to move in the same direction as the loan interest rate.

Now consider the example that was illustrated by Figure 8-17. In this example, the nonbank public increased its supply of deposit funds to banks. This caused an increase in the equilibrium quantity of deposits and a reduction in the equilibrium deposit interest rate.

But this will not really be the end of the story. We know that a bank's marginal cost of making loans is equal to $r_D + MC_D + MC_L$. If the equilibrium deposit rate declines as a result of an increase in the nonbank public's supply of deposits, then each bank's marginal cost of making loans correspondingly falls. As a result, all banks in the loan market will be willing to supply more loans at any given loan interest rate; the market loan supply schedule will shift rightward, and the equilibrium loan rate will fall. Again, the deposit and loan interest rates will move in the same direction.

Why Loan and Deposit Interest Rates Do Not *Always* Move Together   While market interest rates on bank loans and deposits commonly move in the same direction over time, from time to time they do not. There is a good reason for this, which is that the equilibrium quantities and interest rates in these two markets depend both on the behavior of the nonbank public *and* on the real resource cost conditions faced by banks. If bank costs change, then, as we show next, equilibrium interest rates on loans and deposits sometimes can move in opposing directions.

A variety of factors could change the resource costs incurred by banks. For instance, technological improvements could lower banks' marginal resource costs, as could reductions in market wages and salaries that banks must pay their employees. Reductions in governmental regulation of banks also could reduce these costs by decreasing the amount of paperwork and other bureaucratic managerial tasks that banks are required to undertake.

Let us suppose that, for whatever reason, bank marginal resource costs fall. This means that, for any given quantities of loans and deposits, MC_L and MC_D would decrease from initial values, say, of MC_L^0 and MC_D^0 to smaller values, MC_L^1 and MC_D^1. As a result, the marginal cost, $MC_j = r_D + MC_L + MC_D$, incurred by any bank, such as bank j, would decrease, as shown in panel (*b*) of Figure 8-18. This means that the loan supply would increase at each bank, so that the market loan supply schedule would shift rightward from L_0^s to L_1^s, as shown in panel (*a*) of Figure 8-18. The result would be a decrease in the equilibrium loan rate, from $r_L^0 = 0.10$ to $r_L^1 = 0.08$, and an increase in the equilibrium amount of loans, from $L_0 = \$10$ billion to $L_1 = \$14$ billion.

In addition, as shown in panel (*d*) of Figure 8-18, the marginal resource cost reductions would cause a rise in the net marginal return, $NMR_j = r_L - (MC_L + MC_D)$, earned by each bank, such as bank j. Therefore, deposit demand by bank j and all other banks increases, so that the market deposit demand schedule shifts rightward from D_0^d to D_1^d, as indicated in panel (*c*). This causes an increase in the equilibrium deposit rate, from $r_D = 0.05$ to $r_D = 0.07$, and an increase in the equilibrium amount of deposits, from $D_0 = \$10$ billion to $D_1 = \$13$ billion.

As this example indicates, reductions in the real resource costs that banks must incur in their operations cause the equilibrium loan interest rate to fall but cause the equilibrium deposit interest rate to rise. Therefore, the two interest rates can, when banks experience significant resource cost changes, move in different directions.

Of course, because the loan rate has fallen, each bank's net marginal return from deposits—$r_L - (MC_D + MC_L)$—decreases somewhat. This would cause a slightly offsetting *reduction* in banks' total deposit demand (not shown in Figure 8-18) that would tend to counter to some extent—but that would not reverse—the rise in the deposit rate. In addition, because the deposit rate increases on net, each bank's marginal cost of making loans—$r_D + MC_D + MC_L$—rises somewhat. This, in turn, would cause a slightly offsetting *reduction* in the total supply of loans (also not shown) by banks that would tend to counter somewhat—but again that would not reverse—the fall in the loan rate.

Note that although these effects arising from market interdependence do not reverse the directions of the movements in market interest rates, economists interested in understanding the full effects of loan and deposit market changes must take them into account. The reason why this is so can be seen in Figure 8-18. To keep things as simple as possible, we have not shown in this figure all the effects arising from interdependence in the loan and deposit markets that we have discussed above. For this reason, as Figure 8-18 stands, banks' balance sheet constraints are not satisfied; loans do not equal deposits. When we take into account interdependence between the two markets, however, the loan supply schedule will tend to shift rightward in panel (*a*), causing equilibrium bank lending to

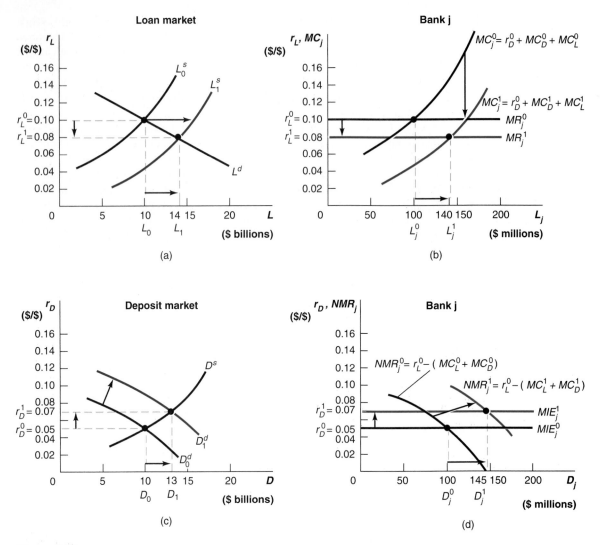

Figure 8-18
The Effects of a Reduction in Bank Marginal Resource Costs.   For given quantities of loans and deposits, MC_L and MC_D decrease. As a result, loan supply would increase at each bank [panel (b)], so that the market loan supply schedule would shift rightward [panel (a)]. The initial result would be a decrease in the equilibrium loan rate, from $r_L^0 = 0.10$ to $r_L^1 = 0.08$, and an increase in the equilibrium amount of loans, from $L_0 = \$10$ billion to $L_1 = \$14$ billion. In addition, the reductions in MC_L and MC_D would cause a rise in the net marginal return on deposits earned by each bank, such as bank j [panel (d)], so that deposit demand by bank j and all other banks increases, and the market deposit demand schedule shifts rightward [panel (c)]. This causes an increase in the equilibrium deposit rate, from $r_D^0 = 0.05$ to $r_D^1 = 0.07$, and an increase in the equilibrium amount of deposits, from $D_0 = \$10$ billion to $D_1 = \$13$ billion.

rise; and deposit demand will tend to shift leftward in panel (c), causing equilibrium deposits to fall. Eventually, loans and deposits will be equated. These effects, then, ultimately will yield loan and deposit market equilibrium quantities that satisfy the banks' balance sheet constraints.

Partial Equilibrium Versus General Equilibrium Analysis   The three examples discussed above have taken into account the interdependence of bank loan and deposit markets. Economists call analysis that completely recognizes this interdependence **general equilibrium analysis.** To be certain that all sources of influence between markets are examined, general equilibrium analysis must be done.

In most circumstances, however, our main concerns, such as understanding the effects of changes in legal regulations on bank behavior and banking markets, can be addressed adequately by looking at one market in isolation from the other, much as we did explicitly in Figures 8-14, 8-17, and 8-18. When we consider one market by itself and abstract from sources of interdependence with other markets, we conduct what economists call **partial equilibrium analysis.** You no doubt will be relieved to learn that we shall concentrate on partial equilibrium analysis in the remaining chapters of this unit.

MONOPOLY BANKING

Another controversy, which we shall discuss in detail in Chapter 11, concerns whether or not the model of competitive banking that we have used throughout this chapter really does a good job of describing real-world behavior. As we shall see in Chapter 10, there are several reasons that the assumptions of perfect competition may not apply readily to the banking industry. Perhaps the most important of these is that, for a number of reasons, laws and regulations have limited freedom of entry and exit in banking, which is one of the most important conditions for competitive markets to exist.

Without providing any further rationales for monopoly banking at this moment—we shall spend much time on possible *reasons* in Chapter 11—let us consider what differences would arise if banking were *monopolized*. That is, how is our basic model of bank behavior changed if there is only one bank in a market, or if there are just a few that jointly seek to maximize their profits?

To answer this question, we shall focus on the effects of monopolistic banking in the market for loans. As shown in Figure 8-19, if there is only one monopoly bank in the loan market, then this bank, which we again refer to as "bank j," faces alone the market loan demand schedule. This means that the bank's marginal revenue is not constant, because the bank can influence the quantity of loans it makes by changing its loan rate, thereby altering the additional revenue it receives for each additional dollar of loans it makes. Indeed, as the bank lowers its loan rate, its marginal revenue from lending declines and lies below the loan rate it charges; hence, the monopoly bank's marginal revenue (MR_j) schedule slopes downward and lies below the market loan demand schedule, as shown in Figure 8-19.

To maximize its profits, the bank makes loans up to the point at which its marginal revenue is equal to the marginal cost it incurs. Consequently, the bank extends loans to the point at which the marginal revenue schedule, MR_j, crosses the marginal cost schedule of the bank, $MC_j = r_D + MC_L + MC_D$. At this point, as depicted in Figure 8-19, bank j desires to make $L_j^* = \$5$ billion in loans. If the bank were to lend less than this, its marginal revenue from lending would exceed the marginal cost it incurs, meaning that the additional revenue received from making more loans would be greater than the additional

DOES THE BEHAVIOR OF BANK DEPOSIT RATES CONFORM WITH THEORY?

As we discuss below and in later chapters, Congress and bank regulators placed restrictions on many bank deposit rates during the 1960s and 1970s. In the 1980s, however, Congress removed most of these restrictions. Most deposit rate regulations effectively were gone by the end of 1983. Hence, our theory of bank behavior with unregulated interest rates should apply best to the period since 1982.

Sluggish and Asymmetric Deposit Rate Behavior

Not surprisingly, economists discovered that, beginning in late 1983, deposit rates tended, in general, to move with other market interest rates. As we discussed above, this certainly is what our theory predicts will

occur if the nonbank public's demand for loans and supply of deposits are the main factors accounting for variations in bank loan and deposit market conditions.

In our model, we considered only the relationship between movements in bank deposit and loan interest rates. According to the theory, however, the same basic relationship should be observed between deposit rates and interest rates earned on other bank assets than loans, such as Treasury securities that banks hold.

An interesting observation following the deposit rate deregulation of the early 1980s, however, was that market deposit rates exhibited considerable *sluggishness* in response to increases in other interest rates. This sluggishness is shown in the accompanying figure, which plots for the post-deposit-rate-deregulation period the 6-month Treasury bill rate, the 6-month interest rate on bank certificates of deposit, and the interest rate on bank money market deposit accounts (see Chapters 3 and 6 for descriptions of these bank deposits). Note

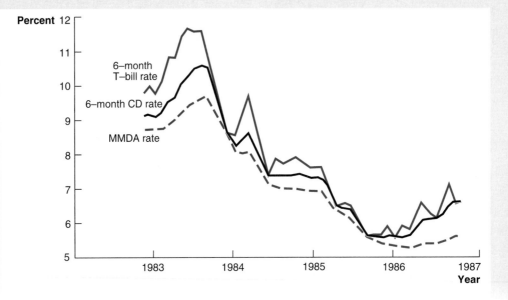

Movements in the 6-Month T-Bill Rate, the 6-Month Interest Rate on Certificates of Deposit, and the Money Market Deposit Account Rate, 1983–1987. This figure illustrates how, following deposit interest rate deregulation in the early 1980s, deposit rates generally moved in the same direction as the interest rates on bank assets, such as the interest rate on T-bills. It also shows that deposit interest rates responded much faster to falls in the T-bill rate than they did to increases in the T-bill rate.

that as the 6-month Treasury bill rate rises, market deposit rates *tend* to increase as well. In addition, market deposit rates decreased in response to reductions in the Treasury bill rate.

What is interesting, though, is that deposit rates fell in response to a decline in the T-bill rate much more rapidly than they rose when the T-bill rate increased. That is, there was *asymmetry* in the responsiveness of deposit rates to changes in interest rates on bank assets. When the T-bill rate declined, market deposit rates also declined almost immediately, as the basic theory we have discussed would predict. When the T-bill rate increased, however, market deposit interest rates rose only with a lag and even then did so *sluggishly*.

What Accounts for Sluggish and Asymmetric Movements in Deposit Rates?

Economists have been somewhat perplexed by this sluggishness and asymmetry in deposit interest rate movements over time. This does not mean that they do not have theories for why this occurs, however.

One possible explanation for deposit rate *sluggishness* is that banks incur *costs of adjustment* when they change the quantities of assets that they hold and liabilities that they issue. For instance, when the T-bill rate rises, the net marginal return from deposits rises at all banks, and so they desire to hold more deposits. If

increasing the quantity of deposits at banks entails its own particular set of costs—costs of deposit adjustment—then the demand for deposits by banks would increase only gradually over time, and the equilibrium deposit rate thereby would rise more slowly than the T-bill rate. In contrast, according to this explanation, the adjustment costs banks incur in *reducing* their deposits might be much smaller; so when the T-bill rate falls, the demand for deposits might fall much more quickly. This would account for the *asymmetry* of deposit rate movements.

Other economists discount this explanation, arguing that adjustment costs aren't really that large and that it is difficult to see why they should differ when a bank increases its deposits as compared to when it reduces its deposits. These economists contend that an alternative explanation for sluggishness and asymmetry of deposit rate movements is that the theory of perfect competition may not best describe bank behavior in loan and deposit markets. According to this view, banks may have *monopoly power* in loan and deposit markets; rather than taking these rates as *given* by forces of market demand and supply that they cannot control, banks instead may be able to *set* their loan and deposit rates to maximize their profits. We have more to say about monopoly banking below and in Chapter 11.

cost it would incur from increasing its lending; hence, it could increase its profits by increasing the amount of loans toward the level $L_j^* = \$5$ billion. If the bank were to make loans beyond this level, it would find that the additional cost it incurred would be greater than the additional revenue earned; therefore, it would reduce its lending back toward the amount $L_j^* = \$5$ billion to increase its profits.

If bank j is truly a monopoly bank, then $5 billion would be the total quantity of loans available to borrowers in this market. What interest rate will borrowers have to pay for this amount of loans? Under perfect competition, the market loan interest rate is determined by the interaction of forces of supply and demand. Under a bank monopoly, however, there no longer is a market supply schedule; the single bank determines its profit-maximizing amount of lending based solely on its own marginal revenue and cost conditions.

Hence, the monopoly bank charges the highest loan rate that borrowers are willing to pay for the amount of loans the bank has chosen to extend to them. As we can see in Figure 8-19, if the amount of lending by the bank is equal to $L_j^* = \$5$ billion, then, according to the market loan demand schedule, the nonbank public is willing and able to pay a loan rate $r_L^* = 0.15$, or 15 percent. This, then, is the market loan rate charged by the monopoly bank.

Many economists have argued that monopolistic banking markets may have been the rule rather than the exception in the United States, at least until fairly recently. There are

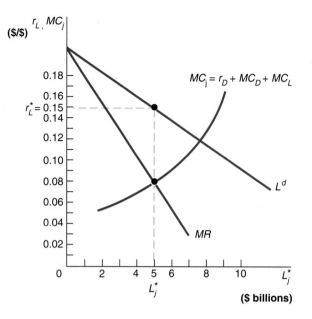

Figure 8-19
A Monopoly Loan Market. If bank j is the only bank in the loan market, then it alone faces the market loan demand schedule. This means that the bank's marginal revenue is not constant; as the bank lowers its loan rate, its marginal revenue from lending declines and lies below the loan rate it charges, so that the bank's marginal revenue (MR$_j$) schedule slopes downward and lies below the market loan demand schedule.

To maximize its profits, the bank makes loans up to the point at which its marginal revenue is equal to the marginal cost it incurs. This is the point at which the marginal revenue schedule, MR$_j$, crosses the marginal cost schedule of the bank, MC$_j$ = r_D + MC$_L$ + MC$_D$. At this point, bank j wishes to make L_j^* = $5 billion in loans.

The bank charges the highest loan rate that borrowers are willing to pay for the amount of loans the bank has chosen to extend to them, which, according to the market loan demand schedule, is equal to the loan rate r_L^* = 0.15.

over 12,000 banks in the United States, so how could this be? We shall address this issue in Chapters 10 and 11. Before examining this issue, however, we need to move away from the pure theory issues considered in this chapter to undertake an investigation of the actual, real-world practices that bank managers have used to achieve maximum profits. That will be our goal in the next chapter.

CHAPTER SUMMARY

1. Any economic theory of bank behavior must recognize the bank balance sheet constraint, which says that assets must equal liabilities and net worth. In a simple model in which the only bank assets are loans and the only bank liability is checkable deposits, the balance sheet constraint requires that loans equal deposits for each bank and for the banking system as a whole.

2. In our basic model of bank behavior, bank revenues are interest earnings on loans that banks make to borrowers. There are two types of bank costs. One is bank interest expenses incurred

through payments on deposits that banks use for lending. The other is real resource costs, which are the expenses that banks incur on labor and other resources used to obtain and service deposits and to make and monitor loans.

3. In a competitive banking market, loans and deposits are each homogeneous financial assets. In addition, there are numerous banks, each of which has a small portion of the total loans and deposits in the banking system. Consequently, each bank takes the market interest rates on loans and deposits as ''given,'' meaning that it cannot influence the magnitudes of these market interest rates via its own actions. For each bank, then, the marginal revenue it receives is equal to the market interest rate on loans, no matter the amount of loans it makes. Likewise, the marginal interest expense it incurs on deposits is equal to the market interest rate on deposits, no matter the amount of deposits it issues.

4. A bank's marginal cost has three components: its marginal interest expense on deposits, the marginal resource cost of loans, and the marginal resource cost of deposits. For a typical bank, marginal cost increases with the amount of lending by the bank. A bank's profits are maximized when the market interest rate on loans is equal to marginal cost. If the market interest rate on loans changes, the bank alters the amount of loans it makes by moving along its marginal cost schedule; hence, the marginal cost schedule is the bank's loan supply schedule. The *market* loan supply schedule is the sum of all banks' loan supply schedules.

5. A bank's net marginal revenue per dollar of deposits is the loan rate it receives per dollar of deposits lent minus the marginal resource cost of loans and the marginal resource cost of deposits. A bank issues deposits up to the point at which the marginal revenue per dollar of deposits is equal to the marginal interest expense it incurs on deposits, which, for a competitive bank, is equal to the market deposit rate. When the market deposit rate changes, the bank changes the amount of deposits it desires, and so its net marginal revenue schedule for deposits is the bank's deposit demand schedule. The market deposit demand schedule is the sum of all banks' deposit demand schedules.

6. In a perfectly competitive banking system, the equilibrium interest rate on loans is determined by the point at which the quantity of loans demanded by the nonbank public is equal to the quantity of loans supplied by banks. The equilibrium interest rate on deposits is determined by the point at which the quantity of deposits demanded by banks is equal to the quantity of deposits supplied by the nonbank public. These equilibrium interest rates will change if there is a change in the nonbank public's supply of deposits or demand for loans, or if there is a change in the real resource costs incurred by banks that cause changes in the banks' demand for deposits or supply of loans.

7. If there is only one, monopoly, bank that makes loans in the loan market, its marginal revenue from lending falls as it increases the amount lent. To maximize its profits, the monopoly bank makes loans up to the point at which marginal revenue is equal to marginal cost. It then charges the highest loan rate that its loan customers are willing to pay for this quantity of loans.

GLOSSARY

Balance sheet constraint: Given that all bank assets are loans and all bank liabilities are deposits, then, if assets must equal liabilities, the value of loans by a bank must equal the value of deposits at the bank.

Economic costs: Both the *explicit costs*, including interest expenses and explicit real resource costs, that a bank must incur in its day-to-day operations and the implicit *opportunity costs* a bank incurs because its owners could be devoting factors of production to alternative uses.

Economic profits: Total revenues less economic costs.

General equilibrium analysis: Analysis of the effects on equilibrium in the loan or deposit market caused by changes in conditions in one of the markets that takes into account the interdependence of that market with the other.

Interest expenses: Costs incurred by a bank through payment of interest in exchange for funds, obtained by issuing deposits, to use in its lending activities.

Nonbank public: Households and firms.

Partial equilibrium analysis: Analysis of the effects on equilibrium in the loan or deposit market caused by changes in conditions in only that market, abstracting from the interdependence of that market with the other.

Real resource expenses: Expenses that a bank must incur in its day-to-day operations in the forms of explicit payments of wages and salaries to employees and payments to owners of other factors of production, and, in addition, in the form of implicit opportunity costs arising from the fact that the bank could be devoting its factors of production to alternative uses.

SELF-TEST QUESTIONS

1. Suppose that there is a *decrease* in the nonbank public's demand for bank loans. Assume that the banking system is perfectly competitive. (*Hint*: In answering the questions below, you may find it helpful to recognize that this example is the reverse case of the one analyzed in the chapter.)

   a. Trace through the *partial equilibrium* effects of this reduction in loan demand, both in the market for loans and with respect to an individual bank j.

   b. Use appropriate diagrams to assist in explaining how the loan market effects you discussed in part a will affect the deposit market behavior of each bank, such as bank j, and equilibrium in the deposit market.

   c. What other *general equilibrium* effects, aside from those you have analyzed in part b above, might be expected to occur before the banking system reaches a final equilibrium? Be specific.

2. Suppose that there is a *decrease* in the nonbank public's supply of bank deposits. Again assume that the banking system is perfectly competitive. (*Hint*: In answering the questions below, you may find it helpful to recognize that this example is the reverse case of the one analyzed in the chapter.)

   a. Trace through the *partial equilibrium* effects of this reduction in deposit supply, both in the market for deposits and with respect to an individual bank j.

   b. Use appropriate diagrams to assist in explaining how the deposit market effects you discussed in part a above will affect the loan market behavior of each bank, such as bank j, and equilibrium in the loan market.

   c. What other *general equilibrium* effects, aside from those you have analyzed in part b, might be expected to occur before the banking system reaches a final equilibrium? Be specific.

3. Suppose that all banks in an unregulated, perfectly competitive banking system find that they must pay higher wages to *all* their employees.

   a. Explain the *partial equilibrium* effects of this wage increase on the loan market behavior of an individual bank and on full loan market equilibrium. Use diagrams to assist you.

   b. Explain the *partial equilibrium* effects of this wage increase on the deposit market behavior of an individual bank and on full deposit market equilibrium. Use diagrams to assist you.

   c. What *general equilibrium* effects might be expected to occur in the loan and deposit markets before the banking system reaches a new, final equilibrium? Explain.

4. Suppose that the United States' banking system can be approximated by the competitive banking model discussed in this chapter. Now suppose that Congress passes laws relaxing restric-

tions on Japanese and German banks that previously limited their ability to compete in U.S. loan *and* deposit markets and, furthermore, that banks of these nations respond by opening branches throughout much of the United States.

a. What would be the *partial equilibrium* effects of this event in the U.S. loan market? What would be the effects on an individual U.S. bank? Use diagrams to assist you in your explanation.

b. What would be the *partial equilibrium* effects of this event in the U.S. deposit market? What would be the effects on an individual U.S. bank? Use diagrams to assist you in your explanation.

c. What *general equilibrium* effects would you expect to occur in the loan and deposit markets following the partial equilibrium effects that you have analyzed in parts a and b above?

5. Suppose that a monopoly bank finds that it must pay higher wages to all its employees. Use a diagram to explain what the effects would be on the amount of loans made by this bank and on the loan interest rate the bank charges.

PROBLEMS

8-1. Suppose that, at its current levels of loans and deposits, a bank that holds loans as its only assets and issues deposits as its only liabilities finds that its marginal resource cost of loans is $0.01 per dollar of lending and that its marginal resource cost of deposits is $0.03 per dollar of deposits. The present market interest rate on deposits is 6 percent. If the banking system is perfectly competitive and if this bank is maximizing its profits, what is the market interest rate on loans? Explain.

8-2. Currently, a bank in a perfectly competitive banking system discovers that its marginal resource cost of loans is equal to $0.02 per dollar of lending and that its marginal resource cost of deposits is $0.04 per dollar of deposits. The market interest rate on deposits is 5 percent, and the market interest rate on loans is 10 percent.

a. Is this bank maximizing its profits? How can you tell?

b. Should this bank increase or decrease its lending? Draw a diagram to help explain your answer.

c. Should this bank increase or decrease its deposits? Draw a diagram to help explain your answer.

8-3. Suppose that in a competitive banking system we observe the equilibrium bank loan rate increase, from 6 percent to 7 percent, while the equilibrium bank deposit rate simultaneously falls, from 4 percent to 3 percent. If the marginal resource cost of loans is unchanged, what has happened to the marginal resource cost of deposits? Explain.

8-4. Consider the following partial equilibrium, algebraic model of the bank deposit market:

Market deposit demand schedule: $D^d = 50 - (500 \times r_D)$

Market deposit supply schedule: $D^s = 10 + (300 \times r_D)$

a. Draw a rough diagram of the market deposit demand and supply schedules.

b. Solve for the equilibrium deposit rate and quantity of deposits.

8-5. Consider the following partial equilibrium, algebraic model of the bank loan market:

Market loan demand schedule: $L^d = 43 - (200 \times r_L)$

Market loan supply schedule: $L^s = 16 + (100 \times r_L)$

a. Draw a rough diagram of the market loan demand and supply schedules.

b. Solve for the equilibrium loan rate and quantity of deposits at the point at which the two schedules cross.

SELECTED REFERENCES

Baltensperger, Ernst, ''Alternative Approaches to the Theory of the Banking Firm,'' *Journal of Monetary Economics*, 6 (1, January 1980), pp. 1–37.

Klein, Michael, ''A Theory of the Banking Firm,'' *Journal of Money, Credit, and Banking,* 3 (2, May 1971), pp. 205–218.

Moore, George, Richard Porter, and David Small, ''Modeling the Disaggregated Demands for M2 and M1 in the 1980s: The U.S. Experience,'' paper presented at the Federal Reserve Board Conference on Monetary Aggregates and Financial Sector Behavior, Washington, D.C., 1988.

Neumark, David, and Steven A. Sharpe, ''Market Structure and the Nature of Price Rigidity: Evidence from the Market for Consumer Deposits,'' *Finance and Economics Discussion Series*, No. 52 (January 1989), Board of Governors of the Federal Reserve System.

Pierce, James, *Monetary and Financial Economics* (New York: John Wiley & Sons, 1984), chap. 7.

Santomero, Anthony, ''Modeling the Banking Firm: A Survey,'' *Journal of Money, Credit, and Banking*, 16 (4, November 1984, pt. 2), pp. 576–603.

Management and Performance of Depository Institutions

1. Why do depository institutions have a liquidity problem?

2. How do depository institutions select their assets?

3. How do depository institutions manage their liabilities?

4. Are asset management and liability management policies interrelated?

5. When do depository institution managers pursue a positive funds gap strategy? A negative funds gap strategy?

6. What are some important measures of depository institution management performance? How have commercial banks and other depository institutions performed in recent years?

In the last chapter, we overviewed the basic economic theory of bank decision making. One of the most common complaints that students have about theories involving concepts such as marginal revenue and marginal cost that were covered in that chapter is their difficulty in believing that banks and other depository institutions really compute these quantities and produce loans or deposits up to the point at which ''marginal conditions'' are satisfied. These students—and you may be one of them—typically perceive that behavior in the real world is not so cut and dried as economic theory appears to make it out to be.

BASIC ASSUMPTIONS OF ECONOMIC THEORY

It is important for you to keep in mind that economic theory describes for us the types of decision making that depository institutions implicitly must undertake if they wish to maximize their profits. Of course, many depository institution managers have never explicitly calculated marginal revenues and marginal costs (although at large banks some economists now are employed to do just that, as economic expertise has become more pronounced). Some depository institution managers may even have forgotten from their economics courses exactly what these terms mean (though *surely* they saved their undergraduate texts to refer to time and again later in life).

Does this mean that the basic theories we discussed in the previous chapter are irrelevant? The answer is a resounding no; even if managers of depository institutions do not explicitly compute marginal revenues and costs, we still can assume that they act as though they do. An analogy from sports and the science of physics may be helpful. When a champion gymnast performs a floor exercise, she does not calculate, using Isaac Newton's laws of gravitation, the various forces at work on her body by the gravity fields projected by the earth, by the floor upon her limbs as she catapults herself in flips and turns, or upon the mat as she somersaults and completes her routine. Yet she still accomplishes her task; not only does she win a championship, but she doesn't even injure herself! Does the fact that she does not *explicitly* compute trajectories, force vectors, and velocities and accelerations mean that the laws of physics do not hold? Certainly not. To have completed her exercise, the gymnast must have behaved *as if* she had understood those laws.

Likewise, just because many managers of depository institutions do not explicitly calculate important quantities such as marginal revenue and marginal cost does not mean that economic laws, such as those governing the forces of supply or demand, do not govern their behavior. Hence, the economic theory of bank behavior developed in the last chapter assumed that depository institution managers must behave *as if* they understood these concepts.

BANKING AS AN ART

Nonetheless, management of a depository institution is a practical art as well as an economic science. In this chapter we focus on the pragmatic, day-to-day aspects of depository institution management. That is, we shall emphasize the means by which depository managers seek to maximize profits.

Depository institution management is considerably more complicated today than it was twenty years ago. For one thing, there is much regulatory uncertainty; in the past ten years we have seen a great deal of deregulation of financial institutions *and* a more recent movement toward increased regulation due to increased financial institution failures. (This topic is explored in Chapters 10, 11, and 12.) Furthermore, depository institution customers—households and businesses on both the lending and borrowing side—have become very sophisticated. They are interest rate conscious and have developed techniques to minimize borrowing costs and maximize interest earnings. (Remember, depository institutions earn profits on the spread between their borrowing rates and their lending rates.) As Chapter 5 indicated, financial innovation has launched a vast array of debt instruments, and markets for such instruments have become internationalized.

These changes have created an environment in which banks (we shall tend to use the term ''banks'' to represent depository institutions generally) face increased competition and increased opportunities. Banks now must decide if they want to enter such areas as investment banking and whether they will provide consumer services for ''free'' or explicitly charge customers for each service. Banks can also select a wider variety of investments, but with such freedom to select comes the mandate to make decisions. The globalization of the financial services industry expands the options for selecting both assets and liabilities. In a very fundamental sense, banks must decide whether to become one-institution shopping and transaction centers or whether to specialize and find one small, highly profitable niche in the financial services industry.

As you read this chapter, always keep in mind that banks are business firms; they hire inputs and produce products or services for sale, and they aim to obtain profits. As financial intermediaries, they create short-term, highly liquid liabilities in the form of transactions and time deposits and ''sell'' these created liabilities to savers. The proceeds obtained are then used by the intermediaries to buy longer-term, less liquid assets (such as bonds, mortgages, consumer loans, and so on) in the financial markets.

Economists have found that they can simplify their analysis, and better predict bank behavior, by assuming that bank managers attempt to maximize shareholders' wealth. In effect, bank managers create both risks and returns for the bank's shareholders when they provide financial services. We can use the same equation that was so useful in Chapter 7 to aid us in this wealth-maximization process. Following the same procedure as was used to find the present value of a bond, we can conceive of the bank as generating profits (the difference between interest received from borrowers and interest paid to obtain funds) through time and then discounting (reducing) those future profits by a proper discount (or interest) rate.

Note that there will be a trade-off between rate of return and risk. That is, a bank manager can select some asset-liability portfolio that has a higher potential return but is more risky, or the manager can select a different asset-liability portfolio that is less risky but earns a lower rate of return.

In this chapter we trace the evolution of bank management theories. We then examine recent trends in management and performance of the banking industry.

THE EVOLUTION OF BANK MANAGEMENT PHILOSOPHY[1]

Early theories of bank management concentrated on bank lending, or asset management, philosophies. More modern approaches to bank management concentrate on bank asset *and* liability management. Modern managers analyze both lending and borrowing in their quest to maximize shareholders' wealth.

THE COMMERCIAL LOAN THEORY, OR REAL BILLS DOCTRINE

A bank has a problem that is best described as the liquidity-earnings dilemma. If a bank desired to be a totally safe haven for all its depositors' funds, it would simply hold all those funds in its vault (i.e., as a perfectly liquid asset). Then, whenever a depositor requested cash from his or her bank, the banker would merely let down the drawbridge, cross the moat to the vault, and return to place the cash in the customer's hand. The problem is that no earnings would be generated for the bank if it were only a storehouse of cash.

Bankers could take a position at the other extreme. They could employ all the funds deposited with them to make a loan to finance a high-risk venture by a company seeking to find a cure for the common cold virus. Such a loan might have a high earnings potential for the bank, but the loan probably will not be liquid. It would be difficult to liquidate (sell) the assets to obtain cash when depositors wanted to make withdrawals.

To resolve the liquidity-earnings problem, bankers long ago recognized the advantage of making *self-liquidating loans* (otherwise known as real bills, or claims on real resources). A loan was considered self-liquidating if it was secured by goods in the process of production or by finished goods in transit to their final destination for resale. When the goods were sold, the loan could be repaid. Loans of this type could ensure the banks continuous liquidity and earn profits. Thus, liquidity and earnings were simultaneously gained. (Note, however, that no loan is truly automatically self-liquidating, because there may not be a market for the goods produced.) Banks that limit themselves to making self-liquidating loans subscribe to the **commercial loan theory** of bank management (or the **real bills doctrine**).

The commercial loan philosophy, however, suffers from the fallacy of composition:

---

[1] This section has drawn on Duane Graddy, Austin Spencer, and William Brunsen, *Commercial Banking and the Financial Services Industry* (Reston, Va.: Reston, 1985).

Such a system can keep one bank liquid, but if all banks follow this procedure, overall liquidity needs will not be met during times of crisis. Thus, a loan secured by goods cannot be repaid if the goods can't be sold. Or if the customer borrows the funds to purchase the goods, the banking system is no more liquid or less liquid than before the transaction. In the absence of a central bank that stands ready to supply needed liquidity to the system as a whole, the commercial loan theory is incomplete.

Although commercial loans continue to be an important component of banks' asset portfolios, the development of other uses of their funds has caused the operating methods of modern banks to change considerably.

THE SHIFTABILITY THEORY[2]

The **shiftability theory** recognized that liquidity could be provided if a certain portion of deposits were used to acquire such assets as loans and securities for which a secondary market exists. Thus, if a bank requires more liquidity to meet depositor withdrawals, increased loan demand, or reserve requirements, these highly liquid assets could be sold. Such securities are called **secondary reserves,** and they include U.S. Treasury bills, commercial paper, and banker's acceptances (see Chapter 5). By adhering to the shiftability theory, bank managers justified the making of longer-term loans, which extended the average maturity of the loan portfolio.

This shifting of assets from less liquid loans to more liquid money market instruments is effective only if all banks are not at the same time selling liquid money market instruments to obtain cash. Everyone cannot be a seller of T-bills simultaneously. Someone must be a buyer. An attempt to increase the total liquidity of the banking system through this process is doomed to failure unless an institution such as a central bank will purchase T-bills when all banks are attempting to increase their liquidity.

The shiftability theory, then, contains the same defect that plagues the commercial loan theory. Both must rely on a third party, such as the Fed, to increase the supply of total liquidity when necessary. For, without the Fed, what will provide instant liquidity for one or a few banks at most cannot provide a source of increased liquidity for the banking system as a whole. The Fed must be a ready buyer of securities from any and all banks for total liquidity to increase.

THE POOL-OF-FUNDS APPROACH

After experiencing the severe liquidity crisis of the Great Depression, bankers adopted an asset-liability portfolio approach that emphasized safety over short-term profitability. Additionally, demand deposits were by far the largest source of bank funds, and so such an emphasis on liquidity was further justified, because these bank liabilities were so short term. The label for this portfolio management technique is the **pool-of-funds approach.**

The pool-of-funds approach begins with the establishment of an overall level of desired liquidity, determined by senior management. In essence, this approach views all the bank's sources of funds (its liabilities) as emanating from a common pool; and this pool is considered to be determined by factors not under the bank's control, such as overall business activity, community income, population, and so on.

The first allocation of this pool of funds goes to primary reserves—vault cash, required

---

[2] This theory was formalized in 1918. See H. G. Moulton, ''Commercial Banking and Capital Formation,'' *Journal of Political Economy* (May–June–July 1918).

deposit reserves at the district Federal Reserve bank, and balances with other depository institutions. The second allocation is to secondary reserves—short-term, highly liquid securities. The average maturity of the secondary reserves is usually less than one year; such funds provide the bank with its primary source of liquidity under this approach.

Once sufficient liquidity has been assured, funds are allocated to finance all legitimate loan requests. Note that the asset structure, or the distribution of credit, is also viewed as a reflection of economic forces in the bank's geographic area; note further that the loan portfolio (the firm's riskier assets) is not considered a source of liquidity.

After the ''legitimate'' credit needs of society are met, any additional funds are used to purchase such long-term securities as Treasury bonds. The objective is to provide income and to supplement secondary reserves as these securities approach maturity.

The pool-of-funds approach is not without its critics. First, there is no objective basis for estimating the ''liquidity standard.'' Second, within the pool of funds, different deposits have different volatility; no indication of the importance of these differences to overall liquidity is considered. Third, the concentration is on liquidity, not profitability; but ultimately the long-run safety of a bank requires adequate earnings. Fourth, it ignores the liquidity provided by the loan portfolio through the continuous flow of funds from principal and interest payments. (We consider this in the next section, which examines the anticipated income theory.) Finally, the pool-of-funds approach disregards the interactive character of assets and liabilities in the generation of liquidity and profit earnings.

THE ANTICIPATED INCOME THEORY[3]

Another theory of bank management of assets was developed in the 1950s in reaction to the apparent insufficient liquidity provided by the making of commercial loans and the holding of money market securities. Using the doctrine of anticipated income, bankers again began to look at their loan portfolios as a source of liquidity. The anticipated income theory encouraged bankers to treat long-term loans as potential sources of liquidity.

How can a banker consider a mortgage loan as a source of liquidity when, typically, it has such a long maturity? Using the **anticipated income theory,** these loans are typically paid off by the borrower in a series of installments. Viewed in this way, the bank's loan portfolio provides the bank with a *continuous* flow of funds that adds to the bank's liquidity. Moreover, even though the loans are long term, in a liquidity crisis the bank can sell the loans to obtain needed cash in secondary markets.

In a sense, mortgage loans (as well as consumer and business loans for some specified period of time) are now considered to be equivalent to short-term business loans that finance inventories. Basically, the anticipated income theory is much like the commercial loan theory except that it embraces a broader base of securities from which liquidity may be obtained. That broader base now includes longer-maturity loans that contribute regularly to liquidity.

CONVERSION-OF-FUNDS APPROACH

Competition from nonbank depository institutions fostered a change in the structure of bank liabilities, as did the innovations in the sources of bank funds: CDs, Eurodollars, repurchase agreements, and so on (see Chapter 6). Consequently, the pool-of-funds approach became less tenable; it became unrealistic to view bank sources of funds as being

---

[3] Developed by Herbert Prochnow, *Term Loans and Theories of Bank Liquidity* (New York: Prentice-Hall, 1949).

a common pool of funds with similar characteristics. Each source had a unique volatility, cost, and legal reserve requirement. Moreover, the upward trend in interest rates induced bankers to become efficient reserve managers. The **conversion-of-funds approach** treats each source of funds individually and matches each source of funds with an asset that has a similar maturity. Demand deposits (which have a high legal reserve requirement and a rapid turnover) are allocated quite differently from funds generated by the bank's sale of long-term bonds. For example, a large proportion of demand deposits are allocated to primary and secondary reserves, while bank bond sales are used to finance long-term loans and fixed assets.

The main advantage of this approach is that it emphasizes profitability, not liquidity. In effect, it reduces the average value of liquid reserves and increases the allocation of funds to loans and investments.

Nevertheless, some problems remain. Liquidity needs are overestimated if one equates deposit turnover (which is indeed high) with deposit volatility (which need not be high if a lot of deposit turnover is self-canceling). Second, the loan portfolio is still assumed to be illiquid. Finally, this approach does not sufficiently stress that asset and liability decisions are interdependent.

THE MODERN APPROACH: ASSET-LIABILITY INTERACTION

In a conceptual sense, asset-liability management involves the coordination of all balance sheet items in a way that maximizes shareholder wealth (present value). Specifically, the asset-liability management approach focuses on the relationship between **variable-rate assets (VRAs)** and **variable-rate liabilities (VRLs).** VRAs and VRLs are those that will be rolled over (renewed), and therefore repriced, during the bank's planning horizon. The asset-liability planning horizon itself can vary from a few days to a year or more, depending on the circumstances.

This approach was doubtless prompted by the high degree of interest rate volatility that existed during the 1970s. For example, from 1950 to 1970, the prime rate changed 32 times; between 1970 and 1980, it changed 139 times.[4]

Three asset-liability management strategies have been developed; each is couched in terms of a *funds gap*, the difference between VRAs and VRLs. This gap measures the sensitivity of a bank's net interest earnings (its profits) to changes in market interest rates. The three strategies developed include the zero funds gap, the positive funds gap, and the negative funds gap.

THE ZERO FUNDS GAP STRATEGY

The first strategy is to pursue a **zero funds gap.** Under this strategy bank managers attempt to equate the proportion of the bank's total assets allocated to variable-rate assets (or assets that change in value as market interest rates change) with the proportion of the bank's total liabilities allocated to variable-rate liabilities (or liabilities that change in value as market interest rates change). In other words, this strategy prompts a bank's managers to hold, say, 40 percent of the bank's assets in VRAs and 40 percent of its liabilities in VRLs. This strategy tends to minimize interest rate risk because interest rates on funds borrowed tend to rise and fall with interest rates on funds lent. This approach minimizes

---

[4] *Supra* Graddy et al., p. 497.

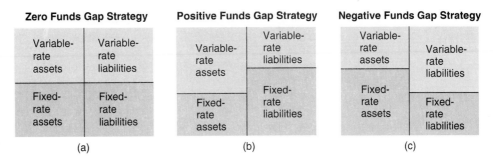

Figure 9-1
Zero, Positive, and Negative Funds Gap Strategies.   Bank managers who attempt to maintain the same spread between interest earnings and interest costs will pursue a zero funds gap strategy. Those willing to take a larger risk will pursue a positive funds gap strategy if they expect interest rates to rise and a negative funds gap strategy if they expect interest rates to fall.

the variability of returns over the planning period, because net interest earnings should be constant over the interest rate cycle, which follows the business cycle.

For example, consider what happens to bank net interest earnings when interest rates rise. The cost of funds to the bank increases as a result, but the bank lends at higher interest rates too, and so its interest earnings rise. To the extent that the spread between borrowing rates and lending rates remains constant over the interest rate cycle, the firm's profits are unaffected too.

Another way to view this strategy is to realize that if a zero funds gap exists, it must also be true that the ratio of the bank's fixed-rate assets (assets whose interest rates do not vary over the life of the loan, such as fixed-rate housing mortgages) to total interest rate assets equals the bank's ratio of fixed-rate liabilities to its total interest rate liabilities. [See Figure 9-1, panel (*a*).] Thus, when interest rates in general rise, the present value of the firm's fixed-rate assets falls, and the present value of its fixed-rate liabilities falls. (Note that fixed-rate assets and liabilities *tend* to be of longer term than variable-rate assets and liabilities; their prices, therefore, are more sensitive to interest rate changes.) To the extent that the spread between them is constant, these present-value changes leave the *market-valued* balance sheet unaltered.

THE POSITIVE FUNDS GAP STRATEGY

A second strategy is to pursue a **positive funds gap**; bank managers obtain a ratio of VRAs to total assets that exceeds the bank ratio of VRLs to total liabilities. For example, if 40 percent of a bank's total interest-earning assets are held in the form of VRAs, then, say, only 20 percent of its total interest-paying liabilities are held in the form of VRLs. As Figure 9-1, panel (*b*), shows, a positive funds gap strategy necessarily entails that the bank hold a lower ratio of fixed-rate assets to total interest-earning assets than its ratio of fixed-rate liabilities to total interest-paying liabilities. Continuing our example, the bank following this strategy will have a ratio of fixed-rate assets to total assets of 60 percent and a ratio of fixed-rate liabilities to total liabilities of 80 percent.

Consider now how the bank fares under such a strategy when market interest rates fall. As a result, the bank's interest earnings fall, as do its interest costs. But because it has a positive funds gap, its interest earnings fall by a greater amount than its interest costs; consequently, its net interest earnings (profits) fall.

When viewed from the *fixed*-interest asset-liability approach, we find that as market interest rates fall, the present value of the bank's fixed-interest assets rise, as does the present value of its fixed-interest liabilities. Because it has pursued a positive funds gap strategy, however, its *net* wealth falls. Although this won't show up on the bank's balance sheet, which values assets and liabilities at their acquisition (historical) values, the bank's stock price will fall as stock market investors realize what has happened.

THE NEGATIVE FUNDS GAP STRATEGY

By now you realize that if the bank pursues a **negative funds gap** strategy, its ratio of VRAs to total assets is less than its ratio of VRLs to total liabilities. And you realize that it must necessarily be true, as Figure 9-1, panel (*c*), shows, that under this strategy the bank's ratio of fixed-rate assets to total assets must exceed its ratio of fixed-rate liabilities to total liabilities.

This strategy is pursued if bank managers expect interest rates to fall. If their expectations prove to be correct, the bank's net interest earnings will rise and its net worth will rise. This latter effect will not show up on the balance sheet, but the bank's stock market price will rise.

Of course, if the bank pursues a negative funds gap strategy and interest rates rise, then its profits will fall and its net worth will fall. The latter effect again will show up in a lower stock market price, but not on the balance sheet.

We conclude our funds gap analysis with the observation that the modern asset-liability interaction approach is superior to the previous approaches in one major respect: It accepts neither the level nor the composition of assets or liabilities as a given. This approach suggests that bank managers have greater control over the fate and profitability of the bank. Note that with the banks' increased control over their destiny comes not only the chance to earn higher profits, but also the possibility of greater losses.

THE SELECTION OF ASSETS AND PORTFOLIO DIVERSIFICATION

In this section we describe another management technique, the diversification of the bank's asset portfolio to reduce risk. Throughout this section we shall assume that, *for a given level of acceptable risk*, bank managers attempt to maximize profits.

ASSET ACQUISITION AND EXPECTED RATES OF RETURN

The determination by banks of which assets to acquire is based on *expected* rates of return rather than on current rates. If interest rates are expected to rise in the near future, it is likely that cash and very short-term assets (such as overnight federal funds) will be held in order to avoid capital losses that would result from holding fixed-money income-earning securities when interest rates rise. (Bank management behavior would be the opposite if interest rates were expected to fall.) A bank holding cash and overnight federal funds, for example, cannot be seriously affected by an increase in market interest rates. But a bank holding 6-month T-bills will be affected adversely by a rise in market rates of interest, because the value of the T-bills will fall.

To minimize risk but still achieve a relatively fixed level of earnings, banks attempt to diversify their asset portfolios. The aim of diversification is to acquire a portfolio consisting of some assets that increase in value when other assets decrease in value, so that the net changes in value approach zero. In the optimal situation, the variable rates of return on diversified assets will act to stabilize the *average overall* rate of return on the total portfolio and thus decrease risk resulting from changes in market activities.

A Numerical Example   Suppose that two assets are available to a portfolio manager. Asset A has a rate of return of 20 percent half the time and 12 percent the other half. Similarly, asset Y has likely returns of 24 and 8 percent. Both assets have an average expected rate of return of 16 percent. The expected rate of return is obtained by multiplying each rate of return by the probability of obtaining it. Therefore, the expected rate of return of asset A equals

$$(0.5 \times 0.2) + (0.5 \times 0.12) = 0.16$$

The expected rate of return of asset Y equals

$$(0.5 \times 0.24) + (0.5 \times 0.08) = 0.16$$

While the average expected rate of return is the same for both assets, the variability (relative to the average) in the rates of return on asset Y is greater than on asset A. Given this greater variability in rates of return, asset Y is said to be riskier than asset A. The point is that a potential investor cannot determine the degree of risk simply by looking at the *expected* rate of return.

Suppose that a recession occurred and the rate of return on one asset increased and the rate of return on the other asset decreased. How would these changes affect the rate of return for a portfolio containing both asset A and asset Y? If the rates of return of two assets change in opposite directions, the change in the average rate of return of a portfolio containing the two will be less than the change in the rate of return from a portfolio consisting of only one of the assets.

Let's assume the following:

1. Asset A has a *high* rate of return (20 percent) during the period when asset Y has a *low* rate of return (8 percent).

2. Asset Y has a *high* rate of return (24 percent) during the period that asset A has a *low* rate of return (12 percent).

3. Given these individual variabilities, a portfolio can be acquired that will have no variability in return (i.e., zero risk) all the time.

That portfolio will consist of two-thirds of asset A and one-third of asset Y ($2 of A for every $1 of Y). It will have a constant return of 16 percent. The calculation is as follows:

$$(\tfrac{2}{3} \times 0.20) + (\tfrac{1}{3} \times 0.08) = 0.13333 + 0.02667 = 0.16, \text{ or } 16\% \text{ (half the time)}$$
$$(\tfrac{2}{3} \times 0.12) + (\tfrac{1}{3} \times 0.24) = 0.08 + 0.08 = 0.16, \text{ or } 16\% \text{ (half the time)}$$

Fully offsetting assets are not, of course, readily available; but to the extent that long-term and short-term assets move in different directions at the same time, asset acquisitions similar to those found in the above example are possible.

ASSET SECURITIZATION BY DEPOSITORY INSTITUTIONS

In Chapter 5, we referred to the recent growth in the use of asset-backed securities. Commercial banks and other depository institutions have participated actively in this growth through the process of **asset securitization.** Asset securitization is a process by which depository institution managers indirectly sell individually illiquid depository institution assets by segregating them into *pools,* or groupings, that depository institution managers use to collateralize securities they sell in financial markets. In turn, the securities sold by the depository institutions may differ from the underlying pools of assets in their interest payments, denominations, and maturities.

Between 1985 and 1993, the total amount of depository institution asset-backed securities increased from over $368 billion to over $1,000 billion. Nearly all these securities were backed by pools of mortgage loans. The amount of asset-backed securities backed by nonmortgage assets of depository institutions grew from just over $1 billion in 1985 to over $60 billion in 1993.

Some observers believe that the current trend toward increased securitization of depository institution assets reflects a major shift in the function of ''banking.'' In the past a key role of depository institutions has been to shoulder interest rate risks—that is, the mismatching of risk of interest rate variations on the asset and liability sides of their balance sheets. This was their ''bread-and-butter'' specialty. Many observers interpret the movement by depository institutions toward more and more asset securitization as an abandonment of that role to other institutions and markets. These analysts argue that depository institutions today are specializing as conservative loan originators and deposit servicers only, leaving the real risks for the less faint-at-heart.

Whether or not this evaluation turns out to be warranted, securitization appears to be here to stay. How much it continues to grow will depend both on the ingenuity of depository institution managers in their continuing efforts to pool loans and to issue market asset-backed securities and on the willingness of regulators to permit them to expand their activities.

TRENDS IN DEPOSITORY INSTITUTION MANAGEMENT AND PERFORMANCE

As you will learn in the remaining chapters in this unit, many of the major issues concerning depository institutions have to do with governmental policies toward these institutions. Nevertheless, there are a variety of issues concerning the management of depository institutions that, although we shall confront them again in the later chapters on regulation, we highlight in the remainder of the present chapter. We do so because they are of particular importance to owners and managers of depository institutions.

BANK HOLDING COMPANIES

In recent decades, the prevailing trend in the corporate structure of depository institutions has been *holding company* ownership of these institutions. Although holding companies own all types of depository institutions, economists and policy makers typically refer to these as bank holding companies. As we shall discuss in more detail, the primary motivation for the growth of holding company ownership of banks and other depository institutions has been a general effort to circumvent various restrictions on the lines of businesses in which these institutions may participate and the extent to which banks can branch within and between states.

There are two basic types of bank holding companies: multi-bank holding companies and one-bank holding companies. The names describe the distinction between the two types of holding companies. As we shall discuss in the next chapter, **multi-bank holding companies**—companies that own and control two or more independently incorporated banks—are a relatively recent development. The multi-bank holding company form of corporate structure typically enables banking corporations to circumvent branching restrictions.

While multi-bank holding companies are of relatively recent origin, the one-bank holding company is not. A **one-bank holding company** is defined as a business organization that is involved in numerous activities, including banking. For example, Macy's Department Store has owned a bank for many years. So, too, have the Goodyear Tire & Rubber Company, Montgomery Ward, and the United Mine Workers. The original purpose of the one-bank holding company was to allow a nonbanking enterprise to engage legally in banking. Since the 1970s, however, this device has been used by commercial banks to enter nonbanking commercial activities.

Over half of the activities of the ''nonbank'' subsidiaries of bank holding companies are related to traditional banking activities, such as commercial finance, mortgage banking, leasing, and consumer finance. Nonetheless, legal restrictions have not specifically prohibited banks from engaging in a multitude of nonbanking commercial activities. Consequently, as one-bank holding companies, commercial banks could engage in bookkeeping and data-processing services, insurance, courier services, management services, securities brokerage, and the like. Perhaps more important, as one-bank holding companies, commercial banks were able to raise funds more easily (instead of attracting deposits) by selling the holding company's commercial paper. Thus, one-bank holding companies could obtain funds in the unregulated commercial paper market and then channel those funds to the parent bank, where they could be used to offset (partially) restrictive Fed actions designed to reduce bank reserves, lending, and the money supply.

We shall have more to say about the regulatory implications of the bank holding company structure in the following chapter. Certainly, a key motivation for the formation of holding companies is to evade or circumvent governmental regulations on banking activities. There is, however, an old-fashioned motive for the holding company structure: profits. In recent years, the average ratio of net income to total assets devoted to nonbanking activities of bank holding companies exceeded the same measure for their banking-related assets. As we shall discuss below, one reason for this experience was that, for the most part, traditional banking activities have not been especially profitable throughout the last several years. The higher relative profitability of nonbanking activities has, as a result, significantly encouraged the growth of bank holding companies.

JOINT VENTURES

There are a variety of activities in which depository institutions can legally join together in pursuit of common interests. One common example is *loan participations*, in which several banks participate in a very large loan to a single borrower. In some instances loan participations may be highly formalized, and sometimes banks can buy or sell shares of the large loan. In many other instances the joint loan arrangements are less formal; contracts simply specify how all banks involved will share in losses from the aggregate loan if the borrower fails to repay as scheduled.

An example of such an arrangement was a large loan made by several banks to the multi-millionaire Donald Trump in the late 1980s. The total amount borrowed by Mr. Trump, which he used to finance the construction of casino-hotels and other investment projects, was too large for any one bank, and so several banks participated in the loan. When, in 1990, several of Mr. Trump's investments turned out to have been poor performers, the banks together had to work out a joint agreement with Mr. Trump, rescheduling his repayment of interest and principal on the loans made by the various banks. Similar situations typically have arisen in recent years with respect to borrowings by Latin American nations that have been ''too big'' for any one bank to tackle but have been made through the participation of several banks simultaneously.

Another form of loan participation by banks has been in the business of credit card lending. Visa International and MasterCard International, Inc., are credit card operations administered by confederations, often called *franchises*, of banks. Individual banks extend revolving accounts to customers, but payments on the accounts typically are processed for all banks in the confederation by central payment clearing centers. This centralized arrangement saves banks that issue credit cards the costs of establishing their own clearing operations for all their credit card transactions.

Another example of a joint venture by depository institutions is *automated teller machine (ATM) networks*. ATM networks are computer-linked teller machines that permit customers of different banks and thrifts to use the same machines for making deposits and withdrawals from their accounts electronically. Although there are some exceptions, depository institutions typically participate in a group ATM network rather than setting up their own networks to help share in the costs of building and maintaining the systems. Most of these networks are confined to regions within states, although in early 1991 there were open discussions by Visa International and MasterCard International, Inc., about the establishment during the 1990s of a *nationwide* ATM network that would facilitate both deposit transactions and ''point-of-sale'' transactions—automatic deductions of retail purchases from depositors' accounts.

An important point to emphasize is that legal restrictions called *antitrust laws* significantly limit formal ties among depository institutions. While depository institutions may share some types of information and processing centers, they cannot work together to price their services to maximize their joint profits. Formation of such explicit pricing coalitions, or cartels, is illegal in the United States. As we shall see in Chapter 11, however, it remains an open question whether or not *implicit* cartel arrangements may have existed in the depository institution industries.

DEPOSITORY INSTITUTION PERFORMANCE AND PROSPECTS

How have depository institutions been doing? This is a difficult question to answer, partly because there are a variety of ways to evaluate their performance. Furthermore, it is a natural feature of a capitalist system that some depository institutions may do very well while others do poorly. In addition, although depository institutions function in a largely capitalistic environment, they nonetheless are subjected to a variety of regulatory restrictions that may assist or impede their performance. Finally, some groups of depository institutions—notably commercial banks and credit unions—have exhibited fair to good performances while others—particularly many savings and loan associations and savings banks—have performed very poorly in recent years. Depository institution performance is the main issue of interest to regulators and shall occupy much of our attention in the remaining chapters of this unit. Nonetheless, we conclude this chapter on depository institution management with a brief overview of how these managers appear to have performed in recent years and of the prospects for the future.

Measures of Performance of Depository Institutions   Perhaps the most widely accepted measure of the performance of depository institutions is their *current profitability*. After all, if depository institutions are profitable, they must not be doing too badly. There are a variety of measures of profitability. Two common measures are return on assets and return on equity. The **return on assets** measure of depository institution profitability measures net income, or profit, as a percentage of total assets. This measure provides an indication of the profitability of depository institutions' assets and therefore is especially useful in making comparisons of the profitabilities of different types of asset categories such as commercial and industrial loans, real estate loans, and so on. The **return on equity** measure of profitability is the ratio of total net income to the depository institution's equity capital; it provides a measure of how profitable are ownership shares of the depository institution and is particularly useful when comparing profitabilities of different depository institutions.

Current profits alone, however, cannot permit one to judge the longer-term performance of a depository institution, because by the nature of their business—lending funds for maturities that extend into the near or far future—current profits could be a misleading indicator if depository institutions have made loans that will perform poorly in the future. Current profits also may be a poor indicator of the growth (or decline) of depository institutions, either alone or as a group. Therefore, a variety of other measures of performance of depository institutions typically are considered along with profitability.

One important measure of performance is **asset growth.** Measuring the growth (or decline) of depository institutions' assets over time provides a reasonable indication, along with their profitability, of both their current and longer-term performance and prospects. Another indicator often considered to gauge the performance of depository institutions is the performance of current loans issued by the banks. Direct measures of loan performance are net loan losses and the proportion of loans that depository institutions categorize as nonperforming loans. **Net loan losses** are the net reductions in income that depository institutions incur when borrowers default on their loans, and **nonperforming loans** are loans on which the borrowers have partially or fully defaulted on their interest and principal payments. Other carefully watched measures of loan performance are loan loss reserves and loan loss provisions. **Loan loss reserves** are cash assets that depository institutions earmark as contingency funds to cover expected losses from partial or full defaults on outstanding loans, and **loan loss provisions** are *additions* to loan loss reserves during a given time interval (usually a year).

Other measures of performance and prospects of depository institutions are the amounts of, prices of, and growth of their equity capital. If investors regard the depository institution industry as currently healthy and potentially profitable in the future, they should be willing to hold shares of ownership in the institutions. If the industry is particularly healthy, the growth of equity capital ownership in the industry should be very strong. Furthermore, the prices of bank shares of equity—that is, *bank stock prices*—should be relatively high and stable. Finally, a depository institution industry should witness relatively few depository institution failures.

Recent Performance and Prospects of Commercial Banks   The overall performance of commercial banks in recent years can best be described as ''interesting to watch.'' The reason is that all of the measures listed above have varied significantly in the past several years. From mid-1986 through mid-1988 and again in late 1989, loan loss

IS THE CREDIT CARD BUSINESS COMPETITIVE?

During 1990 and 1991, the general level of interest rates fell, and this was reflected by a gradual reduction in the interest rates that banks and thrifts paid their depositors for funds that these depository institutions used to make loans, such as credit card loans. Nevertheless, as shown in the figure below, the spread between deposit rates and bank credit card rates widened significantly from late 1989 to early 1991. Even though deposit rates and many loan rates fell during that period, credit card interest rates tended to stay constant or to fall by much smaller magnitudes.

Many observers, including members of Congress and some of their constituents, cried "foul" when this occurred. Bills were introduced on the floor of the House of Representatives and the Senate that would have placed limits on credit card rates to prohibit depository institutions from maintaining high rates on these forms of revolving credit. The justification commonly offered for these bills was that the high rate spreads were concrete evidence of a lack of competition among the issuers of credit cards. Indeed, further apparent evidence of attempts by depository institutions to restrain credit card competition occurred in 1990 when a few banks

participating in Visa International brought suit against AT&T, challenging its indirect entry into the Visa confederation (it had purchased the share of a Visa franchise contract held by a participating bank). These banks claimed, on the basis of their Visa contracts, that only depository institutions should legally be permitted to belong. Many observers argued that the banks had brought the lawsuit because AT&T had offered Visa credit at lower interest rates than other bank credit card issuers and that the banks were counterattacking to keep credit card rates artificially high.

At the same time, however, many depository institutions found that their share of the credit card business fell during the 1980s and early 1990s, even as outstanding balances on credit cards nearly tripled. Between 1986 and 1990, the share of credit card receivables held by credit card issuers other than banks rose from less than 6 percent to over 18 percent. Of the top ten credit card issuers in 1990 (who together had issued nearly 150 million credit cards), half—including some relatively new credit card services offered by Sears and AT&T—were nonbank corporations. By the early 1990s, a typical adult in the United States had 8 credit cards, of which on average only $2\frac{1}{2}$ were bank cards. Furthermore, AT&T was not the only nonbank company getting involved in the Visa and MasterCard business previously

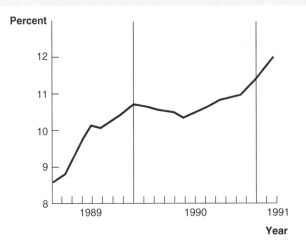

The Credit Card Interest Spread, May 1989–February 1991. Difference between average yields on 1-year certificates of deposit issued by commercial banks and average bank credit card interest rate, in percentage points. (*Bank Rate Monitor*, N. Palm Beach 33408)

"owned" by depository institutions. In 1990 Sears attempted to purchase the Visa franchise of a failed Utah savings and loan association, but Visa refused to fill its order for credit cards. Shortly thereafter, Sears received temporary legal authority to countermand that decision. Furthermore, in early 1991 General Motors' GMAC Capital Corporation expressed interest in issuing Visa cards as well.

According to depository institutions, it is "unfair" to permit Sears, AT&T, GM, and the like to issue the equivalent of bank credit cards, because those companies are not subject to the same set of regulations as depository institutions. Corporations like Sears and AT&T, however, have taken advantage of the outcry against high credit card interest rates by arguing that depository institutions simply wish to limit competition in the credit card business to keep the interest rates artificially high.

Relatively high and inflexible interest rates on credit cards are an interesting economic controversy, because there are so many—about 6,000—issuers of credit cards. With so many competitors, why should the credit card interest rate remain so much above other loan interest rates, whether or not Sears and AT&T join the fray? One possible answer is that credit card rates are high because many who use the cards are poor credit risks; delinquency rates on credit card loans are high, especially during economic recessions, as credit card issuers discovered during the 1990–1992 recession. Good credit risks pay their credit card balances promptly, avoiding most or all interest payments, but poorer credit risks take much longer to repay—or do not repay at all. Hence, the higher credit card interest rates may compensate credit card lenders for the greater risks they incur by issuing credit cards to so many people.

Adapted in part from Larry Light et al., "Top of the News: The War of the Plastic," *Business Week* (April 15, 1991), pp. 28–29; David B. Hilder and Peter Pae, "Rivalry Rages among Big Credit Cards," *Wall Street Journal* (Friday, May 3, 1991), p. B1; and from Neal Lipschultz, "Representative Proposes Legislation on Disclosing Credit Card Rates, Fees," *Wall Street Journal* (Monday, October 14, 1991), p. A7A.

provisions as a percentage of assets actually exceeded the return on assets, as shown in Figure 9-2. Indeed, in 1989 the commercial banking industry's average return on assets was 0.51 percent, the lowest since 1970. It stayed almost unchanged, at 0.50 percent, in 1990.

As shown in Figure 9-3, several measures of the weakness of loan performance—including net loan losses, loan loss reserves, and loan loss provisions—drifted upward throughout the 1980s and early 1990s. As a whole, commercial banks made many loans in the 1980s that, after the fact, turned out to be "nonperformers." Chief among these were loans to Latin American nations. In 1991, for instance, bank regulators required banks to "write down" the value of loans to the Brazilian government to 60 percent of their principal amount; banks were required to discount loans to Argentina's government to 30 percent of their principal amount.

Interestingly, these Latin American loan losses that U.S. banks experienced in the 1980s and 1990s reflected a repeat of past mistakes. As early as 1825 every Latin American nation had defaulted on loan interest payments to banks of that time. Yet in the 1920s U.S. banks rushed to lend to the nations of Central and South America, only to suffer massive defaults on interest and principal payments in the 1930s. Indeed, even by the mid-1940s Latin American nations remained in default on over a third of the loans made to them by U.S. banks. By the late 1970s—a couple of bank management generations later—commercial banks again lined up to make loans to Latin American countries, only to regret them, once again, a decade later. As in the 1930s, when Central and South American loan defaults stemmed from a nosedive in the prices of Latin American export commodities such as copper and other minerals, the defaults of the 1980s and 1990s resulted from significant drops in the price of an export mineral. In the 1980s and 1990s, however, the export mineral whose price fell and produced a loan crisis was oil.

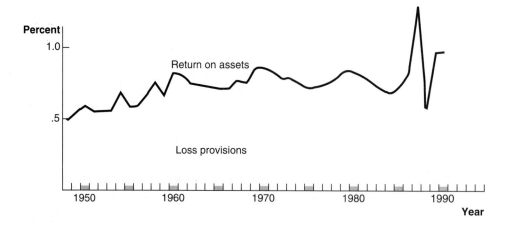

Figure 9-2

Commercial Bank Return on Assets and Loan Loss Provisions as a Percentage of Assets, 1970–1990.   Return on assets is the ratio of net income to total assets of commercial banks. [*Source*: Allan D. Brunner, John V. Duca, and Mary M. McLaughlin, "Developments Affecting the Profitability and Practices of Commercial Banks," *Federal Reserve Bulletin,* 77 (7, July 1991), pp. 505–527.]

Figure 9-3

Measures of Commercial Bank Loan Losses and Loan Loss Provisions, 1977–1990.   Reserves for loan losses, loan loss provisions, and net loan losses as percentages of commercial bank loans. [*Source*: Allan D. Brunner, John V. Duca, and Mary M. McLaughlin, "Developments Affecting the Profitability and Practices of Commercial Banks," *Federal Reserve Bulletin,* 77 (7, July 1991), pp. 505–527.]

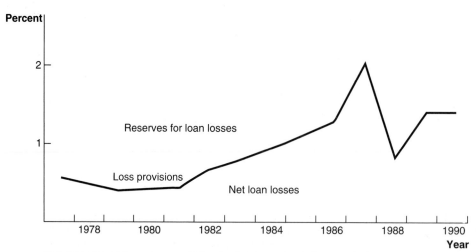

Data for loans and reserves are averages. Losses are net of recoveries.

The annual growth of total loans made by banks was high throughout much of the 1980s, and was as high as 16.1 percent in 1984. As the loans to Latin American and other developing nations turned sour, however, banks cut back significantly on loans; by 1987 growth in total bank lending had fallen to an annual rate of 4.2 percent. Indeed, although total loans and other bank assets have risen in total, as a proportion of total assets held by *all* financial institutions—including pension funds, insurance companies, money market funds, etc.—the asset share held by commercial banks had fallen from over 34 percent in 1960 to nearly 25 percent by 1990.

Another group of nonperforming loans was real estate loans. Figure 9-4 shows how the portion of real estate loans that were nonperforming rose from less than 2.5 percent in early 1988 to nearly 4.5 percent by the end of 1990. Unfortunately for banks, this increase in defaults on real estate loans followed a sharp increase in real estate lending by commercial banks during the 1980s, from under $200 billion in 1984 to over $350 billion in 1990.

Clearly, the late 1980s and early 1990s were not great years for commercial banks. As Figure 9-5 indicates, this led to significant variation in stock prices at two types of large banks—money center banks and regional banks—relative to the prices of other stocks. **Money center banks** are very large banks that engage in national and international lending and deposit businesses, while **regional banks** are somewhat smaller—but still quite large—banks that primarily participate in loan and deposit markets across state lines in the regions around their headquarters locations.

Shares of ownership of small banks do not trade as widely as those of large banks, and so they are not included in Figure 9-5. Nonetheless, their recent experience also has been generally poor. Their return on assets fell from over 0.9 percent in 1982 to under 0.6 percent by the end of the 1980s. Hence, small banks tended to be slightly more profitable—relative to total assets—than large banks, but their performance has generally paralleled that of large banks.

Figure 9-4

Commercial Banks' Nonperforming Real Estate Loans as a Percentage of Total Real Estate Loans, 1984–1990.   In the late 1980s, bank real estate loan losses rose considerably. (*Source:* Office of the Comptroller of the Currency.)

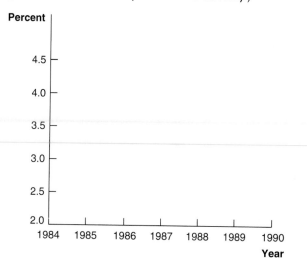

PRIVATE BANKING—A FADDISH THROWBACK TO THE NINETEENTH CENTURY OR A WAVE OF THE FUTURE?

Even as bank profitability declined in the 1980s and early 1990s, bank services for the "upper crust" of society expanded. Known broadly as "private banking," such banking services include attending to mundane details for special customers, such as wiring large sums at a moment's notice, assisting customers with personal financial planning, and providing unusual and innovative loan financing.

An Old Practice

Readers young and old alike have read with thrill the famous story of revenge—and, in part, of a private banking relationship—told by Alexandre Dumas (also the author of *The Three Musketeers* and *The Man in the Iron Mask*) in his novel *The Count of Monte Cristo*. In the story, a nineteenth-century merchant marine is unjustly imprisoned largely through the efforts of a man who later becomes a successful banker. After escaping from prison, discovering a huge fortune, and transforming himself into the "Count of Monte Cristo," the ex-merchant marine arranges years later for private banking services from his former nemesis, who does not recognize him from the earlier time that their paths had crossed. The count exacts his revenge upon the banker by ruining him financially—through the count's manipulation of the private banking agreement he has negotiated with the hated banker.

As this story implies, private banking has existed for a long time. Indeed, the original "House of Morgan," the pre-1935 banking empire whose 1990 biographer Ron Chernow has termed "probably the most formidable financial combine in history,"* got its start by catering to the financial needs of prominent nineteenth-century families of wealth, such as the Astors, du Ponts, and Vanderbilts. Indeed, successors to the original Morgan empire—the J. P. Morgan holding company and its subsidiary bank, Morgan Guaranty Trust; the Morgan-Stanley investment company, and the British banking and investment firm Morgan-Grenfell—largely have continued the practice of treating wealthy individual depositors differently from "the rest of us." Even today, the J. P. Morgan Company, Chernow assures us,

seduces the rich with leather armchairs, grandfather clocks, and polished brass lamps. In private dining rooms, anniversaries of accounts are celebrated, with customers receiving engraved menus as souvenirs. The bank won't soil its white gloves with just anybody's cash, and many depositors bring along corporate connections. Although the bank is bashful about revealing precise figures, it prefers personal accounts of at least $5 million and will occasionally stoop as low as $2 million—as a favor.†

Modern Private Banking

Today, the remnants of the Morgan empire are getting more competition for the right to treat big depositors "like royalty." For depositors with minimum account balances ranging from $250,000 to $5 million, banks such as Chase Manhattan, Citibank, and Harris Trust—which in the mid-twentieth century broke away from the J. P. Morgan style of "white-glove banking" to service the financial needs of the masses of "little people"—recently have rushed to return to this nineteenth-century style of banking. In contrast to the nineteenth-century times when banks courted the dollars of baronial landlords and industrialists, however, today's private-banking arrangements are being marketed to "yuppie entrepreneurs" and corporate executives.

These big banks have plenty of other competition. Recent estimates are that as many as 350 specialized private-banking institutions exist, sometimes in the form of independent "banking boutiques" or special private-banking subsidiaries of bank holding companies, and that at least 5,000 community or regional banks have worked hard to develop first-name, specialized banking relationships with individuals of local or national prominence. Specific targets of their private-banking efforts are 1.8 million households known as the "wealth market": corporate executives who earn at least $100,000 or more a year, entrepreneurs whose companies have book values in excess of $250,000, and households with a net worth of at least $1 million.

A Growth Market?

While some might regard all this hoopla over a banking "wealth market" as a modern-day reemergence of what the famous economist Thorstein Veblen once called a hunger for "conspicuous consumption"—especially given the fact that over a fourth of the lowest-income households in the United States remain too poor to afford to maintain even a single bank account—banks are unabashed in their modern-day pursuit of the wealthy. The reason is that private-banking accounts can be very profitable. Even though the costs of providing personalized banking services are high, the potential return also is significant. A typical annual fee for a private-banking account is 1 percent of the balance in the account. Hence, a $5 million private-banking account would yield a bank total revenues of $50,000 per year, to say nothing of interest revenues earned from loans made to that "special customer." Banks also find that the personal contacts they make with these customers can have positive side effects if the customers steer their friends or their corporate accounts to their "personal banker."

Is this really a new trend or just a perpetuation of an old banking tradition? In all likelihood, the latter is true.

While the business of modern banking perhaps is more "democratic" than it once was, banks have always yearned for the business of the rich and famous. What may have changed in recent years is the willingness of banks to compete openly for private-banking relationships. Naturally, such an increase in competition likely will benefit those who use the services—as if the consumers of this particular service need any extra benefits!

*Chernow, *The House of Morgan* (New York: Atlantic Monthly Press, 1990), p. xi.

†*Ibid.*, p. xiii.

Adapted in part from Arlene Hershman, "Personal Business: Putting a Private Banker at Your Service," *Business Week* (April 8, 1991), pp. 92–93, and Craig Smith, "Banks' Internal Turf Battles Are Costly: Branches Need to Feed Most Profitable Divisions," *Wall Street Journal* (Friday, May 17, 1990), p. B7B. (*Note:* For those students who can meet the minimum-balance requirements of private-banking accounts, the Hershman article also offers evaluations of which banks are "big city-slickers aiming to be small-town-personal," or "safe and yearning to be J. P. Morgan," or "in sync with Southern Californians who have arrived.")

Figure 9-5 indicates that while the stocks of large banks slightly outperformed the Standard & Poor's 500 index of aggregate stock prices in 1988, by the end of 1989 and throughout much of 1990 bank share prices were significantly below the index of aggregate stock prices. This weak performance almost certainly stemmed from the realization by investors that the banking industry's loan losses and profitability had plummeted. In addition to the sharp decline in bank stock prices and earnings in 1989 and 1990, bank equity growth fell significantly as well; few wished to hold bank stock, fearing the industry was in deep trouble. Overall, some analysts judged 1990 itself to have been the worst year for banking since the Great Depression. This poor year followed upon the weak decade of the 1980s, during which 1,086 banks failed, double the total number that failed between 1934 and 1980. Indeed, the situation had begun to look so bad by the early 1990s that the *Wall Street Journal* began printing a regular series on its opinion page entitled "Saving the Banks."

What are the prospects for the commercial banking industry? The best answer at this time probably is "very uncertain." By 1992, bank stock prices had rebounded somewhat, but they remained well below other stock prices. Bank earnings also were up somewhat—interestingly, the common explanation for this was the higher earnings that stemmed from a general *fall* in interest rates in which loan rates fell more slowly than deposit rates—and loan loss reserves and provisions largely had leveled off. Furthermore, equity ownership in commercial banks had increased. It remains to be seen whether the situation really has improved for the banking industry—or whether the rebound in 1991–1992 was a temporary recovery from long-term ills. We shall take up some of the prevailing problems in the banking industry in Chapters 10, 11, and 12.

Performance of the Thrift Industry   We shall devote an entire chapter (Chapter 13) to the massive crisis that afflicted thrift institutions in the 1980s and into the 1990s. Therefore, we shall be brief—and direct—in our coverage here. Rather than focusing on profitability, loan losses, and so on, we shall offer some more stark figures for you to

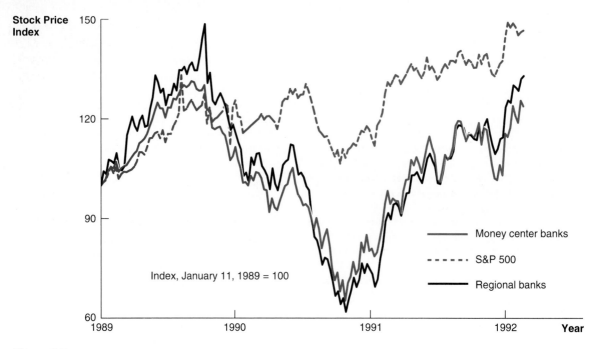

Figure 9-5
Bank Stock Indexes and the Standard & Poor's 500 Index.   Stocks of large money center
and regional banks slightly outperformed other stocks during 1988, plummeted to much lower
levels in late 1989 and 1990, and recovered somewhat through 1992. (*Source*: Board of Governors
of the Federal Reserve System. Weekly data: January 6, 1989 = 100.)

contemplate. The issue in this industry has become this: Irrespective of their recent and
near-term profitability prospects, will very many of these institutions even *survive?*

Between 1980 and 1988, regulators judged to be insolvent and seized and closed 489
thrift institutions (mainly savings and loan associations and savings banks). Between
February 1989 and February 1991, 530 thrifts (that is, 41 more within those two years
than in the previous nine combined) were taken over by regulators, and 432 of these were
closed within that period. By early 1991, governmental regulators had determined that
nearly 2,200 of about 4,000 savings and loan associations that were in existence had
technically failed, and these regulators had estimated that between 600 and 1,100 more
would need to be closed.

A Congressional Budget Office estimate in early 1991 was that between 1,000 and
1,200 savings and loan associations would remain in existence by 1995. Estimates of the
discounted present value (in 1991 dollars) of the total cost of closing the remaining
insolvent thrift institutions ranged anywhere from $130 billion (U.S. Treasury) to $142
billion (General Accounting Office) to $200–$250 billion (Congressional Budget Office).

In short, the thrift industry has become a shadow of its former self, and the source of
a major loss to society (and, as we shall see, particularly to U.S. taxpayers). Things went
very wrong for the thrift industry in the last two decades. We shall have much more to
say on this topic in later chapters. Suffice it to say for now that this is an industry that

literally has experienced a disaster comparable only to the bank failures of the 1930s. Its prospects may have improved somewhat, but the industry's overall prognosis remains very troubled.

CHAPTER SUMMARY

1. Banks create short-term, highly liquid liabilities by accepting demand and time deposits; they then use them to buy longer-term, less liquid assets. As a consequence, banks have a potential liquidity problem: Their liabilities are more liquid than are their assets.

2. There are various theories about how banks should solve their liquidity problem. The commercial loan theory is that banks can solve their liquidity problem by making only short-term, self-liquidating loans that are secured by goods in the process of production or goods in transit. There are two flaws in this theory: (a) No loan is truly automatically self-liquidating, because there may not be a market for the goods produced; and (b) such a policy entails automatic destabilizing changes in credit levels, because total liquidity automatically increases during periods of inflation and contracts during periods of recession.

3. Another theory of how banks can solve their liquidity problem is the shiftability theory. This theory is that banks should purchase assets that are highly liquid. It follows that both bank assets and bank liabilities will then be highly liquid. The problem with this theory is that the entire financial system cannot simultaneously increase its liquidity; a third party such as a central bank is required to increase liquidity for the entire financial community in times of financial crisis.

4. A third theory about how banks can resolve liquidity problems is the anticipated income theory. This theory is that banks will have sufficient liquidity even if they make long-term loans, as long as those loans are repaid in a series of installments that provide banks with predictable inflows of funds. Moreover, these long-term loans can be sold in secondary markets to meet liquidity problems.

5. After the Great Depression, bank managers concentrated on maintaining liquidity, and the pool-of-funds approach was practiced. This approach viewed bank sources of funds as a common pool with similar characteristics; from this pool, primary and secondary reserves were met; then legitimate loans were made; then long-term U.S. bonds were purchased.

6. Innovations in debt instruments and increased competition from nonbank financial institutions induced bank managers to rethink their approach. The conversion-of-funds approach evolved, in which each bank's source of funds was viewed as having unique characteristics that made it more suitable for purchasing specific assets. This approach emphasized profitability over liquidity, but it still did not sufficiently stress that asset and liability decisions are interdependent and that bank managers can affect both the size and the composition of both their assets and their liabilities.

7. The asset-liability integration approach emphasizes bank profits and involves an aggressive pursuit of both assets and liabilities. Such strategies as a zero funds gap, a positive funds gap, and a negative funds gap have been developed; bank managers choose the strategy that is most consistent with their expectation of future interest rates and the degree of risk their stockholders wish to assume.

8. A new trend in depository institution management is asset securitization. Banks and thrifts securitize assets by pooling groups of loans with similar characteristics together and selling securities to investors that guarantee those investors shares of the returns from the pooled groupings of assets.

9. There are a variety of measures of depository institution performance, including return on assets, return on equity, loan loss reserves and provisions, asset and equity growth, and stock prices.

10. Overall, the performance of the commercial banking industry, while varied, has been weak in recent years. The thrift industry, and especially savings and loan associations, has experienced even worse performance.

GLOSSARY

Anticipated income theory: The theory that banks can solve their liquidity problem even by making long-term loans if borrowers repay the loans in a series of continuous installments.

Asset growth: The growth or decline of a depository institution's assets over time.

Asset securitization: A process by which depository institution managers indirectly sell individually illiquid depository institution assets by segregating them into *pools,* or groupings, that the depository institution managers use to collateralize the securities they sell in financial markets.

Commercial loan theory, or real bills doctrine: The theory that banks can provide needed liquidity by making only short-term, self-liquidating loans secured by goods in the process of production or goods in transit.

Conversion-of-funds approach: An approach to bank management that treats each source of funds individually and matches each source of funds with an asset that has a similar maturity.

Loan loss provision: Additions to loan loss reserves by depository institutions within a given interval, such as a year.

Loan loss reserve: Cash assets that depository institutions hold as contingencies against anticipated loan defaults by borrowers.

Money center banks: Very large banks that engage in national and international lending and deposit businesses.

Multi-bank holding companies: Corporations that own and control two or more independently incorporated banks; also called ''group banking.''

Negative funds gap: The situation in which a bank's ratio of variable-rate assets to total assets is less than its ratio of variable-rate liabilities to total liabilities.

Net loan losses: Net reductions in income incurred by depository institutions when borrowers default on their loans.

Nonperforming loans: Loans that a depository anticipates will experience partial or complete default of interest and/or principal payments.

One-bank holding company: A business organization that owns one bank and is involved in other commercial activities.

Pool-of-funds approach: Portfolio management technique that emphasizes safety over short-term profitability; on the basis of a desired level of liquidity, funds are allocated first to primary reserves and then to secondary reserves, loan requests, and finally purchase of long-term securities.

Positive funds gap: The situation in which a bank's ratio of variable-rate assets to total assets exceeds its ratio of variable-rate liabilities to total liabilities.

Regional banks: Banks that primarily participate in loan and deposit markets across state lines in the regions around their headquarters locations.

Return on assets: The ratio of a depository institution's net income relative to the depository institution's assets.

Return on equity: The ratio of a depository institution's net income relative to the depository institution's equity capital.

Secondary reserves: Highly liquid short-term assets that can be used to supplement reserves during times of liquidity strains.

Shiftability theory: The theory that banks can solve their liquidity problem by purchasing assets that are highly liquid.

Variable-rate assets (VRAs):   Assets that can be rolled over (or renewed), and therefore repriced, during the bank's planning horizon.

Variable-rate liabilities (VRLs):   Liabilities that can be renewed, and therefore repriced, during the bank's planning period.

Zero funds gap: The situation in which a bank's ratio of VRAs to total assets equals its ratio of VRLs to total liabilities.

SELF-TEST QUESTIONS

1. Briefly outline and explain the differences between the various fundamental approaches to bank management.

2. At a round-table discussion of top managers of Megabuck National Bank, chief executive Richard (Richie) Rich questions the current policy of the bank, which is to make only short-term, "self-liquidating" loans secured by goods already in production or finished and in transit to ultimate purchasers. Rich argues that the bank should instead make long-term commercial loans to be used by borrowers for various purposes, with the provision that borrowers repay the loans in regular installments that in turn generate income and liquidity for Megabuck National Bank. What management philosophy does Megabuck National Bank presently follow? What approach is Richie Rich promoting?

3. Suppose that your goal as a bank manager is to insulate net interest income of the bank completely from the risk of interest rate fluctuations. What management strategy would best achieve this objective: a positive, negative, or zero funds gap approach? Explain.

4. What are the primary means that bank owners might use to judge a bank's performance? Would some be better indicators of short-run performance versus expected long-run prospects for the bank? Identify those that you feel would fall into each of these two categories.

5. What factors appear to you to explain best the movements of various measures of bank performance during the late 1980s and early 1990s? Is there any "common denominator" behind the generally weak performance of commercial banks during that period?

PROBLEMS

9-1. Suppose that asset A yields 10 percent half the time and 8 percent half the time and asset Y yields 16 percent half the time and 2 percent half the time.
   a. Calculate the expected rates of return on assets A and Y.
   b. Which asset is considered riskier?

9-2. Suppose that the probabilities that security A will provide payoffs of $10,000 and $15,000 are 0.6 and 0.4, respectively. What probabilities that security B will provide payoffs of $8,000 and $18,000 would make the two securities have equivalent expected payoffs?

9-3. If the probabilities that security C will provide nominal yields of 6 percent and 10 percent are 0.5 and 0.5, respectively, and if the probabilities that security D will yield 4 percent and 12 percent are 0.5 and 0.5, respectively, which security would you expect to have the higher market price?

9-4. In 1985, the aggregate return on assets for all commercial banks in the United States was 0.70 percent, and the return on equity was 11.18 percent.
   a. Explain why the return on equity can be so much greater than the return on assets.
   b. What was the ratio of bank equity to total bank assets in 1985? (*Hint:* Think about the

denominators in the return-on-assets and return-on-equity measures, and then try to relate the two measures in some way to compute the equity-asset ratio.)

c. In 1989, the aggregate return on assets for banks was 0.51 percent, and the return on equity was 7.94 percent. Did the equity-asset ratio in the banking system rise or fall between 1984 and 1989? Can you tell for sure from these figures whether the *level* of aggregate net income of banks rose or fell between those years? Why or why not?

SELECTED REFERENCES

Boemio, Thomas R., and Gerald A. Edwards, Jr., ''Asset Securitization: A Supervisory Perspective,'' *Federal Reserve Bulletin,* 75 (10, October 1989), pp. 659–669.

Brewer, E., ''Bank Funds Management Comes of Age,'' Federal Reserve Bank of Chicago *Economic Perspectives* (March/April 1980), pp. 3–10.

Brunner, Allan D., John V. Duca, and Mary M. McLaughlin, ''Recent Developments Affecting the Profitability and Practices of Commercial Banks,'' *Federal Reserve Bulletin,* 77 (7, July 1991), pp. 505–527.

Chernow, Ron, *The House of Morgan* (New York: Atlantic Monthly Press, 1990).

Duca, John V., and Mary M. McLaughlin, ''Developments Affecting the Profitability of Commercial Banks,'' *Federal Reserve Bulletin,* 76 (7, July 1990), pp. 477–499.

Graddy, Duane B., Austin H. Spencer, and William H. Brunsen, *Commercial Banking and the Financial Services Industry* (Reston, Va.: Reston, 1985).

Gup, Benton E., and John R. Walter, ''Top Performing Small Banks: Making Money the Old-Fashioned Way,'' Federal Reserve Bank of Richmond *Economic Review,* 75 (6, November/December 1989), pp. 23–35.

Liang, J. Nellie, and Donald T. Savage, ''The Nonbank Activities of Nonbank Holding Companies,'' *Federal Reserve Bulletin,* 76 (5, May 1990), pp. 280–292.

Moulton, H. G., ''Commercial Banking and Capital Formation,'' *Journal of Political Economy* (May–June–July 1918).

Prochnow, Herbert V., *Term Loans and Theories of Bank Liquidity* (New York: Prentice-Hall, 1949).

Robinson, Roland, *The Management of Bank Funds* (New York: McGraw-Hill, 1962).

Silber, William L., *Commercial Bank Liability Management* (Chicago: Association of Reserve City Bankers, 1978).

Sinkey, J. F., Jr., *Commercial Bank Financial Management* (New York: Macmillan, 1983).

Regulation of Depository Institutions

As we shall emphasize more than once in this chapter, one of the central issues that the United States must resolve in coming years is what is the "best" regulatory structure for depository institutions. Despite key legislative changes in the 1980s, the basic form of the current regulatory structure was constructed by legislation enacted at the height of the Great Depression of the 1930s. This regulatory structure has been severely tested—and has been discovered to be largely inadequate—during the past decade. Hence, the coming decade promises to be one in which tough choices must be made about the goals of banking regulation and the manner in which such regulation should be implemented.

This general topic is much too broad for a single chapter. Consequently, in this chapter our goals are to cover the essential history of the current structure of banking regulation in the United States and to outline the fundamental forms of legal restrictions that federal and state governments have actually placed on depository institutions. Subsequent chapters will build on this broad background to analyze in more detail the crucial issues that must be confronted if the "best" regulatory structure is to be determined.

ISSUES IN THE REGULATION OF DEPOSITORY INSTITUTIONS

Before we embark in this and subsequent chapters on a full examination of the structure of depository institution regulation, we begin here with an overview of the key issues. You should try to keep these issues in mind as you read this and the following three chapters.

GOALS OF BANK REGULATION

Because the United States is a democratic republic with a basically capitalistic economy, we commonly assume that there must be "good" reasons for regulations; otherwise, we would anticipate a preference for "letting markets work." If banking regulators, as duly appointed enforcers of laws passed by elected representatives in our legislatures, do not let the markets work, it must be because we as a society have determined that banking markets, if left to their own devices, would yield socially undesirable outcomes. The *goals of regulation,* then, must be *to correct or improve upon the performance of private markets for banking services.*

Assuring Depository Institution Solvency: Limiting Failures   A normal consequence of unhindered forces of demand and supply in private markets is that businesses often fail (go bankrupt). That is, they become *insolvent:* The combined value of their total liabilities rises above the combined value of their assets so that their net worth positions fall below zero. Businesses fail for many different reasons, and when they do fail, they cause all kinds of hardships to creditors, to owners, to workers, and to customers. But perhaps the greatest hardships result when a *depository institution* fails, because so many individuals depend on the safety and security of banks.

Look at Figure 10-1, which indicates that during the 1920s an average of about 600 banks failed each year. In the early 1930s, that average soared to 2,000 failures each year. It was in 1933, at the height of such bank failures, that the **Federal Deposit Insurance Corporation (FDIC)** was founded; the FDIC insured the funds of depositors and removed the reason for ruinous "runs" on banks. When a bank is forced out of business, the FDIC pays back depositors. Since the FDIC was created, the number of bank failures averaged only twelve per year until relatively recently.

A key objective of depository institution regulation since the 1930s has been to limit the number of failures of these institutions by limiting *risk taking* by managers of these institutions. Until the 1980s, this goal largely was achieved, in large measure through

Figure 10-1
Banks Closed, 1921–1992.   (*Source:* FDIC data.)

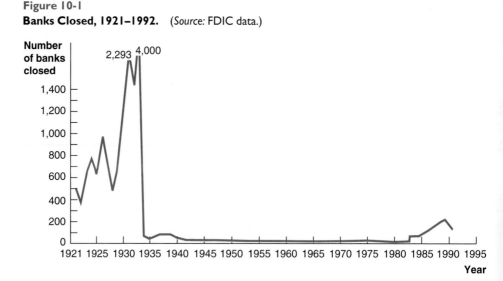

banking regulation. Nevertheless, as noted in the last chapter and indicated in Figure 10-1, commercial bank failures have increased substantially since the early 1980s. We shall explore the reasons for this development in subsequent chapters.

Assuring Depository Institution Liquidity   There can sometimes be a tenuous distinction between liquidity and solvency. If an otherwise solvent depository institution finds itself without enough cash on hand to honor a short-term commitment it has made, it has created a liquidity crunch for itself that ultimately may threaten its solvency. In addition, if enough depository institutions find themselves seriously illiquid simultaneously, a misperception can develop among all depositors that banks are on the verge of insolvency. Then a bank run can commence that can *cause* the institutions to become insolvent.

If left to their own devices, depository institutions might or might not maintain sufficient liquidity to prevent such runs from occurring. Hence, another key objective of depository institution regulation is to ensure that these institutions maintain sufficient liquidity to honor, within a few days if not at a moment's notice, the claims of their depositors.

Promoting Economic Efficiency   Another goal of depository institution regulation is to promote greater efficiency in the performance of the banking industry in particular and in the functioning of the economy in general. With respect to the banking industry—as with any industry—key objectives of regulation are **technical efficiency** and **allocative efficiency.** Depository institutions are technically efficient if they provide their services at the lowest possible cost in terms of the social resources that they expend in the process. They are allocatively efficient if they set the price of their services at the additional cost incurred in providing the last unit of service they produce.

Broader economic efficiencies are gained when depository institutions promote as fully as possible social gains from the financial intermediation process. As we emphasized in Chapter 6, the point of fractional reserve banking is to transform the deposits of savers into loans for investors to use in purchases of productive capital goods. In times past, banks were storehouses of gold, silver, and other precious metals, and used these stocks as a basis for their lending operations; as Adam Smith wrote in the *Wealth of Nations* in 1776, ''The judicious operations of banking, by substituting paper in the room of a great part of this gold and silver, enables the country to convert a great part of this dead stock into active and productive stock.''

In modern times, the same basic function is served by depository institutions: They accept deposits of fiduciary money that otherwise might be ''stuffed into mattresses'' and lend a large fraction of these funds out for use in the accumulation of capital and the production of goods and services. If depository institutions do not perform this basic function smoothly and efficiently, society loses. For instance, if banks accept savings from their depositors and use nearly all those funds to make only long-term loans for which no secondary markets exist, they probably will not have done any favors for society as a whole. If new investment opportunities come along for other potential borrowers, the loaned-up depository institutions will not possess the liquidity needed to grant them the loans they need. A socially costly ''credit crunch'' may result.

THE FUNDAMENTAL REGULATORY PROBLEM: TRADE-OFFS AMONG GOALS

As we shall discuss in the remaining chapters of this unit, bank regulators face a dilemma: Their goals often conflict. For instance, at the heart of the banking regulation initiated during the 1930s was the desire to prevent future bank failures by insuring the liquidity and solvency of the banking system. The experience of the Great Depression induced regulators to trade an efficient, competitive banking system for one that was less technically and allocatively efficient but much safer with respect to depository institution failures and runs on banks.

The problems of regulatory-induced inefficiencies became apparent in the climate of rising interest rates in the 1970s and 1980s, when banks and thrifts often found themselves in more open competition with one another. In response to this development, some regulations were removed to give those depository institutions greater freedom to respond to changing market conditions. In particular, the Depository Institutions Deregulation and Monetary Control Act of 1980 and later laws passed by Congress have put the various depository institutions—commercial banks, savings and loan associations, savings banks, and credit unions—on a more equal footing with one another. The general goal of such legal changes was to promote greater technical and allocative efficiency in the provision of banking services.

Traditional depository institutions also have found themselves facing competition from other financial institutions, such as money market mutual funds that woo away their depositors with the promise of higher potential returns and stock brokerage companies that now offer a variety of banking-type services. Even retail store chains such as Sears have joined forces with brokerage firms to offer investment and banking services to their customers.

A result of these developments—and others—was that many depository institutions found themselves ''squeezed out'' by the competitive frenzy that erupted. Others, in their zeal to compete, did themselves in through their own mistakes. Some were victims of managerial fraud. While banking in many ways became a more competitive—and arguably more efficient—business in the 1980s, it also became a more volatile and risky business as well.

The 1990s have witnessed perhaps the most heated debate about the tensions among the competing goals of banking regulation since the turbulent decade of the 1930s, when many of the current banking regulations first were enacted. One outcome of that debate appears to have been, on the one hand, a movement toward tighter enforcement of existing regulations. Many observers argue that the result was a rapid movement toward a somewhat safer banking system, but others claim it actually has produced a much less efficient industry, as evidenced by a so-called banking credit crunch in 1990–1991. Hence, the debate has led, on the other hand, to calls by some for more significant *deregulation* of banking in the United States. The coming years promise to be a time in which citizens, the representatives they elect, and the regulators that representatives appoint will be asked to sort through these issues and to make some tough choices about which goals should be most important as guiding principles for depository institution regulation.

THE EARLY HISTORY OF DEPOSITORY INSTITUTION REGULATION IN THE UNITED STATES

To understand the evolution of banking regulation in this country, we will quickly review, in roughly chronological order, the more important banking acts and regulations that continue to be important to us in the 1990s. We begin with the banking legislation of the 1930s, because it continues to have very significant implications for banking today.

THE GLASS-STEAGALL BANKING ACT OF 1933

The Banking Act of 1933, known more commonly as the **Glass-Steagall Act,** was passed by Congress and signed into law by President Roosevelt on July 16, 1933. The act was authored by Senator Carter Glass (Democrat, Virginia) and Congressman Henry Steagall (Democrat, Alabama), the chairpersons of the Senate and House Banking Committees, respectively. This landmark legislation did the following:

1. Created the Federal Deposit Insurance Corporation (FDIC). The FDIC was designed to give depositors confidence in a bank, even if the bank appeared to be weak and about to fail.

2. Prohibited deposit-taking banks from being ''principally'' engaged in underwriting ''ineligible'' securities. In effect, this separated commercial banks and investment banks (institutions that offer advising, underwriting, and brokerage services to firms issuing new stocks and bonds).

3. Prohibited commercial banks from paying interest on any (checking) deposit that is payable on demand.

4. Gave the Fed the authority to establish ceilings on interest rates that member banks could pay on time and on savings deposits.

This legislation provided the framework for the regulation of our banking system for the next fifty years.

The Federal Deposit Insurance Corporation   The Federal Deposit Insurance Corporation is a government agency that guarantees the deposits of each depositor (in commercial banks) up to a specified limit, even though the bank that accepts those deposits may fail. Currently, this limit is $100,000. Until late 1989, deposits in savings and loan associations and savings banks were insured up to the same amount by the **Federal Savings and Loan Insurance Corporation (FSLIC);** since that time, they have been insured by the FDIC's Savings Association Insurance Fund (SAIF), as discussed below and in Chapter 12. Credit union deposits usually are insured by the **National Credit Union Administration (NCUA),** which supervises the National Credit Union Shareholders Insurance Fund.

The FDIC was established to mitigate the primary cause of bank failures—the simultaneous rush of depositors to convert their demand or savings deposits into currency (bank runs). Consider the following scenario. A bank begins to look shaky; its assets may not seem sufficient to cover its liabilities. If the bank has no deposit insurance, depositors in this bank (and any banks associated with it) will all want to withdraw their funds from the bank at the same time. Their concern is that this shaky bank will not have enough funds to return their deposits to them in the form of currency.

Indeed, this is what happens in a bank failure when insurance doesn't exist. Just as with the failure of a regular business, the creditors of the bank may not all get paid, or if they do, they will get paid less than 100 percent of what they are owed. Depositors are creditors of a bank because their deposits are liabilities of the bank. In a fractional reserve banking system, banks do not have 100 percent of their depositors' money in the form of vault cash. All depositors, therefore, cannot simultaneously withdraw all their funds. It is therefore necessary to assure depositors that they can have their deposits converted into cash, when they wish, no matter how serious the financial situation of the bank.

The FDIC provided this assurance. By insuring deposits, the FDIC bolstered depositors' trust in the banking system and provided depositors with the incentive to leave their deposits with the bank, even in the face of widespread talk of bank failures. In 1933, it was sufficient for the FDIC to cover each account up to $2,500 (about $30,000 in today's dollars).

Even though the FDIC was created by the federal government and is considered a federal agency, its main source of funds has not been federal taxes. Like any private insurance fund, the total of the insurance premiums paid by the insured is the primary source of the funds. The FDIC insurance is funded by an assessment of insured commercial banks. That assessment presently is 0.23 percent of commercial banks' total deposits.

The Separation of Commercial Banking from Investment Banking   An investment banker underwrites a new issue of corporate or municipal bonds or an issue of a private corporation's shares of stock. By "underwriting," the investment banker guarantees that the entire issue will be sold at a minimum price per bond or per share of stock. A commercial banker, in contrast, accepts deposits of savers and purchases assets from borrowers. Commercial banking is at the heart of the process of financial intermediation between savers and borrowers. Investment banking is a brokerage service.

The separation of commercial and investment banking was mandated because of the then-prevailing opinion that many commercial banks up to 1933 had been involved in the underwriting of risky securities. When some of those securities did not sell at the promised minimum price, the commercial bank that was underwriting the issue simply added the securities to its own asset portfolio. Its asset portfolio might then end up being too risky because it contained too many risky securities. The bank might also have an incentive to purchase bonds it underwrites for portfolios that it manages in trust for its customers. Furthermore, it might be inclined to give investment advice that is not objective; hence a conflict of interest may exist.

The Prohibition of Interest on Demand Deposits   Prohibiting interest on demand deposits seemed reasonable in the early 1930s, when banks were trying to attract customers by paying high interest rates. According to the views of the framers of the legislation banning interest payments on checking deposits, banks had to earn high rates from the assets of their balance sheet to afford to pay high interest rates on deposit liabilities. So, the framers argued, they used depositors' funds in investments that promised high returns, even though high return and high risk go hand in hand. When business activity slowed, it was believed, the value of riskier assets declined substantially, and many banks were not able to sell them at their earlier values when the banks tried to cover deposit withdrawals. The specter of insolvency and bank failure then loomed large. To prevent failures resulting from this kind of competition, the 1933 law forbade banks from paying interest on demand deposits.

The original Glass-Steagall Act placed interest rate ceilings only on commercial banks. These ceilings were extended to thrift institutions, however, by the **Interest Rate Adjustment Act of 1966,** and remained as fundamental restrictions on depository institutions until the 1980s.

RESTRICTIONS ON BANK ENTRY

One of the conditions that results from regulating an industry is the creation of barriers to entry. A convincing case for worthiness or need must be made before a commercial bank can obtain a federal or state charter. Before a bank will be granted a charter, the bank's founders must give proof of their integrity and ability to manage a bank. Additionally, state and federal regulatory banking agencies require evidence of "need" for a new bank before they will issue a charter. Obviously, the term "need" is difficult to define objectively. For many years, "unworthy" would-be bankers were detected and prevented from entering the industry. Existing banks were making higher-than-normal rates of return (in certain geographic areas), while regulatory agencies prevented new competition from entering the industry.

The Dual Banking System   Since the National Banking Act of 1864, commercial bank owners have been able to choose between seeking a state charter (from a state banking authority) or a federal charter (from the federal government through the comptroller of the currency). This option has led to the coexistence of national banks and state banks. Thus, the United States has a dual banking system. About two-thirds of all banks have state charters; however, they account for less than half of the total assets of all banks. To further confuse the issue, membership in the Federal Reserve System and the FDIC is optional for state banks. Yet membership in the Federal Reserve System and the Federal Deposit Insurance Corporation is required for all national banks.

The Overlap of Regulation and Supervision   In principle, the dual banking system allows for an overlapping of supervision and regulation by several authorities. There are four sources of regulation, supervision, and control:

1. The Office of the Comptroller of the Currency
2. The Federal Reserve
3. The FDIC
4. State banking authorities

Figure 10-2 shows the jurisdiction over commercial banks that has prevailed since December 31, 1981.

The three federal agencies listed above each have their own way of examining, scrutinizing, and appraising the activities of a federally chartered bank. In principle, each agency can conduct its own examination of a federally chartered commercial bank, and thus such banks are subject to triple scrutiny. Only state-chartered banks (if they remain outside the Federal Reserve System and the FDIC) can be subjected to the supervision and examination procedures of a single state agency. The Treasury Department's **Office of the Comptroller of the Currency,** in contrast, maintains chartering, supervisory, and examining powers over about 4,000 national banks. Even though the Fed has supervisory power over all national banks and state-chartered member (of the Fed) banks, it examines only about 1,000 state-chartered member banks. National banks are examined by the comptroller of the currency.

Because almost all commercial banks have FDIC insurance, the FDIC has examining powers over most state-chartered banks and all nationally chartered banks. In practice, the FDIC examines only nonmember state-insured banks. These number over 7,000, however.

UNIT AND BRANCH BANKING

Most countries have a few large banks, each bank with many branches located throughout the nation. The United States, on the other hand, has a large number of distinct and separate depository institutions throughout the country.

Various state laws have allowed only **unit banking,** which is a system that permits each bank to have only a single geographic location. Thus, many states have prevented or limited **branch banking.** A branch bank, as its name suggests, is one of two or more banking offices owned and operated by a single banking corporation. Branch banking

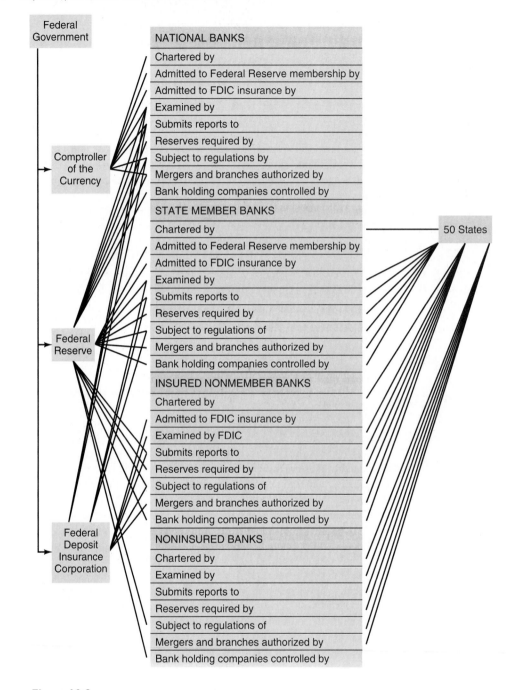

Figure 10-2

The Overlapping Regulation and Supervision of Commercial Banks. [Adapted from hearings on financial structure and regulation, Subcommittee on Financial Institutions of the Senate Committee on Banking, Housing, and Urban Affairs, 93d Congress, 1st Session, 1973. Cited in Murray E. Polakoff, Thomas A. Durkin, et al., *Financial Institutions and Markets,* 2d ed. (Boston: Houghton Mifflin), 1981; and Federal Reserve Bank of Atlanta *Economic Review* (December 1982), p. 46.]

A COMPARISON OF BANKING STRUCTURES—THE UNITED STATES, EUROPE, AND JAPAN

INTERNATIONAL PERSPECTIVE

The twelve nations of the Economic Community (EC) of Western Europe have a combined population about 30 percent greater than that of the United States. Yet together the number of commercial banks in the EC is about *one-sixth* of the number of banks in the United States. In the EC there is one commercial bank for every 150,000 people; in the United States there is one bank for every 20,000 people. In addition, the EC has fewer than half as many savings institutions that are analogous to the United States' thrift institutions. Furthermore, the EC makes do with a much smaller number of depository institutions even though the currency-equivalent value of assets of EC depository institutions significantly exceeds the amount of assets of depository institutions in the United States.

Comparison with Japan is even more striking. The United States has about ten times as many commercial banks as Japan, even though its population is only about twice as large. As a result, in Japan there is one commercial bank for every *850,000* people.

Branching and Bank Size

It would be tempting to conclude from these figures that European and Japanese citizens get "less personalized" financial services than citizens of the United States. This is not necessarily true. Even though there are fewer commercial banks and other depository institutions in Europe and Japan, these institutions have large numbers of branches. Indeed, the number of branches relative to the number of people does not vary a great deal across nations. During the 1980s, for instance, there was about one bank branch for every 2,300 people in the United States, which was almost exactly the same as in the United Kingdom, somewhat more than in Japan (one branch for every 2,800 people) and Italy (one branch for every 4,300 people), and somewhat less than in France and Germany (each with about one branch for every 1,500 people).

Nevertheless, one clear implication that can be drawn from this comparison is that European and Japanese depository institutions are much larger, relative to U.S. institutions. By the beginning of the 1990s, Europe had nearly half of the largest commercial banks in the world, and Japan had over a fourth of that number; in contrast, the United States had about a tenth.

Another possible implication is that there potentially is less "market rivalry" among depository institutions in Europe and Japan as compared with those in the United States. Indeed, the top five depository institutions in Belgium, Denmark, France, Italy, Luxembourg, Portugal, Spain, and the United Kingdom have over 30 percent of the deposits of their nations' citizens; in Greece and the Netherlands the top five institutions have over *80* percent of their nations' deposits. In Japan, the top five depository institutions together account for 20 percent of deposits in the Japanese banking system. These figures compare with a 10 percent share of deposits at the top five banks in the United States.

Universal Banking in Europe

In most parts of Europe, banking is nearly, if not fully, "universal," meaning that there are few, if any, Glass-Steagall-type separations of banking and securities trading. Although Europeans sometimes raise concerns about the potential for conflicts of interest that might result and about the high banking fees they pay, many indicate that they feel they benefit from being able to conduct all their financial dealings at a single bank. One common complaint of customers of European banks is that universal banking makes European banks *too* stodgy and conservative—rather than behaving as "high-flying," risky institutions.

Interestingly, however, the United States and Europe face some parallel problems in the 1990s. Only recently has the United States faced the likely inevitability of cross-state banking and national consolidation of the banking industry. Likewise, only in 1992 did formalized agreements between nations in the EC confederation open the borders of European nations to fuller banking competition. Before then, significant restrictions on cross-border banking existed in several European countries. Hence, during the 1990s and into the next century it seems likely that Europe and the United States will seek to compare their experiences with banking regulation and deregulation. Although the structures of their banking systems have significant differences, they share similar problems and goals.

Source: Jean Dermine, ed., *European Banking in the 1990s* (Oxford: Basil Blackwell, 1990), and Philip Revzin, Terence Roth, and Margaret Studer, "Universal Banks in Europe Win Plaudits for One-Stop Shopping," *Wall Street Journal* (February 26, 1991), p. C1.

comprises a banking corporation having two or more "branches" or offices within a geographic area; branch offices can be newly opened, or they can be existing banks that are acquired and merged into the corporation. As of 1992, fourteen states continued to limit branching within state boundaries (typically within a county or into adjacent counties), and one—Colorado—permits no branching at all (it is a unit banking state).

Under the McFadden Act of 1927, as amended by the Glass-Steagall Act in 1933, state law, not federal law, governs branch banking. Federal law does not prohibit national banks from branching, but national banks must obey the branching law of the states in which they are located. At the federal level, however, some doors to branch banking have been opened in states that prohibit it. For example, in 1974, the comptroller of the currency ruled that customer-bank communications terminals do not qualify as branch banks. Taken in its broadest perspective, this ruling helped spur the development of automated teller machines as "robot branches" with no people as one answer to some states' restrictions on branching.

Bank Holding Companies   In addition to branching, there is another mechanism for establishing multiple-office banking. As you learned in Chapter 9, through multi-bank holding companies (sometimes called "group banking"), a banking corporation can obtain ownership or control of two or more independently incorporated banks.

Multi-bank holding companies have greatly expanded in the last three decades. Table 10-1 shows the rapid growth since 1965 in deposits effectively controlled by these multi-bank companies. This rapid expansion of holding company ownership in banking can be attributed largely to the legal limitations on branching. To a considerable degree, group banking has served as a way to evade the intrastate branching laws; most multi-bank holding companies are located in unit-banking states. Moreover, because state laws often permit these groups to operate across state lines, group banking has become an attractive device for circumventing state rules against interstate banking as well.

While the primary incentive to form multi-bank holding companies was to evade restrictions on bank branching within or between states, a key rationale for formation of a one-bank holding company is to evade regulations on businesses in which banks can legally engage themselves. The Bank Holding Company Act of 1956 did not specifically prohibit banks from engaging in a multitude of nonbanking commercial activities. As we

T A B L E   10-1
Multi-Bank Holding Companies

Year	No. of Multi-Bank Holding Cos.	No. of Banks	No. of Branches	Assets*	Deposits*
1960	47	426	1,037	20	18
1965	53	468	1,486	31	28
1970	121	895	3,260	93	78
1975	289	2,264	9,896	371	297
1981	407	2,607	14,121	678	480
1986	1,314	4,431	28,046	1,827	1,315
1991	910	3,706	32,462	2,605	1,683

* Billions of dollars.

Source: Board of Governors of the Federal Reserve System, *Annual Statistical Digest.* Includes only domestic data.

discussed in the last chapter, one-bank holding companies could engage in a variety of lines of business and could obtain funds in the unregulated commercial paper market to direct to the parent bank. Furthermore, bank holding companies could undertake activities involving securities brokerage, which effectively permitted banking corporations to circumvent (partially) the Glass-Steagall Act. In light of these advantages, the number of one-bank holding companies grew considerably between 1973 and 1990, as shown in Table 10-2.

Regulators and members of Congress shared concern about the activities of one-bank holding companies. They worried that a holding company's sale of unregulated commercial paper might affect the soundness of the bank and that conflicts of interest and increased concentration of financial power might arise. These concerns led to the passage of the 1970 Bank Holding Company Act. This act brought one-bank holding companies under the same restrictions as multi-bank holding companies (pursuant to the 1956 Bank Holding Company Act).

Interstate Banking   Each bank in this country initially served only its own particular community. It was not allowed to extend its services to other communities. As transportation systems improved, communications expanded, and population increased and became more mobile, banks sought to extend their services beyond the limits represented by the geographic boundary of their own community. In the early 1900s, some banks (following their migrating customers) established branches across state lines. As a result, they began to increase in size.

Congress had long wanted to discourage large, "monopolistic" banks. This led it to enact the McFadden Act of 1927 and the 1933 Glass-Steagall amendments that give nationally chartered banks the same statewide branching abilities that are permitted to state-chartered banks. Subsequently, each state has determined its own branching structure,

T A B L E   10-2
One-Bank Holding Companies*

Year	No. of One-Bank Holding Cos.	No. of Banks	No. of Branches	Assets†	Deposits†
1973	1,282	1,282	7,861	262	207
1975	1,419	1,410	8,486	290	230
1977	1,607	1,602	10,241	496	403
1979	2,028	2,019	11,920	693	541
1981	3,093	3,082	14,329	756	587
1986	5,162	4,984	11,670	517	442
1991	4,843	4,843	11,860	679	534

*Prior to 1971, there were only multi-bank holding companies. Following an amendment in 1970 to the Bank Holding Company Act, one-bank holding companies were formed as well. The first year for which the Board of Governors of the Federal Reserve System (in the *Annual Statistical Digest 1971–1975*) distinguished between multi-bank and one-bank holding companies was 1973. We can infer, however, that there were at least 1,316 one-bank holding companies by the end of 1971 and 1,356 by the end of 1972. The estimate was derived as follows: The number of multi-bank holding companies grew from 121 in 1970 to 251 in 1973 and there was a total of 1,567 multi- and one-bank holding companies combined in 1971, and 1,607 in 1972. This suggests there were *at least* 1,316 (that is, 1567 − 251) one-bank holding companies by the end of 1971 and 1,356 (that is, 1607 − 251) in 1972.

†Billions of dollars.

Source: Board of Governors of the Federal Reserve System, *Annual Statistical Digest.* Data after 1975 include foreign data.

and unless states coordinate reciprocal banking arrangements, branch banking has stopped at state lines.

Before the Bank Holding Company Act of 1956, however, banks were able to acquire out-of-state banks through multi-bank holding companies. The 1956 legislation, however, prohibited new interstate bank acquisitions (old acquisitions were ''grandfathered in'') unless the state where the acquired bank was located specifically permitted such entry. Until 1975 no state permitted entry. This was true except for certain subsidiaries of some U.S. commercial banks that were set up under the **Edge Act.** This act was passed in 1919 and allows limited acceptance of deposits by banks, provided these deposits are related to international transactions. Under the law, deposits also may be accepted across state lines if they are used to finance the production of goods intended primarily for export.

TOILS AND TROUBLES: 1960 THROUGH 1989

The various regulations discussed above almost certainly helped promote *stability* of the banking system in the decades immediately following the 1930s. By protecting depository institutions from significant competition, regulations permitted these institutions to be profitable enterprises. (Indeed, a common saying was that ''Banking is a license to steal.'') High profitability, in turn, helped ensure bank solvency, aside from a handful of failures from year to year, and high liquidity, except for scattered problems from time to time.

Nevertheless, beginning in the late 1950s and early 1960s the staid, stodgy world inhabited by boring, conservative bankers began to change. The initial changes were few and came slowly, but the pace accelerated as time passed. The regulatory issues faced today stem from developments that began a generation ago.

THE 1960s AND EARLY 1970s

By the late 1950s major banks were all too aware that major corporations were minimizing their average holdings of non-interest-bearing deposits. Banks reacted to this leakage from their main source of funds by introducing the large negotiable CD in 1961. The CDs earned interest but were initially subject to Regulation Q, which put ceilings on interest rates (resulting from the 1933 Banking Act). These CDs were quite successful in (temporarily) stemming the loss of deposits, and they introduced the concept of liability management described in Chapter 9. Unfortunately, this change exposed banks to the risk of unanticipated swings in the costs of funds as market forces changed.

The original interest rate ceilings from the Glass-Steagall Act and newly instituted ceilings for thrift institutions mandated by the Interest Adjustment Act of 1966 set the stage for the ''credit crunch of 1966.'' In that year, market interest rates rose above the interest rate ceilings, and consequently the steady flow of funds to banks was again disrupted. Banks and thrifts now scrambled for funds not subject to interest rate ceilings.

What ensued has been described as a cat-and-mouse game in which banks would first develop either (1) a new source of funds such as borrowing Eurodollars or (2) new short-term debt instruments, such as commercial paper issued by holding company affiliates or repurchase agreements. Then the Fed would step in and define the instrument as a deposit and subject it to an interest rate ceiling and reserve requirements.

It became clear that the regulatory system was not working, and legal deregulation began. In 1970, interest rate ceilings were lifted for CDs over $100,000, and NOW accounts were introduced in 1972. (Recall from Chapter 3 that NOW accounts are interest-earning checking accounts.)

FINANCIAL INNOVATION: 1975–1983

Technological advances created powerful incentives for nonbank institutions to enter the banking industry—especially because nonbanks were not regulated. An explosion of financial innovation and deregulation of depository markets erupted during the period 1975 to 1983.

One key innovation was the money market mutual funds (MMMFs), which, you will recall from Chapter 5, are pools of liquid assets managed by investment companies that sell shares to the public in small denominations. They are backed by high-quality liquid assets, are not subject to reserve requirements, and permit limited checking. MMMFs were enormously successful; they grew from $3.3 billion in 1977 to $186.9 billion in 1981. Their growth occurred at the expense of depository financial institutions. Customers withdrew funds from their accounts with these institutions in a growing tide of disintermediation—the direct placement, through MMMFs, of their funds in markets for Treasury securities and corporate bonds.

This growth in MMMFs put tremendous pressure on banks, which in turn put pressure on regulatory agencies and Congress for help. In 1970 regulatory agencies authorized money market certificates (MMCs), which had no checking provision but had an interest rate ceiling that floated with the 6-month T-bill rate. Also, unlike MMMFs, the MMCs were covered by deposit insurance. The MMCs were well received, but they did not reduce the growth of MMMFs significantly. In addition, in the late 1970s MMC interest rates actually rose above interest rates on many long-term, fixed-rate assets, such as mortgages, so that some depository institutions—notably savings and loan associations and savings banks—experienced significant reductions in profitability.

THE DEPOSITORY INSTITUTIONS DEREGULATION AND MONETARY CONTROL ACT (DIDMCA) OF 1980

During the 1970s, disintermediation hurt savings and loan associations and the housing industry. During the same time, many state-chartered member banks also abandoned the Federal Reserve System because (1) the Fed required member banks to hold higher reserves than most state banking authorities required of nonmember state-chartered banks and (2) some nonmember state-chartered banks were allowed to hold high-quality interest-earning assets as reserves. As nominal interest rates rose, the cost of Fed membership grew higher for state-chartered banks. The Fed became concerned about its ability to control and regulate the banking sector and the money supply as more banks abandoned the Federal Reserve System. The tremendous growth in money market mutual funds also caused great harm to thrift institutions because the thrift institutions were not allowed to offer market interest rates to depositors.

To eliminate or to reduce these problems and to control the money supply better, the Federal Reserve provided detailed suggestions to Congress for a new financial environment. The result was the Depository Institutions Deregulation and Monetary Control Act (DIDMCA) of 1980. Table 10-3 summarizes the most important effects of this wide-ranging act.

Two provisions in the DIDMCA of 1980 eliminated the Federal Reserve System's problem of declining membership. Because all depository institutions of similar size are now required to hold the same ratio of reserves to deposits with the Federal Reserve System, membership no longer affects a depository institution's profitability. All depository institutions now have equal access to Federal Reserve services, and they pay the same price for services (e.g., check clearing and collection). Note that this provision entailed additional regulation, not deregulation.

T A B L E   10-3

Primary Provisions and Effects of the Depository Institutions Deregulation and
Monetary Control Act of 1980

Provision	Effect
Phased out deposit interest ceilings	Interest rate ceilings on deposits were phased out over a period of 6 years. A depository institutions deregulation committee was set up to do this.
Nationwide NOW accounts permitted	Any depository institution after Dec. 31, 1980, was allowed to offer NOW accounts; that is, interest-bearing checking accounts to individuals and nonprofit organizations. Automatic transfer services (ATSs) were also allowed in all commercial banks. Savings and loan associations can use remote service units, and credit unions that are federally insured can offer share draft accounts (CUSDs).
Reserves required on all transactions accounts at depository institutions	Gradually, reserve requirements were uniformly applied to all transactions accounts which are defined as demand (checking) deposits, NOW accounts, ATS accounts, and credit union share drafts. This required reserve system was phased in over 8 years for all depository institutions that are not Federal Reserve members. For Federal Reserve members, the act meant a reduction in reserve requirements; those reductions were phased in over 4 years.
Increased access to the discount window	All depository institutions issuing transactions accounts and nonpersonal time deposits now have the same borrowing privileges at the Federal Reserve discount window just as if they were member commercial banks.
Fees established for Federal Reserve services	A fee schedule for the Federal Reserve "chores" such as check clearing and collection, wire transfers, and the like was established by Oct. 1, 1981.
Power of thrift institutions expanded	Federally insured credit unions were allowed to make residential real estate loans. Savings and loan associations had higher loan ceilings and some ability to make consumer loans, and the power to issue credit cards.
The imposition of supplemental reserves	The Federal Reserve Board, under extraordinary circumstances, can impose additional reserve requirements on any depository institution of up to 4 percent of its transactions accounts. This supplementary reserve, if imposed, must earn interest.
Increased level of federally insured deposits	Previously, federally insured deposits had a ceiling of $40,000; that ceiling was increased to $100,000.

Source: Economic Review, Federal Reserve Bank of Atlanta, vol. LXV, no. 2, March–April 1980, pp. 4–5.

This law, as Table 10-3 documents, covered a lot of ground. The 1980 act was Congress's mandate to regulatory agencies to simplify all preceding monetary and banking regulations enacted by Congress. Note, however, that although the act did reduce regulation in a number of areas, it also increased regulation in others. Many nonmember state banks were subjected to more regulation than they were before 1980.

THE GARN–ST GERMAIN ACT OF 1982

Reacting to a large number of failures of S&Ls and savings banks, Congress passed the Depository Institutions Act of 1983, also known as the Garn–St Germain Act of 1982.

The main provisions of this act were as follows:

1. Banks and other depository institutions were authorized to offer money market deposit accounts (MMDAs) to compete with MMMFs. The interest rates on these accounts were unregulated. An important advantage that MMDAs have over MMMFs is that they are covered by federal deposit insurance. This provision has done much to restore the competitive position of thrifts and commercial banks. Figure 10-3 shows both the dramatic initial growth of MMMFs and the incredible explosion in MMDAs over the period from 1978 to 1983. Table 10-4 shows how the liabilities of depository institutions changed dramatically during this same period. Note that the importance of demand deposits and savings deposits fell dramatically, and the importance of other checkable deposits, MMDAs (especially), and large time deposits increased. We conclude that banking innovations and the resulting deregulation had a significant impact on both the structure and the cost of bank (and thrift) sources of funds (liabilities).

2. Thrifts were permitted to invest up to 10 percent of their assets in commercial loans, while the maximum percentage of assets held in consumer loans was raised to 30 percent.

3. The FDIC and the FSLIC were given emergency powers to permit troubled institutions to merge across state lines and to permit commercial banks to make interstate acquisitions of closed banks or thrifts with assets of $500 million or more.

THE DECLINING RESILIENCE OF DEPOSITORY INSTITUTIONS AND THE "TOO-BIG-TO-FAIL" POLICY

As indicated in the last chapter, all in all the 1980s were not good years for depository institutions. Some blame the deregulation provisions contained in the 1980 and 1982

Figure 10-3

A Comparison of MMMF and MMDA Growth.   When MMMFs were introduced in 1970, they were extremely successful; they seriously upset depository institution fund sources, as people transferred their deposits to instruments that earned market interest rates. In 1982 depository institutions were permitted to offer MMDAs, which also earned market interest rates and were covered by deposit insurance. The growth of MMDAs was explosive. (*Source:* Board of Governors of the Federal Reserve System.)

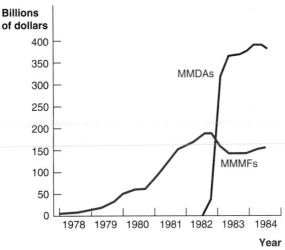

T A B L E 10-4
Principal Liabilities of Depository Institutions, Year-End 1978–1983 (Percentage of Total*)

(1) Year	(2) Demand Deposits	(3) Other Checkable Deposits†	(4) MMDAs	(5) Savings Deposits	(6) Small Time Deposits	(7) Large Time Deposits	(8) Term RPs	(9) Term Eurodollars	(10) Total
1978	16.7	0.6	0.0	31.7	34.4	12.9	1.8	2.1	100.0
1979	16.0	1.0	0.0	25.9	38.9	13.6	1.8	2.7	100.0
1980	15.1	1.6	0.0	22.7	41.3	14.6	2.0	2.8	100.0
1981	12.5	4.1	0.0	18.3	43.7	15.9	2.0	3.6	100.0
1982	11.7	5.0	2.1	17.6	41.7	16.0	2.0	4.0	100.0
1983	10.5	5.5	16.1	13.4	34.0	14.0	2.4	4.0	100.0

* Details may not add to totals due to rounding.

† Other Checkable Deposits include negotiable order of withdrawal (NOW) and automatic transfer service (ATS) accounts at depository institutions, credit union share draft accounts, and demand deposits at thrift institutions.

Sources: Monetary Trends and *Survey of Current Business.*

legislation, while others argue that the laws enacted in those years simply did not go far enough to free up depository institutions to protect themselves from greater problems. Irrespective of which of these opposing views is correct, the 1980s surely seemed to regulators as though they would never end.

The first signs of real trouble were scattered and therefore did not necessarily seem symptomatic of the gathering institutional crisis. In 1982, a large bank, Penn Square, failed. It was not the first failure of a large bank; isolated failures of large depository institutions had occurred from time to time since the FDIC had been established. Several other depository institutions had close connections with Penn Square, however, and for this reason they also were affected adversely. Among these institutions was Continental Illinois Bank of Chicago, then the nation's seventh largest bank, which had purchased, at a combined price of over $1 billion, over 450 energy-related loans from Penn Square— exactly the type of loans whose value had plummeted with declines in energy prices and led Penn Square down the road to insolvency.

Rumors that Continental Illinois was in trouble led to a new type of modern-day bank run in May 1984, conducted by computer and with wire transfers and primarily initiated by the bank's foreign depositors. The bank lost over $10 billion in deposits within 60 days. Because of Illinois state branching restrictions, Continental Illinois depended primarily upon large certificates of deposit as a source of funds for its operations, but holders of its uninsured deposits began selling its CDs and refusing to renew them when they matured. To induce depositors to hold its uninsured CDs, Continental Illinois began offering above-market interest rates, but largely to no avail. The bank resorted to selling more than $5 billion in assets, but ultimately the run took its toll, and the FDIC, with the assistance of the Federal Reserve, felt forced to step in to resuscitate the bank. Even though insured depositors had not yet suffered direct losses, the bank had more than $3 billion in federally insured deposits and over $30 billion in uninsured deposits and borrowings from other sources. In the middle of May, the FDIC purchased $2 billion in subordinated notes from the bank, and the Federal Reserve Bank of Chicago offered continual liquidity assistance.

Following closely on the heels of the Continental Illinois disaster was a more traditional bank run on *state-insured* thrifts in Ohio. When a Florida-based securities dealer called ESM Government Securities, Inc., failed in March 1985, one of the largest state-insured savings associations in Ohio, Home State Savings Bank, suffered massive asset losses. Word of these losses reached the thrift's depositors, who immediately began withdrawing their funds; Home State lost $55 million in deposits in a single day and over $100 million in deposits in the following two days. When it became clear that the Home State loss by itself would wipe out Ohio's deposit insurance fund, a run on *all* Ohio-insured thrifts occurred. These were closed by action of the state's governor and reopened with FSLIC insurance later in the month.

No sooner had the Ohio mess been cleaned up when a similar run occurred in Maryland. Two thrifts there also failed and experienced deposit losses that exceeded the value of that state's insurance fund that had covered them and 100 other state-insured institutions. The Maryland governor placed a temporary $1,000 withdrawal limit on customers of all thrifts covered by the state insurance plan, and that eased the run on the thrifts in that state. Ultimately, state and federal regulators coordinated a transferal of nearly all state-insured institutions to FDIC coverage.

In the meantime, by August of 1985, Continental Illinois Bank had been classified as a "permanent" recipient of $4.5 billion in federal government assistance. Regulators had been forced to "nationalize" the bank; effectively, the FDIC owned nearly 80 percent of the shares in the bank. It did not sell off the last of these shares until 1991.

The Continental Illinois experience led to an important step in federal regulatory policy, which was a "too-big-to-fail" policy enacted by the comptroller of the currency in September 1984. Under this policy, the comptroller announced in congressional testimony that his office had determined that the eleven largest national banks were too large to be permitted to fail. The goal of this policy was to shore up public confidence in these institutions, any one of whose failure certainly would have caused the nation's deposit insurance system to suffer tremendous costs. Another by-product of this policy—quickly pointed out by those banks whose names did not appear on the list of those "too big to fail"—was that the faith and guarantee of the U.S. government was by this act placed behind these banks, giving them a potential advantage over other banks in raising uninsured deposit funds. Smaller banks felt this was inequitable treatment, and nearly everyone—including the regulators themselves—agreed that it was.

Nonetheless, by 1990 the too-big-to-fail policy had become an implicit factor in decision making by all three federal banking regulators—the Office of the Comptroller of the Currency, the FDIC, and the Federal Reserve. For instance, when the Bank of New England was teetering on the verge of failure in 1990, the FDIC provided it with support that effectively guaranteed the funds of both insured and uninsured depositors. In contrast, the FDIC permitted smaller banks—which it did not judge to be "too big to fail"—to collapse. In the spring of 1991, in response to the perceived inequities in this approach, the Financial Institutions Subcommittee of the House Banking Committee approved nearly unanimously a bill that would end the too-big-to-fail policy.

CAPITAL REQUIREMENTS

Concurrent with these developments was a regulatory effort to contain the potential costs of bank failures. This effort focused on the regulation of bank capital relative to total assets. From a regulatory standpoint, **depository institution capital** includes equity shares and other items that assist in protecting the insured deposit accounts of those institutions from losses in the event of failure. **Capital requirements** are legally imposed limitations on the amount of assets that depository institutions may hold in relation to their capital.

CURRENT CONTROVERSY

THE VALUE OF BEING "TOO BIG TO FAIL"

A 1990 study by Maureen O'Hara and Wayne Shaw has explored the effects of the comptroller's too-big-to-fail policy. O'Hara and Shaw looked at stock price data from 64 banks, including those that were on the comptroller's list. They explored how the announcement of the too-big-to-fail policy, reported by the *Wall Street Journal* on September 20, 1984, affected the stock prices of banks both on and off the comptroller's list.

An interesting twist developed from the fact that when the comptroller made his announcement on September 19, 1984, he did not provide the names of the eleven banks covered by the too-big-to-fail policy. The next day the *Wall Street Journal*, in reporting his announcement, identified the nation's eleven largest banks by name, indicating that those eleven were the ones most likely to be covered by the new policy. The *Wall Street Journal* forgot, however, that the comptroller regulates only *national* banks; hence, the article on September 20 incorrectly listed the four largest *state* banks—Manufacturers Hanover Trust, J. P. Morgan, Bankers

Trust, and Chemical Bank—as likely members of the eleven too-big-to-fail banks included in the comptroller's list.

O'Hara and Shaw found that the eleven banks listed in the *Wall Street Journal* article—including the four incorrectly listed as members of the comptroller's too-big-to-fail group of banks—experienced *abnormal* stock price gains that day, by which they meant that the price increases were greater than would have been expected by random variation. In contrast, banks not on the *Wall Street Journal's* list experienced abnormal *losses*. The authors of the study conclude that the too-big-to-fail policy undeniably influences investors' perceptions of the riskiness of banks' shares. Hence, they conclude, those banks that are categorized as "too big to fail" unambiguously gain from the policy, at the expense of those that are not included in this group.

Adapted from Maureen O'Hara and Wayne Shaw, "Deposit Insurance and Wealth Effects: The Value of Being 'Too Big to Fail,'" *Journal of Finance*, 45 (5, December 1990), pp. 1587–1600, and Maureen O'Hara, "From Too Big to Fail to Too Sick to Save," *Wall Street Journal* (Tuesday, February 19, 1991), p. A21.

These requirements are imposed in the form of minimally acceptable ratios of total capital to assets.

Before the 1980s, depository institutions were not required to meet specific capital-asset ratios. Regulators instead typically used implicit pressures—often called ''moral suasion''—to induce managers at institutions they believed to be undercapitalized to increase the institutions' ratios of capital to total assets. This informal approach seemed to work until the late 1960s; after that time there was a gradual decline in capitalization of banks.

Bank regulators first began imposing explicit capital requirements on commercial banks in 1981. Congress ratified this approach in 1983 in a provision of the **International Lending Supervision Act,** which authorized all three primary bank regulators—the Federal Reserve, the FDIC, and the Office of the Comptroller of the Currency—to set and enforce capital requirements. By 1985, these regulators had agreed to subject all banks to the same requirements, using two measures of capital. One of these included equity, loan loss reserves, perpetual preferred stock (stock with no maturity date), and mandatory convertible debt (debt that is converted to stock at a later date). The other added such items as subordinated debt and limited-life preferred stock (stock with a set maturity date).

These actions helped end the decline in bank capitalization, but regulators were soon disappointed if they had hoped that the end to the decline would be followed by an *increase* in the amount of bank capital relative to assets. Indeed, by 1989 the aggregate commercial bank capital-to-asset ratio of 6.4 percent was roughly half the level of 1934 during the Great Depression. In addition, regulators had become concerned about the further risks assumed by banks through their commitment lending. Finally, bank loan losses rose sharply in the 1980s, indicating the potential for significant risks of bank insolvency in the future. In response to these developments, in 1989 the three banking regulators imposed an entirely new set of comprehensive capital requirements.

Measures of Capital and Risk-Adjusted Assets   Under these capital requirements, there again are two types, or "tiers," of bank capital. Tier One, or **core,** capital, is composed of the bank's tangible equity. Under the regulations, **total capital** is equal to Tier One capital plus Tier Two, or **supplementary,** capital. Tier Two capital includes a portion of the bank's loan loss reserves and subordinated debt.

In addition, for purposes of computing a bank's capital-asset ratios, regulators adjust the amounts of assets held by the bank according to risk weights to yield a measure they call **risk-adjusted assets.** This is done as follows. Regulators view cash, U.S. government securities, and government-guaranteed GNMA mortgage-backed securities as safe assets, and so they assign them a risk weighting of zero. They assign a 20 percent risk weighting to assets they believe have a relatively small risk of default, including interbank deposits, general obligation municipal securities, and FNMA and FHLMC mortgage-backed securities that are partially guaranteed by the federal government. They give somewhat more risky assets such as first home mortgages and municipal revenue bonds a risk weighting of 50 percent. They assign a risk weighting of 100 percent to all other bank securities and loans. Finally, they take into account off-balance-sheet activities such as loan commitments by converting them into "credit exposure dollar equivalents," apply the risk weightings just discussed to those amounts, and sum up all the risk-weighted measures that they have calculated. The total amount computed then is the bank's amount of risk-adjusted assets.

The amount of risk-adjusted assets is the denominator of the bank capital ratios the regulators compute. This quantity also is used to compute the amount of loan loss reserves that count toward inclusion in Tier Two, supplementary capital; under the regulations, loan loss reserves in excess of 1.25 percent of risk-adjusted assets may not be included in supplementary capital. The reason is that regulators view particularly large loan loss reserves as a sign of greater risk instead of a larger cushion against loss.

Interestingly, both U.S. regulators and those of other nations simultaneously adopted these measures of risk. Formal adoption of these risk categories occurred in a meeting of representatives of ten central banks, including the Federal Reserve System, in July 1988. Hence, these basic measures of capital and assets are used now by regulators in numerous countries. The purpose of this international coordination of capital standards was to avoid imposing requirements that would seriously weaken the international competitive position of any one nation's banking system.

The Requirements   Under the regulations adopted in 1989, banks were required, by 1992, to maintain minimum acceptable risk-adjusted capital ratios (the specific required ratio for total—core plus supplemental—capital is 8 percent, which was reached in steps between 1989 and 1992). While only about 5 percent of all banks found themselves "failing" these requirements at the time they were enacted, they spurred many banks to issue more equity shares and to sell more subordinated debt. Indeed, *one* reason for the fall in stock prices of banks in 1990 was that so many were supplying more new shares of stock. (Of course, the *main* reason, unfortunately for the banks, was that investors lost confidence in the stocks, causing a fall in demand.)

THE FINANCIAL INSTITUTIONS REFORM, RECOVERY, AND ENFORCEMENT ACT OF 1989

At the time of its passing, the DIDMCA of 1980 was thought to be the solution to the problems that had plagued the depository institution regulatory structure in the 1960s and 1970s. Its passage, proponents hoped, would signal a new era in banking characterized by greater competition among depository institutions and between these institutions and other financial intermediaries.

In large measure, these hopes were dashed by the events of the 1980s. As savings and loan and savings bank failure rates skyrocketed, and as the pace of commercial bank failures picked up significantly, it became increasingly apparent that the DIDMCA of 1980 and subsequent legislation had, at best, placed a "Band-Aid" on underlying weaknesses in the structure of regulation or, at worst, had hastened the collapse of some of the weakest of depository institutions.

The **Financial Institutions Reform, Recovery, and Enforcement Act of 1989,** known as **FIRREA** for short, addressed the regulatory difficulties and institutional failures that became apparent in the 1980s. As we shall discuss in more detail in Chapter 13, congressional passage of FIRREA probably was forced by events as much as by a coalescence of ideas for regulatory reform: The thrift industry was collapsing, and something simply had to be done.

We shall spend much more time discussing FIRREA in Chapter 13. It is important, however, to lay out a brief sketch of the legislation and its provisions at this point, because most current depository institution policy making and regulation presently are influenced by the scope of this legislation.

FIRREA is a lengthy act with fourteen sections. We concentrate here on the provisions of FIRREA with broadest implications for depository institution regulation, which are as follows:

1. The act abolished the original regulator of most thrift institutions, the **Federal Home Loan Bank Board.** Also abolished was the FSLIC. At the same time, the act created a new thrift regulator, the **Office of Thrift Supervision (OTS),** under the administration of the Treasury Department.

2. The act significantly restructured the FDIC, for the first time since its inception in 1933. It created two separate FDIC insurance funds, the **Bank Insurance Fund (BIF)** and the **Savings Association Insurance Fund (SAIF).** SAIF replaced the FSLIC as the insurance fund for most thrift institutions. The act also subjected thrift institutions to the FDIC's conservatorship and receivership powers, broadened those powers, and limited the claims that depository institutions could make against the FDIC.

3. FIRREA increased bank and thrift deposit insurance premiums. BIF premiums were nearly doubled from one-twelfth of 1 percent (0.0833 percent) of insured deposits in 1989 to 0.23 percent in 1991. The act also increased SAIF premiums, raised the maximum premiums the FDIC could charge for both funds, and set targets for replenishing the government's bank and thrift insurance funds, which had been seriously depleted by large numbers of thrift failures.

FIRREA largely was passed to address the thrift institution crisis that we shall discuss in detail in Chapter 13. Nevertheless, the three provisions listed above all had important implications for the entire scope of depository institution regulation. By making the Treasury Department the regulator of thrift institutions, FIRREA involved that department, which already is the home of the Office of the Comptroller of the Currency, much more directly in the regulatory process. In addition, the powers and responsibilities of the FDIC were significantly enhanced—and the regulatory task it faced was significantly enlarged. The increase in deposit insurance premiums paid by both banks and thrifts not only affected all these institutions but signaled a determination by the government to charge them for the higher failure rates the government's insurance funds had experienced.

THE 1990S: DECADE OF DECISION?

This is a textbook in economic and not political science. Nevertheless, it is now widely agreed by bankers, economists, and policy makers alike that one of the major political issues of coming years may be the salvaging and/or restructuring of depository institutions. Of course, changes in the shapes of political landscapes are difficult to foresee; after all, the fortunes of presidential candidates sometimes change swiftly within a matter of weeks or days. It is conceivable that voters and politicians will lose interest in banking problems. Certainly, members of Congress often prefer to avoid such thorny problems—particularly if they cost taxpayers funds that they prefer not to spend. There also is nothing especially glamorous to voters about seeing their representatives and senators conducting committee hearings in a room full of stodgy bankers.

As politicians learned in the 1980s, however, banking problems do not tend to go away of their own accord. Left alone, such problems typically become magnified and clamor for attention. They may be unavoidable in the 1990s, which—whether politicians like it or not—may be the ''decade of decision'' for banking policy in the United States.

MOVEMENTS TOWARD CHANGE IN THE 1990s?

In 1991, the Treasury Department unfurled a proposal for a complete change in the structure of the U.S. banking system. Under the plan, several changes would be made:

1. The Glass-Steagall Act's separation of banks from securities firms would be abolished. Provided that banks met specified capital standards, they could affiliate with securities firms, insurance companies, and mutual funds under a holding company structure. Furthermore, commercial companies would be permitted to own banks through such holding companies.

2. Banks would be permitted to operate nationwide branching systems.

3. The coverage of federal deposit insurance would be reduced, and even more stringent bank capital requirements would be established.

4. A new federal banking regulator within the Treasury Department would be established that would regulate all nationally chartered banks and thrifts. The Federal Reserve would be given responsibility for regulating all state-chartered depository institutions. Direct regulatory responsibilities would be taken away from the FDIC, which would concentrate solely on handling deposit insurance and failures.

As of this writing, it is unclear whether any or all of these proposals will be enacted by Congress. Reactions to the proposals have been mixed. Many lawmakers have appeared ready to support nationwide branching but have expressed concerns about bank ownership by commercial enterprises. According to one senator, ''These proposals are bad medicine for banks and poison for the American public.'' The same senator expressed fear that Japanese and European companies would buy up the nation's banks if commercial firms were permitted to own banks. Some analysts, in contrast, argued that banking and commerce belong together.

Other analysts have argued that reduced deposit insurance coverage could induce many depositors to pull their funds out of the banking system altogether, leading to a collapse of the industry. The FDIC chairman decried the proposal to end the FDIC's direct supervisory responsibilities as ''very dangerous'' because it would ''take away all our powers to protect the insurance fund.'' Many in Congress questioned the Treasury Department's competence to regulate so many banks, and banking lawyers predicted that many state banks would seek to switch to national charters to avoid tougher Federal Reserve regulation.

At the time of this writing, the full Treasury plan is not given much chance to pass, at least in its entirety. Congressional consensus appears to have coalesced around a somewhat more limited scheme in which movements toward nationwide banking would be permitted, bank deposit insurance premiums would be increased further, current regulations on capital lending would be tightened, limits would be imposed on bank real estate lending, and separation of banking and commerce largely would continue. In short, Congress continues to move slowly on major banking reform.

DIFFICULT ISSUES AND TOUGH CHOICES

Which goals of banking regulation—stability through regulated solvency and liquidity, or efficiency via deregulation competition—will society ultimately choose to emphasize? We cannot forecast an answer to this question, although the recent trend is toward stability at the expense of efficiency.

What we *can* do, however, is provide you, the student, with a more concrete framework upon which to base your *own* judgments on these issues. This will be our objective as we move on to the next chapter, which analyzes the economic consequences of governmental regulation of depository institutions.

CHAPTER SUMMARY

1. The failure of a depository institution is an event of special importance because many people depend on the safety and security of such institutions. Moreover, when one bank fails, the soundness of other banks becomes suspect. If all banks are on a fractional reserve system, no bank can survive a situation in which all or most depositors attempt to withdraw their funds at the same time. During the Great Depression, bank runs were contagious and many banks toppled, which contributed to the severity of the Great Depression.

2. The Banking Act of 1933 (the Glass-Steagall Act) was passed as a reaction to the collapse of the banking system during the Great Depression. The key provisions of the Glass-Steagall Act were (a) the creation of the FDIC, (b) the separation of commercial banking from investment banking, and (c) a prohibition of payment of interest on demand deposits.

3. The FDIC has insured the deposits of commercial banks since its formation in 1933. For decades, federal deposit insurance has helped reduce the fragile nature inherent in a fractional reserve banking system; by providing depositor confidence in even shaky banks, the ''bank run'' was largely eliminated.

4. In the 1930s it was deemed important to separate commercial banking from investment banking because investment banking was believed to increase the riskiness of a commercial bank's portfolio; also, possible conflicts of interest are avoided with separation.

5. The preoccupation with excessive competition in the banking industry led to an entry-restricting policy: Potential entrants to the banking industry are required to provide a convincing case for the ''need'' for another bank before they can obtain a charter. This policy may have contributed to reduced competition in the banking industry.

6. The dual banking system in the United States has contributed to overlapping supervision and regulation of banks. There are four sources of regulation, supervision, and control: the Office of the Comptroller of the Currency, the Federal Reserve, the FDIC, and state banking authorities.

7. There is a large number of distinct and separate depository institutions in the United States. Interstate banking has been prohibited, and some states have encouraged a unit banking system and discouraged branch banking. In recent years, technological and legal innovations tended to reverse this trend, however.

8. In 1980 the Depository Institutions Deregulation and Monetary Control Act was passed. Interest rate ceilings on deposits were phased out, nationwide NOW accounts were permitted, reserves were required on all transactions accounts at depository institutions, such institutions all now had access to borrowing from the Fed, and the power of thrifts was expanded.

9. In 1982 the Garn–St Germain Act was enacted, which permitted banks and other depository institutions to offer deposit accounts with unregulated interest rates, allowed thrifts to expand their commercial and consumer lending, and gave the federal deposit insurers emergency power to permit interstate acquisitions of closed banks.

10. In 1981, again in 1985, and once again in 1989 federal banking authorities imposed capital requirements on commercial banks in an effort to shore up their resilience to the risk of asset losses. The latest set of requirements has very specific definitions of bank capital and of risk-adjusted assets. All commercial banks are subject to these requirements.

11. In 1984, the comptroller of the currency announced that some banks were ''too big to fail.'' This policy was successful in restoring the public's faith in the largest depository institutions, but it also was widely viewed as unfair to banks not included in the comptroller's list, because it implicitly placed government guarantees on even the uninsured deposits of the banks that were deemed too large to fail.

12. The Financial Institutions Reform, Recovery, and Enforcement Act was passed in 1989. Among other things, it eliminated the Federal Home Loan Bank Board and replaced it with the Office of Thrift Supervision within the Department of the Treasury, eliminated the FSLIC and made the FDIC chief insurer of the deposits of both commercial banks and thrift institutions, raised deposit insurance premiums for all depository institutions, and ordered the study of further efforts to restructure banking regulation in the United States.

GLOSSARY

Allocative efficiency: Efficiency gained when the prices of bank services are set at the additional cost incurred in providing the last unit of service the bank produces.

Bank Insurance Fund (BIF):   The FDIC's deposit insurance fund for commercial banks.

Branch banking: A system that allows banks to operate at more than one location.

Capital requirements: Legal limitations on the amount of assets that depository institutions may hold in relation to their capital.

Core capital: Capital composed of the bank's tangible equity; called Tier One capital.

Depository institution capital: Most narrowly defined as equity shares in a bank, but more broadly defined by bank regulators as composed of all items, including equity, that help shield insured deposits from losses in the event of a failure by a bank.

Edge Act: Law that allows deposits to be accepted across state lines if they are used to finance the production of goods that are primarily to be exported.

Federal Deposit Insurance Corporation (FDIC): A government agency that insures the deposits held in all federally insured depository institutions. Under the provisions of 1989 legislation, the FDIC maintains separate insurance funds for commercial banks and savings institutions.

Federal Home Loan Bank Board (FHLBB): A committee of three appointed by the President of the United States to regulate members of the Federal Home Loan Bank System. It also regulated FSLIC and the Federal Home Loan Mortgage Corporation. This board was disbanded in 1989.

Federal Savings and Loan Insurance Corporation (FSLIC): A government agency that insured deposits held in member savings and loan associations. It was eliminated in 1989.

Financial Institutions Reform, Recovery, and Enforcement Act (FIRREA): 1989 act with 14 provisions that made major changes in regulations affecting depository institutions.

Glass-Steagall Act: Also known as the Banking Act of 1933, the act created the FDIC, prohibited deposit-taking banks from underwriting ''ineligible'' securities, prohibited commercial banks from paying interest on checking accounts, and authorized the Federal Reserve to establish interest rates on time and savings deposits.

Interest Rate Adjustment Act of 1966: Act that placed interest rate ceilings on deposits in thrift institutions.

International Lending Supervision Act: 1983 act that authorized the Federal Reserve, the FDIC, and the Office of the Comptroller of the Currency to set and enforce capital requirements.

National Credit Union Administration (NCUA): A federal agency that insures credit union deposits.

Office of the Comptroller of the Currency: The office in the U.S. Treasury Department that supervises the regulation and examination of national banks.

Office of Thrift Supervision (OTS): A regulatory authority created in 1989; it is based in the Department of the Treasury and has primary responsibility for regulating savings and loan associations and savings banks.

Risk-adjusted assets: A measure of a bank's actual assets and its off-balance-sheet loan guarantees that accounts for regulators' perceptions of risk and that is used by regulators to compute a bank's capital requirements.

Savings Association Insurance Fund (SAIF): The FDIC's insurance fund for savings and loan associations and savings banks, established in 1989 to replace the FSLIC.

Supplementary capital: Capital that includes a portion of the bank's loan reserves and subordinated debt; called Tier Two capital.

Technical efficiency: Efficiency gained when bank services are provided at the lowest possible cost in terms of the social resources that the banks expend in the process.

Total capital: The sum of core (Tier One) and supplementary (Tier Two) capital.

Unit banking: A restriction preventing banks from operating at more than one location; a prohibition against branch banking.

SELF-TEST QUESTIONS

1. What original Glass-Steagall regulations remain with us today? Which of the original banking restrictions contained in that legislation have since been eliminated or relaxed?

2. What types of regulations limit the entry of depository institutions into the financial services industry? How have depository institutions attempted to evade these regulations? To what extent have they been successful?

3. What were the main provisions of the DIDMCA of 1980? Was its primary purpose to increase or reduce the regulation of depository institutions?

4. What were the key provisions of the Garn–St Germain Act of 1982? What were its main implications for depository institutions?

5. What motivated the "too-big-to-fail" policy? Why was it so controversial?

6. What are capital requirements? How do bank regulators presently measure bank capital? How do they adjust bank assets for riskiness?

7. What were the main provisions of banking legislation enacted by Congress since the late 1980s?

PROBLEMS

10-1. Suppose that a large bank on the "too-big-to-fail" list of regulators pays an annual interest rate of 6.4 percent to holders of its certificates of deposit (CDs), while a smaller regional bank not on the "too-big-to-fail" list pays an annual CD interest rate of 6.5 percent. The large bank has $10 billion in CDs outstanding, while the regional bank has issued $1 billion in CDs.

  a. Based on these data, what is the net per-deposit-dollar value that the large bank derives from being "too big to fail"?

  b. What is the large bank's total profit advantage, relative to the regional bank, if the two banks have identical revenues and incur the same costs otherwise?

10-2. Consider the following balance sheet for Union Federal Bank (amounts in millions of dollars):

Assets		**Liabilities and Capital**	
Cash assets	10	Deposits	180
U.S. government		Subordinated debt	5
securities	60	Equity	10
FNMA mortgage-backed			
securities	20		
Municipal revenue bonds	10		
Loans	100		

In addition, assume that regulators have determined that the "credit-equivalent" amount of off-balance-sheet guarantees made by this bank in the form of loan commitments totals to $41 million, and regulators have decided to treat this amount as risky loans in their evaluation of the bank's assets.

  a. What is the amount of the bank's Tier One, or core, capital? What is the amount of the bank's Tier Two, or supplementary, capital? What is its total capital, for regulatory purposes?

  b. Using the risk weights adopted by bank regulators in 1989, what is the amount of risk-adjusted assets of Union Federal Bank? What is its total risk-adjusted capital ratio? Based on the current capital requirement imposed by regulators, has this bank met the regulatory standard?

10-3. Suppose that American State Bank, like Union Federal Bank in problem 10-2, has $200 million in assets. Its liabilities are the same, but it has $5 million in cash assets, $55 million in securities, no FNMA securities or municipal revenue bonds, $140 million in loans, and $50 million in credit-equivalent loan commitments that regulators classify as risky loans. What is American State's risk-adjusted capital ratio? Does it meet the current requirement?

SELECTED REFERENCES

Broaddus, Alfred, ''Financial Innovation in the United States—Background, Current Status and Prospects,'' *Economic Review*, Federal Reserve Bank of Richmond, 71 (1, January/February 1985), pp. 2–22.

Cargill, Thomas F., and Gillian G. Garcia, *Financial Deregulation and Monetary Control* (Stanford, Calif.: Hoover Institution Press, 1982).

———, *Financial Reform in the 1980s* (Stanford, Calif.: Hoover Institution Press, 1985).

Cooper, Kerry, and Donald R. Fraser, *Banking Deregulation and the New Competition in Financial Services* (Cambridge, Mass.: Ballinger, 1986).

Keaton, William R., ''The New Risk-Based Capital Plan for Commercial Banks,'' Federal Reserve Bank of Kansas City *Economic Review*, 74 (10, December 1989), pp. 40–60.

Munn, Glenn C., F. L. Garcia, and Charles J. Woelfel, *Encyclopedia of Banking and Finance*, 9th ed. (Rolling Meadows, Ill.: Bankers Publishing Company, 1991).

O'Hara, Maureen, and Wayne Shaw, ''Deposit Insurance and Wealth Effects: The Value of Being 'Too Big to Fail,''' *Journal of Finance*, 45 (5, December 1990), pp. 1587–1600.

Economic Consequences
of Bank Regulation

CHAPTER PREVIEW

1. What theories have been offered to explain choices of bank regulation? What are the distinctive features of each theory?

2. What are the societal advantages of competition over monopoly in banking?

3. What are economies of scale and scope in banking, and how do they help economists determine how "big" society might wish for banks to be?

4. Are bank profits higher in markets where a few banks have large market shares? Why or why not?

5. Should banking be separated from other types of business?

6. Do capital requirements really make banks safer?

THEORIES OF REGULATION OF DEPOSITORY INSTITUTIONS

In the last chapter, we discussed three basic goals of bank regulation: solvency, liquidity, and efficiency. We also discussed the fact that regulators face potential trade-offs among these goals. We did not, however, address a related question: How do we explain the choices of regulators about which goals to emphasize, given that there are trade-offs among regulatory goals?

THEORIES OF REGULATION

There are three basic theories of regulator behavior. These are the public-interest theory, the capture theory, and the public-choice theory.

The Public-Interest Theory The first theory of regulation is the **public-interest theory.** According to this theory, regulators seek to maximize the welfare of society as a whole. That is, as officials duly appointed by elected representatives, regulators determine their policies in light of the *public interest.* It is this theory of regulation that supports the establishment of independent regulatory bodies such as public utility commissions. If the market does not work, argue the public interest theorists, regulators intervene and do what is best for both firms and consumers in those markets. According to this view, then, regulators such as the Federal Reserve or the FDIC dispassionately survey the situation faced by the banks they regulate and the consumers of their financial services, conduct careful studies of alternative regulatory policies and their effects on social welfare, and implement only those policies that maximize total welfare. The individual interests of the regulators themselves play no role in their decisions.

The Capture Theory Experience with regulation has led many observers to reject the public-interest view in favor of one that stands in nearly direct contrast. According to the advocates of the alternative view, which economists call the **capture theory** of regulation and generally credit to the Nobel economist George Stigler, society as a whole does not benefit from regulation. Instead, those who benefit from regulation are those who are regulated. Those who lose, typically, are the consumers of their products. Not surprisingly, then, this theory suggests that firms actually may *seek* to be regulated.

This perspective is based in cynicism about governmental processes. Its adherents see regulatory bodies, such as the Federal Reserve or the FDIC, as groups of individuals that the firms they regulate—banks—desire to influence so as to achieve favorable treatment; that is, the regulated firms strive to *capture* their regulator so that they might reap all the benefits from regulation. They might do this by unofficially ''lobbying'' the regulators, by providing ''favors'' (a nice term for bribes), or by standing ready to employ the regulators—and members of their economic staffs—when their terms in government expire.

Indeed, although a few Federal Reserve and FDIC policy makers and staff economists have been known to go into fields such as academics (a generally nonlucrative career, we can assure you) at the end of their time in Washington, many of these individuals complete their careers as officers at financial institutions. According to the capture theory, current Fed or FDIC policy makers and economists recognize that they ultimately may work for the depository institutions they presently regulate. Hence, the last thing they wish to do is regulate them too harshly; they might find out later on that they are out of a job!

The Public-Choice Theory Proponents of the **public-choice theory** of regulation offer a theory that encompasses the public-interest and capture theories as special cases. According to the public-choice perspective, regulators face trade-offs. Other things constant, they might like to do what is best for the society as a whole, but, unfortunately, ''other things constant'' is not the way the world really works. On the one hand, regulators would like to keep the prices charged by the firms they regulate low for the benefit of consumers of those products, who may then be grateful to the regulators and the politicians, who then will raise their salaries and reappoint them. On the other hand, low prices can mean low profits for the firms that supply the products, and that could spell the eventual end of those firms—and an end of the need for the services of the regulators. Therefore, regulators can't have their cake and eat it, too. Either direction they lean, whether toward the interests of consumers or toward the interests of producers, regulators stand to gain *and*, simultaneously, to lose.

As a result, according to the public-choice theory, regulators typically will set regulations on markets that permit firms to earn profits above perfectly competitive profit levels but below those they could earn if they could set their prices at purely monopolistic levels. Hence, the theory predicts that regulators will prefer neither perfectly competitive markets nor completely monopolistic markets. Yet, by not allowing competition regulators will, according to the theory, permit firms to have at least partial ''monopoly power,'' which is the ability to set their prices noncompetitively.

COMPETITION OR MONOPOLY IN BANKING?

If the public-choice theory of regulation is applied to banking, then it predicts that bank regulators typically will not prefer a completely competitive banking system. If this theory is valid, it follows that we should not expect to observe perfectly competitive banking markets in a regulated banking system such as the one that presently exists. Would society lose anything as a result? That is the question to which we turn our attention in this section.

FUNDAMENTAL PROPERTIES OF COMPETITIVE BANKING MARKETS

Let us suppose that regulators were to act solely in the interests of consumers; that is, let us suppose that they design their regulations with an aim to produce a perfectly competitive banking system. From the perspective of society, what would be the important properties of such a perfectly competitive banking system? To consider this question, we shall apply the theory of bank behavior we developed in Chapter 8.

As we discussed in Chapter 8, a bank's short-run marginal cost, MC, has three components: the interest rate on deposits, r_D; the marginal resource cost of deposits, MC_D; and the marginal resource cost of loans, MC_L. Recall that each of these components is measured in units of dollar per dollar, or as fractions (percentages).

In the discussion that follows, we shall simplify by assuming that each of these components is fixed. We shall make an even less realistic assumption by holding MC_D and MC_L *constant*, which means that we shall assume that marginal resource costs do not vary in the short run with changes in the amounts of deposits and loans at banks. We also shall assume that banks incur no fixed costs. Finally, we shall assume that all banks have the same costs. We make these assumptions only to help simplify the diagrams we shall display; the main points we wish to communicate hold true in the absence of these assumptions.

Under our assumptions, the marginal cost schedules of banks are identical and horizontal, as shown by the MC schedule in Figure 11-1. Furthermore, because marginal cost is the same for each dollar of lending by the bank, marginal cost is equal to average total cost (ATC).

Recall that, in a competitive banking industry, the marginal cost schedule is each bank's loan supply schedule. Furthermore, summation of all banks' loan supply schedules yields the total market loan supply schedule. Under our simplifying assumptions, each bank has the same horizontal marginal cost schedule, and so the banking industry's loan supply schedule under competitive banking would be this same marginal cost schedule.

Figure 11-1 depicts a loan market equilibrium under banking competition, given our simplifying assumptions. Point C is the competitive equilibrium. At this point, the quantity of loans demanded is equal to the quantity of loans supplied. The equilibrium loan rate is r_L^C, and the equilibrium quantity of lending by banks is L_C.

Allocative Efficiency   One key property of competitive banking is the fact that the market equilibrium loan rate, r_L^C in Figure 11-1, is equal to marginal cost. This means that the loan rate that bank customers pay just covers the cost that banks incur to produce the last dollar of loans. As we discussed in Chapter 2, economists call this property of a competitive market *allocative efficiency.*

Most economists believe that the attainment of allocative efficiency is a desirable property of perfect competition. If economic goods are priced so that the cost of producing the last unit just compensates the producer of the good for its production, then members of society will use resources as efficiently as possible. This basic tenet of economic theory applies to the market for bank loans as well as it does to markets for any other good or service.

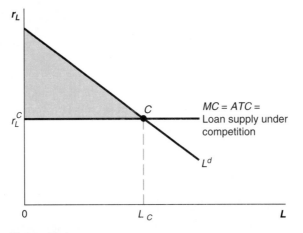

Figure 11-1
Loan Market Equilibrium and Consumer Surplus under Bank Competition. This diagram of loan market equilibrium is drawn under the assumption that marginal cost is constant and of the same magnitude across banks. Point C is the competitive equilibrium. At this point, the quantity of loans demanded is equal to the quantity of loans supplied, the equilibrium loan rate is r_L^C, and the equilibrium quantity of lending by banks is L_C.

The market equilibrium loan rate is equal to marginal cost, and so the loan rate that bank customers pay just covers the cost banks incur to produce the last dollar of loans, implying that the competitive loan market is allocatively efficient.

The total revenues earned by banks in the market for loans is equal to the rectangular region $r_L^C \times L_C$, which also represents the total cost of producing loans. Therefore, banks in this competitive loan market earn zero economic profits.

The shaded triangular region is the total amount of consumer surplus, which represents the aggregate value of interest payments consumers of bank loans do not have to pay that they otherwise would have been willing to pay.

Consumer Surplus   In Figure 11-1, the total revenue earned by banks in the market for loans is equal to the market loan rate times the amount of lending, or $r_L^C \times L_C$, which is the rectangular area shown in the figure. Because marginal cost is constant and, therefore, equal to average cost, this area also represents the total cost of producing loans. Hence, banks in this competitive loan market earn zero economic profits, meaning that they earn accounting profits sufficient to cover the opportunity cost of being in the banking business.

Economists call the shaded triangular region in Figure 11-1 the total amount of *consumer surplus*. Recall from Chapter 4 that, for an individual consumer of a loan, consumer surplus is the amount by which the interest the individual would have been willing to pay for a loan exceeds the market interest that the individual actually has to pay. The triangular region shaded in Figure 11-1 measures the aggregate amount of consumer surplus for all consumers of bank loans. The reason is the fact that the loan demand schedule lies above the loan supply schedule. This tells us that consumers of L_C in total loans would have been willing to pay higher loan rates than the market rate that they actually had to pay, r_L^C, to have obtained this total amount of credit. Specifically, they *would* have been willing to pay the entire dollar amount including *both* the rectangular and the triangular areas, but they in fact only have to pay the rectangular area. Hence, the triangular area is the total amount they do not have to pay as a result of the functioning of a competitive loan market.

It is the total amount of consumer surplus made available as a result of perfect competition in the banking industry.

EFFICIENCY LOSSES AND REDISTRIBUTIONS UNDER MONOPOLY BANKING

Economists typically believe that monopolistic markets have undesirable properties. They refer to these undesirable properties as *efficiency losses, redistribution effects,* and *deadweight losses.*

To illustrate these concepts, we now consider the possibility that a regulator enacts and enforces regulations that restrict the entry of depository institutions into the banking industry to such an extent that existing depository institutions are able to act together as a single monopoly, or *cartel.* In this case, Figure 11-2 would be applicable to the market for bank loans.

In Figure 11-2, banks together maximize joint profits by producing loans to the point at which marginal revenue is equal to marginal cost. Hence, they produce L_M in loans. At this quantity of lending, which corresponds to point M on the loan demand schedule, loan consumers are willing and able to pay the loan rate r_L^M. The total revenue earned by banks is equal to $r_L^M \times L_M$, and the total cost they incur is equal to ATC $\times L_M$, and so the amount of economic profits earned by banks is equal to $(r_L^M - \text{ATC}) \times L_M$, which is the rectangular area marked in Figure 11-2.

Efficiency Loss   The first implication of Figure 11-2 is that, under monopoly banking, the loan rate charged by banks exceeds the marginal cost of lending. Therefore, allocative efficiency is not attained, and so an **efficiency loss due to bank monopoly** occurs. The last dollar of lending by banks does not reflect properly the true (social opportunity) cost of producing that last dollar of loans, which means that resources used for lending by banks are not allocated in the least costly way. Society as a whole loses from this resource misallocation, because the resources could have been put to alternative, and less costly, uses.

An important result of lost efficiency in banking resulting from monopolistic markets is a reduction in bank lending, as compared with the amount of lending that would have occurred under bank competition. This can be seen in Figure 11-2. Under competition, the amount of lending would have occurred at the competitive equilibrium point C and would have been equal to L_C. Under monopoly, however, the amount of loans made by banks falls to the lower quantity, L_M.

Redistribution Effects and Deadweight Loss from Monopoly   Recall from our previous discussion that, in a competitive market, the entire triangular area below the loan demand schedule but above the marginal cost schedule is the total amount of consumer surplus obtained by loan consumers. In a monopolistic banking market, borrowers continue to obtain consumer surplus, because borrowers of loans would have been willing to pay interest rates in excess of r_L^M for the amount of loans L_M but do not have to do so. The total amount of consumer surplus obtained by borrowers is the upper shaded triangle in Figure 11-2.

Part of the consumer surplus that borrowers would have obtained in a competitive market is now the amount of profits earned by the monopolistic banks and shown as the upper rectangular area in Figure 11-2. This means that some of the consumer surplus that would have arisen under competition is *redistributed* to the owners of banks in a monop-

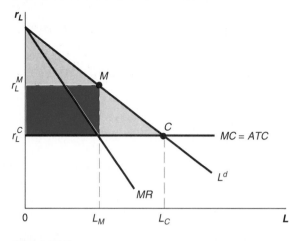

Figure 11-2

The Efficiency Loss, Redistribution Effect, and Deadweight Loss due to Monopoly in Banking.   If a regulator enacts and enforces regulations that enable banks to act together as a single monopoly, or cartel, then banks together would maximize joint profits by producing loans to the point at which marginal revenue is equal to marginal cost. Hence, they produce L_M in loans. At this quantity of lending, which corresponds to point M on the loan demand schedule, the loan rate is r_L^M. The total revenue earned by banks is equal to $r_L^M \times L_M$, and the total cost they incur is equal to $ATC \times L_M$, and so the amount of economic profits earned by banks is the rectangular area $(r_L^M - ATC) \times L_M$.

Because the loan rate charged by banks exceeds the marginal cost of lending, allocative efficiency is not attained, and so an efficiency loss occurs. As a result, there is a reduction in bank lending to L_M, as compared with the amount of lending that would have occurred under bank competition, L_C at point C.

The total amount of consumer surplus obtained by borrowers is the upper shaded triangle. Part of the consumer surplus that borrowers would have obtained in a competitive market is now redistributed to bank owners as profits, the upper rectangular area in the figure.

Another part of consumer surplus that otherwise would have been obtained by borrowers under competitive banking markets but is not under banking is the lower shaded triangle. Because neither loan consumers nor bank owners receive this area under monopolistic banking, it is a deadweight loss incurred by society as a whole.

olistic banking system. Economists call this the **redistribution effect due to bank monopoly.**

Another part of consumer surplus that otherwise would have been obtained by borrowers under competitive banking markets but is not under banking is the lower shaded triangle in Figure 11-2. This amount is no longer obtained by consumers in a monopoly banking market, but it also is not redistributed to owners of banks. No one gets this area under monopolistic banking; consequently, economists refer to this amount as a **deadweight loss due to bank monopoly,** which is incurred by society as a whole.

Estimates of Losses and Redistributions from Banking Monopoly   How large have the losses and redistributions from monopoly in banking markets really been in the United States? One study, published in 1982 and conducted by Stephen Rhoades of the economic staff of the Federal Reserve Board, found evidence of significant effects resulting from monopolistic bank loan markets in the 1970s.[1]

Rhoades estimated that in 1978 the amount of total loans made by banks was significantly below the amount that should have prevailed under perfect competition. Under competition, he found, lending would have been 16 percent greater than it actually was that year. This, he concluded, was evidence of substantial allocative inefficiency in banking.

Rhoades estimated that the amount of additional profits earned by banks as a result of monopolistic banking—the redistribution effect—also was significant. Specifically, he found that bank profits resulting from monopoly amounted to $1.3 billion in 1978 dollars, which was 13 percent higher than they would have been if bank loan markets had been competitive. This means that, according to Rhoades's estimate, about $1 for every $7 or $8 of banks' profits resulted from monopolistic banking.

According to Rhoades's estimates, there also was a deadweight loss as a result of monopoly banking, but he estimated that it was much smaller than the amount of the redistribution effect: about $12 million in 1978 dollars. In a follow-up study, however, two economists argued that Rhoades's estimate of the deadweight loss was between 15 and 45 times too small, depending on what approach they used in reevaluating Rhoades's estimate.[2] Hence, there is not complete agreement on the relative size of the deadweight social loss that monopolistic banking may have caused for U.S. society in the 1970s; it may have been very small, or it may have been significant.

As we discussed in the last chapter, the DIDMCA of 1980 and the Garn–St Germain Act of 1982 were intended to promote greater competition among depository institutions. These efforts developed from a growing public perception that banking markets had been overregulated and, to some extent, too monopolistic. Studies such as those conducted by Rhoades and others in the 1980s concluded that monopolistic banking was inefficient, transferred consumer surplus to the owners of banks, and produced deadweight social losses, which gave further impetus to the movement to deregulate banks and other depository institutions.

ECONOMIES OF SCALE AND SCOPE IN DEPOSITORY INSTITUTIONS: DOES "BIG" MEAN "BAD" IN BANKING?

Does society gain or lose from "bigness" in banking? A large part of this issue, which we shall focus on in this section, concerns whether or not banking becomes a less costly activity as bank size increases. Another related issue, which we shall explore in the following section, is the extent to which domination of banking markets by a few "big" depository institutions affects the degree of competition in those markets.

ECONOMIES OF SCALE

Previously, to simplify our discussion as much as possible, we assumed that there were constant short-run marginal and average costs in banking. Typically, however, we would

---

[1] Stephen Rhoades, "Welfare Loss, Redistribution Effect, and Restriction of Output Due to Monopoly in Banking," *Journal of Monetary Economics*, 9 (1, January 1982), pp. 375–387.

[2] B. M. Craven and R. S. Thompson, "Monopoly Welfare Losses in U.S. Banking: Comment," *Journal of Monetary Economics*, 14 (1, July 1984), pp. 123–126.

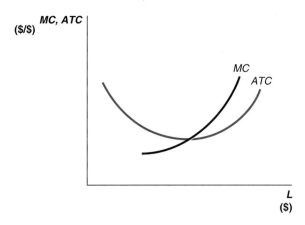

Figure 11-3
The Typical Short-Run Cost Schedules for a Bank. This diagram shows the general shapes of the average and marginal cost schedules for a typical bank of a given size. A typical bank's average total cost schedule is U-shaped. Its marginal cost schedule, which slopes upward over most of its range, crosses through the average total cost schedule at this schedule's minimum point.
    These short-run cost schedules tell us how the bank's marginal and average costs vary with changes in the amount of its lending, given the bank's current overall size, or scale. These schedules would apply for the bank in light of the current size of its home office and its current number of branches, which would be taken as fixed when the cost schedules are constructed.

anticipate that, in reality, marginal and average costs would vary with the amount of lending by banks. Figure 11-3 displays the general shapes of the short-run average and marginal cost schedules for a typical bank of a given size. As for any firm, a typical bank's short-run average total cost schedule is U-shaped, and its short-run marginal cost schedule slopes upward over most of its range, crossing through the average total cost schedule at the latter schedule's minimum point.

    Economists call the cost schedules in Figure 11-3 *short-run* cost schedules because they indicate how a bank's marginal and average costs vary with changes in the amount of its lending, *given* the bank's current overall size, or **scale.** That is, the cost schedules in Figure 11-3 would apply for the bank in light of the current size of its home office and its current number of branches, which would be taken as fixed when constructing the cost schedules in Figure 11-3.

The Long-Run Average Total Cost Schedule   Over a long enough period of time, which economists call the *long run,* the bank would be able to vary all factors of production, including factors that determine its overall scale, such as the number of branches it operates. For instance, if the bank were to increase the number of branches, it would be able to make more loans than it presently could contemplate. In contrast, if it were to close many of its branches, it would have to reduce the scale of its lending sharply.

    Naturally, the general cost of doing business varies with the size, or scale, of the bank. Economists call cost measures that take into account the effects of changing the absolute size of a bank the *long-run costs* of the bank. Of particular interest to economists in this regard is a bank's **long-run average total cost (LRATC) schedule.** Figure 11-4 helps conceptualize this concept. It shows short-run marginal and average total cost schedules for three different bank sizes, labeled *s* for relatively "small," *m* for "medium-sized,"

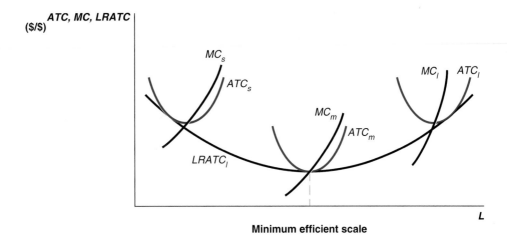

Figure 11-4
A Bank's Long-Run Average Total Cost Schedule.   Shown in this diagram are short-run marginal and average total cost schedules for three different bank sizes, labeled s for relatively "small," m for "medium-sized," and l for relatively "large." These cost schedules trace out, roughly, the bank's long-run average total cost (LRATC) schedule.

Typically, as a bank increases its size, its average cost would tend to fall to some extent, because as it gets larger, it can accomplish some cost savings. Hence, as the bank increases its scale from small to medium-sized, its long-run average total cost declines, and it experiences scale economies.

As a bank grows in size, however, some inefficiencies can also arise, leading to increases in long-run average total cost, as implied by the upward slope of the LRATC schedule as the bank increases its scale from medium-sized to large. Therefore, a typical bank usually experiences diseconomies of scale beyond some size.

Long-run average cost is minimized for a bank of medium size, and so this is the size that would be the minimum efficient scale for the bank, or the scale size at which the bank is technically efficient.

and l for relatively "large." These cost schedules trace out, roughly, the bank's long-run average total cost schedule that is shown in Figure 11-4.

Economies and Diseconomies of Scale   We typically would anticipate that as a bank initially increases its size—say, by operating more branches and increasing the number of automated teller machines it installs—its average cost would tend to fall to some extent. The reason is that as the bank gets larger, it can accomplish some cost savings. For instance, instead of training new college graduates to be branch managers, one at a time, at a few branches, it can set up a special training class for several newly graduated individuals and train them simultaneously, thereby lowering the average cost per branch management trainee. It also can spread the total cost of operating the computer system that links its branches and teller machines over a larger number of branches and machines, which also lowers the bank's average cost of producing loans and other banking services. Economists say that when average cost falls with an increase in the scale size of the bank, the bank has gained **economies of scale,** or **scale economies.** Hence, as the bank increases its scale from small to medium-sized in Figure 11-4, its long-run average total cost declines, and it experiences scale economies.

As a bank gets larger, however, some inefficiencies can also arise. It may open too many branches and automated teller machines for its existing computer system to monitor, leading to more communications breakdowns and delays. Employee training may become a more complicated task, as there are more employees to train and keep track of, with enlarged employee turnover. Bigness may lead to costly bureaucracy as well. All these aspects of further increases in scale, then, may lead to increases in long-run average total cost, as implied by the upward slope of the LRATC schedule as the bank increases its scale from medium-sized to large in Figure 11-4. Economists call a rise in long-run average total cost resulting from an increase in bank size a situation in which the bank experiences **diseconomies of scale** (or **scale diseconomies**).

Minimum Efficient Scale   As drawn, Figure 11-4 implies that long-run average cost is minimized for a bank of medium size, relative to the other extremes that are drawn. If this were the case, then economists would say that this medium size would be the **minimum efficient scale** for the bank. By this they would mean that this is the bank size that would yield the minimum—and hence most efficient—value of long-run average total cost for the bank. This would be the *best* size for the bank to be, both from the perspective of profit-maximizing owners of the bank and from the perspective of the rest of society, which would desire the most efficient allocation of resources throughout the economy. Banks that operate at minimum long-run average cost have achieved **technical efficiency.**

If the bank were larger or smaller than its minimum efficient scale, economists would judge it to be **technically inefficient;** the bank would not be using the technology available to it—its training programs, computer equipment, and so on—in a way that is least costly in terms of resource expense. At the minimum efficient scale, the bank is as technically efficient as it can be, which is in the best interests of the bank's owners and of society as a whole.

We have drawn Figure 11-4 under the *assumption* that the representative bank's LRATC schedule is U-shaped, so that the minimum efficient scale for the bank is medium-sized. In fact, it is possible that the LRATC for banks could be shaped much differently. Panels (*a*) and (*b*) of Figure 11-5 show two alternative shapes that the LRATC schedule might exhibit. In panel (*a*), the LRATC schedule reaches the point of minimum efficient scale very quickly as the bank increases in scale; this would mean that economies of scale are "used up" very quickly as a bank increases its size. Further increases in scale would lead to significant diseconomies of scale, and so the best size for a bank would be relatively small. Panel (*b*) of Figure 11-5, in contrast, shows an LRATC schedule in which long-run average total cost continues to decline even as the bank becomes larger and larger, so that even a very large bank experiences some economies of scale.

We would expect that if the technology used by banks led to an LRATC schedule such as that shown in panel (*a*) of Figure 11-5, the banking system would have numerous *small* banks. In contrast, if the LRATC schedule were shaped like that depicted in panel (*b*) of Figure 11-5, we would anticipate that a few *large* banks would develop. Indeed, if long-run average cost declined without limit as the scale of the bank increased, we might expect that a *single* bank might be most efficient, in which case economists would say that banking is a **natural monopoly;** that is, the technology of banking, much like the technologies of providing water and electricity, would lend itself to services being provided by a single firm.

As we shall discuss below, there is little evidence that banking is a natural monopoly. There is considerable disagreement, however, about the minimum efficient scale in banking.

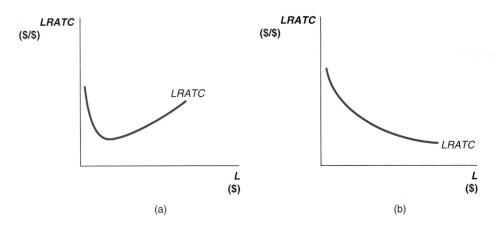

Figure 11-5
Extremely Shaped Long-Run Average Total Cost Schedules.   For banks with an LRATC schedule such as that shown in panel (*a*), economies of scale are used up very quickly. Therefore, the minimum efficient scale for a bank is very small, and we would anticipate that the banking system would have many small banks. For the case of the LRATC schedule depicted in panel (*b*), a bank would continue to experience economies of scale as it grows larger and larger. Hence, we would anticipate that a few large banks would develop or, possibly, that banking might be a natural monopoly in which long-run average cost declines without limit as the scale of the bank increases.

Another important factor influencing the size of a bank is the extent to which there are cost savings that the bank can realize from *diversification.* For instance, a bank that previously had specialized only in making commercial and industrial loans might find that its loan managers and credit analysts could use their specialized skills in making consumer loans as well. As a result, the bank alone might be able to produce the given amounts of both types of loans more cheaply than could two banks that specialized in both types of lending. Hence, the bank could widen the **scope** of its business and, in so doing, increase its overall range of operations. It could thereby lower its average total cost by becoming a *larger* bank, in terms of its mix of products. It would increase its size, however, not necessarily by opening more branches and teller machines, but rather through expanding into more businesses in its existing geographic area.

If a bank is able to experience cost savings by diversifying its product offerings and services, economists say that it experiences **economies of scope** (or **scope economies**). It is important to recognize that economies of scope and economies of scale are separate concepts. The former concept concerns cost reductions from diversifying into different product lines, while the latter concept refers to cost efficiencies made possible by expanding the overall output of the bank, holding its product mix unchanged. A bank potentially could experience the two types of economies separately or simultaneously.

INTERPRETING EVIDENCE ON SCALE AND SCOPE ECONOMIES

In recent years economists have conducted a wide range of studies of economies of scale and scope in banking. They have had a difficult time of it, however, because it turns out that it is a much easier task to define and discuss these concepts than it is to measure them accurately.

Before we lay out the current evidence on scale and scope economies, we shall begin by discussing some of the difficult issues that are involved in attempting to measure these economies. There are several issues that researchers have been forced to address and that we shall consider.

What Costs Matter for Measuring Scale and Scope Economies?

Early studies of economies of scale in banking conducted in the 1960s and 1970s tended to emphasize the importance of a bank's real resource, or operating, costs in determining the relative cost efficiency of different banks. Therefore, they often excluded interest expenses of banks when scale economies were estimated. Experience has convinced economists that interest expenses are a very important part of total bank costs—which should be no surprise, because we saw in Chapter 8 that both types of costs are important. Hence, modern studies of economies of scale and scope consider all aspects of bank costs.

What Exactly Do Banks Produce?

If you think about this question for a while, you will conclude that it is not an easy one to answer. At first pass, it seems straightforward. After all, the output that any firm produces is what it sells. It seems clear, then, that various types of credit extended by a bank should be counted as output of the bank. Nevertheless, banks also provide check-clearing services to holders of demand and other checkable deposits, and they earn fees from providing these services. Does this make checking deposits part of the output of banks as well?

There is no clear-cut answer. Indeed, economists have developed three different ways of defining and measuring bank output. One, which they call the **asset approach,** views bank liabilities such as deposits as the ''raw materials,'' or dollar ''inputs,'' for making loans that yield interest revenues to the bank. Loans and other interest-bearing assets, then, are viewed as the appropriate measure of output, according to this approach. Another perspective is provided by the **user-cost approach** to measuring bank output, under which a particular financial product of a bank is classified as an output of the bank if its net contribution to bank revenue is greater than zero. If its net contribution to revenue is negative, it is classified as an input instead. The third basic approach to measuring bank output is the **value-added approach.** As its name implies, this approach considers bank outputs to be those categories of financial products that contribute the most value to the bank's operations.

Each of these approaches to measuring bank output has advantages and disadvantages. The asset approach seems most sensible from a theoretical standpoint, but it ignores the ''output-like'' features of other bank services. The user-cost approach allows for the possibility that certain deposit services might be forms of outputs provided by banks, but it turns out that because banking is such a regulated industry, accurate measures of user costs can be difficult to construct. The value-added approach does not suffer from this difficulty, and so its popularity has increased in recent years.

On the surface, it would seem that if economists cannot even agree on how to measure the output of banks, it would not be possible to agree on estimates of economies of scale and scope derived from producing bank outputs. We shall see shortly that, nonetheless, general agreement has emerged among economists concerning some aspects of the economies-of-scale-and-scope issue.

Bank-Level versus Branch-Level Economies of Scale

In considering economies of scale, an important issue is whether researchers are able to distinguish between the minimum efficient scale of the entire bank as opposed to the best size of an individual bank office or branch. Early studies were not very successful in making this distinction; indeed, studies conducted in the early 1980s almost uniformly concluded that significant economies of scale existed for banks only below $25 million to $40 million in total deposits. Beyond this range, long-run average cost tended to increase. The evident implication was that it did not pay for banks to grow beyond that size.

While $25 million to $40 million may seem like a lot to the average person, this amount of deposits makes for a relatively small bank. The apparent conclusion that this was the minimum efficient scale for a bank seemed to stand in direct contradiction to the observed fact that numerous banks have *billions* of dollars in deposits. There is now general agreement that these studies actually had discovered estimates for the minimum efficient scale for an individual *bank office* or *branch* but did not answer the larger question concerning the minimum efficient scale for an entire banking operation.

Some Tentative Conclusions about Economies of Scale and Scope in Banking

More recent studies have been able to offer some tentative conclusions about both economies of scale and scope in banking. One very interesting conclusion is that most studies come up with similar answers irrespective of how they measure bank output. Some studies have used single-output measures, such as total assets; others have used multiple outputs along the lines of the user-cost and value-added approaches to output measurement; and still others have used *index* measures of bank output, such as weighted averages of both assets and liabilities, and thereby have sought to strike a happy medium between the two extremes. Somewhat surprisingly, very similar conclusions have been obtained from these differing approaches.

First among these is the general conclusion that, for an entire banking organization, economies of scale are experienced up to a level of about $100 million in deposits. One cannot jump to the further conclusion that this is the minimum efficient scale for a bank, however. The reason is that the empirical evidence also appears to support the conclusion that the long-run average total cost schedule is almost *flat* (though still slightly U-shaped) beyond a scale of $100 million in deposits. The long-run average total cost schedule seems to become upward sloping only for the very largest—multiple billions of dollars in deposits—bank sizes. This result seems to indicate that there is no single minimum efficient scale in banking. Hence, the banking industry could have a variety of sizes of banks—from a few hundred million dollars to a few billion dollars—and still be cost-efficient.

Second, there is relatively little evidence that economies of scope constitute an especially important feature in banking. An exception to this statement is that several studies have found that there may be efficiency gains from producing certain *pairs* of banking products, such as consumer and mortgage loans, simultaneously.

On net, then, it does not appear from the evidence provided in economic studies of bank scale and scope economies that banks would, if left to their own devices, tend to be either especially large or small, simply on the basis of technological efficiency. Most economists would look at these results as suggestive that banking is far from being a natural monopoly and that, in principle, there is little reason that significant numbers of banks could not operate efficiently in an unregulated environment.

Implications for State Restrictions on Branch Banking

One restriction that remains important in the United States is regulation of branch banking. Several studies of economies of scale and scope in banking have examined separately banks in states that have liberal branching laws and banks in states that permit little or no branching (which economists call ''unit banking'' states). Studies have typically found that banks that are not permitted to branch experience *diseconomies of scale*. This means that these banks are forced to have an inefficiently large banking office because they cannot operate branches.

In contrast, studies have tended to conclude that there is little evidence of diseconomies of scale for banks that are subject to fewer branching restrictions. The general implication of these conclusions is that branching restrictions can lead to cost-inefficient banking in the states with such restrictions. Furthermore, most studies have found that branching is not just a costly endeavor by banks to provide customer convenience; up to a point, increased branching lowers banks' average costs. For this reason, many economists believe that branch-banking regulations often are socially costly and should be reduced or eliminated.

BANK MARKET CONCENTRATION AND PERFORMANCE

Banking costs are only a part of the big picture. Banks and their regulators also consider revenues and profits. These, in turn, depend upon the interactions of banks, whether primarily competitive or somewhat monopolistic, in loan and deposit markets.

One of the most important issues in assessing these market interactions among banks is the degree to which **market concentration**—the extent to which the few largest banks dominate the shares of loans or deposits in banking markets—affects **market performance**—the degree to which both allocative and technical efficiencies are attained in banking markets. Economists commonly refer to this as the ''concentration-performance'' relationship in banking, which they seek to understand to help bank regulators to determine how much bank market concentration is acceptable.

There are two basic perspectives on this issue. The first of these, the *structure-conduct-performance* model, views highly concentrated markets (markets in which a few banks are dominant) as undesirable. The second, the *efficient structure* theory, views highly concentrated markets as a natural outcome of rivalry among banks that leads to the most cost-efficient banking system. We shall discuss each of these theories in turn.

THE STRUCTURE-CONDUCT-PERFORMANCE MODEL

Traditionally, economists have based their evaluations of the bank concentration-performance relationship on the **structure-conduct-performance (SCP) model.** According to the SCP theory, the *structure* of a banking market refers to both the number and size distribution of firms in the market. Market structure influences the *conduct* of the banks in the market. Bank conduct, in turn, determines the *performance* of the market.

The SCP model states that the more concentrated a banking market is—that is, the smaller the number of banks competing in the market and the larger the market share of just a few banks—the more likely it is that banking conduct will be monopolistic. This would mean that banks would conduct their business taking into account their monopoly power, and allocative inefficiency and social losses would occur. Bank market performance would be poor. In contrast, banking markets with low measured concentration—markets with a relatively large number of banks that each possess a fairly small share of the market—would be more likely to be nearly perfectly competitive. As a result, banks would conduct themselves as the theory of competition would predict, and bank market performance would be good.

There are a variety of predictions of the SCP model. First, as banking markets become more concentrated, it should be the case that bank profits will be higher. In addition, banks should charge higher loan rates, pay lower deposit rates, and make fewer loans than they would if markets were less concentrated. Hence, most studies of the SCP model have emphasized the possible link between bank market concentration and bank profits. The conclusions of these studies have been very mixed. While many studies found that greater concentration has led to increased bank profits, as the SCP model predicts, several others have not supported this link. Therefore, no unanimous verdict has emerged on the validity of the SCP model. Nevertheless, most economists have agreed that the studies provide qualified support for the idea that the number and size distribution of banks influence bank profits and the interest rates that banks charge on loans and pay on deposits.

THE EFFICIENT STRUCTURE THEORY

As often occurs, however, economists do not agree on *why* the number and size distribution of firms influence bank profits and interest rates. In direct contradiction to the SCP model, another theory offered to explain such relationships is the **efficient structure theory.** According to this approach, large market shares by a few banks result because these banks are more efficient. Because they can provide their services at lower cost than their competitors, these few banks can expand to larger size relative to their rivals. Furthermore, because they are more cost-efficient, says the efficient structure theory, they are more profitable. Consequently, the fact that banks with greater market shares are more profitable makes sense: They are more cost-efficient, and so they have greater profitability.

Support for this theory was provided by several studies conducted in the 1980s. These studies found that bank market concentration was not the ''prime contributor'' to firm profits; indeed, evidence was provided that concentration itself had little to do with profits, that what really mattered was the market share of each firm. In turn, these studies argued, bank market share reflected the relative efficiency of the banks competing in the banking market. Hence, the authors of these studies concluded that the efficient structure theory was preferred to the SCP model.

Proponents of the SCP approach were chastened but not deterred. More recent SCP studies have emphasized the fact that the efficient structure theory *also* predicts that if banks with larger market shares are more cost-efficient, then they also should charge lower loan rates and pay higher interest rates on their deposits—because the banks should be able to provide their services at lower cost, their customers should reap some of the benefits of their efficiency in a competitive marketplace. In fact, the evidence does not appear to support this prediction of the efficient structure theory.

What can we conclude? Unfortunately, the debate as yet appears to be unresolved. Furthermore, another problem with deciding upon the ''winner'' of the debate also seems nearly insurmountable. That issue is exactly how ''banking markets'' should be defined.

DEFINING DEPOSITORY INSTITUTION MARKETS

By definition, banks and other depository institutions trade financial instruments in several markets—such as markets for real estate loans, commercial loans, consumer loans, and federal funds loans—simultaneously. The geographic scope of such markets can vary considerably, however. Consider, for instance, a bank in a small town in an isolated rural area. Its markets for real estate, commercial, and consumer loans certainly are limited to its local area, but it may sell federal funds to a bank in New York. A large regional bank, in contrast, may make real estate and consumer loans to companies hundreds of miles away from its home location—indeed, it might even compete with the small, rural bank just discussed—but it may lend to businesses mainly within a 20-mile radius around its headquarters.

Defining what constitutes the "market" for a given bank, then, generally is an important, but thorny, problem. It is important because measuring such factors as "market concentration" naturally depends crucially upon one's definition of a market. It is thorny because economists disagree about the best way to define a market.

Economists usually define a **market** to be *a group of buyers and sellers whose actions significantly influence the production, quality, and price of specific goods or services.* The **geographic market** of a bank, therefore, is the land area that includes nearly all those buyers and sellers. For a financial instrument such as federal funds, the geographic market is a national one; while for some real estate loans, it may be confined to a very small local area. In contrast, banks may make some commercial loans in markets whose geographic area encompasses much of the world.

Clearly, any definition of a "banking market" must be a compromise, given that banks can simultaneously compete in local, regional, national, and international markets. The compromise definition that most economists who study banking markets have used is the concept of a **primary service area.** Economists define a primary service area to be a geographic area that includes a large percentage of the identifiable buyers and sellers of all banking services. For example, if a large fraction—say, 75 percent—of a bank's loans are made within the formal limits of a city, that city might be defined as the primary service area of that bank, and economists would view that bank as in competition for loans with all other banks for whom the same fraction of customers resided in that city.

Nevertheless, even this compromise measure of banking markets turns out in many instances to be difficult to implement in practice. For one thing, economists differ regarding how a primary service area should be measured; for instance, should it be based on the geographic area encompassing, say, the borrowers of 75 percent of a bank's total loans or the holders of 75 percent of its total deposits? In addition, sufficient data to measure a bank's primary service area may be unavailable even if there is agreement on the proper way to define the concept.

Because of these problems, a common way to measure geographic markets is by assuming that they are the same as the *standard metropolitan statistical areas (SMSAs)* used by statisticians and economists in the Bureau of the Census and elsewhere in the Department of Commerce. SMSAs are areas that statisticians can categorize as "metropolitan" according to agreed-upon criteria. Another common approach is to use even more rough measures of geographic markets, such as legal city limits, state boundaries, or regional groupings of states.

SOME IMPLICATIONS FOR INTERSTATE BANKING

Defining geographic markets, resolving the issue of economies of scale and scope, and determining an outcome to the structure-conduct-performance/efficient structure controversy all are crucial objectives of economists who seek to understand banking markets. The reason is that the social desirability of eliminating interstate banking restrictions depends on the conclusions that economists reach on these issues.

Traditional opposition to interstate banking has been based on the view that opening up local markets within states to out-of-state competition would permit large banks from outside a state to expand even further in size. Moreover, argue those who oppose interstate banking, smaller, in-state banks would be unable to compete with these large banks. As a result, the local banks would fail, and the large, out-of-state banks would gain large shares of local markets for loans or deposits. Eventually only a few banks would dominate these markets on a nationwide basis. This would lead to less rivalry among banks and, ultimately, to worse banking industry performance in terms of economic efficiency.

In contrast, those who promote interstate banking argue that, in fact, over 12,000 banks is a number that is too large for 50 states with less than 300 million people. They agree that if permitted to branch nationwide, out-of-state banks from such urban locations as New York, Chicago, or Los Angeles would begin making loans in ''local'' areas such as Rushville, Indiana; Winslow, Arizona; or Clanton, Alabama. They argue, however, that this would promote banking competition in such localities. If the out-of-state banks gain market share from local banks, that would be because out-of-state banks were more efficient. Better banking industry performance would result, and society would be better off.

The logical foundations of these arguments ultimately rest in the issues we have discussed above. Those who oppose interstate banking contend that there is a natural tendency for banks to become ''big''; therefore, they must believe that economies of scale and scope are important in banking. Furthermore, they believe that ''big'' banks with large market shares constitute a recipe for bank conduct that would produce poor industry performance. Hence, they also subscribe to the structure-conduct-performance model.

In contrast, those who favor reducing or eliminating restrictions on interstate banking are less convinced that scale and scope economies are important in banking. They believe that, to the extent that they *are* important, their existence could lead to ''big'' banks with relatively large market shares. Nevertheless, competition between fewer but more cost-efficient banks would promote better industry performance, as predicted by the efficient structure theory.

As you can see, the issues we have discussed are indeed very important. In the 1990s, Congress almost certainly will make decisions that either will leave interstate banking restrictions in place or will reduce them significantly. Which decision is best for society depends on resolutions of these controversies.

At present, there seems to be significant momentum toward interstate banking. In 1979, thirty of the fifty states did not permit full statewide branching by banks. In contrast, by 1992 only fourteen states still did not allow banks to branch statewide, and, furthermore, only four states did not have laws that permitted some form of interstate activity by banks. The only issue remaining is whether or not the United States Congress will add federal authorization for interstate banking.

DO CAPITAL REQUIREMENTS MAKE BANKS SAFER?

Undoubtedly, as banking spreads across state lines, some depository institutions will become larger. As their asset holdings increase, however, regulators have become concerned that their capital may not keep pace. As we noted in the last chapter, this led regulators to impose capital requirements on banks in the early 1980s. In the late 1980s and early 1990s they stiffened many of these requirements. The overall goal of imposing and toughening bank capital requirements was to make banks safer. There is some disagreement, nonetheless, about whether this intended effect will be realized.

THE INTENT OF CAPITAL REQUIREMENTS

Regulators impose capital requirements in hopes of achieving three related objectives that, together, would make banks safer. One objective of capital requirements, which we emphasized in Chapter 10, is to increase the size of the cushion protecting depositors and, more directly, the federal deposit insurance fund, from losses in the event of bank failure.

In reality, however, this is not the *main* objective of imposing stiff capital requirements on banks. Bank regulators do not want to have to use the higher capital cushion; large bank failures can mean extremely large deposit insurance losses whether capital-to-asset ratios are 5 percent or 8 percent. A more important objective of higher capital requirements, therefore, is to encourage bank managers to behave in less risky ways. As we shall discuss in more detail in Chapter 12, federal deposit insurance can encourage bank managers to make riskier loans than they might otherwise, and regulators hope that higher capital requirements will reduce this incentive. The basic idea is that if owners have larger capital investments in the bank, they have more to lose from bank failure and will keep a closer eye on those they hire to manage the bank. Hence, banks will, if higher capital requirements are successful, voluntarily reduce their risk of failure, which would reduce the number of failures.

A third objective of higher capital requirements is to increase the public's confidence in the banking system. Bank regulators hope that if they impose higher capital requirements on banks, more depositors will regard the banks as less prone to failure. If this perception is shared by enough depositors, the chances of bank runs will be reduced.

DO CAPITAL REQUIREMENTS PROVIDE A FALSE SENSE OF SECURITY?

Not all economists agree that higher capital requirements unambiguously contribute to the general goal of safer banks. Indeed, some have argued that higher capital requirements could have the opposite effect.

Often, these arguments are based on fairly complicated models of portfolio behavior, but it is possible to understand the main point of the arguments without going into much detail. Consider the following examples. One is consumer protection laws. These laws often require companies that manufacture medicines that could be poisonous to children if taken in sufficiently large quantities to "child-proof" the containers of these medicines. Typically, the companies attempt to do this by making pill boxes or bottles difficult for a child to open. Another example concerns automobile safety legislation. Several laws exist mandating that auto manufacturers build only vehicles that meet minimum safety standards in crash tests, and other laws, such as seat-belt-use requirements, govern the conditions under which people may drive cars.

Some economists argue that although such laws are well-intentioned, they may not have intended beneficial effects. For instance, if pill boxes and bottles are not child-proofed, parents will be careful to place them in locations their children cannot reach, but if the parents believe that the boxes and bottles are safe from a child's curiosity, they may be less cautious. Then the children may have easier access to the dangerous medications than they did in the absence of the consumer protection laws. Likewise, if drivers of automobiles believe that their cars are sturdier and that they are well protected by seat belts, they may drive less safely than they would otherwise.

Similarly, say critics of bank capital requirements, these requirements could give bank owners, managers, and depositors a false sense of security. This could induce them to accept *higher* levels of risk than they might have in the *absence* of capital requirements. While capital requirements might lower bank risk on net, the reduction in risk would be significantly less than regulators had intended.

DID BANK REGULATIONS INDUCE A "CREDIT CRUNCH" IN THE EARLY 1990s?

Around the end of 1990, many individuals, firms, and policy makers began to complain that banks were not willing to make loans. In that year, Federal Reserve surveys of bank managers indicated that between 30 and 40 percent of all banks reported toughened lending standards during the prior three months. Many managers reported tightened criteria for real estate lending. Prospective borrowers began quickly to feel the pinch of these changes, as fewer bank loans were forthcoming. This set the stage for the claim that a *credit crunch* was in progress—and calls for the government to do something about it. President George Bush, for instance, joined the fight, saying in his 1991 State of the Union Address, "Sound banks should be making more sound loans now."

Capital Requirements and a Credit Crunch

Many observers in early 1991 argued that stiffened governmental safety and soundness regulations had induced the perceived credit crunch. "To some extent, overzealous bank examiners discouraged some banks from making new loans," said Michael Boskin, the head of the President's Council of Economic Advisors. Others, and particularly bankers, pointed to a more specific regulatory culprit: new, higher bank capital requirements enacted by regulators in the United States and several other nations in 1989 through 1991. According to the vice chairman of Chase Manhattan Bank, "It would be more realistic to lower the level of capital or to push back the date for full implementation [of the new requirements]." An analyst at Salomon Brothers agreed, saying, "Regulators have got to relax the capital standards."

The problem did not appear to be confined to the United States. Because bank regulators from the United States, much of Europe, and Japan had coordinated the new capital requirements, banks in all these nations faced the tougher standards. Large Japanese banks, for instance, almost uniformly reduced their assets, mainly by reducing their lending, in the fiscal year ended March 1991—the first reduction in Japanese bank assets in over fifty years. Managers of many of these banks, like their United States counterparts, pointed to the higher capital requirements as the reason for their reductions in lending. The Japanese cutback did not just affect Jap-

anese borrowers; in early 1991, foreign banks accounted for 21.5 percent of all bank assets in the United States, and Japanese banks held over half that total.

Policy makers were so concerned that they relaxed capital standards somewhat in 1991. For a time, the Fed also considered buying commercial loans directly from banks to free up more of the banks' funds for renewed lending. As you will learn in Chapter 17, this would have been an unprecedented move by the Fed, which sticks almost solely to purchases of U.S. Treasury securities. Even the idea of the Fed doing such a thing created a stir in financial markets.

Making a Mountain out of a Molehill?

In a *Wall Street Journal* editorial opinion in the second week of February 1991, following a pageful of headlines about the credit crunch, Allan Meltzer, an economist at Carnegie Mellon University, announced, "There is no credit crunch." According to Meltzer, all the talk of a credit crunch "is nonsense—plain old-fashioned nonsense. Repetition has not made the story about a credit crunch true, and it will not. Repetition simply spreads disinformation." According to Meltzer, the solution, if one really was needed, was simple. If the Fed were to conduct an expansionary monetary policy to push down interest rates, bank loan rates would fall. Then, Meltzer argued, "borrowing would be higher. The banks would supply more credit, and the empty talk of a credit crunch would disappear."

Who was right? In retrospect, it appears that Meltzer was. Throughout 1991 the Fed, in fact, pursued policies that reduced interest rates (we shall have more to say about this in Units 5 and 6). By June of 1991, bankers were complaining about making too little on their loans, but their lending had expanded. Customers were happy, because the market loan rates they had to pay to borrow from banks had fallen. If there ever had been a credit crunch, by 1992 it largely was over—and without need for a suspension of or significant reduction in the new capital standards.

Sources: David Wessel, "Anatomy of a Credit Crunch: How It Started, What Might Be Done to End It," *Wall Street Journal* (February 11, 1991), p. A2, and "Bank Readiness to Make Loans Fading, Fed Says," *Wall Street Journal* (February 11, 1991), p. A2; Marcus W. Brauchli, "Japan's Big Banks Slash Assets in Rush to Comply with New Capital-Ratio Rule," *Wall Street Journal* (May 29, 1991), p. A5; Paul Duke, Jr., "Fed Weighed Buying Commercial Loans from Banks to Help Ease Credit Crunch," *Wall Street Journal* (February 22, 1991), p. A2; and Allan H. Meltzer, "There Is No Credit Crunch," *Wall Street Journal* (February 8, 1991), p. A12.

CAN BANKS OBTAIN THE REQUIRED CAPITAL?

One of the main issues that banks have had to face in light of the more stringent capital requirements imposed since the 1980s is whether or not they will be able to raise sufficient capital to meet the requirements. Banks faced a particularly difficult dilemma in 1989 and 1990, when new capital requirements were being implemented just as bank stock prices fell significantly. As a result of these simultaneous events, banks were being asked to issue new shares of ownership just as the price per share was falling, making the task of raising funds through stock offerings more difficult. Indeed, increasing the supply of stock shares tended, other things constant, to drive down the prices of shares even further.

Some banks found that one way to meet capital requirements was to reduce lending, rather than raise new capital. Others did a little of both, while many others did in fact issue new shares of stock. This latter effort was aided in early 1991 when bank stock prices recovered significantly. Nevertheless, many banks found the new capital requirements to be poorly timed and have experienced real difficulties in raising sufficient capital to meet the new requirements.

SHOULD BANKING BE SEPARATED FROM "OTHER LINES OF COMMERCE"?

Perhaps one of the key issues that Congress will have to address in the 1990s concerns the Glass-Steagall Act's separation of banking from other lines of commerce. Under the terms of the Glass-Steagall Act, banks are not permitted to hold shares of stock ownership; furthermore, commercial enterprises are not allowed to possess shares of ownership in banks. As we discussed in Chapter 10, the bank holding company structure permits some indirect forms of cross-ownership to exist, but the Bank Holding Company Acts of 1956 and 1970 placed strict limitations on the ability of banking and other forms of commerce to "mix."

This separation of banking from other forms of commerce has been questioned in recent years. Recall from Chapter 10 that the primary justifications for the Glass-Steagall Act's provisions separating the two were the related concerns about the potential conflicts of interest and about centralization of economic power. The decline of the predominance of American banking relative to the rest of the world, and in particular with respect to Europe and Japan (see the International Perspective in Chapter 10), has helped spur arguments in favor of repealing this legal separation, for two reasons. First, banks in Europe and Japan that mix with other forms of business have been very successful, perhaps at the expense of American banks. Proponents of mixing banking and commerce argue that this may indicate that there are economies of scale and scope that are sacrificed by separating the two. Second, as banking markets become more global, these proponents argue, concerns about too much centralization of economic power in the hands of too few American bankers have become less relevant than they were in the 1930s. Indeed, many of those who argue for a repeal of the Glass-Steagall restrictions claim that if they remain in force there may be all too few U.S. banks able to compete in global markets.

Some economists have argued for years that Congress should permit banking and other forms of commerce to mix. They contend that if nonbank firms were permitted to own and operate banks, there would be freer entry into banking. As a result, banking would be a more competitive industry, which would benefit consumers. In addition, they argue, combining banking and commerce would better enable banks to benefit from the mana-

UNIVERSAL BANKING AND FINANCIAL INTEGRATION IN EUROPE IN THE 1990s

INTERNATIONAL PERSPECTIVE

The United States is not the only nation whose banking system must meet numerous regulations. Despite its large size and penetration of world credit markets, the Japanese banking system also faces many governental restrictions. Regulatory rules in Japan greatly constrain the kinds of businesses that banks of various types may undertake, even for those banks that may underwrite stocks and bonds. This is one of the few similarities between American and Japanese banking, and it separates both nations' banking systems from those of Europe.

As we discussed in the last chapter, most European nations permit limited or unlimited forms of **universal banking**—the ability of banks to offer a complete line of banking-related services and to own shares of stock in companies. By the early 1980s, all major European nations, such as Germany, the United Kingdom, France, Belgium, Denmark, and the Netherlands, permitted banks to underwrite securities. Three of these countries, Germany, the United Kingdom, and the Netherlands, had placed no limits whatsoever on the lines of business that banks could undertake.

Beginning in the late 1980s and continuing into the 1990s, the European Community (EC) moved toward a policy of full, though somewhat limited, universal banking by depository institutions within member nations' borders. Provisions of the EC's "Second Banking Coordination Directive" issued in 1988 called for full implementation of this policy by EC member nations no later than 1993.

As part of its coordinated banking policies, the EC issues a "single banking license." This license, the equiv-

alent of a bank charter, automatically permits a bank headquartered in any EC member nation to branch into any other member nation. Provided that a bank's *home country* authorizes it to do so, a bank may provide many financial services, including trading in equities on its customers' accounts—or on its own account.

This rule implies that banks operating out of nations such as the United Kingdom and Germany, which permit universal banking, will be able to trade in stocks and bonds in any other EC nation, including those that in the past prohibited such activities. Naturally, this means that if other EC nations do not relax rules for their own banks, their own banks could operate under a severe competitive disadvantage relative to banks from the United Kingdom and Germany. As a result, most European governments have rushed to reduce restrictions on their own banks. The result, most observers predict, will be a competitive free-for-all among the banks of Europe.

Will American banks lose out as a result of the European movement toward deregulation? Many observers think so. Some American policy makers agree. In fact, the United States Treasury Department's 1991 proposal to move American banks into a world of more universal banking was spurred in part by the changes in Europe. Universal banking appears to be the wave of the future for a big part of the world; it remains to be seen whether or not the United States will join the crowd.

Sources: Herwig Langohr and Anthony M. Santomero, "The Extent of Equity Investment by European Banks," *Journal of Money, Credit, and Banking,* 17 (2, May 1985), pp. 243–252; Rob Dixon, *Banking in Europe: The Single Market* (London: Routledge, 1991); and Allen B. Frankel and John D. Montgomery, "Financial Structure: An International Perspective," Working Paper, Division of International Finance, Board of Governors of the Federal Reserve System (June 1991).

gerial expertise and technological improvements that other industries might have to offer. Finally, they contend that greater diversification of banks into other lines of business would assist in reducing overall bank risk and thereby lead to a decrease in bank failures.

Critics of this view counter that it is hopelessly optimistic. Many of these critics argue that, in fact, other nations have experienced difficulties with their efforts to mix banking with other businesses. They believe that the significant concentration of banking we see in Japan and several European nations, which they contend has been harmful to consumers, has been enhanced by allowing nonbanking firms to own banks, and vice versa.

To some extent, events have forced this issue to the forefront in recent years. Among these events have been the problems that banks have had in raising required capital in recent years, which we discussed in the last section. Indeed, some in Congress have concluded that if banks cannot raise necessary capital, perhaps other firms that possess capital should be permitted to enter banking. This pragmatic view also appears to have motivated, at least in part, the Treasury proposal in the early 1990s to eliminate the Glass-Steagall Act's separation of banking from other lines of commerce.

Even those who favor this form of deregulation as a matter of principle have expressed reservations, however. They have argued that mixing banking and other types of commerce cannot be allowed as long as deposit insurance is available to all firms that offer checking and savings accounts. These analysts, therefore, believe that fundamental changes in banking policy cannot succeed unless they are accompanied by a revamping of federal deposit insurance. This issue is the topic of the next chapter.

CHAPTER SUMMARY

1. According to the public-interest theory of regulation, bank regulators act in the best interest of society as a whole. In contrast, the capture theory of regulation contends that regulators set rules that assist the firms they regulate, so that firms in fact seek out governmental regulation.

2. The public-choice theory of regulation hypothesizes that bank regulators make decisions that are in their own best interests. In doing so, they face a trade-off between inducing (a) a banking industry structure that is competitive and benefits bank consumers or (b) an industry structure that is monopolistic and favors bank owners. The theory concludes that regulators typically prefer banking industry structures between these two extremes.

3. A desirable feature of perfect competition is that it produces allocative efficiency. In contrast, monopolistic banking is allocatively inefficient; it leads to higher loan rates and less lending than under competition. Furthermore, banking monopoly redistributes some consumer surplus to bank owners in the form of higher profits and causes some consumer surplus to be lost completely, meaning that there is a deadweight social loss caused by monopolistic banking.

4. A bank experiences economies of scale when its long-run average total cost declines as the absolute size of the bank increases. It experiences economies of scope when it is cheaper to produce two outputs, such as two different types of loans, simultaneously rather than separately, meaning that the bank can reduce its costs by diversifying into different lines of business. Whether or not large banks are more technically efficient than smaller banks depends upon the extent to which the banks experience economies of scale and scope.

5. There are two fundamental theories of the effects of bank market structure on the performance of the banking industry, as viewed from the perspective of society as a whole. One is the structure-conduct-performance model; this model contends that concentrated banking markets lead to explicit or implicit monopoly arrangements among banks, which causes poor industry performance, which is reflected in high bank profits. The other is the efficient structure theory, which argues that some banks obtain large shares of their markets and earn high profits because they are more efficient.

6. Complicating efforts by economists to evaluate scale and scope economies and theories of market structure and performance in banking are significant measurement problems. One problem concerns the appropriate definition of bank output. The other is that geographic markets are difficult to define in banking.

7. While there is general agreement that capital requirements provide a protective cushion against

depositor losses in the event of a bank failure, some economists argue that increases in capital requirements may actually induce bank managers to take on more risk.

8. One problem for banks in recent years has been to raise sufficient capital to meet higher capital requirements without having to cut back on their lending. Some observers believe that higher capital requirements may have contributed to a credit crunch in the early 1990s.

9. The Glass-Steagall separation of banking from other lines of commerce has been questioned in recent years. Some recent proposals have included provisions for relaxing or eliminating this legal separation.

GLOSSARY

Asset approach: An approach to measuring bank output that views loans and other interest-bearing assets as the appropriate measure of output.

Capture theory: A theory of regulation that proposes that those who are regulated—and *not* society as a whole—benefit from the regulations; the regulators are ''captured'' by the regulated businesses.

Deadweight loss due to bank monopoly: A portion of consumer surplus that would have existed under competition but that is no longer obtained by consumers in a monopoly banking market and also is not redistributed to owners of banks.

Diseconomies of scale (or scale diseconomies): Average cost rises as the scale size of a bank increases.

Economies of scale (or scale economies): Average cost declines as the scale size of a bank increases.

Economies of scope (or scope economies): A situation in which a bank achieves cost savings by diversifying its product offerings and services.

Efficiency loss due to bank monopoly: The nonattainment of allocative efficiency that arises from monopolistic banking, in which the last dollar of lending by banks does not reflect properly the true cost of producing that last dollar of loans; by implication, resources used for lending by banks are not allocated in the least costly way.

Efficient structure theory: The theory that proposes that banks that are more efficient gain a larger market share and are more profitable than other banks.

Geographic market: The land area that includes nearly all the buyers and sellers of a good or service.

Long-run average total cost (LRATC) schedule: A schedule that shows the average costs incurred by a bank in producing various output levels if all factors of production are permitted to vary.

Market: A group of buyers and sellers whose actions significantly influence the production, quality, and price of specific goods or services.

Market concentration: The extent to which the few largest banks dominate the shares of loans or deposits in banking markets.

Market performance: The degree to which both allocative and technical efficiencies are attained in banking markets.

Minimum efficient scale: The bank size that yields the minimum long-run average total cost for the bank.

Natural monopoly: A situation in which the technology of producing a particular good or service implies economies of scale at any output level for a firm, so that the most technically efficient market structure is one large firm.

Primary service area: A geographic area that includes a certain percentage of the identifiable buyers and sellers of all banking services.

Public-choice theory: A theory of regulation that proposes that regulators set rules that permit firms to earn profits above perfectly competitive profit levels but below those they could earn if they could set their prices at purely monopolistic levels.

Public-interest theory: A theory of regulation that proposes that regulators choose policies that maximize the welfare of society as a whole.

Redistribution effect due to bank monopoly: In a monopolistic banking system, bank profits that take the place of some portion of the consumer surplus that would otherwise have arisen under competition.

Scale: A measure of the overall size a bank chooses when it may vary all factors of production.

Scope: The overall range of operations of a business, in terms of the different types of goods and services it produces.

Structure-conduct-performance (SCP) model: The theory that proposes that market structure (which includes the number and size distribution of firms) influences the conduct of banks in the market, and, in turn, bank conduct determines the performance of the market.

Technical efficiency: The production of a good or service at minimum long-run average total cost.

Technical inefficiency: The production of a good or service at more than minimum long-run average total cost.

Universal banking: The ability of banks to offer an almost unlimited array of financial services.

User-cost approach: An approach to measuring bank output that classifies a financial product as output if its net contribution to profits is greater than zero and as input if its net contribution to profits is negative.

Value-added approach: An approach to measuring bank output that considers outputs to be those categories of financial products that contribute most value to the bank's operations.

SELF-TEST QUESTIONS

1. If we measure bank output as total lending by a bank, what approach to bank output measurement would we have adopted? Assume that we use this approach to output measurement for two banks, one with $500 million in loans and the other with $750 million in loans. In light of recent evidence on this issue, would it be possible for both banks to be operating at the minimum efficient scale? Explain.

2. Would it be possible for some banks to experience diseconomies of scale in terms of their present overall size even as their individual branches achieved their minimum efficient scales? Why or why not?

3. Suppose that regulators permit a merger of two banks in the hope that market performance will be improved. They observe that even though loan market demand conditions remain unchanged, the amount of lending by banks decreases, the market interest rate rises, and the long-run average total cost of the new bank is lower than was true for the two banks before the merger. Have the regulators achieved their objective?

4. Compare and contrast the main features of the structure-conduct-performance and efficient structure theories of the relationship between bank market structure and performance. Does one seem to place more emphasis on allocative efficiency relative to technical efficiency than the other, and vice versa? Support your answer.

5. How could higher bank capital requirements increase the risk that a bank might fail?

PROBLEMS

11-1. Consider the following situation. Recently, a merger of two banks in the town of Midwestern Junction has produced a single bank for the community's loan market. Before *and* after the merger, banking in Midwestern Junction is characterized by a fixed marginal cost of $0.06 per dollar of lending. Before the merger, the market loan rate was 6 percent, and the equilibrium quantity of loans was $200 million. After the merger, the market loan rate in Midwestern Junction was 9 percent, and the quantity of lending by the newly formed bank was $100 million. The market demand and marginal revenue schedules in Midwestern Junction are straight lines, and demand and revenue conditions were unchanged by the merger. Use this information to answer the following questions.

  a. What amount of economic profits did the two banks in Midwestern Junction earn before the merger?

  b. What amount of consumer surplus did borrowers in Midwestern Junction earn before the merger? (*Hint:* You have enough information to figure out the vertical intercept of the market loan demand schedule, and the fact that the loan demand schedule is a straight line means that the amount of consumer surplus will be a triangular area.)

  c. What amount of economic profits does the single bank earn after the merger?

  d. Has this merger created a deadweight loss for the town of Midwestern Junction? If so, how much is the loss in dollars? (*Hint:* Because the demand and marginal revenue schedules are straight lines, a deadweight loss is a triangular area.)

  e. What amount of consumer surplus do Midwestern Junction borrowers earn following the merger?

11-2. Suppose that the long-run average total cost schedule for each of the banks in a banking system with $100 billion (which is the same as $100,000 million) in loans is *flat* between $0 and $50 million in loans but slopes upward beyond the latter level of lending. Assuming that the total amount of lending in the banking system is constant, what is the *minimum number* of banks we would expect to observe in this industry, assuming that each bank operates at its minimum efficient scale?

11-3. A monopoly bank incurs a constant marginal cost of $0.10 per dollar of lending. When the marginal revenue it derives from lending is $0.10 per dollar of lending, the bank makes $200 million in loans and charges a loan rate of 20 percent. If it were to charge a loan rate of 10 percent, it would be able to make $400 million in loans. The loan demand and marginal revenue schedules faced by the bank are straight lines.

  a. What amount of economic profits are earned by this bank?

  b. What is the amount of the deadweight loss caused by monopolization of this market? (*Hint:* Make use of the fact that the loan demand schedule is a straight line, so that the deadweight loss is a triangular area.)

11-4. Suppose that new regulations require that a bank have a ratio of capital to total assets of 0.05. Presently, however, the bank has $10 million in capital and $250 million in assets. What are two ways that the bank could meet its new capital requirement? (Give specific dollar amounts of changes it could make in its balance sheet.)

11-5. Bank regulators have created conditions under which Southeastern Township Bank has a monopoly in its local loan market. The bank finds that if it were to charge a loan interest rate of 10 percent, it would have no loan customers. However, if it maximizes its profit from lending, it extends $20 million in loans and charges a loan rate of 6 percent. The loan demand and marginal revenue schedules it faces are straight lines, and its marginal cost is constant and equal to $0.02 per dollar of loans.

  a. What is the maximum profit that may be earned by Southeastern Township Bank?

  b. If Southeastern Township Bank maximizes its profit, what is the amount of consumer surplus in this local loan market?

    c. If Southeastern Township Bank maximizes its profit, what is the amount of deadweight loss due to its monopoly power in its local loan market?

    d. Suppose that bank regulators now require Southeastern Township to make loans *as if* it were a perfectly competitive bank. What dollar amount of loans should it extend?

    e. Given the situation described in part d, what is the amount of consumer surplus in this market?

SELECTED REFERENCES

Berger, Allen, and David Humphrey, "Measurement and Efficiency Issues in Commercial Banking," Finance and Discussion Series no. 151, Board of Governors of the Federal Reserve System (December 1990).

Clark, Jeffrey, "Economies of Scale and Scope at Depository Financial Institutions: A Review of the Literature," Federal Reserve Bank of Kansas City *Economic Review,* 73 (8, September/October 1988), pp. 16–33.

Craven, B. M., and R. S. Thompson, "Monopoly Welfare Losses in U.S. Banking: Comment," *Journal of Monetary Economics* 14 (1, July 1984), pp. 123–126.

Dixon, Rob, *Banking in Europe: The Single Market* (London: Routledge, 1991).

Evanoff, Douglas, "Branch Banking and Service Accessibility," *Journal of Money, Credit, and Banking,* 20 (2, May 1988), pp. 191–202.

Gilbert, R. Alton, "Bank Market Structure and Competition: A Survey," *Journal of Money, Credit, and Banking,* 16 (4, November 1984, part 2), pp. 617–644.

Huertas, Thomas, "Can Banking and Commerce Mix?" *Cato Journal,* 7 (3, Winter 1988), pp. 743–769.

Humphrey, David, "Why Do Estimates of Bank Scale Economies Differ?" Federal Reserve Bank of Richmond *Economic Review,* 76 (5, September/October 1990), pp. 38–50.

Keeley, Michael, and Frederick Furlong, "A Reexamination of Mean-Variance Analysis of Bank Capital Regulation," *Journal of Banking and Finance,* 14 (1, March 1990), pp. 69–84.

Koehn, Michael, and Anthony Santomero, "Regulation of Bank Capital and Portfolio Risk," *Journal of Finance,* 35 (5, December 1980), pp. 1235–1250.

Langohr, Herwig, and Anthony Santomero, "The Extent of Equity Investment by European Banks," *Journal of Money, Credit, and Banking,* 17 (3, May 1985), pp. 243–252.

Mengle, David, "The Case for Interstate Branch Banking," Federal Reserve Bank of Richmond *Economic Review,* 76 (6, November/December 1990), pp. 3–17.

Morris, Charles, "The Competitive Effects of Interstate Banking," Federal Reserve Bank of Kansas City *Economic Review* 69 (9, November 1984), pp. 3–16.

Peltzman, Sam, "Toward a More General Theory of Regulation," *Journal of Law and Economics,* 19 (2, August 1976), pp. 211–240.

Posner, Richard A., "Theories of Economic Regulation," *Bell Journal of Economics,* 5 (2, Autumn 1974), pp. 335–358.

Rhoades, Stephen, "Structure-Performance Studies in Banking: An Updated Summary and Evaluation," Staff Study no. 119, Board of Governors of the Federal Reserve System, Washington, D.C. (August 1982).

———, "Welfare Loss, Redistribution Effect, and Restriction of Output Due to Monopoly in Banking," *Journal of Monetary Economics,* 9 (1, January 1982), pp. 375–387.

Santomero, Anthony, "European Banking Post-1992: Lessons from the United States," in *European Banking in the 1990s,* ed. Jean Dermine (Oxford: Basil Blackwell, 1990).

Smirlock, Michael, "Evidence on the (Non) Relationship between Concentration and Profitability in Banking," *Journal of Money, Credit, and Banking,* 17 (1, February 1985), pp. 69–83.

Stigler, George, "Theory of Regulation," *Bell Journal of Economics,* 2 (1, Spring 1971), pp. 3–21.

Wolken, John, "Geographic Market Delineation: A Review of the Literature," Staff Study no. 140, Board of Governors of the Federal Reserve System, Washington, D.C. (October 1984).

CHAPTER 12

Deposit Insurance: Past, Present, and Future

CHAPTER PREVIEW

1. What are the goals of federal deposit insurance?

2. How is federal deposit insurance structured in the United States?

3. What are the advantages to society of federally insured deposits?

4. Why are financial institutions, in today's environment, encouraged to increase their risk taking?

5. How can bank managers increase their risk taking?

6. What are the key problems of the present federal deposit insurance system?

7. How might federal deposit insurance be reformed in the future?

Banking deregulation in the 1980s turned out to be a mixed blessing for depository institutions and their customers. On the one hand, deregulation increased competition, and U.S. financial institutions became more concerned with providing their financial services at lower cost. On the other hand, deregulation increased the freedom to fail, and many financial institutions have done just that.

The thrift industry has been in crisis since the mid-1980s—or perhaps longer, as we shall see in the next chapter. In addition, the number of commercial bank failures also has increased alarmingly—so much that many observers are wondering if it isn't time to *re*regulate financial institutions and substitute more stability for less efficiency. In this chapter we explore the system designed to provide stability to the financial institution: federal deposit insurance.

THE OBJECTIVES AND STRUCTURE OF FEDERAL DEPOSIT INSURANCE

The United States has a long tradition of fear of big business in general, and big banking in particular; indicative of this fear is the opinion that Thomas Jefferson once expressed in a letter to Elbridge Gerry: "Banking establishments are more dangerous than standing armies." It is in this light that the regulatory structure we surveyed in Chapter 10 can best be understood.

Because many Americans have always been so distrustful of banks, Congress has imposed a variety of restraints on their powers, such as those we discussed in the last two chapters. In addition, Congress has created other safeguards to protect the stability of the financial system. Perhaps the most important of these safeguards is the modern system of federal deposit insurance.

THE ORIGINS OF FEDERAL DEPOSIT INSURANCE

Governments have for some time been involved in providing deposit insurance in the United States. The first governmental involvement in deposit insurance was at the state level and dates back to the early 1800s. The federal government's role as deposit insurer has been fairly recent by historical standards.

At various times in history, states established deposit insurance funds to reduce the likelihood that bank liquidity crises would induce depositors to launch runs on banks and thereby force widespread bank insolvencies. Often, however, these state funds suffered from a difficulty that economists call the **adverse selection problem.** Some states made their system voluntary and permitted banks to withdraw from the system at any time with their full accumulations in the safety fund. Unfortunately, this encouraged only the banks most likely to fail to participate in the system. Because they were the worst risks, these banks chose on their own to participate—they *self-selected* in a way that was *adverse* to the interests of the safety fund—in an effort to shore up their declining fortunes. Those banks in good shape, in contrast, had little reason to participate and chose not to do so. While some state deposit insurance funds avoided the adverse selection problem, many state funds collapsed and thereby failed to halt bank runs.

In 1933, following the worst bank runs in American history, the federal government first became involved in deposit insurance when Congress created the Federal Deposit Insurance Corporation (FDIC) to provide deposit insurance for commercial banks. Almost exactly a year later, in 1934, Congress authorized the formation of the Federal Savings and Loan Insurance Corporation (FSLIC) to insure deposits in savings and loan associations and mutual savings banks. In 1971 it created the National Credit Union Share Insurance Fund (NCUSIF) to insure deposits in credit unions.

As we discussed in Chapter 10, Congress mandated major changes to the organization of federal deposit insurance in the Financial Institutions Reform, Recovery, and Enforcement Act of 1989. Among the most important of these was the abolishment of the FSLIC and the transferal of responsibility for all federal deposit insurance to the FDIC. More changes in deposit insurance may be in the offing in the 1990s.

AIMS OF FEDERAL DEPOSIT INSURANCE

The goals of federal deposit insurance are (1) to protect the savings and transactions balances of small savers and (2) to help stabilize the banking system.

Traditionally, proponents of federal deposit insurance have argued—and Congress has agreed—that providing deposit guarantees to small savers is equitable because the cost of obtaining information about the solvency of a financial institution is higher for small depositors than for large depositors. Lacking information, small depositors have a rational incentive to participate in bank runs—whether an institution is troubled or not. Thus, contend those in favor of federal deposit insurance, governmental insurance for small savers is socially beneficial because it reduces the probability of destabilizing bank runs.

In addition, argue proponents of federal deposit insurance, a single federal deposit insurance agency probably will incur lower information costs than the total cost of the combined efforts of many small depositors. Deposit markets are therefore made more efficient by federal deposit insurance, they argue, because such insurance reduces the society's costs of gathering information.

Hence, concludes this line of argument, federal deposit insurance provides social benefits by reducing the probability of bank runs. If there is less chance of a bank run, then

PARALLEL PANICS OF A.D. 33 AND A.D. 1907

INTERNATIONAL PERSPECTIVE

Some of the greatest bank runs of all time occurred in the United States in the late 1800s, early 1900s, and 1930s, and these runs set the stage for the creation of federal deposit insurance. The most famous single U.S. panic was the Panic of 1907. Yet bank runs have occurred for as long as there have been banks.

A Truly "Classical" Bank Run

In A.D. 33, a massive bank panic took place in the Roman empire. Rumors had circulated in Rome that the Alexandrian firm of Seuthes and Son, which had lost three spice ships in a Red Sea hurricane and had taken sizable losses in Ethiopian caravan trade, was near bankruptcy. Shortly thereafter, the well-known firm of Malchus and Co. of Tyre, which had branches in Antioch and Ephesus, became insolvent as a result of a strike by its Phoenician workmen and fraud committed by a trusted manager. Roman citizens then learned that the Roman banking firm of Quintus Maximus and Lucius Vibo was heavily involved in loans to both Seuthes and Malchus. A run on the bank's deposits ensued. It then spilled over to a larger banking firm, the Pettius Brothers' bank, when its depositors learned that it had sizable dealings with the bank of Maximus and Vibo.

A series of coincidences caused this isolated incident to become much more serious. The Pettius Brothers' bank, by chance, was temporarily strapped for cash, because it held many securities issued by Belgium, whose semi-civilized citizens had recently revolted. Although Maximus and Vibo closed its doors first, Pettius Brothers suspended operations the same day. Also by chance, the Roman senate had recently passed a law, to be enforced with heavy penalties, requiring one-third of each senator's capital to be invested in Italian land. This induced these wealthy men to call in their outstanding loans and reduce their own deposit balances at their banks in Rome just as Maximus and Vibo and Pettius Brothers were failing. Simultaneously, word arrived from Corinth and Carthage of bank failures in those locales. Panic then struck the Roman street of Via Sacra—the Roman equivalent of Wall Street. Ultimately, every banking house in Rome closed its doors.

Shortly, panic was on the verge of sweeping the empire. Gracchus, the praetor (chief magistrate) of Rome, appealed to the Roman senate for aid, and it responded by sending a fast messenger to Emperor Tiberius, who was on a vacation in Capri. Four days later, the messenger returned to meet a huge crowd of Roman senators, citizens, and slaves alike, who gathered in the Roman Forum while the emperor's letter was read. Tiberius ordered the distribution of 100 million sesterces (the Roman currency) from the Imperial Treasury to reliable bankers, who were to lend the funds to needy debtors, with no interest to be collected in three years; he also suspended the decree forcing the investment of senators' funds in Italian land. Within days, the panic in Rome, Carthage, and Corinth had ended, and business as usual resumed on the Via Sacra.

A.D. 1907, or History Repeats Itself

Like the Roman banking panic of A.D. 33, the United States banking panic of October 1907 had no single cause. A key factor behind the panic, nevertheless, was excessive speculation in copper, mining, and railroad stocks by the Wall Street "trusts"—conglomerates that dabbled in both commercial and financial dealings. One particular trust, Knickerbocker Trust, had tried to corner United Copper stock, but its scheme backfired as its own stock plummeted 35 points in only 2 hours. The collapse of Knickerbocker's stock spawned fears that other trusts might soon follow, feeding a self-fulfilling prophecy that led to a collapse of stock prices up and down Wall Street. Fueling those fears was a recent speech by President Theodore Roosevelt that had attacked "malefactors of great wealth" and seemed to indicate an unwillingness in Washington to rescue the now-failing trusts in the event of a panic such as the one under way.

Emergency telegrams providing updates on the extent of the spreading crisis were wired to 23 Wall Street, the home of J. Pierpont Morgan's banking empire. The 70-year-old Morgan, like Emperor Tiberius before him, was away when the panic hit—this chief "malefactor of great wealth" was a lay delegate attending an Episcopal convention in Richmond, Virginia. His home office got word to him quickly, however, and he rushed back to New York, where he huddled with other bankers and U.S. Treasury Secretary George B. Cortelyou at a Manhattan hotel. The day after the meeting, Cortelyou, following Tiberius's example, entrusted $25 million in government funds to Morgan to lend to trusts up and down Wall Street.

In contrast to the Roman case, this government extension of funds did not immediately halt the panic. After Morgan refused to see an official of Knickerbocker Trust, the official shot himself, setting off a rash of suicides among Knickerbocker depositors. For two weeks, depositors sat on camp chairs on Wall Street waiting for banks to reopen. New York police distributed numbers to people to save their places, and some depositors paid people to hold their places in line. As more than fifty brokerage firms teetered on the edge of insolvency, Morgan, with only minutes to spare, mustered a pledge from bank presidents around New York to come up with another $25 million bail-out package. Morgan immediately dispatched a team of messengers to the floor of the stock exchange, where a tumultuous mob reminiscent of the Via Sacra crowd of A.D. 33 waited expectantly. With the announcement, a mighty roar of ovation for Morgan arose that he could hear in the Morgan bank building across Wall Street.

Morgan's efforts had not ended. The next week, he arranged a $30 million rescue of New York City, which had been unable to raise previously promised funds from European investors, who were unconvinced that the financial panic had ended. Morgan's doctor worried about his health throughout the crisis, forcing him to cut his cigar consumption to *only* twenty per day. Morgan caught 30-minute catnaps during meetings in which millions of dollars were at stake—and, in the midst of it all, managed to emerge from the crisis richer than ever. As a price for his efforts to salvage the American financial system from total collapse, Morgan secured Theodore Roosevelt's approval of a takeover of Tennessee Steel by Morgan's pet company and favorite creation: U.S. Steel. Roosevelt agreed, temporarily turning a blind eye to a clear violation of Roosevelt's own pet project: the U.S. government's new antitrust laws.

Adapted from Charles Calomiris, "Deposit Insurance: Lessons from the Record," Federal Reserve Bank of Chicago *Economic Perspectives*, 13 (3, May/June 1989), pp. 10–30, and Ron Chernow, *The House of Morgan* (New York: Atlantic Monthly Press, 1990), chap. 7.

banking institutions can play their roles as safekeepers of deposits, financial intermediaries, and operators of a payments mechanism.

THE STRUCTURE OF FEDERAL DEPOSIT INSURANCE

In spite of the 1989 organizational alterations, the basic structure of federal deposit insurance has not changed significantly since the inception of the federal programs in the 1930s. Banks and most thrifts pay insurance premiums to the agencies that insure their deposits. These premiums go to the FDIC's deposit insurance funds. At present, commercial banks, savings and loan associations, and savings banks pay an FDIC insurance premium of 0.23 percent per dollar of insured deposits.

Federal credit unions are insured by a fund supervised by the National Credit Union Administration (NCUA). The structure of this fund is different from that of the other federal deposit insurance programs. Instead of requiring credit unions to pay an annual assessment, the NCUA mandates that they deposit 1 percent of their deposits with the National Credit Union Share Insurance Fund.

SUCCESSES AND SHORTCOMINGS OF FEDERAL DEPOSIT INSURANCE

In recent years economists, regulators, and members of Congress have berated the inadequacies of federal deposit insurance. Yet just two decades ago economists, regulators,

WHO REALLY PAYS DEPOSIT INSURANCE PREMIUMS?

The FDIC's deposit insurance premiums are assessed against the insured deposits at banks and thrifts. The FDIC uses these premiums to replenish its Bank Insurance Fund (BIF) and Savings Association Insurance Fund (SAIF). Under the 1989 provisions of FIRREA, in the early 1990s the FDIC increased significantly the premiums it charged banks and thrifts for federal deposit insurance.

Certainly, the banks and thrifts themselves write the checks to cover these premiums, but an important economic issue is what portion of those premiums *actually* is paid by depository institutions. From the perspective of depository institutions and their customers, these premiums effectively are *taxes* that are used by the FDIC to provide a government service, deposit insurance. Consequently, the economic effects of an increase in deposit insurance are analogous to the effects of an increase in a tax on a specific product produced by any industry.

The Economic Effects of the Deposit Insurance Premium

To understand this, consider panels (*a*) and (*b*) of Figure 12-1, which depict alternative equilibrium positions in the market for checkable deposits, using the theory we developed in Chapter 8. Recall that, for each depository institution, the net marginal revenue from deposits in our basic model of a competitive banking system was equal to $r_L - MC_D - MC_L$, where r_L represents the prevailing market interest rate on bank loans, MC_D is the marginal resource cost of obtaining and servicing deposits, and MC_L is the marginal resource cost incurred in making and monitoring loans. For each depository institution, this net marginal revenue may be graphed as a downward-sloping *deposit demand* schedule. Recall from Chapter 8 that we may sum these schedules horizontally across all depository institutions in the deposit market to obtain the initial market deposit demand schedules labeled D_0^d in panels (*a*) and (*b*). Alternative market deposit supply schedules for the nonbank public are labeled D_0^s in the panels, and the panels depict the same initial equilibrium deposit rate, r_D^0, and the same initial equilibrium quantity of deposits, D_0. The key difference in panels (*a*) and (*b*), which we shall discuss

shortly, is the slope of the deposit supply schedule of the nonbank public.

If the FDIC requires that, in addition to incurring normal marginal resource costs on deposits and loans, banks and thrifts must also pay a deposit insurance premium, denoted p and measured as a dollar premium per dollar of deposits, then each depository institution's net marginal revenue from deposits declines by the amount p. That is, the new net marginal revenue is equal to $r_L - MC_L - MC_D - p$ for each and every depository institution. This means that, for each institution, its deposit demand schedule *shifts downward* by the vertical distance p, which is the amount of the deposit insurance premium. Because the market deposit demand schedule is the horizontal sum of the deposit demand schedules of all banks and thrifts, it must shift downward by exactly this same amount, as shown in panels (*a*) and (*b*) of Figure 12-1.

Who Pays the Deposit Insurance Premium?

Note that the nonbank public's deposit supply schedule is steeper in panel (*a*) than in panel (*b*). This means that changes in the interest rate that banks pay on deposits have relatively smaller effects on the quantity of deposits demanded by the nonbank public in panel (*a*) as compared to panel (*b*). Although the *interest elasticity of deposit supply* varies along a deposit supply schedule, we may conclude that deposit supply is *relatively less interest-elastic in panel (a) as compared to panel (b)*, within the range of interest rates considered.

In panel (*a*), we can see that the effect of requiring depository institutions to pay deposit insurance premium p is to cause the equilibrium deposit interest rate to fall by very nearly the full amount of the premium p. Hence, if the nonbank public's supply of deposits to the banking industry is relatively interest-inelastic, the members of the nonbank public effectively pay most of the insurance premium, because they receive lower deposit interest payments from banks. As in the case of a government tax imposed on a specific good for which the demand is price-inelastic, the cost of the deposit insurance premium is *shifted forward* by banks and thrifts to their deposit customers, who bear the burden of the premium.

In contrast, in panel (*b*) we can see that if the supply of deposits by the nonbank public is relatively interest-

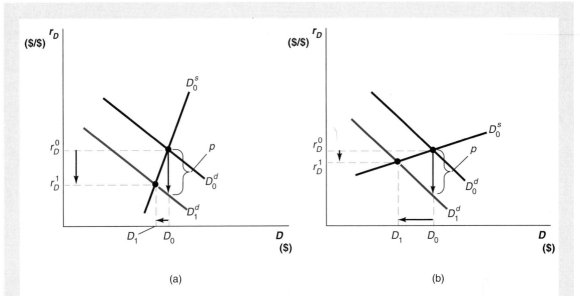

(a)   (b)

Figure 12-1
Possible Effects of an Increase in the Deposit Insurance Premium.   In both panels (a) and (b), initial equilibrium points arise at the deposit rate r_D^0 and the equilibrium quantity of deposits D_0. In panel (a), however, the nonbank public's deposit supply schedule is steeper in the neighborhood around this equilibrium point than is the case in panel (b). This means that, within a range of deposit interest rates around that equilibrium point, deposit supply is relatively more interest-inelastic in panel (a) than in panel (b).

   When there is an increase, by the amount p, in the deposit insurance premiums that all banks must pay, deposit demand shifts downward by that amount. Because deposit supply is relatively inelastic in panel (a), the equilibrium deposit rate falls by nearly the amount p, which means that households and firms effectively pay almost all of the premium increase through receipt of lower interest on deposits. In this case, however, there is little financial disintermediation as a result of the premium increase.

   When the nonbank public's supply of deposits is relatively elastic, as in panel (b), the equilibrium deposit rate falls by a much smaller amount. Hence, depository institutions must effectively pay most of the premium increase. In this case, there is a much larger reduction in the equilibrium quantity of deposits, and so there is greater financial disintermediation.

elastic (so that relatively small changes in the deposit interest rate have relatively large effects on the quantity of deposits supplied to banks and thrifts), imposition of the deposit insurance premium p has a very small effect on the equilibrium interest rate on deposits. Members of the nonbank public in this case would pay very little of the deposit insurance premium, which is *shifted backward* as a cost that must be absorbed by depository institutions.

The Importance of Who Pays the Bulk of the Deposit Insurance Premium
We can see from Figure 12-1 that, in general, both depository institutions and their customers share in pay-

ment of the deposit insurance premium. Depository institutions pay part of the premium as an increase in their cost of doing business, and members of the nonbank public pay part of the premium through receipt of lower deposit interest payments from banks and thrifts.

   We can also see from Figure 12-1, however, that the amount of the change in the equilibrium *quantity* of deposits in the market for deposits, from D_0 to D_1 in both panels, also is related to the issue of who pays the insurance premium. In panel (a), because the nonbank public does not significantly change its quantity of deposits supplied even if there is a relatively large change in the deposit rate, the reduction in the deposit rate that is nearly equal to the amount of the premium causes a fairly small decrease in the quantity of deposits held at banks and thrifts. In contrast, in panel (*b*), in which the nonbank public's quantity of deposits supplied is very sensitive to deposit rate changes, there is a much larger reduction in the equilibrium amount of deposits the nonbank public is willing to hold at depository institutions caused by the fall in the deposit rate stemming from imposition of a deposit insurance premium.

If the diagram in panel (*b*) were more representative of the real-world situation than that in panel (*a*), we could conclude that if the FDIC were to impose higher deposit insurance premiums, members of the nonbank public would be more likely to remove their deposits from banks and thrifts. For an industry that already is in shaky shape—as we shall discuss below and in the following chapter—such disintermediation could be devastating.

What has happened as a result of the sizable increases in FDIC insurance premiums? So far, it appears that the public is paying at least a part of the premium increase. Indeed, when the FDIC increased the BIF premium it charges commercial banks in 1990 and 1991, some banks actually charged their depositors specific "deposit insurance fees" on their accounts, which amounted to effective reductions in the net interest payments they received on their deposits. In general, however, most simply offered lower deposit rates and increased overall service charges for their customers' deposit accounts. There also were few signs of significant disintermediation. Hence, there was little evidence that banks and thrifts were forced to absorb all the costs of the premium increase.

Source: Anita Raghavan, "Banks Pass Along U.S. Insurance Costs," *Wall Street Journal* (May 13, 1991), p. B5B.

and members of Congress praised deposit insurance as a key element of the United States' financial system. Indeed, Congress felt strongly enough about the strengths of deposit insurance in 1980 to raise the coverage limit from $40,000 directly to $100,000. What accounted for the earlier optimism? What motivates the recent pessimism? We attempt to answer these questions in turn.

THE SUCCESSES OF FEDERAL DEPOSIT INSURANCE

From 1934 until the late 1970s, observers widely hailed federal deposit insurance as a remarkable success. The United States had experienced major bank runs in 1837, 1857, 1893, 1907, and 1929 through 1933, but federal deposit insurance appeared to have made those experiences just bad national memories that offered little current or future threat of recurrence.

Indeed, between 1943 and 1975 the number of insured commercial bank failures in any given year never reached double digits, even though the number of insured commercial banks always exceeded 13,000 during this period. Likewise, the number of failures of insured savings associations never was any higher than ten in a given year during the same interval, relative to a total number of insured institutions that ranged from about 2,500 to approximately 4,000 during the period.

Insured deposit losses of the federal insurance funds also were extremely low during the first few decades of federal deposit insurance. The FDIC never lost more than one-hundredth of a cent per dollar of deposits at all insured banks in any given year from 1940 to 1980, and the FSLIC lost no more than two-hundredths of a cent per dollar, with the exception of one year, between 1942 and 1980. In fact, for many years during those periods, the losses of the insurance funds were so minuscule that the FDIC and FSLIC *rebated* some of the premiums paid by banks and savings associations, much as private insurers do when their policy holders have fewer losses than were anticipated.

In short, until the early 1980s federal deposit insurance looked like a true success story in socioeconomic engineering. The provision of deposit insurance had halted bank runs, and to many it appeared to have, in conjunction with prudent federal regulation, reduced even the threat of significant isolated depository institution failures.

THE FLAWS IN THE DEPOSIT INSURANCE SYSTEM

Unfortunately, the way in which these deposit-insuring agencies were set up contained serious flaws. First, Congress set a relatively low price of deposit insurance to individual depository institutions. From 1933 until 1989, the deposit insurance premium was 0.083 percent. Banks and thrifts discovered that this was a small price to pay for the ability to advertise federal insurance to depositors as a means of enticing them to entrust institutions with their funds. Indeed, it is arguable that some depository institutions effectively were subsidized by the federal insurers.

Second, the insurance premium is the same percentage of total deposits for all depository institutions, regardless of the riskiness of the institution's portfolio. Since 1950, bank and savings association insurance agencies have (by government statute) charged the same premiums to all depository institutions they insure irrespective of the type of institution and differences in risk across institutions.

For example, every federally insured commercial bank and savings association pays a flat fee for the FDIC guarantee of the first $100,000 of each deposit account in the bank. Therefore, a bank in Fargo, South Dakota, that makes nearly all local loans pays the same premium rate as a money center bank in New York City with billions of dollars of nonperforming Latin American loans. Likewise, a healthy savings bank in Boston, Massachusetts, pays the same premium per deposit dollar as a savings and loan association in Houston, Texas, that holds multi-million-dollar loans to developers whose projects have collapsed. The flaw in this pricing structure is that an individual depository institution's premium is set without regard to its probability of failure, the riskiness of its portfolio, or the estimated cost to the insurer should the institution fail.

Incentives to Increase Risk Taking   The net result of these two flaws (low price and flat rate) in the deposit insurance scheme is that managers have an incentive to hold more assets of higher yield, and therefore higher risk, than they would if there were no deposit insurance. Thus, the premium rate is artificially low, permitting institution managers to obtain deposits at less than market price (because depositors will accept a lower interest payment on insured deposits); and even if the institution's portfolio becomes riskier, its insurance premium does not rise. Consequently, depository institution managers can increase their net interest margin by using lower-cost insured deposits to purchase higher-yield, higher-risk assets. The gains from risk taking accrue to the managers and stockholders of the depository institutions; the losses go to the deposit insurer.

Economists call this the **moral hazard problem** of deposit insurance. By insuring bank deposits, the government puts its faith in the "moral character" of the managers of the depository institutions it insures. There is, however, a hazard that their moral character cannot be trusted, that the depository institution managers in fact will act in risky, or even fraudulent, ways. If widespread, such behavior could put the entire deposit insurance system at risk.

Regulation as an Answer to the Problems Inherent in Deposit Insurance   To combat the underlying flaws in the financial institution industry and in the deposit insurance system, Congress tried to be careful in 1933 when it created federal deposit insurance. To avoid the adverse selection problem, it did not permit institutions that joined the federal program to leave the system at any time. Congress also installed a vast federal regulatory apparatus. It gave the FDIC and the FSLIC broad regulatory powers to offset the risk-taking temptations—the moral hazard problem—to depository institution managers. These powers included the ability to require higher capital requirements, regulation, examination, supervision, and enforcement.

In short, Congress set up a framework that specifically organized the financial institutions industry to protect firms in the industry from the rigors of competition. Market discipline of the behavior of financial institutions was replaced by regulatory discipline. In many respects the system worked well. Virtually no small saver has lost a penny of insured funds since federal deposit insurance was established. Nevertheless, in recent years the number of depository institution closures and insolvencies has increased to record post-Great Depression highs. We now turn to that issue.

DEPOSITORY INSTITUTION FAILURES AND FEDERAL DEPOSIT INSURANCE

Perhaps at no time in its sixty-year history has federal deposit insurance been as sorely tested as during the period since the mid-1980s. While some believe that it is weathering that test, others contend that it is failing the test miserably. Let us begin by describing the problems that deposit insurance has experienced. Then we shall analyze how deposit insurance works—and whether or not it is working well.

THE MOUNTING FAILURES OF DEPOSITORY INSTITUTIONS

In 1941, thirteen insured thrift institutions failed; from then until 1980, the annual number of such failures reached ten only twice. After 1980, the thrift industry nearly collapsed. Of the total of 890 FSLIC-insured failed thrifts over the period from 1934 to 1983, over half occurred between 1980 and 1983 alone. Thrift failures continued unabated into the 1990s. As might be expected, the resolution of the crisis took a heavy toll on the federal deposit insurance system. We shall have much more to say about the thrift disaster in the next chapter.

The condition of commercial banks also became shaky, particularly in the latter part of the 1980s. Bank failures increased dramatically in the late 1980s and early 1990s. Consider the following data. From 1934 through 1942, 393 banks failed, which amounted to an average of about 44 failures per year. Then, from 1943 through 1984, a total of 362 banks failed, or less than 9 failures, on average, per year—hence the widely hailed "success" of the federal deposit insurance programs. Then, from 1985 through 1991, *1,065* commercial banks failed—an annual average of nearly 163 bank failures per year. This annual average for 1985–1991 was almost *twelve times greater than the average for all the preceding years combined.*

In light of these figures, news articles in recent years have compared the entire depository institutions industry to the dinosaurs—giants on the verge of potential extinction. Although there are many factors that have made success difficult for this industry, the dangers that their problems pose for federal deposit insurance potentially are monumental. Can federal deposit insurance cope with this crisis? Or, conversely, has it been a contributor to the industry's difficulties? Should federal deposit insurance be redesigned—or even be eliminated? These are the questions we address in the remainder of this chapter.

AN ANALYSIS OF DEPOSIT INSURANCE

In this section we critically examine deposit insurance. We first analyze the underlying problems that motivate a potential need for deposit insurance: asset illiquidity and lack of information concerning the financial condition of households and firms. Then we describe the benefits to society of deposit insurance—and the problem for the deposit insurer.

The Heart of the Depository Institution Problem   Depository institutions accept deposits that are extremely liquid; that is, on demand, the institution must be prepared to refund, at a one-to-one exchange rate, amounts held in demand deposit and other checkable deposit accounts. The assets that depository institutions acquire are much less liquid. This situation exposes depository institutions to runs, a situation in which many depositors want their funds at the same time and depository institutions are unable to pay them all.

Because depository institutions expose themselves to such liquidity risks, it is proper to ask why they do so. The answer is that, traditionally, the very nature of the function of depository institutions is to assume this liquidity risk from households and firms—for a fee, of course.

In other words, the ultimate source of the liquidity problem stems from households and firms. Consider a setting in which:

1. Households and firms experience liquidity risks.

2. Lack of information exists concerning the liquidity risk exposure of specific households and firms.

3. Because of item 2, the liquidity risks are uninsurable; that is, no private insurers will emerge because, given imperfect information, insurers may well set deposit insurance premiums in such a way as to induce many households and firms to take liquidity risks.

In such a system, households and firms will undertake less long-term, illiquid investment projects than they otherwise could, because individuals would otherwise bear excessive, uninsurable, risks. Here is where depository institutions emerge. They offer deposit contracts that are convertible into currency at a one-to-one exchange rate upon demand; they thereby substitute their own liquidity risk for nonfinancial firms' liquidity risk, and they do so with the hope of earning profits. While this arrangement leaves everyone better off and promotes economic growth, it also has its disadvantages: Occasionally bank runs arise and depository institutions fail—bringing households and firms down with them.

The Benefits to Society of Deposit Insurance   We have established the fact that by accepting such highly liquid liabilities as demand deposits and savings accounts, banks and thrifts have gone into the business of substituting their own liquidity risk for the liquidity risk of households and firms, in an attempt to earn profits. But this now merely transfers the inherent problem concerning a lack of information about financial strength from individuals and businesses to depository institutions. Individual depositors have imperfect information concerning (1) how risky and how liquid the depository institution's asset portfolio is and (2) when, and how much, other depositors wish to withdraw. Furthermore, depository institutions typically employ a "first-come, first-served" rule in honoring deposit redemption.

Because depositors know that not all depositors can get their funds back, one's place in line matters and runs are possible. Note that runs are quite rational from the individual depositor's point of view. But there are social costs to runs: Runs on insolvent depository institutions may well lead to runs on solvent institutions; and if many banking institutions fail, the total quantity of credit—and of money, because demand and other checkable deposits are part of the quantity of money—will fall dramatically. As a result, the flow of economic activity—national income, national output, and employment—can be adversely affected. Enter the federal deposit insurance scheme.

Now the Insurer Has the Problem   Note, however, that the problem concerning lack of information about a specific enterprise remains. The federal deposit insurer must now be concerned with the solvency of those institutions that it is insuring. The insurer, therefore, incurs the costs of gathering and evaluating information about the condition of depository institutions; those costs exist whether or not a specific institution fails. If an institution does fail, the federal deposit insurer incurs the additional expense of paying the claims of the insured depositors.

Recall an earlier conclusion in this chapter: If the deposit insurer does not price its services properly, then depository institutions have an incentive to increase their profits by taking on additional risk. But in practice it is extremely difficult for even the federal deposit insurer to measure the risk of insured banks. Presumably the risk of an insured bank to the federal deposit insurer is indicated by the variation in the bank's future net income stream; but one cannot directly observe today the future results of specific bank management decisions. In practice, deposit insurers measure a bank's risk by the degree of variability in its past earnings.

STRUCTURAL WEAKNESSES IN FEDERAL DEPOSIT INSURANCE

As we indicated in our review of the history of federal deposit insurance, Congress recognized the need for a large regulatory structure to deal with the moral hazard problem that stems from deposit insurance. Despite its best efforts, however, Congress created a deposit insurance system with two key structural weaknesses. First, the present system has proved to be poorly equipped to adapt itself to efforts of depository institutions— whether intentional or unintentional—to increase the risks they incur. Second, the system has entrusted significant power to regulators without safeguards against the risk that regulators themselves may make bad judgments.

HOW DEPOSITORY INSTITUTIONS CAN INCREASE RISK

Recall that the flat premium charge provides incentives to depository institutions to incur more risk. It is important to realize that as an institution becomes weak, it has even more incentives to take on more risk. For one thing, if the higher risk pays off, the institution can avoid the "troubled" list, which brings with it more regulation and constraints on management behavior. For another, if an institution is insolvent and waiting to be closed, or if it is nearly insolvent, managers have a strong temptation to take a final chance at a big score to avoid bankruptcy. By not closing insolvent institutions, therefore, deposit insurers induce risk taking. But how can depository institutions take on more risk?

Increasing Leverage   One major method of increasing risk is to increase the institution's leverage (debt), by reducing its ratio of capital to assets. One way in which to do that is to increase the size of the institution and finance it by borrowing; another is to issue debt and issue the proceeds to stockholders as dividends, instead of purchasing additional assets. Yet another is what economists call **affiliated-institution risk.** This occurs when a depository institution issues debt backed partly by the value of the capital of an affiliated institution, which commonly is a bank holding company. This effectively permits a depository institution to grow without expanding its own capital, but it simultaneously increases the risk incurred by the institution by linking its safety and soundness to the capital of a separate firm.

Changing the Composition of Assets or Liabilities   A further method by which a firm can incur additional risk (without affecting the leverage of its portfolio) is by increasing its total portfolio risk. This can be done by changing the composition of the institution's assets or the composition of its liabilities used to finance the assets. Figure 6-1 in Chapter 6 shows that since the 1960s, commercial banks in fact have changed the composition of their assets by increasing the ratio of their loans to securities. In effect, the percentage of these banks' portfolios invested in high-credit-risk assets (loans) has increased at the expense of low-credit-risk assets. At the beginning of the 1980s, the share of commercial bank assets in cash and securities was roughly 36 percent of total assets. By the end of the decade, it amounted to just 27 percent. In contrast, the portion of total assets allocated to loans grew from 54 percent to 61 percent.

Portfolio risk can also be raised by increasing the amount of credit risk in a bank's high-credit-risk assets: Bank managers can replace less risky loans with riskier ones. Regulators, in fact, have complained that in recent years the asset quality of many thrifts and banks has declined considerably. Of particular concern has been the growth in real estate lending at the expense of commercial and industrial (C&I) loans. C&I loans made by commercial banks—the traditional bread and butter business of the industry—declined during the 1980s and early 1990s, while real estate loans grew considerably in relative importance.

Decreasing Portfolio Diversification   Bank managers can also increase portfolio risk by decreasing the portfolio's degree of diversification. It is believed that the 1984 failure of Continental Illinois Bank was partly due to that institution's excessive reliance on high-interest borrowing as a source of funds (instead of lower-cost deposits); in effect it increased overall risk by increasing risk on the liability side of its balance sheet.

Finally, total portfolio risk can be increased by mismatching asset maturity and liability maturity—or mismatching interest rate sensitivity of assets and liabilities. In today's environment, deposit-receiving institutions have incentives to increase their leverage, portfolio risk, or both, because such activities are subsidized by deposit insurers: the FDIC, the federal government, and—ultimately—taxpayers. Such subsidization, however:

1. gives insured institutions a competitive advantage over uninsured institutions;
2. induces higher degrees of risk taking than would be the case if there were no subsidies.

Note that if deposit insurance were priced ''properly'' (i.e., to reflect the institution's individual risk), then factors 1 and 2 would not exist.

HOW REGULATORS MAY HAVE WORSENED THE PROBLEM

When Congress created deposit insurance and set up a nationwide regulatory apparatus, it recognized that it could not, as a large political body, effectively ''micro-manage'' the system it had constructed. Therefore, it left most of these details to bank and thrift regulators. Under the law, these regulators have been given significant discretion, although they must operate within the broad guidelines laid out by law.

Hence, depository institution regulators possess the power—and the concomitant responsibility—to influence significantly the course of events in the bank and thrift industries. This means that Congress subjects society to **regulatory risk,** which is the risk that regulators may make decisions that, in retrospect, turn out to have been poor ones.

To understand why regulatory risk is so important, it is necessary to review the nature of the myriad choices that regulators must make on a regular basis. One of these is what to do when a depository institution fails. Another is how to best prevent depository institutions from reaching the point at which failure is unavoidable. On a case-by-case basis, these are not particularly earth-shaking decisions, but when they are multiplied by the number of instances in which they must be reached, these choices are weighty indeed.

Regulatory Responses to Depository Institution Failure   When a depository institution fails, the FDIC has several options:

1. *Direct deposit payoff* In the case of **direct deposit payoff,** the FDIC declares the depository institution insolvent, pays off its depositors, and sells the depository institution's assets. If it can sell the assets for more than the value of the depository institution's liabilities (a *very* rare event), the FDIC suffers no loss. Otherwise, it must draw down its insurance fund to cover any loss.

2. *Purchase and assumption* Under the option of **purchase and assumption,** instead of closing and liquidating the depository institution, the FDIC arranges for the failed depository institution to be merged with another, healthy institution. The merger partner purchases most of the failed institution's assets and assumes responsibility for most of its outstanding liabilities. How many assets the merger partner purchases and how many liabilities it assumes have to be worked out in negotiations with the FDIC. A key advantage of purchase and assumption over a direct deposit payoff is that it often saves the FDIC much effort, time, and money that it otherwise would devote to liquidating all the failed bank's assets and settling all its outstanding liabilities. It also enables the failed institution to remain open, so that it can continue to provide services to its depositors.

3. *Indirect payoff* Under the **indirect payoff** option, the FDIC arranges for another depository institution to assume only the insured deposits of the failed institution. The uninsured depositors, in contrast, receive a direct payment from the FDIC for the amount of their claims that the FDIC's staff estimates are recoverable from sale of the institution's assets that are retained by the FDIC. This option, which was first implemented in 1984, permits the failed institution to remain open but typically is more costly to the FDIC than a purchase and assumption. It sometimes is used when a merger partner for the failed institution is not available.

4. *Direct assistance* The FDIC has congressional authorization, in many circumstances, to give **direct assistance**—to make direct loans (often in coordination with the Federal Reserve) to a failed depository institution. According to the law, the FDIC is supposed to do this only if it can make a case that the failed institution provided "essential" services to its community. In practice, however, the FDIC has stretched this point when very large banks deemed "too big to fail" are tottering on the brink of insolvency and closure. Such banks typically are so large that a purchase and assumption would be difficult to arrange, while either a direct or indirect deposit payoff would be prohibitively costly to the FDIC's insurance fund.

In past years, the FDIC has preferred not to make direct deposit payoffs. In many cases, then, deposit insurers have preferred the route of purchase and assumption, indirect payoff, or direct assistance. In retrospect, argue many critics, decisions not to make a direct deposit payoff may have been misguided, even if they were well-intentioned. The inherent problem, contend these observers, is that the deposit insurance regulators may get so wrapped up in the "here and now" of a situation that they ignore the long-run consequences of their actions.

For instance, the FDIC might decide it is least costly to close smaller banks when they fail, even as it provides direct assistance to large banks because it has judged the large banks to be "too big to fail." By assisting the large banks, permitting them to remain open, and thereby saving their insured depositors the time and trouble they would have experienced if the bank had temporarily been closed, the FDIC may send insured depositors at smaller banks the signal that they should move their funds to large depository institutions. Furthermore, its actions also would help protect the interests of *uninsured* depositors, encouraging these individuals or firms to hold more deposits at large banks to the detriment of their smaller rivals. The long-run consequences of such differential treatment of failed banks, argue FDIC critics, may be very costly in terms of their *future* implications for the banking system, even if they lower the FDIC's short-run dollar losses.

Weaknesses in Safety and Soundness Regulation and Accounting   Without meaning to do so, regulators may not properly accomplish a key task the Congress assigns them, which is to audit and generally supervise the activities in which depository institutions become involved, so as to prevent these institutions from becoming insolvent in the first place. This is a complex task known as **safety and soundness regulation.** It is an area that primarily is the domain of accountants and auditors, but it has important implications for the economic vitality of the depository institutions industry and the health of the federal deposit insurance system.

Proficiency in safety and soundness regulation is an area in which critics have been particularly disdainful of the approach of depository institution regulators. For one thing, these critics argue that regulators have poorly measured the value of assets and liabilities of the depository institutions covered by federal deposit insurance. Mismeasurement of assets and liabilities, naturally, would cause regulators to misjudge the solvency of depository institutions.

In the regulators' defense, however, it should be pointed out that it typically is difficult to rate the financial condition of *any* business enterprise—whether or not it is a depository institution—because **generally accepted accounting principles (GAAP)** value assets and liabilities at their historical, not current market, values. Often, this can lead to an overstatement of the current value of a bank's assets—or its capital. For instance, at the beginning of 1991, the market value of the equity shares of twenty of the twenty-five largest commercial banks in the United States was less than half of the corresponding GAAP value of those shares.

Critics argue that depository institution regulators in the past have made the job even more difficult for themselves by applying **regulatory accounting principles (RAP)** to banks and thrifts. RAP also uses historical, not market, valuation, and it provides even less useful information (for this discussion) than GAAP. RAP is more liberal in defining income and assets; that is, RAP includes as income and assets items that GAAP does not. As a consequence, the income and assets of financial institutions are biased upward—painting a picture that is less dismal than the true situation. For example, in 1982, before the nature of the gathering thrift industry crisis became widely recognized, RAP net worth for the thrift industry was 3.69 percent of total assets, GAAP net worth was only 2.9 percent of total assets, and the estimated market value net worth ratio was a *negative* 12.03 percent!

PROPOSALS FOR SALVAGING DEPOSIT INSURANCE

Deposit insurance in the United States is in trouble. The FDIC's Bank Insurance Fund began the 1990s with low cash reserves and had been nearly depleted by the end of 1991. In the face of projections of a BIF shortfall of over $20 billion by 1995, Congress was forced to divert $70 billion in tax dollars to the FDIC in 1992.

In light of the FDIC's difficulties, nearly everyone agrees that the federal deposit insurance system needs fixing. Furthermore, there is no shortage of proposals for what types of repairs might be made. These fall into four basic categories. One approach is to scrap governmental insurance of deposits altogether, replacing the existing federally supported, taxpayer-backed system with a private program. Another approach is to retain a governmental role in deposit insurance but to reformulate that role significantly. A third idea is to combine elements of the first two approaches. And a fourth approach is to require banks to operate as legally separate insured and uninsured units. We consider each of these proposals in turn.

PRIVATE DEPOSIT INSURANCE

Because federal deposit insurers either cannot or will not price insurance premiums based on the portfolio risk of specific institutions, perhaps a case can be made for private deposit insurance. A small number of economists have advocated precisely that. They maintain that there are several advantages of private, over federal, deposit insurance.

The Case for Private Insurance   According to those economists who favor private deposit insurance:

1. Private deposit insurers are more flexible in monitoring and controlling risks undertaken by individual institutions.
2. Private insurers would be more selective in choosing institutions to insure.
3. Private insurers are not subject to political pressures and consequently are more likely to price premiums differently for different institutions, reflecting different risks— thereby eliminating the temptation for thrifts to take on more risk than is optimal (from society's point of view).

This "private market solution" to the deposit insurance problem has a natural appeal for many economists. Economic theory, beginning with Adam Smith, tells us that markets typically do a good job of allocating and pricing goods and services—*and* risks. Indeed, one of the main functions of existing private life and property and casualty insurers is to do just that. Given that private insurers appear able to manage that task—though not without their own governmental regulatory apparatus, it should be noted—why shouldn't deposit insurance be provided privately as well?

Indeed, since the early 1980s private insurers have provided some forms of deposit insurance. For instance, so-called cash accounts—money market fund accounts—at securities firms such as Merrill Lynch often are covered in part by private insurance guarantees. Some commercial banks also have taken out insurance against the risk of currency nonconvertibility on non-dollar-denominated deposits held by their customers in branches outside the United States. These private policies seem to have protected financial institutions and their customers against risk of loss, without the need for direct governmental involvement.

A Potential for Market Failures?   Of course, such purely private programs have not yet experienced significant losses, making their prospects for long-term success difficult to evaluate. Those who doubt the prospects for success if the United States were to convert to a private deposit insurance system point out the potential for **market failures** in such a system. According to this view, the parties in a private deposit insurance transaction— the private deposit insurer and the owners of a given depository institution—have an incentive only to design a system that covers their own specific concerns in the event of a failure. In such a system, contend critics of private deposit insurance, there likely would be an underallocation of insurance to cover the needs of depositors. Hence, the private market almost certainly would, according to this view, fail to meet the needs of all of society, resulting in the market failure.

Proponents of private deposit insurance respond that this view does not give enough credit to depositors to look out for their own interests. In the absence of federal deposit insurance, they argue, depositors would have a much greater incentive to spend serious time and effort evaluating the riskiness of financial institutions that hold their funds. Depositors also would have an incentive, in the absence of a governmental deposit insurance system, to take out insurance policies protecting the value of their own deposits at banks and thrifts, just as they take out policies to protect their homes and automobiles from the threat of loss.

Critics of the private solution respond to this that it ignores a fundamental problem: Some individuals will find it in their best interest *not* to be insured; a liquidity problem of a large bank could then induce a run on the bank by the uninsured depositors, potentially inducing runs on other banks. It is the threat of a large-scale bank run under private insurance, these critics argue, that ultimately requires direct governmental involvement in deposit insurance. In fact, they point out, it was this recognition that led to the 1934 implementation of a federal insurance program.

PROPOSALS FOR REFORM OF THE CURRENT GOVERNMENTALLY MANAGED SYSTEM

In light of the potential problem of market failures that may arise in a purely private deposit insurance system, most economists and policy makers have advocated reforms of the existing federal insurance program. There are nearly as many proposed reforms as there are economists and policy makers interested in this problem, but we can identify a few proposals that stand out as the most commonly suggested.

Adding More "Market Discipline"   One of the significant advantages of a market-based system for allocating goods, services, and risks is that when people make mistakes, they are ''punished'' by losses. Those who experience such losses learn from their mistakes, and those who are not directly involved but observe others punished by failure and loss learn from them as well. Hence, individuals and firms are *disciplined* by market forces, which improves their ability to withstand ill events in the future.

As we have discussed in this chapter, the vast regulatory apparatus and policies that accompany federal deposit insurance protect depository institutions and their customers from many of the ill effects of their own mistakes. Consequently, by its very nature the structure of deposit insurance lessens the amount of *market discipline* that otherwise would influence the choices that banks, thrifts, and depositors might make. One proposal for reform of deposit insurance is to reinvigorate market discipline while preserving the basic structure of the federal deposit insurance system.

Two central reforms lie at the heart of this proposal. One is to scale back existing deposit insurance guarantees. This could be done by reducing the maximum account balance insured by the federal government or the number of insured accounts that any given individual or household can hold, or both. Another reform would be to end the too-big-to-fail policy first adopted by the Office of the Comptroller of the Currency in 1984 and since followed by the FDIC and the Federal Reserve. Indeed, Congress acted to restrain regulators' use of the too-big-to-fail policy in 1991.

Such reforms, proponents contend, would enhance the disciplining influence of market forces, thereby encouraging depository institutions and their customers to monitor risks more closely. As a result, fewer risks would be taken, and, in the end, there would be fewer failures. Furthermore, they argue, these reforms would move deposit insurance back toward its initial goal—primarily protecting the ''small saver'' who is less informed and therefore is less able to look out for his or her own interests in the complex world of finance.

Switching to Market-Valued Reporting   Another change that economists and some policy makers have proposed is to reform regulatory accounting principles (RAP). As we pointed out earlier, at present RAP uses historical valuations of depository institutions that may understate but all too often have overstated the true value of a depository institution's income, asset, and capital accounts. This leads to a regulatory picture that is ''too rosy'' relative to the harsh realities of the marketplace.

The fundamental reform most commonly proposed is for RAP to be altered so that, if anything, regulators look at an accounting picture that errs toward making depository institutions' prospects seem *worse* than really is true. Erring on the side of caution, argue proponents of this reform, is the appropriate path for regulators to follow. The best way to do this, they contend, is for RAP to use *market-valued* measures of income, asset, and capital accounts of depository institutions. Furthermore, the appropriate market valuations to use would be those that most conservatively state the values of these accounts. Certainly, if such a policy had been in place in the 1970s, the thrift crisis might have been muted significantly, as we shall see in the next chapter.

The problem, of course, is that assigning market values to bank assets and liabilities is a tricky business. Such valuations at best must be estimates, making market valuation accounting difficult for regulators to implement. For this reason, it seems unlikely that such a regulatory approach will be adopted soon.

Enhancing Supervision and Examination and Centralizing Regulatory Responsibility   As part of the regulatory system that has existed since the 1930s, banks and thrifts are subjected to **field examinations,** which are on-site visits to depository institutions by staff accountants and auditors of bank regulators, including the FDIC, the Office of the Comptroller of the Currency, and the Federal Reserve. In recent years, regulators have used these ''bank examinations'' to produce numerical ratings from 1 (good) to 5 (poor) in five separate areas of depository institution performance: capital, assets, management, earnings, and liquidity. This system of numerical ratings is known by the acronym **CAMEL.** Based on the ratings in each category, regulators award a depository institution an overall CAMEL rating. A CAMEL rating of 1 or 2 means that the regulator regards the depository institution as healthy, a rating of 3 causes the regulator to place the institution on its ''watch list,'' and a rating of 4 or 5 indicates that the regulator considers the institution to be in serious trouble.

Depository institution examinations are certainly the heart of the enforcement of the safety and soundness that go with the government's guarantee of deposit insurance. On-site examinations are not inexpensive, however. The annual cost to regulatory agencies of conducting these examinations runs into the hundreds of millions of dollars. Nonetheless, most proposals for deposit insurance reform call for more resources to be devoted to this activity.

Some regulators have proved to be more efficient and credible than others in their examination of depository institutions. For instance, as of 1992 the Federal Reserve had 990 examiners for the 1,000 state-chartered commercial banks that it had responsibility for regulating—almost one examiner per bank—while the Office of the Comptroller of the Currency had 2,350 examiners for just over 4,000 banks—or nearly half the number of examiners, per bank, as the Fed. Not surprisingly, this enabled the Fed to conduct more frequent and thorough on-site examinations of the banks it regulated. Interestingly, 7.1 percent of national banks, which the Office of the Comptroller examined, failed between 1987 and 1990, while 4.2 percent of state banks—supervised in part by the Fed—failed during the same period. In 1990 alone, 2.3 percent of national banks failed, while less than 1 percent of banks regulated solely by the Fed failed.

Some observers argue that these differences together indicate the existence of two related problems. One, they argue, is that some regulators are better at supervisory tasks than others. Another is that some regulators are better funded and less burdened with conflicting responsibilities than others. The best way to end these differences among the supervisory capabilities of the various regulators, these observers contend, would be to place the responsibility for safety and soundness regulation in the hands of a smaller number of regulators—or, perhaps, a single safety and soundness regulator. Reducing the number of regulators would have the added benefit of eliminating problems with overlapping supervisory roles of regulators, such as situations that arise in which the Fed regulates a bank holding company that owns banks that are under the jurisdiction of the FDIC or the Office of the Comptroller of the Currency. This reform, they argue, would further enhance the effectiveness of safety and soundness regulation.

Charging Risk-Related Deposit Insurance Premiums   Perhaps the most often mentioned reform in recent years is the proposal that the FDIC vary the deposit insurance premiums it charges banks and thrifts with the riskiness of those institutions. From 1951 through 1984, the FDIC and FSLIC, at the direction of Congress, set equal deposit insurance premiums for banks and thrifts. Then, in 1985, the FSLIC placed a special premium surcharge on thrift institutions that effectively raised their annual premium to a level roughly $2\frac{1}{2}$ times that of commercial banks. (The FSLIC did not necessarily raise the premium to take into account greater riskiness of thrifts, however—even though effectively that may have occurred; instead, it sought to replenish its insurance fund, as we shall see in Chapter 13.) The FDIC renewed the tradition of equal premiums when it raised commercial bank premiums to a level with thrifts in 1991. As before, all institutions again were paying the same fixed premiums with no accounting for differences in risks.

Until recently, the main drawback in efforts to price deposit insurance premiums based on a depository institution's inherent riskiness was that risk was difficult to measure. Indeed, economists generally agree that the true risk of failure is nearly impossible to measure; instead, regulators would need to use ''proxy'' measures of risk. Recently, however, financial economists have developed **option pricing models** that can be used to assign dollar values to parties involved in financial transactions that entail different contingencies for the interested parties. They do so by using information on the dollar amount of an option available from use of an asset, the current price of the asset, the time remaining to maturity, and the variability of the asset's price to calculate a risk-adjusted valuation of the options available to a party from holding the asset.

One can envision the deposit insurance system as a program in which the government issues a contingent claim, or option—its deposit insurance guarantee—to two parties: depository institutions and depositors. In principle, then, option pricing models could be used to determine the value of deposit insurance to each depository institution. This value would indicate the appropriate premium to charge that institution for deposit insurance.

There are, nevertheless, some unresolved problems with this approach. One is that option pricing models assume that well-specified rules exist that regulate when an option—payment of deposit insurance to deposit holders—may be exercised. As we have already discussed, however, the FDIC has significant discretion over if or when payment will be made. Furthermore, option pricing models typically assume that full, up-to-date information on a bank's or thrift's market value is available to use in computing the value of the deposit insurance guarantee. In fact, such information often is imperfect and needs to be supplemented with detailed accounting data that sometimes are not current or readily available to regulators.

Proponents of risk-based deposit insurance premiums argue that even an imperfect means of pricing according to risk would be preferable to the flat-premium system that Congress has specified since 1934. Furthermore, they argue, regulators could learn about how best to implement a risk-based system by experience. Over time, they could improve their information-gathering capabilities to enable them to calculate more accurate—and, hence, more ''fair''—premiums to charge banks for the deposit insurance guarantee they provide.

COMBINING PUBLIC AND PRIVATE INSURANCE

As a further suggested reform, some have suggested that, even if the market failures that might be inherent in a purely private deposit insurance system argue against it, society could still benefit from some private competition for deposit insurance. These economists envision a system in which public and private insurers would exist side by side. Depository institutions could sign up for insurance from either type of insurer, but all depository institutions would be required to get deposit insurance (to avoid the adverse selection problem discussed earlier). Furthermore, the government would set the standards for private insurers to make certain that they could deal with a major banking crisis.

There are several justifications for such a system, according to its proponents. One is that although the governmental program would continue under this scheme, to serve as an ''anchor'' for the entire system, private competition for deposit insurance would keep the government on its toes. Both the government and the private insurers would have an incentive to set fair but accurate premiums—the private insurers would do so to protect themselves from loss while pursuing maximum profits, and government agencies would do so to preserve their bureaucratic turf. Furthermore, private insurers who pursue profits from their operations might be likely to develop improvements in administering deposit insurance, from which the government's insurance program might benefit.

CORE BANKING

In 1991, a bill was introduced into the Congress that would set up a **core banking** deposit insurance system. Under such a system, a bank effectively would be managed as if it had two separate balance sheets. One part of its balance sheet, the ''core,'' would consist of federally insured deposit liabilities and assets that bank managers purchased with these deposits. Banks would be required to invest insured deposit funds only in very safe assets such as cash and Treasury bills. The bank would be able to manage the remaining part of the assets and liabilities on its balance sheet as it saw fit. If the bank were to fail, insured depositors would be reimbursed out of the bank's cash and security holdings held as ''core assets.'' Other depositors, debt holders, and owners would not be rescued by regulators.

It remains to be seen if Congress will adopt this idea or any of the others we have overviewed. There clearly is much disagreement about what should be done about federal deposit insurance. Nearly everyone agrees, however, that *something* must be done.

CHAPTER SUMMARY

1. The main objective of governmental deposit insurance is to prevent bank runs and panics, but another goal is to protect the deposits of small savers who are ill informed about risks in financial markets.

2. Depository institutions have an inherent liquidity problem that makes them susceptible to runs: They accept deposit contracts that are convertible into currency at a one-to-one exchange rate upon demand. Therefore, depository institutions are in the business of substituting their own liquidity risk for the liquidity risks that exist in the real (nonfinancial) sector.

3. Two key historical problems of deposit insurance have been adverse selection and moral hazard. Federal deposit insurance largely has eliminated the adverse selection problem by requiring all depository institutions to obtain some form of deposit insurance. The fixed-premium system that the FDIC has used since its creation, however, contributes to a significant moral hazard problem under which depository institution managers have an incentive to increase the riskiness of their institutions.

4. Recently, thrifts and banks have possessed the means and the willingness to take on more risk: They can increase their leverage; or given the amount of leverage, they can increase total portfolio risk by mismatching their asset-liabilities maturities, reducing portfolio diversification, and changing the composition of their portfolios so as to increase the proportion of riskier assets.

5. Although federal deposit insurance was successful during its first forty years, the past twenty have presented the federal system with its most difficult test as thrift and bank failures have increased dramatically. For this reason, many economists and policy makers believe that the federal deposit insurance system should be reformed.

6. In theory, private deposit insurance can replace the federal program and potentially could be more efficient and successful. A concern about possible market failures in a purely private deposit insurance system has prevented this option from being followed, however. Nonetheless, many economists continue to advocate some form of private insurance even if the government maintains its federal program.

7. Proposed reforms to the current federal deposit insurance system include providing means for more market discipline by placing greater limits on deposit insurance coverage; using accounting methods that entail market valuation of depository institutions' income, assets, and capital; enhancing and centralizing depository institution regulation; and charging risk-based premiums on deposit insurance.

GLOSSARY

Adverse selection problem: A situation that may arise in a voluntary insurance program, in which only the worst risks choose to participate in an effort to gain from the program.

Affiliated-institution risk: The risk a depository institution incurs when it issues debt backed partly by the value of the capital of an affiliated institution, such as a bank holding company, thereby permitting the depository institution to grow without expanding its own capital.

CAMEL rating: A system of numerical ratings that regulators use to assess the quality of a depository institution's capital, assets, management, earnings, and liquidity.

Core banking: A deposit insurance system that requires a bank to hold a "core" of very safe assets, such as cash and Treasury bills, from which the bank could reimburse insured depositors if it failed.

Direct assistance: The term applied to the FDIC practice of making direct loans to a failed depository institution that it classifies as one that provided "essential" services to its community.

Direct deposit payoff: A situation in which the FDIC declares a depository institution insolvent, pays off its depositors, and sells the depository institution's assets.

Field examinations: On-site visits to depository institutions by staff accountants and auditors of bank regulators.

Generally accepted accounting principles (GAAP): A network of concepts, principles, and procedures developed by the accounting profession to develop and report financial information.

Indirect payoff: A situation in which the FDIC arranges for another depository institution to assume only the insured deposits of a failed institution and makes a direct payment for the estimated recoverable portion of the claims of the failed institution's uninsured depositors.

Market failure: A situation that occurs when a private market benefits only those who participate in the market but fails to meet the needs of other members of society whose welfare is affected by that market.

Moral hazard problem: By insuring bank deposits, the government puts its faith in the "moral character" of the managers of the depository institutions it insures, thereby exposing itself to a hazard that the depository institution managers will undertake risky, or even fraudulent, actions.

Option pricing models: Financial models that can be used to assign dollar values to parties involved in financial transactions, such as the exchange of deposit insurance guarantees, that entail different contingencies for the interested parties.

Purchase and assumption: A situation in which the FDIC arranges for a failed depository institution to be merged with another, healthy institution, which purchases most of the failed institution's assets and assumes responsibility for most of its outstanding liabilities.

Regulatory accounting principles (RAP): Accounting definitions applied to depository institutions that define "income" and "assets" more liberally than GAAP; that is, RAP includes some items in income and assets that generally accepted accounting practices do not.

Regulatory risk: The risk that regulators may make decisions that, after the fact, turn out to have been poor ones.

Safety and soundness regulation: The regulatory task of auditing and otherwise supervising the activities of depository institutions to help prevent these institutions from becoming insolvent.

SELF-TEST QUESTIONS

1. In the Current Controversy in this chapter, you learned that the equilibrium deposit rate generally falls by a fraction of the insurance premium paid by depository institutions. Explain why this fact might help account for the 1950 decision by Congress to charge the same deposit insurance premium to banks and thrifts, which by then were competing against each other for deposit customers.

2. Explain, in your own words, the nature of the adverse selection problem and why it has been a difficulty for deposit insurance systems in the past.

3. Explain, in your own words, the nature of the moral hazard problem. Why does a fixed premium on deposit insurance contribute to this problem?

4. How might the FDIC unintentionally make short-run decisions about dealing with failed depository institutions that seem appropriate in the short run but are bad decisions in the long run?

5. Of the possible deposit insurance reforms discussed in this chapter, which to you seem to have the greatest potential for success? Which seem least likely to succeed? Why?

PROBLEMS

12-1. Suppose that a bank is in a position of likely bankruptcy and is considering two alternative investments with associated payoffs and risk:
Investment A: $500,000 or $900,000 at probabilities 0.5 and 0.5
Investment B: $100,000 or $1,200,000 at probabilities 0.5 and 0.5.
a. Compute the expected values of the payoffs from these alternative investments.
b. Which of the two would you expect the bank to purchase if a $1 million payoff was required to avoid bankruptcy?

12-2. The current market value of a bank is equal to $10 million. The bank presently has a probability of failure equal to 0.5 (hence, the probability the bank remains open with its current value of $10 million is 0.5). If the bank failed at present, its managers believe that the value to the bank's owners of the FDIC deposit insurance system is equal to $2 million; that is, this is how much the bank would be worth to the owners in its present condition. The bank's managers, however, have the option of undertaking a risky investment that they estimate could raise the market value of the bank to $20 million while increasing the probability of failure to 0.75 (so the probability the bank would stay open and retain the $20 million value is 0.25). The value of the FDIC insurance guarantee to the bank's owners would remain constant at $2 million.
a. What is the present expected value of the bank?
b. What would be the expected value of the bank if the bank's managers undertake the risky investment? Compare this amount with the expected value from part a. Do the bank's managers have an incentive to undertake the investment?
c. Suppose that the FDIC adopted risk-based insurance premiums. If so, the bank managers calculate that the value of the bank if it stays open after undertaking the new risky investment would fall to $18 million, because it would have to pay much higher deposit insurance premiums if the bank remains open. The value of the FDIC's guarantee in the event of failure, which does not change, remains constant at $2 million. The probability of failure if the managers undertake the risky investment remains equal to 0.75. What is the bank's expected value under these conditions if it adopts the risky project? Will the bank's managers now have an incentive to undertake the risky investment?

SELECTED REFERENCES

Baer, Herbert, and Elijah Brewer, ''Uninsured Deposits as a Source of Market Discipline: Some New Evidence,'' Federal Reserve Bank of Chicago *Economic Perspectives,* 10 (5, September/October 1986), pp. 23–31.

Barth, James R., John J. Feid, Gabriel Riedel, and M. Hampton Tunis, ''Alternative Federal Deposit Insurance Regimes,'' Federal Home Loan Bank Board, Office of Policy and Economic Research, Research Paper no. 152, Washington, D.C. (January 1989).

Benston, George J., Robert A. Eisenbeis, Paul M. Horvitz, Edward J. Kane, and George G. Kaufman, *Perspectives on Safe and Sound Banking: Past, Present, and Future* (Cambridge, Mass.: MIT Press, 1986).

Calomiris, Charles W., ''Deposit Insurance: Lessons from the Record,'' Federal Reserve Bank of Chicago *Economic Perspectives,* 13 (3, May/June 1989), pp. 10–30.

Flood, Mark D., ''On the Use of Option Pricing Models to Analyze Deposit Insurance,'' Federal Reserve Bank of St. Louis *Review,* 72 (1, January/February 1990), pp. 19–35.

Gilbert, R. Alton, ''Market Discipline of Bank Risk: Theory and Evidence,'' Federal Reserve Bank of St. Louis *Review,* 72 (1, January/February 1990), pp. 3–18.

Kane, Edward J., *The Gathering Crisis in Federal Deposit Insurance* (Cambridge, Mass.: MIT Press, 1985).

Kuester, Kathleen A., and James M. O'Brien, ''Market-Based Deposit Insurance Premiums: An Evaluation,'' Finance and Economics Discussion Series, no. 150, Board of Governors of the Federal Reserve System, Washington, D.C. (January 1991).

Morris, Charles S., and Gordon H. Sellon, Jr., ''Market Value Accounting for Banks: Pros and Cons,'' Federal Reserve Bank of Kansas City *Economic Review,* 76 (2, March/April 1991), pp. 5–20.

Munn, Glenn C., F. L. Garcia, and Charles Woelfel, *Encyclopedia of Banking and Finance* (Rolling Meadows, Ill.: Bankers Publishing Company, 1991).

Pierce, James L., *The Future of Banking* (New Haven and London: Yale University Press, 1991).

Thomson, James B., ''Using Market Incentives to Reform Bank Regulation and Federal Deposit Insurance,'' Federal Reserve Bank of Cleveland *Economic Review,* 26 (1, First Quarter 1990), pp. 28–40.

The Thrift Crisis

CHAPTER PREVIEW

1. How did the thrift industry evolve?

2. In what ways did the federal government contribute to the inflexibility of thrift institutions' portfolios?

3. How did the years before the 1980s set the stage for the thrift crisis of the 1980s and 1990s?

4. How did the thrift crisis unfold in the 1980s?

5. What did Congress do in response to the thrift crisis?

6. How much will the crisis cost? Who is paying the cost?

7. Is there a danger that the crisis could spill over to other financial institutions, such as commercial banks?

The past decade has witnessed the largest financial institution crisis since the bank runs of the Great Depression in the 1930s. This crisis has directly afflicted the thrift industry but, because of federal deposit insurance, also has had immediate effects on all of us as taxpayers. The thrift crisis probably was *the* economic story of the 1980s, and it certainly stands out as at least *one* of the top continuing stories of the 1990s. In this chapter, we explore the nature of this crisis—how it unfolded, what caused it, what has been done in an effort to bring it to a conclusion, and what may be its possible implications for the future.[1]

SAVINGS ASSOCIATIONS FROM 1816 TO 1951

In Chapter 6, we provided a very brief history of the beginnings of savings associations—savings banks and savings and loan associations (S&Ls)—in the United States. As we discussed there, savings banks began in 1816 as mutual organizations dedicated to providing a means for small savers to accumulate some of their wealth as shares in the savings bank. Savings and loan associations originated in 1831. They also began primarily as mutual institutions, and most were ''building and loan associations'' that pooled the savings of individuals to provide members with home mortgage loans.

---

[1] Although all the readings cited in our chapter references assisted us in the preparation of this chapter, much of our discussion is based on James Barth's *The Great Savings and Loan Debacle* (Washington, D.C.: American Enterprise Institute Press, 1991) and on Lawrence J. White's *The S&L Debacle: Public Policy Lessons for Bank and Thrift Regulation* (New York: Oxford University Press, 1991).

THE CONVERGENCE OF S&Ls AND MOST SAVINGS BANKS

In this chapter, we shall not separately distinguish between savings banks and savings and loan associations. Before the 1980s, however, the difference between the two groups of institutions was more clear-cut. Savings banks, which largely were confined to the northeastern and northwestern portions of the United States, provided a variety of financial services that included some mortgage lending, while savings and loan associations were much more involved in such lending.

By the 1980s, however, savings banks had largely separated *themselves* into two groupings. One group began to look more like commercial banks. This group obtained national charters and chose to be insured and regulated by the FDIC; members of this group now are insured by the FDIC's Bank Insurance Fund (BIF), along with commercial banks. The other group of savings banks decided to obtain FSLIC ''savings bank'' charters and to be insured by the FSLIC along with savings and loan associations. This latter group composed the larger number of savings banks, and members of this group became much more like savings and loan associations. They now are insured by the Savings Association Insurance Fund (SAIF) within the FDIC.

Because this latter group of savings banks is so similar to savings and loan associations, we shall follow common practice by referring to both savings and loan associations and savings banks broadly as either *savings associations* or as *S&Ls.* We shall also follow the common, albeit imprecise, practice of referring to the crisis that has afflicted S&Ls as the *thrift crisis.* It is important to keep in mind, however, that one important set of thrift institutions, the credit union industry, so far has not experienced the problems of savings associations.

FEDERAL INVOLVEMENT: 1932 TO 1950

S&Ls grew steadily through the 1920s. The severe decline in real estate values during the Great Depression years seriously damaged the S&L industry, however. Many mortgage borrowers became delinquent in their payments, but even if the S&Ls foreclosed on these members, the market values of the mortgaged houses had fallen to levels far below the amounts of the original loans. In conjunction with the savings withdrawals of members and the commercial banking collapse, this decline in the housing market hastened the failure of large numbers of S&Ls. By the early part of the 1930s, then, the S&L industry was very nearly the basket case that commercial banking had become.

The housing crisis and impending thrift industry collapse induced the federal government to enact a series of sweeping changes in the federal government's role in housing and thrift-related activities. In 1932, Congress enacted the *Federal Home Loan Bank Act,* which created twelve Federal Home Loan Banks (FHLBs)—which it called the Federal Home Loan Bank System—under the supervision of a three-member Federal Home Loan Bank Board (FHLBB). The purpose of the FHLBs was to provide emergency funding for S&Ls during periods of economic downturn and credit disruptions such as those recently experienced at the onset of the Great Depression.

In 1933, Congress passed the *Home Owners' Loan Act (HOLA),* which for the first time established a federal S&L charter, which was issued by the FHLBB. HOLA required that federal S&Ls be mutual institutions and that they provide services only to customers in local communities; like commercial banks, S&Ls were not granted authority to branch beyond boundaries laid out in state laws.

Then, in 1934, Congress enacted the *National Housing Act.* As we discussed in the last chapter, this legislation authorized creation of the Federal Savings and Loan Insurance Corporation (FSLIC). The FSLIC, which was administered by the FHLBB, provided deposit insurance for member thrift institutions. The law required that all federally chartered S&Ls be members of the FSLIC and permitted state-chartered S&Ls to join as well, as long as they submitted themselves to FHLBB oversight.

Because of the services and subsidies provided under the terms of the FHLB Act of 1932, the HOLA of 1933, and the National Housing Act of 1934, many S&Ls were induced to convert to national charters. Furthermore, much of the S&L industry was rejuvenated. By 1955—that is, just over two decades after their industry was on the brink of collapse—S&Ls roughly had tripled their relative share of holdings of financial assets as compared with commercial banks and other financial institutions.

PRELUDE TO CRISIS: 1951–1978

Although it was not apparent to citizens and policy makers at the time, the federal involvement in the S&L industry that was initiated in the 1930s and well in place by the early 1950s had laid the groundwork for the crisis of the 1980s and 1990s. The intervening period of the 1950s, 1960s, and 1970s can, in retrospect, be seen as a gathering together of forces that simultaneously were unleashed to induce the thrift catastrophe that has dominated our recent history.

THE 1950s

For the S&L industry, the year 1951 is notable, as we shall explore in more detail below, because of a significant *tax change* that Congress enacted. The *Revenue Act of 1951* ended a tax-exempt status that S&Ls had enjoyed since their founding, but it laid out a set of special tax deductions for S&Ls. This 1951 tax law change was followed by another in 1962, when Congress reduced the maximum allowable bad debt reduction to 60 percent of taxable income, *provided* that S&Ls hold at least 82 percent of their assets in forms including cash, U.S. government securities, and qualifying mortgage loans.

These tax changes provided S&Ls with a significant financial incentive to concentrate solely on mortgage lending. Of course, S&Ls had traditionally devoted themselves primarily to mortgage-related activities, the FHLB Act and other laws enacted by Congress in the 1930s to stabilize housing markets had provided further inducements to concentrate on this line of business, and the FHLBB had placed direct regulatory restrictions on the amount of nonmortgage activities of federally chartered S&Ls. Nevertheless, this was the first of several tax law changes that followed that were to influence considerably the decisions of *all* S&L managers.

THE 1960s

The 1960s marked the beginning of the thrift industry unraveling that degenerated into the full-fledged thrift crisis two decades later. A key development of the 1960s was growing competition between S&Ls and commercial banks. Although these depository institutions continued to specialize in different areas on the asset side of their balance sheet, they both needed deposit funds to continue growing. Banks, which traditionally had relied on their base of deposits from firms, began to compete aggressively for deposits of households. These deposits, of course, were the foundation of funding for S&Ls.

In addition, while the United States' involvement in the Vietnam conflict in the 1960s grabbed most attention on the political front, the 1960s also saw important economic changes. One of these was a gradual increase in short-term market interest rates. Deposit rates rose faster than mortgage rates, and many thrifts began to show signs of financial stress, though few were in jeopardy of failing.

Congress responded to the narrowing of interest rate spreads at S&Ls with direct action: the *Interest Rate Adjustment Act of 1966.* For the first time, legislation placed legal limits on the interest rates that S&Ls could pay on their savings deposits. Effectively, this act applied the Glass-Steagall ceilings on commercial bank deposit rates to the thrift industry, although it permitted S&Ls to pay three-fourths of 1 percent more on deposits than banks could pay—to ''compensate'' for the fact that Congress did not permit S&Ls to offer the full range of services, such as checking accounts or consumer or commercial loans, that it permitted commercial banks to provide. Congress later reduced this interest differential in the deposit rate ceilings applied to S&Ls to one-half of 1 percent in 1970 and to one-fourth of 1 percent in 1973.

GROWING TURBULENCE: 1970–1978

Congress hoped, through passage of the 1966 Interest Rate Adjustment Act, to eliminate the ''interest squeeze'' problem faced by S&Ls. Indeed, this measure was a ''Band-Aid'' that protected S&Ls for about a decade. The U.S. Treasury also helped out in 1970 by raising the minimum denomination of a Treasury bill from $1,000 to $10,000, making it impossible for a typical ''small saver'' to hold Treasury bills rather than bank or thrift institution deposits.

People can be surprisingly innovative, however, when faced with governmental regulations. A key innovation of the early 1970s, which we discussed briefly in Chapter 5, was the money market mutual fund (MMMF). These funds, which first appeared in 1972, offered individuals a means of *pooling* their savings; although individual small savers alone might not be able to purchase Treasury bills or other high-denomination financial instruments that paid unregulated interest rates, many savers together could do so through MMMFs.

Until the late 1970s, however, MMMF growth was fairly low, because until then market interest rates were only significantly above the S&L and bank ceiling deposit rates for brief periods. For instance, from 1970 until June 1973 the ceiling deposit rate for thrift passbook savings accounts was 5.0 percent; during the same interval the average interest rate on 3-month Treasury bills was 4.96 percent. MMMF assets were only about $100 million by the end of this period.

Nevertheless, thrifts began to become concerned that they would lose deposits if market interest rates continued to move upward. In partial response, NOW accounts—interest-bearing checking accounts intended to compete with the non-interest-bearing demand deposits issued by commercial banks—were introduced by a Massachusetts thrift in 1972. Thrifts in six other northeastern states adopted this idea before Congress put a temporary halt on the further spread of NOW accounts.

In July 1973, the ceiling on thrift deposit rates was increased to 5.25 percent; regulations kept it at that level until June 1979. From 1974 through 1978, however, the average rate on 3-month Treasury bills was equal to 7.80 percent, or 2.55 percent above the ceiling on S&L deposit rates. By the end of 1978, MMMF assets had grown to $9.5 *billion,* and it was clear that unless something changed, thrift depositors would be moving their funds to MMMFs in droves.

Therefore, in June 1978 the FHLBB permitted S&Ls to offer interest rates that were tied to the Treasury bill rate on 6-month certificates of deposit with denominations greater than $10,000. (The Federal Reserve also allowed commercial banks to offer the certificates as well.) Although these ''money market certificates'' became popular, they still did not permit savers with deposits under $10,000 to earn market interest rates. Indeed, the average deposit at an S&L at this time was less than $5,000, and so the "average" saver remained unable to earn market rates of interest *unless* he or she transferred savings to MMMFs.

BEGINNINGS OF THE THRIFT MELTDOWN: 1979–1982

The year 1979 marked the beginning of the end for some thrifts, although, as we shall see, the true thrift disaster occurred in the early 1980s. The reason that hard times for the thrifts began in 1979 was that market interest rates began to rise rapidly in that year. We shall see *why* this happened in Chapter 25. What is important to recognize at this point are the *consequences* of this interest rate increase, which for the thrift industry couldn't have come at a worse time.

THE INTEREST RATE RUN-UP AS THE PRELUDE TO THE THRIFT MELTDOWN

At the end of 1978, the interest rate on 3-month Treasury bills was just over 9 percent; by the end of 1980 it had climbed to nearly 16 percent. Thrifts that had lobbied hard in 1978 for the right to pay market interest rates on money market certificates suddenly found that the rates they were paying on those certificates periodically exceeded the market interest rates on new mortgage loans—they were forced to pay more for deposits than they were making by issuing new mortgages! In addition, of course, the S&Ls were continuing to earn much lower interest rates on old mortgage loans. This was an intolerable situation for these institutions.

It was made worse by the continued loss of depositors. From the end of 1978 until the end of 1980, MMMF assets grew more than fourfold, from $9.5 billion to $42.9 billion. As MMMFs expanded, S&Ls courted disaster. By the middle of 1980 over a third of all FSLIC-insured thrifts, with over a third of all thrift assets, were reporting losses. It was clear that something drastic had to be done.

Intended Reforms of the 1980s   Congress had not stood by idly during this time. Work on legislation to reform the banking and thrift industries had begun as early as 1976, and the pace of Congress quickened noticeably by the beginning of 1979. Finally, in 1980, Congress passed the *Depository Institutions Deregulation and Monetary Control Act (DIDMCA)*. We discussed the broad features of this legislation in Chapter 10; we concentrate here on what it did specifically for—and to—the thrift industry.

First, the DIDMCA for the first time permitted thrifts to offer adjustable-rate mortgages, so that they could in the future protect themselves from the danger of paying deposit rates that exceeded the mortgage loan rates they earned. Second, the legislation set up a timetable for gradual elimination of all deposit rate ceilings, to be accomplished in phases ending in early 1986. Third, the DIDMCA gave thrifts the power to offer trust and other traditional "banking" services. Finally, it authorized thrifts to expand their legal portfolio of assets to include consumer loans and commercial paper (up to a limit of 20 percent of total assets).

Congress intended for all these changes to make thrifts more flexible and more competitive with commercial banks and other financial institutions, such as MMMFs. Of course, these changes could not be implemented by the FHLBB and the thrifts overnight; by the end of 1981, in fact, nearly 85 percent of all FSLIC-insured thrifts, which held over 90 percent of the assets of the industry, were reporting losses. Furthermore, MMMF assets increased by nearly *sixfold* between the end of 1979 and the end of 1981, from $42.9 billion to $236.3 billion.

Recognizing that the S&L problem was not solved by the DIDMCA alone, however, Congress in 1982 passed the *Garn–St Germain Act.* This act had four highly publicized provisions that affected the thrift industry. One was that it, for the first time, authorized thrift institutions to make secured or unsecured *commercial* loans (including holdings of high-yield, high-risk *"junk bonds"* issued by firms in lieu of borrowing directly from commercial banks), up to a limit of 11 percent of total assets. A second provision raised the permitted amount of S&L consumer lending to up to 30 percent of assets. A third granted S&Ls the authority to make commercial real estate loans, up to a maximum of 40 percent of their assets. Fourth, the act created money market deposit accounts (MMDAs)—deposit accounts with limited transfer capability for depositors, no interest rate ceiling, and no reserve requirements.

Evidence that the reforms in the DIDMCA and Garn–St Germain Act might have helped seemed to appear almost instantaneously. MMMF funds *shrank* during 1983 and did not attain their previous asset magnitude again until the end of 1985. While the S&L industry as a whole continued to post losses in 1983, only a third of S&Ls were still in the loss category. Indeed, in 1983 the industry appeared poised for a real rebound.

Reforms, or Recipes for Disaster?   *Not* widely recognized by any but the most perceptive of observers at the time, however, were some hidden problems in the 1980 and 1982 laws. Before 1980 the minimum net worth (capital) requirement for FSLIC-insured thrift institutions was 5 percent. The DIDMCA changed that requirement to a range of 3 percent to 6 percent, but left it up to the FHLBB to set the specific level. Nevertheless, whenever Congress sets a lower range that lies below current standards, that is a signal that it wishes a regulator to lower its standards. The FHLBB took the hint, lowering the thrift net worth requirement to 4 percent in 1980 and to 3 percent in 1982.

It did so even as it switched to a new set of accounting principles. These were the less demanding *regulatory accounting principles (RAP)* that we discussed in the last chapter. Naturally, many thrifts took advantage of this change to lower their net worth relative to assets to levels just consistent with the regulations—and well below those specified by the regulations if their assets had been measured using *generally accepted accounting principles (GAAP)* or market-valued accounting approaches.

In addition, the Garn–St Germain Act of 1982 authorized the FHLBB to issue FSLIC promissory notes to thrift institutions in exchange for **net worth certificates.** Under this "gimmick," the thrift could count the FSLIC note as an asset and the net worth certificate as part of its net worth. In effect, the FHLBB, at the urging of Congress, handed these thrifts FSLIC cash guarantees without adding any additional safeguards for the FSLIC deposit insurance fund.

The FHLBB expanded the danger to the FSLIC even further by encouraging solvent S&Ls to acquire insolvent S&Ls in *purchase and assumption* transactions of the type discussed in the last chapter. As we saw there, these transactions often are less expensive for deposit insurance funds, because healthy institutions can assume many of the insolvent institution's assets rather than the government insurer's incurring the cost of disposing of those assets one by one. In yet another accounting gimmick, however, the FHLBB added another twist to the standard purchase and assumption transactions by permitting the acquiring thrifts in these transactions to create special **goodwill** assets. Goodwill is an accounting value of a firm's "going-concern" or "franchise" value that is commonly used under GAAP, but the FHLBB expanded the concept so that it in most cases made up the difference between the insolvent thrift's assets and liabilities—that is, the FHLBB effectively gave acquiring thrifts more cash guarantees to hold assets, guarantees backed by the FSLIC deposit insurance fund.

THE GREAT S&L DISASTER

By 1983, the thrift industry as a whole was nearly back on its feet, although most thrifts were scrambling to regain the ground they had lost in the previous five years. A turnaround was in the offing—and indeed was in progress—and no one in the thrift industry wanted to be left behind.

SOME NONREGULATORY REASONS FOR THE RECOVERY

Although members of Congress were quick to seize credit for the thrift recovery, other forces were at work as well. One of these, it turned out, was an earlier piece of legislation, the *Economic Recovery Tax Act* of 1981. This law shortened the tax depreciation periods for real estate, making real estate a much more valuable asset after taxes than it had been previously. The legislation created what Congress had hoped—a real estate boom that kicked into high gear in 1983. As the main traditional issuers of mortgages, and now that Congress had freed up many old restrictions, savings and loans stood to benefit significantly from this boom in residential and commercial real estate.

Simultaneously, world oil prices rose in the early 1980s. This was particularly beneficial for thrifts in the southwestern part of the United States. As oil prices increased just as the tax law changes made real estate a more attractive investment—and as a population shift toward that part of the country was in progress—the thrift industry suddenly became attractive to anyone in southwestern states who had the funds to invest.

Assets of the U.S. thrift industry grew by over *18 percent* alone in 1983, as compared with annual growth rates just over 7 percent in the previous three years; in 1984 total thrift assets increased again by almost 20 percent. In the southwestern states, thrift growth was even more pronounced. Thrift assets in California grew by 28 percent in 1983 and over 29 percent in 1984; in Texas they increased by over 33 percent in 1983 and by 38 percent in 1984; in Arizona they grew by over 18 percent in 1983 and by almost *47 percent* in 1984.

There was also an increase in the number of new thrift applications approved by the FHLBB to be insured by the FSLIC. The FHLBB approved 47 new thrifts in 1983 and 133 more in 1984. By 1985, for the first time since 1966, the number of FSLIC-insured thrift institutions in the United States actually increased. This was quite a turnaround for an industry that just a few years before had been on the brink of destruction. Not only were old thrifts doing better, but now new people wanted into the business!

In addition, some of the old hands in the thrift business also wanted to play by new rules. During 1983, 1984, and 1985, 257 FSLIC-insured thrift institutions converted from mutual to stock forms of ownership—more than three times the number of such conversions during the previous three years. Many of these conversions involved new people entering the thrift business, but some were old people wishing to make profitable investments. Clearly, both groups perceived that the thrift industry might be a good bet for high and, in light of deposit insurance, safe profits that under a stock ownership structure could be retained by the owners of S&L stock rather than being distributed to depositors.

THE END OF THE THRIFT RECOVERY AND THE ONSET OF THE CRISIS

The thrift recovery of 1983 to 1985 ended nearly as quickly as it occurred. In many ways, its waxing and waning phases were reminiscent of an old-fashioned gold rush, such as the great Alaskan gold rush just before the turn of the twentieth century. In a gold rush, entrepreneurs typically hurry to the location of new-found gold, mine every profitable ounce, and depart the region, leaving ghost towns in their wake.

The foundation laid by Congress and the FHLBB in 1980 through 1982 formed the catalyst for the waxing phase of the thrift gold rush of 1983 through 1985. The Economic Recovery Tax Act of 1981, the subsequent economic recovery from a severe recession, and the simultaneous rise in oil prices in the early part of the 1980s provided the impetus for the significant growth observed in the thrift industry from 1983 to 1985.

Like many gold rushes, however, this apparent rejuvenation of the thrift industry was a flash-in-the-pan recovery based on short-term factors. In 1984, the Treasury revamped its tax code's treatment of real estate depreciation; as part of its alterations, it lengthened the depreciation period for real estate, which caused the after-tax value of real estate to fall. Furthermore, in 1985 and 1986 oil prices fell considerably, which naturally caused significant economic distress for the southwestern part of the United States—exactly the region where the greatest S&L growth had just occurred.

It did not take long for the waning phase of the thrift gold rush to set in, or for many thrifts to take on aspects not unlike the abandoned ghost towns of gold-rush days. Thrifts began to go under, and quickly. The scope of the disaster was staggering. Even under the permissive RAP measurements, 130 thrifts had become insolvent by the end of 1985; 255 more joined this category in 1986, and 351 more joined those in 1987. The RAP standards, of course, disguised the true scope of the mess. Even as an *apparent* thrift recovery was proceeding in 1983, 1984, and 1985, well over a thousand more thrifts became insolvent under more stringent accounting standards. Hundreds more joined this category after 1985.

We shall discuss the specific numbers and dollar amounts involved in more detail later on in the chapter. First, however, we must consider what brought about this collapse.

WHAT ACTUALLY CAUSED THE THRIFT CRISIS?

We can identify six sets of factors that ''caused'' the savings and loan crisis. We discuss each in turn. In the following section, we seek to identify which of these factors may have been most important.

Portfolio Inflexibility and Managerial Inexperience   Since their beginnings in 1831, savings and loan associations have specialized in using funds from savings deposits for home mortgage lending. Hence, S&Ls initially specialized in mortgage lending as a matter of choice, but after the 1930s they also did so either because of explicit regulations or because of strong tax incentives.

Furthermore, S&Ls overspecialized in producing mortgage loans with fixed interest rates. This exposed them to significant *interest rate risk*. If interest rates on their short-term liabilities—the savings deposits they issued—were to decline, S&Ls stood to gain, but if interest rates on their short-term liabilities were to rise—as occurred in 1979–1982— they could, and did, lose heavily.

Adjustable-rate mortgages largely would have permitted S&Ls to hedge against interest rate risk in their mortgage lending. This was recognized throughout the 1970s, and the FHLBB several times proposed legal changes allowing S&Ls to offer adjustable-rate mortgages. Congress always balked, however, because of concerns that S&Ls would take advantage of loan consumers. Only when the industry was on the verge of collapse in 1980 did Congress for the first time authorize adjustable-rate mortgages—by which time much damage already had been done.

It took a while for the new mortgages to catch on with S&L managers and with the public. It took much less time for S&L managers to begin using their abilities to make consumer and commercial loans and to hold forms of commercial paper. Thrift managers felt the need to help their institutions recover from their precarious positions, but many lacked experience in these lines of business. As a result, many made mistakes in judgment in their lending decisions, and these mistakes turned out to be very costly.

The High and Variable Interest Rates of 1979–1982   Undeniably, the significant run-up in interest rates and unusual variability of interest rates at the end of the 1970s and beginning of the 1980s created the initial set of conditions that led to the S&L industry collapse in the mid-1980s. Given that S&Ls specialized in offering long-term, fixed-rate mortgage loans while issuing short-term, variable-rate deposit liabilities, these high and variable interest rates created conditions through which very few of these institutions could have survived for long.

This period of high and volatile interest rates lasted just over three years. In some ways, that does not seem long, but for many S&L managers it surely must have seemed an eternity. It was certainly long enough to place many S&Ls in jeopardy and to give their managers incentives to try to grow out of the problems quickly when given the chance, which is exactly what many attempted to do.

Financial Deregulation and Increased Competition   Congress made a concerted effort in the early 1980s to deregulate depository institutions, in hopes that markets for financial services would become more competitive. As we discussed in Chapter 11, a key feature of competition is the freedom of firms to enter—or to *exit*—an industry. One way that firms exit an industry is through *failure*. In the face of stiff competition, some firms simply cannot survive. They earn negative profits and must leave the industry.

Following the significant deregulation of depository institutions brought about through the DIDMCA and the Garn–St Germain Act, it was inevitable that thrift and bank failure rates would increase somewhat. This was especially true in light of the development of new computer technologies coincident with the financial deregulation of the early 1980s. These technological developments made highly labor-intensive depository institutions good candidates for extinction in the highly competitive financial services industry. Only those institutions best able to implement these new technologies at the lowest possible cost would have been able to remain competitive in the long run. Those that could not do this were certain to remain too labor-intensive, and some were certain to fail.

Changes in Other External Factors   Two separate factors influencing the perform- ance of the S&L industry were tax law changes and oil prices. Without a doubt, these external factors played key roles in the thrift crisis.

Changes in the tax code in the 1950s and 1960s helped induce S&Ls to become even more heavily involved in mortgage lending than they might have become otherwise. Further changes in tax laws in the 1980s then contributed considerably to the housing boom of the early 1980s and the subsequent housing bust in the mid-1980s.

Adding to the housing market's ups and downs of the 1980s were the wide variations in oil prices during the period. When the after-tax value of real estate climbed nationwide from 1982 to 1985, the effect in the southwestern part of the United States was magnified by generally rising oil prices that caused a regional economic boom. Likewise, when the after-tax value of real estate generally declined somewhat beginning in 1985, the negative effect this had on the values of loans made by thrifts in the southwestern states was magnified by the general decline in that region's economy caused by a fall in oil prices.

Fraud   Fraudulent activities undeniably contributed to the scope of the S&L mess. Several thrift managers and owners were indicted and convicted of breaking laws in their dealings. Estimates about how widespread S&L fraud was during the 1980s vary considerably, however. Estimates of the extent of fraudulent activities in failed S&Ls during the 1980s have ranged anywhere from 3 percent of all S&L failures to 50 percent of all failures.

What accounts for such a wide range of fraud estimates? For one thing, it is difficult to know whether fraud has occurred until thrift owners and managers actually are convicted of crimes. Estimates of fraudulent activities, therefore, really amount to guesses about what judgments might be reached by courts of law.

Moral Hazard   Almost certainly a greater contributor to the crisis than fraud was the *moral hazard problem.* Recall from the last chapter the nature of this problem: By insuring bank deposits, the government puts its faith in the "moral character" of the managers of the depository institutions it insures, which exposes the government's insurance system to the hazard that the depository institution managers will undertake riskier actions than they would otherwise. While fraud is an extreme outcome of the moral hazard problem, the problem of moral hazard can involve risky practices that are entirely legal and legitimate; the difficulty is simply that such practices have a greater likelihood of causing the insured institution to fail.

In the absence of deposit insurance, households and firms would have strong incentives to look out for their own best interests in their dealings with depository institutions. They would be much more likely to pay attention to their depository institution's financial statements; indeed, depositors whose life savings were at a particular bank or thrift would be likely to demand regular reports on the depository institution's condition. In addition, households and firms would be more likely to hold their funds on deposit at more than one depository institution, in case one of them were to fail.

The availability of federal deposit insurance, however, reduces the incentive for households and firms to monitor depository institutions or to diversify their deposits across institutions. Why should they be as cautious as they otherwise might be, when the government is now responsible? Furthermore, if they can hold more than one federally insured deposit in a single depository institution, why should they diversify their deposit holdings as fully as they might otherwise?

From the perspective of S&L managers, the moral hazard problem of deposit insurance was particularly acute. As long as deposit insurance protected the S&Ls' depositors, these managers could feel confident that their attempts to "go for the gold" would have few adverse effects on their institutions' depositors. Even George Bailey, the hero in *It's a Wonderful Life*, might have been tempted to make riskier investments in this environment.

Almost certainly, the actions of Congress and thrift regulators in the early 1980s magnified the scope of the moral hazard problem. All the financial deregulation that occurred assuredly increased the potential size and number of moral hazard difficulties. This deregulation, however, was not accompanied by greater *safety and soundness regulation* to reduce the threat of losses stemming from these problems. If anything, the force of safety and soundness regulation decreased in the early 1980s, especially when the FHLBB, at the urging of Congress, adopted RAP and reduced thrift capital requirements.

Symptomatic of the moral hazard was the increased prevalence of so-called junk bonds in the asset portfolios of many S&Ls. These longer-term, high-yield bonds issued by firms whose risks were rated as significant in financial markets were very attractive to S&Ls seeking quick profits. Their high risk, however, was reflected in the volatility of their yields.

Another symptom of moral hazard problems was the increased use of **brokered deposits** by thrift institutions. Deposit brokers, which include several respected Wall Street securities companies, collect funds from individual investors into $100,000 "bundles" that they sell to banks and S&Ls as deposits in exchange for a fee. The size of the bundle is no accident—it is exactly the limit on deposit insurance for an individual account. The deposit broker keeps track of each investor's share of the total bundle and, for a fee, transfers the interest return from the deposit to the original investors. Although this activity is legal, it helped to fuel the growth of the S&L industry and to expand the size of the industry's pool of insured deposits.

WHAT WAS THE SINGLE MOST IMPORTANT FACTOR IN THE CRISIS?

With so many different causal factors to choose from, it seems somewhat risky for us to name the most important factor that caused the thrift crisis. Certainly, plenty of people have pointed fingers of blame at one another as the crisis has unfolded. Nevertheless, nearly all academic observers and former policy makers have stressed one factor as the most important of all those listed above: the *moral hazard problem caused by the structure of federal deposit insurance.*

Recall, as discussed in the previous chapter, that Congress since 1934 has required fixed deposit insurance premiums for all federally insured depository institutions. In addition, recall that Congress never set these premiums at levels that a private insurer would have calculated. In fact, from the beginning, Congress set deposit insurance at levels that were too low—though there probably were some periods in the 1950s and 1960s in which it is arguable that the premiums were too high. Low, fixed deposit insurance premiums led to a significant moral hazard problem for the federal deposit insurance system. The premiums that S&Ls paid for deposit insurance did not vary with the riskiness of their investments, and so there was no incentive for S&L managers—or S&L depositors—to seek to lower that risk. All risk was assumed by the government as deposit insurer.

Certainly, the structure of federal deposit insurance was not the single cause of the thrift mess; all the factors discussed above came together at one time to produce a full-blown crisis. Nonetheless, it is undeniable that the single common element that was the catalyst for the crisis was the federal deposit insurance system.

THE FINANCIAL INSTITUTIONS REFORM, RECOVERY, AND ENFORCEMENT ACT OF 1989

We emphasized the implications of the *Financial Institutions Reform, Recovery, and Enforcement Act (FIRREA) of 1989* for commercial banks in Chapter 10. Here, we consider its implications for thrift institutions, which were in fact the main factors that motivated its passage by Congress. We begin by providing background on the evolution of the thrift crisis in the years immediately before its passage. We then outline the essential provisions of the legislation and consider how much the thrift crisis has cost—and who has been asked to pay for it.

REGULATORY ACTION AND INACTION BEFORE PASSAGE OF FIRREA

By 1985, it had become clear to all concerned that a thrift industry crisis was under way. It also had become apparent that the FSLIC's insurance fund was struggling to maintain its solvency. At the end of 1985, the fund had a $4.5 billion surplus, but by the end of 1986 that surplus had *fallen* by over 50 percent, to $1.9 billion. The amount of insured deposits at FSLIC-insured thrifts, in contrast, was more than $780 billion at the end of 1985, but had *grown* by over 5 percent by the end of 1986, to nearly $824 billion.

Last-Ditch Efforts to Halt the Crisis   Several regulatory changes were made to try to halt—or at least slow down—the crisis. In 1985, the FHLBB imposed a special deposit insurance premium surcharge that raised the thrift deposit insurance premium by 150 percent. It also enacted regulations to contain the annual growth rates of thrift institutions that were not meeting the FHLBB's capital requirements, and in the fall of 1986 the FHLBB began a policy of gradually phasing in higher capital requirements, from 3 percent to an eventual "target requirement" of 6 percent (the maximum allowed by law). In 1985 the FHLBB also began a **Management Consignment Program,** under which incumbent managers of insolvent thrifts were removed and replaced by a "consigned" group of managers from other thrifts in the same region.

During 1986 the FHLBB also increased the size of its examination and supervision staff by 50 percent, and it increased it by another 14 percent over the following two years. Furthermore, in the spring of 1987 the FHLBB began a gradual phasing-out of its RAP techniques for evaluating the worth of assets, capital, and income of thrifts, in favor of a return to GAAP procedures.

Although these measures all helped significantly to slow the crisis, they did not stop it. The FHLBB and some members of Congress made efforts during 1986 to arrange for the FHLBB to take out emergency loans of up to $15 billion from the federal government so that the FHLBB could rebuild the FSLIC insurance fund and close down currently insolvent thrift institutions. Politics entered the story, however, when operators of thrift institutions (especially in Texas) complained to their representatives in Congress (and particularly to a Texas representative, James Wright, who shortly would become Speaker of the House of Representatives) that FHLBB regulators were being overly harsh in their new policies and that more funds for the FSLIC would "unfairly" close down many thrifts. Wright responded by using his political power to hold up congressional progress on the FSLIC rescue plan.

Zombie Thrifts   As a result, 1986 was a period in which the FHLBB undertook much examination of thrifts but lacked the resources to close them down or merge them with healthier acquirers. These insolvent, *but still open,* S&Ls became known as **zombie thrifts.** For those of you who have never seen a standard "B" horror movie, a "zombie"—a word derived from the name of a voodoo snake god—is a term for a mythical instance in which a voodoo spell imparts new, artificial life to a previously dead body. The term was descriptive, then, of these open but technically insolvent thrifts: They were financially dead, but through regulatory inaction they continued to live. Hundreds of these zombie thrifts continued to operate from 1985 through 1987.

Zombie thrifts also continued to run losses, which meant that the size of the liability faced by the FSLIC's deposit insurance fund continued to mount. After all, additional losses incurred by zombie thrifts were simply dollars that no longer would be available for thrift owners to reimburse insured depositors—and that, therefore, would have to be paid by the FSLIC's insurance fund.

The Day of Reckoning   Finally, in February of 1987, the federal government's General Accounting Office declared that the FSLIC was insolvent by as much as $6 billion. On February 25, 1987, the *Wall Street Journal* ran a page-3 story on the FSLIC deficit in which it quoted one member of the House Banking Committee as saying, "This shows the FSLIC is in even worse shape than our nightmares." In perhaps one of the truly classic congressional understatements, he continued, "It means we have to do something rather soon to help them." The same story also quoted the new House Speaker James Wright as saying, "I anticipate that the Banking Committee will report out an FSLIC bill the first half of March. It [the appropriated dollar amount] will be substantially less than what the administration asked for."

It turned out that the House Speaker was right. The final bill, which Congress passed in late July of 1987, authorized $10.825 billion in total FHLBB borrowing, but with a $3.75 billion annual borrowing cap. The new legislation also contained a "forbearance provision," under which the FHLBB was instructed to permit thrifts with extremely low net worth ratios (as low as 0.5 percent of liabilities) to continue to operate, as long as these thrifts met "good-faith" tests. Essentially, Congress seems at this point to have been concerned that the FHLBB might be too harsh with thrifts, and so it effectively authorized closure of only the worst of the zombie cases.

In 1987, a total of 351 FSLIC-insured thrifts were insolvent under RAP, and many more were insolvent under GAAP. Of the 351 RAP-insolvent thrifts, 109 were in the state of Texas; these Texas thrifts alone had over $39 billion in assets, or nearly 40 percent of the total of $99 billion in assets of all the RAP-insolvent thrifts in the United States. During 1988, the FHLBB used its new funding authority to **resolve**—close or otherwise dispose of—205 thrifts at an estimated cost to the FSLIC of nearly $30 billion. Of these 1988 *thrift resolutions,* 81 were Texas thrifts, and the FSLIC's cost of closing these thrifts amounted to more than $18 billion.

George Bush was elected to the presidency in 1988 and took office in January 1989. The Bush administration announced a new thrift program on Febuary 6, 1989, and on February 7 the *Wall Street Journal* ran a front-page story headlined, "Dinosaur Thrifts: The Bush Bailout Plan for Savings and Loans Could Spell Extinction." The administration's initial plan called for funding of $50 billion borrowed through the sale of long-term government bonds. Under the proposed scheme, thrifts would pay the principal, and taxpayers would pay part of the annual interest on the debt. It called for about 350 more thrifts to be taken over by the government, incorporation of the previously independent FHLBB as a unit of the Treasury, higher deposit insurance premiums, and expenditures of $50 million by the Justice Department for criminal prosecutions of fraudulent activities by S&L owners and managers.

The administration formally proposed its bill to Congress in March of 1989. A full five months later, despite the obvious urgency of the situation—zombie thrifts were continuing to lose money in the meantime—Congress finally passed FIRREA, as the Bush bill became known. It retained essential features of the original bill in its main provisions.

MAIN PROVISIONS OF THE ACT

FIRREA had numerous provisions; the printed version of the act ran to 381 pages. Hence, we highlight only the key aspects of the legislation. We also concentrate on the provisions of the act that were most closely related to resolving the thrift crisis.

A New Regulatory Structure   FIRREA abolished the Federal Home Loan Bank Board. The act replaced the FHLBB with a new agency, the *Office of Thrift Supervision (OTS),* which is a bureau within the United States Treasury Department. Its structure and regulatory powers over federally insured thrifts are similar to those possessed by the Treasury's Office of the Comptroller of the Currency with respect to national commercial banks.

In some instances, however, the OTS's authority is limited. FIRREA gave the FDIC, which replaced the FSLIC as custodian of thrift insurance through the Savings Association Insurance Fund, ultimate authority to authorize enforcement actions against insolvent thrifts. The act also authorized the FDIC to terminate insurance for S&Ls even if the OTS objects. In addition, it added two directors to the board of the FDIC (the comptroller of the currency and the head of the OTS), which increased the board's size from three members to five.

FIRREA created a new independent agency, the *Federal Housing Finance Board,* to oversee the Federal Home Loan Bank system, which the act kept intact. This board has five directors, including the secretary of housing and urban development and four private individuals appointed by the President and confirmed by the Senate. FIRREA required that the FHLB system expand its funding for ''affordable housing'' through subsidized (below-market-interest) loans to thrifts engaged in mortgage lending for low- and moderate-income borrowers.

New Safety and Soundness Restrictions   FIRREA reversed the trend toward financial deregulation in the early 1980s by placing new legal limitations on S&L activities. The act specified that all nonmutual S&Ls are prohibited from holding high-yield, high-risk ''junk'' bonds. It repealed the Garn–St Germain limit on thrift commercial real estate loans of 40 percent of assets and replaced that limitation with a restriction that such lending be less than four times the capital of the institution.

FIRREA also created a new system of capital requirements for federally insured S&Ls, to be administered by the OTS. In addition, the act outlawed depository institutions that fail to meet capital adequacy standards from accepting any brokered deposits. Finally, the act toughened civil and criminal sanctions against fraudulent dealings by S&L owners and managers.

Funding the Resolution of Insolvent Thrifts   A key provision of FIRREA was authorizing the funding of continued thrift resolutions, which the FHLBB had placed on hold as all waited during 1989 for congressional passage of FIRREA. The act specified that funding for these resolutions was to be handled jointly by the Treasury Department and a new agency, the *Resolution Funding Corporation (RFC).*

FIRREA authorized the creation of yet another agency, the *Resolution Trust Corporation (RTC),* to oversee the actual resolution of thrift insolvencies, under day-to-day management by the FDIC. The RTC is headed by a five-member board that includes the secretary of the treasury, the Federal Reserve Board chairman, the secretary of housing and urban development, and two private individuals appointed by the President and confirmed by the Senate.

Largely through the borrowing arranged by the Treasury and the Resolution Funding Corporation, FIRREA authorized expenditures of $50 billion, based on the estimate at the time of a $40 billion cost for the RTC to dispose of old zombies and newly insolvent S&Ls. The additional $10 billion was earmarked to replenish the old bankrupt FSLIC fund, which was converted to the SAIF under the auspices of the FDIC.

Obviously, the ''alphabet soup'' of regulations changed significantly as a result of FIRREA. The FHLBB is a name of the past, although the FHLB system remains. The FSLIC also is gone. Now we have OTS, RFC, and RTC to keep straight. Indeed, those directly involved in these agencies also had trouble keeping all the names organized, which led the RTC to create a schematic diagram of all the interrelationships that FIRREA created, shown in Figure 13-1.

Figure 13-1 ➡
Functional Relationships Established by the Financial Institutions Reform, Recovery, and Enforcement Act of 1989.   [*Source*: Lawrence J. White, *The S&L Debacle* (New York: Oxford University Press), pp. 190–191.]

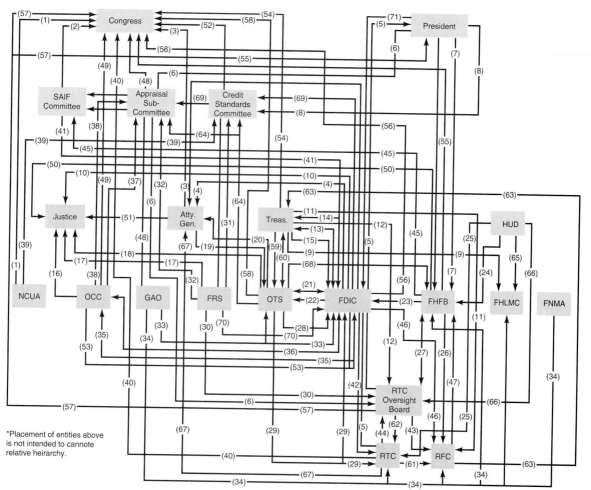

*Placement of entities above
is not intended to cannote
relative heirarchy.

1. Enforce. Report § 918
2. Committee Report § 226
3. Enforce. Report § 918
4. Bridge Bank Activity § 214
5. Annual Reports § 501
6. Approve 2 Board Members § 501
7. Approve 4 Board Members § 702
8. Appoint 6 Comm. Members § 1205
9. Purchase FHLMC Oblig. § 731
10. Crim. Refer. § 918
11. Backup Funds § 511
12. Serve on BOD § 501
13. Preserve Minority Shops § 308
14. Report on Rec/Conserv. Activity § 212;
    Can Borrow 5B with Treasury's OK § 218;
    Quarterly Operating Plans & Forecast § 220
15. Supplement SAIF Funds § 211; FSLIC Fund
    § 215
16. Crim. Refer. § 918
17. Crim. Refer. § 918
18. Crim. Refer. § 918
19. Bridge Bank Activity § 214
20. Info on Holding Co. § 301
21. Approve Corp Debt Activity 222; Preserve
    Minority Shops § 308
22. Notify of Ins. Trans. § 206; Collect Fees/
    Assessments § 208; § 301 New S & L Appl. §
    212; Enforce Action § 912; Subsidiary Activity
    § 220; Reporton Rec./Conserv. Action § 212

23. Help fund SAIF § 211
24. Serve on BOD § 702
25. Reimburse RTC Property § 501
26. Help Fund § 511
27. Dist. Bank Allocation § 511
28. Serve on BOD § 203
29. Appoint Rec./Conserv. § 212
30. Serve on BOD § 501
31. Comm. Member § 1205
32. Comm. Member § 1101
33. Ann. Audit § 301 Audit of BIF, SAIF, FSLIC
    Funds; Old FSLIC Cases Ann. § 219, 501
34. Ann. Audit § 501, 511, 702, 731
35. Report on Rec/Conserv. Activity   212
36. Civil Money Penalty Regs. § 907
37. Comm. Mem. § 1101
38. Comm. Mem. § 1205
39. Comm. Mem. § 1101, 1205
40. Reports and Appearances § 501
41. Report to BODs § 226
42. SAIF Funding Help § 211
43. Set Dir./Dispose Assets § 511
44. Reports/Funding Requests § 501
45. Rep. From Dist. Banks § 226
46. Send FSLIC Fund Money § 215
47. Issue Stocks § 511
48. Report Audit Findings
49. Enforce. Report § 918
50. Crim. Refer. § 918
51. Crim. Refer. § 918

52. Enforce. Report § 918; Bank Ser./Fee § 1002
53. Serve on BODs § 203
54. Ann. Reports on Fed. Financial Asst./Risk
    Assess. § 1403, 1404
55. Ann. Reports on Housing, Enforcement,
    Activities & Advances, Home Mortgage
    Disclosure Act § 721, 918, 1211 Title VII
56. Ann. Report on BIF, SAIF, FSLIC Funds §
    220; Enforce. Report § 918
57. Ann. Report on RFC Activity § 511
58. Ann. Report on Activity § 301; Enforce.
    Report § 918
59. Oversee § 301
60. Preserve Minority Shops § 308
61. Issue Cert. § 501; Pay Under Special Cond. §
    511
62. Oversee Activity § 501
63. Pay Back Assets on Dissolution § 511
64. Comm. Mem. § 1101; § 1205
65. Regulator § 731
66. Serve on BOD § 501
67. Bridge Bank Activity § 214
68. Request Advances § 714
69. Comm. Mem. § 1101; § 1205
70. Bank Holding Co. Approval § 208
71. Appoint 3 Board Members § 203

Source : RTC

HOW MUCH HAS IT ALL COST, AND WHO IS PAYING?

Even as Congress authorized $50 billion in fund-raising and expenditures to clean up the thrift mess, it became obvious that this amount would not be nearly enough to resolve insolvent thrifts. Even in early 1989 while FIRREA was being debated in Congress, the FHLBB estimated that 400 additional S&Ls would have to be closed at an estimated cost—in 1989 dollars—of $40 billion. Added to the earlier estimate of $40 billion in thrift cleanup costs, this produced a total of $80 billion as the estimated cost of the thrift bailout when Congress approved FIRREA.

Overly Rosy Projections Congress recognized that how much the thrift crisis actually would cost depended on a number of factors, many of which were beyond its control. For instance, the health of thrifts depended in large measure on the underlying performance of the economy. Particularly important, given the large thrift holdings of mortgages and mortgage-backed securities, was how well real estate values held up in the early 1990s. None of these factors could be known when Congress passed FIRREA in 1989, and so the Bush administration and Congress used *projections* of future events as guides in structuring the legislation.

Congress based FIRREA on unrealistically positive projections. Among other things, the legislation was based on an assumption that there would be no serious recession for ten years; the recessionary events of 1990 to 1992 quickly proved that projection incorrect. Furthermore, from its inception the plan that became FIRREA assumed that S&L deposits would *grow* by 7 percent each year; in fact, S&L deposits shrank by several billion dollars nearly every month from late 1989 through 1991, as shown in Figure 13-2.

All these projections, of course, turned out to be wrong. Nevertheless, Congress structured FIRREA around these overly optimistic estimates. Doing so lowered the estimated costs of the thrift cleanup as officially recognized in 1989. It did nothing, however, to stop the actual costs from mounting as all the projections failed to be realized.

Measuring the Cost of the Cleanup Before we consider estimates of the true cost of the thrift crisis, we must recognize all the problems involved in measuring the dollar amounts of the cost. Many cost estimates are not very clear, for instance, on *dates*. As we discussed earlier, the thrift problem first began to mushroom in 1985, and the FHLBB closed numerous thrifts between 1985 and 1987. Many official estimates of the total cost of the thrift crisis *exclude* these earlier thrift resolutions and thereby lower the projected total cost of the thrift cleanup.

Second, most estimates of the total cost of the thrift crisis ignore the fact that the United States Treasury has lost billions of dollars in *tax collections* as a result of the crisis. To induce healthy banks and thrifts to acquire insolvent thrifts, Congress and regulators granted them many tax breaks.

Third—and most important—many cost estimates that are quoted in the media ignore the time value of money. Recall from earlier chapters that to compare present values of funds with future values of funds, we must convert the future values into discounted present values of those funds by taking into account the role of the interest rate as a measure of the rate of exchange between the present and the future.

It is helpful to consider an example of misconceptions that can result if we fail to do this. A good example to think of is a state lottery. Many states now have so-called million-dollar lotteries. They claim to give away $1 million in prize money. In fact, they typically give away a *total* amount of $1 million over a period of several years. For example, the state lottery may award the winner $100,000 every year for 10 years. This is $1 million dollars, right? Well, not really. Suppose the interest rate over the next 10 years is 7 percent.

$ Billions

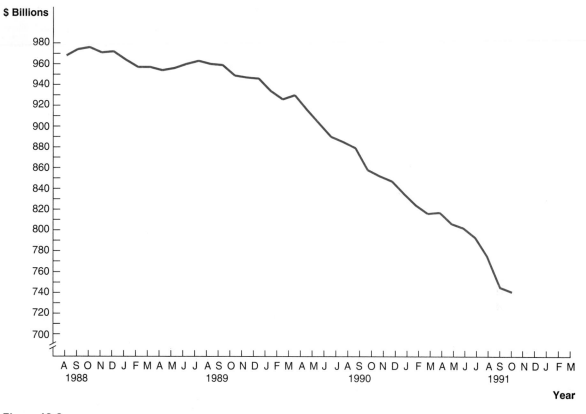

Figure 13-2
Deposits of SAIF-Insured Thrift Institutions. [*Source: Federal Reserve Bulletin.*]

Then the discounted present value of $100,000 installments received each of the next 10 years really is equal to just over $750,000. This would be the amount that the individual who wins a ''$1 million lottery'' has really won, looked at from the perspective of today. Hence, state lotteries, by failing to account for the time value of money, typically *overstate* the *present values* of the amounts that they actually award as prizes.

This has important implications for measuring the cost of the thrift crisis. To make the cost of the thrift cleanup sound more dramatic, the media often release the largest possible magnitudes, which are the amounts that fail to take into account the time value of money. Consider the following example that concerns the initial 1989 FIRREA allotment of $50 billion. The RFC borrowed that amount for repayment over a 30-year term. Some *undiscounted* estimates the media announced at that time then used computations of the amount of funds, plus interest, that the RFC would have to repay over that 30-year span. This amounted to a so-called cost estimate of $250 billion when, in fact, the $50 billion borrowed at that time was the appropriate discounted value of the cost—ignoring the fact that Congress and the administration probably underestimated the *true* discounted value of the cost.

The Estimated Cost Of course, $50 billion by itself is a very large sum that, as we have indicated, turned out to be too little to handle the thrift cleanup. By the early 1990s, in fact, it was clear that *much* more would be needed.

Various groups and individuals have made estimates of the cost of the thrift crisis. Early on, estimates differed considerably; even as late as 1988 there were present-value estimates that differed by as much as $100 billion. There has been more time for a full accounting of the costs to be made, however, and so most estimates now lie much closer together.

Estimates by the Congressional Budget Office, the General Accounting Office, and private and government economists now place the *discounted present value of the entire thrift cleanup cost in a range between $140 billion and $200 billion* (in 1991 dollars). To help put these amounts into perspective, let's do some quick, back-of-the-envelope calculations. For starters, the entire deficit of the federal government for 1991 was equal to $320.9 billion; hence, the amount society lost from the thrift crisis could have offset much of the federal deficit for 1991. Closer to home, note that there are—according to the 1990 census—about 248,710,000 women, men, and children in the United States. This means that the total discounted present value of the thrift cleanup cost is in the range of $562 to $807 for every woman, man, and child.

Furthermore, there is a good chance that, even though cost estimates by different observers are similar, these estimates still may underestimate the magnitude of the cleanup. The estimates are sensitive to the length of time the RTC spends disposing of failed thrifts' assets. They also depend considerably on the market values of those assets, which could rise or fall in the future.

Who Pays?   Naturally, an important issue that Congress had to address was who would actually pay all these costs. Under the original provisions of FIRREA, estimates were that thrifts themselves would pay about one-fourth of the cost of the cleanup, while taxpayers would pay the rest. In fact, thrifts will end up paying a much smaller portion of the amount, for two reasons. First, as we discussed in the Current Controversy in the preceding chapter, one key way that thrifts have paid for some of the costs has been through much higher deposit insurance premiums. A portion of these premiums, however, ultimately is paid by thrift customers, because the market interest rate that depositors receive on their funds falls as a result of higher premiums. Hence, it was inevitable from the outset that thrifts themselves would not pay even one-fourth of the cleanup cost.

A second and more important reason that thrifts will pay only a small portion of the cost is that they simply are unable to pay more. As noted above, the FIRREA assumptions about the overall health of the economy and the thrift industry were very over optimistic, if not plain wrong. Although there are many well-managed and solvent S&Ls, the thrift industry as a whole continues to struggle. It does not have a present-value sum of $140 billion to $200 billion that it can part with at the moment.

Consequently, taxpayers ultimately will pay for most—indeed, nearly all—of the costs of the thrift cleanup. They will do so because their government made a guarantee, through its commitment to federal deposit insurance, to cover these costs. We as citizens may be unhappy about it, but as voters we all agreed to support the deposit insurance system. Of course, we as voters could instruct our representatives to refuse to make good on the deposit insurance guarantee, but we could do this only if we were willing to sacrifice the integrity of the government and the credibility of the entire deposit insurance system. In short, we are stuck with the bill.

Where Did the Money Go?   An important question, aside from who pays, is where all the funds have gone. Certainly, they are gone already—that is why so many thrifts became insolvent. Who got the money?

The answer is that a lot of different people received these funds. For instance, again consider a ''close-to-home'' example. Suppose that you were to make a $500 loan to a friend to help him pay his tuition for the current term. Your friend agrees to repay that amount plus interest of $25 at the end of the term, but when that time arrives your friend (ex-friend?) informs you he can only repay $250 and that you will never see the additional $275 he had promised you. Who gets that $275? Obviously, he does. He has received a **resource transfer** (a transfer of title to resources—the education he received during the term that the $275 permitted) from you. This $275 thereby would amount to a resource loss to you, because you could have used those funds to purchase other goods or services yourself.

Analogously, those who ''gained'' from the S&L mess were those who received loans from those S&Ls in the early and middle 1980s that subsequently plummeted in value or went completely unpaid. Many of these loans went into real estate construction—for instance, new office buildings and shopping malls in places such as California, Arizona, and Texas—that declined considerably in value after the fact. Who got the money—that is, who received resource transfers? The answer is lots of people. One group was composed of the original owners of the land, who were lucky enough to sell it for development before the price of the land fell. Another group consisted of the construction companies and workers who developed the real estate. All these people ultimately received funds for these S&L-funded projects that turned out to be worth considerably less than was paid. This means that those who developed the projects received a significant transfer of resources from the S&Ls and, because of the deposit insurance system, from taxpayers.

CONTINUING CRISIS

In 1991, for the first time since the first quarter of 1986, the thrift industry earned a profit. Still, the thrift crisis is not over yet. Indeed, while the current edition of this text was being written in the early 1990s, federal regulators, citing problems that began in the mid-1980s, took control of the savings bank that held the mortgage loan of one of the authors (unfortunately, that doesn't get him out of making his monthly payments). All of us continue to pay for the crisis, and we will pay for it for many years to come.

WAS FIRREA ENOUGH?

It is easy to be a Monday-morning quarterback concerning economic events. With respect to nearly any economic event, we can easily gather economic data that demonstrate, after the fact, how alternative decisions by policy makers could have yielded benefits—or prevented losses—for society as a whole. What is important, however, is whether policy makers did the best they could *at the time, given the information they had.*

Certainly, once it began, the thrift crisis was difficult to stop and to clean up. FIRREA represented the most important step toward both of these goals. Nevertheless, the FIRREA legislation contained a variety of flaws. We have already discussed one of these: the unrealistic projections around which the legislation was structured. There were other difficulties, however, that many observers believe Congress should have recognized before passing the legislation. To some extent these problems have complicated efforts to end the crisis and may have driven up its cost.

The Matter of Timing   One of these was the contradictory nature of the legislation on the issue of how quickly failed institutions were to be resolved by the RTC. On the one hand, it called on the RTC to dispose of failed thrifts as quickly as possible, with a target date for RTC completion of 1992. This deadline was motivated by a growing understanding by members of Congress that their previous delays might have pushed up the cost of the S&L cleanup. On the other hand, FIRREA required that the RTC not dispose of thrifts so fast as to upset real estate markets. Lying behind this latter stipulation were congressional fears that if the RTC tried to sell too many real estate assets at once, real estate values around the country would plummet. Of course, the RTC could not meet both of these provisions of the legislation simultaneously, and it became clear that the 1992 target date was unlikely to be met.

Indeed, some observers feared that the RTC was given so little specific direction by Congress that it threatened to become an inefficient bureaucracy whose main interest was to perpetuate itself. A few even accused it of ineptness: A joke that began to circulate asked, ''How many RTC bureaucrats does it take to put in a light bulb?'' and then answered, ''Two; one to say that everything is going well, and a second to screw it into the water faucet.''

Certainly, it is taking the RTC some time to dispose of the assets of closed S&Ls. Out of an initial caseload of 454 failed thrifts with $148 billion in assets to be sold, in its first seven months of operation the RTC disposed of only 52 thrifts with $17 billion in assets. In answer to its critics, however, the RTC points out that it is hobbled by other FIRREA stipulations. For instance, before selling certain types of residential properties, the RTC must give at least 90 days' notice to make sure that nonprofit agencies and low-income individuals have a chance to purchase the properties. In addition, FIRREA instructs the RTC not to sell any properties for less than 95 percent of ''appraised'' values, even though such appraisals might have been made when real estate prices were at their height.

Unaddressed Issues   Of greater concern to most observers were questions left unanswered by FIRREA and related legislation. Two in particular stood out. One was the absence of any substantive reform of deposit insurance. As we discussed in the last chapter, Congress debated such reforms in the early 1990s but made little headway. Because most economists and policy makers agree that the moral hazard problem of deposit insurance was perhaps the most important issue that needed to be addressed, the absence of concrete action on this issue was widely perceived to be a major weakness of FIRREA and subsequent congressional action on the thrift crisis. As things currently stand, no really substantive reforms of deposit insurance have yet occurred.

Second, Congress did not deal with the regulatory issue of accounting standards. Although thrift regulators no longer use the RAP approach of the FHLBB, they—and bank regulators—continue to use the historical accounting procedures of GAAP. Neither regulators nor Congress has yet formally adopted techniques of accounting based on measures of current market values. Many observers argue that until adoption of such market-value accounting occurs, thrift and bank regulators likely will continue to learn of impending depository institution failures much later than necessary.

COULD IT HAPPEN AGAIN—AND TO WHOM?

The failure of Congress to address the issues of deposit insurance and regulatory accounting practices has led many observers to conclude that another financial institution crisis could occur in the future. Some prognosticators forecast that a *commercial banking* crisis may be inevitable unless Congress makes fundamental regulatory and depository insurance reforms. Indeed, some pessimists contend that such a crisis may already have begun.

In support of their contention, these doomsayers point to the growing list of commercial bank failures in the 1990s. As we noted in the last chapter, the commercial bank failure rate of 163 per year from 1985 through 1991 was well over ten times greater than the annual average for all previous years of the federal deposit insurance system. Furthermore, in 1992 the FDIC projected that commercial bank failures could average *over 200* per year into 1995.

Clearly, the failure rate of commercial banking institutions is at a level unprecedented since the Great Depression era of the 1930s. There is undeniable cause for concern that they may be the next victims of a flawed deposit insurance system and an unreformed regulatory structure. If the thrift institution mess of the 1980s and 1990s was a crisis, a similar debacle in commercial banking could be a catastrophe. As we shall see in the subsequent chapters, commercial banks and other depository institutions play a key role not only as financial intermediaries but also as channels through which the Federal Reserve conducts monetary policy in the United States. For this reason, a commercial banking catastrophe would have effects far wider in scope than even the massive thrift crisis of the past decade.

CHAPTER SUMMARY

1. A century after the first savings banks and savings and loan associations opened their doors, Congress in the 1930s initiated considerable federal involvement in the affairs of the thrift industry. This was done through the establishment of federal deposit insurance of savings institutions, the creation of a large thrift regulatory apparatus, and indirect and direct restrictions on thrift portfolio compositions.

2. The seeds of the current thrift crisis were sown in the 1950s when Congress left the federal deposit insurance system of the 1930s unaltered and simultaneously enacted tax legislation that encouraged thrifts to devote almost all their energies to housing-related finance. While the moral hazard problem of deposit insurance and the portfolio inflexibility of thrifts posed no significant problems during the thrift heyday of the 1950s, greater competition between banks and thrifts in the 1960s led Congress to impose interest rate ceilings on thrift savings accounts.

3. Through much of the 1970s, interest rates rose and gradually became more variable. At the end of the 1970s, market interest rates rose considerably, and banks and thrifts experienced significant financial disintermediation. Because S&Ls had so many of their assets placed in long-term mortgage-related loans while their deposits primarily were short-term instruments, they experienced particular difficulties when this occurred. A significant portion of the thrift industry was sustaining losses by the beginning of the 1980s, and many thrifts were on the verge of insolvency.

4. In an effort to assist S&Ls in escaping further damage from high and variable interest rates, Congress in the early 1980s passed legislation that deregulated considerably the activities of thrift institutions. These laws also reduced the scope of safety and soundness regulation, setting into motion the forces that produced the thrift crisis in the 1980s.

5. The thrift crisis had several causes, including the high and variable interest rates of 1979 through 1982, certain aspects of the deregulation of the early 1980s, tax law changes that produced a subsequent real estate boom that induced shaky S&Ls to ''go for broke'' in risky real estate investments, a strong economic recovery in the southwestern part of the United States following a deep recession in the early 1980s, and instances of managerial fraud and mismanagement. Most experts agree, however, that the main causal factor in the thrift crisis was the moral hazard problem stemming from the structure of the federal deposit insurance system.

6. The Financial Institutions Reform, Recovery, and Enforcement Act (FIRREA) of 1989 was the major congressional answer to the thrift crisis. The act revised the thrift regulatory structure, placed new restrictions on thrift activities, and provided funding for resolving bankrupt S&Ls.

7. Measuring the total cost of the thrift crisis is complicated by the fact that the crisis has stretched out over several years. Another complication is that future costs are difficult to assess in light of the dependence of thrift performance on economic conditions that will prevail in the future. Early estimates of the cost of the crisis were biased upward by failure to take into account the time value of money, but they were biased downward by use of unrealistic projections about the future health of the economy and of S&Ls themselves. Current present-value cost estimates, which lie in a range between $140 billion and $200 billion, are midway between these extremes.

8. To date, Congress has failed to deal with some of the most important underlying problems—a faulty deposit insurance structure and regulatory overreliance on historical accounting practices—that laid the foundation for the thrift crisis. Many observers fear that continued avoidance of these problems may lead to a future crisis in the commercial banking industry.

Glossary

Brokered deposits: Bundles of funds held by several individuals that are packaged by brokers for sale to banks and S&Ls as deposits.

Goodwill: The accounting value of a firm's "going-concern" or "franchise" value.

Management Consignment Program: FHLBB program that removed incumbent managers of insolvent thrifts and replaced them with a consigned group of managers from other thrifts in the same region.

Net worth certificates: Certificates authorized by the Garn–St Germain Act of 1982 and issued by distressed thrifts to the FSLIC in exchange for promissory notes. The thrift may use promissory notes in computing net worth; therefore, the FSLIC intended for these certificates to help a thrift buy time to strengthen its financial base.

Resolution: The act of closing a failed thrift or otherwise disposing of its assets.

Resource transfer: A transfer of title to resources.

Zombie thrifts: S&Ls that technically are insolvent but that, because of regulatory inaction, continue to operate.

Self-Test Questions

1. In what ways did the federal government induce S&Ls to adopt inflexible asset portfolios before 1980?

2. Explain why the high and variable interest rates of 1979 through 1982 were particularly hard on S&Ls while causing fewer difficulties for commercial banks.

3. What types of deregulation reduced the restrictions on S&L portfolios in the 1980s?

4. In what ways was the scope of safety and soundness regulation reduced in the early 1980s?

5. Some observers have argued that deregulation in the 1980s did not go far enough and that this contributed to the thrift crisis. Do you see any basis for this argument? Explain.

6. Other observers argue that as long as deposit insurance maintains its present structure, further deregulation of depository institutions is a mistake. Do you agree? Explain.

PROBLEMS

13-1. Suppose that estimates of taxpayer costs of the thrift cleanup were equal to $50 billion this year, $55 billion next year, and $60.5 billion the following year. Also, suppose that the average annual interest rate over the next two years is 10 percent.

    a. Ignoring the time value of money, what is the total estimated cost of the thrift cleanup for this 3-year period?

    b. Taking into account the time value of money, what is the total estimated cost of the thrift cleanup for this 3-year period?

    c. How much greater is your answer to part a above as compared with your answer to part b above in dollar terms? In percentage terms?

13-2. Consider the following (fictitious) data. The RTC has assets of failed thrifts that amount to $10 billion at current market values. Any amount that it sells reduces the net cost to taxpayers of the thrift cleanup dollar for dollar. The assets' market values uniformly fall by an annual rate of 50 percent if unsold. Finally, the annual market interest rate is 7 percent. Answer the following questions under the assumption that the RTC sells assets at their market values.

    a. Suppose that the RTC sells only $3.58 billion in assets this year and sells the remaining amount next year. What is the discounted present value of the effective dollar cost to taxpayers resulting from the RTC's inability to sell all the assets this year?

    b. Suppose that, instead, the RTC sells $7.86 billion in assets this year. What is the discounted present value of the effective dollar cost to taxpayers resulting from the RTC's inability to sell all the assets this year?

    c. Compare your answers to parts a and b. How much, in dollars, does the speedier resolution of failed thrifts by the RTC in part b save taxpayers, relative to its slower resolution in part a? How much is saved in percentage terms?

13-3. Suppose that to increase the size of the Savings Association Insurance Fund, the FDIC were to set a premium rate of $0.40 per $100 (0.40 percent) of insured deposits at thrifts.

    a. At the beginning of the year, insured deposits at thrifts are $1,000 billion. Assuming that the FDIC expects failures to reduce the amount in the SAIF by $3.5 billion this year, what will be the net change in the insurance fund this year, ignoring the reduction in thrift deposits resulting from the failures during the year?

    b. Suppose that the FDIC projects that SAIF losses due to failures will actually be $5.0 billion during the year. Ignoring the reduction in thrift deposits resulting from those failures, what deposit insurance premium should the FDIC now set if it wishes for the SAIF to remain unchanged during the year?

SELECTED REFERENCES

Barth, James R., *The Great Savings and Loan Debacle* (Washington, D.C.: American Enterprise Institute Press, 1991).

Kane, Edward J., *The Gathering Crisis in Federal Deposit Insurance* (Cambridge, Mass.: MIT Press, 1985).

————, *The S&L Insurance Mess: How Did It Happen?* (Washington, D.C.: The Urban Institute Press, 1989).

Munn, Glenn, F. L. Garcia, and Charles Woelfel, *Encyclopedia of Banking and Finance,* 9th ed. (Rolling Meadows, Ill.: Bankers Publishing Company, 1991).

White, Alice, "The Evolution of the Thrift Industry Crisis," Finance and Economics Discussion Series no. 101, Board of Governors of the Federal Reserve System (December 1989).

White, Lawrence J., *The S&L Debacle: Public Policy Lessons for Bank and Thrift Regulation* (New York: Oxford University Press, 1991).

Unit 4

Central Banking, Monetary Policy, and the Federal Reserve System

Depository Institutions and the Money Supply Process

CHAPTER PREVIEW

1. What happens when someone deposits in a depository institution a check that is written on another depository institution?

2. What happens when someone deposits in a depository institution a check that is written on the Federal Reserve?

3. How does a depository institution react to an increase in its reserves?

4. What is the maximum deposit expansion multiplier?

5. What reduces the size of the deposit expansion multiplier?

6. How do we determine the magnitude of the multiplier linking the quantity of money to the monetary base?

7. How do we determine the magnitude of the multiplier linking the quantity of credit in the banking system to the monetary base?

Many depository institutions accept transactions deposits, which means that they will hold your funds and pay them out as you order them to do so. These institutions—commercial banks and thrift institutions—need not hold a 100 percent reserve on their transactions-balance liabilities. Rather, they are required to hold only fractional reserves; they lend out part and keep part on reserve at all times. As we show in this chapter, fractional reserves for transactions balances lead to a multiple expansion (or contraction) of the quantity of money when the reserves of these institutions increase (or decrease). For example, when the Fed purchases a U.S. government security from the public, the nonbank public (households and firms) deposits these new funds in depository institutions, but only a fraction of them need be held as reserves. Depository institutions may lend the remainder. In turn, borrowers redeposit those funds in the banking system. Depository institutions hold a fraction of them as reserves and may lend the remainder. Thus, there is a multiple expansion of deposits that are part of the money stock.

In the analysis that follows, we examine the relationship between the level of reserves and the total amount of deposits and the levels of money and credit. Keep in mind that banks are profit-making institutions and that they do not earn interest on reserves; consequently, banks try to minimize reserve holdings. This chapter shows that whatever affects reserves also can affect the quantity of money. We show first that when someone deposits a check in one bank that is written on another bank, the two banks involved are individually affected—but the overall amount of deposits in the banking system does not change. Then we show that when someone deposits a check that is written on the Fed in a depository institution, a multiple expansion in the level of deposits potentially results.

THE RELATIONSHIP BETWEEN RESERVES AND TOTAL DEPOSITS IN DEPOSITORY INSTITUTIONS

To show the relationship between reserves and depository institution deposits, we first analyze a single bank (existing alongside many others).

Under legal requirements, this single bank must hold **required reserves:** reserves, in the form of vault cash or in its reserve account with a Fed district bank, which are equal to a specified percentage of total deposits; any reserves it holds above the required reserves economists refer to as **excess reserves.** Suppose, for example, that you deposit a $1,000 check in bank A, which is subject to a 10 percent reserve requirement. When bank A receives credit for this check by the Fed (the Fed increases bank A's reserve account by $1,000), it receives an increase in reserves of $1,000—$100 of which is required and $900 of which is excess.

A single bank is able to make loans to its customers only to the extent that it has reserves above the level legally required to cover the new deposits. When an individual bank has excess reserves, it can make loans and change the quantity of money. If the bank has no excess reserves, however, it can make no further loans, and so it cannot change the quantity of money. Only the banking system as a whole can alter the amount of deposits and hence the quantity of money. This will become obvious as the **T-accounts** (asset-liability accounts) of an isolated bank are compared with the T-accounts of several banks that we will use to represent the complete banking system.

HOW A SINGLE BANK REACTS TO AN INCREASE IN RESERVES

To examine the behavior of a single bank after its reserves are increased, we begin by making the following assumptions:

1. The **required reserve ratio,** the percentage of total deposits that depository institutions are required to hold, is 10 percent for all transactions deposits: The Fed requires that an amount equal to 10 percent of all transactions deposits be held on reserve in a district Federal Reserve bank or in vault cash.

2. Depository institutions desire to keep their excess reserves at a zero level because reserves at the district Federal Reserve bank do not earn interest. Depository institutions will wish to convert excess reserves into interest-bearing assets such as loans. (Or they can purchase interest-earning securities; this assumption would complicate our analysis, but the conclusions would be the same.)

3. Transactions deposits are the bank's only liabilities; reserves at the district Federal Reserve bank and loans are the bank's only assets. Loans are promises made by customers to repay some amount in the future; that is, they are IOUs.

4. There is such a ready loan demand that the bank has no trouble lending additional money.

5. Every time a loan is made to an individual (consumer or business), the individual puts all its proceeds into a transactions deposit; the public withdraws no cash (paper currency or coins).

We shall adopt assumptions 1 and 2 throughout, but we shall relax the other assumptions later in the chapter.

Look at the initial position of the bank in Figure 14-1. Liabilities consist of $1 million in demand deposits. Assets consist of $100,000 in reserves, which you can see are required reserves in the form of vault cash or in the depository institution's reserve account at the district Federal Reserve branch, and $900,000 in loans to customers. Total assets of $1 million equal total liabilities of $1 million.

Figure 14-1
Bank 1.

Assets		Liabilities	
Total reserves	$ 100,000	Transactions deposits	$1,000,000
Required reserves ($100,000)			
Excess reserves ($0)			
Loans	$ 900,000		
Total	$1,000,000	Total	$1,000,000

Note that we have assumed for simplicity that the bank has zero net worth. Actually, a depository institution rarely has a net worth of more than a fairly small percentage of its total assets (see Chapter 11). Hence, this assumption is not too simplistic, and so we shall use it throughout this chapter.

With a 10 percent reserve requirement and $1 million in transactions deposits, we can see that the bank has required reserves of $100,000 (10 percent of $1 million). Because the bank holds no excess reserves, its **total reserves**—the sum of its required and excess reserves—also equal $100,000.

Assume that a new depositor writes a $100,000 check drawn on another depository institution and deposits it in bank 1. Transactions deposits in bank 1, therefore, immediately increase by $100,000, bringing the total to $1.1 million. At the same time, total reserves of bank 1 increase to $200,000. A $1.1 million total in transactions deposits means that required reserves are now $110,000. Bank 1 now has excess reserves equal to $200,000 minus $110,000, or $90,000. This is shown in the T-account in Figure 14-2.

Figure 14-2
Bank 1.

Assets		Liabilities	
Total reserves	$ 200,000	Transactions deposits	$1,100,000
Required reserves ($110,000)			
Excess reserves ($90,000)			
Loans	$ 900,000		
Total	$1,100,000	Total	$1,100,000

Look at excess reserves in Figure 14-2. Excess reserves were zero before the $100,000 deposit, and afterward they are $90,000—that's $90,000 worth of assets not earning any income. Bank 1 will now lend out the $90,000 in excess reserves in order to obtain interest income. Loans will increase to $990,000. The borrowers who receive the loans will not leave them on deposit in bank 1. They borrow funds to spend them. As they spend them, actual reserves eventually will fall to $110,000 (as required), and excess reserves will again become zero, as shown in Figure 14-3.

Figure 14-3
Bank 1.

Assets		Liabilities	
Total reserves	$ 110,000	Transactions deposits	$1,100,000
Required reserves ($110,000)			
Excess reserves ($0)			
Loans	$ 990,000		
Total	$1,100,000	Total	$1,100,000

In this example, a person went into bank 1 and deposited a $100,000 check drawn on another bank. That $100,000 became part of the reserves of bank 1. Because that deposit immediately created excess reserves, further loans were possible for bank 1. Bank 1 lent the excess reserves to earn interest. A bank will not lend more than its excess reserves because, by law, it must hold a certain amount of required reserves.

WHAT HAS HAPPENED TO THE QUANTITIES OF DEPOSITS AND MONEY?

A look at the T-accounts for bank 1 might give the impression that the total amounts of deposits and money increased because of the new customer's $100,000 deposit. Remember, though, that the deposit was a check written on another bank. Therefore, the other bank suffered a decline in its transactions deposits and its reserves. While total assets and liabilities in bank 1 have increased by $100,000, they have decreased in the other bank by $100,000. *Thus, the total amount of money and credit in the economy is unaffected by the transfer of funds from one depository institution to another.*

Each depository institution can create loans (and deposits) only to the extent that it has excess reserves. In the above example, bank 1 had $90,000 of excess reserves after the deposit of the $100,000. In contrast, the bank on which the check was written found that its excess reserves were now a negative $90,000 (assuming it had zero excess reserves previously). That bank now has less reserves than required by law; it is deficient in its reserve holdings. It will have to call in loans in order to make actual reserves meet required reserves (or not relend when other loans are paid)—or it will have to borrow funds from another source.

The thing to remember is that new reserves are not created when checks written on one bank are deposited in another bank. The Federal Reserve System, however, can create new reserves; that is the subject of the next section.

THE FED'S DIRECT EFFECT ON THE TOTAL RESERVES IN THE BANKING SYSTEM

This section examines the Fed's direct effect on total bank reserves. Following it is an explanation of how a change in the level of reserves causes a multiple change in the total amount of bank deposits. First consider the Federal Open Market Committee (FOMC), whose decisions essentially determine the level of reserves in the monetary system.

FEDERAL OPEN MARKET COMMITTEE

Open-market operations are the buying and selling of U.S. government securities in the open market (the private secondary U.S. securities market) by the FOMC (a committee of Federal Reserve officers—see Chapter 15) in order to change the quantity of money. If the FOMC decides that the Fed should buy or sell bonds, it instructs the New York Federal Reserve Bank **Trading Desk** (the term for the office that actually conducts securities trading on the Fed's behalf) to do so.

THE MECHANICS OF A SAMPLE OPEN-MARKET TRANSACTION

In practice, the FOMC does not give the Trading Desk at the New York Fed a specific dollar amount to purchase or sell; instead, it leaves the decision on how much to trade to the judgment of the Trading Desk's manager. The manager, however, must attempt to meet the general intent of the policies the FOMC establishes. Let us suppose that to do so, the Trading Desk must purchase $100,000 worth of U.S. government securities.

The Fed pays for these securities by writing a check on itself for $100,000. It transfers this check to the bond dealer in exchange for the $100,000 worth of bonds. The bond dealer deposits a $100,000 check in its transactions account at a bank, which then sends the $100,000 check back to the Federal Reserve for payment. When the Fed receives the check, it adds $100,000 to the sending bank's reserve account at its Federal Reserve district bank. Thus, the Fed has created $100,000 of reserves. The Fed can create reserves because it has the ability to ''write up'' (that is, add to) the reserve accounts of depository institutions whenever it buys U.S. securities. When the Fed buys a U.S. government security in the open market, it expands total reserves and the quantity of deposits and money (initially) by the amount of the purchase.

Using T-Accounts Consider the T-accounts of the Fed and of the depository institution receiving the check. Figure 14-4 shows the T-accounts for the Federal Reserve after the bond purchase and for the depository institution after the bond dealer deposits the $100,000 check. The Fed's T-account (which here deals only with changes) shows that after the purchase, the Fed's assets have increased by $100,000 in the form of U.S. government securities. Liabilities have also increased by $100,000, in the form of an increase in the reserves the depository institution holds on deposit in its own Federal Reserve bank account. The T-account for the depository institution shows an increase in assets of $100,000 in the form of reserves with its district Federal Reserve bank. The depository institution also has an increase in its liabilities in the form of $100,000 in the checking account of the bond broker; this is an immediate $100,000 increase in the quantity of money, because checking account balances are a component of the money stock.

Figure 14-4
T-Accounts for the Federal Reserve and the Depository Institution
When a U.S. Government Security Is Purchased by the Fed.

FEDERAL RESERVE SYSTEM		DEPOSITORY INSTITUTION	
Assets	Liabilities	Assets	Liabilities
+$100,000	+$100,000	+$100,000	+$100,000
U.S. government securities	Depository institution's reserves	Reserves	Transactions deposit owned by broker

THE SALE OF A $100,000 U.S. GOVERNMENT SECURITY BY THE FED

We must reverse the process described above when the account manager at the New York Fed Trading Desk sells a U.S. government security from the Fed's portfolio. When the individual or institution buying the security from the Fed writes a check for $100,000, the Fed reduces the reserves of the depository institution on which the check was written. Thus, the $100,000 sale of the U.S. government security leads to a reduction in reserves in the banking system.

Using T-Accounts   Figure 14-5 shows the T-accounts for the sale of a U.S. government security by the Fed. On the left-hand side, the T-account for the Federal Reserve is shown. When the $100,000 check goes to the Federal Reserve System, the Federal Reserve reduces by $100,000 the reserve account of the depository institution on which the check is written. The Fed's assets are also reduced by $100,000, because it no longer owns the U.S. government security. The depository institution's liabilities are reduced by $100,000 when that amount is deducted from the account of the bond purchaser, and the money supply is thereby reduced by that amount. The depository institution's assets are also reduced by $100,000 because the Fed has reduced that institution's reserves by that amount.

Figure 14-5
T-Account Changes after the Fed Has Sold $100,000 of U.S. Government Securities.

FEDERAL RESERVE SYSTEM		DEPOSITORY INSTITUTION	
Assets	Liabilities	Assets	Liabilities
−$100,000	−$100,000	−$100,000	−$100,000
Reduction in U.S. government securities	Depository institution's reserves	Reserves	Transactions account balances

Adjusting the Price of U.S. Government Securities   No one is forced to deal with the Fed; it sells or purchases government securities in the open market. The Fed merely adjusts the price it offers or asks until it can buy or sell what it wants. For example, if the Fed wants to sell a U.S. government security for $100,000 and no one wants to buy it, the Fed can lower the selling price (thereby increasing the yield). If the Fed wants to buy a $100,000 U.S. security and no one wants to sell it, it can raise its offered price until sellers are willing to sell at the price offered (thereby reducing the yield).

Remember that the Fed can purchase as many U.S. government securities as it wishes because it—unlike any of the rest of us—can pay for them by writing a check on itself. Also, it can adjust the price of bonds to achieve its objective because, unlike private securities dealers, it does not have to worry about minimizing capital losses or maximizing capital gains. The Fed's duty is to operate for social benefit, not for private gains. In any event, every time the Fed purchases U.S. government securities, it increases reserves in the system. We shall now consider the relationship between the resulting quantity of deposits and reserves.

DEPOSIT EXPANSION BY THE BANKING SYSTEM

Consider now the entire banking system. For all practical purposes, we can look at all depository institutions (we shall refer to them as banks) taken as a whole. While their different deposit liabilities do not necessarily have the same reserve requirements, for the purpose of exposition, we shall for the moment ignore these real-world details. To understand how money is created, we must understand how depository institutions respond to Fed actions that increase reserves in the entire system.

THE FED PURCHASES U.S. GOVERNMENT SECURITIES

Assume that the Fed purchases a $100,000 U.S. government security from a bond broker. The bond broker deposits the $100,000 check in bank 1 (which started out in the position in Figure 14-1). The check, however, is not written on another depository institution. Rather, it is written on the Fed itself.

Look at the T-account for bank 1 shown in Figure 14-6. If this figure looks familiar, it is because it is exactly the same as Figure 14-2. The Fed's security purchase has increased reserves by $100,000 to $200,000, and it also has initially increased transactions deposits by $100,000. Because required reserves on $1.1 million of transactions deposits are only $110,000 (i.e., $1,100,000 \times 0.10 = $110,000$), there are $90,000 (i.e., $200,000 - $110,000 = $90,000$) of excess reserves.

Figure 14-6
Bank 1.

Assets		Liabilities	
Total reserves	$ 200,000	Transactions	
Required reserves		deposits	$1,100,000
($110,000)			
Excess reserves			
($90,000)			
Loans	$ 900,000		
Total	$1,100,000	Total	$1,100,000

Effects on the Quantity of Money The major difference between this example and the one given previously is that here the amount of deposits in the banking system increased by $100,000 immediately. Why? Because transactions deposits held by the public—the bond brokers—are part of the money stock, no other bank has lost reserves, *and,* by assumption, the bond brokers withdraw no currency from their deposit accounts. (We shall take up *this* latter complication later.) Thus, the purchase of a $100,000 U.S. government security by the Federal Reserve from the public increases the quantity of money imme-diately by $100,000.

The Continuing Process   The process of money creation does not stop here. Look again at the T-account in Figure 14-6. Bank 1 has excess reserves of $90,000. No other depository institution (or combination of depository institutions) has negative excess re-serves of $90,000 as a result of the Fed's bond purchase.

Bank 1 will not wish to hold non-interest-bearing excess reserves. It will expand its loans by $90,000, as shown in Figure 14-7. Figure 14-7 is exactly like Figure 14-3, but there has been no corresponding reduction in loans at any other depository institution.

Figure 14-7
Bank 1.

Assets		Liabilities	
Total reserves	$ 110,000	Transactions	
Required reserves		deposits	$1,100,000
($110,000)			
Excess reserves			
($0)			
Loans	$ 990,000		
Total	$1,100,000	Total	$1,100,000

The individuals who have received the $90,000 of new loans will spend these funds, which will then be deposited in other banks. To make this example simple, assume that the $90,000 in excess reserves was lent to a single firm for the purpose of buying a Burger King franchise. After the firm buys the Burger King franchise, Burger King deposits the $90,000 in its account at bank 2. For the purpose of simplicity, ignore the previous assets and liabilities in bank 2 and concentrate only on the T-account *changes* resulting from this new deposit, as shown in Figure 14-8. A plus sign indicates that the T-account entry has increased, and a minus sign indicates that the entry has decreased. For bank 2, the $90,000 deposit, after the check has been sent to the Fed, becomes an increase in reserves (assets) as well as an increase in transactions deposits (liabilities). Because the reserve requirement is assumed to be 10 percent, or $9,000, bank 2 will have excess reserves of $81,000. But, of course, excess reserves are not income-producing, and so bank 2 will reduce them to zero by making loans of $81,000 (which will earn interest income), as Figure 14-9 shows.

Figure 14-8
Bank 2.

Assets		Liabilities	
Total reserves	$90,000	New transactions	
Required reserves		deposits	$90,000
($9,000)			
Excess reserves			
($81,000)			
Total	+ $90,000	Total	+ $90,000

Figure 14-9
Bank 2.

Assets		Liabilities	
Total reserves	+$9,000	Transactions deposits	+$90,000
Required reserves ($9,000)			
Excess reserves ($0)			
Loans	+$81,000		
Total	+$90,000	Total	+$90,000

Remember that in this example the original $100,000 deposit was a check issued by a Federal Reserve bank. That $100,000 constituted an immediate increase in the quantity of money of $100,000. The money-creation process (in addition to the original $100,000) occurs because of the fractional reserve banking system, coupled with the desire of depository institutions to maintain zero excess reserves (given a sufficient loan demand).

A Continuation of the Deposit Expansion Process Assume that another firm has received an $81,000 loan from bank 2 because it wants to buy into an oil-drilling firm. This oil-drilling firm has an account at bank 3. Look at bank 3's simplified T-account in Figure 14-10, where, again, only increases in the assets and liabilities are shown. When the firm borrowing from bank 2 pays the $81,000 to the oil-drilling firm's manager, the manager deposits the check at bank 3. Total reserves at bank 3 go up by that amount when the check is sent to the Fed.

Figure 14-10
Bank 3.

Assets		Liabilities	
Total reserves	+$81,000	New transactions deposits	+$81,000
Required reserves ($8,100)			
Excess reserves ($72,900)			
Total	+$81,000	Total	+$81,000

Because the reserve requirement is 10 percent, required reserves rise by $8,100, and excess reserves are therefore $72,900. Bank 3 also will want to lend those non-interest-earning assets (excess reserves). When it does, loans will increase by $72,900. Total reserves will fall to $8,100; excess reserves become zero as the oil-drilling firm's manager writes checks on the new deposits. The total amount of deposits—and the quantity of money—has thereby increased by another $72,900, as shown in Figure 14-11.

Figure 14-11
Bank 3.

Assets		Liabilities	
Total reserves	$8,100	Transactions deposits	$81,000
Required reserves ($8,100)			
Excess reserves ($0)			
Loans	$72,900		
Total	$81,000	Total	$81,000

The Process Continues to Banks 4, 5, 6, and so on   This process will continue. Each bank obtains smaller and smaller increases in deposits because 10 percent of each deposit must be held in reserve; therefore, each succeeding depository institution makes correspondingly smaller loans. Table 14-1 shows the new deposits, possible loans and investments, and required reserves for the remaining depository institutions in the system.

What Has Happened to the Total Amounts of Deposits and Money?   In this simple example, the total amount of transactions deposits, and, hence, the total quantity of money, increased initially by the $100,000 that the Fed paid to the bond broker in exchange for a bond. The transactions deposits increased further following a $90,000 deposit in bank 2. And they again increased after an $81,000 deposit in bank 3. Eventually the levels of deposits and money will increase by a total approaching $1,000,000. This is shown in Table 14-1 and represented graphically in Figure 14-12.

TABLE 14-1
The Maximum Potential Effect on the Money Supply of an Increase in Reserves of $100,000 with a 12% Required Reserve

Bank	New Deposits	Possible Loans and Investments (Excess Reserves)	Required Reserves
1	$100,000	$ 90,000	$ 10,000
2	90,000	81,000	9,300
3	81,000	72,900	8,100
4	72,900	65,610	7,290
5	65,610	59,049	6,561
6	59,049	53,144	5,905
7	53,144	47,830	5,314
8	47,830	43,047	4,783
All other banks	$430,467	$387,420	$ 43,047
Total	1,000,000	$900,000	$100,000

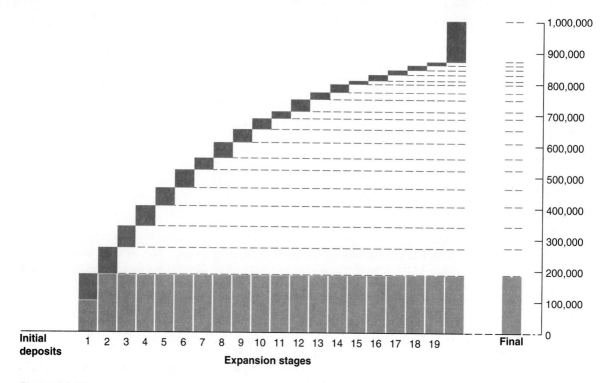

Figure 14-12

The Multiple Expansion in the Money Supply due to $100,000 in New Reserves, When the Required Reserve Ratio Is 10 Percent. The banks are all aligned in decreasing order of new deposits created. This is merely a graphical representation of Table 14-1.

TOTAL RESERVES MUST INCREASE FOR THE MULTIPLE EXPANSION TO OCCUR

Even with fractional reserve banking and zero excess reserves, the quantities of deposits and money cannot multiply unless total reserves increase. The original new deposit in bank 1 in the previous example was in the form of a check written on a Federal Reserve district bank. It therefore represented *new* reserves to the banking system. Had that check been written on bank 3, for example, nothing would have happened to the total amount of transactions deposits; there would have been no change in the total money supply. To repeat: Checks written on banks within the system represent assets and liabilities that simply cancel each other out. Only when excess reserves are created by the banking system can the money supply potentially increase.

The example would work the same way if depository institutions used their excess reserves to acquire interest-earning securities instead of to make loans. The owners of those securities would receive checks from the purchasing depository institution; the securities sellers would then deposit these checks into their own depository institutions. The deposit expansion process would continue in the same manner.

THE SIMPLEST DEPOSIT (MONEY) EXPANSION MULTIPLIER

In the example just given, a $100,000 increase in excess reserves generated by the Fed's purchase of a security yielded a $1,000,000 increase in the amounts of transactions deposits and money; they increased by a tenfold multiple of the initial $100,000 increase in total reserves.

We can derive the relationship between the *maximum* increase in transactions deposits and the change in reserves mathematically. Again assume that there are only transactions deposits in the banking system and that banks hold zero excess reserves. Consider the following equation, where the Greek delta letter (Δ) denotes a ''change in'' a variable:

$$\Delta TR = d \times \Delta D \qquad\qquad (14\text{-}1)$$

where ΔTR = change in total reserves
$\ d$ = required reserve ratio for transactions deposits
ΔD = change in transactions deposits

In other words, the change in total reserves in the banking system equals the required reserve ratio times the change in total transactions deposits, given our assumptions so far that banks hold no excess reserves, that the public makes no currency withdrawals, and that there are no other types of deposits in the banking system.

Now divide each side of equation (14-1) by the required reserve ratio d:

$$\frac{\Delta TR}{d} = \frac{d \times \Delta D}{d} \qquad\qquad (14\text{-}2)$$

The right-hand side of this equation can be simplified by recognizing that $\Delta TR/d = (1/d)\Delta TR$ on the left-hand side of equation (14-2) and that $d/d = 1$ on the right-hand side of the equation, so that

$$\frac{1}{d} \times \Delta TR = \Delta D \qquad\qquad (14\text{-}3)$$

Equation (14-3) shows that a change in total reserves will, under our assumptions, increase demand deposits by the factor $1/d$ times the change in reserves; $1/d$ is the **deposit expansion multiplier.** Under our assumption that transactions deposits are the only form of money, the deposit expansion multiplier also is a **money multiplier,** or a number by which a reserve measure is multiplied to obtain the total quantity of money for the economy. The deposit expansion multiplier is the number by which a change in reserves is multiplied in order to calculate the ultimate change in total deposits in the banking system. Consider the example used earlier. The Fed increased reserves by $100,000, and the required reserve ratio was 10 percent (0.10). Putting those values into equation (14-3) yields

$$\frac{1}{0.10} \times \$100,000 = 10 \times \$100,000 = \$1,000,000 \qquad\qquad (14\text{-}4)$$

In this example, the money multiplier was 10: $1/0.10 = 10$.

The deposit expansion multiplier given in equation (14-3) can also be used for deposit *contraction.* If the Fed *sells* a $100,000 T-bill, reserves in the system fall by $100,000. Given a required reserve ratio of 10 percent, transactions deposits (and hence the quantity of money) will decrease by $1,000,000.

This formula gives the *maximum* that the quantities of deposits and money will change for a specific change in reserves, or the *maximum deposit expansion and money multipliers.* It is a formula for a very simplified world in which all deposits are transactions deposits that are subject to the same reserve requirement, the public wants neither more nor less cash on hand, and banks always hold zero excess reserves. In reality, groupings of transactions deposits at banks are subject to different reserve ratios. As of April 1992, for instance, the reserve requirement for the *first* $42.2 million in transactions deposits at any bank *actually* was 3 percent; the 10 percent requirement applied to all deposits in excess of $42.2 million at each depository institution.

Also, banks may wish to hold positive levels of excess reserves, even though they bear no interest income. Furthermore, when the nonbank public wants to hold more or less cash, the value of the money multiplier actually will change. We now turn to a discussion of complete money and credit multipliers that take into account these factors.

COMPLETE MONEY AND CREDIT MULTIPLIERS

In the real world, several of the assumptions we made when we derived the *maximum* value of the money multiplier fail to hold. Banks *do* hold some—though not many—excess reserves. The nonbank public *does* make currency withdrawals. (In addition, the Fed *could* impose a reserve requirement on time deposits; presently, however, it does not do so, and hence we may ignore this additional theoretical complication.) We need to consider these factors to understand fully how the money multiplier is determined in the real world.

Furthermore, the quantity of money is not the only variable that the Fed may wish to influence. The Fed also is interested in the amount of lending banks do, which is the **total credit** they extend. As we shall see, we can also analyze this issue using the multiplier approach.

CURRENCY LEAKAGE AND POSITIVE EXCESS RESERVE HOLDINGS

For starters, we shall relax *two* of our earlier assumptions. First, we shall suppose that, in fact, individuals wish to make currency withdrawals from the banking system. In the real world, the total quantity of money, of course, consists of both *bank-supplied* money (transactions deposits) and part of the *government-supplied* money (currency). As we shall discuss below, the aggregate amount of government-supplied money consists of bank reserves and currency. Currency therefore is an important part of the story, and so we must take its existence into account. Second, we shall assume that banks desire to hold positive quantities of excess reserves. In fact, banks do hold such reserves, and so we need to understand the implications of that fact.

T-Account Mechanics   Let's reconsider our earlier example of a $100,000 security purchase by the Fed. Bank 1, as shown in Figure 14-13, receives an initial $100,000 deposit from the broker from whom the Fed purchased the security. This step is identical to our earlier example, and so Figure 14-13 shows the same levels of total reserves, loans, and deposits as Figure 14-6.

Figure 14-13
Bank 1.

Assets		Liabilities	
Total reserves	$ 200,000	Transactions	
		deposits	$1,100,000
Required reserves			
($110,000)			
Excess reserves			
($90,000)			
Loans	900,000		
Total	$1,100,000	Total	$1,100,000

Now, however, suppose that all members of the nonbank public, including the broker, desire to hold an amount of currency that is a constant fraction of their transactions deposit holdings. This is a simplifying assumption, but it makes sense if people typically make currency transactions whose combined value is a stable fraction of checking transactions. Furthermore, suppose specifically that members of the nonbank public desire to hold currency in a ratio to transactions deposits equal to $1/4$, or 25 percent. If so, the broker wishes to withdraw $20,000 shortly after the initial $100,000 deposit with bank 1. (This is not unrealistic timing, because Fed funds transfers for security purchases typically are *direct deposits* into the broker's account, as we shall discuss in Chapter 16.)

Once the broker makes this withdrawal, his remaining transactions deposit balance will have fallen to $80,000. Therefore, total deposits at bank 1 on net will equal $1,080,000, as shown on the right-hand side of the T-account in Figure 14-14. That is, the *net* increase in deposits at bank 1 is $80,000, and the ratio of currency to transactions deposits will equal $20,000/$80,000 = 0.25; the broker then will attain his desired holdings of currency in proportion to transactions deposits. When bank 1 honors the broker's currency withdrawal, the bank's total reserves fall by the amount of the withdrawal, or by $20,000, as shown on the left-hand side of the T-account in Figure 14-14. Its total transactions deposits now equal $1,080,000, and so its required reserves are equal to $108,000 (total transactions deposits times the required reserve ratio, or $1,080,000 × 0.10), and its excess reserves are equal to $72,000 (total reserves less required reserves, or $200,000 − $108,000).

Figure 14-14
Bank 1.

Assets		Liabilities	
Total reserves	$ 200,000	Transactions	
		deposits	$1,100,000
− Currency		− Currency	
withdrawal	20,000	withdrawal	20,000
Net total		Net transactions	
reserves	$ 180,000	deposits	$1,080,000
Required reserves			
($108,000)			
Excess reserves			
($72,000)			
Loans	900,000		
Total	$1,080,000	Total	$1,080,000

Economists call such a currency withdrawal by the name **currency leakage**. If we visualize the deposit expansion process as a flow through depository institutions, then the broker's currency withdrawal represents an immediate leakage from that flow. We ignored the possibility of currency leakage, which must reduce the deposit expansion multiplier, in our earlier example.

The other factor we ignored was the possibility that depository institutions may desire to keep positive excess reserves (sometimes called **prudential reserves**). They may do so, for example, when they fear significant future rises in interest rates (which would lower the value of bonds they purchase), or if the economy appears to be headed for a recession (which would increase the risk of borrower default on principal and interest and induce depositors to draw down their accounts).

To keep things simple, suppose that banks desire to hold excess reserves in constant proportion to any new transactions deposits that they receive. Specifically, suppose that all banks wish to maintain excess reserve holdings equal to 5 percent of any additional transactions deposits. This means that of its current holdings of excess reserves equal to $72,000, bank 1 *desires* to hold only $4,000 (transactions deposits times the desired excess reserves ratio, or $80,000 × 0.05). This leaves $68,000 in *undesired* excess reserves that bank 1 wishes to lend.

This is the amount of the initial deposit that bank 2 would receive in the absence of currency leakage. Its depositor, Burger King, now wishes to hold currency as a fraction equal to one-fourth of its deposits, however. This means that bank 2 actually receives a net deposit of $54,400, following a currency leakage of $13,600, so that Burger King's ratio of currency to deposits will equal $13,600/$54,400 = 0.25.

Thus, in the first step following the Fed's $100,000 security purchase, the initial increase in deposits in the banking system is bank 1's increase in deposits of $80,000, as compared with a $100,000 increase in our earlier example, which ignored the possibility of currency leakage. In the second step, the net deposit increase at bank 2 is equal to $54,400, as compared with $90,000 in the earlier example.

Clearly, the amount of deposit expansion in our example is significantly reduced when there is currency leakage and positive holdings of excess reserves by banks. This makes sense. If there is currency leakage, banks have fewer reserves left over to lend. They also lend fewer reserves if they hold more than they are required to hold.

Calculating the New Deposit Expansion Multiplier   Because deposit expansion is lower in our new example, it must be the case that the banking system's deposit expansion multiplier is smaller as well. Note now that total reserves in the banking system changed by the amount

$$\Delta TR = (d \times \Delta D) + (e \times \Delta D) \\ = (d + e) \times \Delta D \qquad \text{(14-5)}$$

where e is the bank's desired ratio of excess reserves to transactions deposits, which in our example was equal to 0.05 (5 percent). The first term on the right-hand side of equation (14-5) is the change in required reserves resulting from a change in transactions deposits, and the second term is the change in excess reserves that occurs; the sum of the two, then, is the change in total reserves on the left-hand side of the equation.

In our example, the amount of currency leakage was equal to

$$\Delta C = c \times \Delta D \qquad \text{(14-6)}$$

where C = currency holdings and c = the public's desired ratio of currency to transactions deposits. Currency in the United States consists of Federal Reserve notes, and so the amount on the left-hand side of equation (14-6) represents Federal Reserve notes supplied through the banking system's allocation of reserves to meet currency demands of the nonbank public.

Together, then, equations (14-5) and (14-6) tell us how much the amount of government money issued by the Fed increases following the Fed's open-market purchase. The total amount of the increase in government-supplied money, then, is the sum of equations (14-5) and (14-6), which is

$$\Delta\text{TR} + \Delta C = [(d + e) \times \Delta D] + (c \times \Delta D)$$
$$= (d + e + c) \times \Delta D \qquad \textbf{(14-7)}$$

The left-hand side of equation (14-7) is the total change in government-supplied money. The right-hand side tells us that this change depends upon the change in deposits in the banking system, based on the required reserve ratio, the excess reserves ratio desired by banks, and the currency-to-transactions-deposit ratio desired by the nonbank public.

Under our fiat money system with fiduciary money, the amount of government-supplied money is the economy's **monetary base,** which economists sometimes call by the name "high-powered money," because it forms the basis for the economy's monetary system. As we discussed in Chapter 2, the monetary base under a gold standard was the amount of specie. In our fiduciary system, however, it is equal to

$$\text{MB} = \text{TR} + C \qquad \textbf{(14-8)}$$

where MB = monetary base. Therefore, the change in the monetary base is

$$\Delta\text{MB} = \Delta\text{TR} + \Delta C \qquad \textbf{(14-9)}$$

That is, the monetary base changes as a result of changes in total reserves and in the quantity of currency held by the nonbank public. Equation (14-9) is the left-hand side of equation (14-7), and so we can rewrite equation (14-7) as

$$\Delta\text{MB} = (d + e + c) \times \Delta D \qquad \textbf{(14-10)}$$

If we divide both sides of equation (14-10) by the quantity $(d + e + c)$, we get

$$\frac{1}{d + e + c} \times \Delta\text{MB} = \Delta D \qquad \textbf{(14-11)}$$

Equation (14-11) tells us that the amount of deposit expansion in the banking system (the right-hand side of the equation) is equal to a multiple of the change in the monetary base (the left-hand side). The deposit expansion multiplier now is $1/(d + e + c)$. Using the data from our example ($d = 0.10$, $e = 0.05$, and $c = 0.25$), we find that the multiplier is equal to $1/(0.10 + 0.05 + 0.25) = 1/0.40 = 2.5 = 2\frac{1}{2}$.

Recall that the deposit expansion multiplier in our previous example was simply equal to $1/d = 1/0.10 = 10$. That was true because we ignored currency leakage and assumed that banks wished to hold no excess reserves; that is, we *assumed* that e and c both were equal to zero. In fact, in the real world this typically is not the case (although the value of e is usually smaller than the value of 0.05 that we chose for our example). Hence, in the real world the deposit expansion multiplier generally is much smaller than the maximum multiplier, $1/d$.

THE COMPLETE MONEY MULTIPLIER

In our earlier example, in which there was no currency leakage and banks desired no excess reserves, the deposit expansion multiplier could tell us how much the *total* quantity of money would increase following a $100,000 security purchase by the Federal Reserve. Now, however, we need to recognize that the total quantity of money, according to the Fed's M1 definition of money (see Chapter 3), is equal to

$$M = C + D \tag{14-12}$$

where M = money stock. This means that a change in the total quantity of money must equal

$$\Delta M = \Delta C + \Delta D \tag{14-13}$$

That is, the money stock changes in response to changes in the nonbank public's holdings of currency and transactions deposits.

Calculating the Money Multiplier   Now we can calculate the complete money multiplier for our much more realistic banking system. We shall call this money multiplier m. The multiplier tells us how much the quantity of money changes in response to a change in the monetary base resulting, for instance, from an open-market purchase or sale by the Federal Reserve. Therefore, the money multiplier belongs in the equation

$$\Delta M = m \times \Delta \text{MB} \tag{14-14}$$

That is, a change in the quantity of money is equal to the money multiplier times a change in the monetary base.

From equation (14-13), we know that we may rewrite the left-hand side of equation (14-14) as equal to $\Delta D + \Delta C$. Also, from equation (14-10), we know that we may rewrite the right-hand side of equation (14-14) as $m \times (\Delta \text{TR} + \Delta C)$, and so (14-14) may be rewritten as

$$\Delta D + \Delta C = m \times (\Delta \text{TR} + \Delta C) \tag{14-15}$$

We can make one more set of substitutions by using equation (14-6) to substitute $\Delta C = c \times \Delta D$ on the left-hand side of equation (14-15) and by using equation (14-7) to substitute $\Delta \text{TR} + \Delta C = (d + e + c) \times \Delta D$ on the right-hand side. This gives us

$$\Delta D + (c \times \Delta D) = m \times (d + e + c) \times \Delta D \tag{14-16}$$

We may now divide both sides of equation (14-16) by ΔD to get

$$1 + c = m \times (d + e + c)$$

which, after we divide both sides by $(d + e + c)$, gives us

$$\frac{1 + c}{d + e + c} = m \qquad \text{(14-17)}$$

Thus, the value of the complete money multiplier is equal to $(1 + c)/(d + e + c)$.

In our example, we had $c = 0.25$, $d = 0.10$, and $e = 0.05$. Therefore, the value of the complete money multiplier for our hypothesized economy was equal to $(1 + 0.25)/(0.10 + 0.05 + 0.25) = 1.25/0.40$, which is equal to 3.125 (or, because $0.40 = 40/100 = 2/5$, the multiplier may be expressed as $(1\frac{1}{4})/(5/2) = 3\frac{1}{8}$, which is 3.125).

The Money Multiplier Model We now have deduced that, in our model of the real world, a change in the total quantity of money is equal to

$$\Delta M = \frac{1 + c}{d + e + c} \times \Delta MB$$

Because we have accounted for all important factors that influence changes in the money stock, we now can drop the Δ notation from this equation. Doing so gives us

$$M = \frac{1 + c}{d + e + c} \times MB \qquad \text{(14-18)}$$

Equation (14-18) says that the actual *level* of the quantity of money (M) equals the money multiplier times the *level* of the monetary base (MB), which in turn equals total reserves (TR) plus currency (C), or total government-supplied money.

Economists call equation (14-18) a *money multiplier model* of the determination of the quantity of money in the economy. If we had a good idea what values c, d, and e would exhibit in the future, we could, in principle, use equation (14-18) to calculate the economy's money multiplier. Then, if we worked for the Fed as staff economists, we could tell the Fed what level the monetary base needs to be to achieve a particular quantity of money.

This is a nice model for two reasons. First, it isn't too difficult to understand, once you get the hang of deriving equation (14-18)—and we'll give you some practice doing this in the end-of-chapter questions. Second, it doesn't require a great deal of information to calculate the multiplier.

We must point out, however, that the money multiplier model has its limitations. It is tempting to view the money multiplier, $m = (1 + c)/(d + e + c)$, as a constant fraction. This is not the case. Only the required reserve ratio d is approximately constant—except that its effective value can vary a little because in reality the first $42.2 million or so in deposits at any bank is subject to a 3 percent reserve requirement while the remaining deposits are subject to a 10 percent reserve requirement. Nonetheless, most transactions deposits are subject to the 10 percent reserve requirement.

The values of the other two ratios, e and c, depend completely on the behavior of the banking system and of the nonbank public, respectively. If banks become more "conservative,'' perhaps because they anticipate an economic downturn ahead, the value of e can increase, causing the value of the money multiplier to fall. Likewise, if the nonbank public holds more currency relative to transactions deposits, perhaps because it loses some confidence in the stability of the banking system, the value of c can rise, which also causes the size of the money multiplier to fall. [For instance, in our example, the money multiplier was $3\frac{1}{8}$, or 3.125, for $c = 0.25$. If c rises to a value of 0.30, then the new value of the money multiplier would be equal to $(1 + 0.30)/(0.10 + 0.05 + 0.30) = (1.30)/(0.45) = 2.889$, which is smaller than 3.125.]

Empirical Measures of the Money Multiplier   Because the components of the money multiplier vary with the behavior of the banking system and of the nonbank public, we can never know with complete certainty what the size of the money multiplier will be from one period to the next.

Economists can get exact measures of *past* money multipliers by calculating the ratio of the quantity of money (either the M1 or M2 definition of money) to the monetary base (MB), or the sum of total depository institution reserves (TR) and currency (C) that support this money supply. Thus,

$$m_1 = \frac{M1}{MB} \quad \text{and} \quad m_2 = \frac{M2}{MB}$$

are the money multipliers for the M1 and M2 measures of the quantity of money.

Figure 14-15 shows empirical estimates of M1 and M2 money multipliers from 1959 to 1992. As is to be expected, the M2 multiplier is greater than the M1 multiplier (it has a larger numerator and the same denominator); the M2 multiplier is rising through time, while the M1 multiplier is somewhat more stable.

Note that the M1 multiplier typically has fallen in a range between roughly $2\frac{1}{2}$ and 3. This is close to our own calculation from our simple multiplier model, where we computed a value of 3.125. Hence, while our model is not completely realistic, it isn't too far off.

If we make the simplifying assumption that the reserve requirement ratio was 10 percent for all deposits during that period, the maximum money multiplier would have been 10. Cash withdrawals and excess reserves are important inhibitors of deposit expansion. Since 1983 the M1 multiplier has increased significantly; the M2 multiplier has fallen since mid-1984. As we discuss in Chapter 24, if the money multipliers are unstable, the quantity of money is a potentially less useful policy variable for the Fed.

Also, it is important for you to realize that these empirical money multipliers are observed *after the fact (ex post);* monetary policy requires information about the value of such multipliers *before the fact (ex ante).* The more volatile are money multipliers, therefore, the more difficult is monetary policy to conduct, if the Fed's goal is to control the quantity of money. Consequently, if the money multiplier model is to be useful as a policy-making tool, the multiplier must be both stable and predictable.

THE TOTAL CREDIT MULTIPLIER

In addition to movements in quantity of money, the Federal Reserve typically is interested in the behavior of total lending by banks. Our money multiplier model, it so happens, implies a model of the determination of total bank lending, or of total credit issued by the banking system.

In our model, the amount of loans, $L,$ is the total amount of credit extended by the

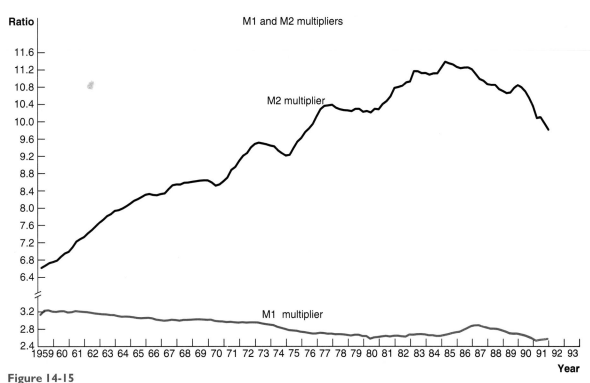

Figure 14-15
Estimates of M1 and M2 Multipliers.   [*Source:* Federal Reserve Bank of St. Louis.]

banking system (we could also allow for security holdings by banks without changing things much). If banks hold only reserves and loans as assets and issue only transactions deposits as liabilities, then, from the banks' consolidated T-accounts, it must be true that

$$L + \text{TR} = D \qquad (14\text{-}19)$$

Equation (14-19) simply says that bank assets must equal bank liabilities. It also implies that $L = D - \text{TR}$, so that a change in total bank credit (loans) must equal

$$\Delta L = \Delta D - \Delta \text{TR} \qquad (14\text{-}20)$$

According to equation (14-20), a change in total bank credit results from a change in transactions deposit liabilities of banks minus a change in total bank reserves.

We now can develop a straightforward multiplier model of bank credit determination. Suppose that bank credit expansion is related by a multiplier to a change in the monetary base:

$$\Delta L = m_L \times \Delta \text{MB} \qquad (14\text{-}21)$$

where m_L is the bank credit multiplier. We can use equation (14-21) to substitute $\Delta L = \Delta D - \Delta R = \Delta D - [(d + e) \times \Delta D]$ on the left-hand side of equation (14-21). In addition, we know from our earlier work that $\Delta \text{MB} = \Delta \text{TR} + \Delta C = (d + e + c) \times$

ΔD, and so we can substitute this quantity on the right-hand side. After these substitutions, we get

$$\Delta D - [(d + e) \times \Delta D] = m_L \times (d + e + c) \times \Delta D$$

If we divide both sides of this expression by ΔD, we get

$$1 - (d + e) = m_L \times (d + e + c)$$

Finally, we can divide both sides of this latter equation by the quantity $(d + e + c)$ to get

$$\frac{1 - (d + e)}{d + e + c} = m_L \tag{14-22}$$

as the expression for the total credit multiplier. Therefore, the money multiplier model we developed earlier also implies a *total credit multiplier model* represented by the equation

$$\Delta L = \frac{1 - (d + e)}{d + e + c} \times \Delta MB \tag{14-23}$$

An open-market purchase of securities by the Fed increases the size of the monetary base, and so equation (14-23) indicates that this action would increase total bank credit by that amount times a multiplier. In our numerical example above, in which $d = 0.10$, $e = 0.05$, and $c = 0.25$, the value of the total credit multiplier would be equal to $[1 - (0.10 + 0.05)]/(0.10 + 0.05 + 0.25) = (0.85)/(0.40)$, which is approximately equal to 2.125. This means that a $1 purchase of securities by the Fed would induce banks to lend about $2.13 more.

As we shall discuss in later chapters, the Fed has not always felt that it should precisely control the quantity of money. In fact, some economists have argued that total bank credit is a better variable for the Fed to attempt to control precisely. Nonetheless, both variables are determined by multiplier processes that are interrelated, as this analysis makes clear. Arguments for concentrating on controlling one variable or the other rest on arguments concerning their effects on the economy as a whole. We shall discuss some of these in Unit 6. At this point, however, we next turn our attention to why and how central banks such as the Federal Reserve System have been created to control these variables.

CHAPTER SUMMARY

1. A fractional reserve banking system leads to the possibility of a multiple expansion (contraction) of the quantity of money as a result of an increase (decrease) in reserves.

2. When a depository institution receives an increase in reserves over and above its required reserve level, it has an incentive to increase its lending or to purchase interest-earning securities. It can do so only to the extent that it has excess reserves.

3. No new reserves are created when checks written on one depository institution are deposited in another; one depository institution gets an increase in reserves that is offset by the other's loss in reserves.

4. The Fed can create or destroy depository institution reserves; as a consequence, the Fed can change the quantity of money in the economy. If the Fed purchases T-bills from a depository institution or from a household that deposits the Fed's check in a depository institution, total reserves in the banking system will rise by the amount of the purchase. Excess reserves rise (by a smaller amount), and depository institutions have an incentive to increase lending by creating transactions deposits. As a result, the money stock increases.

5. If the Fed sells T-bills to a depository institution or to a household that pays for them with a check written on a depository institution, total reserves in the banking system decrease. If, before this transaction, excess reserves were zero for the depository institutions involved, then this transaction will cause excess reserves to be negative; actual reserves will be less than required reserves. The depository institution must call in loans and not renew maturing loans. As a consequence, the money stock falls.

6. No one is forced to deal with the Fed when the Fed wishes to buy or sell in the open market; the Fed induces households and depository institutions to buy from it (or sell to it) by offering a lower price (or a higher price) for the securities. Because it is not concerned with profit maximization (and because it can purchase government securities merely by writing a check on itself), the Fed can perform as many open-market operations as necessary to achieve its objectives.

7. Fed open-market transactions directly change total reserves in the banking system; therefore, the Fed can change the money supply. The relationship between changes in total reserves and changes in the public's deposits is defined by the deposit expansion multiplier. In order to determine the maximum deposit expansion, the change in reserves is multiplied by the reciprocal of the required reserve ratio; the reciprocal of the required reserve ratio is called the maximum deposit expansion multiplier. Because the United States has a fractional reserve banking system, the required reserve ratio is less than 1 and the maximum deposit expansion multiplier is greater than 1. In other words, it is possible for the money supply to change by a multiple of a change in total reserves.

8. The real-world money multiplier is less than the maximum money multiplier, partly because depository institutions actually hold some excess reserves, but mostly because currency leakages (withdrawals) occur. A currency leakage occurs when the public does not deposit the entire amount of a check in a depository institution; the public withholds some of the check in the form of currency.

9. By its nature, bank deposit expansion also implies bank credit expansion. Consequently, there is a multiplier relationship between total bank credit and the monetary base, just as there is one between the quantity of money and the monetary base.

GLOSSARY

Currency leakage: Withdrawal of currency from depository institutions by the nonbank public.

Deposit expansion multiplier: The number by which a change in reserves is multiplied to calculate the ultimate change in total deposits in the banking system.

Excess reserves: Reserves that a depository institution, or the whole banking system, holds above required reserves; total reserves minus required reserves.

Monetary base: The amount of government-supplied money, which forms the basis for the economy's monetary system; equals currency held by the nonbank public plus total bank reserves.

Money multiplier: A number by which a reserve measure, such as the monetary base, is multiplied to obtain the total quantity of money in the economy.

Prudential reserves: Reserves that depository institutions voluntarily hold above required reserves to remain liquid to prepare for troubled times.

Required reserve ratio: The percentage of total deposits that the Fed requires depository institutions to hold in the form of vault cash or in a reserve account with the Fed.

Required reserves: The value of reserves that a depository institution must hold in the form of vault cash or in a reserve account with the Fed; required reserves are equal to some percentage of total deposits.

T-account: A simplified balance sheet that includes only the assets and liabilities (or their changes) under discussion.

Total credit: The total amount of lending that all banks do.

Total reserves: The sum of a bank's required and excess reserves.

Trading Desk: The term that refers to the office in the New York Federal Reserve Bank that conducts securities trading for the Fed.

SELF-TEST QUESTIONS

1. Explain, in your own words, whether you can change the total quantity of deposits in the banking system by writing a check on your own account for deposit in another bank.

2. Explain, in your own words, whether the Federal Reserve System can change the total quantity of deposits in the banking system by writing a check on its own account that a securities dealer deposits in her account in a private bank.

3. Economists like to point out that the Fed could conduct open-market operations to control the quantity of money by buying or selling bottles of ketchup, or even spaceships (if enough of them existed). Explain why this statement is justified.

4. In a true "free-banking" economy, there are no reserve requirements. Does this necessarily mean that deposit expansion has no limit in such a system? Explain your answer.

5. Explain, in your own words, without reference to any equations or formulas, why an increase in the amount of currency leakage from the banking system reduces the multiplier effect of an open-market purchase or sale by the Fed.

6. Explain, in your own words, without reference to any equations or formulas, why an increase in the amount of excess reserves that banks desire to hold, other things constant, reduces the value of the total credit multiplier.

PROBLEMS

14-1.   Assume a 5 percent required reserve ratio, zero excess reserves, no currency leakages, and a ready loan demand. The Fed buys a $1 million T-bill from a depository institution.
   a. What is the maximum money multiplier?
   b. By how much will total deposits rise?

14-2.   The Fed purchases a $1 million T-bill from Mr. Mondrone, who deposits the proceeds in bank 1. Using T-accounts, show the immediate effects of this transaction on the Fed and bank 1.

14-3.   Continuing the example from problem 14-2:
   a. Indicate bank 1's position more precisely, using a T-account, if required reserves equal 5 percent of demand deposits.
   b. By how much can bank 1 increase its lending?

14-4. Consider the balance sheet of a single bank (among many) below (in millions).

Assets		Liabilities	
Reserves	$ 400	Demand deposits	$1,000
Loans	1,600	Savings deposits	1,000

Assume that required reserves are 20 percent of demand deposits *and* 20 percent of savings deposits. If a customer withdraws $100 from demand deposits, what will be the expected response of this single bank?

Consider below the consolidated balance sheet of all commercial banks.

Assets		Liabilities	
Reserves	$ 4,000	Demand deposits	$10,000
Loans	16,000	Savings deposits	10,000

For the same initial action (i.e., a withdrawal of $100) that is immediately redeposited in another commercial bank, how would the consolidated balance sheet look?

14-5. Suppose that required reserves are, instead, 25 percent of demand deposits and 15 percent of savings deposits. If a customer deposits $100 in demand deposits, what will be the expected response of the single bank?

If the proceeds of the loans are eventually distributed 60 percent into demand deposits and 40 percent into savings deposits, determine the expected changes in the consolidated balance sheet.

14-6. Until 1990, the Federal Reserve imposed a reserve requirement on nonpersonal (i.e., nonhousehold) time deposits. If the quantity of nonpersonal time deposits is denoted N, and the nonbank public's desired ratio of nonpersonal time deposits is denoted n, calculate the value of the money multiplier, assuming that d, e, and c are positive constants. [*Hint:* The point is to give you practice deriving the money multiplier. Replace equation (14-5) with $\Delta TR = (d \times \Delta N) + (t \times \Delta N) + (e \times \Delta N)$, and redo the algebra. To check your work, make sure that you get our earlier answer if $t = 0$.]

14-7. Consider an economy in which there is no currency, banks hold no excess reserves, and banks issue a single type of deposit, which is a transactions deposit. If the quantity of transactions deposits is $200 million and the quantity of bank reserves is $50 million, then what is the required reserve ratio for transactions deposits?

14-8. Consider an economy in which there is no currency and banks issue only a single transactions deposit. Banks presently are satisfied holding $200 million in excess reserves, and the required reserve ratio is 10 percent. If the value of the money multiplier is 5.0, then what is the total quantity of deposits in the banking system?

14-9. Consider an economy in which the only type of bank liability is transactions deposits, and banks never desire to hold excess reserves. The required reserve ratio for transactions deposits is 0.50 (50 percent). In addition, the monetary base is $100 billion, and the total quantity of money is $150 billion. What is the nonbank public's desired ratio of currency to transactions deposits?

14-10. The year is A.D. 2310. Residents of an earth colony on Titan (the largest moon of the planet Saturn) use transactions deposits at banks as the only form of money. Banks on Titan always wish to hold 10 percent of deposits as excess reserves. There are no other deposits in the banking system. If the banking system on Titan has $300 million in total reserves and the total quantity of money is $1,500 million, what is the required reserve ratio set by the Titan colony's central bank?

SELECTED REFERENCES

Board of Governors of the Federal Reserve System, *The Federal Reserve System: Purposes and Functions,* 7th ed. (Washington, D.C., 1984).

Crick, W. F., "The Genesis of Bank Deposits," *Economica* (1927).

Humphrey, Thomas, "The Theory of Multiple Expansion of Deposits: What It Is and Whence It Came," Federal Reserve Bank of Richmond *Economic Review,* 73 (2, March/April 1987), pp. 3–11.

Nichols, Dorothy M., *Modern Money Mechanics: A Workbook on Deposits, Currency, and Bank Reserves,* Federal Reserve Bank of Chicago, 1961; revised in 1968, 1971, 1975, and 1982.

Tobin, James, "Commercial Banks as Creators of Money," in D. Carson (ed.), *Banking and Monetary Studies* (Homewood, Ill.: Irwin, 1963), pp. 408–419.

U.S. Central Banking and the Federal Reserve System

CHAPTER PREVIEW

1. Why did the First Bank of the United States end in the midst of controversy?

2. What factors accounted for the rise and fall of the Second Bank of the United States? Was its demise harmful to the American economy?

3. How did free banking function in the United States in the middle part of the nineteenth century?

4. Why did the Civil War alter the course of money and banking in the United States?

5. How did economic and political turbulence of the late nineteenth and early twentieth centuries lead to a coalition favoring formation of a United States central banking arrangement?

6. What is the history of the Federal Reserve System?

7. How is the Federal Reserve System presently structured?

To carry out affairs of state—military conquests, exploration, and so on—governments have often required the assistance of a financial agent, such as a bank. Many economic historians believe, consequently, that the main impetus for central banking institutions such as the Federal Reserve System stems from the needs of governments.

The proper role and functions of government has always been a highly charged issue in the United States. Because of the interconnection of the federal government and a central bank, this has, at various times in our nation's past, made central banking a political controversy. Our ancestors argued vehemently about how to structure central banking institutions, and some spent much of their lives fighting the very existence of such institutions. Indeed, although we often take the Federal Reserve System for granted today, it has existed for only just over a third of our nation's history.

In this chapter, we have three objectives. We begin by providing a brief chronology of central banking in the United States from the eighteenth century until the twentieth century. We then discuss the forces that came together to create the Federal Reserve System. Finally, we conclude by describing the structure of today's Federal Reserve System.

A SHORT HISTORY OF CENTRAL BANKING IN THE UNITED STATES

Probably because of their experiences with the Bank of England's near-monopoly powers, the U.S. Founding Fathers were mostly against the establishment of a central bank—be it privately or publicly run. Added to this was a desire of existing banks to avoid dominance by a strong national bank and a presumption of state preeminence over a federal government. Consequently banking was regulated by individual states until 1863—with the exceptions of the First and Second National Banks of the United States.

THE FIRST BANK OF THE UNITED STATES

As we discussed in Chapter 6, Congress chartered the First Bank of the United States in 1791. To some extent, the First Bank of the United States took on many of the functions of a central bank. It was able to control the power that state banks had to issue notes and to lend funds. When the First Bank decided to lend more to private parties, the reserves of state banks expanded. When it reduced its loans, the reserves of state banks contracted. It also exerted power over state banks in another way. If the First Bank of the United States possessed state bank notes, it could hold the notes (or pay them out), and therefore the issuing state banks were not required to draw down on their reserves of gold or silver. In contrast, if the First Bank presented state bank notes for redemption at the banks that issued them, the issuing banks had to pay in gold or silver; thus their reserves fell.

The First Bank of the United States was profitable, averaging a rate of return of 8 percent per year for its investors. When its charter came up for renewal in 1811, however, Congress did not renew it. There were many reasons for this action. One of the most important reasons was that during its twenty-year existence, the ownership of some of the bank's stock had shifted to foreigners. As today, Americans feared excessive foreign control over the economy. This view was particularly prevalent during the attempt to make the First Bank a central bank. Opponents also contended that the First Bank of the United States would discourage the growth of state banks by regularly presenting state bank notes for redemption in specie.

THE SECOND BANK OF THE UNITED STATES

During the War of 1812, many leaders became convinced that the United States government needed a central banking institution in times of crisis. Hence, in 1816 the federal government gave a twenty-year charter to the Second Bank of the United States. The Second Bank provided commercial banking services to the economy as well as central banking services to the banking system. Like the First Bank, it regulated state banks by presenting their notes for redemption in specie and by varying the credit it created.

Many Americans looked with suspicion upon the powerful Second Bank. Further, some people blamed it for a financial panic that occurred in 1819. More resentment against the bank arose during the term of the vain and powerful Second Bank president, Nicholas Biddle. Toward the end of Biddle's appointment, there were strong political forces at work to make sure that the charter of the Second Bank lapsed. The election of Andrew Jackson (1767–1845) to the presidency of the United States in 1828 magnified the Second Bank's troubles. The fact that the Tennesseean ''Hero of New Orleans'' had defeated the Second Bank's supporter Henry Clay in the election was only part of the difficulty. In addition, during the campaign the majority of the directors and officers of the Second Bank had publicly opposed Jackson and his party. Also important was the fact that Jackson—who earlier in his life had nearly become bankrupt as a result of speculative land dealings and thereby had developed a strong distrust of banks—believed the national bank to be the most corrupting influence in American life. Jackson accused the Second Bank of monopolizing American finance. This set the stage for a ''bank war'' between Jackson and Biddle.

Ultimately, Biddle's biggest political mistake was to apply for a recharter four years before the 1836 expiration date of the original charter. His intention was to secure a recharter and at the same time embarrass Jackson in the 1832 election. Congress apparently saw rechartering the Second Bank as a good thing, and Jackson's attempt to use the ground of unconstitutionality failed to block a congressional vote on July 3, 1832, to recharter the bank.

Jackson's response was characteristic of him and perhaps is one of his more famous utterances; to Vice President Martin Van Buren, he said, "The bank, Mr. Van Buren, is trying to kill me, *but I will kill it.*" On July 10, 1832, Jackson vetoed the bill renewing the charter, and Congress failed to override his veto. The recharter of the Second Bank became the major campaign issue in the 1832 election, which Jackson won resoundingly. After the election, Jackson withdrew all federal deposits from the bank and placed them in selected state banks, called "pet" banks.

INFLATION AFTER THE DEMISE OF THE SECOND BANK OF THE UNITED STATES

The demise of the Second Bank of the United States in 1836 brought with it many changes on the American banking scene. Inflation increased and continued from 1834 to 1837. A depression occurred from late 1839 to 1843. Many historians believe that the inflation and subsequent economic downturn were caused by the fall of the Second Bank of the United States. They feel that the absence of the Second Bank's restraining forces on state banks led to a rapid increase in the amount of paper currency available (resulting from the proliferation of "wildcat banks," so called because their locations were said to be so remote that only wildcats frequented them).

Historically, large increases in the quantity of money have led to a reduction in the price of money. But recall from Chapter 2 that the price of money is its purchasing power, and so large increases in the quantity of money typically have led to increases in the rate of inflation. Figure 15-1 shows that the quantity of money did increase after Jackson's veto of the act to recharter the Second Bank in 1832.

The increase of wildcat banking was not the major cause of the increase in the money stock from 1832 to 1836. The ratio of bank-held reserves to credit outstanding did not fall during that period because, on the whole, banks were fairly cautious. The increase in the quantity of money resulted largely from an increase in the amount of specie—gold and, to a much lesser extent, silver—in the U.S. economy. After all, the United States was part of an international economy. It adhered to a specie standard that involved shipments of specie into and out of the country, and gold and silver formed the basis of the circulating money stock. During this time, there was a large increase in specie imports from Mexico as well as from Europe.

The bottom curve of Figure 15-1 shows that the amount of specie flowing into the United States increased dramatically from 1832 until about 1837. This inflow of specie is attributed largely to three causes:

1. The increase in U.S. exports of cotton to England.

2. Foreign investment in the developing U.S. transportation system.

3. The reestablishment of Anglo-American commercial ties that had been interrupted by the War of 1812 between the United States and England. From 1821 to 1837 the British invested more than $125 million in U.S. transportation and other social overhead facilities.

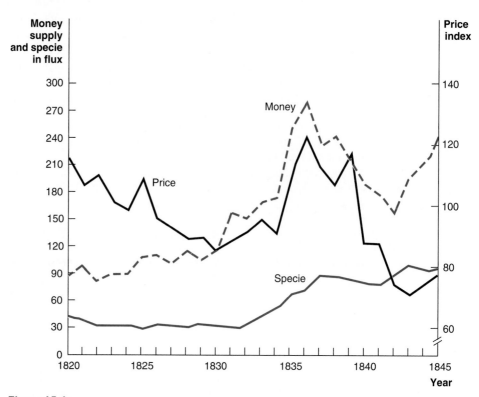

Figure 15-1

Prices and the Money Stock during the Demise of the Second Bank.   Prices rose sharply during 1835 and from 1829 to 1836. Although this price rise generally has been attributed to the demise of the Second Bank and the proliferation of money emanating from wildcat banks, much of it was due to the influx of specie into the United States, as indicated on the bottom curve. A 100 percent increase in specie took place in the eight years before 1835. [*Source:* Hugh Rockoff, "Money, Prices, and Banks in the Jacksonian Era," in R. W. Fogel and S. L. Engerman (eds.), *The Reinterpretation of American Economic History* (New York: Harper & Row, 1971), table 1, p. 451.]

Thus, the demise of the Second Bank of the United States alone was not responsible for the inflation from 1834 to 1836.

THE ABSENCE OF A CENTRAL BANK AND THE PANIC OF 1837

Shortly after the expiration of the charter of the Second Bank, there was a major banking panic. As shown in Figure 15-1, accompanying and following this panic were significant declines in the quantity of money and in the level of prices; the inflation of the first half of the 1830s was followed by deflation in the latter part of the decade and into the 1840s. This deflation was accompanied by a large decline in economic activity—a severe recession.

Could a central bank, such as the Second Bank of the United States, have prevented the Panic of 1837 and subsequent depression? This is an important question, because a key rationale for a central bank is its potential role in economic and financial stabilization. There have been two traditional views on this issue. One is that the panic, deflation, and recession resulted from the demise of the Second Bank and the lack of caution by newly unregulated banks around the country that induced them to become too illiquid and ill-prepared for economic weakness. Another view is that the Jacksonian bank war and end of the Second Bank had nothing to do with the subsequent recession. According to this view, events overseas were responsible for the decline of American economic fortunes. There was a major credit crunch in Britain in late 1836, and British banks rushed to redeem the American bank notes they held for specie, which, according to this view, pulled the rug from under the American banking system.

Another explanation, developed in part by Marie Sushka of Arizona State University, lies between these extremes.[1] By the early 1830s, according to this perspective, the public had developed great confidence in banks—perhaps because the Second Bank had helped maintain sound banking practices throughout the nation. This confidence led to a sharp reduction in the proportion of money that individuals and businesses held in specie; during the 1830s the amount of specie held in banks increased. Paper money would serve just as well, people believed, as long as the banks were sound.

But after the demise of the Second Bank, public confidence in banks again declined. The proportion of money that individuals wished to hold in specie increased. At the same time, most banks became more cautious and conservative, which induced them to increase their holdings of specie relative to the much lower levels of specie they had held in previous years. The **Specie Circular Act of 1836** required that (most) federal land purchases be paid for in gold, and this also increased specie holdings by individuals. Furthermore, the government began redistributing its deposits among banks around the country, reducing the immediate availability of specie. Then, at the end of 1836, the specie redemption sought by desperate British bankers was the final blow. The high demand for specie at this time put great strains on the banking system. When depositors requested specie from the banks and some banks could not or would not redeem bank notes with specie, a banking panic—known now as the Panic of 1837—occurred on a scale previously unprecedented. The end result was the worst depression of the century; the depression lasted from 1839 to 1843.

The modern view, then, is that there were a number of causes of the Panic of 1837 and the subsequent depression. While it is possible that the Second Bank could have moderated some of the ill effects of the panic, many economic historians question whether it could or would have fully prevented the downturn.

STATE BANKING AND ITS ALLEGED ABUSES BEFORE THE CIVIL WAR

Between 1836 and the establishment of the national banking system in 1863, there were two sets of banks in the United States. There were first the private, unincorporated banks, and second the banks that were incorporated with charters from state governments. The private banks (companies) acted in a manner similar to the incorporated banks throughout this period.

Free Banking   State legislatures in Michigan and in New York passed free-banking laws in 1837 and 1838, respectively. After these dates, many other states followed suit. Before this time, a bank could obtain a corporate charter from a state only by an act of

---

[1] Marie Sushka, ''The Antebellum Money Market and the Economic Impact of the Bank War,'' *Journal of Economic History,* 36 (4, December 1976), pp. 804–835.

the legislature of that state. **Free-banking laws** ended this practice; anyone or any group could now secure a corporate charter and engage in banking if it complied with the provisions of the general bank incorporation law. Requirements for obtaining a charter varied from state to state. Table 15-1 lists the states with and without free-banking laws by 1860.

According to critics of the day, the requirements were inadequate to protect depositors and the general public. Critics of free banking claimed that state banks had inadequate capital and inadequate reserves against their notes and deposits. Many state banks at that time made risky loans. Problems with state banks resulted in the practice of circulating state bank notes of different values. Some state bank notes could be redeemed in gold and silver; they circulated at face value. That is, if a state bank note had $10 printed on it, it was just as good as having $10 in gold or silver. Other state bank notes circulated at small discounts; still others circulated at huge discounts. Not an insignificant portion of circulating state bank notes became completely worthless. Counterfeiters often made particular state bank notes valueless. By the end of the 1860s, for example, there were more than 5,000 types of counterfeit notes in circulation. For the Bank of Delaware alone, there were approximately three dozen counterfeit issues in circulation.

New York enacted and implemented a highly restrictive banking law to avoid such

T A B L E   15-1
States with and without Free-Banking Laws by 1860

States with Free-Banking Laws	Year Law Passed	States without Free-Banking Laws
Michigan	1837[a]	Arkansas
Georgia	1838[b]	California
New York	1838	Delaware
Alabama	1849[a]	Kentucky
New Jersey	1850	Maine
Illinois	1851	Maryland
Massachusetts	1851[b]	Mississippi
Ohio	1851	Missouri
Vermont	1851[b]	New Hampshire
Connecticut	1852	North Carolina
Indiana	1852	Oregon
Tennessee	1852[b]	Rhode Island
Wisconsin	1852	South Carolina
Florida	1853[b]	Texas
Louisiana	1853	Virginia
Iowa	1858[b]	
Minnesota	1858	
Pennsylvania	1860[b]	

[a] Michigan prohibited free banking in 1840 and allowed it again in 1857.

[b] According to Rockoff, very little free banking was done under the laws in these states.

Source: Reprinted from A. J. Rolnick and W. E. Weber, "Inherent Instability in Banking: The Free Banking Experience," *Cato Journal,* 5 (3, Winter 1986). Their source was Hugh Rockoff, *The Free Banking Era: A Re-Examination* (New York: Arno Press, 1975).

abuses. Banks in that state were supervised and examined. It is not surprising, then, that legislation that established a national banking system in 1863 was modeled to a large extent on New York law.

A Closer Look at the Free-Banking Era   What you have read above is the traditional view of the free-banking experience in the United States. In recent years some economists have reanalyzed the 1836–1863 free-banking era and have qualified that interpretation significantly.

The first thing to note is that the era was not a period of laissez-faire banking. Free banking got its name from the free-entry provision: Any group was allowed to open a bank, issue its own currency (bank notes), accept deposits, and make loans. It is significant to note, however, that states with free-banking laws placed important restrictions on banks:

1. Free banks were mandated to deposit state bonds (from any state), some of which were very risky, with the state banking authority. Because the market price on such bonds fluctuated, sometimes violently, they were not liquid, and this increased the inherent instability of the system. Also, these bond-collateral requirements forced banks to hold an undiversified portfolio.

2. Free banks had to pay specie for notes on demand; failure to redeem even one note meant that the bank would be closed and its assets used to pay off note holders, who had prior legal claims over other bank creditors. And if the public desired to increase its ratio of currency to deposits, this requirement forced banks to offer reserves (specie) even if the public would have preferred bank notes; this could have precipitated bank failures.

3. Because unit banking existed in most states, intrastate branching was not possible; free banking did not allow for interstate banking either. As under the bond-collateral requirement, banks were prevented from obtaining an optimal asset portfolio; unit banking made the solvency of a bank too dependent on the particular industries located near the bank.

Recently, revisionist economic historians such as Arthur Rolnick and Warren Weber of the Federal Reserve Bank of Minneapolis also have questioned the traditional view. According to these revisionists:

1. Very few free-bank closings (which admittedly were numerous in some states) involved losses to note holders.

2. Free-bank notes were quite safe.

3. Most of the free banks were not short-lived.

4. Free-bank failures were quite localized; that is, runs did not spread to banks in other states or to banks within a state that were not holders of the bonds or bad investments that failed and caused the problem.

Critics of this revisionist view point out that Rolnick and Weber's statistics indicate that about 48 percent of all free banks closed and that about 15 percent of all free banks became insolvent, causing losses for bank note holders; hence, these critics question whether notes of free banks really were "quite safe." Nonetheless, even these critics admit that earlier views that "free" (almost unregulated) banking was unsuccessful may have been overstated, particularly in light of the recent catastrophe in the U.S. thrift industry, which was heavily regulated (see Chapter 13).

THE CIVIL WAR AND THE BEGINNING OF THE END OF FREE BANKING

If not for the outbreak of the Civil War, the United States undoubtedly would have continued down the free-banking path for a longer period. The wartime breakup of the country, however, permanently changed the course of the nation's banking and monetary affairs. During the war, the Union and the Confederacy had separate currencies and banking systems. Both suffered from inflation during the war, as the two governments printed money to finance their efforts. Inflation was particularly pronounced in the Confederacy; tremendous inflation in the southern states virtually rendered the Confederate currency worthless even before the Army of Virginia surrendered in 1865.

As the Union government became more confident of victory in 1863 and 1864, the Union Congress enacted legislation that changed the face of American monetary and banking arrangements. In 1864, Congress enacted the **National Banking Act.** This legislation contained the following important provisions:

1. Branching was prohibited, except for those state banks that changed to a national charter and already had some intrastate branches.

2. Required reserves were imposed on deposit liabilities and were to be held either in vault cash or as deposits in reserve-city banks or central reserve-city banks (New York, Chicago, St. Louis), which themselves had to hold their entire 25 percent reserves in vault cash. Eligible reserves were gold, gold certificates, greenbacks (more on these below), or other Treasury currency—not national bank notes. Because these reserves could not be used, they became frozen assets in a crisis, precipitating financial panics. The pyramiding of reserves in this unit bank system also worsened the problem, because in a time of crisis each bank pulled its reserve deposits from its reserve-city banks.

3. State bank notes were taxed out of existence; national banks therefore gained the sole privilege of issuing bank notes. To compensate for having established thousands of unit banks, the federal government printed uniform bank notes that were to be issued by national banks when they made loans. Such notes were homogeneous and were received and paid at par by national banks throughout the nation—thereby creating a federal currency.

4. Each national bank was required to deposit, with the comptroller of the currency, $100 of special 2 percent government bonds for every $90 of bank notes issued. This provided an incentive for national banks to issue credit in the form of deposits rather than notes; the banks frequently charged a higher interest rate to borrowers who demanded loan proceeds in notes (currency). This led to an underissuance of notes, which is alleged to have been the cause of several liquidity crises in the United States: In a crisis banks could not pay out one liability for another (deposits for bank notes), but had to pay out legal tender cash (gold or greenbacks) from their assets.

In short, this reserve system had its problems. Periodically, the smaller rural banks would call upon the larger city banks for cash to satisfy their own depositors' liquidity needs. The larger city banks, finding that their reserves fell correspondingly, cut back on their own lending, thereby contributing to a general scarcity of credit. As a consequence, this system that allowed a pyramiding of reserves caused financial crises to spread quickly throughout the financial community. Under the national banking system there was no ''lender of last resort'' to supply additional funds during such credit crunches; because holders of reserves (large city banks) were themselves commercial banks, they were subject to the identical credit crunches that the smaller banks were. That is one reason that led to a change in public attitudes about central banking and the eventual creation of the Federal Reserve System in 1913, which are the subjects of the remainder of this chapter.

PRELUDE TO THE FED

Most of us in our day and age take the existence of the Federal Reserve for granted. The Fed is rooted deeply in history, however. The Federal Reserve did not materialize overnight; its creation stemmed from decades of agitation over the subject of this text: money and banking issues.

The Greenback Era During the Civil War, the Union issued a fiduciary, nonredeemable paper money, popularly known as **greenbacks** (for the obvious reason that one side was printed in green ink). After the Civil War, three-fourths of the quantity of money in the United States consisted of greenbacks and related notes issued by the U.S. government. Hence, the bulk of the money supply in the United States was composed of financial instruments that had not existed before the Civil War. Yet when Congress had authorized the creation of greenbacks, it had done so with the express intent of removing them from circulation after the conclusion of the Civil War. Its aim also had been to resume a full gold standard as soon as possible following the conclusion of hostilities.

Although Congress first authorized greenbacks in 1862, the *Greenback Era* of United States economics and politics typically is dated as beginning with the end of the Civil War. This period, which stretched to 1879, was marked by deep political divisions over the issue of continuing or ending the use of greenbacks as a national currency. Keep in mind that national involvement in monetary and banking affairs had been limited in scope since the demise of the Second Bank of the United States over half a century before; to many of the generation of the 1860s and 1870s, greenbacks were a federal intrusion into private and state affairs.

A banking panic in 1873 considerably changed the political complexion of the greenback issue. Some who had previously doubted the worth of federal greenbacks lost faith in the worth of private national bank notes. Agitation grew for an expansion of the federal government's issue of greenbacks, and in 1874 the Republican-controlled Congress passed a bill that would have authorized such an expansion—known as the "Inflation Bill"—only to see it vetoed by Republican President Ulysses Grant (1822–1885). In a political compromise, Congress then enacted a law holding constant the quantity of greenbacks already issued, thereby postponing the previously planned elimination of the national currency. Then, in 1875, following a solid defeat at the polls, the lame-duck Republican Congress finished its session by passing the **Resumption Act of 1875,** which authorized resumption of a full gold standard in 1879.

Political lines of the nation then split into "hard money" and "soft money" camps. The hard money proponents, which included eastern business people and bankers—and most academic economists—supported the resumption of the gold standard and eventual elimination of the national currency. Soft money advocates of the western regions of the nation—farmers and other western laborers and small-business people—lobbied against the gold standard and in favor of continuation and expansion of the issuance of greenbacks. Because the Republican party was solidly in the gold resumption camp while the Democrats wavered on the issue, many in the west formed independent political parties; among these, in fact, was a party called the "Greenbackers" that single-mindedly pursued monetary issues at the polls in the 1876 election.

Populism and the Free-Silver Movement   Despite the efforts of the soft money advocates, the Republicans won the 1876 election. Greenbackers dissolved as a formal political entity in 1882. Those previously allied with the Greenbackers adopted a new idea: **free silver.** This term is somewhat misleading; it referred broadly to a proposal to permit unlimited coinage of silver as dictated by the monetary needs of the American economy. Those who favored silver coinage began the "free-silver movement" and wedded their interests to the broader interests of the political and economic movement called **populism** that developed in the 1880s and culminated with the formal formation of the Populist party in 1892.

Prospectors found large deposits of silver in the western regions of the United States as the nation expanded, and beginning in 1872 there was a lengthy decline in the price of silver relative to other goods and services. In 1873, Congress passed a law, which the free-silver movement later termed "The Crime of 1873," that ended the coinage of silver dollars, which up to that time had been a legal practice; significant quantities of silver coins had been produced in the 1830s and 1850s. Proponents of the use of silver as money felt this law disbanding the silver dollar had resulted from a conspiracy of the eastern hard money interests to promote the gold standard even though silver was a less expensive commodity to use as money.

Behind the free-silver movement lay concerns about periods of price *deflation* that the United States had experienced. For instance, between 1882 and 1885 the level of prices of goods and services *fell* by about 13 percent. For many western farmers and others who borrowed from banks, this had resulted in an unexpected increase in the real magnitudes of their debts that, not too surprisingly, they did not like. These individuals composed the heart and soul of the free-silver movement.

The greatest success of the free-silver movement was the **Treasury Note Act of 1890,** otherwise known as the Sherman Silver Purchase Act. Congress enacted this legislation with the support of President Benjamin Harrison (1833–1901), who had defeated the hard money advocate Grover Cleveland (1837–1908) in 1888. Harrison had promised to "do something for silver," and the 1890 act sponsored by Senator John Sherman did just that. It authorized annual Treasury purchases of silver and the issuance of U.S. notes backed by the silver the Treasury purchased.

The free-silver movement did not seek to replace gold as the basis for the nation's monetary system; rather, it promoted **bimetallism,** in which *both* gold and silver would stand side by side as the metals backing the nation's money. Proponents of bimetallism argued that a combined gold-silver system would strengthen the nation's money, because if one metal fluctuated in value, they claimed, stability of the other metal's value automatically would lend stability to the quantity of money. Opponents of bimetallism argued that, in fact, a decline in the price of one metal, such as silver, would cause individuals to hoard the more highly valued money backed by the other metal—gold—driving money backed by gold out of use. Economists argue to this day about which of these views was correct.

The bimetallists of the free-silver movement had great hopes for their monetary plan. They envisioned the eventual internationalization of the bimetallic standard and a period of economic harmony and stability. These hopes were dashed by the Panic of 1893 and the economic depression of the 1890s.

Panics, Studies, and Central Banking Proposals   Bimetallism really never got off the ground. The American people reelected Grover Cleveland, the champion of the hard money interests, as President in 1892. A general decline in stock prices through 1892 and early 1893 was followed by a financial panic in May of 1893. Individuals began to hoard

WAS *THE WIZARD OF OZ,* LIKE SEEMINGLY EVERYTHING ELSE IN THIS WORLD, ALL ABOUT *MONEY?*

Believe it or not, the answer to this question probably is yes. Undeniably, the creator of the Land of Oz, L. Frank Baum, wrote his classic *The Wonderful Wizard of Oz,* published in 1900, as a child's story; yet he filled it with symbolism concerning the monetary issues of his day. Consider the following interpretation, which has been offered by the economist Hugh Rockoff. Oz, the name of the fictitious land visited by Dorothy, the little girl from Kansas, also happens to be the abbreviation for *ounces,* as in ounces of *gold.* The city inhabited by the Wizard of Oz, the Emerald City (symbolic of Washington, D.C.), happens to be all green-colored—the color of money. The same is true of the Emerald Palace (representing the White House) the Wizard inhabits; indeed, before entering the Emerald City and Palace, Dorothy and her friends—the Scarecrow, the Tin Woodman, and the Cowardly Lion—all put on green-colored glasses with gold buckles. The people of the Emerald City they meet most likely represent Washington bureaucrats, and the yellow brick road that led to the Emerald City could be nothing but a pathway of gold bars leading to Washington.

Who is Dorothy supposed to be? According to Rockoff, she broadly represents the United States but probably is modeled more narrowly after Elizabeth Lease, a populist orator from Kansas known in her time as the "Kansas Tornado." Indeed, the tornado that carries Dorothy to the Land of Oz most likely is symbolic of the free-silver movement that swept out of the western United States to shake the political foundations rooted in the eastern part of the nation. Her dog Toto may represent the "teetotaler," or prohibitionist, wing of the populist movement—a group that, like Toto, continually pulls Dorothy (America) in the wrong directions. The Munchkins probably represent the "small-minded inhabitants" of the east, while the Scarecrow, who thinks he has no brains but really does, represents western farmers who fail to give themselves enough credit for their innate common sense. The Tin Woodman symbolizes the urban workingman who has lost both heart and soul. The Cowardly Lion, according to Rockoff, is William Jennings Bryan, the "roaring orator" and presidential candidate who decried gold but backed off—in a way Frank Baum evidently found cowardly—from that stand for political reasons. Indeed, the poppy field that puts the Cowardly Lion to sleep in the story probably symbolizes the political issues that distracted Bryan from the free-silver movement.

Who were the Wicked Witches of the East and West? According to Rockoff, they are Presidents Grover Cleveland and William McKinley, who, against the wishes of the populists, stuck with the gold standard. The Wizard of Oz, Rockoff theorizes, is a man named Marcus Alonzo Hanna, a close adviser to McKinley, head of the Republican National Committee, and widely viewed by Frank Baum and many other United States citizens as a political powerhouse who manipulated members of Congress and Presidents.

In the movie version of the classic story, Dorothy wears ruby slippers. In the book, however, her slippers were cast from *silver.* Recall from the story that her slippers were Dorothy's key to returning to home and happiness—she tapped them together, repeated over and over (in the movie version) "There's no place like home," and magically was transported back to Kansas. The symbolism here should be clear—silver as a component of the nation's monetary standard was viewed by Frank Baum as the answer to the nation's economic problems.

Naturally, any work of art such as *The Wizard of Oz* can be perceived by different people in different ways. We hope that this description of the monetary symbolism one can find in the book will not ruin the story for you the next time you read it or see it on the screen. After all, what *really* matters to the child in all of us is that Dorothy made good friends and eventually found her way home.

Adapted from Hugh Rockoff, "The 'Wizard of Oz' as a Monetary Allegory," *Journal of Political Economy,* 98 (4, August 1990), pp. 739–760.

gold, and stocks of the less-valued silver began to build at the U.S. Treasury. In the summer of 1893, during which yet another wave of bank panics occurred, Cleveland called a special session of Congress to reconsider the annual silver purchases required by the Sherman Silver Purchase Act of 1890. Congress responded by repealing the act.

The grand finale of the free-silver movement was the election of 1896, which pitted the Democratic party's William Jennings Bryan (1860–1929) against the Republican William McKinley (1843–1901). McKinley was a hard money proponent and a solid favorite to win the election. By this time, the Democratic party had absorbed most of the free-silver advocates, and at the Democratic National Convention in Chicago Bryan championed their cause. In a speech that many present there compared to an emotional earthquake, Bryan decried McKinley's hard money views, saying,

> You shall not press down upon the brow of labor this crown of thorns, you shall not crucify mankind upon a cross of gold.

Bryan's speech-making abilities made him a public sensation. Nevertheless, he lost the election, which sounded the final death knell for the free-silver movement.

In fact, a general economic recovery followed in the late 1890s and early 1900s. Just when national financial and economic stability seemed assured, however, another panic swept Wall Street and the nation in 1907 (see the International Perspective in Chapter 12 for a description of the Panic of 1907). This panic occurred at a precipitous time—the apparent success of a strong central government during the presidency of Theodore Roosevelt (1858–1919) had convinced many citizens and leaders that centralized policy making could work. Roosevelt and Congress called for studies of central banking arrangements. One, the *Warburg Plan,* proposed establishment of a centralized banking system overseen by a forty-two-member ''Board of Managers'' composed of the secretary of the Treasury, the comptroller of the currency, the United States treasurer, six members of Congress, twenty chairmen of central bank branches, twelve members voted by stockholding member banks, and a salaried board governor. All appointed members would serve one-year terms under this plan. Another study, the *Fowler Plan,* advocated a similar system governed by a ''Court of Finance,'' to be composed of seventeen members, all appointed by the President, representing specific regions of the nation.

The Aldrich-Vreeland Act   In response to the Panic of 1907 and some of the recommendations made by the Warburg and Fowler plans, Congress passed the Aldrich-Vreeland Act in 1908. This act required that Congress appoint a National Monetary Commission. Congress directed the commission, which was headed by Senator Nelson Aldrich (1841–1915), to recommend reforms necessary for the establishment of a central bank. Nine congressional representatives and nine senators held extensive hearings, which culminated in 1911 in the *Aldrich Plan* for a United States central bank.

Some of the more important recommendations from the National Monetary Commission were:

1. The creation of a central institution that would hold and create bank reserves through its credit-creating powers.
2. The establishment of a coordinated system of check clearing and collection.
3. The creation of an efficient fiscal agent to assist the Treasury in its debt management and with its receipts, disbursements, and foreign exchange transactions.

The Aldrich Plan specifically recommended one central bank with fifteen branches for different regions of the country. The members of the National Monetary Commission remained suspicious of too much centralization. Therefore, they proposed that the central bank be governed by a "Reserve Association Board." This board would be composed of forty-five members including the secretaries of the Treasury, commerce, labor, and agriculture; the comptroller of the currency; fourteen members elected by boards of directors of the central bank's branches; twelve members elected by holders of stock in the central bank; twelve members representing agriculture and business; and a governor and deputy governor.

Ultimately, a greatly revised version of the Aldrich Plan was pieced together through the efforts of President Woodrow Wilson (1856–1924), Senator Carter Glass (1858–1946), and Senator Robert Owen (1856–1947). The more streamlined plan they put together, which became the 1913 *Owen bill* for a central bank, called for a centralized banking system overseen by a seven-member "Board of Governors of the National Currency" who would "serve at the pleasure of the president." Three of these would be the secretaries of the Treasury and agriculture and the comptroller of the currency, and four would be presidential appointees who would represent the views of national interests in commerce, manufacturing, transportation, and banking and credit.

This plan formed the basis for legislation ultimately enacted by Congress later that year. This legislation was the Federal Reserve Act.

THE FED FROM ITS ORIGINS TO THE PRESENT

As our chronology has made clear, the people at the end of the nineteenth century took for granted the *absence* of central banking arrangements. For almost a century—from 1833 through 1913—the United States had no formal central bank. The turnabout during the second decade of the twentieth century ushered in the *presence* of central banking that we—at the tail end of that century—now take for granted.

THE FEDERAL RESERVE ACT AND THE EARLY FEDERAL RESERVE

Even after the Panic of 1907 and the recommendations of the 1908 National Monetary Commission, strong opposition to a central bank continued. From the inception of the United States as a nation, antifederalist sentiment often prevailed. When it became apparent that a central bank was to be established, there was controversy about who should control it. Naturally, the federal government wanted control. So, too, did the business sector and potential member banks (i.e., national banks). The Owen bill and successive alterations of that bill represented a compromise reached among these contending factions. Under the final bill introduced by Glass and Owen, which became the **Federal Reserve Act,** the federal government, the business community, and member banks would each have representation in the control of the U.S. central bank. There was to be a division of control between the central authorities in Washington, D.C., and twelve regional district Federal Reserve banks.

To accomplish this goal, the original Federal Reserve Act of 1913 established the seven-member **Federal Reserve Board,** which was composed of the secretary of the Treasury, the comptroller of the currency, and five members appointed by the President and confirmed by the Senate. Each of the five appointees was to represent separate geographic, commercial, and industrial interests, and at least two members of the Board were to be experienced in banking and finance. The *Federal Reserve System* the act authorized also was intended to represent diverse interests, as we shall discuss in more detail below.

The historic legislation creating the U.S. central banking system was signed into law on December 23, 1913, by President Woodrow Wilson. As originally conceived, the Federal Reserve System was to be a type of cooperative among businesses, consumers, bankers, and the federal government. Its originators hoped that the Fed, as it has come to be called, was now empowered to prevent financial panics—such as the one that occurred in 1907—because it could lend funds (and thereby provide liquidity) to banks during monetary crises. The Fed was not conceived as an institution that would control the money supply, interest rates, and credit. Rather, it was to give "elasticity" to money and bank reserves. Money elasticity existed if the money supply could change substantially, over short periods of time, in response to the public's changes in the demand for it. Thus, the Fed was not viewed as an institution that would actively alter the money supply to achieve economic goals, but rather as an institution that would change the money supply at the public's will.

Elasticity was to be obtained via a discounting, or lending, mechanism. Through this mechanism, member banks were allowed to borrow funds temporarily from the Fed. In the United States no such discounting mechanism existed at that time. The amount of elasticity actually providable by the Fed was limited, however, because the Federal Reserve Act was very specific in terms of assets that could be rediscounted. The term **rediscounting** applies to the process of central banks lending reserves on the basis of collateral that may have already been discounted. For example, if a depository institution is in need of reserves and has in its asset portfolio private paper that it has already discounted, the Fed will extend a loan to the institution (in the form of reserves) at a discount—thus the notion of Fed rediscounting. The process of discounting and rediscounting is discussed in greater detail in Chapter 17.

The Federal Reserve Act specified what collateral would be eligible for rediscounting. Eligible collateral consisted mostly of high-grade, self-liquidating commercial paper (recall this concept from Chapter 6). Over the years, however, the eligibility for discounting has been expanded—as specified in Regulation A of the Federal Reserve Code. Most important, a 1916 amendment authorized advances (loans) to member banks on the bank's own 15-day notes, secured either by eligible paper or by government securities. In 1932, the Fed was authorized to make advances to member banks on any asset. The Federal Reserve Act also defined reserves to member banks in a way different from the way in which they had been defined for national banks up to that time. Only deposits of member banks in Federal Reserve district banks were to be used as reserves in the Federal Reserve System.

For the most part, the Fed was viewed as a passive service agency. Its services include providing check clearing and collection, regulating member banks, and providing currency. At its inception, the Fed's function did not include engaging in countercyclical monetary policy—that is, the Fed was not expected to expand the money supply in order to counteract a recession and decrease the money supply in order to counteract a period of inflation.

The Question of Capitalization for the Federal Reserve Banks   Who should provide the capital for the Federal Reserve banks? Recall that the First and Second Banks of the United States were owned in part (20 percent) by the federal government, and the remainder was owned by the private sector. Many argued that a similar system should be used for the new central bank. Others favored selling stock to the general public. Still others thought stock should be sold only to member banks. Ultimately, each member bank (national bank) at that time was required to subscribe to (buy) the stock of its district Federal Reserve bank. A mandatory subscription was to equal 3 percent of each national bank's net worth (called capital and surplus). Another 3 percent was due at the Fed's request. In actuality, each member bank paid only the 3 percent of its net worth as a subscription to the Federal Reserve System. Because the member banks own the stock of each Federal Reserve district bank, these district banks are properly designated as wholly owned by the member banks. Ownership does not mean, however, that private banks control the Fed or even receive its earnings (except for an insignificant amount—no more than 6 percent of the value of the Fed stock held by the bank).

The Relationship between the Twelve Federal Reserve Banks and the Board of Governors   The Federal Reserve Act of 1913 left much unsaid about what should be the relationship between the twelve Federal Reserve district banks and the Federal Reserve Board (renamed the Board of Governors of the Federal Reserve System pursuant to the Banking Act of 1935) in Washington, D.C. To a large extent, the district banks handled their chores independently of each other. Additionally, they engaged in discounting (almost) independently of each other. At that time, the New York Fed was still the most important district bank because it held the largest percentage of the Federal Reserve System's total reserves. This is still the case today.

World War I provided an immediate test for the Federal Reserve. The international gold standard nearly collapsed entirely with the outbreak of war in Europe, disrupting United States' financial and commodity markets. In August of 1914, before the Federal Reserve really had begun full operations, Treasury Secretary William McAdoo invoked the Aldrich-Vreeland Act and authorized national and state banks to issue emergency currency, which kept panic from sweeping the banking system. The quantity of money grew by about 70 percent between the opening of the Federal Reserve banks in November 1914 and the signing of the Armistice that concluded World War I in November 1918, and the price level nearly doubled during that period.

Although Congress had intended for the Federal Reserve System to be nearly independent from government to shelter its operations from partisan politics, the outbreak of the war placed much power in the hands of Treasury Secretary McAdoo. When the other members of the Federal Reserve's Board of Governors objected to Federal Reserve purchases of Treasury bonds for war finance at artificially low prices, McAdoo threatened to invoke congressional legislation that had authorized him to gain immediate control over all U.S. banking reserves in an emergency. In effect, he threatened to become Federal Reserve Board ''dictator'' and, when the rest of the Board gave in, effectively carried out his threat.

Irrespective of McAdoo's power over centralized strategy of the Federal Reserve, until 1922 most day-to-day Fed policy was determined by the officials of the twelve district banks. In other words, the Federal Reserve Board—aside from Secretary McAdoo during the war—had relatively little power. Indeed, the most powerful leadership came from the head of the Federal Reserve Bank of New York, Benjamin Strong, who had solid connections with J. Pierpont Morgan and other Wall Street barons as well as with political leaders. During much of this period, there was a conflict between the Federal Reserve Board and the twelve Federal Reserve banks because the Board wanted to dominate policy making. Nonetheless, Strong was the dominant force in the Federal Reserve System during the 1920s until his death in 1928.

The Great Depression   Nearly everyone agrees that the great debacle of the Fed's history was its handling of the stock market crash of 1929 and the subsequent waves of bank panics throughout much of the nation. To this day, however, there continues to be little agreement about whether these panics were a cause or a symptom of the Great Depression that followed on the heels of the ''great crash.'' Irrespective of this latter issue, nonetheless, most economic historians concur that the Federal Reserve System utterly failed to meet the key objective that Congress had set out for it in the Federal Reserve

Act: namely, to provide for the economy's need for an ''elastic'' currency in times of crisis.

Initially, the Federal Reserve responded to the banking crisis that followed the 1929 crash by releasing more reserves into the banking system. Then the power vacuum created by the death of Benjamin Strong was not quickly filled, and the result was a policy of inaction. Between 1929 and 1933, one-third of all commercial banks had ceased to exist, and the quantity of money had also *fallen* by about a third—the largest decline in the nation's history.

Many economic historians argue that this decline in the money stock contributed to the severity of the Great Depression. Some go further, contending that it both *induced* and *perpetuated* the economic catastrophe. We shall have more to say about views on the effects of the quantity of money on economic activity in Unit 6, where we shall see that there still is much disagreement on this issue. Nevertheless, to this day all observers recognize that Federal Reserve officials committed significant errors of judgment in the early 1930s. (For a contest at the 1988 Christmas party of Federal Reserve Board staff members, a few economists set up a display called ''You Make the Call'' for judging by members of the Board; among other questions, it asked the 1988 members of the Board what *they* would have done in the 1930s—as a *joke*, it indicated that cutting the money stock was the ''right call'' for a Board member confronted with a stock market crash and a declining economy.)

LANDMARK DATES AT THE FED: 1935, 1951, AND 1980

The experience of the Great Depression called into question the significant reform that the Federal Reserve System had represented. It is interesting to compare the reaction of the generation of the 1930s with the judgment of the generation of the 1830s in regard to the Second Bank of the United States. In the 1830s, the answer to perceived misjudgments by central bankers was to eliminate the central bank and decentralize the monetary and banking affairs of the nation. In the 1930s, the answer that citizens and their lawmakers reached was just the opposite. It took the form of new legislation that *centralized* the powers of the Federal Reserve System.

The Banking Act of 1935   By the mid-1930s, a widespread perception had formed that *private* financial interests had led to and perpetuated the Great Depression, to the detriment of the public good. Additionally, the public and their representatives attached much of the blame for the economic crisis to the previous President, Herbert Hoover (1874–1964), and his administration. Consequently, Congress acted by passing a host of banking laws that extended the scope of federal oversight of the financial system, such as the Glass-Steagall Act of 1933 and other legislation that we discussed in Unit 3. One other important law Congress enacted in the 1930s was the **Banking Act of 1935.** The Federal Reserve structure that exists today is that specified by this legislation.

Among other things, the Banking Act of 1935 significantly amended the Federal Reserve Act. First, it gave the Federal Reserve Board the new, official title, **Board of Governors of the Federal Reserve System,** so that members of the Board are formally ''governors'' of the system. To avoid confusion, Congress renamed the chief officers of the Federal Reserve banks, who previously were ''governors'' of the district banks; they became ''presidents'' of the banks instead.

Second, Congress removed the secretary of the Treasury and the comptroller of the currency from the Board. Henceforth, the president had the power, subject to Senate confirmation, to appoint all Federal Reserve governors, with due regard to regional diversity and variation in background of the appointees. Not more than four of the seven members of the Board of Governors could belong to the same political party.

Third, the 1935 law lengthened the term of appointment of Board governors to 14 years; members of the original Federal Reserve Board served 10-year terms. Congress specified that the terms of the governors' appointments were to overlap in such a way that a new governor was appointed every 2 years. Congress further authorized the President to appoint, from existing governors or through a new appointment, both a Board chairman and vice chairman. Each of these officials would serve 4 years in these positions before being reappointed to another 4-year term.

Fourth, the 1935 law permitted the Board of Governors to vary reserve requirements within ranges set by Congress. This change gave the Board in Washington significant power not shared by the district Federal Reserve bank presidents.

Fifth, in another move to centralize power over policy making with the Board of Governors, the law gave the Board of Governors final say concerning Federal Reserve bank discount rates. While the Federal Reserve banks could individually propose changes in their discount rates, it was up to the Board in Washington to approve or veto such changes.

Finally, in an effort to formalize the Federal Reserve's trading of government securities (which we shall discuss in more detail below and in greater depth in Chapter 17), Congress created a twelve-member Federal Reserve committee, the **Federal Open Market Committee (FOMC).** This committee, as we address later on, is composed of the Board of Governors and five of the Federal Reserve bank presidents.

Following the passage of the Banking Act of 1935, there was a gradual shift of power within the Federal Reserve System from the district banks to the Board of Governors. Today that power primarily is centralized in the Board of Governors, although the Federal Reserve bank presidents continue to exercise considerable power within the Federal Reserve System.

The Fed-Treasury Accord of 1951   During World War II, the Board of Governors of the Federal Reserve System, under the leadership of Board Chairman Marriner Eccles from 1934 to 1948, implicitly became an arm of the United States Treasury. To help in the Treasury's efforts to finance the massive war effort, the Fed assisted by buying and selling government securities in sufficient quantities to "peg" the interest rate on Treasury bills at a nearly constant, and low, level.

The Fed's cooperation and assistance during the war also aided its image within and outside the government. By the end of the 1940s, however, some concern had developed within the Federal Reserve System that too much cooperation threatened the Fed's cherished independence. The Fed reached an amicable agreement with the Treasury Department in March 1951, known as the *Federal Reserve–Treasury Accord*, to end this practice. Most economists mark this date as the advent of truly independent monetary policy making in modern times.

The DIDMCA of 1980   We shall discuss Federal Reserve policy making in the 1960s, 1970s, and 1980s in detail in Chapter 26. Yet the Depository Institutions Deregulation and Monetary Control Act of 1980 made important changes in the Fed's structure that are appropriate for us to explore in this chapter. Before 1980, only national commercial banks and state commercial banks that chose to do so were *member banks* in the Federal Reserve System. This membership, which required that a member bank hold shares of ownership in the Federal Reserve System, subjected the member bank to Fed regulatory oversight and required the bank to hold reserves with the Federal Reserve bank in its district.

Membership also qualified it for access to Federal Reserve services, however, such as check clearing, and for access to Federal Reserve discount loans, at subsidized prices and interest rates. State authorities regulated all remaining commercial banks that were not Fed members, and other state and federal authorities regulated thrift institutions; these nonmember depository institutions thereby had no direct access to Fed services and loans. To obtain these services indirectly, they maintained correspondent relationships with commercial banks that belonged to the Federal Reserve System.

The DIDMCA ended this structure. It stipulated that *all* federally insured depository institutions must meet the Federal Reserve's reserve requirements. In return, the DIDMCA granted *all* these same depository institutions access to Federal Reserve services (though Congress instructed the Fed to charge ''market prices'' for these services) and to its discount loans. Hence, the act expanded considerably the scope of the Fed's authority over total reserves in the banking system, thereby tightening its ability to influence the quantity of money.

THE PRESENT FED: STRUCTURE AND ORGANIZATION

As discussed above, the ''center'' of the seven-member Federal Reserve System is the Board of Governors in Washington, D.C. It would be a mistake, however, to assume that the Board of Governors is the *only* important entity within the Federal Reserve System. The Fed is a creature of many parts.

Currently the Federal Reserve System consists of:

1. The Board of Governors
2. Twelve Federal Reserve district banks
3. Member banks
4. Other depository institutions

Within the system itself, there are other important groups:

1. The Federal Open Market Committee
2. The Federal Advisory Council (FAC)
3. The Federal Reserve staff

The Board of Governors Under the terms of the Banking Act of 1935, the Board of Governors consists of seven members, and each member serves a 14-year term. The terms are staggered so that one of the seven members is retired at the end of every 2 years. The governors are appointed by the President. Neither the comptroller of the currency nor the secretary of the Treasury is eligible to be a governor. No member of the Board can be reappointed if he or she has served a full term. At any one time, no more than one member can be selected from any of the twelve Federal Reserve districts. One of the members is designated by the President as chairman and another as vice chairman. Each appointment of the seven members is accomplished with the advice and consent of the Senate. Although each governor can serve a 14-year term, the chairman of the Board of Governors serves a 4-year term.

The Board of Governors does not need to go to Congress to obtain its operating revenues. Nor does the General Accounting Office (GAO) perform a full audit of the Board's activities, because the Board's operating funds are obtained from the ''earnings'' of the twelve Federal Reserve banks and therefore are presumably not under the control of Congress or the GAO.

In principle, the Federal Reserve System maintains its independence on three levels: (1) the Board's independent source of revenues, (2) the staggered terms of the governors, and (3) freedom from accountability to the GAO. Congress decided that in order for the Fed to carry out its functions effectively, it should be independent of both the executive and the legislative branches of government. Whether this independence has been abused and should be terminated is the subject of the Current Controversy at the end of this chapter.

Among its many powers, the Board of Governors can:

1. Approve or disapprove discount rates established by the various district banks.
2. Establish within the limits set by Congress reserve requirements for all depository institutions.
3. Permit one district Federal Reserve bank to lend to another, and require such a loan if at least five members of the Board agree.
4. Determine the types of loans that the Federal Reserve district banks shall make.
5. Supervise the Federal Reserve district banks by examining their accounts.

Federal Reserve District Banks   The original Federal Reserve Act authorized twelve separate Federal Reserve districts, each with its own Federal Reserve bank. Figure 15-2 shows the locations of the Fed banks and the twenty-five branches.

Each Federal Reserve district bank is a federally chartered corporation. It has stockholders, directors, and a president. In each of the twelve geographic districts, the member banks are the stockholders of the Reserve bank. They select six of the nine directors for each district bank. Currently, each member bank purchases stock in the Federal Reserve bank equal to 3 percent of its net worth. As the net worth of the member bank increases, it must purchase more Federal Reserve bank stock.

The nine directors of each Federal Reserve district bank are categorized as class A in the banking sector, class B in the business sector, and class C in the public sector. Class A directors are elected by the member banks. Of the class A directors, one is supposed to represent a small bank, one a medium-sized bank, and one a large bank. Member banks also elect the class B directors, who are not necessarily bankers. Rather, they typically are prominent individuals from the business or agricultural sector.

Finally, class C directors are appointed directly by the Board of Governors of the Federal Reserve System in Washington, D.C. These directors cannot be officers of any bank; they are to be from the public sector. Each director serves a 3-year term. These terms are staggered such that one director of each of the three categories is elected or appointed each year.

An important power of the Board of Governors is to select the chairman and the deputy chairman of the board of directors of each Federal Reserve district bank. These two individuals are selected from the three class C directors.

The Federal Reserve district banks are privately owned by the member banks; however, control by member banks is limited. Also, the degree to which the district banks' profits are remitted to the member banks is strictly controlled. The Federal Reserve district banks are not chartered to earn profits, but rather to supervise member banks and to engage in the implementation of the monetary policy set forth by the Board of Governors of the Federal Reserve System.

In this age of rapid communications technology, there has been some discussion about the actual need for district banks. Is their continuing existence simply another case of a government agency outliving its usefulness? It is safe to say that the vested interests of

Figure 15-2
Geographical Locations of Federal Reserve District Banks.   [*Source:* Board of Governors of the Federal Reserve System, *Federal Reserve Bulletin* (April 1992).]

those who work for and with each district bank would remain sufficiently strong to prevent the demise of district banks, even if they were no longer needed.

Member Banks   The United States has a dual banking system consisting of nationally chartered banks and state-chartered banks. All national banks are required to be members of the Federal Reserve System. State banks can become members if they wish. Before the passage of the Depository Institutions Deregulation and Monetary Control Act of 1980, membership in the Federal Reserve System offered major benefits. Member banks were allowed to use the Fed's check-clearing facilities as well as its transfer wire service for transferring funds from one bank to another. In order to be a depository of the U.S. Treasury (to have a U.S. Treasury tax and loan account), a bank had to be a member of the Federal Reserve System. There was and perhaps continues to be some prestige attached to membership in the Federal Reserve System.

Since 1981, however, all depository institutions have been able to obtain the Fed's services if they pay the fees charged by the Fed. In other words, any depository institution can use the Fed's check-clearing and collection process if it is willing to pay a service charge. All depository institutions are now required to hold non-interest-bearing reserves with Federal Reserve district banks; this diminishes but has not eliminated the distinction between nonmember and member banks; the latter continue to have a role in the Federal Reserve System not shared by the former.

Nonmember Depository Institutions   The diagram of the Federal Reserve System in Figure 15-3 shows no category labeled ''nonmember depository institutions.'' This category has no formal role in the organizational structure of the Fed. Nonetheless, all depository institutions must hold reserves with Federal Reserve district banks.

The Federal Open Market Committee   In the Banking Act of 1935, Congress created the FOMC to formulate and to execute policies with respect to the purchase and sale of government securities (to pursue monetary policies) for the Federal Reserve System as a whole. These transactions in government securities are normally referred to as **open-market operations.** After the FOMC was put into operation, individual district Reserve banks were no longer allowed to pursue their own transactions in government securities without FOMC permission. Because the seven Federal Reserve governors constitute a

Figure 15-3
Organizational Structure of the Federal Reserve System.   (*Source:* Board of Governors of the Federal Reserve System.)

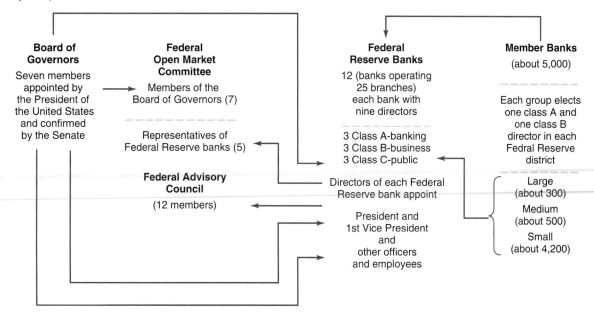

JUST HOW POWERFUL IS THE FED CHAIRMAN?

Several past chairmen of the Federal Reserve's Board of Governors—Marriner Eccles (1934–1948), William McChesney Martin (1951–1970), Arthur Burns (1970–1978), and Paul Volcker (1979–1987)—left their personal stamps on the Federal Reserve System. Eccles rescued the Fed from political demise following its poor performance at the onset of the Great Depression, and Martin became synonymous with the institution during his 20-year reign as chairman. Martin also provided the Fed with its most memorable quotes, such as "The Federal Reserve's job is to take away the punch bowl just when the party gets going," and with its operating cliché, that the Fed's proper monetary policy entailed "leaning against the wind," meaning that it should expertly counter the directions of business cycles. Within the Fed, Burns was known as a hard taskmaster whose goal seemed to be to bring staff economists to their knees.

Volcker and the Test of the Chairman's Power over the Board

Volcker followed in that tradition. A joke that made the rounds within the Fed toward the end of his period there concerned his apparent lack of respect for some of his fellow Board governors. In the early 1980s, Volcker, whose career was wedded to the Fed and who had been appointed by a Democratic President, Jimmy Carter, seemed to hold disdain for appointments to the Board by Republican President Ronald Reagan in the early 1980s. According to the joke, he and the other Board governors went to dine at a high-class Washington restaurant. The waiter went first to Volcker and ran down the list of special entrees available, including a steak dinner with a choice of vegetables. Volcker chose the steak dinner. The waiter then said, "And the vegetables?" After a long look at his colleagues around the table, Volcker then replied, "Oh, they'll all have the same."

The depth of the public's perception of the power of the Federal Reserve Board chairman was evidenced in 1987 when Volcker departed. Stock prices dipped,

bond market prices plummeted, and the dollar's value on world exchange markets took a beating. Ironically, however, it was during Volcker's term as Board chairman that the true power of that position was tested severely. In February 1986, Volcker faced a Board that included four appointees of Ronald Reagan who were convinced that market interest rates were too high and that the Fed should respond by lowering its discount rate. Volcker refused, arguing that "My colleagues from the other central banks weren't ready to move and I had no interest in moving without them." Nonetheless, when it came to the Board vote, Volcker lost, 4–3. Reportedly, he went afterward to a scheduled luncheon with then-Treasury Secretary James Baker, where he expressed anger and threatened to resign his position. Baker and others convinced Volcker to stay on to avoid destabilizing financial markets, but Volcker spent the next year of his term as chairman mindful of the fact that he could be outvoted at any time.

Has Democracy Arrived at the Fed?

Volcker's loss of power over the Board set a new precedent for his 1987 successor, Alan Greenspan, to confront. Greenspan quickly developed a reputation as a consensus builder rather than a dictator, and he gained credibility with the public as a result of the Fed's handling of the stock market crash of October 1987. Nevertheless, Greenspan faced his own political crisis in 1991. In early February of that year, he became convinced that market interest rates should be reduced through appropriate policy actions by the Fed's New York account manager. Greenspan followed protocol by telephoning the members of the FOMC to inform them of his decision to instruct the account manager to undertake these actions.

Two members of the FOMC—presidents at the Federal Reserve's district banks in St. Louis and Kansas City—disagreed with this policy change and requested that Greenspan take up the matter at the FOMC's next meeting, scheduled for the following week. Greenspan, however, refused, claiming that the Fed's internal rules permitted him to take his planned action. The district bank presidents persisted in their dissent, which induced

Greenspan to ask the Fed's legal staff for advice on the matter. They responded with an opinion that the rules were too murky on the issue for an unambiguous legal judgment.

In the end, Greenspan had his way on the interest rate cut, but he ultimately backed down, saying, "The Fed cannot effectively be run by executive fiat. If the Fed chief executive officer cannot persuade his colleagues of the rightness of his policies and recommendations, he cannot prevail." His colleagues welcomed the change. Board Governor Wayne Angell said, "It's [the Board and FOMC] now a more collegial group, rather than a school-marm lecturing third graders."

The *Wall Street Journal* and other financial publications trumpeted this dispute and change in direction with front-page headlines and stories. Clearly, the Fed had become a more democratic institution. As former Fed Governor Martha Segar pointed out, however, "Democracy is messier than dictatorship."

Is More Democracy Good or Bad for the Fed?
There are mixed views on the desirability of greater openness of debate and reduction in the chairman's power at the Fed. Not surprisingly, the other Board governors and the district bank presidents applauded the change, which increased their own power within the Fed. According to Governor Angell,

We have to remember that we are an independent central bank in a democracy. It's important that the Congress and the public and the financial markets have some notion what we are trying to do, and that we have some semblance of debate.

A former president of the Dallas Federal Reserve Bank offered a similar judgment:

There's a lot of institutional memory among the presidents. Not to put Washington down . . . but I don't think we're totally dumb. We d——— sure know what's going on in the hinterlands, and I think it's important somebody can go to Washington and say, "Hey, here's what's going on in the boondocks."

A respected economist expressed an editorial opinion in the *Wall Street Journal* that "the passing of the auto-

cratic era of Arthur Burns and Paul Volcker should not be lamented."

Not all observers agreed, however. Many participants in financial markets felt that the internal squabbling at the Fed caused it to respond too slowly to needs for changes in its policies. One *Wall Street Journal* reporter claimed that

. . . [i]t was a startling defeat for Alan Greenspan. With the economy in trouble, monetary policy, a potent stimulus, was put on hold for four critical weeks. Credit remained costly. Layoffs mounted. Instead of combating the recession, the Fed's lack of action exacerbated it.

Economics Nobel laureate Paul Samuelson agreed:

Greenspan got behind. He's got three or four colleagues who are zealots, and he didn't lean on them. You can't be both a good guy and a powerful leader. He was a good guy.

A key member of Congress, Indiana Representative Lee Hamilton, expressed somewhat different concerns:

The bank presidents, as I understand it, are participating in an important economic-policy decision without being either appointed by the president or confirmed by the Senate. I'm not aware of any other agency where major policy decisions are made by individuals who are not government officials.

Hamilton also indicated possible new legislation to amend the role of the district bank presidents.

As we discussed earlier, the early history of the Fed was replete with instances in which internal bickering at the Fed occurred. It will be interesting to see how the story of Fed democracy versus autocracy unfolds in the 1990s and beyond.

Adapted from William Greider, *Secrets of the Temple: How the Federal Reserve Runs the Country* (New York: Simon and Schuster, 1987); Alan Murray, "Dispute Flares Up at Fed over Greenspan's Authority," *Wall Street Journal* (April 4, 1991), p. A3; "Democracy Comes to the Central Bank, Curbing Chief's Power," *Wall Street Journal* (April 5, 1991), p. A1; "Fed Fight Could Work to Delay Cut in Rates," *Wall Street Journal* (April 15, 1991), p. A1; and Jerry L. Jordan, "Strong Chairmen Weaken the Fed," *Wall Street Journal* (April 26, 1991), p. A14.

majority of the twelve-member FOMC, establishment of the FOMC further strengthened the leadership role of the Board of Governors.

The chairman of the Board of Governors is also the chairman of the FOMC. The president of the Federal Reserve Bank of New York is the only permanent member of the FOMC and is always the FOMC vice chairman. The four remaining positions on the FOMC are rotated among the presidents of the district banks. In reality, all twelve presidents attend virtually every meeting of the FOMC. They all take part in discussions, but only five of them are voting members. The FOMC meets eight times a year in Washington, D.C. A much more detailed discussion of FOMC operating procedures is provided in Chapter 17.

At the meeting of the FOMC, its members do not rigidly set the actual quantity and nature of future open-market operations. The FOMC gives a general *FOMC directive* to the person in charge of the Trading Desk at the New York Fed. This person is the FOMC account manager, or simply the account manager. The account manager confers daily by telephone with some of the FOMC members.

The New York Fed makes its purchases and sales of U.S. government securities through a system of dealers. Note that the Fed deals in the *secondary* U.S. government securities market. That is, it buys and sells already existing securities.

The Federal Advisory Council   The Federal Reserve Act of 1913 established the Federal Advisory Council. Its establishment was part of the compromise concerning who should control the Federal Reserve System. The FAC is composed of twelve individuals, one from each of the twelve Federal Reserve districts. Congress originally designed it to promote communication between the banking industry and the Fed. Virtually all members of the FAC have been prominent bankers.

The FAC meets quarterly with the Board of Governors of the Federal Reserve System. As its name implies, the FAC's role is strictly advisory; the Board of Governors is under no obligation to follow FAC advice. Although Fed insiders say that the FAC is virtually powerless, outsiders remain unconvinced. Indeed, a 1990 study by Thomas Havrilesky found evidence that the FOMC directive may be influenced by recommendations of the FAC.[2]

The Professional Staff   Not often discussed, but definitely important, is the Federal Reserve System's professional staff. The Board of Governors and the district banks rely heavily on the professional staff to interpret economic events and to predict the impact of potential monetary policy changes. Many senior staff members have been with the Federal Reserve System for decades, and several governors have been appointed from the professional staff, although none has been chosen as chairman. They are the permanent bureaucracy of the Fed and have been known to have great influence on the thinking of Board members. At every meeting of the FOMC, staff personnel make written and oral presentations about the state of the economy and policy issues.

Federal Reserve staff members, the Board of Governors, and members of the FOMC have considerable responsibilities. As we discussed in earlier chapters, they regulate a sizable portion of the commercial banking industry. In addition, however, the Fed has a prominent role in the nation's payments system, and it conducts monetary policy in the United States. We examine each of these areas of responsibility in the following two chapters.

---

[2]Thomas Havrilesky, ''The Influence of the Federal Advisory Council on Monetary Policy,'' *Journal of Money, Credit, and Banking*, 22 (1, February 1990), pp. 37–50.

CHAPTER SUMMARY

1. The First Bank of the United States lasted from 1791 to 1811. Congress did not renew its charter.

2. The nation's lack of a central bank weakened considerably its ability to finance the war effort in the War of 1812. This experience convinced leaders of the time to support the charter of the Second Bank of the United States for the period 1816–1836.

3. As a result of the "bank war" between President Andrew Jackson and political proponents of the Second Bank, the charter of the Second Bank was not renewed in 1836. Considerable economic and financial fluctuations occurred immediately before and after the Second Bank's demise. So many different factors contributed to these events, however, that it is difficult to reach a conclusion concerning whether continuation of the Second Bank would have been better for the American economy.

4. From 1837 until the Civil War, the United States experienced a period of "free banking" with little federal government involvement. The traditional historical view of this period was that banking was unstable, but recent research has questioned this conclusion.

5. The Civil War largely ended the free-banking experiment. Near the end of the Civil War, in 1864, Congress passed the National Banking Act that created a national banking system and that, through a tax on state bank notes, induced most banks to convert to national charters. State banks emerged again thereafter, leading to the dual banking system that exists in the present day.

6. The existence of the national currency issued by the Union government—greenbacks—at the conclusion of the Civil War led to squabbling between hard money interests that favored removal of the greenbacks and soft money advocates that preferred retention and expansion of the federal government's money issues. This led to the Greenback Era, which died out shortly after resumption of the gold standard in 1879.

7. Replacing the greenback coalition was the free-silver movement, which joined forces with the populist political movement that developed in the 1880s and 1890s to promote a bimetallic monetary standard for the United States. For a brief interval, from 1890 until 1893, the United States had a bimetallic standard.

8. In the 1890s the United States suffered from a wave of banking panics and a depression. A recovery that waxed and waned in the early 1900s was nearly ended by the Panic of 1907. In 1908 Congress enacted the Aldrich-Vreeland Act, permitting the government to use emergency authority to stop panics.

9. After several years that witnessed a variety of studies and proposals for a central bank, Congress in 1913 passed the Federal Reserve Act, which created a Federal Reserve System composed of member banks in twelve districts, whose Federal Reserve district banks were to be overseen by a Federal Reserve Board in Washington.

10. The present structure and powers of the Fed stem from the provisions of the Banking Act of 1935, the Fed-Treasury Accord of 1951, and the Depository Institutions Deregulation and Monetary Control Act of 1980.

GLOSSARY

Banking Act of 1935:   Act that amended the Federal Reserve Act. Among other things, it removed the secretary of the Treasury and the comptroller of the currency from the Board, it lengthened Board governors' terms to 14 years, it permitted the Board of Governors to vary reserve requirements within ranges set by Congress, and it gave the Board of Governors final say concerning Federal Reserve bank discount rates.

Bimetallism: A monetary system in which both gold and silver back the nation's money supply.

Board of Governors of the Federal Reserve System: New name given to the Federal Reserve Board, in accordance with the Banking Act of 1935; Board governors are appointed by the President and confirmed by the Senate.

Federal Open Market Committee (FOMC):   A major policy-making unit of the Federal Reserve System that directs its open-market operations.

Federal Reserve Act: Act passed in 1913 that established a central banking system. Control was to be divided between central authorities in Washington, D.C., and twelve regional banks. The federal government, business sector, and member banks were to share in control.

Federal Reserve Board: Seven-member board, created by the original Federal Reserve Act and composed of the secretary of the Treasury, the comptroller of the currency, and five other members; the five members were to represent separate geographic, commercial, and industrial interests.

Free-banking laws: Laws during the 1800s that facilitated the formation of banks; businesses could obtain banking charters by complying with a general incorporation law; an act of government legislation was not necessary to create a bank.

Free silver: A term in the late nineteenth century that referred broadly to a proposal to permit unlimited coinage of silver as dictated by the monetary needs of the economy.

Greenbacks: A fiduciary, nonredeemable paper money issued by the United States (the Union) during the Civil War.

National Banking Act: An act passed in 1864 that, among other things, prohibited branch banking, imposed required reserves, taxed state banks out of existence, and required national banks to deposit $100 of special 2 percent government bonds for every $90 of bank notes.

Open-market operations: The purchase or sale of U.S. Treasury securities or federal agency securities by the Fed; a method of monetary control.

Populism: A political movement of the late nineteenth century that became aligned with the free-silver movement.

Rediscounting: The process of discounting by central banks to private banks that borrow reserves on the basis of collateral that already has been discounted once.

Resumption Act of 1875:   Act that authorized a full resumption of the gold standard in 1879.

Specie Circular Act of 1836:   A law that required most federal land purchases to be paid for in gold.

Treasury Note Act of 1890:   Also known as the Sherman Silver Purchase Act. The act required the Treasury to purchase silver annually and to issue U.S. notes backed by the silver.

SELF-TEST QUESTIONS

1. Briefly outline the history of U.S. central banking from 1791 to 1836. What were the key issues concerning central banking that arose during this period?

2. Would you argue that free banking was successful or unsuccessful? Explain.

3. Were there any fundamental differences between the objectives of the ''Greenbackers'' of the 1870s and of those who promoted the free-silver movement in the 1880s and 1890s? Support your answer.

4. Compare the early proposals for the Federal Reserve System and its governing board with the actual structure the Banking Act of 1935 specified. What are key differences and similarities?

5. Explain ways that the Federal Reserve might be viewed as a private institution. Explain how it might also be viewed as a governmental institution. How might these contrasting aspects of the Fed create conflict and controversy?

PROBLEMS

15-1. Assume that when first issued, each greenback $1 bill was equal in value to one-half of $1's worth of a paper dollar that was redeemable in gold. Assume further that $20 of redeemable paper money had a market value of 1 ounce of gold.
  a. What was the exchange rate of greenbacks per $1 of gold-redeemable money?
  b. How many greenbacks were required to purchase 1 ounce of gold?

15-2. Continuing problem 15-1, assume now that the quantity of greenbacks supplied increases twice as fast as the quantity of redeemable paper currency supplied, and that the quantity of redeemable paper currency supplied doubles while the quantity of gold remains constant. Other things constant, calculate:
  a. The gold price of redeemable paper currency
  b. The exchange rate of greenbacks for redeemable paper currency
  c. The number of greenbacks required to purchase 1 ounce of gold

15-3. Suppose that during the early period of U.S. banking, all state banks required reserves in the form of specie to be equal to 20 percent of total deposits. Suppose that the First Bank of the United States experienced a $10 withdrawal of specie that then was deposited in a state bank.
  a. Determine the immediate change in total reserves and in excess reserves.
  b. Determine the immediate change in the quantity of money.
  c. Determine the final change in the quantity of money following maximum possible expansion.

15-4. Suppose that the First Bank of the United States receives a $10 loan repayment in the form of state bank notes that then are redeemed for specie.
  a. How much would the quantity of state bank notes change?
  b. How much would the quantity of loans previously provided by state banks have to change?
  c. What would be the change in the quantity of money?

15-5. Franklin National Bank purchases a 1-year, $100,000 Treasury security for $90,000. What is the discount rate on this security?

15-6. Continuing problem 15-5, assume that Franklin National then borrows $100,000 in reserves from the Fed. The Fed credits Franklin National's account with $95,000. What is the rediscount rate that the Fed charged Franklin National? (Assume a 1-year borrowing term for simplicity.)

15-7. Let member banks be required to subscribe to Fed bank stock at a rate of 3 percent of net worth. Consider the following depository institution balance sheet (in millions):

Assets		Liabilities and Net Worth	
Cash	$100	Deposits	$500
Securities	200	Net worth	50
Loans	250		

  a. How many dollars' worth of Fed bank stock must be purchased by the member bank?
  b. If Fed bank profit distributions are limited to 6 percent of the value of Fed bank stock, how many dollars' worth of Fed bank profits can the member bank receive?

Selected References

Baum, L. Frank, *The Wonderful Wizard of Oz* (New York: Hill, 1900).

Clarke, M. St. Clair, and D. A. Hall, *Legislative and Documentary History of the Bank of the United States* (1832; reprinted in New York: Augustus M. Kelley, 1967).

Crabbe, Leland, "The International Gold Standard and U.S. Monetary Policy from World War I to the New Deal," *Federal Reserve Bulletin*, 75 (6, June 1989), pp. 423–440.

Dykes, Sayre Ellen, and Michael A. Whitehouse, "The Establishment and Evolution of the Federal Reserve Board: 1913–1923," *Federal Reserve Bulletin*, 75 (4, April 1989), pp. 227–243.

Friedman, Milton, and Anna J. Schwartz, *A Monetary History of the United States, 1867–1960* (Princeton, N.J.: Princeton University Press, 1963).

Greider, William, *Secrets of the Temple: How the Federal Reserve Runs the Country* (New York: Simon and Schuster, 1987).

Hammond, Bray, *Banks and Politics in America* (Princeton, N.J.: Princeton University Press, 1957).

Havrilesky, Thomas, "The Influence of the Federal Advisory Council on Monetary Policy," *Journal of Money, Credit, and Banking*, 22 (1, February 1990), pp. 37–50.

Kahn, James A., "Another Look at Free Banking in the United States," *American Economic Review*, 75 (4, September 1985), pp. 881–885.

Kettl, Donald F., *Leadership at the Fed* (New Haven: Yale University Press, 1986).

Mann, Glenn G., F. L. Garcia, and Charles J. Woelfel, *Encyclopedia of Banking and Finance* (Rolling Meadows, Ill.: Bankers Publishing Company, 1991).

Remini, Robert V., *The Life of Andrew Jackson* (New York: Penguin Books, 1990).

Rockoff, Hugh, "New Evidence on Free Banking in the United States," *American Economic Review*, 75 (4, September 1985), pp. 886–889.

———, "The 'Wizard of Oz' as a Monetary Allegory," *Journal of Political Economy*, 98 (4, August 1990), pp. 739–760.

Rolnick, Arthur J., and Warren E. Weber, "Inherent Instability in Banking: The Free Banking Experience," *Cato Journal*, 5 (3, Winter 1986), pp. 877–890.

Sushka, Marie E., "The Antebellum Money Market and the Economic Impact of the Bank War," *Journal of Economic History*, 36 (4, December 1976), pp. 809–835.

Timberlake, Richard H., *The Origins of Central Banking in the United States* (Cambridge, Mass.: Harvard University Press, 1978).

Unger, Irwin, *The Greenback Era* (Princeton, N.J.: Princeton University Press, 1964).

The Federal Reserve: Custodian of the Financial System

CHAPTER PREVIEW

1. What are the primary roles for a central bank?
2. Why is the issue of economic externalities important in justifying a need for a central bank?
3. What are the Fed's assets and liabilities?
4. In what ways is the Fed the U.S. government's fiscal agent?

5. In what ways is the Fed the U.S. economy's lender of last resort?
6. In what ways is the Fed the "custodian of the financial system"?
7. What are the major payments systems in the United States, and what function does the Fed play in those payments systems?

THE ROLES OF A CENTRAL BANK

We began the previous chapter by noting how the development of many central banks has been promoted by the governments of their nations. Certainly, this was the manner in which the Federal Reserve's founding and growth occurred. Before we embark on a discussion of the various functions of the Federal Reserve in this chapter and the one that follows, however, it is important that we consider some of the key roles that the Fed and other central banks have occupied in our history.

THE GOVERNMENT'S BANK

As we pointed out at the beginning of Chapter 15, governments throughout history have recognized that banking can be a profitable endeavor. Therefore, many governments have sought to establish central banks as a means of raising funds to pay for governmental expenses on internal improvements, military hardware, and so on. In short, governments sometimes have used central banks as a means of imposing indirect taxes on their citizens. Governments typically have extracted these indirect taxes through seigniorage earnings from their central banks' exclusive (monopoly) right to create money and from positive economic profits that central banks have gained from their monopolistic provision of banking services to individuals and firms.

Another important function of a central bank throughout history, however, has been its role as **fiscal agent** for governments. Even if a government is benevolent and nonprofit-maximizing in its banking and monetary policies, it may need a central banking system to enable it to conduct financial transactions related to its affairs of state. For instance, governments typically require means of depositing funds that they have collected from taxpayers, rather than allowing the funds to lie idle before ultimate disbursement for expenditures on public services. Governments also need a centralized system for issuing debt instruments—for instance, Treasury bills or bonds—in financial markets. The role of a central bank typically has been to serve as a depository institution for the treasury of a government and to coordinate its debt transactions during a *financial fiscal period,* such as a year, hence the term ''fiscal agent.''

The Federal Reserve System is the fiscal agent for the United States Treasury. The Fed is the central depository for Treasury deposits. Additionally, the Fed oversees the mechanisms and procedures by which the Treasury sells new securities to the public. The Fed, in short, is the bank of the federal government, and it has occupied that position since its inception in 1913.

THE BANKER'S BANK

Some economists contend that central banks would not exist without governmental involvement. They argue that, in fact, there is no need for a single central bank to act as fiscal agent for the government. They contend, for instance, that the so-called pet banks of, during, and after the time of Andrew Jackson's presidency (see Chapter 15) in the nineteenth century were adequate in accomplishing this task. The ''real'' reason for governments to promote one central bank, these economists argue, is to use them to extract resources from their citizens. This, of course, is the familiar refrain sung by Jefferson, Madison, Jackson, and the other opponents of central banking in our nation's history.

Externalities and Governmental Involvement   Other economists counter that, in fact, private banks *need* a central bank. The reason, they argue, is that banking markets, like markets for other goods and services, may experience **externalities.** A market externality occurs when market transactions between one set of individuals or firms affects the economic well-being of a group of individuals or firms that was not a party to those transactions. Air pollution is the classic example of an externality. For instance, an individual who smokes a cigar inside a plane on an overseas flight has paid the airline the market price for a ticket giving him the right to a seat on that flight, and so both he and the airline are satisfied with the terms of the transaction. The smoke from his cigar, however, may considerably reduce the utility derived from the long flight by other passengers aboard the plane. In this instance, the cigar smoke produces a **negative externality;** the actions of the cigar smoker *reduce* the economic well-being of other individuals.

Not all externalities are negative. Consider another example related to the air we breathe. A corporation recently has bought a large tract of land in the Pacific Northwest. It plans to lease the land to loggers, who remove trees for use in producing wood for construction and for paper production. In years past, a previous company had permitted some of the land to be ''clear-cut,'' meaning that nearly all the trees were removed without any replacement with new trees. To make the land more productive and profitable in the long run, the corporation signs agreements with loggers who will clear timber in the future, requiring them to plant new trees in the clear-cut area and in any areas in which trees are removed in the future. The corporation and the loggers agree to this arrangement because it is in their own best interest; but indirectly, because the new trees will absorb carbon dioxide and produce oxygen that we all breathe, the timber market transaction benefits society at large. Hence, this would be an example of a **positive externality,** in which market transactions *increase* the well-being of otherwise uninvolved individuals or firms.

The existence of market externalities is a common justification for governmental involvement in the workings of private markets; indeed, some economists view externalities as the underlying reason that individuals in society form governments. One key role for governmental institutions, according to this view, is to arbitrate and regulate when disputes arise from the presence of externalities. For instance, the restrictions on smoking by passengers on airline flights within the continental United States stem from a governmental decision to ban the activity to remove the negative externality that smoking creates for nonsmoking passengers.

Externalities and the Need for a Central Bank   It is possible that banking markets are subject to externalities. The reason is that banks, by their nature, are in the business of processing financial transactions that represent payments from one party to another. If a transaction involving exchange of funds between one party and another does not occur properly, other individuals not involved in this transaction may suffer.

Consider a simple example. Suppose that a college student has worked full-time the previous two years to save for college, and she has placed all her funds in her hometown credit union, 100 miles distant. The student waits until the last minute to pay her tuition, which is due to her college on September 1. On that day, she calls her hometown credit union, asking that it wire a payment to her college to cover her tuition. Unbeknownst to her, however, on that day the credit union has almost no cash reserves for use in making such payments but has relied on the fact that it has a security that will mature that day, which will provide it with funds it can use to honor last-minute requests for funds. Nevertheless, by chance on the afternoon of September 1 the issuer of the single multi-million-dollar security due to the credit union suffers a computer problem that makes it impossible to make payment to the credit union on that day, leaving the latter institution unable to forward the college student's funds until the next day. While the college student will still be able to register for classes, she now will have to pay a late fee and go through a late registration. Even though she was not a party to the credit union's transaction with the issuer of the security, she suffers an economic loss.

This is a somewhat contrived example, but it is one that many analysts think could be commonplace if a central bank such as the Federal Reserve were not around to make loans to depository institutions that find themselves solvent but illiquid, such as the credit union in the example above. Such instances of illiquidity that can arise from unexpected payments glitches that sometimes occur in banking transactions, along with other possible reasons payments may not be made or received on time, are strong arguments in favor of a central bank that stands ready to provide liquidity to depository institutions in a liquidity crunch, these observers argue. In this capacity, the central bank would be society's **lender of last resort,** ready to make last-minute loans to illiquid but otherwise solvent institutions that accidentally find themselves unable to meet their payment obligations. It would do so not only for the institutions themselves, but also for the benefit of their customers. Indeed, in extreme cases the existence of a lender of last resort might be needed to prevent bank runs that would be harmful to all members of society. This, in fact, was a key rationale for the Fed following the Panic of 1907, as we discussed in the last chapter.

Many analysts—and nearly all proponents of central banks—go a step further. They argue that a central bank also is needed to oversee and regulate the process by which individuals, firms, and depository institutions exchange financial payments. According to this view, a central bank should do more than just lend in the last resort in times of stress; society also needs a central bank to keep the financial system running smoothly on a day-to-day basis and to clean up messes when they occur, much as a building custodian oils machinery to keep it from breaking down and cleans spills on hallway floors so that the unaware passerby does not slip and fall. Economists and policy makers often call this a central bank's role as **custodian of the financial system.** This argument is based on the idea that a poorly functioning financial system creates a negative externality for everyone, including individuals who have few if any dealings with banks, because breakdowns in the financial system could have repercussions for the economy as a whole.

In its role as lender of last resort and/or financial system custodian, a central bank effectively functions as a bank for other banks, or a *banker's bank*. Just as we count on our own depository institution to make us a loan if we really become illiquid and need it desperately (perhaps through our access to a credit card), a depository institution would depend on a central bank to extend it credit in a time of need. Likewise, just as we presume that the depository institution where we hold our checking accounts will clear our checks for us, a depository institution would count on the central bank to make certain that the check-clearing system will properly distribute and allocate payments and receipts across all institutions that participate in the check-clearing process.

THE NATION'S MONETARY AUTHORITY

A third possible role for a central bank is to serve as a country's monetary policy maker. Certainly, this has been a primary role of the Federal Reserve System. It is such an important role, however, that we defer further discussion on this topic to Chapter 17.

In the present chapter, we focus on the first two rationales for a central bank that are discussed above: the central bank as the government's bank and the central bank as a bank for bankers. Throughout, we focus on these issues as the concern of our nation's central bank, the Federal Reserve System. We begin with an overview of the Fed's balance sheet and then consider the Fed's relationship to the United States Treasury Department. The remainder of the chapter considers the Fed's role as a bank for other depository institutions in the nation's financial system.

THE FED AS THE TREASURY'S FISCAL AGENT

In the last chapter, we discussed the overall structure of the Federal Reserve System. We barely skimmed the surface of the Fed's duties and responsibilities, however. Furthermore, we said nothing about the Fed's own assets and liabilities. We begin our discussion of the Fed's roles as a central bank by reviewing the components of the Fed's own balance sheet.

THE FED'S CONSOLIDATED BALANCE SHEET

Table 16-1 displays the consolidated balance sheet of the Federal Reserve System as of January 31, 1992. Keep in mind as we discuss the Fed's balance sheet that actual dollar values vary over time. What is important in the table are the sizes of different items relative to total assets, which are indicated by the percentages in parentheses.

Fed Assets   The primary asset held by the Federal Reserve System is United States government securities, which typically account for over three-fourths of its total assets. Most securities the Fed holds are Treasury bills and notes, although over a tenth typically are Treasury bonds. At any given time, the Fed holds a fraction of its Treasury securities under repurchase agreements (RPs), and much of its trading of securities is done via RP transactions. We shall have more to say about this in the following chapter.

Like any other bank, the Fed makes loans. Key borrowers are private depository financial institutions. The amount of loans to these institutions, made through the discount windows of the Federal Reserve banks, usually is small relative to the Fed's total assets

TABLE 16-1
The Fed's Consolidated Balance Sheet*
($ millions, as of January 31, 1992)

Assets			Liabilities and Net Worth		
U.S. Treasury securities	$266,148	(79.9%)	Federal Reserve notes	$280,117	(84.1%)
Loans to depository			Reserve deposits of		
institutions	112	(0.1%)	depository institutions	29,195	(8.8%)
Federal agency			U.S. Treasury deposits	10,828	(3.3%)
obligations	6,095	(1.8%)	Foreign official deposits	321	(0.1%)
Gold certificate account	11,058	(3.3%)	Deferred credit items	4,788	(1.4%)
Special drawing rights			Other liabilities	2,808	(0.8%)
certificate account	10,018	(3.0%)	Total liabilities	$327,427	(98.5%)
Assets denominated					
in foreign currencies	26,928	(8.1%)			
Items in process					
of collection	5,034	(1.5%)	Capital	5,072	(1.5%)
Other assets	7,736	(2.3%)	Total liabilities		
Total assets	$333,129		and net worth	$333,129	

* Percentages are relative to total assets.
Source: Federal Reserve Bulletin (April 1992), p. A11.

(typically less than 1 percent of total assets). Nonetheless, discount window lending is an important feature of the Fed, as we shall also discuss in more detail in the next chapter.

Along with U.S. Treasury securities, the Fed holds some debts issued by other federal agencies. These holdings generally constitute a small portion (usually 2 or 3 percent) of the Fed's total assets, however.

Although the United States officially left the gold standard in 1971, remnants of the gold standard are reflected by the presence of **gold certificates** in the Fed's balance sheet. Under the gold standard, the Treasury formally would sell gold to the Fed in exchange for money. It would continue to hold the government's stocks of gold, however, and instead issue gold certificates to the Fed, giving it formal title to the gold. Consequently, these certificates are assets of the Federal Reserve System. These certificates are valued at official governmental dollar-gold exchange rates instead of market rates of exchange.

Special drawing rights (SDRs) certificates also are Fed assets. The International Monetary Fund (IMF), a cooperative international financial institution owned and operated by over 150 nations, issued SDRs as a type of international currency in the 1970s, in part to supplement the declining international gold standard. Indeed, SDR certificates are Fed assets much like gold certificates. As part of the United States' membership in the IMF, the Treasury maintains shares in the IMF through SDRs, which is financed through issuance of the SDR certificates to the Fed.

The amounts of gold or SDR certificate holdings rarely change. Indeed, both of these asset items have remained constant for some time. This means that as the size of the Fed's total assets increases over time, the relative importance of gold and SDR certificates continually declines.

The Federal Reserve holds large amounts of assets denominated in foreign currencies. These are securities valued in terms of other nations' currencies, such as Japanese yen or

German deutschemarks. As we shall discuss in Unit 7, the Fed sometimes trades these assets to influence the exchange value of the dollar.

Recall from Chapter 6 that cash items in the process of collection are checks or other types of cash drafts deposited with a financial institution for immediate credit but subject to cancellation of credit if they are not paid after the fact. As a financial institution, the Fed also holds such uncollected items at any given time.

Fed Liabilities and Capital   The main liability of the Federal Reserve is Federal Reserve notes. What are these? As a hint, take out your billfold or purse and, if you have any currency on hand, take a look at the face of a bill: You will see the words "Federal Reserve Note" imprinted boldly across the top. Federal Reserve notes constitute the circulating currency of the United States. These notes generally are over 80 percent of the Fed's total liabilities and net worth.

The Fed has three types of deposit liabilities. The first of these is the reserve deposits of private depository institutions, including both those reserves held by these institutions toward their reserve requirements and any excess balances they may wish to hold as well.

The second deposit liability of the Fed is the deposit accounts of the United States Treasury. As we discuss below, these are the "working balances" of the Treasury; that is, most of these funds are checking account funds upon which the Treasury draws when it needs to make payments.

The third type of deposit account at the Fed consists of **foreign official deposits,** which are accounts of foreign governments or official financial institutions, such as foreign central banks. Most of these accounts are checking accounts of these foreign institutions, which they draw upon when they need to make dollar-denominated payments in the United States.

A final liability of the Fed is deferred-availability cash items. These represent payments by the Fed to another party that have not yet been made but are promised, or that have been made but have not yet been "cleared." The difference between the Fed's cash items in process of collection and its deferred-availability cash items is known as **Federal Reserve float.** Federal Reserve float, then, is the net difference between funds it has not yet collected from others and funds others have not yet collected from the Fed.

THE FED'S INTERACTION WITH THE U.S. TREASURY

As indicated in our discussion above, the U.S. Treasury holds its principal checking accounts at the twelve Federal Reserve banks and their branches. In its capacity as the Treasury's bank, the Federal Reserve System maintains and services these Treasury deposits, processing the receipts and disbursements from those accounts that are associated with the federal government's taxation and spending policies. As the primary fiscal agent of the Treasury, the Federal Reserve handles most of these duties, although private depository institutions may become "special depositories" of the Treasury (shades of the "pet banks" of the Jacksonian era) provided that they pledge enough of their own holdings of Treasury securities or other acceptable collateral (which then are called **pledged assets**) to secure fully the Treasury's accounts with these institutions. In fact, the Treasury holds most of its deposits with private banks, from whom it earns market interest rates.

The Federal Reserve also handles much of the paperwork and legwork associated with issuing and redeeming Treasury securities. When the Treasury offers a new issue of securities, the Federal Reserve banks receive the applications of depository institutions, dealers, and others who wish to purchase them. The Fed, on instructions from the Treasury, separates the securities into allotments for delivery to purchasers, and it processes their payments for deposit into the Treasury's accounts.

The Fed also redeems government securities from the Treasury's accounts when they mature. It also makes periodic interest coupon payments from the Treasury's accounts. Furthermore, it issues and redeems U.S. savings bonds and notes and assists private depository institutions that apply for and receive designation to act as agents for disbursing and redeeming these Treasury instruments.

As we discuss in more detail later, more than paperwork is entailed in the Fed's securities services to the Treasury. Much of the trading in primary and secondary markets for Treasury securities now is conducted on electronic networks. The Fed operates and supervises much of this trading activity, thereby ensuring that the markets for government securities remain active and liquid, which generally benefits the Treasury by lowering potential investors' perceptions of riskiness from holding or trading the Treasury's debt. This and other forms of electronic trading networks are important features of today's payments system.

THE U.S. PAYMENTS SYSTEM

A central feature of banking is that a large part of the liabilities of banks and other depository institutions—demand deposits and other checkable deposits—function as means of payment. For instance, when you write a check in payment for groceries, you use your checking deposit with a depository institution as a form of payment for the groceries. The grocer is willing to accept your check provided that he is convinced you are the person authorized to draw funds from that account and that your check is not likely to bounce.

As far as you are concerned, once you have your groceries, you are satisfied with the transaction. The transaction is far from over, however. Indeed, it has just begun. From the grocery, your check ultimately will make its way to the grocer's bank, which, in turn, will begin your check's route toward eventual "clearing" with your own depository institution.

The clearing of checks is a function of the nation's **payments system.** The payments system is the institutional structure through which financial transactions among households, firms, and financial institutions are completed. In the United States, there are a variety of ways that these agents make and receive payments, and so our payments system is fairly complex. Much of it now is computerized, and many payments take place without the necessity for parties to transactions to be in the same location when exchanging funds. In terms of numbers of payments, however, most still take the form of cash or check transactions such as the grocery exchange described above.

A key rationale for the Fed when it was founded just after the beginning of the twentieth century was for it to occupy a position of prominence within the payments system. As we shall see, the Fed has fulfilled this objective of its founders; its role in the payments system is pervasive.

THE EVOLUTION OF THE U.S. PAYMENTS SYSTEM

Of course, the Fed has only existed for just over three-quarters of a century, while the United States has constituted an independent nation for over two centuries. Hence, we should begin by considering how the U.S. payments system functioned before the Fed was on the scene up to the present.

The Payments System from 1791 to 1836   For nearly all the period from 1791 to 1836, the first two central banks of the nation (the First and Second Banks of the United States) played central roles in the payments system. Recall that specie (measured monetary gold and gold coins) was the basis of the nation's monetary system during most of this period. Nevertheless, the notes of private banks also functioned as media of exchange, as long as individuals were willing to accept these notes in payment for goods and services.

The bank notes themselves represented titles to specie. For instance, a $1 note issued by a bank in Fayetteville, North Carolina, constituted a title to a dollar's worth of specie from that bank. Notes of this bank might change hands in financial transactions many times, but ultimately one of the holders of a note might decide that she would like payment in gold for the note. What would happen, however, if she had received the note in payment for goods or services from a fairly distant location (by horse or carriage in the late 1700s and early 1800s), such as Charlottesville, Virginia? How would she collect payment in specie from a bank in Fayetteville, North Carolina?

She would do so indirectly. Instead of going all the way to Fayetteville for payment, she would take the Fayetteville bank note to her own bank in Charlottesville. Provided that her bank was willing to accept the note—banks kept track, by mail circulars, of which banks in the general vicinity had recently failed—she could obtain the dollar's worth of gold from her own bank. Her own Charlottesville bank, then, would redeem the note for specie, in return for a fee for the service. In fact, her bank, like most others of the time, generally would build up inventories of notes of other banks that it then would redeem at regular intervals. This might be done directly, by sending by carriage the notes of all Fayetteville banks that were in its possession to Fayetteville for redemption for specie.

Alternatively, the Charlottesville bank itself might choose to redeem the Fayetteville notes indirectly. This could be done through the nearest branch office of the Second Bank of the United States, in Richmond, Virginia. Because this central bank had branch offices in each of the states, it was able to *internalize* much of the process of note redemption. Once the central bank's Richmond office had received the Fayetteville bank note from the Charlottesville bank, it could redeem the note through its *own* branch office in Fayetteville. Of course, the central bank would charge the Charlottesville bank a fee for this service, but the Charlottesville bank could gain significant savings in time and effort by redeeming the Fayetteville notes in this manner rather than directly.

Note redemption was the primary payments system service provided by the First and Second Banks of the United States. This central banking service—a crucial aspect of the nation's payments system—ended, however, with the demise of the Second Bank in 1836.

Private Clearing Houses from 1836 to 1913   Even though central banks had provided note redemption services until the end of the Second Bank's charter, this had not prevented the development of private systems for redeeming bank notes. In 1819, the Suffolk Bank of Massachusetts initiated a bank note redemption system. It and other banks in the Boston area had deduced that some banks were taking advantage of an interesting feature of bank notes. Banks could issue more notes relative to the amount of specie backing those notes if the chances the notes would be redeemed were small. This makes sense; if very few people were to try to redeem a bank's notes (or if it were difficult for them to do so), then a bank would be able to issue many more notes without fear that it would face a liquidity crisis caused by too many simultaneous attempts to redeem notes for specie.

Some New England banks, which came to be known at the time as "country banks," began locating their offices in places far distant from the business centers in the state. This purposeful strategy lessened the likelihood that households and firms would try to redeem the notes of these country banks. As a result, they could issue more notes with less specie on hand to back them. These country bank notes, because they were so rarely redeemed, dominated the circulation of notes in Boston.

The Suffolk note redemption system undercut this strategy. The Suffolk Bank made arrangements with many of the New England country banks to hold specie deposits with the Suffolk Bank that it could use to redeem notes of those banks. In addition, it went to great efforts to seek redemption of the notes issued by country banks that would not participate in the Suffolk system. Effectively, the Suffolk Bank shouldered for the New England region the payments system responsibilities that a governmental central bank might otherwise have assumed.

The Suffolk system became a model for **clearing-house associations** that developed in the 1840s and 1850s. A clearing-house association was a group of banks that agreed to establish a central location—a clearing house—for clearing payments made on accounts held by their depositors. Initially, as in the Suffolk system, the clearing house was the central bank of the association. Over time, as clearing-house associations became larger and more popular, the associations established separate clearing-house locations.

Another innovation, which was stimulated in large part by a banking panic in 1857, was the development of **clearing-house certificates,** which were titles to the specie deposits of associations' member banks. Rather than actually exchange gold deposits when their notes cleared, member banks would exchange the paper certificates instead. Effectively, these certificates were ''money'' for the clearing-house members. Some clearing-house associations—notably the New York Clearing House Association—went a step further. When the Panic of 1857 forced country banks to draw down their specie reserves, New York City banks floated the country banks loans by issuing them more clearing-house certificates. This meant that these alternative certificates—**clearing-house loan certificates**—joined specie as part of the monetary base for the banking system.

Clearing-house loan certificates became more popular with each successive panic: 1873, 1884, 1890, and then the ''big'' Panic of 1893. Clearing-house associations around the country issued so many of these certificates—in denominations as low as $10—that some banks actually began to pay them out to depositors when the latter made deposit withdrawals. In some locales, then, clearing-house certificates became part of the general quantity of money. These certificates were not eliminated until 1908, when the federal government began to question the widespread use of the certificates, which technically were not legal tender even though people used them alongside other bank notes. By this time, passage of the Aldrich-Vreeland Act had fully injected the federal government into the nation's financial system, and passage of the Federal Reserve Act five years later changed the entire complexion of the payments system.

THE CURRENT PAYMENTS SYSTEM

Obviously, our present payments system includes no role for bank notes and specie redemption. Bank notes passed out of general use in the 1930s, which also marked the beginning of the end—if not the effective finale—of the gold standard era. Checking deposits, which already had become more popular as the twentieth century progressed, began to supplant bank notes before their demise in the 1930s. The reason was that telegraph and telephone communication and significant technological improvements in transportation facilitated speedier clearing of checks.

Currency and Checks   As we discussed in Chapter 3, about 80 percent of all payments are made in currency. The total number of estimated currency transactions in the 1990s was about 300 billion annually. Most of our day-to-day payments continue to be made with pieces of paper, except now we use a national currency—Federal Reserve notes—instead of bank notes or greenbacks.

Checks continue to be an extremely important means of payment in the United States. As we discussed in Chapter 3, between 15 and 20 percent of all payments are made by check in the United States. We estimate that banks in the 1990s will process over *60 billion* checks *each year.* This figure is only about a fifth of the number of currency transactions, but when one thinks of how much more is involved in a check-clearing transaction, the number is staggering. Like the redemption of the bank notes of old, bank clearing-house systems must clear the accounts of many institutions simultaneously, every single day. Nowadays, thousands of institutions are involved, each of which has thousands of depositors.

To get a feeling for the magnitude of check clearings that banks deal with, consider this. If checks were cleared continuously (which they are not), banks would have to clear about *2,000 checks every second of every day* to clear 60 billion checks in a single year. One is reminded of the PBS show with astronomer Carl Sagan intoning ''billions and billions'' when one contemplates the scope of the check-clearing problem.

How do depository institutions manage to clear so many checks? The answer is that necessity has bred invention. As the volume of check clearings increased in past decades, depository institutions centralized the check-clearing process at clearing houses, just as the Suffolk Bank system centralized the bank note redemption process. Furthermore, much of the check-clearing process became automated as communications technology improved. Checks now are encrypted with magnetic ink that machines can read directly, which permits automatic sorting, computer crediting, and machine-assisted distribution of checks. Thus, ''billions and billions'' of checks may be cleared in a year when there is access to technology that permits ''thousands and thousands'' of checks to be processed each minute at a fairly low cost per check.

Electronic Payments by and to Consumers   As we saw in Chapter 3, electronic means of payment make up an extremely small fraction of the total quantity of payments in the United States. Yet electronic payments account for more than 80 percent of the total *dollar value* of all financial transactions. Although electronic means of payment have not supplemented currency or checks in the typical day-to-day pattern of transactions for a typical individual, some individuals and institutions clearly make use of electronic payments mechanisms.

One important type of electronic payments mechanism is the **automated clearing house (ACH).** ACHs are consumer-oriented payments systems that process payments within one or two days after they are initiated by a payor to a payee. A good example of an ACH system is automatic payroll deposit systems used by many businesses to make salary payments to their employees' bank accounts directly rather than issuing them paper checks. Another example is the Social Security System's ACH system that directly deposits payments into the deposit accounts of Social Security beneficiaries.

Automated teller machine (ATM) networks are another type of consumer-oriented electronic payments system. Bank depositors largely use these systems for cash withdrawals from their accounts. Another consumer-oriented set of systems is **point-of-sale (POS) networks,** which permit consumers to pay for purchases through direct deductions from their deposit accounts at financial institutions.

Recently, the federal government initiated a new system, called **electronic benefits transfer (EBT),** which disperses cash payments to individuals who qualify for government benefits such as Aid to Families with Dependent Children (AFDC) or food stamps. This system performs the function of an ACH system but works much like an ATM system because it disburses currency rather than making direct deposits into bank accounts. The reason the government has opted for EBT over an ACH is that, by definition, those who qualify for governmental benefits are low-income individuals. These people often do not have bank accounts—three-fourths of all AFDC and food stamp recipients do not have checking accounts—making a more standard ACH system for distributing the funds infeasible. Therefore, the government has adopted an ATM-type system, complete with special machines for disbursing cash or food stamps.

Large-Dollar Electronic Payments Systems   Individual consumers like you and the authors of this text account for small fractions of the total payments made in the United States. Financial and nonfinancial firms initiate the really big-dollar electronic transactions. They do so primarily through the use of two **large-dollar payments systems**—systems that specialize in processing payments that typically have very large dollar values. One of these large-dollar systems is the **Clearing House Interbank Payment System (CHIPS),** which is privately owned and operated by the New York Clearing House Association. The other is **Fedwire,** which is owned and operated by the Federal Reserve System.

CHIPS links about 140 United States depository institutions. Most of these are among the largest depository institutions in the nation. This private system transmits an average of roughly $1,000 billion *($1 trillion)* in payments *every day.* The average size of a single CHIPS transaction is about $6 million.

All depository institutions that are required to hold reserves at the Fed have access to Fedwire, although they must pay fees for wire transfer services. Hence, Fedwire has more participants—and, consequently, makes more individual funds transfers—than CHIPS. Nevertheless, the dollar volume of payments made on Fedwire is somewhat smaller, at about $950 billion per day, than the volume of CHIPS transfers. The average payment on Fedwire also is smaller, averaging about $3.5 million.

The two wire transfer systems tend to specialize in different types of funds transactions. On the CHIPS network most wire transfers are associated with foreign exchange trading and Eurocurrency transactions. On Fedwire the primary types of transactions are (1) transfers of federal funds between depository institutions and (2) purchases and sales of government securities. The federal funds transactions arise from interbank purchases and sales of federal funds (see Chapter 6) as well as third-party payments by corporations and nonbank financial institutions.

Federal funds transfers on Fedwire concern the exchange of balances held on deposit at Federal Reserve banks by depository institutions. A depository institution making a payment using Fedwire asks the Federal Reserve bank to transfer funds from its own reserve account at the Fed to the Fed account of the institution receiving the funds. Upon receipt of this request, which is made on the wire system itself, the Federal Reserve bank reduces the account balance of the sending bank and increases the account balance of the receiving bank. Consequently, transfers of large sums may be made over large distances within a few minutes.

Financial institutions and investors also use Fedwire for **book-entry security transactions,** which are purchases and sales of government securities such as Treasury bills and bonds. These agents set up book-entry security accounts at Federal Reserve banks for this purpose. When one institution purchases a government security from another institution, the Federal Reserve bank electronically deducts the security from the seller's book-entry account and adds the funds to the seller's Fed deposit balance. The Federal Reserve bank then increases the book-entry security account of the purchaser of the security and reduces the purchaser's reserve account balance with the Fed.

AUTOMATED FINANCIAL TRADING IN MARKETS THAT NEVER SLEEP?

INTERNATIONAL PERSPECTIVE

What do "CORES," "MATIF," and "CATS" all have in common? They are fully automated trading systems that exist in Japan, France, and Canada, respectively. CORES, in Tokyo, is the Computer-Assisted Order Routing and Execution System; MATIF is the Marché à Terme International de France, based in Paris; and CATS is the Toronto-based Computer-Assisted Trading System that has links in Spain, Belgium, and Brazil. The United States has a system known as "Globex," and Switzerland has its own system called "Soffex."

All these trading systems, plus others in the United Kingdom, Singapore, Sweden, Denmark, and elsewhere in the world, share the common feature that they permit traders in financial markets to place orders for purchases and sales of securities via computers. At a minimum, these automated trading systems promise to reduce the amount of pushing and shoving in the trading pits of markets in futures, commodities, and so on. Ultimately, their development and growth could lead to the demise of direct interaction among people in these markets.

Mechanics of Automated Trading

Most nations' automated trading systems have their own special features, and so we describe the U.S. Globex system as an example. This system, which is operated by the Chicago Mercantile Exchange (CME), promises to be a standard for the future. Indeed, several other nations' systems, such as the French MATIF, joined in a partnership with Globex. Hence, it is perhaps the best one to single out for description.

Individuals conduct trades on Globex via computer terminals. For a given financial instrument, such as a typical futures contract, Globex displays on the computer screen the best bid and offer with the amounts involved, the most recent sale price and quantity traded, and related spot market prices for reference. An individual may use the computer's keyboard to interact with the system to attempt to make trades via appropriate commands.

For instance, if an individual sees a bid for a futures

contract that he would like to accept, he can place a sell order into the system. The system automatically checks to see that this sell order is at a price equal to or less than the buy order and that it is for the same contract for which the earlier bid was made. If these conditions are met, then the system also automatically checks to be certain that the quantities of the bid and offer to sell are compatible and that earlier offers to sell have not been received by the system (if so, the system automatically places orders "in line" according to the time they were sent into the system). Finally, the system transmits information on the trade it has arranged to the clearing houses of individual exchanges (in the case of a futures contract, the CME) to be executed. Then, the trade is accomplished.

Important Implications

We have all become so accustomed now to the use of computers that there is perhaps nothing surprising about the fact that computerized financial market trading is becoming more commonplace. Nevertheless, this innovation promises to change many aspects of the institutional structures of financial markets around the globe.

The most obvious implication of automated trading is that, without the need for human beings to process transactions, there is no technical reason that individuals should not be able to trade financial instruments at any time of the day—or night. For example, a person who tunes into Globex at 9 P.M. central time, when the CME is closed, may see a bid price on the system that is acceptable to him and may arrange a trade on the system. In fact, providing an individual with this ability was one of the key reasons that the CME set up the Globex system.

If a person can trade at 9 P.M., why should he confine himself to trading in a Chicago exchange? Why not trade, for instance, in an exchange in Tokyo, where 9 P.M. in the midsection of the U.S. is mid-morning in Japan? Alternatively, why not trade in an exchange in Sydney, Australia, or instead think of waiting for a short time until exchanges open in Singapore or Hong Kong? The possibilities for *fully globalized trading* that automated trading opens up should be apparent.

It is globalization of financial markets that is the most important implication of computer-assisted trading. As more nations expand their automated trading systems, the hours that trading can take place around the world undoubtedly will overlap to a greater extent. Eventually, 24-hour trading across the globe promises to be commonplace.

Policy Issues

The potential globalization of financial markets heralded by the advent of automated trading raises a host of issues for policy makers. The most glaring of these is that every nation has its own rules for securities trading. These rules typically are similar but not identical. Nations with more demanding requirements for trading in their securities exchanges may incur fewer risks to their trading systems as globalization continues; they also may see their exchanges lose business to those in nations with less stringent rules. Consequently, the growing use of automated trading promises to force policy makers around the globe to coordinate their policies much more than they have in the past.

Second, even in areas in which policy makers have shared views on the proper functioning of financial markets and payments systems, the advent of automated trading raises some thorny issues. For example, nearly all nations' policy makers agree that financial markets should be structured so that both "small" (that is, individuals) and "large" (that is, institutional) traders have the same access to transactions. Clearly, it is impossible for an individual who trades on his own account to literally stay awake 24 hours a day, glued to his computer console. For large institutions, however, it is simply a matter of employing people in shifts. Consequently, automated trading has the potential to give institutional traders some advantages they previously had not possessed. When the New York Stock Exchange implemented after-hours electronic trading in June 1991, many observers hailed the move as pathbreaking, but others feared that the advantage gained by institutional traders would produce a "two-tiered" stock market that would benefit large traders at the expense of the little guy.

A third issue concerns the growing linkages between payments systems throughout the world. If there is a payments system foul-up or a market crash in, say, Hong Kong at 3 P.M., it would occur at about 2 A.M. eastern time in the United States. This would be about 7 A.M. in London, however. If a large number of individual traders on London exchanges are affected by the hypothesized Hong Kong problem, this could slow or even halt trading in London. If the problem is not ironed out within a few hours, it could influence trading activity when markets open in New York. The effects of a catastrophe in one market, then, could spill over to other markets throughout the world—literally "As the World Turns."

These are the types of possibilities that cause policy makers to lie awake at night. One solution, in fact, may be for policy makers to stay up all night. Proposals already are on the table at the Fed to extend its operating hours for Fedwire. Someday in the not-too-distant future, central bankers may never sleep.

Sources: Herbert Baer and Douglas D. Evanoff, "Payments System Issues in Financial Markets That Never Sleep," Federal Reserve Bank of Chicago *Economic Perspectives,* 14 (6, November/December 1990), pp. 2–15; Ian Domowitz, "The Mechanics of Automated Trade Execution Systems," Working Paper, Northwestern University (June 1990); Kevin G. Salwen and Craig Torres, "Big Board After-Hours Trading May Lead to a Two-Tier Market," *Wall Street Journal* (June 13, 1991), p. C1; and A. Patricia White, "The Globex Trading System," *Finance and Economics Discussion Series,* no. 157, Board of Governors of the Federal Reserve System (April 1991).

Electronic transfers of funds on CHIPS occur in a similar manner, although the Fed is not a party to these transactions. A depository institution that belongs to the CHIPS network maintains an account balance with CHIPS; when it transfers funds to another institution, it does so by requesting that the CHIPS network automatically reduce its CHIPS account balance and increase the CHIPS account balance of the receiving institution.

SOURCES OF RISK IN THE PAYMENTS SYSTEM

Any payments system involves risks. For instance, any "average" Western television show or movie trumpeted the risks of shipping specie payments by coach or train from a bank in one location to a bank in another under the gold standard of the nineteenth century. Here, there was an obvious payments system risk: The coach or train could be robbed, and John Wayne or the Lone Ranger might not always be around to save the gold.

In general, however, there are a variety of types of risk experienced by participants in any payments system. These basic categories of risk apply to transactions made using *any* payments system in any day and age. In our discussion, we consider these risks as viewed from the perspective of a depository institution to which funds are due and are to be transmitted via a payments system of which the institution is a participant.

Liquidity Risk   This is the risk that arises from the possibility that a payment, even if made in full, may not be made when due. Instead, it may be forthcoming at a later time than originally contracted. This means that a depository institution may not receive funds when it had counted on those funds being available, making the institution less liquid until the belated payment arrives, hence the term **liquidity risk.**

CHIPS and Fedwire represent the modern answer to the problem of liquidity risk. In the days of the ''Old West'' depicted in Western shows and movies, liquidity risk was substantial, because poor weather and other inconveniences, such as robberies, could significantly slow the transmission of payments between parties in a transaction. The development of modern mail systems lessened that risk considerably. As we all know, however, check transactions over delivery systems such as the U.S. Postal Service may or may not always be delivered to a recipient promptly. This fact, coupled with the development of modern communications systems and computers, inevitably has led to the development of wire transfer systems as the means to reduce liquidity risks for the largest transactions.

Credit Risk   Credit commonly is extended in many transactions. For instance, if you purchase an item through the mail by sending a check for payment along with your order, you effectively have granted credit to the mail-order company until the time that you receive the item you order. As another example, if you mail in an order form for a magazine subscription and check the box that says ''bill me,'' the time between when the company mails your first magazine and the time that you pay for your subscription is a period during which the magazine company extends credit to you.

Such extensions of credit entail **credit risk** for one of the parties to a transaction. Economists commonly split credit risk into two categories. One concerns the **market risk** that a debt is not repaid because the borrower defaults on the original transaction, requiring both parties to strike a new agreement. This causes the lending party to incur a loss that typically is less than the full credit it extended to the borrower, because the lender usually receives at least part of the full amount of the loan it had extended. Another category of credit risk is **delivery risk,** which is the risk that a party in a funds transaction fulfills its agreement but that the other party fails entirely to do so. In the case of a loan, the lender in this transaction loses the entire value of the transfer.

Risk for the System as a Whole   Institutions in a payments system are interlinked. For instance, on a large-dollar electronic funds transfer network such as CHIPS, if bank A agrees to wire funds to bank B at 10 A.M. on a given day, bank B, in anticipation of that payment, may agree to wire funds to bank C at 10:30 to fulfill an obligation with that bank. Furthermore, bank C may plan to use the funds it receives at 10:30 to wire payment of a debt to bank D at 11, and so on.

The risk that bank A may fail completely or partially to honor its obligation to bank B is a credit risk to bank B. For banks C and D, which—without even knowing it—depend on successful completion of the transaction between banks A and B, there are no direct liquidity or credit risks, because banks C and D are not parties to agreements with bank

A. Nevertheless, the situation in the payments system is such that, *indirectly,* they *are* parties to that agreement. Therefore, these institutions experience an *indirect* risk that economists call **systemic risk.** In a world with no lender of last resort, failure of bank A to honor its 10 A.M. obligation to bank B theoretically could cause an unraveling of the entire stream of payments across many banks, causing liquidity problems for some and outright credit losses for others.

Systemic risk involves *externalities* in payments systems. In the example outlined above, banks C and D did not have a say in the terms of the funds transfer arranged between banks A and B; yet they may lose if bank A fails to live up to its agreement with bank B. Hence, they stand to suffer possible negative externalities if bank A reneges on its agreement. It is this externality inherent in the systemic risk of payments systems that many economists and policy makers believe provides a rationale for the existence of a central bank such as the Federal Reserve System.

THE FED'S ROLE IN THE PAYMENTS SYSTEM

Systemic risk lies behind the problem of bank runs, which periodically plagued the United States throughout the nineteenth century and the first half of the twentieth century. A main purpose in forming the Federal Reserve System was to stem bank runs. That is, a key objective of the Fed, as a central bank, is to reduce or eliminate the problem of systemic risk in the payments system.

THE FED AS LENDER OF LAST RESORT

A key responsibility of the Federal Reserve is to serve as lender of last resort to solvent but illiquid depository institutions. To give you an idea how important the Fed views this responsibility, consider the following information. The Fed has many regulations, to which, as a good bureaucratic agency, it has chosen to assign letters identifying regulations, such as Regulation D, Regulation F, and so on. Over time, it has developed so many regulations that it has had to assign names such as Regulation BB and so on, much as astronomers long ago ran out of letters to denote stars of varying brightness discovered in distant galaxies, forcing them to use double or triple lettering systems as they developed larger telescopes that enabled them to see more stars. Of all its regulations, the one that deals with its lender-of-last-resort function is the Fed's first one, which is Regulation A.

The Fed's Official View on Its Lender-of-Last-Resort Role   According to Regulation A,

> Federal Reserve credit is available on a short-term basis to a depository institution under such rules as may be prescribed to assist the institution, to the extent appropriate, in meeting temporary requirements for funds, or to cushion more persistent outflows of funds pending an orderly adjustment of the institution's assets and liabilities.

If you read over this statement, which forms the heart of the regulation, two or three times, you will conclude that it is not very specific. On the one hand, it uses the words "short-term" and "temporary," which seems to imply that the Fed intends for its discount window loans to depository institutions to have short maturities. On the other hand, Regulation A refers to "cushion[ing] more persistent outflows of funds," which leaves open the possibility the Fed could make longer-term loans.

DAYLIGHT OVERDRAFTS AND THE ROLE OF THE FED

In recent years, a pressing issue concerning the nation's payments system has stemmed from a phenomenon the Fed calls **daylight overdrafts.** Daylight overdrafts are overdrawals of Federal Reserve or CHIPS accounts that occur before the end of each day, at which time all depository institutions settle their Fedwire and CHIPS accounts. The Fed views such overdrafts as unsecured loans that expose both the Fed and other depository institutions to potentially significant risks, considering that transactions on these large-dollar payments systems typically involve millions or even billions of dollars.

The Mechanics of a Daylight Overdraft

To understand how daylight overdrafts occur, it is simplest to consider an example involving Fedwire. At the end of a day, all depository institutions must have a positive balance in their reserve accounts at the Fed. During the course of the day, as institutions wire funds to others or receive funds from others on the Fedwire network, mismatches in these electronic payments can cause depository institutions' balances in their Fed accounts to fall below zero. Figure 16-1 illustrates a depository institution daylight overdraft of its Federal Reserve deposit account that stretches from approximately 10 A.M. until nearly 4 P.M.

The mismatching of transmittals and receipts of funds that causes a daylight overdraft for a depository insti-

tution may be *unintended.* For example, if the institution pays funds out of its Fed account at 10 A.M. because it anticipated receipt of funds via a wire transfer from another source before 10 A.M. but then did not receive that transfer, a daylight overdraft such as that illustrated in Figure 16-1 could be initiated accidentally. Such unintended overdrafts could arise from poor planning of payments and receipts, mistaken communications between institutions, or computer hardware or software problems. Book-entry security transactions on the Fedwire network are particularly prone to unintended overdrafts, because the seller of a security, rather than the purchaser, typically has discretion over when delivery of the security will take place. Usually, the only stipulation in a security agreement is that the transfer occur by the close of business that day. Hence, the seller may initiate the transaction at an unexpected time during the day, causing the buyer of the security to wire funds earlier than it expected would be necessary, causing a daylight overdraft of its reserve account at its Federal Reserve bank.

Unintentional overdrafts typically do not have lengthy durations. Figure 16-1, therefore, would be most representative of an *intentional* daylight overdraft. An example of how the overdraft illustrated in Figure 16-1 might arise would be a situation in which a bank consistently borrows federal funds each day to maintain positive end-of-day balances in its reserve account with the Fed. In the example shown in Figure 16-1, for instance, the bank enters the day with a positive reserve

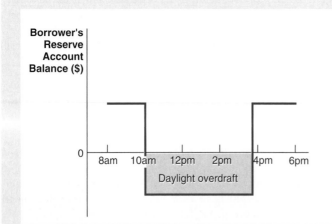

Figure 16-1
Creation of a Daylight Overdraft. A depository institution begins the day with a positive balance in its reserve account with the Federal Reserve. At about 10 A.M. the depository institution sends funds to another party over the Fedwire system that exceeds the balance in its account, and so it creates a daylight overdraft of its account. Toward the end of the day, around 4 P.M., the depository institution either receives funds from another party or borrows funds to bring its account balance up to a positive level.

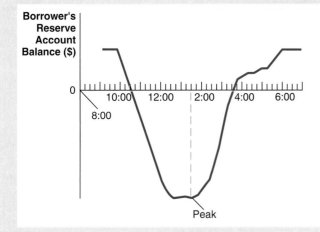

Figure 16-2
A Typical Daily Pattern for Total Overdrafts by a Depository Institution. Normally, a depository institution that overdraws its reserve deposit account at the Federal Reserve does so gradually through sending funds electronically to various other parties during the course of a day. Toward the middle of the day, the depository institution then begins to be a net recipient of funds. By the end of the day, its reserve account balance again is positive.

balance because it had borrowed federal funds from another depository institution the previous day. It repays the federal funds loan at 10 o'clock, and when it does so, its reserve balance at the Fed falls below zero; it runs a daylight overdraft. Toward the end of the day, just before 4 o'clock, the bank arranges a new federal funds loan, which causes its Fed reserve account balance to become positive once again.

The pattern of overdrafts shown in Figure 16-1 is unrealistically "smooth." Depository institutions typically generate more and more overdrafts as the day progresses from early morning hours until early afternoon, when *peak overdrafts,* or maximum overdraft amounts, usually occur. Then the institutions begin to arrange for federal funds loans and other means of increasing their reserves, causing their reserve balances gradually to increase. Figure 16-2 shows a possible— and typical—pattern of overdrafts for a depository institution.

CHIPS daylight overdrafts are analogous to those that occur via Fedwire, but in the case of CHIPS, overdrafts do not entail negative balances in the Federal Reserve bank accounts of depository institutions. Instead, the CHIPS account balances of CHIPS participants fall below zero during the day and reach positive values again only as the day progresses.

Magnitudes of Daylight Overdrafts
Daylight overdrafts would not have become an issue of Federal Reserve policy making if they were infrequent and small. In fact, they are both common and large. Daylight overdrafts on the Fedwire system rose from a daily average peak of about $75 billion in early 1985 to

roughly $125 billion by 1990. This amount was roughly *twice the size of the aggregate reserve balances of all depository institutions!* Daylight overdrafts are not "small potatoes."

CHIPS overdrafts generally have been smaller; the average daily peak overdrafts on the CHIPS network typically hover in the range of $50 billion. This also is a fairly sizable amount of dollars, however.

Daylight overdrafts have been widespread. More than 1,000 depository institutions have been known to overdraw their accounts on a given day. Over the course of a three-month period, as many as 5,000 depository institutions may incur daylight overdrafts.

Fed Policies on Daylight Overdrafts
In recent years, the Fed has sought to contain the growth of daylight overdrafts. It has adopted a "two-pronged" approach to this task. First, it has imposed direct limitations, or *caps,* on the maximum amounts of Fedwire or CHIPS overdrafts that depository institutions can incur without penalty. Second, it has initiated a policy of charging interest on the Fedwire overdrafts. Both of these policies appear to have slowed the growth of daylight overdrafts. Nonetheless, overdraft volumes are still substantial, and the Fed continues to evaluate further policy approaches to the issue.

Source: David D. VanHoose and Gordon H. Sellon, Jr., "Daylight Overdrafts, Payments System Risk, and Public Policy," Federal Reserve Bank of Kansas City *Economic Review,* 74 (8, September/October 1989), pp. 9–29, and the Board of Governors of the Federal Reserve System.

The regulation also says that the Fed will make loans to depository institutions "under such rules as may be prescribed." That statement also is not very specific. Indeed, the more detailed discount window rules published by the Fed also tend to be unspecific. Furthermore, some of the written procedures that Fed officers actually follow when deciding whether or not to extend loans to depository institutions are not available to the depository institutions themselves!

Views on the Proper Role of the Lender of Last Resort   Clearly, the Fed permits itself significant *discretion* in its function as the financial system's lender of last resort. This does not mean, however, that there is no intellectual guidance available to the Fed in its administration of this duty. In fact, there is a long tradition of views on the proper role of a lender of last resort.

British economists of the late nineteenth century, Henry Thornton and Walter Bagehot (pronounced "badge-it") developed "rules" that they felt central banks, such as the Bank of England, should follow in their roles as lenders of last resort. First and foremost, they argued that all forms of liquidity provided by central banks should be temporary, that central bank loans should be collateralized, and that central banks should extend loans only to solvent depository institutions; this approach would keep a central bank from becoming entangled in a long-lasting bailout of failed institutions.

These economists also contended that if a poorly managed institution did happen to fail, a central bank should cushion the effects of the failure that otherwise might be experienced by the rest of the payments system to prevent panics from developing. This would require making loans, as needed, to other solvent institutions that might be exposed to systemic risks related to that failure. In a true crisis, argued these British economists, a central bank should make as many loans as necessary to solvent institutions to stem the crisis.

Furthermore, in Thornton and Bagehot's view, a central bank should never let the liquidity assistance it provides in this function conflict with its broader duties related to the nation's payments system and to its monetary policy responsibilities. It should never let concerns with a single institution's problems predominate over its responsibility to the financial system as a whole.

Finally, these economists believed that central banks should extend credit to depository institutions only at **penalty rates,** or interest rates that are higher than market interest rates and that thereby penalize the borrowing institution. Otherwise, these economists argued, the central bank might become a lender of *first resort* instead of the lender of last resort.

Early in the history of the Federal Reserve System, the Fed indicated that it intended to follow most of these "classic" rules on the concept of lender of last resort. Yet, over time, the Fed has relaxed or violated several of these policy prescriptions, as we shall discuss in more detail in our analysis of the operation of the Fed's discount window in Chapter 17. Specifically, it now makes many long-term loans, and the discount rates it charges on its short-term loans to depository institutions typically are *below* market rates of interest. From time to time—notably in the case of the Continental Illinois Bank failure in 1984 (see Chapter 11)—it also has made discount window loans to insolvent depository institutions.

Nonetheless, the Fed undeniably is the nation's lender of last resort, and it stands ready to halt systemic failures before they can progress. For instance, the day after the stock market crash of October 1987 an unidentified spokesperson for the Fed issued a statement guaranteeing that the Fed stood ready to provide credit when needed, and the Fed did so. Most observers believe that this immediate response to the crash kept it from turning into a greater panic that might have caused great damage to the banking system and to the economy.

THE FED AS CUSTODIAN OF THE FINANCIAL SYSTEM

Many economists contend that the Fed's lender-of-last-resort function is sufficient to protect the financial system from the effects of crashes or other reverses. Since its founding, though, the Fed has not been content to limit its role in this way. It also has taken on the task of financial system custodian. In this role, it monitors and supervises many of the activities of the nation's payments system.

In light of our discussion of large-dollar electronic payments systems, one area of Federal Reserve direct involvement in the payments system is its operation and regulation of the Fedwire network. This network, which actually began its operations in 1918, well before the computer age, connects all the Federal Reserve district banks, their branches, and other depository institutions. The Fed both operates this network and determines the rules by which depository institutions may use this service. The Fed also sets the fees that institutions must pay to use Fedwire.

The Fed performs a major function in the nation's check-clearing system. Roughly half of the checks written in the United States clear through the Fed's check-clearing operations, which connect banks of most medium-to-large cities in the nation. Depository institutions in smaller cities or rural areas obtain access to the Fed's check-clearing services (as well as to its other services, such as Fedwire) through their correspondent relationships with the banks that maintain direct access.

The Fed charges fees for its check-clearing services, and as mandated by the DIDMCA of 1980, it attempts to charge fees that would have arisen in a competitive market for these services. Congress mandated Fed fees for check-clearing services for two basic reasons. One was that Congress wanted the Fed to increase its earnings so that more of its excess earnings (net of the Fed's costs of operations) could be passed along to the Treasury; in days of federal budget deficits, the government wants to scrounge up every available source of revenue. A second reason was that private clearing houses process nearly half of all checks written in the United States, and these institutions felt that the Fed previously had charged below-market fees for its services. This, the private clearing houses argued, placed them at a competitive disadvantage, much as taxpayer-subsidized U.S. Postal Service rates can make the task of competing more difficult for the United Parcel Service or Federal Express.

THE FEDERAL FINANCIAL SAFETY NET

The Fed views its roles as custodian of the financial system and lender of last resort to be the first two layers of the **federal financial safety net,** which is a term for the various federal government protections against widespread financial failures and panics. From this perspective, the Fed's function as financial system custodian permits it to maintain a day-to-day involvement in the nation's payments system, both through its own payments system operations (check clearing and Fedwire) and through its supervisory role. As a result of its custodial role, the Fed is able to observe problems as they initially arise and, at least in principle, can respond to those problems with appropriate adjustments in its services and supervision. This, then, is the first layer of a federal ''safety net'' of protection for the financial system.

The second layer is the Fed's role as lender of last resort. If, by chance, the Fed's custodial operations are insufficient to prevent events that might precipitate instances of illiquidity and systemic breakdown, the Fed is there to provide liquidity, through discount window loans, to solvent but temporarily illiquid depository institutions.

The Fed has no direct responsibility for the third, and final, layer of the federal financial safety net. This last layer is the federal deposit insurance system. In cases in which institutions' illiquidity is permanent, rather than temporary, because they have become insolvent, deposit insurance is available to protect the ''small'' depositors. As we discussed in Chapters 12 and 13, however, the nation's deposit insurance system has been in a precarious state for the past several years, and so the strength of this third and final layer of protection against systemic breakdown is significantly weakened. Naturally, this has placed greater pressure on the first two layers—both of which are the responsibility of the Fed.

This chapter has concentrated on the Federal Reserve's role as the central banking authority of the United States. Yet the Fed's responsibilities extend beyond those we have discussed in this chapter. Congress also has delegated to the Fed the task of conducting U.S. monetary policy. We turn our attention next to this important function of the Federal Reserve System.

CHAPTER SUMMARY

1. Traditionally, central banks have adopted three basic roles: fiscal agent for the government, banker's bank, and monetary policy maker.

2. As fiscal agent for the government, a central bank typically serves as the government's depository and as an agent in the disbursement of funds and in the issuance of governmental debts.

3. As the bank for private bankers, the central bank typically acts as lender of last resort and/or as the custodian of the nation's financial system.

4. The primary rationale for a central bank to serve as a lender of last resort and/or as financial system custodian is the possibility that payments systems are subject to externalities, which occur when the actions of agents that engage in a payments transaction affect the well-being of an agent not involved in that transaction.

5. Like any bank, the Federal Reserve System has a balance sheet composed of assets, liabilities, and a capital account. The main asset of the Fed is U.S. government securities; another important, though quantitatively small, asset is Fed loans to depository institutions. The main liabilities of the Fed are Federal Reserve notes (currency) and reserve deposits of depository institutions.

6. The Federal Reserve plays an important role in the United States' payments system. Before the Fed, however, the First and Second Banks of the United States performed analogous roles through their clearing of bank notes redeemable in gold. Between the demise of the Second Bank and the founding of the Fed, depository institutions worked out ingenious schemes for clearing payments that typically involved private clearing houses.

7. Although most payments in the United States are made via currency and checks, the largest payments are made on the electronic wire transfer systems Fedwire and CHIPS.

8. Participation in any payments system subjects a party to a payments transaction to a variety of potential risks. Among these is systemic risk, which is the possibility that a party may not receive a payment due from another party because of the latter's inability to collect from a third party. Because it is a third-party source of risk, systemic risk represents a payments system externality.

9. Through its roles as lender of last resort and custodian of the financial system, the Federal Reserve System is a key part of the federal financial safety net in the United States.

Glossary

Automated clearing house (ACH):   Payments networks that process payments within one or two days after they are initiated by a payor to a payee.

Automated teller machine (ATM) networks: Payments systems that bank depositors typically use to make cash withdrawals from their accounts.

Book-entry security transactions: Purchases and sales of government securities such as Treasury bills and bonds that are made through use of the Fedwire network.

Clearing-house association: A group of banks that agree to set up a central location—a clearing house—for clearing payments made on accounts held by their depositors.

Clearing-house certificates: Titles to the specie deposits of clearing-house associations' member banks that these banks exchanged to redeem bank notes in the nineteenth century.

Clearing House Interbank Payment System (CHIPS):   A large-dollar electronic payments network that is privately owned and operated by the New York Clearing House Association.

Clearing-house loan certificates: Titles to specie deposits that banks loaned to other banks that actually did not have specie on deposit; these certificates joined specie as part of the monetary base for the banking system in the latter half of the nineteenth century.

Credit risk: The risk that a debtor will not fully repay a loan to a creditor.

Custodian of the financial system: A central bank function under which it supervises a nation's payments system to ensure that the financial system operates smoothly.

Daylight overdrafts: Depository institutions' overdrawals of their Federal Reserve or CHIPS accounts for terms of a few minutes or a few hours.

Delivery risk: The risk that a party in a funds transaction may fulfill its end of a credit agreement but that the other party completely fails to follow through on its obligation.

Electronic benefits transfer (EBT):   A government-operated network that disburses cash payments to individuals who qualify for government benefits such as Aid to Families with Dependent Children or food stamps.

Externality: The term for a situation in which the economic transactions between one set of individuals or firms affect the well-being of other individuals or firms that are not involved in those transactions.

Federal financial safety net: The various federal government safeguards against widespread financial failures and panics, including the Fed's custodial role in the financial system, the Fed's function as lender of last resort, and the federal deposit insurance system.

Federal Reserve float: The difference between the Fed's cash items in process of collection and its deferred-availability cash items.

Fedwire: A large-dollar electronic payments network that is owned and operated by the Federal Reserve System.

Fiscal agent: A central bank's role as depository for government funds raised from taxes and borrowings and as coordinator of the mechanisms and procedures by which the government issues debt instruments when it borrows.

Foreign official deposits: Deposit accounts that foreign governments or official financial institutions hold with the Fed, usually as checking accounts that they use to make dollar-denominated payments in the United States.

Gold certificates: Titles to stocks of gold issued by the United States Treasury to the Federal Reserve System and held by the Fed as an asset.

Large-dollar payments systems: Payments networks that specialize in processing payments that typically have very large dollar values.

Lender of last resort: An institution that stands ready to make a loan to any and all illiquid but solvent depository institutions in the face of an impending bank run or analogous crisis.

Liquidity risk: The risk that arises from the possibility that a payment, even if made in full, may not be made when due.

Market risk: The risk that a creditor may not receive full payment on a debt because the borrower defaults on the original transaction, requiring both parties to strike a new agreement.

Negative externality: A market transaction that reduces the economic well-being of other individuals or firms not involved in the transaction.

Payments system: The institutional structure through which households, firms, and financial institutions exchange funds.

Penalty rates: Interest rates, such as the Fed's discount rate, that are set above market interest rates and that thereby penalize the borrowing institution.

Pledged assets: Assets, usually in the form of Treasury securities or municipal bonds, that depository institutions must hold as collateral against deposits made by federal, state, and local governments.

Point-of-sale (POS) networks: Payments systems that permit consumers to pay for purchases through direct deductions from their deposit accounts at financial institutions.

Positive externality: A market transaction that increases the economic well-being of other individuals or firms not involved in the transaction.

Special drawing rights (SDR) certificates: Assets held by the Fed that are Treasury obligations to the Fed for its share of financing of special drawing rights; these, in turn, are a type of international currency established in the 1970s.

Systemic risk: The risk that some institutions in a payments system, because their transactions are interlinked with those of other institutions, may be unable to honor credit agreements as a result of failures in otherwise unrelated transactions between the other institutions; a form of negative externality in a payments system.

SELF-TEST QUESTIONS

1. List and define in your own words the key roles of a central bank. Which of these roles seems to you to be most important? Why?

2. In light of the material in Chapter 14, which Federal Reserve assets and liabilities are most important from a monetary policy perspective? Explain your reasoning.

3. Define, in your own words, the meaning of the term "externality." List at least one real-world example of both negative and positive externalities unrelated to banking. Then list at least one example of both types of externality that concern banking markets.

4. Many economists in the 1960s forecast that today's volume of check clearing could never be sustained. Hence, they contended that our society eventually would abandon checks and paper currency. Yet these forms of payment persist. What factors would you guess the economists of the 1960s may have overlooked when they made their forecasts? Explain your reasoning.

5. List and define payments system risks. Which of these risks justifies most clearly the Fed's potential role as lender of last resort? Explain why.

PROBLEMS

16-1. In a bank credit market, the demand schedule for bank credit (C) is

$$C = 10 - 15r$$

and the market supply schedule for bank credit is given by

$$C = 5 + 35r$$

    a. Draw a rough diagram of these demand and supply schedules.
    b. What is the equilibrium market interest rate?
    c. What is the equilibrium quantity of credit extended by banks?

16-2. Suppose that the market supply schedule given in problem 16-1 fails to account for systemic risks that banks create for society when they extend credit. If the supply curve properly accounted for these risks, it would be given by $C = 35r$.
    a. Draw the new supply schedule on your rough diagram from part a of problem 16-1.
    b. Calculate the interest rate that would arise in the market if the market properly accounted for systemic risks. On the basis of your answer, by how much is the market interest rate you computed in part a (of this problem) ''too low'' because it fails to account for systemic risks?
    c. Suppose that the Federal Reserve wishes, through imposing a set of supervisory regulations, to induce the banking system to supply an amount of credit that would account for systemic risks that arise from extension of credit. By how much will the Fed desire to restrict total bank credit, in comparison to the amount that would have arisen from the market equilibrium you examined in part a of problem 16-1?

SELECTED REFERENCES

Baer, Herbert L., and Douglas D. Evanoff, ''Payments System Issues in Financial Markets That Never Sleep,'' Federal Reserve Bank of Chicago *Economic Perspectives,* 14 (6, November/December 1990), pp. 2–15.

Domowitz, Ian, ''The Mechanics of Automated Trade Execution Systems,'' Working Paper, Northwestern University (June 1990).

Federal Reserve Payments System Policy Committee, *Proposals for Modifying the Payment System Risk Reduction Policy of the Federal Reserve System,* Board of Governors of the Federal Reserve System (May 1989).

Federal Reserve Task Force on Controlling Payments System Risk, *Controlling Risk in the Payments System,* Board of Governors of the Federal Reserve System (August 1988).

Garcia, Gillian, and Elizabeth Plautz, *The Federal Reserve: Lender of Last Resort* (Cambridge, Mass.: Ballinger, 1988).

Gilbert, R. Alton, ''Payments System Risk: What Is It and What Will Happen If We Try to Reduce It?'' Federal Reserve Bank of St. Louis *Review,* 71 (1, January/February 1989), pp. 3–17.

Goodfriend, Marvin, ''Money, Credit, Banking, and Payments System Policy,'' Federal Reserve Bank of Richmond *Economic Review,* 77 (1, January/February 1989), pp. 7–23.

Goodhart, Charles, *The Evolution of Central Banks* (Cambridge, Mass.: MIT Press, 1988).

Smith, Vera C., *The Rationale of Central Banking and the Free Banking Alternative* (1936; reprinted in Indianapolis: Liberty Press, 1990).

Summers, Bruce J., ''Clearing and Payment Systems: The Role of the Central Bank,'' *Federal Reserve Bulletin,* 77 (2, February 1991), pp. 81–90.

Timberlake, Richard H., ''The Central Banking Role of Clearinghouse Associations,'' *Journal of Money, Credit, and Banking,* 16 (1, February 1984), pp. 1–15.

VanHoose, David D., and Gordon H. Sellon, Jr., ''Daylight Overdrafts, Payments System Risk, and Public Policy,'' Federal Reserve Bank of Kansas City *Economic Review,* 74 (8, September/ October 1989), pp. 9–29.

Wood, John C., and Dolores S. Smith, ''Electronic Transfer of Government Benefits,'' *Federal Reserve Bulletin,* 77 (4, April 1991), pp. 203–217.

The Federal Reserve: Instruments of Monetary Policy

CHAPTER PREVIEW

1. What are open-market operations?

2. What are the three ways that open-market operations affect the economy?

3. What are dynamic open-market operations and defensive open-market operations, and what is the distinction between them?

4. What is Fed discount window policy?

5. Why has the discount rate not been an important Fed monetary policy tool?

6. How should the Fed structure its role as lender of last resort?

7. What types of funds are eligible to satisfy reserve requirements?

8. Why are depository institutions required to hold reserves?

9. How should reserve requirements be structured?

According to the United States Constitution, the Congress has ultimate authority over the production and regulation of the quantity of money. When it passed the 1913 Federal Reserve Act and subsequent amendments, however, Congress delegated this authority to the Federal Reserve System. Hence, the Fed has responsibility for conducting monetary policy in the United States. As we discuss in this chapter, the Fed has three key policy tools, or **instruments,** that it may use to pursue this task. These are open-market operations, discount window policy, and reserve requirements.

OPEN-MARKET OPERATIONS

The single most important instrument of monetary policy in the United States is **open-market operations.** Open-market operations are the Fed's purchase and sale of U.S. government securities. As we noted in Chapter 5, United States government securities are Treasury bills, Treasury notes, and Treasury bonds. Actually, the Fed typically conducts open-market operations via the purchase and sale of Treasury bills. Additionally, open-market operations involve the purchase and sale of federal agency securities, such as those issued by the Federal National Mortgage Association (so-called Fannie Mae) and, in minor amounts, banker's acceptances.

THREE DIRECT EFFECTS OF OPEN-MARKET OPERATIONS

When the Fed purchases or sells securities on the open market, the economy is affected in three direct ways:

1. Depository institution reserves change.
2. The price (and, therefore, the yield) of securities changes.
3. Economywide expectations change.

Changes in Reserves   Chapter 14 pointed out how Fed purchases of Treasury bills from a depository institution change that depository institution's reserves. Briefly, if the Fed purchases $1 million worth of T-bills from a depository institution, the Fed eventually pays by increasing the reserve account of that institution. That means that the depository institution changes its asset portfolio's structure. It now has $1 million less in T-bills and $1 million more in reserve deposits at the Fed. The Fed has a $1 million increase in its assets (T-bills) and in its liabilities (deposit obligations to the selling depository institution).

A depository institution's reserves also increase if the Fed purchases the $1 million T-bill from the private sector. Thus, whenever the Fed purchases U.S. government securities, depository institution reserves increase by exactly the amount of the purchase. Furthermore, other things being constant, the quantity of money will expand by some multiple of the original Fed purchase. This increase in the money stock may, ultimately, lead to an increase in the level of economic activity.

Complementary reasoning indicates that the sale of a T-bill by the Fed to a depository institution or to the nonbank public decreases overall depository institution reserves and normally leads to a multiple contraction in the quantity of money. This contraction in the money stock eventually *may,* as we shall discuss in Unit 6, lead to a reduction in economic activity.

Interest Rate Changes   As indicated in Chapter 7, as the price of a bill or bond changes, so, too, does its yield. An increase in the purchase of bonds will cause bond prices to rise, which amounts to a decrease in bond yields. A decrease in bond purchases causes bond prices to fall and bond yields to rise.

Because the Fed is a large buyer/seller relative to all other buyers/sellers of U.S. government securities, the Fed can (usually) affect the price of a bill or bond directly. It follows that the Fed can also influence interest rates. In principle, the Fed could, if inflation expectations were constant (see below), change short-, medium-, or long-term interest rates by buying or selling securities aggressively in any of these markets. To maintain a given price (and therefore interest rate) for a bill, all the Fed need do is to be prepared to buy or to sell as much as the rest of the traders care to sell or to buy at that ''going'' security price (interest rate).

Changes in Expectations   An ''announcement effect'' exists for open-market operations, as well as for the other monetary tools. ''Fed watchers''—stock market analysts, brokerage house employees, general investors, corporate treasurers, and a host of other individuals, including university professors—monitor open-market operations and make their predictions about the future effects of open-market operations on such economic variables as interest rates and inflation. Unfortunately, complete agreement does not exist among economists about how expectations change specifically when specific open-market operation changes occur. On the one hand, one might interpret an increase in Fed purchases of securities as an expansionary monetary policy that will cause lower interest rates, increased business production and investment, and increased consumer spending. On the other hand, expansionary monetary policy might induce expectations of still higher future increases in the money stock and the anticipation of inflation. The expectation of higher rates of inflation will encourage money lenders to place an inflationary premium on interest rates; nominal interest rates will then rise. Moreover, an expectation of increased inflation may well discourage business investment and consumer spending.

Nonetheless, the view that open-market purchases are expansionary, even accounting for expectational adjustments, remains the dominant view within the economics profession. In this text, we generally shall view them in that way. It is important to recognize, however, that changes in open-market operations necessarily lead to expectational changes, but all expectational changes cannot be predicted in light of possible differences in interpretation across agents in the economy.

THE EFFECTS OF OPEN-MARKET OPERATIONS ON RESERVES, MONEY, AND CREDIT

At this point we do not possess all the tools necessary to analyze fully the interest rate effects of open-market operations (see Chapter 25). We can, however, use the money and total credit multiplier models we developed in Chapter 14 to explore the effects of open-market operations on the quantities of money and total credit.

Defining Different Types of Reserves and the Monetary Base   The Fed's key to monetary policy is its ability to affect depository institution reserves and/or the money multiplier process. Total reserves, however, do not tell the whole story. For this reason, the Fed has developed several reserve measures:

1. *The monetary base (MB)* Economists also call the monetary base, or simply the base or the reserve base, by the name "high-powered money." The **monetary base** consists of total depository institution reserves (TR) plus currency in circulation (*C*). Currency in circulation is currency in the hands of the public and not in the Fed, the U.S. Treasury, or bank vaults. Economists sometimes call this sum (MB = TR + *C*) high-powered money because a dollar's worth of it can support several dollars for transactions accounts in a fractional reserve system, as you will recall from Chapter 14. The higher the required reserve ratio, the less "power" each dollar in the monetary base has; the lower the required reserve ratio, the more "power" each dollar in the monetary base has. In other words, the monetary base consists of those assets available to the public that, if held by depository institutions, could be used to satisfy Federal Reserve reserve requirements. (Remember that currency in the vaults of depository institutions can be used to satisfy reserve requirements.)

2. *Excess reserves* **Excess reserves (ER)** are those reserves above the reserves required by law. Excess reserves by definition are total reserves minus required reserves (RR); that is, ER ≡ TR − RR.

3. *Borrowed reserves* **Borrowed reserves (BR)** are those reserves that depository institutions have borrowed from the Fed.

4. *Nonborrowed reserves* **Nonborrowed reserves (NBR)** are, by definition, equal to total reserves minus borrowed reserves (NBR ≡ TR − BR). We analyze borrowed and nonborrowed reserves in more detail below and in Chapter 25.

5. *Nonborrowed base* The **nonborrowed base** is the monetary base minus borrowed reserves, or, equivalently, nonborrowed reserves plus currency held by the nonbank public. Some economists prefer this measure to the full monetary base, believing that the nonborrowed base better reflects the potential maximum money supply than does the monetary base.

6. *Free reserves* **Free reserves (FR)** equal borrowed reserves minus excess reserves ($FR \equiv BR - ER$). Depository institutions tend to repay the Fed the amount of reserves borrowed from the Fed before they purchase securities or make loans. If so, then free reserves are a good measure of the degree to which depository institutions are able to expand their assets.

When the Fed purchases a security, it adds to its own assets. It does so by writing a check on its own account, and when this check is deposited in a depository institution, it causes an expansion in total reserves in the banking system. Consequently, the immediate effect of an open-market purchase is an increase in bank reserves.

The Effects of an Open-Market Operation on Reserves and the Quantity of Money   Unless the Fed makes reserves available to depository institutions through discount window loans, however, borrowed reserves do not change as a result of an open-market purchase. This means that it is the nonborrowed reserves component of total reserves that increases following an open-market purchase. An open-market sale, in contrast, reduces the nonborrowed part of total reserves in the banking system.

Recall from Chapter 14 that the money multipler model tells us that

$$\Delta M = m \times \Delta MB \tag{17-1}$$

A change in the quantity of money is equal to the money multiplier times a change in the monetary base. From our definitions above, the monetary base is equal to $MB = TR + C$. Or $MB = NBR + BR + C$, because total reserves by definition must be the sum of nonborrowed reserves and borrowed reserves. Therefore, in general, $\Delta MB = \Delta NBR + \Delta BR + \Delta C$. Other things equal, an open-market purchase or sale causes only nonborrowed reserves to change, and so $\Delta BR = \Delta C = 0$ (provided that ''other things equal'' holds). Therefore, an open-market operation causes the monetary base to increase by an increase in nonborrowed reserves; that is, $\Delta MB = \Delta NBR$, so that equation (17-1) may be rewritten as

$$\Delta M = m \times \Delta NBR \tag{17-2}$$

Equation (17-2) says that the change in nonborrowed reserves has a full multiplier effect on the quantity of money. Hence, we may conclude that an open-market *purchase,* which would cause the change in nonborrowed reserves to be *positive,* would, other things equal, cause the quantity of money to *rise* by the increase in nonborrowed reserves times the money multiplier. In contrast, an open-market *sale,* which would cause the change in nonborrowed reserves to be *negative,* would, other things equal, cause the quantity of money to *fall* by the decrease in nonborrowed reserves times the money multiplier.

The Effects of Open-Market Operations on Total Bank Credit   Recall that, in our basic model of the banking system in Chapter 14, we assumed that all bank credit consisted of loans (L). We showed in Chapter 14 that a change in the quantity of bank credit also could be expressed as a multiple of a change in the monetary base:

$$\Delta L = m_L \times \Delta MB \tag{17-3}$$

where m_L is the total credit multiplier.

Holding all other things, including currency and borrowed reserves, equal, we know from our reasoning above that $\Delta MB = \Delta NBR$ following an open-market purchase or sale. Therefore, we may rewrite equation (17-3) by

$$\Delta L = m_L \times \Delta NBR \tag{17-4}$$

Equation (17-4) says that a change in nonborrowed reserves following an open-market operation is multiplied times the total credit multiplier to cause a change in the quantity of total bank credit. If the Fed *purchases* securities in the open market, the change in nonborrowed reserves will be *positive,* and total bank credit will *rise* by a multiple of this change in nonborrowed reserves. If the Fed *sells* securities in the open market, the change in nonborrowed reserves will be *negative,* and total bank credit will *fall* by a multiple of this change in nonborrowed reserves.

We can see, then, that open-market operations represent a direct means for the Federal Reserve System to influence the quantities of *both* money and credit in the economy. It is this direct effect of open-market operations that makes this instrument of monetary policy one that the Fed uses most often. Indeed, the Fed conducts open-market operations each day. Doing so is a little more involved than our simple equations imply, however. Many officials and Federal Reserve staff members coordinate the Fed's efforts in this regard.

THE MECHANICS OF OPEN-MARKET OPERATIONS

The Federal Open Market Committee (FOMC) meets eight times each year in Washington, D.C. Its staff briefs the committee on current economic conditions and future projections in what is referred to as the ''chart show.'' The FOMC then issues a directive, which is an instruction to the two managers of the open-market accounts. One manager heads domestic operations; the other heads foreign operations. Both managers are vice presidents of the New York Fed. The New York Fed serves as the agent of the twelve Federal Reserve banks in conducting open-market operations, and the two managers take their orders from the FOMC.

The FOMC Directive   The **FOMC directive** to the account managers consists of three parts:

1. Part A contains the qualitative statements of the stabilization goals, for example, higher employment, lower inflation, stable growth of real output, and a balance-of-payments improvement.

2. Part B includes the specific target ranges for the next year (from the current quarter to the corresponding quarter one year later). These targets have varied over the years, but usually they are stated in terms of credit conditions, interest rates, or monetary aggregates (the various money supply measures such as M1 and M2).

3. Part C lists short-term targets that take into account special calendar events (such as Christmas, when currency leakages are unusually large) but are consistent with the goals in part B.

It is important to realize that the FOMC directive does not set specific targets for reserves in the system. It is up to the account managers to decide the dollar value of the securities to be bought or sold on the open market to achieve the results mandated in the directive. Of course, the discretionary power of the managers is not unlimited. If the FOMC changes its mind or feels that its directives are not being carried out properly, it can issue additional verbal instructions to the account managers before the next meeting of the FOMC.

Although the directive eventually is made public (currently at the end of 30 days), it is not made public immediately. The reason the Fed gives for keeping the directive secret for three or four weeks is that it believes some people are in a position to act upon this information more rapidly than others and thus can earn profits at the expense of others. Carrying this policy of secrecy to the extreme, the domestic account manager at the New York Fed actually places buy and sell orders simultaneously with different dealers, so that it is not immediately apparent whether the Fed is a net buyer or a net seller. This attitude of secrecy is not without its critics; some feel that in this day of modern electronic communications, the Fed should announce its directive immediately and publicly. It is difficult to understand how immediate disclosure could help some and hurt others in any systematic fashion. But it is easy to see how a policy of secrecy places high premiums on inside information.

Day-to-Day Operations   Once the account managers have received their directive, they brief the members of their trading staffs and the action begins. In particular, the domestic account manager contacts the three dozen or so special dealers in government securities who are located in New York City; the securities dealers in turn deal with the public. Because the Fed is a semipublic institution (it is owned by member banks, but its top officials are governmental appointees), its activities are under scrutiny; therefore, it strives to sell at the highest price and buy at the lowest price in its open-market operations.

It is often true that no physical paper check is necessary for an open-market transaction. As we discussed in the last chapter, Fedwire links the district Reserve banks to commercial banks, which act as clearing agents for the special dealers in government securities. Computers linked through Fedwire debit and credit transactions to the security book-entry accounts of the depository institutions in question, typically on the same day as the transaction. The open-market operations of any day last only about a half hour.

As we discuss in the Current Controversy below, the Fed buys and sells many times the volumes of the net changes in the monetary base that its open-market operations produce. Individual open-market purchases or sales typically involve millions of dollars in securities; the $100,000 purchase we considered in Chapter 14 was a nice, round number but was not particularly realistic.

TYPES OF OPEN-MARKET OPERATIONS

Whatever the aim of open-market operations, the Fed uses two basic types of open-market transactions:

1. Outright purchases or sales
2. Purchases under repurchase agreements (RPs) and sales under matched sales-purchase agreements (reverse RPs, also known as matched transactions)

Outright Purchases or Sales   Outright purchases or sales are what you might expect—the Fed buys or sells securities in the open market with no strings attached to the transactions. If the Fed purchases a security, it is not obligated to sell it back at a later date. If the Fed sells a security to a buyer, the buyer is not obligated to resell it to the Fed at a later date.

Repurchase Agreements and Reverse Repurchase Agreements   In a repurchase agreement the Fed buys securities from a dealer and the dealer agrees to repurchase the securities at a specified date and price. In effect, such a transaction is a loan by the Fed to the dealer; the interest rate is set by auction among the dealers. A Fed purchase under a repurchase agreement by the dealer is referred to as an RP transaction.

The counterpart to the RP is the reverse RP, or matched sales-purchase transaction. In such a transaction, the Fed sells securities to a dealer and also agrees to buy back the securities at a specified price and date. This amounts to a loan to the Fed by the dealer.

RPs and reverse RPs are typically very short-term contracts. The Fed usually conducts RPs for fewer than 15 days (usually 7 days), and it typically terminates reverse RPs in 7 days or less. Originally, large commercial banks and government securities dealers primarily used RPs as an alternative means of financing their government securities inventories. Now, however, a variety of institutional investors regularly use RPs, and the Federal Reserve Bank of New York uses RP transactions to implement monetary policy directives and to make investments for foreign officials and monetary authorities.

The duration of RPs and reverse RPs indicates that they are used only when the Fed wants to alter depository institution reserves temporarily. Table 17-1 shows that RPs and reverse RPs are by far the greatest part of the gross volume of Fed open-market transactions. Furthermore, they are becoming an increasingly higher percentage of the gross value of open-market operations.

DEFENSIVE AND DYNAMIC OPEN-MARKET TRANSACTIONS

At first sight, Table 17-1 appears rather startling. The net change in Fed holdings of governmental securities (and to a lesser extent, banker's acceptances) is a very small percentage of the total transactions. In terms of the volume of gross transactions, RPs and reverse RPs are more than 115 times greater than outright purchases or sales of government securities and agency obligations.

To understand Table 17-1, it is crucial to distinguish between dynamic and defensive open-market operations. The Fed uses **dynamic open-market operations** to *change* the level of depository institution reserves. Outright purchases or sales of government securities or federal agency obligations, which are more or less permanent, will accomplish that end. In contrast, **defensive open-market operations** are balancing adjustments intended to *maintain* the current level of total depository institution reserves. From time to time, the economy encounters foreseen and unforeseen events that automatically and temporarily change total reserves and/or the quantity of money. To keep the economy on an even keel and to maintain the desired level of total reserves, short-term defensive actions are necessary. RPs and reverse RPs, because of their short-term nature, are designed to do precisely that. RPs provide temporary reserves, and reverse RPs sop up temporary excess reserves.

Consider two examples. At Christmas time, there are enormous currency leakages from depository institutions, causing depository institution reserves to shrink—as Chapter 14 indicated. The Fed counters currency leakages via RP transactions; the Fed buys securities with the arrangement that it can sell them back after Christmas. The initial Fed purchase creates reserves for the Yuletide season; then, in early January, the Fed sells back the

TABLE 17-1
Federal Reserve Open-Market Transactions—1991

Types of Transactions*

Outright transactions:	
Gross purchases	$ 31,439
Gross sales	120
Redemptions	1,000
Matched transactions:	
Gross purchases	1,570,456
Gross sales	1,571,534
Repurchase agreements:	
Gross purchases	310,084
Gross sales	311,752
Total change in system:	
Open-market account from 1990	29,729

* In millions of dollars. Includes U.S. government securities and federal agency obligations and excludes banker's acceptances.

Source: Board of Governors of the Federal Reserve System, *Federal Reserve Bulletin.*

securities to offset the huge quantity of currency that the public redeposits in depository institutions.

Similarly, around April 15, when income-tax-payment time rolls around, the reserve position of depository institutions falls, and the quantity of money falls with it, as taxpayers send checks to the IRS (which is a branch of the U.S. Treasury). The Treasury's account at the Fed therefore increases by the same amount by which public deposit accounts in depository institution reserves decrease. This temporary reduction in the public's total deposits and depository institution reserves can be, and often is, offset by RPs.

DISCOUNT WINDOW POLICY

Open-market operations change the quantity of nonborrowed reserves in the banking system, thereby altering the level of total reserves and, through the money multiplier process, the quantities of money and credit. This is not the only way that the Fed can change reserves, money, and credit, however. By definition, total reserves equal nonborrowed reserves plus borrowed reserves; the latter are reserves the Fed lends directly to depository insitutions. Hence, Fed lending to depository institutions is another means of conducting monetary policy.

THE THEORY OF DISCOUNT WINDOW POLICY

Discounting is the process of lending by the Federal Reserve System to depository institutions. The term ''discounting'' gets its name from the method by which depository institutions obtain loans from the Fed. Depository institutions discount securities or commercial loans that are eligible by selling those loans to the Fed for a short time, in exchange for an increase in the depository institution's reserve account. The Fed ''discounts'' the asset (loan) by increasing the depository institution's reserve account by a value that is less than the amount of the IOU. The depository institution then buys the asset back at the face value of the loan.

In practice, however, the most common type of depository institution borrowing from the Fed is in the form of an **advance,** which is a promissory note signed by an official of the depository institution with U.S. government securities as collateral. Nonetheless, all Fed lending to member banks is usually called discounting. In practice, each Fed district bank provides loans through what is figuratively known as the ''discount window.''

Discount Window Policy   Economists refer to the terms and conditions under which the Fed lends to depository institutions as **discount window policy.** The Fed's **discount rate** is the rate the Fed charges on its loans to depository institutions. If the Fed were ready to lend unlimited quantities of reserves at any given discount rate, it could directly control (even dictate) short-term interest rates. For example, if the Fed wished to lower short-term interest rates, through its discount policy it could agree to lend unlimited reserves to depository institutions at a discount rate below market rates. Depository institutions would be able to obtain reserves at an interest rate below the rate at which they could lend those reserves. Competition among depository institutions would then cause all short-term interest rates to fall when all depository institutions were allowed to borrow from the Fed at below-market interest rates. The Fed thus could make borrowing from it a more profitable source of funds for a depository institution than such alternatives as selling CDs, selling the securities it owns, or borrowing in the federal funds market.

Discount window policy also refers to the amount of reserves the Fed is willing to lend at any given discount rate to depository institutions. Because the Fed can lend whatever amount it wishes and because increased lending directly increases reserves, the Fed can choose the quantity of money it prefers by selecting the amount it will lend. For example, if the Fed knew the amount of currency that the public desired to hold and if it knew the amount of excess reserves that depository institutions were prepared to hold (prudential reserves), then (given the required reserve ratios) it could determine the quantity of money or its rate of growth simply by adjusting its quantity of lending. But in so doing, it would give up control over the interest rate. The Fed would have to increase or decrease its lending regardless of what happened to interest rates if it wanted to affect the money supply in a particular way.

The Effect of Changes in Discount Window Borrowing on Bank Reserves and the Quantity of Money   According to the law of demand, a reduction in the price of a good or service increases the quantity demanded; likewise, an increase in price decreases the amount of the good or service that is demanded. Analogously, because the Fed's discount rate is the ''price'' of reserves that depository institutions borrow from the Fed, a decrease in the discount rate induces depository institutions to borrow more reserves from the Fed. An increase in the discount rate induces them to borrow fewer reserves. Consequently, a change in the discount rate causes a change in borrowed reserves in the banking system.

When the Fed extends a discount window loan to a depository institution, it does so by crediting the institution's reserve deposit account at the Fed; thus, the Fed gains a liability in the transaction, and total reserves in the banking system increase. The Fed also gains an asset: the loan to the depository institution.

Recall from equation (17-1) that $\Delta M = m \times \Delta MB$. Recall also that $\Delta MB = \Delta NBR$

THE THORNY QUESTIONS OF FED "CHURNING" AND OPEN-MARKET SECRECY

Some people make a career of criticizing the Fed. A congressman named Wright Patman, for instance, spent over a decade attacking William McChesney Martin and the rest of the Federal Reserve in the 1950s and 1960s. More recently, the Fed has been criticized—often by economists more expert in their criticisms than Patman could have been—for two reasons. First, some economists believe that the Fed conducts altogether too many open-market operations. Second, some economists (a few of these also participate in the first criticism as well) contend that the Fed also is much too secretive about the aims of its open-market operations.

The Issue of Open-Market Churning

As Table 17-1 indicates, the Fed engages in a large number of open-market operations designed to change the total level of reserves by relatively small amounts. This process is aptly referred to as **churning.** Churning has generated a considerable amount of controversy. Some have complained that the only beneficiaries of churning are three dozen or so special securities dealers that earn enormous brokerage fees. (Note that when stockbrokers encourage excessive buying and selling of securities in order to increase their own profits, they are subject to prosecution.)

Federal Reserve officials claim that much of the supposed churning is really not churning at all. They contend that temporary transactions and those arranged on behalf of foreign central banks do not constitute churning. In particular, to provide reserves on a temporary basis, the Fed engages in repurchase agreements with dealers. When there is a "need" to drain reserves temporarily, the Fed arranges reverse repurchase agreements. Federal Reserve officials believe that such transactions should not be included in the computation of the gross open-market purchases indicated in Table 17-1.

Officials at the Federal Reserve System maintain that the bulk of their open-market operations are defensive in nature and do no more than accommodate seasonal variations in the demand for currency and deposits. The churning is necessary to accommodate these seasonal variations in currency and deposit demand. The reso-

lution of this controversy is therefore not straightforward. Any fixed rate of growth of reserves in the banking system would eliminate the defensive nature of open-market operations. Because seasonal swings in the demand for cash balances are quite large over a one-year period, however, depository institutions might find themselves with temporary large short-run changes in reserves. For example, if the Fed did not engage in defensive open-market operations, there would be a sharp contraction in the supply of deposits each December and a sharp expansion each January, just the opposite of what would happen to the demand for cash balances.

Excessive Secrecy at the Fed?

The Fed is indeed a secretive place. Innocent-looking documents at the Fed commonly carry labels such as "confidential" or "highly confidential." Up to 1966, the Fed could attach such labels to any document it wished. In 1966, however, Congress passed the Freedom of Information Act, which empowered any United States citizen to request a government document and placed the burden of proving a need for secrecy upon the government agency that possessed the document.

In 1975, a Georgetown law student filed suit against the FOMC under terms of the Freedom of Information Act. His complaint was that the FOMC was keeping its open-market directives secret for 90 days following their adoption. He requested a court ruling to force the FOMC to reveal the contents of its directive immediately following its meeting. In May 1976, a U.S. district court ruled in the student's favor and ordered the FOMC to release the directive within one business day following its adoption.

From 1976 to 1979, the Federal Reserve System pursued an appeal to the Supreme Court, in which it argued, among other things, that an absence of FOMC secrecy could contribute to "unfair speculation" in financial markets, to market reactions to Fed policies that the Fed had not desired, and to harm to the government's commercial interests through greater interest rate variability that a lack of secrecy might cause. The Supreme Court sent the case back to the district court for further review. In the end, the Fed won the case, although it did shorten its time of release of the directive to the day after the next FOMC meeting (about six weeks later).

If there is one group that really dislikes not getting in on secrets, however, it is politicians. Beginning in 1989, several members of Congress, led by House member Lee Hamilton, introduced legislation requiring an end to Fed secrecy. Their efforts might have been successful if not for the fact that they complicated things by attempting to make other changes at the Fed, such as putting the secretary of the Treasury back on the Federal Reserve Board. As of this writing, secrecy at the Fed continues, even though most economists doubt that prompt release of the FOMC directive could be nearly as harmful as the Fed claimed in court.

Fed release of information might not be all that beneficial, either. A 1991 study by David Simon, a Fed staff economist, determined that participants in financial markets are very adept in their efforts to figure out the Fed's policy intentions. This study concluded, in fact, that interest rate forecasts by individuals effectively take into account the information content of the FOMC directive within a single day after the FOMC meeting, even though the directive is not disclosed. The reason, according to the study, is that the Fed's open-market operations quickly signal to financial markets the intent of Fed policy, and the "Fed watchers" in the markets immediately deduce what the FOMC decided at its meeting.

Sources: Milton Friedman, "Monetary Policy: Theory and Practice," *Journal of Money, Credit, and Banking,* 14 (1, February 1982), pp. 98–118; Fred J. Levin and Ann-Marie Meulendyke, "Monetary Policy: Theory and Practice, A Comment," *Journal of Money, Credit, and Banking,* 14 (3, August 1982), pp. 399–403; Marvin Goodfriend, "Monetary Mystique: Secrecy and Central Banking," *Journal of Monetary Economics,* 17 (1, January 1986), pp. 63–92; Louis Uchitelle, "Moves On in Congress to Lift Secrecy at the Federal Reserve, *New York Times* (Sept. 16, 1989), p. 1; Lindley H. Clark, Jr., "Remaking the Fed: Maybe It's Time," *Wall Street Journal* (Sept. 18, 1989), p. 1; and David P. Simon, "Secrecy, Signalling, and the Accuracy of Expectations during the Borrowed Reserves Operating Regime," *Journal of Banking and Finance,* 15 (2, April 1991), pp. 329–341.

$+ \Delta BR + \Delta C$. Assuming that all other things, including currency and nonborrowed reserves, are constant, it follows that $\Delta MB = \Delta BR$ following a change in the Fed's discount rate. Therefore,

$$\Delta M = m \times \Delta BR \tag{17-5}$$

Equation (17-5) says that a change in borrowed reserves induced by a change in the Fed's discount rate has a full multiplier effect on the quantity of money. For instance, a *reduction* in the discount rate would cause an *increase* in borrowed reserves, which would cause a multiple *positive* effect on the quantity of money. In contrast, an *increase* in the discount rate would cause a *decrease* in borrowed reserves, which would cause a multiple *negative* effect on the quantity of money.

If we look only at equation (17-5), we might be tempted to conclude that discount window policy works just like open-market operations. Discount window policy, however, is a less direct instrument of policy than open-market operations. The reason is this: If the Fed would like the quantity of money to change by a particular amount, equation (17-5) tells it how much borrowed reserves should change, but it does *not* tell the Fed exactly how much to change the discount rate to *induce* the needed change. This less direct linkage between discount window policy and reserves has made it a less useful monetary policy instrument, as have other factors we discuss below.

Discount Window Policy and Total Bank Credit From equation (17-3), we know that a change in the monetary base causes a multiple change in the quantity of total credit extended by the banking system: $\Delta L = m_L \times \Delta MB$. Furthermore, we know that $\Delta MB = \Delta NBR + \Delta BR + \Delta C$. Finally, we also know, from our reasoning above, that a change in the discount rate, holding other factors—including currency holdings and open-market operations—constant, induces a change in borrowed reserves. Hence,

$$\Delta L = m_L \times \Delta BR \tag{17-6}$$

is the equation that tells us the effect of a discount-rate-induced change in borrowed reserves on the quantity of total bank credit.

According to equation (17-6), a change in borrowed reserves causes a multiple change in total credit. A rise in borrowed reserves induced by a decrease in the discount rate would cause total credit to increase by a multiple amount; a fall in borrowed reserves induced by an increase in the discount rate would cause total credit to decrease by a multiple amount. As in the case of the effects of discount window policy on the quantity of money, the effects of discount window policy are less direct than those of open-market operations, although the linkage from reserve changes to quantity changes works in the same way.

Anatomy of Fed Lending Under provisions of the 1980 Depository Institutions De-regulation and Monetary Control Act, all depository institutions that must hold reserves with the Fed may apply for loans from their Federal Reserve district bank. If the Fed grants a loan, the loan falls into one of three categories:

1. *Adjustment credit* These loans allow depository institutions to adjust their portfolios to unanticipated deposit and loan activity.

2. *Seasonal credit* These loans permit certain institutions (e.g., farm banks) special access to the discount window to fund such seasonal activities as vacations, planting, and harvesting. Seasonal credit loans exist for those depository institutions that do not have ready access to national money markets.

3. *Extended credit* This program is designed to fulfill the longer-term credit needs of troubled depository institutions resulting from prolonged cash flow problems.

According to the guidelines established by Regulation A and its amendments, banks must have an appropriate reason for borrowing and must have sought alternative sources of funding first. Reasons that are considered appropriate under these guidelines include (1) liquidity needs arising from unanticipated deposit or loan activity, (2) the avoidance of overdrafts in reserve accounts, and (3) liquidity needs arising from outside forces, such as wire transfer failures.

Reasons that are considered inappropriate include (1) borrowing to take advantage of a favorable spread between the discount rate and the interest rate on alternative sources of funds and (2) borrowing to support loan and investment activities. Additionally, the Fed sets guidelines regarding the appropriate amount, frequency, and duration of borrow-ing for banks of different sizes.

Despite these regulations, in practice adjustment and seasonal borrowing are sensitive to the spread between the federal funds rate and the discount rate.

An interesting development in recent years has been the significant growth of Fed discount window loans classified as seasonal and extended credit. Figure 17-1 shows the portions of Fed lending classified as adjustment, seasonal, and extended credit. As you can see, the latter categories have eclipsed adjustment credit—the traditional type of loan made by a lender of last resort—in recent years. The Fed now appears to be in the business of long-term lending.

What accounts for this change? As we discussed in the last chapter and in Chapter 12, the federal deposit insurance system has experienced many problems in recent years. This leaves it to the Fed, as the other main participant in the federal financial safety net, to take up the slack in that net. It has done so by opening up the discount window to more and more problem banks. Critics of the Fed believe that this violates the classic role of lender of last resort, but the Fed continues its policy of longer-term lending.

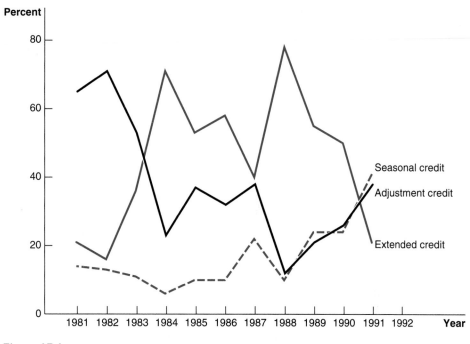

Figure 17-1
Distribution of Discount Window Borrowing by Type, 1970-1991. (*Source: Federal Reserve Bulletin*; percentages computed from annual averages of monthly dollar amounts.)

In defense of the Fed, we should point out that extended credit becomes more expensive to a depository institution the longer it borrows. Since 1987 the Fed has charged depository institutions a progressively higher discount rate as they extend the time horizons of their borrowing from the Fed. For institutions that borrow for more than a few months, the discount rate can, in fact, be a penalty rate.

DISCOUNT RATE POLICY RECONSIDERED

It has been noted that a change in the discount rate can directly affect depository institution reserves and the quantities of money and bank credit. It can have some subsidiary effects as well.

The Announcement Effect   Another possible effect of a change in the discount rate is referred to as the **announcement effect.** This means that by changing the discount rate the Fed can signal its intentions and the financial community will react accordingly. It is not clear, though, what "reacting accordingly" entails. A Fed increase in the discount rate could be interpreted as either (1) the intent of the Fed to tighten monetary policy or (2) an admission by the Fed that it is unable to contain inflation and that it is keeping the discount rate in line with increases in other short-term rates. So-called Fed watchers therefore often have a difficult time anticipating the Fed's intended "announcement effect." An act that can be interpreted in two entirely different ways can hardly be useful as an "announcement effect" tool. Moreover, it would appear that the Fed could demonstrate its intentions by using its other tools or by simply stating its intentions without using any of its tools. Because a change in the discount rate will be interpreted in at least two different (and contradictory) ways, any announcement effect often is likely to be, on net, quite small.

A Sluggish Discount Rate Policy   When the Fed changes the discount rate, it is usually criticized. If it raises the discount rate, the press and politicians invariably interpret this as a tight money policy; and a tight money policy is usually quite unpopular. Indeed, some observers blamed a discount rate increase for the stock market crash of 1987. It is not surprising, therefore, that for the most part the discount rate has been sluggish in response to changes in economic conditions. The Fed in the past has not wanted to rock the boat.

During boom times, interest rates normally rise along with most other prices. If the Fed does not raise the discount rate, its ''price'' for borrowed reserves will be relatively lower than other short-term rates. The Fed, therefore, will be lending at precisely the time a policy to counter inflation (countercyclical policy) calls for a restrictive monetary stance. At best, a lagging, or sluggish, discount rate change interferes with monetary policy; at worst, it is destabilizing. Nonetheless, it is probably safe to say that most economists do not worry about this problem because the Fed does not have to lend a specified quantity at the discount window. And even if it does lend, such lending can be offset by open-market sales of T-bills.

Changes in the Discount Rate   The board of directors of each Federal Reserve bank is required either to reestablish or to change the current discount rate every 14 days. The recommended change (usually it's a nonchange) is reported to the Board of Governors, who may either approve or veto it. Consider the following data on discount rate changes: From January 1, 1960, to January 1, 1970, the New York Fed changed its discount rate thirteen times. Then, from January 1, 1970, to January 1, 1980, the New York Fed changed the rate thirty-six times.

This increase in the frequency of discount rate changes did not, however, reflect a more aggressive use of discount policy. Close examination reveals that these changes in the discount rate followed changes in the federal funds rate. Figure 17-2 indicates that borrowing by member banks is indeed responsive to relative changes in the discount rate. Despite the fact that the Fed allegedly disallows borrowing for profit, member borrowings are closely and positively related to the difference between the federal funds rate and the discount rate. As this difference rises, the discount rate falls relative to the federal funds rate and depository institutions react predictably: They borrow more from the Fed. This indicates that in practice it is difficult to allow borrowing only for specific needs. Institutions apparently ''need'' to borrow more when doing so is more profitable.

In actuality, the observed changes in the discount rate that have followed changes in the federal funds rate represent passive actions on the part of the Fed. The Fed typically prefers to keep the *relative* discount rate constant.

Other Costs of Using the Discount Window   It should be noted that the discount rate does *not* reflect the *full cost* of discount window borrowing by depository institutions. Fed regulations limit the use of discount window credit and limit the volume, frequency, and duration of borrowing. Consequently, if a bank borrows today, it may be unable to borrow later, when the federal funds rate may be well above the discount rate. In addition, depository institutions must consider that excessive borrowing could bring greater scrutiny from federal regulators. Also, if word got out that a particular bank was using the discount window, it might be perceived as a sign of weakness.

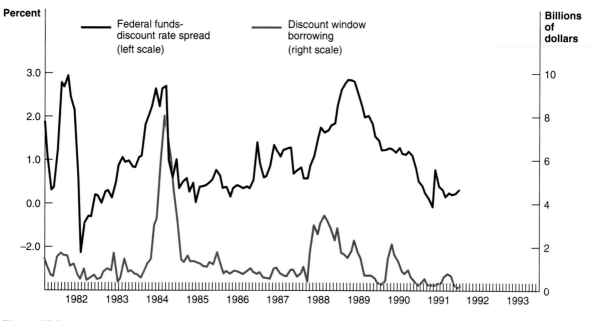

Figure 17-2
Discount Window Borrowing and the Rate Spread.   These graphs indicate that when the spread between the federal funds rate and the discount rate (black curve) rises, the total amount of discount window borrowing (color curve) also tends to rise. In general, when the spread falls, so does bank borrowing from the Fed. (*Source: Federal Reserve Bulletin, various issues.*)

RESERVE REQUIREMENTS

The third, but least used, instrument of monetary policy is reserve requirements. As we discussed in Chapter 14, the Fed enforces reserve requirements by requiring depository institutions to hold reserves in proportion to transactions deposits. These required proportions are required reserve ratios.

REQUIRED RESERVES

Congress gives the Fed the power to set legal reserve requirements—within limits—for depository institutions. Only a depository institution's vault cash and its deposits at the Fed are eligible to satisfy these legal reserve requirements.

The Effects of Reserve Requirement Changes on the Quantities of Money and Credit   Changes in reserve requirements do not change the level of total reserves in the economy. The Fed determines the amount of nonborrowed reserves through its open-market operations, and it sets the quantity of borrowed reserves via discount window policy. Therefore, reserve requirement changes leave the size of the monetary base unaffected.

Recall, however, that the money multiplier in our basic model developed in Chapter 14 was $m = (1 + c)/(d + e + c)$, where c is the nonbank public's desired ratio of currency to transactions deposits, e is depository institutions' desired holdings of excess reserves relative to transactions deposits, and d is the required reserve ratio for transactions deposits. A change in the required ratio, therefore, changes the value of the money multiplier. A decrease in the required reserve ratio increases the size of the multiplier; an increase in the required reserve ratio decreases the size of the multiplier.

According to our money multiplier model, $M = m \times MB$; that is, the quantity of money is equal to the money multiplier times the monetary base. A change in reserve requirements changes the value of the money multiplier but, other things equal, does *not* change the monetary base. Therefore, we have

$$\Delta M = \Delta m \times MB \qquad (17\text{-}7)$$

Equation (17-7) says that a change in the money multiplier caused by a change in the required reserve ratio is multiplied by the monetary base to cause a change in the quantity of money. Because a reduction in the required reserve ratio *increases* the size of the multiplier, a *decrease* in reserve requirements *increases* the quantity of money. Because an increase in the required reserve ratio *decreases* the size of the multiplier, an *increase* in reserve requirements *decreases* the quantity of money.

Equation (17-3) tells us that there is also a multiplier effect of the monetary base on total credit: $\Delta L = m_L \times \Delta MB$. We saw in Chapter 14 that the total credit multiplier is $m_L = [1 - (d + e)]/(d + e + c)$. A decrease in the required reserve ratio increases the numerator of the total credit multiplier [when e falls, the quantity $1 - (d + e)$ becomes larger] while decreasing its denominator (the quantity $d + e + c$ becomes smaller as e falls), and so a decrease in reserve requirements raises the size of the total credit multiplier. In contrast, an increase in reserve requirements reduces the size of this multiplier.

We may conclude that

$$\Delta L = \Delta m_L \times MB \qquad (17\text{-}8)$$

As in the case of the effect of reserve requirements on the quantity of money, a change in reserve requirements alters the value of total bank credit by changing the size of the multiplier relating it to the monetary base. Therefore, a reserve requirement *decrease* causes the total credit multiplier to *rise* and thereby *raises* total bank credit. A reserve requirement *increase,* in contrast, causes the total credit multiplier to *fall* and thereby *reduces* total bank credit.

In principle, then, the Fed could vary reserve requirements to influence the quantities of money and credit. It rarely does so, however. The reason is that reserve requirements are a *blunt* instrument of monetary policy. The system of computing reserve requirements is not simple, as we shall discuss below. Changes in required reserve ratios require changes in planning and management by both the Fed and the depository institutions that must hold required reserves. Therefore, the Fed changes reserve requirements very infrequently. Between 1980 and 1992 it changed required reserve ratios a grand total of *three* times.

Calculating Reserve Requirements Depository institutions do not have to satisfy reserve requirements on a daily basis; instead their reserves are averaged over a longer period. Before 1968, a member bank calculated its reserve requirements using a **contemporaneous reserve accounting (CRA) system.** The CRA system required Fed member banks to calculate their required reserves in any week on the basis of their total net deposits in the same week. Net demand deposits are gross demand deposits minus the sum of cash items in the process of collection and demand balances due other banks. Deposits and

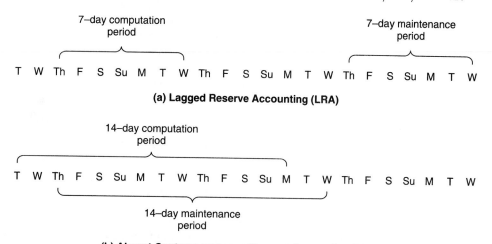

(a) Lagged Reserve Accounting (LRA)

(b) Almost Contemporaneous Reserve Accounting (ACRA)

Figure 17-3

Reserve Accounting Systems.   From 1968 until February 1984, depository institutions were subject to a lagged reserve accounting (LRA) system. (*a*) Under this system, depository institutions calculated their deposits for reserve requirement purposes during a lagged "computation week" that stretched from a Thursday (Th) to the following Wednesday (W), and they held reserves to meet the reserve requirement during the "maintenance week" that ran from the Thursday a week hence until the following Wednesday.

(*b*) Under the almost contemporaneous reserve accounting (ACRA) system adopted in February 1984, the reserve computation period now is 14 days long, from a Tuesday (T) until the Monday (M) two weeks hence. During this two-week period, depository institutions calculate their average levels of deposits for purposes of meeting reserve requirements. The reserve maintenance period also lasts 14 days, from the Thursday immediately after the beginning of the computation period until the Wednesday two weeks later. Therefore, the maintenance period overlaps the computation period by two days.

required reserves were calculated on a weekly basis, but the so-called statement week ran from each Thursday through the following Wednesday. During any statement week, the daily average of required reserves was equal to a percentage of the average net deposits in the bank during that week.

From 1968 until February 1984, member banks (all depository institutions today) were subject to a **lagged reserve accounting (LRA) system.** Depository institutions calculated the required reserves for the current week by using average net deposits two weeks earlier; they met these requirements by adding the amount of cash that was in the vault two weeks before to the average net reserve deposit balance at the Fed district bank for the current week. The upper part of Figure 17-3 shows the timing of reserve requirement *computation* and *maintenance* under the LRA system. Depository institutions calculated their deposits for reserve requirement purposes during the lagged ''computation week,'' and they held reserves to meet the requirement during the ''maintenance week.''

The Fed designed the lagged reserve accounting system to allow depository institutions to reduce their excess reserves and thereby increase their earnings. The idea was that if depository institutions could always predict precisely what their required deposits at the Fed would be in two weeks, they could make sure they did not have an overabundance of non-interest-earning excess reserves in two weeks. The LRA system seemed to be effective; the average excess reserves of all member banks fell from $400 million in 1978 to approximately $250 million by 1980.

Criticism of LRA   While the institution of lagged reserve accounting may have benefited depository institutions by reducing average excess reserves, it seemed to hamper monetary policy when the Fed shifted in 1979 to a stronger effort to control the growth of nonborrowed reserves and the quantity of money. Because required reserves for depository institutions already were preset under LRA, based on deposits they held two weeks earlier, the Fed found that it was forced to supply enough reserves to enable reserve requirements to be met in the depository institutions' reserve maintenance week. In turn, this made it difficult for the Fed to reduce total reserves when necessary to cut monetary growth.

In response to heavy criticism of LRA, the Fed agreed to return to a form of **almost contemporaneous reserve accounting (ACRA),** and this went into effect in February 1984. The lower part of Figure 17-3 shows the timing of ACRA. The reserve computation period now is 14 days long; during this 2-week period, depository institutions calculate their average levels of deposits for purposes of meeting reserve requirements. The reserve maintenance period also lasts 14 days but overlaps the computation period by 2 days. This 2-day overlap gives depository institutions time to raise or lower their average reserve balance for the reserve maintenance period, once they know the average reserve balance they must hold to meet their reserve requirements.

MEETING RESERVE REQUIREMENTS

At present, the Fed imposes a 3 percent reserve requirement on the first few dozen million dollars of transactions deposits at each depository institution. The deposits *above* this threshold at each depository institution are then subject to a reserve requirement of 10 percent. This means that the bulk of the hundreds of billions of dollars of total transactions deposits at depository institutions are subject to the 10 percent requirement.

A depository institution can obtain funds to meet its reserve requirements by selling securities (or other assets) to other depository institutions or by borrowing from other depository institutions in the federal funds market. Note, however, that while one depository institution can avail itself of these opportunities to increase reserves, all depository institutions cannot simultaneously satisfy their reserve requirements by doing so. The total amount of reserves in existence cannot be changed by one depository institution, or even by all depository institutions exchanging assets and reserves with each other.

Depository institutions can, however, increase overall reserves by borrowing from the Fed or by selling securities to the Fed. Depository institutions also have the option of meeting reserve requirements by making fewer loans and by not renewing loans as they mature.

WHY A RESERVE REQUIREMENT?

Early in the banking history of this country, certain states imposed reserve requirements on state-chartered banks. National banks also have had a reserve requirement since 1864. Today virtually all depository institutions have some type of reserve requirement. Why does the Fed impose reserve requirements?

One way to determine how important something is, is to try to determine what life would be like without it. What would be the economic effects of a zero required reserve system? It might appear that such a system would be disastrous. Actually, it seems likely that depository institutions would *voluntarily* hold reserves based on some percentage of their deposits. Depository institutions have sufficient experience to anticipate the amount of funds they need to have on reserve to meet cash and deposit withdrawals. Continued profitability would require sufficient liquidity to satisfy depositors. Thus, depository institutions would doubtless hold reserves to cover normal expected net withdrawals; these are **prudent reserves.** So, even if there were no reserve requirements, prudent reserves would not be zero.

Can the Fed and Congress determine for all institutions in general "the best" reserve ratio better than each depository institution can determine what its own "best" reserve ratio should be? Can the Fed and Congress determine the appropriate reserve ratio during abnormal times?

Do Reserve Requirements Protect the Depositor?   Only if the required reserve ratio were set at 100 percent could depositors be assured of liquidity on demand. The closing of so many banks that met the Fed's reserve requirements during the Great Depression is proof that even with required reserves (at less than 100 percent), banks can and do fail.

Actually, the argument that reserve requirements are necessary to protect depositors is irrelevant today. Deposit insurance has eliminated the concern of a run on banks by most depositors. Why, then, do we have reserve requirements?

The Reason for Reserve Requirements   Reserve requirements must be viewed as a monetary policy tool of the Fed. The Fed can directly alter required reserves (within the limits set by Congress) and, as we discussed above, alter the size of the quantity of money. The argument in favor of required reserves relates to the stability of the money multiplier. If required reserves are stable, then the money multiplier will, within certain bounds, be stable. This means that the Fed can control the money stock with greater accuracy when it engages in open-market operations. A voluntary reserve ratio would certainly be less stable than a required reserve ratio, and control over the money stock would therefore be more difficult.

Because higher reserve requirements strengthen the relationship between the monetary base and the quantity of money, some critics of Federal Reserve policy making maintain that its decision to eliminate reserve requirements on all time deposits in 1990 and to cut the reserve ratio for transactions deposits in 1992 showed that it does not intend to control the quantity of money. Indeed, one of the authors of this text participated in a staff meeting in 1988 in which senior members of the Federal Reserve Board staff could not think of any good reasons, under their policy procedures in place at that time, for reserve requirements. One opinion that a staff member expressed, however, was that removing the requirements might be bad, because doing so might reduce the "prestige of the Fed."

In 1990, the Fed made a major change in reserve requirements by eliminating entirely reserve requirements on time deposits; before that year, it had imposed reserve requirements on both transactions and time deposits. Now, it assesses reserve requirements solely on transactions deposits at depository institutions. Critics of this 1990 reserve requirement reduction and the one that followed in 1992 contend that these actions were mistakes, because they believe that the quantity of money has important effects on economic activity. Before we can evaluate this issue in later chapters, we must first understand more fully the relationship between money and the rest of the economy. That will be our goal in the chapters that follow this one.

OTHER MISCELLANEOUS MEANS OF CONDUCTING MONETARY POLICY

The three policy instruments discussed above—open-market operations, the discount rate, and required reserve ratios—are the primary means by which the Federal Reserve conducts monetary policy in the United States. It has some other instruments in its tool kit, however, that it uses from time to time.

MORAL SUASION

Another Fed tool is moral suasion, in which the Fed uses its influence, or power of persuasion, to induce financial institutions to behave more in the public's interest. In effect, the Fed employs moral suasion to convince financial institutions to be more concerned with their own long-run interests and less with their own short-run interests. For example, during an inflation the Fed may suggest to financial institutions that they reduce their lending and help to cool down an overheated economy.

In practice, moral suasion can be transformed into arm-twisting; for example, on occasion the Fed lets it be known that it will remember who has cooperated and who has not when it lends at the discount window. And because the Fed can prohibit bank mergers, it has the power (for good or ill) to use moral suasion to attain monetary policy objectives.

SELECTIVE CONTROLS

To this point we have analyzed Fed tools that directly affect total reserves and/or interest rates. Selective controls, however, concentrate on specific markets that may be unaffected by overall monetary policy.

Margin Requirements   Margin requirements are specific down payments for stock purchases; in effect, margin requirements limit the percentage of the price of stocks that can be borrowed. For example, a margin requirement of 20 percent prohibits stock buyers from borrowing more than 80 percent of the price of the stock they purchase. Congress empowers the Fed to raise margin requirements to 100 percent of the price of stock, if necessary, in order to control a speculative stock market situation. Before the stock market crash of 1987 the perception was that margin requirements were unnecessary, and the Fed had asked Congress to abolish its power to set margin requirements. Now everyone is not so sure that such Fed power should be eliminated.

Credit Controls   During World War II and the Korean War, the Fed set minimum down payments and maximum loan maturity dates on loans for consumer durables. The Credit Control Act of 1969 empowers the President to authorize the Fed to regulate and control ''any or all extensions of credit'' to fight inflation. More recently, in 1980 President Carter induced the Fed to impose on banks a 15 percent reserve requirement on unsecured consumer loans. Many believe that such controls contributed to reduced credit extension, and to the 1981–1982 recession.

The Fed has several monetary policy instruments with which to influence the quantity of money. Seemingly, the Fed is able to exert very powerful effects on the nation's economy. Nevertheless, you will learn in the chapters that follow that many economists question the extent of the Fed's ability to predictably influence the economy over long-run periods. In contrast, others believe it may be the most important economic policy-making institution in the United States. How monetary policy ultimately affects economic activity is a major issue in economics, and we shall spend the next several chapters exploring this issue in some detail.

CHAPTER SUMMARY

1. Open-market operations are the purchase and sale by the Fed of U.S. government securities; in practice, the Fed conducts open-market operations through Fed purchases and sales of Treasury and federal agency securities.

2. When the Fed conducts open-market operations, it affects the economy in three ways: depository institution reserves change, interest rates on securities change, and economywide expectations change.

3. The FOMC directive to account managers consists of three parts: a qualitative stabilization goal; specific target ranges for credit conditions, interest rates, and monetary aggregates over the next year; and short-term targets that take into account special seasonal events. The account managers decide on the specific quantity of securities to be bought and sold in order to comply with the general directive. The FOMC directive is not made public immediately, although the benefits of such a policy are not obvious.

4. There are two basic types of open-market operations: (a) outright purchases or sales and (b) RPs and reverse RPs. Because RPs and reverse RPs are very short-term agreements, the Fed uses them only when it wants to alter depository institution reserves temporarily; the Fed uses RPs and reverse RPs when it engages in defensive open-market operations. RPs provide temporary reserves, and reverse RPs sop up temporary excess reserves; the Fed intends for defensive open-market operations to maintain the current level of depository institution reserves. Dynamic open-market operations, in contrast, are intended to change the level of depository institution reserves, and outright purchases or sales of Treasury securities by the Fed are best suited for that function.

5. The Fed extends credit to depository institutions by a process called discount window lending. In principle, discount window lending can be an important monetary policy tool, but the Fed traditionally has not used the discount rate as its key policy instrument.

6. Discount window policy refers to the terms and conditions under which the Fed lends to depository institutions. Such policy has a price dimension (the discount rate) and a quantity dimension (the amount of lending that the Fed chooses to do).

7. The practice of setting the discount rate below the market rate of interest and discouraging member banks from borrowing has helped to eliminate discount window policy as a major policy tool.

8. Currently there are three categories of loans to depository institutions by the Fed: (a) adjustment credit, which is routine but short-term; (b) seasonal borrowing loans for smaller- and medium-sized banks that reside in resort or farm areas; and (c) extended credit loans in case of severe, long-term liquidity problems of individual institutions.

9. Each depository institution is obligated to calculate its required reserves based on the Fed's requirement. Before 1968, a contemporaneous reserve accounting system was used. Under a CRA system, during any given statement week the daily average of required reserves must equal the required percentages of average net deposits held by the bank. From 1968 until February 1984, depository institutions were allowed to use a lagged reserve accounting system, so that they could better predict their reserve requirements and thereby hold fewer costly (non-interest-earning) excess reserves. Since February 1984, depository institutions have been required to use an "almost contemporaneous" system.

10. A depository institution can meet its reserve requirement by selling securities to the Fed or other depository institutions, borrowing from other depository institutions in the federal funds market, making fewer loans, not renewing loans that mature, and borrowing from the Fed.

GLOSSARY

Advance: A promissory note signed by an official of a depository institution; the depository institution uses U.S. government securities and other assets that qualify as collateral to borrow from the Fed.

Almost contemporaneous reserve accounting (ACRA):   The present required reserve accounting system, in which banks calculate average deposits over a two-week period and then hold required reserves based on those average deposits over an overlapping two-week period.

Announcement effect: The effect on economic activity of changes in, say, the discount rate that results when individuals view the changes as a sign of a change in monetary policy.

Borrowed reserves: Reserves borrowed by depository institutions from the Fed through the discount window.

Churning: The process of engaging in a large number of offsetting open-market operations that change the total level of reserves by relatively small amounts.

Contemporaneous reserve accounting (CRA) system: A method of calculating a depository institution's required reserves in any week based on the institution's daily average of net deposits for the current week.

Defensive open-market operations: Fed purchases or sales of government securities in which it uses RPs and reverse RPs to maintain the current level of depository institution reserves.

Discount rate: The rate of interest the Fed charges on its loans to depository institutions.

Discount window policy: The terms and conditions under which the Fed lends to depository institutions.

Dynamic open-market operations: Open-market operations in which the Fed intends for outright purchases and sales to change the level of depository institution reserves.

Excess reserves: Total reserves minus required reserves.

Federal funds: Deposits, usually held at the Fed, that one depository institution borrows from another.

FOMC directive: Federal Open Market Committee instructions to account managers that include (1) a qualitative stabilization goal; (2) specific target ranges in terms of credit conditions, interest rates, and monetary aggregates; and (3) targets that take into account special calendar events.

Free reserves: Excess reserves minus borrowed reserves.

Instruments: Policy tools used by the Fed, such as open-market operations.

Lagged reserve accounting (LRA) system: A method of calculating a depository institution's current required reserves at the Fed based on the institution's average daily net deposits two weeks earlier.

Monetary base: Total bank reserves plus currency in circulation outside depository institutions; also called the reserve base, or high-powered money.

Moral suasion: A monetary policy tool of the Fed in which it uses its power of persuasion to induce financial institutions to behave in the public interest.

Nonborrowed base: The monetary base minus borrowed reserves.

Nonborrowed reserves: Total reserves minus borrowed reserves.

Open-market operations: The Fed's purchase and sale of U.S. government securities.

Prudent reserves: Reserves held by depository institutions to cover normal expected net withdrawals.

SELF-TEST QUESTIONS

1. Define and explain the relationships between the following concepts: excess reserves, required reserves, borrowed reserves, nonborrowed reserves, free reserves, total reserves, and the monetary base.

2. Explain, in your own words, the distinction between dynamic open-market operations and defensive open-market operations.

3. Why does it make sense that open-market operations are a useful monetary policy instrument mainly in nations with large, well-developed financial markets?

4. Why does the Fed use open-market operations as its primary instrument of day-to-day monetary policy, even though open-market operations and discount window policy exert their effects through similar economic mechanisms? Explain your reasoning.

5. Explain why it is that changes in reserve requirements change the quantity of money through a different mechanism than either open-market operations or changes in the Fed's discount rate. Give both verbal and algebraic explanations.

6. Why might depository institution managers prefer lagged reserve requirements to contemporaneous reserve requirements?

PROBLEMS

17-1.   Let the consolidated balance sheet of depository institutions be given by the following table.

Assets		Liabilities	
Vault cash	$ 100	Demand deposits	$2,000
Deposits at Fed	300	Time deposits	4,000
Loans	4,000	Net worth	500
Securities	2,000		
Other assets	100		

Required reserves must be equal to 10 percent of demand deposits and 5 percent of time deposits.

a. Determine excess reserves.

b. If the Fed sells $100 of government securities exclusively to the nonbank public, which pays for them out of demand deposits, what immediate changes occur in the balance sheet?

c. Determine the change in excess reserves.

d. What final change would occur in the balance sheet under the assumption that a call-in of loans would be associated with a 50-50 split in demand deposit and time deposit account reductions?

17-2.   Continuing problem 17-1, suppose that the Fed purchased $10 of government securities from commercial banks.
  a. What immediate changes would occur on the consolidated balance sheet?
  b. Determine excess reserves now.
  c. Determine the maximum change in M1 that may result.
  d. Determine the maximum change in M2 that may result.

17-3.   Suppose that bank A makes a $1,000 loan when it has zero excess reserves; it must satisfy a 12 percent reserve requirement. What happens to bank A's (a) liabilities, (b) actual reserves, (c) required reserves, and (d) reserve position (excess or deficit)?

17-4.   Continuing problem 17-3, suppose that bank A sells $120 of securities to one of its customers in order to pay back its Federal Reserve bank. Immediately after it sells $120 of securities, what happens to bank A's (a) liabilities and (b) assets?

17-5.   Suppose that a bank's balance sheet is given by the accompanying table.

Assets		Liabilities	
Vault cash	$ 1	Demand deposits	$20
Deposits at Fed	3	Time deposits	40
Loans	40	Loans from Fed	0
Securities	20	Net worth	5
Other assets	1		

Required reserves must equal 10 percent of demand deposits and 5 percent of time deposits.
  a. Determine excess reserves.
  b. If the Fed reduced the discount rate to member banks so that the bank borrowed $2, what immediate changes would occur in the bank's balance sheet?
  c. Determine the excess reserves after the change.
  d. How much could the bank lend to a customer under the assumption that the loan value would return to this member bank as demand deposits?
  e. How much could the bank lend if the proceeds were to be withdrawn?

17-6.   The Bound Brook Bank has daily net deposits that average $10 million and daily vault cash that averages $10,000 during a statement week. Under a lagged reserve accounting system, what must be the Bound Brook Bank's deposits at the Fed two weeks hence, assuming that it is subject to an average reserve requirement of 12 percent?

17-7.   Study the T-account below and answer the following:
  a. What is the required reserve ratio for this bank?
  b. If all depository institutions were subject to this required reserve ratio, what is the value of the maximum money expansion multiplier?

Assets		Liabilities	
Loans and invest- ments	$176,000	Deposits	$200,000
Reserves (Required $24,000, excess $0)	24,000		

17-8. Assume that the bank in problem 17-7 is suddenly subject to an 8 percent required reserve ratio.

   a. What happens immediately to the bank's total reserves?

   b. What is the value of the bank's excess reserves?

   c. What is the bank likely to do now?

   d. If all depository institutions are now subject to an 8 percent required reserve ratio, what is the value of the maximum money expansion multiplier?

17-9. Consider the consolidated balance sheet of depository institutions below. Let required reserves be equal to 10 percent of demand deposits plus 5 percent of time deposits.

Assets		Liabilities	
Vault cash	$ 100	Demand deposits	$2,000
Deposits at Fed	300	Time deposits	4,000
Loans	4,000	Net worth	500
Securities	2,000		
Other assets	100		

   a. Determine excess reserves.

   b. If the Fed reduces required reserves to 8 percent of demand deposits plus 4 percent of time deposits, determine excess reserves.

   c. What would be the maximum increase in M1?

SELECTED REFERENCES

Federal Reserve Bank of Kansas City, *Operation of the Federal Reserve Discount Window under the Monetary Control Act of 1980* (August 3, 1982).

Friedman, Milton, "Monetary Policy: Theory and Practice," *Journal of Money, Credit, and Banking,* 14 (1, February 1982), pp. 98–118.

————, *A Program for Monetary Stability* (New York: Fordham University Press, 1960).

Gilbert, R. Alton, "Benefits of Borrowing from the Federal Reserve When the Discount Rate Is below Market Interest Rates," Federal Reserve Bank of St. Louis *Review,* 61 (3, March 1979), pp. 25–32.

Goodfriend, Marvin, "Monetary Mystique: Secrecy and Central Banking," *Journal of Monetary Economics,* 17 (1, January 1986), pp. 63–92.

————, and Monica Hargraves, "A Historical Assessment of the Rationales and Functions of Reserve Requirements," Federal Reserve Bank of Richmond *Economic Review,* 69 (2, March/April 1983), pp. 3–21.

Levin, Fred J., and Ann-Marie Meulendyke, "Monetary Policy: Theory and Practice, A Comment," *Journal of Money, Credit, and Banking,* 14 (3, August 1982), pp. 399–403.

Lumpkin, Stephen A., "Repurchase and Reverse Repurchase Agreements," Federal Reserve Bank of Richmond *Economic Review,* 13 (1, January/February 1987).

Mengle, David L., "The Discount Window," Federal Reserve Bank of Richmond *Economic Review,* 72 (3, May/June 1986), pp. 2–10.

Meulendyke, Ann-Marie, *U.S. Monetary Policy and Financial Markets* (New York: Federal Reserve Bank of New York, 1990).

Roth, Howard L., ''Federal Reserve Open Market Techniques,'' Federal Reserve Bank of Kansas City *Economic Review,* 71 (3, March 1986), pp. 3–15.

Simon, David P., ''Secrecy, Signalling, and the Accuracy of Expectations during the Borrowed Reserves Operating Regime,'' *Journal of Banking and Finance,* 15 (2, April 1991), pp. 227–470.

Monetary and Macroeconomic Theory

The Classical Foundations of Monetary Theory

CHAPTER PREVIEW

1. Why did the classical economists believe that the full-employment level of output is the amount that firms and workers produce and consume?

2. According to the classical economists, under what conditions will an economy produce output below the full-employment level?

3. What is the classical theory of the demand for money?

4. How is the level of prices determined in the classical theory?

5. How are interest rates determined in the classical model?

$\mathbf{H}$enry Ward Beecher (1813–1887), in *Proverbs from Plymouth Pulpit,* wrote: ''Money is like snow. If it is blown into drifts it blocks up the highway, and nobody can travel; but if it is diffused over all the ground it facilitates every man's travel.'' By this, he meant that, up to a point, providing more money improves the performance of the economy, but too much of it can be harmful. Indeed, a pragmatic view shared by many economists is that too much money in the economy can cause inflation, while too little can depress real economic activity. The optimal amount of money, however, is very difficult to determine, as we shall learn throughout the remainder of this text.

A successful monetary policy requires at least two elements:

1. A theory, or model, of how the economy works. The key first step in determining the optimal amount of money is to understand how the national levels of output, employment, expenditures, and prices are *determined* and, in addition, how these economic variables are *interrelated.*

2. A theory that explains how changes in the current-dollar quantity of money (amount of money in present-year units, unadjusted for price changes) affects these economic variables.

A PROLOGUE TO UNIT 5

As you will learn in this unit, economists have not always reached a consensus about what role money does, or should, play in the economy. This lack of consensus continues to plague the economics profession, whose members have developed a variety of models of the economy.

THE CLASSICAL MODEL

The classical model was the first systematic and rigorous attempt to explain the determinants of such important economy-wide, or *aggregate,* economic variables as the price level and the national levels of output, employment, and expenditures. The classical model also attempted to show how these variables were interrelated and how and where money fit in.

Classical economics was the predominant school of thought from the 1770s until the 1930s. Included in the ranks of the classical economists are such intellectual giants as Adam Smith (1723–1790), David Hume (1711–1776), David Ricardo (1772–1823), James Mill (1773–1836) and his son John Stuart Mill (1806–1873), Thomas Malthus (1766–1834), Karl Marx (1818–1883), and A. C. Pigou (1877–1959) and other later ''neoclassical'' (''neo'' means *new*) economists as Walras (1834–1910), Marshall (1842–1924), and Wicksell (1851–1926). Even Copernicus (1473–1543), the astronomer, contributed to the classical model, and there is strong evidence that Malthus influenced Charles Darwin's thinking about evolution. The classical model, as presented in this chapter, is a combination of the Cambridge University oral tradition of macroeconomics and a reconstruction by John Maynard Keynes, whom we shall discuss later.

By and large, the classical economists concluded that capitalism is a self-regulating economic system. They argued that the mechanisms inherent in the capitalist system naturally drive the economy toward full employment of such economic resources as household labor. Classical economists recognized that temporary unemployment might exist in the form of frictional unemployment, in which people are between full-time jobs, but felt that *eventually* there would be no involuntary labor unemployment. Workers would perceive the existence of any widespread unemployment, or a condition of surplus labor in the market for labor services. Ultimately, this would cause wages to fall, and unemployment would disappear as businesses hired more labor services and workers offered less of these services.

As a result, workers and firms would produce a full-employment level of output. Households also would purchase this level of output. As firms supply goods, the income to purchase the goods automatically would be forthcoming in the form of wages, rents, interest payments, and profits. If households saved ''too much''—a surplus of saving—interest rates would fall and thereby would induce households to reduce saving and business firms to increase investment expenditures. The classical economists summarized their conclusion that workers and firms would produce a full-employment level of output that households would purchase in the dictum, ''Supply creates its own demand.''

Naturally, such an outlook left little or no role for governmental intervention in the economy. Because a capitalistic economy equilibrates at the full-employment level of output, monetary policy cannot influence the level of output. Thus there is a **neutrality of money.** That is, money is ''neutral'' in its effects on real economic activity. Changes in the quantity of money would alter the amount of desired transactions by households but could not affect the full-employment level of output produced. Only prices could adjust. Consequently, the classical economists theorized that increases in the quantity of money cause the level of prices to rise proportionately. Decreases in the quantity of money, they believed, cause the price level to fall proportionately.

Classical economists recognized that this theory was only a model of the economy. They understood that various institutional features present in real-world economies, such as short-term constraints in households' abilities to gather and process information, minimum wage laws, long-term labor contracts, and unionization of some industries, could inhibit the flexibility of wages, prices, and interest rates assumed by the model. They felt, however, that the existence of these institutional structures did not significantly affect the underlying power of their theory to predict the performance of the economy.

THE KEYNESIAN REVOLUTION AND A NEW TRADITION

The Great Depression of the 1930s did much to make classical economics appear less useful, if not invalidated. The general levels of prices and wages fell significantly during the Depression, but so did output and labor employment. Real national income fell by 25 percent from 1929 to 1933, and the unemployment rate rose to nearly 17 percent of the labor force at the depths of the Depression. Led by the great economist John Maynard Keynes, economists of the post-Depression period sought to establish a new tradition of thought about how the economy functions and about what role monetary policy plays in influencing national output, employment, expenditures, and price levels.

According to this new tradition, capitalistic economies were not self-regulating. Instead, Keynes and his followers felt that capitalistic economies were plagued by problems of insufficiently flexible prices, wages, and interest rates and of imperfectly available information for workers and firms. Hence, the economy was unlikely to produce the full-employment output level. These problems required active governmental stabilization policies to assure the attainment of full employment. Indeed, in its extreme form this new tradition of economic thought turned the classical dictum upside down. It argued that "Demand creates its own supply."

It is not an overstatement to regard much economic policy making of the post-World War II period, especially from the early 1960s through the late 1970s, as a social experiment in **demand management**—the use of fiscal and monetary policies to "fine-tune" the economy's total level of desired expenditures—that tested the validity of this new tradition developed by Keynes and his followers. These followers included, among many others, Nobel laureates Paul Samuelson, James Tobin, Franco Modigliani, and Robert Solow. Whether or not this experiment was successful is a topic of continual debate.

THE STAGFLATION PROBLEM AND RETHINKING THE KEYNESIAN TRADITION

Events beginning in the mid-1970s caused many economists to question the post-classical tradition of Keynes and his followers. A particularly bothersome development was the problem of **stagflation,** which is the simultaneous existence of high levels of inflation and unemployment. The new tradition had not predicted this problem and, indeed, appeared ill-suited for offering means for its solution. For this reason, the stagflation problem of the 1970s may have been as damaging to the postwar tradition in economics as the Great Depression was to the classical model.

The 1970s and 1980s ushered in an ongoing period of sharp disagreement among economists about the best model of the economy and the best theory of the proper role for monetary policy. (By "best," economists mean "most successful at predicting.") Although various economists have promoted several specific theories, the views of most economists in the 1990s fall into two basic groupings. One set of economists seeks to rejuvenate the essential elements of the original classical model while incorporating some features of the postwar tradition that they regard as useful. Central among this group of economists are those known as "new classical" economists. These economists follow in the footsteps of the original classical theorists; they argue that the assumption of flexible prices, wages, and interest rates is the foundation for a successful model of the economy and of the role of money.

The new classical economists accept the traditional view of the postwar economists that informational constraints sometimes interfere with the economy's self-adjustment process. Yet they do not see such informational constraints as a significant impediment to the attainment of full-employment output. Nor do they accept the view that systematic—that is, predictable—monetary policy changes are nonneutral in their effects on real economic activity. The key reason, according to the new classical economists, is that individuals rationally act in their own best interest, thereby finding their own way to full employment without need for governmental action. An extreme version of this view, which is known as "real business cycle theory," implies that monetary policy is always neutral and that "Supply creates its own demand," just as in the original classical model.

PRESERVING THE KEYNESIAN TRADITION

The second group of economists presently is at work to preserve the essential elements of the postwar tradition. Like Keynes and other earlier proponents of this tradition, these economists believe that informational imperfections and rigidities in prices, wages, and interest rates are central to understanding and predicting economic performance. They argue that theories incorporating these elements are necessary for a successful monetary policy. These economists, however, recognize the flaws of the postwar tradition. Thus, they have sought to develop their modern theories using some of the views of classical economists that they believe remain relevant. Consequently, this modern group of Keynesian theorists has developed theories in which price, wage, and interest rate rigidities result from rational decision making by self-interested individuals. These modern theories also have led to the development of a "new Keynesian" economics that promotes the view that "Demand creates its own supply."

Naturally, this prevailing lack of consensus about the working of the economy and the proper role of monetary policy can make this a challenging and potentially frustrating topic for money and banking students, instructors, and textbook authors alike. Yet this unsettled state of affairs also makes the topic both intellectually stimulating and exciting. The issues we shall discuss in this unit are those that will continue to dominate the time and efforts of economists and policy makers throughout the 1990s. Economists almost certainly will debate them into the next century. As you read the chapters in this unit, keep this fact in mind. Furthermore, if you feel that you are losing your perspective anywhere in your readings in this unit, you may wish to reread this overview.

SOME BASIC CONCEPTS

Before we undertake a full study of the role of money in the economy, we need to begin by defining some basic concepts. These concepts will be used throughout this unit.

NATIONAL INCOME AND PRODUCT

National income is the sum of all income receipts in the economy. Because households own all the factors of production whose services may be sold for wages and salaries, rents, interest and dividends, and profits, households earn all these income receipts. The amount of income earned over the course of a given time period, measured in the prices that prevail during that period, is denoted Y. All the income earned by households ultimately is spent on the goods and services produced by firms. It is spent directly, in the form of household consumption, or indirectly by either the government or business firms. The government spends by imposing taxes on households and by borrowing household saving. Firms spend (invest) by purchasing goods and services produced by other firms; they do so by borrowing household saving. The total value of output produced by firms in a given time period, measured in terms of prices that prevail during that period, also equals Y. That is, the value of firms' product, or output, in terms of a current period's prices is the income, measured in those prices, received by households during that period.

THE PRICE LEVEL

The value of income and output for different periods can vary either because firms produce more or fewer goods and services or because the prices of those goods and services rise or fall. If we denote the quantity of *real* goods and services produced by firms within a given period by y, then the level of prices of those goods and services, denoted P, must equal Y/y. Economists call this measure of the price level, P, the **income price deflator.** Because Y/y by definition is equal to P, it is true by definition that Y is equal to P times y.

Economists define a *base period* to be a period in which $Y = y$, so that $P = 1$. Within the base period, current-period income, Y, is equal to the base-period *real* (price-level-adjusted) income, y, and the price level is $P = 1$. For a period other than the base period, however, current-period income Y could exceed *real* income during that period, y, in which case $P > 1$. In addition, current-period income Y in a period other than the base period could be less than *real* income during the period, y, in which case $P < 1$. The income price deflator thereby permits us to measure whether changes in current-period income Y result from changes in the real amount of income and product, y, or from changes in the level of prices, P, or both.

Because we define P to be Y/y, it follows that y is by definition equal to Y/P. This means that real income, y, is equal to nominal income, Y, *deflated* by the income price deflator, P. The way that economists typically convert from nominal income to real income is by measuring Y in current, nominal dollars while measuring P as an index that converts current, nominal prices to real, base-period prices. That is, the units of measurement of P are nominal, current-dollar values relative to real, base-period dollar values. Dividing Y by P therefore yields real, base-period dollars as the unit of measurement, which is the appropriate unit of measurement for real income, y.

A key goal of monetary economics is to understand how changes in the quantity of money may affect real output, y, and the level of prices, P. Because y and P are aggregate, economywide measures, they are examples of **macroeconomic variables.** Macroeconomic variables are aggregate quantities that give us information about economywide changes. Much of monetary theory aims to explain how these macroeconomic variables are determined and what role money plays in this process.

THE FOUNDATION OF MONETARY THEORY

The basic conclusion of the classical model, and, indeed, the starting point for a foundation of monetary theory, is the phrase ''Supply creates its own demand.'' This phrase, in honor of its popularizer, Jean Baptiste Say (1767–1832), is known as **Say's law.** Whether or not this phrase actually describes an economic ''law'' is the issue of division among economists interested in understanding the workings of the economy and in determining the optimal quantity of money.

Underlying Say's law and much of classical economics are the premises that wants are unlimited and that the primary economic goal of each of us, as self-interested individuals, is maximum satisfaction. In addition, we are *rational;* that is, we always do as well as possible to look out for our own interests. We do so by making the best use of our time and of the information available to us when we make economic decisions.

This model of the behavior of individual economic agents—all of us individually and collectively—implies that an increase in the supply of one commodity or service implies an increase in the demand for another. It also implies that, without governmental interference, we all will voluntarily change the prices we bid or offer for goods or services. As a result, prices, wages, and interest rates are flexible. Together, these implications of the classical perspective imply that, in general, the economy will tend toward full employment. Money will be neutral. We shall devote the remainder of this chapter to explaining these classical conclusions.

ASSUMPTIONS OF THE CLASSICAL MODEL

Three key assumptions underlie the classical model:

1. Economic agents (that is, workers, consumers, and business persons) are motivated by the *rational pursuit of self-interest.* As workers and consumers, households want to maximize their total economic well-being. As owners of business firms, households always want to increase the total profits earned by businesses. Classical economists referred to these household goals as ''utility-maximizing behavior.'' This means that households do all that they can to maximize their levels of satisfaction derived from all endeavors.

2. *Pure competition* exists in markets for goods and services and for factors of production. No single buyer or seller of an output or productive factor can influence the output or factor price that will prevail in the marketplace. As a consequence, each economic agent takes prices as ''given''; each is a *price taker.* No single *individual* trades enough goods or factors to affect the prices of these goods or factors. Nevertheless, *as a group,* buyers or sellers in these markets can cause prices to rise or to fall to any equilibrium level. That is, the forces of total demand and total supply in markets for produced goods or for factors of production determine the prices of these goods and factors.

3. Economic agents do not suffer from **money illusion.** That is, in general, buyers and sellers correctly perceive and react only to changes in *real* (that is, *relative,* or price-level-adjusted) prices, wages, and interest rates. They do not alter their desired trades of real quantities of produced goods and factors of production simply because of *nominal* price changes. For example, suppose that a given household had purchased a specific basket of goods and services and had provided a given level of labor and other factor services (services flowing from productive inputs such as land and capital) during a year. An absence of money illusion means that a household would have traded the same quantities of goods and services and of factor services if the individual's income tripled during the year while all the prices of the traded goods also had tripled. Because real, or relative, prices have not changed, the classical model assumes that the household will transact the same market quantities, all other things constant; that is, it will not suffer from money illusion.

CLASSICAL THEORY OF PRODUCTION, EMPLOYMENT, AND AGGREGATE SUPPLY

Any model of the economy must begin with a theory of how goods and services are produced, and in what quantities. Hence, a theory of production, of employment of resources like labor, and of the supply of goods and services by firms was the natural starting point for the classical model.

THE AGGREGATE PRODUCTION FUNCTION

A **production function** tells us how much output of goods or services workers and firms will produce given various possible quantities of factors of production, or inputs and the current state of arts or technology. In equation form (a bar over a letter indicates that the variable in question is constant), a production function is expressed as

$$y = f(\overline{K}, N, \overline{A}) \tag{18-1}$$

where y = real output per unit of time
$\overline{K}$ = stock of capital goods (goods that may be used in the production of other goods)
N = quantity of labor services per unit of time
$\overline{A}$ = quantity of land services

Equation (18-1) tells us that the amount of output of goods and services is a function of the stock of capital, the amount of labor services employed, and the quantity of land services used.

Short-Run Production If we concern ourselves with the *short run,* then we consider a time horizon short enough that firms cannot vary all factors of production. In macro-economics, the capital stock and the quantity of land services are taken as fixed in the short run. The quantity of labor services, N, may vary, though. Economists can measure the quantity of labor as the number of persons employed, as the amount of time people work, or as a combination of the two measures, called *person-hours* (expressed in constant-quality units).

In the short run when capital and land services are fixed, it is simplest to write the production function as a short-run relationship between N and y,

$$y = f(N) \tag{18-2}$$

while keeping in mind that other factors and technology are important for the long run. The level of output y represents the total production of goods and services in the economy.

A Sample Production Function As a very simple example, suppose for a moment that the production function is a square-root function; that is, $y = N^{1/2}$ (where $N^{1/2}$ is the square root of N, or $\sqrt{N}$). Naturally, if $N = 0$, no output is produced. (Even if our capital stock included robots, someone would have to switch their switches to the "on" position.) If firms employ $N = 1$ unit of labor during a given time interval, they produce 1 unit of output. Furthermore, an increase in the amount of labor to $N = 4$ (a nice choice, because it is the square of 2) would increase output to 2 units, an increase to $N = 9$ would increase output to 3 units, an increase to $N = 16$ would increase output to 4 units, and so on.

This very simple example illustrates a key economic assumption, that the aggregate production function should satisfy the **law of diminishing marginal returns.** In our example, each successive increase in N yielded one more unit of output per period. But each increase in output required successively *larger* increases in the quantity of labor N. That is, increasing output production from $y = 0$ to $y = 1$ required the addition of only 1 unit of labor, but successive 1-unit increases in output production required successively larger—3 (4 minus 1), 5 (9 minus 4), and 7 (16 minus 9)—increases in the units of labor employed. Hence, according to the law of diminishing marginal returns, which our square-root production function satisfies, it takes more labor to generate each whole-unit increase in output production.

An equivalent way of visualizing the law of diminishing marginal returns is to measure the effects on output production of successive unit increases in the quantity of labor. For instance, $N = 1$ in our square-root production function again yields $y = 1$ unit of output; $N = 2$ yields $2^{1/2}$, or just about 1.41, units of output; $N = 3$ yields $3^{1/2}$, or about 1.73 units of output; and $N = 4$ yields 2 units of output. Therefore, increasing N from 0 to 1 unit raises output 1 unit; increasing N from 1 to 2 units raises output by 0.41 (1.41 minus 1) unit; increasing N from 2 to 3 units raises output by 0.32 (1.73 minus 1.41) unit; and increasing N from 3 to 4 units raises output by 0.27 unit. An increase in output resulting from a 1-unit increase in labor is a measure of the **marginal product of labor,** or MP_n. The marginal product of labor is the gain in output from employing an additional unit of labor. The law of diminishing marginal returns implies that the marginal product of labor— that is, the derived gain in output—eventually declines as output production increases. This condition is satisfied by our square-root example.

Drawing the Production Function and the Marginal Product of Labor   Panel (*a*) of Figure 18-1 shows a general production function. As illustrated in the figure, any general aggregate production function that exhibits the law of diminishing marginal returns has a *concave,* or bowed, shape. The square-root function used in our sample numerical computations is just one example of a family of many possible functions that have this property. The diagram in panel (*b*) of the figure shows that, for such a production function, the marginal product of labor will decline as it did in our numerical example. Economists call the schedule in panel (*b*) a *marginal-product-of-labor schedule.* The downward slope of this schedule is simply a reflection of the law of diminishing marginal returns.

THE AGGREGATE DEMAND FOR LABOR

In sophisticated, highly specialized economies, most laborers work for an employer. A comparatively small portion of the population is self-employed. Consequently, a labor market evolves in which buyers (business firms) and sellers (households) of labor transact voluntarily. Also, people use money in sophisticated economies, and so firms pay a money wage rate W, measured in current, nominal dollars per unit of labor per unit of time, to workers. Workers and firms only value those wage payments in terms of the prices of goods that workers consume and that firms produce. The reason is that workers care about the amount of goods and services their wages can buy, whereas firms care about the real payment made to workers in exchange for their production of goods and services. This implies that both workers and firms make economic decisions based upon the real, price-level-adjusted wage rate, as you will see below.

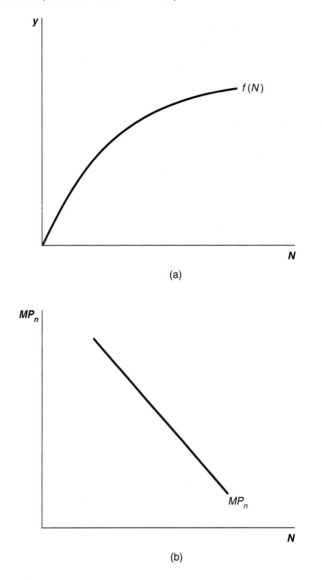

(a)

(b)

Figure 18-1
The Production Function and MP$_n$ Schedule. In the short run, higher levels of output require increased employment of labor because technology and other factors of production are held constant [panel (a)]. The production function is concave (bowed) because of the law of diminishing marginal returns, which says that total output increases at a decreasing rate as employment is increased by equal amounts. This means that the marginal product of labor declines [panel (b)].

For ease of exposition, it is easiest to assume there is a composite good/service produced by all firms in the economy and that only one labor skill exists. These assumptions imply that there will be national markets for the composite output and the single type of labor service. (We could relax these assumptions to make the story more realistic, but doing so also makes the story much harder to tell and understand.) These markets determine a single composite good/service price, which consequently measures the level of prices in the economy, and a single national wage rate.

As in any market, we can derive the aggregate demand-for-labor schedule by summing the individual firm labor demand schedules.

The Firm's Demand for Labor   A profit-maximizing, competitive firm always produces output up to, but not beyond, the point at which marginal revenue (MR) is equal to marginal cost (MC). In addition, because each firm in a competitive market cannot influence the price of its output, each output unit by definition yields the same marginal revenue, which is the price per unit. This implies that each firm produces to the point at which

$$\text{MR} \equiv P = \text{MC} \tag{18-3}$$

It is, however, also the case that, by definition, marginal cost equals the ratio of wage rate (W) to the marginal product of labor (MP_n); that is,

$$\text{MC} \equiv W / \text{MP}_n \tag{18-4}$$

To see this, consider the following example. Suppose that, within a given interval, the nominal wage rate is $W = \$10$ per unit of labor and that the marginal product of labor at the current output level is $\text{MP}_n = 5$ units of output per unit of labor. Then the marginal cost of producing the present level of output is $\text{MC} = \$2$ per unit of output.

Also, recall that a firm's marginal cost schedule usually is upward-sloping. The relationship in equation (18-4) is consistent with—indeed, implies—this fact. We know that because of the law of diminishing marginal returns, a rise in output causes a fall in the marginal product of labor. For a given value of W, (18-4) then implies that as output rises, MP_n must fall and MC must rise. Therefore, the marginal cost schedule for the firm will slope upward, from left to right.

If we use equation (18-4) in equation (18-3), we find that a profit-maximizing firm will hire units of labor to the point at which

$$P = W/\text{MP}_n$$

or, by multiplying both sides of that equation by MP_n,

$$W = \text{MP}_n \times P \tag{18-5}$$

where $\text{MP}_n \times P$ is the valuation of labor's marginal product at the firm's output price. Economists call this quantity the **value of the marginal product of labor,** $\text{VMP}_n \equiv \text{MP}_n \times P$.

The VMP_n schedule slopes downward, as panel (a) of Figure 18-2 shows. The firm takes its output price P as given, and so it views the price as a constant. Because of the law of diminishing marginal returns, MP_n declines as the firm increases its output. Hence, VMP_n also falls as the firm's output rises.

Equation (18-5) shows that the firm employs units of labor up to the point at which the wage rate it pays (the market nominal wage rate W) is equal to the value of labor's marginal product. Panel (b) of Figure 18-2 illustrates this condition for two different nominal wage rates, W_0 and W_1. At the wage rate W_0, the amount of labor desired by the firm is N_0. At the higher wage rate W_1, however, the value of marginal product must

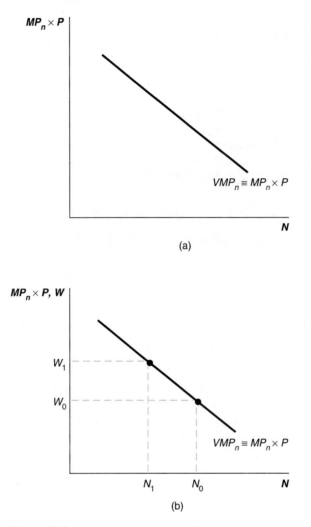

(a)

(b)

Figure 18-2

The VMP$_n$ Schedule and the Demand for Labor. The schedule depicting the relationship between the value of the marginal product of labor slopes downward [panel (a)] because of the law of diminishing marginal returns. Because a profit-maximizing firm hires labor services to the point at which the value of labor's marginal product is equal to the nominal wage, a rise in the market nominal wage rate causes a decrease in the firm's quantity of labor demanded [panel (b)]. This represents an upward movement along the firm's labor demand schedule.

increase if the firm is to maximize its profits, and so the firm desires to employ fewer (N_1) units of labor. The VMP$_n$ schedule gives combinations of nominal wage rates and employment levels desired by the firm. Therefore, it is the *firm's labor demand schedule,* as graphed with the nominal wage on the vertical axis.

Note that equation (18-5) can be rearranged into the form

$$W/P = MP_n \qquad\qquad (18\text{-}6)$$

where W/P is the real, price-level-adjusted wage rate. Written in this way, the firm's profit-maximizing condition for hiring labor says that the firm desires to employ workers up to the point at which the marginal product of labor (the real output gain from employing a unit of labor) equals the real wage rate (the real value of the resources expended by the firm in employing the unit of labor). Note, though, that equations (18-5) and (18-6) are just different versions of the same condition. This means that both imply the same desired quantities of labor for the same values of W, P, and MP_n.

For instance, consider Figure 18-3. Panel (a) is the same as panel (b) from Figure 18-2, at which the $VMP_n \equiv MP_n \times P$ schedule is graphed against the nominal wage rate. Panel (a) depicts two different nominal wage-desired employment combinations. In panel (b), the same combinations are shown where all variables are divided by P. That is, the

Figure 18-3

Alternative Depictions of Labor Demand.   A profit-maximizing firm hires labor services to the point at which the value of labor's marginal product is equal to the *nominal* wage, and so a rise in the nominal wage rate lowers the firm's quantity of labor demanded [panel (a)]. Equivalently, the firm hires labor services to the point at which the marginal product of labor is equal to the *real* wage. A rise in the nominal wage rate, with the price level unchanged, causes a rise in the real wage and a fall in the quantity of labor demanded [panel (b)].

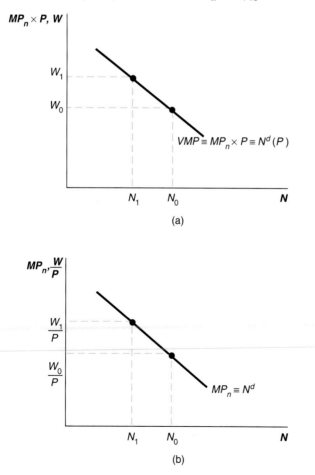

figure shows the MP_n schedule graphed against the real wage W/P. For the same values of P, W_0, and W_1, however, the same desired employment levels must arise for either diagram. Hence, if we measure the nominal wage W vertically, the $VMP_n \equiv MP_n \times P$ schedule is the firm's labor demand schedule. But on a graph where we measure the real wage W/P vertically, the MP_n schedule is the firm's labor demand schedule. Therefore, the schedule in panel (b) is simply labeled N^d, but the schedule in panel (a) is labeled $N^d(P)$. We do this to indicate that labor demand as graphed against the nominal wage depends on output prices. Both schedules are equivalent representations of the firm's desired employment levels at various wages and a given output price.

Figure 18-4 illustrates the effects of an increase in the marginal product of labor. This increase could arise from a technological improvement. Or it could arise from an increase in the amount of capital or land services available for workers to use in the production of output. As shown in panel (b) of the figure, the marginal product of labor is higher at every given output level, and so the MP_n schedule shifts upward, from MP_n^0 to MP_n^1. This means that although the price level has not changed, the VMP_n schedule must shift upward

Figure 18-4
The Effect of a Rise in the Marginal Product of Labor on the Firm's Demand for Labor.   A rise in the marginal product of labor increases the value of labor's marginal product for any given price level [panel (a)]. At a given nominal wage rate, the firm will desire to employ more labor services. Equivalently, the rise in the marginal product of labor also implies that, at a fixed real wage, the firm will wish to employ more workers [panel (b)].

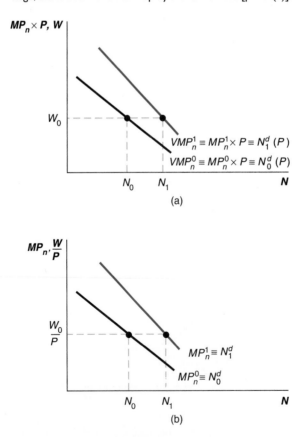

(a)

(b)

in panel (*a*). Even if we hold the wage rate fixed at W_0, the firm's desired level of employment will rise as a result. The reason is commonsensical: Workers now are more productive. So if the nominal wage rate does not change, the firm desires to hire more of their labor services. Furthermore, the desired level of employment rises by the same amount using either diagram, from N_0 to N_1.

Figure 18-5 shows the effects of a rise in the price level. In panel (*a*), the rise in the firm's output price, from P_0 to P_1, causes the VMP_n schedule to *shift* upward. At the market wage W_0, the firm now desires to employ N_1 rather than N_0 units of labor. In panel (*b*), because we measure the real, price-level-adjusted wage on the vertical axis, the rise in the price level lowers the real wage along that axis. As a result, there is a rightward *movement along* the MP_n schedule. But because this diagram is an equivalent representation of the firm's employment decision, the same increase in the quantity of labor demanded by the firm must result.

The Economy's Total Demand for Labor   For either means of graphing labor demand, the horizontal summation of all demand curves for labor yields the aggregate labor

Figure 18-5
The Effect of a Rise in Prices on the Firm's Demand for Labor.   A rise in prices increases the value of labor's marginal product at any given level of employment. If the nominal wage is unchanged, the firm will desire to employ more labor [panel (*a*)]. Equivalently, the real wage falls if prices rise while the nominal wage rate stays the same, and so the firm wishes to employ more labor [panel (*b*)].

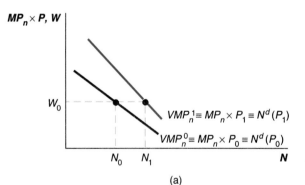

(a)

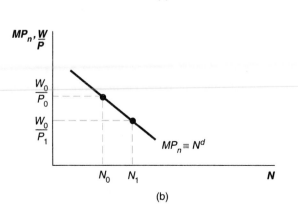

(b)

demand schedule in our simplified economy. In general, this schedule therefore just looks like those displayed in Figure 18-3. Furthermore, the effects of changes in technology and the availability of other factors of production and in the level of prices are the same as those shown in Figures 18-4 and 18-5.

THE AGGREGATE SUPPLY OF LABOR

According to the classical theoreticians (and most of us, too), work is irksome. Indeed, a laborer experiences *increasing marginal disutility* (or irksomeness) as he or she works more hours per day, per week, or per month. If this is so, then why do people work? Because they receive wage income that they can use to purchase goods and services. Consumption of goods and services provides people utility (satisfaction) that compensates them for the irksomeness they experience in working.

A Worker's Supply of Labor   The rational seller of labor (someone like you, your instructor, or one of the authors of this textbook), therefore, compares the marginal disutility (or cost) of working one more unit of time with the marginal utility (or benefit) that he can obtain by spending (or saving) the wage income gained from working one more unit of time at the present nominal wage rate. In equilibrium, the rational worker will supply labor time up to the quantity at which the marginal utility obtained from the market nominal wage rate is just equal to the marginal disutility incurred by working that last unit of time.

It is the real, price-level-adjusted wage rate that matters to a worker. This is so because that is the measure of the purchasing power of the worker's wage income. Suppose the worker receives a 50 percent wage increase. If the prices of goods and services he may purchase with that wage income also rise by 50 percent, then the worker will be no better off working more or less than he presently does. To behave otherwise would imply that the worker suffers from money illusion. The classical model explicitly rules out money illusion.

The only way that a rational worker in the classical model can be induced to provide more units of labor per unit of time is for the *real* wage rate to increase. The real wage rate can rise under two sets of circumstances. It can rise because (1) the nominal wage rises with prices unchanged or (2) the price level falls with the nominal wage unchanged. Figure 18-6 illustrates the effect of a rise in the nominal wage from W_0 to W_1, holding prices fixed at a level P_0. As depicted in panel (*a*), this causes a rise in the real wage that induces laborers to supply more labor services. Therefore, the figure depicts the labor supply schedule, N^s, as upward-sloping. Panel (*b*) shows the same result, but with only the nominal wage graphed on the vertical axis. The amount of labor supplied rises by the same amount, but labor supply depends on output prices, and so we label this version of the labor schedule $N^s(P_0)$, which is uniquely associated with the price level P_0. For either representation of the labor supply schedule, the individual worker *moves along* the schedule when the nominal wage rises.

Figure 18-7 illustrates the effects of a fall in the price level, holding the market, nominal wage rate fixed. In panel (*a*) of the figure, a fall in the price level, from P_0 to a lower level P_1, causes a worker's real wage to rise. Thus, she supplies more labor services, as shown by a movement along the N^s schedule. In panel (*b*), though, a rise in the level of prices means that, at the given nominal wage rate, the worker is more willing to supply as much labor as before (since her real wage is higher). Viewed differently, she is willing to accept a lower nominal wage to work any given number of hours. Viewed from either perspective, the labor supply schedule graphed against the nominal wage must *shift* right-

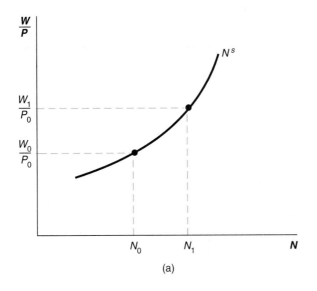

(a)

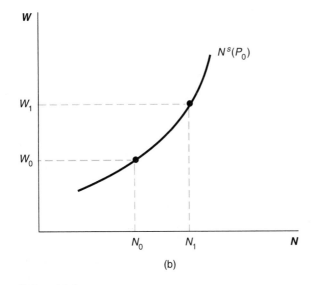

(b)

Figure 18-6
The Supply of Labor by Workers.   Workers supply more labor as the real wage increases, and so the labor supply schedule slopes upward against the real wage [panel (*a*)]. Equivalently, when the nominal wage rises with prices unchanged at P_0 [panel (*b*)], a worker is willing to supply more labor services.

ward when the price level falls, from $N^s(P_0)$ to $N^s(P_1)$. Both panels, nonetheless, are representations of the same choices, and so desired employment by this laborer increases by the same amount in each case.

The Economy's Supply of Labor   By summing the individual supply-of-labor sched-ules horizontally, we can derive an aggregate labor supply schedule. We can do this using

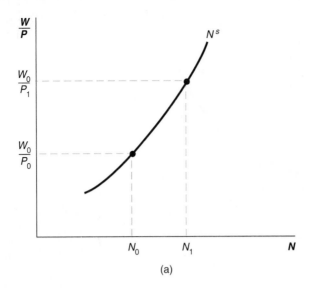

(a)

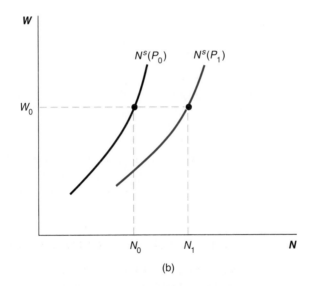

(b)

Figure 18-7
The Effect of a Fall in Prices on the Supply of Labor by Workers. A fall in the level of prices, from P_0 to P_1, with the nominal wage unchanged, causes the real wage to rise, and so workers desire to supply more labor services [panel (a)]. Equivalently, with the nominal wage rate unchanged, workers increase their supply of labor services [panel (b)].

either type of graph (that is, against the real wage or against the nominal wage alone). These schedules would shift for the same reasons previously discussed for the individual worker. Changes in nominal wages or the level of prices affect all workers' real wages identically. Either version of the total labor supply schedule—that is, the version graphed against the real wage rate or the version graphed against the nominal wage rate—also could shift if other factors changed. Examples of such changes would be variations in all

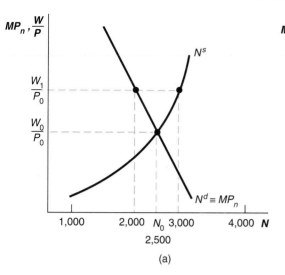

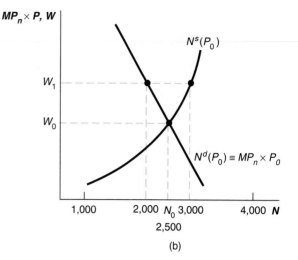

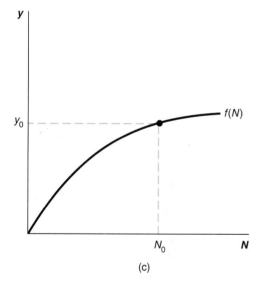

Figure 18-8
Determining Aggregate Output.   The level of employ-ment is established by labor market equilibrium [panel (*a*) or (*b*)]. The production function then indicates the level of out-put produced by this level of labor employment [panel (*c*)].

At the higher-than-equilibrium nominal wage W_1, a below-full-employment situation exists. National output will be less than the full-employment level. There will be temporary sur-plus labor, or unemployment.

laborers' attitudes toward work, labor force participation rates of the population, or tax rates applied to workers' wage incomes.

LABOR MARKET EQUILIBRIUM AND THE AGGREGATE SUPPLY SCHEDULE

Figure 18-8 shows both the total supply of labor and the total demand for labor for each possible diagrammatic representation of the labor market, depending upon whether we measure the real wage or the nominal wage on the vertical axis. In both diagrams, the equilibrium *nominal wage,* labeled W_0, is determined when the quantity of labor demanded by firms is equal to the quantity of labor supplied by workers, labeled N_0 (assumed to be equal to 2,500 units of labor), *given* the level of prices, P_0.

Consider the real wage rate W_1/P_0 in panel (a) of Figure 18-8. At this real wage rate, firms in the economy desire to hire only 2,000 total units of labor. But laborers desire to provide 3,000 units. This means there is a surplus of 1,000 units of labor at the real wage W_1/P_0. Economists more commonly call this surplus of unemployed labor the amount of labor *unemployment.*

What will happen? In the classical model, the answer is that the nominal wage will be driven downward as workers with unemployed labor skills compete with fully employed laborers for time on the job (or for jobs, period). They will compete by offering to work at lower wages. This will drive nominal wages downward in the labor market. Unemployment will only be temporary.

The same basic story applies in panel (b) of Figure 18-8. Here, however, we measure only the money wage on the vertical axis. Nevertheless, this diagram represents the same labor market equilibrium at the nominal wage W_0 and level of employment N_0, given the price level P_0. Also, an above-equilibrium nominal wage of W_1 must produce the same level of unemployment in this diagram, since the diagram depicts the same market behavior. The same forces would drive the nominal wage downward. Unemployment again is at worst a temporary condition.

We shall call the equilibrium level of employment in the market for labor *full employment.* That is, we define full employment of labor by the intersection of the labor demand and labor supply schedules in either diagram. At this level of employment, both workers and firms are at their desired levels of labor employment given the nominal wage rate and the price level.

Panel (c) of Figure 18-8 measures the amount of output produced by the amount of labor N_0. Because the labor market is in equilibrium, we call this output level, y_0, the *full-employment level of output.*

The classical theory predicts that changes in the general level of prices do not affect the full-employment output level. To see why this is so, consider the example illustrated in Figure 18-9. Suppose that the labor market initially is in equilibrium in panels (a) and (b). The nominal wage is W_0, and the level of labor employment is N_0, given the price level P_0. Given this quantity of labor, the full-employment level of output is y_0, as panel (c) shows. In the final diagram, in panel (d), the level of output is on the horizontal axis and the price level is on the vertical axis. In this diagram, the labor market–production equilibrium occurs at the price-output combination P_0 and y_0.

Now suppose that the price level falls by 50 percent, to $P_0/2$. As a result, given the money wage W_0, in panel (a) of the figure the real wage doubles, to $W_0/(P_0/2) = 2(W_0/P_0)$. At this new, higher real wage there is surplus labor, or unemployment. This causes the nominal wage to be driven downward. The labor market reaches equilibrium only when the nominal wage falls by 50 percent, to $W_0/2$. Then the new real wage is $(W_0/2)/(P_0/2)$, which is equal to W_0/P_0. This is the market-clearing real wage rate. In the end, the equilibrium real wage and employment level do not change.

Panel (b) tells the same basic story but from a different perspective. In this representation of the labor market only the nominal wage appears on the vertical axis. Now, a 50 percent fall in the price level causes demand for labor by firms to fall, because the value of labor's marginal product falls by 50 percent. In addition, however, workers do not suffer from money illusion. They realize that a 50 percent increase in their real wage has taken place, and they respond by raising their supply of labor. As a result, the equilibrium nominal wage falls to $W_0/2$. The equilibrium employment level remains unchanged at N_0.

Because employment remains the same, the amount of output does not change in panel (c). But in panel (d), the price level falls by one-half. Therefore, the economy finds itself in a new equilibrium at the same full-employment level of output. This happens even though the price level is 50 percent lower.

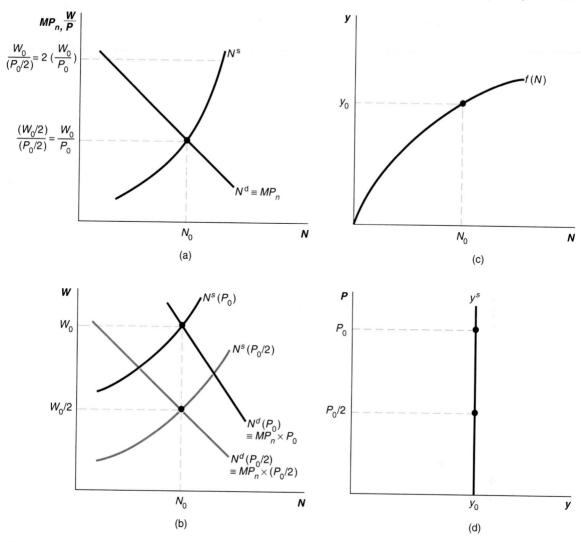

Figure 18-9
Deriving the Classical Aggregate Supply Schedule.   If the price level falls by one-half, the real wage doubles if the nominal wage rate stays equal to W_0 [panel (a)]. At the higher real wage, $W_0/(P_0/2) = 2W_0/P_0$, there is surplus labor. The nominal wage is bid downward until labor market equilibrium is reestablished at the full-employment quantity of labor, N_0. Equivalently, when the price level falls by one-half, the value of labor's marginal product is reduced and labor demand falls [panel (b)]. Laborers recognize that their real wage is higher, and so they increase their labor supply. On net, employment remains at the level N_0. Output produced does not change [panel (c)] in equilibrium. Therefore, a fall in the level of prices has no effect on the production of real output; the aggregate supply schedule is vertical [panel (d)].

Indeed, the equilibrium output level would not change in response to any given change in the price level. This means that both of the equilibrium points we have derived in panel (*d*) of Figure 18-2 actually lie on a *schedule* of combinations of output and price levels for which the labor market is in equilibrium. Economists call this schedule the economy's *aggregate output supply schedule.* We shall refer to it by the shorthand name, the **aggregate supply schedule.**

The classical aggregate supply schedule is vertical at the full-employment level of output. As a result, output is "supply-determined." In the classical model, once we know the position of the economy's aggregate supply schedule we know the short-run level of output produced in the economy, irrespective of any other factors.

Unemployment in the Classical Model   In the classical model, unemployment is only temporary. If there is a surplus in the labor market, the nominal wage rate will adjust to eliminate that surplus. The classical economists recognized, though, that we sometimes observe persistent unemployment in the real world. Does this mean there is something wrong with the classical model? The classical economists did not believe this to be the case. Persistent unemployment, they argued, can occur only if some external factor, such as minimum wage laws or other legal impediment, like forced unionized wage setting, causes the nominal wage rate to be rigid in the face of price changes. The classical theorists did not believe that these factors were significant enough to consider in their model. Moreover, they did not believe that such institutional restrictions on the flexibility of nominal wages were desirable or that, if enacted, they would be long-lasting. As we shall see in later chapters, modern economists continue to debate these points.

THE QUANTITY THEORY OF MONEY AND AGGREGATE DEMAND

An important feature of our derivation of the aggregate supply schedule was that we determined equilibrium wages and labor employment taking the price level as "given"; we did not consider how the price level was determined. That does not necessarily mean that we are not interested in how to determine the level of prices. Indeed, understanding how prices are determined in the classical model is crucial to understanding the very limited role that classical economists prescribed for monetary policy.

THE CLASSICAL THEORY OF THE DEMAND FOR MONEY

The classical economists believed that the crucial determinant of the level of prices in an economy was the quantity of money in circulation. This meant that the key to ascertaining the magnitude of the price level was to understand how much money all households desired to hold. Consequently, the classical theorists began their analysis of price level determination by constructing a theory of the *demand for money.*

The Quantity Theory of Money   The cornerstone of the classical theory of price level determination was the **quantity theory of money**—that people hold money for transactions purposes. Although many classical economists understood the quantity theory of money, modern economists credit the American economist Irving Fisher (1867–1947) of

Yale University with much of its development. The simplest form of the quantity theory of money is based upon the **equation of exchange:**

$$MV \equiv Py \qquad (18\text{-}7)$$

where M is the nominal quantity of money (the current-dollar value of currency and demand deposits held by the nonbank public) and V is the income velocity of money (the average number of times people spend each unit of money on final goods and services per unit of time). Therefore, the left-hand side of equation (18-7) is the value of current-dollar monetary payments for final goods and services. The right-hand side of the equation multiplies the price level for final goods and services by the quantity of output of goods and services. This quantity also is the current-dollar value of monetary payments for final goods and services. Because both measures must be the same, equation (18-7) is an accounting definition, or identity.

The Cambridge Equation   Alfred Marshall and his colleagues at Cambridge University in England proposed a *behavioral* version of the quantity theory of money. They developed the **Cambridge equation,** which states that

$$M^d = kPy \qquad (18\text{-}8)$$

where M^d is the total quantity of money all individuals in the economy desire to hold and k is a fraction ($0 < k < 1$). The output produced in the economy generates income of an equal amount for all households in the economy (because they own all factors of production). Hence, the amount Py is the nominal value of output and also is the nominal income earned by households. Therefore, equation (18-8) represents a simple theory of the demand for money by households. It says simply that households desire to hold some fraction of their nominal income as money.

The idea behind this theory is that the key function of money is its usefulness as a *medium of exchange.* To conduct planned transactions in the markets for goods and services in a money economy, households need nominal money balances. According to equation (18-8), k is equal to $M^d/(Py)$. This means that k is the public's desired holdings of nominal money balances relative to total nominal income. The classical economists believed that k was a stable ratio that they could regard as a constant (in the long run) for their theory.

This theory of money demand, which the classical economists called a theory of the **transactions motive** for holding money, obviously is very simple. People often hold money balances not only for planned transactions in markets for goods and services but also for emergencies. For instance, what would they do if they were making some planned purchases at a K-Mart store and saw a flashing blue light over some specially priced merchandise if they kept no extra dollars on hand?. Both Fisher and Marshall recognized the existence of a **precautionary motive** for holding money for contingencies like K-Mart blue-light specials. Nevertheless, for ease of exposition, economists typically lump these two motives together and refer only to the transactions motive.

AGGREGATE DEMAND AND PRICE LEVEL DETERMINATION

So far, we have discussed only the classical theory of the demand for money. It turns out that it is a short step from the Cambridge equation to a theory of the aggregate demand for output produced in the economy. From there it is a shorter step still to a theory of the determination of the level of prices.

The Aggregate Demand Schedule   Suppose that the quantity of nominal money balances supplied through the actions of a central bank is $M^s = M_0$. In equilibrium, all individuals in the economy desire to hold this quantity of money balances; that is, $M^d = M^s$. This means that, using the Cambridge equation (18-8), when households in the economy desire to hold the nominal quantity of money that the central bank supplies, it will be the case that $kPy = M_0$. This yields the equation

$$y^d = M_0/(kP) \qquad\qquad (18\text{-}9)$$

This is an equation for the economy's **aggregate demand schedule.** The aggregate demand schedule is all combinations of real output and prices for which households are satisfied holding the quantity of nominal money balances M_0, given their average desired ratio of money holdings k.

Figure 18-10 depicts the aggregate demand schedule. As shown in equation (18-9), as the price level rises, the quantity of real output that households desire to purchase declines. The reason is that as the price level increases, so does nominal income to households. According to the Cambridge equation (18-8), households will desire to hold more money balances. This means that they use less of their income to purchase real goods and services. Consequently, the quantity of real output demanded declines when the price level increases. This is a leftward movement along the aggregate demand schedule.

Price Level Determination   Panel (*a*) of Figure 18-11 shows both aggregate demand and aggregate supply together on the same diagram. In the classical model, output is supply-determined, and so $y^s = y_0$, the full-employment output level. The diagram depicts equilibrium in the *market for output,* which occurs when $y^s = y^d$, or where the aggregate supply schedule crosses the aggregate demand schedule. At this point on the aggregate

Figure 18-10
The Classical Aggregate Demand Schedule.   The aggregate output demand schedule is derived from the Cambridge equation. The aggregate demand schedule is negatively sloped. It indicates that lower price levels, with the nominal money supply and the Cambridge k held unchanged, increase the quantity of output demanded.

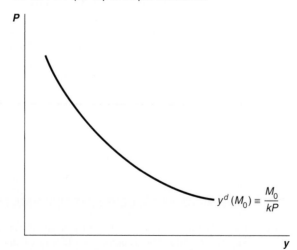

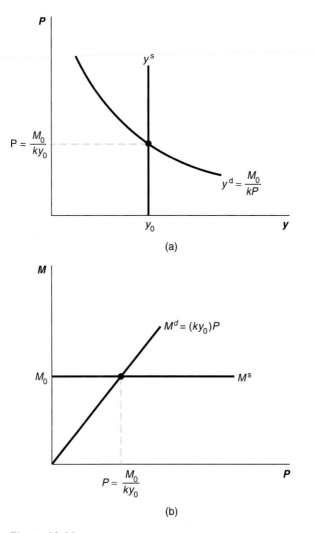

Figure 18-11
Determining the Price Level in the Classical Model.   The equilibrium price level is determined at the point at which the quantity of real output supplied by firms, $y^s = y_0$, is equal to the
quantity of real output demanded by consumers, $y^d = M_0/(kP)$. This is the point at which the
aggregate supply and aggregate demand schedules cross, at the price level $P = M_0/(ky_0)$ [panel (a)].
Equivalently, the equilibrium price level is determined at the point at which the quantity of money
demanded, $M_d = (ky_0)P$, is equal to the quantity of money supplied, $M^s = M_0$. This is the point at
which the money demand and money supply schedules cross [panel (b)], at the same equilibrium
price level.

demand schedule, $y^d = y_0$, the amount of output supplied equals the quantity of output
demanded ("Supply creates its own demand!"). From equation (18-9), this means that,
at this point, $y_0 = M_0/(kP)$. So the equilibrium price level is

$$P = M_0/(ky_0) \qquad (18\text{-}10)$$

Panel (*b*) of the figure depicts an alternative way of viewing price level determination in the classical model. In equilibrium, households desire to hold the nominal quantity of money, M_0, given the amount of real output produced, y_0. The Cambridge equation (18-8) says that $M^d = kPy$, and so at the supply-determined level of output this equation is

$$M^d = (ky_0)P \qquad \text{(18-11)}$$

We may graph this equation as a straight-line demand schedule with slope ky_0, as depicted in panel (*b*). The quantity of money supplied is equal to the constant amount M_0. At the intersection of these two schedules, the price level is $P = M_0/(ky_0)$. This is the same value determined in the market for real output and given in equation (18-10).

In short, both of these diagrams are equivalent representations of price level determination in the classical model. The reason is that, in the classical model, households either hold some of their income as money or spend it on real output. Because output is supply-determined in the classical system, when households wish to purchase the amount of output supplied [the output market equilibrium depicted in panel (*a*) of Figure 18-11], they also wish to hold the quantity of nominal money balances supplied by the central bank [the money market equilibrium depicted in panel (*b*) of Figure 18-11]. It is most common currently for economists to work with the output market diagram in panel (*a*) of Figure 18-11. Either diagram is acceptable since either one gives us the same answer.

Velocity in the Classical Model   Note that equation (18-11) may be rearranged to say that for any given quantity of money supplied, M,

$$M/k = Py \qquad \text{(18-12)}$$

holds when the money market is in equilibrium. Because the quantity equation (18-7) tells us that it is always true that

$$MV \equiv Py$$

equation (18-12) implies that, in the classical model, it is always true that $k \equiv 1/V$ or, identically, that

$$V \equiv 1/k \qquad \text{(18-13)}$$

Recall that the classical theorists assumed that k is constant in the long run. Equation (18-13) tells us that this assumption means that the classical model we have constructed implicitly assumes that the income velocity of money (the average rate of turnover of a dollar of money in exchange for goods and services) is constant. Fisher and other classical theorists did not really believe that income velocity is always constant. (It rarely is for any economy.) However, they did believe that it was *stable* (predictable) over long periods relevant for their theory.

The Relationship between Money and Prices   Suppose that an economy's central bank decided to change the money stock from an initial amount M_0 to a new amount αM_0, where α (pronounced ''alpha,'') is a constant not equal to 1. Figure 18-12 illustrates the

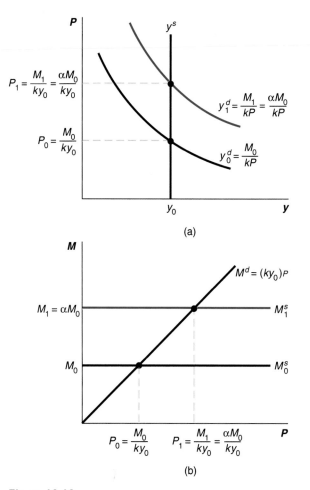

Figure 18-12
The Effect of a Rise in the Nominal Money Supply on the Equilibrium Price Level.   If the nominal quantity of money is multiplied by a factor greater than unity, the aggregate demand schedule shifts outward [panel (*a*)], and the money supply schedule shifts upward [panel (*b*)]. The equilibrium price level rises to an amount equal to the same factor multiplied by the original price level.

effects of such a change for the case in which $\alpha > 1$. In this case, the new quantity of money would exceed the initial quantity. As shown in panel (*a*) of the figure, a rise in the quantity of money would increase the aggregate demand for output. Panel (*b*) of the figure shows the rise in the quantity of money as an upward shift of the money supply schedule.

As shown in both panels of the figure, the equilibrium price level must rise, from P_0 to P_1, following the increase in the quantity of money. The question we would like to answer is, by how much? We can determine the answer in the following manner. From equation (18-10) we know that the initial price level was $P_0 = M_0/(ky_0)$. The new price level, after the money stock rises by the factor α, must be $P_1 = \alpha M_0/(ky_0)$.

Therefore, the absolute change in the level of prices caused by the change in the quantity of money is $P_1 - P_0 = (\alpha - 1)[M_0/(ky_0)]$. The *proportionate change* in the price level, relative to its initial value, is therefore equal to

$$\frac{P_1 - P_0}{P_0} = (\alpha - 1)\left(\frac{M_0}{ky_0}\right) \bigg/ \left(\frac{M_0}{ky_0}\right) \tag{18-14}$$
$$= \alpha - 1$$

Suppose that α equals 2. Then, in the example illustrated in Figure 18-12, the money stock was doubled from M_0 to $2M_0$. As a result, the price level rose from $P_0 = M_0/(ky_0)$ to $P_1 = 2M_0/(ky_0) = 2P_0$. The price level doubled, and so prices rose in equal proportion with the rise in the quantity of money. Equation (18-14) tells us that the classical model implies that this doubling of the money stock causes a proportionate change in the price level of 1. That is, the price level rises by 100 percent, which is the percentage increase implied by a doubling of prices.

We can conclude that the classical model predicts that, at the supply-determined, full-employment level of output, changes in the quantity of money have equiproportionate effects on the level of prices of goods and services. Changes in the quantity of money cannot influence the full-employment level of output. This is true because such changes affect only the level of aggregate demand and not aggregate supply. Dramatic changes in the quantity of money, nonetheless, can have dramatic effects on the level of prices. Hence, the classical economists felt that the key role of monetary policy should be to stabilize the level of prices.

INTEREST RATE DETERMINATION IN THE CLASSICAL MODEL

One of the economic variables of greatest interest to monetary economists is the interest rate. So far we have had nothing to say about the classical theorists' approach to understanding the determination of the equilibrium rate of interest. Let us turn now to this final issue.

An aggregate demand–aggregate supply equilbrium in the output market implies that all output produced in an economy ultimately is purchased in equilibrium. We all know that many people save some of the real incomes they earn; they do not use all their incomes to purchase output. Yet although many people in an economy save, the classical model tells us that, in equilibrium, people purchase all output that is produced. On the surface, there appears to be a contradiction here, because this saving represents a *leakage* from the flow of expenditures on output by households. It is the role of the interest rate to resolve this apparent contradiction.

SAVING AND INVESTMENT

Individuals save output through some form of storage. In modern economies, people store output indirectly by creating titles to output in the form of financial claims such as bank deposits and bonds. When you make a deposit in a savings account, you store a title to some output that you otherwise could have purchased. Effectively, it is as if you were storing real goods and services until some future time. Indeed, saving is by its nature an act of forgoing current consumption so that you can undertake more consumption at a future date.

The Soviet Union Met the Quantity Theory

INTERNATIONAL PERSPECTIVE

There were repeated efforts in the Soviet Union during the late 1980s to move from a government-controlled, socialistic economy toward a "mix" of both governmental and private production and pricing of goods and services. However, until the demise of the U.S.S.R. on Christmas day, 1991, nearly all Soviet output was produced by governmental enterprises. Also, almost all prices remained strictly government-controlled. Shortages of many goods developed, and "black-market" trading (trading of goods and services at nongovernmental, illegal prices) increased dramatically. In early 1991, in an effort to reduce the amount of black-market trading, the Soviet leadership decided to declare all 50- and 100-ruble currency notes worthless. The central Soviet government granted its citizens only three days to convert these large notes into smaller-denomination notes, and many citizens found that deadline impossible to meet.

There probably were two rationales for this policy. The Soviet government's "official" intention was to make black-market transactions more difficult to undertake. The government cited evidence that illegal traders often used large-denomination ruble currency notes in their transactions. By eliminating large-denomination currency notes the government hoped to make these trades more difficult to conduct.

The intended total reduction in large-denomination Soviet currency notes amounted to 26 billion rubles, or nearly a 20 percent reduction in nominal cash balances supplied by the Soviet government. Economists in the West theorized that Soviet policy makers had adopted the classical hypothesis of a stable, if not constant, income velocity of money. These Western economists speculated that Soviet leaders hoped that the reduction in the nominal money stock would, with a stable velocity, decrease aggregate demand and lessen the upward pressure on prices. As a result, incentives to undertake black-market trades would disappear. This, these econ-

omists believed, was a second and probably more important rationale for the 1991 Soviet policy action.

Note that the quantity theory of money tells us that, for the former Soviet Union, it would be true that $MV = Py$, where P represents the government-controlled price level and y represents the government-determined output level. (Of course, black markets continued to function, and so the price level was not *completely* fixed, but this is a useful simplifying assumption.) We can immediately predict, from the quantity theory, that the reduction in the nominal money supply would have to cause an offsetting increase in the income velocity of money. Both terms on the right-hand side of the quantity equation were fixed, and so a change in M in one direction would be offset by a change in V in the opposite direction. Hence, the income velocity of Soviet rubles would not remain stable as in the classical economic model. The reason would be that the former Soviet government's control of prices violated a key element of the classical model, which is the assumption of pure competition and flexibility of prices.

Indeed, the income velocity of Soviet rubles accelerated in 1990 and 1991. As a result, aggregate demand did not fall significantly following the reduction in the nominal money supply. In contrast, large amounts of wealth that Soviet citizens held as money were "expropriated" (taxed away) by the elimination of large-denomination ruble notes that many citizens had saved for years. Upward pressure on prices of goods and services continued, largely unabated, and black markets flourished. It is unclear whether or not the ex-Soviets learned a lesson from their experiment in drastic money supply reduction. However, there is an important lesson for all of us: The classical model is a poor guide to policy making if any of its key assumptions—like flexibility of prices under pure competition—fail to hold in the real world.

Based on an article by Keith Crane, "How Not to Cure a Monetary 'Hangover,'" *Wall Street Journal* (January 28, 1991), p. A10.

Not all individuals save, though. Many would like to spend more now than their incomes would otherwise allow. This is particularly true for individuals who own business firms. Owners of these firms often wish to purchase capital goods with which to produce goods and services at a profit, using the acquired capital together with labor and land services. But capital purchases can be expensive and require expenditures that exceed the real incomes of individuals who own these firms. As a result, these individuals, through the firms they own, borrow output from those individuals who save. In modern economies, this borrowing occurs when borrowers trade titles to output in a future period for the titles to current output presently owned by savers.

Often, business firms borrow the saved income, on behalf of the firms' owners. Business firms then *invest this borrowed income:* The firms purchase capital goods to use in the production process. That is, the saving that represents an initial *leakage* from the flow of income and expenditures is *reinjected* into that flow in the form of investment spending on goods and services by business firms.

The Aggregate Saving Schedule   Given real income, the main determinant of saving per unit of time is the real rate of interest. According to the classical economists, there is a direct relationship between the real interest rate, r_r, and the amount that households save out of a given level of income, other things constant. (Recall our discussion of the real interest rate in Chapter 7.) If the real interest rate rises, households will save more of and consume less out of a given level of income. If the real interest rate falls, households will save less and consume more out of a given level of income.

Figure 18-13 illustrates this direct relationship between real saving (the amount of real income that households save) and the real interest rate. This schedule is a supply schedule. The amount of saving done by households in the economy represents titles to real output; the classical economists called these financial claims **loanable funds.** The real interest rate is the *price* of these loanable funds, and the saving schedule is an upward-sloping *supply schedule for loanable funds,* also known as the *aggregate saving schedule.* As the

Figure 18-13
The Saving Schedule.   For a given level of national income, individuals will save more and consume less as the real interest rate rises. The saving schedule is the loanable funds supply schedule. It shifts rightward if the level of real income increases or if individuals now wish to substitute more future consumption for less present consumption. It shifts leftward if the level of real income falls or if individuals now wish to substitute more present consumption for less future consumption.

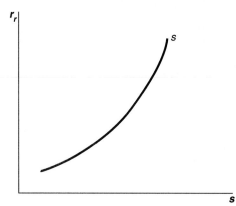

real interest rate rises, the quantity of saving in the form of loanable funds supplied increases. As the real interest rate falls, the amount of saving in the form of loanable funds supplied decreases.

The Aggregate Investment Schedule   According to classical economists, given profit expectations of owners of businesses, the most important determinant of business investment spending on capital goods is the rate of interest. The classical economists theorized that the amount of desired investment spending depended inversely upon the real interest rate.

Recall from Chapters 4 and 7 that we measure the rate of exchange between present and future by the discount factor, $1/(1 + r_r)$. When a firm computes the discounted present value of an investment in a capital good today, it applies the discount factor to the profit that this investment is expected to yield in the future. If the real interest rate rises, the discount factor falls. As a result, the discounted value of the capital investment falls, making the investment less profitable from today's perspective. Less investment spending will be undertaken.

For example, suppose that a business firm this year considers purchasing a machine that would cost \$9,300 to purchase and install in a factory by the end of the year. Also suppose, for simplicity, that the machine does not depreciate until the end of next year, when it stops working. (This is a strange machine, but it is an easy one to think about.) The expected gross profit gain *next year* from using the machine is \$10,000. But the business is purchasing the machine *this year* and needs to make a comparison that considers the time value of money. If the prevailing annual real interest rate is 5 percent, then the discounted present value of the gross profit gain from purchasing this machine is \$10,000/$(1 + 0.05)$ = \$9,523.81. The net profit, from today's perspective, of this machine therefore is equal to \$9,523.81 − \$9,300 = \$223.81.

If the real interest rate rises to 10 percent, the firm must recompute the machine's net profitability. The gross profit gain now is equal to \$10,000/$(1 + 0.10)$ = \$9,090.91, which implies a net *loss* to the firm of \$9,090.91 − \$9,300 = −\$209.09. The rise in the interest rate has made this investment unprofitable, and so the firm will not make the investment. The firm's investment spending for this year will fall.

The inverse relationship between desired investment spending and the interest rate is shown in Figure 18-14. The downward slope of this *aggregate investment schedule* is reminiscent of the law of demand, and for good reason. Businesses obtain funds used for investment spending by borrowing from savers at the real interest rate r_r. The aggregate investment schedule also (in the absence of a government, which we shall bring into our story shortly) is the *demand schedule for loanable funds.* As the real interest rate rises, the demand for loanable funds for capital investment declines. As the real interest rate falls, the demand for loanable funds for capital investment rises.

THE LOANABLE FUNDS MARKET AND INTEREST RATE DETERMINATION

Consider Figure 18-15, which shows the aggregate saving (loanable funds supply) schedule and the aggregate investment (loanable funds demand) schedule together on the same coordinate axes. They intersect at the real interest rate r_r^0. At this real rate of interest, the quantity of loanable funds supplied is equal to the quantity of loanable funds demanded. Stated in a different way, desired saving is equal to desired investment. This real interest rate r_r^0 is the rate at which the market for loanable funds is in equilibrium. It also is the

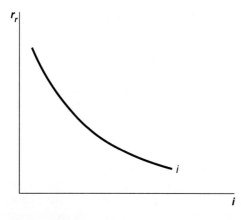

Figure 18-14

The Desired Investment Schedule. As the interest rate rises, the discounted present value of future flows of profits to firms falls, and so firms wish to reduce current investment spending. Therefore, the desired investment schedule depicts an inverse relationship between the interest rate and desired real investment by business firms. This schedule is, ignoring government, the economy's loanable funds demand schedule.

The aggregate real investment schedule shifts rightward if firms anticipate higher future profits. It shifts leftward if they anticipate lower future profits.

real interest rate at which the market for real output is in equilibrium, because at this real interest rate the equality of saving and investment means that all leakages from the flow of real income (saving) are reinjected into that flow as investment expenditures. That is, all the income that some households save is spent as investment by firms when the interest rate is r_r^0. Therefore, at this real interest rate households and firms purchase the full-employment level of output.

Suppose that the real interest rate were higher than r_r^0, at the rate r_r^1 in Figure 18-15. In this case, the quantity of loanable funds supplied would exceed the quantity demanded; desired saving would exceed desired investment. There would be a surplus quantity of loanable funds supplied, and leakages from the income-expenditure stream would exceed reinjections. Savers would compete against one another for interest earnings, and the real interest rate would fall back to its equilibrium level.

In contrast, suppose that the interest rate fell to r_r^2 in Figure 18-15. At this interest rate, the quantity of loanable funds demanded would exceed the quantity of loanable funds supplied; desired investment would exceed desired saving. There would be a shortage of loanable funds, and leakages from the income-expenditure stream would be too low relative to desired reinjections. Borrowers would bid against each other to obtain scarce loanable funds, and the real interest rate would rise to its equilibrium level.

To this point, our version of the classical model has assumed that saving is used only to finance business investment spending. In the model, firms do all the borrowing. In the real world, governments also borrow loanable funds. For simplicity's sake, we have ignored the existence of governmental taxation and spending in our discussion of the classical model. The classical theorists recognized that the government often is an important participant in the economy, and so they included it in their model. Government expenditures and taxes influence an economy, argued the classical theorists, through their effects on the equilibrium interest rate and the equilibrium quantity of loanable funds.

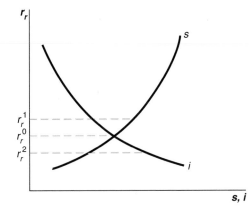

Figure 18-15
Determination of the Real Interest Rate.   The interest rate adjusts to the point at which the quantity of loanable funds demanded (desired investment) is equal to the quantity of loanable funds supplied (desired saving). If the interest rate is equal to r_r^1, there will be an excess quantity of loanable funds supplied; saving will exceed desired investment. Household savers will offer lower rates of interest to induce firms to borrow their loanable funds, and the interest rate will fall toward equilibrium at the interest rate r_r^0. If the interest rate is equal to r_r^2, there will be an excess quantity of loanable funds demanded; desired investment will exceed saving. Business firms will offer to pay higher rates of interest to induce households to save loanable funds, and the interest rate will rise toward equilibrium at the interest rate r_r^0.

Fiscal Policy in the Classical Model   *Fiscal policy* refers to governmental policies with respect to government spending and taxation. Let us denote the amount of real government spending on output per unit of time as g. Suppose that the amount of output that the government obtains via taxes per unit of time is t. If government spending exceeds taxes, then the government's budget over the given period will be in deficit by the amount $g - t$. Economists often call this amount the *primary deficit.* The primary deficit is the simplest measure of the government's deficit; it abstracts from other factors such as interest payments on any existing government debt.

The government must initially finance any deficit by borrowing. Let us suppose that the government determines the amounts of its spending and taxation independently of any other economic variables, so that g and t are *lump-sum quantities.* This implies that the government must borrow a lump-sum amount of loanable funds in order to finance its deficit.

Figure 18-16 shows the effect of an increase in the government's budget deficit from an initial value of zero (a balanced budget) to a new, lump-sum value of $g - t$. This is a fixed amount of loanable funds that the government desires to borrow at any given interest rate. It is the government's demand for loanable funds. In Figure 18-16, we add this lump-sum demand for loanable funds by the government horizontally to the private loanable funds demand of business firms. This produces a new, total (private and public) loanable funds demand schedule. At the original real interest rate r_r^0, there would now be an excess quantity of loanable funds demanded, and the real interest rate would rise to a new equilibrium level of r_r^1.

At this new equilibrium interest rate, the amount of saving will be higher, rising from s_0 to s_1. This rise in saving out of existing output implies an equal-valued decline in

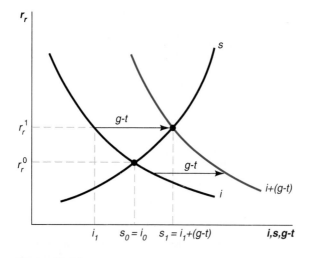

Figure 18-16

The Effects of Governmental Deficit Spending.   The government must borrow loanable funds to finance an excess of spending, g, over taxes, t. If the amount it needs to borrow is fixed at $g - t$, then this amount represents the government's demand for loanable funds. If this is added to the demand for loanable funds by firms, then $i + (g - t)$ is the total demand for loanable funds.

If the interest rate without a government deficit ($g - t = 0$) was equal to r_r^0, then the increase in the demand for loanable funds caused by a rise in the deficit to the amount $g - t$ results in an increase in the equilibrium rate of interest, to r_r^1. The rise in the interest rate causes private investment to fall, from i_0 to i_1. The amount of saving rises, from s_0 to s_1. Because real income is equal to the full-employment level in the classical model, real income is unchanged, and so a rise in saving means there is a decline in private consumption by an equal amount. The combined reductions in private investment and private consumption are equal to the amount of the deficit. Therefore, the increase in the government's deficit *crowds out* an equal amount of private spending.

consumption. In addition, the amount of private investment by businesses falls from i_0 to i_1. The combined magnitude of the fall in consumption (rise in saving) and the fall in private investment is exactly equal to the increase in the lump-sum deficit, $g - t$.

Thus, classical theory predicts that an increase in the government's deficit, which could arise from an increase in government spending, from a decrease in taxes, or from both, has two effects. First, a rise in the deficit causes an increase in the real rate of interest. Second, this rise in the real interest rate causes a fall in private spending (reductions in private consumption and investment). This fall in private expenditures is exactly equal to the increase in the deficit. Economists call this second effect the **crowding-out effect.** In the classical model, deficit-financed government spending policies ''crowd out'' an equal amount of private spending. In effect, the government consumes a larger share of the full-employment level of output on behalf of its citizens, leaving less for them to consume privately.

Money and Interest Rates   In the classical model of the loanable funds market and real interest rate determination, the nominal quantity of money plays no role. The quantity of money has no effect on the real interest rate, which is determined solely by the real income allocations of savers and borrowers of loanable funds.

We know, though, from Chapter 7 that the *nominal interest rate* (r_n) is approximately equal to the real interest rate (r_r) plus the expected rate of price inflation. Before, we

C U R R E N T
CONTROVERSY

THE RETURN OF A CLASSICAL ECONOMIST

The classical model rests on a foundation of ideas that date back many years. For this reason, it often is tempting to jump to the conclusion that those "old ideas" have little current relevance. A good counterexample to this concerns some ideas of a particular classical theorist, David Ricardo (1772–1823). Ricardo argued that many tax changes would in fact have little or no effect on macroeconomic variables. For example, Ricardo felt that a cut in lump-sum taxes would have no effect on aggregate consumption. The reason, he argued, was that the government must finance a tax cut today by issuing more bonds. The government must pay interest on these bonds in the future, and taxes eventually will have to be raised to pay these future interest payments. Therefore, Ricardo concluded, taxpayers will recognize that a tax cut today implies a tax increase in the future. As a result, rational, self-interested individuals will respond to a tax cut today by saving the "proceeds" of the cut (the enlargement of disposable, after-tax income) until the future date at which the government increases taxes to make interest payments on governmental debts resulting from today's tax cut. Consequently, today's tax cut need not result in higher current consumption.

Until recently, modern economists had largely ignored or dismissed Ricardo's argument. They assumed (as we shall see in the next chapter) that a current tax cut unambiguously would increase present after-tax income and cause a rise in current consumption. However, several economists have rejuvenated Ricardo's logical argument to help explain why this modern theory of taxes and consumption has not always fit the facts. Indeed, these modern economists have concluded that Ricardo was right all along and that it is recent theorists who were wrong in ignoring Ricardo's theory.

This idea, that individuals realize that current tax cuts imply future tax increases and consequently save for future bond interest repayments rather than increasing their consumption, implies that a tax cut that results in a budget deficit today is equivalent to a tax increase in the future. For this reason, economists call Ricardo's theory the "Ricardian equivalence proposition." This proposition is now a major subject of study and debate in economics. Many economists continue to doubt that households are so farsighted as to save all proceeds from current tax cuts for future interest repayments. Other doubters of Ricardian equivalence point out that because people know that they may die before they actually will have to pay taxes for bond interest repayments, these individuals will in fact increase their consumption when the government cuts taxes.

Nonetheless, the promoters of the Ricardian equivalence proposition maintain that rational, self-interested individuals will be farsighted. They also argue that individuals who care about the welfare of their offspring may transfer proceeds of tax cuts that they have received to their children either before their deaths, as gifts, or after their deaths, as bequests, so that their children will be able to pay higher future taxes needed by the government to fund bond interest payments. This has led economists to explore motives behind individuals' bequests to their offspring. How much people care about their children in the aggregate may be crucial to how tax policies affect the macroeconomy!

Ricardo developed many other theories, especially concerning labor market behavior and wages, but his theory of tax policy continues to be a significant source of controversy in economics—nearly two centuries after his death. Perhaps the Ricardian equivalence proposition was Ricardo's most enduring bequest to the generations that followed him.

learned that changes in the quantity of money have equiproportionate effects on prices. Therefore, in the classical model, an increase in the rate of money growth of, say, 3 percent will cause the rate of inflation to rise by 3 percent. A sustained inflation causes a rise in the nominal rate of interest of approximately 3 percentage points. In contrast, a decrease in the rate of growth of the quantity of money of 3 percent would cause the nominal interest rate to fall by about 3 percentage points.

In the classical model, then, monetary policy has no effect on the real rate of interest. But an increase in the rate of growth of the money stock causes the nominal interest rate to rise, while a decrease in the growth rate of the quantity of money causes the nominal interest rate to fall, other things constant.

CHAPTER SUMMARY

1. The classical model is an edited and modernized version of the writings of eighteenth-, nineteenth-, and early twentieth-century economists.

2. Three key assumptions that underlie the classical model are (a) economic agents are motivated by rational self-interest, (b) pure competition exists in all markets, and (c) economic agents do not suffer from money illusion.

3. Flexibility of prices, wages, and interest rates assures that full employment of labor will be attained in the classical model. Unemployment, or a surplus of labor, causes nominal wage rates to fall relative to the price level. This reduction in the real wage rate will restore labor market equilibrium to full employment.

4. Through the production function, the full employment of labor generated in the labor market determines the full-employment output level, which does not depend on output prices. Consequently, the aggregate supply schedule is vertical in the classical model, and output is supply-determined. This notion lies behind Say's law, that "Supply creates its own demand."

5. The quantity theory of money, which was the dominant macroeconomic theory for several centuries, maintains that individuals hold money for transactions purposes. Specifically, the Cambridge equation assumes that desired money balances are a constant proportion to nominal income.

6. The aggregate demand schedule can be derived from the Cambridge equation. This curve shifts if the quantity of money changes.

7. The price level is established by an aggregate demand–aggregate supply equilibrium in the market for output. Because output is supply-determined in the classical model, the price level is demand-determined. Changes in the quantity of money do not influence the full-employment output level but do cause equiproportionate changes in the price level.

8. The real rate of interest adjusts to assure that leakages from the stream of income and expenditures in the form of saving are reinjected into that stream in the form of investment expenditures. According to the classical model, deficit-financed increases in government spending cause higher real interest rates and crowd out an equal amount of private expenditures.

9. The real rate of interest is determined independently of the quantity of money, but changes in the growth rate of money directly influence nominal interest rates.

GLOSSARY

Aggregate demand schedule (y^d):   Combinations of various price levels and levels of output for which individuals are satisfied with their consumption of output and their holdings of money.

Aggregate supply schedule (y^s):   The relationship between various price levels and levels of national output that workers and firms will produce voluntarily.

Cambridge equation: An equation developed by Alfred Marshall and other economists at Cambridge University, England, which indicates that individuals desire to hold money for planned transactions, in proportion to the nominal value of income.

Crowding-out effect: Condition that occurs when there is an increase in the government's deficit. A rise in the real interest rate, caused by an increase in the deficit, causes a fall in private spending. In the classical model, this fall is exactly equal to the increase in the deficit; in essence, government deficit spending "crowds out" an equal amount of private spending.

Demand management: The use of monetary and fiscal policies to vary the level of aggregate desired expenditures in pursuit of socially desired levels of real income, employment, and prices.

Equation of exchange: An accounting identity that states that the nominal value of all monetary transactions for final goods and services is equal to the nominal value of the output of goods and services purchased; discussed most fully by the American economist Irving Fisher.

Income price deflator: A measure of the level of prices of goods and services in terms of prices in a base year; by definition, P is equal to Y/y, where Y is the current output valued in current prices and y is real output produced.

Law of diminishing marginal returns: The law that states that each successive addition of a unit of a factor of production, such as labor, eventually produces a smaller gain in output produced, other factors hold constant.

Loanable funds: The term that classical economists use to refer to the amount of real income that households save, representing titles to real output.

Macroeconomic variables: Quantities, such as national income or the price level, that are economywide measures of economic performance.

Marginal product of labor: The change in total output resulting from a 1-unit increase in the quantity of labor employed in production.

Money illusion: State that exists when economic agents change their behavior in response to changes in nominal values, even if there are no changes in real (price-level-adjusted) values.

Neutrality of money: The idea that money is neutral if changes in its quantity affect only nominal values, and if real variables like employment, national output, and the composition of national output do not change when the quantity of money varies.

Precautionary motive: Rationale for people to hold money as a contingency in case a need should arise to make unplanned expenditures.

Production function: A relationship between possible quantities of factors of production and the amount of output of goods and services that firms can produce with current technology.

Quantity theory of money: The theory that people hold money for transactions purposes.

Say's law: J. B. Say's dictum that supply creates its own demand.

Stagflation: The simultaneous existence of high levels of inflation and unemployment.

Transactions motive: Rationale for people to hold money because they want to make planned purchases of goods and services.

Value of the marginal product of labor: The valuation of labor's marginal product at current market prices, measured as the marginal product of labor times the selling price of output per unit.

SELF-TEST QUESTIONS

1. Draw a fully labeled diagram of the aggregate production function $y = f(N)$. Briefly explain why the slope of this function is the marginal product of capital. Draw a diagram of the marginal-product-of-labor (MP_n) schedule implied by your production function.

2. Explain why the marginal-product-of-labor schedule is the labor demand schedule for a competitive firm. What factors cause this schedule to shift?

3. What factors cause the aggregate labor supply schedule to shift? Why?

4. Use appropriate diagrams to derive at least two points along the classical aggregate supply schedule.

5. Aggregate output increases as the economy improves its technological know-how. The only way that this can occur in the classical model is if the aggregate supply schedule shifts rightward as technology improves. Prove to yourself that this actually is what the classical theory implies.

6. During the last two decades, many more women have entered the labor force, which has increased the supply of labor. Use the classical model to predict the implications of greater female labor force participation upon (a) the equilibrium real wage rate, (b) the equilibrium level of labor employment, (c) the full-employment level of output and the position of the aggregate supply schedule, and (d) the level of prices, assuming that the money stock and the income velocity of money are unchanged.

7. Many economists have found evidence that, in most major industrialized economies around the world, the "productivity of labor" has declined.
   a. One measure of labor productivity is the *average product of labor,* which is the ratio of the level of output produced to the level of labor employment. Use the classical model of production to reason out different possible causes of a decline in the average product of labor.
   b. Another measure of labor productivity is the marginal product of labor. What would cause a fall in the marginal product of labor?
   c. Compare your answers with those for parts b and c. Discuss why economists must be very careful to stress what measures of "labor productivity" they have used when they discuss the issue of falling labor productivity.

8. Suppose that conditions in the labor market are static but that major developments in payments technology greatly increase the average rate of turnover of money in exchange. What are the effects, if any, on the level of output, the price level, and the real rate of interest?

9. Suppose that the federal government increases its spending on real goods and services while holding taxes constant. Also assume that it initially had a balanced budget. Finally, suppose that a central bank purchases all bonds used to finance a governmental budget deficit with new money that it prints to pay for the bonds.
   a. What will be the effect of this policy action on the equilibrium real interest rate? Explain. What specific policy action accounts for this effect: the rise in real government spending or the increase in the quantity of money, or both?
   b. What will be the effect on the nominal interest rate? Explain. What specific policy action accounts for this effect: the rise in real government spending or the increase in the quantity of money, or both?
   c. What will be the effect on private real spending? Explain.

PROBLEMS

18-1.   Assume that Mr. Colacci has an income of $100 per week and that he saves $10 and spends $90 on consumer goods. He works 38 hours per week. Assume now that *all* prices double; all goods and services cost twice as much, wages are two times higher, and nominal interest rates rise by exactly 100 percent.
   a. Will Mr. Colacci save a higher percentage of his income?
   b. Will he work more than 38 hours per week now?
   c. Under what conditions would he save more than 10 percent of his income and work more than 38 hours per week, assuming that the price level has doubled?

18-2.   Let the aggregate demand for labor be given by $W_R = 25 - N$, and let the aggregate supply of labor be given by $W_R = -5 + 2N$, where W_R is shorthand notation for the real wage rate and N is the quantity of labor.
   a. Determine the equilibrium real wage rate.

    b. Compute the equilibrium quantity of labor.

    c. Suppose that prices of all goods doubled. Write out the labor demand and labor supply equations in nominal terms after the price change.

    d. Determine the equilibrium nominal wage rate and the equilibrium quantity of labor.

18-3. Assume that the values for k are (a) 0.2, (b) 0.25, and (c) 0.333. What are the corresponding values of V? When k rises, what happens to V? What is the reason for this?

18-4. Suppose that Ms. Smith receives a monthly income of $1,000 at the first of each month, spends all her income every month, and spends the same amount each day. What is the average value of her cash balances over the course of a month? What is her average k? Now suppose that she gets paid the same annual income, but she receives $500 on the first of the month and $500 in the middle of each month. What is her average cash balance during the month? What is her k? What happens to k when people get paid more often?

18-5. Suppose that the Cambridge equation is the correct theory of money demand and that $k = 0.2$, $P = 4.0$, and $y = \$100$ billion in base-year dollars.

    a. What are desired nominal money balances?

    b. What are desired real money balances?

    c. Show that real money balances equal a constant portion of real income, using these figures.

18-6. In the equation of exchange, $MV = Py$, assume that $V = 5$ and $y = \$100$ billion in base year dollars. Determine P for each of the following:

    a. $M = \$80$ billion   **c.** $M = \$160$ billion

    b. $M = \$100$ billion   **d.** $M = \$200$ billion

    What can you conclude from your answers to this question?

18-7. Suppose that the price level has a value of 2 units, real output is 100 units, and the income velocity of money is 4 units.

    a. What is the nominal quantity of money?

    b. What fraction of nominal income is held as money; that is, what is the value of k in the Cambridge equation?

    c. Suppose that the money stock and the income velocity of money are unchanged but that the quantity of real output rises to 200 units. What is the price level?

    d. Use your answers from parts a and b to assist in plotting a rough diagram of the classical aggregate demand schedule that includes these values for the income velocity and the stock of money.

18-8. Suppose that the demand for loanable funds (l) is given by $r_n = 20 - (0.5)l$, where r_n is the nominal interest rate, while the supply of loanable funds is given by $r_n = 2 + l$.

    a. What is the equilibrium nominal rate of interest?

    b. Compute the equilibrium value for l.

    c. If the prices of all goods doubled, write the new nominal demand for and supply of loanable funds after the change.

    d. Determine the new equilibrium rate of interest.

    e. Determine the new equilibrium quantity of loanable funds.

SELECTED REFERENCES

Barro, Robert, ''The Ricardian Approach to Budget Deficits,'' in *Macroeconomic Policy* (Cambridge, Mass.: Harvard University Press, 1990).

Fisher, Irving, *The Theory of Interest* (New York: Macmillan, 1930).

Froyen, Richard T., *Macroeconomics: Theories and Policies,* 3d ed. (New York: Macmillan, 1990).

Hicks, John R., *Theory of Wages* (London: Macmillan, 1932).

Keynes, John Maynard, *The General Theory of Employment, Interest, and Money* (London: Macmillan, 1936).

Marshall, Alfred, *Money, Credit, and Commerce* (London: Macmillan, 1925).

————, *Principles of Economics* (New York: Macmillan, 1925).

Mill, John S., *Principles of Economics* (London: J. W. Parker, 1848).

Patinkin, Don, *Money, Interest, and Prices,* 2d ed. (New York: Harper & Row, 1965).

Ricardo, David, "Funding System," in *The Works and Correspondence of David Ricardo,* ed. P. Sraffa (Cambridge: Cambridge University Press, 1951).

Say, Jean B., *A Treatise on Political Economy* (London: Longmans, 1821).

Wicksell, J. G. K., *Interest and Prices,* trans. R. F. Kahn (London: Macmillan, 1936).

Macroeconomic Nuts and Bolts

Economic events have a way of changing economic theory. The Great Depression, which was worldwide and lasted from 1929 until the late 1930s, appeared to provide incontrovertible evidence that there were no mechanisms within capitalism that automatically brought the economy back to full employment—at least, not in any time frame that one could call short run. Indeed, in Great Britain a deep recession and high unemployment existed for approximately five years *before* the worldwide Great Depression began.

In 1936, the British economist John Maynard Keynes published a book, *The General Theory of Employment, Interest, and Money,* that was to revolutionize economic thinking. In his book (commonly called *The General Theory*), Keynes sought to replace the classical model with his own version of how the macroeconomy works. This chapter and the two that follow will focus on Keynes's criticisms of the classical model and will develop simplified versions of his general macroeconomic theory. This theory replaced the classical paradigm in the hearts and minds of many (but certainly not all) economists during the years following the Great Depression.

KEYNES'S CRITICISMS OF THE CLASSICAL MODEL

The intellectual revolution that Keynes initiated has dominated much of the macroeconomic theorizing that followed his time. Indeed, the foundations of his attack on classical economic thinking continue to be the key issues that divide economists today. According to Keynes:

1. The classical theory of the market for labor and of aggregate output supply is at best a first step toward a full theory; fundamental flaws exist in the classical theory of the supply side of the economy.

2. The classical theory of the demand for money is too simple. There are several motives for holding money, and the classical economists overemphasized the transactions motive.

3. The classical treatment of saving and investment viewed the interest rate as the economic variable that ensured ultimate equality of the demand for and supply of loanable funds, but the interest rate does not fulfill this role.

4. The classical economists felt that, without governmental interference in the economy, departures of labor employment and output from their full-employment levels would at most be temporary and certainly would not persist over the long run. Keynes took issue with the classical theorists' view of the short run and questioned whether their model even stood the test in the long run.

5. Finally, the classical theory of aggregate demand depended upon the quantity theory of money. Keynes felt that this was not the correct approach to deriving the aggregate demand for output. His approach was to develop separate theories of desired expenditures of different *sectors* of the economy and then to put these theories together to construct a combined theory of the aggregate demand for output.

THE LABOR MARKET

Keynes had no serious quarrel with the classical theory of labor demand. He agreed that buyers of labor (employers) suffer from no ''money illusions'' and, therefore, concern themselves only with the money wage rate *relative* to output prices (their real wage rate). Yet Keynes rejected the classical theory of labor supply. Recall from Chapter 18 that classical theory states that the aggregate labor supply schedule is upward-sloping against both the nominal and the real wage rates, depending upon which is chosen for analytical purposes. This formulation predicts that during periods when nominal wage rates are relatively constant and prices are rising, some laborers will withdraw some (or all) of their labor because the *real* wage is falling. Keynes argued that actual observation did not support this prediction.

According to Keynes, the existence of unions, minimum wage laws, and long-term legal contracts between workers and firms within or outside unionized environments all are *real-world* factors that potentially explain downward ''stickiness'' (inflexibility) of nominal wage rates. Such stickiness makes involuntary labor unemployment a distinct possibility. In his simplified model, therefore, Keynes assumed downward rigidity of wages, as you will see in Chapter 21.

THE DEMAND FOR MONEY

Recall that both the supply of and the demand for money determine the price level in the classical model. This is true because the annual output of final goods and services, y, is constant at a point in time and is equal to the full-employment output level. In addition, the classical model assumes that the income velocity of money, V, is constant, at least with respect to the payments technology and habits of society. This assumption shows up in the treatment of the ''Cambridge k,'' which is equal to $1/V$, as a constant in the classical money demand equation.

If both money and output are constant, then it follows that $MV = Py$, and so P changes in equal proportion with variations in M. If we reject the assumption of a constant y, however, then there is no longer a proportionate relationship between M and P. Changes in M may change either P or y, or both, as long as V is nearly constant (or moves predictably). This is the tenet of a modern quantity theory of money, called *monetarism,* which we shall discuss in Chapter 21.

Actually, Keynes also believed that V was not constant. Indeed, he developed a theory of how changes in M may lead to changes in V in the opposite direction, so that changes in the quantity of money may have smaller effects on nominal income than the classical theory would predict. Besides treating money as a medium of exchange, Keynes's theory also emphasizes money's role as a *financial asset,* or a means of holding wealth, so that a *speculative motive* for holding money exists. Hence, the amount of money that households desire to hold depends upon speculation about movements in bond prices and interest rates. It is this theory of the demand for money, which we shall discuss in Chapter 20, that leads to the conclusion that M may be inversely related to V.

SAVING, INVESTMENT, AND THE INTEREST RATE

In the classical model, it is the interest rate that brings desired saving and desired investment into equality. Therefore, changes in the interest rate ensure that "leakages" from the flow of income and expenditures (the amount of saving) ultimately are reinjected into that flow. The interest rate performs the crucial role of equalizing saving and investment in the classical system. This is because saving depends directly on the real interest rate, while investment depends negatively on the real interest rate.

Saving and the Interest Rate   According to Keynes, the real interest rate is not the primary determinant of an individual's saving and consumption. Instead, he argued that saving and consumption primarily depend upon an individual's real income. In Keynes's view, the classical economist held constant the most important determinant of the consumption-saving decision—real income. If full employment prevails, as in the classical model, then it is legitimate to hold income constant and to claim saving and consumption depend mainly on the interest rate. But because the *issue* is whether or not there can be full employment, it is not proper to hold income constant. To assume a constant national income because one assumes full employment is, according to Keynes and his followers, to assume one's conclusions.

Thus, every time total real income changes, the classical saving (and consumption) function will shift. In short, Keynes argued that the classical saving schedule is volatile (it fluctuates) because the most important determinant of saving—real income—is not constant. When we discuss the traditional "Keynesian model" later in this chapter, you will see that real saving and real consumption are functions of real disposable income and not the real interest rate.

Investment and the Interest Rate   Here, again, said Keynes, the classical economist held constant the most important determinant of desired investment spending—profit expectations. An inverse relationship exists between investment and the real interest rate, *other things constant.* What the classical theorists held constant are profit expectations, but profit expectations are subject to quick and violent changes. As a result, the desired investment schedule also fluctuates; it shifts every time profit expectations change. Thus, Keynes argued that a capitalistic economy is unstable in large part because the investment function is unstable.

Saving, Investment, and Equilibrium   In the traditional Keynesian framework, interest rates *primarily* determine neither saving nor investment, and so interest rate variations cannot bring saving and investment into full equality. If both the saving and investment schedules are volatile, can one be sure that saving-investment equality assures full employment? Keynes answered no. For example, assume there is a rise in the general level of "thriftiness" by citizens, who for some reason increase their saving significantly.

The result is that real consumption spending will fall. Holding the prices of goods and services fixed, individuals will purchase less real output, implying a fall in production and incomes, or a recession.

According to the classical model, increases in investment that result from a decline in the real interest rate offset increases in saving. But it is not legitimate to hold profit expectations constant during a recession. If profit expectations fall, business owners might ignore significant interest rate reductions. In short, will businesses invest more in plant and equipment at precisely the time they have excess capacity due to a recession? To Keynes the answer to this question was evident. In this chapter we shall see that, in the traditional Keynesian model, a saving-investment equality can hold even in deep recessions.

THE LONG RUN VERSUS THE SHORT RUN

On an even deeper philosophical level, Keynes and his followers criticized the patience (some would say the insensitivity) of classical (and many modern) economists who were prepared to wait for changes in relative prices, real wage rates, and real interest rates to move the economy toward full employment. In the meantime, what about all the human suffering endured by the unemployed, by the bankrupt, and by their families? This is a question guaranteed to discomfit those who believe in a self-regulating economy. How long do people have to wait? How long is the long run? Frustrated with classical prescriptions to leave the economy to its own devices and to wait for long-run adjustments, particularly during the long years of the Great Depression, Keynes offered his oft-quoted dictum: ''In the long run we are all dead.'' This dictum has become almost as famous as Say's law.

In light of this philosophical perspective, the traditional framework stemming from Keynes's original theories focused on the macroeconomic *short run.* As we shall discover in this chapter, this approach can provide us with a deeper understanding of how the economy can depart from full employment in the short run. It also can help us to understand why there is a potential role for fiscal stabilization policies in the traditional Keynesian system. In later chapters we also shall see, however, that this nearly exclusive focus on the short run may have been an overreaction to the apparent overreliance on long-run adjustments in the classical model.

A SHIFT IN THE FOCUS OF ANALYSIS

Another philosophical issue that divided Keynes from the classical theorists was his basic approach to constructing a macroeconomic model. In the classical model, equilibrium employment of labor determines the quantity of aggregate output *supplied,* given levels of capital and land utilization—and given the state of technology. The quantity of money in circulation is the main determinant of the quantity of aggregate output *demanded.* The adjustment of saving and investment (given the government's deficit, if one exists) determines the distribution of output among owners of business firms, households, and the government sector of the economy. When household saving is equal to the sum of business investment and the governmental deficit, then households, firms, and the government are satisfied with their shares of the amount of real output produced. This adjustment achieves an equality of leakages from and reinjections into the economy's flow of income and expenditures.

Keynes turned this chronology completely around. In so doing, he greatly changed the manner in which his contemporaries and most modern economists approach the development of models of the economy. Keynes believed that economists should begin their study of how the economy works by starting with groupings of economic agents, or *sectors,* within the economy. According to Keynes, the best way to do this is to begin by considering separately the investment decisions of owners of business firms, the consumption and saving behavior of other households, and the setting of government spending and taxes. Once one understands the behavior within each of these sectors, one can then construct an aggregate model of income and spending flows. One then can integrate the role of money, interest rates, and the aggregate supply of output to build a full theory of the workings of the economy.

This Keynesian approach has for many years now been the *traditional* approach to macroeconomic model building. The remainder of this chapter provides an introduction to this traditional Keynesian model. Also discussed are the traditional Keynesian perspective on the role of saving and investment, the short-run determination of aggregate income and expenditures, and the possibility that actual output will not equal full-employment output in the short run.

THE "BUILDING-BLOCKS" APPROACH TO AGGREGATE INCOME AND EXPENDITURES

THE CIRCULAR FLOW OF INCOME AND EXPENDITURES

A key contribution of the traditional model we shall study in this chapter is that it brings to the forefront the flows of income and spending. We can examine these flows in the **circular flow diagram,** which is a conceptualization of the basic flows of income and spending in the economy during a given period of time. Figure 19-1 is a circular flow diagram. The economic agents are households and the legal entities they own, business firms. Via the markets for factors of production, households provide factor services (labor, capital, land, and entrepreneurship) to firms in exchange for factor payments (wages and salaries, interest and dividends, rents, and profits). The total amount of price-level-adjusted factor payments is **real national income,** y.

Households distribute real national income to four uses. First, households use a portion of real income to pay taxes to the government. **Real net taxes,** denoted t, are the amount of real taxes paid to the government by households, net of any *transfer payments* to households by the government. Transfer payments, such as Aid to Families with Dependent Children (AFDC) or Social Security benefits, are really flows of income that the government does not retain for its own use, but rather redistributes among households. Second, households purchase real goods and services in domestic product markets (markets for goods and services in the households' home country). The real flow of spending by households on goods and services is **real household consumption,** which we denote as c. Third, households may purchase goods and services from other countries, which is real import consumption, or just **real imports,** m. Finally, households save through financial markets the amount of real income they do not use for consumption of domestic or foreign goods or for payment of net taxes. This is called **real household saving** and is denoted as s.

NATIONAL INCOME AND PRODUCT IDENTITIES

Hence, households, *by definition,* split aggregate real income into these four categories. This implies the **national income identity,**

$$y \equiv c + s + t + m \tag{19-1}$$

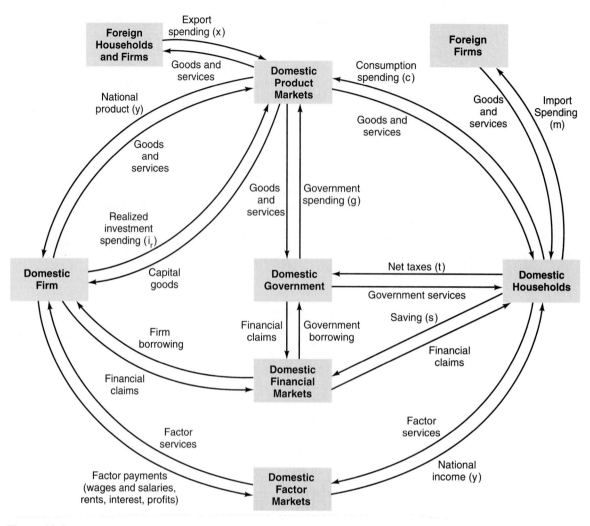

Figure 19-1

The Circular Flow of Income and Expenditures. Firms' earnings from goods and services produced and supplied through product markets ultimately flow to households, which own the firms and the factors of production. Households consume domestic and foreign goods and services, save, and pay taxes. The goods and services produced by firms are purchased by households, firms, the government, and foreign residents.

Recall that we use the "three-bar" symbol to indicate that this relation *always* must be true, whether or not our economy is in equilibrium.

Owners of business firms borrow a portion of real household saving to use in financing firm purchases of goods and services from other firms or inventories of finished goods not yet sold. Economists call actual real firm expenditures in the product markets **real realized investment,** i_r. The government borrows the remainder of household saving to fund its deficit, which will exist if its spending on goods and services, g, exceeds the real net taxes it receives from households.

Therefore, actual expenditures on goods and services produced by firms arise mainly from household consumption (c), realized investment (i_r), and government spending (g). Foreign residents, however, may also purchase goods and services produced by domestic firms. The purchases of these goods and services exported by firms to other countries are called **real export spending** (x). Consequently, total expenditures on the real output of firms in the economy *must, by definition,* be divided into these four categories of expenditures:

$$y \equiv c + i_r + g + x \qquad \text{(19-2)}$$

Equation (19-2) is the **national product identity,** which holds whether or not the economy is in equilibrium.

Note that output, y, is equal to income, y. The real aggregate expenditures that flow to firms necessarily flow, ultimately, to households, which own the firms and provide all the factors of production used to produce the firms' aggregate output.

THE BEHAVIOR OF HOUSEHOLDS AND FIRMS

Traditional macroeconomic analysis views these flows between household, firm, and government sectors of the economy, and the national income and product identities that they imply, as fundamental *building blocks.* We can use these building blocks to construct a simple model of the determination of equilibrium aggregate income and spending.

We will postpone full discussion of international issues until Unit 7. Therefore, throughout this chapter we shall assume that we have a **closed economy.** This means that there is no trade by this nation with other nations around the world. We make this assumption not because it is realistic, because it is not. What is important for now is to understand the essential features of how the economy works. We can best accomplish this goal in a closed-economy framework. (We consider how our model can account for exports and imports in the International Perspective on page 496.)

In a closed economy there are no imports or exports, and so m and x are equal to zero in Figure 19-1. This means that our national income identity becomes $y \equiv c + s + t$. The national product identity for a closed economy is $y \equiv c + i_r + g$.

The national income and product identities tell us nothing that the classical economists had not already figured out, at least on a conceptual level. To put together a truly distinguishable alternative model of the economy, we need theoretical foundations for the behavior of the household, firm, and government sectors of the economy.

HOUSEHOLD CONSUMPTION AND SAVING

The best place to begin is with the largest (typically about two-thirds) component of national income and expenditures: household consumption. The basic proposition of traditional macroeconomic analysis is that real household consumption is a function of **real disposable** (after-tax) **income.** This is a commonsensical idea, as can be seen by referring to Figure 19-1. Households receive their real income from firms in the form of wages and salaries, dividends and interest, rents, and profits. In modern economies, the government taxes wages and salaries immediately, and households pay taxes on most other forms of income with some immediacy. Hence, households *really* receive the after-tax income $y - t$, which is real disposable income, y_d.

As we can also see in Figure 19-1, a household in a closed economy can allocate this disposable income to two uses—consumption and saving. That is, we can rearrange the income identity $y \equiv c + s + t$ as $y_d \equiv y - t \equiv c + s$. The source of households' ability to consume or save is the disposable income that they earn. So it makes sense that a key determinant of their consumption and saving must be their disposable income.

Because $y_d \equiv c + s$ in a closed economy, it follows that

$$\Delta y_d \equiv \Delta c + \Delta s \qquad (19\text{-}3)$$

where the symbol Δ denotes ''change in.'' Equation (19-3) tells us that an increase in disposable income by definition is spent or saved by households. If we divide both sides of this identity by Δy_d, we find that

$$1 \equiv \frac{\Delta c}{\Delta y_d} + \frac{\Delta s}{\Delta y_d} \qquad (19\text{-}4)$$

Equation (19-4) says that the sum of the change in consumption resulting from a change in disposable income and the change in saving resulting from a change in disposable income must be equal to 1. Keynes first emphasized the two ratios on the right-hand side of equation (19-4). Keynes called the first ratio, $\Delta c/\Delta y_d$, the **marginal propensity to consume (MPC).** The marginal propensity to consume is a change in consumption induced by a change in disposable income. Keynes defined the second ratio, $\Delta s/\Delta y_d$, as the **marginal propensity to save (MPS),** because it is a change in saving induced by a change in disposable income. Equation (19-4) says that households either spend or save a 1-unit change in real disposable income, and so the MPC and the MPS must sum to 1.

Because $y_d \equiv c + s$, it is also true that (dividing both sides by y_d)

$$1 \equiv \frac{c}{y_d} + \frac{s}{y_d} \qquad (19\text{-}5)$$

Keynes termed the first ratio on the right-hand side of equation (19-5) the **average propensity to consume (APC),** and he called the second ratio the **average propensity to save (APS).** Again, because households may only spend or save disposable income in a closed economy, the APC and the APS must sum to 1.

The Consumption Function   Keynes's theory of consumption, which we shall see is a key element of the traditional model of aggregate expenditures, states that real consumption spending by households has two components. One is known as **induced consumption,** or an amount of consumption spending induced by household disposable income. The other is **autonomous consumption,** or the amount of consumption spending by households irrespective of the amount of disposable income they earn.

A simple representation of this theory is the mathematical function

$$c = c_0 + b y_d \qquad \text{where } c_0 > 0 \text{ and } 0 < b < 1 \qquad (19\text{-}6)$$

Equation (19-6) says that consumption equals a fixed amount plus an amount that depends on disposable income. This is a straight-line function with an intercept c_0 and a slope b. Both c_0 and b are positive constants. An example of this function appears in Figure 19-2. In general, even if y_d were equal to zero, this consumption function says that there would

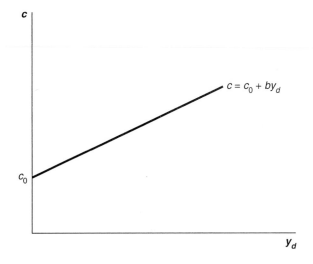

Figure 19-2
The Consumption Function.   The consumption function $c = c_0 + by_d$ has two components. *Autonomous consumption,* the amount of consumption that would occur even if households earned no disposable income, is the amount c_0. This is the vertical intercept of the consumption function. *Induced consumption,* the amount of consumption induced by disposable income, is the amount by_d. The slope of the consumption function is b, which is the marginal propensity to consume.

still be consumption of an amount c_0. Indeed, this amount of consumption takes place no matter the level of disposable income. Hence, c_0 is the real value of autonomous consumption. The amount of consumption by_d is the amount induced by disposable income, or induced consumption. As disposable income y_d increases, so does the amount of induced consumption.

Note that because c_0 is a constant, Δc_0 must equal zero. Therefore, equation (19-6) tells us that $\Delta c = b \Delta y_d$, or that $b = (\Delta c / \Delta y_d) \equiv \text{MPC}$. *The slope of this straight-line consumption function is the MPC.*

The Saving Function   Because disposable income is split between consumption and saving, Keynes's theory of household consumption automatically implies a theory of household saving. If we substitute our straight-line consumption function into the definition of disposable income, $y_d \equiv c + s$, we have $y_d = c_0 + by_d + s$ (where an equals sign, not an identity, now applies because we have substituted in an hypothesis which may or may not be true). We may rearrange this to get a straight-line function,

$$s = -c_0 + (1 - b)y_d \qquad (19\text{-}7)$$

Note that if $y_d = 0$, according to this saving function there is *dissaving* of an amount c_0. (For instance, some college students do not have jobs during the academic year, and so their disposable income is zero; they dissave by making withdrawals from their wealth to pay their expenses during the year.) Households would use this dissaving for their autonomous consumption. In general, y_d is a large positive value, and the amount of saving $(1 - b)y_d$ is the saving induced by earnings of disposable income.

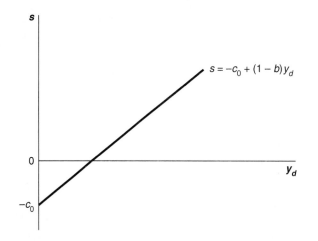

Figure 19-3

The Saving Function.   The saving function is $s = -c_0 + (1-b)y_d$. It has two components. The first, $-c_0$, is *autonomous dissaving*, or the amount that households must draw from their existing wealth to consume if they earn no disposable income. The second, $(1-b)y_d$, is *induced saving*, or the amount of saving induced by disposable income. The slope of the saving function is $1-b$, which is the marginal propensity to save. Because b is the marginal propensity to consume, this implies that the sum of the marginal propensity to consume and the marginal propensity to save is equal to 1.

Figure 19-3 depicts an example of this straight-line saving function. The slope of the saving function, $(1-b)$, is the MPS, or $1 - \text{MPC}$. Note that $b + (1-b) = 1$, and so these straight-line consumption and saving schedules imply that $\text{MPC} + \text{MPS} = 1$.

FIRM INVESTMENT BEHAVIOR

Another key component of expenditures in the economy is investment spending. Investment spending by firms occurs in two ways. One is expenditures by firms on new capital goods used by the firms to produce new goods and services. Another is expenditures by firms on *inventories* of newly produced goods that the firms have not yet sold. *Actual* capital goods and inventory expenditures, however, may turn out to be different, in light of actual economic conditions, than what firms had *intended* when they first planned their investment spending. On the one hand, total *actual* real expenditures on capital goods and on inventories of newly produced goods sum to the amount of *realized* investment, i_r that showed up in the circular flow diagram in Figure 19-1. On the other hand, the amount of *desired* real expenditures on capital goods and inventories, denoted i, may or may not equal actual realized investment. As we shall see shortly, realized firm investment and desired firm investment are equal only when the economy achieves an equilibrium flow of total income and expenditures.

As you already learned in Chapter 18, the classical economists theorized that changes in the real interest rate influence firms' desired real investment expenditures, i. The reason is that a higher real interest rate lowers the discounted present value of a given expected future stream of returns yielded by a capital good. This makes an investment expenditure on a given capital good less desirable for any given current real cost of purchasing and installing the capital good. Therefore, a firm desires to reduce its investment spending

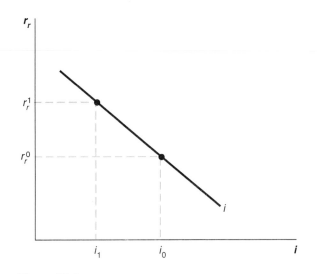

Figure 19-4
The Desired Investment Schedule.   Because the discounted present value of future returns that firms earn from current capital investment spending falls when the real interest rate rises, an increase in the real interest rate reduces real desired investment by firms. Hence, the desired investment schedule slopes downward.

when the real interest rate increases. In contrast, a lower real interest rate increases the discounted present value of a given expected future stream of returns yielded by a capital good. This makes an investment expenditure more desirable, so that a firm desires to increase its investment spending when the real interest rate falls, other things constant.

The Desired Investment Schedule   The inverse relationship between investment and the real rate of interest is shown in Figure 19-4. As shown in the figure, variations in the rate of interest between r_r^0 and r_r^1 cause the level of desired investment to vary between i_0 and i_1. Hence, there is a movement along the **desired investment schedule,** or combinations of real interest rates and corresponding levels of desired investment, when the rate of interest changes.

The Role of Profit Expectations   Keynes and his followers accepted the essential elements of this theory. Indeed, they took the theory a step further. According to the theory, an increase in the rate of interest induces lower desired investment, given the expected stream of returns from the investment. A decrease in the rate of interest induces greater desired investment, given the expected stream of returns. But it is also true that, holding the rate of interest unchanged, the valuation of a current investment expenditure depends positively upon the expected future stream of returns, or profits, that the investment project will yield in the future. If firms anticipate that business conditions will worsen in the future, then expected future profitability falls, and firms will place a lower present value on investment expenditures. Current desired investment will fall. In contrast, if firms anticipate that business conditions will improve in the future, then expected profitability rises. Firms will place a higher present value on investment expenditures, and so cuurent desired investment will rise.

Figure 19-5 illustrates that desired investment is sensitive to *both* the real interest rate *and* profit expectations of firms. The negative slope of the desired investment schedule

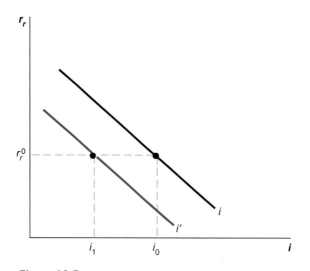

Figure 19-5

The Effect of Reduced Firm Profit Expectations on Desired Investment.   If firms anticipate that future profits will be lower, then for any given real interest rate their expectation is that the discounted stream of returns from current investment spending will be smaller. They will undertake less investment at any given real interest rate. The desired investment schedule shifts leftward, and desired real investment falls.

stems from the influence that the real rate of interest has on desired real investment. Desired investment, however, can vary even if the real interest rate remains unchanged, as shown in the figure. Increased future expected firm profitability would cause the investment schedule to shift to the right, causing desired investment to equal the amount i_0. Lower future expected firm profitability would cause the investment schedule to shift to the left, causing desired investment to equal the lower amount i_1.

Variations in Desired Investment   From a comparison of Figures 19-4 and 19-5, it is clear that observed real-world variations in investment could arise *either* from changes in the real interest rate *or* from changes in firm profit expectations. For the remainder of this chapter, we shall not seek to disentangle these separate reasons that investment might vary. We shall simply recognize that changes in either factor could cause such variations.

There are potential reasons that desired investment might vary with the aggregate level of real income (in which case, we could have some *income-induced investment*). However, we shall assume, as did Keynes, that the predominant determinants of variations in investment are variations in interest rates or in firm profit expectations. Such variations, which would cause desired investment to vary, as between i_0 and i_1 in Figures 19-4 and 19-5, could also be shown on a diagram relating real desired investment to the level of real income. As long as changes in real income have *in*significant effects on investment expenditures, desired investment is **autonomous investment**—desired investment is autonomous with respect to income. Thus, the investment function as graphed with income measured horizontally in Figure 19-6 is horizontal. Furthermore, variations in the real interest rate or in firm profit expectations that cause autonomous desired investment to vary between i_0 and i_1 would cause the autonomous investment schedule to lie somewhere between the two schedules shown in Figure 19-6.

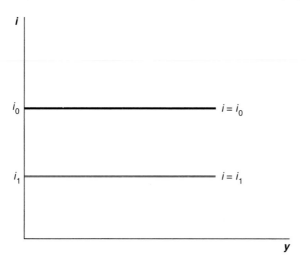

Figure 19-6
A Fall in Autonomous Desired Investment.   Because real desired investment by business firms does not depend on real income in the traditional Keynesian model, the desired investment schedule is horizontal as graphed with real income measured on the horizontal axis. Desired investment spending is *autonomous*. If real investment falls, either because of a rise in the real rate of interest or because of a fall in firms' profit expectations, autonomous investment falls, and the desired investment schedule shifts downward.

EQUILIBRIUM INCOME IN A CLOSED ECONOMY WITH NO GOVERNMENT

Obviously, governments play important roles in today's economies. Nonetheless, it often is best to begin economic models as simply as possible. We can make them more realistic once the essential elements of the models are well understood. That is the approach we shall follow. Specifically, we shall begin by assuming that the economy has no government sector.

If there is no government, then there is no government spending or taxes, and so $g = t = 0$. It follows, from the national income identity, that $y_d = y \equiv c + s$ and, from the national product identity, that $y \equiv c + i_r$ for this economy.

THE AGGREGATE EXPENDITURES SCHEDULE

Aggregate *desired* expenditures in this economy will be the sum of desired expenditures by households, which is the amount of household consumption c, and by firms, which is the amount of desired investment, i. We can determine the aggregate level of desired real expenditures at any given real income level by summing vertically the consumption function and the autonomous desired investment schedule, as illustrated in Figure 19-7. By assumption, desired investment is autonomous, so that the desired investment schedule graphed against income is horizontal (see Figure 19-6); it has a slope of zero. This means that the slope of the resulting **aggregate expenditures schedule,** $c + i$, is the same as the slope of the consumption function, which is $b = \text{MPC}$.

The aggregate expenditures schedule in Figure 19-7 tells us the level of *desired* aggre-

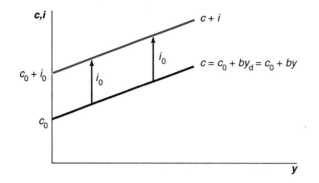

Figure 19-7

The Aggregate Expenditures Schedule in a Closed, Private Economy.   In an economy with no government, aggregate desired real expenditures are equal to household consumption spending plus desired real investment spending by firms. Therefore, if we add autonomous investment vertically to the consumption function, we obtain a schedule of levels of aggregate desired real expenditures for any given level of real income. This is the *aggregate expenditures schedule, c + i.*

gate real expenditures by households and firms corresponding to any given level of real national income. For any particular amount of real income measured on the horizontal axis of Figure 19-7, we can read up to the aggregate expenditures schedule and over to the vertical axis to find the total amount of desired expenditures by households and firms. Because the aggregate expenditures schedule tells us the total amount of real desired spending at each level of real income, it would be more accurate to call it the "real aggregate desired expenditures schedule." This would be a rather lengthy name, however, and so we shall use the shorter form, "aggregate expenditures schedule," throughout this chapter.

EQUILIBRIUM NATIONAL INCOME

The equilibrium flow of real national income is that level at which households and firms desire to spend all income earned. That is, in equilibrium, households and firms both are satisfied with the actual flow of real income and expenditures. If the flow of income and expenditures differed from the level desired by households and firms, they would have an incentive to change their spending, which in turn would change the income-expenditure flow. In equilibrium, therefore, there is no tendency for the flow of real income and expenditures to change.

Given this definition of equilibrium, we can define the equilibrium level of real national income to be the level at which aggregate desired expenditures are equal to real output produced. From the income and product identities, this is the total amount of real income received by households.

A Schedule of Equilibrium Income-Expenditure Combinations Figure 19-8 shows a schedule of all the possible combinations for which aggregate desired expenditures, measured on the vertical axis, can equal aggregate real income, y. We call this schedule the **45-degree line,** because it cuts in half the 90-degree angle of the coordinate axes in the diagram. At any given level of real income, y, it is possible to read up to the

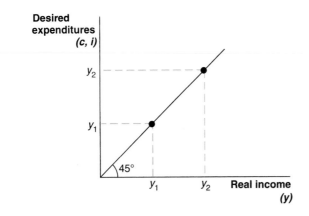

Figure 19-8
The 45-Degree Line: Schedule of Income-Expenditure Equilibrium Points. The economy is in equilibrium when aggregate desired expenditures equal aggregate real income. This will be true all along the 45-degree line. If aggregate desired expenditures equal the amount y_1, then if we read over to the 45-degree line and downward to the horizontal axis, we find that this level of spending is equal to the level of income y_1. The same would be true for a higher level of desired expenditures y_2. Therefore, any point along the 45-degree line is a possible equilibrium point for the economy.

45-degree line and over to the same level of aggregate desired expenditures. Hence, all along the 45-degree line the economy will satisfy our equilibrium condition that spending equals total income.

In our economy with no government, households and firms are the only purchasers of final goods and services. So, in equilibrium, households and firms purchase the amount of real output produced, y. Therefore,

$$y = c + i \qquad (19\text{-}8)$$

must hold in equilibrium. Attainment of this equilibrium condition is shown graphically in Figure 19-9, which superimposes Figures 19-7 and 19-8. The aggregate expenditures schedule, $c + i$, gives all possible combinations of real income and of desired aggregate household and firm expenditures (Figure 19-7). Further, the 45-degree line (Figure 19-8) gives all possible combinations of aggregate real income levels that could be equal to aggregate expenditures. Therefore, the single point at which the two schedules intersect is the single point that satisfies the equilibrium condition $y = c + i$.

Saving and Investment in Equilibrium Recall that, in the classical model, desired saving and investment were equal when the economy was in equilibrium. This means that leakages from the flow of income and expenditures in the form of household saving were, in equilibrium, reinjected into that flow in the form of business investment spending. It turns out that the economy achieves this same condition when our Keynesian economy has achieved an equilibrium level of real income.

To see this, recall first that the national income identity for this simplified economy is $y \equiv c + s$. Our condition for equilibrium national income is $y = c + i$. Substituting the

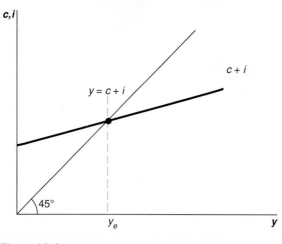

Figure 19-9
Determining Equilibrium Real Income: y = c + i.   Equilibrium real income occurs when
aggregate desired real expenditures, $c + i$, equal the aggregate level of real income, y. This will be
true at the single point where the aggregate expenditures schedule crosses the 45-degree line. The
equilibrium level of real income is y_e.

income identity for y in this equilibrium condition then tells us that, in equilibrium, $c +$
$s = c + i$, or, after subtracting c from both sides of this equality,

$$s = i \qquad\qquad (19\text{-}9)$$

That is, desired household saving is equal to desired investment expenditures when the
economy attains equilibrium real income.

Figure 19-10 shows this graphically. It displays a single autonomous investment schedule and the household saving schedule. Desired saving equals desired investment where
the schedules cross, which determines the equilibrium level of real income.

A Full Depiction of Equilibrium Real Income   To summarize, there are two equivalent (that is, one implies the other) conditions for the attainment of equilibrium real
income in our simple, government-free economy. Households and firms spend all real
income ($y = c + i$), and saving equals investment ($s = i$). Both equilibrium conditions
are shown simultaneously in Figure 19-11, in which we graph desired consumption (c),
desired saving (s), and desired investment vertically and real income horizontally. We
superimpose Figures 19-9 and 19-10 to show that both equilibrium conditions must indeed
yield the same equilibrium level of real income, y_e.

Finally, recall the national product identity, which in our simplified economy says that
$y \equiv c + i_r$, where i_r is the amount of realized, or actual, investment spending by business
firms. In equilibrium, $y = c + i$. If we substitute the national product identity for y in
the equilibrium condition, we obtain $c + i_r = c + i$, or, after subtracting c from both
sides of this equation,

$$i_r = i \qquad\qquad (19\text{-}10)$$

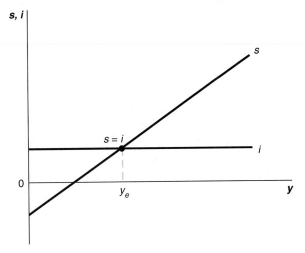

Figure 19-10
Determining Equilibrium Real Income: *s* = *i*.   Another way of expressing equilibrium for the economy is to say that real household saving (leakages from the flow of income and expenditures) must equal desired real investment spending by firms (reinjections into the flow of income and expenditures). This will occur at the income level at which s = i, which is where the saving and desired investment schedules intersect. The equilibrium level of real income is y_e.

Equation (19-10) is a third and final way that we can think of equilibrium. It says that firms must actually undertake the amount of investment spending that they *desire* to undertake. That means that, in equilibrium, firms do not purchase more capital goods or hold more inventories of finished goods than they desire to hold. Likewise, firms do not

Figure 19-11
Determining Equilibrium Real Income: *y* = *c* + *i* and *s* = *i*.   Equilibrium real income is obtained both when aggregate desired real expenditures, *c* + *i*, equal real income, *y, and* when saving, *s*, equals investment, *i*. Both equilibrium conditions yield the same equilibrium income level, y_e.

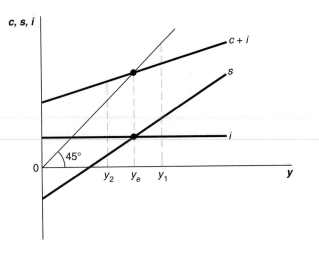

purchase less capital goods or hold fewer inventories of finished goods than they desire to hold when the economy is in equilibrium.

In Figure 19-11, if real income somehow were temporarily equal to y_1, real income (output) would exceed the level of aggregate desired expenditures ($y > c + i$), desired saving would exceed desired investment ($s > i$), and realized investment would exceed desired investment ($i_r > i$). Firms would have purchased too many capital goods and would see inventories of unsold goods accumulate above desired levels. They would reduce their purchases of new capital goods and lower their inventories. This would cause real income (output) to fall toward the equilibrium level y_e.

In contrast, if real income somehow were temporarily equal to the amount y_2, aggregate desired expenditures would exceed the level of real income, or output ($c + i > y$), desired investment would exceed desired saving ($i > s$), and desired investment would exceed realized investment ($i > i_r$). Firms would not have purchased enough capital goods and would observe their inventories of finished goods fall below desired levels. Therefore, they would begin to increase their purchases of new capital goods and raise their inventories of finished goods. This would cause equilibrium real income (output) to rise back toward the equilibrium level y_e.

RECESSIONARY AND INFLATIONARY GAPS

As discussed earlier, the traditional model we are constructing illustrates Keynes's claims that the economy could reach an *equilibrium* level of real income and output that differs from the full-employment level. While we are not yet in a position to explain fully how this may occur (we reserve this issue for Chapter 21), we *can* explore this possibility using the simple model we have constructed.

Consider Figure 19-12. Displayed in the figure are three possible levels of real income. One, labeled y_f, is the level of real income (output) at full employment. The other two,

Figure 19-12

Recessionary and Inflationary Gaps.   If the full-employment level of real income is y_f but the economy finds itself in equilibrium at point *C*, then the distance $A - B$ is a *recessionary gap*. This is the amount by which aggregate desired expenditures would have to increase for the economy to be at the full-employment income level. In contrast, if the economy is in equilibrium at point *E*, then the distance $D - A$ is an *inflationary gap*, which is the amount by which aggregate desired expenditures would have to fall for the economy to be at the full-employment income level.

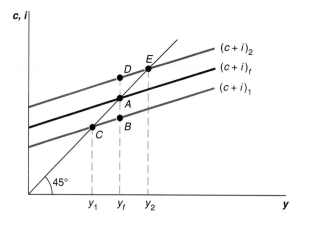

labeled y_1 and y_2, show *equilibrium* levels of real national income, given the desired levels of aggregate expenditures, $(c + i)_1$ and $(c + i)_2$, that lie below and above the full-employment income level.

When the economy finds itself at an equilibrium at point C with equilibrium real income y_1, it is producing an output level that has fallen below full employment, and so a recession exists. More precisely, in Figure 19-12, a **recessionary gap** equal to the distance $A - B$ exists. We define a recessionary gap as the amount by which the quantity of national real income (output) exceeds the quantity of aggregate desired expenditures at the full-employment level of real income. If the economy found itself in this situation, unemployment would exist.

Recall that *nominal* income is equal to Y, which by definition is the product of real income y and the level of prices P. Although we have maintained the assumption of fixed prices throughout this chapter, note we could have measured nominal, rather than real, income on the horizontal axis in Figure 19-12, and we could have measured nominal, rather than real, expenditures on the vertical axis. In fact, followers of Keynes often made no distinction between the two. For this reason, they argued that in a recessionary gap there also is a tendency for nominal income to be too low in comparison to the full-employment level. From this perspective, it is natural to think of a recessionary gap as a situation in which there is a natural tendency for prices to fall.

In contrast, when the economy is at point E, with equilibrium real income level y_2, equilibrium desired expenditures are greater than the amount of output that firms can produce when they fully employ all resources. If we had instead measured nominal income and spending on the horizontal and vertical axes, this also would have implied higher nominal income than would be consistent with the value of output produced. Viewed from this alternative perspective that traditional Keynesian theorists commonly adopt, there would be significant upward pressure exerted on the prices of goods and services. Therefore, traditional Keynesian theorists call the distance $D - A$ an **inflationary gap.** Thus, as we shall explore more fully in Chapter 21, in the traditional Keynesian model inflation is only likely to be a significant problem when the economy is at or very near its full-employment level of output.

Suppose that the economy were in either a recessionary gap or inflationary gap situation. In either case, the problem would be the existence of a mismatch of actual desired expenditures with the level of desired expenditures, labeled $(c + i)_f$, needed to attain the full-employment level of real income, y_f, as the actual equilibrium level for the economy. The implication is that, in a recessionary gap, the economy would need to experience some increase in autonomous expenditures to increase the aggregate level of desired expenditures. In an inflationary gap, a reduction in autonomous expenditures would be necessary.

MULTIPLIER ANALYSIS

The existence of recessionary or inflationary gaps suggests the justification for and the proper direction for governmental policies. Indeed, Keynes's belief that the nearly laissez-faire (at least, by today's "big-government" standards) economy during the Great Depression was trapped in a sizable recessionary gap was the reason that he promoted a more direct governmental role in seeking to end the Great Depression.

It is one thing to construct graphs such as that in Figure 19-12 and then to envision "eliminating" undesirable gaps by shifting aggregate expenditure schedules in a textbook or on a blackboard. It is quite another to determine the proper "real-world" *quantities* involved. This section deals only with the theoretical relationship between shifts in the aggregate expenditures schedule and changes in the equilibrium level of real national income. Clearly, before policy makers can construct a successful monetary policy or fiscal policy, they must have a firm grasp of the amounts by which variations in aggregate expenditures actually change equilibrium national income.

As Figure 19-12 indicates, changes in the position of the aggregate expenditures schedule clearly will alter the equilibrium level of real national income. The issue, of course, is the magnitude of the effect of a shift of the aggregate expenditures schedule upon real income. In general, as we shall see, a given 1-unit change in the position of the aggregate expenditures schedule has a greater-than-1-unit (multiple) effect on equilibrium income.

Aggregate Autonomous Expenditures and Shifts of the Aggregate Expenditures Schedule   What causes a shift of the aggregate expenditures schedule? To answer this question, it is helpful to take a look at the *equation* for the aggregate expenditures schedule. Suppose that the amount of autonomous investment is equal to a level i_0. Also, keep in mind that because there is no government in our simple model of an economy, y_d is equal to $y;$ disposable income is the same as total income if there are no taxes. Because the aggregate expenditures schedule is constructed by adding the consumption function together with autonomous investment, the level of aggregate expenditures then is equal to

$$c + i = (c_0 + i_0) + by \qquad (19\text{-}11)$$

where $c = c_0 + by_d$ is the consumption function, and because real income (y) and disposable income are the same, $c = c_0 + by$. Also, we have substituted $i = i_0$, the level of real autonomous desired investment, for i on the right-hand side of equation (19-11). Equation (19-11) is a straight-line equation. Figure 19-3 is a graph of this equation. The slope of the schedule is equal to b, which is the MPC. The vertical intercept of the schedule is $c_0 + i_0$. This latter amount is the sum of autonomous consumption and autonomous investment, which we shall call **aggregate autonomous expenditures.** The quantity $b \times y$ in equation (19-11) is **income-induced consumption,** the amount of household consumption spending induced by real income that households receive.

The only way that a straight-line function can shift upward or downward is if the vertical intercept of the function changes. Likewise, the only way that the autonomous expenditure schedule can shift upward or downward to yield a new equilibrium level of real income is if the intercept of the schedule, the amount of aggregate autonomous expenditures, increases or decreases.

Figure 19-13 illustrates an example of a downward shift in the autonomous expenditures schedule. In the example, this downward shift results from a fall in aggregate autonomous expenditures caused by a reduction in autonomous investment ($\Delta i_0 < 0$). This reduction in autonomous investment, as we discussed earlier, could arise from an increase in the real rate of interest or from a fall in firms' profit expectations.

The Multiplier Effect   As we can see in Figure 19-13, the fall in aggregate autonomous expenditures (given by the distance $A - C = \Delta i_0$) causes equilibrium real income to fall (by the distance $D - B = y_1 - y_2 = \Delta y$). The decrease in real income (Δy) exceeds the value of the reduction in aggregate autonomous expenditures (Δi_0). This means that the reduction in autonomous expenditures has a **multiplier effect** on equilibrium income. That is, a given 1-unit reduction in aggregate autonomous expenditures has a greater-than-1-unit effect, in the same direction, on equilibrium real income.

To see why this is true, recall that our condition for equilibrium real income in our simple economy is $y = c + i$. From equation (19-11), the total amount of desired

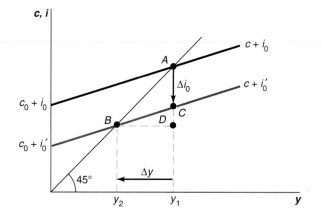

Figure 19-13
The Effect on Equilibrium Income of a Fall in Autonomous Desired Investment.   A reduction in autonomous desired investment, which could be caused by a higher real interest rate or a fall in firms' profit expectations, would reduce aggregate desired expenditures. The aggregate expenditures schedule would shift downward by the distance $A - C$, which would be the amount of the reduction in desired investment. Equilibrium income would be reduced by the distance $D - B$, or $y_1 - y_2$.

expenditures, $c + i$, is equal to $(c_0 + i_0) + by$ for this economy. Substituting this quantity for $c + i$ on the the right-hand side of our income equilibrium condition then tells us that $(c_0 + i_0) + by$. We can subtract the quantity by from both sides to get an equivalent representation of our equation, which is $(1 - b)y = (c_0 + i_0)$. Finally, we can divide both sides of this last equation by $(1 - b)$ to derive *an expression for equilibrium real income,* which is

$$y_e = \frac{1}{1 - b} (c_0 + i_0) \qquad\qquad \textbf{(19-12)}$$

Recall that the MPC is the portion of an additional unit of disposable income that households use for consumption. Therefore, b, the MPC, is a fraction between zero and 1. It follows that $1/(1 - b)$ must be the reciprocal of a fraction, or an amount greater than 1. From equation (19-12), this means that equilibrium income in our laissez-faire economy is always a multiple of aggregate autonomous expenditures, $c_0 + i_0$.

Furthermore, any change in aggregate autonomous expenditures is multiplied by $1/(1 - b)$ to cause a change in the equilibrium level of real income. In the diagram in Figure 19-12, for instance, the amount of the fall in equilibrium real income (the distance $D - B = \Delta y$) must be equal to $1/(1 - b)$ times the fall in aggregate autonomous expenditures (the distance $A - C = \Delta i_0$), or, in equation form,

$$\Delta y = \frac{1}{1 - b} \Delta i_0 \qquad\qquad \textbf{(19-13)}$$

Economists call the factor $1/(1 - b)$ the **autonomous expenditures multiplier.** It is a measure of the size of the multiplier effect on equilibrium real national income of a change in the level of autonomous expenditures. Because b is the MPC, the amount of this multiplier in this economy is equal to $M = 1/(1 - \text{MPC}) = 1/\text{MPS}$ (because MPC + MPS = 1). Hence, the autonomous expenditures multiplier M is equal to 1 divided by 1 minus the marginal propensity to consume. Because the marginal propensities to consume and to save sum to 1, the multiplier also is the inverse of the marginal propensity to save.

Consider the following example. Suppose that the value of the MPC is equal to 0.75, so that each dollar increase in disposable income induces an increase in consumption of 75 cents, or that each dollar reduction in disposable income induces a decrease in consumption of 75 cents. Suppose that autonomous net investment falls by $\Delta i_0 = \$1$ million, perhaps because the real interest rate increases or firms' expectations of future profitability fall. If this fall in autonomous investment implies a reduction of $1 million in firms' purchases of machines, then the real incomes of machine builders fall by $1 million. But this is not the only effect on real incomes in the economy as a whole. Because machine builders' incomes fall by $1 million, they must also reduce their consumption spending by $750,000 (because the MPC is equal to 0.75). Their saving must fall by $250,000 (because the MPS is equal to $1 - \text{MPC}$, or 0.25). The $750,000 reduction in consumption expenditures by machine builders is a fall in the incomes of groups from whom machine builders would have purchased goods and services. Thus, aggregate income now falls by an additional $750,000, and so aggregate income is now lower by $1.75 million.

At this point, a $1 million decrease in aggregate autonomous expenditures has caused national income to fall by $1.75 million. Moreover, the process is not yet complete, because the group whose income has fallen by $750,000 now will spend less ($0.75 \times \$750,000 = \$562,500$ less) and will save less ($0.25 \times \$750,000 = \$187,500$ less) than before. Furthermore, the reduced amount that it spends on consumption will be an income reduction for still another group, and so on. The total amount of the reduction in income will be a large sum ($\$1,000,000 + \$750,0000 + \$562,500 + \ldots$) of income reductions across groups within the economy.

Using the autonomous expenditures multiplier, $M = 1/(1 - \text{MPC})$, we may compute the amount of this total reduction in income. This reduction is equal to $[1/(1 - 0.75)] \times -\$1$ million $= (1/0.25) \times -\$1$ million $= 4 \times -\$1$ million $= -\$4$ million.

The fact that a fall in autonomous aggregate expenditures generates a multiple reduction in equilibrium real income was, according to Keynes, a possible explanation for the Great Depression. For instance, if y_1 in Figure 19-12 had been the full-employment level of real income, then the fall in autonomous investment spending Δi_0 would cause a recessionary gap to exist at the new, lower equilibrium level of real income y_2. One way that the economy could recover from this recession would be for autonomous investment to rise back to its original level. Another would be for autonomous consumption, by some coincidence, to rise by exactly the amount that autonomous investment originally fell. Keynes and his followers did not believe that a laissez-faire economy was capable of such coincidentally offsetting changes in autonomous spending. This is why they argued that there was a key role for governmental action in the economy.

ADDING THE GOVERNMENT SECTOR

By taking into account the activities of the government, the basic Keynesian model changes in two ways. First, the government purchases goods and services in an amount equal to g. Second, the government raises revenues, net of any transfer payments it makes, by assessing a net amount of taxes equal to t.

EQUILIBRIUM REAL INCOME WITH A GOVERNMENT SECTOR

Government expenditures influence the aggregate expenditures schedule directly, while taxes affect the schedule indirectly through the consumption function. For ease of exposition, let's assume that g and t are autonomous with respect to national income, so that aggregate desired expenditures are equal to

$$c + i + g = c_0 + b(y - t_0) + i_0 + g_0 \qquad \text{(19-14)}$$

where $g = g_0$ is the amount of autonomous government spending and $t = t_0$ is the amount of autonomous net taxes. We assume here that taxes are an autonomous lump sum. This is a little unrealistic, because many government taxes are collected on income earnings of households and firms, but autonomous, lump-sum taxes are much easier to consider in an economic model.

Equation (19-14) shows that the consumption function must take into account the effects of taxes, because disposable income, y_d, is defined to be total income y less net taxes t. Rearranging equation (19-14) gives us

$$c + i + g = (c_0 - bt_0 + i_0 + g_0) + by \qquad \text{(19-15)}$$

That is, real aggregate desired expenditures by households, firms, and the government have two components. One is **net aggregate autonomous expenditures,** $c_0 - bt_0 + i_0 + g_0$. Net aggregate autonomous expenditures are equal to autonomous consumption, c_0, net of the consumption-reducing effect of taxes, bt_0, or **net autonomous consumption,** plus autonomous desired firm investment, i_0, plus autonomous government spending, g_0. The other component of aggregate desired expenditures in our more realistic economy with a government sector, again, is *income-induced consumption, by,* which is the amount of spending by households that is induced by real income.

A comparison of this equation with the previous equation for aggregate expenditures in the traditional model *without* government,

$$c + i = (c_0 + i_0) + by \qquad \text{(19-11)}$$

indicates that

1. The introduction of government expenditures causes the aggregate expenditures schedule to shift upward by the amount g_0, because the vertical intercept, which is the amount of *net aggregate autonomous expenditures,* rises by that amount. Furthermore, changes in autonomous government expenditures (Δg_0) cause the vertical intercept to shift dollar for dollar, just like changes in autonomous consumption (Δc_0) and autonomous investment (Δi_0).

2. The introduction of net autonomous taxes causes the aggregate expenditures schedule to shift downward by the amount bt_0, or by the MPC times the amount of net autonomous taxes. This is true because the vertical intercept, which is the amount of *net aggregate autonomous expenditures,* falls by that amount. Furthermore, a change in autonomous net taxes (Δt_0) causes the aggregate expenditures schedule to shift in the *opposite* direction from the tax change. This is true because an increase in net autonomous taxes reduces net autonomous consumption, $c_0 - bt_0$.

Equilibrium Real Income   Our equilibrium condition is still that all real income ultimately is spent, even for our closed economy *with* a government sector, and so this condition is

$$y = c + i + g \tag{19-16}$$

Substituting equation (19-5) into the right-hand side of equation (19-16) and solving for y yields the equilibrium level of real income when there is a government sector:

$$y = \frac{1}{1 - b}(c_0 + i_0 + g_0 - bt_0) \tag{19-17}$$

According to this expression, the autonomous government spending multiplier M_g will be equal to $1/(1 - b)$, which is also the autonomous investment multiplier and the autonomous consumption multiplier, $M = 1/(1 - \text{MPC})$.

Multipliers deal with shifts in the aggregate expenditures schedule, and changes in net taxes shift the aggregate expenditures schedule by *less* than \$1 for each \$1 tax change. To compute the tax multiplier (M_t), we use equation (19-17) to calculate the change in income resulting from a change in taxes, with autonomous consumption, investment, and government spending constant. A change in t would then be multiplied by $-b$ and by $1/(1 - b)$, to give us the resulting change in income. Hence, the tax multiplier is equal to $-b/(1 - b)$, or $-\text{MPC}/(1 - \text{MPC})$, which is negative (because an increase in net taxes shifts the aggregate expenditure schedule *downward*) and less than $1/(1 - b)$.

To summarize, three multipliers are important in the traditional Keynesian model. One is the autonomous expenditures multiplier, $M = 1/(1 - \text{MPC})$. This multiplier tells us how much equilibrium real income changes following any given change in net aggregate autonomous expenditures by households, firms, and the government. Changes in government spending cause a multiplier effect exactly equal to the value of this autonomous expenditures multiplier, and so the government expenditures multiplier is $M_g = M = 1/(1 - \text{MPC})$. Changes in autonomous, lump-sum taxes reduce net autonomous expenditures, and so the tax multiplier is negative and equal to $M_t = -\text{MPC}/(1 - \text{MPC})$.

Equilibrating Leakages and Reinjections with a Government Sector   Note that, from the national income identity, $y \equiv c + s + t$. Substituting this identity into the left-hand side of the equilibrium condition, $y = c + i + g$, implies that $c + s + t = c + i + g$, or that, in equilibrium,

$$s + t = i + g \tag{19-18}$$

This condition says that *total net leakages* from the flow of income and expenditures, in the form of voluntary saving by households and taxing by governments, are, in equilibrium, reinjected into the economy via firm investment spending and government expenditures. We can rearrange equation (19-18) slightly, by subtracting t from both sides of the equation, so that $s + t - t = i + g - t$, which tells us that $s = i + (g - t)$ in equilibrium. This equation is reminiscent of the classical condition that household saving is equal to desired investment plus the government deficit. In this traditional Keynesian model, however, this condition is just an alternative way of determining the equilibrium level of real income rather than a means of determining the interest rate.

IS ALL GOVERNMENT SPENDING THE SAME?

In our simple version of the traditional Keynesian model, the government expenditures multiplier, M_g, has the same value, $1/(1 - MPC)$, no matter what type of government expenditures are undertaken. Not all economists agree that this is a realistic result. Indeed, some contend that the size of the government expenditures multiplier varies with the type of expenditures undertaken by the government.

Federal, state, and local governments purchase a wide variety of goods and services. For instance, the federal government purchases military goods, provides services, and pays for *infrastructure capital*, which consists of goods such as roads and highways, dams and sewer systems, aircraft traffic control centers, and waterway navigation and port facilities. State and local governments typically make similar types of expenditures, although their military commitments are much smaller.

Some economists, including David Aschauer, argue that the true multiplier effect of government expenditures on infrastructure capital is much greater than the multiplier effect of government military and service expenditures. The argument that Aschauer puts forward is that expenditures on infrastructure capital have positive *complementary* effects on private investment. By this, he means that greater availability of good roads, airports, waterways, and fresh water and sewage systems improves the long-term productive capability of private firms that use these goods. Spending on military and public services, in contrast, are once-and-for-all expenditures with smaller, if any, lasting benefits, according to Aschauer.

On the one hand, Aschauer has estimated that, for the period 1945–1985, the government expenditures multiplier associated with spending on infrastructure capital in the United States had a value of about 4. That is, each real-dollar increase in expenditures on goods such as roads, dams, and so on caused a fourfold increase in the economy's equilibrium level of real income, according to his measurements. On the other hand, Aschauer found that changes in other types of government spending, such as military spending and public service expenditures, had little measurable multiplier effect on real income. Aschauer interprets these results as consistent with his hypothesis that only government spending on infrastructure capital has an important, sustained multiplier effect on real income.

There are possible weaknesses in Aschauer's conclusions. For instance, military expenditures might not produce a *measurable* gain in output, but there might be an *implicit* gain from the fact that a country's military protects its economy from harm or, in the nuclear age, destruction by a malevolent foreign power. This implicit gain would be nearly impossible to measure. In addition, public service expenditures that include direct outlays to manage and sustain transfer programs may constitute public investments in *human capital,* which is the economic term for the abilities, skills, and health of the people in an economy. Benefits arising from human capital gains that public service spending yields also would be hard to measure. For this reason, Aschauer's results are certain to generate heated debate among economists.

Source: David Alan Aschauer, "Is Government Spending Stimulative?" Contemporary Policy Issues, 8 (4, October 1990), pp. 30–46.

STABILIZING AGGREGATE INCOME

This traditional model implies that recessionary gaps and inflationary gaps are common and that a full-employment, price-stable equilibrium is an unlikely (barring extreme coincidences) situation. The reason is that equilibrium real income will be equal to the amount that is consistent with the level of aggregate desired expenditures. It will not necessarily be equal to the full-employment level of real income.

We can think of governmental stabilization policy making in the traditional model as the discretionary activity of policy makers with respect to changes in autonomous government expenditures *g* and net autonomous taxes *t*. **Fiscal policy** actions, which are variations

OPENING UP THE MODEL— INTERNATIONAL TRADE

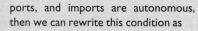

To keep the analysis simple in this chapter, we assumed that the model economy was "closed"—that there were no exports (x) or imports (m). Until the 1970s, this was a very good approximation for the United States, because until that decade exports and imports each were rarely much more than 5 percent of U.S. GDP. Since the mid-1970s, however, these relative magnitudes have roughly doubled. Let's briefly consider, therefore, how to modify our simple Keynesian model to account for international trade.

We know from equation (19-1) that real national income by definition is equal to $y \equiv c + s + t + m$, and we know from equation (19-2) that real national product (output) by definition is equal to $y \equiv c + i_r + g + x$. In *equilibrium*, however, all income is spent: real income, y, is equal to total aggregate desired expenditures by U.S. citizens. Total desired expenditures in an *open economy* (one with international trade) include household consumption on domestic output (c), firm investment (i), government spending (g), *and* net spending by foreign residents on American goods. The latter quantity is the amount of export purchases by foreigners (x) less the amount of import purchases by Americans (m), or *net exports* ($x - m$).

Hence, the real income equilibrium condition for an open economy with international trade is given by

$$y = c + i + g + (x - m)$$

If the economy's consumption function is $c = c_0 + b(y - t)$ and if investment, government spending, ex-

ports, and imports are autonomous, then we can rewrite this condition as

$$y = c_0 + b(y - t_0) + g_0 + (x_0 - m_0)$$

where x_0 is the amount of autonomous export spending by foreigners and m_0 is the level of autonomous import spending by Americans. We can solve the above equation for y to get

$$y = [1/(1 - b)][c_0 + i_0 + g_0 - bt_0 + (x_0 - m_0)]$$

as a revised expression for equilibrium real income in an open economy.

From this expression, we can see that as long as exports and imports are autonomous, the autonomous expenditures multiplier is still equal to $1/(1 - b)$, or $1/(1 - MPC)$. We can now see, however, that autonomous changes in international trade also exert multiplier effects on equilibrium real income. For instance, an increase in exports of American goods and services to other nations raises equilibrium real income in the United States by the amount $\Delta y = [1/(1 - MPC)]\Delta x_0$, while an increase in imports of foreign goods and services into the United States *reduces* American real income by $\Delta y \equiv -[1/(1 - MPC)]\Delta m_0$.

We can see from this elaboration of our basic Keynesian model one reason why American citizens and policy makers recently have become so concerned about the fact that American exports generally have *fallen* while foreign imports have increased during the last decade (see Chapter 28). These changes in American flows of international trade both tend to have *negative* multiplier effects on aggregate American real income.

in g or t (or both), can shift the aggregate expenditures schedule in desirable directions. In principle, fiscal policy actions can eliminate recessionary and inflationary gaps.

COUNTERCYCLICAL FISCAL POLICY

In principle, fiscal policy actions may be used to eliminate recessionary or inflationary gaps. If fiscal policy actions are to eliminate a recessionary gap, the aggregate expenditures schedule must shift upward by a sufficient amount. Some combination of increased government spending or reduced net taxes can do precisely that. If a **balanced budget** for the government (governmental purchases of goods and services are equal to taxes net of public transfer payments, or $g = t$) initially existed, then a **budget deficit** ($g > t$) would now exist. Thus, government must undertake **deficit spending** (financed by borrowing) to eliminate recessionary gaps.

In contrast, if an inflationary gap exists, the government must shift the aggregate expenditures schedule downward to bring the economy to a full-employment, price-stable equilibrium. Fiscal policy requires some combination of decreased g and increased t. In other words, a **budget surplus** ($g < t$) or a smaller deficit is appropriate in times of inflation, in order to cool down the economy. In practice, politicians have been more enthusiastic about engaging in deficit spending than they have been about running budget surpluses. The facts are that since the 1950s the United States government has increased taxes *and* government purchases of goods and services dramatically.

We may conclude that our traditional model of the determination of aggregate real income suggests that a key role for governmental policy makers is to conduct a **countercyclical fiscal policy.** Under this approach, the government runs budget deficits (or reduces budget surpluses) when autonomous investment or net autonomous consumption falls below the levels consistent with full employment, causing recessionary gaps. The government runs budget surpluses (or reduces budget deficits) when autonomous investment or net autonomous consumption rises above the levels consistent with full employment, causing inflationary gaps. This is the primary policy recommendation that Keynes drew from this theoretical approach.

We have derived this traditional Keynesian recommendation for a countercyclical fiscal policy from a model of the short run in which a role for price-level adjustments has been ignored in our discussion of recessionary and inflationary gaps. Keynes and his followers argued, nonetheless, that following short-run discretionary policy from period to period is consistent with doing what is best for the economy over the long haul. In short, Keynes and his followers felt this countercyclical fiscal policy was consistent with achieving both the best possible short-run *and* long-run outcomes for the economy.

Of course, this is a textbook in money and banking, and so far we have had nothing to say about the role of monetary policy in the traditional Keynesian framework. This is because we have not yet treated the role of money explicitly in the traditional model. We turn to that topic in the next chapter, in which we also discuss Keynes's views on monetary policy.

CHAPTER SUMMARY

1. The Great Depression undermined the classical model and paved the way for the Keynesian model.

2. Keynes disputed five features of the classical theorists' approach, including their views on the functioning of the labor market, on the demand for money, on the determinants of saving and investment, on the role of short-run analysis versus long-run analysis, and on the best way to construct a theory of aggregate income and expenditures.

3. In the basic traditional model, which emphasizes the short run, the role of price-level adjustments largely is ignored, and the model determines the equilibrium level of real national income at levels less than and up to the full-employment income level.

4. Aggregate desired expenditures, which represent the amount of desired spending by all rele-

vant sectors of the the economy at each level of national income, are the primary determinant of the equilibrium level of national income.

5. Desired real investment spending by business firms depends upon *both* the real interest rate *and* firms' profit expectations. Because profit expectations can vary considerably over time, desired investment can be quite volatile even if the real interest rate is constant.

6. In the traditional model, household consumption is a stable function of real disposable (after-tax) income. Total consumption is the sum of autonomous consumption, which is independent from the level of income, and induced consumption, which varies positively with disposable income.

7. The aggregate expenditures schedule in a closed economy is the sum of desired consumption, investment, and government spending. The intercept of this schedule is equal to net aggregate autonomous expenditures by consumers, firms, and the government. When investment, government spending, and net taxes are autonomous, the slope of the aggregate expenditures schedule is equal to the slope of the consumption function, the marginal propensity to consume, which is a fraction.

8. When the economy is in equilibrium, all real income is spent, and so aggregate real expenditures are equal to aggregate real income, which occurs at the single point at which the aggregate expenditures schedule crosses the 45-degree line.

9. Changes in aggregate autonomous expenditures change the value of the intercept of the aggregate expenditures schedule, which causes it to shift vertically and to yield multiple changes in the level of equilibrium national income. The main determinant of the multiplier is the slope of the aggregate expenditures schedule.

10. Inflationary gaps and recessionary gaps occur when the aggregate expenditures schedule does not intersect the 45-degree line at the full-employment income level. A full-employment, price-stable equilibrium requires that such gaps be eliminated. In principle, such gaps can be reduced by countercyclical fiscal policy.

GLOSSARY

Aggregate autonomous expenditures: Aggregate desired expenditures, including autonomous consumption and autonomous investment, that are independent of the level of national income.

Aggregate expenditures schedule: A schedule that represents total desired expenditures by all the relevant sectors of the economy at each and every level of real national income during some period of time.

Autonomous consumption: Household consumption spending that is independent of the level of national income.

Autonomous expenditures multiplier: A measure of the magnitude of the multiplier effect on equilibrium real income caused by a change in aggregate autonomous expenditures; in the simple traditional model, $1/(1 - MPC) = 1/MPS$.

Autonomous investment: Desired investment that is independent of the level of national income.

Average propensity to consume (APC): Total household consumption divided by total disposable income; the portion of disposable income devoted to consumption spending.

Average propensity to save (APS): Total household saving divided by total disposable income; the portion of disposable income devoted to saving.

Balanced budget: Budget that results when government purchases of goods and services (g) are equal to taxes net of public transfer payments (t); $g = t$.

Budget deficit: Condition that exists when government spending exceeds net taxes.

Budget surplus: Condition that exists when government spending is less than net tax revenues.

Circular flow diagram: A conceptualization of the basic flows of income and spending in the economy during a given period of time.

Closed economy: An economy in which there are no imports or exports. In an economic model, this asumption allows the study of essential features of the economy without having to account for complicating (though more realistic) factors.

Countercyclical fiscal policy: An approach that encourages the government to run budget deficits when there is a recession and to run budget surpluses when inflation occurs.

Deficit spending: Spending financed by borrowing.

Desired investment schedule: Combinations of real interest rates and corresponding levels of desired real investment spending.

Fiscal policy: A short-hand term for intentional variations in expenditures and/or net taxes by governmental policy makers to stabilize national income.

Forty-five-degree line: A schedule of points for which an amount measured on the horizontal axis is equal to the corresponding amount measured on the vertical axis; in the traditional Keynesian model, a schedule of combinations of aggregate desired expenditures and real national income for which the economy is in equilibrium.

Income-induced consumption: The amount of household consumption spending induced by real income that households receive.

Inflationary gap: The amount by which aggregate desired expenditures exceed real output at the full-employment level of real national income.

Marginal propensity to consume (MPC):   The additional consumption caused by an increase in disposable income; a change in consumption spending divided by a corresponding change in disposable income; the slope of the consumption function as graphed against disposable income.

Marginal propensity to save (MPS):   The additional saving caused by an increase in disposable income; a change in saving divided by a corresponding change in disposable income; the slope of the saving function as graphed against disposable income.

Multiplier effect: The ratio of a change in the equilibrium level of national income to an increase in autonomous aggregate expenditures. When the aggregate expenditure schedule shifts vertically, the equilibrium level of national income changes by a multiple of the amount of the shift.

National income identity: An identity that states that real national income equals real household consumption plus real household saving plus real net taxes plus real imports, or $y \equiv c + s + t + m$.

National product identity: Identity that states that real national product equals household consumption plus real realized investment plus government spending plus real export spending, or $y \equiv c + i_r + g + x$.

Net aggregate autonomous expenditures: Expenditures equal to autonomous consumption, net of the consumption-reducing effect of taxes, plus autonomous desired investment and autonomous government spending.

Net autonomous consumption: Autonomous consumption, net of the consumption-reducing effect of taxes.

Real disposable income: A household's after-tax income.

Real export spending: Real value of goods and services produced by domestic firms and exported to other countries.

Real household consumption: The real flow of spending by households on goods and services.

Real household saving: The amount of income that households save through financial markets.

Real imports: The flow of spending by households for the purchase of goods and services from other countries.

Real national income: The total amount of price-level-adjusted factor payments (wages and salaries, interest and dividends, rents, and profits).

Real net taxes: The amount of real taxes paid to the government by households, net of any transfer payments (such as Social Security benefits) to households by the government.

Real realized investment: Actual real firm expenditures in the product markets.

Recessionary gap: The amount by which equilibrium real income exceeds aggregate desired expenditures at the full-employment level of real income.

SELF-TEST QUESTIONS

1. A simple representation of the Keynesian consumption function is $c = c_0 + by_d$. Define and briefly explain each of the two components of desired consumption incorporated into this function. Draw a diagram of the consumption function. What is its slope? What is the economic interpretation of the value of its slope?

2. Suppose that real investment spending is observed to fall. More than one factor could have caused this reduction in investment. List some possible explanations.

3. Use an appropriate diagram to show how the aggregate desired expenditures schedule is derived. On the same diagram, show the equilibrium level of real national income implied by the position of the schedule you have constructed. Why is this the equilibrium income level?

4. Prove that, in an economy with no government, the equilibrium condition $y = c + i$ can also be written as $s = i$ and as $i_r = i$, where i_r represents realized, or actual, investment.

5. In the basic Keynesian model of real income determination, equilibrium occurs where the level of national income is equal to the amount of aggregate desired spending by households, firms, and the government. However, it is possible for desired spending to exceed national income. Explain how equilibrium is reattained if this occurs.

6. Suppose that there was a change in aggregate behavior such that all households save a larger fraction of their incomes than previously was the case. Using whatever diagrams are helpful, illustrate the effects that this behavioral change would have on the consumption function and on equilibrium national income.

PROBLEMS

19-1. In the simple Keynesian model, suppose that MPC $= 0.8$. If disposable income increased from $80 billion to $100 billion, by how much would consumption rise? By how much would saving rise? Is the sum of your two answers equal to the change in income?

19-2. The simple Keynesian consumption function can be written as $c = c_0 + by_d$. Although the MPC is constant, show algebraically how the APC, which is equal to c/y_d, nevertheless would change as y_d changed if $c_0 > 0$.

19-3. If the consumption function is $c = \$20 + (0.8)y_d$, determine the level of consumption and the level of saving for $y_d = \$50$, 150, and 250. Compute the associated values of the APC.

19-4. If there is no government, if the consumption function is $c = \$20 + (0.8)y_d$, and if the level of desired investment is $i = \$10$, then determine the level of aggregate desired expenditures for $y = \$50, \$150$, and $\$250$. Determine the level of real income that satisfies the condition that saving is equal to desired investment.

19-5. Suppose that the consumption function is $c = \$20 + (0.8)y_d$, and the level of desired investment is $i = \$10$. Finally, suppose that there is no government. If i changed to $\$12$, what variables would change in the simple Keynesian model? Determine the ratio of the change in equilibrium real income to the change in desired investment that caused the change in real income. Is your answer consistent with the value of the multiplier?

19-6. Suppose that the consumption function again is $c = \$20 + (0.8)y_d$ and that the level of investment is $i = \$10$. Also suppose that the levels of government expenditures and net taxes are $g_0 = t_0 = \$5$. Determine the level of real national income that is equal to the level of aggregate desired expenditures. As compared with your answer to problem 20-4, what is the effect on the equilibrium level of real national income of adding this amount of government spending and net taxes to the model?

19-7. Suppose that the level of government spending is equal to $\$100$ billion (in base-year dollars) and that the level of real net taxes is equal to $\$50$ billion. In equilibrium, will saving be equal to real desired investment? Why or why not?

19-8. Suppose that equilibrium real income, in base-year dollars, is $y = \$500$ billion. The consumption function is $c = \$50 + (0.75)y_d$. Real net taxes are equal to $\$100$ billion, and real government spending is equal to $\$125$ billion.
   a. What is the equilibrium level of consumption? Of saving?
   b. What is the amount of real desired investment?

19-9. Suppose that the consumption function is $c = \$50 + (0.75)y_d$ and that real net taxes are equal to $t = \$40 + (0.20)y$. Real desired investment is $i = \$140$, and real government spending is held constant at $g_0 = \$40$.
   a. Calculate the equilibrium level of real income.
   b. At the equilibrium level of real income, what is the amount of real net taxes? What is the equilibrium level of disposable income?
   c. What is the equilibrium level of consumption? Of saving?
   d. Show that $s + t = i + g$ at the equilibrium real income level, using the figures you have computed.

19-10. Suppose that real national income, in base-year dollars, is $\$600$ billion, full-employment national income is $\$500$ billion, and the marginal propensity to save is 0.25. Outline a single fiscal policy action that could be used, in the Keynesian model, to achieve the full-employment income level. Be specific about the dollar amount that you would prescribe.

SELECTED REFERENCES

Branson, William, *Macroeconomic Theory and Policy* (New York: Macmillan, 1978).

Dillard, Dudley, *The Economics of John Maynard Keynes* (Englewood Cliffs, N.J.: Prentice-Hall, 1948).

Froyen, Richard T., *Macroeconomics: Theories and Policies,* 3d ed. (New York: Macmillan, 1990).

Hansen, Alvin H., *A Guide to Keynes* (New York: McGraw-Hill, 1953).

Harris, Laurence, *Monetary Theory* (New York: McGraw-Hill, 1981).

Hicks, John R., "Mr. Keynes and the Classics: A Suggested Interpretation," *Econometrica,* 5 (2, April 1937), pp. 147–159.

Keynes, John Maynard, *The General Theory of Employment, Interest, and Money* (New York: Harcourt Brace Jovanovich, 1964).

Klein, Lawrence R., *The Keynesian Revolution,* 2d ed. (New York: Macmillan, 1966).

LeKachman, Robert, *The Age of Keynes* (New York: Random House, 1966).

———, (ed.), *Keynes and the Classics* (Boston: Heath, 1965).

Money in the Traditional Macroeconomic System

CHAPTER PREVIEW

1. According to the traditional Keynesian view, there are three motives for holding money. What are they?

2. How does the traditional Keynesian theory of interest rate determination differ from the classical theory?

3. What is the Keynesian transmission mechanism for monetary policy?

4. What is the *LM* schedule? What is the *IS* schedule? What is an *IS-LM* equilibrium?

5. How do monetary and fiscal policy actions affect national income and the nominal rate of interest in the *IS-LM* model?

6. Can monetary and fiscal policy makers coordinate their actions? Should they coordinate their policies?

In the previous chapter, we constructed a simple version of the traditional Keynesian model that was intended to capture the essential elements of Keynes's criticisms of the classical theory. That model is, nevertheless, an incomplete representation of Keynes's theory, for several reasons. First, the model includes no role for money and other financial assets, for interest rates, or for monetary policy. A second neglected feature is a role for some flexibility in price adjustment. We shall consider the first of these issues in the present chapter, and we shall spend much time on the latter issue in Chapters 21, 22, and 23.

In the Keynesian framework, there are linkages between the interest rate, money, and real income that do not exist in the classical model. These new linkages stem from Keynes's contributions to the theory of the demand for money. Learning about the Keynesian theory of the demand for money and about the expanded role of money and interest rates in influencing real economic activity will involve a significant ''cost'' in intellectual effort. But the time and study effort that you put into this task will yield a high return. In this chapter we will construct a version of the traditional Keynesian model that will provide an efficient means to:

1. Analyze *simultaneous* attainment of both equilibrium real income and the equilibrium interest rate.

2. Examine the effects of monetary policy and fiscal policy actions, and their interaction, on equilibrium real income and the equilibrium interest rate.

3. Compare the traditional Keynesian model with the classical model.

THE MONEY DEMAND FUNCTION

One of the key areas of interest of classical theorists such as Irving Fisher and Alfred Marshall was the demand for money. These economists felt that the demand for money arose predominantly from the *transactions motive* for holding money as a medium of exchange in planned exchanges. In a world of uncertainty, of course, the classical theorists recognized that there also would be a *precautionary motive* for holding money in the event of a need to undertake unplanned transactions. Both motives relate to the same basic idea: that individuals desire to hold money as a readily available form of purchasing power. Because both motives concern the role of money as an exchange medium, the classical economists theorized that the primary determinant of the demand for nominal money balances was an individual's nominal income level. They summarized this theory in the *Cambridge equation,*

$$M^d = kY \qquad\qquad (20\text{-}1)$$

where $M^d \equiv$ the desired nominal quantity of money
$\quad k \equiv$ the desired ratio of nominal cash holdings to nominal
$\qquad$ income, with $0 < k < 1$
$\quad Y \equiv$ nominal national income, equal to Py

Several classical economists recognized that the Cambridge equation was just a simple representation of the demand for money. For instance, some realized that higher interest rates increase the opportunity cost of holding money, because individuals otherwise could hold bonds and earn interest income. Nevertheless, those classical economists who discussed this issue argued that the interest rate played a limited role as a factor influencing the demand for money. They instead emphasized the level of income as the key determinant of the demand for money.

One of the significant contributions to economics provided by Keynes and his followers was a theory of the demand for money that highlights the role of interest rates. This theory of money demand also implies a mechanism for interest rate determination that contrasts sharply with the classical model. It also indicates that monetary policy works much differently from the mechanism developed by the classical economists.

THE PORTFOLIO DEMAND FOR MONEY

As already noted, the classical economists emphasized transactions-based motives for holding money that stressed its medium-of-exchange properties. Keynes followed the classical tradition (indeed, Keynes learned his economics from classical scholars). Therefore, he adopted both the transactions motive and the precautionary motive for holding cash balances as part of his own general theory of the demand for money.

When Keynes looked at the world around him during the 1920s and 1930s, he observed behavior that apparently contradicted the classical hypothesis that the level of income was the single key determinant of money demand. He saw wealthy individuals who, before the stock market crash of 1929, had accumulated large portfolios of stocks and bonds but held few cash balances. Keynes noticed that after the crash, these same individuals were holding much smaller amounts of stocks and bonds. They had significantly increased their pools of cash balances. This observation started him thinking about an entirely new motive for holding money that focused on the role of money as a *financial asset,* whose quantity individuals vary as they adjust their portfolios of wealth to changing economic conditions—including variations in the rate of interest.

Money, Other Financial Assets, and Wealth   As we saw in Chapter 6, financial assets are available in such forms as bonds, common stocks, savings accounts, certificates of deposit, and so on. Between the 1930s and the 1980s, Americans could not earn interest on money balances. This is *still* the case for currency and demand deposit balances, but interest earnings now are possible for some transactions accounts (for example, negotiable-order-of-withdrawal, or NOW, accounts). Nonetheless, it is typically true that the interest rate that individuals can earn on transactions accounts is less than that which they can earn on nonmoney financial assets. It is therefore meaningful to distinguish between money and nonmoney financial assets.

A famous conversation once occurred between the American authors F. Scott Fitzgerald (1896–1940) and Ernest Hemingway (1899–1961). Reportedly, Fitzgerald commented to Hemingway, ''You know, Ernest, the rich are different from us.'' Hemingway replied, ''I know. They have more money than we do.'' Surely, money is a component of a person's wealth. Defined broadly, however, wealth includes any asset that has value to the individual who owns it. This is a definition that is too broad for our purposes. We shall restrict ourselves to consideration of *financial wealth,* or the portion of an individual's wealth held as financial assets.

In the model below, we simplify our terminology by supposing that, at a moment in time, the financial wealth an individual allocates is split only between money, M, and a single nonmoney financial asset, which we shall call ''bonds,'' B. In using the term ''bonds'' to describe all nonmoney assets, we follow Keynes's appoach. You should keep in mind that we are using this term in a much wider context than we used it earlier in this text.

The key distinction between money and bonds (nonmoney financial assets) is that money is, by definition, the most *liquid* of financial assets. The nominal price of money is always equal to 1 unit of money (for instance, $1, 1 franc, 1 yen, etc.). The nominal price of a nonmoney financial asset, a bond, can vary over time, however. This means that it is possible to reap a capital gain if the nominal price of a bond increases over a given interval in time. It also is possible to incur a capital loss if the nominal price of a bond decreases over a given interval. In contrast, a $1 bill of United States currency has the same $1 nominal value over any given interval, and so nominal capital gains or losses cannot occur if individuals hold only non-interest-bearing money.

Naturally, individuals' stocks of wealth vary over time as flows of saving or dissaving occur. To keep things simple, let us consider an individual's decision making about distributing wealth between money and bonds at a *given point in time.* Suppose that, at some given instant, an individual's nominal financial wealth is equal to some amount W. The individual allocates wealth in only two possible ways. First, she may hold money balances, M, which we shall assume is non-interest-bearing cash. Second, she may hold bonds, B, which earn a nominal rate of return, r_n. Thus, at this point in time, it is true that

$$W = M + B \tag{20-2}$$

At a point in time, no flows of saving or dissaving occur, and so wealth is constant. This means that ΔW by definition is equal to zero. From equation (20-2), it follows that $\Delta M + \Delta B = 0$, or

$$-\Delta B = \Delta M \tag{20-3}$$

On the one hand, equation (20-3) says that, at a point in time, any change in an individual's desired holdings of bonds must correspond to a change in the individual's money holdings of an equal and opposite amount. On the other hand, any change in an individual's desired holdings of money must also correspond to a change in the individual's holdings of bonds of an equal and opposite amount. This fact forms the basis for a relationship between desired money holdings (the demand for money) and the interest rate, because bonds earn interest.

For simplicity's sake, let us suppose that all bonds (that is, all nonmoney assets) are **consols,** or perpetual, nonmaturing bonds. As we discussed in Chapter 7, the English government supplies consols on British bond markets. These consols offer a continual, unending stream of fixed nominal payments to their holders. The nominal discounted present value of a consol is given by R/r_n, where R is the fixed nominal payment received every period and r_n is the nominal, per-period market rate of interest. If the consol pays $R = \$1,000$ per year forever, and if the market rate of interest in the economy, r_n, is 10 percent, then the discounted present value of the consol is \$10,000.

In a world of uncertainty and such transactions costs as brokerage fees, an individual usually will only pay an amount somewhat less than the bond's nominal discounted present value when purchasing the bond. As a final simplification, however, let us assume that these factors are insignificant in determining the amount individuals will be willing to pay to purchase a consol. Under this final assumption, the price of the consol will be equal to the amount that individuals will be willing to pay, which will in fact be the consol's nominal discounted present value, so that

$$P_B = R/r_n \qquad\qquad (20\text{-}4)$$

is the price of this perpetual bond.

Equation (20-4) tells us that, all other factors unchanged, there will be an inverse relationship between the prices of existing bonds and interest rates. If the interest rate falls, bond prices by definition will rise, and individuals who hold these bonds will reap a nominal capital gain. If the interest rate rises, bond prices will fall, and individuals who hold these bonds will incur a nominal capital loss. But if individuals hold only money, they will neither reap a capital gain nor incur a capital loss when the interest rate changes, because the nominal value of money does not change.

The Portfolio Demand for Money   We now have all the elements we need to understand why changes in interest rates may influence the quantity of money demanded in an economy. Because the price of existing bonds varies inversely with changes in the interest rate, a fall in the interest rate in the future would cause the price of the perpetual bond to rise in the future; hence, individuals who hold these bonds would earn capital gains. In contrast, a rise in the interest rate in the future would cause the price of the perpetual bond to fall, and so individuals who hold these bonds would earn capital losses. Therefore, anticipations about future capital gains or losses from bond holdings depend directly upon *speculations* about whether interest rates will rise or fall in the future. In light of these speculations, an individual adjusts the composition of her *portfolio* of money and bonds.

Now suppose that the interest rate *falls,* in the *present,* to a level that a given individual believes is *low* by historical standards. If this individual perceives that the interest rate has fallen to a historically low level, then she also believes that the interest rate will rise in the future. Therefore, she also anticipates that bond prices will fall, which would cause her to incur capital losses on her bond holdings. To avoid some of these anticipated future losses, she then could sell bonds in the *present.* From equation (20-2), we can see that if she sells bonds, this individual reallocates this portion of her fixed wealth from holdings of bonds to holdings of money. So for this individual, *the present fall in the rate of interest causes a present increase in desired money holdings.*

Suppose instead that the interest rate *rises,* at *present,* to levels that an individual perceives to be *high* by historical standards. If this individual believes that the interest rate has risen to a historically high level, then she also believes that the interest rate will fall in the future, and so she expects bond prices to rise. This would allow her to earn capital gains from her bond holdings. To increase her earnings further, this individual would then purchase bonds in the *present.* From equation (20-2), we can see that if she buys bonds, this individual reallocates this portion of her fixed wealth from holdings of money to holdings of bonds. Therefore, for this individual *the present rise in the interest rate causes a present reduction in desired money holdings.*

Certainly, perceptions concerning whether current levels of interest rates are historically high or low may vary across individuals in the economy. When interest rates rise to particularly high levels, more people are likely to agree that interest rates will fall in the future. They will respond by reducing the quantities of money they desire to hold. Similarly, when interest rates fall to low levels, more people are likely to agree that interest rates will rise in the future. They will respond by increasing the quantities of money they wish to hold.

In Keynes's original theory, an individual speculates by holding either all her wealth as money or all her wealth as bonds. Hence, Keynes called his theory a model of the **speculative demand for money.** Followers of Keynes, such as the Nobel economist James Tobin, have extended this basic theory to settings in which individuals hold both money and bonds but adjust their wealth portfolios in light of interest rate changes. Nowadays, therefore, this is called a theory of the **portfolio demand for money.**

Figure 20-1 illustrates the portfolio demand for money, labeled M^d_{port}. The schedule

Figure 20-1

The Portfolio Demand for Money.   As the nominal interest rate rises, the amount of financial wealth that individuals hold as money falls. Hence, the portfolio demand for money is inversely related to the nominal interest rate.

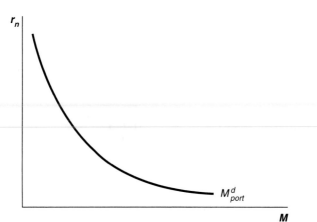

depicted in the figure is downward-sloping because of the inverse relationship between the interest rate and desired money holdings. The portfolio money demand schedule is drawn as convex with respect to the origin. The reason is that, as discussed above, as the interest rate reaches ever-higher levels, more and more individuals have an incentive to reallocate wealth holdings to bonds rather than money. Hence, desired holdings of money drop off more and more quickly as the interest rate rises. And as the interest rate falls to ever-lower levels, more and more individuals have an incentive to reallocate wealth holdings to money rather than bonds. Thus, the public eventually reaches a point at which it will hold limitless amounts of money instead of holding any bonds.

The degree to which the portfolio money demand schedule is convex, or bowed, depends on how the subjective notions of "historically high or low" interest rates are spread across individuals in the economy. If all individuals have very nearly the same notions on historical highs and lows, then the portfolio demand-for-money schedule is very bowed, because when interest rates rise above a certain level, nearly all individuals will reduce their money holdings at the same time. Likewise, when interest rates fall below a certain level, nearly all individuals will increase their money holdings at the same time. In contrast, if everyone has very different ideas about historical highs and lows for interest rates, there will be gradual changes in total portfolio money holdings as the interest rate rises or falls, and the portfolio money demand schedule is less convex, or more nearly linear.

THE TOTAL DEMAND FOR MONEY

Of course, there is another important determinant of desired nominal money holdings, which is the level of nominal income earned by households. As household income in-

Figure 20-2
The Transactions and Precautionary Demands for Money.   In our simple version of the Keynesian theory of the demand for money, neither the transactions demand for money nor the precautionary demand for money depends on the nominal interest rate. Hence, in panels (a) and (b) both schedules are vertical as graphed with the nominal interest rate on the vertical axis. An increase in nominal income, however, increases both the amount of money individuals hold for transactions purposes and the amount they hold as a precaution. Therefore, a rise in nominal income shifts both schedules rightward.

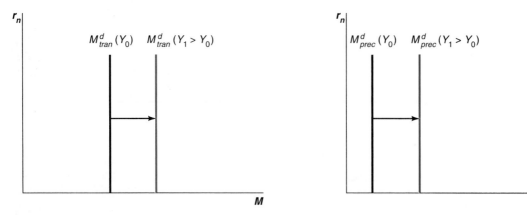

(a)   (b)

creases, individuals will plan to undertake more transactions and, in addition, will hold more money balances as a contingency for unplanned transactions. Thus, both the transactions demand for money, labeled M_{tran}^d in Figure 20-2 in panel (*a*), and the precautionary demand for money, M_{prec}^d in panel (*b*), increase as nominal income rises. Although there are ways that the transactions and precautionary demands for money can be influenced by changes in interest rates, for the sake of simplicity we assume that only income, and not the rate of interest, influences M_{tran}^d and M_{prec}^d. Therefore, we shall assume that these schedules are vertical.

The Total Demand for Nominal Money Balances   Panel (*a*) of Figure 20-3 shows the construction of a total demand-for-money schedule. The sum of M_{tran}^d and M_{prec}^d is added to M_{port}^d horizontally. This is done at a given level of nominal national income, Y_0, to yield the total demand-for-money schedule, labeled simply $M^d(Y_0)$. The *negative slope* of the total money demand schedule results from the speculative motive for holding money. The level of nominal income, in contrast, determines the *position* of the schedule.

Panel (*b*) of Figure (20-3) shows the effect on the total demand for money of a rise in the level of nominal national income. Because a rise in income (from Y_0 to some higher income level Y_1) causes an increase in the demand for money for transactions and precautionary purposes (see Figure 20-2), the total demand for money increases, as shown by a rightward *shift* of the money demand schedule, from $M^d(Y_0)$ to $M^d(Y_1)$.

The Demand for Real Money Balances   Up to now, our discussion of the demand for money has considered only the demand for nominal, or current-dollar, nominal money balances. What all of us really care about, however, is the *real purchasing power* of the money we hold. As a very simple but concrete example, suppose that you began the day with $5 of cash on hand with which to purchase lunch. Suppose also that the price of a sandwich is exactly $2.50. This means that you could, if you wished, purchase two sandwiches at lunchtime. Now suppose that, during the morning, the general level of prices, including the price of a sandwich, rises by a factor of 2. The same lunchtime sandwich now will be twice as expensive ($5 per sandwich), and so the real purchasing power of the $5 in cash that you have on hand will be half what it was before. To purchase the same number of sandwiches at lunchtime, you will have to double your nominal money balances to $10. That is, a doubling of prices will require a doubling of nominal money balances to keep your real lunchtime purchasing power the same.

This simple example shows that households' nominal cash balances have meaning only if adjusted for price-level changes. That is, what any rational individual really cares about is his **real money balances,** or the amount of his price-level-adjusted holdings of money. In recognition of this fact, Figure 20-4 depicts the demand for real money balances, $m^d \equiv M^d/P$, where $m \equiv M/P$ is the quantity of price-level-adjusted, real money balances and P is the current level of prices. Because of the portfolio motive for holding money, the demand-for-real-money-balances schedule is negatively sloped.

An individual's demand for real purchasing power, however, depends upon the *real* income that he receives. The reason is that real purchasing power is necessary for the individual to undertake real-valued planned and unplanned transactions, and the amount of planned and unplanned transactions will increase with the amount of real income. Hence, a rise in real income, from some initial level y_0 to a higher level y_1, causes a rise in the demand for real, price-level-adjusted money balances, as shown in Figure 20-4.

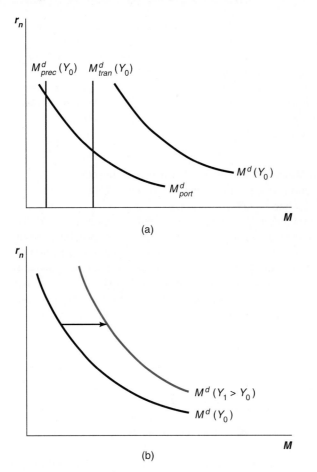

(a)

(b)

Figure 20-3
The Total Demand for Money. The total demand for money in the economy is the sum of the portfolio, transactions, and precautionary demands for money. This is done by adding the three schedules horizontally to obtain the total money demand schedule, M^d [panel (a)]. This schedule slopes downward because of the negative slope of the portfolio demand-for-money schedule. Its position depends on the level of nominal income, and so it is labeled $M^d (Y_0)$. The effect of a rise in nominal income is depicted in panel (b). A rise in income increases the transactions and precautionary demands for money, and so the total demand for money must rise at any interest rate when income increases.

INTEREST RATE DETERMINATION

THE SUPPLY OF MONEY

In earlier chapters, we investigated in some detail how the Federal Reserve can influence the quantity of nominal money balances supplied. We also discussed the fact that part of the nominal money stock contains interest-bearing deposits such as NOW accounts. For the present, we shall keep the analysis as simple as possible and assume that the

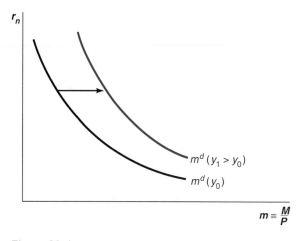

Figure 20-4
The Demand for Real Money Balances.   The demand for real money balances, $m = M/P$, is the total demand by individuals for real purchasing power. The demand for real money balances slopes downward, because of the portfolio motive for holding real money balances. It shifts rightward when real income increases, because of the transactions and precautionary motives for holding real money balances.

central bank supplies all money in the form of non-interest-bearing cash and deposits. We shall also assume that the quantity of money supplied does *not* depend upon the nominal interest rate, so that the nominal money supply function is vertical, as graphed in Figure 20-5.

The Federal Reserve can—through open-market operations, discount rate policy actions, and changes in reserve requirements—influence the nominal quantity of money supplied. An open-market purchase, a decrease in the discount rate, or a reduction in reserve requirements shifts the nominal money supply schedule to the right. An open-market sale, an increase in the discount rate, or an increase in reserve requirements shifts the nominal money supply schedule to the left. The Federal Reserve, therefore, can determine the position of the nominal money supply function, other things equal.

Nevertheless, as we discussed earlier, it is the real purchasing power of money (M/P) that actually is important. From the Federal Reserve's perspective, it would be nice if it could precisely control the quantity of real money balances. This is not possible, however, though we shall see later on that the Federal Reserve's actions ultimately have a large influence on the real purchasing power of money.

A diagram of the *real supply of money, M^s/P,* appears in Figure 20-6. As shown, it is the price-level-adjusted version of Figure 20-5. We must keep in mind that the Federal Reserve's policy actions (open-market operations, discount rate policy actions, and reserve requirement changes) directly affect only the nominal supply of money, M^s. On the one hand, if the price level is constant, Federal Reserve policy actions that increase the nominal money supply will shift the real money supply schedule to the right, and policy actions that reduce the nominal money supply will shift the real money supply schedule to the left.

On the other hand, the price level can change without the Federal Reserve undertaking any policy actions. A rise in the level of prices shifts the real money supply schedule leftward. A fall in the level of prices shifts the schedule rightward.

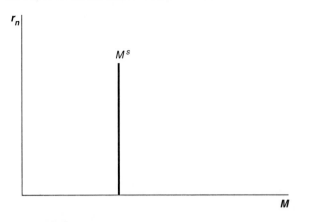

Figure 20-5
The Nominal Money Supply.   We assume that the Federal Reserve is able to control completely the quantity of nominal money balances in the economy and that the supply of money is independent of the interest rate. Hence, the nominal money supply schedule is vertical.

THE EQUILIBRIUM INTEREST RATE

Figure 20-7 superimposes the demand schedule for real money balances on the real money supply schedule. At the point where the two schedules cross, all individuals in the economy are satisfied holding the quantity of money balances supplied by the Federal Reserve, M_0, valued in real terms by adjusting for the current price level, P_0. Thus, at this point the quantity of real money balances demanded is equal to the quantity of real money balances supplied.

The interest rate r_n^0 is the nominal interest rate at which this *market for real money*

Figure 20-6
The Supply of Real Money Balances.   The supply of real money balances is the nominal money supply, M^s, deflated by the price level, P, or (M^s/P). The supply of real money balances shifts rightward, or increases, if M^s rises with P unchanged, if P falls with M^s unchanged, or if M^s otherwise rises relative to P.

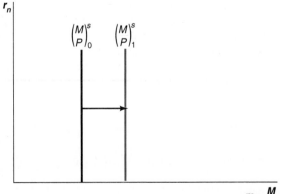

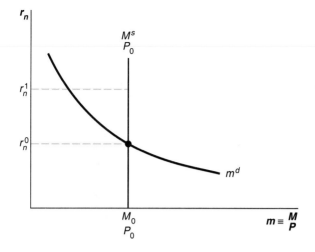

Figure 20-7
Equilibrium in the Market for Real Money Balances.   In equilibrium, the quantity of real money balances demanded is equal to the quantity of real money balances supplied. This occurs where the supply and demand schedules cross, at the interest rate r_n^0. At the rate r_n^1, there is an excess quantity of real money balances supplied, which means that there is an excess quantity of bonds demanded. Bond prices will rise, which means that the nominal interest rate will fall to its equilibrium level.

balances is in equilibrium. Indeed, the role of the nominal interest rate is to adjust as needed to ensure that this market reaches an equilibrium. To see how this adjustment process works, suppose that the nominal interest rate were equal to r_n^1 in Figure 20-7. At this higher interest rate, there would be an excess quantity of real money balances supplied; that is, in the aggregate, individuals desire to hold less real money balances than the Federal Reserve has supplied.

Because the total wealth of all individuals is fixed at a point in time, no new bonds are issued; only *existing* bonds may be traded. At the nominal interest rate r_n^1, individuals desire to hold more existing bonds than are available. Consequently, there is an excess quantity of bonds demanded, which will cause bond prices to rise. Recall that there is an inverse relationship between bond prices and nominal rates of interest. As bond prices rise, the interest rate falls toward the equilibrium level r_n^0. We can conclude that, at this equilibrium interest rate, both the market for bonds and the market for real money balances are in equilibrium.

Figure 20-8 shows the effect of an increase in the nominal quantity of money supplied by the Federal Reserve, from M_0 to a larger amount M_1, holding the price level unchanged at a level P_0. This increase in the nominal money supply causes the real money supply schedule to shift rightward. At the initial equilibrium interest rate r_n^0, there now is an excess quantity of money supplied. Therefore, as discussed above, there is an excess quantity of bonds demanded. Bond prices will be bid upward, and the rate of interest will begin to fall to a new equilibrium level, r_n^1.

The fall in the interest rate caused by a constant-price increase in the nominal quantity of money supplied (that is, an increase in the quantity of money, assuming prices are unchanged) is the **liquidity effect** of monetary policy. This term gets its name from the fact that an increase in the nominal quantity of money amounts to an increase in the

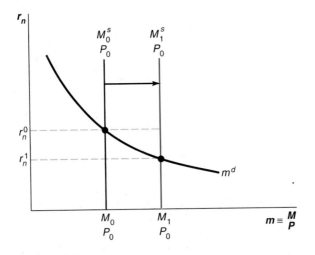

Figure 20-8
The Liquidity Effect of an Increase in the Nominal Money Supply.   An increase in the
nominal money supply with a constant price level causes a rise in the supply of real money balances.
At an original equilibrium nominal interest rate r_n^0, there is now an excess quantity of money supplied. This implies that there is an excess quantity of bonds demanded. Bond prices rise, and the
interest rate falls to a new equilibrium level of r_n^1. The fall in the equilibrium interest rate caused by a
constant-price rise in the nominal money supply is called the *liquidity effect.*

amount of liquidity in the economy. For individuals to be satisfied with this enlarged
amount of cash, the equilibrium interest rate must fall.

Figure 20-9 shows the effect of an increase in the level of prices, from P_0 to a higher
level P_1, holding the nominal money stock unchanged. This rise in the price level lowers
the quantity of real money balances supplied; in other words, there is a reduction in the
purchasing power of the nominal quantity of money. At the initial equilibrium interest
rate r_n^0, there now is an excess quantity of real money balances demanded, meaning that
at this interest rate individuals would prefer to have more real purchasing power. They
desire to hold fewer bonds at this rate of interest, and so there is an excess quantity of
bonds supplied; hence people will sell bonds, and bond prices will begin to fall. As
existing bond prices fall, the interest rate rises. Eventually, the interest rate rises to the
new equilibrium level, r_n^1.

This change in the nominal interest rate caused by a constant-nominal-money-stock
increase in the level of prices of goods and services is called the **real balance effect.**
Naturally, it gets its name from the fact that changes in the level of prices cause changes
in the price-level-adjusted quantity of money balances, or real money balances, in the
economy.

Changes in the equilibrium interest rate also can result from shifts in the position of
the demand schedule for real money balances. Figure 20-10 shows the effect of a fall in
the public's demand for real balances. If, in the aggregate, individuals desire to hold fewer
real money balances at any given interest rate, then at the initial equilibrium rate of interest
r_n^0 there will immediately be an excess quantity of real money balances supplied. The
implied excess quantity of bonds demanded will cause bond prices to be driven upward,
and the equilibrium rate of interest will be driven downward to r_n^1.

The fall in the public's demand for real money balances, or reduced demand for real

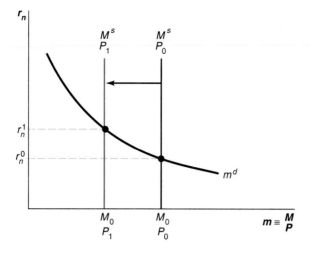

Figure 20-9
The Real Balance Effect of a Rise in the Price Level.   A rise in the price level with a fixed quantity of nominal money balances supplied reduces the real supply of money. At an initial equilibrium nominal rate of interest r_n^0, there is now an excess quantity of money demanded, which means that there is an excess quantity of bonds supplied. Bond prices fall, and the nominal interest rate rises to a new equilibrium value of r_n^1. This rise in the interest rate caused by an increase in the price level is the *real balance effect.*

Figure 20-10
The Effect of a Fall in the Demand for Money.   A reduction in the quantity of money demanded at any given interest rate means that, at an initial equilibrium interest rate r_n^0, there now will be an excess quantity of money supplied, or an excess quantity of bonds demanded. Bond prices will rise, and the nominal interest rate will fall to a new equilibrium level of r_n^1.

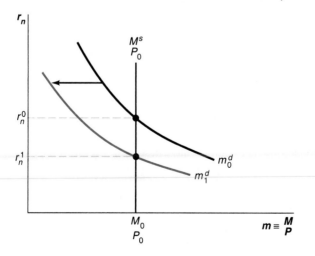

purchasing power, could have occurred because there was a fall in real income in the economy. Such a fall would cause individuals to undertake fewer planned and unplanned transactions, which would induce them to reduce transactions and precautionary real money balances. On the other hand, other factors unrelated to real income also could have changed that would have caused the fall in the demand for real money balances shown in Figure 20-10. For instance, there could have been an improvement in payments system technology, such as the introduction of a new credit card payments system, that reduced households' needs for immediately available purchasing power. This sort of event also could result in a fall in the transactions and precautionary demands for real money balances even if real income were unchanged.

THE *LM* SCHEDULE

The equilibrium interest rate depends on several factors, including the nominal supply of money, the level of prices, and factors that influence the public's demand for real purchasing power (M^d/P). One of these latter factors, as discussed above, is the level of real income. In our discussion of the functioning of the market for real money balances, the level of real income has been taken as given. We know, though, from our discussion of the simple traditional model in Chapter 19, that the equilibrium level of real income is determined by the level of desired expenditures in the economy. In that simple model, in contrast, the interest rate was taken as given.

Our goal in the remainder of this chapter is to understand how both the equilibrium nominal interest rate and the equilibrium level of real income are *simultaneously* determined. It turns out that we now have everything we need to put these concepts together. Let us begin this task by taking our understanding of money market equilibrium one step further, by considering something called the *LM* schedule.

THE DERIVATION OF THE *LM* SCHEDULE

The **LM schedule** is a locus of combinations of real income levels and nominal rates of interest for which the market for real money balances is in equilibrium. Figure 20-11 depicts the derivation of the *LM* schedule; note well that we derive an *LM* schedule holding the real money supply constant. As we saw previously, a fall in real income, say from y_0 to a smaller amount y_1, causes the demand schedule for real money balances to shift from $m^d(y_0)$ to the leftward position $m^d(y_1)$, so that the equilibrium interest rate must fall from r_n^0 to r_n^1, as shown in panel (*a*) of the figure. This means that the economy would move from a real income–nominal interest rate combination y_0 and r_n^0 for which the market for real money balances initially was in equilibrium to a new combination y_1 and r_n^1 that preserves money market equilibrium. These new combinations are representative points of money market equilibrium along the *LM* schedule in panel (*b*).

John Hicks first derived the *LM* schedule in 1937. He called it the ''*LM*'' schedule because it is the set of points at which desired holdings of money balances, or liquidity, *L*, equals the quantity of money balances supplied by the Federal Reserve, *M*.

In the *LM* schedule that we have derived in Figure 20-11, the notation for the schedule is $LM(M_0/P_0)$. We use this notation to make clear that we have derived this schedule of points given the nominal quantity of money supplied M_0 and the price level P_0. That is, we have derived this particular *LM* schedule given the quantity of real money balances supplied equal to M_0/P_0. If there had been a different quantity of real money balances

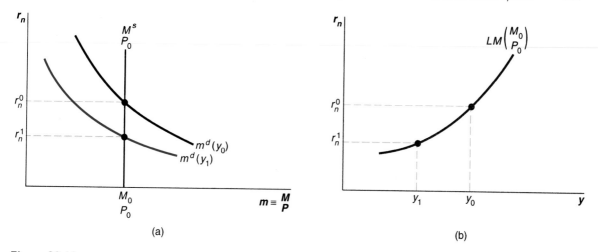

Figure 20-11

Deriving the LM Schedule.   If real income falls from y_0 to a smaller amount y_1, then the demand for real money balances will fall, causing the equilibrium nominal interest rate to decline from
r_n^0 to r_n^1 [panel (a)]. This means that both of these real income–interest rate combinations maintain
equilibrium in the market for real money balances. A schedule of points containing these two real
income–interest rate combinations [panel (b)] is the LM *schedule*. The LM schedule is all combinations of real income and the interest rate for which the market for real money balances is in
equilibrium. Note that the real money supply is held constant when the LM schedule is derived.

supplied, this locus of combinations of real income and the nominal interest rate would
not have been in the same position.

THE SLOPE OF THE *LM* SCHEDULE

In Figure 20-11, the *LM* schedule is somewhat convex (bowed), and it has a slope that is
neither particularly steep nor particularly shallow. It is possible, however, that the *LM*
schedule may be very steep or very shallow. We must understand why this may be so.
Figure 20-12 shows a derivation of the *LM* schedule when the demand schedule for real
money balances is very steep. As shown in the figure, when the money demand schedule
has a steep slope, so does the *LM* schedule.

Why is this so? The answer is that when the demand schedule for real money balances
is steep, this means that the demand for money is relatively insensitive to changes in the
interest rate. Along a steeply sloped money demand schedule, a comparatively large change
in the interest rate causes a comparatively small change in the quantity of real money
balances that individuals desire to hold. In this case we say there is a relatively **interest-
inelastic demand for money,** meaning that the interest sensitivity, or interest elasticity,
of the demand for real money balances is low. When a fall in the total demand for money
causes a leftward shift in this interest-inelastic schedule, the fact that individuals' money
holdings are relatively unaffected by changes in the interest rate means that the interest
rate must fall by a comparatively large amount to bring the quantities of real money
balances demanded and supplied back into equality. As shown in Figure 20-12, this means
that the *LM* schedule, like the money demand schedule, will be steeply sloped.

The more steeply sloped is the demand schedule for real money balances, the more
steeply sloped will be the *LM* schedule. In contrast, as the demand for real money balances

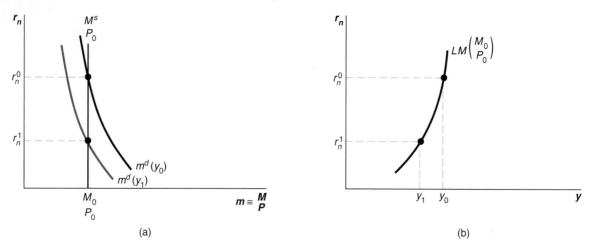

(a)   (b)

Figure 20-12
Determining the Slope of the LM Schedule.   The slope of the *LM* schedule depends on the
interest elasticity of the demand for real money balances. If money demand is very interest-inelastic,
so that the money demand schedule is very steep over most of its range [panel (*a*)], then the *LM*
schedule derived by reducing real income also is steep over most of its range [panel (*b*)].

becomes comparatively more shallow (less steep), the *LM* schedule also will become more
shallow. Along a more shallow money demand schedule, there is an **interest-elastic
demand for money;** the demand for real money balances is relatively more interest-
sensitive.

We can conclude that the relative steepness or shallowness of the *LM* schedule tells us
about the **interest elasticity of money demand**—the relative responsiveness, or sensitivity, of the demand for real money balances to changes in the interest rate. We shall see
later that this is an important point to understand about the *LM* schedule.

SHIFTS IN THE *LM* SCHEDULE

We already know that the position of the *LM* schedule depends upon the quantity of real
money balances. The reason is that we have derived the *LM* schedule by varying real
income while holding the quantity of real money balances unchanged. Now suppose that
the Federal Reserve increases the nominal money supply while real income and the price
level remain fixed. As shown in Figure 20-13, the real quantity of money rises from
M_0/P_0 to M_1/P_0. Even though real income is unchanged at y_0, the equilibrium nominal
interest rate now must fall, as a result of the liquidity effect, from r_n^0 to r_n^1. This means
that there is a new real income–interest rate combination, y_0 and r_n^1, that is consistent with
money market equilibrium and, therefore, must lie on an *LM* schedule below and to the
right of the original *LM* schedule. The constant-price rise in the nominal money supply
has shifted the *LM* schedule downward and to the right. A constant-price reduction in the
nominal money supply would shift the *LM* schedule upward and to the left.

On the other hand, Figure 20-14 shows the effect of a rise in the price level, holding
the nominal supply of money and real income unchanged. An increase in the prices of
goods and services, from P_0 to a higher level P_1, causes a reduction in the real purchasing

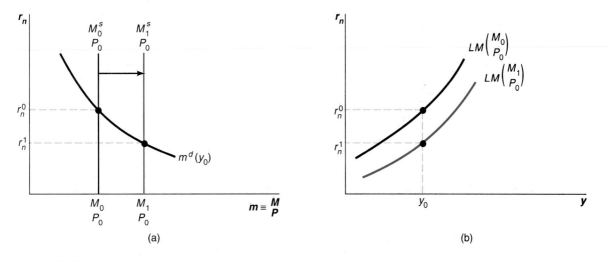

Figure 20-13

The Effect on the _LM_ Schedule of an Increase in the Nominal Money Supply.   A constant-price-level increase in the nominal money supply results in a liquidity-effect reduction in the equilibrium nominal interest rate even though real income is unchanged. This means that the money market is in equilibrium at the same level of real income but at a lower interest rate [panel (a)]. Because the economy is on an _LM_ schedule when the money market is in equilibrium, this implies that there is a new _LM_ schedule below and to the right of the original _LM_ schedule [panel (b)] following a rise in the nominal money supply.

Figure 20-14

The Effect on the _LM_ Schedule of an Increase in the Price Level.   An increase in the level of prices with no change in the nominal money supply results in a real-balance-effect increase in the equilibrium nominal interest rate even though real income is unchanged. This means that the money market is in equilibrium at the same level of real income but at a higher interest rate [panel (a)]. Because the economy is on an _LM_ schedule when the money market is in equilibrium, this implies that there is a new _LM_ schedule above and to the left of the original _LM_ schedule [panel (b)] following a rise in the price level.

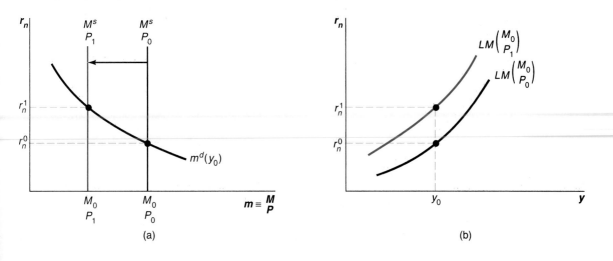

power of money, from M_0/P_0 to the lower amount M_0/P_1. This results in a leftward shift of the real money supply schedule. The real balance effect causes the equilibrium nominal interest rate to rise from r_n^0 to r_n^1, even though the level of real income is unchanged. This yields a new real income–interest rate combination that preserves equilibrium in the money market but now lies above the original equilibrium combination. Therefore, the *LM* schedule shifts upward and to the left. In contrast, a fall in the price level causes a real balance effect on the interest rate that is reflected in a downward and rightward shift in the *LM* schedule.

Finally, suppose that the payments system technology improves, so that the public reduces its demand for real money balances at any given interest rate. As shown in Figure 20-15, this would reduce the desired quantity of real money balances at any given interest rate, including the initial equilibrium rate, r_n^0, even though the quantity of real money balances supplied, M_0/P_0, and the level of real income, y_0, would not have changed. Thus, the money demand schedule shifts from $m_0^d(y_0)$ to $m_1^d(y_0)$, and the equilibrium interest rate is driven downward to r_n^1. This means that the money market is in equilibrium at a new real income–interest rate combination below the original *LM* schedule. The *LM* schedule shifts downward and to the right as a result of this constant-income fall in the demand for real money balances. A constant-income rise in the demand for real money balances would, in contrast, shift the *LM* schedule upward and to the left.

We may conclude that the *LM* schedule shifts if any of three possible events occur: (1) a constant-income, constant-price change in the nominal money supply (a liquidity effect), (2) a constant-income, constant-nominal-money-supply change in the level of prices of goods and services (a real balance effect), or (3) a constant-income, constant-real-money-balances change in the demand for real money balances.

Figure 20-15

The Effect on the *LM* Schedule of a Constant-Income Reduction in the Demand for Money.   A decrease in the demand for money with no change in the level of real income causes a reduction in the equilibrium nominal interest rate even though real income is unchanged. This means that the money market is in equilibrium at the same level of real income but at a lower interest rate [panel (*a*)]. Because the economy is on an *LM* schedule when the money market is in equilibrium, this implies that there is a new *LM* schedule below and to the right of the original *LM* schedule [panel (*b*)] following a constant-income reduction in the demand for real money balances.

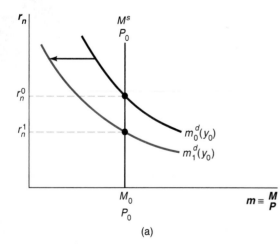

(a)

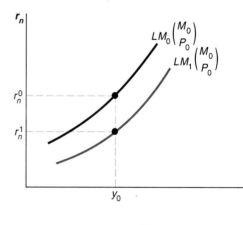

(b)

THE *IS* SCHEDULE

In the previous chapter, we saw that equilibrium real income must satisfy the condition that all real income is spent in the forms of household consumption, desired business investment, and government expenditures. Alternatively, it must be true that leakages from the flow of income and expenditures, in the form of saving and taxes, must be equal to reinjections of expenditures, in the form of investment and government spending. We also discussed the fact that desired investment spending depends inversely upon the real rate of interest. This implies that desired investment depends negatively on the nominal interest rate (because the real rate by definition approximates the nominal rate less the expected rate of inflation).

As we shall see below, this inverse relationship between desired investment and the interest rate implies that changes in the rate of interest affect equilibrium real income. Hence, there are combinations of real income and the nominal interest rate for which equilibrium real income is obtained. This set of real income–interest rate combinations is the *IS* **schedule.**

THE DERIVATION OF THE *IS* SCHEDULE

The derivation of the *IS* schedule entails a straightforward extension of the simple traditional model of Chapter 19. Figure 20-16 depicts the derivation. Panel (*a*) of the figure is investment as plotted against the nominal interest rate, which is a downward-sloping schedule, because of the negative dependence of real investment spending, i, on the interest rate. At an initial nominal interest rate r_n^0, the desired level of real investment spending is equal to i_0. We can sum this level of desired real investment spending, consumption, and government spending to construct the aggregate desired expenditures schedule shown in panel (*b*). Equilibrium real income is located where this schedule crosses the 45-degree line and is equal to y_0. Therefore, at the interest rate r_n^0, we have a real income–interest rate combination r_n^0 and y_0 for which real income is at its equilibrium level. This yields a point in panel (*c*).

If the interest rate were to fall to r_n^1, then the discounted present value from the stream of returns to real investment would rise. Thus, firms would have an incentive to increase the amount of autonomous (unrelated to the level of real income) real investment from i_0 to the larger amount i_1 in panel (*a*) of Figure 20-16. In panel (*b*), there would be a rise in aggregate desired expenditures that, in turn, would result in a multiplier-effect increase in equilibrium real income, from y_0 to y_1. This implies a new equilibrium real income–interest rate combination below and to the right of the original combination in panel (*c*).

The locus of points including the two points shown in Figure 20-16 is the *IS* schedule. As in the case of the *LM* schedule, it was given its name in 1937 by John Hicks, who first derived the schedule by assuming a simple economy with no government sector. Because income is equal to desired expenditures all along the *IS* schedule, it is also true that, with no government, saving "leakages" from the income-expenditure flow equal investment "reinjections." Therefore $i = s$; hence the term "*IS*."

THE SLOPE OF THE *IS* SCHEDULE

The relative slope of the *IS* schedule shows the **interest elasticity of desired investment**—the relative responsiveness of desired investment spending to changes in the interest rate. In the *IS* schedule derivation in Figure 20-16, the desired investment schedule was neither

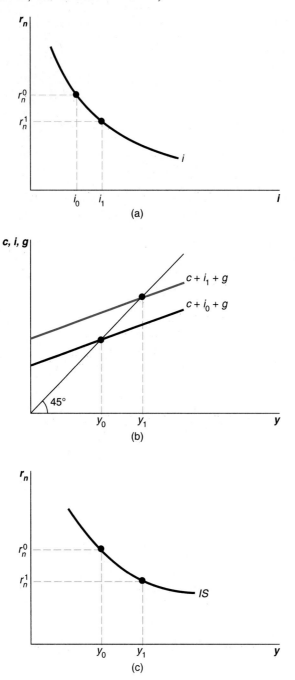

Figure 20-16

Deriving the *IS* Schedule.   A fall in the nominal interest rate causes an increase in real desired investment by firms [panel (*a*)]. This causes the aggregate expenditures schedule to shift upward by the amount of the rise in autonomous investment spending [panel (*b*)], resulting in a rise in equilibrium real income. This yields two interest rate–real income combinations that are contained in the downward-sloping *IS* schedule [panel (*c*)]. Along the *IS* schedule, aggregate desired real expenditures are equal to real income.

particularly shallow nor particularly steep. It is possible, however, that one or the other may be the case. If the desired investment schedule is very shallow, then there is relatively **interest-elastic desired investment.** This means that comparatively small changes in the interest rate generate comparatively large changes in the amount of desired investment.

Figure 20-17 derives the *IS* schedule when desired investment is relatively interest-elastic. Because a comparatively small fall in the interest rate causes a comparatively large increase in desired investment spending, the aggregate expenditures schedule shifts upward by a comparatively large magnitude, causing a large multiplier-effect increase in real income. Therefore, the derived *IS* schedule is relatively shallow, or more nearly flat, than it otherwise would have been.

If desired investment were relatively interest-insensitive—in other words, if there were **interest-inelastic desired investment**—then comparatively large changes in the interest rate would cause comparatively small changes in desired investment, in aggregate desired expenditures, and in equilibrium real income. In this case, the derived *IS* schedule would be relatively steep.

SHIFTS IN THE *IS* SCHEDULE

We derive the *IS* schedule by changing only the nominal interest rate and holding all other factors that affect autonomous desired expenditures unchanged. These factors include autonomous consumption, government expenditures, and autonomous net taxes. An increase in real autonomous consumption or in real government spending would, for any given interest rate, result in an increase in aggregate desired expenditures, as shown in Figure 20-18. The result would be an increase in equilibrium real income. This yields a new real income–interest rate combination that lies to the right of the original combination. Thus, a rise in autonomous consumption or government spending (or an autonomous tax reduction) will shift the *IS* schedule rightward and upward.

Another way that a rightward shift of the *IS* schedule could occur would be if the desired investment schedule itself shifted outward and to the right. This type of increase in desired investment could occur, for instance, because of a rise in profit expectations by business firms. Such a rise would also increase aggregate desired expenditures and equilibrium real income at any given interest rate, thereby shifting *IS* to the right.

Of course, reductions in autonomous consumption, autonomous investment, and autonomous government spending or an increase in autonomous lump-sum taxes would shift the *IS* schedule downward and leftward. The reason is that reductions in net autonomous expenditures would shift the aggregate expenditures schedule downward, lowering equilibrium real income at any interest rate.

IS-LM EQUILIBRIUM AND DISEQUILIBRIUM

The *IS* schedule represents all real income–interest rate combinations for which real income is in equilibrium, while the *LM* schedule represents all real income–interest rate combinations for which the market for real money balances is in equilibrium. Although it would be possible to draw several diagrams (the investment schedule, the 45-degree-line/aggregate expenditures diagram, and the market for real money balances) to explore the interactions between these sets of equilibrium combinations, it is much more efficient to use the *IS* and *LM* schedules. The reason is that, by combining the two schedules on one diagram, we can find the *single* combination of real income and the interest rate that

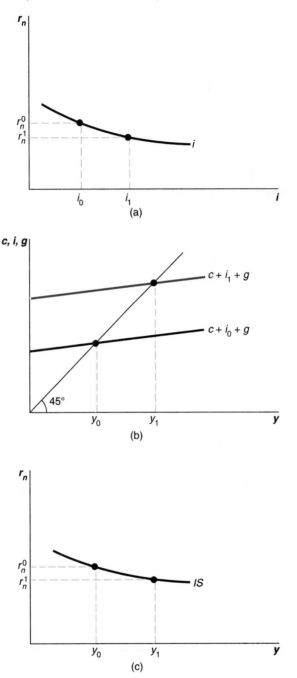

Figure 20-17
Determining the Slope of the *IS* Schedule.   If desired real investment is very interest-elastic, so that the desired investment schedule is very shallow over most of its range, then a relatively small reduction in the interest rate causes a relatively large increase in investment spending by firms [panel (*a*)]. Therefore, there is a comparatively large upward shift in the aggregate expenditures schedule and a relatively large increase in equilibrium real income [panel (*b*)]. As a result, the *IS* schedule is very shallow over most of its range.

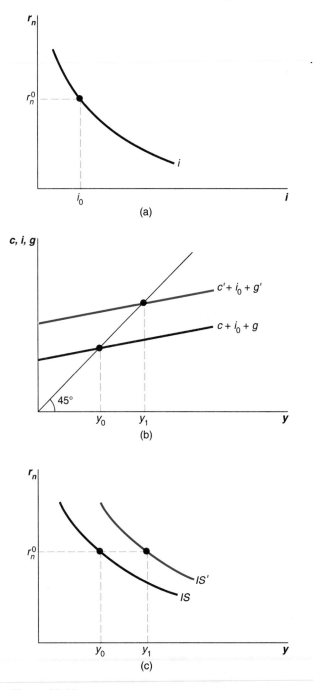

Figure 20-18

The Effect of a Rise in Net Aggregate Autonomous Expenditures on the *IS* Schedule.

If net aggregate autonomous expenditures rise at any given rate of interest, perhaps because of a rise in autonomous consumption, an increase in autonomous government spending, or a reduction in autonomous lump-sum taxes, equilibrium real income will increase [panel (*b*)]. This occurs even if the interest rate is constant [panel (*a*)]. Therefore, equilibrium real income is now higher at the same interest rate, and so the economy must be on a new *IS* schedule to the right of the original *IS* schedule. A rise in net aggregate autonomous expenditures shifts the *IS* schedule to the right.

achieves equilibrium real income and equilibrium in the market for real money balances. This combination is known as ***IS-LM* equilibrium.**

PUTTING *IS* AND *LM* TOGETHER

Figure 20-19 depicts the achievement of this simultaneous equilibrium. It shows both the *IS* schedule and the *LM* schedule crossing at a point, labeled *E*. At this point, because the economy is on its *IS* schedule, real income is equal to real desired expenditures at the quantity y_0. In addition, because point *E* is on the *LM* schedule, the money market is in equilibrium at the interest rate r_n^0.

Why is this *IS-LM* diagram such an *efficient* way of modeling the economy? The answer is that we have captured a significant amount of information on this single diagram. No longer will we have to draw, over and over, money market and 45-degree-line diagrams. Instead, we now can use *IS* and *LM* together to analyze the same issues that we previously used these diagrams to examine.

IS-LM EQUILIBRIUM AND DISEQUILIBRIUM

If we are to term the single point where *IS* and *LM* cross an *equilibrium point,* it should be the case that, if the economy were to depart somehow from that point, there should be forces that would automatically push the economy back toward that point. In fact, this is the case.

Consider first a disequilibrium position that would exist at point *A* in Figure 20-19. Recall that, along the *LM* schedule, the market for real money balances is in equilibrium for any given level of income. At point *A,* above the *LM* schedule at the interest rate r_n^1 and income level y_1, the interest rate is too high to achieve equilibrium in the market for

Figure 20-19

***IS-LM* Equilibrium and Disequilibrium.** At point *E*, at which the *IS* and *LM* schedules cross, the market for real money balances is in equilibrium, and aggregate real desired expenditures equal aggregate real income. At points *A* and *D*, the economy is on its *IS* schedule but is not on its *LM* schedule, and so the market for real money balances is not in equilibrium; the interest rate will move back toward the equilibrium level r_n^0 at point *E*. At points *B* and *C*, the economy is on its *LM* schedule but is not on its *IS* schedule, and so aggregate desired real expenditures are not equal to aggregate real income; real income will move toward the equilibrium level y_0 at point *E*.

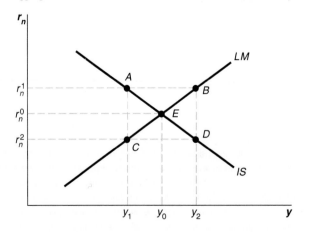

real money balances. This implies there is an excess quantity of money supplied at this interest rate. Therefore, the interest rate will tend to fall toward r_n^0. And as the interest rate falls, equilibrium real income rises. This causes a movement along the *IS* schedule toward point *E* and the real income level y_0.

Similar logic implies that at point *D*, below the *LM* schedule at the interest rate r_n^2 and income level y_2, the interest rate is too low to achieve equilibrium in the market for real money balances. This would result in an excess quantity of real money balances demanded at this interest rate, which would cause the interest rate to rise toward r_n^0. As the interest rate rises, equilibrium real income will fall, causing a movement up along the *IS* schedule toward point *E* and real income y_0.

Also, we know that the *IS* schedule plots all possible equilibrium real income levels for any given rate of interest. Therefore, at point *B*, to the right of the *IS* schedule at real income level y_2, real income is above its equilibrium level; that is, real income exceeds aggregate desired expenditures at the interest rate r_n^1. This means that, at this point, actual output, which by definition is $c + i_r + g$, exceeds aggregate desired expenditures, $c + i + g$. Therefore, $i_r > i$; actual, realized firm investment exceeds desired firm investment. As a result, undesired investment expenditures on capital goods and inventories will accumulate for firms. Firms will reduce their real investment, causing real income to fall toward its equilibrium level, y_0. As real income falls, the demand for real money balances falls. This causes a fall in the interest rate that shows up as a movement along the *LM* schedule from point *B* toward the equilibrium point *E*.

Finally, at point *C*, the opposite situation exists. The level of real income, y_2, is too low relative to desired real expenditures at the interest rate r_n^2. Because output equals $c + i_r + g$ while aggregate desired expenditures equal $c + i + g$, it is true that $i_r < i$ at point *C*. Firms desire to do more investment spending than presently is undertaken, and so they will increase real investment, and thus real income will rise toward y_0. As real income rises, so does the demand for real money balances, which causes an upward movement along the *LM* schedule as the interest rate is driven upward toward r_n^0 at point *E*.

MONETARY POLICY IN THE *IS-LM* MODEL

We are now (finally!) able to understand how monetary policy affects economic activity in the traditional Keynesian system. As a further dividend from all this intellectual effort that we have marshaled to put together the *IS-LM* model, we also can say much more about the effects of fiscal policy in the traditional model. It is, though, best to begin by considering the way that monetary policy works in the *IS-LM* framework.

MONETARY POLICY IN *IS-LM*

Suppose that the Federal Reserve conducts an open-market purchase (it could also, as we discussed in Chapter 17, reduce the discount rate or cut reserve requirements), thereby causing an increase in the nominal supply of money. Suppose further that the price level remains unchanged. (As we shall see in the next chapter, this is a heroic assumption.) Then, as shown in Figure 20-20, the *LM* schedule shifts downward and to the right, from $LM(M_0/P_0)$ to $LM(M_1/P_0)$.

Before the shift in the *LM* schedule, the initial *IS-LM* equilibrium point was *E*. After the shift, at the initial level of real income y_0, the nominal interest rate r_n^0 now lies above the new *LM* schedule and cannot be consistent with a new *IS-LM* equilibrium. At this interest rate, there is now an excess quantity of money supplied, and the interest rate will

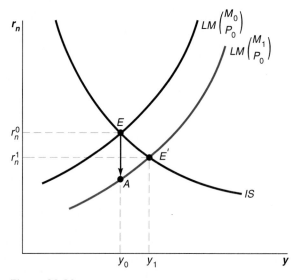

Figure 20-20

The Effect of an Increase in the Nominal Money Supply. A constant-price increase in the nominal money supply causes a liquidity-effect reduction in the nominal interest rate, and so the *LM* schedule shifts downward by the distance *E* − *A*. As the interest rate falls, desired real investment rises, causing equilibrium real income to increase. The rise in real income causes an increase in the demand for real money balances, resulting in a rise in the interest rate. On net, the nominal interest rate falls, and real income rises, as shown by a new equilibrium point *E'*.

be driven downward toward point *A*. As the interest rate falls, aggregate desired investment and, therefore, aggregate desired expenditures will increase. This causes a movement down along the *IS* schedule from point *A* toward point *E'*. Point *E'* is the new *IS-LM* equilibrium. The net effect of a constant-price increase in the nominal money supply is an increase in equilibrium real income and a reduction in the equilibrium nominal interest rate.

If the nominal money supply is instead reduced while the price level remains unchanged, the discussion above would be reversed. Equilibrium real income falls, and the equilibrium nominal rate of interest increases.

THE KEYNESIAN TRANSMISSION MECHANISM FOR MONETARY POLICY

The example depicted in Figure 20-20 and discussed above illustrates the **Keynesian monetary policy transmission mechanism.** This is the essential Keynesian theory of how changes in the quantity of money are transmitted to other variables in the economy. According to the traditional Keynesian model, changes in the quantity of money induced by alterations in Federal Reserve policy instruments influence equilibrium real income through two linkages. First, a change in the nominal money supply causes a liquidity effect, in the opposite direction from the nominal money supply change, on the equilibrium nominal interest rate. Second, a change in the interest rate causes a change, in the opposite direction, in desired real investment and aggregate desired expenditures. On net, this chain of events, summarized in Figure 20-21, results in a change in equilibrium real income in the same direction as the change in the nominal money supply.

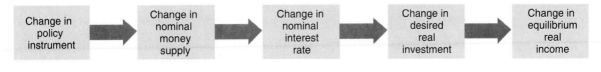

Figure 20-21
The Keynesian Monetary Policy Transmission Mechanism.   Changes in monetary policy instruments cause a change in the nominal money supply. According to the traditional Keynesian model, this, in turn, causes a liquidity effect on the nominal interest rate. A change in the interest rate then causes a change in real desired investment and a resulting change in equilibrium real income.

According to this mechanism for the transmission of monetary policy actions, the size of the effect of a change in the nominal money supply depends on two factors. First, if the liquidity effect, or the effect of the change in the nominal supply of money on the nominal interest rate, is large, then the ultimate effect on real income is more likely to be large. If the liquidity effect is small, then the ultimate effect of monetary policy changes on real income is more likely to be small.

What governs the size of the liquidity effect? Recall that the relative steepness or shallowness of the *LM* schedule depends on the interest sensitivity, or elasticity, of the demand for real money balances. If the demand schedule for real money balances is relatively more interest-elastic (shallow), then a given constant-price change in the nominal money supply causes a relatively smaller change in the nominal interest rate. The liquidity effect in this case will be comparatively small, and the result is a shallow *LM* schedule. In contrast, if the demand schedule for real money balances is relatively more interest-inelastic (steep), then a given constant-price change in the nominal money supply causes a relatively larger change in the nominal interest rate. The liquidity effect in this case will be comparatively large, and the *LM* schedule is steep. Thus, the more interest-inelastic (less interest-elastic) is the public's demand for real money balances—that is, the steeper is the *LM* schedule—the greater will be the liquidity effect of a given nominal money supply change.

Second, if the effect of a given interest rate change on the amount of desired real investment spending is relatively small, meaning that investment is relatively interest-insensitive, or interest-inelastic—so that the *IS* schedule is comparatively steep—then the ultimate effect of monetary policy actions on real income is more likely to be comparatively small as well. If the effect of a given interest rate change on the amount of desired real investment spending is relatively large, meaning that investment is relatively interest-elastic—so that the *IS* schedule is comparatively shallow—then the ultimate effect of monetary policy actions on real income is more likely to be comparatively large. Thus, the more interest-elastic is desired investment spending by firms—that is, the more shallow is the *IS* schedule—the greater will be the ultimate effects of a monetary policy action on equilibrium real income.

We can conclude that, according to the Keynesian monetary policy transmission mechanism, a constant-price increase in the nominal money supply will cause the equilibrium nominal interest rate to fall and the equilibrium level of real income to rise. A constant-price decrease in the nominal money supply will cause the equilibrium nominal interest rate to rise and the equilibrium level of real income to fall. The size of the effect on real income will be larger when the demand for real money balances is relatively more interest-inelastic, so that the *LM* schedule is more steep. When desired investment spending is relatively more interest-elastic, the *IS* schedule is more shallow.

FISCAL POLICY IN THE *IS-LM* MODEL

In the simple model we considered in Chapter 19, we saw that fiscal policy actions, such as changes in government spending or in taxes, had multiplier effects on equilibrium real income. Further, there is no guarantee in the traditional Keynesian model that real income will equal the full-employment income level. Hence, because fiscal policy actions can influence real income, some possible justification exists for using fiscal policies to stabilize real income. This analysis was, however, oversimplified. The reason is that throughout that discussion we ignored the effects of fiscal policy actions on economic variables other than real income. In fact, one of the key disputes about the effectiveness of fiscal stabilization policies concerns how such policies also may influence interest rates.

FISCAL POLICY IN *IS-LM*

We can best understand the effects of fiscal policy in the *IS-LM* model by considering an example. Suppose that real government spending rises, holding all other things (including taxes) constant. If taxes are unchanged, then the government would finance this increase in government spending out of any previously existing government budget surplus or, more likely, from an increase in an already existing budget deficit.

Figure 20-22 illustrates the effects of this fiscal policy action in the *IS-LM* framework. The increase in government expenditures causes the *IS* schedule to shift rightward. At the initial equilibrium interest rate r_n^0, real income will rise. How much will income rise? Recall that in Chapter 19, in which we held all factors other than real income constant, a rise in government spending increased real income by a multiple amount. The per-dollar multiplier was equal to $M_g = 1/(1 - \text{MPC})$. This amount is, in fact, the amount by which the *IS* schedule shifts rightward, toward point *A* from the initial equilibrium point *E*.

We must now consider the fact that the demand for real money balances will increase

Figure 20-22
The Effect of an Increase in Government Spending. A constant-price increase in the level of government spending shifts the *IS* schedule rightward by the distance *A − E*. As real income rises, the demand for real money balances rises, causing the equilibrium interest rate to increase. This in turn causes desired real investment to fall; there is partial *crowding out*. Real income falls somewhat as a result. On net, the nominal interest rate and real income both increase, as shown by a new equilibrium point *E'*.

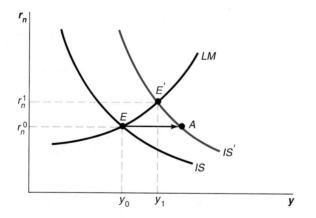

in response to this rise in real income. This causes a rise in the equilibrium interest rate from from r_n^0 to r_n^1 that is shown by an upward movement along the *LM* schedule from point *A* to point *E'*. As the equilibrium interest rate rises, real autonomous investment falls, causing real income to decrease somewhat, to y_1.

How much is the decrease in real income caused by the fall in investment? Recall that in Chapter 19 we determined that, holding the interest rate constant, a reduction in investment spending would cause a fall in real income equal to the autonomous expenditures multiplier, $1/(1 - MPC)$, times the fall in investment. Here, we again have a decline in investment spending; in the present instance, though, this fall in investment resulted from a rise in the interest rate. Yet the multiplier effect is still $1/(1 - MPC)$ times the fall in investment. Thus, although the rise in government spending initially causes real income to rise by a multiple amount, the induced rise in the interest rate causes investment to fall. This causes real income again to fall by a multiple amount.

In general, the *net effect* of the increase in real government expenditures on equilibrium real income is positive, as shown in Figure 20-22. The equilibrium interest rate also rises. If government spending had fallen, equilibrium real income would have fallen, and the equilibrium interest rate also would have decreased.

Suppose that, instead of an increase in government spending, there had been a reduction in taxes. In this case, the *IS* schedule again would have shifted to the right. The amount of the shift in this event would have been the amount of the tax reduction multiplied by the tax multiplier, $M_t = -MPC/(1 - MPC)$. Thus the equilibrium level of real income would increase. Nevertheless, the final amount of the increase would be smaller than the amount of the shift in the *IS* schedule. The reason would be that as real income rose, so would the demand for real money balances and the equilibrium interest rate. As a result, real income would fall somewhat. On net, a tax reduction therefore causes both the equilibrium nominal interest rate and the equilibrium real income level to rise. A tax increase causes the opposite effects.

THE CROWDING-OUT EFFECT

The reason that the equilibrium level of real income in the *IS-LM* model rises by less following an expansionary fiscal policy action—a rise in government spending or a reduction in taxes—than the traditional multiplier effect would predict is simple. When real income starts to rise, so does the demand for real money balances and the equilibrium nominal interest rate. The induced rise in the interest rate causes real desired investment spending by firms to fall. As a result, real income falls by an amount that is a multiple of the reduction in desired investment expenditures.

The rise in government spending or reduction in taxes consequently causes, through induced interest rate changes, decreased private spending by business firms. Economists call this the **crowding-out effect.** This crowding-out effect is reminiscent of the prediction of the classical model that increases in government deficits completely crowd out an equal amount of private expenditures on goods and services. In the traditional Keynesian model, however, there is not generally complete crowding out. Rather, equilibrium real income rises, on net, when government spending rises or when taxes fall.

What determines the relative size of the crowding-out effect? Suppose that Figure 20-22 had been drawn with a very steep *IS* schedule (so that desired investment is relatively interest-inelastic) and with a very shallow *LM* schedule (so that the demand for real money balances is relatively interest-elastic). If the schedules were shaped in this way, the amount of the final increase in equilibrium real income would have been very nearly the same as the amount of the rightward shift in the *IS* schedule. The crowding-out effect would have

CURRENT

CONTROVERSY

HAS THERE EVER BEEN A "LIQUIDITY TRAP"?

Traditionally, many observers have associated Keynesian economics with the view that fiscal policy has an important role to play in macroeconomic stabilization. The reason for this dates back to Keynes's own writings and statements. During the Great Depression, Keynes became convinced that the economy was in a **liquidity trap.** A liquidity trap is a situation in which interest rates are so low that nearly everyone anticipates that they will rise in the future. To avoid the implied capital losses on bond holdings, nearly all individuals in the economy choose to hold most of their wealth as money.

In the traditional Keynesian model, a liquidity trap occurs along the horizontal portion of the money demand schedule. This corresponds to a horizontal region along the economy's *LM* schedule. Hence, in a liquidity trap the economy finds itself in a situation in which *LM* is extremely shallow. Monetary policy is almost completely ineffective as an instrument for influencing real income. Increases in the nominal money supply cannot significantly raise output or reduce the rate of interest; the economy is "trapped" in a situation in which it is awash in desired liquidity. However, fiscal policy changes such as increases in government expenditures or tax cuts shift the *IS* schedule rightward and, with a horizontal *LM* schedule, have comparatively large effects on equilibrium real income.

Keynes speculated about whether the liquidity trap was a theoretical curiosity or a situation that might actually arise in the real world. Many followers of Keynes concluded, following the Great Depression, that the Great Depression itself might have been an example of a liquidity trap. They maintained that sufficiently expansionary fiscal policy actions during the Great Depression might have ended the deep recession. Although Keynes himself did not claim that the Great Depression was a liquidity trap situation (indeed, in the *General Theory* he noted that he knew of no example of a liquidity trap[*]), he was adamant that government expenditure programs were needed. In a 1930 radio broadcast, he said, "If we just sit tight, there will be still more than a million men unemployed six months or a year hence. That is why I feel that a radical policy of some kind is worth trying, even if there are risks about it."

As we know, the Great Depression did end, and governments' shares of expenditures increased significantly after the 1930s. There has been significant disagreement among economists, nevertheless, about whether or not a liquidity trap ever really existed during the 1930s, or, for that matter, at any other period in history. Several studies have concluded that a liquidity trap has *not* existed in the United States, at least not during the twentieth century.[†]

Examination of actual data on the real quantity of money and long-term interest rates for the period 1929–1941 also leads one to conclude that no liquidity trap existed in this country during the Great Depression. Casual observation, or graphical exposition, of those data indicate a negative relationship between those variables; the curve relating them does not become parallel to the horizontal axis, but appears negatively sloped throughout.

H. W. Pifer decided to test the liquidity trap hypothesis more directly.[‡] Pifer tested the proposition that the demand for money approaches infinity when the rate of interest approaches some minimum value, using a nonlinear estimating technique. He concluded that the minimum interest rate value that generates a demand for money that approaches infinity is not significantly different from zero and doubts that a liquidity trap exists at a positive interest rate.

Lest you think that for once empirical studies provide conclusive evidence, we hasten to point out that Robert Eisner maintains that Pifer used an incorrect statistical test; Eisner subjected Pifer's model to other statistical criteria. Eisner estimates that a liquidity trap, in the sense that the demand for money approaches infinity, exists at a real interest rate of approximately 2 percent.

Although on balance there seems to be little evidence of a liquidity trap, we cannot rule out completely the possibility of its existence.

[*] John Maynard Keynes, *The General Theory of Employment, Interest, and Money* (London: Macmillan, 1936), p. 207.
[†] See Martin Bronfenbrenner and Thomas Mayer, "Liquidity Functions in the American Economy," *Econometrica,* 28 (October 1960), pp. 810–834, and David Laidler, "The Rate of Interest and the Demand for Money: Some Empirical Evidence," *Journal of Political Economy,* 74 (December 1966), pp. 543–555.
[‡] H. W. Pifer, "A Non-Linear, Maximum Likelihood Estimate of the Liquidity Trap," *Econometrica,* 37 (April 1969), pp. 324–332.

been very small. In contrast, if Figure 20-22 had been drawn with a very shallow *IS* schedule (so that desired investment is relatively interest-elastic) and with a very steep *LM* schedule (so that the demand for real money balances is relatively interest-inelastic), the amount of the final increase in equilibrium real income would have been very nearly equal to zero. There would have been very nearly complete crowding out. We may conclude that the crowding-out effect grows larger as the interest elasticity of desired investment increases. The crowding-out effect also rises as the interest elasticity of the demand for real money balances falls.

Note that the extreme case of complete crowding out would occur when the *IS* schedule is horizontal (desired investment is completely interest-elastic) and the *LM* schedule is vertical (the demand for real money balances is completely interest-inelastic). In this case, a rise in government spending would shift the *IS* schedule horizontally along itself, causing no change in the equilibrium real income level. This means that real investment spending falls by exactly the same amount as the rise in government spending—crowding out is indeed complete. This special case, then, is the *IS-LM* analogue to the classical model. This makes sense, because the classical model emphasized the interest sensitivity of desired investment but had absolutely no interest sensitivity of money demand. In this view, as the *IS-LM* model makes clear, crowding out must be complete.

THE CASE FOR AND AGAINST MONETARY-FISCAL COORDINATION

Fiscal policy actions can influence the position of the *IS* schedule, while monetary policy actions affect the position of the *LM* schedule. In principle, fiscal and monetary policy making could jointly achieve target levels of both real income and the rate of interest. Fiscal policy actions could place the *IS* schedule in a position consistent with a desired level of income. Monetary policy actions then could move the *LM* schedule to a position at that income level and at a desired rate of interest. The result would be monetary and fiscal **policy coordination.**

Should monetary and fiscal policy makers coordinate their actions? Like many questions in economics, it turns out that the answer to this one is difficult to resolve. Coordination of policy making potentially can improve upon noncoordinated policy making if "coordination" means "agreeable cooperation." If both the Federal Reserve and the government share the same goals, and if those goals are truly what is best for the economy, then from a theoretical standpoint society could gain from policy coordination.

It is possible, however, that monetary and fiscal policy makers may desire to achieve different goals. For instance, the Federal Reserve might seek greater financial stability, while the the President and Congress might desire greater real income stability. It is likely that different real income–interest rate combinations would be consistent with these differing policy goals. This would generate tensions between the policy makers.

Indeed, it is arguable that such tensions might be desirable. An overemphasis by the President and Congress on achieving stability around a "high" level of real income might produce financial instability if the Federal Reserve were to coordinate its monetary policy making with fiscal policy actions. In contrast, an overemphasis on financial stability on the part of the Federal Reserve might cause significant instability of real income if the President and Congress were to coordinate fiscal policies with the Federal Reserve's monetary policies. For this reason, noncoordinated policy making might be the best way to "split the difference" between potentially competing objectives. Coordinated policies might be undesirable.

MONETARY-FISCAL COORDINATION IN EUROPE?

INTERNATIONAL

PERSPECTIVE

In 1958, six Western European nations formed the *European Community,* or EC, which is an institutional structure intended to promote various forms of economic cooperation. Since that time the EC has added several members, all of whom in 1992 dropped many restrictions on trade across the borders of their nations. Also, in 1978 a group of nations within the EC formed the *European Monetary System,* or EMS. The EMS tries to coordinate monetary policies within the member group of nations. The consistent goal of this subgroup of nations within the EC has been to induce all EC members to join the EMS. Another, more controversial goal has been to turn the EMS, ultimately, into a single monetary policy-making authority that has euphemistically been termed a "EuroFed." Finally, many proponents of this plan have argued that if it is to be successful, there must be greater harmonization of fiscal policy making within the EC. In short, these proponents of a EuroFed claim that monetary and fiscal policy coordination would be desirable not only within individual European nations but also *between* these nations. A debate on this issue has been ongoing since the formation of the EMS.

In light of our discussion of the issues involved in coordinating monetary and fiscal policies within a single nation like the United States, it should not be too surprising that the European debate has not yet reached a conclusion. Obviously, the interests of policy makers within a single nation may differ, and perhaps for legitimate reasons. In Europe, the added problem is that *national interests* may differ, making coordination of policy making potentially desirable for some nations but potentially undesirable for others.

There is a historical precedent for optimism on the part of proponents of European monetary coordination. That precedent is the history of monetary policy of the United States. Through the late eighteenth century and much of the nineteenth century, individual states tried to conduct their own banking and monetary policies, often placing state interests above the interests of the United States. As we saw earlier, ultimately Congress established a single federal monetary authority, the Federal Reserve System. It effectively coordinates monetary policy for all the states within the United States. In principle, European governments could duplicate this institutional change.

Of course, the United States also offers another historical precedent that may dampen the hopes of the promoters of European policy coordination. It is apparent that divided aims of monetary and fiscal policy makers have made close monetary-fiscal coordination in the United States at best a fleeting achievement and at worst a nonexistent ideal for some American economists who believe such coordination would be desirable. The national interests that divide European nations necessarily would complicate European monetary-fiscal coordination whether or not Europe ever forms a EuroFed. This is likely to be an issue in Europe for some time to come.

Some economists argue that another reason that policy coordination might not be a good idea is that coordinated monetary and fiscal policy efforts to expand real income could place upward pressure on the level of prices in the economy. That is, economists sometimes argue that greater monetary-fiscal coordination could have inflationary consequences. However, we are not yet able to discuss this issue, because to this point we have assumed that the level of prices is fixed. We shall investigate the determination of the price level in the traditional Keynesian model in the next chapter.

CHAPTER SUMMARY

1. By incorporating the transactions and precautionary motives into his general theory of the demand for money, Keynes followed in the footsteps of the classical economists. However,

Keynes's central contribution was the theory of the speculative motive for holding money, which focuses on money's role as a financial asset.

2. Under the speculative motive for holding money, individuals respond to current increases in the rate of interest and corresponding reductions in current bond prices by allocating more of their financial wealth to holdings of bonds and less to money holdings. They do so in hopes of capital gains when bond prices rise in the future and interest rates fall.

3. The total demand for money is the sum of the amounts held for transactions, precautionary, and speculative purposes. Because the speculative demand for money varies inversely with the interest rate, so does the total demand for money. Because the transactions and precautionary demands for money depend positively on income, so does the total demand for money.

4. Individuals concern themselves with the real purchasing power of their nominal money holdings, which are their real money balances.

5. In the traditional Keynesian model, the equilibrium nominal interest rate is determined by the equalization of the quantity of real money balances demanded with the quantity of real money balances supplied.

6. As real income rises, so does the demand for real money balances and the equilibrium nominal rate of interest. This positive relationship between real income and the money-market-equilibrium interest rate generates the *LM* schedule.

7. The *LM* schedule is a locus of all combinations of real income and the nominal rates of interest for which the market for real money balances is in equilibrium. The *LM* schedule is more shallow when the demand for real money balances is more interest-elastic. It steepens when the demand for real money balances becomes more interest-inelastic.

8. An increase in the nominal money supply causes a liquidity effect on the nominal interest rate and shifts the *LM* schedule downward and to the right. An increase in the price level causes a real balance effect on the interest rate and shifts the *LM* schedule upward and to the left. Finally, a reduction in the demand for real money balances that is unrelated to the level of real income shifts the *LM* schedule downward and to the right.

9. As the rate of interest rises, desired real investment spending declines, causing a fall in aggregate desired expenditures and a reduction in equilibrium real income. This negative relationship between the rate of interest and equilibrium real income generates the *IS* schedule.

10. The *IS* schedule is a locus of all combinations of real income levels and interest rates for which aggregate desired expenditures are equal to real income. The slope of the *IS* schedule is more shallow when desired real investment is more interest-elastic. The *IS* schedule steepens when desired real investment becomes more interest-inelastic.

11. The *IS* schedule shifts upward and to the right whenever a rise in aggregate autonomous expenditures occurs that is unrelated to changes in the interest rate. This could result from a rise in autonomous consumption, an increase in autonomous investment not caused by a fall in the interest rate, an increase in autonomous government expenditures, or a lump-sum autonomous tax cut. In contrast, the *IS* schedule shifts downward and to the left whenever a fall in aggregate autonomous spending takes place.

12. An *IS-LM* equilibrium occurs when both equilibrium real income and money market equilibrium are attained simultaneously. This occurs at the single point where the *IS* and *LM* schedules cross. By varying the positions of the *IS* and *LM* schedules, fiscal and monetary policy makers can alter the equilibrium levels of real income and the rate of interest.

13. In principle, monetary and fiscal policy makers might coordinate policy actions designed to influence the positions of the *IS* and *LM* schedules. However, such coordination would be difficult to achieve if the policy makers have different goals. Furthermore, different goals could be deemed desirable, making noncoordinated policy making preferable in some instances to policy coordination.

GLOSSARY

Consol: A perpetual, or nonmaturing, bond.

Crowding-out effect: A reduction in private spending resulting from a higher interest rate caused by a fiscal-policy-induced rise in real income.

Interest-elastic demand for money: Demand for money that is relatively sensitive to changes in the interest rate.

Interest-elastic desired investment: Desired investment that is relatively sensitive to changes in the interest rate.

Interest elasticity of desired investment: A measure of the relative responsiveness of desired investment spending to changes in the interest rate.

Interest elasticity of money demand: A measure of the relative responsiveness of desired holdings of money balances to changes in the interest rate.

Interest-inelastic demand for money: Demand for money that is relatively insensitive to changes in the interest rate.

Interest-inelastic desired investment: Desired investment that is relatively insensitive to changes in the interest rate.

IS schedule: A locus of all combinations of real income levels and interest rates that are consistent with the attainment of equilibrium real income.

IS-LM equilibrium: The single point where the IS and LM schedules intersect; at this point, the economy attains equilibrium real income and simultaneously achieves money market equilibrium.

Keynesian monetary policy transmission mechanism: Essential Keynesian theory of how changes in the quantity of money are transmitted to other variables in the economy. A constant-price increase in the nominal money supply reduces the nominal interest rate via a liquidity effect, and this fall in the interest rate stimulates a rise in desired investment spending and aggregate desired expenditures that causes equilibrium real income to increase.

Liquidity effect: A reduction in the nominal rate of interest that results from an increase in the nominal quantity of money supplied, holding the level of prices unchanged.

Liquidity trap: The very shallow ranges of the money demand and LM schedules along which virtually everyone agrees that market interest rates are likely to rise in the future and that money is an asset far superior to bonds; in a liquidity trap, the demand for real money balances is nearly completely interest-elastic.

LM schedule: A locus of all combinations of real income levels and interest rates that are consistent with the attainment of equilibrium in the market for money.

Policy coordination: The joint determination of policy actions by separate policy authorities, such as different governmental agencies within a country or between countries, in pursuit of common economic goals.

Portfolio demand for money: Term for a simplified version of Keynes's model of the speculative demand for money. In the simplified model, individuals hold both money and bonds but adjust the composition of their wealth portfolios in light of their speculations about interest rate movements.

Real balance effect: An increase (decrease) in the nominal rate of interest that results from an increase (decrease) in the level of prices of goods and services, holding the nominal quantity of money supplied unchanged.

Real money balances: The price-level-adjusted value of the nominal, current-dollar quantity of money, defined as the ratio of the nominal money stock to the price level; the real purchasing power of the nominal quantity of money.

Speculative demand for money: Keynes's theoretical motivation for an inverse relationship between the nominal interest rate and desired money holdings.

SELF-TEST QUESTIONS

1. Of the classical and Keynesian theories of the demand for money, which would you argue is the more *general* theory? Why?

2. Keynes's theory of the demand for money classifies three motives for holding non-interest-bearing money. Name and briefly describe these motives. Which hypothesized rationale for money demand represents the greatest departure from the classical theory of money demand? Explain.

3. Show graphically how the *LM* schedule is derived from equilibrium in the market for real money balances.

4. Show graphically how the *IS* schedule is derived from the condition for equilibrium real national income.

5. Use graphs of the market for real money balances and of the *LM* schedule to explain how a decline in the demand for real money balances that is *unrelated* to national income (arising perhaps from the increased use of credit cards) affects the position of the *LM* schedule. In addition, use a separate, full *IS-LM* diagram to determine the effects of such a decline in money demand on the equilibrium levels of real income and the rate of interest, holding all other factors unchanged.

6. Suppose that government spending is increased while taxes are simultaneously reduced, so that the government runs a budget deficit. In addition, suppose that this deficit is financed by selling government bonds to the Federal Reserve, which creates new money to purchase these bonds. Use the *IS-LM* model to explain the possible effects of this ''money-financed'' increase in the government's deficit. Is the crowding-out effect of deficit spending made larger or smaller by selling government bonds to the Federal Reserve? Why?

7. Draw an *IS-LM* diagram. Label the *IS-LM* equilibrium point E.
   a. Mark a point on the *IS* schedule below and to the right of point E, and label this point C. Is equilibrium real income attained at point C? Is money market equilibrium attained at point C? Explain.
   b. If the economy is at point C, what direction on your diagram will it tend to move? Why?
   c. Mark a point on the *LM* schedule below and to the left of point E, and label this point B. Is equilibrium real income attained at point C? Is money market equilibrium attained at point C? Explain.
   d. If the economy is at point B, what direction on your diagram will it tend to move? Why?

8. Draw an *IS-LM* diagram. Label the equilibrium point on your diagram E. Now suppose a tax increase is enacted by Congress. Show the effect of this action on your diagram. After the tax increase, is real income still attained at point E? Is the money market in equilibrium at point E after the tax increase? Explain your answers, and explain how equilibrium will be reattained by the economy after the tax increase.

9. Draw an *IS-LM* diagram. Label the equilibrium point on your diagram E. Now suppose that there is a nominal money supply reduction by the Federal Reserve. Show the effect of this action on your diagram. After the money supply reduction, is real income still attained at point E? Is the money market in equilibrium at point E after the money supply reduction? Explain your answers, and explain how equilibrium will be reattained by the economy after the money supply reduction.

PROBLEMS

20-1. Suppose that the speculative demand for real money balances is given by the equation $m_{spec}^d = 1000 - 50r_n$. Also, suppose that the transactions and precautionary real money balances are given by $m_{tran}^d = 2500$ and $m_{prec}^d = 500$.

    a. What is the equation for the total demand for real money balances?

    b. What is the total quantity of real money balances demanded when r_n is equal to (a) 20, (b) 10, (c) 5?

    c. What is the quantity of real money balances held for speculative purposes when r_n is equal to (a) 20, (b) 10, (c) 5?

    d. What is the quantity of real money balances held for transactions purposes when r_n is equal to (a) 20, (b) 10, (c) 5?

    e. What is the quantity of real money balances held for precautionary purposes when r_n is equal to (a) 20, (b) 10, (c) 5?

20-2. Refer to your answer to part a in the previous question to assist in answering the questions below.

    a. Suppose that the price level is equal to 2 and the nominal money supply is 7,000. What is the equilibrium value of r_n?

    b. If the nominal money supply is increased to 7,500, what is the new equilibrium value of r_n? What is the name of this effect on the equilibrium interest rate following an increase in the nominal money supply?

    c. Suppose that the nominal money supply is at its new level of 7,500 but that the price level now rises to a value of 2.5. What is the new equilibrium value of r_n? What is the name of this effect on the equilibrium interest rate arising from a rise in the price level?

20-3. Suppose that the equation for the total demand for real money balances is given by $m^d = 100 - 5r_n + 10y$. In addition, suppose that the nominal money supply is equal to 40 and that the price level is equal to 0.5.

    a. What is the equation for the *LM* schedule?

    b. Draw a rough diagram of the *LM* schedule. What is its slope? What are its horizontal and vertical intercepts?

20-4. Consider the following equations for consumption, desired investment, and government spending: $c = 50 + (0.8)y_d$, $i = 25 - (0.2)r_n$, $g = 25$, $t = 0$.

    a. What is the equation for the *IS* schedule?

    b. Draw a rough diagram of the *IS* schedule. What is its slope? What are its horizontal and vertical intercepts?

20-5. Solve the *LM* equation from problem 20-3 and the *IS* equation from problem 20-4 jointly for the equilibrium interest rate and the equilibrium level of real income.

SELECTED REFERENCES

Branson, William, *Macroeconomic Theory and Policy* (New York: Macmillan, 1978).

Froyen, Richard T., *Macroeconomics: Theories and Policies,* 3d ed. (New York: Macmillan, 1990).

Hansen, Alvin H., *A Guide to Keynes* (New York: McGraw-Hill, 1953).

Harris, Laurence, *Monetary Theory* (New York: McGraw-Hill, 1981).

Hicks, John R., "Mr. Keynes and the Classics: A Suggested Interpretation," *Econometrica,* 5 (2, April 1937), pp. 147–159.

Keynes, John Maynard, *The General Theory of Employment, Interest, and Money* (New York: Harcourt Brace Jovanovich, 1964).

Robertson, Dennis H., ''Mr. Keynes and the Rate of Interest,'' in *Essays in Monetary Theory,* ed. Dennis H. Robertson (London: Staples Press, 1940).

Schinasi, Garry J., ''European Integration, Exchange Rates, and Monetary Reform,'' *The World Economy,* 12 (4, December 1989), pp. 389–413.

Swann, Dennis, *The Economics of the Common Market,* 6th ed. (London: Penguin, 1988).

chapter 21

The Traditional Theory of Money, Prices, and Real Output

The last two chapters have pieced together crucial elements of the traditional Keynesian theory of the functioning of the economy and of the roles of monetary and fiscal policies. This chapter concludes our discussion of the traditional theory by exploring the most crucial issues that separated Keynes and his followers from the intellectual foundations first laid by the classical theorists. Why might equilibrium real income and output differ from the full-employment level of real income and output? If this can happen, what factors could account for it? What, if any, role is there for monetary and fiscal policies to return the economy to full employment once it leaves that state?

These are the central issues that divide economists in the ways that they approach discussions of the roles of monetary and fiscal policies. Ultimately, the diverging stands that economists take on these issues explain why they sometimes reach contradictory conclusions about the effects of policy actions and, indeed, about whether active monetary and fiscal policies are at all desirable. Because these issues are so important, we shall have a lot of ground to cover in this chapter.

We shall demonstrate in this chapter that the traditional Keynesian theory of aggregate demand is significantly different from that of the classical theorists and that this dissemblance can partially explain the wide gulf between economists influenced by Keynes and his followers and other economists who follow in the footsteps of classical theorists. We shall also show that an even wider intellectual gulf separates these groups when it comes to the theory of labor market behavior and the supply side of the economy. In this and the following two chapters we shall seek to explore and understand why this is so.

THE TRADITIONAL KEYNESIAN THEORY OF AGGREGATE DEMAND

In the classical theory, the aggregate demand for real output depended largely on the quantity of money supplied by a central bank such as the Federal Reserve. The classical theorists indicated the level of aggregate demand for goods and services by the position of an aggregate demand schedule relating the desired quantity of real output consumption in the economy to the prevailing level of prices of goods and services. The traditional Keynesian model also implies an aggregate demand schedule that relates real output to the price level.

THE AGGREGATE DEMAND SCHEDULE

Recall that in the *IS-LM* framework the intersection of the *IS* schedule and the *LM* schedule determines equilibrium real income. At this point, aggregate desired expenditures are equal to real income, and the market for real money balances is in equilibrium. In addition, exactly where this equilibrium point lies on the *IS-LM* diagram depends on the position of the *IS* schedule, which is determined by the levels of autonomous consumption, investment, government spending, and taxes, and the position of the *LM* schedule, which is determined by the quantity of real money balances supplied.

An increase in the level of prices from an initial level P_0 to a higher level P_1, holding the nominal money supply constant, causes a *real balance effect* on the nominal interest rate that shifts the *LM* schedule vertically upward. This effect is measured by the distance from the initial equilibrium point E to point A in panel (*a*) of Figure 21-1. When the nominal interest rate rises, equilibrium real income falls, from y_0 to y_1, as desired investment spending and aggregate desired expenditures decrease. Consequently, this real balance effect caused by a rise in the level of prices results in a fall in real income.

As shown in panel (*b*) of the figure, this means that we can plot two real income–price level combinations, y_0 and P_0, and y_1 and P_1, that are consistent with *IS-LM* equilibrium. In turn, both of these real income–price level combinations therefore must be consistent with equilibrium real income and with equilibrium in the market for real money balances. This will be true for all points on a schedule of combinations of points that include the two we have plotted. This schedule of points is the **aggregate demand schedule** for the traditional Keynesian model. All along this schedule lie combinations of real income and levels of prices that maintain *IS-LM* equilibrium.

As the derivation in Figure 21-1 indicates, the factor that accounts for the downward slope of the aggregate demand schedule is the real balance effect of price changes on the nominal interest rate. Changes in the interest rate induced by changes in the price level cause variations in aggregate desired expenditures and, thus, in real income.

MONETARY POLICY AND AGGREGATE DEMAND

Figure 21-1 derived the aggregate demand schedule under the assumption that the nominal quantity of money supplied was constant, at M_0. Now consider what happens to the aggregate demand schedule if the nominal money supply rises from an initial amount M_0

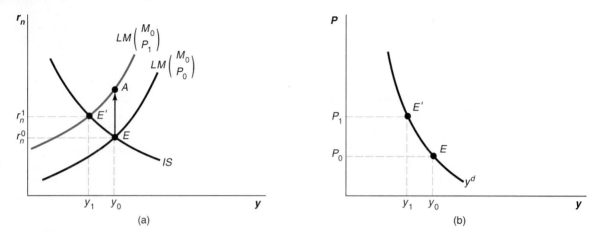

(a) (b)

Figure 21-1
Deriving the Aggregate Demand Schedule. A rise in the level of prices causes a real-balance-effect increase in the equilibrium nominal interest rate of the amount $A - E$ in panel (a). This
is the amount by which the LM schedule shifts upward from an initial equilibrium point E. The final
IS-LM equilibrium is at point E' at a higher nominal interest rate and a lower level of real income
after a decline in desired real investment induced by the rise in the interest rate. Because equilibrium real income falls when the price level rises [panel (b)], the *aggregate demand schedule* slopes
downward.

to a larger amount M_1. As shown in panel (a) of Figure 21-2, at a given real income–price
level combination y_0 and P_0, this increase in the nominal money stock causes the LM
schedule to shift rightward along the IS schedule. Equilibrium real income rises, to y_1.

There is now a new IS-LM equilibrium, however. Recall that the aggregate demand
schedule is a locus of real income–price level combinations that preserve IS-LM equilibrium. It must now be the case that the real income–price level combination y_1 and P_0 lies
on a new aggregate demand schedule in panel (b) that lies to the right of the original
aggregate demand schedule. This means that a rise in the nominal money supply shifts
the aggregate demand schedule to the right. A rise in the nominal money supply *increases*
aggregate demand.

In contrast, a reduction in the nominal money supply would have shifted the LM
schedule upward and to the left, causing real income to fall at any given price level. The
aggregate demand schedule would have shifted leftward following a decrease in the
nominal money supply. Thus, a fall in the nominal money supply *reduces* aggregate
demand.

Note that the size of the effect of a constant-price change in the nominal money supply
depends crucially upon the size of the liquidity effect of the nominal money supply change
on the nominal interest rate. The size of the effect also depends upon the responsiveness
of desired investment to a given change in the interest rate. That is, it depends upon the
strengths of the linkages in the Keynesian monetary policy transmission mechanism. As
we saw in the last chapter, this mechanism weakens considerably as the LM schedule
becomes more shallow (the demand for real money balances becomes more interest-
elastic). It also weakens as the IS schedule becomes more steep (desired investment
spending becomes more interest-inelastic). Consequently, the effects of monetary policy
actions on aggregate demand become smaller as the LM schedule becomes shallower and
as the IS schedule steepens. In the extreme case when the LM schedule is horizontal,

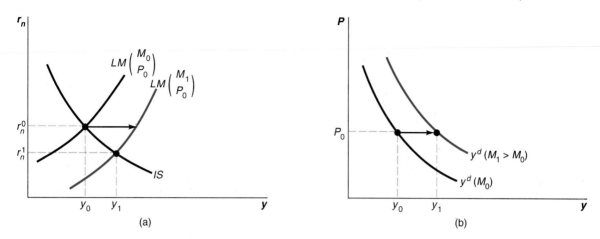

Figure 21-2
The Effect on Aggregate Demand of an Increase in the Nominal Money Supply. A
constant-price increase in the nominal money supply causes the LM schedule to shift downward and
to the right. Equilibrium real income rises [panel (a)]. Because the economy is at a new IS-LM
equilibrium at the same price level with a higher level of real income, it now is on a new aggregate
demand schedule that lies to the right of the original aggregate demand schedule [panel (b)]. A
constant-price rise in the nominal money supply causes an increase in aggregate demand.

monetary policy actions have no effect whatsoever on aggregate demand. This case, of
course, is an extreme version of the *liquidity trap,* in which monetary policy has little, if
any, influence on aggregate demand for goods and services.

FISCAL POLICY AND AGGREGATE DEMAND

In the classical model, fiscal policy played a role in the extent to which government deficit
spending affected the real interest rate. Deficit-financed government spending completely
crowded out an equal-sized amount of private spending. This meant that fiscal policy
actions caused a redistribution of output between the government and the private sector
of the economy. Therefore, the classical theorists concluded that fiscal policy actions had
no effect on aggregate demand.

As we saw in the last chapter, the traditional Keynesian model also indicates that
increases in government deficits can crowd out private desired expenditures. In this framework crowding out is not, however, complete. This means that fiscal policy affects aggregate demand in traditional Keynesian theory.

Figure 21-3 shows why this is the case. Panel (a) shows the effects of an increase in
real government spending, from g_0 to a larger amount g_1, holding the level of prices of
goods and services unchanged at P_0. The IS schedule shifts rightward by the amount of
the spending increase times the government spending multiplier, $1/(1 - \text{MPC})$. As real
income rises, however, the demand for real money balances increases, driving up the
equilibrium nominal interest rate. In response, desired real investment expenditures
decline. There is not complete crowding out, and so, on net, real income rises, from
y_0 to y_1.

The economy is at a new IS-LM equilibrium in panel (a), and so by definition it must
be operating on an aggregate demand schedule to the right of the real income–price level
combination y_0 and P_0, at the new real income–price level combination y_1 and P_0. This

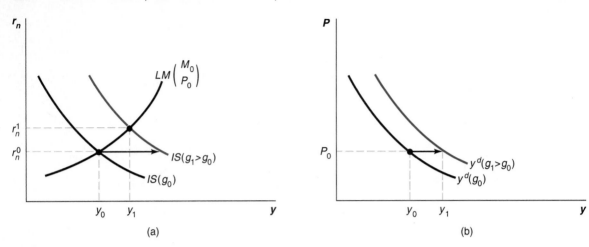

Figure 21-3

The Effect on Aggregate Demand of an Increase in Government Spending. A constant-price increase in real government spending causes the *IS* schedule to shift rightward. Equilibrium real income rises [panel (*a*)]. Because the economy is at a new *IS-LM* equilibrium at the same price level with a higher level of real income, it now is on a new aggregate demand schedule that lies to the right of the original aggregate demand schedule [panel (*b*)]. A constant-price rise in real government spending causes an increase in aggregate demand.

means that the rise in government spending shifts the aggregate demand schedule outward and to the right, as shown in panel (*b*) of the figure. An increase in real government expenditures causes an increase in aggregate demand.

Note that a reduction in taxes would have had the same basic effects. The only difference would have been that the *IS* schedule would have shifted rightward by the amount of the tax reduction times the tax multiplier, $-MPC/(1 - MPC)$. Therefore, a reduction in taxes also causes an increase in aggregate demand.

Finally, an increase in any other component of aggregate desired expenditures also would raise aggregate demand. For instance, increases in autonomous consumption or in autonomous investment cause the *IS* schedule to shift rightward, thereby causing a rightward shift in the aggregate demand schedule. (In addition, as you saw in the International Perspective in Chapter 19, an increase in exports or a reduction in imports would have these same effects.)

If there had been a reduction in real government expenditures or an increase in real taxes, there would instead have been a leftward shift in the *IS* schedule. The equilibrium nominal interest rate would have fallen as the resulting fall in real income caused a reduction in the demand for real money balances. This would have induced a rise in desired investment spending that would have partially, but not fully, offset the fall in equilibrium real income. Because real income would fall, on net, holding the price level constant, aggregate demand would have shifted to the left. Reductions in government spending or increases in taxes reduce aggregate demand.

Note that the magnitudes of the aggregate demand effects of changes in government spending or taxes depend crucially upon how much crowding out occurs. Furthermore, as we saw in the last chapter, the crowding-out effect becomes larger as the *LM* becomes more steep (as the demand for real money balances becomes more interest-inelastic) and as the *IS* schedule becomes more shallow (as desired investment spending becomes more interest-elastic). Therefore, the steeper is the *LM* schedule and the shallower is the *IS* schedule, the smaller will be the effects of fiscal policy actions on aggregate demand. In the extreme case when the *LM* schedule is vertical and the *IS* schedule is horizontal, crowding out is complete, and fiscal policy has no influence on aggregate demand in the economy. In this extreme case, therefore, the traditional Keynesian model produces the same conclusion about the role of fiscal policy as that obtained by classical theory.

THEORIES OF AGGREGATE SUPPLY

The most radical departures of the traditional Keynesian model from that proposed by the classical theorists have to do with the supply side of the economy. As we saw in Chapter 18, the classical economists made three important assumptions when they examined the market for labor and derived the classical aggregate supply schedule:

1. Rational self-interest
2. Pure competition, with completely flexible wages and prices
3. No money illusion

Keynes and his followers had—and continue to have—quarrels with the latter two of these assumptions. The traditional Keynesian model attempted to demolish the assumption of flexible wages and prices and of a complete absence of money illusion. Consequently, we shall focus our attention on these latter two issues in the present chapter.

Our approach in this chapter will be to examine the effects of dropping each of these two assumptions individually. In the next chapter we shall see how we can handle both at the same time, which is the approach taken in modern Keynesian theories.

THE CASE OF STICKY MONEY WAGES

One of the most bothersome things about the classical theory, according to Keynes, was its assumption that all wages and prices are completely flexible. The assumption of complete flexibility of prices clearly failed to hold during the Great Depression. For instance, the prices of agricultural products declined by 63 percent during the period 1929–1933, while the prices of implements used in agricultural production fell by only 6 percent (which obviously squeezed the profitability of the agricultural industry—mainly small family farms at that time—considerably). The prices of petroleum products fell by 56 percent during the same period, but motor vehicle prices declined by only 16 percent. To Keynes, the notion that the economywide level of prices adjusted as fully as the classical model predicted was obviously incorrect.

Another problem with the classical model, according to Keynes and many of his followers, was its assumption that nominal wages were completely flexible. During the Great Depression, wages in many industries fell little, if at all, and yet many people were out of work and could not find jobs. According to the classical theory, this surplus of available labor services should have been eliminated as the nominal wage was bid downward. Unemployment should have been temporary. The lengthy duration of the Great Depression, said Keynes, represented clear evidence that nominal wages were not flexible enough to end unemployment.

To see what wage inflexibility, or ''stickiness,'' implies for labor employment and the economy's output of goods and services in the face of falling prices, as during the Great Depression, consider Figure 21-4. Panel (*a*) of the figure shows a labor market diagram

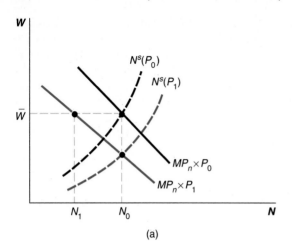

(a)

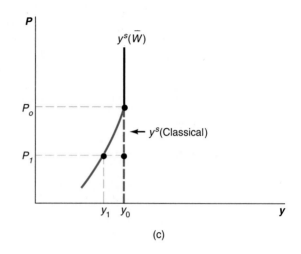

(c)

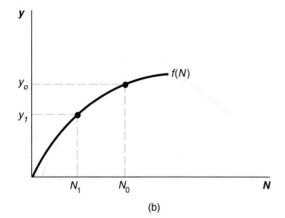

(b)

Figure 21-4

**Deriving Aggregate Supply with a Fixed Nominal
Wage Rate.**   If the nominal wage is fixed, a fall in the price
level causes a reduction in $MP_n \times P$, or a fall in the demand for
labor. At the fixed nominal wage, less labor services are desired by firms, and so employment falls [panel (a)]. The reduction in employment causes a decline in real output produced
by firms [panel (b)]. Hence, the fall in the price level has caused
a reduction in real output produced; the aggregate supply
schedule slopes upward [panel (c)].

in which we measure the nominal wage on the vertical axis, panel (b) depicts the economy's aggregate production function, and panel (c) shows the derivation of alternative
aggregate supply schedules for the economy. Consider panel (a). As the level of prices
falls, from an initial price level P_0 to a lower price level P_1, the demand for labor, MP_n
$\times P$ (the value of labor's marginal product) decreases. If wages were completely flexible,
then workers would also be willing to supply more labor as they recognize that the real
wage rises following the fall in prices. This is shown as the shift in the dashed labor supply
schedule from $N^s(P_0)$ to $N^s(P_1)$. The nominal wage would decrease in proportion to prices,
and, on net, employment would stay unchanged, at N_0. From panel (b), this implies that
real output produced would remain at its full-employment level, y_0, following the fall in
the price level. The aggregate supply schedule in panel (c) would be vertical.

Suppose, however, that the nominal wage is ''sticky,'' so that it cannot fall to a new
equilibrium level. If the nominal wage remains fixed at the level W in panel (a), then the
fall in labor demand caused by the reduction in output prices from P_0 to P_1 causes firms'
demand for labor to fall. As a result, actual employment in the economy will fall *below*
the full-employment level N_0 to the lower level N_1. This means that there will be unemployed workers. From panel (b), it follows that real output will fall below the full-
employment level y_0 to the smaller amount y_1. As shown in panel (c), the implication is

that, with a ''sticky'' nominal wage, the fall in the price level from P_0 to P_1 causes real output produced to fall from y_0, the full-employment level, to y_1. The **aggregate supply schedule** containing these two real output–price level combinations is upward-sloping as a result of the stickiness of the nominal wage rate. Furthermore, along the upward-sloping portion of this schedule the economy experiences real output–price level combinations that yield output levels below full employment. Unlike the vertical classical aggregate supply schedule that we discussed in Chapter 18, rises in prices cause increases in real output produced along this Keynesian aggregate supply schedule, denoted $y^s(W)$ because we derived it given the fixed wage W.

The reason that the aggregate supply schedule is convex, or bowed upward, if the nominal wage rate is fixed, is because the production function is concave, or bowed downward. In turn, this follows from the law of diminishing marginal returns. Successive increases in the price level stimulate increases in labor demand and in employment. But these successive rises in employment result in smaller and smaller gains in real output produced.

What could account for stickiness of the nominal wage? According to Keynes and his followers, one explanation was the development of labor organizations, such as craft or trade unions. These organized groups of laborers would seek to keep the nominal wages of their members at desired levels relative to other occupations. Moreover, in a highly unionized environment, **explicit contracts**—contracts in which the terms of relationships between workers and firms are written and legally binding upon both parties—would directly fix wage rates over given intervals of time, such as a year or more. These contracts usually would permit wages to rise above desired levels but would not allow wages to fall below those levels, even if some workers must be laid off. As a result, there would be *downward stickiness* of the nominal wage like that considered in Figure 21-4. Explicit contracts need not occur only in unionized settings; for instance, most college professors are not represented by unions but have explicit contracts with the university.

In addition, a notion that economists have developed since Keynes is that firms and workers may adopt **implicit contracts.** Implicit contracts are tacit understandings between employers and employees that the employees' wages will not be lowered by employers in poor economic conditions. In return, employers will not increase wages as much as economic conditions might normally indicate when times are good. Under this arrangement, workers essentially have the equivalent of an insurance policy that their wages will not be cut.

Any one of these reasons, plus the possibility that governments may enact minimum wage laws, is sufficient to cause some stickiness, particularly in the downward direction, in the nominal wage rate. As we noted in Chapter 18, the classical economists recognized several of these possible reasons for wage stickiness and labor unemployment, but they argued that the normal functioning of free markets would make such stickiness unsustainable. Therefore, unemployment eventually would end. In the eyes of most economists of that time and of the decades that followed, the experience of the Great Depression severely weakened the strength of this argument.

THE CASE OF IMPERFECT INFORMATION

One of the themes of the work of Keynes was that expectations about future events play an important role in affecting the current behavior of economic agents such as households and firms. This theme shows up clearly in Keynes's theory of the speculative demand for money. The reason that Keynes, and those economists that followed him, emphasized the role of expectations was that he sought to consider the fact that economic agents must make decisions in a world of uncertainty about the future. That is, they possess *imperfect information* when they make current decisions. As we shall see, the existence of imperfect information leads to an upward-sloping aggregate supply schedule even if nominal wages are flexible.

Consider the decision by laborers to supply labor services today. They may have a good idea about what is happening to some specific prices of goods and services today, but they do not have perfect information about how all prices may be changing. Indeed, reliable price index numbers appear widely in newspapers and on television only on a monthly basis, after the fact.

This means that when workers make decisions about how much labor to supply to firms, they base their decisions on their *perceptions* of what the current real wage actually is. That is, they must form an *expectation* of the value of the real wage. Of course, they know the nominal wage rate that firms are paying for their labor services, but they do not know the exact value of the price level, which they must *forecast*.

According to the traditional Keynesian model, time lags in the arrival of information compound the problem of imperfect information. As noted above, most government price indexes are widely published or publicly announced only on a monthly basis. During the month, workers must rely on their own devices; they must form price expectations that determine their estimate of the real wage they earn.

To formalize this idea, let P^e denote the price level expectation of workers. Also, suppose that, at a given time, the specific value of this price expectation is $P^e = P_0$, where P_0 is a specific value. This means that if the current nominal wage they earn, which we shall now assume is completely flexible, is W_0, they estimate their real wage to be $W_0/P^e = W_0/P_0$. Figure 21-5 displays a diagrammatic example. In panel (*a*), if workers' expectations are correct, then labor demand of firms is equal to the value of the marginal product of labor, $MP_n \times P_0$. The equilibrium nominal wage is equal to W_0, where this labor demand schedule crosses the workers labor supply schedule $N^s(P^e = P_0)$. Employment is equal to N_0, and the production function in panel (*b*) yields the amount of output produced, y_0. This gives the output–price level pair y_0 and P_0 in panel (*c*).

Suppose, however, that the price level falls below the amount P_0 that workers had expected, to a smaller value of P_1. Because information about this change is not readily available, workers will not know this has occurred and will keep their price expectation unchanged at $P^e = P_0$. Therefore, the labor supply schedule in panel (*a*) of the figure will stay fixed in position. As the prices that firms receive for goods and services fall, the value of labor's marginal product, or labor demand, will fall to $MP_n \times P_1$, and the resulting equilibrium nominal wage falls to W_1. Workers, not yet recognizing that prices have fallen to P_1 (because of a lack of information about aggregate price changes), *perceive* that their real wage has fallen from W_0/P_0 to W_1/P_0. Hence, they are less willing to provide labor services, as shown by a movement down along the labor supply schedule to the new equilibrium employment level N_1. As shown in panel (*b*), this fall in labor employment causes a fall in real output produced, from y_0 to y_1. Therefore, the economy experiences a new real output–price level combination y_1 and P_1 that lies below and to the left of the original combination in panel (*c*). The schedule containing both these points is the economy's aggregate supply schedule. We label this schedule $y^s(P^e = P_0)$ because we have derived it for this given price level expectation of workers.

As in the case of sticky nominal wages, the imperfect-information aggregate supply schedule slopes upward. In this case, however, we have allowed nominal wages to vary; it was workers' *price expectations* that were sticky. The justification for this stickiness of expectations mentioned above was the idea that information about aggregate price movements is available to workers only with a lag. What this means is that, in contrast to the

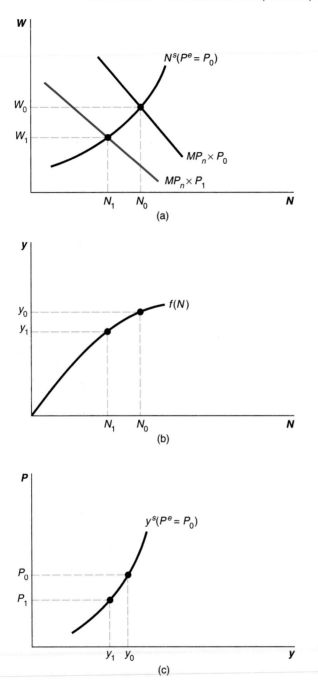

Figure 21-5
Deriving the Aggregate Supply Schedule with Flexible Nominal Wages and Imperfect Information.   If workers have imperfect information about prices that is received with a lag, then labor supply does not shift in response to a change in the price level. A fall in the price level reduces labor demand, and so there is a movement along the labor supply schedule to a lower employment level [panel (a)]. As employment falls, so does the amount of real output produced [panel (b)]. Therefore, the aggregate supply schedule slopes upward [panel (c)].

assumption of the classical theorists that workers do not suffer money illusion, it is as if worker illusion about the real value of their nominal wage had occurred.

Recall that the classical theorists felt that money illusion existed only if individuals were irrational. Keynes and his followers rejected this idea. They believed that money illusion, particularly concerning the real value of nominal wages, was pervasive. The reason, they argued, was not worker irrationality but rather the fact that information is not always freely available to workers in an uncertain world.

THE MARKET FOR REAL OUTPUT

We now have assembled the essential elements of traditional Keynesian theories of the aggregate demand for and aggregate supply of real output in the economy. We represent the level of aggregate demand for goods and services in the economy by the aggregate demand schedule, which is all combinations of real income (output) and levels of prices for which aggregate desired expenditures equal real income and the quantity of real money balances demanded equals the quantity of real money balances supplied. The level of aggregate demand for goods and services—that is, the position of the aggregate demand schedule—depends on the nominal money supply and on factors that influence aggregate autonomous expenditures, such as fiscal policy instruments like government spending and taxation.

The aggregate quantity of real output of goods and services usually increases as the price level rises, provided either that nominal wages are sticky or that workers have imperfect information about the level of prices. Under either view, this means that the aggregate supply schedule is upward-sloping. From here onward, we shall simply draw the aggregate supply schedule as upward-sloping and emphasize a specific rationale for the upward slope only when this is relevant to the issues at hand.

PUTTING AGGREGATE DEMAND AND AGGREGATE SUPPLY TOGETHER

Figure 21-6 is a diagram of the *market for real output,* in which we graph both the aggregate demand schedule and the aggregate supply schedule together. They cross at the equilibrium price level, labeled P_0, at which several conditions hold. The economy is on its aggregate demand schedule, which implies that aggregate real expenditures are equal to the level of real income y_0 (the economy is also on its *IS* schedule) and that the quantity of real money balances demanded at this real income level y_0 is equal to the real value of the quantity of money balances supplied, evaluated at the price level P_0 (the economy is on its *LM* schedule). Furthermore, the economy also is on its aggregate supply schedule, and so workers and firms are satisfied producing the amount of real output y_0 at the price level P_0. That is, this prevailing real output–price level combination is consistent with prevailing labor market conditions and with the productive capabilities of the economy as reflected by the position of the aggregate production function.

Figure 21-6 therefore depicts an equilibrium for the economy's market for real output as visualized by traditional Keynesian economists. In contrast, Figure 21-7 shows the analogous output market equilibrium as visualized by the classical theorists and discussed in Chapter 18. We can now make a straightforward comparison of the implications of the two theories. As shown in Figure 21-6, the aggregate supply schedule is upward-sloping in the traditional Keynesian model, either because nominal wages are sticky or because workers have imperfect information about aggregate prices. The classical aggregate supply

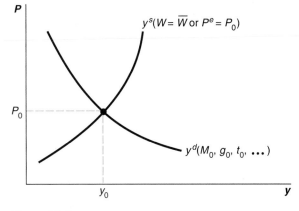

Figure 21-6

The Keynesian Market for Real Output.   In the traditional Keynesian model, the equilibrium level of prices and the equilibrium quantity of real output are determined by the intersection of the aggregate demand and supply schedules. The position of the aggregate demand schedule depends upon the nominal money supply and the amount of net autonomous aggregate desired expenditures, including government spending and taxes. The aggregate supply schedule is upward-sloping, either because the nominal wage rate is sticky or because workers have imperfect information about prices.

schedule in Figure 21-7 is, in contrast, vertical, because the classical theorists assumed that nominal wages were flexible and that information about prices was freely available with no time lags.

Furthermore, the position of the aggregate demand schedule in the traditional Keynesian model illustrated by Figure 21-6 depends on a number of factors, including the nominal

Figure 21-7

The Classical Market for Real Output.   In contrast to the traditional Keynesian model, the classical aggregate supply schedule is vertical at the full-employment output level. This is true because nominal wages are flexible and workers have perfect information about prices. In addition, with a constant velocity the position of the aggregate demand schedule depends only on the nominal money supply. Real output is supply-determined, and the price level is determined by the nominal money supply alone.

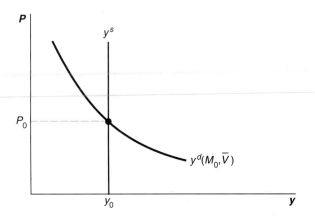

quantity of money, the prevailing levels of real government expenditures and taxes, and other factors that change aggregate autonomous expenditures. The classical determinants of aggregate demand in Figure 21-7 are much more limited. They are the quantity of money and the income velocity of money.

THE EFFECTS OF MONETARY POLICY ACTIONS

In the classical model, the fact that the aggregate supply schedule was vertical meant that monetary policy actions could have no effect on real output produced in the economy. The classical theorists therefore said that money was *neutral*. In contrast, in the traditional Keynesian model money is *nonneutral*. To see why this is so, consider Figure 21-8. At an initial equilibrium with the nominal quantity of money M_0, price level P_0, and real output y_0, shown at point A in panel (b), the economy must also be at an *IS-LM* equilibrium, at point A in panel (a). This is so because the economy is on its aggregate demand schedule. An increase in the nominal quantity of money supplied to a larger amount M_1 causes the *LM* schedule to shift to the right in panel (a) and causes a movement to a new *IS-LM* equilibrium at point B at the higher real income level y'. This initial change from y_0 to y' is the amount by which the aggregate demand schedule shifts rightward, from point A to point B, in panel (b).

After the rightward shift in aggregate demand, it is now the case that, at the initial equilibrium price level P_0, workers and firms will produce only an amount of real output y_0. More output will be forthcoming only if the price level increases toward the new equilibrium level of P_1, causing a movement upward along the aggregate supply schedule in panel (b), from point B to point C. As the price level rises, real money balances fall, and the *LM* schedule shifts back to the left somewhat, from point B to point C in panel

Figure 21-8
The Effect on Prices and Output of an Increase in the Nominal Money Supply.   An increase in the nominal money supply causes a liquidity effect that shifts the *LM* schedule downward along the *IS* schedule [panel (a)]. The amount of the immediate rise in real income, from y_0 to y', is the amount by which the aggregate demand schedule shifts rightward [panel (b)]. Firms are willing to produce more output than the amount y_0, however, only if the price level rises. The rise in the price level, P_0 to P_1, causes a real balance effect that shifts the *LM* schedule upward [panel (a)], resulting in a fall in real income to its final equilibrium level, y_1 [panels (a) and (b)].

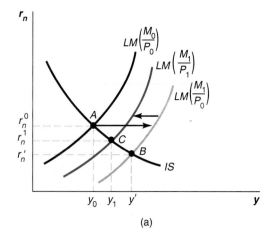

(a)

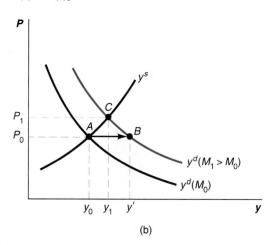

(b)

(*a*). This causes a movement back along the new aggregate demand schedule and a fall in the quantity of real output demanded, to y_1, which is the final equilibrium level of output in both panels of the figure.

The result that the price level rises with an increase in the nominal money supply mirrors the conclusion reached by the classical theorists that expansionary monetary policy actions can be inflationary. The increase of the nominal quantity of money, however, also causes a rise in the quantity of real output produced. Monetary policy actions therefore are nonneutral in their effects on the economy. They cause changes in real output and, by implication, in the quantity of labor employment (holding other factors constant, more output cannot be produced unless firms employ more labor services).

THE EFFECTS OF FISCAL POLICY ACTIONS

Fiscal policy actions also affect equilibrium real income and prices in the model. Consider Figure 21-9, which illustrates the effects of an increase in real government spending from an initial amount g_0 to a larger amount g_1. As shown in panel (*b*) of the figure, the economy begins with an equilibrium price level of P_0 and equilibrium real output y_0 at point A. This implies the *IS-LM* equilibrium at point A shown in panel (*a*). The increase in government expenditures shifts the *IS* schedule rightward in panel (*a*), and real income rises toward y' at point B. The magnitude of this rise in real income on the *IS-LM* diagram is the amount by which the aggregate demand schedule shifts rightward, from point A to point B, in panel (*b*).

At the initial price level P_0, workers and firms will not produce all the output demanded by households, firms, and the government, and so the price level rises toward a new equilibrium of P_1, which is a movement upward along the aggregate supply schedule in

Figure 21-9
The Effect on Prices and Output of an Increase in Government Spending.   An increase in real government spending shifts the *IS* schedule rightward along the *LM* schedule [panel (*a*)]. The amount of the immediate rise in real income, from y_0 to y', is the amount by which the aggregate demand schedule shifts rightward [panel (*b*)]. Firms are willing to produce more output than the amount y_0, however, only if the price level rises. The rise in the price level, P_0 to P_1, causes a real balance effect that shifts the *LM* schedule upward [panel (*a*)], resulting in a fall in real income to its final equilibrium level, y_1 [panels (*a*) and (*b*)].

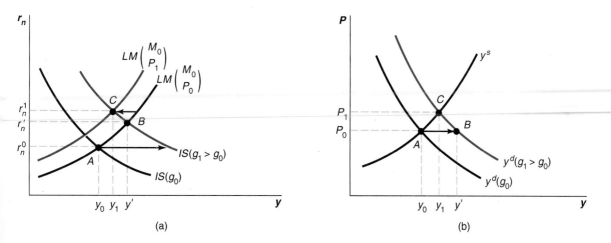

panel (*b*), from point *B* to point *C*. As the price level increases, real money balances fall, which causes the *LM* schedule to shift to the left in panel (*a*); this corresponds to a movement upward along the new aggregate demand schedule in panel (*b*), from point *B* to point *C* and toward the final equilibrium level of real output, y_1.

On net, then, an increase in real government expenditures causes a rise in both the equilibrium real output and the equilibrium price level. Indeed, any increase in net autonomous aggregate expenditures resulting, say, from a rise in autonomous investment, a rise in autonomous consumption, or a fall in taxes would have caused the same effects. In contrast, a reduction in net autonomous aggregate expenditures caused by a fall in government spending, a fall in autonomous investment, a reduction in autonomous consumption, or an increase in taxes would have effects opposite to those shown in Figure 21-9.

CONDUCTING MONETARY POLICY IN THE TRADITIONAL MACRO SYSTEM

Because monetary policy is nonneutral in the traditional Keynesian model, it is common for economists who identify with this position to prescribe expansionary or contractionary monetary policy actions to stabilize real economic activity. Indeed, about once every week or so in the *Wall Street Journal* or in other financial news publications there is some kind of speculation about "what the Fed might do" in order to stabilize the economy in the face of changes in autonomous consumption or investment. The article usually is couched in terms of changes in "consumer confidence" or "business expectations."

The idea that the Federal Reserve has an important role to play in stabilizing employment and real output is firmly grounded in the Keynesian tradition. It is the antithesis of the classical position, which viewed the maintenance of stable prices as the limited role of monetary policy. The traditional Keynesian theory goes even further by arguing for monetary stabilization of labor employment and real economic activity. According to this model, monetary policy can *reduce* unemployment. The cost of doing so, as we shall see, is higher inflation.

THE PHILLIPS CURVE

A Keynesian theory of the aggregate supply schedule implies an inverse relationship between inflation and unemployment. To see why this is so, consider Figure 21-10. Panel (*a*) of the figure shows a Keynesian aggregate supply schedule with several possible positions of the aggregate demand schedule, panel (*b*) depicts the economy's aggregate production function, and panel (*c*) depicts the rate of price inflation on the vertical axis and the labor unemployment rate on the horizontal axis.

Suppose that aggregate demand is in relatively low positions such as y_0^d and y_1^d in panel (*a*). These low levels of aggregate demand could result, for instance, because both autonomous consumption and autonomous investment have fallen to particularly low levels. Note that a shift of aggregate demand from y_0^d to y_1^d causes a nearly insignificant rise in the level of prices, from P_0 to P_1. The rate of price inflation is the proportionate change in the level of prices per unit of time, or $(\Delta P/P)/\Delta t$; and so for these low levels of aggregate demand, ΔP and, hence, inflation are small. Denote this low rate of price inflation as $\dot{p}_0$. What is also true is that output is low relative to the scale on the horizontal axis in panel (*a*). Reference to panel (*b*) thus implies that, at the low output levels, labor employment is also low, which means that labor unemployment is high. Economists measure the "unemployment rate" as the ratio of unemployed (those who wish to be employed but cannot find a job) to the labor force (all those in the population who wish to be employed),

(a)

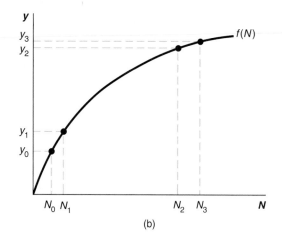

(b)

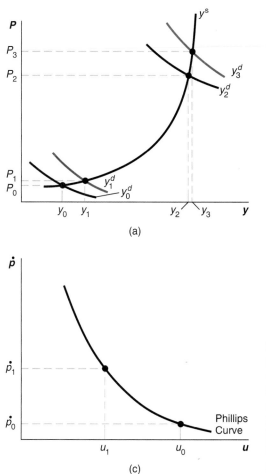

(c)

Figure 21-10

Deriving the Phillips Curve.   A given shift in the aggregate demand schedule has a much larger effect on the price level for high levels of output than it does at lower output levels [panel (*a*)]. Therefore, inflation is greater at higher levels of output. At higher output levels it also is true that employment is higher [panel (*b*)], and so unemployment is lower. This implies that there is an inverse relationship between the inflation rate and the unemployment rate, which is the Phillips curve [panel (*c*)].

and so this ratio, which we shall denote as u, is high. We denote the average unemployment rate for these low levels of aggregate demand as u_0. We now have constructed an inflation rate–unemployment rate combination $\dot{p}_0$ and u_0 in panel (*c*).

Now consider the much higher levels of aggregate demand, labeled y_2^d and y_3^d in panel (*a*). Note that the rise in aggregate demand from y_2^d to y_3^d is similar in size to the increase from y_0^d to y_1^d, but it causes a much larger increase in the level of prices and, therefore, in inflation. Denote the rate of inflation caused by the movement from P_2 to P_3 by $\dot{p}_1$. At such high levels of aggregate demand, the economy is in equilibrium along the steepest portion of the aggregate supply schedule. This is where the law of diminishing returns implies that employment-raising increases in the price level have very small effects on the quantity of real output. This means that, in panel (*b*), the economy is operating along the less steep portion of its aggregate production function. Along this portion of the production function, labor employment is high, which implies that labor unemployment is low. Denote the average unemployment rate in this range of high output levels u_1. We now have constructed another inflation rate–unemployment rate combination $\dot{p}_1$ and u_1 in panel (*c*).

We could continue this process and derive a locus of points described by the smooth, convex (bowed inward) curve shown in panel (*c*). Economists call this schedule of points a **Phillips curve,** in honor of its discoverer, A. W. Phillips. Phillips actually conducted a study of British data that showed an inverse relationship between nominal *wages* and unemployment rates, but nowadays the term most often is used to describe the theoretical relationship between price inflation and unemployment.

Is there really a Phillips curve? Certainly, there has been in the past. Figure 21-11 shows a plot of inflation rates and unemployment rates for the United States for the period 1961–1969. Clearly, the curve implied by these data points looks very much like the Phillips curve derived from a Keynesian aggregate supply function (as in Figure 21-10). As we shall see shortly, in more recent times the data yield a less Keynesian-looking Phillips curve.

A POSSIBLE ROLE FOR MONETARY POLICY

The fact that the traditional Keynesian model yields an inverse, Phillips curve, relationship between price inflation and unemployment rates immediately implies a theoretical role for monetary policy. That role is to reduce unemployment by increasing aggregate demand as needed, through expansionary monetary policy actions, such as sustained open-market operations, discount rate cuts, or reserve requirement reductions. Also implied is a role for fiscal policy. Sustained expansionary government spending or tax policies also would raise aggregate demand. In turn, as aggregate demand rises, the economy marches upward along its Phillips curve, according to the theory, to lower, and more desirable, labor unemployment rates (see Figure 21-10). The cost of such policy making, which Figure 21-11 shows was borne in the 1960s, is higher rates of inflation.

Most traditional Keynesian theorists believe that higher inflation is a cost worth incurring in order to reduce unemployment. For instance, the famous Keynesian economist

Figure 21-11

Inflation and Unemployment Rates in the United States, 1961–1969. During the 1960s, there was a smooth, downward-sloping Phillips curve, as predicted by the traditional Keynesian model.

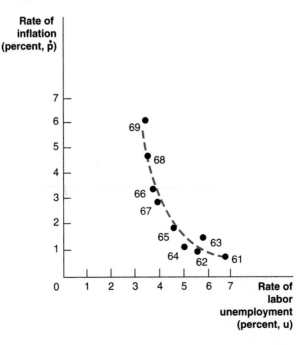

Joan Robinson (1903–1983) once said, "Unemployment is a reproach to democratic government." Such judgments are, of course, normative ones. For those who held such views, however, the experience of the 1960s proved the worth of the traditional Keynesian model and justified policies that raised inflation when policy makers thought that unemployment rates were too high.

A Blending of Classical and Traditional Systems: Monetarism

The 1960s were the heyday of the basic version of the traditional Keynesian model. They were the times in which economists became renowned as "fine-tuners" of the economy. Taken literally, the Phillips curve implied by the traditional model indicated that policy makers could tell economists what unemployment rate they desired; economists could then tell policy makers the inflation cost that would be necessary in order to reach the desired amount of unemployment. Of course, everyone recognized that zero unemployment was not achievable, because even at "full employment" there are some people between jobs. Nonetheless, very low rates of unemployment were the widely recognized goal of governmental policy making, and both monetary and fiscal policy makers largely oriented their policy actions toward this aim.

Despite the apparent successes in reducing unemployment during the 1960s, some economists, known as **monetarists,** were not convinced that the traditional Keynesian model and its Phillips curve were suitable guides for policy. This group of economists, which included Milton Friedman, Karl Brunner, and Allan Meltzer, among others, went even further, arguing that the Phillips curve was an inherently *unstable* relationship. Furthermore, these economists claimed that fiscal policy actions had little effect on the economy, while monetary policy actions had pronounced effects. It is this latter claim that earned these individuals the name "monetarists."

Most economists did not accept this monetarist perspective in the 1960s because, as Figure 21-11 indicates, traditional Keynesian theory appeared to do so well. In the 1970s, though, the real world departed completely from the predictions of the traditional model. Figure 21-12 makes clear that the simple Phillips curve relationship broke down entirely.

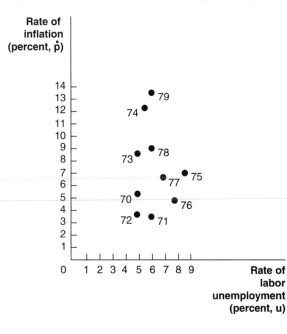

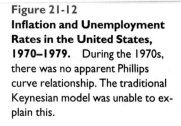

Figure 21-12
Inflation and Unemployment Rates in the United States, 1970–1979. During the 1970s, there was no apparent Phillips curve relationship. The traditional Keynesian model was unable to explain this.

No smooth, inverse relationship between inflation and unemployment existed in the decade of the 1970s. This experience made the previously unconvinced economists pay much more attention to the monetarists, even if not all of them completely adopted the monetarists' theories and policy suggestions.

Another factor that seemed to support the monetarist view was accumulating evidence that fiscal policy changes had more muted effects on the economy than the standard Keynesian model would have predicted. Because the monetarists had also made this forecast, the economics profession really began to sit up and take notice. As we shall see, the monetarist view of the functioning of the economy did not imply the wholesale rejection of the traditional Keynesian *theory,* but it did cause many Keynesian economists to take the theory less literally.

THE END OF THE PHILLIPS CURVE?

INTERNATIONAL PERSPECTIVE

The United States was not the only nation for which the Phillips curve broke down in the 1970s and 1980s. Nations around the world shared this experience. The apparent breakdown of the traditional Keynesian theory was not isolated to the United States.

The diagrams on the facing page show actual inflation rates and unemployment rates in the 1970s and 1980s for Germany, France, Italy, the United Kingdom, Japan, and the United States. One conclusion that we can reach after examining these diagrams is that the relationship between inflation and unemployment has differed considerably across countries. For instance, while unemployment and inflation have alternately risen and fallen in apparent cyclical patterns in the United States, unemployment in France has continuously increased almost irrespective of inflation changes (though France has experienced significant inflation reductions in recent years). Indeed, unemployment generally rose, though with some variation across nations, throughout Europe during the 1970s and 1980s. Inflation generally fell.

The Japanese experience is particularly interesting. For Japan, the Phillips curve was slightly downward-sloping but very steep throughout the 1970s and 1980s. Wide variations in inflation had little effect on unemployment in Japan. In contrast, Germany experienced wide variations in unemployment with little change in inflation. Italy, France, and especially the United Kingdom witnessed considerable variability in both inflation and unemployment. No one nation's experience was the same.

During the 1970s and some parts of the 1980s, there was no apparent relationship between inflation and unemployment in the United States and Europe. Many economists have argued that breakdowns of the Phillips curve in the United States and in Europe signal the end of the Phillips curve as a policy guide. They contend that it was never a useful guide to policy in Japan. Indeed, these economists, many of whom are monetarists, argue that there never was a stable Phillips curve that policy makers could exploit.

Other economists point out that over some periods the Phillips curve relationship seems stable. For instance, there was a fairly smooth, downward-sloping relationship between inflation and unemployment in France, Italy, and the United Kingdom throughout much of the 1980s. In addition, while the relationship between inflation and unemployment in Japan was weak, it still was an inverse relationship, as traditional Keynesian theory would predict. These economists conclude that the most notable and inexplicable exception to the Phillips curve relationship implied by the traditional Keynesian theory remains the United States.

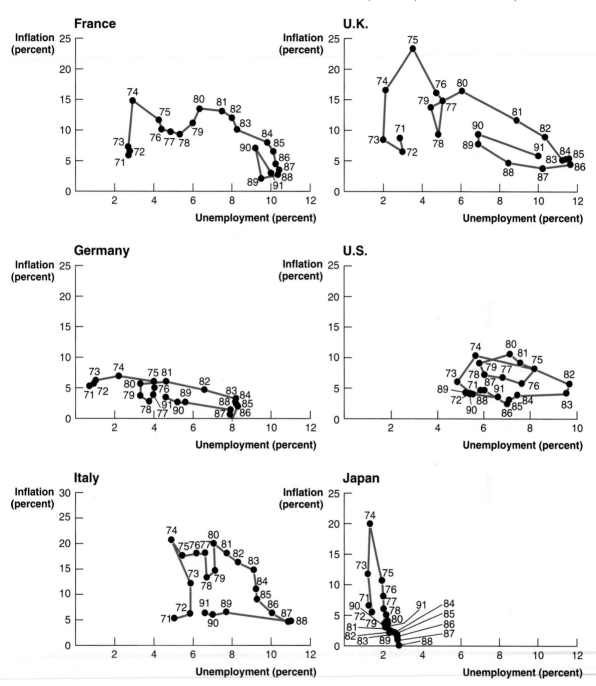

Inflation and Unemployment Rates in the United States, Japan, and Selected European Nations, 1971–1991.

THE QUANTITY THEORY OF MONEY REVISITED

The monetarists do not deny the usefulness of much of Keynesian theory; indeed, the leading monetarist, Milton Friedman, has said:

> I believe that Keynes's theory is the right kind of theory in its simplicity, its concentration on a few key magnitudes, its potential fruitfulness. I have been led to reject it, not on these grounds, but because I believe that it has been contradicted by evidence: its predictions have not been confirmed by experience. This failure has not isolated what are ''really'' the key factors in short-run economic change.
>
> . . . Rereading [Keynes's] *General Theory* has . . . reminded me of what a great economist Keynes was and how much more I sympathize with his approach and aims than with those of many of his followers.[1]

The monetarist argument, then, is that Keynes's followers misinterpreted Keynes's views on the determinants of real economic activity and on the relative importance of various factors that influence the economy's performance.

The key determinant of *nominal* national income, according to the monetarists, is the nominal money supply. The reason for this conclusion is that the monetarists believe that the quantity theory of money, as represented in the Cambridge equation, $M^d = kY$, is a very good approximation to actual economic behavior. While Friedman and other monetarists recognize that the factor k in the Cambridge equation can vary somewhat with changes in interest rates, due to the speculative motive for holding money, they do not believe that the speculative motive is an *empirically* important determinant of money demand behavior.

This means that monetarists feel that the classical theory of aggregate demand is a good representation of real-world behavior. That is, they, like Irving Fisher, are comfortable viewing the Cambridge k, and hence the income velocity of money, as nearly constant or at least predictable. As we saw in Chapter 18, once we make this assumption, the aggregate demand for real output depends predominantly upon the nominal money supply.

THE MONETARIST THEORY OF AGGREGATE DEMAND

We can view the monetarist *theory* of aggregate demand as a more narrow representation of the Keynesian model, as shown in Figure 21-13. In panel (*a*) of the figure, the *LM* schedule is drawn as very steep, implying that the demand for real money balances is very interest-inelastic. The *IS* schedule is very shallow, indicating that desired investment is very interest-elastic. A leftward shift of the *LM* schedule caused by a rise in the level of prices—the real balance effect—produces a lower equilibrium level of real income, y_1, and a movement from y_0 to y_1 in panel (*b*), which yields a downward-sloping aggregate demand schedule. But, as we discussed earlier in this chapter, if the *LM* schedule is very steep while the *IS* schedule is very shallow, the main determinant of the position of the aggregate demand schedule is the nominal money supply. Therefore, the main determinant of the position of aggregate demand is the nominal quantity of money M_0.

---

[1] Quoted in Robert Gordon, ed., *Milton Friedman's Monetary Framework: A Debate with His Critics* (Chicago: University of Chicago Press, 1974), p. 134.

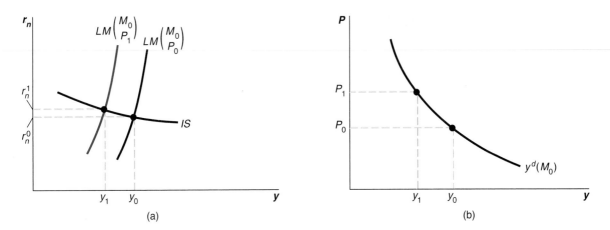

Figure 21-13
The Monetarist Version of IS-LM and Aggregate Demand.   According to the monetarists,
desired investment is very interest-elastic, and the demand for real money balances is very interest-
inelastic. Therefore, the IS schedule is shallow, and the LM schedule is steep [panel (a)]. It follows
that the nominal money supply is the main determinant of equilibrium real income in IS-LM and, as a
result, that the nominal money supply is the main factor influencing the position of the aggregate
demand schedule [panel (b)].

MONETARY POLICY IN THE SHORT RUN
AND IN THE LONG RUN

The view that the nominal quantity of money is the main determinant of aggregate demand
is a key factor separating the monetarists from traditional Keynesian theorists. The other
important division between them, however, is their view of short-run and long-run equilibrium positions for the economy. As we discussed earlier in this unit, Keynes strongly
criticized the classical theorists' emphasis of long-run adjustments of the economy. Keynes
summarized his view that the classical theorists overemphasized the long run in the famous
dictum we mentioned earlier: "In the long run, we are all dead."

Milton Friedman and other monetarists have argued that Keynes went too far and
overemphasized the short run. Their approach, and, indeed, their view of the "correct"
interpretation of Keynes's general theory of economics, emphasizes the fact that a short-
run equilibrium can differ from a long-run equilibrium. Of the two, they argue, the latter
is the more important to consider. This perspective places the monetarists more firmly in
the classical camp even though they use the foundations of traditional Keynesian theory
to support their arguments.

THE NATURAL RATE OF UNEMPLOYMENT AND THE LONG-RUN
PHILLIPS CURVE

The starting point for the monetarists' argument is their definition of the "long run."
Monetarists define the long run as a period of time long enough that workers become so
well-informed about actual developments in the economy that their price level expectations

and, thus, inflation rate expectations correspond to actual prices and inflation rates. In the long run, then, workers have *full information.* The monetarists do not claim that the economy is always in a long-run state; rather, they argue that it tends to reach that state over time even though it can depart from this full-information state over short-run time periods.

The Natural Rate of Unemployment If the economy is in a situation of full information, so that expected prices equal actual prices and expected inflation equals actual inflation, monetarists argue that the economy will then tend toward a **natural level of employment.** This level of employment is the employment level that the classical model would predict, in which workers have perfect information about price levels and movements and, therefore, about the real wage they earn and how it is changing over time. This would be the level of employment at which labor demand and labor supply cross, as in the classical model. Variations around this level of employment could occur, causing temporary unemployment as workers are between jobs. On average, the unemployment rate would be at a fairly low average level in the long run, called the **natural rate of unemployment.**

Figure 21-14 diagrammatically summarizes the monetarist perspective. The monetarists believe that, in the aggregate, nominal wages are flexible, so that labor demand and labor supply determine the equilibrium nominal wage, as shown in panel (*a*) of the figure. In the full-information long run, expected and actual prices and inflation are equal. Therefore, P^e is equal to the actual price level P_0 under full information, and the full-information, natural level of employment, N_0, is determined where the labor demand schedule at this actual price level ($\text{MP}_n \times P_0$) crosses the labor supply schedule [$N^s(P^e = P_0)$]. At this natural, full-information employment level, the **natural level of output** is equal to the amount y_0 in panel (*b*).

The Short Run and the Long Run In the short run, argue the monetarists, the traditional Keynesian theory is correct in its assumption that workers have incomplete information about aggregate prices and price changes. For instance, if the price level rises from P_0 to a higher level P_1, the demand for labor will rise in panel (*a*) of the figure. Because workers do not perceive this actual change in prices, as they see the nominal wage rise they will misinterpret this rise as an increase in the real wage and offer more labor services. The level of employment will rise to N_1, above the full-information, natural employment level, and output will be at the level y_1 in panel (*b*).

In contrast, a fall in the price level to a lower level P_2 causes labor demand to fall to $\text{MP}_n \times P_2$ and, in the short run, causes reductions in the employment and output levels to N_2 and y_2, below their natural levels. The three real output–price level combinations y_0 and P_0, y_1 and P_1, and y_2 and P_2 lie along an upward-sloping Keynesian aggregate supply schedule, graphed in panel (*c*) of Figure 21-14. But, according to the monetarists, this is only the *short-run aggregate supply schedule.* In the long run, when information becomes available, the economy will find itself at the natural level of output y_0. This will happen because as more information becomes available to workers, they will adjust their labor supply behavior, causing an eventual return to the natural employment and output levels consistent with the natural levels.

Therefore, the *full-information aggregate supply schedule* is vertical in panel (*c*), at the natural level of output. Like the classical aggregate supply schedule, the full-information aggregate supply schedule is vertical because, along this locus of real output–price level

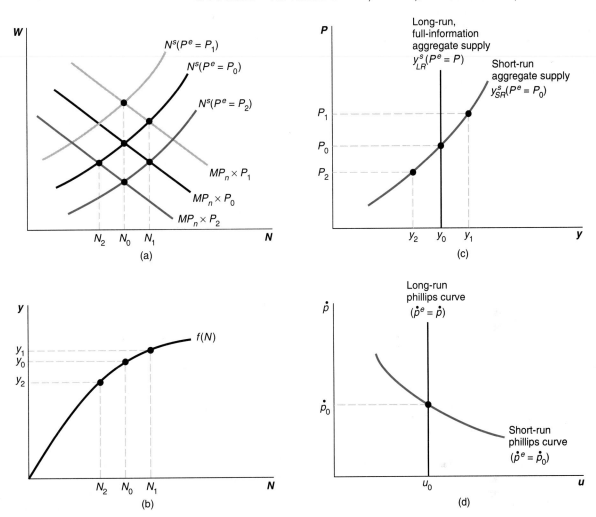

Figure 21-14

Long-Run, Full-Information Aggregate Supply and the Long-Run Phillips Curve.   If price and inflation expectations are constant, then an increase or decrease in the price level causes employment to change [panel (a)], which causes a change in output [panel (b)] and a change in unemployment [panel (d)]. Therefore, with fixed price and inflation expectations, the short-run aggregate supply schedule slopes upward [panel (c)], and the short-run Phillips curve slopes downward [panel (d)]. If full information is available about prices and inflation, however, equilibrium employment, unemployment, and output do not vary with changes in the price level. The long-run aggregate supply schedule and the long-run Phillips curve are vertical at the natural, full-information level of output (y_0) and unemployment (u_0).

combinations, wages are flexible and workers have full information. In the short run, full information is not necessarily available, and so the economy can move off this full-information supply schedule to points along the short-run supply schedule. Movements upward or downward along the short-run schedule, however, generally would be short-lived, according to the monetarists; they would last only as long as information about prices and inflation is imperfectly available.

The Long-Run Phillips Curve   Panel (d) of Figure 21-14 depicts the Phillips curves corresponding to the short-run and long-run, full-information aggregate supply schedules graphed in panel (c). If workers are fully informed, as we might expect over a long enough time horizon, then the economy will be at its natural output level y_0. This implies that the economy will be at its corresponding natural rate of unemployment, denoted u_0. At this natural rate of unemployment, in which expected price inflation is equal to actual price inflation, the *long-run Phillips curve* (LRPC) is vertical. Only in the short run in which workers have imperfect information will the short-run Phillips curve (SRPC) of the traditional Keynesian model be relevant. The economy can move upward or downward along this short-run Phillips curve only when it moves upward or downward along its short-run aggregate supply schedule; in turn, this occurs only in the short run when workers have imperfect information.

THEORIES OF STAGFLATION

How long is the ''short-run'' time horizon over which workers have imperfect information? What is the magnitude of the natural rate of unemployment? Clearly, these are the obvious, crucial questions. Unfortunately, the answers are not always so clear. Nevertheless, even many ''Keynesian'' economists have adopted the monetarist elaboration of traditional Keynesian theory as a useful explanation of why the economy may experience **stagflation,** the simultaneous occurrence of high labor unemployment rates and high inflation rates.

The Cost-Push Theory of Stagflation   Suppose the natural rate of unemployment for the economy is equal to u_0 (which might be, say, $4\frac{1}{2}$ percent). This is the unemployment rate at which the economy's Phillips curve would be vertical in panel (b) of Figure 21-15. At this unemployment rate, the economy would be at its natural level of output, labeled y_0 in panel (a), where its full-information aggregate supply schedule would be located. If the current price level is equal to P_0 and the current rate of price inflation is equal to $\dot{p}_0$, then short-run aggregate supply (y_0^s) and Phillips curves (SRPC$_0$) cross through the long-run schedules at P_0 and $\dot{p}_0$, respectively. We label this initial equilibrium point E.

Suppose that, for some reason, there is a decrease in productive capabilities in the economy, so that both the short-run and long-run aggregate supply schedules shift to the left, to y_1^s and $y_{LR,1}^s$ in panel (a). We know that we derive the short-run Phillips curve from the short-run aggregate supply schedule, while the long-run Phillips curve corresponds to the long-run aggregate supply schedule. Therefore, if the supply schedules shift leftward, the short-run and long-run Phillips curves must shift rightward, to SRPC$_1$ and LRPC$_1$. The magnitude of the shift in each set of schedules is given by the distance $E - A$ in each panel. In the short run, for a given level of aggregate demand, real output would fall, unemployment would rise, and the price level and the inflation rate would increase. The short-run equilibrium positions for the economy would be at the points labeled B in each panel of the figure.

What could account for such a reduction in productive capability and these short-run effects? Recall that the aggregate supply schedule's position depends on a number of factors, including such supply-side factors as the state of prevailing technology, the size of the economy's capital stock, and the availability and cost of this and other economic

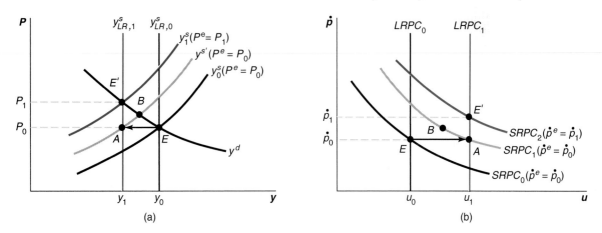

Figure 21-15
The Cost-Push Theory of Stagflation.   If there is a rise in firms' real costs of producing goods
and services, then the short-run and long-run aggregate supply schedules shift leftward by the distance $A - E$ in panel (a). In the short run, real output falls to the level at point B. In panel (b), there
is a rightward shift of the short-run and long-run Phillips curves by the amount $A - E$. In the short
run, unemployment rises, as does inflation.
   In the long run, however, price expectations adjust to the higher level of prices, and the short-
run aggregate supply schedule shifts further to the left, to a final long-run equilibrium at point E'
[panel (a)]. Output is at its new, lower, natural level. As inflation expectations increase with the
long-run recognition of higher prices and inflation, the short-run Phillips curve shifts further to the
right to a long-run position at point E' [panel (b)]. Unemployment is at its new, higher, natural level.

resources. An example of a factor that could shift the aggregate supply schedule upward
and to the left, as illustrated in our example, would be a sharp rise in the relative (real,
price-level-adjusted) prices of energy resources, such as the sharp rise in relative oil prices
caused by the Persian Gulf crisis and war in 1990–1991. Indeed, these events caused the
price level and the inflation rate to rise. In the short run, real output fell, and unemployment
rose.
   The points labeled B in the figure cannot be long-run equilibrium points for the economy, because the economy is still above its *new* natural output level y_1 in panel (a) and
below the corresponding *new* natural rate of unemployment u_1 in panel (b). The long-run
adjustment to a final equilibrium takes place as information about higher prices and
inflation becomes available. This causes workers to increase their price and inflation
expectations and, thereby, to lower their perceptions of the real wage rate. When this
occurs, there is another leftward shift in the short-run aggregate supply schedule and a
corresponding outward shift of the short-run Phillips curve. The economy's final long-run
equilibrium position is at points labeled E'.
   According to the monetarists, the natural output level falls permanently following this
loss in productive capability. The only way that a recovery could take place would be if
the reason for the sharp energy price increase (such as the political crisis and war in 1990–
1991) ceased to exist, causing relative energy prices to fall to previous levels. The short-
run and long-run aggregate supply schedules would then shift back toward their original
positions, and the price level and inflation rate would fall.
   Economists sometimes call the theory of short-run stagflation caused by such factors

as higher energy costs the **cost-push theory of stagflation.** According to this theory, higher costs of factors of production cause a fall in aggregate supply. Prices and inflation increase, and, simultaneously, real output falls and unemployment rises.

The Demand-Pull Theory of Stagflation Monetarists believe that stagflation can result from sustained increases in aggregate demand arising from continued growth of the nominal supply of money. Consider Figure 21-16. If the economy starts from an initial position at a natural employment level and natural unemployment rate of y_0 and u_0, respectively, at initial equilibrium points labeled E in panels (a) and (b), then a sustained increase in the nominal supply of money would cause aggregate demand to shift outward. In the short run, the level of prices rises from P_0 to P' as the economy moves to a new short-run equilibrium in the market for real output, shown by the movement along the short-run aggregate supply schedule to point A in panel (a). At this point, the real output level would be above the natural level, at y'. There would be a corresponding movement upward along the short-run Phillips curve $SRPC_0$ to a lower rate of unemployment u_0 at point A, and inflation would rise from $\dot{p}_0$ to $\dot{p}_1$ in the short run.

In the long run, however, as workers recognized the higher prices and inflation rates, they would correctly perceive that these changes had reduced their real wages. They would supply less labor. This would cause the short-run aggregate supply schedule to shift back to the left, to $y^s(P^e = P_1)$. In addition, the short-run Phillips curve would shift outward to $SRPC_1(\dot{p}^e = \dot{p}_1)$. Real output would fall, and unemployment would rise until the

Figure 21-16
The Demand-Pull Theory of Stagflation. If there is an increase in the nominal money supply, then the aggregate demand schedule shifts rightward, and there is a rise in the price level and a short-run increase in real output at point A in panel (a). Inflation increases and unemployment falls in the short run at point A in panel (b).

In the long run, the rise in prices and inflation is recognized by workers, and the short-run aggregate supply schedule shifts leftward as workers' price and inflation expectations increase. Real output falls to its natural level, y_0, at a long-run equilibrium at point E' in panel (a). As inflation expectations rise in the long run, the short-run Phillips curve also shifts rightward, and the economy reaches a long-run equilibrium at the natural rate of unemployment u_0 in panel (b). During this long-run adjustment, real output falls and unemployment rises as prices and inflation continue to increase. Stagflation would be observed during this adjustment.

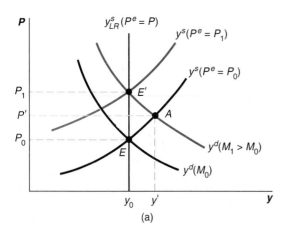

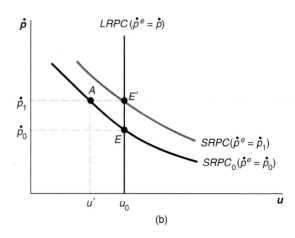

(a)

(b)

MONETARISM AND POLITICAL BUSINESS CYCLES

Economists sometimes call the monetarist hypothesis of a vertical long-run Phillips curve the "natural rate theory." The reason is that the theory implies that there is a natural rate of unemployment. However, if there is indeed a natural unemployment rate toward which the economy tends in the long run, policy makers by implication have limited, or perhaps nonexistent, abilities to influence output and labor unemployment over long time spans.

Nevertheless, most policy makers in democratic republics either are elected politicians or are in their positions because they were appointed by elected politicians. Many observers feel that, as a result, policy makers desire to influence the performance of the economy in hope of achieving political gains when the economy performs favorably (higher output and lower unemployment). The monetarist natural rate theory implies that, at best, politicians may obtain short-run political gains from such activities. However, short-run economic gains that translate into more votes for incumbent politicians can yield long-run victories for these individuals if they are reelected to lengthy terms in office.

If the hypothesis that politicians seek to influence macroeconomic activity for their own benefit is correct, then one determinant of short-run cycles in the behavior of prices, real output, unemployment, and interest rates should be the lengths of elected terms of politicians, or the "electoral cycle." This idea that cycles in economic activity may depend on political cycles is known as the *political business cycle theory*. The political business cycle theory has become an area of study in which the interests of both economists and political scientists have overlapped considerably.

One aspect of this line of inquiry that has been of particular interest to monetary economists is the possibility that Federal Reserve behavior might be influenced by political aims. Indeed, in the last two decades there has been considerable economic research investigating whether or not the Federal Reserve brings about temporary increases in the nominal money supply to achieve short-run output and employment gains immediately before the elections of incumbent presidents. The final verdict on this issue is still uncertain. Nevertheless, there is evidence that some Federal Reserve Board chairmen, such as Arthur Burns during the presidency of Richard Nixon, may have pursued such politically motivated policies.

If Federal Reserve policy making is somewhat motivated by political considerations, then the political business cycle theory may offer at least a partial explanation for the twentieth-century tendency for most democratic republics to experience sustained inflation. The terms of politicians in most democratic republics range from two to six years in length. The political business cycle theory therefore implies that every two to six years there should be an incentive for central banks to increase nominal money supplies to achieve short-run economic gains. However, there is no political incentive to reduce the nominal supplies of money after elections; the politicians and central banks permit their economies to revert, on their own, to natural levels of employment and output. Therefore, the nominal money supplies in these countries would, according to the political business cycle theory, tend only to grow over time, bringing about sustained inflationary trends in these economies. Hence, this theory potentially can explain inflation.

economy reached a new long-run equilibrium at points E' in panels (a) and (b) of the figure. Note that, during the course of this long-run adjustment, we would see the levels of prices and inflation rise even as real output was falling and unemployment was rising. We would observe stagflation for a period of time during the period of adjustment of price and inflation expectations.

This theory of stagflation is a **demand-pull theory of stagflation.** According to this theory, which is a natural extension of the monetarist distinction between short-run and long-run effects of expansionary monetary policies, monetary policies that stimulate aggregate demand (recall that monetarists believe that only the nominal money supply has a significant influence on aggregate demand) have at best short-lived real effects. Sustained increases in the nominal money supply can raise real output and lower unemployment for short periods but cannot have long-run real effects, because as information becomes available and expectations adjust, the economy returns to its natural equilibrium levels of real output and unemployment.

Again, we return to the key questions. First, how long is the "long run"? The answer, according to the monetarists, is that the long run is however long it takes information to become available and price and inflation expectations to adjust. This is not a very specific answer, but a more specific answer is hard to come by. As we shall see in the next chapter, one modern group of economists that follows the more classical extreme of the monetarist philosophy believes that the long run is very short if workers form very quickly adjusting, "rational" expectations. Another modern group, which follows the Keynesian tradition, believes that the long run is more closely determined by the lengths of wage contracts, which they believe largely determine the short-run behavior of workers and firms. We turn to these modern offshoots of monetarist, and more broadly Keynesian, theories in the next two chapters.

CHAPTER SUMMARY

1. In the traditional Keynesian model, the aggregate demand schedule is a locus of all combinations of real income and levels of prices for which both equilibrium real income and money market equilibrium are maintained.

2. There are several determinants of the level of aggregate demand in the traditional Keynesian model, including the nominal money supply, government spending, real net taxes, and autonomous consumption and investment.

3. The relative importance of the effects of monetary policy actions on the level of aggregate demand depends upon the relative strength of the Keynesian monetary policy transmission mechanism.

4. The relative importance of the effects of fiscal policy actions on the level of aggregate demand depends upon the amount of the crowding-out effect, which generally is not complete in the Keynesian model.

5. One possible explanation for an upward-sloping Keynesian aggregate supply schedule is that nominal wages may be fixed over intervals of time.

6. Another possible explanation for an upward-sloping Keynesian aggregate supply schedule is that information about aggregate price changes may be imperfect over intervals of time.

7. The traditional Keynesian model implies that there is an inverse relationship between inflation and unemployment, at least in the short run. A relationship between inflation and unemployment is known as a Phillips curve.

8. Monetarists argue that the primary determinant of the level of aggregate demand is the nominal money supply.

9. Monetarists follow the traditional Keynesian model by assuming that imperfect information makes the short-run aggregate supply schedule upward-sloping. However, they assert that in the long run expectations adjust in light of new information, so that there is a natural level of output and a vertical long-run aggregate supply schedule.

10. Monetarism provides possible explanations of stagflation that extend the Keynesian model in some ways but are similar to the classical model in others.

GLOSSARY

Aggregate demand schedule (y^d): In the traditional Keynesian model, a locus of combinations of real income and price levels that maintain *IS-LM* equilibrium.

Aggregate supply schedule (y^s): The relationship between various price levels and levels of national output that workers and firms will produce voluntarily.

Cost-push theory of stagflation: Simultaneous rising short-run inflation and unemployment rates, stemming from reduced availability of or higher relative prices of factors of production.

Demand-pull theory of stagflation: Simultaneous rising short-run inflation and unemployment rates, stemming from a long-run adjustment of the economy following a sustained increase in aggregate demand.

Explicit contracts: Contractual arrangements in which the terms of relationships between workers and firms, especially concerning wage payments, are written and legally binding upon both parties.

Implicit contracts: Unwritten agreements between workers and firms concerning terms like wage payments that may or may not be legally binding.

Monetarists: Economists who believe that monetary policy actions have pronounced effects on the economy—but that fiscal policy actions do not.

Natural level of employment: As predicted by the classical model, the level of employment toward which the economy tends when workers have perfect information about price level movements and, thus, about the real wage they earn and how it is changing over time. At the natural level of employment, the natural level of output is produced.

Natural level of output: Level of output that occurs when there is full information.

Natural rate of unemployment: An average level of unemployment around the natural level of employment; a state toward which the economy tends if full information about prices and inflation is available. At the natural level of employment, the natural level of output is produced.

Phillips curve: A curve that shows an inverse relationship between inflation and unemployment rates.

Short run: According to the monetarists, the short run is a period of time short enough that workers do not have complete information about aggregate prices and inflation, so that expected prices and inflation may differ from actual prices and inflation.

Stagflation: The simultaneous observation of rising inflation rates and of declining real output and rising unemployment rates.

SELF-TEST QUESTIONS

1. Diagrammatically derive the Keynesian aggregate demand schedule. Explain why its position depends on the amount of autonomous consumption.
2. It often is claimed that the crucial distinction between the classical and traditional Keynesian macroeconomic theories is that they are constructed using differing assumptions about labor market behavior.
   a. Briefly explain the classical view of the labor market. What are two ways that traditional Keynesian theorists have disagreed with this view of the labor market?
   b. Derive graphically a Keynesian aggregate supply schedule, using either one of the Keynesian assumptions about the operation of the labor market.
   c. Compare the aggregate supply schedule you derived in part b with the classical aggregate supply schedule. Why is it that the usefulness of Keynesian aggregate demand policies depends upon a Keynesian perspective on labor market behavior?

3. During the 1970s and again briefly in 1990–1991, the United States economy was affected adversely by events that economists have called "supply shocks," in which large increases in the relative prices of energy resources occurred. Use the traditional Keynesian aggregate demand–aggregate supply framework to illustrate the effects on real output and the price level of such an event. Also, explain why this type of macroeconomic disturbance makes it difficult to know whether it would be best for the Federal Reserve to respond by increasing or reducing the nominal money supply.

4. Key contributions to macroeconomic theory are the traditional Keynesian theories of aggregate demand and aggregate supply. As discussed in this chapter, the monetarist approach to aggregate demand and supply also can be discussed from a Keynesian perspective.
   a. Economists of a monetarist persuasion have a particular perspective on aggregate demand that is based on their beliefs concerning the interest elasticity of desired investment and the interest elasticity of money demand. Draw an *IS-LM* diagram that illustrates this view, and explain the associated monetarist elasticity assumptions.
   b. To explain how the monetarists get their name, illustrate with another *IS-LM* diagram the monetarist view of the effect on real income of an expansionary monetary policy. On a separate graph, illustrate the monetarist view of the effect on real income of an expansionary fiscal policy. Which is larger? Why?

5. Explain how a short-run Phillips curve is derived, using appropriate diagrams.

6. A key point of contention between the monetarists and traditional Keynesian theorists has been their views of the long-run effects of expansionary aggregate demand policies. Use either the aggregate demand–aggregate supply framework or the Phillips curve diagram to assist in explaining how the two groups disagree on this point.

7. Until the early 1970s, it commonly was agreed that policy choices were constrained by a trade-off between inflation and unemployment called the Phillips curve. However, policies designed to lower unemployment rates during the 1970s tended to produce high inflation and high unemployment simultaneously. Explain concisely, but as fully as you can, how this may have occurred.

PROBLEMS

21-1. Consider the following equations for a fictitious economy, which has no government. Demand for real money balances:

$$r_n = 40 - (0.5)(M/P) + 2y$$

Supply of real money balances: $M/P = 40$

IS schedule: $r_n = 40 - 2y$

   a. Derive an equation for the *LM* schedule.
   b. Use your answer from part a to solve for equilibrium real income given that $M/P = 40$.
   c. Suppose now that the price level is cut in half but that the nominal money supply is unchanged. What is the new value of the real money supply?
   d. Use your answer from part c to redo parts a and b.
   e. Based on your answers to parts b and d, what happens to equilibrium real income when the price level is cut in half? What is the economic term for this effect of a change in the price level on the level of real income? What does this effect imply about the slope of the aggregate demand schedule?

21-2. Suppose that the labor demand equation for a fictitious economy is $W/P = 100 - (0.5)N$, where W is the nominal wage rate, P is the price level, and N is the quantity of labor. Also, suppose that the nominal wage rate is fixed at $W = 10$. Compute the employment levels that will arise if (a) $P = \frac{1}{2}$, (b) $P = 1$, (c) $P = 2$. What happens to employment as the price level rises? What then will happen to real output produced, holding all other things constant? What can be concluded about the slope of the aggregate supply function?

21-3. Suppose that the labor demand function is given by $W/P = 180 - (0.5)N$. However, now suppose that nominal wages are flexible but that workers have imperfect information about the price level; workers' aggregate labor supply is given by $W/P^e = 20 + (0.5)N$, where P^e is the workers' expectation of the price level.

   a. If the actual price level and workers' expectation of the price level turn out to be the same and equal to 1, then what is the equilibrium employment level? What is the equilibrium nominal wage rate?

   b. Suppose that workers expect the price level to equal 1 but that the actual price level is equal to $\frac{1}{2}$. What is the equilibrium level of employment? What is the equilibrium nominal wage rate?

   c. Based on your answers to parts a and b, what happens to labor employment when workers' price expectations are unchanged but the actual price level falls? What does this imply about the slope of the aggregate supply schedule?

21-4. For the sake of simplicity, suppose that the aggregate demand and supply schedules are straight-line functions, where the aggregate demand schedule is given by $P = 6M + 2g - 5t - 2y$ (where M is the nominal quantity of money, g is real government spending, and t is real net taxes) and the aggregate supply schedule is given by $P = 5 + 3y$.

   a. What is the equilibrium level of real output if $M = 5$, $g = 10$, and $t = 3$? What is the equilibrium price level?

   b. Suppose that M rises to 10 but g and t are unchanged. What is the new equilibrium level of real output? What is the new equilibrium price level?

   c. Suppose that M stays unchanged at $M = 5$ but that t increases to $t = 5$. What is the new equilibrium level of real output? What is the new equilibrium price level?

21-5. Monetarists believe that the main determinant of the demand for real money balances is the level of real income. Suppose that the demand for real money balances is given by the equation $M/P = (0.25)y$. Also, suppose that the aggregate supply schedule for the economy is given by $P = 10y$.

   a. If the quantity of money is 1,000, what is the equilibrium level of real output? What is the equilibrium price level?

   b. If the quantity of money is reduced to 250, what is the new equilibrium level of real output? What is the new equilibrium price level?

   c. Based on your answers to parts a and b, is monetary policy neutral in its short-run effects on the economy?

21-6. If the short-run Phillips curve is given by the equation $\dot{p} = 20/u$, where $\dot{p}$ is the rate of price inflation and u is the unemployment rate, then what is the value of $\dot{p}$ if u is equal to (a) 20, (b) 10, (c) 5, (d) 2? Plot these four inflation-unemployment combinations and connect them with a smooth schedule. Does this schedule satisfy a normal Phillips curve relationship? Explain.

21-7. This question is an extension of the question above. Suppose that the natural rate of unemployment is $u = 5$. In light of your answer to the previous question, what can you conclude is the expected rate of inflation along the Phillips curve given by the equation $\dot{p} = 20/u$?

21-8. This question is an extension of questions 21-6 and 21-7. Consider another Phillips curve with the equation $\dot{p} = 40/u$. What inflation rates arise when u is equal to (a) 20, (b) 10, (c) 5, (d) 2? If the natural rate of unemployment is $u = 5$, then what can you conclude is the expected rate of inflation along this Phillips curve?

SELECTED REFERENCES

Branson, William, *Macroeconomic Theory and Policy* (New York: Harper & Row, 1979).

De Grauwe, Paul, ''The Cost of Disinflation and the European Monetary System,'' *Open Economies Review,* 1 (2, 1990), pp. 147–173.

Friedman, Benjamin, ''The Theoretical Non-Debate about Monetarism,'' *Kredit und Kapital,* 9 (1974), pp. 347–365.

Friedman, Milton, ''Comments on the Critics,'' in *Milton Friedman's Monetary Framework: A Debate with His Critics,* ed. Robert J. Gordon (Chicago: University of Chicago Press, 1974).

Froyen, Richard T., *Macroeconomics: Theories and Policies,* 3d ed. (New York: Macmillan, 1990).

Hicks, John R., ''Mr. Keynes and the Classics: A Suggested Interpretation,'' *Econometrica,* 5 (2, April 1937), pp. 147–159.

Hoover, Kevin D., ''Two Types of Monetarism,'' *Journal of Economic Literature,* 22 (1, March 1984), pp. 58–76.

Keynes, John Maynard, *The General Theory of Employment, Interest, and Money* (New York: Harcourt Brace Jovanovich, 1964).

Laidler, David, ''The Legacy of the Monetarist Controversy,'' Federal Reserve Bank of St. Louis *Review,* 72 (2, March/April 1990), pp. 49–64.

Mayer, Thomas (ed.), *The Political Economy of American Monetary Policy* (Cambridge: Cambridge University Press, 1990).

Mayer, Thomas (ed.), *The Structure of Monetarism* (New York: Norton, 1978).

Means, Gardner C., ''Industrial Prices and Their Relative Inflexibility,'' U.S. Senate Document 13, 74th Congress, 1st Session (Washington, D.C., 1935).

Meltzer, Allan H., ''On Keynes' *General Theory,*'' *Journal of Economic Literature,* 19 (1, March 1981), pp. 34–64.

Smith, Warren, ''A Graphical Exposition of the Complete Keynesian System,'' *Southern Economic Journal,* 23 (4, October 1956), pp. 115–125.

Rational Expectations and Modern Monetary Theory

CHAPTER PREVIEW

1. What is an adaptive expectation? What are problems with the use of adaptive expectations in economic models?

2. What is the rational expectations hypothesis? Why is it that many economists find the rational expectations hypothesis useful in their macroeconomic models?

3. What are the key elements of the new classical theory?

4. What is the new classical policy ineffectiveness proposition? Why is it implied by the new classical model?

5. In what ways have traditional Keynesian theorists reacted to the new classical theory and its predictions?

6. What are the important features of modern Keynesian contracting models?

7. How does wage indexation affect the economy?

8. Why is it difficult to distinguish among the new classical and modern Keynesian theories in order to test their real-world validity?

In the last four chapters, we have surveyed the classical and traditional Keynesian macroeconomic theories of how monetary (and fiscal) policy actions influence the economy. The classical theorists developed their model of the economy from the assumptions of pure competition, flexible wages and prices, and the absence of money illusion. A key conclusion forthcoming from the classical model was that, even though the nominal money supply is the main determinant of the aggregate demand for goods and services, monetary policy actions are neutral in their effects on real economic activity.

In contrast, Keynes and his followers developed a body of theory in which both monetary and fiscal policy actions affect the aggregate demand for goods and services. They also based their theory of the economy on foundations that violated the assumptions of flexible wages and the absence of money illusion. According to the traditional model that summarizes these key elements of the Keynesian theory, monetary policy actions can be nonneutral.

A more recent contribution to macroeconomic theory is monetarism. Monetarists, like the classical theorists, believe that the quantity of money is the main determinant of the aggregate demand for goods and services in the economy. In this respect, monetarism is a throwback to the classical theory, but it retains key aspects of the Keynesian tradition. According to monetarist thought, the traditional Keynesian model is a useful depiction of the *short-run* effects of monetary policy actions. That is, monetarists argue that, in the short run, changes in the money stock can indeed influence real variables like employment and output. In the *long run,* however, the real effects of monetary policy actions dissipate, and the only economic variable that ultimately responds is the level of prices. In the short run, then, the predictions of monetarist theory look ''Keynesian,'' while in the long run the predictions of monetarist theory look ''classical.'' Monetarists invariably walk a tightrope spanning the two larger bodies of theory.

This tension inherent in the monetarist approach reflects the broader stresses that divide modern economists. As we noted at the end of the last chapter, two key questions arise in light of the monetarist attempt to reconcile the Keynesian short run with the classical long run. First, *how long* does it take to get to the long run? Second, what is the *natural rate of unemployment* toward which the economy tends in the long run?

Most modern economists would agree that the monetarist revolution against the simple Keynesian model was the crucial first step toward breaking away from a narrow reliance upon *only* the Keynesian model or *only* the classical model. They have attempted to resolve the tension with which the monetarists have grappled. In the process, these theorists had to address the most thorny of issues raised by the monetarists in their efforts to separate the short run from the long run: the formation of price and inflation expectations.

THE RATIONAL EXPECTATIONS HYPOTHESIS

In the last chapter we saw that, for the monetarists, an adjustment to a long-run equilibrium occurs when information about actual movements in prices and inflation rates becomes available to workers. Workers then suffer from no money illusion about the real wage, they attain the natural unemployment rate, and they produce the natural level of output. Until the economy reaches this point, however, the imperfect availability of information causes workers' price and inflation expectations to deviate from the actual price levels and inflation rates. This causes workers' perceptions of their real wage earnings to be incorrect. The result is unemployment below or above the natural rate and a level of output production below or above the natural level; there is short-run instability in real economic activity.

The crucial element in this monetarist elaboration of traditional Keynesian short-run theory and classical long-run theory is the role of expectations of prices and inflation. In the real world, all of us make decisions not only on the basis of things we presently observe immediately around us—for instance, prices of items we happen to purchase from day to day in our own town or city, information on prices of goods and services that we see in ads in the local newspapers, or bits and pieces of information we may see on regional or national television news shows—but also on the basis of our anticipations about future prices and rates of inflation.

Each of us can make ''best guesses'' about the present economywide inflation rate based on changes in the prices of some of the goods and services we consume. We also can try to form our own forecasts of how the rate of inflation will change in the future. If asked, each of us, though, would be hard-pressed to explain how we make our ''best guesses'' or put together our forecasts. Unless we are statisticians by training, none of us is likely to use sophisticated computer modeling to undertake these tasks. We simply do the best we can given the information available to us.

There most likely is widespread agreement among economists that this is the case. Economists have not always agreed, however, about how to *model* the process of expectation formation. Just saying that people do the best they can with limited information isn't very specific. Nonetheless, economic models need to be specific. Consequently, in recent years economists have developed precise notions of expectation formation processes.

ADAPTIVE EXPECTATIONS

One way to form expectations is to do so "adaptively." The simplest way to illustrate what is meant by this is by considering an example. Suppose that someone were to ask you to forecast future economywide annual inflation rates over the next 5 years. One approach would be to go to back issues of the *Wall Street Journal* or relevant government publications and examine the performance of the annual inflation rate over, say, the past 20 or 30 years. You could plot points on a graph with these inflation rates measured vertically and time measured horizontally, and you could then draw a rough "trend line" between these points and beyond through the 5 years into the future. Along that trend line would lie your forecasts for inflation rates for the next 5 years.

If you had just finished a basic college statistics course, you could even be a little more sophisticated. Instead of plotting a rough trend line on a diagram, you could use statistical methods to calculate exactly the specific location where your trend line should lie. Indeed, you could come up with an algebraic equation for the trend line. You could substitute different years into your equation, and your equation would tell you, for each year, the forecast for the inflation rate. If you used this more sophisticated approach, you could actually make forecasts beyond a 5-year time horizon, using your past data.

Both of the above approaches actually would be somewhat sophisticated. Another less sophisticated approach you might take to forecasting annual inflation rates for the next 5 years (especially if you don't want to take the time to go to the library, to draw graphs, or to calculate equations) would simply be to guess that inflation over the next 5 years might be equal to the average inflation rate over the last 5 years.

ADAPTIVE EXPECTATIONS PROCESSES

All these approaches to forecasting inflation are known as **adaptive expectations** processes. This means that, under each approach to forming an inflation expectation, you would have used only *past* information. Whether we drew a trend line, used statistical techniques, or calculated rough averages, all that we would have brought to bear on our problem of forming an expectation was past annual inflation rates. That means that we made our expectation as an *adaptation* of past data.

As we saw in the last chapter, one way to derive a Keynesian aggregate supply schedule is to assume that workers form expectations about prices and inflation that turn out, after the fact, to be wrong. This assumes that it takes time before workers recognize that they were wrong. During this period, which is the monetarist "short run," workers do not perceive that a rise in labor demand by firms may be caused by a rise in the level of prices. Therefore, they are willing to work more, and produce more, as the nominal wage rises, because they misperceive this rise in the nominal wage as a rise in their real wage.

Consistent with the idea that it takes time for expectations to adjust to current events is the idea that individuals form expectations adaptively. If workers use an adaptive expectations process to make their price level or inflation forecasts, then they must always wait for new information on prices and inflation rates to become available before they alter their forecasts. This reasoning implies that over fairly lengthy periods of time workers cannot help but suffer from money illusion concerning their wages. As a result, policy actions that increase aggregate demand and push up the aggregate price level always will cause workers to misperceive their true real wages and to work and produce more than the long-run, natural levels.

PROBLEMS WITH ADAPTIVE EXPECTATIONS

Many economists find this implication of adaptive expectations a troubling one, because it does not give people much credit for having common sense about the future. Consider an extreme example. Suppose that someone again were to ask you to make a forecast of inflation rates for the next 5 years but *also* informed you that the Federal Reserve planned to increase the annual growth rate of the money stock by a factor of 10, relative to this year's rate of money growth, over the next 5 years. Would you still base your forecast only on past inflation rate data, even though this text now has exposed you to a variety of theories that indicate that higher money growth rates imply higher prices? Most economists believe that you would not do this. If, however, economists were to use a model that assumed that people form their expectations adaptively, the model implicitly would assume exactly that kind of noncommonsensical behavior.

Another bothersome feature of adaptive expectations is that any specific adaptive expectations process may be as good as any other specific adaptive expectations process. For instance, one person might draw a graph of 30 years of past annual inflation data to plot a trend line for his future inflation forecasts, while another person might draw a similar graph using data from the previous 40 years. The trend lines that result will be similar but almost certainly will not be the same. How are we as economists to choose which of these adaptive approaches is the better one? An inability to decide about what specific adaptive expectations process to use makes the use of adaptive expectations in economic models problematic.

To summarize, implicit in the traditional Keynesian, imperfect-information model of aggregate supply is the assumption that individuals form expectations adaptively, meaning that individuals use only past information to make forecasts about the future. This adaptive view of how people form expectations has two crucial problems when it comes to incorporating price level and inflation expectations into models of the economy. First, the assumption of adaptive expectations does not give people enough credit for recognizing (when doing so is appropriate) that *currently available* as well as past information, *as well as their own understanding* of how the economy works, can yield better forecasts than just using past data. Second, there are an infinite number of different adaptive schemes for forming expectations, and there is no good way to sort out any one adaptive expectations process for a model of the economy.

RATIONAL EXPECTATIONS

The problems inherent in the use of adaptive expectations processes for constructing models of the economy have led modern economists to a broader theory of how individuals form expectations. These economists base their theory on what is known as the **rational expectations hypothesis.** This hypothesis states that an individual bases his best forecast of the future value of an economic variable such as the price level or inflation rate on all past *and current* information available to him, *plus* his current understanding of how the economy works. Whereas an adaptive forecast looks backward, because it mainly uses past information, a *rational* forecast looks forward.

Consider, for instance, the example used earlier, in which someone asked you to make a forecast of annual inflation rates for the next 5 years, given the further information that the Federal Reserve plans to increase the rate of growth of the nominal money supply by a factor of 10 over the course of that future period. If you truly formed an adaptive 5-year inflation forecast, you would, like a mindless robot, follow some adaptive procedure, such as averaging inflation rates from some arbitrary point in the past up to the present to calculate your forecast. But if your behavior were consistent with the rational expectations hypothesis, you would not do this; instead, you would make use of the information that the rate of money growth will be 10 times higher in the future. Using your own model of how changes in the nominal money supply affect the economy, you would forecast how such changes, relative to the present situation, will work their way through the economy to produce higher rates of inflation.

THE RATIONAL EXPECTATIONS HYPOTHESIS

The rational expectations hypothesis is more general than the hypothesis of adaptive expectations because it is less restrictive. An adaptive expectations process restricts people to use only past (before and right up to the present) information. The rational expectations hypothesis asserts that if a person can do better than an adaptive forecast, he will do so. He will do so because doing better than the adaptive forecast, if that can be done, is the *rational* thing to do, meaning only that the individual will then have made his truly *optimal* forecast.

This does not preclude the possibility that an individual's best, rational forecast may, as a special case, be adaptive. Suppose that all the information you had was inflation data for last year, that you had no idea what the Federal Reserve—or any other agent in the economy, for that matter—was likely to do in the future, and that you had absolutely no idea how the economy worked, and yet someone still asked you to make your best forecast of next year's inflation rate. Given this very constrained set of information, your best, rational forecast might very well be to use the last year's inflation rate as your estimate of the coming year's inflation rate. (We cannot say *for sure* that this would be the case, because we cannot know how your mind might process this information, plus we realize that you may have studied this text carefully and therefore understand several theories of how the economy works.) In this case, your *rational* forecast of inflation would be an *adaptive* forecast.

In many, if not most, situations, however, it would not be unreasonable to think that we all make price level and inflation forecasts using every bit of information we can bring to bear on the problem. Furthermore, it is sensible to think that bits and pieces of information about what may be happening in the economy at this instant (or may yet occur in the future) may be useful to us in that endeavor. That perspective is at the heart of the rational expectations hypothesis. It appears to be such a reasonable view to take on how expectations are formed that it has won over most modern theorists, whether they are of Keynesian or classical persuasion.

QUESTIONS ABOUT RATIONAL EXPECTATIONS

The rational expectations hypothesis does suffer from some problems, however. One difficulty is that it is so general that it can be difficult to incorporate into a theory of how the economy works. For instance, you have been reading this textbook and listening to lectures by your professor, and so you may have a better idea than others about how to interpret current information about possible future monetary policy actions. You might also spend some time reading the *Wall Street Journal* regularly, while another of your classmates may choose instead to spend the same time watching MTV. Obviously, you, another of your classmates, or someone outside your class all are likely to form different, but individually rational, expectations about the future level of prices and future price inflation. Does this mean that economists need to model each person's rational expectations formation procedure? Could this even be done?

Second, if everyone forms his or her own rational expectation about future levels of prices and future inflation rates, then each person will make decisions *today* based on those expectations. For instance, if you were deciding whether or not to take a part-time job or whether to work more or fewer hours in a part-time job you presently have, you would form a perception about the real wage earnings from that employment based on your rational price level expectation. But everyone else in the economy presumably would be making the same kinds of decisions, and those decisions would, in the aggregate, affect what the future level of prices will turn out to be. Does this mean that you must try to form expectations about *others'* expectations if your own expectation is to be a "rational" one? If so, doesn't that also mean that others will also try to forecast *your* expectation as well? Does the rational expectations hypothesis then lead to hopeless logical circularity that produces no single answer about how to model "rational" expectations?

These are thorny philosophical problems. As we shall see, part of what divides modern economists is the manner in which economists seek to address them. Some economists conclude that the rational expectations hypothesis is so open-ended and hopelessly circular in its logical implications that economists cannot legitimately incorporate it into models of the economy. These economists largely have continued to identify with the classical or traditional Keynesian bodies of theory and have given up on including theories of expectation formation and expectation adjustment.

Most modern theorists, however, believe that the role of price level and inflation expectations is too important to ignore in their models. These theorists have instead chosen to make expectations central to their models of how the economy works and of what role money plays in influencing economic activity. Among this modern group, the rational expectations hypothesis therefore is a key feature of the models that they have proposed and are continuing to develop.

In this chapter, we shall discuss two separate bodies of theory that have used the rational expectations hypothesis. The first now commonly is known as the "new classical" theory of macroeconomics. As its name implies, it has rejuvenated many of the ideas and conclusions commonly associated with classical theory. The second body of theory has, in contrast, sought to incorporate the rational expecations hypothesis into the traditional Keynesian model. This approach has produced what we shall term the "modern Keynesian model." As we shall see, these two approaches share several features, the most important of which is the rational expectations hypothesis. They yield, however, strikingly different predictions about the behavior of important economic variables and about the usefulness of monetary (and fiscal) stabilization policies.

THE NEW CLASSICAL MODEL

We shall begin with the "new classical" theory for two reasons. First, the economists who initiated this intellectual approach to modeling the economy were in fact the first to use the rational expectations hypothesis. This hypothesis, which the economist John Muth of Indiana University first developed in an article published in 1961, has since been used by macroeconomists such as Robert Lucas of the University of Chicago, Thomas Sargent of Stanford University, and Neil Wallace of the University of Minnesota to try to make sense out of the breakdown of the short-run Phillips curve relationship in the 1970s. These individuals, among others, paved the way for what became known in the late 1970s and early 1980s as the ''new classical revolution'' against traditional Keynesian economics. Because the new classical theorists first used the rational expectations hypothesis, it is reasonable to begin with their theory.

Second, as was the case in our comparison of the classical and traditional Keynesian theories, in which the classical model was the ''benchmark'' for comparisons, the new classical theory provides a nice ''benchmark'' for comparisons to the modern Keynesian theory discussed later in this chapter and to other developments that we shall survey in the next chapter.

Because the new classical theorists were the first to adopt rational expectations, during much of the latter 1970s and the 1980s there was much confusion among economists about what portion of the new classical theory's conclusions stemmed directly from use of that hypothesis. Indeed, some observers, such as Lester Thurow of the Massachusetts Institute of Technology, referred to the new classical theorists as ''rational expectation- ists,'' and many criticisms of their theory failed to distinguish between separate key assumptions that form the foundation of what is truly ''new classical economics.''

KEY NEW CLASSICAL ASSUMPTIONS

The new classical theorists adopt three key assumptions:

1. Rational self-interest.
2. Pure competition with flexible wages and prices.
3. Information is imperfect, but all individuals form rational expectations, meaning specifically that they use all available past and current information and that they understand how the economy functions.

The first two of these assumptions are not new to us. They correspond exactly to the first two assumptions used by the classical theorists to construct their model of the economy. The third assumption, however, recognizes an essential, and undeniable, point made by Keynes and developed more fully by his followers—namely, that information is imperfect, and so individuals must make decisions based on expectations they form about current and future movements in economic variables such as prices and inflation rates. In contrast to the traditional Keynesian model that implicitly assumes adaptive expectations, the new classical theorists explicitly make the assumption that expectations are formed *rationally.* Furthermore, the new classical model takes a particular philosophical view on what *rational expectations* really means. Their view is that it means that individuals fully use all available past and current information *and,* further, that individuals have a basic understanding of how the economy works. It is this last provision that makes it possible to incorporate the rational expectations hypothesis into a full model of the economy. The reason is that this provision means that we, as economists, shall assume that the individuals in our model know that the economy works the way our model says it works. That is, we assume that all expectations formed by the individuals whose behavior we intend our model to depict behave *as if* they understand and agree with our economic model.

The new classical economists, and others who use the rational expectations hypothesis in constructing economic models, believe that this is a reasonable way to incorporate the rational expectations hypothesis. After all, they argue, if the hypothesis is correct *and* the proposed theory is also correct, then our model will permit us to make predictions that evidence from the real world should support or reject. Economists still debate this issue, but henceforth we shall follow the new classical theorists in adopting this assumption— so that we can understand how theories with rational expectations work.

ESSENTIAL ELEMENTS OF THE NEW CLASSICAL MODEL

Recall that, in the traditional Keynesian model, workers form adaptive expectations of current and future price levels and inflation rates. As a result, a monetary policy action that increases the nominal quantity of money and, hence, aggregate demand will cause the level of prices to rise. The rise in prices induces a rise in labor demand by firms and an increase in labor employment. According to the new classical theorists, such behavior on the part of workers is *irrational* unless workers face severe constraints on their ability to observe actions of the Federal Reserve and to understand how its actions are likely to affect the level of prices and the rate of inflation.

In general, the new classical theorists argue, the behavior of workers that is presumed in the traditional Keynesian model cannot occur if workers pay any attention to current policy activities of the Federal Reserve, say, by reading the newspaper or by watching television from time to time. In addition, such behavior cannot occur if workers have even the most basic understanding of how changes in the nominal money supply by the Federal Reserve can cause changes in the level of prices. Therefore, the new classical economists believe that individual workers base their aggregate price and inflation expectations upon their anticipations of *future* monetary (or, possibly, fiscal) policy actions, using their own understanding of the way that policy makers conduct policies at present or will conduct policies in the future. The new classical economists also argue that workers recognize that an increase in the nominal money supply will result in an increase in the level of prices. These economists argue further that workers understand that an increase in the growth of the nominal money supply over time will cause higher price inflation over time.

Therefore, the new classical economists propose that the price expectation of workers, P^e, actually depends upon their expectation of the Federal Reserve's behavior regarding the nominal money supply, denoted M^e. Furthermore, their expectation of inflation, $\dot{p}^e$, actually depends upon their expectation of the future rate of growth of the money stock.

This notion, that each of us conditions our price and inflation forecasts to our forecasts of what the Federal Reserve might do in the future, appears rather straightforward (especially to anyone who reads constantly about ''Fed watchers'' in publications such as the *Wall Street Journal*). Nevertheless, the new classical economists argue that it is a fact of life that the adaptive-expectations-based, traditional Keynesian model ignores, making the latter model incorrect in most of its conclusions. This is a strong claim, but as we shall see, it follows directly from the new classical assumptions.

ANTICIPATED MONETARY POLICY AND SHORT-RUN NEUTRALITY

To understand the substance of the new classical argument, consider Figure 22-1. Panel (*b*) of the figure illustrates the labor market; at an initial equilibrium, labor demand of firms depends on the actual output price P_0, and labor supply of workers depends upon the *nominal money supply expectation of workers*, $M^e = M_0$. This means that workers expect the Federal Reserve to set the nominal money stock equal to a quantity M_0, and this anticipation governs their expectation of the price level and, thus, their perception of the real wage they will earn. Given these initial positions of labor demand and labor supply, the equilibrium nominal wage is W_0, and the equilibrium level of employment is N_0.

Panel (*a*) depicts a corresponding equilibrium in the market for real output, where the intersection of aggregate demand and aggregate supply determines the initial price level P_0 and the initial level of real output y_0. We shall assume that at this initial equilibrium

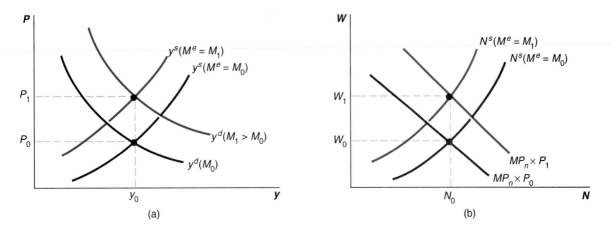

Figure 22-1

The Effects of a Fully Anticipated Increase in the Nominal Money Supply in the New Classical Model.   A rise in the money stock would cause aggregate demand to rise, causing a rise in the price level [panel (a)]. The increase in the price level results in a rise in the demand for labor by firms [panel (b)]. If the increase in the nominal money supply is fully anticipated by workers, they will recognize that their real wages will fall when the price level increases, and so they will reduce their supply of labor [panel (b)]. On net, the equilibrium level of labor employment is unchanged. Aggregate supply shifts leftward with the higher expectation of the nominal money supply and the resulting rise in the expected price level [panel (a)]. On net, the equilibrium level of real output is unchanged. Hence, in the new classical model a fully anticipated increase in the nominal money supply has no real (output or employment) effects.

the actual money stock is equal to the amount that workers expected, M_0. The price expectation of workers determines the position of the aggregate supply schedule. Their price expectation, in turn, depends on their money stock expectation $M^e = M_0$.

Suppose now that the Federal Reserve were to preannounce (say, via a press conference or through a press release) that it planned to increase the nominal money supply to a larger amount, M_1. Furthermore, suppose that it follows through exactly with this promise. This causes the aggregate demand schedule to shift rightward in panel (a) of Figure 22-1. *Other things held constant,* the price level rises, causing labor demand and employment to rise in panel (b) and a resulting rise in real output produced in panel (a).

In the new classical model, however, expectations are not constant. Because the Federal Reserve preannounced its policy in our example, workers know that the money stock will rise, and they raise their expectation of the nominal money supply to $M^e = M_1$. They also understand how the economy works, and so they know that the price level will rise, and by how much. Therefore, they raise their price expectations, resulting in a leftward shift of the labor supply schedule in panel (b) and, therefore, in a leftward shift of the aggregate supply schedule in panel (a). These shifts occur simultaneously with the rise in labor demand and increase in aggregate demand. On net, the equilibrium price level increases in the short run, but labor employment and real output remain at their natural levels, N_0 and y_0. Monetary policy is neutral, even in the short run.

In a way, this is hardly surprising, because in our example the Federal Reserve gave out precise, believable information about its policy intentions. Therefore, workers effectively had full information: They *fully anticipated* the rise in the nominal money supply and the resulting rise in the price level. As a result, our example really replicated the classical model.

Nevertheless, new classical theorists argue that less stringent assumptions about information availability also will produce conclusions consistent with those arising from our example. For instance, the Federal Reserve realistically does not preannounce all of its policy actions, but many of its policy actions are in fact predictable. The Federal Reserve often settles into routines, and reporters and other Fed watchers often inform the public about these routines and what they imply about likely Federal Reserve policy.

When the Federal Reserve follows set routines, or is *systematic*, in its policy making, argue the new classical theorists, workers will be able to anticipate monetary policy actions. If so, workers will adjust their expectations and their labor supply behavior to neutralize their effects on the economy. According to the new classical model, *individuals will anticipate systematic monetary policy actions, and these systematic policy actions will have* neutral *effects on the economy, even in the short run.*

UNANTICIPATED MONETARY POLICY AND SHORT-RUN NONNEUTRALITY

Of course, people aren't perfect in their ability to predict the future. Furthermore, the Federal Reserve sometimes is unpredictable. Sometimes it says it is going to follow a particular policy but either is unsuccessful or, argue some cynics, is insincere. Either way, from time to time it is inevitable that some Federal Reserve policy actions will be unsystematic. If so, people will not anticipate these actions.

Figure 22-2 illustrates the effects of an unanticipated increase in the nominal money supply, from M_0 to a larger quantity M_1. Aggregate demand rises in panel (*a*), causing a rise in the price level that stimulates an increase in labor demand in panel (*b*). Because workers had anticipated that the money stock would only be equal to M_0, they misperceive the rise in the nominal wage as indicating a rise in the real wage and increase the quantity of labor services supplied. Employment rises to N_1 in the short run, and real output increases to y_1. Hence, in the new classical model, *monetary policy actions can have short-run real effects only if monetary policy is unsystematic and, therefore, is unanticipated.*

What would happen in the long run? According to the new classical theorists, in the long run people figure out that the Federal Reserve either accidentally increased the nominal money supply or intentionally increased it without "fair warning." They eventually adjust their expectations accordingly; price expectations rise, and labor supply and aggregate supply shift leftward as in Figure 22-1. In the long run, money still is neutral, as argued by the monetarists.

THE POLICY INEFFECTIVENESS PROPOSITION

The examples considered above illustrate the key elements of the new classical argument. Systematic, predictable monetary policy actions have no short-run effects on real variables, and unsystematic, unpredictable monetary policy actions have short-run real effects that are dissipated in the long run.

We have emphasized the new classical view of monetary policy effects because most new classical theorists, like the monetarists, typically have attributed to money the predominant role in influencing aggregate demand and prices. If, however, fiscal policy actions affect aggregate demand, identical arguments would apply to their effects. Systematic fiscal policy actions would have no short-run real effects, and unsystematic fiscal policy actions would have real effects only in the short run that ultimately "wash out" in the long run.

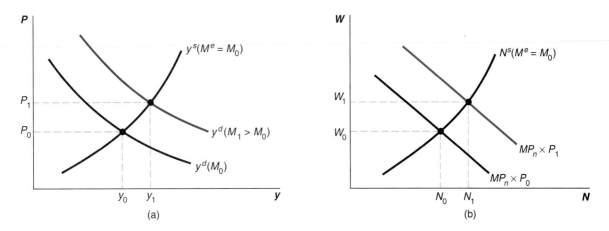

Figure 22-2
The Effects of a Completely Unanticipated Increase in the Nominal Money Supply in the New Classical Model.   A rise in the money stock would cause aggregate demand to rise, causing a rise in the price level [panel (a)]. The increase in the price level results in a rise in the demand for labor by firms [panel (b)]. If the increase in the nominal money supply is completely unanticipated by workers, they will fail to recognize the price level will rise, and so their supply of labor is unchanged [panel (b)]. As a result, the equilibrium level of labor employment rises. Equilibrium real output increases as well [panel (a)]. Hence, in the new classical model a completely unanticipated increase in the nominal money supply has real, expansionary effects in the short run.

The new classical conclusion that monetary and fiscal policy actions have no long-lived effects in a flexible-wage, flexible-price, rational expectations environment is known as the **policy ineffectiveness proposition.** It is this proposition that economists most commonly have associated with the new classical theory, because it has such extreme implications. Effectively, it implies that any policy actions intended to stabilize real output and employment through changes in aggregate demand ultimately cannot achieve their objectives.

To some Keynesian economists, such as Franco Modigliani and Robert Solow of the Massachusetts Institute of Technology and James Tobin of Yale University, the policy ineffectiveness proposition is an unrealistic, extreme version of monetarism. Tobin, for instance, has termed the monetarist arguments of Milton Friedman and others ''Mark I Monetarism'' and the theory of the new classical theorists ''Mark II Monetarism.'' Even some monetarists are not fully convinced that the policy ineffectiveness proposition is correct. Indeed, the explanation that Friedman and other monetarists have offered for the Great Depression is that it resulted from a significant (over one-third) decline in the nominal money supply between 1929 and 1933 that greatly reduced aggregate demand. It would seem that if the new classical theory were unambiguously correct, people should have adjusted their expectations about monetary policy at some point within this four-year time span. It is difficult to believe, both monetarists and Keynesians argue, that people would not eventually have perceived and anticipated this massive decline in the money supply, in which case the new classical theory implies that the Great Depression should have *automatically* ended within no more than a couple of years if not more quickly. Instead, it perpetuated for several more years following 1933.

Indeed, if the new classical theory is correct, it is difficult for Keynesians and some monetarists to see how any recessions could persist for long periods of time. The new classical theorists often have argued that such persistence (such as the severe persistence seen in the Great Depression) is owed to misguided governmental policy making. For instance, common new classical explanations for the severity and prolonged nature of the Great Depression are that monetary policy was often very unsystematic during that period, making expectation formation a complicated task, and that the absence of governmental bank deposit insurance in the 1930s led to extremely large wealth losses that had adverse effects on economic behavior.

MODERN KEYNESIAN THEORY: RATIONAL CONTRACTING

Traditional Keynesian economists have been particularly unwilling to accept the new classical theory and the policy ineffectiveness proposition it implies. An initial line of attack pursued by economists of a Keynesian persuasion was against the rational expectations hypothesis. Many early Keynesian observers questioned the reasonableness of the hypothesis, arguing that it implied an unrealistic ability to gather information easily and to learn rapidly.

There have been two reactions to this view by those who would like to salvage remnants of the traditional Keynesian theory. One has been to deny the validity of the rational expectations hypothesis. Another has been to develop theories that incorporate rational expectations but that also recognize the existence of constraints on the capability of individuals to gather, process, or act upon information. Those who have developed such *modern Keynesian theories,* such as Stanley Fischer of the Massachusetts Institute of Technology, Jo Anna Gray of the University of Oregon, and John Taylor of Stanford University, have become convinced that the rational expectations hypothesis is preferable to the assumption of adaptive expectations formation. But they deny that wages and prices are as flexible as is assumed by the new classical theory.

The reason that wages and prices might be inflexible, according to these modern Keynesians, is that workers and firms in the real world often agree to contracts that set the terms, such as wages and benefits, that govern the employment of workers with firms over a given time period. The existence of such long-term contracts, argue modern Keynesians, can make the instantaneous adjustments of expectations to monetary policy actions moot even if such adjustments are possible. If workers agree to wage contracts with firms, for instance, they cannot adjust their behavior to changed expectations even if they wanted to do so. As a result, as we shall see, modern Keynesian theories conclude that monetary policy has real effects.

WHY WOULD WORKERS AND FIRMS USE CONTRACTS?

As we discussed in the last chapter, there are many types of labor contracting agreements in the economy, including both *explicit* (legally binding) and *implicit* (unstated) contracts between workers and firms. Explicit contracts that set wages certainly are commonplace in unionized industries. Explicit employment contracts also exist in various occupations outside of unionized industries. Certainly, most college students discover that firms that hire them after graduation often have clearly stated initial salaries and set policies about the timing of initial and annual salary reviews and changes. Implicit contracts vary significantly across industries, and because they are implicit, economists argue over whether or not they exist.

No one disagrees, however, on the fact that wage contracts are important in some parts of the economy. The issue that arises, nonetheless, is why such contracts exist. After all, firms would prefer to pay lower, market-based wages if the demand for their products falls, and workers would prefer to earn higher, market-based wages if the demand for their skills rises. Why should either party to a wage contract agree to fix the nominal wage rate at a level that later may not be consistent with demand and supply conditions in the labor market?

This is an issue that continues to occupy the time and research efforts of numerous economists, but we can point to two key reasons that economists have identified to date. First, for nominal wages to rise or fall with the forces of supply and demand in the labor market, workers and firms must agree to engage in ''auctioning'' workers' skills. Indeed, the classical labor market theory, by assuming that wages and employment adjust almost instantaneously to changes in demand and supply conditions, implicitly assumed that workers auction their skills continuously to the highest bidders among firms. Still, it is difficult to envision how the labor market could really work so quickly without posing some severe hardships on people. Suppose, for instance, that you studied hard to become an architect specializing in construction of office buildings. If the market for architects were a continuous auction market for architects' skills, then architects would be willing to relocate themselves and their families at a moment's notice between cities around the country. Doing so would impose severe personal costs (disutility) upon architects. These costs, which economists call labor market *transaction costs,* could be high enough to induce architects to prefer to negotiate a long-term contract with an employer in a single city. Their employer might also desire such a contract, because otherwise the employer would have to scour the country from day to day for available architects specializing in buildings currently under construction. Hence, the existence of transaction costs is one reason that workers and firms may enter into binding or implicit wage contracts.

Another possible reason for the existence of contracts is *risk aversion* by workers and firms. The world is an uncertain place, and as a result, market wages could rise or fall at any time. If they rise, workers are better off while firms are not; if wages fall, firms are better off while workers are not. Workers and firms may agree to fix the wage rate, via a contract, for an interval of time to share in the risk that one or the other might lose from variability of the market wage rate.

A THEORY OF RATIONAL CONTRACTING

The modern Keynesian theory of macroeconomics in a world with wage contracts combines both wage stickiness and imperfect information from the traditional Keynesian model. It follows in the footsteps of the new classical economists by adopting the rational expectations hypothesis. Hence, modern Keynesian contract models retain one element of the new classical framework—the rational expectations hypothesis—while rejecting the other—the assumption of market clearing under competition.

In the traditional ''sticky-wage'' model discussed in the previous chapter, we assumed that workers and firms simply set the nominal wage at a constant value over an interval of time. We provided no explanation of how workers and firms determined *that* fixed wage, however. It is as if workers and firms tossed a coin to determine the nominal wage. Indeed, this ''arbitrariness'' inherent in the traditional sticky-wage theory of aggregate supply in the traditional Keynesian framework represented a serious weakness that the new classical theorists have consistently attacked.

One key goal of modern contracting theory has been to provide an explanation of exactly what nominal wage workers and firms would choose to set in a contractual agreement. The main requirement of this theory has been that the chosen wage should be consistent with the rational behavior of workers and firms. That is, workers and firms agree to set a wage rate that is consistent with their underlying preferences and that is the best possible choice they can make given the information available to them when they sign contracts. This last requirement means that both workers and firms choose a wage based on their *rational expectations* of what economic conditions will be during the period in which the wage contract is in force.

There are a variety of specific theories of rational contracting. The most sophisticated of these attempt to capture as many real-world elements of contracting as possible. For instance, contracts of different firms and industries are of different lengths, so that they *overlap.* Some unionized industries have two-year contracts or three-year contracts, while nonunionized industries often have one-year contracts. Also, modern theories of contracting consider the possibility that some industries may be perfectly competitive, while others may have less competitive market structures.

Note, though, that the more economists account for real-world features, the more complex their models become. Our goal here is not to make things complicated by seeking to incorporate every relevant feature of real-world contracting. For this reason, we shall make the simplifying assumption that industries are perfectly competitive and that workers and firms *synchronize* all wage contracts, meaning that all workers and firms sign their contracts at the same time and that all contracts have the same duration.

Expected Labor Market Clearing The place to begin constructing our contracting model is with a consideration of what would happen if there were no wage contracts at all, if there were flexible prices, and if there were full information. If this were the case, then in any given time interval, the labor market would ''clear.'' That is, the nominal wage rate would adjust to the point at which the quantity of labor demanded would be equal to the quantity of labor supplied. At this market-clearing wage, labeled W^* in Figure 22-3, the equilibrium quantity of labor services supplied by workers and demanded by firms is N^*. These values of the nominal wage and of the level of employment would be the full-information, or natural, values.

It is important to recall the desirable properties of this classical labor market equilibrium. At the full-information, market-clearing wage rate W^*, laborers wish to supply the same quantity of labor services that business firms desire to purchase. That is, the desires of both the providers and consumers of these services are satisfied at this nominal wage rate. As a result, there is no labor unemployment at this wage rate; N^* is the natural, full-information quantity of labor.

Of course, the hallmarks of the Keynesian challenge to this classical labor market equilibrium were that institutional features such as contracts often fix wages and that information is not fully available to workers. The modern Keynesian theory of wage contracting seeks to combine these Keynesian tenets into a theory that recognizes the desirable, albeit unattainable, properties of the classical labor market theory.

According to this modern theory of contracting, workers and firms in competitive industries would very much like to be in the classical world with all its desirable properties, including the absence of unemployment. Nevertheless, because it is so costly to undertake instantaneous adjustments in the labor market via a continuous labor auctioning process, both workers and firms agree to sign wage contracts with lengthy durations. The duration of the contracts can vary, but we shall assume that all contracts are for one year. When workers and firms sign these contracts that fix the nominal wage rate, they do not know exactly what economic conditions will prevail during the contract year. Nonetheless, according to the theory, they will do the best that they can to set a wage that would hold, on average, in the absence of contracts. That is, at the time that workers and firms negotiate a wage contract, they will try to *replicate* the nominal wage rate that they *expect* the

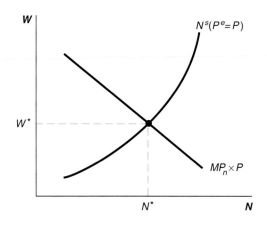

Figure 22-3
Full-Information Employment and the Market-Clearing Nominal Wage Rate.   If workers and firms have full information about prices, $P^e = P$, then the equilibrium quantity of employment is the natural, full-information level, N^*. The wage rate W^* is the market-clearing nominal wage rate at which the quantity of labor demanded is equal to the quantity of labor supplied at this natural employment level.

classical labor auction market would have produced, if left to its own devices, during the upcoming period of the contract. They would like to achieve this wage rate because that is the wage rate at which there is no labor unemployment, and both workers and firms are satisfied.

The Contracted Wage and the Aggregate Supply Schedule   Therefore, workers and firms will agree to set the contracted wage rate equal to the *expected value of the classical, market-clearing nominal wage rate, W**. Figure 22-4 illustrates this situation. When wage contracts are negotiated, workers and firms do not know the actual level of prices that will arise for the duration of the contracts, the upcoming year. They can, though, form their best expectation, or rational expectation, of what the level of prices will turn out to be, labeled P^e. Thus, both workers and firms anticipate that the labor supply schedule of workers will be in the position $N^s(P^e)$ during that next year, *on average*. They also anticipate that the average level of labor demand by firms during the coming year will be given by the labor demand schedule $MP_n \times P^e$. This means that they expect that if the labor market were to clear during the coming year, the average level of the nominal wage rate would be W^{*e}. At this anticipated market-clearing wage, the average amount of unemployment would be zero, because the labor market would be in equilibrium at this nominal wage rate.

Both workers and firms would prefer not to observe either labor shortages or surpluses (unemployment) during the period the wage contract is in force, because at full employment workers operate on their supply schedule while firms operate on their demand schedule. Therefore, they will set the contract wage, labeled W^c, equal to the anticipated market-clearing wage W^{*e}. This means that workers agree to provide labor services at this contracted wage, as shown by the horizontal schedule labeled W^c.

Once the contract wage is set, the level of prices may or may not actually turn out to be equal to the level that workers and firms anticipated. Figure 22-5 shows three possibilities. One is that the actual price level P_0 is equal to the expected price level P^e, in which case the level of prices turns out to be exactly equal to the price level that workers

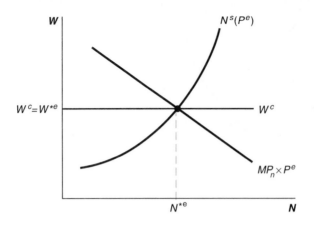

Figure 22-4
Determining the Contractual Wage Rate.   At the time a wage contract is signed, workers and firms form an expectation of the price level, P^e, that they think will exist during the period of the contract. They anticipate that, at this expected price level, the level of employment will be N^{*e}. The wage rate W^{*e} is the expected market-clearing nominal wage rate at which the quantity of labor demanded is equal to the quantity of labor supplied at this expected natural employment level. Workers and firms desire to obtain this level of employment during the term of the contract, and so they set the contract wage W^c equal to the expected market-clearing wage rate W^{*e}.

and firms expected when they set contract wages. As shown in panel (a) of the figure, the position of the labor demand schedule at this price level then determines the level of employment, N_0. At this quantity of employment, workers and firms produce output level y_0, as depicted in panel (b). This yields the price-output combination shown as the point P_0 and y_0 in panel (c). Because workers and firms exactly realize their expectations in this situation, N_0 is the natural employment level, and y_0 is the natural output level.

In general, however, it is unlikely that workers and firms will be exactly ''on the money'' in their price predictions. For instance, the price level could actually turn out to be higher than they anticipated when they negotiated their contracts. If so, then the price level actually will turn out to be equal to a value P_1 that exceeds P^e, and labor demand will in fact be greater than workers and firms had anticipated, given by the MPN $\times$ P_1 schedule in panel (a) of Figure 22-5. Nevertheless, workers must honor the contracts they signed, and so they find themselves providing more labor services than they had anticipated, given by the amount N_1 in panel (a), and producing more output, y_1 in panel (b). (Of course, real-world contracts might specify overtime pay above some threshold number of hours and might place upper limits on amounts of hours worked, but for simplicity of exposition we avoid considering these additional complications.) This yields the price-output combination P_1 and y_1 in panel (c).

If the price level actually turned out to be lower than workers and firms had anticipated, then labor demand would have fallen below its anticipated level, to MP$_n$ $\times$ P_2, where P_2 is a price level lower than the expected level of prices P^e. Firms would employ less labor services, N_2 in panels (a) and (b), than workers and firms had anticipated when they negotiated their wage contracts. They would produce less output, y_2 in panel (b). This would yield the price-output combination P_2 and y_2 in panel (c).

A schedule defined by the three points that we have constructed is the economy's aggregate supply schedule under wage contracting. We have derived the schedule for the

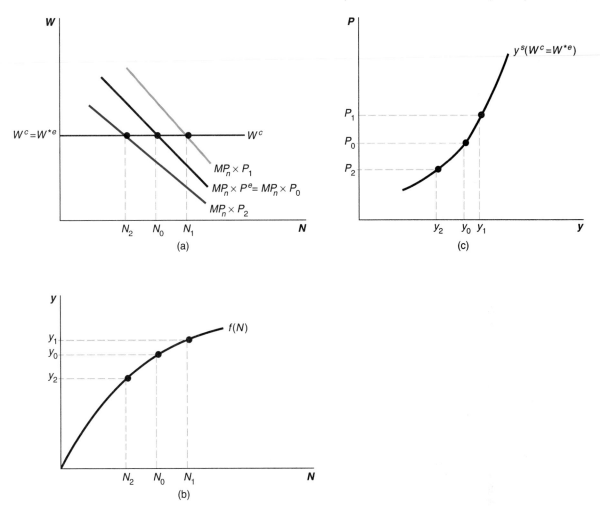

Figure 22-5
Deriving the Aggregate Supply Schedule for the Wage Contracting Model.   During the term of the wage contract between workers and firms, the contracted nominal wage rate W^c is set equal to the market-clearing nominal wage rate W^{*e}. Workers and firms expected that this would be the market-clearing wage rate based on their price expectation when they signed the contract. If the price level varies during the term of the contract, however, the demand for labor by firms will rise or fall, causing employment to vary [panel (a)]. As a result, the amount of real output produced will vary with price changes that were not anticipated when the contract was signed [panel (b)]. Therefore, the aggregate supply schedule will slope upward in the modern Keynesian contracting model [panel (c)]. Monetary policy actions that shift the aggregate demand schedule will be nonneutral during the period the wage is held fixed at W^c.

contract wage W^c; hence we use the notation $y^s(W^c)$ to denote the schedule. Changes in this contract wage would shift the aggregate supply schedule. Specifically, a higher contract wage would have yielded an aggregate supply schedule above and to the left of the schedule depicted in panel (c) in Figure 22-5. A lower contract wage would have yielded an aggregate supply schedule below and to the right of the schedule that is shown. Of course, changes in the marginal product of labor arising from real technological changes or in variations in the amounts of other real resources like capital or land services also could shift the aggregate supply schedule to the left or right as well.

This derivation of aggregate supply, of course, is very similar to the aggregate supply derivation for the case of sticky wages in Chapter 21. It goes far beyond the arbitrary stickiness that we assumed in that derivation, however, because rational contracting decisions of workers and firms determined the fixed wage. Laborers and business firms may turn out to be wrong in their choice of a contract wage that they hope will be consistent with full employment, but in making their selection of this contract wage they do the best that they can with the information available to them. Consequently, this theory of contracting maintains the rational expectations hypothesis but allows for fixed nominal wages during an interval of time.

WAGE INDEXATION

In fact, some contracts in the economy do not require completely fixed nominal wages during the term of the contract. These contracts set a "base wage" that laborers will earn but permit this base wage to vary with changes in other economic variables. A common example of this, especially in some union contracts, is known as a "cost of living adjustment," or COLA. Under a COLA contract, rises in the price level automatically cause the wage paid to workers to rise, usually at set intervals of time, such as every three months. COLA clauses in wage contracts are examples of what economists call **wage indexation,** in which wages are "indexed to" (meaning that they adjust automatically to) changes in prices.

Another common way that contracts index wages is to tie them to the performance of an employing firm, through contract features such as commission pay, bonus plans, or profit-sharing agreements. In this way, when the firm's prices rise, workers share indirectly in the revenues that are generated. Their effective wage rises (or, possibly, falls) automatically.

It turns out that considering all forms of wage indexation in the economy is a daunting modeling task, and so we shall try to keep things simple. Let's first suppose that all contracts in our model index wages one-for-one to movements in prices, so that every time the price level rises by one unit, the contracted nominal wage rises by one unit. Let's also suppose that wages are adjusted continuously during the term of the wage contract, even though this would rarely be done in practice. In addition, let's assume that wages move freely upward or downward as prices change in either direction (which also is rarely the case).

Under these assumptions, Figure 22-6 illustrates what would occur if prices turned out to be higher or lower than workers and firms anticipated when they set the "base" contract wage W^c. As in our basic contracting model, W^c is set equal to the expected market-clearing wage rate W^{*e}. In panels (a) and (c) of the figure, we assume that, initially, the price level P_0 is the level of prices expected when workers and firms agreed to the contract base wage; that is, $P^e = P_0$. At this price level, N_0 is the full-information, natural employment level, and y_0 is the natural level of output in panel (b). This yields the real output-price combination y_0 and P_0 in panel (c).

Under a fully indexed wage contract, the actual wage will vary from the base wage W^c in equal proportion whenever the price level rises or falls. For instance, if the price level rises from P_0 to a higher level P_1, then the actual wage paid to workers will be equal to W^c *plus* an amount equal to the rise in the price level, or $W^c + (P_1 - P_0)$. When the price level rises, labor demand increases, but firms now also must pay a wage that has

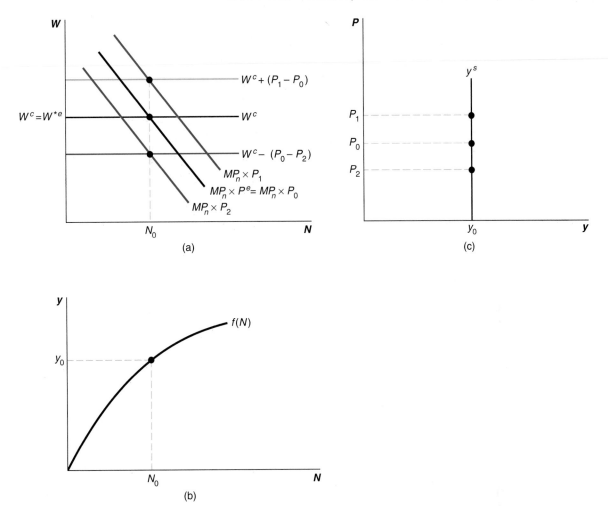

Figure 22-6
Deriving the Aggregate Supply Schedule When Wages Are Fully Indexed to Price Changes.   During the term of the wage contract between workers and firms, the *base* contracted nominal wage rate W^c is set equal to the market-clearing nominal wage rate W^{*e}. Workers and firms expected that this would be the market-clearing wage rate based on their price expectation when they signed the contract. If the price level varies during the term of the contract, the demand for labor by firms will rise or fall, causing employment to vary [panel (*a*)]. But if the contract wage is fully indexed to price changes, the nominal wage will rise or fall directly with the variations in the price level. Equilibrium employment will not change. This implies that the amount of real output produced will be unchanged as well [panel (*b*)]. Therefore, the aggregate supply schedule will be vertical in the modern Keynesian contracting model with fully indexed wages [panel (*c*)]. Monetary policy actions that shift the aggregate demand schedule will be neutral during the period the wage is indexed.

THE INDEXATION PUZZLE

INTERNATIONAL

PERSPECTIVE

For reasons discussed in this section, workers and firms typically will not elect to index wages fully to price changes that were not expected when they signed wage contracts. As long as there is some variability in aggregate demand, it should nonetheless be the case, according to the contracting theory, that they should desire partial, if not full, wage indexation. For instance, even if contracts did not call for wages to rise one-for-one with unexpected price changes, they could require that wages rise, say, by a specified part of each unit increase in the price level.

While wages appear to be partially, if not nearly completely, indexed in European nations such as Germany and the United Kingdom, most studies agree that the degree of aggregate wage indexation in the United States is very low. Some studies have found little evidence of any significant aggregate wage indexation in the United States. This low degree of indexation of nominal wages is a puzzle.

One possible reason that wage indexation could be lower in the United States than in other nations would be if aggregate demand variability were smaller in the United States. However, studies that consider this factor still find that United States wage indexation remains surprisingly low.

Another possible reason that wage indexation appears to be so low in the United States is that indexation may be costly. Just saying in a contract that wages must be indexed is not enough. Firms must monitor price changes and must make automatic wage adjustments for their workers. Personnel must be hired just to undertake this task, and they must be paid wages as well. If the costs of indexing become too high, firms may not agree to even partial indexation of wages. The problem with this explanation is that it does not explain why wage indexation is more widespread in European countries.

A third possible reason for lower wage indexation in the United States is that pension plans, commission pay, bonus plans, profit sharing, and employee stock ownership have become more widespread in the United States than in many other nations. All these contractual arrangements are ways of indexing wages to firm profits, which in turn depend in part on the prices that firms charge. While wages may not be indexed directly to the aggregate level of prices, these other forms of indexation may amount to indirect ways of indexing wages to price changes.

It also is possible that studies measuring wage indexation in the United States and other countries have some weaknesses. Some economists believe that recent studies are at best a step in the right direction toward measuring the amount of wage indexation across nations. They argue that economists need to work harder at determining the actual levels of aggregate wage indexation before concluding that the degree of indexation is either high or low.

Finally, a few economists have accepted the conclusion that wage indexation in the United States is low and have argued further that it is too low relative to a level that would be best for society as a whole. Other economists disagree sharply with this view. They contend that low indexation of wages is anti-inflationary, and that one reason that inflation has been higher in some European nations than it has been in the United States may be because wages in much of Europe are almost fully indexed. We shall have more to say in Unit 6 about how greater wage indexation might have an effect on inflation.

In short, there is an indexation puzzle. Wages appear to be indexed partially, if not fully, to price changes in some countries. But there is little or no wage indexation in others. This is a phenomenon that economists have not yet fully explained.

increased in equal proportion to the rise in prices. As shown in panel (a), this means that employment will not change, and from panel (b), neither will output. Thus, the economy is at a new output-market combination y_0 and P_1 in panel (c).

In contrast, if the price level were to fall to a value P_2 below the anticipated price level P_0, labor demand would fall, as shown in panel (a). But the actual wage paid under the fully indexed contract would be $W^c - (P_0 - P_2)$, which would be less than the base wage W^c in proportion to the fall in prices. Firms would demand fewer labor services at the lower price level, but they would pay a proportionately lower nominal wage, and so actual employment would not change. Hence, output would not change in panel (*b*). The economy would now be at the real output–price level combination y_0 and P_2 in panel (*c*).

The schedule containing the three output-price combinations in panel (*c*) of Figure 22-6 would be the economy's aggregate supply schedule if complete COLA agreements indexed all contracts fully to price changes. This is a familiar-looking vertical schedule reminiscent of the classical model. The reason it is vertical is that, as in the classical model, wages under a full COLA contract adjust equiproportionately to changes in the price level. This "Keynesian" contracting model basically duplicates the classical conclusions when nominal wages are fully and flexibly indexed under the terms of contracts.

In some industries in the United States, nominal wages are determined by contracts not indexed at all, as in the simpler contracting model we discussed earlier. In other industries, COLA arrangements are common but are rarely as full or flexible as we assumed in the example above. Consequently, a modern Keynesian theorist would argue that, in the aggregate, there is "partial" indexation of wages in the United States. This means that the aggregate supply schedule would not be vertical, but its slope would not be as shallow as a fixed-wage theory would imply.

Note that in our example in Figure 22-6 the implication is that changes in prices caused by fluctuations in aggregate demand stemming, say, from changes in autonomous consumption or investment—or from monetary policy actions—would have no effects on output and employment. This means that full indexation of all wages in the economy would be optimal if aggregate demand variability were the only source of economic fluctuations. If that were the case, then by fully indexing wages to price changes workers and firms could assure themselves that they would always maintain the natural, full-information levels of employment and output.

Why aren't all contracted wages fully indexed? The reason is that the economy can also experience variability in the aggregate supply schedule caused by volatility of relative prices of key resources such as oil or by sudden technological changes. Figure 22-7 shows that if both shallow and vertical aggregate supply schedules shift leftward by the same amount, then for a given position for the aggregate demand schedule the effect on real output (and, hence, employment) is larger when the aggregate supply schedule is vertical. Because full indexation of nominal wages makes the aggregate supply schedule vertical, it follows that full wage indexation is not always optimal for the economy.

COMPARING THE NEW CLASSICAL AND MODERN KEYNESIAN THEORIES

Both of the theories that we have discussed in this chapter share a single common element, which is the rational expectations hypothesis. The new classical theory, however, assumes that pure competition ensures flexibility of all wages and prices, while the modern Keynesian theory assumes that contracts make the nominal wage at least partially rigid.

Another feature that both theories share is the implication that there is a full-information, natural level of employment toward which the economy tends in the long run, if not in the short run. We may regard the fact that both modern versions of classical and Keynesian theories reach such a conclusion as an ultimate victory of sorts for the monetarists. The adoption by some modern Keynesians of the idea that there is a natural employment level, and hence a natural rate of unemployment, is a major departure from the traditional Keynesian model.

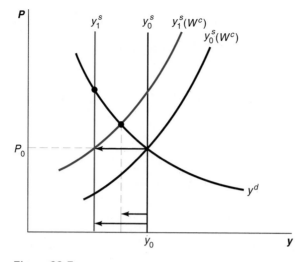

Figure 22-7

The Effects of Aggregate Supply Reductions with Nonindexed and Fully Indexed Contract Wages.   If aggregate supply schedules that arise under nonindexed and fully indexed wage contracts shift leftward by the same amount, then the effect on equilibrium real output is greatest in the case of fully indexed contract wages. Increased output variability under full wage indexation implies that there will be greater variability of labor employment. Therefore, full wage indexation is less desirable to workers and firms if aggregate supply is variable.

In spite of these similarities, however, the two theoretical approaches imply very different mechanisms by which monetary policy may be nonneutral, or have real effects. It is important to keep these features of the theories straight.

NEW CLASSICAL CONCLUSIONS

In the new classical theory, aggregate demand policies (monetary or fiscal policies) are ineffective in influencing the levels of labor employment or real output production. Indeed, this is true in the short run if policy actions are systematic and, therefore, predictable. Rational expectations by workers automatically take into account such systematic policy actions, and workers alter their labor supply behavior in ways that yield the natural level of employment and the natural level of output. Only unsystematic policy actions can have short-lived real effects on economic activity. Nevertheless, even these dissipate in the long run.

MODERN KEYNESIAN CONTRACTING THEORY

In the modern Keynesian model of wage contracts, there also are natural employment and output levels. But workers and firms agree to fix the nominal wage rate, via contracting agreements, for an interval of time. During this interval, monetary (or fiscal) policy actions can cause price-level changes that will cause variations of labor employment and real output from their full-information, natural levels. As a result, recessions or expansions of real output could be persistent. In our simple model, they could last only as long as the duration of the contracts, but in more realistic settings, where contracts in numerous industries overlap, much more persistence is possible.

ARE CONTRACTING MODELS RELEVANT?

The economists Stanley Fischer, Jo Anna Gray, and John Taylor first developed the earliest forms of the modern Keynesian contracting models in the 1970s. Many traditional Keynesians quickly embraced these models as the Keynesian answer to the new classicals' use of the rational expectations hypothesis. However, during the late 1970s and 1980s the contracting models came under attack from several directions. One reason was that it is difficult for economists to develop theories of why such contracts should exist in the first place. If contracts fix actual wages, then when market wages turn out to be different from those that workers and firms had anticipated when contracts were signed, it would be optimal for workers and firms to recontract their nominal wages. Indeed, because labor market conditions continuously change, it would be logical that eventually such contracts would cease to exist. Workers and firms would find it desirable to "recontract" every day, which would amount to letting the nominal wage move flexibly with variations in labor demand and supply.

In fact, one piece of evidence that this criticism of contracting models might be borne out was the sharp decline in unionization of industries in the United States in the late 1970s and 1980s. Union membership as a share of total nonagricultural employment in the United States rose from under 15 percent in 1935 to over 30 percent after World War II and stayed in that range until around 1975. From 1975 through 1992 union membership's share of nonagricultural employment proceeded to dip down to nearly 15 percent. Of course, nonunionized workers often have explicit or implicit wage contracts with firms, but some economists believed that the decline in unionization of the work force was evidence that the contracting models were losing what relevance they might have had for the United States economy.

In addition, evidence accumulated during the 1980s indicating that not all the predictions of these models squared with real-world observations. Several economic studies conducted during the early 1980s cast doubt on the idea that real output changes occurred because workers and firms had been mistaken in their predictions about the price level, in contradiction to the predictions of the contracting models. Later studies of unionized industries also questioned whether the observed behavior of contracted wages conformed with the predictions of the contracting models. Finally, perhaps most damaging was the fact that, in contrast to the prediction forthcoming from Keynesian contracting theories, measured real wages seemed to move *procyclically*. That is, the aggregate real wage rate often would rise when labor employment was high and fall when labor employment was low. The contracting theories of the 1970s predict the opposite: With fixed nominal wages, high levels of aggregate demand should raise employment, output, and prices and reduce real wages, while low levels of aggregate demand should reduce employment, output, and prices and increase real wages.

Some economists have responded to these criticisms of the modern contracting theories by eschewing them and developing alternative Keynesian theories or by abandoning Keynesian theorizing altogether (see the next chapter). Others, however, have sought to defend the contracting theories. These economists have argued that theoretical difficulties in explaining why wage contracts exist do not alter the fact that they do indeed exist. They also have pointed out that declining union membership has not necessarily reduced the frequency of wage contracting in the economy. In addition, in the early 1990s many of these economists published research studies showing that earlier studies casting doubt on the predictions of contracting models may have been incorrect on conceptual or measurement grounds. Some of these more recent studies also have questioned the earlier conclusion that real wages have moved procyclically. These studies conclude that, when properly measured, real wages actually move countercyclically as the contracting theories suggest. This debate is not yet resolved, and so the relevancy of contracting models has yet to be proved or disproved.

THE OBSERVATIONAL EQUIVALENCE PROBLEM

Economists like to think that they are good social scientists. As such, they try to use the scientific method, which entails formulating theories and then testing them using real-world data. Therefore, it would seem on the surface that it would be a straightforward proposition to apply this approach to verifying either the new classical model or the modern Keynesian theory.

Unfortunately, doing so turns out to be more difficult than one might expect. Both predict that real employment and output variations will occur when unanticipated changes in prices, or "price-level surprises," occur. In the new classical model, this can occur, for instance, when the Federal Reserve makes mistakes, is misunderstood, or is insincere in its policy announcements. In the modern Keynesian model, this occurs when prices differ from the level that workers and firms had anticipated when they negotiated their wage contracts.

Because each theory tells us that real output will differ from the full-information, natural level as a result of price surprises, this basic, and most easily testable, prediction of the theories is the same. That is, both theories are "observationally equivalent" in their predictions, which makes it difficult to separate one theory from the other when economists conduct empirical tests. Economists call this the **observational equivalence problem** that often occurs in models based on the rational expectations hypothesis.

Research by economists in the 1980s found little evidence that price-level surprises had real-output effects, and this conclusion was for a time regarded as significant evidence against *both* the new classical and modern Keynesian theories. Additional economic research in the early 1990s that used more advanced measures of the natural levels of employment and output have provided more support for both theories. Nevertheless, testing one theory against the other has proved an elusive task.

CHAPTER SUMMARY

1. Under adaptive expectations, individuals base expectations about prices and inflation only on past information.

2. There potentially are an infinite number of ways that individuals might form adaptive expectations of prices and inflation. In addition, if individuals use only past information to form adaptive expectations, then under many circumstances their expectations could be more accurate if they used current information, along with their understanding of how the economy works. For these reasons, many economists believe that the assumption of adaptive expectations is not a useful one to use in modeling the economy.

3. Under the rational expectations hypothesis, individuals form price and inflation expectations using both past and current information. They also use their knowledge of how the economy works.

4. The new classical theorists assume that individuals have rational expectations and that pure competition exists, so that wages and prices are flexible and market determined.

5. According to the new classical model, only unsystematic, unpredictable monetary policy actions can influence the level of real output and the amount of labor employment. Systematic, predictable monetary policy actions have no real effects. This latter prediction of the new classical theory is known as the policy ineffectiveness proposition.

6. There have been two key Keynesian responses to the new classical theory. One has been to argue that the rational expectations hypothesis is incorrect and that the traditional Keynesian model, and its use of adaptive expectations, is correct. Another has been to adopt the rational

expectations hypothesis but to deny the policy ineffectiveness proposition, on either theoretical or empirical grounds.

7. Modern Keynesian models assume rational expectations but assume that pure competition does not hold, so that wages or prices are inflexible and are not always market determined. Modern Keynesian contracting models emphasize the possibility of wage stickiness caused by rational contracting of nominal wages.

8. If contracts set wages, monetary policy actions can influence real output and employment even if all individuals in the economy have rational expectations.

9. Indexation of wages to unanticipated changes in the price level through contract features such as cost-of-living-adjustment clauses steepens the aggregate supply schedule and reduces the extent to which monetary policy actions influence the levels of real output and employment.

10. Both the new classical and modern Keynesian contracting theories imply that unanticipated changes in the price level cause changes in real output and employment. This similarity in predictions, which is known as observational equivalence, makes testing the models against one another a difficult task.

GLOSSARY

Adaptive expectations: Expectations that are based only on information from the past up to the present.

Observational equivalence problem: The difficulty that occurs, when two theories have the same predictions about the economy, in testing whether one theory is better than the other.

Policy ineffectiveness proposition: The new classical conclusion that policy actions have no real effects in the short run if the policy actions were anticipated, and not in the long run even if the policy actions were unanticipated.

Rational expectations hypothesis: The idea that individuals form expectations based on all available past and current information and on a basic understanding of how the economy works.

Wage indexation: The pegging of wages to prices, so that wages automatically adjust to changes in prices.

SELF-TEST QUESTIONS

1. Explain, in your own words, the distinction between adaptive expectations and rational expectations.

2. Briefly explain the rational expectations hypothesis as first put forward by the new classical economists.

3. Explain the main objections to the use of adaptive expectations in economic models.

4. Explain the main objections to the use of rational expectations in economic models.

5. Use the aggregate demand–aggregate supply framework to demonstrate the effects on output and the price level of a fall in the nominal money supply that is fully and correctly anticipated by economic agents, assuming that the new classical model is correct. What are the implications for systematic attempts to influence real output via monetary policy actions?

6. Use the aggregate demand–aggregate supply framework to demonstrate the effects on output and the price level of a fall in the nominal money supply that is completely unanticipated by economic agents, assuming that the new classical model is correct. What are the implications for unsystematic attempts to influence real output via monetary policy actions?

7. In light of your answers to questions 5 and 6, what are some possible situations in which

monetary policy actions have nonneutral effects on the economy, according to the new classical theory?

8. Explain why the modern Keynesian economists theorize that fixed-nominal-wage contracts may be rational undertakings.

9. Derive an aggregate supply schedule implied by the modern Keynesian theory of rational contracting. Now suppose that there is a sudden increase in expected labor force participation by teenaged workers. What would happen to the position of the aggregate supply schedule? Why?

10. Explain why the aggregate supply schedule under fully indexed nominal wage contracts is vertical. Why is full wage indexation by workers and firms not necessarily optimal?

PROBLEMS

22-1.   Suppose that all individuals' adaptive expectations are simple averages of past information. If inflation rates for the past three years were 4.8 percent, 7.5 percent, and 7.7 percent, then what is the expected inflation rate for the current year?

22-2.   Suppose that the expected price level today (time t) is given by

$$P_t^e = (0.5)P_{t-2} + (0.5)P_{t-1}$$

a. What type of expectations formation process is this?
b. Suppose that absolutely no current information is available and that individuals have no knowledge of how the economy works. Is this then a rational or an adaptive expectations process, or both?
c. Suppose that the price level two periods ago had a value of 2 and that last period's price level was 4. According to this expectations formation process, what is the expected current-period price level?

22-3.   Suppose that an individual forms her expectation of this year's (time t) inflation rate using the rule

$$\dot{p}_t^e = (0.1)\dot{p}_{t-3} + (0.3)\dot{p}_{t-2} + (0.6)\dot{p}_{t-1}$$

a. What type of expectations formation process is this?
b. Explain in your own words the rationale this person might have used to make up this rule for determining her expectation of this year's inflation rate.
c. Suppose inflation three years ago was 9 percent, that two years ago it was 10 percent, and that last year it was 5 percent. What is this individual's inflation expectation for this year?
d. Suppose inflation for each of the last three years actually was constant and equal to 7 percent. What then is this individual's inflation expectation for this year?

22-4.   Suppose that the real economy is classical in nature, with the exception that current information about monetary policy actions is imperfect. The economy's full-employment, natural output level has been equal to $1,000 billion (in base-year dollars) for the past three years and cannot change during the current year, and the income velocity of money has been, and is, constant and equal to 4. For the past three years, the money stock has been constant and equal to $500 billion.

a. What has the price level been each of the last three years?
b. What is the adaptive expectation of the money stock for the current year?
c. Suppose that the Federal Reserve makes a believable announcement to all individuals in the economy that the money stock will be increased to $1,000 billion during the

current year. What is the adaptive expectation of the level of prices for the current year? What is the rational expectation of the price level for the current year? Which seems the most likely to be used by these individuals?

d. Suppose that even though, as in part c above, all individuals received information that led them to anticipate that the money stock would rise to $1,000 billion, it actually stayed the same. Which form of price expectation would have actually been "correct"? By how much (in percentage terms) would the other expectation have been "wrong"? Does this mean that the "wrong" expectation would have been irrational? Why or why not?

22-5. Suppose, for the sake of simplicity, that the equation for the aggregate supply schedule is linear and is given by $y = y_n + a(P - P^e)$, where y_n and a are positive constants.

a. Draw a diagram of this supply function, with P on the vertical axis and y on the horizontal axis. What is the supply function's horizontal intercept? What is its slope?

b. Suppose that individuals in the economy are able to predict exactly any movements in the actual price level. In this case, what is the level of real output? What is the economic term for this output level? Draw a diagram of the aggregate supply function for this special case.

c. Based on your answers to parts a and b, will unanticipated changes in the price level cause real output to change? Will fully anticipated changes in the price level cause real output to change?

22-6. Suppose that the demand for labor is given by $W/P = 65 - (0.25)N$ and that the supply of labor is given by $W/P^e = 5 + (0.75)N$, where W is the nominal wage rate, P is the actual price level known by firms, and P^e is the price expectation of workers.

a. Suppose that the actual price level and the workers' expectation of the price level are both equal to 1. What is the equilibrium level of employment? What is the equilibrium nominal wage rate?

b. Suppose that workers expect that the price level will equal 1 but the actual price level turns out to equal 2. What is the equilibrium level of employment? What is the equilibrium nominal wage rate?

c. Based on your answers to parts a and b, what is the effect on equilibrium employment of a rise in the price level from 1 to 2 that is not anticipated by workers?

22-7. Suppose that the demand for labor is given by $W/P = 50 - (0.5)N$ and that the supply of labor is given by $W/P = 10 + (0.5)N$, where W is the nominal wage rate and P is the price level.

a. What is the equilibrium quantity of labor? What is the equilibrium real wage rate?

b. Suppose that workers and firms agree to fix the nominal wage rate rather than letting the market determine the wage, but that they desire to achieve the market-clearing real wage rate and employment level. If they all expect the price level to be equal to 1, what nominal wage rate will they set in the contract? If they set this contract wage and the actual price level turns out to be equal to 1, what will be the amount of employment? Is this the natural level of employment?

c. If workers and firms turn out to be wrong in their price-level expectation and, in fact, the actual price level during the period of the contract is equal to 2, what will the value of the actual real wage be? What quantity of labor services will firms actually employ under the terms of the contract? Is this above or below the natural level of employment?

22-8. Suppose again that labor demand is given by $W/P = 50 - (0.5)N$ and that labor supply is given by $W/P = 10 + (0.5)N$. However, now suppose that workers and firms agree to set the nominal wage equal to the market-clearing level plus an automatic, complete adjustment for changes in the price level. If the price level doubles, the contracted nominal wage is doubled, and if the price level falls by one-half, the contracted nominal wage is reduced by one-half.

    a. If the price level is expected to be equal to 1, what nominal wage will workers and firms specify in the wage contract? What is the level of employment if the price level actually turns out to be equal to 1 during the term of the contract?

    b. If the price level actually turns out to be equal to 2 during the term of the contract, what will be the value of the contracted wage? What will be the level of employment under this indexed contract?

SELECTED REFERENCES

Ball, Laurence, "Is Equilibrium Indexation Efficient?" *Quarterly Journal of Economics,* 103 (2, May 1988), pp. 299–311.

Barro, Robert J., *Macroeconomic Policy* (Cambridge, Mass.: Harvard University Press, 1990).

Card, David, "Unexpected Inflation, Real Wages, and Employment Determination in Union Contracts," *American Economic Review,* 80 (4, September 1990), pp. 669–688.

Fethke, Gary C., "The Conformity of Wage Indexation Models with the 'Stylized Facts,'" *American Economic Review,* 75 (4, September 1985), pp. 856–861.

Fischer, Stanley, *Indexation, Inflation, and Economic Policy* (Cambridge, Mass.: MIT Press, 1986).

Geary, Patrick T., and John Kennan, "The Employment–Real Wage Relationship: An International Study," *Journal of Political Economy,* 90 (3, August 1982), pp. 854–871.

Gordon, Robert J., "What Is the New-Keynesian Economics?" *Journal of Economic Literature,* 28 (3, September 1990), pp. 1115–1171.

Gray, Jo Anna, "Wage Indexation: A Macroeconomic Approach," *Journal of Monetary Economics,* 2 (2, April 1976), pp. 221–235.

———, and David E. Spencer, "Price Prediction Errors and Real Activity: A Reassessment," *Economic Inquiry,* 28 (4, October 1990), pp. 658–681.

Lucas, Robert E., Jr., *Studies in Business Cycle Theory* (Cambridge, Mass.: MIT Press, 1981).

Sargent, Thomas, and Neil Wallace, "Rational Expectations and the Theory of Economic Policy," *Journal of Monetary Economics,* 2 (April 1976), pp. 169–183.

Taylor, John, "Aggregate Dynamics and Staggered Contracts," *Journal of Political Economy,* 88 (1, February 1980), pp. 1–23.

Tobin, James, *Asset Accumulation and Economic Activity* (Chicago: University of Chicago Press, 1980).

Weiner, Stuart E., "Union COLAs on the Decline," Federal Reserve Bank of Kansas City *Economic Review,* 71 (6, June 1986), pp. 10–25.

Recent Developments in Monetary Theory

CHAPTER PREVIEW

1. What might account for rigidities of the aggregate price level? Do we observe evidence of price level inflexibility in the real world?

2. What are small menu costs? In what way might the existence of small menu costs help explain why prices might be sticky?

3. Why might worker productivity vary with the real wage rate? How would a dependence of productivity upon the real wage rate possibly lead to monetary nonneutrality?

4. What is the insider-outsider theory of labor market behavior? Why does this theory provide a possible explanation for persistent unemployment?

5. How might the complexities of the economy's input-output table assist in explaining why relative, price-level-adjusted prices and wages might be inflexible?

6. What are common features of the various new Keynesian macroeconomic theories? How have these theories been criticized?

7. What are the essential elements of the real business cycle theory of macroeconomic fluctuations?

8. How has the real business cycle theory been criticized?

9. In what directions is monetary theory headed?

If our economy were one in which pure competition always prevailed, wages and prices were completely flexible, and all individuals were rational, suffered from no money illusions, and made very quick use of any available information, nearly all economists by now would have adopted the classical model. Information is, nonetheless, imperfect in the real world, and so most economists who might otherwise have been attracted to the classical model tend to identify with the new classical framework. According to either theory, systematic monetary policy actions have no real effects. If not always neutral at every instant in time, money is neutral "on average." Under pure competition among rational, well-informed economic agents, money cannot have long-lived real effects. Perhaps John Stuart Mill (1806–1873) best summarized this position:

> There cannot, in short, be intrinsically a more insignificant thing, in the economy of society, than money; except in the character of a contrivance for sparing time and labor. It is a machine for doing quickly and commodiously, what would be done, though less quickly and commodiously, without it; and like many other kinds of machinery, it only exerts a distinct and independent influence of its own when it gets out of order.[1]

---

[1] John Stuart Mill, *Principles of Economics* (London: J. W. Parker, 1848).

If the classical or new classical theories were correct, it would be the case that, over reasonably short spans of time, changes in nominal, current-dollar output would be reflected almost fully as changes in the level of prices. Because firms and workers would determine the levels of labor employment and output irrespective of changes in the price level, the aggregate supply schedule would be vertical at the economy's natural level of output. Variations in aggregate demand caused by monetary policy actions would thereby cause only price variations, which would be reflected in a rise in the nominal value of the real output produced. Real output, however, would not change.

Many economists, however, are convinced by the evidence that prices and aggregate nominal income do not generally move together. That is, these economists believe that there is evidence of short-run price stickiness. The traditional Keynesian theorists and many modern Keynesian economists have narrowly focused their attention on the possible stickiness of the prices of labor services (that is, wage rigidities). As we saw in the last chapter, this form of price stickiness can lead to nonneutrality of money, at least over the time span in which wages are fixed. Monetary policy actions can have real effects.

Other modern Keynesian theorists have gone even further. According to these economists, the theory of rational contracting that we studied in Chapter 22 is only a first step toward understanding why money may be nonneutral. These economists argue that, indeed, many prices, including the prices of numerous goods and services, are rigid in the short run. The best-known example of such rigidity, discussed in Chapter 21, was the experience of the Great Depression. The significant fall in aggregate demand that occurred during the 1929–1933 period generated very small price declines in many markets. For instance, during that period of time there was only a 6 percent decline in the prices of agricultural implements and a 16 percent decline in motor vehicles prices. In contrast, real production of both types of goods fell by 80 percent during that period. This and other past evidence, maintain many Keynesian theorists, indicate price-level rigidities that imply nonneutrality of money.

Of course, not all economists agree with this interpretation. Indeed, many, including classical, monetarist, new classical, and even some Keynesian, theorists disagree. This makes it tempting to conclude either that economists cannot find any common ground or that they simply like to argue with one another. Hence the old saying commonly credited to George Bernard Shaw (1856–1950): "If all economists were laid end to end, they would not reach a conclusion." Nevertheless, the issue of money neutrality is so important that it really should not be surprising that it continues to create great friction among the economists of our time, much as it did throughout most of the nineteenth and twentieth centuries.

At present, economists, for better or worse, are very much divided on the role of money in the economy and, indeed, on the workings of the economy itself. Furthermore, economic theories at present have tended to move toward extremes that depart from the limited "common ground" of the new classical and modern Keynesian contracting theories, which both conclude—for differing reasons—that real output movements are caused by price-level misperceptions. Although many economists still identify with either the new classical or contracting theories, others have pursued alternative theoretical explanations of how the economy functions.

One modern group of theorists has developed economic models that take Keynesian economics to the opposite extreme from the classical "supply-creates-its-own-demand" models. According to several of these Keynesian theories, "demand creates its own supply." In these and related models, which have been developed by economists now known as **new Keynesian theorists,** the classical assumption of pure competition is abandoned. These economists believe that markets determine prices and output quantities but that these markets are not competitive. Some of these new Keynesian economists also have questioned the assumption of purely rational behavior that so many economists traditionally have taken for granted.

Another group of economists has taken theory toward another extreme. These theorists have argued that, in fact, ''supply creates its own demand'' with a vengeance. According to the models developed by this group of economists, aggregate demand variability has no effect whatsoever on real output and employment. The single factor accounting for cyclical movements in real variables, according to these economists, is the variability of the supply side of the economy. Thus, these economists are known as **real business cycle theorists.**

Of the two groups of economists, the new Keynesians have developed the largest array of potential macroeconomic theories. For this reason, much of this chapter will focus on new Keynesian models. The real business cycle approach is more self-contained and straightforward, and so it will require less space. Both theories are important, however, as we shall see.

ARE PRICES RIGID?

This question is not easily answered. The reason is that while the prices of some goods and services appear to be sticky, prices of other goods and services seem to be very flexible. The key issue is whether the *aggregate* price level is rigid or flexible. If the aggregate level of prices is sticky, then changes in the nominal value of output produced may result when the nominal money supply is varied.

Recently estimates have been made of the degree of price flexibility across several countries. One way that price-level stickiness might occur is if the price level is slow to change over time. Table 23-1 displays estimates of the degree to which the rate of change of the price level in a given year depends upon the rate of price change in the previous year, for the United States, the United Kingdom, France, Germany, and Japan. A value of 1 for this measure would indicate that the rate of price level change depends completely on the rate of price change in the previous year, which would imply full **price inertia,** or the tendency of the growth of prices to resist change. In contrast, a value of 0 for this measure indicates that the rate of price level change in a given year adjusts independently relative to the rate of change of prices in the previous year, so that no price inertia is present. As Table 23-1 indicates, of the five nations for which recent estimates are avail-

T A B L E   23-1
Measures of Annual Inertia in the Price Level for Five Nations

Country	Period of Time	Estimated Value of Inertia Measure
United States	1954–1987	0.87
United Kingdom	1960–1986	0.57
France	1960–1986	0.55
Germany	1960–1986	0.73
Japan	1960–1986	0.15

Source: Robert J. Gordon, "What Is New-Keynesian Economics?" *Journal of Economic Literature,* 28 (3, September 1990), p. 1131.

able, the United States has shown the greatest price-level inertia, while Japan has shown the smallest. This provides some evidence of price rigidities in the United States but relatively little in Japan. For other nations, there is partial inertia of prices.

Another possible measure of price-level flexibility is how much the growth rate of the price level for a given year changes in response to variations in the growth of real output during the same year. If the value of this measure is equal to 0, then the growth of the price level is not affected by changes in output growth, which could be interpreted as evidence that the aggregate level of prices is rigid. If this measure has a value of 1, then price-level growth responds fully to changes in the growth of real output, which could be viewed as evidence that prices are flexible.

Table 23-2 displays estimates of this measure for the same five countries. There is much less variability of this measure of the degree of price-level flexibility across the countries, and the estimated values of this measure are neither particularly large nor particularly small.

A final way to measure the degree of price-level flexibility is to relate the responsiveness of the growth of aggregate prices to changes in the growth of real output relative to its long-run, or trend, growth rate, where the trend growth rate could be interpreted as a measure of the natural rate of output growth for an economy. A zero value for this measure would imply that the growth of prices is entirely unresponsive to changes in the deviation of output growth from its long-run trend, which could be interpreted as evidence that prices are rigid. In contrast, a value of unity for this measure would indicate that the rate of price change is fully responsive to deviations of output growth from its long-run trend, which could be viewed as an indication that prices are flexible.

Table 23-3 lists values of this measure of the degree of price-level flexibility for the same five countries. According to this measure, differences across countries are much more striking. The United States has a much lower value than the other countries. This indicates that price-level growth in the United States is much less responsive to variations in output growth rate deviations relative to the long-run trend growth rate. Japan's value is higher than that estimated for the other nations, implying that its price-level growth rate has been more responsive to deviations of output growth rates relative to the trend rate of growth. The other nations lie between the United States and Japan, as was the case in Table 23-1.

Clearly, the evidence on the degree of aggregate price-level flexibility is mixed, both for the United States and for the other four countries for which these recent estimates are

---

T A B L E 23-2
Measures of the Responsiveness of Annual Price-Level Growth to Changes in Real Output Growth for Five Nations

Country	Period of Time	Estimate of Responsiveness Measure
United States	1954–1987	0.28
United Kingdom	1960–1986	0.35
France	1960–1986	0.26
Germany	1960–1986	0.21
Japan	1960–1986	0.39

Source: Robert J. Gordon, "What Is New-Keynesian Economics?" *Journal of Economic Literature,* 28 (3, September 1990), p. 1131.

T A B L E   23-3
Measures of the Responsiveness of Annual Price-Level Growth to Deviations of
Output Growth from Trend Growth for Five Nations

Country	Period of Time	Estimate of Responsiveness Measure
United States	1954–1987	0.17
United Kingdom	1960–1986	0.43
France	1960–1986	0.47
Germany	1960–1986	0.33
Japan	1960–1986	0.64

Source: Robert J. Gordon, "What Is New-Keynesian Economics?" *Journal of Economic Literature,* 28 (3, September 1990), p. 1131.

available. The general indication of these estimates is that prices are relatively more flexible in Japan than in some other countries, while those of the United States are relatively more rigid. To the extent that the aggregate level of prices in the United States is rigid, the assumption of flexible prices that is adopted in the classical, traditional Keynesian, monetarist, new classical, and modern Keynesian contracting theories of the previous chapter becomes more difficult to justify.

THEORIES OF PRICE RIGIDITY: THE NEW KEYNESIAN ECONOMICS

The new Keynesian theorists believe that the assumption of complete price-level flexibility in the United States is unwarranted in light of the evidence of inflexibility or, at least, of partial rigidities in the price level. They argue further that a correct theory of the economy must account for the existence and relevance of these rigidities.

In the 1960s and early 1970s, several economists attempted to develop a general Keynesian theory based on the assumption of rigid prices. In the models that these economic theorists developed, this assumption was the cornerstone. Prices were fixed, and real output adjusted to changes in market conditions. Output was demand determined, rather than supply determined as in the classical model.

These theories largely were abandoned in the late 1970s and early 1980s, however. There were two reasons that this happened. First, although it was straightforward for economists to construct models based on the sticky-price assumption, it was very difficult to explain *why* prices would stay rigid over the prolonged time periods required for quantity adjustments to occur in markets. Firms' costs of changing prices seemed small in comparison to the costs of adjusting the production and sale of output, and so keeping prices fixed appeared to be irrational business behavior. Second, the rational expectations hypothesis was also developed in the 1970s, and it seemed to offer a stronger hope for understanding why short-run and long-run price and output adjustments might differ. The Keynesian models with rigid prices seemed to have little to offer in the way of explanation for short-run versus long-run issues.

Beginning in the mid-1980s, however, many economists rejuvenated theories based on price rigidities. These economists are now collectively referred to as the new Keynesian theorists. Unlike the Keynesian theorists of the 1960s and 1970s, however, these econo-

SURVEY EVIDENCE ON RIGID PRICES

Because different measures of aggregate price rigidity imply different degrees of price stickiness, whether or not prices are rigid is in the eye of the beholder. Most economists agree that prices are not completely flexible, but most also agree that they are not entirely rigid. So what is the answer to this dilemma?

Some economists believe that the place to start is with the firms themselves. A few, including Alan Blinder, conducted surveys in the late 1980s, in which they asked firms how often they changed prices and why they sometimes did so slowly. One clear conclusion from Blinder's study was that firms themselves believe that they leave their prices unchanged for lengthy intervals. Among the set of seventy-two firms that Blinder had interviewed by 1990, he found that typically firms said that they changed their prices only about once a year. He also found that firms claimed not to raise prices any faster than they lowered them. Firm managers interviewed by Blinder said that, rather than raising or lowering their prices, they sometimes changed the level of service or product quality instead.

Firms in Blinder's survey also felt they had good reasons for not changing their prices. As reasons for why they delayed changing their prices, firms mentioned that they usually waited until other competitors changed their prices, that they waited until their own costs changed, or that they waited as long as possible to avoid breaking implicit understandings with customers. Firms also mentioned costs of price adjustment as a reason for not changing prices (see the section on small menu costs later in this chapter).

Some economists are skeptical of surveys of firms' attitudes. Managers of firms, these economists contend, have no incentive to tell the truth in interviews. It is also possible that firms believe that they hold prices fixed for lengthy time periods because that is what their price lists and catalogs say. In reality, it could be that the firms often shave a little off their published prices as necessary to woo customers, which would imply more price flexibility than fixed price lists and catalogs might otherwise imply. Finally, skeptical economists contend that surveys are based on small samples that may not be adequately representative of all firms in the economy.

Many economists contend that surveys have no place in economics. Their argument is that people do what they do, not what they say they do. These economists are unlikely to be convinced by surveys of firms' prices that aggregate price rigidities are significant. It is likely that other ways of measuring price-level inflexibility will have to be developed before either side in this controversy will concede its ground.

Source: Alan Blinder, "Why Are Prices Sticky? Preliminary Results from an Interview Study," *American Economic Review*, 8 (2, May 1991).

mists have sought to develop sticky-price theories in which the reasons for price rigidities are fully explained. Although not all economists accept these theories, most agree that they have more to offer than the earlier theories that *assumed* rigid prices at the outset instead of *explaining* why holding prices fixed might represent rational firm behavior.

Since the mid-1980s, the new Keynesians have constructed several possible explanations for why prices might be rigid and what implications such price rigidity would have for the economy and for the effects of monetary policies. While the various theories are not necessarily mutually exclusive, we shall discuss them individually.

SMALL-MENU-COST MODELS

If prices are somehow held fixed even as market demand conditions change, then business firms in the economy must, for some reason, choose not to change their prices over perceptible intervals of time. Furthermore, it must also be the case that these firms are capable of setting their own prices irrespective of changing market conditions. It must be possible for them to maximize their profits and remain in business even if they do not change their prices as often as normally would be required in competitive conditions.

In order for this to be the case, conditions of pure competition must not prevail. That is, firms in the economy must have some *monopoly power.* Each firm must face a set of customers that somehow is unable to, or chooses not to, trade with firms that produce similar, but nonidentical, goods or services. Given the customers' demand for the firm's output, the firm is able to set its own price to maximize profits.

Nevertheless, as we have seen elsewhere in this text, profit-maximizing monopoly pricing generally means that a firm will change the price of its product when the demand for its product rises or falls. The reason is that marginal revenue (the additional revenue received per additional unit produced and sold) varies with the position of the firm's demand schedule. Profit maximization requires that output adjust to the point at which marginal revenue equals marginal cost; and so if demand rises or falls without any change in the firm's costs, it will benefit the firm, in terms of profitability, to adjust the amount of output it produces and the price it charges for each unit of output. Therefore, price inflexibility does not necessarily follow from the existence of monopoly power by firms.

Nevertheless, the idea that prices might be inflexible as a result of monopoly power by firms certainly is not new. For instance, in the 1930s the economist Gardiner Means promoted the **administered pricing hypothesis.** Under the broad interpretation of Means's hypothesis, firms undertake discretionary rather than competitive pricing of their products; more narrowly, Means also asserted that there is a tendency by firms with monopoly power to hold prices fixed over fairly long time intervals. This idea was widely criticized in the 1940s but resurfaced again in the 1950s, only to be widely debunked again in the 1960s.

To some extent, then, the notion that prices may be rigid as a result of monopolistic price setting can be regarded as an old idea again brought back to life. However, a key reason that the administered pricing hypothesis continually was discarded by many economists in the past was that economists who promoted the hypothesis were unable to explain why it might be rational for firms to hold prices constant even as demands for their products varied. This seemed inconsistent with profit-maximizing behavior and, therefore, irrational.

The new Keynesian *small-menu-cost theory* developed in the late 1980s and 1990s has sought to provide an explanation of why rational business managers might choose to hold prices fixed over relatively long intervals of time. As the name of the theory implies, it is based on the idea that firms incur costs—**small menu costs**—when they change their prices. Many of these costs, such as the costs of printing new price tags, menus, and catalogs, may not be very large in magnitude. Some of the costs of changing prices, however, such as those incurred in bringing together business managers from points around the nation or world for meetings on price changes or in renegotiating deals with customers, may be significant.

Figure 23-1 depicts the logic of the small-menu-cost argument.[2] The figure is drawn under the assumption that a firm's marginal cost is constant and equal to average total cost. It also assumes that the demand schedule for the firm's output, labeled D, is a straight line. This implies that the marginal revenue schedule also is a straight line.

Two sets of demand and marginal revenue schedules are shown in Figure 23-1. When demand is at D_0, the marginal revenue schedule is at the position MR_0. The profit-

---

[2] This figure is adapted from Robert J. Gordon, "What Is New-Keynesian Economics?" *Journal of Economic Literature,* 28 (3, September 1990), p. 1146.

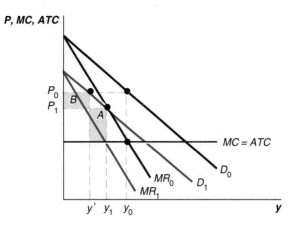

Figure 23-1
The Profit Effects for a Monopoly Firm That Leaves Its Price Unchanged When Demand Falls. If demand and marginal revenue shift downward, a firm interested in maximizing profits normally would reduce its price from P_0 to P_1. If the firm does not lower its price, its profit gain is equal to area B. But if the firm lowers its price to P_1, it reaps a profit gain given by area A. $A - B$ is an amount greater than zero, because the price P_1 would yield maximum profit. Therefore, if there are no costs of price adjustment, the firm will reduce its price. If there is a cost of adjusting its price that exceeds the amount $A - B$, however, the firm will leave its price unchanged at P_0.

maximizing quantity of output produced by this monopoly firm is where marginal revenue is equal to marginal cost, at y_0. The profit-maximizing price charged for this quantity of output is P_0. The amount of profit earned by the monopoly firm is $(P_0 - \text{ATC})$ times y_0. This is the maximum possible profit if demand is at the level D_0.

Now suppose that demand falls to the level D_1. Then the marginal revenue schedule shifts to MR_1. In the absence of costs of price adjustment, the firm would respond by reducing output to y_1 and charging a lower price P_1. Its maximum possible profit would be $(P_1 - \text{ATC})$ times y_1.

Consider what happens if this firm does not change its price when demand falls. If it keeps its price at P_0, then at the new, lower level of demand D_1 the firm will be able to sell only the level of output y'. Its profit then will be $(P_0 - \text{ATC})$ times y'.

In the absence of small menu costs of price adjustment, the firm would lower its price, because the constant-price level of profit $(P_0 - \text{ATC})$ times y' is less than the flexible-price profit level $(P_1 - \text{ATC})$ times y_1. We can figure out how much lower the constant-price profit level is by examining the diagram. If the firm produces the output level y', then charging the price P_0 rather than the true profit-maximizing price P_1 yields a profit increase given by the area labeled B. In contrast, at the profit-maximizing price P_1, producing y' units of output rather than the true profit-maximizing level of output y_1 yields a profit reduction given by the area labeled A. The net reduction in firm profits caused by producing y' units of output at the price P_0 rather than the true profit-maximizing output level y_1 at the price P_1 is $A - B$.

Because y_1 and P_1 are consistent with maximum profit when demand is equal to D_1, we know that the firm would lose profits by keeping its price constant at P_0 when demand falls. Therefore, $A - B$ must be a positive number. There is a net fall in profits if the firm does not change its price. If it were costless to change its price, the firm would do so in order to earn higher profits.

Suppose, however, that there is a cost that the firm must incur to lower its price from P_0 to P_1. If so, then the firm will lower its price only if the profit gain from doing so, the amount $A - B$, is greater than the cost of lowering the price. If the profit gain from changing its price, $A - B$, is less than the cost of lowering the price of its output, then the firm will leave its price unchanged at P_0. Its price will be rigid, and most of the reaction to reduced demand will be reduced output.

Most economists, including the new Keynesians, believe that the costs of price adjustment are comparatively small. If this is true, then the price charged by the firm will be rigid only if the amount of the profit gain from changing the price, $A - B$, is even smaller. It so happens that if the marginal cost schedule is horizontal, as in Figure 23-1, then the amount $A - B$ is as small as possible. Therefore, for firms with fairly shallow marginal and average cost schedules, profit gains from changing prices are small. It follows that small menu costs can induce these firms not to change their prices when demands for their products vary; the adjustment will be mostly in output changes.

Firms in different industries will have differently shaped marginal and average cost schedules and will experience diverse menu costs. Therefore, the extent to which firms hold their prices constant in the face of changes in demands for their products will vary across industries. Not all prices will be rigid. Several new Keynesian theorists argue that many, and even most, firm prices are sticky over fairly long time intervals. As a result, the aggregate level of prices could be very nearly rigid because of small menu costs.

Not all economists agree with this assessment. Several have criticized the small-menu-cost theory. One problem with the theory that these critics have identified is that it emphasizes only the small costs of changing prices when the costs of adjusting output production levels may be more significant. If it is costly for a monopolistic firm to keep its price the same by lowering its output when demand for its product falls, then these costs may dominate the costs it saves by keeping its price fixed. Its product price would be flexible rather than fixed; the firm will react to demand changes by changing price more than output.

Another possible problem with the theory is that it assumes that the firm seeks to maximize profits only for a single period. However, in the real world firms receive flows of profits continuously over time. To see why this is a problem, consider Figure 23-1 once again. Suppose that the marginal cost schedule is fixed over time. Also suppose that demand falls to D_1 and stays at this level from this point in time onward. If the firm leaves its price unchanged at P_0, then its profit loss from doing so is equal to area A minus area B. The firm will incur this profit loss every period from now into the future. That is, its total profit loss from today's perspective actually will be the discounted sum of all future values of $A - B$, which is much larger than the single-period loss $A - B$. The small menu cost of price adjustment is, in contrast, a once-and-for-all fixed cost that the firm would incur only this period. This means that a firm that is interested in maximizing the discounted value of current and future profits will leave its price the same when demand falls only if the size of $A - B$ is *very* small, if the demand changes are believed to be *temporary,* or if the small menu costs are not *too* small.

THE EFFICIENCY WAGE THEORY

Whereas the small-menu-cost theory focuses on price stickiness in firm product markets, other new Keynesian approaches follow the modern contracting theory by considering rigidities that arise in the market for labor. One of the chief among these new Keynesian hypotheses is the **efficiency wage theory.** Elements of this theory stem from the argument advanced in the late 1950s by Harvey Leibenstein that higher real wage payments in developing countries led to better nutrition and education for workers, which in turn improved labor productivity in those countries. In the 1980s, new Keynesian theorists extended this idea by arguing that higher real wage payments by firms encourage laborers to work harder, improve their efficiency, increase their morale, and raise their loyalty to the firms. All these effects of higher real wages, claimed the new Keynesian economists, raise the marginal product of labor.

This rather simple idea is, from the standpoint of economic theory, somewhat revolutionary. The reason is that the traditional theory of the aggregate production function and the marginal product of labor adopted by classical, traditional Keynesian, monetarist, new classical, and modern Keynesian theorists alike, does not consider such real wage effects on worker productivity.

It turns out that when firms consider the productivity effects of real wage payments, there is an incentive for firms to hold the real wage fixed, even under conditions bordering on pure competition. Given labor market conditions, there will be an optimal real wage, below which firms' cost reductions are more than offset by lost worker efficiency, or productivity. Above this optimal real wage, firms would achieve worker efficiency gains, but they would be less than the increase in the total wage bill. Therefore, firm profits are maximized when firms set the real wage at this optimal, *efficiency* wage.

According to this theory, firms will set rigid real wages, even in otherwise competitive labor markets. If real wages are inflexible, the amount of labor employment will not necessarily be equal to the full-employment level. Hence, the efficiency wage theory can explain the existence of labor unemployment.

There are possible difficulties with this theory, however. One is that while the theory can potentially explain labor unemployment, it does not tell us much about why prices might be sticky. Indeed, with a fixed real wage it turns out that the aggregate output supply schedule is vertical. (Recall from Chapter 22 that if the nominal wage moves unit for unit with price changes—which implies a fixed real wage—the aggregate supply schedule is vertical.) This means that unless we add some other assumption to the efficiency wage model, it yields complete price-level flexibility.

Another problem is that efficiency wage theorists assume from the outset that the only way firms can affect the behavior of their workers is through the real wage payment the firms make. In fact, there are a variety of ways that firms can give workers incentives to be more efficient. They can provide rewards like bonuses, pension plans, commissions, shares of firms' profits, or even shares of ownership in the firms. Once these types of labor compensation are permitted, complete rigidity of efficiency wage payments becomes less likely.

THE INSIDER-OUTSIDER THEORY

Another new Keynesian theory that focuses on labor market behavior is known as the **insider-outsider theory.** The basis for this theory is the notion that current employees of a given business have the ''inside track'' to maintaining their positions in the firm because the firm would have to incur costs in order to replace them. These employee insiders thereby are able to exercise some control over the terms under which new employees are hired by the firm, which would keep other potential workers from offering to work for the firm at a real wage rate that is lower than the insiders'.

Although it is easiest to envision the insider-outsider theory applying most directly to unionized settings, many new Keynesian economists argue that it has relevance for non-unionized environments as well. Costs of hiring and firing workers are not insignificant; to hire a worker a firm often must undertake significant advertising and search costs, and to fire a worker the firm may be forced to offer termination wages, help retrain the terminated worker, or battle with the worker and the worker's attorney in the courts if the employee feels the termination was unjustified. All these costs could contribute to the development of insider-dominated labor markets that contain significant barriers to entry by worker ''outsiders.'' These outsiders, some new Keynesians argue, find themselves involuntarily unemployed or underemployed even though they may be willing to work at lower real wages.

This new Keynesian hypothesis is attractive to some economists primarily because it potentially may assist in explaining persistent unemployment. In contrast to models that rely on explicit contractual arrangements to explain levels of labor employment below the natural level, the insider-outsider theory directly implies this outcome. The theory also helps explain differences in wages within and across industries and countries as well as the segmentation of many labor markets.

A criticism of the theory offered by many economists and some other new Keynesians alike is that it does not really explain how insiders *become* insiders. These economists also claim that the theory fails to explain why outsiders should not be able to lower their real wage offers sufficiently not only to become insiders but also to lessen considerably the ability of existing insiders to maintain control over the ability of firms to hire other outsiders. Critics of the insider-outsider theory have argued that the theory at best may help explain why it may take real wages time to fall in response to a surplus of labor but that it cannot fully explain persistence of unemployment. Indeed, a common criticism of the theory is that an entrepreneurial outsider could, rather than remaining unemployed and discouraged, gather together other unemployed outsiders, form a firm that pays lower real wages, and drive insider-dominated firms out of business!

THE INPUT-OUTPUT TABLE APPROACH

All the above new Keynesian theories, like the modern contracting theory, focus on rigidities in nominal prices or in real wages. The *input-output table approach,* in contrast, considers the possibility that *both* nominal and relative, price-level-adjusted, prices may be rigid. An **input-output table** takes into consideration all elements that figure into the production and pricing decisions of all workers and firms in the economy. The foundation for the input-output table approach to macroeconomic modeling is based on the idea, first promoted by the economist Arthur Okun, that there are high search costs that customers—households or other firms—of a given firm must incur if they decide to change suppliers. These costs, Okun argued, make the firm's customers willing to continue purchasing goods or services from that firm even if the firm's price is relatively higher—even if their desires for the firms' product decline somewhat or if their own costs of doing business increase. Consequently, according to Okun, firms that supply goods and services may find that they can leave the prices of their products fixed relative to those of other firms over fairly lengthy periods of time. If all firms behave in this way, both nominal and relative prices will tend to be rigid.

Modern new Keynesian extensions of this basic idea have emphasized that, in a modern economy in which many firms supply needed inputs to other firms, the sort of customer relationships stressed by Okun and others mean that the economy faces a complex input-output table of relative prices. All these relative prices, in turn, are determined by conditions in markets in a large number of diverse industries, each of which has imperfect information about these market conditions. Given the complexities of these interdependencies among firms and their customers that exist throughout the economy and the lack of complete information about the nature of these complexities, firms are slow to change their absolute and relative prices.

The input-output table approach can be viewed as a combination of both the other new Keynesian sticky-price theories discussed earlier in this chapter and the new classical/modern contracting theories considered in the previous chapter. The approach puts together the idea of rigid prices with the imperfect-information arguments advanced by the other modern theories that use the rational expectations hypothesis.

This combining of theories, unfortunately, implies a very complicated approach to macroeconomic modeling that is still being developed by economists. Many current new Keynesian theorists believe, nonetheless, that it may ultimately provide a full theory of macroeconomic behavior and of the role of money.

COMMON FEATURES OF THE "NEW KEYNESIAN ECONOMICS"

Although there are some clear distinctions between the new Keynesian theories, there also are several features that they share in common. One of these is the use of models that slightly relax or drop the classical assumption of pure competition among individuals and firms in the economy. Although some of the new Keynesian models, such as the efficiency wage theories, possess elements of competitive behavior, monopoly power of firms or workers generally is a prominent feature of these theories. Many economists criticize the idea that monopoly is possible in a long-run equilibrium. Nevertheless, this is a central feature of most new Keynesian theories.

Another common feature of new Keynesian models is the existence of **coordination failures.** Coordination failures are inabilities of workers and firms to plan and implement desired production and pricing decisions as a result of changes in macroeconomic variables such as inflation or aggregate real income. The basic idea behind coordination failures is that changes in macroeconomic variables have *spillover effects* on the decision making of individual economic agents. For instance, a widespread business recession lowers the real incomes of nearly all households, including those that might otherwise have undertaken significant amounts of consumption, and thereby lowers the sales of nearly all firms, including those firms that would have been very profitable otherwise. Hence, a recession causes spillover effects on individual households and firms and changes the decisions that they make about production, employment, and pricing. The alterations in individual decision making caused by such macroeconomic spillover effects in turn cause market outcomes to vary and, in the aggregate, influence inflation, employment, and real output.

The idea of coordination failures in macroeconomics is in many ways an extension of the theory of market **externalities,** which are spillover effects that arise when the behavior of individuals or firms in one market unintentionally influences the behavior of individuals or firms in other markets. Just as pollution of natural resources by some industries affects the profitability of industries that rely on natural resources for their success, the new Keynesians argue, movements in macroeconomic variables affect individual decision making and, thereby, aggregate, macroeconomic outcomes.

Indeed, claim the new Keynesian theorists, it is the existence of market imperfections and of coordination failures that underlies a need for active policy involvement in the economy. To the new Keynesians, the economy is an inherently unstable system that must be carefully watched and regulated by the actions of monetary and fiscal authorities.

Other economists, such as classical or new classical adherents, remain unconvinced. They have trouble seeing how market imperfections could persist or how coordination failures could be as significant as the new Keynesians claim—or whether either element of the new Keynesian theories really exists in the economy. These remain fundamental points of disagreement within the economics profession.

THE ANTITHESIS OF KEYNESIAN ECONOMICS: REAL BUSINESS CYCLE THEORY

Simultaneous with the development of the new Keynesian sticky-price theories during the late 1980s and 1990s has been work by other economists to extend and, to a large extent, amend the theories constructed by the new classical economists in the 1970s and early 1980s. This research has extended the new classical theory by continuing the new classical emphasis on the assumptions of pure competition with price and wage flexibility and market clearing and of rational expectations. It has amended the new classical theory, however, by removing any role for aggregate demand effects on real output. In this body of theory, which is now known as the **real business cycle theory,** money is neutral both in the long run and in the short run. Only real, supply-side factors matter in influencing labor employment and real output.

This certainly is a familiar-sounding theme, because the conclusions of the real business cycle theorists parallel very closely those of the classical economists. One key difference between the two approaches is that the real business cycle theorists follow other modern theorists by recognizing explicitly the fact that information is imperfect. Following in the footsteps of the new classical economists, the real business cycle proponents use the rational expectations hypothesis.

As in the classical model, the aggregate supply schedule for the real business cycle theory is vertical. The reason is that labor supply shifts in response both to actual price-level changes and to changes in actual employment and production. According to the theory, households plot out a set of optimal paths of labor versus leisure over their life spans, choosing whichever path is best in light of currently observed changes in firm production and labor demand. Whenever conditions in the economy change, labor supply adjusts immediately, so that employment remains at its natural level.

The natural levels of employment and real output, in turn, vary only in response to unanticipated shocks to the productive technology of firms. These could be negative shocks, such as those caused by rises in relative prices of energy or other productive inputs, by wars, or by agricultural famines or natural disasters; or they could be positive shocks, such as inventions of new technologies or reductions in the relative prices of energy or other productive inputs. Such unanticipated disturbances to firm productive technology shift the aggregate supply schedule to the right or left, causing real output to vary cyclically over time.

Real business cycle theory differs from the classical model in a very important respect. Recall that in the classical model the aggregate nominal money supply was assumed to be under complete control of a government agency or central bank. In contrast, in the real business cycle theory the nominal money supply is determined entirely by the interaction of the depository financial institutions and the public. According to this theory, when the public's real income rises, the demand for transactions services from unregulated banks and other depository financial institutions rises as well (as in the Keynesian transactions motive for holding money). Banks respond by producing more transactions services and, thus, more transactions deposit money. The aggregate quantity of bank deposit money—

often called **inside money,** because its quantity is determined by the interactions of banks and the public—moves directly with real income and is not fully controlled by a central bank like the Federal Reserve.

Furthermore, in the real business cycle model, bank deposit money plays no role in determining the price level. The price level instead is determined solely through the interaction of the demand for and supply of currency and bank reserves—called **outside money,** because its magnitude is outside of the control of banks and the public—issued by the government. According to this theory, this is the only component of the nominal money supply that can be controlled at all by the government and, through the quantity equation, this is the part of the nominal money supply that determines the price level. That is, in the new classical theory the position of the aggregate demand schedule is determined solely by the nominal quantity of currency and reserves supplied by the Federal Reserve System. In short, the only money that matters in the real business cycle model is the monetary base (outside money), and the monetary base matters only to the extent that the amount supplied determines the level of prices of goods and services.

Many economists have been attracted to the real business cycle model because it is so firmly grounded in microeconomic principles. As in the classical model, all economic agents are rational, in that they pursue their own best interests and that pure competition prevails with market clearing through price and wage flexibility. Further, all households respond to available information in a way that the theory says is optimal. These are assumptions that many economists like; hence, many economists have adopted this model as their own.

According to Gregory Mankiw, a new Keynesian theorist,

> It is impossible to overemphasize how radical this development [the real business cycle theory] is. At no time in the history of economic thought has the complete irrelevance of monetary policy been so widely and so seriously debated.
>
> . . . As a matter of the sociology of science, the coincidence of the [1980s] disinflation of [former Federal Reserve Board Chairman] Paul Volcker and the rise of real business cycle theory is a puzzle. Economists are fond of saying that our discipline is not cloistered in an ivory tower, that it is driven by events in the world at large. Surely there are many cases in which this is true, such as the rise of Keynesian economics in the Great Depression. But the rise of real business cycle theory in the 1980s shows that our profession has its own internal dynamic that is independent of current events in the outside world.[3]

Mankiw's perspective on the real business cycle theory is shared by many Keynesians as well as by economists of other persuasions. Nevertheless, the internal consistency and, indeed, elegance of the real business cycle theory continues to attract new adherents. As Mankiw himself indicates, real business cycle theorists have raised an important scientific question: Can all macroeconomic observations be explained by changes in technology? That is, can business cycles actually be explained solely by *real,* supply-side factors? The economics profession continues to debate this question.

FUTURE DIRECTIONS IN MONETARY THEORY

Where is monetary theory headed? The answer to this question is not entirely clear, but certain trends are evident. First, traditional Keynesian theory has largely been replaced by

---

[3] N. Gregory Mankiw, ''Commentary,'' in *Monetary Policy on the 75th Anniversary of the Federal Reserve System,* ed. Michael T. Belongia (Boston: Kluwer Academic Publishers, 1991), pp. 275–276.

the new classical and modern Keynesian theories that emphasize the role of a natural level of output toward which the economy tends over time; this basic claim of the monetarists has won over most (but not all) modern economists. Second, the new classical and modern Keynesian contracting theories have been very difficult to verify using real-world evidence because they yield similar predictions. Unlike the Ptolemaic and Copernican theories of astronomy, which had similar predictions but which can be rejected (in the case of Ptolemy's theory of the earth as the center of the universe) or verified (in the case of Copernicus's theory of the earth as a satellite of the sun) on the basis of physical observation (we can send satellites of our own into orbits around the earth and the sun), these modern theories apply to an economy that cannot be subjected to experimentation and observation.

Dissatisfaction with this state of affairs has helped spur the development of new theories of the economy and of the role of money. The new Keynesian and real business cycle theories discussed in this chapter represent very different alternative approaches that economists currently are exploring. The new Keynesian theories uniformly indicate that money is nonneutral in its effects on economic activity. In direct contrast, money is always neutral in the real business cycle model.

Some newcomers to the study of monetary theory are tempted to throw their hands up in complete disgust at this state of affairs. Others find themselves attracted to one view or another. Some even become so fascinated that they become economists in an attempt to figure out which theory best captures the ''economic truth.''

Among practicing economists, there has been another reaction to the present state of affairs in which there is no shortage of theories but little clear evidence that any one of the theories is unambiguously correct. Some economists have argued that perhaps the real problem in monetary theory has been the presumption that only one theory must be correct. Perhaps, these economists argue, more than one theory may apply to real-world economies that are composed of a variety of individuals, markets, and industries. In such a **multisector economy,** goes this alternative argument, more than one theory may be correct, depending on which sector it applies to.

Indeed, a combination of more than one theory can help explain why no single monetary or macroeconomic theory generally bears up to all the available evidence. For instance, as was discussed in the Current Controversy in the previous chapter, there is some evidence (albeit contradictory evidence) that the real wage moves procyclically (that is, the real wage rises as employment, output, and prices increase) even though modern Keynesian contracting models imply that the opposite should be the case. Yet procyclical movements are consistent with some new Keynesian sticky-price models, which in turn are inconsistent with evidence that there is some aggregate price-level flexibility. If some sectors of the economy experienced nominal wage contracting but had flexible product prices while other sectors observed price rigidity but had flexible nominal wages, then the observed behavior of *aggregate* real wage and price levels for the economy as a whole would indeed be both partially consistent and partially inconsistent with predictions of both theories.

If different economic theories apply to different parts of a large, modern economy, then any single classical, traditional Keynesian, monetarist, new classical, modern Keynesian, new Keynesian, or real business cycle theory would be inadequate as a guide to understanding the determination of economic activity and the levels of prices. Any single theory would, by itself, be a poor guide to effective policy making.

As one might expect, combining more than one theory into a more general multisector model of the economy is a complicated undertaking. The reason is that all the sectors of modern economies are interdependent, while monetary policy is conducted on an economywide basis. Nonetheless, theories of this type help explain why the Federal Reserve often complains that it cannot stabilize all parts of the economy at the same time. In a multisector theory, for instance, a ''contracting'' sector might benefit from a particular monetary policy action, while a ''classical'' sector might not gain or might even lose from that action. Furthermore, multisector theories may assist in explaining why some sectors do not have wage contracts, why some sectors do, and why some sectors that have wage contracts do not index wages. A likely reason is that there are spillover effects, or new Keynesian coordination failure problems, that influence the behavior of workers and firms across sectors of the economy. For instance, if it is costly to index wages, workers and firms in many industries may choose not to use indexed labor contracts, which would tend to make nominal wages more rigid than they otherwise would be, thereby reducing the variability of the price level. This would create a spillover effect on those workers and firms in industries that *do* have indexed wage contracts, causing some of them to reduce their degree of wage indexation—or perhaps not to index their wages at all.

Monetary theory clearly has a long way to go. However, it also has come a long way. The situation, again, is analogous to the state of the science of astronomy. Although the Ptolemaic model of the apparent motion of the stars has given way to the Copernican model of the actual motion of the earth and more recently to Newton's theory of gravitation and to Einstein's relativistic theory of matter and energy, astronomers still do not understand how our universe, with all its stars and galaxies, came to assume its present form. Astronomers have come a long way since Ptolemy's theory of earth as the center of the universe, but they still are far from their ultimate objective. Likewise, monetary theorists have progressed considerably from the simple classical model with its assumptions of pure competition and perfect information, but they have much more work yet to do. As in the science of astronomy, the continuing failure to reach final conclusions about the neutrality or nonneutrality of money sometimes makes monetary theory a frustrating field. Yet frustration also provides the field with a dynamism that continues to drive monetary economists to develop new theories and conduct further studies of money and the economy.

CHAPTER SUMMARY

1. The aggregate price level in some countries, including the United States, shows evidence of less than full flexibility. This fact has motivated some economists to develop new Keynesian, sticky-price models of the economy. These models share some similarities to the administered pricing hypotheses advanced in the 1930s and again in the 1950s, but they differ in that they provide possible *explanations* for why firms might choose not to change their prices over relatively long time intervals.

2. If prices are rigid, monetary policy generally is nonneutral. Consequently, new Keynesian theories of the economy and of the role of money have focused on price rigidities as potential explanations for why money may be nonneutral.

3. One new Keynesian explanation for alleged rigidities in product prices is that small menu costs, which are the costs of making price changes, may more than offset the profit gains that firms might otherwise receive if they were to change their prices in reaction to variations in market conditions.

4. Another new Keynesian theory of rigidities in wages and prices assumes that an increase in the real wage encourages greater labor productivity. This efficiency wage hypothesis implies that employment varies with changes in the nominal money supply, so that money is nonneutral.

5. The insider-outsider theory of labor market behavior provides a possible explanation for the persistence of labor unemployment and for the nonneutrality of money. According to this

theory, relatively high costs associated with hiring and firing workers discourage firms from doing so, which gives current employees (insiders) the ability to keep potential employees (outsiders) from being hired even if the potential employees would be willing to work at a lower real wage rate.

6. Under the input-output table approach to macroeconomic theory, the complexities of interactions among numerous workers and firms and the imperfect availability of information about all market conditions throughout the economy lead to real, relative (price-level-adjusted) price rigidities as well as rigidities in nominal prices and wages. Money is nonneutral, according to this approach.

7. The various new Keynesian models share two common features. One common element is the abandonment of the classical assumption of pure competition. The other is the existence of coordination failures, or macroeconomic spillover effects that inhibit the abilities of individual workers and firms to carry out otherwise optimal decisions.

8. In direct opposition to the new Keynesian monetary and macroeconomic theories is the real business cycle theory. According to real business cycle theorists, variations in real output arise only from technological changes in the economy caused by events such as wars, famines, changes in relative prices of factors of production, or technological improvements. Money is always neutral.

9. In the real business cycle model, bank deposit money (inside money) has no effect on either real variables or the price level. The price level is determined by the demand for and supply of currency and bank reserves (the monetary base, or outside money).

10. One recent approach to monetary and macroeconomic theorizing has been to consider multi-sector models, in which sectors within a single, aggregate economy exhibit behavior that is best described by different economic models.

GLOSSARY

Administered pricing hypothesis: The idea that firms with some measure of monopoly power will set prices in a discretionary way and hold them constant over relatively lengthy periods of time.

Coordination failures: Spillover effects between workers and firms that arise from movements in macroeconomic variables that make it difficult for these individual economic agents to plan and implement their production and pricing decisions.

Efficiency wage theory: The hypothesis that the productivity of workers depends on the level of the real wage rate.

Externality: A spillover effect that arises when behavior by an individual or firm in one setting or market indirectly causes changes in the behavior of individuals or firms in another setting or market.

Input-output table: A tabulation of all elements that figure into the production and pricing decisions of all workers and firms in the economy.

Inside money: Money held in the form of bank deposits.

Insider-outsider theory: The idea that ''insider'' employees, by virtue of the costs involved in replacing them, are able to keep potential ''outsider'' workers from being hired at a lower real wage rate than the insiders earn.

Multisector economies: Economies that are composed of sectors within which economic behavior is best represented by different economic theories, making no single theory the best description of the economy as a whole.

New Keynesian theorists: Economists who have developed economic models based on the idea that ''demand creates its own supply.''

Outside money: Money in the form of currency and bank reserves; the monetary base.

Price inertia: A tendency for the level of prices to resist change with the passage of time.

Real business cycle theorists: Economists who have developed economic models based on the idea that "supply creates its own demand."

Real business cycle theory: An extension and modification of the theories of the new classical economists of the 1970s and 1980s, in which money is neutral and only real, supply-side factors matter in influencing labor employment and real output.

Small menu costs: The costs firms incur when they make price changes, which include both the costs of changing prices in menus or catalogs and the costs of renegotiating agreements with customers.

SELF-TEST QUESTIONS

1. According to the new Keynesian small-menu-cost theory, is there an aggregate supply schedule for the economy as a whole? Why or why not? (*Hint:* Is there an industry supply schedule under monopoly?)

2. Draw a diagram with demand and marginal revenue schedules faced by a profit-maximizing monopolist. Suppose that the monopolist's marginal cost is constant. Explain how to measure the firm's profit loss that occurs if it does not raise its price in response to an *increase* in the demand for its product.

3. Suppose that the marginal product of labor depends positively upon the real wage that workers earn. What happens to the production function if the real wage rises? Explain.

4. Explain, in your own words, the essential elements of the insider-outsider theory of labor market behavior.

5. Explain, in your own words, the major aspects of the input-output approach to macroeconomic modeling.

6. Suppose that a new firm had plotted out a strategy for significant long-term growth but discovers that a major economywide recession has made that plan impossible to implement. In response, it cuts back on its expansion plan and fires some of its employees. Is this a coordination failure? Explain.

7. Explain the distinction between inside money and outside money.

8. Draw a short-run Phillips curve that would be applicable to the new classical theory if monetary policy actions are unanticipated. On the same diagram, draw a short-run Phillips curve implied by the real business cycle theory. Are they the same? Why or why not?

PROBLEMS

23-1. Suppose that prices are rigid, so that the price level is constant and equal to $\overline{P} = 5$. Also, suppose that the income velocity of money is constant and equal to $\overline{V} = 2$. What is the level of real output when the nominal money supply is equal to (a) 50, (b) 100, (c) 150? Is money neutral?

23-2. Consider the following situation faced by a monopolistic firm. Its marginal cost of producing output is constant and equal to $2 per unit. At an initial level of demand for its product, the firm produces the profit-maximizing level of output equal to 400 units and charges a price of $8 per unit. However, the firm experiences a fall in the demand for its product that causes the profit-maximizing level of output to fall to 300 units. The price that the firm should charge to maximize its profits is $6 per unit. If the firm were instead to leave its price unchanged at $8 per unit, it could sell 200 units of output. The firm has calculated that lowering its price from $8 per unit to $6 per unit would force it to incur a $225 cost to print and replace price catalogs. Will this firm change its price? Explain, and show your work.

23-3.   Suppose that a firm determines that a 1-unit increase in its real wage rate would cause, at its current employment level, a 1-unit increase in worker effort and productivity that, in turn, yields a 1-unit gain in output produced. The firm also determines that a 1-unit increase in its real wage rate would generate a cost equal to 1 output unit. Would this firm change its real wage? Why or why not?

SELECTED REFERENCES

Akerlof, George A., and Janet L. Yellen (eds.), *Efficiency Wage Models of the Labor Market* (Cambridge: Cambridge University Press, 1986).

Ball, Laurence, and David Romer, ''Are Prices Too Sticky?'' *Quarterly Journal of Economics,* 104 (3, August 1989), pp. 507–524.

Barro, Robert J., ''Second Thoughts on Keynesian Economics,'' *American Economic Review,* 69 (2, May 1979), pp. 54–59.

———, and Herschel Grossman, *Money, Employment, and Inflation* (Cambridge: Cambridge University Press, 1976).

Blinder, Alan S., and N. Gregory Mankiw, ''Aggregation and Stabilization Policy in a Multi-Contract Economy,'' *Journal of Monetary Economics,* 13 (1, January 1984), pp. 67–86.

Clarkson, Kenneth W., and Roger LeRoy Miller, *Industrial Organization: Theory, Evidence, and Public Policy* (New York: McGraw-Hill, 1982).

Clower, Robert W., ''The Keynesian Counterrevolution: A Theoretical Appraisal,'' in *The Theory of Interest Rates,* ed. F. H. Hahn and F. Brechling (London: Macmillan, 1965), pp. 103–125.

Cooper, Russell, and Andrew John, ''Coordinating Coordination Failures in Keynesian Models,'' *Quarterly Journal of Economics,* 103 (3, August 1988), pp. 441–463.

Duca, John V., ''The Spillover Effects of Nominal Wage Rigidity in a Multisector Economy,'' *Journal of Money, Credit, and Banking,* 19 (1, February 1987), pp. 117–121.

———, and David D. VanHoose, ''Optimal Monetary Policy in a Multisector Economy with an Economy-Wide Money Market,'' *Journal of Economics and Business,* 42 (4, November 1990), pp. 253–264.

——— and ———, ''Optimal Wage Indexation in a Multisector Economy,'' *International Economic Review,* 32 (4, November 1991), pp. 859–868.

Froyen, Richard T., and Roger N. Waud, ''Real Business Cycles and the Lucas Paradigm,'' *Economic Inquiry,* 26 (2, April 1988), pp. 183–201.

Gordon, Robert J., ''What Is New-Keynesian Economics?'' *Journal of Economic Literature,* 28 (3, September 1990), pp. 1115–1171.

Leibenstein, Harvey, *Economic Backwardness and Economic Growth* (New York: John Wiley & Sons, 1963).

Leijonhufvud, Axel, *On Keynesian Economics and the Economics of Keynes* (New York: Oxford University Press, 1968).

Lindbeck, Assar, and Dennis Snower, *The Insider-Outsider Theory of Employment and Unemployment* (Cambridge, Mass.: MIT Press, 1988).

Mankiw, N. Gregory, ''Commentary,'' in *Monetary Policy on the 75th Anniversary of the Federal Reserve System,* ed. Michael T. Belongia (Boston: Kluwer Academic Publishers, 1991), pp. 275–276.

————, ''A Quick Refresher Course in Macroeconomics,'' *Journal of Economic Literature* 28 (4, December 1990), pp. 1645–1660.

————, ''Real Business Cycles: A New Keynesian Perspective,'' *Journal of Economic Perspectives,* 3 (3, Summer 1989), pp. 79–90.

————, ''Small Menu Costs and Large Business Cycles: A Macroeconomic Model of Monopoly,'' *Quarterly Journal of Economics,* 100 (2, May 1985), pp. 529–538.

Mason, Edward S., *Economic Concentration and the Monopoly Problem* (Cambridge, Mass.: Harvard University Press, 1957).

Means, Gardiner C., *The Structure of the American Economy,* Part I (Washington, D.C.: National Resources Committee, 1939).

Mill, John S., *Principles of Economics* (London: J. W. Parker, 1848).

Neal, Alfred C., *Industrial Concentration and Price Inflexibility* (Washington, D.C.: Temporary National Economic Committee, 1941).

Okun, Arthur M., *Prices and Quantities: A Macroeconomic Analysis* (Washington, D.C.: Brookings Institution, 1981).

Patinkin, Don, *Money, Interest, and Prices,* 2d ed. (New York: Harper & Row, 1965).

Plosser, Charles I., ''Money and Business Cycles: A Real Business Cycle Interpretation,'' in *Monetary Policy on the 75th Anniversary of the Federal Reserve System,* ed. Michael T. Belongia (Boston: Kluwer Academic Publishers, 1991), pp. 245–274.

————, ''Understanding Real Business Cycles,'' *Journal of Economic Perspectives,* 3 (3, Summer 1989), pp. 51–79.

Monetary
Stabilization Policy

Objectives and Targets
of Monetary Policy

CHAPTER PREVIEW

1. What are ultimate objectives of monetary policy?

2. What is an intermediate target of monetary policy?

3. Why might the Fed use an intermediate target?

4. What characteristics should an intermediate target possess?

5. What economic variables might be useful intermediate targets?

6. What are the advantages and disadvantages of alternative strategies for intermediate targeting by the Fed?

The previous unit may have convinced you that economists share little common ground in their views about money's role in the economy. Certainly, there is no shortage of theories—classical, traditional Keynesian, monetarist, new classical, modern Keynesian, new Keynesian, real business cycle—from which the Fed may choose in its quest for the best monetary policy. Yet even economists who share the same view on how the economy works often disagree about the *specific approaches* that the Fed should take toward achieving its ultimate economic goals.

We shall see in this unit that even if economists might reach some general agreement about the appropriate *ends* of monetary policy, they still would not necessarily share the same perspectives on the best *means* toward those ends. In this chapter, we consider the Fed's choice of ultimate economic goals and review specific approaches that the Fed might take toward achieving these goals. In the following chapters we analyze the Fed's day-to-day conduct of monetary policy in light of its policy objectives and the issue of whether the Fed should adopt hard-and-fast "rules" or use its own discretion in its ongoing efforts to achieve its goals for the economy.

ULTIMATE OBJECTIVES OF MONETARY POLICY

In the previous unit you learned that the quantity of money is a key determinant of prices and inflation in nearly any theory of the functioning of the economy. According to several economic theories, the quantity of money also plays a significant role in determining the economy's levels of real output and labor employment. Given that the Federal Reserve System has the ability to influence the quantity of money, we begin by considering the two ultimate economic goals, or **ultimate objectives,** that the Federal Reserve most strongly pursues when it formulates its monetary policies.

ACHIEVING HIGH AND STABLE OUTPUT LEVELS

One key goal of the Fed is to lay the best monetary policy foundation for the nation to attain high and stable levels of production of goods and services. A nation that produces more output per person than other nations is often assumed more likely to have happier and more productive citizens. A nation that can achieve higher and more stable growth in its production of real output also has the better foundation for long-run prosperity for its citizens.

The economy's aggregate production function indicates that if real output is high, labor unemployment rates are low, holding other factors unchanged. For this reason, an ultimate aim by the Federal Reserve to attain high and stable growth of real output essentially is the same as a goal to achieve low and stable unemployment rates.

MAINTAINING LOW INFLATION AND STABLE PRICES

The second fundamental goal of the Fed is to achieve low and stable inflation rates. High inflation, in the absence of fully indexed nominal contracts, imposes a variety of potential costs on individuals, firms, and financial institutions. For one thing, greater inflation encourages individuals and firms to find ways to economize on their holdings of currency and demand deposits, which entails expenditures of real resources. It also entails more frequent price changes and associated *menu costs* (see Chapter 23). Individuals and firms may also be induced to change the terms of wage and other contracts much more frequently, which is costly in time and effort, or to index contracts to inflation to a larger extent, which also may entail resource costs.

Unanticipated inflation also has *redistribution effects,* because it effectively transfers wealth from creditors to debtors. Another possible redistribution effect arises if income taxes are not fully indexed, because inflation increases nominal incomes and thereby pushes people and firms into higher tax brackets, effectively raising their taxes without any actual income tax rate increases. To the extent that individuals and firms seek to avoid such redistribution effects, they also incur direct real costs.

Finally, inflation *variability* also may be costly, because it forces economic agents to determine whether *aggregate* or *relative* prices have changed, thereby complicating consumption and production decisions.

INTERMEDIATE TARGETS OF MONETARY POLICY

Although the Federal Reserve could, in principle, conduct open-market operations, vary the discount rate, or adjust reserve requirements with an aim to achieve its output and inflation objectives directly, it rarely has done this. Instead, the Fed typically has used **intermediate targets** of monetary policy. An intermediate target is an economic variable whose value the Fed chooses to control because it feels that doing so is consistent with its ultimate objectives. That is, an intermediate target is an objective distinguishable from the Fed's ultimate output and inflation goals—and one the Fed would not wish to control by itself—but closely enough linked to its ultimate goals that the intermediate target can serve as a "stand-in" or "proxy" for the ultimate objectives of its policies.

As we shall discuss shortly, there are a variety of variables that the Fed might consider as possible intermediate targets. In fact, conceivably there is almost no limit to the listing of economic variables from which the Fed might select an intermediate target of its policies. For instance, the Fed might decide to buy or sell college textbooks in sufficient quantities to keep the average price of a textbook at a fixed, target level. It probably would not ever do this, however, because it is unlikely that college textbooks will ever bear a close enough relationship to aggregate economic activity to justify Fed involvement in that market.

The need for a potential intermediate target to be closely related to the Fed's ultimate goals, then, stands out as a key element in limiting the set of variables that the Fed might consider as a possible intermediate target variable. Nevertheless, several economic variables still remain on the Fed's list of candidates, as we shall discuss below. First, however, we need to consider why the Fed might wish to use an intermediate target in the first place.

THE RATIONALE FOR INTERMEDIATE TARGETS

There are two parts to the rationale for the Fed's use of intermediate targets. The first is that it may be difficult, if not impossible, to understand all the interrelationships among economic variables sufficiently to aim the Fed's instruments of monetary policy directly at its ultimate policy objectives. The second is that even if the Fed were to understand completely how the economy works, it typically does not have enough information on hand to make the best possible decisions about how to attain its ultimate goals directly. Let's consider each individually.

Problems in Aiming Directly at Ultimate Policy Objectives   As we discussed in the chapters of the previous unit on monetary and macroeconomic theory, there are several alternative theories of how the quantity of money influences other economic variables. Furthermore, while one theory may be more or less widely accepted at any given time, disagreement about the relative validity of the various theories continues.

Interestingly, academic economists are not the only ones who argue about the relevance of the theories. In the 1960s and 1970s economists in some parts of the Federal Reserve System—notably economists associated with the Federal Reserve Bank of St. Louis—were strong adherents of the monetarist theory, even though economists in other parts of the Federal Reserve System—notably the Federal Reserve Board in Washington—tended to favor Keynesian-type explanations of economic activity. In the 1980s and 1990s, another split became apparent when some Fed economists—particularly those associated with the Federal Reserve Bank of Minneapolis—promoted the real business cycle theory.

Clearly, if Fed economists and policy makers themselves cannot agree about exactly how monetary policy actions affect economic variables, it is difficult to envision how the Federal Reserve System as a whole could settle on the best means of, say, conducting day-to-day open-market operations to stabilize real output and the price level.

From this perspective, an intermediate target might be viewed as a *compromise* means of conducting policy, in the absence of full agreement among policy makers concerning the best way to aim directly at ultimate policy goals. For instance, as we shall discuss below, one intermediate target the Fed has used in the past has been the nominal quantity of money. While not all economic theories indicate that the money stock affects all economic variables, nearly all theories indicate that a change in the quantity of money should cause the price level to move in the same direction, if not necessarily in the same proportion. Federal Reserve adherents of a wide variety of theories might agree that, in the absence of any other area of agreement, a policy that aimed to achieve an intermediate monetary target might be better than any other policy option for which no basis of agreement exists. To the extent that price stabilization and low inflation might be ultimate monetary policy objectives, using the money stock as an intermediate target might then be a means for the *pragmatic* Federal Reserve conduct of monetary policy.

Informational Problems   The above argument in favor of an intermediate monetary target really focuses on a *political,* rather than an *economic,* justification. Although disagreements about economic theory might favor the use of a broad intermediate target as a political compromise among policy makers, there is a strong economic argument to be made in favor of using an intermediate target in monetary policy even if everyone agreed on the ''true'' model of the economy.

The basis of this argument is the problem of imperfect information in the conduct of monetary policy. Some economic variables, such as interest rates and quantities of money or credit, can be measured on a week-to-week or even day-to-day basis. Others, such as nominal output, may be estimated on a weekly basis but generally are known only on a monthly basis; and some, such as price level data or real output measurements, are available almost solely on a monthly basis. Furthermore, it is not uncommon for these latter variables to be established only approximately at monthly intervals; government statisticians fairly commonly revise their monthly calculations of these variables after the fact.

Hence, up-to-date information about prices and real output typically is least likely to be available readily to policy makers. In contrast, information about financial variables, such as interest rates, money, or credit, is available much more quickly. Information about nominal income is less readily available, but policy makers typically may obtain this information more quickly and accurately than data on ultimate policy goals.

The fact that some economic variables other than those directly related to ultimate policy objectives may be measured more accurately over shorter periods of time leads naturally to the idea of using these other variables as intermediate targets. The basic idea is that by aiming its policy instruments at an intermediate target, the Fed can receive almost immediate feedback about whether or not the general thrust—if not the precision—of its policy actions is on the mark. In contrast, if it were to undertake a certain set of open-market operations to change the direction of a variable such as real output or the price level, at the present time it would do so largely in an informational vacuum. The Fed would have no way of knowing until a few weeks or usually months later whether its actions were having their intended effects.

IMPLEMENTING AN INTERMEDIATE TARGET

How can the Fed choose a target variable that it normally would not care about, yet which helps it achieve its ultimate objectives? The answer to this question is lengthy, which is the reason that we shall devote the rest of this chapter to the intermediate targeting issue. Let's begin by overviewing some basic concepts concerning the choice of an intermediate monetary policy target.

Criteria for Selecting Intermediate Targets   There are several conditions that the Fed would like an intermediate target variable to satisfy. They are as follows.

1. *Consistency with the Fed's ultimate goals*   This is the paramount condition that any intermediate target variable must meet. If the Fed's ultimate objectives are, say, stabilization of real output and the level of prices, then the Fed presumably would normally regard other economic variables as secondary to those ultimate goal variables, or even irrelevant. Hence, the Fed will care about achieving an intermediate target *only* if doing so assists it in pursuing its ultimate policy objectives.

2. *Measurability* If an intermediate target variable is to be useful to the Fed, it must be a variable that the Fed can measure accurately and precisely. The Fed must have little or no doubt about the magnitudes of the variable it uses as an intermediate target. Otherwise, problems in measuring this economic variable will adversely affect the Fed's ability to achieve its ultimate goals.

3. *Timeliness* Accurate information about an intermediate target variable must be available to the Fed on a timely basis. An economic variable that the Fed can measure only infrequently is not likely to be particularly helpful as an intermediate target, given that this is the problem that the Fed also has with its *ultimate* goal variables. If information on the value of a potential intermediate target variable is available no more frequently than information about ultimate objectives of policy, the Fed might as well forget using an intermediate target.

4. *Controllability* For an intermediate economic variable to be useful to the Fed as an intermediate target variable, the Fed must be able to influence the magnitude of the variable. Furthermore, there needs to be a strong and clearly understood linkage between the Fed's policy instruments and the intermediate variable, so that the Fed can control its magnitude and achieve a target value for that variable.

Meeting each of these conditions is a tall order. Nevertheless, if an intermediate targeting strategy is to be successful, the Fed must do all that it can to satisfy each of these criteria. Otherwise, the Fed is unlikely to meet its ultimate objectives for monetary policy.

Aggregate Demand Stabilization and Intermediate Targets As we discussed in Chapter 21, monetary policy actions are transmitted to the economy through their effects on money market equilibrium and the position of the *LM* schedule. Furthermore, the position of the economy's aggregate demand schedule stems from equilibrium of the *LM* and *IS* schedules. Consequently, monetary policy actions influence the position of the economy's aggregate demand schedule. Although Fed policy makers might like to be able to influence firm production and worker labor supply behavior, they are unable to affect directly such supply-side variables. Aside from the effects that worker and firm expectations of Fed behavior may have on labor supply and production decisions by workers and firms (see Chapter 22), the Fed has no means of influencing the position of the economy's aggregate supply schedule.

Therefore, a monetary policy intended to achieve output and price level stability generally must operate through its effects on the economy's aggregate demand schedule. It follows that choosing the "best" intermediate target for monetary policy typically involves targeting a variable that is a key determinant of the position of the aggregate demand schedule. In this way, the Fed's intermediate target choice will be consistent with the Fed's ultimate objectives.

Figure 24-1 provides a diagrammatic illustration of this point. It shows an initial aggregate demand–aggregate supply equilibrium at point A, at which the price level is P_0 and real output is y_0. In addition, y_0 is the economy's natural, full-information level of output, and so the economy's long-run aggregate supply schedule is vertical at this output level (recall this concept from Chapter 21).

Suppose that the Fed's ultimate goals are to stabilize real output relative to its natural, full-information level and to minimize variability of the price level. If the aggregate supply schedule is stable, then the only way that real output and the price level will vary is if the aggregate demand schedule is variable, as shown in the diagram. Such volatility in aggregate demand could result from a number of factors unrelated to Federal Reserve actions,

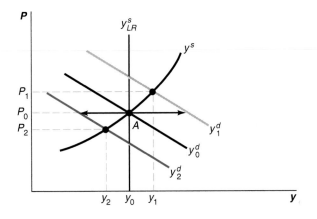

Figure 24-1

Stabilizing Aggregate Demand via Intermediate Targeting.   Variations in the position of
the economy's aggregate demand schedule cause short-run variations in the level of real output
from its natural, full-information level, which is equal to y_0 at the location of the economy's long-run
aggregate supply schedule. Such aggregate demand variations also cause variability in the level of
prices and of inflation. One purpose of an intermediate targeting strategy is to stabilize aggregate
demand and thereby eliminate such variability in real income and inflation.

such as changes in household consumption, firm desired investment, government spending
or taxation policies, or variations in the public's demand for money.

A key role for an intermediate targeting procedure in monetary policy, therefore, is to
reduce such volatility in aggregate demand. For this reason, as we shall see below, most
approaches to intermediate targeting focus on stabilizing real income determined by the
economy's *IS-LM* equilibrium. After all, as you learned in Chapter 21, the economy's
aggregate demand schedule is a locus of *IS-LM* equilibrium points. Stabilization of the
level of real income forthcoming from *IS* and *LM* equilibrium thereby implies stabilization
of aggregate demand and, as a result, real output and price level stabilization.

Note that this discussion abstracts from the destabilizing effects that would result from
variability in the economy's aggregate supply schedule. As you will see later on, aggregate
supply volatility also complicates the choice of an intermediate target. For the time being,
however, we shall concentrate on the aggregate demand stability properties of alternative
intermediate targets.

The Menu of Intermediate Targets   The Fed conducts its policies in financial markets: markets for government bonds, for interbank loans, and for central bank credit.
Consequently, because the Fed must choose an intermediate target that it can effectively
control, financial market variables stand out as the most likely candidates for the role of
intermediate target.

Key variables in financial markets are *interest rates.* Not surprisingly, then, interest
rates are on the list of potential intermediate targets of monetary policy, and the Fed may
have used interest rate targeting policies in the 1950s and 1960s. (It is difficult to make
an unambiguous claim on this point, because the Fed was rather coy about the role of the
interest rate in its strategies during those years.) Another important variable, of course, is
the *quantity of money,* and as we shall discuss below and in the next chapter, the Fed used
the rate of growth of the quantity of money as an intermediate target during the 1970s

and early 1980s. As we shall discuss later in the chapter, another possible intermediate target in financial markets would be a measure of *credit* in the economy. The Fed has used such measures as indicators in the past but has not officially adopted credit aggregates as intermediate monetary policy targets.

Although the Fed can most directly control financial market variables, it need not be limited specifically to such variables as potential intermediate targets. One economic variable to which Federal Reserve and other economists have become attracted recently is *nominal income*. Yet another is *commodity prices,* and some have advocated an adaptation of interest rate targeting that would entail targeting the *spread* between long- and short-term interest rates implied by the term structure of interest rates.

In our discussion below, we shall concentrate on those intermediate targets that the Fed either has used in the past or has considered most seriously. We shall discuss all the above possibilities, however. In recent years the Fed has shown a propensity to change intermediate targets as conditions warrant, and so to ignore all the most likely possibilities for intermediate targets would not be prudent. To evaluate which intermediate target may be most desirable, it is important to understand the essential features of each.

THE NOMINAL INTEREST RATE AS AN INTERMEDIATE TARGET

Among all possible intermediate target variables, nominal interest rates stand out for several reasons. First, interest rates may be observed frequently by the Fed. Average data on interest rates on financial instruments are available to the Fed daily, and the Fed can track some interest rates by the hour. As we noted above, measurability and timeliness are key criteria for an intermediate target, and so nominal interest rates clearly fit the bill on these points.

The Fed also has considerable ability to influence nominal interest rates through purchases and sales of government securities. Consequently, the Fed may be able to exercise significant control over nominal interest rates, at least in the short run. In principle, then, nominal interest rates appear to be potentially controllable by the Fed.

The key issue, then, is whether or not a nominal interest rate target is consistent with the Fed's ultimate goals. That is the issue we concentrate on now.

IMPLEMENTING A NOMINAL INTEREST RATE TARGET

Let's begin our analysis by first considering how the Fed can target the nominal interest rate. Consider panel (*a*) of Figure 24-2, in which we assume that the Fed has already chosen a target level for the interest rate, given by r_n^*. (At this point we shall not worry about how the Fed determines that target r_n^*; once we understand how the Fed can keep the interest rate at the level r_n^*, we shall consider this issue more thoroughly.)

First consider point A, in panel (*a*) of Figure 24-2, at which the demand schedule for real money balances, $m_0^d(y_0)$, crosses the supply schedule for real money balances, which is vertical at the quantity of real money balances M_0/P_0. Recall from Chapter 21 that the position of the demand schedule for real money balances depends upon the public's demand for real purchasing power, which in turn depends on the public's aggregate real income (which we assume is constant and equal to y_0) and tastes and preferences (among other things). Furthermore, the Fed can influence directly the quantity of nominal money balances, M_0, but the quantity of real money balances supplied varies with changes in the price level even if the Fed undertakes no policy actions. For now we shall assume that the price level is fixed at P_0.

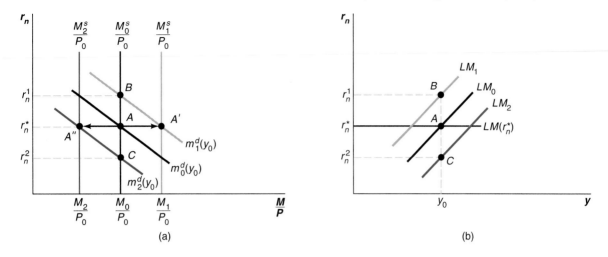

Figure 24-2
Implementing a Nominal Interest Rate Target.   If the public's demand for real money balances varies between $m_1^d(y_0)$ and $m_2^d(y_0)$, as shown in panel (a), then equilibrium points in the
market for real money balances will range between points B and C. The Fed can vary the quantity of
money supplied as needed, however, to keep the nominal interest rate constant at a target level r_n^*.
As shown in panel (b), targeting the interest rate effectively makes the LM schedule horizontal at
$LM(r_n^*)$. If the Fed did not target the interest rate, however, the economy's typically positively sloped
LM schedule would shift upward or downward with variations in the demand for real money balances, between points B and C.

Keeping the Interest Rate on Target   Point A in panel (a) of Figure 24-2 depicts an
initial equilibrium in the market for real money balances at which the equilibrium nominal
interest rate is equal to r_n^*, the Fed's target. Suppose, however, that the public's demand
for real money balances inexplicably were to increase to $m_1^d(y_0)$. That is, the public's
demand for real purchasing power increases even though real income remains unchanged.
If the Fed were to do nothing in response, and the price level remained unchanged (by
assumption), then the equilibrium nominal interest rate would rise to r_n^1, at point B. This,
of course, would violate the Fed's aim to keep the interest rate at the target level of r_n^*.
What should the Fed do in this situation? The answer is simple; the Fed would need to
undertake a policy action, such as an open-market purchase, to increase the quantity of
money. This would shift the supply schedule for real money balances rightward (again,
assuming that the price level is unchanging) and return the equilibrium interest rate to r_n^*
at point A'. The Fed thereby would keep the nominal interest rate at the targeted level.

  In contrast, suppose that the public's demand for real money balances instead were to
decline suddenly relative to the initial position $m_0^d(y_0)$, to the new position $m_2^d(y_0)$ shown
in panel (a) of Figure 24-2. If this were to occur, then the equilibrium nominal interest
rate, in the absence of any Fed actions, would fall to r_n^2 at point C. The Fed could prevent
this fall in the nominal interest rate, however, by conducting policy actions to *reduce* the
quantity of money it supplies, from M_0 to M_2. As shown, this would keep the interest rate
in equilibrium at the target value of r_n^*, at point A''.

  Panel (b) of Figure 24-2 shows the implications of interest rate targeting for the
economy's LM schedule. The typically upward-sloping LM schedule for the economy
initially was in the position LM_0 at point A, at which the equilibrium interest rate in the
market for real money balances was equal to r_n^* at the level of real income y_0. A rise in

the demand for real money balances normally would have caused the *LM* schedule to shift upward, to LM_1, as shown by the vertical movement from point *A* to point *B* and the rise in the interest rate from r_n^* to r_n^1. In contrast, a fall in the demand for real money balances normally would have caused the *LM* schedule to shift downward, to LM_2, as shown by the vertical movement from point *A* to point *C* and the decline in the interest rate from r_n^* to r_n^2.

Under nominal interest rate targeting, however, the Fed does not permit the economy's *LM* schedule to shift in either direction shown in panel (*b*) of Figure 24-2. Instead, it always responds to variations in the demand for real money balances by increasing or reducing the quantity of money supplied as needed to keep the nominal interest rate at its target level, r_n^*. If this is the way that the Fed conducts monetary policy, then it is *as if* the *LM* schedule actually were *horizontal* at the interest rate target r_n^*. In fact, *effectively* the *LM* schedule *is* horizontal if the Fed always adjusts the quantity of money as needed to keep the interest rate at the target level. Hence, the horizontal *LM* schedule labeled $LM(r_n^*)$ in panel (*b*) of Figure 24-2 is the **effective *LM* schedule** when the Fed uses an interest rate target.

Choosing the Interest Rate Target   Now that we have shown how the Fed would target the interest rate, plus the implications of such a policy for the *LM* schedule, we need to consider how the Fed would choose its interest rate target. This process is explained in Figure 24-3. Suppose that the Fed chooses the real income level *y** as an ultimate target. If so, and if the *IS* schedule is in the position shown in Figure 24-3, then all the Fed has to do is calculate the interest rate needed to yield this level of real income from the aggregate expenditures equilibrium implied by the *IS* schedule.

That is, the Fed would simply have to estimate the position of the *IS* schedule and, given its ultimate objective for the level of real income *y**, determine the intermediate interest rate target, r_n^*, that it needs to "hit" to achieve its ultimate goal for real income. As shown in Figure 24-3, the Fed would then target the interest rate at this level. In so

Figure 24-3
Choosing the Nominal Interest Rate Target.   Given an ultimate objective for real income, *y**, the Fed estimates the position of the economy's *IS* schedule. It then calculates the nominal interest rate, r_n^*, needed to yield the level of income, *y**, based on the level of aggregate desired expenditures implied by the *IS* schedule. The Fed then keeps the nominal interest rate at this target level using the approach described in Figure 24-2.

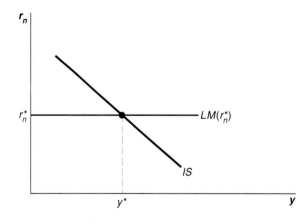

doing, it would effectively make the *LM* schedule horizontal at $LM(r_n^*)$, as we explained earlier.

THE ADVANTAGES AND DISADVANTAGES OF USING THE NOMINAL INTEREST RATE AS AN INTERMEDIATE TARGET

As depicted in Figure 24-3, using the nominal interest rate as an intermediate target appears to be a fairly straightforward proposition. Indeed, the apparent simplicity of nominal interest rate targeting is one of its key advantages. There are, however, others that are more important.

Advantages of Interest Rate Targeting A key advantage of using the nominal interest rate as an intermediate target in fact is already depicted by Figures 24-2 and 24-3. Therefore, let's begin by reconsidering the implications of those two figures. As shown in Figure 24-2, if the Fed did *not* act to keep the interest rate at its target level r_n^*, the *LM* schedule would shift upward or downward with increases or decreases in the public's demand for real money balances. But Figure 24-3 indicates that as long as the *IS* schedule is not variable, such shifts in the *LM* schedule would not be desirable, because then the Fed's ultimate real income target, y^*, would not be maintained.

We can see this clearly in Figure 24-4, which superimposes panel (*b*) of Figure 24-2 onto Figure 24-3. As you can see in Figure 24-4, if the Fed were to permit the *LM* schedule to move vertically upward or downward from point *A*, between points *B* and *C*, then equilibrium real income also would vary, between y_1 and y_2. As a result, the level of real income would not stay constant at y^*, the Fed's ultimate real income objective.

In contrast, if the Fed were to target the nominal interest rate at r_n^*, it would make the effective *LM* schedule horizontal at $LM(r_n^*)$, as we discussed earlier. Hence, the interest rate would not vary in response to changes in the public's demand for real money balances.

Figure 24-4
An Advantage of Interest Rate Targeting.   A key advantage of interest rate targeting is that it automatically stabilizes real income when there is variability in the demand for real money balances. Such variability normally would cause the economy's *LM* schedule to vary between points *B* and *C*, thereby causing the nominal interest rate to fluctuate and resulting in variations in equilibrium real income. By targeting the nominal interest rate at r_n^*, however, the Fed keeps the economy in equilibrium at point *A*, thereby preventing such real income volatility, *provided that the* IS *schedule is stable.*

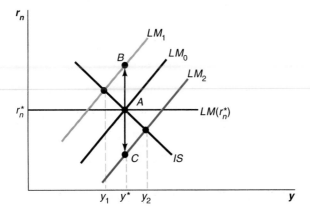

Real income thereby would *automatically* remain constant at the ultimate objective y^* in the face of such volatility in money demand. Effectively, by using the interest rate as an intermediate target the Fed automatically offsets the effects of money demand variability on real income.

Another advantage of using the nominal interest rate as an intermediate target is that doing so also automatically offsets the effects of variability in the economy's *money supply* process. As we discussed in Chapter 14, the economy's money multiplier is not really constant. It depends on several things, including the required reserve ratio, the public's desired holdings of currency relative to transactions deposits, and depository institutions' desired holdings of excess reserves relative to transactions deposits. The latter two factors, in turn, typically vary with the expectations and tastes and preferences of households, firms, and depository institutions. Consequently, the money multiplier and, thus, the quantity of money can vary without any policy actions by the Fed.

In turn, variations in the quantity of money caused by money multiplier volatility would cause the equilibrium interest rate to rise or fall, thereby inducing upward or downward shifts in the *LM* schedule. By targeting the nominal interest rate, however, the Fed can, just as in the case of money demand variations, keep such shifts in the *LM* schedule from occurring. Therefore, using the nominal interest rate as an intermediate target automatically offsets the real income effects of variations in the nominal quantity of money supplied. This permits the Fed to achieve its real income objective, given the position of the *IS* schedule.

In sum, the key advantage of nominal interest rate targeting is that it automatically offsets the real income effects of variability in the market for real money balances. By keeping the nominal interest rate at the target level, the Fed keeps the economy at an *IS-LM* equilibrium that is consistent with its ultimate objective for real income.

Furthermore, recall that the economy's aggregate demand schedule stems from *IS-LM* equilibrium. Therefore, by maintaining *IS-LM* equilibrium, interest rate targeting automatically stabilizes aggregate demand in the face of volatility in money demand or in the money multiplier. As we noted in our discussion of Figure 24-1, this implies that as long as aggregate supply is stable, interest rate targeting also may be consistent with a goal of minimizing inflation.

Disadvantages of Interest Rate Targeting A cliché among economists is that "there is no such thing as a free lunch." This statement is true for the use of the interest rate as an intermediate target just as it is true for everything else in life. If you have carefully followed our discussion up to this point, you surely noted that we maintained three assumptions throughout: The price level was constant, aggregate supply was fixed, and the *IS* schedule was not variable.

We shall take up the issue of aggregate supply variability and price level flexibility later on. For now, let's consider the issue of *IS* variability, because this is the most glaring disadvantage of using the interest rate as an intermediate target. To see this, consider Figure 24-5.

Figure 24-5 shows the effects of variability in the *IS* schedule, which could arise from changes in autonomous household consumption spending, autonomous investment, or government spending or taxation policies. As Figure 24-5 indicates, when the effective *LM* schedule is horizontal [as it is under interest rate targeting, at $LM(r_n^*)$], rightward or leftward shifts in the *IS* schedule (between IS_1 and IS_2) cause the largest possible variability in equilibrium real income, between points D and E. Consequently, equilibrium real income will vary between y_1 and y_2, rather than remaining at the Fed's objective y^*. This, in turn, will cause the economy's aggregate demand schedule to become more variable,

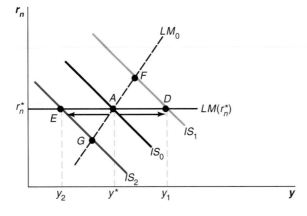

Figure 24-5

A Disadvantage of Interest Rate Targeting.   If variations in autonomous consumption, investment, government spending, or taxes cause fluctuations in the position of the economy's *IS* schedule, the result under interest rate targeting is the maximum possible volatility of equilibrium real income, between y_1 at point *D* and y_2 at point *E*. If the Fed did not target the interest rate, the *LM* schedule would be LM_0 instead, and there would be less variability in equilibrium real income, between point *F* and point *G*.

given that the level of real income determined by *IS-LM* equilibrium is variable at the fixed price level, P_0.

Also displayed in Figure 24-5 is a dashed *LM* schedule that has a typical positive shape. This is the shape the *LM* schedule would have if the Fed did not target the nominal interest rate. As Figure 24-5 indicates, if the *LM* schedule displayed its normal upward slope, equilibrium income would vary instead between points *F* and *G* when the *IS* schedule shifts to the right or left. *Hence, in the presence of* IS *variability the Fed could be better off if it did not use the nominal interest rate as an intermediate target.* Large variability in autonomous consumption, investment, government spending, and taxes, therefore, all would represent drawbacks to targeting the interest rate.

As noted above, the problem of *IS* variability is the most obvious disadvantage of nominal interest rate targeting. There are other possible problems, however. One that many monetarist economists have pointed out is that once the Fed begins targeting the interest rate, it may lose track of the original *purpose* in targeting the interest rate, which is to achieve ultimate objectives involving real income and prices. After a period of targeting the interest rate, Fed critics often complain, the Fed may forget that the interest rate is an *intermediate* target, treating it instead as if it were an ultimate objective.

A second, more technical, problem is that the Fed may not be able to keep the nominal interest rate fixed for an extended period of time. When the Fed conducts policy actions to keep the nominal interest rate constant for a long interval, it **pegs** the nominal interest rate. Economists are divided about whether or not a long-term interest rate peg is feasible. The reason is that, as we discussed in Chapter 7, the nominal interest rate is approximately equal to the real interest rate plus the expected rate of inflation. Many economists contend that the real rate of interest depends only on real factors and therefore cannot be influenced by the Fed in the long run. If so, trying to peg the nominal interest rate amounts to attempting to fix expectations of the future inflation rate at a particular level, which may not be feasible.

Economists are divided on this latter issue, however. Some point out that the Fed successfully pegged the nominal interest rate on Treasury securities for an extended period during and after World War II. Others argue that there is no theoretical reason that interest rate pegging should not be feasible, because the Fed can influence price expectations as needed through its interest rate pegging policies.

THE MONEY STOCK AS AN INTERMEDIATE TARGET

During most of the 1970s and part of the 1980s the Federal Reserve claimed to use monetary aggregates such as M1 and M2 as intermediate targets. As we shall discuss in the following chapter, the Fed pursued a variety of strategies in targeting the quantity of money during that period. Here we shall concentrate on the desirable and undesirable properties of using the quantity of money as an intermediate target of monetary policy.

IMPLEMENTING A MONEY STOCK TARGET

When the Fed uses the quantity of money as an intermediate target, it adjusts the position of the money supply schedule as needed to keep the nominal quantity of money at a targeted level, M^*. For a given level of prices, this keeps the supply schedule for real money balances from varying. (The price level, of course, can vary, but for now we shall continue to assume that the price level is fixed.)

Keeping the Quantity of Money on Target   For instance, as shown in panel (a) of Figure 24-6, under money stock targeting the Fed always offsets variations in the value of the money multiplier that cause the nominal quantity of money to change, say, from M^* to M_1 or from M^* to M_2. As depicted in panel (b), such variations would, in the absence of monetary targeting, cause the position of the LM schedule to vary between LM_1 and LM_2. By keeping the money stock at a target level M^*, however, the Fed would respond to variability in the money multiplier by keeping the LM schedule in the fixed position shown as $LM(M^*)$ in panel (b) of Figure 24-6.

Choosing the Money Stock Target   As in the case of interest rate targeting, when the Fed uses an intermediate monetary target, it selects the target to be consistent with its ultimate objectives. If this entails stabilizing real income near a target level y^*, then the Fed chooses its intermediate monetary target M^* to position the LM schedule at an IS-LM equilibrium at this real income objective, as depicted in Figure 24-7.

   Again, as when the Fed uses an interest rate target, to choose the best value of an intermediate monetary target the Fed would need to estimate the position of the IS schedule to be certain that IS and LM would intersect at an equilibrium level of real income equal to y^*. In contrast to interest rate targeting, however, when the Fed uses an intermediate money stock target, it also must take into account factors that affect the LM schedule, so that it can be certain to place the LM schedule in the correct position [such as $LM(M^*)$ in Figure 24-7]. This, in turn, would stabilize aggregate demand for the economy.

ADVANTAGES AND DISADVANTAGES OF A MONEY STOCK TARGET

Because the Fed must take into account all factors that affect the position and shape of the LM schedule when it uses the quantity of money as an intermediate variable, you

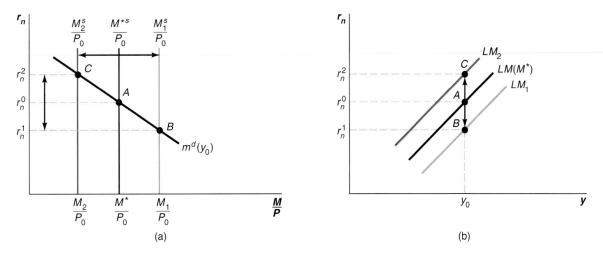

Figure 24-6
Implementing an Intermediate Monetary Target.   If the Fed targets the quantity of money
at a level M*, it does not allow variability in the quantity of money, between M_1 and M_2, which
would result from changes in the money multiplier, to cause the shifts in the money supply schedules that are shown in panel (a). It instead would take appropriate policy actions to keep the money
stock equal to M*. As shown in panel (b), in the absence of monetary targeting the position of the
LM schedule would vary between points B and C as a result of money multiplier variability. Under
monetary targeting, however, the Fed eliminates the effects of money multiplier variability on the
LM schedule and attempts to keep the LM schedule in the position shown by LM(M*).

might think that monetary targeting would be a less desirable policy strategy. This is not
necessarily the case, however. Monetary targeting has definite advantages, although it has
some clear disadvantages as well.

Advantages of Money Stock Targeting   The key advantage of money stock targeting
is that it deals with the disadvantage of interest rate targeting. You will recall that under
interest rate targeting, *IS* variability has its largest possible effects on equilibrium real
income. This problem of interest rate targeting is reduced, however, by targeting the
quantity of money, as Figure 24-8 indicates.

In the Fed conducts policy to keep the quantity of money equal to M*, then, as Figure
24-8 shows, the economy's *LM* schedule will be in the location depicted by *LM(M*)*. As
long as the Fed correctly estimates the position of the economy's *IS* schedule and chooses
the right monetary target, the equilibrium level of real income, determined at point *A*, will
be y*, the Fed's objective. Of course, the Fed's estimate of the position of the *IS* schedule
may, after the fact, turn out to be incorrect, and so there will be some variability of real
income, between points *B* and *C*.

If the Fed had targeted the interest rate, however, the economy's effective *LM* schedule
would have been the dashed, horizontal schedule $LM(r_n^*)$ depicted in Figure 24-8. In this
case, real income would have varied between points *D* and *E,* entailing greater variability
of real income than the Fed instead may obtain by using the money stock as an intermediate
target.

We may conclude, then, that a key advantage the Fed may gain using an intermediate
monetary target is that this approach better shields equilibrium real income, and, hence,

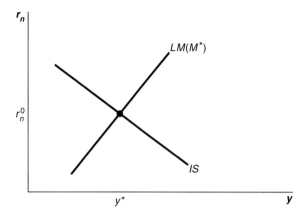

Figure 24-7
Choosing the Intermediate Monetary Target.   To select its monetary target, the Fed must estimate the position of the economy's *IS* schedule. Taking into account its understanding of how the quantity of money affects the economy's *LM* schedule, the Fed would then choose the target quantity *M** that is consistent with its ultimate real income target *y**.

aggregate demand, from the effects of variability of the economy's *IS* schedule. This is most clearly an advantage as the *LM* schedule becomes more steeply sloped. In fact, as shown in Figure 24-9, money stock targeting *completely* shields equilibrium real income from variability in response to *IS* volatility if the *LM* schedule is *vertical.*

Recall from Chapter 21 that the *LM* schedule is vertical, as depicted in Figure 24-9, if the public's demand for real money balances is completely interest inelastic. If this is the

Figure 24-8
An Advantage of Monetary Targeting.   The Fed gains a key advantage of monetary targeting, as compared with interest rate targeting, when the economy's *IS* schedule is variable. Such variabil- ity in the *IS* schedule, as shown by shifts between IS_1 and IS_2, does cause variability in real income under monetary targeting, from y_1 at point B to y_2 at point C. Nevertheless, the variability in real income is much lower than if the Fed were to target the nominal interest rate, effectively making the *LM* schedule horizontal at $LM(r_n^*)$; under interest rate targeting, real income would have varied between the levels associated with points D and E instead.

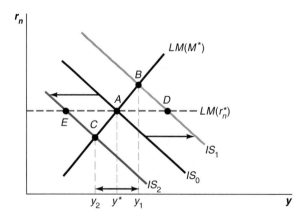

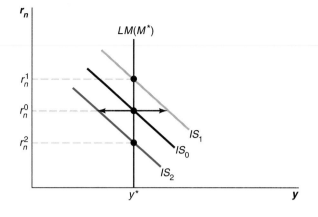

Figure 24-9
Intermediate Monetary Targeting with a Vertical *LM* Schedule.   If the public's demand for real money balances is completely interest inelastic, then volatility in the position of the economy's *IS* schedule has no effect on real income. As long as the Fed chooses the correct target level for the money stock, *M**, it can ensure that equilibrium real income will remain at its target level, *y**.

case, then *IS* variability causes the equilibrium interest rate to vary, as shown in Figure 24-9 by variation between the equilibrium interest rates of r_n^1 and r_n^2, but equilibrium real income will remain at the Fed's ultimate objective *y**. In this special case, shifts in the *IS* schedule resulting from changes in autonomous consumption, investment, and government spending and taxes have no effect on the level of real income; intermediate monetary targeting fully insulates real income from *IS* volatility.

Not surprisingly, economists with a monetarist bent favor using the quantity of money as an intermediate target, because they feel that the quantity of money is the primary determinant of changes in real income in the short run and of prices in the long run (see Chapter 21). According to monetarist economists, therefore, a further advantage the Fed can gain from targeting the quantity of money is that it can stabilize the level of prices as well as the equilibrium level of real income.

Disadvantages of Monetary Targeting   Two important drawbacks, however, are associated with using the quantity of money as an intermediate target. One of these is the potential difficulty in measuring money. As we discussed in Chapter 3, a variety of financial innovations in years past have made it difficult for economists to reach agreement about exactly what financial assets should be included in measures of money. Those who adopt the *transactions approach* to measuring money emphasize money's role as a medium of exchange. In contrast, those who subscribe to the *liquidity approach* prefer to focus on money's role as a financial asset that functions as a store of value.

Disagreements about the best way to measure money can significantly complicate the procedure of using the quantity of money as an intermediate target. The natural solution, it would seem, would be to choose the approach to measuring money that is most consistent with the Fed's ultimate objectives. The problem, however, has been that different measures of the quantity of money have been most consistent with the Fed's ultimate policy goals at different times. For instance, for some time periods M1 seems to best relate to real income and the level of prices, while at others M2 appears to be most consistent with these two economic variables. During some intervals neither measure has done very well, and others, such as divisia index measures of money (see Chapter 3), seemed to be more closely related to the Fed's ultimate goals.

Aside from the money measurement problem, a disadvantage of monetary targeting is that it exposes real income and aggregate demand to variability arising from volatility in the public's demand for real money balances. To see this, consider Figure 24-10. Panel (a) of Figure 24-10 shows the effects of variability in the demand for real money balances, between m_1^d and m_2^d, caused, perhaps, by changes in household spending patterns or in households' tastes and preferences. If the Fed keeps the quantity of money at its target level M^* even as the demand for real balances rises or falls, then the equilibrium interest rate will vary between r_n^1 and r_n^2.

This, in turn, will cause the economy's LM schedule to vary between $LM_1(M^*)$ and $LM_2(M^*)$, as depicted in panel (b) of Figure 24-10. As a result, equilibrium real income will vary between y_1 and y_2, even though the Fed keeps the quantity of money constant at the target level M^*. By targeting the quantity of money, the Fed will not achieve its ultimate real income objective, y^*.

Note that if the Fed had instead targeted the nominal interest rate, the Fed would have automatically offset the effects of money demand variability. We showed this, as you will recall, in Figure 24-2. Hence, we may conclude that, on the one hand, money demand variability is a disadvantage of intermediate monetary targeting that can be dealt with by interest rate targeting. On the other hand, as we just discussed above, IS variability is a disadvantage of interest rate targeting that intermediate monetary targeting can address.

Hence, determining which of the two targeting approaches—interest rate targeting or money stock targeting—to follow hinges on the variability of money demand as compared with the variability of the IS schedule. Furthermore, deciding which of these two inter-

Figure 24-10
A Disadvantage of Monetary Targeting. If the Fed targets the quantity of money at M^*, then variations in the public's demand for real money balances between points B and C result in changes in the nominal interest rate, as shown in panel (a). Such interest rate volatility, in turn, is reflected by changes in the position of the LM schedule between points B and C in panel (b), even though the Fed achieves its intermediate monetary target M^*. Consequently, equilibrium real income can vary around the Fed's ultimate objective, between y_1 and y_2.

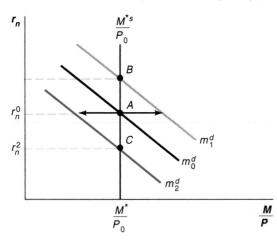

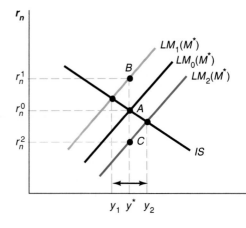

(a)   (b)

mediate targets is more appropriate also depends on the slopes of the schedules. As we noted earlier, monetary targeting better offsets the effects of *IS* volatility when the demand for money is more interest inelastic.

In comparing the two intermediate targeting procedures, we may now summarize the following conclusions:[1]

1. Interest rate targeting is preferable to money stock targeting if money demand is very volatile, if the demand for real money balances is more interest elastic, and if there is relatively little variability in the economy's *IS* schedule.

2. Money stock targeting is preferable to interest rate targeting if the position of the *IS* schedule is very volatile, if the demand for real money balances is less interest elastic, and if there is relatively little variability in the public's demand for real money balances.

In general, of course, we might expect that there will be some variability in both the *IS* schedule and the money demand schedule. Furthermore, although empirical evidence indicates that the demand for money is relatively interest inelastic, we would not expect the *LM* schedule to be either vertical or horizontal. Determining which variable to use as an intermediate target—the interest rate versus the quantity of money—consequently can be a tricky undertaking.

NOMINAL INCOME AS AN INTERMEDIATE TARGET

There is a disadvantage for both interest rate targeting and monetary targeting that we have avoided in our discussion to this point. Throughout our discussion, we have maintained the simplifying assumptions that the economy's aggregate supply schedule is stable and that prices are fixed. Of course, we know that these assumptions are unrealistic. While interest rate targeting or monetary targeting may stabilize aggregate demand, they do nothing to offset automatically real income and price level changes that can occur because of variability in the aggregate supply schedule.

To see this, consider Figure 24-11. Suppose that the Fed selects one of the two policy approaches we have discussed so far. Furthermore, suppose that it chooses one that works so well that it *completely* stabilizes the aggregate demand schedule by ensuring that, for a given level of prices, the economy stays at the same *IS-LM* equilibrium level of real income, y^*.

In the absence of aggregate supply variability, such an outcome would lead to no variability of real income relative to y^* and to no inflation; the economy would remain at point *A* in Figure 24-11, given our assumption that the Fed's policy choice makes aggregate demand perfectly stable. Aggregate supply variability, however, changes the story considerably. If there is considerable variation in the position of the aggregate supply schedule, as shown by variation between y_1^s and y_2^s, then the equilibrium level of real income will continue to vary, between y_1 and y_2, as will the economy's price level, between P_1 and P_2, as depicted in Figure 24-11. This will occur even though the Fed may have perfectly stabilized aggregate demand.

Hence, the potential problem of aggregate supply variability is a weakness that both approaches share. It can be an important weakness. From time to time, a variety of events

---

[1] These results were first derived by William Poole, ''Optimal Choice of Monetary Policy Intruments in a Simple Stochastic Macro Model,'' *Quarterly Journal of Economics,* 84 (2, May 1970), pp. 197–216.

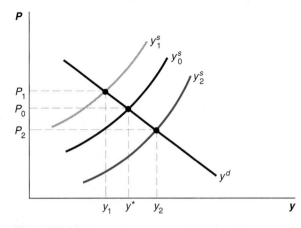

Figure 24-11

The Problem of Variability in Aggregate Supply.   When the Fed uses financial intermediate targets such as the nominal interest rate or the quantity of money, it typically does so to stabilize aggregate demand automatically. If aggregate supply is volatile, this is not necessarily the optimal policy strategy, however. Changes in the position of the economy's aggregate supply schedule can induce variability both in real output and in the level of prices.

can cause the economy's aggregate supply schedule to shift. Examples are variations in world oil prices, wars, famines, widespread union strikes, or other events that change the prices or availability of important resources used by firms in producing goods and services. Therefore, while interest rate targeting or money stock targeting may enable the Fed to stabilize aggregate demand, either of these approaches faces a problem when aggregate supply variability occurs.

Because the position of the economy's aggregate supply schedule does vary from time to time, and sometimes by large amounts, many economists have argued that the Fed should adopt a broader approach, rather than just trying to stabilize aggregate demand. The strategy that some have recommended is nominal income targeting. Under this proposed monetary policy strategy, the Fed would treat nominal national income, $Y = P \times y$, as its intermediate target.

IMPLEMENTING NOMINAL INCOME TARGETING

To see how the Fed would implement a nominal income target, we use the explanation provided in a 1989 article in the Federal Reserve Bank of St. Louis *Review* by Dennis Jansen of Texas A&M University and Michael Bradley of George Washington University.[2] If the Fed were to target nominal national income, it would vary its policy instruments as needed to keep nominal income constant at a target level Y^*. This means that it would conduct policy to ensure that $P \times y = Y^*$ always holds. Suppose, for example, that the Fed's goal was to keep nominal national income at a target level of, say, $Y^* = \$4,000$ billion; then a variety of price level–real income combinations would be consistent with this target. Examples are $P_0 = 4$, $y_0 = 1,000$; $P_1 = 5$, $y_1 = 800$; and $P_2 = 8$, $y_2 = 500$.

---

[2] Michael D. Bradley and Dennis W. Jansen, "Understanding Nominal GNP Targeting," Federal Reserve Bank of St. Louis *Review,* 71 (6, November/December 1989), pp. 31–40.

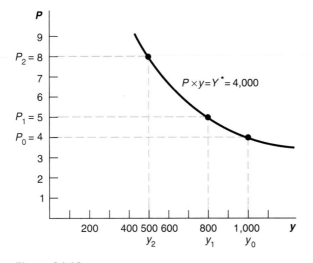

Figure 24-12
Targeting Nominal Income.   If the Fed has an intermediate nominal income target of $Y^* = 4,000$, this means that it tries to ensure that the economy reaches an equilibrium at a price level–real output combination for which $P \times y = Y^* = 4,000$. The locus of all such combinations is a schedule called a rectangular hyperbola.

All these and an infinite number of other possible price level–real income combinations would lie along the schedule depicted in Figure 24-12 that is labeled $P \times y = Y^*$. This schedule, like the classical aggregate demand schedule we discussed in Chapter 18, is a *rectangular hyperbola.*

Now consider Figure 24-13, which shows an aggregate demand–aggregate supply equilibrium at point A at the price level $P_0 = 4$ and the level of real output $y_0 = 1,000$. In addition, the natural, full-information level of output in Figure 24-13 is $y^* = 1,000$, which implies that the economy's market for real output is in equilibrium at the natural output level, along the long-run aggregate supply schedule y_{LR}^s, at point A. In addition, this equilibrium point A lies along the $P \times y = Y^*$ schedule we derived in Figure 24-12. Hence, equilibrium nominal income at the equilibrium point A is $Y_0 = P_0 \times y_0 = 4 \times 1,000 = 4,000$, which is equal to Y^*, the Fed's intermediate nominal income target.

Under nominal national income targeting, whenever there is a shift in aggregate demand or in aggregate supply as a result of some external event, the Fed adjusts its policy instruments to vary the quantity of money and shift the aggregate demand schedule back to an aggregate demand–aggregate supply equilibrium that lies on the $P \times y = Y^*$ schedule. Let's consider a couple of examples of how this would work.

Targeting Nominal Income When Aggregate Demand Falls   Figure 24-14 displays the response of the Fed to a fall in aggregate demand under nominal income targeting. Initially, the economy's aggregate demand schedule is at the position y_0^d. After a fall in aggregate demand resulting, say, from a reduction in autonomous consumption, the aggregate demand schedule shifts leftward to y_1^d. The equilibrium price level falls to $P' = 2$, and equilibrium real income falls to $y' = 800$.

In the long run, we can predict that the price expectations of workers and firms would fall, causing aggregate supply to shift downward and to the right until a new long-run equilibrium was reached along the vertical y_{LR}^s schedule. Under nominal income targeting,

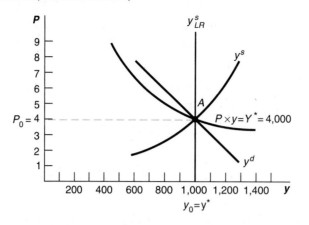

Figure 24-13
Fed Achievement of a Nominal Income Target.   If the Fed is able to ensure that the economy is in a long-run equilibrium at its target level for nominal income, $P \times y = Y^* = 4,000$, then the economy's aggregate demand, aggregate supply, and long-run aggregate supply schedules all intersect on the $P \times y = Y^*$ schedule. Hence, the equilibrium price level, $P_0 = 4$, times the equilibrium and natural level of output $y_0 = y^* = 1,000$, is equal to $4,000 = Y^*$, and the Fed achieves its intermediate nominal income target.

however, the Fed would not wait around for such long-run adjustments to occur. Instead, by targeting nominal income it would automatically increase the quantity of money and thereby shift the aggregate demand schedule back to the right so that the economy would again find itself on the $P \times y = Y^*$ schedule. Hence, by conducting monetary policy to

Figure 24-14
Achieving a Nominal Income Target When Aggregate Demand Declines.   If there is a fall in aggregate demand, from y_0^d to y_1^d, in the short run the equilibrium real output level falls to y' = 800, and the equilibrium price level falls to $P' = 2$. Therefore, equilibrium nominal income would fall toward $P' \times y' = 1,600$. To keep nominal income from falling below $Y^* = 4,000$, however, the Fed would need to increase aggregate demand. Indeed, it would reposition the aggregate demand schedule at its original location, y_0^d. Hence, nominal income targeting entails Fed stabilization of aggregate demand when the aggregate demand schedule tends to vary in its position.

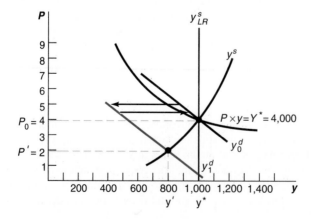

keep nominal income at the intermediate target level of $Y^* = 4,000$, the Fed automatically would stabilize aggregate demand, just as would be true if it optimally chose interest rate targeting or monetary targeting.

Targeting Nominal Income When Aggregate Supply Falls   Now consider Figure 24-15, which depicts the effects of a reduction in aggregate supply. An event such as a worldwide increase in oil prices, a war, or an agricultural famine would cause the natural, full-information level of output for the economy to fall, as shown by the reduction in the natural output level from $y^* = 1,000$ to $y^{*\prime} = 800$. Both the long-run and short-run aggregate supply schedules would shift leftward by this amount, as shown in Figure 24-15. Barring a change in the position of the aggregate demand schedule, the equilibrium price level would rise from $P_0 = 4$ to $P' = 7$ at point B in Figure 24-15. Equilibrium real income would fall to $y' = y^{*\prime} = 800$. Consequently, the economy's level of nominal income would rise to $Y' = P' \times y' = 7 \times 800 = 5,600$; even though real income would have fallen, the price level would have risen enough that nominal income would *rise* from the initial level $Y_0 = P_0 \times y_0 = 4 \times 1,000 = 4,000$.

Under nominal income targeting, however, the Fed would not allow nominal national income to rise. An increase in nominal income would indicate to the Fed that it should reduce aggregate demand to keep the economy on the $P \times y = Y^*$ schedule in Figure 24-15. As a result of such an action by the Fed, a new equilibrium point would be reached on the $P \times y = Y^*$ schedule at point C. Real income would still fall from $y_0 = y^* = 1,000$ to $y' = y^{*\prime} = 800$, because the Fed's aggregate demand policies can do nothing to improve the productive abilities of workers and firms. Note, however, that the price level at point C, the equilibrium point that would arise if the Fed targets nominal income,

Figure 24-15
Achieving a Nominal Income Target When Aggregate Supply Declines.   If a rise in energy prices, a war, or a famine causes the economy's natural level of output to fall from $y^* = 1,000$ to $y^{*\prime} = 800$, then the economy's aggregate supply and long-run aggregate supply schedules shift leftward. If the Fed were to stabilize aggregate demand at $y^d(M_0)$, the result would also be an eventual long-run price level increase from $P_0 = 4$ to $P' = 7$, and equilibrium nominal income would tend to rise from $Y^* = 4,000$ to $Y' = P' \times y' = 7 \times 800 = 5,600$. To keep nominal income from rising, however, the Fed would, under nominal income targeting, respond automatically by reducing aggregate demand. As a result, the equilibrium price level would rise by much less, to $P_1 = 5$.

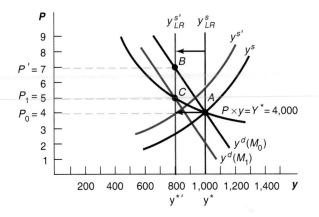

would be equal to $P_1 = 5$, rather than $P' = 7$ at point B, the equilibrium point that would occur if the Fed kept aggregate demand stable. Thus, nominal income targeting leads to less inflation than would arise if the Fed simply stabilized aggregate demand through some alternative intermediate targeting procedure.

ADVANTAGES AND DISADVANTAGES OF NOMINAL INCOME TARGETING

Like other monetary policy strategies, nominal income targeting has both advantages and disadvantages. Let's take a look at each in turn.

Advantages of Nominal Income Targeting   The key advantage of nominal income targeting is shown by the example depicted in Figure 24-15. In the face of a fall in aggregate supply, interest rate targeting and monetary targeting typically would entail stabilizing aggregate demand. As a result, equilibrium real output would fall, and the equilibrium price level would rise. Under nominal income targeting, in contrast, the Fed would respond to a fall in aggregate supply by reducing aggregate demand as well. Real output would fall by the same amount as if the Fed had simply stabilized aggregate demand, but the price level would rise by a smaller amount as a result of the Fed's action. The economy would still be worse off than it was before the aggregate supply reduction, but it would be better off than if the Fed had failed to target nominal income.

In the face of changes in aggregate demand, nominal income targeting is no better or worse than would typically be the case under other intermediate targeting strategies. To keep nominal income at its target level, the Fed would stabilize aggregate demand at its initial level. This would be the same basic outcome that would arise under successful interest rate targeting or monetary targeting. Hence, the Fed would not ''give up anything'' by using nominal income as an intermediate target rather than the interest rate or the money stock.

Disadvantages of Nominal Income Targeting   It is the ability of nominal income targeting to handle aggregate supply variability better than other alternative intermediate targeting strategies that has recently made it so attractive to many economists inside and outside the Fed. This does not mean that nominal income targeting is flawless, however.

First, recall that a key reason to use an intermediate target rather than aiming monetary policy actions directly at the Fed's ultimate objectives is that data on the intermediate target variable should be available in a more timely manner than data on prices and real output. Indeed, nominal income data generally are available to the Fed at least once a month. Nevertheless, nominal income data are much less timely than information about the quantity of money, which typically is available on a weekly basis, and about interest rates, which usually are known day by day. Therefore, nominal income fails to satisfy as well as other possibilities the ''timeliness'' requirement for an intermediate target variable.

Second, to know how much to change the quantity of money to shift the aggregate demand schedule sufficiently to keep nominal income at its targeted level, the Fed needs to understand completely the linkages between money, aggregate demand, and nominal income. This means that nominal income targeting by the Fed would require a significant amount of information. Included among the needed information would be data on the shapes of the aggregate demand and supply schedules and on the amounts by which each may have shifted.

Both of these difficulties make nominal income less attractive as an intermediate target than it might otherwise appear in theory. This does not mean that the Fed has not or will not ever use a nominal income targeting strategy. What it does mean, however, is that the Fed would have to work hard to make such a strategy successful.

OTHER POSSIBLE INTERMEDIATE TARGETS

We have concentrated on interest rate, monetary, and nominal income targets only because they either have been used by the Fed in the past or have attracted the most attention of economists. There are a number of other possible intermediate targets for monetary policy, however, that some economists and policy makers have promoted. We shall consider the three of these that have been the most discussed in recent years.

TARGETING THE SPREAD BETWEEN LONG- AND SHORT-TERM INTEREST RATES

The argument in favor of using the **spread** between the interest rate on a long-term security and the interest rate on a short-term security is similar, though not identical, to the argument promoting the use of a single interest rate as an intermediate target. The basic idea, as under simple interest rate targeting, is for the Fed to attempt to determine a specific setting of interest rates that is consistent with its ultimate objectives. The distinction, however, is that if the Fed were to target a long-short interest rate spread, it would not care so much about the *levels* of either long- or short-term interest rates; rather, it would concern itself with the *difference* between the two.

The rationale for targeting the interest rate spread is that a variety of interest rates potentially influence real investment and aggregate desired expenditures. By targeting the spread, therefore, the Fed can focus on more than just one interest rate. In addition, as you know from our discussion of the *yield curve* in Chapter 7, the difference between interest rates on financial instruments with differing terms to maturity depends largely on expectations about future short-term interest rates. Therefore, proponents of spread targeting contend, if the Fed were to target on the spread between long-term and short-term interest rates, it implicitly would be conducting monetary policy actions that would keep expectations of interest rates from varying.

You also know, of course, from our discussion of real and nominal interest rates in Chapter 7, that the nominal interest rate is approximately equal to the real interest rate plus the expected rate of inflation. According to those who favor spread targeting, it follows that if the Fed can pin down interest rate expectations through spread targeting, it also can, in the process, stabilize inflation expectations. This, in turn, would assist the Fed in following a low-inflation policy that is consistent with real output stability.

Several potential pitfalls, however, are associated with targeting the spread between long- and short-term interest rates. One of these is that economists do not fully understand the relationship between monetary policy actions and the yield curve. As we discussed in Chapter 21, a contractionary monetary policy action can have both a *liquidity effect* and a *real balance effect* on interest rates. The liquidity effect of a monetary tightening is an increase in nominal interest rates. In contrast, if a monetary tightening causes inflation expectations to fall, the actual price level can fall as a result of the increase in aggregate supply that results, causing a real balance effect that implies an offsetting *reduction* in nominal interest rates. Disentangling these potentially offsetting effects on *both* short-term and long-term interest rates is a complex undertaking that has generated little agreement among economists.

Furthermore, the relationship between the long-short rate spread on economic activity presently is unclear. Robert Laurent of the Federal Reserve Bank of Chicago has documented strong predictive power of the spread for economic activity over some periods, but the long-term prospects for a continued strong relationship between the spread and ultimate Fed objectives remain uncertain. This is an ongoing agenda of research for numerous economists.

TARGETING COMMODITY PRICES

Another intermediate targeting proposal that has gained attention in recent years is commodity price targeting. Commodity prices are the dollar prices of specific goods, such as gold, silver, copper, and so on. Most proposals for using commodity prices as indicators or targets of monetary policy would entail focusing on an *index* of prices for a "basket" (weighted bundle) of commodities. Some proposals, however, single out the price of a single commodity—gold—as a potential target.

Under a true commodity price targeting strategy for monetary policy, the Fed would vary its instruments of monetary policy as needed to keep an index of commodity prices within some fixed range thought to be consistent with the Fed's ultimate policy objectives. In a sense, such a scheme would not be unlike a gold standard, in which the level of prices of goods and services would vary inversely with the price of gold. If the Fed were to target an index of commodity prices, the general level of prices instead would tend to vary inversely with the index of commodity prices.

As you might guess, the idea behind commodity price targeting is to try to obtain some of the price stability that can be gained from a commodity standard, such as a gold standard. By tying monetary policy to an *index* of commodities, however, a commodity price targeting procedure would not expose the economy's level of prices to potential variations in the price of a single commodity. Indeed, if the Fed kept the commodity price index stable, then the general price level likely would be stable, according to proponents of this monetary policy strategy.

The problems associated with commodity price targeting are, however, similar to those that would arise in targeting the spread between long- and short-term interest rates. The link between monetary policy instruments and commodity prices is uncertain and potentially weak, and the relationship between commodity prices and ultimate economic objectives is unclear.

Because of these problems, much of the immediate focus that economists have placed on commodity prices is their role as a potential **policy indicator.** As such, movements in commodity prices might provide the Fed with valuable information concerning possible future movements in the general level of prices of goods and services. This is a far cry from using this variable as a *target*, however. At present it seems unlikely that commodity prices will be a full-fledged intermediate target anytime soon.

TARGETING CREDIT AGGREGATES

There are a variety of measures of credit—that is, the amount of loans extended in the economy. Two of these, however, have attracted most attention. One is *bank credit,* which is the total amount of lending solely by depository institutions. Another is *total credit,* or the amount of total lending in the economy as a whole.

There are several reasons that promoters of credit targeting have offered for the use of credit measures as intermediate targets. One is that, as we learned in Chapters 14 and 17, the quantity of credit, and in particular bank credit, responds to changes in Fed policy instruments through a multiplier process just as the quantity of money does. In addition, it is possible to envision the quantity of credit influencing economic activity through a variety of channels. After all, a large amount of private and public consumption and investment is financed through extensions of credit.

On the one hand, some economists also question the wisdom of focusing on a single intermediate target, such as the quantity of money. They contend that using more than one intermediate target would be preferable. These economists promote using *both* money and credit aggregates as intermediate targets, placing different weights on the two in the monetary policy process.

On the other hand, other economists have argued that the relation between the quantity of money and other ultimate Fed objectives has been highly variable, if not poor, in recent years. This group of credit targeting proponents argues in favor of scrapping monetary or interest rate targeting entirely and using a credit aggregate as the single intermediate target.

Some support for this latter view was provided in the 1970s and early 1980s by evidence provided by Harvard economist Benjamin Friedman and others that credit aggregates were more closely related to price and output movements in the 1970s and early 1980s than other variables such as monetary aggregates. Further support was provided by studies by Princeton economist Ben Bernanke and others that showed a strong relationship between bank credit and the Great Depression.

The problem, however, was that Friedman and others tended to promote the use of broad credit aggregates, while the work of Bernanke and still others indicated that a narrower aggregate such as bank credit would be a better intermediate policy target. An additional, and more telling, problem occurred in the 1980s: The relationship between credit aggregates and other measures of economic activity broke down, just as occurred with respect to most monetary aggregates during the same period. This left proponents of credit aggregates in the same boat as those who had argued in favor of monetary targeting—and has spelled a decline, though not a complete end, of the interest in credit targeting in recent years.

As you can see, there are a variety of potential intermediate targets for monetary policy. In recent years the Fed certainly has focused on interest rates and the quantity of money, and some believe it may have used nominal income targeting as well. This is a very interesting and evolving area in the economics of monetary policy. So is the topic to which we turn our attention in the next chapter. In this chapter, we have really just scratched the surface concerning real-world problems in monetary policy making. In the chapter that follows we consider the nitty-gritty difficulties of deciding how best to conduct monetary policy today, tomorrow, and the day after that. As we shall see, this issue rivals intermediate targeting as an area of concern for the Fed.

CHAPTER SUMMARY

1. Key ultimate objectives of monetary policy include maintaining high and stable real income and low and stable prices and inflation rates.

2. A key problem the Fed faces in its attempts to achieve many of its objectives is that data on many economic variables are available only with relatively long time lags. Furthermore, the relationship between the Fed's policy instruments and the ultimate policy objectives may be complicated, making it difficult for the Fed to aim its policy instruments directly at its final objectives. For this reason, the Fed may decide to use an intermediate target.

3. An intermediate target is an economic variable that the Fed seeks to control in hopes that it may thereby achieve its ultimate objectives. An intermediate target therefore needs to be con-

sistent with the Fed's ultimate objectives, and it needs to be measurable and controllable. Finally, to be most useful, data on an intermediate target variable should be available to the Fed on a timely basis.

4. One possible intermediate target is the nominal interest rate. An advantage of using the nominal interest rate as an intermediate monetary policy target is that doing so automatically stabilizes real income and aggregate demand if the demand for money or the money multiplier is volatile. A key disadvantage, however, is that targeting the nominal interest rate exposes real income and aggregate demand to the greatest possible variability resulting from variations in desired spending that shift the economy's *IS* schedule. In addition, the Fed may get so wrapped up in targeting the interest rate that the interest rate may become an ultimate objective. Finally, some economists contend that targeting the nominal interest rate is infeasible in the long run.

5. Using the money stock as an intermediate target has the advantage that it better stabilizes real income and aggregate demand, as compared with an interest rate target, when real expenditure volatility shifts the *IS* schedule rightward or leftward. A key disadvantage of monetary targeting, however, is that it exposes real income and aggregate demand to greater variability arising from money demand volatility, as compared with an interest rate targeting strategy. Economists also remain in disagreement about the best way to measure and control monetary aggregates, and the relationship between monetary aggregates and other economic variables has not been stable in recent years.

6. Interest rate targeting or monetary targeting primarily work by stabilizing the economy's aggregate demand schedule. This is the best policy strategy, however, only if the economy's aggregate supply schedule is not variable. Nominal income targeting by the Fed potentially could reduce inflation and inflation variability arising from such volatility in aggregate supply, as compared with other possible intermediate targeting strategies. Difficulties with nominal income targeting are that the linkage from monetary policy instruments to the level of nominal income may be complicated and that nominal income data are available to the Fed fairly infrequently, as compared with financial market data on interest rates and monetary aggregates.

7. Other possible intermediate targets are the spread between long- and short-term interest rates, commodity price indexes, and credit aggregates. Targeting the interest spread may be preferable to targeting a single interest rate, because doing so takes into account the effects of both long-term and short-term interest rates on economic activity. Nevertheless, the linkage from monetary policy to this spread through the economy's yield curve is not well understood. Targeting commodity price indexes promises some of the price stability that a commodity standard might yield if optimally operated plus the added stability of including more than one commodity in the standard. The strength of the linkage from monetary policy instruments to commodity prices also is uncertain, as is the relationship between commodity prices and real income and unemployment rates. Finally, targeting credit aggregates seems at least as appealing to some as targeting monetary aggregates, though this proposal suffers from similar problems—measurement difficulties and possible inconsistencies with ultimate objectives—as monetary targeting.

GLOSSARY

Effective *LM* schedule: The horizontal *LM* schedule that effectively is produced when the Fed uses an interest rate target.

Intermediate target: An economic variable whose value the Fed chooses to control only because it feels that doing so is consistent with its ultimate objectives.

Peg: To fix a rate, such as the nominal interest rate, at a certain level. When a rate is pegged, policy actions are implemented to keep that rate constant (pegged).

Policy indicator: An economic variable whose changes imply possible future movements in an ultimate objective of monetary policy.

Spread: The difference between the interest rate on a long-term security and the interest rate on a short-term security with (otherwise) similar characteristics.

Ultimate objectives: The end economic goals that the Fed seeks to achieve through its monetary policies.

SELF-TEST QUESTIONS

1. Summarize the contrasting views on how the Fed chooses its ultimate objectives. Why is it such a potentially difficult task to decide which of the potential ultimate objectives of Fed policy really are its true ultimate objectives?

2. Review the rationales for the Fed's use of an intermediate target. Which seems to you to be most important? Explain.

3. List the key criteria for choosing among alternative intermediate targets of monetary policy. Does any one of these seem to you to be more important than the others? Why?

4. Compare and contrast the advantages and disadvantages of interest rate targeting versus money stock targeting. Why is it that economists often view the Fed as stuck in a situation where there is no clearly "best" choice to make between these two approaches?

5. Explain why nominal income targeting deals with aggregate supply shocks better than monetary policy strategies that simply stabilize aggregate demand. Explain both verbally and through use of a diagram.

6. Briefly summarize other alternative intermediate targeting strategies we discussed in this chapter, along with their key advantages and disadvantages.

PROBLEMS

24-1. Assume that the Fed has determined that there is no variability in the economy's *IS* schedule. Both the money demand schedule and the money multiplier are highly variable, however, and are equally likely to rise or fall. Use appropriate diagrams to explain which policy—an interest rate target or a monetary target—is optimal in this situation.

24-2. The Fed's nominal income target is $Y^* = 2{,}000$. At present, the economy's market for real output is in equilibrium at the natural, full-information level of income, which is equal to $y^* = 500$. Furthermore, the Fed has achieved its nominal income target at this equilibrium point.

   a. What is the current equilibrium price level?

   b. The economy's aggregate demand schedule is given by the linear equation $y^d = (2 \times M) - (50 \times P)$, and the current quantity of money is $M = 350$. Show that your answer to part a is consistent with this equation and the data.

   c. A reduction in aggregate supply causes the economy's natural, full-information level of real output to fall to $y^{*\prime} = 400$. If the Fed keeps the money stock unchanged, what will the new *long-run* equilibrium price level be?

   d. Suppose that the Fed targets nominal income following the reduction in the natural level of real output to $y^{*\prime} = 400$. What price level is needed if the Fed is to obtain its nominal income target?

   e. Use your answer from part d to determine the needed quantity of money to be consistent with the Fed's nominal income target and the new natural output level $y^{*\prime} = 400$.

Should the Fed cause aggregate demand to rise or fall? Does the Fed thereby add to or subtract from the long-run inflationary effect of the aggregate supply reduction?

SELECTED REFERENCES

Benavie, Arthur, and Richard T. Froyen, "Price Level Determinacy and Nominal Interest Rate Pegging," *Oxford Economic Papers,* 40 (4, December 1988), pp. 634–645.

Bernanke, Ben S., "Nonmonetary Effects of the Financial Crisis in the Propagation of the Great Depression," *American Economic Review,* 73 (3, June 1983), pp. 257–276.

Bradley, Michael D., and Dennis W. Jansen, "Understanding Nominal GNP Targeting," Federal Reserve Bank of St. Louis *Review,* 71 (6, November/December 1989), pp. 31–40.

Cacy, J. A., "The Choice of a Monetary Policy Instrument," *Issues in Monetary Policy* (Kansas City: Federal Reserve Bank of Kansas City, 1980), pp. 30–47.

Cover, James P., and David P. Schutte, "The Stability of Money-Supply Policies That Peg the Rate of Interest," *Southern Economic Journal,* 57 (2, October 1990), pp. 330–339.

Federal Reserve Bank of New York, *Intermediate Targets and Indicators for Monetary Policy: A Critical Survey* (New York, 1990).

Fischer, Stanley, "Toward an Understanding of the Costs of Inflation: II," in *Indexing, Inflation, and Economic Policy,* ed. Stanley Fischer (Cambridge, Mass.: MIT Press, 1986), pp. 35–69.

———, and Franco Modigliani, "Toward an Understanding of the Real Effects and Costs of Inflation," in *Indexing, Inflation, and Economic Policy,* ed. Stanley Fischer (Cambridge, Mass.: MIT Press, 1986), pp. 7–33.

Friedman, Benjamin, "The Role of Money and Credit in Macroeconomic Analysis," in *Macroeconomics, Prices, and Quantities: Essays in Honor of Arthur M. Okun,* ed. James Tobin (Washington, D.C.: Brookings Institution, 1983), pp. 161–199.

———, "Targets, Instruments, and Indicators of Monetary Policy," *Journal of Monetary Economics,* 1 (2, October 1975), pp. 443–473.

Froyen, Richard T., *Macroeconomics: Theories and Policies,* 3d ed. (New York: Macmillan, 1990).

Furlong, Frederick T., "Commodity Prices as a Guide for Monetary Policy," Federal Reserve Bank of San Francisco *Economic Review* (1, Winter 1989), pp. 21–38.

Garner, C. Alan, "Commodity Prices: Policy Target or Information Variable?" *Journal of Money, Credit, and Banking,* 21 (4, November 1989), pp. 508–514.

Kahn, George A., "Nominal GNP: An Anchor for Monetary Policy?" Federal Reserve Bank of Kansas City *Economic Review,* 73 (9, November 1988), pp. 18–35.

Laurent, Robert D., "An Interest Rate-Based Indicator of Monetary Policy," Federal Reserve Bank of Chicago *Economic Perspectives,* 12 (1, January/February 1988), pp. 3–14.

———, "Testing the Spread," Federal Reserve Bank of Chicago *Economic Perspectives,* 13 (4, July/August 1989), pp. 22–34.

McCallum, Bennet T., "Some Issues Concerning Interest Rate Pegging, Price Level Determinacy, and the Real Bills Doctrine," *Journal of Monetary Economics,* 17 (1, January 1986), pp. 135–160.

Poole, William, "Optimal Choice of Monetary Policy Intruments in a Simple Stochastic Macro Model," *Quarterly Journal of Economics,* 84 (2, May 1970), pp. 197–216.

Monetary Policy Implementation and Federal Reserve Operating Procedures

CHAPTER PREVIEW

1. What are the two components of the total demand for reserves by depository institutions?

2. What are the two components of the total supply of reserves by the Fed?

3. How is the equilibrium federal funds rate determined?

4. What are alternative Federal Reserve operating procedures for monetary policy?

   How do they work, and how can we evaluate the relative success of alternative operating procedures?

5. What different operating procedures has the Fed used in the past? When did it use them, and why has it switched operating procedures several times?

6. What is the Fed's current operating procedure?

$\mathbf{A}$s we discussed in the last chapter, there are several ultimate targets of monetary policy. Whatever broad policy strategies and targets the Fed may choose to pursue, however, it faces yet another policy problem. This concerns how to conduct monetary policy on a day-to-day basis, given its selections of intermediate targets and ultimate policy objectives. That is, the Fed must figure out how to *implement* the policy strategy that it elects to pursue. The manner in which the Fed actually executes its policy strategy from day to day is known as the Fed's monetary policy **operating procedure.** As we discussed in the previous chapter, intermediate targets must be consistent with the Fed's ultimate objectives. Likewise, its operating procedure must be consistent with both its intermediate and its ultimate policy targets, as we shall seek to make clear below.

In principle, the Fed could conduct monetary policy in a wide variety of ways. Typically, however, the Fed's primary means of conducting monetary policy is through purchases and sales of United States government securities, or *open-market operations.* Consequently, our discussion of Fed operating procedures largely will focus on how the Fed has conducted—and should conduct—open-market operations in an effort to achieve its objectives. Nevertheless, we shall also show that other instruments of policy—the discount window and reserve requirements—play important roles.

Recall from Chapters 14 and 17 that Federal Reserve open-market operations exert effects on the quantity of money through their effects on reserves in the banking system. As we shall emphasize below, you must understand the *market for bank reserves* before you can fully understand issues concerning choices among different Fed operating procedures. Therefore, we begin this chapter with the theory of the market for reserves held by banks. We then apply this long-standing theory, which has been developed over the years by many Federal Reserve economists, to the problem of Fed operating procedures. After you finish this chapter, you will be able to analyze Federal Reserve policy making using the same tools that an economist at the Fed would use.

THE MARKET FOR BANK RESERVES

The equilibrium quantity of reserves in the banking system is determined in the **market for bank reserves.** This is a nationwide market in which the Fed, as the nation's monetary authority, supplies reserves through open-market operations and via the discount window. Banks, in contrast, demand reserves to meet reserve requirements and to satisfy additional reserve needs they may have.

THE DEMAND FOR BANK RESERVES

Let's begin with the demand side of the market for bank reserves. As noted above, there are two separate components of the total demand for reserves by all depository institutions that participate in the nation's banking system.

Required Reserves   The largest component of the total demand for bank reserves is the *demand for required reserves.* Depository institutions are legally bound to hold reserves, based on the required reserve ratio established by the Fed. Hence, if the required reserve ratio is a fraction equal to d, and if the total quantity of transactions deposits in the banking system is a dollar amount equal to D, then the demand for required reserves by depository institutions, RR^d, is a fixed amount, given by

$$RR^d = d \times D \qquad \text{(25-1)}$$

For example, if the required reserve ratio is $d = 0.10$, and if the total quantity of transactions deposits in the banking system is $D = \$120$ billion, then $RR^d = 0.10 \times \$120$ billion $= \$12$ billion; depository institutions desire to hold $12 billion in reserves to meet their legal reserve requirements.

Excess Reserves   As we discussed in Chapter 14, however, many depository institutions typically hold some excess reserves as *prudential reserves.* Thus, excess reserves effectively ensure a depository institution against the possibility that it may experience unanticipated withdrawals by its customers or that it may need the reserves to honor other customer agreements, such as loan commitments (see Chapter 6).

Depository institutions earn no interest on excess reserves that they hold in their vaults or at a Federal Reserve bank. This means that, by holding excess reserves, depository institutions incur an *opportunity cost:* They could lend out those reserves and earn interest income.

The most liquid of all loans that a depository institution might make would be a 1-day loan. Such a loan would be the most attractive alternative to holding excess reserves, because after a 1-day loan matures, the reserves again would be available to cover unexpected contingencies. For depository institutions, the most important 1-day-loan market is the *federal funds market.* Recall that the federal funds market is a market for interbank loans, in which some depository institutions lend to others. Typically the lending arrangements entail maturities of 1 day, although some federal funds loans have longer maturities.

The nominal interest rate on federal funds loans is the *federal funds rate,* which we shall denote r_f. Because r_f is the rate that depository institutions could earn on 1-day loans of their excess reserves to other depository institutions in need of reserves, this rate is the best measure of the opportunity cost of excess reserves.

The Demand for Excess Reserves   Let's think about what would happen if the federal funds rate initially were equal to 6 percent but then rose to 7 percent. At the initial federal funds rate of 6 percent, an individual depository institution, say, bank 1, might desire to hold, say, $25 million in excess reserves. If the federal funds rate rises to 7 percent, however, the opportunity cost to bank 1 of holding excess reserves would rise. For this depository institution, the rise in the federal funds rate would induce it, therefore, to *reduce* its holdings of excess reserves. Bank 1 would do so by lending some of its excess reserves to other depository institutions in the federal funds market. As a result, bank 1's excess reserves might fall to, say, $15 million; that is, it is induced by the rise in the federal funds rate to lend out $10 million more as federal funds loans to other depository institutions.

Figure 25-1 illustrates the effects just discussed for bank 1. A rise in the federal funds rate from $r_f^0 = 0.06$ to $r_f^1 = 0.07$ causes bank 1's excess reserve holdings to fall from $25 million to $15 million. These two federal funds rate–excess reserve combinations, therefore, lie on bank 1's *excess reserves demand schedule,* which slopes downward in the diagram.

Figure 25-1

The Total Demand for Excess Reserves in the Banking System.   To the far left of the diagram is bank 1's demand schedule for excess reserves; when the federal funds rate rises from $r_f = 0.06$ to $r_f = 0.07$, bank 1 reduces its holdings of excess reserves from $25 million to $15 million. Also depicted is the demand for excess reserves by bank 2; when the federal funds rate rises from $r_f^0 = 0.06$ to $r_f^1 = 0.07$, the rise in the opportunity cost of excess reserve holdings induces bank 2 to decrease its excess reserve holdings from $75 million to $35 million. The third schedule from the left is the horizontal summation of the excess reserve demand schedules of bank 1 and bank 2. Finally, adding the quantities of excess reserves demanded by all other banks ($7,900 million if the federal funds rate is equal to $r_f^0 = 0.06$ and $5,950 million if the federal funds rate rises to $r_f^1 = 0.07$) yields the total demand for excess reserves by all banks, ER^d, which is the schedule on the far right.

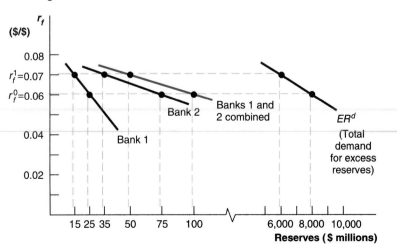

Likewise, other depository institutions that hold excess reserves, such as bank 2, would be induced to hold fewer excess reserves when the federal funds rate increases. As shown also in Figure 25-1, bank 2 responds to the rise in the federal funds rate from $r_f^0 = 0.06$ to $r_f^1 = 0.07$ by reducing its own excess reserves from \$75 million to \$35 million.

We may sum the quantities of excess reserves demanded by these two banks at each interest rate. At the federal funds rate $r_f^0 = 0.06$, the total quantity of excess reserves demanded by banks 1 and 2 is equal to \$100 million = \$25 million + \$75 million; at the higher federal funds rate $r_f^1 = 0.07$, the total quantity of excess reserves the two banks wish to hold is equal to \$50 million = \$15 million + \$35 million. Hence, we may trace out a combined excess reserves demand schedule for the two banks.

Finally, we may add to this latter excess reserves demand schedule the excess reserve demand schedules for all other depository institutions that may wish to hold excess reserves. If the total quantity of excess reserves that all depository institutions other than bank 1 and bank 2 wish to hold when $r_f^0 = 0.06$ is equal to \$7,900 million, then the total quantity of excess reserves that all institutions desire to hold at this federal funds rate is equal to $ER_0 = \$100 \text{ million} + \$7,900 \text{ million} = \$8,000$ million, or \$8 billion. Likewise, if the total quantity of excess reserves that all depository institutions other than bank 1 and bank 2 wish to hold falls to \$5,950 million when the federal funds rate rises to $r_f^1 = 0.07$, then the total quantity of excess reserves held by all depository institutions falls to $ER_1 = \$50 \text{ million} + \$5,950 \text{ million} = \$6,000$ million, or \$6 billion.

The final schedule traced out in Figure 25-1 is the *total excess reserves demand schedule* for all depository institutions, or ER^d. The reason that ER^d slopes downward is that each depository institution that holds excess reserves views the federal funds rate as the opportunity cost of excess reserves. As this opportunity cost rises, all depository institutions reduce their desired holdings of excess reserves.

The Total Demand for Bank Reserves   The *total demand for bank reserves* is the sum of the total demand for required reserves by depository institutions and the total demand for excess reserves by these same institutions. Figure 25-2 shows the construction of the total demand schedule for bank reserves.

The excess reserves demand schedule, ER^d, is the same schedule we constructed in Figure 25-1. As before, when the federal funds rate rises from $r_f^0 = 0.06$ to $r_f^1 = 0.07$, depository institutions reduce their desired excess reserve holdings from $ER_0 = \$8$ billion to $ER_1 = \$6$ billion. A rise in the federal funds rate does not necessarily influence the deposits held at banks, however. (For instance, even though the average federal funds rate is published every day in the *Wall Street Journal,* do you change your deposit holdings at your bank every time it changes each day?) Therefore, the required reserves of banks are not directly responsive to such a change in the federal funds rate.

As in our discussion above, we suppose that the required reserve ratio is equal to $d = 0.10$ and that the quantity of transactions deposits subject to reserve requirements is equal to $D = \$120$ billion. It follows that the quantity of required reserves demanded at any given federal funds rate is equal to $RR_0 = d \times D = 0.10 \times \$120 \text{ billion} = \$12$ billion.

By definition, banks demand reserves to meet reserve requirements and to hold as excess, prudential, reserves. Therefore, the total-demand-for-bank-reserves schedule, TR^d, must be the sum of the ER^d and RR^d schedules. For instance, at the federal funds rate $r_f^0 = 0.06$, the total quantity of reserves demanded by all depository institutions is equal to $TR_0 = ER_0 + RR_0 = \$8 \text{ billion} + \$12 \text{ billion} = \$20$ billion. In contrast, at the higher federal funds rate $r_f^1 = 0.07$, the total quantity of reserves demanded by all institutions is equal to $TR_1 = ER_1 + RR_0 = \$6 \text{ billion} + \$12 \text{ billion} = \$18$ billion. The rise in the federal funds rate raises the opportunity cost of holding excess reserves and thereby induces

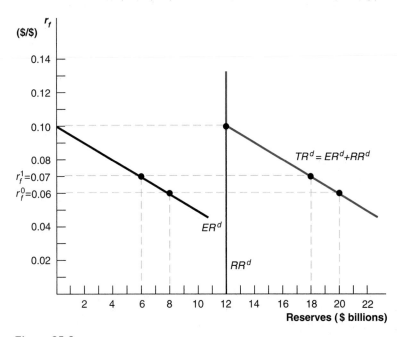

Figure 25-2

The Total Reserves Demand Schedule.   If the required reserve ratio is equal to 0.10 and the total quantity of deposits in the banking system is equal to $120 billion, then the quantity of required reserves demanded by banks is equal to $12 billion; hence, the required reserves demand schedule, RR^d, is vertical at this quantity. The excess reserves demand schedule for the banking system, which was derived in Figure 25-1, is ER^d. The total reserves demand schedule, TR^d, is the horizontal sum of the RR^d and ER^d schedules.

depository institutions to reduce their excess reserves, which causes their desired holdings of total reserves to decline.

It follows that, over most of its range, the total demand schedule for reserve holdings of banks slopes downward. Note, however, that if the federal funds rate rises sufficiently, then no depository institution will desire to hold any excess reserves. In Figure 25-2, for instance, at a federal funds rate equal to $r_f^2 = 0.10$, or higher, the quantity of excess reserves demanded by depository institutions falls to zero. At this rate or above, the opportunity cost of excess reserve holdings is so high that no depository institution wishes to hold excess reserves, and so depository institutions desire to hold only required reserves. Hence, at a federal funds rate at or above $r_f^2 = 0.10$, the TR^d schedule becomes vertical.

THE SUPPLY OF BANK RESERVES

It is crucial for you to keep in mind throughout our discussion of the market for reserves one very important fact. This is that, in our economy, the *Federal Reserve System supplies all bank reserves.* Furthermore, as we now explain, the Fed supplies reserves to depository institutions in two ways: through open-market operations and via the discount window.

Nonborrowed Reserves   The Fed can supply new reserves to depository institutions via purchases of government securities. Recall from Chapters 14 and 17 that such purchases

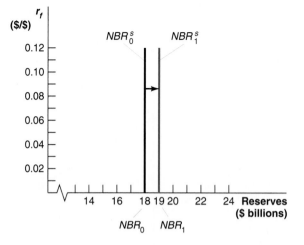

Figure 25-3
The Supply of Nonborrowed Reserves and the Effect of an Open-Market Purchase. The Fed varies the quantity of nonborrowed reserves supplied through its open-market operations. Hence, the Fed can control directly the quantity of nonborrowed reserves in the banking system, depicted as $NBR_0 = \$18$ billion. In the absence of any further open-market purchases or sales by the Fed, this is the quantity of nonborrowed reserves supplied irrespective of the federal funds rate, and so the nonborrowed reserves supply schedule NBR^s is vertical at $NBR_0 = \$18$ billion.

A Fed open-market purchase of $1 billion increases the quantity of nonborrowed reserves supplied from $NBR_0 = \$18$ billion to $NBR_1 = \$19$ billion. Therefore, the nonborrowed reserves supply schedule shifts rightward by the amount of the open-market purchase.

by the Fed inject new funds into the banking system in the form of bank reserves that did not exist before the Fed's security purchases. Reserves that it creates in this manner, rather than through direct discount window loans to banks, are *nonborrowed reserves supplied by the Fed.*

To keep things as simple as possible, we shall assume that the Fed uses open-market operations to determine a desired amount of nonborrowed reserves supplied without regard to the level of the federal funds rate. For instance, in Figure 25-3, the Fed may supply a quantity of nonborrowed reserves equal to $NBR_0 = \$18$ billion; if so, this is the quantity of nonborrowed reserves supplied whether the federal funds rate is equal to 0.06 or 0.07. This means that the *nonborrowed reserves supply schedule,* NBR^s, is vertical at $NBR_0 = \$18$ billion.

Figure 25-3 also shows the effects of a $1 billion open-market purchase by the Fed. Such a purchase would immediately inject $1 billion more into the banking system; nonborrowed reserves supplied by the Fed would rise from $NBR_0 = \$18$ billion to $NBR_1 = \$19$ billion. That is, the open-market purchase would cause the supply schedule for nonborrowed reserves to shift *rightward,* from NBR_0^s to NBR_1^s. Note that an open-market sale of securities by the Fed would reduce the quantity of nonborrowed reserves supplied at all possible federal funds rates and thereby would shift the NBR^s schedule leftward.

Borrowed Reserves Although the Fed supplies most reserves to the banking system via open-market operations, it supplies *borrowed reserves* to depository institutions by granting them discount window loans. The amount of borrowed reserves the Fed supplies to depository institutions depends upon how willing it is to make loans to these institutions—and at what discount rate it is willing to make these loans.

The Fed typically has set the discount rate it charges on its loans to banks *below* the market interest rates on alternative sources of funds for banks that wish to borrow. To see what this policy implies, consider Figure 25-4. The best alternative source of funds that banks might use instead of the discount window is the federal funds market: Those banks that need to borrow funds could borrow federal funds from depository institutions that otherwise would hold excess reserves. Consequently, the market rate of interest faced by banks as an alternative to borrowing from the Fed at the discount rate is the federal funds rate, r_f.

Suppose that the market federal funds rate is $r_f^1 = 0.07$. Now suppose that the Fed sets the discount rate, which we shall denote by r_d, at the level $r_d = 0.04$. In addition, suppose that the Fed announces that it is willing to lend an unlimited amount of reserves to any bank that wants a loan at this discount rate of $r_d = 0.04$. How many banks would you expect to borrow from other banks in the federal funds market? Naturally, the answer is that every bank would then desire to borrow from the Fed rather than from other banks. This would be true for any market federal funds rate above $r_d = 0.04$, including, for instance, a lower market federal funds rate of $r_f^0 = 0.05$. Either the federal funds market would dry up at market federal funds rates in excess of the Fed's discount rate, or the market federal funds rate somehow would have to fall to $r_f = r_d = 0.04$.

Figure 25-4
The Borrowed Reserves Supply Schedule.   If the Fed permits unlimited borrowing at the discount rate, then the borrowed reserves supply schedule would be horizontal, as depicted by the borrowed reserves supply schedule labeled BR_1^s. In contrast, if the Fed were to place significant constraints on permitted borrowing of reserves by banks, the borrowed reserve supply schedule would be nearly vertical, as shown by the schedule BR_2^s. Current Fed policy is to restrict access to discount window borrowing to some degree, and so the borrowed reserves supply schedule typically slopes upward, as depicted by the intermediate-sloped schedule BR_0^s, which indicates that the Fed permits banks to borrow $2 billion in reserves when the federal funds rate is equal to 6 percent while the discount rate is equal to 4 percent. If the federal funds rate rises to 7 percent while the discount rate remains unchanged, the Fed allows banks to increase their discount window borrowings to $3 billion.

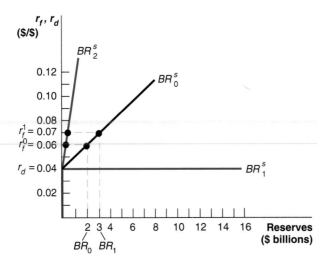

Therefore, in this example in which the Fed places no limits on borrowing at a subsidy discount rate, the *borrowed reserves supply schedule* would be the horizontal schedule labeled BR_1^s in Figure 25-4.

An alternative to a policy of unlimited borrowing would be for the Fed to restrict severely the number of discount window loans. It would supply only a very small amount of discount window loans when the market interest rate on federal funds is slightly above its discount rate, at a rate such as $r_f^0 = 0.06$. If the federal funds rate rises to a level such as $r_f^1 = 0.07$, then the Fed might allow somewhat more borrowing, but not much more. The borrowed reserves supply schedule would be very steep, as shown by BR_2^s in Figure 25-4.

Note that if the federal funds rate were to fall *below* the discount rate, it would be cheaper to borrow reserves from other banks in the private federal funds market than to borrow them directly from the Fed. Few if any banks would borrow from the Fed in this instance. Hence, over the range of possible federal funds rates below the discount rate, the schedule BR_2^s is *vertical,* as shown in Figure 25-4, and the borrowed reserves supply schedule is "kinked" at the discount rate $r_d = 0.04$.

As we discussed in Chapter 17, traditionally the Fed has in fact restricted access to the discount window. It has not, however, placed severe restrictions on the ability of banks to increase their discount window borrowings when the market interest rate on federal funds increases. Consequently, we may regard the most likely shape of the borrowed reserves schedule as lying between the extremes given by BR_1^s and BR_2^s in Figure 25-4, such as the schedule labeled BR_0^s. According to this schedule, a rise in the market federal funds rate from $r_f^0 = 0.06$ to $r_f^1 = 0.07$ induces depository institutions to increase their total borrowings of reserves from the Fed from $BR_0 = \$2$ billion to $BR_1 = \$3$ billion, and the Fed permits this increase.

As before, however, if the federal funds rate were to lie below the discount rate, the amount of reserves that banks would borrow from the Fed would be negligible, and so the borrowed reserves supply schedule BR_0 would be vertical below the discount rate. Hence, the borrowed reserves supply schedule BR_0^s would overlap with the schedule BR_2^s if the federal funds rate happened to lie below the discount rate, as shown in Figure 25-4.

The Total Supply of Bank Reserves   By definition, the total quantity of reserves supplied is equal to the amount of nonborrowed reserves the Fed supplies via open-market operations plus the quantity of borrowed reserves it supplies through the discount window. Hence, to obtain the *total reserves supply schedule,* we must sum the nonborrowed reserves supply schedule and the borrowed reserves supply schedule. This is illustrated in Figure 25-5 by summing the nonborrowed reserves supply schedule NBR_0^s from Figure 25-3 with the borrowed reserves supply schedule BR_0^s from Figure 25-4.

As shown in Figure 25-5, if the federal funds rate is equal to $r_f^0 = 0.06$, then, based on our above discussion, the total quantity of reserves supplied by the Fed is equal to $TR_0 = NBR_0 + BR_0 = \$18$ billion $+ \$2$ billion $= \$20$ billion. If the federal funds rate rises to $r_f^1 = 0.07$, then the total quantity of reserves the Fed supplies increases to $TR_1 = NBR_0 + BR_1 = \$18$ billion $+ \$3$ billion $= \$21$ billion.

For the range of federal funds rates below the discount rate $r_d = 0.04$, there are no discount window borrowings, and the amount of total reserves is simply the amount of nonborrowed reserves, as shown in Figure 25-5. The total reserves supply function, TR^s, is kinked at the discount rate just as the borrowed reserves supply function is kinked at this rate.

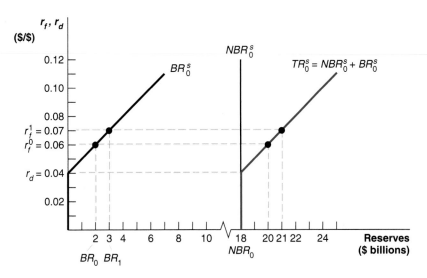

Figure 25-5
The Total Reserves Supply Schedule.   The total reserves supply schedule, TR_0^s, which tells the quantity of reserves that the Fed will supply to banks at each possible federal funds rate, is derived by summing horizontally the borrowed reserves supply schedule, BR_0^s, and the nonborrowed reserves supply schedule, NBR_0^s.

RESERVE MARKET EQUILIBRIUM

Equilibrium in the market for bank reserves occurs at the point at which the total quantity of reserves supplied by the Fed is demanded by depository institutions. Figure 25-6 depicts such a reserve market equilibrium.

The total quantity of reserves supplied is equal to the total quantity of reserves demanded at the point at which the total reserves demand schedule, TR^d, crosses the total reserves supply schedule, TR^s. At this point, the total quantity of reserves supplied is equal to the total quantity of reserves demanded at $TR_0 = \$20$ billion.

Note that at this equilibrium point the federal funds rate is equal to $r_f^0 = 0.06$. This interest rate, then, is the *equilibrium* federal funds rate. Suppose that the federal funds rate instead were equal to $r_f^1 = 0.07$. In this case, the total quantity of reserves supplied by the Fed would equal $21 billion, but the total quantity of reserves demanded by banks would equal $18 billion. There would be an excess quantity of reserves supplied, which would cause the federal funds rate to be bid downward toward the equilibrium level of $r_f^0 = 0.06$.

Likewise, if the federal funds rate were equal to $r_f^2 = 0.05$, Figure 25-6 indicates that the total quantity of reserves supplied by the Fed would equal $19 billion, while the total quantity of reserves demanded by banks would equal $22 billion. Then there would be an excess quantity of reserves demanded by depository institutions, and so the federal funds rate would be bid upward toward the equilibrium level of $r_f^0 = 0.06$.

Note that we can use the diagram of the reserves market to determine several other quantities. We know that the total quantity of required reserves demanded by depository institutions is equal to the quantity defined by the vertical portion above the kink in the total reserves demand schedule. Hence, we can see from the diagram in Figure 25-6 that the quantity of required reserves for this banking system is equal to $12 billion. In addition,

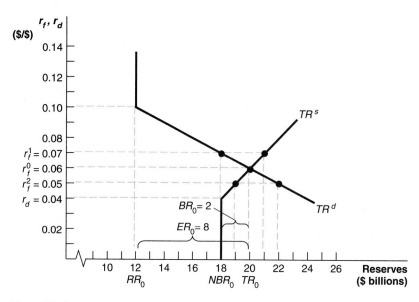

Figure 25-6

Equilibrium in the Market for Bank Reserves.   Above r_f^0, at the federal funds rate $r_f^1 = 0.07$, there is an excess quantity of total reserves supplied by the Fed equal to $21 billion − $18 billion = $3 billion. Below r_f^0, at the federal funds rate $r_f = 0.05$, there would be an excess quantity of reserves demanded by banks equal to $22 billion − $19 billion = $3 billion. Equilibrium in the market for bank reserves occurs at the federal funds rate $r_f^0 = 0.06$, at which the equilibrium total quantity of reserves supplied and demanded is equal to $TR_0 = $20 billion.

Equilibrium total reserves (TR_0) minus nonborrowed reserves (NBR_0) would equal the equilibrium amount of borrowed reserves (BR_0), or $20 billion − $18 billion = $2 billion = BR_0. Equilibrium total reserves (TR_0) minus required reserves (RR_0) would equal the equilibrium quantity of excess reserve holdings (ER_0), or $20 billion − $12 billion = $8 billion = ER_0.

we also know that, by definition, the quantity of excess reserves held by banks may be computed by subtracting the $12 billion in required reserves from the $20 billion in total reserves, and so the equilibrium amount of excess reserves in Figure 25-6 is equal to $20 billion − $12 billion = $8 billion.

Finally, we also know that, by definition, the amount of borrowed reserves in the banking system is equal to the $20 billion in total reserves minus the $18 billion in nonborrowed reserves. Therefore, the equilibrium quantity of borrowed reserves supplied by the Fed must be equal to $20 billion − $18 billion = $2 billion.

The Effects of Open-Market Operations   We can now use our theory of the market for bank reserves to analyze the effects of Federal Reserve open-market operations. Consider, for instance, the effect of an open-market purchase by the Fed. As shown in Figure 25-3, a Fed open-market purchase increases the quantity of nonborrowed reserves supplied by the amount of the purchase. The total reserves supply schedule is the sum of the supply of nonborrowed reserves and the supply of borrowed reserves, and so an open-market purchase must cause the total reserves supply schedule to shift rightward, as shown in Figure 25-7, leaving the borrowed reserves supply schedule fixed in its initial position.

Before the open-market purchase, Figure 25-7 indicates that the equilibrium federal funds rate was equal to r_f^0, where the initial total reserves supply schedule, TR_0^s, crossed

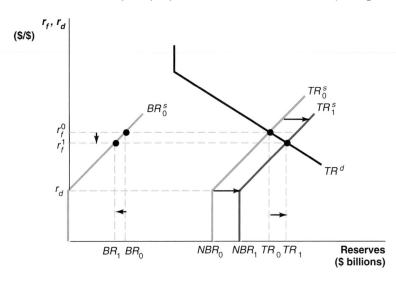

Figure 25-7

The Effect of a Fed Open-Market Purchase on Reserve Market Equilibrium.   A Fed open-market purchase, as shown in Figure 25-3, increases the quantity of nonborrowed reserves in the banking system from NBR_0 to NBR_1. Therefore, the total reserves supply schedule shifts rightward by the amount of the open-market purchase. At the initial equilibrium federal funds rate r_f^0, there is now an excess quantity of reserves supplied, and so the equilibrium federal funds rate falls to r_f^1, causing borrowed reserves of banks to decline somewhat, from BR_0 to BR_1. On net, equilibrium total reserves in the banking system increase, from TR_0 to TR_1.

the total reserves demand schedule, TR^d. *After* the Fed's purchase, however, the total quantity of reserves supplied by the Fed now must exceed the total quantity of reserves demanded by banks at the federal funds rate r_f^0. Thus, there is now an excess quantity of reserves supplied at this federal funds rate, and the federal funds rate must be bid downward to a new equilibrium rate r_f^1. At this federal funds rate, the total quantity of reserves demanded is equal to the total quantity of reserves supplied, TR_1.

Note that even though the Fed's open-market purchase *initially* causes the quantity of reserves in the banking system to rise by the amount of the purchase (the amount by which the total reserves supply schedule shifts rightward), the *equilibrium* increase in total reserves in the banking system, from TR_0 to TR_1, shown in Figure 25-7, turns out to be somewhat smaller. The reason is that when the equilibrium federal funds rate declines, depository institutions are induced to borrow less reserves from the Fed's discount window. Consequently, the Fed supplies less reserves through the discount window than it did before, as illustrated by a backward movement along the borrowed reserves supply schedule in Figure 25-7. On net, then, equilibrium total reserves increase, but by somewhat less than the amount of the Fed's open-market purchase. Furthermore, the equilibrium federal funds rate falls.

The Effects of a Change in the Discount Rate   Now think about what our model implies about the effects of a reduction in the Fed's discount rate. By reducing the discount rate, as illustrated in Figure 25-8 by the fall in the discount rate from r_d^0 to r_d^1, the Fed lowers the point at which the borrowed reserves supply schedule kinks. This effectively

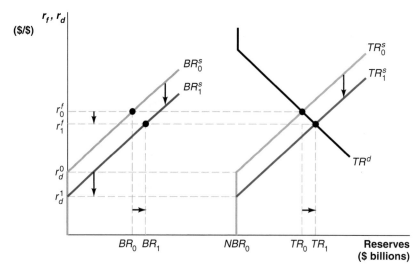

Figure 25-8
The Effect of a Fed Discount Rate Cut on Reserve Market Equilibrium. A Fed discount rate reduction has no effect on the quantity of nonborrowed reserves, NBR_0, but it shifts the kink in the borrowed reserves schedule downward. Therefore, the kink in the total reserves supply schedule shifts downward by the amount of the discount rate cut. At the initial equilibrium federal funds rate r_f^0, there is now an excess quantity of reserves supplied, and so the equilibrium federal funds rate falls to r_f^1. On net, equilibrium borrowed reserves increase from BR_0 to BR_1, and equilibrium total reserves in the banking system also increase, from TR_0 to TR_1.

shifts the borrowed reserves supply schedule rightward, from BR_0^s to BR_1^s. We know that the total reserves supply schedule is the sum of the borrowed reserves supply schedule and the nonborrowed reserves supply schedule; hence, the total reserves supply schedule also must shift right, as shown by the movement from TR_0^s to TR_1^s in Figure 25-8.

The initial equilibrium federal funds rate was equal to r_f^0 in Figure 25-8. After the discount rate reduction, however, the total quantity of reserves supplied by the Fed exceeds the total quantity of reserves demanded by depository institutions. There is an excess quantity of reserves supplied, and the equilibrium federal funds rate will be bid downward to r_f^1, as depicted in Figure 25-8. On net, the equilibrium quantity of reserves rises from TR_0 to TR_1.

We may conclude that a reduction in the discount rate has effects that are similar to those induced by an open-market purchase. The equilibrium federal funds rate declines, and the equilibrium quantity of reserves in the banking system increases.

The Effects of a Change in the Demand for Required Reserves Not all changes in the equilibrium federal funds rate and the equilibrium quantity of total bank reserves are induced by actions of the Federal Reserve System. Such changes also can be caused by variations in the behavior of depository institutions. For example, consider Figure 25-9, which depicts the effects of an increase in the demand for required reserves by depository institutions. Such an increase could arise for one of two possible reasons. The Fed could increase the required reserve ratio, d, or, alternatively, the amount of transactions deposits in the banking system, D, could increase. In either case, the result would be an

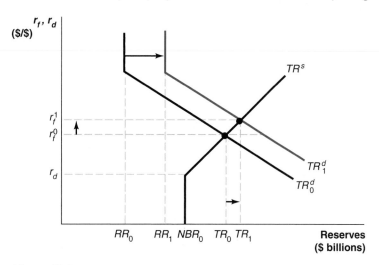

Figure 25-9

The Effect on Reserve Market Equilibrium of a Rise in the Demand for Required Reserves.   A rise in the demand for required reserves causes the entire total reserves demand schedule to shift rightward. At the initial equilibrium federal funds rate r_f^0, there is now an excess quantity of reserves demanded, and so the equilibrium federal funds rate rises to r_f^1, and equilibrium total reserves in the banking system also increase, from TR_0 to TR_1.

increase in the demand for required reserves by banks, which is shown in Figure 25-9 by the rightward shift of the total reserves demand schedule, from TR_0^d to TR_1^d, holding the demand for excess reserves unchanged.

In Figure 25-9, r_f^0 is the initial equilibrium federal funds rate. Following the rise in the demand for total reserves, however, an excess quantity of reserves is demanded by depository institutions at this federal funds rate. Therefore, the federal funds rate must be bid upward to a new equilibrium level, shown by r_f^1. Furthermore, the equilibrium quantity of total reserves increases, from TR_0 to TR_1.

POLICY TRANSMISSION FROM THE MARKET FOR BANK RESERVES TO THE ECONOMY

How do Fed policy actions that have their immediate effects in the market for bank reserves have anything to do with broader targets and objectives of monetary policy? This is the last question we need to address before thinking about how the Fed might conduct monetary policy on a day-to-day basis. As you will see, the linkage from Fed policies in the market for bank reserves involves straightforward extensions of ideas we already have seen in earlier chapters.

THE YIELD CURVE AND THE RISK PREMIUM

You know now that day-to-day policy actions by the Fed have their immediate effects on the very short-term (1-day) interest rate at which depository institutions exchange reserves: the federal funds rate. It may be hard, right off the bat, to see why any of us should ever care about an interest rate on a financial instrument with only a 1-day maturity. After all, that doesn't seem to have much to do with broader issues such as investment spending or the demand for money. Or does it?

Recall from Chapter 7 that even if we abstract from issues such as default risk, liquidity, and tax treatment differences among bonds, it is very often the case that bonds with different terms to maturity earn different rates. Specifically, financial instruments of different maturities tend to have higher yields as the time to maturity rises. Hence, there is a *term structure of interest rates* that implies that the *yield curve* typically slopes upward for financial assets with similar risk, liquidity, and tax characteristics.

Likewise, there is a *risk structure of interest rates.* Holding term to maturity constant, other factors—default risk, liquidity properties, and tax-treatment characteristics—make some financial instruments more risky than others. For instance, it typically is the case that a security with higher default risk pays a higher market interest rate.

One-day federal funds have a much shorter maturity than financial instruments involved in determining the opportunity costs relevant to firms' decisions concerning real investment and money holdings. Furthermore, unsecured federal funds loans are riskier than U.S. Treasury securities. Nevertheless, the theories of the term structure and risk structure of interest rates we discussed in Chapter 7 imply that the 1-day federal funds rate must be related to other longer-term interest rates.

Yield Curves for Federal Funds and Other Instruments   Recall from Chapter 7 that once we have controlled for all factors other than term to maturity, it is possible to construct a yield curve for financial instruments of different terms to maturity. Indeed, the generally upward-sloping yield curve relationship we find for financial instruments such as T-bills also holds for other instruments, including federal funds. Just as a yield curve for Treasury securities slopes upward, so does the yield curve for federal funds of 1-day and longer terms.

Figure 25-10 shows a possible *federal funds yield curve,* which is the upper curve on the diagram. The dashed portion of the federal funds yield curve is an imaginary portion that would apply to interbank ''federal funds'' loans with maturities longer than a few weeks. Such loans do not take place, but the dashed portion of the federal funds yield curve indicates possible yields that would be implied for such loans if they did occur.

Relating the Federal Funds Rate to Other Interest Rates   The United States Treasury does not issue 1-day bills, nor does it issue bills with maturities of just a few weeks or less. If it *did* issue such very short-term bills, however, the interest rates on such government securities would be *lower* than those on federal funds loans. Federal funds loans are not collateralized, while U.S. Treasury bills are backed by the taxing power of the government and are therefore free of default risk.

Indeed, the interest rate that the Treasury would pay on its bills and bonds would be lower than that for federal funds loans of any given maturity. Therefore, Figure 25-10 also displays a possible yield curve for Treasury securities that lies *below* the federal funds yield curve. The lower part of this yield curve for Treasury securities also is dashed, to indicate that we do not directly observe these yields. (Note that one can, however, *infer* this portion of the Treasury yield curve from the prices of Treasury securities that are within days of maturity.)

Suppose, as shown in Figure 25-10, that the equilibrium 1-day federal funds rate r_f, which is determined in the market for bank reserves, is equal to 0.08 (8 percent). As long as the term- and risk-structure relationships implied by the sample yield curves in Figure 25-10 prevail, the 6-month Treasury interest rate may be determined by reading up from

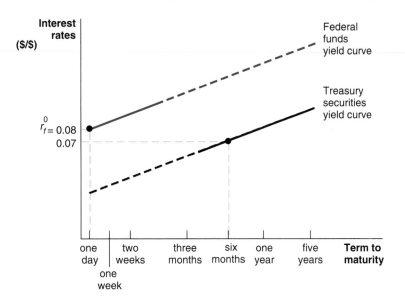

Figure 25-10
Federal Funds and Treasury Security Yield Curves.   Federal funds loans have terms to maturity ranging from a day to a few weeks. The dashed portion of the federal funds yield curve is an extrapolation that most likely would hold if federal funds loans had terms longer than a week. The Treasury security yield curve also typically slopes upward. The dashed position of the Treasury security yield curve is an extrapolation that most likely would hold if Treasury securities with shorter terms to maturity existed. Federal funds are riskier than Treasury securities. Hence, for any term to maturity the federal funds rate typically would exceed the Treasury security rate in light of the higher risk of federal funds lending, and the federal funds yield curve lies above the Treasury security yield curve.

If the federal funds rate is $r_f^0 = 0.08$, then the term structure and risk structure of interest rates implied by the shapes and positions of the yield curves indicate that the interest rate on a 6-month Treasury security will equal 0.07 (7 percent).

a 6-month maturity on the horizontal axis of the diagram and over to the vertical axis. Hence, the interest rate on a 6-month Treasury security that is consistent with the term structure and risk structure of interest rates is equal to 0.07 (7 percent).

DETERMINATION OF THE EQUILIBRIUM MONEY STOCK

We now can explain how day-to-day policy actions of the Federal Reserve System may or may not affect broader economic variables. Let us begin with the determination of the equilibrium quantity of money. This is displayed in Figure 25-11. Panel (*a*) shows an equilibrium in the market for bank reserves, in which the equilibrium federal funds rate is equal to $r_f^0 = 0.08$. At this federal funds rate, the total quantity of reserves supplied and demanded is equal to $TR_0 = \$15$ billion. Panel (*b*) is the same as Figure 25-10; it shows the term- and risk-structure relationships between federal funds loans and Treasury securities. As in Figure 25-10, panel (*b*) of Figure 25-11 indicates that the longer-term (6-month) nominal interest rate on Treasury securities is equal to $r_n^0 = 0.07$. Finally, panel (*c*) is a diagram of the economy's money demand schedule that we developed in Chapter 20. If we assume that the 6-month Treasury security rate is the interest rate relevant for

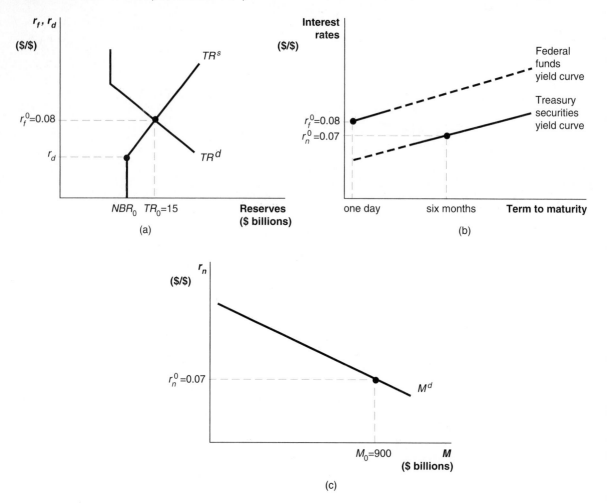

Figure 25-11
Determining the Equilibrium Quantity of Money.   As shown in panel (*a*), the equilibrium federal funds rate, $r_f^0 = 0.08$, is determined by equilibrium in the market for bank reserves. Given the term structure and risk structure of interest rates implied by panel (*b*), the equilibrium nominal interest rate on a 6-month Treasury security is $r_n^0 = 0.07$. If this is the interest rate applicable to the public's demand for nominal money balances, *M*, panel (*c*) indicates that the equilibrium quantity of money demanded is equal to $M_0 = \$900$ billion.

money demand decisions, then we can see that, according to panel (*c*) of Figure 25-11, the quantity of money demanded at $r_n^0 = 0.07$ is equal to $M_0 = \$900$ billion. This quantity, then, is the equilibrium quantity of money in the economy.

Open-Market Operations and the Equilibrium Quantity of Money   Suppose that the Fed wishes to increase the quantity of money. To increase the equilibrium quantity of money demanded by the public, the Fed would need to induce a reduction in the longer-term interest rate, r_n. This could be accomplished if the Fed could induce a *sustained* reduction in the federal funds rate.

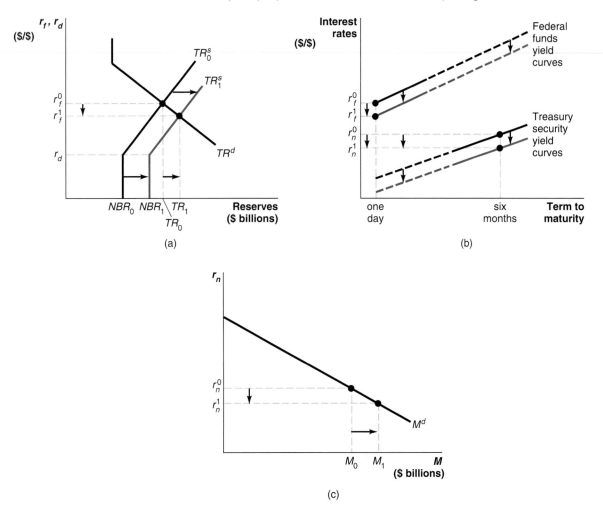

Figure 25-12
The Effects of an Open-Market Purchase on the Equilibrium Quantity of Money.   An open-market purchase causes a reduction in the equilibrium federal funds rate (see Figure 25-10), from r_f^0 to r_f^1 in panel (a). As long as the open-market purchase was an outright purchase and was expected to be "permanent," expectations of future federal funds rates also will fall, and the federal funds yield curve will shift downward in panel (b). In addition, as long as the risk structure of interest rates is unaffected by Fed policy, the Treasury security yield curve also must shift downward, and the equilibrium nominal interest rate on a 6-month Treasury security will fall, from r_n^0 to r_n^1. This, in turn, will cause the equilibrium quantity of money demanded to increase, from M_0 to M_1 in panel (c).

Figure 25-12 shows how this could be done. An *outright purchase* of securities by the Fed would increase the supply of nonborrowed reserves, thereby shifting the supply schedule for total reserves rightward. If all other factors are unchanged, this action would reduce the equilibrium federal funds rate from r_f^0 to r_f^1, as shown in panel (a). The equilibrium quantity of reserves also would increase, from TR_0 to TR_1.

Note that a *repurchase agreement* by the Fed also could reduce the 1-day federal funds rate, as shown in panel (*a*) of Figure 25-12. Yet a repurchase agreement transaction would not represent a *sustained* change in Fed policy that would generate a change in the federal funds rate that individuals would perceive as long lasting, so that they would expect future 1-day rates to fall as well. As we know from the expectations theory of the term structure of interest rates (see Chapter 7), if individuals expect both the current and future interest rates on a short-term financial instrument to fall, then the interest rate on a longer-term instrument of similar characteristics also will fall. The reason, according to the expectations theory of the term structure, is that the longer-term rate is an average of current and expected future short-term interest rates.

Therefore, as long as the Fed conducts open-market purchases via outright (not repurchase) transactions, the fall in the equilibrium federal funds rate in panel (*a*) of Figure 25-12 also will induce a downward shift of the federal funds yield curve in panel (*b*). Not only does the current 1-day federal funds rate fall, as shown in panel (*a*), but, in addition, individuals anticipate then that future 1-day federal funds rates also will be lower. Hence, rates on term federal funds also must fall, and so the federal funds yield curve shifts downward in panel (*b*).

We know that the risk structure of interest rates relates the yield curve for Treasury securities to the federal funds yield curve. Assuming that this risk structure is unchanged (which is a reasonable assumption), it follows that the Treasury yield curve also shifts downward, as shown in panel (*b*) of Figure 25-12, following the Fed's outright purchases of securities. Consequently, the interest rate on a longer-term security falls from r_n^0 to r_n^1, as shown in panel (*b*).

Finally, as panel (*c*) of Figure 25-12 depicts, a fall in the longer-term interest rate induces an increase in the quantity of money demanded. The equilibrium quantity of money thereby increases, from M_0 to M_1.

The Money Multiplier Revisited   We spent some time in Chapters 14 and 17 working with the money multiplier relating total bank reserves, as a component of the monetary base, to the total quantity of money. In the money multiplier model, the money stock, M, is equal to the money multiplier, m, times the monetary base, $MB = TR + C$.

According to the money multiplier model, then, the rise in total reserves from TR_0 to TR_1, as in panel (*a*) of Figure 25-12, should induce an increase in the quantity of money. This is exactly what we see happen in panel (*c*) of Figure 25-12; the equilibrium quantity of money does indeed rise, from M_0 to M_1. Consequently, we may conclude that our more advanced model of money stock determination gives us predictions that accord with our basic multiplier model.

Nevertheless, there is a crucial difference between our new model and the multiplier model. In Figure 25-12, the crucial channel between a change in total bank reserves and a resulting change in the quantity of money involves interest rates. Yet interest rate effects were absent in our basic money multiplier model, which we developed by ignoring any interest rate influences on the relationship between total bank reserves and the quantity of money.

Our analysis in Figure 25-12 implies, therefore, that we actually would expect the money multiplier process to be influenced by interest rate variations. Such variations, in turn, could cause changes in the size of the money multiplier that links changes in total reserves to changes in the money stock. Indeed, because interest rates do vary, our theory developed in the present chapter predicts that the money multiplier should vary over time. As we discussed in Chapter 14, this is exactly what we observe.

MONETARY POLICY OPERATING PROCEDURES

We finally have all the tools we need to understand the essential elements of alternative operating procedures used by the Federal Reserve in carrying out monetary policy. As we indicated early in the chapter, the Fed has done us an unintended favor, because at various times it has used nearly all possible operating procedures that economists have envisioned. This means that we can explain Fed operating procedures in a historical context, which permits us to explain the theory of different operating procedures as we trace the actual history and Fed experience with these procedures.

FEDERAL FUNDS RATE TARGETING, 1970–1979

Most monetary economists regard the 1970s as the beginnings of the "modern" era of Federal Reserve policy making. It was during this period that the Fed first sought to apply economic theory directly to monetary policy. The Fed, under the leadership of Federal Reserve Board Chairman Arthur Burns, did this in two ways. First, it established a firm intermediate target of monetary policy. Second, it developed a well-defined operating procedure.

The Fed adopted the quantity of money as its intermediate policy target. During most of the 1970s the specific measure of money that the Fed used was M1, although at various times it also used M2 as an intermediate target. The Fed used monetary aggregates as intermediate objectives because it believed that the quantity of money best satisfied the criteria for an intermediate target that we discussed in the last chapter.

Although the Fed's intermediate goal in the 1970s was to target specific values for a monetary aggregate, it settled on a monetary policy operating procedure that emphasized interest rate channels. Specifically, the Fed focused on the federal funds rate. Indeed, the Fed *targeted* the federal funds rate in the 1970s, and so its operating procedure of that period was known as **federal funds rate targeting.**

Targeting the Federal Funds Rate   It may seem strange to you to think of the Fed trying to target a market *interest rate* to aim at a specific *quantity of money.* If so, you may count yourself in good company, because some very well known economists criticized the Fed for following this policy. Nonetheless, this was indeed the operating procedure that the Fed followed.

The operating procedure theoretically can accomplish what the Fed intended. Figure 25-13 shows how. Panel (*a*) displays the market for bank reserves, panel (*b*) depicts possible federal funds and Treasury security yield curves, and panel (*c*) shows the demand for money. Even though the transmission of Fed monetary policy actions works from panel (*a*) to panel (*b*) and then to panel (*c*), let's begin, as the Fed would, by first considering panel (*c*).

The reason the Fed would have begun with panel (*c*) of Figure 25-13 is that its intermediate target was the quantity of money. As shown in panel (*c*), the Federal Open Market Committee would first choose a target level of the money stock, labeled M^*. As we discussed in the previous chapter, the FOMC would choose a target quantity of money that it felt was consistent with its ultimate economic objectives. Federal Reserve staff economists would, in addition, *estimate* the position of the money demand function. Once Fed economists had accomplished this task, the FOMC could deduce what longer-term nominal interest rate was needed to achieve the target quantity of money M^*. This interest rate is labeled $r_n(M^*)$ in panel (*c*) of Figure 25-13. (You should read this notation as "the

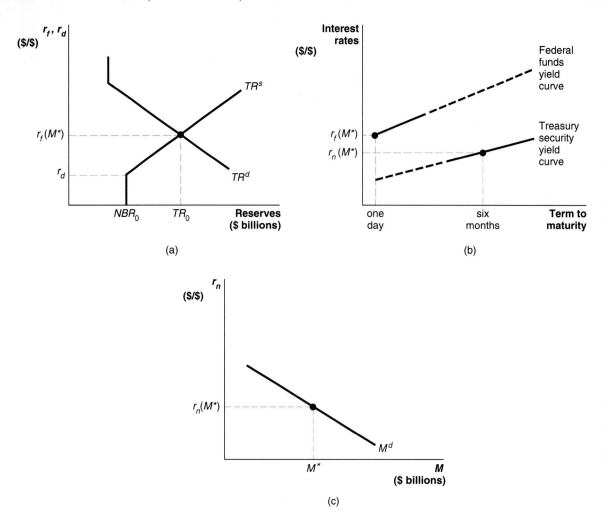

Figure 25-13
Choosing a Federal Funds Rate Target to Achieve a Money Stock Target. If the Fed's intermediate target is the quantity of money M^*, then the nominal interest rate needed to induce the public to demand this quantity of money is $r_n(M^*)$, as shown in panel (c). Given the term structure and risk structure of interest rates displayed by the yield curves in panel (b), the federal funds rate consistent with the intermediate monetary target therefore is equal to $r_n(M^*)$. Hence, this is the federal funds rate target that the Fed seeks to target in the market for bank reserves [panel (a)].

value of the longer-term nominal interest rate consistent with achieving the intermediate monetary target M^*.'')

Other Fed staff economists would be responsible for estimating the term-structure and risk-structure relationships of interest rates such as those depicted by the yield curves shown in panel (b) of Figure 25-13. This would help the FOMC to determine what specific federal funds rate it should target to achieve its intermediate monetary objective. This *target* federal funds rate, then, is labeled $r_f(M^*)$ in panel (b).

Therefore, the FOMC would instruct the New York Fed's Trading Desk to conduct open-market operations in the market for bank reserves, depicted in panel (a) of Figure 25-13, with an aim to keep the federal funds rate at, or near, $r_f(M^*)$. As long as the Fed's economists were not too far off in their money demand and yield curve estimates, the FOMC would then have done its best to achieve the intermediate monetary target.

Note that, in practice, the FOMC did not really instruct the Trading Desk to keep the federal funds rate *constant*. The FOMC instead specified a federal funds rate target *range,* because the FOMC recognized that the Trading Desk could not always hold the federal funds rate constant in the face of changing conditions in the market for bank reserves. Nevertheless, the FOMC's target range for the federal funds rate usually was very narrow, and so we shall simplify our discussion by treating the FOMC's federal funds rate target as a constant value.

Figure 25-14 illustrates how the Trading Desk implemented federal funds rate targeting. As in Figure 25-13, the Fed targets the federal funds rate at $r_f(M^*)$ in an effort to achieve its intermediate money stock target, M^*. Panel (a) of Figure 25-14 shows the Fed's response to an unexpected increase in the demand for excess reserves by depository institutions. This would cause a rightward shift in the demand schedule for total reserves, from TR_0^d to TR_1^d, and, in the absence of any Fed policy response, an increase in the federal funds rate, to r_f^1.

If allowed to persist, this rise in the federal funds rate ultimately would raise the future interest rate expectations of financial market participants. This, in turn, would cause the federal funds and Treasury security yield curves to shift upward in panel (b) of Figure 25-14 (not actually shown), and longer-term interest rates also would rise. A rise in the longer-term interest rate, r_n, would then cause the equilibrium quantity of money demanded to fall in panel (c); the Fed would not achieve its intermediate monetary target.

To nip in the bud such an event, the Trading Desk would undertake the action shown in panel (a) of Figure 25-14. Instead of permitting the federal funds rate to rise with the increase in reserve demand, the Trading Desk would buy an amount of securities sufficient to increase the supply of reserves from TR_0^s to TR_1^s in panel (a). This action would keep the federal funds rate unchanged at $r_f(M^*)$ and, provided that all other factors remained unchanged, would maintain the quantity of money at the target quantity M^*.

Advantages and Disadvantages of Federal Funds Rate Targeting   The example illustrated in Figure 25-14 depicts the key advantage of federal funds rate targeting. Namely, this Fed operating procedure *automatically* offsets the effects of variability in the demand for excess reserves by depository institutions. As we discussed in Chapter 14, excess reserve holdings by depository institutions typically are very small relative to total reserves. *Variability* of depository institutions' excess reserve holdings, however, can be substantial. Targeting the federal funds rate helped permit the Fed in the 1970s to keep such variability from causing it to miss its money stock targets.

A similar advantage was the fact that, in the real world, the borrowed reserves supply function is not always stable. By allowing banks to borrow reserves at a subsidy rate, the Fed opens up the reserve supply process to variability that results from changes in the borrowing preferences of banks. This means that the supply schedule for total reserves sometimes can shift even when the Fed conducts no open-market operations and keeps the discount rate constant. Under a federal funds rate targeting procedure, however, the Fed automatically would shift the supply schedule for total reserves back again, thereby offsetting such effects.

As in all things, federal funds rate targeting has its downside. First of all, individuals' expectations about future interest rates depend on many factors; when such factors may

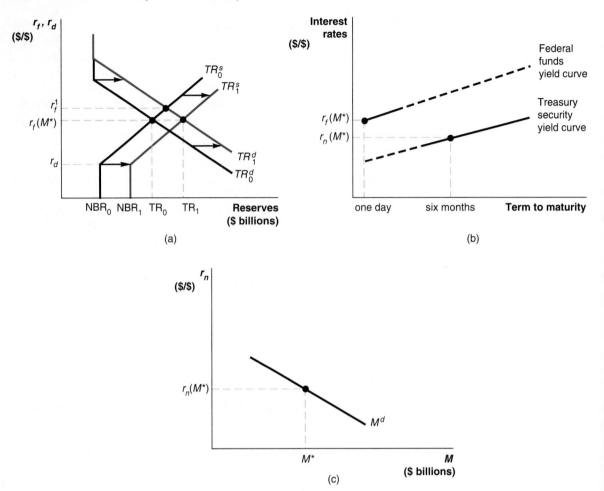

Figure 25-14
Implementing a Federal Funds Rate Target to Maintain a Money Stock Target.   If
there is an increase in the demand for excess reserves that causes the demand for total reserves by
banks to rise from TR_0^d to TR_1^d, then, in the absence of Fed policy actions, the federal funds rate
would tend to rise to r_f^1 [panel (a)], which is above the target consistent with the intermediate
monetary target M^* [panels (b) and (c)]. To keep this from occurring, the Fed would need to
conduct a sufficient amount of open-market purchases to increase nonborrowed reserves enough
to shift the total reserves supply function far enough to the right to keep the federal funds rate at
the Fed's target level, as shown in panel (a).

change, they alter expectations and the shapes of interest rate yield curves. And the Fed
cannot always predict when such factors may change.

Second, and perhaps more important, the Fed cannot always accurately forecast the
position of the money demand schedule. An interest rate targeting procedure yields the
target quantity of money *only* if money demand is stable. If the monetary demand schedule
shifts to the left or right, then the equilibrium quantity of money will end up below or
above the Fed's target.

Experience with Federal Funds Rate Targeting   The Fed stuck with the federal funds rate targeting procedure for roughly a decade. Initially, federal funds rate targeting seemed to work fairly well. Things began to go awry, however, in the mid-1970s, when the models of the demand for money that Fed economists used began to substantially overpredict money demand. The problem was not inadequacies in the Fed economists' abilities. Models of money demand used by private forecasters and academic economists also suffered from this problem, which came to be known among monetary economists as the "Case of the Missing Money."

Unfortunately for the Fed, this occurrence was a sign of a rocky road ahead. For the rest of the 1970s, the demand for money was more variable than it had been in previous years. The Fed continued to miss its monetary targets, and this problem worsened as the decade progressed. Furthermore, in the latter part of the 1970s the Fed's procedure more often allowed the money stock to grow *faster* than was consistent with its intermediate monetary targets.

By 1979, growth in the money stock had accelerated. So had inflation. It was clear to the Fed that something had to be done; that "something" was a change in operating procedures.

NONBORROWED RESERVES TARGETING, 1979–1982

Many observers, and in particular monetarists, had for years argued that the Fed's federal funds rate targeting procedure was a mistake. These critics contended that the Fed had become so wrapped up in targeting the federal funds rate that this had become a Fed *goal* instead of a *means* to achieving the goal of monetary targeting. They further argued that controlling the level of bank reserves would achieve much closer control of monetary aggregates than focusing solely on an interest rate. The unraveling of monetary control in the latter part of the 1970s seemed to be hard evidence that the critics were right.

Somewhat surprisingly, a Fed shift in the monetarist direction did not come under the direction of a monetarist leader of the Fed. Instead, it occurred under the leadership of Federal Reserve Board Chairman Paul Volcker, who served in that capacity from 1979 until 1987. Volcker was a consummate Fed "insider" who had spent almost his entire career in the Fed, and he had never been strongly attached to monetarist principles.

Nevertheless, on October 6, 1979, Volcker and the Fed abruptly announced a newly gained adherence to the monetarist philosophy. The Fed abandoned federal funds rate targeting. In its place, it adopted a new operating procedure, called **nonborrowed reserves targeting.**

Targeting Nonborrowed Reserves   Under the nonborrowed reserves targeting procedure, the Fed conducted open-market operations with an aim to keep the growth of nonborrowed reserves on a set path. This meant that, at a given time, the Fed sought to attain a target level of nonborrowed reserves, which, in turn, it intended to be consistent with its intermediate goal of controlling the quantity of money.

Figure 25-15 depicts the essential elements of nonborrowed reserves targeting. Panel (*a*) displays the market for bank reserves, panel (*b*) shows federal funds and Treasury security yield curves, and panel (*c*) illustrates the economy's money demand schedule. The Fed's policy decision-making process began with its intermediate monetary target, M^* in panel (*c*).

Just as was true under federal funds rate targeting, interest rate relationships played a role in linking the Fed's policy actions to the quantity of money. Panel (*c*) indicates that, on average, the nominal interest rate on Treasury securities consistent with the Fed's

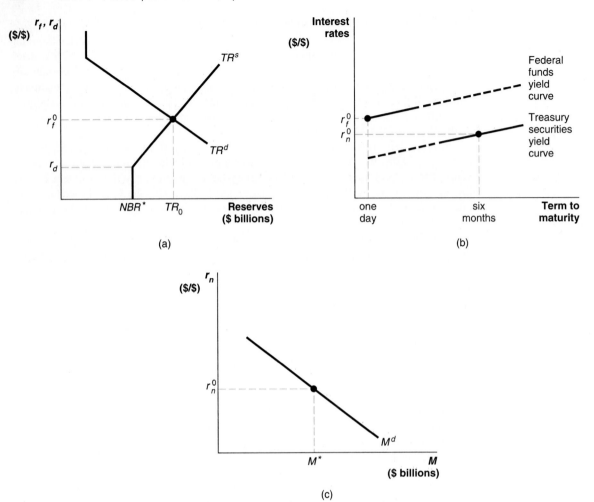

Figure 25-15

Choosing a Nonborrowed Reserves Target to Achieve an Intermediate Monetary Target. If the Fed's intermediate target for the quantity of money is equal to M^* [panel (c)], then, given the risk structure and term structure of interest rates [panel (b)], the Fed needs to set its nonborrowed reserves target equal to NBR* [panel (a)] to achieve the federal funds rate consistent with the monetary target. If money market conditions change, however, the Fed does not alter its nonborrowed reserves target but instead permits interest rates to adjust.

money stock target would be equal to r_n^0. Furthermore, the term and risk structures of interest rates implied by panel (b) indicate that the federal funds rate that would be consistent, on average, with the Fed's money stock target would be r_f^0. If the Fed were to exactly achieve the target quantity of money M^*, therefore, it would need to conduct open-market operations designed to set nonborrowed reserves at just the right level to achieve the r_f^0 as the equilibrium federal funds rate.

Let's suppose that the Fed selected just the right level of nonborrowed reserves to do this, given by NBR*, so that the demand and supply schedules for total reserves, TR^d and TR^s, intersected at the federal funds rate r_f^0. Under nonborrowed reserves targeting, however, the Fed made no effort to keep the federal funds rate from varying in response to changes in reserve market conditions. Indeed, the Fed literally kept the level of nonborrowed reserves fixed (at least, in the short run) at NBR*, no matter what else might happen.

Advantages and Disadvantages of Nonborrowed Reserves Targeting   The key advantage of nonborrowed reserves targeting was that this Fed operating procedure *automatically* stabilized the quantity of money in the face of unanticipated variations in the money demand schedule, such as those that occurred in the 1970s. To see that this is so, consider Figure 25-16, which begins with the same equilibrium points as in Figure 25-15 but goes a step further by analyzing the effects of an unpredicted rise in the demand for money. As shown in panel (c), an increase in the demand for money would, at the initial Treasury security rate r_n^0, cause the equilibrium quantity of money to rise to M_1, well above the target level M^*.

Under federal funds rate targeting, absent changes in the term or risk structure of interest rates, there would be no interest rate adjustment to offset this large rise in the quantity of money above the Fed's target. In contrast, under a nonborrowed reserves targeting procedure the Fed permits interest rates to vary. And vary they must, because we are not at the end of our story in Figure 25-16. When the quantity of money starts to rise, a large part of that increase occurs through a rise in transactions deposits in the banking system, because the larger component of the quantity of money is bank deposits. In turn, a rise in transactions deposits in the banking system causes required reserves to increase as well, which means that the total demand for required reserves by depository institutions shifts to the right, as shown in panel (a) of Figure 25-16. This, in turn, causes a rise in the federal funds rate, from r_f^0 to r_f^1.

Under a nonborrowed reserves targeting procedure, the Fed does not vary nonborrowed reserves to keep the federal funds rate from increasing. Financial market participants realize that this is the case. Therefore, if they believe that the rise in money demand that caused the increase in the federal funds rate will be long lasting, they also will expect that the rise in the federal funds rate will be sustained. This means that the interest rates on term federal funds must rise, and the federal funds yield curve will shift upward, as shown in panel (b) of Figure 25-16. As long as the risk structure of interest rates stays the same, the Treasury security yield curve must shift upward as well; hence, the longer-term security rate relevant to money demand decisions also must rise, from r_n^0 to r_n^1. As the interest rate rises, the equilibrium quantity of money demanded falls back to M_2, which is closer to the amount of the Fed's monetary target, M^*, as shown in panel (c).

As this example illustrates, the Fed cannot always exactly achieve its monetary target under nonborrowed reserves targeting. It can, however, automatically mute the effects of money demand variability, which a federal funds rate targeting procedure is incapable of doing. (*Remember:* Under a federal funds rate targeting approach, the quantity of money would have ended up at M_1 instead of M_2 in panel (c) of Figure 25-16.) This is the advantage of nonborrowed reserves targeting and the rationale for its adoption by the Fed in 1979.

An operating procedure that targets nonborrowed reserves has two potential disadvantages. One drawback is that it is not the best procedure if money demand is very stable while (a) the demand for total reserves varies with changes in banks' demands for excess reserves and (b) the supply of total reserves varies with changes in banks' preferences concerning borrowing from the Fed. Federal funds rate targeting definitely is a better operating procedure in this latter situation, as we showed earlier.

Another potential disadvantage of nonborrowed reserves targeting is that its success as a means of controlling the quantity of money hinges on letting interest rates vary. If

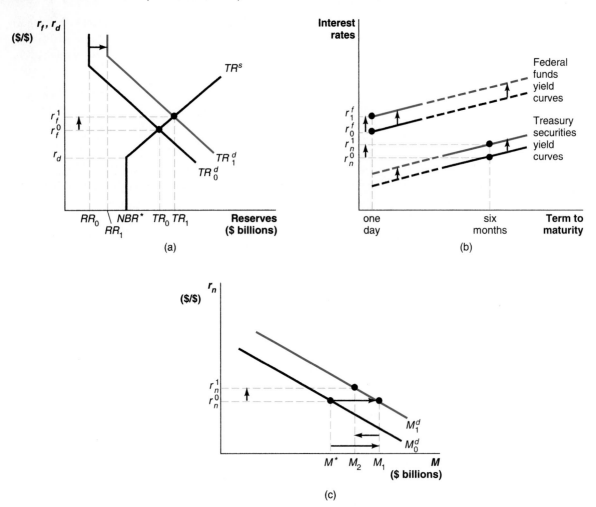

Figure 25-16

Nonborrowed Reserves Targeting as an Automatic Monetary Stabilizer. If there is a rise in the public's demand for money [panel (c)], then at a given nominal interest rate the equilibrium quantity of money demanded by the public will increase to M_1, well above the Fed's intermediate monetary target, M^*. Part of the rise in the quantity of money will result from an increase in deposits at banks, which will lead to a rise in the demand for required reserves by banks. Hence, the total reserves demand schedule shifts rightward in panel (a). This causes a rise in the equilibrium federal funds rate, from r_f^0 to r_f^1, and, if this change is expected to be long-lasting, an upward shift in the federal funds yield curve and in the yield curve for Treasury securities [panel (b)]. The resulting increase in the nominal interest rate on these securities, from r_n^0 to r_n^1, causes the equilibrium quantity of money to fall back to M_2, closer to the Fed's target, M^*. Consequently, by targeting nonborrowed reserves the Fed lets interest rate adjustments automatically stabilize the quantity of money in the face of money demand variability.

interest rate volatility is socially undesirable, then nonborrowed reserves targeting is not necessarily the best operating procedure.

Experience with Nonborrowed Reserves Targeting   When the Fed embarked on its new procedure in 1979, many economists—and especially those of a monetarist bent— had high hopes. Nonborrowed reserves targeting promised to improve monetary control considerably, thereby providing economic stability that, in the midst of double-digit infla- tion, seemed to have been lost.

In general, these hopes were not realized. Certainly, inflation did fall shortly after the change in operating procedures; by 1980 it was in the single-digit range, and within just a few years it was holding fairly stable between 3 and 6 percent. Nothing else seemed to work out as anticipated, however. For one thing, the quantity of money became *more,* instead of less, variable after 1979. Furthermore, even though theory indicated that some increase in interest rate volatility might occur, few economists predicted the very wide swings in interest rates that occurred from 1979 to 1981.

Finally, something else unexpected occurred. The whole point of nonborrowed reserves targeting was to improve the Fed's ability to control monetary aggregates, which in turn appeared to be closely related to ultimate economic goals such as prices and output. Beginning in 1981, however, this relationship broke down. The income velocity of money, the ratio of nominal income to the quantity of money (see Chapter 18), had steadily and *predictably* risen since the end of World War II, and so there appeared to be a systematic relationship between money and nominal income that the Fed could attempt to exploit by using a monetary aggregate as an intermediate target. In 1981, in a sharp departure from this previous relationship, the income velocity of money began to *decline.* Suddenly, the rationale for using money as an intermediate target, and for using nonborrowed reserves targeting to control money, was dashed. By 1982, the Fed had given up on nonborrowed reserves targeting.

BORROWED RESERVE TARGETING, 1982–1989

From 1982 until roughly 1989, the Fed experimented with yet another monetary policy operating procedure, called **borrowed reserves targeting.** The Fed's immediate aim in using borrowed reserves targeting was to keep the level of reserves that banks borrow from the discount window near a selected target level. Before we consider what, if anything, the Fed might achieve from using this operating procedure, let's see how it works.

Targeting Borrowed Reserves   Figure 25-17 illustrates how the Fed can target bor- rowed reserves. Panel (a) of Figure 25-17 depicts the borrowed reserves supply schedule by itself. Panel (b) shows the total reserves supply schedule obtained by adding nonbor- rowed reserves to the borrowed reserves supply schedule from panel (a), along with the total reserves demand schedule.

As the procedure's name implies, the Fed chooses a desired target level of *borrowed* reserves, denoted BR* in panel (a) of Figure 25-17. The Fed's problem then is to figure out how to induce depository institutions to borrow this amount of reserves. As panel (a) indicates, the way to do this is to make certain that the market for bank reserves produces just the right federal funds rate to induce depository institutions to borrow the amount BR* from the Fed. This federal funds rate, which is consistent with the Fed's borrowed reserves target, is denoted $r_f(\text{BR*})$.

DID THE FED REALLY TARGET NONBORROWED RESERVES AND THE QUANTITY OF MONEY FROM 1979 TO 1982?

When the Fed switched to nonborrowed reserves targeting in 1979 and simultaneously announced a renewed emphasis on the quantity of money as an intermediate target, many observers concluded that monetarism had finally triumphed over traditional Keynesian orthodoxy. Within just a few months after the announcement, however, many monetarists renounced the approach the Fed had taken toward achieving the goals it had announced. Indeed, some accused the Fed of falsely professing an interest in targeting nonborrowed reserves and attaining a monetary target.

Did the Fed Really Change Its Operating Procedure in 1979?

At the time of the policy change, there were insufficient data to evaluate this view. In a couple of studies in the late 1980s, however, Dennis Jansen of Texas A&M University, together with Michael Bradley of George Washington University and Thomas Cosimano of the University of Notre Dame, sought to determine whether or not the Fed really changed its operating procedure. They used sophisticated statistical procedures to do this, but it is easy to explain the basic idea behind their analyses. If the Fed really shifted to a nonborrowed reserves targeting procedure in 1979, then between that time and 1982 nonborrowed reserves should not have been influenced by changes in interest rates; furthermore, interest rates should have become more variable.

In fact, the studies by these authors found that before 1979 nonborrowed reserves varied with interest rate movements, but this reserve aggregate did not do so after 1979. In addition, the variability of the federal funds rate increased by about twenty times after 1979 as compared with the period in which the Fed targeted the federal funds rate. Consequently, these studies indicate that the Fed really did switch procedures in 1979.

Did the Fed Ever Really Care about Monetary Targets?

Most bothersome to the monetarists who had argued for adoption of the nonborrowed reserves procedure in 1979 was their belief that, in fact, the Fed adopted monetary targets in name only. In their view, this was a Fed claim, but not a reality. In the words of Milton Friedman, in a 1985 *Wall Street Journal* opinion column,

> There is an old story about a farmer who used his barn door for target shooting. A visitor was astounded to find that each of the numerous targets on the door had a bullet hole precisely in the center of the bull's-eye. He later discovered the secret of such remarkable accuracy. Unobserved, he saw the farmer first shoot at the door and then paint the target.
>
> That is the precise counterpart of the way in which the Federal Reserve System hits its monetary bull's-eye. It simply repaints its target. . . .
>
> Monetary targets that meant something would contribute to both monetary and economic stability. Monetary targets that are repainted whenever the Fed regards it as convenient to do so serve only to conciliate short-sighted congressmen and *Wall Street Journal* commentators.

To see why Friedman reached the conclusion that the Fed did not take monetary targets seriously, consider the accompanying figure. The solid path in the figure is the actual path of a measure of M1 from late 1975 through the end of 1984. Along that path are *target ranges* for M1 established by the Fed at various points in time. Note that the Fed would always determine its target ranges using the actual money stock as a starting point, even if the money stock had risen above or fallen below the earlier target range. This led the money stock to *drift* over time, usually upward but sometimes downward. This entailed drift in the monetary base as well, and so such monetary drift is called **base drift.** Also permitted to drift were the Fed's monetary target ranges, as shown in the figure, hence Friedman's conclusion that the Fed simply repainted its targets.

Why would the Fed permit base drift to occur? Marvin Goodfriend, an economist from the Federal Reserve Bank of Richmond, offered a theory in a 1987 study that base drift results because the Fed has other objectives besides monetary and price stability. According to Goodfriend, the problem is that the Fed also desires to smooth interest rates, but it can't do that and simultaneously smooth the money stock and price level as well.

Goodfriend's hypothesis can explain base drift, but other hypotheses can as well, and these alternative theories do not require that the Fed has any objectives

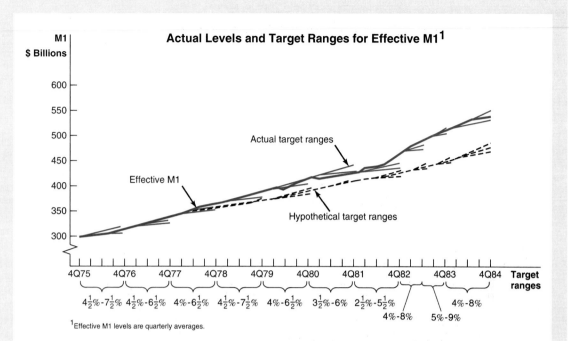

Actual Levels and Target Ranges for Effective M1[1]

[1]Effective M1 levels are quarterly averages.

Base Drift of a Measure of M1.   During the 1979–1982 period in which the Fed targeted monetary aggregates, critics contended that the Fed adjusted its targets after the fact. Base drift, or the tendency of the money stock to depart from an original target path, never to return, is apparent evidence that the critics may have had a point. The Fed commonly readjusted its target ranges for the quantity of money after allowing the actual quantity of money to move to the edges of, or even beyond, previous target ranges, as shown above. [*Source:* Alfred Broaddus and Marvin Goodfriend, "Base Drift and the Longer Run Growth of M1: Experience from a Decade of Monetary Targeting," Federal Reserve Bank of Richmond *Economic Review,* 70 (6, November/December 1984), pp. 3–14.]

other than monetary and price level stability. For instance, base drift is the best policy if there are permanent shifts in the economy's money demand schedule; such shifts require permanent shifts in the Fed's supply of money as well if the Fed is to maintain stable prices. Furthermore, if the quantity of money is not perfectly controllable by the Fed, the process of targeting money itself may cause base drift, again even if the Fed cares nothing about interest rate smoothing.

So, did the Fed really care about monetary targets in the 1970s and early 1980s? Perhaps only the Fed knows for sure. The problem is that people at the Fed disagree. For instance, in his 1987 book about the Fed entitled *Secrets of the Temple,* William Greider quotes some former Fed officials as saying they never took monetary targeting seriously. Nonetheless, many officials not quoted by Greider took exception to his claim that the

Fed did not care about monetary targets; according to them, they and others at the Fed at that time were serious about monetary targets, even if a few others weren't. We may never know for certain whose views really dominated at the Fed.

Sources: Michael D. Bradley and Dennis W. Jansen, "Federal Reserve Operating Procedures in the Eighties: A Dynamic Analysis," *Journal of Money, Credit, and Banking,* 18 (3, August 1986), pp. 323–335; Thomas F. Cosimano and Dennis W. Jansen, "Federal Reserve Policy, 1975–1985: An Empirical Analysis," *Journal of Macroeconomics,* 10 (1, Winter 1988), pp. 27–47; Milton Friedman, "The Fed Hasn't Changed Its Ways," *Wall Street Journal* (August 20, 1985), editorial page; Alfred Broaddus and Marvin Goodfriend, "Base Drift and the Longer Run Growth of M1: Experience from a Decade of Monetary Targeting," Federal Reserve Bank of Richmond *Economic Review,* 70 (6, November/December 1984), pp. 3–14; and Marvin Goodfriend, "Interest Rate Smoothing and Price Level Trend-Stationarity," *Journal of Monetary Economics,* 19 (2, May 1987), pp. 335–348.

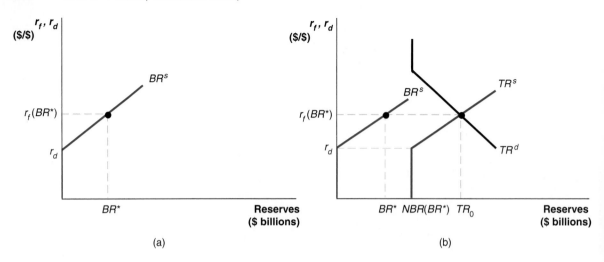

Figure 25-17

Targeting Borrowed Reserves.   Under borrowed reserves targeting, the Fed selects a target level of borrowed reserves, BR*. Based on its knowledge of the shape and position of the borrowed reserves supply function [panel (a)], the Fed determines the federal funds rate that allows it to achieve this target. In turn, attaining the needed federal funds rate, $r_f(M^*)$, requires that the Fed set the level of nonborrowed reserves, NBR(M^*), to position the total reserves supply schedule in an intersection with the total reserves demand schedule at that federal funds rate [panel (b)].

As shown in panel (b) of Figure 25-17, the way for the Fed to attain this needed equilibrium federal funds rate is to conduct open-market operations to achieve the right quantity of nonborrowed reserves, labeled NBR(BR*). This places the total reserves supply schedule in the position needed to attain the equilibrium federal funds rate, r_f(BR*).

To summarize, a borrowed reserves targeting procedure is implemented in the following way. The Fed conducts open-market operations to vary nonborrowed reserves as necessary to yield an equilibrium federal funds rate that, in turn, induces depository institutions to borrow the amount of reserves that is consistent with the Fed's target.

Advantages and Disadvantages of Borrowed Reserves Targeting   If this seems like a somewhat convoluted operating procedure, you are not the only one who feels this way. Nevertheless, Federal Reserve policy makers and economists offer an alleged advantage of this procedure as compared with alternatives. The advantage is that, under this procedure, *neither* the federal funds rate *nor* the level of nonborrowed reserves is fixed. The Fed must let both adjust to achieve its borrowed reserves target from one time period to the next. This, according to Fed officials, means that this procedure is more flexible than alternatives.

A problem that economists had after 1982 was evaluating the usefulness of the borrowed reserves procedure when the Fed's intermediate policy targets were unclear. After 1982, Fed officials sometimes appeared to focus on a range of policy indicators, including nominal income, the term structure of interest rates, international trade flows, commodity prices, and, lately, of all things, the quantity of money! Hence, it was very difficult for economists to evaluate this procedure fully. Sometimes it appeared to be federal funds rate targeting, while other times it appeared to be borrowed reserves targeting. Only the Fed knew for sure.

CURRENT CONTROVERSY

WAS THE BORROWED RESERVES TARGETING PROCEDURE A SMOKESCREEN FOR FEDERAL FUNDS RATE TARGETING?

Under the borrowed reserves targeting procedure described above and illustrated in Figure 25-17, the Fed conducted open-market operations to achieve an equilibrium federal funds rate that induced depository institutions to borrow an amount of reserves that the Fed desired. Therefore, this procedure necessarily entailed targeting a quantity of reserves via an *indirect federal funds rate target*. Some observers have contended, however, that the Fed's *true* target under its procedure was not really borrowed reserves at all; instead, they have argued, the Fed returned to a procedure that had the *actual* objective of limiting variability of the federal funds rate.

Those who have been cynical about the Fed's motives point to a rather interesting fact: The Fed changed its borrowed reserves target very frequently. For instance, during the first four years in which the Fed used the borrowed reserves targeting procedure, it changed its borrowed reserves target *twenty-one times in a forty-four-month period*. Hence, the Fed changed its borrowed reserves target almost once every two months, or nearly as often as the FOMC met during the period. One obvious reason why the Fed might change a *nominal* borrowings target, of course, might be to increase it gradually to adjust for inflation. Of the twenty-one adjustments mentioned above, however, eleven were *decreases*, while the remaining ten were increases. Indeed, it has not been uncommon for the Fed to increase its borrowed reserves target one month, reduce it once or twice in the following two or three months, and then increase it again.

Why would the Fed change its borrowings target so often? A cynical answer to this question is that perhaps the "borrowings target" really was a smokescreen for a policy procedure that really smooths variations in the federal funds rate. According to this view held by many Fed critics, what the Fed *really* did was not unlike the behavior of a high school chemistry student who begins by looking up coefficient values in the *Handbook of Chemistry and Physics,* boils some water to make it look like he really is doing his project, makes up data to fit the answer he knows he should get, and signs out of the lab. The Fed, in like manner, knew what federal funds rate it wanted, according to its critics. It then made up a borrowed reserves "target" that was consistent with this desired federal funds rate. As a result, it actually varied its borrowed reserves "target" to be certain it attained its *true* target: a particular value for the federal funds rate. Indeed, at some intervals during the borrowed reserves targeting period the federal funds rate was at least as stable as it was during the time when the Fed explicitly targeted the federal funds rate.

Certainly, this cynical view appears to explain the Fed's behavior. There is an alternative explanation, however. This is that, in fact, the Fed targeted borrowed reserves as it claimed. Nonetheless, it found that it needed to vary its borrowed reserves target in an effort to achieve *other* objectives. For instance, if the Fed were to use nominal income as an intermediate target, as some believe it has done on an informal basis in recent years, then Fed efforts to stabilize nominal income would require periodic adjustments in the Fed's borrowed reserves target in the market for bank reserves. Furthermore, oscillating upward and downward Fed adjustments of the borrowed reserves target might be optimal in such a situation, and these would appear to coincide with less variability of the federal funds rate even if stabilizing the federal funds rate were not a Fed objective.

Sources: Daniel L. Thornton, "The Borrowed-Reserves Operating Procedure: Theory and Evidence," Federal Reserve Bank of St. Louis *Review,* 73 (1, January/February 1988), pp. 30–54, and David D. VanHoose, "Borrowed Reserves Targeting and Nominal Income Smoothing," *Journal of Macroeconomics,* 12 (2, Spring 1990), pp. 263–278.

Experience with Borrowed Reserves Targeting   This does not mean that monetary policy was unsuccessful under borrowed reserves targeting. If a policy procedure is judged solely on the Fed's performance with respect to its *ultimate* goals, then Fed policy making from 1982 through 1989 was not too bad. In general, inflation was lower than in the 1970s and not too much higher than in the 1950s and 1960s. Real output growth during that period was high and stable.

Most economists doubt, however, that the Fed's borrowed reserves targeting procedure was responsible for these fairly positive economic outcomes. Many observers have argued that the Fed simply was lucky. According to this view, the borrowed reserves targeting procedure was inherently flawed, but external events such as falling oil prices at just the right times in the 1980s and the U.S. success in the Persian Gulf War in 1991 saved the Fed from mistakes that this operating procedure otherwise would have caused.

RECYCLING IN THE 1990s: THE RETURN OF FEDERAL FUNDS RATE TARGETS

As if to verify this view, in the 1990s the Fed has made yet another change in its operating procedure. Although this change was not widely publicized, the Fed again began to target the federal funds rate. It did so for two reasons. First, the linkages between borrowed reserves and its ultimate goals weakened. Second, the relationship between monetary aggregates and its final output and price level goals seemed to recover.

Indeed, the Fed's policy strategy in the 1990s is almost a throwback to the 1970s. The Fed has begun to pay more attention to monetary aggregates again, though now it places more emphasis on M2 instead of M1. It also is willing to tolerate greater variability in monetary aggregates in the 1990s than it did in the 1970s. Yet the Fed appears to have come full circle in its policy making, as it again targets an interest rate in an effort to achieve monetary, price, and output goals. We shall all see in the coming years if this renewed federal funds rate operating procedure is a success.

CHAPTER SUMMARY

1. Depository institutions desire to hold reserves for two purposes. One is to meet reserve requirements, which depend upon the required reserve ratio and the quantity of bank deposits subject to reserve requirements. The other is to hold prudential, excess reserves. Because the opportunity cost of holding excess reserves is the federal funds rate, depository institutions desire to hold more excess reserves when the federal funds rate falls and less excess reserves when the federal funds rate rises. Therefore, the total reserves demand schedule slopes downward over most of its range.

2. The Fed supplies reserves to the banking system in two ways. First, it supplies nonborrowed reserves via open-market purchases. Second, it supplies borrowed reserves through the discount window. The Fed generally sets the discount rate below the federal funds rate, and so it restricts the amount of reserves that depository institutions may borrow. Nonetheless, it typically permits them to borrow more reserves as the federal funds rate rises relative to the discount rate. Consequently, the total reserves supply schedule slopes upward over most of its range.

3. The equilibrium federal funds rate is the federal funds rate at which the total quantity of reserves demanded by banks is equal to the total quantity of reserves supplied by the Fed, so that the market for bank reserves is in equilibrium. In addition, banks are satisfied with the amount

of reserves they exchange at this federal funds rate in the private federal funds market. Hence, when the reserves market is in equilibrium, so is the federal funds market.

4. Other things equal, an open-market purchase or reduction in the Fed's discount rate reduces the equilibrium federal funds rate and increases the equilibrium quantity of total reserves in the banking system. An open-market sale or increase in the discount rate increases the equilibrium federal funds rate and reduces the equilibrium quantity of total reserves, assuming that all other factors are unchanged.

5. Because of the risk structure and term structure that relates interest rates of financial instruments with differing characteristics and terms to maturity, the Fed can influence other interest rates in the economy by using its policy instruments to induce variations in the equilibrium federal funds rate. It is this mechanism that constitutes the ''money supply process'' and through which the Fed can influence the quantity of money.

6. Under the federal funds rate targeting of the 1970s, the Fed sought to keep the equilibrium federal funds rate at a constant value that the Fed deemed to be consistent with its intermediate monetary targets. This policy procedure seemed to be successful initially because it automatically offset the effects of variability in reserve market conditions. It was less successful when money demand became more volatile as the 1970s progressed.

7. In the face of declining control of monetary aggregates and worsening inflation, the Fed in 1979 adopted a nonborrowed reserves targeting procedure. While this procedure appeared to assist the Fed in its efforts to contain inflation, monetary and interest rate variability actually increased. The relationship between money and other economic variables broke down in the early 1980s, eliminating the rationale for the new procedure. Consequently, the Fed stopped using it in 1982.

8. From 1982 until roughly 1989, the Fed used a borrowed reserves targeting procedure. Economists found the advantages and disadvantages of this procedure to be difficult to evaluate. Nonetheless, the Fed used it with no apparent ill effects.

9. Since 1989, the Fed has returned to federal funds rate targeting and has given renewed attention to monetary aggregates.

GLOSSARY

Base drift: A tendency for actual and targeted levels of monetary aggregates to shift over time.

Borrowed reserves targeting: A monetary policy operating procedure used by the Fed from October 1982 until 1989, in which the New York Fed's Trading Desk bought and sold securities in quantities sufficient to attain an equilibrium federal funds rate that, in turn, induced banks to borrow a target level of reserves from the Fed's discount window.

Federal funds rate targeting: A monetary policy operating procedure under which the New York Fed's Trading Desk conducted sufficient open-market purchases and sales to keep the federal funds rate at or very near a target level that the FOMC judged to be consistent with achieving an intermediate monetary target; used by the Fed throughout the 1970s until October 1979.

Market for bank reserves: The nationwide market in which the Federal Reserve System supplies reserves through its open-market operations and via the discount window; depository institutions demand these reserves for use in meeting reserve requirements and in holding prudential, excess reserves.

Nonborrowed reserves targeting: A monetary policy operating procedure under which the New York Fed's Trading Desk bought and sold securities in sufficient quantities to keep the level of nonborrowed reserves on or near a target growth path; adopted because of its automatic-stabilizing properties in the face of money demand variability that caused the money stock to deviate from the Fed's target, this procedure was used from October 1979 until roughly October 1982.

Operating procedure: The manner in which the Fed conducts monetary policy on a day-to-day basis.

SELF-TEST QUESTIONS

1. Draw a diagram of the total reserves demand schedule, and answer the following questions.
   a. There should be a kink in the schedule. Explain why the schedule is vertical above this kink and how to interpret the quantity of reserves corresponding to this vertical portion of the schedule.
   b. Why does the total reserves demand schedule slope downward to the right of the kink?
2. Draw the total reserves supply schedule, and answer the following questions.
   a. Who supplies reserves: the Fed, private depository institutions, or both?
   b. There should be a kink in the schedule. Explain why the schedule is vertical below the kink and how to interpret the quantity of reserves corresponding to the vertical portion of the schedule.
   c. Why does the total reserves supply schedule slope upward to the right of the kink?
3. Why do the federal funds and Treasury securities yield curves typically slope upward? Why does the federal funds yield curve generally lie above the Treasury securities yield curve?
4. Why is it that the interest rate on a financial instrument with a term to maturity of a few weeks or a few months has much more direct effect on the demand for money than the 1-day federal funds rate?
5. Suppose that the Fed uses an operating procedure in which it seeks to target the federal funds rate. If the Fed decides that it must, for some reason unrelated to monetary policy, increase its discount rate, should the New York Fed's Trading Desk purchase or sell U.S. government securities? Use a fully labeled diagram of the market for bank reserves to assist in explaining your answer.
6. Suppose that there is a large and persistent fall in the demand for money. If the Fed wishes to minimize differences between the actual equilibrium quantity of money and a monetary target M^*, would it be more likely to achieve its goal by using a federal funds rate target or a nonborrowed reserves target? Use appropriate diagrams to justify your answer.
7. Suppose that the Fed's operating procedure entails achieving a borrowed reserves target, BR^*. If there is a signficant and persistent decline in transactions deposits in the banking system, should the New York Fed's Trading Desk buy or sell U.S. government securities? Use diagrams to assist you in explaining your answer.
8. Explain, in your own words, why the equilibrium federal funds rate is consistent both with reserves market equilibrium and with federal funds market equilibrium.

PROBLEMS

25-1.   Consider the diagram on the facing page when answering the questions below. Explain how you obtain your answers.
   a. What is the quantity of required reserves?
   b. What is the discount rate?

c. What is the level of nonborrowed reserves?

d. What is the equilibrium value of the federal funds rate?

e. What is the equilibrium quantity of borrowed reserves?

f. What is the equilibrium quantity of excess reserves?

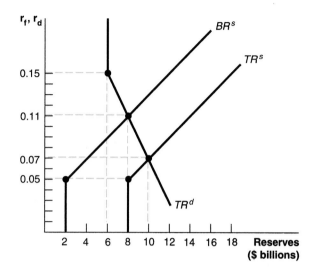

25-2. Suppose that the Federal Reserve presently targets nonborrowed reserves at a level of $50 billion and that it has achieved its target. Required reserves are equal to $40 billion. Equilibrium total reserves are equal to $60 billion. Answer the following questions, and show your work.

a. What is the equilibrium quantity of borrowed reserves, assuming that depository institutions do not borrow from the Fed when the federal funds rate is less than the discount rate?

b. What is the equilibrium quantity of excess reserves?

25-3. Suppose that the Fed presently targets borrowed reserves at a level of $5 billion and that it has achieved its target. Required reserves are equal to $60 billion, and equilibrium excess reserves are equal to $10 billion. Answer the following questions, and show your work.

a. What is the equilibrium quantity of total reserves?

b. What is the level of nonborrowed reserves, assuming that depository institutions do not borrow from the Fed when the federal funds rate is less than the discount rate?

25-4. Suppose that reserve market equilibrium occurs at a federal funds rate of 6 percent. A few depository institutions borrow from the Fed when the federal funds rate is below the discount rate; these depository institutions have no source of funds other than the Fed and maintain a constant level of borrowing of $5 billion. The equilibrium level of total reserves is equal to $100 billion, and required reserves are equal to $90 billion. Finally, the Fed's discount rate is 8 percent. Use all the information above to draw a rough diagram of this situation in the market for bank reserves. Then answer the following questions.

a. Is the discount rate a subsidy rate or a penalty rate?

b. What is the equilibrium quantity of borrowed reserves?

c. What level of nonborrowed reserves has the Fed supplied via open-market operations?

d. What is the equilibrium quantity of excess reserves?

SELECTED REFERENCES

Bradley, Michael D., and Dennis W. Jansen, ''Federal Reserve Operating Procedures in the Eighties: A Dynamic Analysis,'' *Journal of Money, Credit, and Banking,* 18 (3, August 1986), pp. 323–335.

Broaddus, Alfred, and Marvin Goodfriend, ''Base Drift and the Longer Run Growth of M1: Experience from a Decade of Monetary Targeting,'' Federal Reserve Bank of Richmond *Economic Review,* 70 (6, November/December 1984), pp. 3–14.

Bryant, Ralph C., *Controlling Money: The Federal Reserve and Its Critics* (Washington, D.C.: The Brookings Institution, 1983).

Cosimano, Thomas F., and Dennis W. Jansen, ''Federal Reserve Policy, 1975–1985: An Empirical Analysis,'' *Journal of Macroeconomics,* 10 (1, Winter 1988), pp. 27–47.

Gilbert, R. Alton, ''Operating Procedures for Conducting Monetary Policy,'' Federal Reserve Bank of St. Louis *Review,* 67 (2, February 1985), pp. 13–21.

Goodfriend, Marvin, ''Interest Rate Smoothing and Price Level Trend-Stationarity,'' *Journal of Monetary Economics,* 19 (2, May 1987), pp. 335–348.

Greider, William, *Secrets of the Temple: How the Federal Reserve Runs the Country* (New York: Simon and Schuster, 1987).

Heller, Robert, ''Implementing Monetary Policy,'' *Federal Reserve Bulletin,* 74 (7, July 1988), pp. 419–429.

Meltzer, Allan H., ''The Fed at Seventy-Five,'' *Monetary Policy on the 75th Anniversary of the Federal Reserve System,* Michael T. Belongia, ed. (Boston: Kluwer Academic Publishers, 1991), pp. 3–66.

Meulendyke, Ann-Marie, *U.S. Monetary Policy and Financial Markets* (New York: Federal Reserve Bank of New York, 1989).

Roth, Howard L., ''Has Deregulation Ruined M1 as a Policy Guide?'' Federal Reserve Bank of Kansas City *Economic Review,* 72 (6, June 1987), pp. 24–37.

Stone, Courtenay C., and Daniel L. Thornton, ''Solving the 1980s Velocity Puzzle: A Progress Report,'' Federal Reserve Bank of St. Louis *Review,* 69 (5, August/September 1987), pp. 5–23.

Thornton, Daniel L., ''The Borrowed-Reserves Operating Procedure: Theory and Evidence,'' Federal Reserve Bank of St. Louis *Review,* 73 (1, January/February 1988), pp. 30–54.

VanHoose, David D., ''Borrowed Reserves Targeting and Nominal Income Smoothing,'' *Journal of Macroeconomics,* 12 (2, Spring 1990), pp. 263–278.

———, ''Monetary Targeting and Price Level Non-Trend-Stationarity,'' *Journal of Money, Credit, and Banking,* 21 (2, May 1989), pp. 232–239.

Walsh, Carl, ''In Defense of Base Drift,'' *American Economic Review,* 76 (September 1986), pp. 692–700.

———, ''Issues in the Choice of Monetary Policy Operating Procedures,'' *Monetary Policy for a Changing Financial Environment,* William S. Haraf and Phillip Cagan, eds. (Washington, D.C.: The AEI Press, 1990), pp. 8–37.

chapter 26

Rules Versus Discretion in Monetary Policy

U p to this point in the text, we have concentrated on what monetary policy might or might not be *able* to do for, or to, the economy. We have not, however, tackled another important issue, which is whether or not the Fed *should* actively attempt to use its policy instruments in efforts to improve economic performance. This issue, which is central to the field of money and banking, is the subject of the present chapter.

RULES VERSUS DISCRETION

Essentially, arguments about Fed policy must begin by tackling a single question. Should the Fed use policy *rules* or should it use its own *discretion* when it determines its monetary policies? This has long been a key topic of debate in money and banking, and it promises to remain so for years to come.

MONETARY POLICY RULES

Before we begin our analysis of economic arguments about rules versus discretion in monetary policy, we must be certain to define our terms carefully. Let's begin by defining a **monetary policy rule.** This is a policy strategy to which a central bank such as the Federal Reserve might *bind* or *commit* itself. By this we mean that the Fed would, if it adopted a monetary policy rule, follow that rule no matter what occurs in the economy, such as an economic expansion or an economic contraction.

There are many possible rules for monetary policy. In fact, the potential number of rules is infinite. For instance, the Fed could commit itself to keeping the federal funds rate constant at 6 percent indefinitely. Alternatively, it could commit itself to increasing the quantity of money by 10 percent for every 1-percentage-point increase in the federal funds rate. Or it could maintain a 2-percentage-point spread between the federal funds rate and the discount rate. Or it could commit itself to increasing the quantity of money at a rate of 2 percent annually.

Note that a monetary policy rule does not necessarily require that the Fed keep an instrument, intermediate target, or ultimate policy goal at some constant level. What a rule involves is making a precommitment to follow a particular strategy and sticking with that strategy irrespective of what may happen to economic variables. A monetary policy rule need not be simple; what makes it a rule is that the Fed commits to the rule and does not depart from it whether the economy does well or poorly.

MONETARY POLICY DISCRETION

Now that we have defined a monetary policy rule, defining monetary policy discretion is straightforward. Simply stated, monetary policy discretion allows for Federal Reserve policy making in the absence of a monetary policy rule.

For instance, we know from Chapter 15 that the Fed's Federal Open Market Committee meets eight times each year. Between meetings, a few FOMC members and staff officials confer daily. One type of discretionary monetary policy would entail day-to-day variations of Fed policy in light of economic events as they transpire, with minimal constraints on open-market operations, discount window policy, or reserve requirements.

More generally, Fed discretion occurs whenever the Fed decides to respond to economic events in ways it had not previously planned. Most policy makers, including the Fed, plot out broad strategies for their policies. If they stick closely to these strategies, then they follow policy rules. If they depart from them, however, they use their discretion. They respond to economic events as they occur, rather than turning a blind eye to temporary economic fluctuations.

THE TRADITIONAL CASE FOR MONETARY POLICY RULES: TIME LAGS IN POLICY MAKING

Economist Milton Friedman provided the classic argument in favor of rules over discretion in macroeconomic policy making in 1953.[1] The essence of Friedman's argument was that monetary policy makers may have very good intentions but still may worsen economic performance through discretionary attempts to stabilize the economy. Although Friedman is a monetarist (see Chapter 21) who does not believe that the Federal Reserve System can exert any long-run effects on real economic activity, he is willing to concede the possibility that monetary policy might have a potential stabilizing role. Nevertheless, Friedman concludes, discretionary monetary policy making more often than not makes things worse for the economy.

THE NEED FOR COUNTERCYCLICAL MONETARY POLICY

To understand the basis of Friedman's reasoning, suppose for the sake of argument that the Federal Reserve's main goal is to stabilize the price level. By definition, then, monetary

---

[1] Milton Friedman, ''The Effects of a Full-Employment Policy on Economic Stability: A Formal Analysis,'' in *Essays in Positive Economics* (Chicago: University of Chicago Press, 1953).

policy actions would stabilize prices if the level of prices is less variable in the presence of policy actions than it would have been if there had been no policy actions at all. That is, successful Federal Reserve stabilization policies must make the price level less variable than it would have been if the Fed had undertaken no policies in the first place.

Clearly, then, the very worst policy that the Federal Reserve could follow would be to undertake actions either that increase the price level when it already is rising or that reduce the price level during a time when it already is declining. If the Fed did this, it would be conducting **procyclical monetary policy,** meaning that its actions would *reinforce* existing tendencies for prices to rise or fall over time. Because a procyclical policy would add to variability of the price level, this would be a wrongheaded policy for the Fed to pursue.

Instead, successful Federal Reserve stabilization policies require that the Fed conduct **countercyclical monetary policy** actions when they are needed. Countercyclical monetary policy actions automatically offset movements in real output that otherwise would have occurred in the absence of Fed policy making. Consequently, countercyclical policy making by the Fed requires the Fed to contract the quantity of money when prices are rising and to increase the quantity of money when prices are falling.

THE PROBLEM OF TIME LAGS IN MONETARY POLICY

Milton Friedman and other economists question whether discretionary monetary policy making typically will be countercyclical. The main reason is that they believe that policy making is plagued by various **policy time lags,** which, when summed together, constitute an interval of time between a need for a countercyclical policy action and the actual effect of that policy action on an economic variable.

One type of time lag in policy is the **recognition lag.** This is the interval that passes between the time that the need for a countercyclical policy action arises and the time this need is recognized by a policy maker. For instance, if the Fed's goal is to stabilize the price level, and prices begin a prolonged increase today, the Fed may not have sufficient data for several weeks. Consequently, the Fed likely will fail to recognize the need for a policy action intended to cause an offsetting reduction in the level of prices. The time it takes for the Fed to realize it needs to do this is the Fed's recognition lag. This lag, therefore, could be weeks or months.

A second type of policy time lag is the **implementation,** or **response, lag.** This is the time between recognition of a need for a countercyclical policy action and actual implementation of the policy action. For example, for the Fed the implementation lag could be the time between realization of a need to change its policies and the time of the next FOMC meeting, at which a new, appropriately countercyclical policy action could be initiated. As we noted in Chapter 17, Fed staff officers and a few FOMC committee members confer each day, and so the implementation lag for the Fed in theory could be very short. Nevertheless, major shifts in monetary policy must be approved by the full FOMC, and so the implementation lag for the Fed may stretch to weeks in length. Furthermore, disagreements among FOMC members could push monetary policy decisions farther into the future, lengthening the implementation lag.

Finally, monetary policy is subject to a **transmission lag.** This is the time that elapses between implementation of an intended countercyclical policy and its ultimate effects on an economic variable. The common analogy to think of is the transmission of a rear-wheel-drive automobile. When the driver moves the gearshift lever to a new position, this action causes internal parts to move that, in turn, actually move the gears. The effects of this gear shift then are transmitted, through the drive shaft, to the rear wheels of the automobile, causing them, say, to change direction. All this happens quickly unless you are in a hurry (or own an old, used car). Then the lag sometimes may seem interminable.

Likewise, when the Fed decreases the quantity of money in an effort to offset counter-cyclically a rise in prices, everything doesn't happen instantaneously. As we discussed in Chapter 17, the Fed must vary an instrument of monetary policy; for example, it must sell government securities. Then the resulting decrease in nonborrowed reserves must bring about, through the money multiplier effect, the reduction in the quantity of money. Finally, the fall in the money stock must reduce aggregate demand and cause the equilibrium level of prices to decline.

Time lags significantly complicate the Fed's efforts to conduct countercyclical monetary policies. Consider the following example. Suppose that the level of prices suddenly rises, perhaps because of a sudden increase in autonomous household consumption that increases aggregate demand. Because of the recognition lag, it will take some time for the Fed to realize that this event has occurred. Furthermore, by the time the Fed has decided to reduce the quantity of money to offset the rise in aggregate demand, autonomous household consumption may have returned to its previous level, reducing the upward pressure on prices without the need for Fed action. Yet the Fed already will have reduced the money stock. By the time that this policy action has been transmitted through the economy, some other event, such as a reduction in government spending, may have pushed prices down further; the Fed's action then will simply worsen the situation. Indeed, by the time its policy action has been transmitted to the level of prices, that action may have unintentionally become a procyclical policy.

According to Milton Friedman, well-meaning policy makers at the Fed often create problems by trying to follow up on their good intentions. Consequently, Friedman concludes that the Fed should abandon discretionary policy making in favor of a monetary *rule*. If the Fed could design a perfectly countercyclical rule, Friedman would be all for it. Otherwise, however, Friedman has argued for years that the best Fed policy strategy is to do as little as possible to influence the direction of economic activity. As a result, policy makers would transmit no additional variability to prices (or real output) through their well-intentioned, but potentially misguided, actions.

DISCRETIONARY MONETARY POLICY AND INFLATION[2]

Many economists find Friedman's argument persuasive. Nevertheless, most believe that the Fed conducts discretionary monetary policies. Indeed, economists at the Fed—a few of whom even had Milton Friedman as a professor in years past—commonly defend Fed discretion, arguing that the Fed has done much to reduce the durations of the various time lags. If the time lag problem is, or has been, solved, they contend, discretion is preferable to fixed policy rules.

In light of Friedman's model that we discussed above, this view has its merits. If the Fed could always learn quickly about the need for a policy action and respond quickly to that need, it might be able to conduct truly countercylical monetary policies.

It turns out, however, that there is another potential problem with discretionary policy making by the Fed. As we explain below, monetary policy discretion may contribute to inflation. That is, a discretionary monetary policy maker may adopt inflationary policies

---

[2] This section is adapted from the literature initiated by the work of Finn Kydland and Edward Prescott, "Rules Rather Than Discretion: The Inconsistency of Optimal Plans," *Journal of Political Economy,* 85 (3, June 1977), pp. 473–492, and Robert J. Barro and David B. Gordon, "A Positive Theory of Monetary Policy in a Natural Rate Model," *Journal of Political Economy,* 91 (4, August 1983), pp. 598–610.

that would result from a lack of a monetary rule. Furthermore, this could happen even if the Fed does not want high inflation. Hence, rules still may be better than discretion.

THE BASIC FRAMEWORK: THE MODERN KEYNESIAN CONTRACTING THEORY

Why would the Fed ever conduct inflationary monetary policies if it doesn't desire high inflation? To understand this, we shall need to consider another model below. This model, however, is not a new one. We first encountered the model—the modern Keynesian contracting model—in Chapter 22.

A Review of the Keynesian Contracting Model   Recall from Chapter 22 that the modern Keynesian theory incorporates the rational expectations hypothesis into a model with sticky wages. In this model, the nominal wage rate that workers and firms set via contracts is consistent with the rational behavior of these agents. That is, workers and firms agree to set a wage rate that reflects their preferences and that is the best choice they can make given the information available when they sign contracts.

We shall, as in Chapter 22, make the simplifying assumptions that industries are perfectly competitive and that all workers and firms synchronize their wage contracts. That is, we assume that all workers and firms sign their contracts simultaneously and that all contracts last the same length of time.

Recall that, according to the modern contracting theory, the goal of workers and firms is to set a nominal wage contract that replicates the nominal wage that they anticipate a competitive labor market would have produced under conditions of complete information. When workers and firms sign contracts that fix the nominal wage rate, however, they do not know exactly what economic conditions will prevail during the upcoming contract period. Hence, they will do the best that they can to set a wage that would hold, on average, in the absence of contracts. Their objective is to achieve this wage rate because that is the wage rate at which there is no labor unemployment.

Therefore, as shown in panel (a) of Figure 26-1, workers and firms will agree to set the contracted wage rate, W^c, equal to the expected value of the classical, market-clearing nominal wage rate, which is labeled W^{*e}. Nevertheless, when they negotiate wage contracts, workers and firms do not know the actual level of prices that will arise for the duration of the contracts. According to the theory, however, workers and firms form their best, rational, expectation of what the level of prices will turn out to be, labeled P_0^e. Thus, both workers and firms anticipate that the average level of labor demand by firms during the contract period will be given by the labor demand schedule $MP_n \times P_0^e$. This means that at this anticipated market-clearing wage, the average amount of unemployment would be zero, because at the expected wage rate W^{*e} the labor market would be in equilibrium.

Once the wage is set by contracts at W^c, the level of prices may or may not actually turn out to be equal to the level that workers and firms anticipated. Three possibilities are shown in Figure 26-1. One is that the actual price level P_0 is equal to the expected price level P_0^e. If so, the level of prices actually equals the price level that workers and firms expected when they set their contract wage. As shown in panel (a) of the figure, the position of the labor demand schedule at this price level then determines the level of employment, N_0. At this quantity of employment, workers and firms produce the output level y_0, as shown by the aggregate production function in panel (b). This yields the price-output combination shown as the point P_0 and y_0 in panel (c). Workers and firms exactly realize their expectations in this situation, and so N_0 is the natural employment level and y_0 is the natural output level.

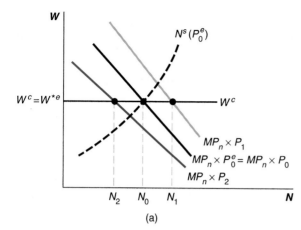

(a)

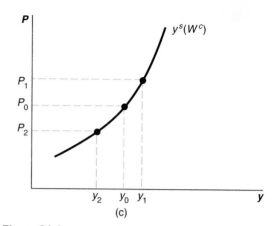

(c)

Figure 26-1

A Review of Aggregate Supply in the Modern Keynesian Contracting Theory.   As we discussed in Chapter 22, the modern contracting theory hypothesizes that workers and firms set a nominal contract wage (W^c) that replicates their expectation of the full-information, labor-market-clearing wage rate (W^{*e}). Once this contract wage is determined, workers are bound to work at this wage based on firms' demand for their labor. If the price level is P_0, which equals the price level that workers and firms expected when they negotiated the contract wage (P_0^e), then they attain the full-information levels of employment [N_0 in panels (a) and (b)] and output [y_0 in panels (b) and (c)]. If the actual price level turns out to be greater than or less than the expected price level, however, equilibrium employment and output will be above or below the full-information levels. Hence, the aggregate supply schedule in panel (c) slopes upward.

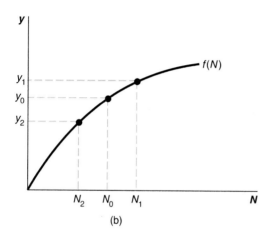

(b)

In general, however, it is unlikely that the price expectations of workers and firms will be fully correct. On the one hand, the price level could actually turn out to be higher than they anticipated when they negotiated their contracts. For instance, the actual price level could turn out to be equal to a level P_1 that is greater than P_0^e. In such a case, labor demand will be higher than workers and firms had anticipated, as shown by the MPN $\times$ P_1 schedule in panel (a) of Figure 26-1. Workers must honor the contracts they signed, and so they find themselves providing more labor services than they had anticipated, given by the amount N_1 in panel (a), and producing more output, y_1 in panel (b). This yields the combination P_1 and y_1 in panel (c).

On the other hand, the price level could turn out to be lower than workers and firms had anticipated. Then, as shown in panel (a) of Figure 26-1, labor demand would fall below its anticipated level, to MP$_n \times P_2$, where P_2 is a price level lower than the expected level of prices P_0^e. As a result, firms would desire fewer labor services, N_2 in panels (a) and (b), than workers and firms had anticipated when they negotiated their wage contracts. They would produce less output, y_2 in panel (b). This would yield the combination P_2 and y_2 in panel (c).

As we discussed in Chapter 22—and now have reviewed for you once again—the schedule defined by the three points that we have constructed is the economy's aggregate supply schedule under wage contracting. We have derived the schedule for the contract wage W^c; consequently, we have used the notation $y^s(W^c)$ to denote the schedule. Changes in this contract wage would shift the aggregate supply schedule. Specifically, a higher contract wage would have produced an aggregate supply schedule above and to the left of the schedule depicted in panel (c) in Figure 26-1. A lower contract wage would have yielded an aggregate supply schedule below and to the right of the schedule that is depicted in panel (c).

Macroeconomic Equilibrium and the Fed's Ultimate Objectives   To complete the contracting model of the economy's market for real output, we must include an aggregate demand schedule with the aggregate supply schedule derived in Figure 26-1. This is done in Figure 26-2, which displays an output market equilibrium implied by the contracting model. The aggregate demand schedule is labeled $y^d(M_0)$ to indicate that the position of the aggregate demand schedule depends, among other things, on the quantity of money, say, M_0. We are interested solely in monetary policy, and so we shall assume that all other factors that might influence the position of the aggregate demand schedule are constant.

Also shown in Figure 26-2 is the economy's long-run aggregate supply schedule, y_{LR}^s, which is vertical at the natural, full-information level of output, y_0. Figure 26-2 depicts a situation in which short-run equilibrium and long-run equilibrium coincide, and the aggregate demand schedule, aggregate supply schedule, and long-run aggregate supply schedule all cross at the same equilibrium price level, P_0.

Finally, Figure 26-2 also includes a level of output labeled y^*. We assume that this level of output, at which we have shown a vertical, dashed line to make it stand out in the

Figure 26-2
Output Market Equilibrium in the Contracting Model.   A full long-run equilibrium in the economy's market for real output occurs at a point at which the aggregate demand, aggregate supply, and long-run aggregate supply schedules intersect at the natural, full-information level of output, given by y_0. At this equilibrium point, the price level is equal to P_0.

The output level y^* is the economy's full-capacity output level. This is the level of real output that the economy is capable of producing but presently does not because other factors, such as income taxes and costs of regulation, reduce the economy's natural output level below its full-capacity level.

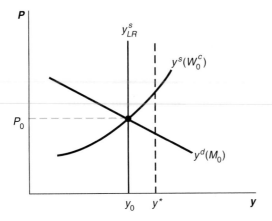

diagram, is an *ultimate target* level of output for the Fed. That is, we assume that one of the Fed's ultimate goals is to achieve a level of output *above* the economy's full-information, natural output level, y_0.

Why would the Fed have such an objective? After all, isn't the natural output level the largest amount that the economy can produce in the long run? The answer to the latter question is yes, but that does not mean that the Fed might not attempt to push the economy above its natural output level. The reason is that the natural, full-information level of output does *not* necessarily correspond to the **full-capacity output** level of the economy. The full-capacity output level is the amount of goods and services that the economy could employ if all resources were employed to their utmost.

There are numerous reasons why the economy's natural, full-information output level typically lies below its full-capacity level. One of the most important is taxes. For instance, taxes on the real wage incomes of workers typically cause them to work less than they otherwise might have wished, meaning that they produce less output than they otherwise would have produced in the absence of income taxes. Another reason that the natural output level usually is less than the full-capacity level of output arises from the existence of governmental regulations. For example, it is now common for governments to place restrictions on how firms may produce some goods and services as a means of protecting the environment from the by-products (such as carbon monoxide or other pollutants) of some means of production. High-polluting production processes, however, may be the lowest-cost means of producing goods and services. Therefore, such governmental regulations often raise the costs of producing goods and services, thereby lowering output relative to what it would have been in the absence of regulations.

Federal Reserve economists routinely estimate the economy's full-capacity output. We assume in Figure 26-2 and in our later discussion that they do so for a reason: The Fed would like, if possible, to use its monetary policies to achieve this level of output, y^*, rather than the lower, natural output level, y_0.

We shall also assume, however, that the Fed has one other ultimate objective: It wishes to keep inflation low. This means that although it would like to raise aggregate demand to expand real output, it also would not wish to overdo any such increase in aggregate demand, because such an action would raise prices above P_0 in Figure 26-2, causing inflation.

A MONETARY POLICY "GAME" AND A THEORY OF INFLATION

We now have all the elements that we need to describe what economists call a monetary policy "game." The thought of games typically conjures up board games, such as Monopoly, or card games, such as poker. People play such games using **strategies,** which are the approaches they take to winning these games, each of which has its own special structure. Furthermore, the strategies that people use in such games typically take into account in some way the behavior of their opponents.

Likewise, the macroeconomic setting depicted in Figure 26-3 leads workers and firms, on the one hand, and the Fed, on the other hand, to form strategies for the economic decisions they make. Specifically, workers and firms must form price expectations so that they may optimally choose their contract wage and, in so doing, must take into account the strategies they expect the Fed to follow in its monetary policy making. The Fed, in turn, must decide on its monetary policy, taking into account the way that workers and firms form their expectations for purposes of setting their contract wage. Effectively, then, private agents (workers and firms) and the Fed are "opponents" in a monetary policy game in which their economic behavior, which stems from their own strategies, interacts to produce a macroeconomic equilibrium.

Potential and Possible Outcomes of the Monetary Policy Game   Figure 26-3 depicts four *potential* monetary policy game outcomes that we might consider, labeled points A, B, C, and D, respectively. We shall explain each of these points below. We shall also show that only *two* of these points are viable, or *possible,* equilibrium positions for the economy that are consistent with the strategies of both private agents and the Fed. Let's consider each of these points in turn.

Point A is the economy's initial equilibrium point that corresponds to the equilibrium point shown earlier, in Figure 26-2, where W_0^c denotes an initial contract wage set by workers and firms. According to the diagram, equilibrium occurs on the economy's long-run aggregate supply schedule at the natural output level, y_0. Therefore, the actual price level, P_0, is equal to the price level initially expected by workers and firms, again denoted P_0^e.

Because the Fed desires to expand the economy's output of goods and services beyond the full-information, natural level of y_0, and toward the full-capacity level of y^*, however, it may be tempted to expand aggregate demand by increasing the quantity of money, from M_0 to M_1. Such a *discretionary* Fed policy action would shift the aggregate demand schedule from $y^d(M_0)$ to $y^d(M_1)$.

If the Fed actually were to increase aggregate demand, it would not typically raise

Figure 26-3
Potential and Possible Outcomes of a Monetary Policy Game.   Point A is an initial equilibrium point for which the economy is at its natural output level, y_0. A *discretionary* Fed policy action
to raise output toward the full-capacity level of y^* shifts the aggregate demand schedule from $y^d(M_0)$
to $y^d(M_1)$. One potential outcome would be a movement along the economy's aggregate supply
schedule to a new short-run equilibrium at point B, with higher output and relatively low inflation.
Yet if workers and firms recognize that the Fed has an incentive to shift the aggregate demand
schedule, they would be unhappy with point B and would raise their expectation of the price level.
This, in turn, would cause the aggregate supply schedule to shift leftward, yielding point D. Point B
would not be a possible equilibrium.

Point C, with output level y_1, might arise if the Fed actually does not attempt to expand output
above its natural level but workers and firms nevertheless anticipate that the Fed will increase the
quantity of money. The Fed, however, would not settle for point C as a macroeconomic equilibrium, and so it also is not a possible outcome. If the Fed did not increase the quantity of money, and
if workers and firms did not believe that it would do so, then the economy would not move from
point A. Point A is a possible equilibrium but is unlikely because of the time inconsistency problem.

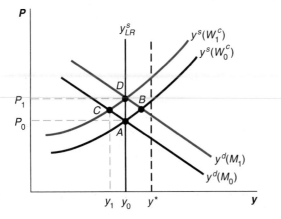

aggregate demand all the way out along the economy's aggregate supply schedule, $y^s(W_0^c)$, to the level of full-capacity output, y^*. If it were to do this, it would increase inflation substantially. Hence, we would expect the Fed to increase aggregate demand by less than this, as shown in Figure 26-3. How much less would depend upon how costly the Fed would view inflation, as compared with how much the Fed desires to expand output toward the full-capacity level.

If the Fed were to increase aggregate demand from $y^d(M_0)$ to $y^d(M_1)$, there are two outcomes that might conceivably occur. One would be a movement along the economy's aggregate supply schedule, $y^s(W_0^c)$, to a new short-run equilibrium at point B. If the Fed could attain point B, it would achieve its goals: Output would expand with low inflation.

If workers and firms understand the Fed's objectives, however, they would be unhappy with a macroeconomic equilibrium at point B. At this equilibrium point, the price level is higher than workers and firms had anticipated when they set the contract wage W_0^c. Therefore, the real wage earned by workers would be less than the full-information real wage they desire, and output would exceed the full-information, natural level that workers and firms wish to produce. Consequently, while point B is a *potential* short-run equilibrium, it is not one that is consistent with the contracting strategy of workers and firms.

In fact, as long as workers and firms understand the Fed's ultimate objectives, they will recognize that the Fed has an incentive to shift the aggregate demand schedule as depicted in Figure 26-3. Indeed, if they were to anticipate that the Fed actually will raise the money stock from M_0 to M_1, they would raise their expectation of the price level, because they know that an increase in aggregate demand would increase the equilibrium price level. But if workers and firms were to expect a higher price level, they would expect that labor demand would increase, causing the full-information wage rate W^* to rise. This means that if workers and firms were to believe that the Fed would increase aggregate demand, they would raise the contract wage, from the initial level W_0^c to a higher level W_1^c. This, in turn, would cause the aggregate supply schedule to shift leftward, from $y^s(W_0^c)$ to $y^s(W_1^c)$, which would yield a macroeconomic equilibrium at point D in Figure 26-3.

The equilibrium at point D is consistent with the strategy of workers and firms, because at this point they have chosen the contract wage optimally, taking into account the behavior they expect from the Fed. In addition, point D is consistent with the Fed's strategy, which is to raise aggregate demand in an attempt to raise output while keeping inflation low (even though, after the fact, the Fed fails in its attempt). Therefore, point D is a *possible* point of equilibrium of the monetary policy game between the Fed and workers and firms.

There are two other potential equilibrium points in our monetary policy game, however. One of these is point C. This equilibrium point might arise if the Fed actually decides that it does not wish to attempt to expand output above its natural level. We know that the Fed would like to do this, so why wouldn't it? The answer is that the Fed presumably is not managed by incompetent policy makers; if they understand how the economy works, they would recognize that if they *did* try to expand output by increasing the money stock, the only possible equilibrium in the monetary policy game is point D in Figure 26-3. In light of this fact, the Fed rationally may decide that the best it can do is keep aggregate demand unchanged, at $y^d(M_0)$. Note that this would effectively represent a Fed policy *rule,* because it would entail a Fed commitment to the particular quantity of money M_0.

Point C conceivably could arise, however, if the Fed does not increase the quantity of money but workers and firms, who realize the Fed may have an incentive to do so, believe that it *will* do so. As we discussed above, if workers and firms anticipate that the Fed will increase the quantity of money and raise the level of prices, they will increase their contract wage, causing the aggregate supply schedule to shift upward and to the left, from $y^s(W_0^c)$ to $y^s(W_1^c)$ in Figure 26-3. In this case, point C would result, at the level of output y_1.

Although point *C* is a *potential* macroeconomic equilibrium, it is *not* a *possible* equilibrium in our monetary policy game. The reason is that this equilibrium point is inconsistent with the Fed's strategy. The last thing the Fed would like to see is both inflation and a *fall* in output to a level below the natural level of output. After all, the Fed's ultimate goals are to *expand* output, if possible, while keeping inflation low. Therefore, the Fed would not settle for point *C* as a macroeconomic equilibrium.

There is one other *possible* equilibrium point, aside from point *D,* in our monetary policy game. This is point *A,* the initial equilibrium point. *If* the Fed did not increase the quantity of money, and *if* workers and firms did not believe that it would do so, then the economy would not move from point *A.* Hence, point *A,* along with point *D,* is a possible point of macroeconomic equilibrium in the monetary policy game.

The Time Inconsistency Problem and an Inflation Bias of Monetary Policy

Figure 26-4 is another version of Figure 26-3 but differs in that it shows only the *possible* equilibrium points of the monetary policy game we have considered. As discussed above, one of these is point *D.* At point *D,* the Fed increases aggregate demand in a *discretionary* manner in an effort to expand output while raising inflation as little as possible; at the same time, private agents recognize that the Fed has an incentive to do this and raise their price expectations and, therefore, their contract wage. Hence, point *D* is a *discretionary monetary policy equilibrium.* The other is point *A.* At this point, the Fed does not increase the money stock to raise aggregate demand, thereby following a monetary *rule;* workers

Figure 26-4

The Inflation Bias of Discretionary Monetary Policy.   Points A and D, which are taken from Figure 26-3, are possible final equilibrium points in the monetary policy game between workers and firms and the Fed, because they are consistent with the strategies of both sets of "players" in the game. Point A is more desirable than point D because, while both yield the natural output level, point D yields a higher price level. Point A may not be obtainable, however, because of the time inconsistency problem of monetary policy, which is that workers and firms know the Fed may take back a promise to stay at point A. Knowing this, they have an incentive to raise the contract wage, shifting the aggregate supply schedule leftward as shown. To keep output from falling, the Fed thereby has an incentive to increase the quantity of money and aggregate demand. Point D, the discretionary equilibrium for the economy, thereby arises if such Fed promises to follow a policy rule and stay at point A lack credibility with workers and firms. The result is a monetary policy inflation bias, $P_1 - P_0$.

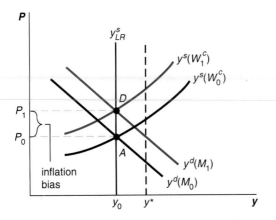

and firms believe that the Fed will stick to this rule and keep the money stock and aggregate demand unchanged. Therefore, point A is an equilibrium that corresponds to a *monetary policy rule.*

Which point will actually emerge in the real world, assuming that the monetary policy game we have described fits reality: the discretionary equilibrium or an equilibrium with a monetary rule? Many economists believe that the actual equilibrium point of the monetary policy game will be point D instead of point A; that is, they contend that the *discretionary* equilibrium typically will be the actual outcome of the monetary policy game.

The reason that many economists reach this conclusion is the existence of a **time inconsistency problem** in monetary policy. This is a fancy term for a simple idea that we figured out in our discussion of the potential equilibrium points B and C when we analyzed Figure 26-4. As we explained, if the Fed tries to follow a monetary rule by keeping the quantity of money unchanged, in hopes of keeping the economy at point A and avoiding inflation, there is no guarantee that workers and firms will *believe* the Fed. Take another look at Figure 26-3. If workers and firms believe that the Fed will follow a monetary rule and keep aggregate demand unchanged, they will leave their contracted wage unchanged; this means, however, that the Fed could successfully get to point B in Figure 26-3, which would make workers and firms unhappy, as we discussed earlier.

Therefore, if workers and firms do not believe that the Fed actually will follow a monetary rule, they always will raise their contract wage in anticipation of an expansion of the quantity of money by the Fed. Because both private agents and the Fed know that point A is a preferable point to point D, workers and firms recognize that once they set their contract wage, the Fed may have an incentive to expand the quantity of money. Because workers and firms cannot necessarily believe the monetary policy rule, the rule is *time-inconsistent.* That is, while a monetary rule that keeps the economy at point A is consistent with the desires and strategies of both private agents and the Fed, it becomes inconsistent with those strategies if the Fed can change the money stock at a later time, after contract wages are set. If the Fed can do this, then monetary policy is subject to a time inconsistency problem.

As we discussed in our analysis of Figure 26-3, a Fed failure to expand demand would yield point C, which the Fed would never desire. Hence, if the Fed actually wishes to follow a monetary rule but knows that workers and firms do not believe that it would pursue a rule, it knows that it will be worse off. Its best choice, in light of the time inconsistency problem that induces workers and firms to raise their contract wages, is to *validate* the expectations of workers and firms; that is, the best thing the Fed can do, in the presence of the time inconsistency problem, is to produce the inflation that workers and firms expect that the Fed will produce!

Effectively, the time inconsistency problem of monetary policy can ''trap'' the Fed into conducting monetary policy according to discretion rather than rules. If this occurs, point D, the discretionary equilibrium point, will be the outcome of the monetary policy game, and the economy will move from the initial point A to this new point D. As a result, the price level will rise, from P_0 to P_1, even though the economy will remain at the natural output level. Economists call the difference between the new and initial price levels, given by $P_1 - P_0$ in Figure 26-4, the **inflation bias** that arises from discretionary monetary policy caused by the time inconsistency problem of monetary policy. Furthermore, they conclude that because output is unchanged at point D and inflation is higher, society is worse off as a result. Society would be better off with a monetary rule, but the time inconsistency problem yields policy discretion and higher inflation.

This, then, represents a theory of inflation. According to this theory, the time inconsistency problem of monetary policy results from the existence of wage contracts. Once workers and firms set their contract wage, the Fed has an incentive to increase the quantity of money to expand output above its natural level. To keep this from occurring, workers and firms, in turn, have an incentive to raise the contracted wage, which causes output to stay at its natural level but adds to the amount of inflation. As a result, monetary policy is discretionary instead of based on a rule, and there is an inherent inflation bias.

CAN DISCRETION BE AVOIDED?

As you can see, the theory we discussed above provides explanations for two features that seem to characterize monetary policy making. First, it explains why discretionary monetary policy may occur. Effectively, says the theory, the time inconsistency problem forces the Fed into honoring the expectations by workers and firms that it will succumb to the temptation to create unexpected inflation to increase output.

Second, the theory provides a possible explanation for why inflation continues despite consistent statements by the Fed that it does not like inflation. And we have seen plenty of inflation during the past several decades, as Figure 26-5 indicates. Furthermore, all this inflation has occurred even though the Fed persistently has contended that its goal is to reduce or eliminate inflation.

If the theory of time inconsistency, discretion, and the inflation bias is correct, is it

Figure 26-5
Two Measures of the Price Level: The GDP Price Deflator (1983 = 100) and the Consumer Price Index (1982–1984 = 100)   (*Source:* 1991 Economic Report of the President)

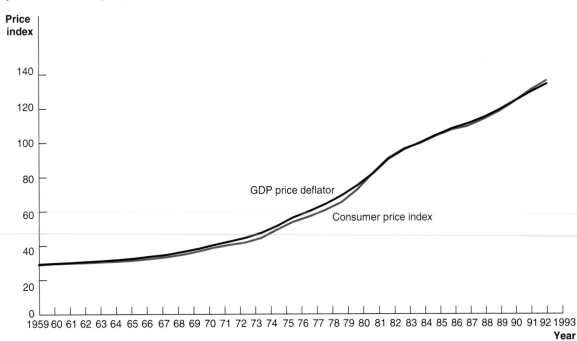

impossible for the Fed to tie itself down to rules? Are discretionary policy making and continual inflation unavoidable?

Economists do not yet have complete answers to these questions. They do have a good start, however. We devote the remainder of this chapter to considering these issues.

MAKING MONETARY POLICY RULES CREDIBLE

There are two reasons that the time inconsistency problem leads to discretion and inflation. First, the fact that the economy's full-capacity output level typically lies above the natural, full-information level of output gives the Fed an incentive to try to expand aggregate demand by increasing the quantity of money unexpectedly. Second, a Fed pronouncement that it will not yield to any temptations to raise the money stock after workers and firms have signed their contracts will not necessarily be believed by workers and firms. The **credibility of** its **monetary policy** is in doubt. That is, Fed claims that it will not induce inflation may not be *credible*.

If the Fed has a credibility problem, then, it may announce as often as it wants that it intends to follow a rule, but workers and firms will not believe the Fed is serious. This problem will only get worse if the Fed permits an inflation bias to develop and perpetuate. Everyone, including the Fed, may recognize a rule would be better, but unless the Fed can announce a rule, be believed by the public, and stick with its rule, discretion and inflation may be inevitable.

Wage Indexation, Discretion, and Inflation   Presumably, no one likes sustained and variable inflation. When inflation has increased in the past, it typically has become a major political issue, with candidates on both sides decrying higher prices as "public enemy number one."

Given that the Fed may not be credible, isn't there anything that the rest of us can do to keep the Fed from creating an inflation bias? In fact, there is. Recall from Chapter 22 that if workers and firms fully *index* nominal wages to unexpected inflation, the economy's aggregate supply schedule becomes vertical. The reason is that when wages are fully indexed to inflation, a rise in the level of prices automatically causes the nominal wage to rise in equal proportion. As a result, the real wage rate remains unchanged, and, in the absence of variations in supply-side factors, the quantity of real output supplied stays constant at the natural, full-information level.

Consider the situation of full wage indexation shown in Figure 26-6. Because wages are completely indexed to unexpected inflation, the economy's aggregate supply schedule is vertical at the natural, full-information output level, y_0. Nevertheless, because of income taxes, regulations, or other factors, the economy's full-capacity output level, y^*, is greater than the full-information level of output.

Now consider the equilibrium position at point A in Figure 26-6, at which the economy's aggregate demand schedule, $y^d(M_0)$, crosses the aggregate supply schedule at the equilibrium price level P_0. The Fed would like, if possible, to move the economy to its full-capacity output level while keeping inflation as low as possible. Does the Fed have an incentive to increase the quantity of money to expand aggregate demand?

The answer is no. The reason is that if the aggregate supply schedule is vertical, the Fed knows that it cannot, even in the short run, induce an increase in equilibrium real output through expansionary aggregate demand policies. If the Fed were to increase aggregate demand, as shown by the dashed schedule $y^d(M_1)$ in Figure 26-6, the only result would be a higher price level, which the Fed does not want. Hence, the Fed will not create

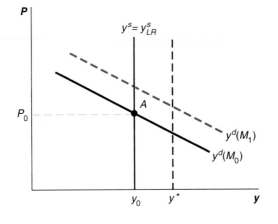

Figure 26-6
Discretionary Policy with Full Wage Indexation.   If workers and firms fully index nominal wages to unexpected changes in the level of prices, the economy's aggregate supply schedule is vertical, as we discussed in Chapter 22. This means that, even if the Fed acts in a discretionary manner, it has no incentive to increase the quantity of money. The reason is that by doing so the Fed cannot induce an increase in real output beyond its natural, full-information level, y_0, in the direction of the full-capacity level, y^*. Hence, the economy remains at point A, and there is no inflation bias.

an inflation bias if wages are fully indexed. Holding other things constant, the economy will remain at point A in Figure 26-6.

In fact, the overall degree of wage indexation in the United States is low; indeed, it is lower than in many other countries. If full wage indexation could solve the inflation bias problem, then why aren't all wages in the United States fully indexed? There are three possible answers.

First, wage indexation is not costless. Workers must negotiate fully indexed contracts with firms, and they may have to give up something, such as some health benefits or "perks," in exchange for full wage indexation. If the direct or opportunity costs of fully indexed contracts are sufficiently large, many contracts may not have indexation clauses.

Second, as we discussed in Chapter 22, full indexation is fine if the only source of variability in the economy's market for real output arises from shifts in the aggregate demand schedule. If the aggregate supply schedule is variable, however, real output and, hence, employment can be volatile as well. In general, neither workers nor firms wish for this to occur, so for this reason full indexation of wages may not take place.

Finally, the slope of the aggregate supply function is influenced by the *aggregate* amount of indexation of all wages in the economy. Hence, it is the combined decisions of all workers and firms in the economy that influence the slope of the aggregate supply schedule; if workers and firms were to make the aggregate supply schedule vertical and remove the Fed's incentive to create an inflation bias, they would have to work together. In general, however, there is no easy way, unless all workers were to join a few large, coordinating unions, to do this. Thus, even though all workers and firms together can determine the slope of the aggregate supply schedule, there is little incentive for workers at individual firms to try to do this. After all, if only a few workers and firms agree to fully indexed contracts while no one else does, they alone must incur costs and experience adverse effects of supply variability—all to no avail, because their individual actions have negligible effects on the aggregate degree of wage indexation in the economy.

A Monetary Policy Constitution, or Monetary Policy by Computer? How else might citizens constrain the Fed's temptation to generate inflation? One possibility is a "direct approach": Society could, through collective action such as the democratic process, make it illegal for the Fed to increase the quantity of money "too rapidly." For instance, a constitutional convention, Congress, and/or voters could enact an amendment to the United States Constitution barring the Fed from letting the quantity of money increase faster than, say, 3 percent per year.

In fact, some economists, such as Milton Friedman, have proposed such constitutional limitations. Some have even gone so far as to suggest abolishing the Federal Reserve System and replacing it with a computer. The computer would be programmed to conduct open-market operations to ensure adherence to a policy of limited money growth and zero inflation.

The objective of such proposals, of course, is to force policy makers to follow rules instead of using discretion. Making inflationary monetary policy illegal and subject to specific punishments (such as firing the members of the Federal Reserve Board), proponents contend, is the only way to make monetary rules credible.

The Importance of a Good Reputation At present, no nation has constitutional prohibitions on excessive monetary growth and inflation. Yet most central banks, including the Federal Reserve System, would like to maintain low inflation. The Fed and other central banks know that, to achieve this objective, they must somehow gain credibility with workers and firms. The issue is how to accomplish this objective in the presence of the time inconsistency problem.

One possible answer is for a central bank, such as the Fed, to establish a "good reputation." To reduce, or even avoid, the credibility problem, the Fed could simply announce a rule and stick with it, even when a temptation to inflate arises. If workers and firms do not believe the Fed, they will raise the nominal wage rate and, as a result, experience lower employment and output. As we discussed in Figure 26-3, we typically would rule out this possibility (which corresponded to point C in that figure). Nevertheless, the Fed might be willing for society to experience this cost in the short run if it can thereby gain long-run credibility that it will follow a rule no matter what. Many believe this is exactly what the Fed did in 1979 when it shifted its operating procedure and announced a new strategy of adhering closely to its monetary targets (see Chapter 25). The result was a sharp recession in 1980 and 1981, but inflation fell dramatically in later years, and so the Fed got a long-term payoff from following—and sticking with—its anti-inflation stand.

Of course, a good reputation is not a panacea for the monetary policy credibility problem. For one thing, a situation might arise in which the Fed judges economic times to be so bad that it is willing to sacrifice its reputation to create unexpected inflation. Once it does this, of course, workers and firms will not believe its promises not to do the same thing again later, and the inflation bias in following years necessarily will be higher.

In addition, it is possible that inflation may rise for reasons that have nothing to do with intentional efforts by the Fed. For instance, the demand for money may fall, which would shift the economy's LM and aggregate demand schedules rightward (see Chapter 21) even if the Fed does nothing. Workers and firms might then blame the resulting inflation on the Fed, unjustifiably lowering its reputation and credibility.

MONETARY POLICY INDEPENDENCE AND INFLATION

As we discussed in Chapter 15, the Federal Reserve System is a quasi-governmental institution. On the one hand, private depository institutions are members of the Fed and elect some of the officers of the Federal Reserve district banks. Furthermore, the Fed's budget is not subject to direct congressional oversight. On the other hand, the President appoints, subject to Senate approval, members of the Fed's Board of Governors. In addition, Congress has enacted various laws that spell out Fed responsibilities as a central bank.

A common description that monetary economists provide of the Fed is that the Fed is an institution that is *independent within the government.* That is, the Fed is part of the government, but the structure of the Fed spelled out in the Federal Reserve Act of 1913 and the Banking Act of 1935 (see Chapter 15) insulates the Fed considerably from other officials of the government. Hence, the Fed has a considerable capability to exercise its own authority separate from other governmental institutions.

The Role of Central Bank Independence   The theory of discretion and inflation we have discussed in this chapter helps explain why some measure of central bank independence might be desirable. As we discussed, this theory indicates that an inflation bias may arise from the monetary policy process because of the time inconsistency problem and as a result of Federal Reserve desires to raise real output above its natural, full-information level. It is possible that central bank independence lessens the importance of both of these factors, thereby reducing the inherent inflation bias of monetary policy.

As we discussed above, one way to lessen the scope of the time inconsistency problem is for the Fed to gain credibility by establishing a strong reputation for sticking to its policy commitments. A needed factor for establishing a strong Fed reputation, however, is for the public to believe that the Fed can independently make and keep its promises. If Federal Reserve officials could be overruled by other members of government, workers and firms would almost certainly doubt the Fed's capability to maintain a reputation as an "inflation fighter." Consequently, it would be very difficult in such circumstances for the Fed to establish credibility if it were simply an agency of the government.

Furthermore, if the Fed could be made entirely immune from the mundane political pressures that influence other governmental officials, it is less likely that it would have a desire to expand real output beyond its natural level. This, in turn, would automatically reduce the potential inflation bias of monetary policy, irrespective of the Fed's reputation.

The Conservative Central Banker   There is another strong argument in favor of Fed independence: The existence of the time inconsistency problem implies that society can gain from the appointment of a **conservative central banker** (or bankers). This is a person (or persons) who dislikes inflation more than an average citizen in society and who thereby is less willing to induce discretionary increases in the quantity of money in an effort to cause unexpected inflation.

To see why society could gain from the appointment of a conservative central banker, take a look back at Figure 26-4. As we discussed, using that figure, the inflation bias from monetary policy arises from the efforts by a central banker to increase the quantity of money and aggregate demand in an attempt to expand real output. Nevertheless, workers and firms recognize that the Fed has an incentive to do this, and so they raise their nominal wages; as a result, equilibrium real output remains at its natural level, and only the price level increases.

The extent to which a central bank tries to raise aggregate demand, however, is tempered by the central banker's dislike of inflation. The less a central banker desires inflation, the

DISCRETION, SECRECY, AND CHEAP TALK AT THE FED

In a Current Controversy in Chapter 15, we touched on the issue of Fed secrecy. As we discussed there, the Fed maintains many secrets, although it does so for much shorter periods of time than it once did. Nevertheless, the Fed is very secretive.

Although members of Congress have offered several proposals to reduce the permitted amount of secrecy at the Fed, most of these proposals have languished. Indeed, many of us seem not to mind Fed secrecy, even though we live in a democratic society. (Have any of you organized campus protests against it lately?) Why is it that society appears willing to accept secretive behavior by the Fed?

Secrecy and Discretion

There are two key reasons that Fed secrecy may in fact be accepted, if not desired, by society. For one thing, it is awfully difficult to get ingenious people such as central bankers to give up secrets they want to keep. For instance, when there was a lawsuit threatening to force the FOMC to release its secretary's recorded minutes immediately after each of the FOMC's meetings, the FOMC found a direct way to deal with the threat to its secrets. It decided that if the lawsuit turned out to be successful, the FOMC secretary just wouldn't keep minutes anymore. In short, efforts to stop secrecy often just lead to new ways for the Fed to keep secrets.

Second, society may *gain* from time to time because of Fed secrecy. Recall that the Fed can minimize the inflation bias of discretionary monetary policy by maintaining a reputation as a hard-nosed inflation fighter. If everyone thinks this reputation is well deserved, then workers and firms typically will not adjust contracted nominal wages upward very much from year to year. They will begin to place a lot of credibility on the Fed's pronouncements that it is really serious about low inflation. Suppose, however, that in reality the Fed really isn't "deep-down serious" about fighting inflation. It generally would pay for the Fed to keep this fact secret. For one thing, the Fed has its reputation to uphold if it is to keep inflation low over the long term. In addition, how-

ever, the Fed knows that a time may come in which a serious economic event may occur; in such a situation, it may wish to surprise the economy with unexpected inflation to raise output to offset the adverse event. Indeed, society could benefit from such an inflation surprise. Yet there could be no surprise unless the Fed could keep its true aims secret. Hence, society may like giving the Fed the power to be secretive, at least to a degree not too much at odds with democratic ideals.

Cheap Talk and Time Inconsistency

The Fed is not just secretive; sometimes it seems to make pronouncements or release forecasts that seem incredibly rosy in comparison with privately held views on the economy's prospects. This is known as Fed "cheap talk." That is, the Fed officials often say things that they know cannot be true or that they really do not believe to be true.

To understand why the Fed might do this, consider what would happen if Alan Greenspan, the Federal Reserve Board chairman, shocked Congress tomorrow by testifying that he anticipated a stock market crash the next day. What would happen? Well, our guess is that many holders of stocks would sell their stocks as fast as they could immediately after his testimony. After all, Alan Greenspan is not only a respected economist; he is a key Fed policy maker who might be able to engineer a stock market crash even if he is wrong that one will occur of its own accord.

What this example illustrates is a time inconsistency problem in the release of information and forecasts by the Fed. Because the Fed itself can directly influence many of the variables that it forecasts (such as interest rates, the quantity of money, the unemployment rate, etc.), any forecasts it releases to the public might be interpreted as indicators of goals the Fed has for these variables. Hence, if the Fed actually thinks that the unemployment rate is likely to rise considerably, but really does not wish for it to increase that much, the last thing it wants to do is tell the world about its unemployment estimate. That might scare everyone so much that unemployment would rise by even more than the Fed expects it will. Consequently, there is a time inconsistency problem in the release of information and forecasts by the Fed. The Fed is likely to release rosier forecasts of the unemployment rate than it really has computed. That is, it will engage in cheap talk.

Most sophisticated individuals realize that the Fed (along with other governmental institutions such as the executive branch and Congress) has an incentive to release overly rosy information and forecasts. Consequently, they take Fed and other governmental economists' public pronouncements and forecasts with a grain of salt. Cheap talk, like secrecy, is just a fact of life at the Fed.

Sources: Karen K. Lewis, "Why Doesn't Society Minimize Central Bank Secrecy?" *Economic Inquiry,* 29 (3, July 1991), pp. 403–415, and Jeremy Stein, "Cheap Talk and the Fed: A Theory of Imprecise Policy Announcements," *American Economic Review,* 79 (1, March 1989), pp. 32–42.

less a central bank such as the Fed would try to raise aggregate demand. As we saw in Figure 26-4, rational contracting by workers and firms keeps output from rising above its natural level even if the Fed increases aggregate demand. Therefore, workers and firms—that is, members of society—would be better off if they made certain that people appointed to lead the nation's central bank do not like inflation. This would lead to smaller increases in aggregate demand and, consequently, a lower monetary policy inflation bias.

By definition, however, a conservative central banker has different preferences than has the typical member of society. Therefore, political tension is bound to develop if a conservative central banker is appointed. For instance, it is common for officials of government, such as the secretary of the Treasury or sometimes even the President, to complain about Federal Reserve policies that keep interest rates ''too high'' or monetary growth ''too low.'' If conservative central bankers were appointed to the Federal Reserve Board but had to give in to these political pressures, society would fail to gain from their conservatism. Therefore, society may gain from insulating them from such pressures.

How can this be done in our highly politicized society? It turns out that economic theory indicates that a crucial means of ensuring the independence of conservative central bankers is to appoint them to lengthy terms and to stagger their terms of office. Other actions that can insulate central bankers from political pressures are formal independence of central banks from the instructions of other governmental authorities, legal prohibitions on direct governmental borrowing from central banks, and protection from removal from office.

In fact, the Federal Reserve Act of 1913 and the Banking Act of 1935 contain provisions addressing these issues. As we discussed in Chapter 15, the term of a Federal Reserve Board governor is much longer, at 14 years, than typical political terms of office, such as 2 or 4 years. In addition, the terms of Board governors overlap, so that only one governor must be replaced at one time (barring simultaneous resignations). The Fed's budget is not directly controlled by Congress or the President, and so the Fed largely is immune from direct instructions of governmental authorities. Although the Fed legally can lend funds directly to the government in cases of extreme urgency, it is not obliged to do so on a regular basis. Furthermore, Congress must follow lengthy legal procedures to remove a Federal Reserve Board governor from office. We may conclude that, in the United States, many measures already are in place to ensure a large measure of central bank independence.

Limitations on Central Bank Independence   This does not mean, however, that the Federal Reserve is entirely independent of political pressures. For instance, by law, appointees to the Fed's Board of Governors represent separate regions of the nation, and an appointee from a particular part of the country may receive considerable political support from members of Congress from that region. As a result, the appointee may feel some pressure to reciprocate by promoting policies that would benefit that part of the nation, either out of loyalty to the "people back home" or in return for their support. The fact that members of Congress perceive benefits from this feature of the Board's structure became evident in 1991 when Senator Terry Sanford of North Carolina fought President Bush's nomination of Lawrence Lindsey to the Federal Reserve Board. Lindsey, a White House staff economist, claimed residence in Virginia, where he had lived for just a few years in connection with his position in Washington, D.C. Sanford, however, criticized the validity of Lindsey's claim to be a representative of that part of the nation after residing in the area for such a short time. (Eventually, the Senate confirmed Lindsey's appointment.)

Most important, because the Federal Reserve System was not created by the United States Constitution, Congress and the President could dismantle the Fed if sufficient political support existed for so doing, and Fed officials know this. This means that the Fed must pay *some* attention to statements by Congress and the President criticizing its decisions. Such attempts at congressional and presidential coercion of the Fed commonly are called "Fed bashing." In a 1988 study, Thomas Havrilesky of Duke University provided evidence that Fed bashing signals the desires of Congress and the President for an easing or tightening of monetary policy.[3] Interestingly, Havrilesky argues that Fed bashing by the President and other members of the executive branch of government are more important than efforts by members of Congress in influencing monetary policy. The reason he offers is that a member of Congress individually has less to gain or lose from Fed policies in terms of vote gains or losses, whereas the entire economic plan of a President's administration may hinge on whether or not the Fed is cooperative. In fact, Havrilesky used an index of signals from the administration and Congress to the Fed, which was compiled from press reports about Fed bashing between 1979 and 1984, to study the effects that such signals had on Federal Reserve monetary policies. He concluded that presidential Fed bashing had significant effects on Fed policies but that congressional attempts to coerce the Fed did not.

What does Fed bashing by a presidential administration accomplish? In a 1991 study, Christopher Waller of Indiana University argued that Fed bashing might be beneficial to an administration if the President feels strongly that the administration is "right" or if, by bashing a pseudo-independent agency such as the Fed, it can set an example for other government agencies.[4] He also contended, however, that bashing of the Fed by a politically strong administration can potentially make the Fed appear to be a puppet of the President, thereby significantly reducing its credibility. Hence, while a strong President may be good for the nation in many ways, one that consistently tries to coerce the Fed may, in fact, worsen social welfare by increasing the inflation bias arising from discretionary monetary policy.

As we noted in a Current Controversy in Chapter 15, in recent years there have been even more direct efforts to limit the Fed's independence. Some proposals in Congress, for instance, would return the secretary of the Treasury to the Federal Reserve Board, reversing the provision of the Banking Act of 1935 that removed the Treasury secretary from the Board. Such measures would strengthen the influence of the administration on monetary policy and, if recent theories are valid, likely would add momentum to inflation.

---

[3] Thomas Havrilesky, "Monetary Policy Signaling from the Administration to the Federal Reserve," *Journal of Money, Credit, and Banking,* 20 (1, February 1988), pp. 83–101.

[4] Christopher J. Waller, "Bashing and Coercion in Monetary Policy," *Economic Policy,* 29 (1, January 1991), pp. 1–13.

GLOBAL EVIDENCE ON CENTRAL BANK INDEPENDENCE

Theory is interesting, but just how important is central bank independence in explaining the inflation performances of different countries? Recent economic research indicates that it may be very important.

For example, a 1990 study by Richard Burdekin and Mark Wohar examined the behavior of the central banks of eight nations from the 1960s through the mid-1980s. Of these, the authors concluded that the three with central banks that the authors regarded as nearly independent—those in Switzerland, the United States, and Germany—were the only countries in which central banks exhibited behavior that appeared truly independent. The authors determined that the central banks of the other five nations they studied (Canada, France, Italy, Japan, and the United Kingdom) were much more likely to accommodate higher government budget deficits with greater increases in the quantity of money. Central banks of these latter five nations also were much less likely to vary their monetary policies countercyclically to variations in inflation.

In a more ambitious 1991 study, Vittorio Grilli, Donato Masciandaro, and Guido Tabellini sought to determine exactly which nations' central banks actually are the most independent and how much difference their relative degrees of independence made. The authors developed two measures of central bank independence. One of these they termed "political independence." This measure was an index of the extent of political independence of a central bank's governing board resulting from the procedure for appointing central bankers, the relationship between the central bank's governing body and the government, and the legal responsibilities of the central bank. The other the authors called "economic independence." This measure was an index of the constraints on the government's ability to borrow from a central bank or to influence its monetary policy instruments.

Of eighteen countries that Grilli, Masciandaro, and Tabellini examined, they concluded that only the central banks of five—Canada, the Netherlands, Switzerland, the United States, and Germany—are both politically and economically independent of their governments. The authors concluded that in four nations—Greece, New Zealand, Portugal, and Spain—the central banks are completely dependent on their governments, both politically and economically. The central banks of the remaining nine nations—Australia, Austria, Belgium, Denmark, France, Ireland, Italy, Japan, and the United Kingdom—were either politically or economically dependent upon their governments, meaning that they could not be classified as fully independent central banks.

Grilli, Masciandaro, and Tabellini also examined what difference central bank independence made for nations' experiences with inflation and real output growth from 1950 to 1987. They concluded that greater economic independence definitely tended to lessen a nation's inflation rate during periods of high worldwide inflation. Greater political independence also seemed to do the same, but mainly during the high-inflation period of the 1970s. These conclusions, of course, support the theories we discussed in this chapter.

Further support for the theory was provided by the authors' finding that the degree of economic or political independence of central banks had no significant effects on countries' real output levels. This conclusion squares with the theory's implication that economies tend to return to their natural output levels irrespective of central banks' efforts to raise aggregate demand to expand their countries' levels of output. It also indicates that nations may have little to lose, in terms of real output growth, by making their central banks more independent.

Sources: Richard C. K. Burdekin and Mark E. Wohar, "Monetary Institutions, Budget Deficits, and Inflation: Empirical Results for Eight Countries," *European Journal of Political Economy*, 6 (4, 1990), pp. 531–551, and Vittorio Grilli, Donato Masciandaro, and Guido Tabellini, "Political and Monetary Institutions and Public Financial Policies of the Industrial Countries," Working Paper (1991).

In sum, discretionary monetary policy tends, because of the policy time inconsistency problem, to produce an inflation bias. Economic theory indicates that this tendency toward inflation can be reduced by greater wage indexation, direct constitutional establishment of monetary rules, enhancements of central bank credibility through reputation effects, or appointment of central bankers who dislike inflation more than others in society. The importance of a strong central bank reputation and of conservatism explains why societies may wish to insulate central banks from political pressures through intricate central banking structures designed to ensure monetary policy independence.

CHAPTER SUMMARY

1. A monetary policy rule is a policy strategy that the Fed plans and follows, irrespective of economic events. Monetary policy discretion is the failure to follow such a rule, or the departure from one that the Fed originally had intended to follow.

2. Monetary policy actions stabilize the economy only if they are sufficiently countercyclical. This means that the effects of policy actions on economic activity must be negatively correlated with economic activity for policy to be stabilizing.

3. A hindrance to the Fed's ability to conduct effective countercyclical monetary policies is the presence of time lags in monetary policy making. These include the recognition lag between the need for a policy action and the realization of that need, the implementation lag between recognition and a policy action, and the transmission lag between the action and its ultimate effects on the economy.

4. Proponents of discretionary monetary policy recognize that time lags are a problem but believe it can be mitigated by finding ways to reduce the lengths of the lags. Those who favor monetary policy rules contend that the time lag problem is largely insurmountable, and so discretionary policy is more likely to destabilize, rather than stabilize, the economy.

5. The economy's full-capacity level of real output typically exceeds its natural, full-information output level. Nonetheless, it is possible, in an environment of rational wage contracting, for the Fed to cause short-term increases in real output toward the full-capacity level by increasing the quantity of money and causing unexpected increases in the price level. This means that if the Fed would like to push the economy toward its full-capacity output level, there is a temptation for it to increase the quantity of money and cause some inflation in exchange for greater real output.

6. If the Fed has an incentive to cause unexpected inflation through discretionary increases in the quantity of money, rational workers and firms will realize this and will raise the contracted wage by the amount that they expect inflation will increase as a result of expansionary monetary policies of the Fed. Indeed, even if the Fed does not actually wish to expand the quantity of money, workers and firms will expect it to; so if the Fed does not do so, real output may actually fall. Hence, the Fed can feel obliged to increase the quantity of money as workers and firms expect that it will, just to keep output from falling, even though this causes inflation. This is the essence of the time inconsistency problem of monetary policy.

7. The inflation bias caused by discretionary monetary policy can be reduced by greater wage indexation, but costs of indexation, concern about variability of aggregate supply, and the failure of individual workers and firms to coordinate their aggregate indexation decisions may make wage indexation too low to constrain the Fed's incentive to inflate.

8. A direct approach to eliminating discretionary monetary policy and the inflation bias would be to implement a monetary policy rule through a change in the nation's constitution. Under such a constitutional provision, monetary policy effectively could be conducted by computer, because a set monetary rule always would be followed.

9. The size of the discretionary inflation bias in monetary policy can be limited if the Fed works to maintain a reputation as a credible inflation fighter. This keeps expectations of inflationary policies by the Fed low, thereby reducing the extent to which workers and firms will increase their contract wages.

10. Society can lower the inflation bias that arises from discretionary monetary policy by arranging an institutional structure in which political leaders appoint conservative central bankers who dislike inflation more than others.

11. Greater central bank credibility and more conservatism by central bankers can best be promoted by ensuring that central banks are independent from political pressures felt by other government officials. This helps explain the convoluted structure of the Federal Reserve System that insulates it from many of these pressures.

GLOSSARY

Conservative central banker: A person, appointed to manage a central bank, who dislikes inflation more than an average citizen in society and who thereby is less willing to induce discretionary increases in the quantity of money in an effort to cause unexpected inflation.

Countercyclical monetary policy: Monetary policy actions that offset movements in economic variables such as real income and thereby generally reduce real income variability.

Credibility of monetary policy: Believability of Fed commitments to follow particular monetary policy rules.

Full-capacity output level: The amount of goods and services that the economy could employ if all resources were employed to their utmost.

Implementation (or response) lag: The interval between the recognition of a need for a countercyclical policy action and the actual implementation of the policy action.

Inflation bias: A tendency for the economy to experience continuing inflation as a result of discretionary monetary policy that takes place because of the time inconsistency problem of monetary policy.

Monetary policy discretion: Monetary policy actions that the Fed makes in response to economic events as they occur, rather than in ways it might previously have planned in the absence of those events.

Monetary policy rule: A policy strategy to which a central bank commits, meaning that it will follow that strategy no matter what happens to other economic variables.

Policy time lags: Time intervals between the need for a countercyclical monetary policy action and the ultimate effects of that action on an economic variable.

Procyclical monetary policy: Monetary policy actions that reinforce movements in economic variables such as real income and that thereby add to real income variability.

Recognition lag: The interval that passes between the need for a countercyclical policy action and the recognition of this need by a policy maker.

Strategy: The approach one takes to accomplishing an objective, such as winning a game.

Time inconsistency problem: Monetary policy problem that can result from the existence of wage contracts. Although a monetary rule that achieves zero inflation is consistent with the desires and strategies of both private agents and the Fed, it becomes inconsistent with those strategies if the Fed can change the money stock at a later time, after contract wages are set.

Transmission lag: The interval that elapses between the implementation of an intended countercyclical policy and its ultimate effects on an economic variable.

SELF-TEST QUESTIONS

1. List and define the three types of policy time lags. Which do you think is likely to be *least* problematical for monetary policy? Which do you think is likely to be the *greatest* problem? Explain your reasoning.

2. Fiscal policy also is subject to the same types of time lags. Of the three, which do you think is likely to be the greatest problem for fiscal policy, keeping in mind that *Congress* and the *executive branch* formulate and enact fiscal policies? Explain your reasoning.

3. Explain, in your own words, the time inconsistency problem that makes policy rules difficult for the Fed to implement.

4. Suppose that the Fed finds inflation *extremely* distasteful. Furthermore, suppose that workers and firms know this. Use your own version of Figure 26-4 to explain why this should lower the inflation bias of discretionary monetary policy.

5. The German central bank, the Bundesbank, traditionally has had an even stronger reputation as an inflation fighter than the Federal Reserve System. When West Germany and East Germany reunited during the early 1990s, however, the German government enacted a currency reform, overruling some strong objections by leaders of the Bundesbank, that caused higher inflation for Germany than it had experienced in some time. Based on our theory of discretionary monetary policy, do you think that this action would have led to a higher inflation bias in the German monetary policy process? Explain.

6. Explain, in your own words, why full wage indexation may not be a viable solution to the time inconsistency problem.

PROBLEMS

26-1. Suppose that the aggregate supply and aggregate demand schedules for the economy are straight-line functions whose equations presently are given by the following:
Aggregate demand: $y = 2W - 5P$
Aggregate supply: $y = 2M + 5P$
where M is the quantity of money, which presently is $M = 10$, and W is the nominal wage, which presently is $W = 5$. Suppose that, in addition, the current equilibrium output level is equal to the economy's natural, full-information level of output. Finally, suppose that the economy's full-capacity output level is $y^* = 20$. Draw a rough (but large, to give yourself some room for labeling) diagram to help interpret your answers. (*Hint:* You likely will find it helpful to refer to Figure 26-4 to assist in answering this question, because your diagram will look a lot like this figure when it is finished.)

   a. What is the current equilibrium price level? Label this price level as P_0 on your diagram.

   b. What is the current equilibrium level of output, which by assumption also is the natural output level? Label this amount as y_0 on your diagram, and draw the economy's long-run aggregate supply schedule.

   c. Suppose that the Fed's goal is to increase aggregate demand sufficiently to achieve the economy's full-capacity output level. Use the aggregate supply equation to determine what new price level, P', is needed to achieve this level of output, assuming that workers and firms do not change the nominal wage.

   d. Use your answer to part c in the aggregate demand equation to determine what quantity of money the Fed must supply to shift the aggregate demand schedule sufficiently to yield the price level computed in part c as an equilibrium value for the economy. Show this shift on your diagram.

26-2.   Suppose that the workers and firms in the setting discussed in problem 26-1 recognize that the Fed has a desire to increase the money stock sufficiently to obtain the full-capacity output level. As a result, they adjust their wages to keep the equilibrium level of output at its natural level, thereby shifting the aggregate supply schedule to an equilibrium point along the *new* aggregate demand schedule (taking into account the change in the quantity of money you computed in part d of problem 26-1).

    a. Use the new aggregate demand schedule to determine the value of the final equilibrium price level, labeled P_1 on your diagram, that will be consistent with this level of output.

    b. Use the aggregate supply equation to compute the new value of the nominal wage that will shift the aggregate supply schedule to a final equilibrium at the natural level of output and at the price level you computed in part a.

    c. What is the inflation bias for the economy, expressed in percentage terms, computed by comparing the final price level P_1 with the initial price level P_0?

SELECTED REFERENCES

Backus, David, and John Driffill, ''Inflation and Reputation,'' *American Economic Review,* 75 (3, June 1985), pp. 530–538.

Ball, Laurence, ''Is Equilibrium Indexation Efficient?'' *Quarterly Journal of Economics,* 103 (2, May 1988), pp. 299–311.

Barro, Robert J., and David B. Gordon, ''A Positive Theory of Monetary Policy in a Natural Rate Model,'' *Journal of Political Economy,* 91 (4, August 1983), pp. 598–610.

———— and ————, ''Rules, Discretion, and Reputation in a Model of Monetary Policy,'' *Journal of Monetary Economics,* 12 (1, July 1983), pp. 101–121.

Burdekin, Richard C. K., and Mark E. Wohar, ''Monetary Institutions, Budget Deficits, and Inflation: Empirical Results for Eight Countries,'' *European Journal of Political Economy,* 6 (4, 1990), pp. 531–551.

Canzoneri, Matthew, ''Monetary Policy Games and the Role of Private Information,'' *American Economic Review,* 75 (5, December 1985), pp. 1057–1070.

Carlson, John B., ''Rules versus Discretion: Making a Monetary Rule Operational,'' Federal Reserve Bank of Cleveland *Economic Review* (Quarter 3, 1988), pp. 2–13.

Devereux, Michael, ''The Effect of Monetary Variability on Welfare in a Simple Macroeconomic Model,'' *Journal of Monetary Economics,* 19 (3, May 1987), pp. 427–435.

Friedman, Milton, ''The Effects of a Full-Employment Policy on Economic Stability: A Formal Analysis,'' in *Essays in Positive Economics* (Chicago: University of Chicago Press, 1953).

————, *A Program for Monetary Stability* (New York: Fordham University Press, 1959).

Grilli, Vittorio, Donato Masciandaro, and Guido Tabellini, ''Political and Monetary Institutions and Public Financial Policies of the Industrial Countries,'' Working Paper (1991).

Havrilesky, Thomas, ''Monetary Policy Signaling from the Administration to the Federal Reserve,'' *Journal of Money, Credit, and Banking,* 20 (1, February 1988), pp. 83–101.

Kydland, Finn, and Edward Prescott, ''Rules Rather Than Discretion: The Inconsistency of Optimal Plans,'' *Journal of Political Economy,* 85 (3, June 1977), pp. 473–492.

Lewis, Karen K., ''Why Doesn't Society Minimize Central Bank Secrecy?'' *Economic Inquiry,* 29 (3, July 1991), pp. 403–415.

Neumann, Manfred, ''Precommitment by Central Bank Independence,'' *Open Economies Review,* 2 (2, 1991), pp. 95–112.

Rogoff, Kenneth, ''The Optimal Degree of Commitment to an Intermediate Monetary Target,'' *Quarterly Journal of Economics,* 100 (4, November 1985), pp. 1169–1189.

Sibert, Anne, and Stuart E. Weiner, ''Maintaining Central Bank Credibility,'' Federal Reserve Bank of Kansas City *Economic Review,* 73 (8, September/October 1988), pp. 3–15.

Stein, Jeremy C., ''Cheap Talk and the Fed: A Theory of Imprecise Policy Announcements,'' *American Economic Review,* 79 (1, March 1989), pp. 32–42.

VanHoose, David D., and Christopher J. Waller, ''Discretion, Wage Indexation, and Inflation,'' *Southern Economic Journal,* 58 (2, October 1991), pp. 356–367.

Waller, Christopher J., ''A Bargaining Model of Partisan Appointments to the Central Bank,'' *Journal of Monetary Economics,* forthcoming.

———— ''Bashing and Coercion in Monetary Policy,'' *Economic Inquiry,* 29 (1, January 1991), pp. 1–13.

————, ''Monetary Policy Games and Central Bank Politics,'' *Journal of Money, Credit, and Banking,* 21 (4, November 1989), pp. 422–431.

————, and David D. VanHoose, ''Discretionary Monetary Policy and Socially Efficient Wage Indexation,'' *Quarterly Journal of Economics,* 107 (1992), forthcoming.

International Money and Finance

chapter 27

Foreign Exchange Markets and International Finance

CHAPTER PREVIEW

1. What are the three main economic transactions that people in different nations make with each other?

2. What transactions lead to a change in the demand for and the supply of a particular currency?

3. Why is the supply curve of a particular currency positively sloped? Why is the demand curve for a particular currency negatively sloped?

4. How is the equilibrium exchange rate determined? How can a central bank influence the equilibrium exchange rate?

5. What is the difference between the spot exchange rate and the forward exchange rate?

6. What are foreign exchange swaps, futures, and options?

7. What is foreign exchange risk, and in what ways does it arise?

8. How do individuals and firms gain from foreign asset diversification?

9. Where does international banking fit into the world's financial system?

Many citizens in the United States have little or no personal experience in international dealings. The United States is a large nation with a great deal of trade that flows among the fifty states. All these interstate trade flows are transacted in the same national currency (dollars). Therefore, most Americans have never converted dollars into currencies of other nations, and those who have typically have done so to make a foreign vacation trip or two. Many of us just have never had a strong personal incentive to develop an "international" outlook on day-to-day economic issues.

In contrast, citizens of many other nations must, through the necessity of daily living, keep up with international economic news. In several nations in South America, for example, the American dollar may substitute very closely—or may even be a preferred currency—relative to home currencies in many market transactions. Citizens in such nations therefore constantly must keep alert to the prices of the dollar in terms of their own nations' currencies. Hence, they have a natural reason to wish to understand international economic issues; their personal stake in international developments is apparent.

Furthermore, in many other nations international trade has been much more important than it traditionally has been in the United States. This is not to say that exports and imports of goods and services have not increased relative to total production in the United States since the 1960s. For instance, U.S. exports of goods and services as a percentage of U.S. *gross domestic product (GDP)*—the value of goods and services actually produced using factors of production owned by U.S. citizens—were equal to 5.2 percent in 1960; by 1975 this had risen to 8.5 percent, and in 1992 the percentage of U.S. GDP allocated to exports stood at over 10 percent. U.S. imports also have grown. In 1960, U.S. imports as a percentage of its GDP were equal to 4.4 percent; by 1975 this had risen to 7.6 percent, and in 1992 U.S. imports as a percentage of its GDP stood at almost 11 percent.

Nevertheless, international trade relative to total production and income in the United States pales by comparison to many other nations of the world, such as those in Europe. For instance, for 1991 in Germany, exports as a percentage of its GDP were approximately equal to 38.0 percent, and imports relative to GDP stood at 31.4 percent. In the United Kingdom, for the same year, these percentages were equal to 23.7 percent and 24.6 percent, respectively. In the Netherlands, these percentages in 1991 were approximately equal to 56.0 percent and 51.0 percent, respectively, while in Belgium they stood at 70.9 percent and 68.1 percent. Clearly, international economic considerations loom with greater prominence, in relation to sizes of national economies, in Europe as compared to the United States. For this reason alone, citizens of Europe tend to have a much greater stake in understanding international economic affairs than do citizens of the United States.

Does this mean that Americans can permit themselves to be ignorant of international economic considerations? The answer is that they do so only at their own expense. For one thing, as we have discussed in the numerous International Perspective sections in previous chapters, there is much that Americans might learn from the experiences of other nations. In addition, the growth of international trade relative to U.S. home production is inescapable even if the relative magnitudes of U.S. international trade remain fairly small as compared with other nations of the world; Americans who ignore international issues may be placing themselves at a competitive disadvantage in the future. Many American industries, such as those specializing in the production of automobiles, consumer electronics, and commercial aircraft, have learned through some hard competitive knocks that it can pay to keep abreast of developments outside the United States and to understand the economic interactions between the United States and the rest of the world.

Our goal in the remaining chapters is to explain the essential facts, theories, and current issues in international monetary and financial economics. It is in the sphere of money and banking that increased **international integration**—the development of strong ties, linkages, and interactions—among world economies has been the greatest in the past few decades. Hence, there is much for you to learn about this topic, and you are certain to find what you read in these chapters relevant in the coming years.

SOME CURRENT INTERNATIONAL ISSUES

Even though international trade in the United States remains fairly small compared with that of other nations, the American public in recent years generally has become more interested in international financial transactions in general and foreign exchange rates in particular. This is true for at least four reasons: record-breaking U.S. trade deficits, a volatile price of the dollar relative to foreign currencies, greater economic integration in Europe, and the continuing globalization of financial markets. Before we consider broader background issues in international money and finance, let's begin by highlighting some of these more specific areas of controversy.

LARGE TRADE DEFICITS IN THE LATE 1980s AND EARLY 1990s

Newspapers and TV news shows have indicated, on numerous occasions, that the United States is ''suffering'' from enormous trade deficits. Such deficits reached record U.S. highs in the late 1980s and into the 1990s (see Figure 27-1). We analyze trade deficits in detail

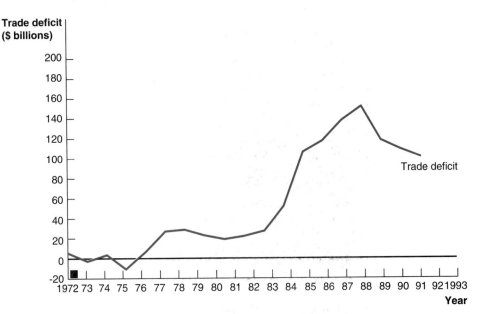

Figure 27-1
U.S. Trade Deficits. The U.S. trade deficit soared in the mid-1980s and stayed above $100 billion into the beginning of the 1990s. (*Source: 1991 Economic Report of the President.*)

in Chapter 28; here we merely point out that it is a matter of heated controversy about (1) whether such trade deficits are ''real'' or due to faulty measurement; (2) whether these deficits are related to our huge federal government budget deficits; and (3) whether such trade deficits justify protectionism in the form of **tariffs,** or taxes on goods imported from foreign countries, and **import quotas,** or restrictions on the quantities of goods imported from foreign countries.

EXCHANGE RATE VOLATILITY

In recent years the **exchange rate,** the price of foreign currency in terms of a unit of domestic currency, has fluctuated tremendously. In particular, as Figure 27-2 shows, from the first quarter of 1984 to the first quarter of 1985 the value of the dollar relative to the currencies of fifteen industrial countries **appreciated** dramatically—the dollar increased in value; when **currency appreciation** occurs, fewer dollars are needed to purchase a given quantity of other currencies. The dollar then **depreciated,** or decreased in value, even more drastically than it had increased, from then until the end of 1987; when **currency depreciation** occurs, more dollars are required to purchase a given quantity of foreign currencies. The dollar generally has trended downward slightly since 1989. U.S. residents who have traveled to foreign countries in recent years have noted that a depreciated dollar buys fewer and fewer foreign goods; and residents who have remained in the United States have noted that the prices of imported goods are getting higher.

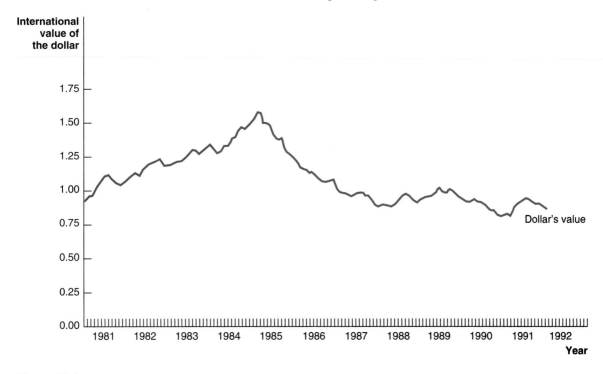

Figure 27-2
The Dollar's Value.   The international value of the dollar has fallen in recent years. This graph
shows the trade-weighted (1970–1972 = $1.00) value of the U.S. dollar relative to the currencies
of ten industrial countries. (*Sources: Federal Reserve Bulletin,* various issues.)

ECONOMIC INTEGRATION IN EUROPE

Since the 1957 Treaty of Rome, Western European nations gradually have moved nearer
to economic and financial integration through the formation and development of the
European Economic Community (nowadays commonly shortened to just "European Community," or EC). The EC began as a collection of six nations (Belgium, France, Germany,
Italy, Luxembourg, and the Netherlands), but since has added six more nations (Denmark,
Greece, Ireland, Spain, Portugal, and the United Kingdom). It seems likely that other
Western European nations may join in the future, and some Eastern European nations
have expressed interest in participating in the EC in the future. By necessity, several
nonmembers, such as Finland, Sweden, and Switzerland, have adopted many of the same
policies as EC nations.

During 1992, the EC eliminated in principle nearly all legal barriers to trade among
member states, thereby accomplishing after a thirty-five-year adjustment period a key goal
enunciated in the Treaty of Rome. For many citizens whose nations are participants of the
EC, an ultimate objective is to emulate as much as possible the federal system of the
United States, thereby producing an economic giant in Europe on a par with the United
States. Pursuit of this goal has been reinforced by efforts to coordinate European monetary
and financial policies. Since 1979, some of the EC nations have experimented with
monetary coordination through the European Monetary System (EMS), and a stated goal

of the EMS is to develop a common currency for Europe issued by a single European central bank, or ''Eurofed.''

As the task of European integration continues in the 1990s, American citizens have begun to contemplate its implications for the economic and geopolitical position of the United States in world affairs. Undeniably, a unified Europe would represent a formidable economic force. The EC began issuing bonds denominated in terms of a new European currency, the European Currency Unit (ECU), in the late 1980s. Some analysts already project that the ECU, which is equal to just over a dollar in value, could become the dominant European currency by the beginning of the twenty-first century and ultimately could rival the U.S. dollar as the world's dominant currency.

In light of this rapid change in one of the most developed and industrialized parts of the world, many U.S. citizens are beginning to recognize that they can no longer sit back complacently, acting as though the world's economic affairs will continue to center on the U.S. economy and the dollar. Indeed, many are waking up to the fact that they cannot *afford* to remain ignorant of the implications of international economic developments such as the integration of Europe. The world has become a competitive place in the 1990s, and global competition for international predominance shows few signs of abating.

GLOBALIZATION OF FINANCIAL MARKETS

As was pointed out in Chapter 16, payments systems innovations have made financial markets more globalized. When the New York Stock Market crashed in October 1987, stock and bond markets in the world's other financial centers (London, Tokyo, Frankfurt, and others) were immediately affected; likewise, when those markets are affected, our markets are similarly changed.

It can be more difficult for a nation to conduct its own monetary policy in a globalized financial system. If the dollar is truly a world currency, then Fed actions to change the rate of growth of the domestic money stock can be largely offset by international financial transactions. For these reasons (and for others that we will introduce as we proceed), it is important to analyze the foreign exchange market. In this chapter we first discuss how nations transact internationally—and how such transactions affect the supply of and demand for international currencies. Then we derive a demand curve for a foreign currency, indicating a relationship between dollar prices of foreign currency and the corresponding quantities demanded for such currency, other things constant. We follow this analysis by deriving a supply curve for the foreign currency, showing the relationship between the dollar prices of foreign currency and the corresponding quantities supplied of such currency.

As you might expect, we then show how the market exchange rate is determined at the intersection of the supply curve and the demand curve for foreign currency. After considering examples of how specific (nonprice) changes in the demand for and the supply of foreign currency change the exchange rate, we discuss how governments might seek to influence market exchange rates. We then turn our attention to the wide variety of foreign exchange instruments that exist in the world's financial markets, and we consider the implications of exchange rate movements for individuals and firms that wish to reduce risk via such financial instruments and markets.

We conclude this chapter with a discussion of the role of depository institutions in the world's financial and monetary system. In the chapters that follow, we explore the ways that economists measure the flows of exchange among nations, the theory and history of central bank exchange rate policies, and the pros and cons of international monetary and financial policy coordination.

INTERNATIONAL ECONOMIC TRANSACTIONS

Residents of different nations transact with each other by trading goods and services, by purchasing or selling financial assets, and by giving and/or receiving gifts. In addition, governments of different nations transact with each other (and with residents of foreign countries) in the same ways.

TRADING GOODS AND SERVICES

Residents of the domestic country **import** goods and services when they purchase those goods and services from residents of other countries; they **export** goods and services when they sell those goods and services to residents of other countries. These transactions are made more difficult because different nations use different currencies; U.S. exporters of goods and services to (say) Japan eventually want to receive dollars, not yen (the Japanese currency). Japanese residents who import U.S. goods receive their incomes in yen, which must be converted into dollars to satisfy U.S. exporters. Similarly, when U.S. residents import Japanese VCRs and automobiles, they must convert their dollars into yen so that Japanese exporters can benefit from the transaction.

More specifically, when U.S. residents buy foreign goods, they exchange bank deposits denominated in U.S. dollars for bank deposits denominated in foreign currency. Such transactions eventually are conducted in the foreign exchange market, in which several hundred (mostly bank) dealers stand ready to buy and sell bank deposits denominated in the various world currencies. Total foreign exchange transactions in the major world markets exceed $1,500 billion a day.

If you wish to vacation in Japan, you must go to your local bank to buy yen with your currency or checking account deposits. In turn, your bank probably will purchase yen from other U.S. banks—unless it is a large bank, in which case it will buy yen directly from a Japanese bank.

Note that when domestic residents wish to import more Japanese-made goods, this leads to a simultaneous increase in the demand for yen and an increase in the supply of U.S. dollars in the foreign exchange market. Similarly, if the Japanese wish to import more U.S.-made goods, this leads to a simultaneous increase in the demand for the U.S. dollar and an increase in the supply of Japanese yen.

BUYING AND SELLING ASSETS

U.S. residents may choose to advance funds to the Japanese by acquiring Japanese-issued assets in the form of common stocks, bonds, commercial paper, and so on. Of course, their Japanese counterparts may well wish to acquire U.S. assets. If U.S. residents wish to acquire more Japanese assets, they must convert dollars into yen; this leads to a simultaneous increase in the supply of dollars and an increase in the demand for yen. Parallel reasoning suggests that if the Japanese wish to acquire more U.S. assets, then they must convert yen into dollars; this leads to an increase in the demand for dollars and an increase in the supply of yen.

GIVING AND RECEIVING GIFTS

If Americans wish to bestow more gifts on friends and relatives in Japan, they must convert dollars into yen; this leads to an increase in the supply of dollars and an increase in the demand for yen. If Japanese residents wish to extend more gifts to U.S. residents, then they must convert yen to dollars. By now you realize that this transaction leads to an increase in the supply of yen and an increase in the demand for dollars.

HOW EXCHANGE RATES ARE DETERMINED

Now that you understand how international transactions lead to changes in the supply of and the demand for currencies in the foreign exchange market, you are in a position to see how exchange rates are determined. Because exchange rates are a price—the price of one currency in terms of another—they are determined through interaction of the competitive forces of supply and demand.

DERIVING A DEMAND CURVE FOR THE YEN

By way of example we will derive a demand curve for the yen; we can, however, use this same procedure to derive a demand curve for the U.S. dollar or any other currency.

Demand curves relate various prices to various quantities demanded, per unit of time, other things constant. In the example that follows, the "price" of the yen will be the exchange rate. Specifically, on the price axis of Figure 27-3 we indicate dollars per yen. For example, one exchange rate is "$0.010 (or 1 penny) is equivalent to 1 yen"; stated differently, "100 Japanese yen are equivalent to $1.00." Thus, the exchange rate of $0.008 per yen indicates that eight-tenths of 1 cent is valued at 1 yen; from another point of view, at that exchange rate 125 yen are equivalent to 1 dollar ($1.00 / $0.008 = 125). Note that as we move up the vertical axis, it takes more and more U.S. currency to be equivalent to 1 yen. Thus, as we move up the vertical axis, the dollar depreciates, and the yen, of necessity, appreciates, because it costs more U.S. currency to buy 1 yen.

Note that the demand curve for the yen slopes downward; as the dollar price of 1 yen

Figure 27-3
A Demand-for-Yen Schedule. As the price per yen falls, other things constant, Americans are inclined to purchase more Japanese-made goods, to lend more to the Japanese, and to extend more gifts to the Japanese. To do so they must convert more dollars into yen, which increases the quantity of dollars supplied and increases the quantity of yen demanded on the foreign exchange market. The demand-for-yen schedule is, therefore, negatively sloped.

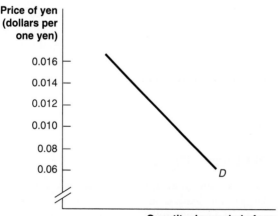

falls (other things constant), the quantity of yen demanded rises. Why does the demand for yen follow the general law of demand? For similar reasons: substitution effects and real income effects.

The Substitution Effect As the price of the yen falls (i.e., it takes fewer pennies to purchase 1 yen, and we move down the vertical axis in Figure 27-3), this yen depreciation (or dollar appreciation) decreases the relative price of Japanese goods to U.S. residents (other things constant). Given domestic U.S. prices, U.S. residents will now wish to substitute Japanese-made goods for American-made goods. For example, suppose that the yen price of a Japanese-made car is 1 million yen. If $0.010 = 1$ yen, then the U.S. price for that car is ($0.010/1$ yen) $\times$ 1,000,000 yen $= \$10,000$.

Suppose now that the price of the yen falls so that $0.008 = 1$ yen. That same Japanese car, which still costs 1,000,000 yen, *now* costs U.S. residents only $8,000. At a lower dollar price for Japanese-made autos (and other Japanese-made goods and services), the quantity of Japanese goods demanded will rise. This will increase the quantity of yen demanded (and increase the quantity of dollars supplied) in the foreign exchange markets.

Note also that a depreciated yen permits Americans to purchase larger quantities of such Japanese assets as common stocks, bonds, and so on, per one U.S. dollar. Because the relative price of Japanese assets has fallen, U.S. residents will desire to substitute such assets for similar U.S. assets. This increased American desire to lend to the Japanese will, at once, increase the quantity of yen demanded and increase the quantity of dollars supplied: in the foreign exchange markets.

The Real Income Effect If the yen depreciates, other things constant, then Americans will be richer. This is because, given American money incomes and given the U.S. price level, Americans will be able to purchase more Japanese goods than before. This higher real income may well induce them to purchase more Japanese-made (and more American-made) goods and services. Also, because they feel richer, Americans may wish to purchase more Japanese (and American) assets. Moreover, now that they feel richer, U.S. residents may well be willing to bestow more financial gifts on their friends and relatives in Japan.

We conclude that the real income effect, which induces Americans to import more goods and services from Japan and to lend more to and give more gifts to the Japanese, increases the quantity of yen demanded. And that will automatically increase the quantity of dollars supplied.

Our main conclusion is that the substitution effect *and* the real income effect both imply a negatively sloped demand curve for Japanese yen (or any other currency).

DERIVING A SUPPLY CURVE FOR THE YEN

To derive the yen's supply curve relating the dollar price per yen to the quantity of yen supplied by the Japanese (mostly), we must consider the Japanese resident's point of view. Let's consider how the Japanese are likely to react to a rise in the dollar price of yen from, say, $0.010 = 1$ yen to $0.012 = 1$ yen. Note that now that it takes more U.S. dollars (pennies, really) to purchase 1 yen, the yen has appreciated in value and the dollar has depreciated.

Assume that in the United States a personal computer sells for $2,000. When the exchange rate is $0.010 = 1$ yen, the U.S.-made personal computer costs the Japanese (1 yen/0.010) $\times$ $2,000 = 200,000$ yen (ignoring transportation costs for simplicity). But if we suppose that the yen appreciated to $0.012 = 1$ yen, then a U.S.-made personal computer now costs only (1 yen/0.012) $\times$ $2,000 = 166,667$ yen. Because U.S. personal computers and all other U.S.-made goods are now relatively cheaper to yen holders, the law of demand predicts that the Japanese will wish to purchase more. Indeed, we predict that the Japanese will also wish to substitute U.S. vacations for Japanese vacations, and substitute American assets for Japanese assets. Too, we expect that the now richer Japanese will also wish to give more gifts to their friends and relatives living in the United States.

In short, substitution and real income effects occur in Japan in the same way that they occur in the United States. Therefore, if the dollar price of the yen rises, we predict that the quantity of yen supplied will rise—and the quantity of dollars demanded will rise—on the foreign exchange market. As Figure 27-4 shows, the supply-of-yen curve slopes upward.

THE FORCES OF SUPPLY AND DEMAND DETERMINE THE EXCHANGE RATE

Consider Figure 27-5, which indicates that the demand-for-yen curve and the supply-of-yen curve establish an equilibrium exchange rate at $0.010 = 1 yen. At any other exchange rate, either a surplus or a shortage of yen will result.

A Surplus of Yen   Consider the exchange rate $0.012 = 1 yen. By inspection of Figure 27-5 you can see that the quantity of yen supplied exceeds the quantity of yen demanded at that exchange rate. This means, essentially, that at that relatively high exchange rate the Japanese are quite anxious to purchase U.S.-made goods, to lend to Americans, and to give gifts to their friends and relatives in the United States. Their competition for the U.S. dollar, which takes place on foreign exchange markets by their buying dollars with yen, will force the yen to depreciate to $0.010 = 1 yen.

A Shortage of Yen   Consider the exchange rate $0.008 = 1 yen in Figure 27-5. That below-equilibrium price of yen is relatively low, and the quantity of yen demanded is very

Figure 27-4
A Supply-of-Yen Schedule.   As the price of 1 yen rises, other things constant, the Japanese are induced to buy more goods from, lend more to, and give more gifts to U.S. residents. To do so they must increase the quantity of yen they offer for the purchase of dollars. The supply-of-yen schedule, therefore, is positively sloped.

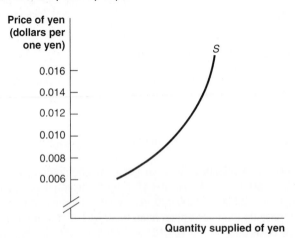

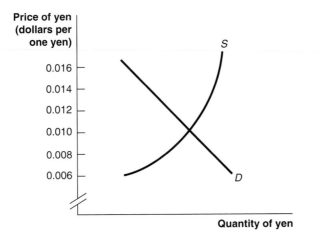

Figure 27-5
The Equilibrium Exchange Rate.   Given these schedules, the equilibrium exchange rate will be set at 0.010 dollar = 1 yen. At a higher exchange rate, such as 0.012 dollar = 1 yen, a surplus of yen (i.e., a shortage of dollars) exists. Competition for dollars among yen sellers will drive the price of 1 yen toward 0.010 dollar. At a lower exchange rate, such as 0.008 dollar per yen, a shortage of yen (i.e., a surplus of dollars) exists; buyers of yen will compete and drive its price up toward 0.010 dollar per yen.

high on the part of Americans wishing to purchase goods and services from and lend to and bestow gifts on the Japanese. Therefore, the quantity of yen demanded to permit such transactions is correspondingly high. In contrast, at that relatively low price for yen, the Japanese are not quite as anxious to purchase from, lend to, and give gifts to the Americans. Therefore, the Japanese will not be as anxious to purchase dollars with the yen they can supply.

The net effect is that the quantity of yen demanded by the Americans will exceed the quantity of yen supplied by the Japanese. There will, therefore, be a shortage of yen (or, viewed alternatively, a surplus of U.S. dollars) on the foreign exchange market. American yen demanders, competing with each other for yen, will force the dollar price of yen up toward $0.010 = 1 yen.

We conclude that, given the supply curve and the demand curve in Figure 27-5, the equilibrium, or market-clearing, exchange rate will be set at $0.010 = 1 yen on the foreign exchange market. At that dollar price for yen, the quantity of yen supplied equals the quantity of yen demanded.

CHANGES IN SUPPLY AND DEMAND CHANGE THE EQUILIBRIUM EXCHANGE RATE

We continue our Japanese-American example. The demand for yen will rise if (among other things):

1. Real incomes in the United States rise relative to real incomes in Japan.

2. American tastes change in favor of Japanese-made goods and services and away from American-made goods and services.

3. After-tax, risk-adjusted real interest rates fall in the United States relative to Japan.

4. The U.S. inflation rate becomes higher than the Japanese inflation rate; this increases the demand for yen because, other things constant, the price of U.S. goods rises relative to the price of Japanese goods.

5. The expected U.S. inflation rate rises relative to the expected Japanese inflation rate. The demand for yen will rise in this situation because the profits on investments in Japan include the expected appreciation of the yen (as well as actual interest income) that will occur if the actual U.S. inflation rate exceeds the actual Japanese inflation rate.

Note that situations 1 through 5 will lead to an increase in the demand for yen by Americans, who will want more yen at every exchange rate. That is, situations 1 through 5 above are *nonprice* determinants of the demand for yen. An increase in the demand for yen is represented by a rightward shift in the demand curve for yen.

A moment's reflection will indicate to you that situations 1 through 5 above will also lead automatically to an increase in the supply of U.S. dollars. Note that we can also conduct our analysis from the Japanese point of view. Situations 1 through 5 would induce the Japanese to buy fewer goods from, lend less to, and give less to Americans. Thus, the supply of yen by the Japanese will fall. In either analysis, the dollar price of the yen will rise; that is, the yen will appreciate relative to the dollar.

We now consider an increase in the demand for yen, and then an increase in the supply of yen, to show how the equilibrium exchange rate can change.

A U.S. CHANGE IN TASTES IN FAVOR OF JAPANESE GOODS

Consider Figure 27-6, which shows an increase in the demand for yen, from D to D', because U.S. residents have had a change in tastes in favor of Japanese goods and services.

Figure 27-6
An Increase in the Demand for Yen.   If tastes change in favor of Japanese-made goods, the demand for the yen increases from D to D'. This creates a shortage of yen (a surplus of U.S. dollars) on the foreign exchange market. Americans competing for the now-scarcer yen will force its dollar price up to the new equilibrium exchange rate of 0.014 dollar = 1 yen; at any lower exchange rate a shortage of yen exists, and at any higher exchange rate a surplus of yen exists.

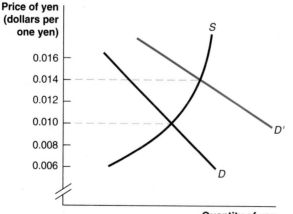

At the previous equilibrium exchange rate of $0.010 = 1 yen, a shortage of yen (i.e., a surplus of U.S. dollars) exists. U.S. residents competing for the now scarcer yen will drive the market price of the yen higher, toward $0.014 = 1 yen. At any exchange rate less than $0.014 = 1 yen, a shortage of yen exists; at any exchange rate above that value, a surplus of yen exists.

THE AFTER-TAX, RISK-ADJUSTED REAL INTEREST RATE RISES IN THE UNITED STATES RELATIVE TO JAPAN

Consider now a situation in which the after-tax, risk-adjusted real interest rate rises in the United States relative to that in Japan. Some Americans who had purchased Japanese assets previously will now wish to sell those assets and substitute similar (higher-yielding) U.S. assets. These Americans will sell their Japanese assets for yen and use those yen to buy the dollars necessary to purchase U.S. dollar-denominated assets. This will increase the supply of yen. Also, we expect that many Japanese investors will now wish to substitute American investments for Japanese investments. Those who do must convert yen into dollars; the supply of yen (from the Japanese) rises.

Figure 27-7 indicates that an increase in the supply of yen, by Americans and Japanese, occurs at every exchange rate; the supply of yen rises from S to S'. At the former equilibrium exchange rate a surplus of yen now exists; Americans and Japanese competing to convert yen into dollars must accept a smaller quantity of dollars per yen. That is, the equilibrium exchange rate falls; the yen depreciates relative to the dollar.

You should be aware that this analysis describes how exchange rates would be set by the forces of supply and demand. But it is seldom the case that central banks permit private supply and demand schedules to determine exchange rates.

FIXED AND FLOATING EXCHANGE RATES

Our discussion to this point has considered the determination of exchange rates through market forces without intervention by central banks. In the real world of the past and present, central bank efforts to keep exchange rates from getting ''too high'' or ''too low'' have in fact been common. We shall have much more to say about the history of governmental efforts to influence exchange rates in the following chapter. In this section, we concentrate on understanding the economics of alternative means of determining the actual exchange rate.

Floating Exchange Rates   Although central banks have commonly sought to influence exchange rates, there have been periods, such as the last twenty years, in which **floating exchange rates** have been the rule rather than the exception. A floating exchange rate is a currency price that is determined by the forces of supply and demand in the foreign exchange market with little or no governmental interference. Our analysis to this point in the chapter has described floating exchange rates.

Fixed Exchange Rates   If central banks undertake actions to peg exchange rates at particular values over periods of time, then there is a system of **fixed exchange rates.** To understand how a central bank may keep an exchange rate fixed, consider Figure 27-8, which again depicts a diagram of the market for yen.

In Figure 27-8 the equilibrium dollar-yen exchange rate is equal to $0.010 = 1 yen at the intersection of the privately determined yen supply (S) and demand (D) schedules. Suppose that this exchange rate of $0.010 = 1 yen is the exchange rate desired by the

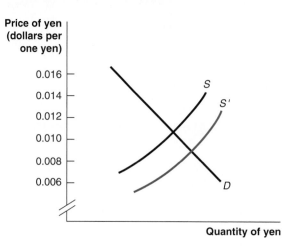

Price of yen (dollars per one yen)

0.016

0.014

0.012

0.010

0.008

0.006

S

S'

D

Quantity of yen

Figure 27-7
An Increase in the Supply of Yen.   If the U.S. after-tax, risk-adjusted real interest rate rises relative to Japan's, then the supply of yen will increase, from S to S'. At the former equilibrium exchange rate a surplus of yen now exists. Japanese (and American) suppliers of yen who wish to purchase U.S. dollar-denominated assets will compete with each other and accept a lower dollar price for yen. The yen will depreciate relative to the dollar.

Fed. Then, as long as private market conditions remain unchanged, there would be no need for Fed actions to keep the exchange rate at this value.

In fact, however, conditions in foreign exchange markets can be very volatile. For instance, there might be a fall in Americans' demand for yen, from D to D', as a result of a reduced desire by Americans to purchase Japanese-made automobiles. In the absence of any Fed actions, the equilibrium exchange rate would fall to $0.080 = 1$ yen; the yen would depreciate, and the dollar would appreciate. If the Fed views the original equilibrium exchange rate of $0.010 = 1$ yen as the best exchange rate, however, the Fed would wish to keep the dollar's value from rising against the yen and thereby causing the dollar to be overvalued relative to the Fed's objective.

Note that, at the initial equilibrium exchange rate of $0.010 = 1$ yen, Figure 27-8 indicates that the amount of yen exchanged was equal to 40 billion yen. After the fall in the demand for yen, however, 38 billion yen are demanded at that initial equilibrium exchange rate. After the fall in the demand for yen, therefore, there is an excess quantity of yen supplied of 2 billion yen (40 billion yen $-$ 38 billion yen) at the initial exchange rate. It is the existence of this excess quantity supplied that would cause the dollar-yen exchange rate to be bid downward in the absence of Fed actions.

If the Fed wishes the exchange rate to remain fixed at $0.010 = 1$ yen, it follows that it must do something to eliminate this excess quantity of yen supplied in the foreign exchange market. The solution to the Fed's problem is straightforward: It needs to eliminate the excess quantity of yen supplied by purchasing the excess amount of yen with dollars. That is, to keep the exchange rate fixed at $0.010 = 1$ yen, the Fed must purchase the 2 billion yen surplus that would exist following the fall in yen demand. The Fed would buy the 2 billion yen at the dollar-yen exchange rate of $0.010 = 1$ yen, and so it would use ($0.010/1$ yen) $\times$ 2 billion yen $= $200 million to purchase the excess quantity of yen supplied.

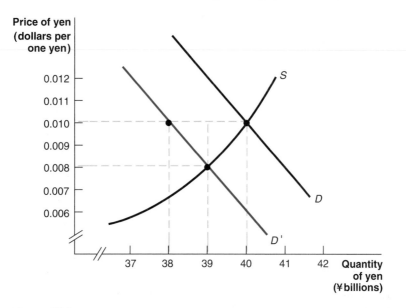

Figure 27-8

Keeping the Dollar-Yen Exchange Rate Fixed in the Face of a Fall in the Demand for Yen.   If Americans' desired levels of spending on Japanese products were to decline, from *D* to *D'*, then there would be an excess quantity of yen supplied of 2 billion yen at the initial equilibrium exchange rate of 0.010 dollar = 1 yen. Unless there are artificial legal restrictions on the exchange rate, there would be a fall in the demand for yen, and the equilibrium dollar-yen exchange rate would tend to decline from 0.010 dollar = 1 yen to 0.008 dollar = 1 yen. Barring legal restrictions or central bank actions, the dollar would appreciate, and the yen would depreciate.

   To keep the exchange rate at its initial level of 0.010 dollar = 1 yen, however, the Federal Reserve could use 200 million dollars to purchase the excess quantity of 2 billion yen that is supplied at the exchange rate of 0.010 dollar = 1 yen. In so doing, it would shift the yen demand schedule back to its original position at *D*.

   By purchasing this quantity of yen, the Fed would add to the total demand for yen. Hence, it would shift the total yen demand schedule rightward by 2 billion yen, or from *D'* back to *D,* the original position of the yen demand schedule. This action therefore would keep the dollar-yen exchange rate fixed at the Fed's desired level of $0.010 = 1 yen.

   We hope that this example will help you to recognize that fixed exchange rates do not ever remain "fixed" of their own volition. Central banks must actively trade foreign currencies to keep exchange rates from changing. This is the reason that most of the world's major central banks maintain portfolios of assets denominated in other nations' currencies. Such assets come in handy if the central banks feel that they need to keep their currencies from becoming "overvalued" or "undervalued."

Capital Controls   What can a nation's government do if its central bank does not have sufficient foreign currency assets to keep the exchange rate pegged at a level the government desires? There are two options. The obvious one would be to give up on pegging the exchange rate. Some governments, however, have opted instead to enact legal controls on their currency's rate of exchange when their central banks are unable to keep the market exchange rate at a desired level. Under this approach, governments make it illegal for their citizens to exchange the national currency for currencies of other nations at any exchange rate except the *official,* or legal, rate, even if the market exchange rate differs from the official rate of exchange.

To see the problems that such legal rules present, reconsider Figure 27-8 and think about the following fictitious—and, given the financial prominence of Japan in today's world, not especially realistic—example. Suppose that the Japanese Diet (Japan's national legislature) were to pass a law making the official dollar-yen exchange rate in Japan equal to $0.010 = 1 yen. Furthermore, suppose that the Japanese central bank has insufficient dollar reserves to influence the equilibrium dollar-yen exchange rate. As long as the yen demand and supply schedules are given by D and S in Figure 27-8, the official and market exchange rates will be equal. If the demand for yen falls to D', however, the dollar-yen exchange rate at market equilibrium will fall to $0.008 = 1 yen; the dollar would appreciate, and the yen would depreciate.

By law, however, individuals and firms in Japan would not be permitted to obtain dollars with yen at the new market exchange rate, even though that is what holders of dollars outside Japan would require and that holders of dollars within Japan would prefer. Traders of dollars and yen inside Japan would be obliged legally to trade yen for dollars at the official exchange rate of $0.010 = 1 yen even though the demand for yen has fallen to D'. So there would be, holding other things constant, an excess supply of yen at the official Japanese dollar-yen exchange rate; that is, there would be too many yen offered in exchange for dollars, or, equivalently, too few dollars offered for yen.

Naturally, in the fictitious situation we have described, many Japanese individuals and firms that would like to obtain dollars at the official exchange rate would be stymied. As a result, many would be tempted to violate the law by trading yen for dollars at the *market* exchange rate instead of the official rate. That is, they would be induced to engage in *black-market,* or illegal, trading of dollars and yen. To reduce such incentives, the Japanese government might enact one more legal restriction, called **capital controls.** In general, capital controls are restrictions on domestic holdings of foreign assets or liabilities or on the ability of foreign residents to obtain (Japanese) domestic assets or liabilities. Specifically, in our fictitious situation the Japanese government might make holding dollars or dollar-denominated assets or liabilities illegal, thereby reducing the potential scope for black-market trading.

These may seem to be extraordinary lengths to take to peg an exchange rate. And, indeed, neither the United States nor Japan recently has taken such measures. In other nations, such as France, South Korea, the former Soviet Union, and countries in Eastern Europe, however, capital controls have been used in the recent past or continue to remain in place. For the governments of such nations the costs to their citizens of an artificially fixed exchange rate apparently are overshadowed by the perceived gains of a fixed exchange rate.

We shall have much more to say about fixed and floating exchange rates in the following chapter, after we discuss international payments flows and actual world experiences with both types of systems. As you can see from our simple examples, however, a system of fixed exchange rates differs from one of floating exchange rates in one important respect: In the former system, central banks typically must trade large amounts of currencies to keep exchange rates from varying in the normally volatile conditions of foreign exchange markets; alternatively, national governments must enact complex controls on holding and trading foreign currencies. In a floating-rate system, in contrast, an active need for central bank or governmental actions is much more limited, or even nonexistent.

FORWARD EXCHANGE, SWAPS, AND FUTURES[1]

Our discussion to this point has simplified matters by examining ''the'' exchange rate between the currencies of two nations. In fact, there are several exchange rates that traders must consider. Of these, we have focused our attention only on the **spot exchange rate,** which is the rate of exchange between two currencies traded for immediate delivery in the **spot exchange market.** Markets for spot exchanges of currencies are a natural place to start, which is why we began with them, but there is much more to foreign exchange markets than spot trades.

Forward Exchange Markets   One common type of foreign exchange transpires in **forward exchange markets,** which are markets for currency trades in which delivery of a currency exchanged occurs at a later time. To understand how a forward exchange transaction works, consider a realistic problem faced by a U.S. importer of Japanese computer microchips. The import company plans to sell the microchips to a U.S. computer manufacturer in a month, according to a contract it has with the manufacturer. Hence, it has arranged for Japanese microchips to be shipped to the United States in four weeks, at which time it must pay for the microchips in yen.

An issue that the U.S. importer must address, however, is how to purchase the yen to make its exchange a month from now. The U.S. importer *could* settle an immediate purchase of the microchips by purchasing yen with dollars in the spot market. The importer then would have to find the best means of saving the yen, perhaps in a yen-denominated bank deposit, until it needs to make payment. The importer also would have to come up with dollars *today* to make the spot market purchase of yen.

Alternatively, the U.S. importer could wait until a month from now when it actually needs the yen, and it could then make a spot market purchase. An advantage of this timing is that it would enable the importer to arrange to have the dollars available four weeks hence instead of immediately. A disadvantage, however, is that a month from now the spot exchange rate may change; the dollar might depreciate against the yen during the coming month.

Rather than carry out either of these spot market transactions, the U.S. importer could instead enter into a *forward* exchange contract. It could offer the *future* delivery of dollars, four weeks from now, in exchange for delivery of yen to the importer at that time. The importer would pay (now) the *present* equilibrium **forward exchange rate** for this transaction. Hence, it would know *today* what exchange rate it would need to pay to obtain the needed yen four weeks from now. This would keep it from having to find the best way to hold yen-denominated assets for four weeks if it makes a spot trade today, or prevent it from potentially experiencing a loss from dollar depreciation versus the yen if it waits for a month to make a spot transaction.

It is possible that the U.S. importer will have to pay a forward exchange rate that is higher than today's spot exchange rate. If so, then the U.S. importer must pay a **forward premium** by obtaining yen with dollars via a forward exchange market transaction. It is also possible, however, that the importer will find that the forward exchange rate is below the current spot exchange rate, in which case the yen may be obtained with dollars at a **forward discount.**

---

[1] This section draws on the discussion provided by Michael Melvin, *International Money and Finance,* 2d ed. (New York: Harper & Row, 1989).

Currency Swaps We have not exhausted the list of possible dollar-yen transactions from which the U.S. importer of Japanese microchips may choose. Suppose that the importer already has inventories of yen available but that it needs to obtain more dollars *today* for some other purpose while ensuring that it can get access to the yen it will need again four weeks from now for its microchip trade. One way to do this, of course, would be to borrow dollars today directly from a depository institution. Another would be to trade some of its yen holdings for dollars today in the spot market and then trade dollars for yen again in a month. Yet another, however, would be for the importer to make a **swap** exchange transaction that combines elements of both spot and forward exchanges. In such an arrangement, the importer could trade yen for dollars today in the spot market and dollars for yen in the forward market. The U.S. importer then can cover both its current need for more dollars and its known future need for yen with a single arrangement.

Only importers with large currency inventories are likely to conduct many swap transactions such as that described above. These transactions are much more common among depository institutions that maintain significant foreign currency deposits and that need access to foreign currencies on a daily basis to meet the needs of their customers. Furthermore, depository institutions and other financial institutions sometimes transact foreign currency swaps on a regular basis as part of speculative strategies aimed at obtaining trading profits from a series of swaps. Others make such trades as *brokers* between other parties and earn commissions from these activities.

Foreign Exchange Futures and Options Recall from Chapter 5 that the use of financial futures and options has grown steadily in the United States. A *futures market,* you will recall, is a highly organized market for the exchange of specific commodities for a specified price on specific future dates. An *option* is a financial contract that grants the holder the right to buy and/or sell specified securities or goods in specific amounts and at specific prices for a specific period of time. The use of both futures and options in foreign exchange transactions has become much more commonplace than it had been both in the United States and throughout the world.

A foreign exchange futures contract is similar to a forward contract, in that the contract calls for future delivery of currencies. Economists and market practitioners use the term **foreign exchange futures** more narrowly than the term ''forward exchange contracts,'' however. Foreign exchange futures are *standardized* forward contracts tailored to the use of a few widely traded currencies; that is, the terms of exchange of two such currencies, say, the pound and the yen, would be preset regarding the amounts and the delivery date. A key standardization of a futures contract that distinguishes it from typical forward contracts is that cash flows between traders take place on a daily basis, based on their ''bets'' about which way currency exchange rates will move relative to the initially agreed-upon price. Actual delivery of currencies at expiration of the futures contract occurs only if the holders keep the contract until expiration. In contrast, under a forward contract no cash flows occur until the actual expiration date of the forward contract.

Firms and individuals also trade foreign exchange futures in specific geographical locations, such as the largest currency futures market, the International Money Market of the Chicago Mercantile Exchange. These markets typically are governmentally regulated. Forward contracts, in contrast, have negotiable terms, often involve less widely traded currencies, are traded among geographically dispersed locations, and typically are subjected to less direct governmental oversight.

Foreign exchange options are contracts that give the holder the right to buy or sell a fixed amount of a currency at a predetermined exchange rate. If the holder may exercise the right any time before the maturity of the option, then the option is called an *American* *option;* if the option is available only at maturity, then the option is a *European option.* Foreign currency options, like foreign currency futures, typically are standardized contracts involving widely traded currencies that are transacted in a few centralized markets.

FOREIGN EXCHANGE RISK, HEDGING, AND INTERNATIONAL DIVERSIFICATION

Why are there so many different kinds of foreign exchange markets? The reason is that firms and individuals use the wide variety of foreign exchange transactions—spot transactions, forward transactions, swaps, futures, and options—as ways to hedge against **foreign exchange risk** (also called *currency risk*). This is the risk an individual or firm incurs by holding and trading foreign currencies.

Types of Foreign Exchange Risk   There are three basic forms of foreign exchange risk:

1. *Accounting risk* **Accounting risk** arises from a difference in a firm's or an individual's holdings of foreign currency assets and foreign currency liabilities. Recall that the difference between total assets and total liabilities is net worth. If the foreign currency exchange rate varies, then the dollar valuations of assets and liabilities denominated in that foreign currency also change. As a result, the dollar measure of the net worth of a firm or individual can be affected. Hence, measured dollar wealth could decline simply because exchange rates change.

   For instance, suppose that the U.S. importer in our earlier example had $500,000 in dollar assets, 10 million yen in yen-denominated assets, and 50 million yen in yen-denominated liabilities. If the exchange rate initially is $0.010 = 1 yen, then the assets of the importer, measured in dollars, would be equal to $500,000 + [($0.010/1 yen) × 10 million yen] = $500,000 + $100,000 = $600,000, and the importer's liabilities, measured in dollars, would be equal to ($0.010/1 yen) × 50 million yen = $500,000. Hence, when the exchange rate is equal to $0.010 = 1 yen, the dollar value of the importer's net worth is equal to $100,000.

   Now suppose that the exchange rate changes to $0.015 = 1 yen, so that the dollar depreciates against the yen. Then the new dollar value of the importer's total assets is equal to $500,000 + [($0.015/1 yen) × 10 million yen] = $500,000 + $150,000 = $650,000. The new dollar value of the importer's liabilities is ($0.015/1 yen) × 50 million yen = $750,000. Hence, in this extreme example, the dollar-denominated net worth of the importer falls to a *negative* value, −$100,000, solely because of a depreciation of the dollar.

2. *Transaction risk* When an individual or firm commits to an import or export contract that involves credit extended for any period of time, such agreements typically entail extension of credit measured in terms of a single currency. By their nature, however, export or import arrangements also involve currency transactions for one of the parties involved, and so that party runs a risk of exchange rate variations during the time of the credit agreement. For example, suppose the Japanese microchip manufacturer in our earlier example ships the microchips to the U.S. importer under an agreement that payment in *dollars* will be forthcoming in, say, two weeks, taking upon itself the responsibility for converting the dollar payment to yen. During the two weeks of credit extension to the U.S. importer, the Japanese firm incurs **transaction risk,** because the dollar could appreciate against the yen during that time; as a result, the Japanese firm could receive less in yen when payment is due.

3. *Profitability risk* A key way to measure the value of any firm is as the discounted present value of the sum of current and all future anticipated profits of the firm. A firm that has significant foreign dealings must take into account its **profitability risk**—the risk that its underlying profitability can be affected by its foreign exchange transactions. A firm—or a depository institution—that is particularly adept at using swaps and forward, futures, and options instruments may be able to add to its underlying profitability through foreign exchange operations. That is, these transactions by themselves, irrespective of the underlying international business trades the exchange operations are associated with—may make the firm more or less profitable in the long run.

Hedging Against Foreign Exchange Risk   Just as the existence of forward, futures, and options markets in the United States economy allows individuals and firms that trade in those markets to hedge against risk, such markets in foreign exchange provide analogous opportunities. Individuals or firms may hedge against foreign exchange risk by making spot trades in conjunction with other transactions, such as forward contracts, swaps, futures, or options.

Consider the following intentionally simplified example. Suppose that an Italian bank lends lira (the Italian currency) to a United States construction company, under an agreement that the construction company will repay the Italian bank in dollars, at the forward dollar-lira exchange rate, when the loan matures a month hence. The Italian bank thereby exposes itself to accounting risk, because it now has a dollar-denominated asset (the dollar repayment it will receive for its lira-denominated loan). It also exposes itself to transaction risk, because the credit it extends as lira will be repaid in dollars that may depreciate against the lira in the spot exchange market. Finally, the Italian bank, as a depository financial institution that commonly trades in foreign exchange markets, also faces profitability risk in its foreign exchange trading.

To hedge against these risks, all the Italian bank needs to do is match the maturity structure of a dollar *liability* that will mature at the same time as its loan to the U.S. construction company matures. It could do this by borrowing dollars from an American bank, to be repaid in lira, in a forward contract at the same market forward exchange rate as applies to its loan. That is, it could set up a *swap* by combining its forward lending transaction with a forward borrowing transaction.

Hence, any exchange rate variability that occurs between the signing of the contracts and the simultaneous maturity of both contracts will affect both the bank's assets and liabilities equally, meaning that its net worth measured in lira will be unaffected. Furthermore, the transaction risk of loss it faces as a lender of lira to be repaid in dollars will be balanced by the potential for gain as a borrower of dollars to be repaid in lira. Finally, because the bank has insulated itself from risk of gain or loss via the swap, its lending transaction will have no foreign exchange profitability implications for the bank, which can concentrate on profiting from the known interest terms in the underlying lira loan. The bank's position thereby is *fully hedged* with respect to its forward loan contract with the U.S. construction firm.

The above example was particularly simple because it entailed a single hedging transaction via a swap with forward exchange instruments of identical maturities. In reality, individuals and firms must deal with risks that arise from the *mismatching* of asset and liability maturities. For this reason, sophisticated international traders often must use the full variety of financial instruments that are available to them, including foreign exchange futures and options, to hedge against foreign exchange risks.

This is not to say that forward, swap, futures, or options market transactions cannot be used to *speculate* about future exchange rate movements in hopes of earning foreign exchange trading profits. Indeed, one reason to hold a futures contract would be to regard it as a "bet" on future exchange rate movements. If the bet goes sour, the holder of a futures contract loses, either through continuing cash flow losses or through a capital loss upon sale of the contract, but if the bet turns out to be correct, the holder earns speculative profits.

Whether an individual or firm chooses to use these alternative foreign exchange transactions and instruments as means of hedging or speculating naturally depends upon attitudes toward risk. As we have noted earlier, exchange rates can be very volatile. We would expect that the most risk-averse investors would hedge against the potentially adverse effects of such exchange rate variability, while we would anticipate that those less averse to risk would seek to earn speculative profits when exchange rates rise or fall by amounts not expected by most other traders.

FOREIGN ASSET DIVERSIFICATION AND INTERNATIONAL BANKING

As we shall discuss in the next chapter, flows of goods and services among countries typically entail reverse flows of payments denominated in foreign currencies (unless the transactions are gifts or transfers). Indeed, our examples above concerning a U.S. microchip importer implicitly involved flows of goods or services and of payments between the United States and Japan. That is, those examples involved currency transactions related to international trade in goods and services.

It is also common, however, for residents in one nation to purchase financial assets of other nations, thereby generating flows of payments among nations and inducing foreign exchange transactions. As we have discussed, many purchases or sales of foreign financial instruments are undertaken to hedge against or speculate about foreign exchange risks. Many purchases or sales of assets denominated in foreign currencies, however, do not arise directly from a concern about foreign exchange risk per se. These asset exchanges occur because individuals and firms choose to hold foreign assets as part of a general strategy of asset diversification. Among those firms that diversify their balance sheets through foreign asset purchases or sales are depository financial institutions, as we shall discuss shortly. First, however, let's consider why a strategy of foreign asset diversification makes sense for many investors in the United States and elsewhere.

INTERNATIONAL ASSET DIVERSIFICATION

People in the United States purchase most of the stocks and bonds that U.S firms and government agencies issue. Foreigners also purchase some of these stocks and bonds, however. Furthermore, American individuals and firms purchase stocks and bonds of foreign companies and nations as well. Why do individuals and firms in a given nation purchase securities issued in nations other than their own?

For one thing, most world financial markets are open to citizens of other nations. Furthermore, although the U.S. stock and bond markets are very large, the volumes traded in foreign securities markets are not insignificant. For instance, the total U.S. stock market capitalization now is less than half that of the world's total, with Far Eastern markets accounting for about one-fourth and European markets composing the remaining fourth. The ratios for U.S., Far Eastern, and European bond markets are similar magnitudes. In short, there are well-developed securities markets around the world.

Asset Returns and International Arbitrage But U.S. citizens do not hold foreign financial assets simply because foreign markets exist. Rather, they do so because they feel that there is something to gain by purchasing international securities. For example, a U.S. investor may believe that the return on securities in another part of the world may, on average, exceed those available within the United States. For this reason, she and other Americans might choose to hold foreign stocks or bonds.

Such differences in average returns across nations certainly may be *potential* explanations for why some individuals may hold foreign assets. We would not expect these differences to persist for very long, however, because market **arbitrage**—buying an asset at its market price in one nation's asset market and then selling it or its equivalent at the higher price in another nation's asset market—should eventually eliminate these differences. In days gone by in which information about asset return and price differences traveled slowly, arbitrage might take time, but in today's highly interconnected financial systems, analysts constantly watch for differences in asset returns and prices across national markets. Hence, differences in returns typically last only for brief intervals nowadays, which limits considerably such differences as a reason to hold securities issued in other nations.

Risk Diversification through International Holdings The primary rationale—aside from the goal of reducing foreign exchange risk that we have already discussed—for holding assets issued in other nations is that doing so helps reduce risk of variation in the overall financial wealth of an individual or a firm. That is, international asset diversification can reduce the overall risk exposure incurred by an individual or firm.

To understand why this might be true, consider an extreme case. Suppose that a Kuwaiti citizen had, before 1990, decided to hold all her wealth in bonds issued by Kuwaiti firms and by the Kuwaiti government. As it turned out, 1990 and 1991 were very bad years for both private firms and the government of that nation as a result of the Iraqi invasion and subsequent war. Even if the Kuwaiti citizen's financial portfolio was well diversified among stocks and bonds issued by a variety of Kuwaiti firms and government agencies, all the returns on these financial instruments would have been affected adversely by the terrible conflict that swept through much of Kuwait in the early 1990s. Even an otherwise well-diversified portfolio of Kuwaiti financial instruments would have suffered severe losses.

Suppose instead that this Kuwaiti citizen had elected to hold financial instruments issued in a *mix* of countries, including, say, Kuwait, the United States, Japan, Italy, and France. The Iraqi conflict and subsequent economic recession in 1991 undeniably had some negative effects on asset returns in these nations. Nevertheless, the overall loss on a portfolio consisting of securities from this larger group of nations would have been much lower than that sustained on a portfolio consisting solely of Kuwaiti securities. Hence, it is easy to see via this extreme example that it might pay to hold assets from more than one nation.

In short, the basic idea of international asset diversification is that the returns on securities issued in a single nation may be subject to disturbances specific to that nation that have little or no effects on the returns on securities issued in some other nation. As a less extreme example, suppose that unexpectedly high U.S. government budget deficits cause interest rates on most American financial instruments to rise, so that their prices tend to fall. The effects of such an unexpected event largely would be isolated to the United States. Therefore, American investors could have reduced the risk of capital losses on their wealth portfolios by having held foreign as well as American stocks and bonds.

To balance risks across nations, many investors seek to hold securities of nations whose

THE ORIGINS OF THE EUROCURRENCY MARKET

INTERNATIONAL

PERSPECTIVE

The Eurocurrency market was first known as the *Eurodollar market,* because most activity in these markets pertained to dollar-denominated deposits and loans by banks with offices in European nations. Only since the 1980s has the term "Eurocurrency market" come into prevalent use as the dollar's importance has declined somewhat relative to other currencies such as the Japanese yen and German deutschemark.

Interestingly, the origins of the Eurodollar market may be traced to the financial dealings of the two post-World War II bulwarks of anticapitalism, the former Soviet Union and China. Following World War II, both nations needed dollars to conduct trade, because the dollar was the key currency in which most international trade was conducted. Both nations feared holding dollar deposits in the United States' banking system, however, because they were concerned that cold war tensions potentially could induce the American government to seize Soviet or Chinese deposits in retaliation. Some bankers based in Europe—and primarily in London—were only too happy to serve as conduits for these nations' dollars, as long as the price was right. Hence,

the Soviet and Chinese governments had their dollar-denominated deposits, and British banks earned profits.

It did not take long for the Eurodollar market to expand considerably. Because Eurodollar lending was a profitable business for London banks, the market interest rate on Eurodollar deposits became attractive to a variety of individuals and firms in the late 1950s and early 1960s. Multinational American firms found such deposits attractive as well; their subsidiaries could hold dollar-denominated deposits at London banks, or in banks in other nations when the market expanded geographically, rather than going to the trouble to send dollars back to the United States for deposit in U.S. banks.

By this time, the residents of democratic republics of Western Europe, the United States, and Japan forgot who deserved the real credit for getting the market started—the opponents of private markets and capitalists who resided in the former Soviet Union and China. Ironically, the enemies of free markets had spurred the development of one of the largest private financial markets in the world.

Source: Jeffrey A. Frieden, *Banking on the World: The Politics of International Finance* (Oxford: Basil Blackwell, 1987).

returns are not directly related to one another. Hence, if the return on a security issued in one country falls, there would be less likelihood that returns would decline for the securities issued in another nation. Some investors, for instance, develop **world index funds,** which are groupings of assets of different national origin whose variations in returns tend to be offsetting. Naturally, these investors also try to include high-yield instruments in their world index funds, because risk diversification is not their only objective. Nonetheless, such diversification is the primary motivation for constructing such global portfolios.

INTERNATIONAL BANKING

Depository institutions play a very important role in the process of international financial diversification and reduction of foreign exchange risks, both on their own behalf and for the benefit of their customers. They do this through interactions in the **Eurocurrency market,** which is an asset market in which banks raise deposit funds and make loans denominated in currencies of various nations, but *outside* the countries that issued those currencies.

The Eurocurrency market's origins were based in cold war politics, as we discuss in the International Perspective above. Most analysts, however, credit the growth of the

Eurocurrency market to attempts by governments to regulate the international activities of their banking systems. Indeed, the first big wave of growth in the Eurocurrency market occurred in the latter half of the 1960s and resulted primarily from banking and monetary restrictions in the United States. By the early 1960s the dollar was so important in financing international trade around the world that New York had fully eclipsed London as the center for international finance. It also became the center for a major flow of dollars to other nations.

In 1963, out of fear that these dollar flows out of the country would damage the prosperity of the United States, the U.S. government placed a tax on most foreign bonds purchased by Americans. Shortly thereafter it imposed limits on the amounts that American banks could lend to foreigners and that U.S. corporations could invest outside the United States. That is, the United States government imposed limited *capital controls.*

These controls lasted until 1974, and they effectively pushed much of the international dollar lending away from New York to locations outside the United States. Besides causing a renewed boom for British banks that traded dollar-denominated assets, or *Eurodollars,* the controls induced *American* banks to beef up their branches in London and in other overseas locations. Despite legal restrictions on movements of funds from U.S. branches of American banks to their overseas offices, the dollar deposits of the overseas branches ballooned as these branches actively solicited such deposits from overseas customers. Between 1970 and 1973 alone, the net size of the Eurocurrency market more than doubled as American, European, and Far Eastern banks scrambled to compete in the new offshore market. Banks began trading in deposits and loans denominated in a variety of currencies, and the Eurocurrency market was born.

Comparing Interest Rates in Domestic and Eurocurrency Markets   With the advent of the Eurocurrency market and the simultaneous development of more sophisticated communications technologies, funds began to flow around the world in magnitudes and at speeds never previously contemplated. Indeed, corporations and depository institutions began to respond to very small interest rate differentials across nations by shifting funds among deposits in domestic banks and Eurocurrency deposits in other locales around the world. They did so because the amounts shifted were so large that even tiny interest rate differentials could yield significant absolute differences in returns, thereby justifying the costs of transferring the funds.

Eurodollar trading has continued to account for the majority of transactions in the Eurocurrency market. Nevertheless, the existence of financial assets denominated in so many currencies at so many different rates of interest made interest rate comparisons across different financial assets exceedingly complicated for all concerned. Therefore, traders adopted the convention, which continues today, of quoting interest rates on alternative Eurocurrency *loans* in terms of percentage points above the **London Interbank Offer Rate (LIBOR).** LIBOR is the interest rate at which six large London banks would lend to or deposit with each other each morning when market trading opens. Eurocurrency *deposit* interest rates typically are quoted in reference to either LIBOR or the market interest rate on large, negotiable certificates of deposit in the United States. By adopting such conventions, the frames of reference for interest rate comparisons became much less complicated.

The Economic Functions of the Eurocurrency Market   The Eurocurrency market is a common financial ''meeting place'' of individuals, firms, and depository institutions from around the globe. As such, the market performs a variety of economic functions.

1. *Focus of world arbitrage* Differences in returns among world securities are "arbitraged away" very quickly and efficiently through the Eurocurrency market. Effectively, this market links domestic markets around the world. For instance, if the returns on dollar-denominated assets traded in the United States fall, funds flow quickly to dollar-denominated assets in London and elsewhere, lowering returns on those assets. This can induce traders to shift funds to asset holdings denominated in other currencies, causing their rates to adjust as well, until a new worldwide interest rate equilibrium is attained.

2. *Center for world lending* By the early 1980s, it had become clear that legal restrictions on the foreign lending and deposit-gathering activities by U.S. banks had become ineffective. By this time, in fact, numerous American banks had circumvented the regulations by setting up "front" offices technically outside United States territory, typically in the Caribbean Islands, and thereby outside the scope of U.S. government interference. The banks used these nearby and inexpensive offices as locations for booking Eurocurrency transactions.

   The Fed finally halted the growth of this charade at the end of 1981 when it permitted American banks to engage in Eurocurrency trading inside the United States through **International Banking Facilities (IBFs).** In spite of their name, IBFs do not indicate actual construction of new "physical facilities"; rather, they are a legal mechanism for banks to maintain separate accounting ledgers for international loans and deposits.

   The establishment of IBFs, plus urgings by the U.S. government to make more loans to developing nations, hastened the growing involvement of American banks in lending to other nations through the Eurocurrency market. Many of these Eurocurrency loans are **syndicated loans,** which are loans negotiated by a typically small group of managing banks that later sell shares of the loans to other banks that they recruit into the "syndicate" of banks that participate in the loan agreement.

   As we discussed in Chapter 6, American banks have not had particularly good experience with many of the international loans they made through the Eurocurrency market in the 1980s. For many of them, the growth of Eurocurrency lending drastically failed to fulfill the earlier high expectations that had induced these banks to become active Eurocurrency lenders. Most of the banks had expected the loans to have high returns; furthermore, they failed to anticipate the fall in oil prices in the early 1980s that affected nearly all developing nations adversely, meaning that the loans contributed less to risk diversification of the banks' loan portfolios than the banks had expected.

3. *Channel of depositor diversification* While many banks found to their dismay that the Eurocurrency *loan* market did not allow them to diversify risks as they had hoped, many *depositors* have found that the Eurocurrency market has been a major blessing. Multinational corporations in particular benefit from the presence of the Eurocurrency market, which they use to spread their funds among a wide variety of deposit holdings, either as dollar-denominated deposits held at a variety of banks or as deposits denominated in several currencies at a few banks.

4. *Facility for foreign exchange risk reduction* As we noted earlier in this chapter, banks often protect themselves from foreign exchange risk by engaging in currency swaps. Such swaps commonly take the form of forward purchases of foreign-currency-denominated assets matched by forward sales of foreign-currency-denominated liabilities.

The highly developed nature of the Eurocurrency market facilitates such swaps. Because banks around the world are linked through the Eurocurrency market, a large number of parties engage in swap transactions at any given time. As a result, the market for such transactions is very competitive; both borrowing and lending banks, and their customers, can benefit from the extent to which the Eurocurrency market serves as a facility for such risk-reducing transactions.

To summarize, the Eurocurrency market is the hub of international finance. It makes financial markets of nations around the world more efficient by linking traders in those markets, and it is the conduit for portfolio diversification by individuals, firms, and financial institutions. Finally, transactions in the Eurocurrency market enable depository institutions to hedge against foreign exchange risks incurred by them either on their own behalf or on behalf of their customers.

Large amounts of the funds that flow between nations are channeled through the Eurocurrency market. These funds flows, as we shall discuss in the next chapter, reflect the underlying waxing and waning of trade and finance among nations. Helping you to understand the nature of these flows, therefore, is the task we must tackle next.

CHAPTER SUMMARY

1. People in different nations make the following economic transactions with each other: trading goods and services (exporting-importing), buying and selling each other's assets, and giving and receiving gifts.

2. Exchange rates are the price of one currency in terms of another. Like all prices, the interacting forces of supply and demand determine the equilibrium exchange rate.

3. The demand curve for a particular currency is negatively sloped; as the dollar price of the yen falls (i.e., it takes fewer dollars to buy 1 yen), this yen depreciation induces U.S. residents to buy more Japanese-made goods and yen-denominated assets, and to bestow more gifts on friends and relatives living in Japan.

4. The supply curve of a particular currency is positively sloped; as the dollar price of 1 yen rises, other things constant, the Japanese will want to sell more yen to purchase dollars, in order to buy more American-made goods and U.S. dollar-denominated assets, and to give more gifts to friends and relatives in the United States.

5. The equilibrium exchange rate is established at the intersection of the supply of and the demand for a currency. At an exchange rate above equilibrium a surplus exists, and competitive currency sellers will drive the exchange rate down; at an exchange rate below the equilibrium rate a shortage exists, and competing buyers will drive the currency price upward.

6. The demand for a particular country's currency rises if (other things constant) (a) real incomes rise in other countries; (b) the after-tax, risk-adjusted, real interest rate rises in that country; (c) tastes change in favor of that country's exports; (d) its inflation rate is lower than other nations' inflation rates; (e) that country's future inflation rate is expected to be below the inflation rates in other countries.

7. If U.S. tastes change in favor of Japanese-made goods and services, then the demand for yen will rise, causing the yen to appreciate relative to the U.S. dollar.

8. If the after-tax, risk-adjusted real interest rate rises in the United States, the supply of yen will increase; this will cause the yen to depreciate relative to the dollar.

9. If a nation wishes to keep the exchange rate between its currency and that of another nation fixed, then its central bank must be able to trade its currency for that of the other nation in sufficient amounts to eliminate any surpluses or shortages that otherwise would result from

variations in demand or supply in the foreign exchange market. Otherwise, the nation must abandon fixed exchange rates or must resort to capital controls that inhibit the ability of its citizens to exchange their currencies for those of the other nation at the market exchange rate instead of the official fixed exchange rate.

10. There are a variety of foreign exchange transactions. These include spot transactions, forward contracts, swaps, futures, and options. Individuals or firms may use different transactions depending upon their relative costs and benefits, and depending upon their implications for foreign exchange risk that individuals or firms incur.

11. There are three types of foreign exchange risk: (a) accounting risk arising from variations in net worth measured in terms of one currency because of exchange rate changes, (b) transaction risk arising from variations in exchange rates that alter the gains derived from a particular exchange contract, and (c) profitability risk resulting from general profits derived or losses incurred from foreign exchange transactions in the course of international business.

12. Individuals and firms hold assets issued in other nations largely because doing so diversifies their financial wealth. The returns on stocks and bonds in a single nation often may be influenced by factors specific to that country, and so holding securities of several nations permits individuals and firms to protect themselves from losses caused by such country-specific factors.

13. An important conduit for international asset diversification and foreign exchange risk-reducing transactions is the Eurocurrency market. Depository institutions are key participants in this market; they make loans and issue deposits denominated in a number of currencies, although the dollar remains the predominant currency traded in the Eurocurrency market. The Eurocurrency market also facilitates international arbitrage that thereby channels funds to assets with the highest returns and equalizes rates of return on identical assets across nations.

GLOSSARY

Accounting risk: Risk of change in measured net worth arising from a difference in holdings of foreign currency assets and foreign currency liabilities.

Appreciate: Increase in value.

Arbitrage: The act of purchasing an asset at a given price in one market and then selling it or its equivalent at a higher price in another market.

Capital controls: Legal restrictions on holdings of foreign assets or liabilities by domestic residents or on holdings of domestic assets or liabilities by foreign residents.

Currency appreciation: A situation in which it now takes more foreign currency to purchase a unit of domestic currency.

Currency depreciation: A situation in which it now takes less foreign currency to purchase a unit of domestic currency.

Depreciate: Decrease in value.

Eurocurrency market: An asset market in which banks raise deposit funds and make loans denominated in currencies of various nations, but located *outside* the countries that issued those currencies.

Exchange rate: The price of foreign currency in terms of a unit of domestic currency.

Export: Sell goods and services to other countries.

Fixed exchange rate: A currency price that a central bank pegs at a particular value over a period of time.

Floating exchange rate: A currency price that is determined by the forces of supply and demand in the foreign exchange market, with little or no governmental interference.

Foreign exchange futures: Standardized forward exchange contracts used for a few widely traded currencies in highly developed market locations.

Foreign exchange options: Financial contracts giving the holder the right to buy or sell a fixed amount of a currency at a predetermined exchange rate.

Foreign exchange risk: The risk an individual or firm incurs by holding and trading foreign currencies; also called currency risk.

Forward discount: The amount by which the current spot exchange rate for a currency exceeds the current forward exchange rate.

Forward exchange markets: Markets for currency trades in which deliveries of currencies exchanged occur at designated future times following agreements on terms of transactions.

Forward exchange rate: The current price of a currency to be delivered at a future time.

Forward premium: The amount by which the current forward exchange rate for a currency exceeds the current spot exchange rate.

Import: Purchase goods and services from other countries.

Import quotas: Restrictions on the quantity of imports.

International Banking Facilities (IBFs): Legal mechanisms under which banks maintain separate accounting ledgers for recording international loans and deposits.

International integration: The development of strong ties, linkages, and interactions among individuals, firms, markets, and governments of different nations.

London Interbank Offer Rate (LIBOR): The interest rate at which six large London banks would lend funds to or deposit funds with each other each morning when market trading opens.

Profitability risk: The risk that a firm's underlying profitability may be affected by its foreign currency transactions.

Spot exchange market: The market for transactions in currencies that take place immediately after traders reach agreement on the rate of exchange.

Spot exchange rate: The price of a currency to be delivered immediately.

Swap: A foreign exchange transaction that combines elements of both spot and forward exchanges into a single trade.

Syndicated loan: A common type of loan in Eurocurrency markets, in which the terms of the loan are negotiated by a small group of banks that later sell shares of the loans to other banks that they recruit into the ''syndicate'' of banks participating in the loan agreement.

Tariffs: Taxes imposed on imports.

Transaction risk: The risk a party to a long-term currency credit contract incurs that the currency's exchange rate could change during the time of the credit agreement.

World index funds: Groupings of financial assets of different national origin whose variations in returns tend to offset one another.

SELF-TEST QUESTIONS

1. Explain, in your own words, why the demand for French francs is negatively related to the dollar price of the franc.

2. Explain, in your own words, why the supply of French francs is positively related to the dollar price of the franc.

3. Suppose that Japanese citizens continue to experience significant increases in their real incomes while the real incomes of Americans remain unchanged. As a result, Japanese consumers desire to import more goods from other nations, including the United States. Would you predict that the dollar would appreciate or depreciate against the yen as a result? Use a diagram of the market for yen to explain your reasoning.

4. Suppose that the government of Denmark, whose currency is the Danish krone (DKr), decides that it wishes to maintain a fixed exchange rate between the krone and the dollar of U.S. $0.10 = DKr 1. Initially, the market demand and supply schedules for the Danish krone intersect at that exchange rate. A rise in the demand for the Danish krone resulting from an increased desire for American imports from Denmark occurs, however. At the initial, desired exchange rate, will there be a shortage or surplus of DKr after this occurrence? What policy should the Danish central bank follow to keep the dollar-krone exchange rate fixed at the desired level? Is it hindered in this policy if it has very few dollar reserves? Explain.

5. List the differences between a forward exchange contract and a foreign exchange futures contract.

6. Explain why the restrictions on American lending to other nations imposed in the 1960s and 1970s were forms of capital controls.

7. List the key economic functions of the Eurocurrency market.

PROBLEMS

27-1.   The figure below shows the supply of and the demand for British pounds (£) as a function of the exchange rate—expressed in U.S. dollars per pound. Assume that Britain and the United States are the only two countries in the world.

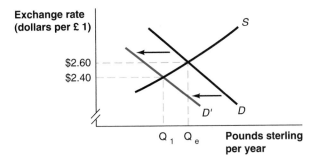

a. How might the shift from D to D' be accounted for?
b. Given the shift from D to D', what exists at U.S. $2.60 = £1$?
c. Will the pound now appreciate, or will it depreciate?
d. What could cause the supply curve of pounds to shift rightward (increase)?

27-2.   Which of the following will cause the yen to appreciate? Explain.
a. U.S. real incomes increase relative to Japanese real incomes.
b. It is expected that in the future the yen will depreciate relative to the dollar.
c. The U.S. inflation rate rises relative to the Japanese inflation rate.
d. The after-tax, risk-adjusted real interest rate in the United States rises relative to that in Japan.
e. U.S. tastes change in favor of Japanese-made goods.

27-3.   Suppose that the demand for and supply of German marks are given by $P_m = 100/q_d$ and $P_m = 2q_s$, where P_m is the price of marks in terms of dollars, q_d is quantity demanded, and q_s is quantity supplied.
a. Determine the equilibrium quantity and price of marks.
b. What is the equilibrium quantity of dollars and price in terms of marks?
c. If the demand for marks shifted such that $P_m = 120/q_d$, what would be the new price of marks?

SELECTED REFERENCES

Dornbusch, Rudiger, and Stanley Fischer, *Macroeconomics* (New York: McGraw-Hill, 1987).

Frankel, Allen B., and John D. Montgomery, "Financial Structure: An International Perspective," *Brookings Papers on Economic Activity* (1, 1991), pp. 257–297.

Frieden, Jeffrey A., *Banking on the World: The Politics of International Finance* (Oxford: Basil Blackwell, 1987).

Grabbe, J. Orlin, *International Financial Markets* (New York: Elsevier, 1986).

Krugman, Paul, *The Age of Diminished Expectations* (Cambridge, Mass.: MIT Press, 1990).

Madura, Jeff, *International Financial Management* (St. Paul, Minn.: West Publishing Co., 1986).

Markusen, James R., and James R. Melvin, *The Theory of International Trade* (New York: Harper & Row, 1988).

Melvin, Michael, *International Money and Finance,* 2d ed. (New York: Harper & Row, 1989).

Miller, Roger L., *Economics Today,* 7th ed. (New York: Harper & Row, 1991).

Solnik, Bruno, *International Investments* (Reading, Mass.: Addison-Wesley Publishing Company, 1988).

Yarbrough, Beth V., and Robert M. Yarbrough, *The World Economy: Trade and Finance* (New York: The Dryden Press, 1988).

The International Monetary System

CHAPTER PREVIEW

1. What is an international payments disequilibrium?

2. What economic mechanisms assure an international payments equilibrium?

3. How do fixed-exchange-rate systems assure an international payments equilibrium?

4. How do floating-exchange-rate systems assure an international payments equilibrium?

5. How and why do governments play a role in the process of payments equilibrium under the alternative exchange rate systems?

6. What types of exchange rate systems have existed in past years?

7. What kind of exchange rate system is predominant today?

In Chapter 27 we described how people in different nations transact economically; they buy and sell goods and services, exchange assets, and give and receive gifts. Because different countries use different monetary units, exchange rates among the different currencies must somehow be established. In that chapter we indicated how the forces of supply and demand can establish equilibrium, or market-clearing, exchange rates.

This chapter is concerned with how economic transactions between nations are financed. Its essential insight is that, ultimately, a nation's expenditures on foreign-made goods and services, its purchases of foreign assets, and its gift giving to foreigners are constrained by its "budget," in the form of its income and wealth. Just like families, nations must eventually come to grips with their budgets when they spend, borrow, and give gifts. When the total of a nation's economic transactions with the rest of the world remains within the nation's budget, we say that it is in a **balance-of-payments equilibrium;** when it is not able to sustain its overall expenditures volume indefinitely, we say that it is in a **balance-of-payments disequilibrium.**

In this chapter we analyze the various monetary systems that have evolved and that force nations toward a balance-of-payments equilibrium. We also make the important distinction between (1) accounting *identities* among international transactions and (2) international balance-of-payments *equilibrium.*

ACCOUNTING IDENTITIES

As you are aware, accounting identities exist for financial institutions and other businesses. In this section we begin with simple accounting identities that must hold for families, and then we describe international accounting identities.

If a family unit is spending more than its current income, such a situation necessarily implies that the family unit must be doing one of the following:

1. Drawing down its wealth. The family must reduce its money holdings, or it must sell stocks, bonds, or other assets.
2. Borrowing.
3. Receiving gifts from friends or relatives.
4. Receiving public transfers from a government, which obtained the funds from taxing others. (A transfer is a payment, in money or in goods or services, without the receipt of a good or service in return.)

In effect, we can use the above information to derive an identity; if a family unit is currently spending more than it is earning, it must draw on previously acquired wealth, borrow, or receive either private or public aid. Similarly, an identity exists for a family unit that is currently spending less than it is earning: It must increase its wealth by increasing its money holdings or by lending and acquiring other financial assets; or it must pay taxes or bestow gifts on others.

Additional identities crop up when we consider *all* the household units. For example, given the quantity of money supplied, the amount by which some households reduce their money holdings must equal the amount by which other households increase their money holdings. A moment's reflection indicates that when we consider businesses and governments, each unit and each group faces its own identities or constraints. For example, net lending by households must equal net borrowing by businesses and governments.

Even though our individual family unit's accounts must "balance"—in the sense that the identity discussed previously must hold—sometimes the item that brings about the balance cannot continue indefinitely. *If family expenditures exceed family income and this situation is financed by borrowing, the household may be considered to be in* disequilibrium *because such a situation cannot continue indefinitely.* Or if such a family deficit is financed by drawing on previously accumulated assets, the family may also be in disequilibrium because it cannot continue indefinitely to draw on its wealth; eventually, it will become impossible for that family to continue such a life-style. (Of course, if the family members are retired, they may well be in equilibrium by drawing on previously acquired assets to finance current deficits; this example illustrates that it is necessary to understand circumstances fully before pronouncing an economic unit in disequilibrium.)

Individual households, businesses, and governments, as well as the entire group of households, businesses, and governments, must eventually reach equilibrium. Certain economic adjustment mechanisms have evolved to assure equilibrium. Deficit households must eventually increase their incomes or decrease their expenditures; they will find that they have to pay higher interest rates if they wish to borrow to finance their deficits. Eventually their credit sources will dry up, and they will be forced into equilibrium. Businesses, on occasion, must lower costs and/or prices—or go bankrupt—to reach equilibrium.

When nations transact with each other, certain identities or constraints also must hold. Nations buy goods from people in other nations; they also lend to and present gifts to people in other nations. If a nation transacts with others, an accounting identity assures a "balance" (but not an equilibrium); this topic is discussed in the next section.

As is true *within* nations, economic adjustment mechanisms evolve to assure that economic equilibrium eventually exists *between* a nation and the rest of the world. Eventually, interest rates, prices, and income levels change until international equilibrium is restored. In the next section we describe international accounting identities; then we analyze the adjustment mechanisms (economic forces) that drive nations to international payments equilibrium.

INTERNATIONAL ACCOUNTING IDENTITIES

A country, like a person, also must balance its accounts. A country is different from a family unit, however, in that (1) a country's accounts must take into consideration the actions of a central bank, and (2) different countries use different currencies to settle their accounts.

The **balance of payments** is a record of all the transactions between the households, firms, and government of one country and the rest of the world. Any transaction that leads to a *payment* by a country's residents (or government) is a deficit item—a deficit item will be identified by a negative sign (−) when we use actual numbers. Deficit items include the following transactions: imports of merchandise, gifts to foreigners, use of foreign-owned transportation, tourism expenditures abroad, military spending abroad, interest and dividends paid to foreigners, purchases of foreign assets (such as stocks, bonds, and real estate), deposits made in foreign depository institutions, and purchases of foreign gold and foreign currency. Note that deficit-item transactions lead to an increase in the demand for foreign currencies and an increase in the supply of the domestic currency on the foreign exchange market.

Any transaction that leads to a *receipt* by a country's residents (or government) is a surplus item and is identified by a plus sign (+) when actual numbers are considered. Surplus items include exports of goods and services, expenditures made by foreigners touring the domestic country, services rendered by the domestic country's transportation facilities, interest and dividends received from abroad, gifts from abroad, foreign military spending in the domestic country, and asset purchases by foreigners, such as foreign purchases of domestic securities, increases in foreign bank loans to domestic companies, and increases in foreign holdings of the domestic currency. Also included are domestic sales of gold to foreigners. Note that surplus-item transactions lead to an increase in the demand for the domestic currency and an increase in the supply of foreign currency. Surplus-item transactions "earn" foreign exchange for a nation. See Table 28-1.

T A B L E   28-1
Surplus (+) and Deficit (−) Items on the International Accounts

Surplus Items (+)	Deficit Items (−)
Exports of merchandise	Imports of merchandise
Private and governmental gifts from foreigners	Private and governmental gifts to foreigners
Foreign use of domestic-owned transportation	Use of foreign-owned transportation
Foreign tourist expenditures domestically	Tourism expenditures abroad
Foreign military spending domestically	Military spending abroad
Interest and dividend receipts from foreigners	Interest and dividends paid to foreigners
Sales of domestic assets to foreigners	Purchases of foreign assets
Deposits in domestic depository institutions made by foreigners	Deposits made in foreign depository institutions
Sales of gold to foreigners	Purchases of gold from foreigners
Sales of domestic currency to foreigners	Purchases of foreign currency

THE CURRENT ACCOUNT

The **current account,** sometimes called the *open account,* tracks ongoing international trades and transfers of goods and services. Therefore, current account transactions include:

1. Exports and imports of merchandise (goods). If for a nation the value of merchandise exported exceeds the value of merchandise imported, a **merchandise trade surplus** (or simply a *trade surplus*) exists; if for a nation the value of merchandise imported exceeds the value of merchandise exported, a **merchandise trade deficit** exists for that nation.

2. Expenditures on sales of services (examples include shipping, brokerage, and insurance services) from other nations.

3. Unilateral transfers (such as foreign aid or private gifts) between nations.

The **current account balance** tracks the value of a country's exports of goods and services (including military receipts and income on investments abroad) and transfer payments (private and government) relative to the value of that country's imports of goods and services (including military payments) and transfer payments (private and government). For ease of exposition, let us refer to the current account balance as the excess of exports over imports. As long as you understand that these terms actually include items that are not normally considered exports or imports, no harm is done.

If exports exceed imports, a **current account surplus** is said to exist; if imports exceed exports, a **current account deficit** (a negative number) is said to exist. A current account deficit must be financed by increasing liabilities to the rest of the world or by selling assets (reducing net claims on the rest of the world). A current account surplus necessarily leads to a purchase of foreign assets (increasing net claims on the rest of the world) or a reduction in net liabilities (repayment of foreign-owned debt).

THE CAPITAL ACCOUNT

The **capital account** records all transactions in assets between the domestic country and the rest of the world. The **capital account balance** is the amount by which the value of a country's sales of such assets as stocks, bonds, and real estate to foreigners compares with the value of that country's purchase of such assets from abroad. If the value of such sales is greater than purchases, then a **capital account surplus** (a positive number) exists; if the value of such sales is less than purchases, then a **capital account deficit** (a negative number) exists. A capital account surplus implies a net capital inflow; a capital account deficit implies a net capital outflow.

An identity relates the current account and the capital account, assuming no intervention by the central banks of nations. Thus

$$\text{Current account} + \text{capital account} \equiv 0 \qquad \textbf{(28-1)}$$

Stated differently,

$$
\begin{aligned}
\text{Current account surplus} &= \text{capital account deficit} \\
&= \text{increase in net foreign assets} \qquad \textbf{(28-2)}
\end{aligned}
$$

Equation (28-2) indicates that if a nation is experiencing a current account surplus, then it must also be running a capital account deficit; for that year that nation must be a net international lender, and the value of assets it purchases from foreigners must exceed the value of assets that foreigners purchase from it. Over the past decade Japan has run current account surpluses and consequently has reaped the benefits of its export sales by acquiring the assets of its trading partners.

Equation (28-1) also implies that

$$\text{Current account deficit} = \text{capital account surplus}$$
$$= \text{decrease in net foreign assets} \qquad \textbf{(28-3)}$$

Equation (28-3) indicates that if a nation is experiencing a current account deficit, it must be running a capital account surplus; for that year that nation, therefore, is a net international borrower. It is financing its current account deficit, in effect, by selling more assets to foreigners than it is acquiring from them. Since 1983 the United States has experienced a current account deficit and, largely as a result, has become an international debtor nation. Although there is some controversy about the measurement of the current account deficit, the United States is widely considered to be the world's largest debtor nation. (See the Current Controversy later in this chapter.)

THE OFFICIAL SETTLEMENTS BALANCE

The **official settlements balance** is the sum of the current account balance and the capital account balance. Because of the existence of central banks this sum need *not* be zero. If, on net, the capital account and the current account are in deficit, the official settlements balance will be negative. That is, in such a situation the domestic country pays more foreign currency to foreigners than it receives. The official settlements balance must itself be financed by official reserve transactions, such as:

1. Increases in liabilities to foreign governments.

2. Gold sales.

3. Use of special drawing rights (SDRs) with the International Monetary Fund (IMF). As we discussed in Chapter 16, SDRs are a type of IMF-issued currency.

4. Sales of foreign currencies.

5. Use of reserves with the IMF.

By definition, the official settlements balance must equal the value of the official reserve transactions. In practice, the numbers don't correspond perfectly because of the existence of some private international transactions that are not recorded. Because we know that the sum of the current account balance and the capital account balance must equal the value of the official reserve transaction (a number we can determine with certainty), a term labeled ''errors and omissions'' (statistical discrepancy) is included to reconcile the differences.

Table 28-2 shows the values of the current account balance, the capital account balance, errors and omissions, and official reserve transactions of the United States for selected years. If there were no central banks, a current account deficit would have to be financed by a capital account surplus: If the residents of the United States spent and gave more than they earned and received in gifts, this deficit would have to be made up by borrowing from the rest of the world. The existence of deficits or surpluses in the official settlements balance of the United States shows that central banks have intervened in the balancing process.

T A B L E 28-2
The U.S. Balance-of-Payments Accounts (In billions of dollars)

	1960	1965	1970	1975	1980	1985	1989	1990
Current account balance	2.8	5.4	2.3	18.1	0.4	−116.4	−106.3	−92.1
Plus								
Capital account balance	−5.4	−6.3	−12.4	−30.2	−38.5	103.5	104.6	−1.7
Plus								
Errors and omissions	−1.0	−0.5	−0.2	5.9	29.5	17.9	18.4	63.5
Equals								
Official settlements balance	−3.6	−1.4	−10.3	−6.2	−8.6	5.0	16.7	−30.3
Official reserve transactions	3.6	1.4	9.4	6.2	8.6	−5.9	−17.0	28.6

Note: Numbers may not add due to rounding. Negative sign denotes deficit.
Sources: Economic Report of the President (various editions); *Economic Indicators;* and *Federal Reserve Bulletin.*

A surplus or deficit in the official settlements balance must be made up by official reserve transactions among the central banks. Table 28-3 shows how the U.S. official settlements surplus or deficit was balanced by official reserve transactions during selected years from 1975 to 1990. In general, a deficit in the U.S. official settlements balance can be financed by a reduction in U.S. assets claims on foreign central banks or by an increase in borrowing from foreign central banks (an increase in liabilities to foreign central banks). Table 28-3 shows that, for the most part, our official settlements deficits have been made up by borrowing from foreign central banks—the foreign official assets entries are positive in all years but 1985 and 1989, when a U.S. official settlements surplus existed. In fact, Table 28-3 shows that for most years the U.S. official reserve assets change was *negative*— the United States was increasing its official reserves, not reducing them. As a consequence, this activity also had to be financed by borrowing from foreign central banks.

ADJUSTMENT MECHANISMS

The last section indicated that the United States currently has an international balance-of-payments disequilibrium; the United States is in a disequilibrium position with respect to its international transactions. It typically has a deficit in its official settlements balance because its current account deficit is not completely financed by a capital account surplus, and this deficit is financed mostly by borrowing from foreign central banks. If individual family units or businesses have "payments deficits," eventually they must do one of two things: increase earnings or decrease expenditures. In this section we discuss the adjustment mechanisms that would—in the absence of central bank manipulations—move a country toward an overall international balance-of-payments equilibrium. The available adjustment mechanisms are changes in income, changes in prices, and changes in interest rates. These three economic mechanisms would continue to change until a balance-of-payments equilibrium were restored among nations.

T A B L E   28-3
Official Reserve Transactions between the Fed and Other Central Banks
(In billions of dollars)

	1975	1976	1977	1980	1982	1985	1989	1990
Official settlements balance	− 6.2	− 15.1	− 36.4	− 8.6	− 1.8	5.0	16.7	− 30.3
Financed by U.S. official reserve assets	− 0.8	− 2.6	− 0.4	− 8.1	− 0.5	− 3.9	− 25.3	− 2.2
Plus Foreign official assets	7.0	17.7	36.8	15.6	3.1	− 2.0	8.3	30.7
Plus Allocations of special drawing rights	0.0	0.0	0.0	1.2	0.0	0.0	0.0	0.0
Equals	6.2	15.1	36.4	8.7	− 1.9	− 5.9	− 17.0	28.6

Note: Numbers may not add due to rounding.
Sources: Economic Indicators, Council of Economic Advisers, and *Federal Reserve Bulletin.*

Two basic international monetary systems would allow these three adjustment mechanisms to work: a **fixed-exchange-rate system,** in which exchange rates are pegged at some official level and only minor fluctuations are allowed, and a **floating-exchange-rate system,** in which exchange rates are permitted to rise and fall in response to supply and demand. Recall that we discussed some of the theory of these alternative systems in Chapter 27. We now discuss implementation of these systems.

FIXED-EXCHANGE-RATE SYSTEMS

From 1821 until 1971, the world used exchange rate systems known as the classical gold standard (1821–1914), the gold exchange standard (1925–1931), and the Bretton Woods system (1946–1971). We shall discuss each of these fixed-exchange-rate systems. First, however, we consider the pure gold standard.

The Pure Gold Standard[1]   Let's consider first a domestic pure gold standard (also see our earlier discussion in Chapter 2), in which we ignore international transactions. In order to establish a pure gold coin system, three things are necessary:

1. Only official gold coins minted by the government are used as money.
2. The government commits itself to purchase gold from the public on demand at a fixed price and to convert the gold into gold coins. For instance, if you discover gold, you can sell it to the government and get a predetermined value of officially stamped gold coins.

---

[1] See Michael Bordo, "The Classical Gold Standard: Some Lessons for Today," *Federal Reserve Bank of St. Louis Review,* 63 (5, May 1981), pp. 2–17, for more on what is in the next few sections.

3. The government will sell gold to the public at the fixed price. If you are concerned about the value of your gold coins, you can sell them to the government for a predetermined quantity of gold—uncoined, and, therefore, not money.

Under such a system, the supply of gold, in the long run, is determined by the opportunity cost of producing gold. The supply of gold coins (money) is determined by the total supply of gold and the amount of gold used for nonmonetary purposes (jewelry, etc.). The fraction of the total gold supply devoted to nonmonetary uses depends on the purchasing power of gold in terms of all other commodities. If the price level rises, the purchasing power of gold coins falls; this fall in the relative price of gold coins will induce people to increase the use of gold for nonmonetary purposes. A fall in the price level increases the relative price of gold coins, and a higher proportion of the gold stock will be converted into gold coins—money. In the short run, the stock of gold is limited due to high production costs. The demand for gold coins is determined by the community's wealth, tastes, and the opportunity cost of holding money (the interest rate). The supply of and demand for gold coins will determine the price level.

A pure international gold standard is established when a number of countries are on a gold coin standard. Under such a system, each government agrees to buy and to sell its particular gold coins (the Americans might call them ''dollars''; the British, ''pounds sterling''). Of course, the coins can be of different weight, shape, and value. Under a pure international gold standard, exchange rates between countries are necessarily fixed. An exchange rate is, you recall, the price of a foreign currency in terms of domestic currency. Thus, if the United States values its currency at 1 ounce of gold per 20 dollars, and Great Britain sets the price of its currency at 1 ounce of gold per 4 pounds sterling, then the exchange rate will be 1 pound = $5, or, conversely, $1 = 1/5 pound.

Adjustment Mechanisms under a Pure International Gold System   Suppose that, in our two-economy world, both the United States and England are on a pure gold standard and that there is a balance-of-payments equilibrium. One way for such an equilibrium to exist is for the value of exports to equal the value of imports in each country. Now assume that U.S. residents increase their demand for British goods, other things constant. This action will cause a current account deficit for the United States and (necessarily) a current account surplus for Great Britain.

This will cause a flow of gold from the United States to England, because the increased U.S. demand for British goods will lower the value of the dollar in terms of the pound sterling. At some lower price of the dollar gold coin (the ''gold point''), U.S. importers will benefit from converting dollar gold coins into gold bullion and shipping the bullion to England—where it can be converted to pound sterling coins to pay for British goods. Because gold can be converted into money, the British money supply will rise; the U.S. money supply will fall correspondingly. The price level will fall in the United States and will rise in Great Britain. British goods will be relatively dearer and U.S. goods relatively cheaper; as a consequence, the United States will export more and import less, and Great Britain will import more and export less. These actions will help to establish a payments equilibrium.

A decrease in the U.S. money supply will also induce a recession in the United States; an increase in Great Britain's money supply will cause an expansion in Great Britain. As a consequence, real incomes will fall in the United States and will rise in Great Britain. This relative income change will lead to an increase in British imports (an increase in U.S. exports) and a decrease in U.S. imports (a decrease in British exports). These income effects will also help to restore international payments equilibrium.

Finally, under a pure gold standard, central banks are supposed to follow the "rules of the game," which leaves very little indeed for central bankers to do. A central bank is supposed to allow its country to fall into a recession when it is in a payments deficit and to allow it to expand or inflate when it is in a payments surplus. A central bank should raise the discount rate (the rate it charges banks to borrow) when the country is experiencing a payments deficit and lower the discount rate when the country is experiencing a payments surplus. In our example, such actions will cause U.S. interest rates to rise relative to British interest rates. This interest rate differential causes short-term capital seeking higher interest earnings to flow to the United States from England—thereby lessening the required movement of gold from the United States to Great Britain and economizing on the use of gold.

In short, under the pure international gold standard, an international payments equilibrium is established by relative price level changes, relative interest rate changes, and relative income level changes. Moreover, central banks allow these adjustment mechanisms to work.

THE CLASSICAL GOLD STANDARD (1821–1914)

The pure gold standard described in the previous section has never existed. It has problems. For one thing, such a system is extremely costly to operate. Discovering, mining, and minting gold are very costly activities. The economist Milton Friedman estimated that the cost of maintaining a full gold coin standard for the United States in 1959 would have been more than 2.5 percent of its GNP![2] It is not surprising that nations sought ways to economize on the use of gold for their domestic and international gold standards. The most obvious way to economize on gold was to find substitutes for gold to act as money. These substitutes included government-provided paper money and privately produced bank notes and bank deposits. In practice, therefore, during the period of the classical gold standard, a nation could be on a *modified* gold standard by maintaining a *fixed ratio of its paper currency to gold* and by requiring its commercial banks to keep a fixed ratio of bank liabilities to gold—or (to save on gold again) a fixed ratio of bank liabilities to government notes and gold (see Chapter 2).

During the classical gold standard period, gold was economized internationally as well. International trade was financed by credit; by receiving short-term loans, a current account deficit could be financed by a capital account surplus, and the use of gold could be economized. Similarly, long-term loans—investments by developed nations in less developed nations, for instance—also provided a means whereby a developing nation could finance a current account deficit by a capital account surplus for long periods. In such a case, a prolonged current account deficit is not necessarily a sign of a payments disequilibrium. Nations also economized on gold by using the currency of certain reliable countries as reserves; certain "key currencies" were used as a substitute for gold for international reserves. Thus, payments adjustments didn't actually require gold flows; in many cases, transfers of pound sterling or other key currencies were made in the money markets of the major cities (London, New York, Paris, and Berlin).

In short, the classical gold standard that existed between 1821 and 1914 evolved into a modified gold standard where paper currency and deposits substituted for gold domestically and key currencies substituted for gold internationally. Also, current account deficits were financed temporarily by a short-term capital account surplus and, for long periods,

---

[2] Milton Friedman, *A Program for Monetary Stability* (New York: Fordham University Press, 1959).

by long-term borrowing that led to capital account surpluses. This financing also economized on gold transfers.

Another way in which the classical gold standard differed from the pure international gold standard was that nations weren't always prepared to abide by the rules of the game. Some countries simply were not willing to induce a domestic recession or to allow inflation in order to eliminate a payments disequilibrium. Central banks could **sterilize** gold flows—that is, keep them from affecting domestic prices—by open-market operations. For example, a deficit nation could sterilize gold outflows by purchasing government securities on the domestic open market; a surplus nation could sterilize gold inflows by selling government securities on the domestic open market. Such actions, of course, prolonged the payments disequilibrium. Eventually, a policy of sterilizing gold flows became infeasible, and countries would have to either start abiding by the rules or go off the gold standard completely.

THE GOLD EXCHANGE STANDARD (1925–1931)

The classical gold standard broke down during World War I. Only the United States remained on a gold standard, and even then the Fed frequently sterilized gold flows. Other nations did not commit themselves to maintain a fixed price of gold.

From 1925 to 1931, the gold standard was restored internationally, as the major trading countries established a gold exchange standard. Under this standard, most countries held gold, dollars, or pound sterling as reserves; the United States and the United Kingdom held only gold reserves. Under this standard, most countries sterilized gold flows in order to insulate their economies from the consequences of adjusting to international payments disequilibria.

In 1931, Great Britain, facing massive gold and capital flows, went off the gold standard, and the gold exchange standard eventually collapsed.

THE BRETTON WOODS SYSTEM (1946–1971)

In 1944, representatives of the major trading nations met in Bretton Woods, New Hampshire, to create a new payments system to replace the gold standard that had been abandoned in the early 1930s. The conference had two main objectives:

1. To create a monetary system that would provide for the relief and reconstruction of the countries that were devastated by World War II

2. To devise a system of fixed exchange rates and a means of correcting international payments disequilibria

A compromise was finally adopted, and President Truman signed the Bretton Woods Agreement Act on July 31, 1945. The articles of that agreement created the **International Monetary Fund (IMF)** to administer the articles and to lend foreign exchange to member countries with balance-of-payments deficits. Each fund member, with the exception of the United States, would establish a par value for its currency in dollars or gold.

Member governments were obligated to intervene to maintain the value of their currencies in foreign exchange markets within 1 percent of the declared par values. The United States, which owned most of the world's already mined gold stock, was similarly obligated to maintain gold prices within a 1 percent margin of U.S.$35 per ounce. Except for a transitional arrangement permitting a one-time adjustment of up to 10 percent in par values, thereafter members could alter par values on exchange rates only with the approval of the IMF. The articles stated that such approval would be given only if the country's balance of payments was in "fundamental disequilibrium." This term, however, was never officially defined.

The Adjustable Peg   The foreign exchange system established at Bretton Woods was based on the concept of the adjustable peg. Par, or pegged, values for each currency were established in 1944 in terms of the U.S. dollar or gold. The term "par value" meant the "appropriate" foreign exchange values that were set at that time. And exchange rates were pegged to those par values. For example, if it were decided that the par value of the French franc would be 5 francs to 1 dollar, or 20 cents per French franc, then the foreign exchange rate would be pegged at that level. Exchange rates were, however, allowed to fluctuate under the influence of supply and demand within a narrow band. From 1944 to 1971, the band was 1 percent above and below par value. From 1971 until 1973, the band was 2.25 percent above par to 2.25 below par value.

Under the rules established at Bretton Woods, governments were supposed to intervene to prevent the values of their currencies in foreign exchange markets from falling below the lower limits. When there was an excess quantity supplied of its currency, that is, when the lower limit was reached, the deficit country's government was obligated to buy the surplus with U.S. dollars in order to support the price of its own currency.

Other Duties of the International Monetary Fund   The IMF could also lend funds to member countries with balance-of-payments deficits. Such loans could come from IMF holdings of gold and currency obtained from the subscriptions of IMF members according to a system of quotas. Each member's quota was set by a formula that reflected its importance in the world economy.

A Brief History of the Bretton Woods System   Immediately after the Bretton Woods system was organized, the rest of the world used about $6 billion of its gold and silver reserves to finance its deficits with the United States. Threatened with a reduction of imports, European countries were faced with a decline in their standards of living, zero economic growth, deflation, and devaluation. The United States solved Europe's balance-of-payments problems by voluntarily lending billions of dollars to Europe under the Marshall Plan (formally called the European Recovery Program). Between mid-1948 and mid-1952, the United States provided $11.6 billion in the form of grants and $1.8 billion in the form of loans to Europe. These voluntary loans averted a "dollar shortage" and allowed European countries for the most part to avoid the problems mentioned above.

From Dollar Deficits to Dollar Surpluses   During the late 1950s and early 1960s the rest of the world wanted to increase its U.S. dollar reserves. The fact that other countries did not convert those dollar holdings into gold indicates that they did not want the United States to correct its balance-of-payments deficit by reducing its rate of inflation, which would have allowed U.S. exports to be more competitive in the world market; it would have also induced U.S. citizens to import less. By the mid-1960s, the U.S. deficit was no longer matched by a desire of the rest of the world to increase dollar reserves. Dollar reserves were being forced on the rest of the world as a result of accelerating inflation in the United States, an inflation that was due largely to American financing of the Vietnam War.

If there had not been any government intervention in the foreign exchange market, the excess quantity of dollars supplied would have caused the price of the dollar to fall against the pound and other currencies. Under the IMF's fixed-exchange-rate system, however, foreign central banks were required to buy the excess quantity of dollars supplied (see the theory of fixed exchange rates in Chapter 27). To prevent the pound from appreciating, for example, the Bank of England had to sell pounds to buy the surplus dollars.

If the foreign central banks had allowed the purchase of dollars to increase their money supplies, the U.S. inflation would have been exported to other countries. If this adjustment mechanism (increase in the money supply of surplus nations, decrease in the money supply of deficit nations) had been allowed to operate, the U.S. trade deficit would have been less because the rest of the world would have had a rate of inflation similar to that of the United States. But this would have required that other countries allow the Fed to determine their monetary policies. No country would have had an independent monetary policy; a country's inflation rate would have been determined by the U.S. rate of inflation.

Some central banks, notably in Germany, France, and Japan, did not permit their rates of monetary growth to accelerate. Instead, they *sterilized* the effects of purchasing dollars in the foreign exchange market by selling bonds in domestic open-market operations. Inflation was not imported by these countries, and American trade deficits with these countries thereby continued.

Purchase of U.S. Government Bonds   Because most of the dollars obtained by these countries (to stabilize foreign exchange rates) were used to purchase U.S. government bonds, foreign governments were in fact borrowing from their own citizens by open-market sales of bonds. This was done so that they could buy the U.S. government bonds that were being issued to finance U.S. budget deficits resulting from the Vietnam War. (In fact, all the growth in federal debt found its way into the portfolios of monetary authorities from 1966 to 1979. The Federal Reserve absorbed $43 billion, and foreign central banks bought $51 billion.) Under the Bretton Woods agreement, though, foreign central banks did have the option of buying gold from the United States at $35 an ounce.

The Demise of the Bretton Woods System   The United States took actions to insulate its gold stock. Although it was illegal for U.S. citizens to own gold, private foreign investors could buy gold at a constant price of $35 an ounce in world gold markets; the United States guaranteed that it would intervene with gold sales in those markets if the price rose above $35 an ounce. This created a potential threat to the U.S. gold stock. Aside from the fact that the gold stock was used to meet obligations to member central banks, private speculators betting on a rise in the dollar price of gold also had claims on U.S. gold. In March 1968, the United States announced that it would no longer sell gold to private holders of dollars. The gold market was divided into two tiers: gold held by foreign central banks (and treasuries) and gold held privately. The United States continued to honor its commitments to buy and sell gold in transactions with other central banks, but it no longer pegged the price of privately held gold. From 1968 until August 1971, the United States "lost" very little of its gold. The United States continued to sell gold to foreign central banks at $35 an ounce *provided that they did not ask for any!*

To ensure further that the United States would not have to deflate and induce a recession to protect its gold reserves, the United States supported an amendment to the articles of the IMF that permitted the creation of **special drawing rights (SDRs),** reserve assets that countries could use to settle international payments. This turned the IMF into a world central bank with the potential to create international reserves.

In addition to threatening the convertibility of the dollar into gold, the "overvalued" dollar also put the American-traded-goods industries at an increasingly serious competitive disadvantage. Labor costs were rising, as wages kept up with inflation. While the non-traded-goods industries could pass those higher labor costs on in the form of higher prices, export industries could not. If they raised prices, they would lose sales to foreign producers. Producers of exports and of goods competing with foreign imports put increasing political pressure on the Nixon administration to do something about the loss of sales to foreign producers.

The European and Japanese governments were reluctant to let their currencies appreciate too far against the dollar. European and Japanese export industries enjoyed their competitive advantage in the world market (partially the result of the overvalued dollar), and they used all their influence to resist the revaluation of their currencies. As long as foreign nations refused to let their currencies appreciate, the United States could do little about it. After all, under the IMF articles, responsibility for pegging exchange rates rested with foreign central banks. The United States had the responsibility to peg only the dollar price of gold.

Nixon's Bombshell   On Sunday evening, August 15, 1971, President Nixon dropped a bombshell on America's trading partners. Nixon announced a radically new economic program to deal with the overvalued dollar; this program included:

1. A suspension of the convertibility of dollars into gold
2. An import surcharge of 10 percent
3. A 90-day freeze on wages and prices to break inflationary expectations

Because the United States no longer honored its IMF obligations to sell gold at $35 an ounce, Nixon put the world officially on a "dollar standard," instead of a gold/dollar standard.

The Smithsonian Agreement   What finally came out of this new policy was the Smithsonian Agreement of December 18, 1971, which officially devalued the dollar by an average of 12 percent against the currencies of fourteen major industrial nations. Even this devaluation of the dollar, however, was not sufficient to eliminate the excess supply of dollars on the foreign exchange market. The U.S. balance-of-payments deficit was still a substantial $10.4 billion during 1972. In early 1973, partly in reaction to the rapid expansion of the money supply in the United States during 1972, private speculators sold large amounts of dollars in the foreign exchange market. Foreign central banks purchased about $10 billion in the first three months of the year alone—compared with a deficit of $10.4 billion for the whole year of 1972—in an attempt to support the dollar. When this massive intervention failed to stabilize the dollar (even after an additional devaluation of the dollar in February), fixed exchange rates were abandoned.

THE FLOATING-EXCHANGE-RATE SYSTEM

On March 16, 1973, the finance ministers of the European Community announced that they would let their currencies float against the dollar. (Japan had let the yen float against the dollar on February 12.) The communiqué argued that official interventions in exchange markets might be useful at appropriate times in order to facilitate the maintenance of "orderly" conditions. Each nation in the European Community stated that it "will be prepared to intervene at its initiative in its own market, when necessary and desirable, acting in a flexible manner in the light of market conditions and in close consultation with the authorities of the nation whose currency may be bought or sold." In other words, the international monetary system was now on a managed float or, as it is sometimes called, a **dirty float.**

Establishing the Equilibrium Exchange Rate in a Pure Floating-Exchange-Rate System   Unlike a fixed-exchange-rate system, a system of pure floating exchange rates allows exchange rates to be set by supply and demand. In Chapter 27 we described in detail how the competitive forces of supply and demand can determine the equilibrium exchange rate, and how changes in the demand for or the supply of a currency can change exchange rates.

Under a system of pure floating exchange rates, in which governments do not intervene in the foreign exchange market to stop their own currency from appreciating or depreciating, a country moves automatically toward a balance-of-payments equilibrium. Assume that the United States and Great Britain are the only two countries in the world and that equilibrium is suddenly disturbed because U.S. tastes change in favor of British-made goods. As Chapter 27 indicated, this leads to an increase in the demand for the British pound and an increase in the supply of dollars. Note that as a consequence of a change in tastes in favor of British-made goods, the following all exist:

1. A shortage of British pounds sterling
2. A surplus of U.S. dollars
3. A balance-of-payments surplus in Great Britain, which finds its exports rising relative to its imports
4. A balance-of-payments deficit in the United States, which finds its imports rising relative to its exports

Note that if there is a shortage of a country's currency on the foreign exchange market, then that country is experiencing a payments surplus; and if there is a surplus of a country's currency on the foreign exchange market, then that country has a payments deficit. Continuing our example, the dollar will depreciate and (following Chapter 27) this causes British-made goods to rise in price relative to American-made goods; Americans will then substitute some American-made goods for British-made goods. A depreciating dollar also causes real incomes to fall in the United States, and so Americans will buy fewer British-made goods (import less)—and fewer American-made goods. Thus, a price effect and a real income effect reduce the U.S. payments deficit.

Parallel reasoning implies that an appreciating pound sterling causes the price of British-made goods to rise relative to American-made goods; an appreciating pound also causes real incomes to rise in Great Britain. The net result is that in Britain exports fall, imports rise, and the British payments surplus declines.

In short, exchange rates will change until each nation is in a balance-of-payments equilibrium situation. We conclude that under a pure floating-exchange-rate international payments standard, countries automatically move toward a balance-of-payments equilibrium. Note that, unlike the situation under a fixed-exchange-rate system, a country's money supply is not affected by a payments disequilibrium. This is because exchange rates will change until the quantity demanded of a given currency exactly equals the quantity supplied of that currency. Thus, under a pure floating-exchange-rate system, changes in exchange rates lead to changes in relative prices and incomes; under a fixed-exchange-rate system, changes in each country's money supply lead to changes in relative prices, incomes, and interest rates.

The Floating U.S. Dollar   Figure 28-1 shows how the dollar has fared relative to a weighted (by the extent of trade) average of ten other currencies (Belgium, Canada, France, Germany, Italy, Japan, the Netherlands, Sweden, Switzerland, and the United Kingdom). Note that immediately following the March 1973 decision to float the dollar, the dollar

Figure 28-1
The Dollar Afloat.   This graph shows the real value of the dollar relative to an index of a weighted average of ten foreign currencies. Note that from early 1980 to 1985 the dollar appreciated dramatically, and that afterward it depreciated equally dramatically. (*Source: Economic Report of the President,* 1992.)

depreciated relative to the other ten currencies, confirming the belief that the dollar was overvalued. From late 1974 to early 1976, the dollar appreciated, and then it plunged rapidly during 1977. Note that from late 1980 to 1985, the dollar appreciated substantially. Although the reason for this appreciation is not totally clear, it is generally agreed that the dollar appreciation occurred, at least partly, because real interest rates were relatively high in the United States and because political and economic instability had increased in much of the rest of the world—especially in Europe, Latin America, and the Middle East. The second explanation implies that the United States was considered a safe haven for investors and had become a financial refuge in troubled times. If so, this could account for the fact that, during 1982 and 1983, the United States enjoyed (1) a large current account deficit that was financed mostly by a capital account surplus (if we include errors and omissions) and (2) an appreciating dollar on the foreign exchange markets. In effect, American citizens were benefiting from a current account deficit because their country was relatively stable politically and economically.

Figure 28-1 also indicates that from February 1985 the dollar generally depreciated relative to other currencies, although it went through periods of appreciation, such as during 1988–1989 and again in early 1991. The general depreciation of the dollar during the 1980s reflected the fact that the United States experienced large merchandise trade deficits. The dollar's general decline, along with the variability in its value relative to other currencies, was due, in part, to a conscious policy on the part of U.S. and foreign (Japanese and West German) policy makers to depreciate the dollar in order to solve the U.S. current account deficit. The fact that American merchandise deficits persisted despite

THE U.S. TRADE DEFICIT—WHAT CAUSES IT, AND SHOULD WE CARE?

The two questions asked in the title of this Current Controversy are central issues in the United States today. Let's consider each question, but let's start with the latter question before we think about the former.

Are Trade Deficits "Bad"?

A common argument is that high trade deficits cost Americans jobs. This argument has problems, however. Flows of funds between nations in payment for trade simply veil the fact that, ultimately, Americans pay for imports with exports, either today or in the future. Even if the United States could shut off all trade today, by doing so it would end its own export business in the long run, costing whatever jobs might be gained in the short run.

In his 1990 book, *The Age of Diminished Expectations,* MIT economist Paul Krugman points out that even short-run increases in employment from reduced trade deficits are unlikely. Suppose that, at prevailing unemployment rates between 5 and 7 percent, the United States Congress decided to impose quotas that effectively shut out all trade from other nations. Naturally, this would produce an immediate trade surplus—though it might be short-lived if other nations responded by shutting out U.S. exports. The issue is, would eliminating the trade deficit create a lot more jobs in the short run? The answer is, probably not. Most economists believe that the natural rate of unemployment in the United States is *at least* 5 percent and likely is somewhat higher. If quotas shut out international trade, where would the workers come from to make up the difference? A likely result of such a drastic effort to remove the trade deficit, Krugman argues, would be higher inflation.

This does not mean that continued U.S. trade deficits are costless. To perpetually buy more goods from foreigners than U.S. citizens sell to others abroad requires that U.S. citizens somehow come up with the cash to make up the difference. They do this by borrowing abroad. As we noted earlier, for this reason the United States in 1983 became a net debtor to other nations. As a result, American residents on net must make interest payments to citizens of other nations who lend to them; that is, they transfer some of their incomes abroad. This is the primary cost of high trade deficits.

What Has Caused the High U.S. Trade Deficit and the Associated Increase in U.S. Indebtedness?

Most economists give a three-part answer to this question. The first part of the answer is that, as we noted in Chapter 4, the national saving rate in the United States is very low relative to other nations. A reflection of this low saving rate is that Americans consume relatively more of their incomes than do foreigners, which places foreigners in a position to lend to Americans, who can then buy more foreign goods.

Some observers blame households and firms for the low national saving rate, arguing that they issue too much debt. This is a questionable point, however. Although the *level* of firm and household debt issued in the United States undeniably has increased in recent years, measured relative to output produced in the United States the debt of private Americans is not much greater than it has been in previous years. For instance, consider the figure, which shows nonfinancial debt as a percentage of gross national product over the years 1970–1990 for the United States, Germany, and Japan. This ratio has been *lowest* in the United States during that entire period, and recent increases in that ratio have been at least as great in Germany and Japan as in the United States.

If the American private sector isn't so easily blamed for the high trade deficit and the growing U.S. indebtedness to other nations, then that potentially leaves the U.S. government as the main culprit. Indeed, many economists believe that the blame lies at this doorstep. A key reason that the total national saving rate of the United States is so low is that the federal government continually runs deficits; by so doing, it effectively captures a lot of funds that would have gone into national saving. In turn, this leads to the trade deficit; lacking accumulated savings to invest at home, households and firms borrow from foreigners and purchase goods from abroad. This relationship between the federal deficit and the trade deficit commonly is called the *twin deficit problem.*

Not all economists concur that the federal government is completely to blame for the high American trade deficits. In fact, some economists believe that U.S. trade deficits aren't really as high as official figures indicate. For one thing, U.S. exports to other countries are understated because (1) exporters have a strong incentive to underreport sales because their taxable income is thereby reduced; and (2) export licenses are required,

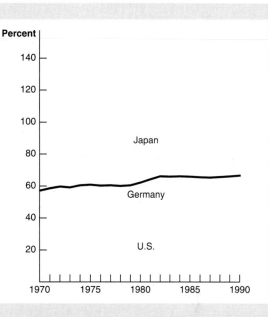

Nonfinancial Corporate Debt as a Percentage of Gross National Product in Germany, Japan, and the United States.   Although many have contended that American firms issue too much debt, aggravating the problem of growing U.S. indebtedness, the ratio of total nonfinancial corporate debt to GNP remained relatively stable in the United States from 1970 through 1990. This ratio also was well below the same ratios in Germany and Japan, which have experienced much more growth in total firm debt relative to GNP.

and in some cases outright bans exist, on the sales of "sensitive" national security–related machinery—hence nonreporting, underreporting, and smuggling result. In contrast, import data are collected directly by a single governmental agency, which collects revenues from tariffs. Thus, U.S. import data are reliable, and U.S. export data are understated. Indeed, using 1987 data, St. Louis Fed economist Mack Ott estimated that the U.S.

trade deficit may be overstated by between 10 and 15 percent annually. This may not solve the problem, but it indicates that its scope may not be as great as some have feared.

Sources: Paul Krugman, *The Age of Diminished Expectations* (Cambridge, Mass.: MIT Press, 1990), chap. 4, and Mack Ott, "Is Trade Deficit as Big as It Seems?" *Wall Street Journal* (December 12, 1987), p. 14.

such persistent depreciation in the dollar was a matter of concern to both policy makers and economic theoreticians.

Economists have long been aware that a time lag exists between a nation's gradual currency depreciation and the elimination of its trade deficit, but the American trade deficit seems to be unusually durable and troublesome. Figure 28-2 shows the U.S. trade deficit through early 1992. As Table 28-4 shows, U.S. trade deficits with specific nations generally have risen, and its trade surpluses with others simultaneously have narrowed. For example, the U.S. trade deficit with Japan rose from about $3.5 billion in early 1991 to over $3.8 billion in early 1992. At the same time, the American trade surplus with Western Europe narrowed by about half a billion dollars, and the American trade deficit with Canada narrowed slightly.

WHICH IS BETTER—FIXED OR FLOATING EXCHANGE RATES?

Under a fixed-exchange-rate international payments system, disequilibrating changes (such as gold discoveries or changes in tastes or technology) require that resources be reallocated until a new equilibrium is restored. Such disequilibrating changes also require that resources be reallocated under a floating-exchange-rate system. Under both systems, the

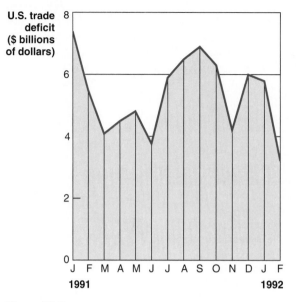

Figure 28-2
The U.S. Trade Deficit. Despite the fact that value of the U.S. dollar has trended downward since its dramatic fall in 1985, U.S. trade deficits have persisted since then. In 1991 and early 1992 they were still sizable. (*Source: Economic Indicators.*)

basic economic mechanisms that bring about resource allocation and restore equilibrium in international payments are essentially the same: price effects, income effects, and interest rate changes.

Evaluating Fixed versus Floating Exchange Rates   What is different about the two systems is the process by which equilibrium is restored. Under a gold or modified gold fixed-exchange-rate system, gold must flow from the deficit nation to the surplus nation; under a Bretton Woods–type system, ultimately the deficit country must experience a reduction in the money supply and the surplus country must experience an increase in the

T A B L E   28-4
The United States' Merchandise Trade Balance
with Respect to Specific Nations or Groups of Nations
(In billions of U.S. dollars)

	Jan. 1992	Dec. 1991	Jan. 1991
Japan	− 3.82	− 4.46	− 3.46
Canada	− 0.19	− 0.92	− 0.44
Western Europe	1.69	1.11	1.10
NICs*	− 1.31	− 1.15	− 1.00

* Newly industrialized countries: Singapore, Hong Kong, Taiwan, South Korea
Source: U.S. Department of Commerce.

money supply. Under any fixed-exchange-rate system, then, surplus countries must inflate and deficit countries must experience recession; these are the rules of the game under a fixed-exchange-rate structure. In periods of a payments disequilibrium, under a fixed-rate standard, monetary and fiscal policies must be geared to achieve a payments equilibrium; other ultimate goals, such as price stability and less unemployment, must become of secondary importance.

Even if an international payments equilibrium currently exists, monetary and fiscal policy actions to attain other goals must be carried out with an eye toward how these actions will affect the balance of payments. For example, if an international payments equilibrium currently exists but unemployment is high, an expansionary monetary policy may well lead to an international payments deficit. Under a fixed-exchange-rate standard, therefore, monetary policy and fiscal policy are carried out in order to achieve one goal— an international payments equilibrium. Policy makers, therefore, are not very free to pursue other goals. Moreover, the rules of the game require that individual trading partners are not free to carry out monetary and fiscal policies that are independent of the other trading partners. Under a fixed-exchange-rate system, a nation that is determined to pursue inflation domestically will ''export'' inflation to other nations; a nation in the throes of a recession will export its recession to other countries.

In short, a fixed-exchange-rate system requires that each nation's other ultimate goals become secondary to one ultimate goal—an international payments equilibrium. If nations are not willing to play by the rules of the game—if they sterilize gold flows by refusing to inflate or deflate their money—a fixed-exchange-rate system will not work smoothly. Such a system will be characterized by prolonged and chronic payments disequilibria and occasional (and sometimes not so occasional) official exchange rate adjustments. Figure 28-3, however, indicates that members of the European Monetary System (EMS), which is made up of many countries with different and independent central banks, have been able to coordinate their policies. The exchange rates of all these countries move together; to do so, each nation must coordinate its stabilization policies.

When a disequilibrating change occurs under a floating-exchange-rate system, an international payments equilibrium will be restored automatically, without any governmental or central bank intervention. Deficit nations will find that their currency depreciates; surplus nations experience currency appreciation. Note that *only one* price—the exchange rate—has to change, and not the price level of each country. Moreover, because a payments imbalance will eventually disappear under a pure float system, nations can pursue other ultimate goals. And nations can do so independently of each other.

While a floating-exchange-rate system seems superior on paper, in practice it has problems. Under a floating-exchange-rate system there are rules of the game too. A nation must *allow* its currency to inflate or deflate. Nations do not always wish for their currency to float, because doing so is costly.

A deficit nation will experience a currency depreciation; it will take more units of the local currency than before to import the same quantity of goods and services. This means that the price of imports will rise and, other things constant, the standard of living will fall in the deficit country. This reduction in living standards also occurs because a currency depreciation means that local producers have an incentive to export more, further reducing the local availability of goods and services. There will be a strong temptation for policy makers to cushion (or offset) such a reduction in living standards by intervening in the exchange market; policy makers may put pressure on the central bank to support the deficit nation's currency by purchasing it with foreign exchange reserves (gold or foreign currency reserves).

The surplus nation, on the other hand, will experience a currency appreciation. The

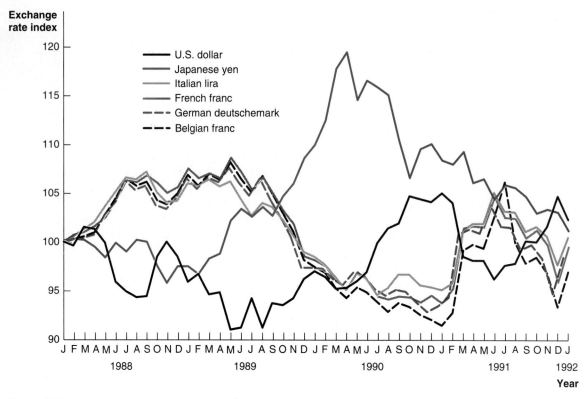

Figure 28-3

The Exchange Rates of Four Representative EMS Nations as Compared with Those of Japan and the United States.   This figure shows that nations in the EMS, such as Belgium, France, Germany, and Italy, have been able to coordinate their economic policies so that the values of their national currencies move together. In contrast, the currency values of the Japanese yen and the American dollar have behaved much differently. (*Source: IMF International Financial Statistics,* various issues. Exchange rates are valued in terms of SDRs; January 1988 = 100.)

nation will increase its imports and decrease its exports, and the surplus will eventually be eliminated. Such events, however, may well be interpreted as putting local producers at a competitive disadvantage in international markets for goods and services. Domestic producers (and their unions) may well put pressure on policy makers to make their goods more competitive on national markets by selling their currency on international exchange markets, thereby forestalling currency appreciation. Such considerations are doubtless of concern in Japan and Germany today.

Another potential problem with a floating-exchange-rate system is that if payments-surplus nations (i.e., Japan and Germany) refuse to allow their currencies to inflate, deficit countries may view this as being unfair to their domestic industries, which are less able to export to surplus nations. Hence a move toward protectionism, in the form of higher tariffs and import quotas, is quite likely. Indeed, support for protectionism seems to be ever present in the United States as we proceed through the 1990s.

In short, there are strong political pressures for central banks to intervene in the foreign exchange markets under a floating-exchange-rate system.

Do Central Bank Efforts to Intervene in Exchange Markets Really Accomplish Very Much?

INTERNATIONAL PERSPECTIVE

In January 1985, President Ronald Reagan's White House chief of staff and Treasury secretary proposed at a meeting of the Group of Five (G5) nations (France, Germany, Japan, the United Kingdom, and the United States—see the next chapter for more details) to increase the efforts by those nations' central banks to stabilize their exchange rates. After nearly nine months of discussion, on September 22 of that year the finance ministers and central banks of those nations made an announcement that "in view of the present and prospective change in fundamentals, some orderly appreciation of the main non-dollar currencies against the dollar is desirable. We stand ready to cooperate more closely to encourage this when to do so would be helpful." In nonbureaucratic language, the G5 nations agreed to try to push down the dollar's value relative to other currencies.

The G5 announcement was made at the Plaza Hotel in New York, and so it was known as the Plaza Agreement. It was followed by a reaffirmation of the Plaza principles at the Louvre Palace in Paris called the Louvre Accord. Much official rhetoric during and since the announcements of these policy agreements has indicated that the G5 nations believe they largely accomplished their stated goals of stabilizing exchange rates at "desired" levels. Some economists, however, believe this represents a strong overstatement. Among these are Michael Bordo of Rutgers University and Anna Schwartz of the National Bureau of Economic Research. In their view, central bank interventions really didn't accomplish much except to distort exchange markets and to subject central banks to excessive risks of loss.

The Extent of Foreign Exchange Interventions

Bordo and Schwartz tabulated data on the foreign exchange interventions coordinated by the Federal Reserve and U.S. Treasury between 1985 and 1989. Bordo and Schwartz reach two conclusions from their analysis of these interventions. First, the interventions were sporadic and variable. Second, they were very small in size relative to the magnitudes of total trading in foreign exchange markets. Bordo and Schwartz note, for instance, that in April 1989 total foreign exchange trading amounted to $129 *billion* per day; yet the Fed purchased only $100 *million* in marks and yen in that entire month, on a single day. In fact, Fed purchases of marks and yen for *all of 1989* amounted to about $17.7 billion, or the equivalent of less than 14 percent of the amount of an average *day's* trading in April of that year.

In light of the tiny relative size of foreign exchange trading by any given central bank, Bordo and Schwartz question the likelihood that central bank exchange market interventions really have significant, long-lived effects on exchange rates. According to these two economists:

> Authorities could learn from King Canute (995–1035, king of Britain, Denmark, Norway). They decided at the Louvre, on the advice of some economists who flattered the authorities' ability to manipulate the market for currencies, that further movement of exchange rates was not desirable. Canute rebuked the flattery of his courtiers by noting that the advancing waves paid no heed to his command that they halt, thus demonstrating his powerlessness.

Potential Drawbacks of Currency Interventions

Bordo and Schwartz believe that the attempts by central banks to manipulate exchange rates is undesirable as well as generally ineffective. First of all, they contend that volatile—and therefore often unexpected—central bank exchange market interventions that do from time to time have effects on exchange rates may cause individuals and firms to experience unintended wealth transfers. For example, a party to a forward exchange transaction might incur an unexpected transaction loss (see Chapter 27) that is an unexpected gain to the other party in the transaction. Further, the increased risk of such transfers induces traders to undertake more efforts to hedge against the risks of unexpected central bank interventions, which is a costly activity.

In addition, Bordo and Schwartz argue that efforts by central banks to manipulate exchange rates expose them—and, hence, their governments and ultimately their taxpaying citizens—to risks of foreign exchange losses. For instance, they point out that while the Federal Reserve and Treasury combined for over $1 billion in realized gains from foreign exchange transactions in 1985 through 1989, the Netherlands lost 600 million Dutch guilders on dollar interventions in 1986 and 1987, and Germany reportedly lost 9 billion deutschemarks in the fourth quarter of 1987 alone. Bordo and Schwartz question the wisdom of central bank gambles with such large stakes in light of their limited abilities to achieve their exchange rate goals.

Can Central Banks Influence Exchange Rates over the Long Haul?

While Bordo and Schwartz make a strong case that central banks cannot manipulate exchange rates over long time horizons, many economists believe that the central banks can and do influence exchange rates from time to time. They argue that looking at the foreign exchange transactions of any single central bank is mis-

leading, because *coordinated* actions by several central banks are likely to have the most pronounced effects on exchange rates. They also argue that the announced *willingness* of central banks to influence exchange rates commonly can cause self-fulfilling prophecies; if traders believe that central banks can influence exchange rates and expect them to do so, then the traders themselves will act on their expectations in ways that push exchange rates in the directions central bankers desire.

Central bank efforts to manipulate exchange rates have been somewhat more muted in the 1990s. This may be because central banks have less desire to influence exchange rates, or because they cannot reach agreement on how to do so. Or it may be that today's central bankers have become more like King Canute; they may have less interest in trying to halt the waves of foreign exchange trading.

Source: Michael D. Bordo and Anna J. Schwartz, "What Has Foreign Exchange Market Intervention Since the Plaza Agreement Accomplished?" *Open Economies Review,* 2 (1991), pp. 39–64.

When everything is said and done, fixed exchange rates become somewhat flexible, and flexible exchange rates become somewhat fixed, because political pressures exist to resist the resource reallocations that are necessary to adjust to shocks that cause disequilibrium in the international balance of payments. In that respect, if nations are not willing to "pay the price" to adjust to change, it doesn't make any difference whether the world is on a fixed-exchange-rate system or a floating-exchange-rate system.

Key Issues   The real issues are:

1. Do floating exchange rates cause unnecessary changes in exchange rates (and, therefore, unnecessary changes in resource allocation, which generate changes in exports and imports) because speculation is greater under flexible exchange rates than under fixed exchange rates?

2. Are interferences with free trade such as tariffs, import quotas, and currency restrictions more likely under a fixed-exchange-rate system (when governments wish to insulate their economies from world changes that cause disequilibria in international payments) than under a floating-exchange-rate system, where currency depreciation is an option (but causes other problems)?

Ultimately, these are empirical questions that only time will answer. If policy makers refuse to play by the rules of the game under either payments system, we may never know the answer to the first question. The second question really asks: Which payments system presents the greatest temptation to policy makers to resist the winds of change?

In recent years, the winds of change have blown at high velocities. Much of Eastern Europe has moved away from central planning in favor of more market-based economies, and the former republics of the Soviet Union have initiated tentative steps toward capitalism and other economic reforms. Germany has reconstituted itself as a single polity and economic unit, and Western Europe as a whole debates the merits of abandoning individual national currencies in favor of a common European currency. Japan has taken on an unprecedented prominence in the world economic system. Although the position of the United States as the dominant nation in the world's economy continues, it shows signs of strain. Undeniably, the global economic system faces a new set of challenges as the world faces the next century.

CHAPTER SUMMARY

1. If a nation is spending more (on imports or gifts) than it is currently receiving (in exports or gifts), then it must finance this activity by borrowing or selling assets.

2. When a nation is in a position in which it cannot continue its current transactions with other nations (due to borrowing constraints or due to dwindling, limited international reserve assets), it is said to be in an international payments disequilibrium. An international payments equilibrium is one of the Fed's ultimate goals.

3. The economic mechanisms that drive a nation into a payments equilibrium are interest rate changes, price changes, and income changes.

4. The international payments systems that have been developed to assure a balance-of-payments equilibrium are fixed-exchange-rate systems and floating-exchange-rate systems. An exchange rate is the price of foreign currency in terms of a unit of domestic currency.

5. An international gold standard is one form of a fixed-exchange-rate system. Each nation on a gold standard (a) imposes a fixed ratio between gold held by the government and currency in circulation (the ratio is 1:1 on a pure gold standard) and (b) agrees to buy and sell gold in unlimited quantities at "official" rates in terms of currency. Because each nation fixes the price of its currency to a given quantity of gold, in effect each country's currency has a fixed value relative to other countries' currencies.

6. If a nation has an international payments deficit under a gold standard, gold (which is money) will flow out of that country and into those countries that are (of necessity) experiencing international payments surpluses. As a consequence, deficit nations experience reductions in their price levels and income levels and increases in their interest rates. Surplus nations experience increases in their price levels and income levels and decreases in their interest rates. These actions create an international payments equilibrium.

7. The rules of the game under the gold standard require that deficit and surplus nations do not offset gold flows by sterilizing gold movements.

8. The Bretton Woods system (1946–1971) was another fixed-exchange-rate system. It established the IMF to help nations adjust to short-term disequilibrium in their international payments. The IMF lent reserves to countries that suffered from short-term liquidity, in order to induce those countries to keep their exchange rates fixed in terms of other countries. When a "fundamental disequilibrium" (never defined precisely by the IMF) existed, a nation was allowed to change its official exchange rate significantly.

9. The basic reserve under the Bretton Woods system was the U.S. dollar; all countries except the United States were allowed to use the dollar as a reserve and as a means of settling international payments. Such a system required that the United States continually run a deficit on its payments. While this system worked for a while, eventually nations accumulated more dollars than they wanted to and everyone became concerned about "financing U.S. deficits." Some nations attempted to exchange their acquired dollars for gold owned by the United States.

10. Not wanting to sell its gold at the official price—which was artificially low in terms of dollars—the United States abandoned the Bretton Woods system in 1973 and allowed the U.S. dollar to float with respect to other currencies.

11. Since 1973, most of the world technically has been on a floating-exchange-rate system. Although central banks sometimes seek to influence exchange rates, many exchange rates fluctuate to reflect the supply of and the demand for the currencies of individual countries.

12. Most nations are not willing to allow their currency to appreciate or depreciate very much in the short run. Therefore, they intervene in the international exchange market to support their currency; they buy it with reserves when it is depreciating or sell it when it is appreciating. Such government intervention generates a ''dirty float'' payments system and causes a payments disequilibrium.

GLOSSARY

Balance of payments: A record of all the transactions between the households, firms, and government of one country and the rest of the world.

Balance-of-payments disequilibrium: A circumstance in which a nation cannot continue its current international transactions indefinitely; a surplus or a deficit in a nation's balance of payments that cannot continue.

Balance-of-payments equilibrium: A circumstance in which a nation can continue its current international transactions indefinitely.

Capital account: A record of all transactions in assets between the domestic country and the rest of the world.

Capital account balance: The amount of a country's sales of assets such as stocks, bonds, and real estate to foreigners relative to the value of that country's purchases of such assets from abroad.

Capital account deficit: A situation in which the value of a country's sales of such assets as stocks, bonds, and land to foreigners is less than the value of that country's purchase of such assets from the rest of the world; a net lending situation.

Capital account surplus: A situation in which the value of a country's sales of such assets as stocks, bonds, and land to foreigners exceeds the value of that country's purchase of such assets from the rest of the world; a net borrowing situation.

Current account: Account that tracks ongoing international trades and transfers of goods and services; also called the open account.

Current account balance: The amount of a country's exports of goods and services (including military receipts and income on investments abroad) and transfer payments (private and government) relative to the value of that country's imports of goods and services (including military payments) and transfer payments (private and government).

Current account deficit: A situation in which the value of a nation's exports of goods and services (and public and private transfers from the rest of the world) is less than the value of its imports of goods and services (and public and private transfers to the rest of the world).

Current account surplus: A situation in which the value of a nation's exports of goods and services (and public and private transfers from the rest of the world) exceeds the value of its imports of goods and services (and public and private transfers to the rest of the world).

Dirty float: Managed floating-exchange-rate system that occurs when governments intervene in a floating-exchange-rate system in order to keep their own currencies from appreciating or depreciating.

Fixed-exchange-rate system: An international payments system in which exchange rates are pegged at some official level and only minor fluctuations are permitted.

Floating-exchange-rate system: An international payments system under which exchange rates are allowed to rise or to fall as supply and demand conditions dictate.

International Monetary Fund (IMF):   An international agency, created by the Bretton Woods Agreement, to help nations that have temporary liquidity problems.

Merchandise trade deficit: Situation that occurs when the value of a nation's merchandise imports exceeds the value of its merchandise exports.

Merchandise trade surplus: Situation that occurs when the value of a nation's merchandise exports exceeds the value of its merchandise imports.

Official settlements balance: The sum of the current account balance and the capital account balance, plus errors and omissions.

Special drawing rights (SDRs):   A reserve asset created by the IMF, which countries can use to settle international payments.

Sterilization: Actions by central banks to offset international currency flows with domestic open-market operations.

SELF-TEST QUESTIONS

1. Explain, in your own words, the meaning of the terms ''balance-of-payments equilibrium'' and ''balance-of-payments disequilibrium.''

2. Many observers focus much of their attention on changes in the American merchandise trade deficit. In recent years, however, the United States has become more of a service-oriented economy than it was previously. Could the merchandise trade deficit thereby be misleading as a key indicator of U.S. international trade flows? Explain.

3. What are the key distinctions between the the current account balance and the capital account balance? Why must they necessarily sum to zero in the absence of central bank interventions?

4. Explain in your own words why official reserve transactions necessarily must offset surpluses or deficits in the official settlements balance.

5. What is a dirty float? Based on the discussion in this chapter, do you believe a dirty float has existed in recent years? Support your answer.

6. Why do some economists believe that the United States suffers from a ''twin deficit problem''?

PROBLEMS

28-1.   Suppose that the United States, England, and Germany adopted a gold standard and defined the value of their currencies as follows: 1 ounce of gold is equivalent to $35, 10 pounds, or 100 marks. What is the exchange rate between (a) the dollar and the pound, (b) the dollar and the mark, and (c) the mark and the pound?

28-2.   The diagram below shows the supply of, and the demand for, British pounds, as a function of the exchange rate—expressed in U.S. dollars per pound. Assume that these are the only two countries in the world.

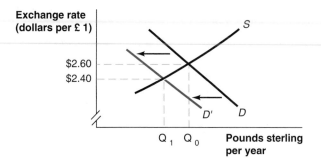

    a. How might the shift from D to D' be accounted for?

    b. If the exchange rate were pegged at $2.60 per pound, what would now exist?

    c. What would cause the supply curve to shift rightward (increase)?

28-3.   Assume that the United States and England are the only two countries in the world. If the exchange rate between the pound and the dollar is $3 per pound, and the United States experiences severe inflation (relative to England), what would happen under (a) a flexible-exchange-rate system and (b) a gold standard?

SELECTED REFERENCES

Bordo, Michael D., ''The Classical Gold Standard: Some Lessons for Today,'' Federal Reserve Bank of St. Louis *Review,* 63 (5, May 1981), pp. 2–17.

———, and Anna J. Schwartz (eds.), *A Retrospective on the Classical Gold Standard, 1821–1931* (Chicago: University of Chicago Press, 1984).

Boyd, J. H., D. S. Dahl, and C. D. Line, ''A Primer on the International Monetary Fund,'' Federal Reserve Bank of Minneapolis *Quarterly Review,* 7 (3, Summer 1983), pp. 6–15.

Bryant, Ralph C. (ed.), *Global Macroeconomics: Policy Conflict and Cooperation* (New York: St. Martin's Press, 1988).

Friedman, Milton, *A Program for Monetary Stability* (New York: Fordham University Press, 1959).

International Monetary Fund, *Final Report of the Working Party on the Statistical Discrepancy in World Current Account Balances* (1987).

Madura, Jeff, *International Financial Management* (St. Paul, Minn.: West Publishing Co., 1986), chaps. 2 and 11.

Markusen, James R., and James R. Melvin, *The Theory of International Trade* (New York: Harper & Row, 1988).

Mundell, Robert A., ''International Monetary Options,'' *Cato Journal,* 3 (1 , Spring 1983), pp. 189–210.

Salerno, Joseph T., ''Gold Standards: True or False,'' *Cato Journal,* 3 (1 , Spring 1983), pp. 239–267.

Yarbrough, Beth V., and Robert M. Yarbrough, *The World Economy: Trade and Finance* (New York: The Dryden Press, 1988).

Yeager, Leland B., ''Stable Money and Free Market Currencies,'' *Cato Journal,* 3 (1, Spring 1983), pp. 305–326.

International Monetary and Financial Policy Coordination

Most nations strive both for self-reliance and for pursuit of the interests of their citizens. According to Johann Wolfgang von Goethe (1749–1832), the German poet, scholar, statesman, and author of *Faust,* "Nothing is good for a nation but that which arises from its own core and its own general wants, without apish imitation of another." Likewise, John F. Kennedy (1917–1963) proclaimed late in his foreshortened presidency that "We must recognize that every nation determines its policies in terms of its own interests."

At the same time, however, during the past half century there has been a gradual recognition that nations also share common interests. Woodrow Wilson (1856–1924) argued early in his presidency in 1913, "Our interests are those of the open door—a door of friendship and mutual advantage," and again in a Senate address in 1917, "There must be, not a balance of power, but a community of power; not organized rivalries, but an organized peace." Wilson's presidency witnessed the formation of the ill-fated League of Nations, the forerunner to today's United Nations and to organized international economic organizations, such as the International Monetary Fund, the World Bank, and the Organization for Economic Cooperation and Development.

Should nations go their own ways in economic affairs, or should they work together? Economic philosophers have contemplated this question for centuries. It is a complicated question with no easy answers, as we shall learn in this chapter. Yet it is a question that has taken on even greater importance in today's world, which increasingly has become more fully linked by communications and transportation technologies. The world is no smaller than it ever was, but the interrelationships among nations have grown, and this trend shows no signs of diminishing.

In this chapter, we explore the implications of interactions among nations and how

769

nations' monetary and financial policy makers might respond. In particular, we focus on the desirability of economic policy makers working together for common goals, as opposed to conducting policy actions aimed at achieving purely nationalistic goals. We also consider recent efforts by monetary and financial authorities of some nations, including the United States, to determine their policies jointly. Finally, we try to evaluate factors that might cause such efforts to continue, or to evaporate.

SOME BASIC INTERNATIONAL POLICY RELATIONSHIPS AND TERMINOLOGY

Before we tackle the tough question of whether purely nationalistic policy making or international-based policy making is most desirable, it is important to consider some basic concepts involving relationships among nations and their economic policies. The natural place to begin is with a discussion of why nations might have a reason to work together in the first place. We follow this with a discussion of ways in which nations might work together in their economic policy making.

IMPLICATIONS OF INTERNATIONAL INTERDEPENDENCE

In a world in which nations trade sizable quantities of goods and services, their economies are **structurally interdependent.** This means that the economic systems of nations are interlinked, so that positive or adverse events and stimulative or contractionary policies in one country have effects on the economic performance in other nations. Therefore, while structurally interdependent nations may be separate political entities, the economic policy strategies of one nation's independent government can influence the well-being of citizens in other nations.

International Policy Externalities   Hence, widespread structural interdependence implies that there are **international policy externalities.** Recall that an externality occurs when the actions of one agent have unintended spillover effects on the economic welfare of others. Because of structural interdependence, such spillovers may occur when a government's policies that were intended only to improve the performance of its own economy influence the performance of the economies of other nations.

International externalities arising from economic policy making can be *positive* or *negative.* A positive international policy externality occurs when an action by a nation's policy maker that was intended to improve the well-being of citizens in that nation also raises the welfare of residents of another country. In contrast, a negative international policy externality arises if a policy maker's action that was meant to raise the welfare of citizens in the policy maker's own country reduces the well-being of residents of another nation.

Beggar-Thy-Neighbor Policy Making and Strategic Behavior in Economic Policy Making   Sometimes, policy makers recognize that their national economies are structurally interdependent and seek to take advantage of that fact, to the detriment of their neighbors. That is, policy makers may intentionally seek to enhance the economic welfare of their own nation's citizens at the expense of the well-being of citizens in other countries, thereby following **beggar-thy-neighbor policies.**

A problem that arises from structural interdependence is that beggar-thy-neighbor policies may help one nation at the expense of others, but pursuit of such policies by governments of all nations tends to make everyone worse off. Consider the beggar-thy-neighbor situation that arises from **protectionist** trade policies—policies that restrict imports of goods and services to protect domestic industries that produce those goods and services, for example, automobile import restrictions. For instance, suppose that the United States government tightens quotas on the number of autos that Japanese and European manufacturers sell in the United States, because it believes that such quotas raise the *net* welfare of U.S. citizens. (The welfare effects are both positive and negative; American auto manufacturers and their employees benefit from auto import quotas, but American consumers face fewer choices and less competition as a result.) While such policies may indeed raise net American welfare in the short run, they also have negative effects on the welfare of Japanese and European auto manufacturers and their employees. Governments in Japan and Europe may respond with their own beggar-thy-neighbor policies, such as import restrictions on, say, American beef or computer products.

The end result of worldwide beggar-thy-neighbor policies may, in the case of trade protectionism, be virtual ''trade wars,'' in which nations seek to promote their own exports by shutting off imports. In the long run, no one gains from such policies.

Beggar-thy-neighbor policies represent a particular type of *strategic policy making*. If international structural interdependence is recognized by governmental policy makers, then these policy makers have an incentive to adopt policy strategies—approaches to achieving objectives for their own nations—that take into account this interdependence. Furthermore, they may have incentives to formulate policy strategies that take into account the strategies they anticipate policy makers of other nations may follow.

INTERNATIONAL POLICY COOPERATION AND COORDINATION

An alternative to the beggar-thy-neighbor strategy is for nations to work together to achieve their goals. There are two basic ways that nations might do this. One is through **international policy cooperation,** a term we use to refer to the act of sharing information concerning national objectives, policy procedures, economic data, and so on. A more ambitious way that nations can work together is by going a step further and undertaking **international policy coordination.** Via international coordination, nations' governments actively determine their policy actions for their *mutual* benefit, rather than with only their own nations' levels of well-being in mind.

International policy *cooperation* has become more commonplace in recent years, particularly in Western nations. For instance, the **Group of Five (G5)** nations—France, Germany, Japan, the United Kingdom, and the United States—and the **Group of Seven (G7) nations**—the G5 nations plus Canada and Italy—have for some time shared information on their policy objectives and procedures. They do so through regular meetings between economic policy secretaries, ministers, and staff members of the various nations.

Many economists believe that international policy cooperation is desirable. Everyone benefits from access to greater information and from a complete understanding of all nations' intentions and goals. Economists share much less agreement, however, about the desirability of international policy *coordination*. As you will learn in the remainder of this chapter, weighing the gains and losses from international policy coordination is a difficult undertaking. It also is a potentially divisive subject. Many believe strongly that policy coordination is desirable, while others disagree just as strongly. We shall try not to take a firm stand one way or the other on the issue; our goal will be to help you understand the issues concerning international policy coordination so that you can make your own informed judgment.

POLICY COORDINATION: PROS AND CONS

Full international policy coordination has perhaps never been achieved. This fact indicates that nations must perceive drawbacks in coordinating their economic policies. Nevertheless, as we shall discuss below, there have been recent efforts to increase the amount of policy coordination among nations. This implies that there also must be some perceived gains from coordination. Let's begin by considering these potential gains from policy coordination, and then let's think about the drawbacks that have discouraged so many nations from setting the policies jointly.

ARGUMENTS IN FAVOR OF INTERNATIONAL POLICY COORDINATION

There are three key justifications for international policy coordination. Of these, the first is the most fundamental argument in favor of greater coordination, but the remaining two also are important justifications.

Internalizing International Externalities   As we noted earlier, structural interdependence among nations means that the economies of nations experience spillover effects as a result of economic events in other nations. As a result, policy actions undertaken in one nation to improve the well-being of citizens of that nation may indirectly reduce the welfare of residents of another nation. Residents of the latter nation thereby would experience a negative international externality resulting from the lack of coordination of policies by the two nations.

By coordinating their policies, policy makers in two such nations would jointly determine their policy actions in light of mutual objectives. Effectively, they would behave as if the two nations together represented a single entity, thus *internalizing,* or recognizing in advance, the spillover effects their policy actions might create for *both* nations. Together, the policy makers would conduct policies that would thereby minimize the significance of these negative spillover effects, and residents of both nations would benefit.

To make the idea of internalizing spillover effects more concrete, consider a hypothetical example concerning international trade. The United States for years has imposed quotas on foreign auto imports, while Japan has restricted foreign beef imports. The U.S. auto import restrictions help the American auto industry and U.S. auto workers but hurt auto manufacturers and workers in Japan, while the Japanese beef import restrictions aid Japan's farmers and meat packers. Hence, the trade policies of both nations cause negative spillover effects. By working together to coordinate their trade policies concerning autos and beef, the two nations could, in principle, reduce the extent of these spillover effects.

Hence, the primary justification for international policy coordination is that such coordination takes into account the interaction among nations' economies that results from structural interdependence arising from trade linkages among nations. In essence, policy coordination treats structurally interdependent nations as parts of a single economic system. Coordinating policy makers then work together to stabilize this larger system of nations.

Making the Most of a Few Policy Instruments   By working together in this manner, policy makers can achieve another possible gain from international policy coordination, which is that they potentially can achieve a larger number of goals given their available policy instruments. Suppose, for instance, that a nation has a level of aggregate demand that is "too low" given the position of its aggregate supply schedule, so that real income lies below the target level of the nation's central bank. To raise aggregate demand, the central bank would need to increase the quantity of money. The central bank has determined, however, that such a policy action would be inconsistent with another central bank objective, which is to keep the value of its currency stable relative to other nations' currencies. By itself, then, this central bank cannot achieve both of its policy objectives with its single instrument of policy, the quantity of money.

If this central bank and those of other nations coordinate their policies, however, together they can resolve the conflict among competing policy goals. As a simple example, suppose that each nation in a group of policy-coordinating countries has the same goal of achieving a target real output level while minimizing exchange rate volatility, yet finds itself in the predicament just described. If the nations' central banks coordinate increases in their money stocks, they each can raise their levels of aggregate demand and potentially achieve their target levels of output. Furthermore, because each increases the supply of its currency, changes in exchange rates among the nations' currencies may be minimized.

The above example is very simplified, but it illustrates the basic idea. If each nation's policy maker has few policy instruments but several goals, and if the various goals of each policy maker are the same, then by working together to coordinate their instrument choices, a group of policy makers potentially can do a better job of achieving their individual objectives. As a result, international monetary policy coordination can make everyone better off.

Strength in Numbers   The third justification for international policy coordination is that policy makers of different nations may gain strength to withstand domestic pressures when they receive support, or, alternatively, counteracting pressure, from their policy-making peers in other countries. That is, in the absence of international policy coordination a domestic policy maker might break down in the face of national political pressures to undertake a policy action the policy maker knows will be counterproductive in the long run. Under international coordination, however, the policy maker may hold firm against such internal disputes, to the benefit of the nation's citizenry as a whole.

For example, suppose that key members of Congress pressure the Fed to undertake policy actions that the Fed believes to be misguided and potentially inflationary. If the Fed is part of a coalition of nations that coordinate their monetary policies, then it can respond to the members of Congress that it must decline to initiate their recommended policy actions, because doing so would be inconsistent with its obligations under its international agreements. Indeed, central bankers of other nations might publicly come to the Fed's defense, causing the Fed's congressional critics to back down.

ARGUMENTS AGAINST INTERNATIONAL POLICY COORDINATION

Many find the above arguments in favor of international policy coordination self-evident and overwhelming. Not everyone agrees, however. Indeed, it is possible to construct a long list of problems that coordinating nations might encounter. Those who favor greater policy coordination view these problems as obstacles to be overcome, while those who oppose coordination perceive them as reasons that nations' policy makers should pursue their economic policies independently.

The Problem of Retaining National Sovereignty   Full policy coordination entails working together to maximize the *joint* welfare of nations. Hence, nations that agree to coordinate their policies implicitly agree to pursue common *international* objectives, rather than more limited national goals. That is, they promise to seek to attain common, rather than selfish, aims. By definition, then, international policy coordination requires that nations' governments sacrifice much of their sovereignty in policy making.

Suppose, for example, that successful policy coordination among three nations requires that the exchange rates among the nations be fixed. The government of one of the nations, however, determines that its citizens could gain from permitting its currency to appreciate relative to the other two countries. Nevertheless, that nation's government must sacrifice its sovereign discretion and not allow its currency to appreciate.

Not surprisingly, some nations rebel at the idea of sacrificing their sovereignty to policy coordination agreements. In a democratic republic, for instance, politicians typically campaign for leadership positions on platforms that promise to raise the welfare of their constituency—the voters in their *nation*. A politician who wins an election after promising ''a chicken in every pot'' in his nation but who afterward tells the nation's voters that deals struck with other countries may in fact produce only half a chicken in every pot may find himself or herself boiling in a pot when the next election rolls around.

The Problem of Commitment and Credibility Another problem with international coordination is that there commonly are incentives for nations to cheat on policy-coordinating agreements. Figure 29-1 illustrates an example in which this is the case. As indicated in the upper-left-hand cell of Figure 29-1, if country A and country B each conduct independent, sovereign policies, they each derive a level of welfare equal to 20 units (to simplify, we pretend that welfare for each nation actually can be measured). In contrast, if both nations coordinate their policy making, then, as shown in the lower-right-hand cell of Figure 29-1, they both reach levels of welfare equal to 40 units. Hence, we consider in Figure 29-1 a situation in which coordination unambiguously would improve the welfare of both nations in the absence of cheating by policy makers.

Suppose, however, that country A's government were to agree to coordinate its policies with the government of country B. After the agreement is concluded, though, staff economists at country A advise its leaders that if country B follows through on the agreement but country A cheats by altering its policies, country A can raise its welfare level to 50

Figure 29-1

Hypothetical Welfare Levels under Different Behaviors by Policy Makers in Countries A and B. If policy makers in both nations fail to coordinate their policies, then their combined welfare is 40 units. If both work together to coordinate policy actions, however, their total welfare is 80 units. The problem is that if either nation "cheats" and fails to coordinate as promised, it can raise its own welfare to 50 units. The result would be a fall in the other nation's welfare, to 10 units, if the other nation honors the coordination agreement.

	Country B does not coordinate	Country B coordinates
Country A does not coordinate	Country A welfare = 20 Country B welfare = 20 Total welfare = 40	Country A welfare = 50 Country B welfare = 10 Total welfare = 60
Country A coordinates	Country A welfare = 10 Country B welfare = 50 Total welfare = 60	Country A welfare = 40 Country B welfare = 40 Total welfare = 80

units, while the welfare of country B will fall to 10 units. This outcome is shown in the upper-right-hand cell of Figure 29-1.

At the same time, country B's governmental economists reach an analogous conclusion about country B's prospects if it cheats on the coordination agreement with country A. They determine, as depicted in the lower-left-hand cell of Figure 29-1, that if country A follows through on the agreement while country B cheats, then country B's welfare level will rise to 50 units while country A's welfare will fall to 10 units.

While joint welfare is highest (40 units + 40 units = 80 units) under full policy coordination between country A and country B, we can see that, in our example, each nation individually could gain from cheating on the coordinating agreement, as long as the other nation does not cheat. That is, a beggar-thy-neighbor policy pays for one of the nations if the other honors its agreement. Total welfare for the two countries is lower (50 units + 10 units = 60 units) when one country or the other cheats on an agreement to coordinate policies.

If both nations cheat on the policy-coordinating agreement, however, total welfare for the nations is at its lowest possible level (20 units + 20 units = 40 units). Yet each nation is better off than it would be if it were to agree to coordinate only to have the other nation cheat on the agreement.

In this example, therefore, both nations agree to coordinate their policies, and stick to that agreement, only if each *trusts* the other. That is, each nation's commitment to the policy-coordinating agreement must be *credible* to the other nation. Otherwise, each nation knows that it can potentially be worse off by agreeing to coordinate and exposing itself to cheating by the other nation, rather than simply conducting noncoordinated policies without regard to the welfare of the other country's citizens. In the absence of mutual credibility, the two nations jointly reach the lowest possible level of welfare, however.

Can the Credibility Problem Be Solved?   It can be extremely difficult for nations to enter into credible commitments to coordinate their economic policies. This international policy credibility problem is not unlike that faced by a potentially discretionary monetary policy maker in the *monetary policy game* we considered in Chapter 26. A possible solution, which is the development of a strong reputation for keeping international commitments, also was discussed in that earlier chapter.

Many economists have concluded that it is impossible for nations to commit to perpetual coordination agreements, because circumstances nearly always arise in which purely sovereign policy making—that is, cheating on the agreements—could make countries better off than if they coordinated. Therefore, these economists conclude that nations weigh the gains from coordination against the losses that coordination may entail, along with losses in future reputation they may incur if they break or fail to renew policy-coordinating agreements. As a result, nations may never settle into a state in which they always coordinate policies or never coordinate policies. Instead, they may alternately coordinate or fail to coordinate over time, depending upon the relative costs and benefits of the alternative policies.

The Problem of Different Outlooks   An essential problem in achieving international policy coordination is that nations may have different perspectives on what they want from policy coordination. For instance, nations may have different objectives that they wish to achieve from coordination. Observers often emphasize that Germany, because of its experience with hyperinflation in the 1920s, has a strong dislike of inflation, and that the United States, as a result of its memory of the Great Depression of the 1930s, has a distaste for high unemployment rates. While both nations might feel that they could gain, in principle, from policy coordination, differences in their social preferences could make coordination of policy making difficult, if not impossible.

Even if nations agree on their fundamental policy objectives, however, they may have technical difficulties coordinating their policies. For example, suppose that the Federal Reserve and the Bank of England were to decide to coordinate their monetary policy actions. If the Fed's economic staff believed strongly that interest rates should be used as intermediate targets while the staff economists at the Bank of England firmly promoted money stock targets, then there would be a serious roadblock to effective coordination. Hence, differences in perspectives on how their nations' economies work and about the best course of policy making also can hinder international policy coordination.

Could Coordination Enhance the Negative Qualities of Policy Makers?   Many opponents of international policy coordination believe that greater coordination among nations' policy makers actually could accentuate weaknesses in the abilities of each nation's policy makers to achieve their objectives. This position essentially is the opposite of the "strength in numbers" argument in support of greater coordination. To illustrate the point of this argument against coordination, consider the following example.

Suppose that monetary policy makers of several nations all share a common desire to follow discretionary monetary policies aimed at increasing their nations' levels of real output above the natural, full-information levels. As we discussed in Chapter 26, this implies that unless each nation's policy maker can establish credibility as an inflation fighter, each nation will tend to suffer from an "inflation bias" in monetary policy.

In the absence of coordination, however, each nation's monetary policy authority must take into account the possibility that it may produce a greater inflation bias than other monetary authorities, which would weaken its country's currency, potentially affecting its trade flows adversely. This concern tends to limit the inflation bias that each nation's monetary authority will produce. If nations *coordinate* their discretionary monetary policies, however, each monetary authority can rest assured that its nation's currency will not depreciate, because under coordination it knows that there will be a shared inflation bias in all other nations as well. Hence, monetary policy coordination actually could induce *higher* inflation in all countries.

MONETARY AND FINANCIAL POLICY COORDINATION MECHANISMS

As you can see, there are a variety of perspectives on the desirability of international policy coordination. Nevertheless, in recent years there has been a growing interest in policy coordination. So far, aside from a few examples to illustrate these perspectives, we have not been very specific about what types of policies might be coordinated among nations. In this section, we consider proposals for some general forms of international monetary and financial coordination. In the section that follows, we discuss some actual efforts to achieve international policy coordination on a few of these fronts.

COORDINATED REGULATION OF BANKING AND FINANCIAL MARKETS

As we noted in the International Perspectives in Chapters 5 and 16, world banking and financial markets have undergone significant changes in recent decades. The worldwide position of United States banks relative to banks of other nations has declined precipitously. Simultaneously, the linkages between U.S. financial markets and those of the rest of the world have improved significantly the ability of financial firms to shift the location of their transactions to less regulated portions of the globe. For instance, as we noted in our Chapter 27 discussion of the growth of the Eurocurrency market, U.S. capital controls in the 1960s and 1970s induced American banks to move much of their dollar-denominated business with overseas firms offshore, to places such as London and the Caribbean.

In effect, development of new computer, telecommunications, and transportation technologies has enabled financial institutions to engage in **regulatory arbitrage.** This is the effort by financial institutions to limit the effects of regulatory differences across nations by shifting funds from highly regulated locales to countries whose authorities impose less stiff restrictions on banking and financial activities. In effect, regulatory arbitrage permits financial institutions to seek out placements for their funds that subject them to the fewest regulations, thereby circumventing those nations with the harshest restrictions on financial activities.

There have been two consequences of regulatory differences and the subsequent regulatory arbitrage. One is that the importance of American banks in international financial affairs has declined considerably. For instance, between 1985 and 1989 alone the percentage of international assets held in American banks declined from 20.1 percent to 14.6 percent. The reason this occurred was that American banking and monetary authorities made strong efforts to clamp down on regulatory arbitrage by U.S. banks. At the same time, Japanese banking authorities actively encouraged international involvement by their nation's banks, and the percentage of international assets held in Japanese banks increased from 23.0 percent to 38.2 percent. Although the efforts by U.S. regulators ultimately failed to halt completely the regulatory arbitrage undertaken by American banks, their restrictions slowed it sufficiently that many of the international funds held at U.S. banks flowed elsewhere—primarily to banks based in Japan.

A second consequence of regulatory arbitrage was that the Eurocurrency market mushroomed between the end of the 1960s and the 1980s. Now, in the 1990s, the payments system that links the banks in the Eurocurrency market has developed sufficiently that there is a much greater likelihood than ever before that financial failures or systemic breakdowns that previously would have been isolated in a single country may be transmitted throughout the world (see Chapter 16's discussion of systemic risk).

Promoting Integrated Banking and Financial Markets   In response to the decline in global prominence of American banks, many American bankers and policy makers have clamored for the establishment of a "more level playing field" in international banking and financial arrangements. They have not been alone in this suggestion; bankers and policy makers in several European nations, such as Britain and France, also have argued in favor of equal access to international markets and equitable treatment by regulators across nations.

Hence, one area in which international policy coordination has been advocated in recent years is the system of legal constraints on the financial activities permitted around the globe. The goal of such efforts, according to their proponents, would be to open banking and financial markets to equal access to international competition. This would, of course, further strengthen the international linkages among these markets, aggravating the global systemic risk problem highlighted above; but those who favor equal access and regulatory treatment believe that this problem could be overcome with sufficient international regulatory coordination.

Coordinated Banking and Financial Regulations Proponents of the international integration of banking and financial markets argue that national regulators should coordinate nearly every aspect of their legal restrictions on financial transactions. Most of these proponents contend that regulatory arbitrage is an effective but costly way to avoid cross-country differences in regulations, and so they propose eliminating such distinctions as completely as possible. For instance, they encourage the elimination of differences in capital requirements, interest rate regulations, and restrictions on the separation of banking from commerce. Furthermore, proponents of international regulatory coordination also propose opening nations' banking markets to equal opportunities for entry by domestic and foreign banks. They typically oppose capital controls entirely.

This is not to say that most proponents of regulatory coordination believe that banking and financial regulations should be entirely ended. Indeed, many who favor coordination by bank regulators believe that such regulations should be stiff. Their key point, however, is that *differences* in regulations should be ended.

To minimize the growth in world exposure to systemic risk that would result from greater integration of global financial markets, those in favor of regulatory coordination believe that national regulators must adopt common policies for dealing with financial crises that might spread beyond national borders. Furthermore, they argue in favor of equal application of those policies across nations, so that systemic risks are shared equally among countries.

MONETARY POLICY COORDINATION

Although proposals for international banking and financial coordination have received much attention, it is the topic of international monetary coordination that has generated more excitement and disagreement in recent years. It is not difficult to get most economists to agree that markets for financial services should be opened to greater competition or that regulatory differences should be minimized. This is so because nearly all economists agree that more competition is good for consumers and that regulatory arbitrage resulting from cross-country regulatory differences is wasteful. In contrast, discussions of monetary coordination inevitably involve choices among competing macroeconomic theories, and as you learned in Unit 5, economists share few agreements in the area of macroeconomic theory.

Nevertheless, evaluating the desirability of international monetary policy coordination became one of the main areas of economic research in the mid-1980s and has continued as one of the hottest topics in economics into the 1990s. Before the 1980s, economists knew they disagreed about the merits of international monetary policy coordination, but they did not really understand fully the basis of much of their disagreement. Now, in the 1990s, the foundations for debate are pretty well understood. They revolve around three basic issues: reestablishing fixed exchange rates, targeting a measure of the world stock of money, and coordinating national monetary policy rules and/or discretion.

A Return to Fixed Exchange Rates? One proposed form of international coordination is to reestablish fixed exchange rates. This proposal has been championed by many, ranging from respected economists such as Ronald McKinnon of Stanford University to the *Wall Street Journal*'s main editorial writers, for years. These writers argue that the experiment with floating exchange rates conducted by the United States since the breakdown of the Bretton Woods system (see Chapter 28) has failed. In a 1984 book, *An International Standard for Monetary Stabilization,* McKinnon goes so far as to say that "the American cycle of boom and bust over the past dozen years is primarily due to instability in the demand for dollar assets and the failure of the Fed to accommodate these demands by adjusting U.S. money growth toward stabilizing the dollar exchange rate.''

McKinnon and others have proposed that the United States, Japan, and Europe coordinate a gradual reestablishment of a fixed-exchange-rate system. Their views diverge on the best means of doing this, however. While some analysts argue for a return to a gold-based exchange rate system, others such as McKinnon promote a system based on joint control of a basket of reserve currencies including, say, the American dollar, Japanese yen, and German deutschemark.

World Money Stock Control   An alternative coordination strategy, also proposed by McKinnon (as an intermediate step toward his final proposal of fully fixed exchange rates), is for central banks around the world to coordinate control of a *world monetary aggregate.* Such a monetary aggregate might be a weighted average of similar monetary aggregates of different nations, such as international equivalents of M1 or M2 measures of money used in the United States (see the International Perspective in Chapter 3 for a discussion of monetary aggregates in different nations). Alternatively, it might be a measure of the stock of dollars throughout the world, such as an aggregate called the ''World Dollar Base,'' developed by the private economists Lewis Lehrman and John Mueller. This measure is equal to total United States currency and bank reserves (the U.S. monetary base) plus the dollar-denominated assets of foreign central banks.

Those who promote coordinated control of a world monetary aggregate argue that the world has become so integrated that central banks should think in broader terms than their own domestic money supplies. In an integrated world, these analysts contend, the quantity theory of money relates the *world* quantity of money to the *world* price level. In support of this position, proponents of world money stock control point to evidence such as that presented in Figure 29-2, which shows a strong positive relationship between percentage increases in the Lehrman-Mueller World Dollar Base and in an index of world food and energy prices, albeit with a lag of just over two years.

Coordinated Monetary Policy Rules   Many economists who otherwise favor international monetary coordination disagree with both the proposal to peg exchange rates and the idea of world money stock control. They contend that a system of fixed exchange rates is too inflexible, while a policy of targeting the world money stock is subject to the same problem of volatile and unpredictable monetary velocity as domestic money stock targeting, such as that experienced by the Fed in the United States in the late 1970s and early 1980s. Instead, these proponents of international monetary coordination argue, national monetary policies should be related via a system of rules. They propose that such rules, in turn, should take into account the structural relationships that vary across nations, as well as shared objectives of the nations that coordinate these monetary policy rules. A truly optimal rule, these observers contend, would be much more flexible than pegged exchange rates or the establishment of world monetary targets. For instance, such a rule might entail coordinated adjustments of national monetary aggregates to variations in nations' price levels, interest rates, or exchange rates with an aim to attainment of joint objectives of participating nations.

Of the proposals for international monetary policy coordination, this latter proposal is the most broad, and it also is the most elusive in terms of its implementability. Certainly, most economists agree that there is much to gain from flexibility in monetary policy. Nevertheless, many argue that ''flexible rules'' often degenerate into discretionary policy actions. The latter, in turn, may not be consistent with maintaining an agreement to

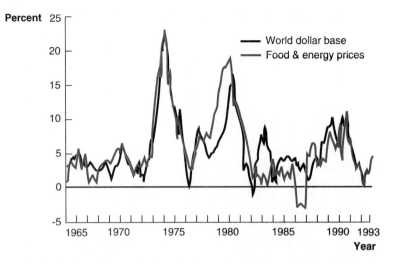

Figure 29-2
**Year-to-Year Changes in World CPI Food and Energy Prices and the World Dollar
Base Lagged about Two Years.**   There is a strong positive relationship between percentage
increases in an index of world food and energy prices and percentages in the World Dollar Base
(the U.S. monetary base plus dollar holdings by foreign central banks) about two years earlier.
[*Source:* John Mueller, "The World's Real Money Supply," *Wall Street Journal* (March 5, 1991),
editorial page.]

coordinate monetary policies. After all, these critics contend, isn't it a short step from
policy discretion to a beggar-thy-neighbor policy strategy?

Nonetheless, many economists continue to study the properties of broad international
policy rules. Their hope is that, one day, a policy coordination strategy may be developed
that would enable central banks around the globe to stabilize their economies without
reliance on inflexible schemes such as fixed exchange rates or a world monetary target.
One specific area of research along these lines concerns the idea of using exchange rate
target zones. Target zones are bands within which central banks would permit their
nations' exchange rates to vary; if exchange rates rise above the upper limits of the bands,
or fall below the lower limits, however, central banks would intervene in exchange markets
to bring their exchanges back within the bands. The idea behind this policy is to retain
some flexibility in exchange rates while simultaneously limiting the extent of permitted
exchange rate volatility.

RECENT EXPERIMENTS WITH POLICY COOPERATION AND COORDINATION

History has shown that international cooperation and coordination are difficult prospects;
the savageries and inhumanities that nations have heaped upon one another in past centuries
and decades are abundant evidence that this is so. Nevertheless, recent years have witnessed some undeniable movements toward world economic cooperation and coordination.
Most of these efforts remain experimental, but several show signs of growing permanence
in their influence on the affairs of nations.

THE BANK FOR INTERNATIONAL SETTLEMENTS

The **Bank for International Settlements (BIS)** is one of the earliest surviving experiments in international cooperation and coordination in the sphere of money and banking. It arose in 1930 under terms of the Young Plan for World War I reparation payments to Great Britain, France, and other nations by Germany. Therefore, its designers originally planned for the BIS to assist in the settlement of financial claims among the nation-states of Europe. The U.S. Congress refused to become involved in German war reparation dealings, and so the Federal Reserve owns no shares in the BIS, although central banks of other nations continue to own shares in the organization. Interestingly, private American banks, including Citibank, J. P. Morgan, the First National Bank of Chicago, and the First National Bank of New York, participated in the founding of the BIS, and these private banks continue to own shares in the bank, which is based in Basle, Switzerland.

Following World War II, representatives to the Bretton Woods conference in 1944 passed a resolution recommending liquidation of the BIS. Nevertheless, in 1948 the BIS became the technical agent for clearing credits and debits of nations participating in the postwar European Recovery Program. Since that time, the BIS has become a bank for central banks in Europe, the United States, Canada, Japan, Australia, and South America. It acts as an agent or trustee for international loan agreements and manages portions of the reserve accounts of some central banks, which it places in world financial markets. That is, some central banks hold deposits at the BIS, which it uses to purchase securities. The BIS also lends to some central banks.

An international board of directors oversees the activities of the BIS. This board includes the governors of the central banks of Belgium, France, Germany, Italy, and the United Kingdom, plus five individuals appointed by each of these central bank governors as representatives of commerce, finance, and industry. These ten directors, in turn, traditionally have selected governors of the central banks of the Netherlands, Sweden, and Switzerland as additional members of the BIS board of directors.

A key function of the BIS is that it is a clearing house for information for central banks around the world; that is, it is a center of international *cooperation* in both banking and monetary affairs. Staff members of the BIS organize periodic meetings of experts to brief central bankers on financial and monetary conditions and conferences for central bank staff economists and regulators from participating nations. The BIS also maintains a statistical data base covering international banking issues for use by the **Group of Ten (G10)** nations—the Group of Seven plus Belgium, the Netherlands, and Sweden—as well as by Switzerland.

THE BASLE BANKING AGREEMENTS

In July 1988, the BIS became the setting for the **Basle Agreement,** which established risk-based capital adequacy standards for commercial banks in the United States, Western Europe, and Japan. As we discussed in Chapter 11, these are the capital standards used by the Federal Reserve, the Office of the Comptroller of the Currency, and the FDIC in their evaluations of the adequacy of capitalization of all commercial banks in the United States. Under terms of the Basle Agreement, these standards apply to banks throughout the most advanced nations of the world.

In 1988, many observers heralded the Basle Agreement as a first step toward truly worldwide coordination of banking regulations. As we discussed earlier, many had promoted eliminating international differences in bank capital requirements as a key step toward integration of world banking markets. And, indeed, so far it seems to have been a clear step in this direction. All nations to date have kept their capital regulations within the Basle Agreement's framework, applying them equally and impartially to their nations' banks.

This does not mean, however, that additional coordination of international banking regulations is inevitable, nor does it mean that integration of banking markets around the world necessarily will occur. Indeed, significant differences still exist among the financial structures of different nations. For instance, in a 1991 study of the 1970s and 1980s, Federal Reserve staff economists Allen Frankel and John Montgomery computed index measures of the ratios of assets of the largest banks in Germany, Japan, the United Kingdom, and the United States relative to each respective nation's gross domestic products. Their results are displayed in Figure 29-3. They show that the largest banks in both Germany and Japan more than doubled their size in the twenty-year period they studied, while British banks grew by much less in relative terms and the relative growth of American banks failed to change significantly.

Furthermore, Frankel and Montgomery document that German, Japanese, and British businesses finance significantly larger shares of their investment through loans from banks than is the case in the United States. In the United Kingdom, for instance, nearly 70 percent of funds raised by businesses at the onset of the 1990s were through borrowings from banks; the proportions for Germany and Japan were on the order of 50 percent and 65 percent, respectively. For the United States, however, a little less than 30 percent of business funds were raised through bank loans.

There also are differences in market structures across nations' banking systems. Figure 29-4 shows Frankel and Montgomery's tabulation of the distribution of assets (measured in dollar terms) among banks in the United States, the United Kingdom, Germany, and

Figure 29-3
Index Measures of the Ratios of the Assets of the Largest Banks to the Gross Domestic Products of Four Industrialized Nations.   While the importance of banking remained relatively small in the United States in the 1970s and 1980s, banking's importance in Germany, Japan, and the United Kingdom grew by much greater amounts. [*Source:* Allen B. Frankel and John D. Montgomery, "Financial Structure: An International Perspective," *Brookings Papers on Economic Activity* (1, 1991, pp. 257–297.]

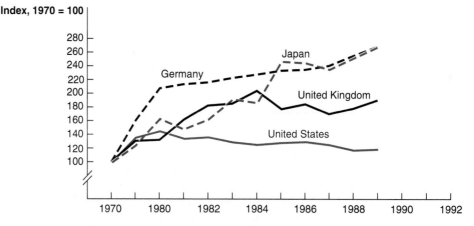

Note: Data for U.S., U.K., and Germany are end of calendar year; Japanese data are for the end of March.

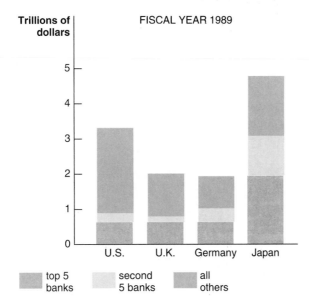

Figure 29-4

Total Assets (Measured in Trillions of Dollars) and Asset Concentrations among Banks in Four Industrialized Nations.   Although total assets of U.S. banks, measured in dollar terms, are greater than those of German and British banks, the portions of total assets at the largest five and largest ten banks in Germany, Japan, and the United Kingdom significantly exceed these relative portions for the United States. [*Source:* Allen B. Frankel and John D. Montgomery, "Financial Structure: An International Perspective," *Brookings Papers on Economic Activity* 1991(1), pp. 257–297.]

Japan at the beginning of the 1980s. It is easy to see from this figure that the top ten banks in Britain and in Germany have similar shares of total assets (roughly between one-half and two-thirds of the total amounts of assets). The degree of asset concentration among banks in Japan is much higher (roughly two-thirds of all assets are at the top ten Japanese banks), however, and the degree of concentration in the United States banking system is much smaller (less than one-third of total assets are at the top ten banks).

There also is little evidence that there is fully open international financial market competition. For example, Figure 29-5 displays ratios of outstanding commercial loans made by foreign banks in each of these same nations, relative to total domestic commercial bank loans in each country, for the years 1980, 1985, and 1990. While foreign banks made many loans to American and British individuals and firms in those years in relation to total lending by banks based in those countries, foreign banks had barely penetrated the German and Japanese loan markets. Note that this is not conclusive evidence that German and Japanese markets are not open to foreign banking competition; we pointed out in the International Perspective in Chapter 4 that saving rates in Germany and Japan exceed those in the United Kingdom and the United States, which implies that German and Japanese citizens probably desire to borrow relatively less than British and American residents. Nonetheless, in fully integrated banking markets we would not expect the magnitudes of the discrepancies in foreign market penetration shown in Figure 29-5 to persist for such lengthy periods.

We may conclude that the Basle Agreement probably is a tentative step toward more

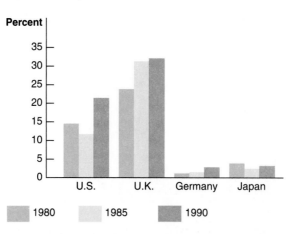

Figure 29-5

Outstanding Commercial Loans by Foreign Banks as a Percentage of Total Domestic Commercial Loans in Four Industrialized Nations.   While foreign banks have captured significant shares of the domestic commercial lending businesses of the United States and the United Kingdom, this has not been the case in Germany and Japan, where domestic banks dominate these nations' commercial loan markets. [*Source:* Allen B. Frankel and John D. Montgomery, "Financial Structure: An International Perspective," *Brookings Papers on Economic Activity* (1, 1991, pp. 257–297.]

complete international coordination of banking regulations. The world has a long way to go, however, before one could claim that regulations are fully coordinated or that banking and financial markets are completely integrated.

THE EUROPEAN SINGLE BANKING MARKET

Beginning in January 1993, the European Community (EC) authorized a "single banking license" valid in any member nation. Among other things, this license permits a bank based in an EC member nation to issue deposits; make loans; trade on its own account or on the accounts of customers in securities, foreign exchange, futures, and options markets; and provide portfolio management and trust services to customers in *any* EC nation. Banks meet their single licensing requirement by maintaining minimum capital requirements denominated in the European Currency Unit (ECU); all EC banks are subject to the same capital requirements.

The degree of regulatory cooperation and coordination in the EC at present is unprecedented. Under terms of the establishment of the single EC banking license, a bank based in any EC nation must meet only the regulatory requirements of its home nation, and such requirements have been made nearly harmonious across nations. Further, the home-country regulator of any EC bank may undertake on-the-spot audits of bank branches in other EC member nations, as long as it notifies the other nations in advance. Likewise, the regulatory authority in any EC member nation may audit a branch within its territory of a bank based in another EC nation.

Proponents of the single banking license believe that its establishment will hasten the nearly complete integration of European banking regulatory requirements, thereby promising the development of a European-wide banking system. They also contend that these steps herald a level of regulatory cooperation and coordination that in many ways parallels developments achieved through the federal structure of the United States, which eventually evolved into the almost fully nationalized banking structure the United States possesses today.

Hence, in banking at least there is some promise that a ''United States of Europe'' may be in the offing. At least this one part of the world has achieved a level of banking integration that a couple of decades ago was merely a dream. In spite of the initial successes of the new EC policies, however, most economists agree that obstacles to true European banking integration remain. Banks in some European nations have been protected from competition for so long that adjustment to an integrated European banking system also promises to be a painful process that some observers fear could generate attempts to circumvent some elements of the EC single banking license. The coming years will provide a true test of this area of international coordination.

MONETARY POLICY COORDINATION BY THE GROUPS OF FIVE, SEVEN, AND TEN

Another dream of those who envision a future world of economic harmony has been worldwide coordination of macroeconomic policies. Central to this objective, for those who have promoted it, is the coordination of monetary policy actions by the major nations of the world. A key first step was the establishment of the Groups of Five, Seven, and Ten, respectively.

These groupings of nations presently exist primarily to foster greater international policy cooperation. The heads of the central banks of the Group of Five maintain regular telephone and face-to-face contact, and the staffs of the central banks of all three groups of nations share information about national objectives, procedures, and statistics through the Bank of International Settlements and other formal and informal means.

In recent years there also have been efforts to establish more direct coordination of monetary policy actions. As we noted in Chapter 28's International Perspective, key examples were the 1985 Plaza Agreement and the 1987 Louvre Accord that increased the scope of G5 central bank interventions in foreign exchange markets. These coordinated central bank interventions, designed to smooth movements in exchange rates, represented the most significant efforts to coordinate monetary policy actions since the breakdown of the Bretton Woods system over a decade before. Many observers in the 1980s viewed these agreements as tentative steps toward more complete international coordination of monetary policies.

Certainly, in retrospect it is clear that these were important experiments in monetary policy coordination. It is also true, however, that events since the Louvre Accord in 1987 reduced the scope for agreement on G5 policy coordination. Of these events, which included G5 disagreements about appropriate levels of economic assistance to the former republics of the Soviet Union and about political matters such as the conflict with Iraq in 1990–1991, the most important certainly was the breakup of the Warsaw Pact in Eastern Europe that led to the reestablishment of a single German nation in 1990. Coping with the costs of reunification of formerly communist East Germany with the capitalist western part of the country made it difficult for Germany to coordinate its monetary policies with the other G5 nations. In the early 1990s, for example, U.S. Treasury Secretary Nicholas Brady publicly requested a coordinated cut in interest rates by the G5 central banks, but this request, which later was echoed by President Bush, fell on deaf ears at the German Bundesbank, which at that time was struggling with the highest German inflation rate in years. While it is possible that G5—or even G7 or G10—coordination may begin anew in the near future, the Plaza and Louvre experiments are on hold—if not ended.

THE EUROPEAN MONETARY SYSTEM

The European Monetary System, or EMS, includes all the members of the EC except Spain and Portugal. These latter two nations are weighing joining the EMS. In addition, although the United Kingdom is a member, it has not always chosen to participate in all aspects of the EMS.

The EMS essentially is an agreement among the participating EC nations to minimize variations of exchange rates among these nations. The functioning of the EMS is overseen by the European Council of Ministers, which created the new monetary unit, the European Currency Unit, as a central feature of the system. The ECU is a **composite unit of account,** which means that it is a weighted basket of the currencies of all the EC nations. The German deutschemark has the largest weight in the basket, at roughly one-third. The French franc has close to 20 percent of the weight, followed by the British pound at nearly 14 percent, the Netherlands guilder at about 10 percent, and the Italian lira at close to 10 percent. The remaining EC currencies together account for the remainder of the weight of the ECU, or roughly 14 percent.

The ECU has two key functions in the EMS. First, it is a settlement instrument for all central banks in the EC; that is, central banks denominate mutual debits or credits in ECUs. Second, the ECU is the pillar of the EMS exchange rate system. It serves as a common unit of account for measuring each nation's currency at the going ECU exchange rate. Hence, each EC nation's exchange rate is measured relative to the ECU.

EMS participants commit themselves to the system's *exchange rate intervention mechanism,* which is a framework of rules spelling out when a nation's central bank needs to intervene to stabilize its country's currency value relative to the ECU. For most nations in the EMS, intervention must occur if their exchange rate relative to those of other nations (measured via ECU exchange measurement conversions) moves more than 2.25 percent above or below the official EMS target. To assist EC central banks in meeting this obligation, the EMS includes a central credit facility through which short-term ECU credit is granted and exchange settlements take place.

The express purpose of the EMS is to limit exchange rate volatility within the EC. There are two rationales for this objective. First, less volatility in exchange rates limits foreign exchange risks (see Chapter 27), which significantly reduces the costs associated with trade among EC nations. Second, reduced exchange rate variability inhibits expected exchange rate changes from causing interest rates to vary among EC member nations, thereby simplifying financial market integration.

Many observers have argued that the EMS has been a great success. Certainly, inflation rates among EMS nations have converged in recent years, and the general level of inflation for the EMS as a whole has declined. Many believe that the performance of the EMS has been so successful that Europe should contemplate a bigger step: the adoption of the ECU as a common currency throughout Europe, to be used by firms and workers as well as by central banks. Indeed, in late 1991 most EC nations agreed to establish a European central bank by the end of the century.

SHOULD NATIONS USE DIFFERENT CURRENCIES?

The proposal to adopt a single European currency to be issued by a European central bank has stimulated economists to evaluate circumstances under which EC nations would gain from such an arrangement. This is a very interesting issue, because its implications extend far beyond Europe. After all, if Europe could get along with just one currency, why shouldn't the rest of the world join the crowd?

OPTIMAL CURRENCY AREAS

Every day, the *Wall Street Journal* publishes exchange rates for about *fifty* separate national currencies. Even this is not a full listing, because the newspaper reports exchange rates only for those currencies that people and firms trade in large volumes. Surely there must be good reasons for so many currencies to exist.

The theory of *optimal currency areas,* developed by Robert Mundell of Columbia University, seeks to address the issue of why there should be—or, perhaps, shouldn't be—so many currencies in the world. A narrow definition of an optimal currency area is that it is a region within which it is least costly to adopt a currency specific to that region. As we shall make clear shortly, this is a somewhat incomplete definition, but let's start with this definition and expand it slightly later on.

To explain the basic idea behind the theory of optimal currency areas, consider a simple example of a large island that is split into two nations of roughly equal size. In each nation, labor wages and capital rental rates are sticky, at least in the short run (more modern versions of the theory relax this traditional Keynesian assumption, but we shall adopt it as a simplification). One nation is country A, and the other is country B. Each of these nations specializes in producing different goods and services, and each nation's government issues its own currency. Suppose that, perhaps because the leader of one of the island's nations offended the leader of the other nation, there are border posts on the island that effectively keep citizens of both nations from selling factors of production outside of their own nations. That is, workers in country A cannot sell labor services or lease capital goods to firms in country B, and vice versa. There are no restrictions, however, on flows of goods and services between citizens of the two nations.

Consider now what happens if there is a sudden fall in the demands by citizens of both nations for the goods and services produced by country B. As a result, firms in country B will demand less labor and capital. Because wages and rental rates on capital are sticky, however, labor and capital unemployment will result in country B, and inflation will occur in country A. In the absence of restrictions on flows of factors of production, citizens in country B could supply more labor and capital to firms in country A, thereby alleviating the unemployment pressures in country B and the inflation problem for country A. Because legal restrictions on mobility of factors of production exist, however, this means of adjustment cannot occur. Instead, country A's currency must fall in value relative to the currency in country B; thus, the prices of goods and services in country A rise relative to the prices of goods and services in country B, eliminating the balance-of-trade disequilibrium that otherwise would take place.

Note that, for adjustment in relative prices of the two nations to occur, the exchange rate between the two currencies must be able to adjust. This means that having separate currencies with a floating exchange rate is advantageous. The underlying reason is that factors are immobile between the two nations, and so the exchange rate between the nations' currencies absorbs the full burden of adjustment.

In our example, then, country A and country B are optimal currency areas. Citizens in both nations gain from having separate currencies, so that the exchange rate between the two nations can play the role of "shock absorber" when market conditions on the island change. Surely, they must incur costs, such as those that arise from foreign exchange risk or from hedging against it, as a result. They gain on net, however, from the relative price adjustments that variation in the exchange rate among separate currencies makes possible, because such variation relieves unemployment and inflation pressures in the face of changes in product demands.

GAINS FROM FIXED EXCHANGE RATES OR CURRENCY UNIFICATION

Now suppose that the leaders of the island nations make up and, indeed, become good friends. They order the border posts torn down, and they permit their citizens to trade freely both their outputs and their factors of production. Shortly thereafter, there once again is a general fall in island demand for goods and services produced by firms in country B. Now, however, residents in country B may respond by supplying more factor services to country A's firms, so that unemployment and inflation pressures are eliminated. In this newly linked island economy, there is no reason for the exchange rate to adjust. That is, the exchange rate between the two nations' currencies might as well be fixed.

Technically speaking, the entire island is an optimal currency area, as economists broadly use the term, when factors of production are very mobile throughout the island. Hence, our earlier definition of an optimal currency area was too narrow. *The full definition of an* **optimal currency area** *is that it is a geographical region within which fixed exchange rates may be maintained without harming international adjustments* and, in some cases, *in which it may be least costly to use a single currency.* Because countries A and B might as well have a fixed exchange rate, they clearly satisfy this full meaning of the term "optimal currency area" and hence fall into that classification.

When would it be optimal for the two nations to take one last step and actually switch to using a single currency? The answer is that they will choose to do so when the cost of converting between currencies in international trade on the island becomes greater than any perceived gain from having separate currencies. If, for example, the islands' citizens are so nationalistic that they receive great satisfaction from using pieces of paper with their own nations' names printed on them and thereby are willing to incur currency conversion costs when they conduct cross-nation trade, then they will continue to use separate currencies. If currency conversion costs within an optimal currency area become large enough, however, residents within that region will choose to use a common currency.

PROBLEMS IN UNIFYING CURRENCIES

We now have a theory of why nations might use different currencies. First of all, they definitely will do so if they are separate optimal currency areas, so that factors of production do not flow freely among nations. Reasons that productive factors might not freely flow among nations are constraints such as immigration restrictions, tariffs, and high costs of moving factors geographically. Second, even if barriers to the free flow of factors of production between different nations are very small, so that nations can adopt fixed exchange rates, the nations still may not adopt a single, common currency if costs of converting from one currency to another are very small relative to perceived benefits of maintaining separate currencies.

What are some possible gains that nations might perceive from having their own currencies? Our example above in which citizens are so nationalistic that they simply derive high utility from using currency printed with their nation's name—and perhaps with a painting or photo of a "founding father or mother"—is conceivable. People commonly are nationalistic and have trouble sacrificing their nations' traditions. There are, however, other reasons that surely play a role.

Lack of Fiscal Integration One of these is that nations typically follow separate fiscal—government spending and taxation—policies. It is the taxation side of the fiscal policy issue that has a bearing on the issue of when nations might use separate currencies. Recall from Chapter 2 that governments have used seigniorage revenues, which are the profits earned from producing money whose market value exceeds its cost of production, as a means of taxation. While seigniorage typically is a relatively small portion of any nation's tax revenues, for some nations it is more important than it is for others. As a result, some nations may value having a separate currency more than their trading partners.

For instance, suppose that the island containing countries A and B is an optimal currency area, so that the nations may maintain a fixed exchange rate without experiencing problems in adjustment of their balance of trade. If the government of country A relies on seigniorage revenues to a greater extent than does country B's government, then country A may be unwilling to adopt a common island currency. The two countries will then keep their separate currencies, but they will maintain a fixed exchange rate.

A common reason given for why the European Community has not adopted a common currency is that some nations, particularly in the southern part of Europe, rely on seigniorage as a significant form of taxation. As we noted in the International Perspective in Chapter 2, however, seigniorage rates have been converging in the EC in recent years. As a result, this rationale for separate currencies in Europe has lost much of its force.

Removal of Currency Competition Another reason that separate currencies might be preferred by residents of European nations is that it is possible that national currencies can *compete,* to the benefit of the citizens of Europe. This notion of beneficial currency competition is due to the economic philosopher F. A. Hayek. He argued that a central bank may be hesitant to issue too much money, and thereby cause inflation, if by so doing it reduces the exchange value of its nation's currency relative to those of other nations. Continual declines in the value of its currency, in turn, would ultimately induce people to prefer to hold less of the nation's currency. That is, it would lose in a currency competition. Eventually, the central bank could ''go out of business''; its currency ultimately could lose its value, because no one would hold it.

Hence, having many national currencies effectively in competition with each other could be advantageous to citizens of all nations. In this case, they could lose an important benefit if governments, such as those in the European Community, banded together to adopt a common currency. Such a move would reduce the extent of currency competition and could, therefore, remove the check on temptations by the common central bank (that is, a Eurofed) to produce inflation in nations using the common currency.

At present, an official goal of the EMS is to form a central bank that would issue the ECU as a common currency for the EC nations. Despite the 1991 accord on a 1999 goal of currency union, however, the future is uncertain. Some nations, such as France and Italy, seem dedicated to the goal, but others, such as Germany and the United Kingdom, are more hesitant. It remains to be seen if the dream of a Eurofed will ever come to pass.

FUTURE DIRECTIONS IN WORLD MONETARY COORDINATION

What are the prospects for expansion of ongoing experiments in monetary and financial policy coordination? At present, the verdict on this issue seems mixed. Even as there are forces pushing nations of the world in the direction of increased cooperation and coordination, other forces work in opposition.

FORCES FAVORING POLICY COORDINATION

Perhaps the key factor that presently tends to move nations in the direction of coordinating their policies is the growing integration of the world's economy. This increased economic integration is particularly noticeable in the world's financial markets. It is perhaps for this reason that central banks adopted the Basle Agreement linking the capital requirements of banks in Europe, Japan, and the United States, and that Europe has moved so quickly toward a single banking market.

Markets for goods and nonfinancial services also have become somewhat more globally integrated, although less so than in markets for financial services. Many nations continue, for example, to impose protectionist import restrictions and tariffs on imports, while complaining that their exports are subjected to similar protectionist policies by other nations. Nevertheless, there has been a noticeable increase in exports and imports for many nations, including the United States, that first occurred in the 1970s and has continued, albeit at a slow pace, since that time. In turn, increased international trade raises the significance of structural interdependence and associated spillover effects among nations' policies, thereby increasing the potential gains from policy coordination.

It is in Europe that mutual real and financial trade flows have increased the most in the past two decades. For this reason, it perhaps is not surprising that policy coordination efforts have flourished in that part of the world. How much the level of coordination expands—with perhaps the ultimate level of coordination being the formation of a Eurofed to issue a single European currency—depends considerably upon the extent to which market integration in Europe continues. Likewise, the extent to which *worldwide* attempts at policy coordination continue or stagnate will be influenced greatly by whether or not the rest of the world eventually shares in the European experience of greater integration.

FORCES DISSUADING POLICY COORDINATION

Despite the hopes and dreams of many proponents of international policy coordination, several forces in today's world are working against active policy coordination. Protectionist policies that inhibit the flows of trade among nations are widespread, and so world output markets have not become integrated quickly. For instance, despite long-standing freezer technologies the United States maintains import restrictions on ice cream, and in spite of a lack of grazing space for cattle Japan perpetuates similar restrictions on beef imports. France keeps out many Japanese consumer electronics goods, and the United States shuts out some French, Japanese, and German automobiles. The list of restrictions on trade around the world goes on and on. Some people gain from such restrictions, while others lose; the point is that protectionist policies slow the rate of world market integration, making policy coordination less useful.

Further, some nations have experienced tremendous changes in recent years. For some, such as those in Eastern Europe, this has encouraged greater interest in trade and integration. For others, however, such as Germany and China, internal changes have reduced interest in international cooperation and coordination. There has even been concern, which may or may not be founded, that the European Community may feel internal pressures to adopt a beggar-thy-neighbor approach to trade and monetary policy interactions with Japan and the United States.

The coming years should show which of these forces ultimately will predominate in the world economy. The approaching end of this century promises to be an exciting time for those captivated by events on the world's economic stage.

CHAPTER SUMMARY

1. If nations trade sizable amounts goods and services, their economies are structurally interdependent, meaning their economic systems are interlinked. Even though they may have separate political structures, the economic policy strategies of one nation's government can influence the well-being of citizens in other nations.

2. The existence of structural interdependence implies that there are international externalities, or spillover effects, in economic policy making. Such spillovers occur when a government's policies aimed at improving the performance of its own economy also affect the performance of the economies of other nations.

3. If national policy makers recognize that their national economies are structurally interdependent, they may undertake strategic behavior intended to assist their own economies to the detriment of those of their neighbors. If so, the policy makers follow beggar-thy-neighbor policies.

4. International policy cooperation is the act of sharing information with other nations concerning national objectives, policy procedures, economic data, and so on. International coordination, in contrast, refers to the determination of joint policy actions intended mutually to benefit those nations involved.

5. There are three basic arguments in favor of international policy coordination. One is that if two nations coordinate their policies, they behave as if the two nations together represented a single entity, thus internalizing the spillover effects their policy actions might create for both nations. A second is that if each nation's policy maker has few policy instruments but several goals, then by working together to coordinate their instrument choices, a group of policy makers potentially can do a better of job of achieving their individual objectives. Finally, policy makers of different nations may gain strength to withstand domestic political pressures when they receive either support or counteracting pressures from their policy-making peers in other countries.

6. Several problems arise from efforts to coordinate policies. One is that it is possible that nations can gain by cheating on their policy-coordinating agreements, so that such agreements may be difficult to form unless all involved governments have sufficient credibility to be trusted. Further, governments may disagree about how their economies work and interact, and they may have different goals. In addition, in some cases it is possible that coordination can bring out the worst in all policy makers, so that their nations' economies could be better off without coordination.

7. Financial institutions undertake regulatory arbitrage by shifting funds from highly regulated locales to countries whose authorities impose less severe restrictions on banking and financial activities, thereby circumventing those nations with the harshest restrictions on financial activities. In recent years, regulatory arbitrage has induced many nations to reduce differences in their banking and financial regulations and to encourage greater worldwide integration of financial markets.

8. Monetary policy coordination can take several forms. Two common proposals for nations to coordinate their monetary policies are for nations (1) to fix their exchange rates or (2) to target a weighted average of their quantities of money, or the world money stock. Some economists recommend broader and more flexible coordinated rules for monetary policy, however.

9. The Bank for International Settlements is a center for monetary and financial cooperation by the G10 nations and Switzerland. Financial integration and banking and monetary policy coordination have increased in much of Europe in recent years, primarily through the European Community and European Monetary System. While tentative efforts have been made toward

greater worldwide coordination of monetary policies, most broad success in coordinating global policies has been in the area of banking regulations, as in the case of the Basle Agreement equalizing capital standards in most developed nations.

10. Nations in the European Monetary System agree to coordinate efforts to stabilize their nations' exchange rates. When nations in a region such as Europe find it advantageous to fix their exchange rates, they feel that their region of the world is an optimal currency area. This means that factors of production can flow fairly freely among nations, so that factor movements can absorb adjustments to changes in the nations' output market conditions. Whether or not European nations should adopt a common currency is an unresolved issue, however, because there are costs and benefits associated with having separate currencies.

GLOSSARY

Bank for International Settlements (BIS): Bank created in 1930 to assist in the settlement of financial claims among the nation-states of Europe. It functions now as an agent or trustee for international loan agreements and manages portions of the reserve accounts of some central banks, which it places in world financial markets.

Basle Agreement: A 1988 agreement that established risk-based capital adequacy standards for commercial banks in the United States, Western Europe, and Japan.

Beggar-thy-neighbor policies: Policies under which policy makers may intentionally seek to enhance the economic welfare of their own nation's citizens at the expense of the well-being of residents of other countries.

Composite unit of account: A weighted basket of the currencies of several nations, such as the European Currency Unit.

Group of Five (G5): Five nations—France, Germany, Japan, the United Kingdom, and the United States—that periodically cooperate in economic policy making.

Group of Seven (G7): The G5 nations plus Canada and Italy.

Group of Ten (G10): The G7 nations plus Belgium, the Netherlands, and Sweden.

International policy cooperation: The sharing of information about national policy objectives, procedures, and data.

International policy coordination: Actions taken by the governments of nations for the mutual benefit of those nations.

International policy externalities: Policy spillover effects from one nation to another that occur when the nations are structurally interdependent and nations do not consider the implications of their own policies for the well-being of citizens in other nations.

Optimal currency area: A geographical region within which fixed exchange rates may be maintained without hindering international adjustments and, under some circumstances, in which it may be least costly to have a single, common currency.

Protectionism: The use of national policies to restrict imports of goods or services to improve the prospects of domestic industries that produce those goods or services.

Regulatory arbitrage: A process by which financial institutions seek to limit the effects of regulatory differences across nations by shifting funds from highly regulated nations to nations whose authorities impose weaker restrictions on banking and financial activities.

Structural interdependence: A situation in which the economic systems of two or more nations are interlinked, and so economic events and policy actions in one of the nations have effects on economic performance in the others.

Target zones: Bands within which central banks permit their nations' exchange rates to vary; the central banks intervene in foreign exchange markets to stabilize their exchange rates only if the exchange rates move outside the upper or lower limit of the target zone.

SELF-TEST QUESTIONS

1. Explain, in your own words, the meaning of the term "structural interdependence." What factors might contribute to greater structural interdependence between two nations?

2. Based on the discussion in this chapter, would you conclude that the G5, G7, and G10 are primarily cooperative arrangements or coalitions of nations that coordinate their policies? Support your answer.

3. Economists sometimes like to say that international policy coordination is a means of internalizing international policy externalities. Explain in your own words what this means.

4. Although the United Kingdom technically is a member of the European Monetary System, it has been hesitant to commit to the exchange rate intervention rules adopted by the other EMS member nations. Can you provide possible rationales for why the United Kingdom might prefer not to fix its exchange rate relative to other nations in the European Community?

5. Explain why most nations of Europe might agree to fix their exchange rates but still might continue to use their own separate currencies. Support your answer with examples.

6. Explain why some regions of the world might be optimal currency areas while others might not. Use concrete, real-world examples to assist in your explanation.

SELECTED REFERENCES

Bryant, Ralph, *Money and Monetary Policy in Interdependent Nations* (Washington, D.C.: The Brookings Institution, 1980).

De Cecco, Marcello, and Alberto Giovannini (eds.), *A European Central Bank?* (Cambridge: Cambridge University Press, 1989).

Dixon, Rob, *Banking in Europe: The Single Market* (London: Routledge, 1991).

Folkerts-Landau, David, "The Case for International Coordination of Financial Policy," in *International Policy Coordination and Exchange Rate Fluctuations,* William H. Branson, Jacob A. Frenkel, and Morris Goldstein, eds. (Chicago: University of Chicago Press, 1990).

Frankel, Allen B., and John D. Montgomery, "Financial Structure: An International Perspective," *Brookings Papers on Economic Activity* (1, 1991), pp. 257–297.

Frenkel, Jacob A., Morris Goldstein, and Paul R. Masson, "The Rationale for, and Effects of, International Economic Policy Coordination," in *International Policy Coordination and Exchange Rate Fluctuations,* William H. Branson, Jacob A. Frenkel, and Morris Goldstein, eds. (Chicago: University of Chicago Press, 1990).

Giavazzi, Francesco, and Alberto Giovannini, *Limiting Exchange Rate Flexibility: The European Monetary System* (Cambridge, Mass.: MIT Press, 1989).

Giovannini, Alberto, and Colin Mayer (eds.), *European Financial Integration* (Cambridge: Cambridge University Press, 1991).

Goodhart, Charles A. E., "International Considerations in the Formulation of Monetary Policy," in *International Financial Integration and U.S. Monetary Policy* (New York: Federal Reserve Bank of New York, 1990), pp. 119–162.

Hayek, F. A., *Denationalization of Money* (London: Institute of Economic Affairs, 1976).

Humpage, Owen F., "A Hitchhiker's Guide to International Macroeconomic Policy Coordination," Federal Reserve Bank of Cleveland *Economic Review* (1990, Quarter 1), pp. 2–14.

Kahn, George A., "International Policy Coordination in an Interdependent World," Federal Reserve Bank of Kansas City *Economic Review,* 72 (3, March 1987), pp. 14–32.

McKinnon, Ronald I., *An International Standard for Monetary Stabilization* (Washington, D.C.: Institute for International Economics, 1984).

Mundell, Robert, "A Theory of Optimal Currency Areas," *American Economic Review,* 51 (4, September 1961), pp. 657–665.

Munn, Glenn G., F. L. Garcia, and Charles J. Welfel, *Encyclopedia of Banking and Finance,* 9th ed. (Rolling Meadows, Ill.: Bankers Publishing Company, 1991).

Niehans, Jurg, *International Monetary Economics* (Baltimore: Johns Hopkins University Press, 1984).

Rogoff, Kenneth, "Can International Monetary Policy Cooperation Be Counterproductive?" *Journal of International Economics,* 18 (3/4, May 1985), pp. 199–217.

Swann, Dennis, *The Economics of the Common Market* (London: Penguin Books, 1988).

GLOSSARY

Accounting risk: Risk of change in measured net worth arising from a difference in holdings of foreign currency assets and foreign currency liabilities.

Adaptive expectations: Expectations that are based only on information from the past up to the present.

Adjustable-rate mortgages (ARMs): Mortgages that permit the lender to vary the interest rate during the period of the loan.

Administered pricing hypothesis: The idea that firms with some measure of monopoly power will set prices in a discretionary way and hold them constant over relatively lengthy periods of time.

Advance: A promissory note signed by an official of a depository institution; the depository institution uses U.S. government securities and other assets that qualify as collateral to borrow from the Fed.

Adverse selection problem: A situation that may arise in a voluntary insurance program, in which only the worst risks choose to participate in an effort to gain from the program.

Affiliated-institution risk: The risk a depository institution incurs when it issues debt backed partly by the value of the capital of an affiliated institution, such as a bank holding company, thereby permitting the depository institution to grow without expanding its own capital.

Aggregate autonomous expenditures: Aggregate desired expenditures, including autonomous consumption and autonomous investment, that are independent of the level of national income.

Aggregate demand schedule (y^d): Combinations of various price levels and levels of output for which individuals are satisfied with their consumption of output and their holdings of money. In the traditional Keynesian model, a locus of combinations of real income and price levels that maintain *IS-LM* equilibrium.

Aggregate expenditures schedule: A schedule that represents total desired expenditures by all the relevant sectors of the economy at each and every level of real national income during some period of time.

Aggregate supply schedule (y^s): The relationship between various price levels and levels of national output that workers and firms will produce voluntarily.

Allocative efficiency: A situation in which the price that members of society pay to purchase a good or service is just equal to the marginal cost of producing the last unit of that good or service; in banking, the efficiency gained when the prices of bank services are set at the additional cost incurred in providing the last unit of service the bank produces.

Almost contemporaneous reserve accounting (ACRA): The present required reserve accounting system, in which banks calculate average deposits over a two-week period and then hold required reserves based on those average deposits over an overlapping two-week period.

Announcement effect: The effect on economic activity of changes in, say, the discount rate that results when individuals view the changes as a sign of a change in monetary policy.

Anticipated income theory: The theory that banks can solve their liquidity problem by making long-term loans if borrowers repay the loans in a series of continuous installments.

Appreciate: Increase in value.

Arbitrage: The act of purchasing an asset at a given price in one market and then selling it or its equivalent at a higher price in another market.

Asset: Title to receipt of a payment at some future date.

Asset approach: An approach to measuring bank output that views loans and other interest-bearing assets as the appropriate measure of output.

Asset-backed securities: Securities that represent shares of the market value of a pooled grouping of assets.

Asset growth: The growth or decline of a depository institution's assets over time.

Asset securitization: A process by which depository institution managers indirectly sell individually illiquid depository institution assets by segregating them into *pools,* or groupings, that the depository institution managers use to collateralize the securities they sell in financial markets.

ATS accounts: Automatic-transfer-system accounts; a combination of interest-bearing savings accounts and non-interest-bearing checking accounts, in which funds are automatically transferred from savings accounts to checking accounts when the latter are overdrawn.

Automated clearing houses: Electronic processing intermediaries that transmit payments between senders of funds and ultimate receivers, typically within one or two days after they are initiated by a payor to a payee.

Automated teller machine (ATM) networks: Payments systems that bank depositors typically use to make cash withdrawals from their accounts.

Automated teller machine bill payment: Transfers of funds from an individual's account at a depository institution to another individual or firm, initiated at an automated teller machine, which is commonly known as a ''bank machine.''

Autonomous consumption: Household consumption spending that is independent of the level of national income.

Autonomous expenditures multiplier: A measure of the magnitude of the multiplier effect on equilibrium real income caused by a change in aggregate autonomous expenditures; in the simple traditional model, $1/(1 - MPC) = 1/MPS$.

Autonomous investment: Desired investment that is independent of the level of national income.

Average propensity to consume (APC): Total household consumption divided by total disposable income; the portion of disposable income devoted to consumption spending.

Average propensity to save (APS): Total household saving divided by total disposable income; the portion of disposable income devoted to saving.

Balance of payments: A record of all the transactions between the households, firms, and government of one country and the rest of the world.

Balance-of-payments disequilibrium: A circumstance in which a nation cannot continue its current international transactions indefinitely; a surplus or a deficit in a nation's balance of payments that cannot continue.

Balance-of-payments equilibrium: A circumstance in which a nation can continue its current international transactions indefinitely.

Balance-sheet constraint: Given that all bank assets are loans and all bank liabilities are deposits, then if assets must equal liabilities, the value of loans by a bank must equal the value of deposits at the bank.

Balanced budget: Budget that results when government purchases of goods and services (g) are equal to taxes net of public transfer payments (t); $g = t$.

Bank for International Settlements (BIS): A bank created in 1930 to assist in the settlement of financial claims among the nation-states of Europe. It functions now as an agent or trustee for international loan agreements and manages portions of the reserve accounts of some central banks, which it places in world financial markets.

Bank Insurance Fund (BIF): The FDIC's deposit insurance fund for commercial banks.

Bank note: A piece of paper that represents a liability on the part of the issuing bank to the holder—and not to a specific payee.

Banker's acceptance: A loan that is usually used by a firm to finance shipments or storage of goods and that may be sold by the original lending bank to other banks.

Banking Act of 1935: Act that amended the Federal Reserve Act. Among other things, it removed the secretary of the Treasury and the comptroller of the currency from the Board, it lengthened the terms of the Board governors to 14 years, it permitted the Board of Governors to vary reserve requirements within ranges set by Congress, and it gave the Board of Governors final say concerning Federal Reserve bank discount rates.

Barter: The trading of a good or service for another without the use of money.

Base drift: A tendency for actual and targeted levels of monetary aggregates to shift over time.

Basle Agreement: A 1988 agreement that established risk-based capital adequacy standards for commercial banks in the United States, Western Europe, and Japan.

Beggar-thy-neighbor policies: Policies under which policy makers may intentionally seek to enhance the economic welfare of their own nation's citizens at the expense of the well-being of residents of other countries.

Bimetallism: A monetary system in which both gold and silver back the nation's money supply.

Board of Governors of the Federal Reserve System: The new name given to the Federal Reserve Board, in accordance with the Banking Act of 1935; Board governors are appointed by the President and confirmed by the Senate.

Bond: Evidence that a corporation has received a loan and has promised to pay the lender a specific amount of money at specific future dates.

Book-entry security transactions: Purchases and sales of government securities such as Treasury bills and bonds that are made through the use of the Fedwire network.

Borrowed reserves: Reserves borrowed by depository institutions from the Fed through the discount window.

Borrowed reserves targeting: A monetary policy operating procedure used by the Fed from October 1982 until 1989, in which the New York Fed's Trading Desk buys and sells securities in quantities sufficient to attain an equilibrium federal funds rate that, in turn, induces banks to borrow a target level of reserves from the Fed's discount window.

Branch banking: A system that allows banks to operate at more than one location.

Brokered deposits: Bundles of funds held by several individuals that are packaged by brokers for sale to banks and S&Ls as deposits.

Budget deficit: The condition that exists when government spending exceeds net taxes.

Budget surplus: The condition that exists when government spending is less than net tax revenues.

Cambridge equation: An equation developed by Alfred Marshall and other economists at Cambridge University, England, which indicates that individuals desire to hold money for planned transactions in proportion to the nominal value of income.

CAMEL rating: A system of numerical ratings that regulators use to assess the quality of a depository institution's *c*apital, *a*ssets, *m*anagement, *e*arnings, and *l*iquidity.

Capital account: A record of all transactions in assets between the domestic country and the rest of the world.

Capital account balance: The amount of a country's sales of assets such as stocks, bonds, and real estate to foreigners relative to the value of that country's purchases of such assets from abroad.

Capital account deficit: A situation in which the value of a country's sales of such assets as stocks, bonds, and land to foreigners is less than the value of that country's purchase of such assets from the rest of the world; a net lending situation.

Capital account surplus: A situation in which the value of a country's sales of such assets as stocks, bonds, and land to foreigners exceeds the value of that country's purchase of such assets from the rest of the world; a net borrowing situation.

Capital controls: Legal restrictions on holdings of foreign assets or liabilities by domestic residents or on holdings of domestic assets or liabilities by foreign residents.

Capital good: A good that may be used in the present to produce other goods or services for future consumption.

Capital market: A market in which securities with a maturity of one year or more (long term) are exchanged.

Capital requirements: Legal limitations on the amount of assets that depository institutions may hold in relation to their capital.

Capture theory: A theory of regulation that proposes that those who are regulated—and *not* society as a whole—benefit from the regulations; the regulators are "captured" by the regulated businesses.

Cash asset: An asset that functions as a medium of exchange.

Cash items in the process of collection: Checks or other types of cash drafts that are deposited with a bank for immediate credit but that are subject to cancellation of credit if they are not subsequently honored by the issuer.

Checkable account: A bank deposit that can be exchanged immediately for the goods and services that an individual wishes to buy.

Churning: The process of engaging in a large number of offsetting open-market operations that change the total level of reserves by relatively small amounts.

Circular flow diagram: A conceptualization of the basic flows of income and spending in the economy during a given period of time.

Clearing-house association: A group of depository institutions that agree to set up a central location—a clearing house—for clearing payments made on accounts held by their depositors.

Clearing-house certificates: Titles to the specie deposits of clearing-house associations' member banks that these banks exchanged to redeem bank notes in the nineteenth century.

Clearing House Interbank Payment System (CHIPS): A large-dollar electronic payments network that is privately owned and operated by the New York Clearing House Association.

Clearing-house loan certificates: Titles to specie deposits that banks loaned to other banks that actually did not have specie on deposit; these certificates joined specie as part of the monetary base for the banking system in the latter half of the nineteenth century.

Closed economy: An economy in which there are no imports or exports. In an economic model, this assumption allows the study of essential features of the economy without having to account for complicating (though more realistic) factors.

Collateralized mortgage obligations (CMOs): Structured debt financing secured by an asset such as car loans, commercial mortgages, credit card debt, and lease receivables.

Commercial and industrial (C&I) loans: Bank loans to businesses.

Commercial bank: A depository institution that is relatively unrestricted in its ability to make commercial loans and that is legally permitted to issue checking accounts.

Commercial loan theory, or **real bills doctrine:** The theory that banks can provide needed liquidity by making only short-term, self-liquidating loans secured by goods in the process of production or goods in transit.

Commercial paper: Unsecured short-term promissory notes issued by banks, corporations, and finance companies.

Commodity monies: Physical commodities such as wool, corn, or livestock that have equivalent monetary and nonmonetary values.

Commodity standard: The use of standardized tokens as money whose value is fully or partially backed by the value of a physical commodity such as gold or silver.

Common stock: A certificate of part ownership in a corporation that entitles the owner to certain voting privileges and to a share in profits.

Compensating balance: Funds that a borrower agrees to maintain in a checking account (earning no interest) as a condition for obtaining a loan; a way to charge a rate of interest higher than the apparent rate.

Composite unit of account: A weighted basket of the currencies of several nations, such as the European Currency Unit (ECU).

Confirmed line of credit: An informal type of bank loan commitment in which not all terms of the loan are fully worked out and in which either party has significant latitude to cancel the agreement before a loan actually is extended.

Conservative central banker: A person, appointed to manage a central bank, who dislikes inflation more than an average citizen in society and who thereby is less willing to induce discretionary increases in the quantity of money in an effort to cause unexpected inflation.

Consol: A perpetuity, or nonmaturing, bond, issued (usually) by the British government, that pays coupon interest but is not redeemable.

Consumer loans: Bank loans to individuals.

Consumer surplus: The amount by which the interest an individual would have been willing to pay for a loan exceeds the market interest that the individual actually has to pay.

Consumption opportunities set: All possible consumption possibilities an individual faces over a given time interval.

Contemporaneous reserve accounting (CRA) system: A method of calculating a depository institution's required reserves in any week based on the institution's daily average of net deposits for the current week.

Controllable liabilities: Liabilities whose quantities a bank can determine in the near term.

Conversion-of-funds approach: An approach to bank management that treats each source of funds individually and matches each source of funds with an asset of similar maturity.

Convertible bonds: Bonds that firms issue that may be converted to shares of stock ownership at a specified price after a specified period of time.

Coordination failures: Spillover effects between workers and firms that arise from movements in macroeconomic variables and that make it difficult for these individual economic agents to plan and implement their production and pricing decisions.

Core banking: A deposit insurance system that requires a bank to hold a "core" of very safe assets, such as cash and Treasury bills, from which the bank could reimburse insured depositors if it failed.

Core capital: Capital composed of the bank's tangible equity; called Tier One capital.

Correspondent balances: Bank deposits held with other banks, called correspondents.

Cost-push theory of stagflation: Simultaneous rising short-run inflation and unemployment rates, stemming from reduced availability of or higher relative prices of factors of production.

Countercyclical fiscal policy: An approach that encourages the government to run budget deficits when there is a recession and to run budget surpluses when inflation occurs.

Countercyclical monetary policy: Monetary policy actions that offset movements in economic variables such as real income and thereby generally reduce real income variability.

Coupon yield equivalent: The yield on a T-bill when it is adjusted for a 365-day year, using the bond's market price instead of its face value.

Credibility of monetary policy: Believability of Fed commitments to follow particular monetary policy rules.

Credit: Provision of goods, services, or funds in exchange for a promise of repayment in the future.

Credit cards: Cards used to initiate automatic loans to a customer, enabling the customer to purchase a good or service from a firm without need for cash or check.

Credit risk: The risk that a debtor will not fully repay a loan to a creditor.

Credit union: A depository institution that accepts deposits from and makes loans to only a closed group of members.

Crowding-out effect: Condition that occurs when there is an increase in the government's deficit. A rise in the real interest rate, caused by an increase in the deficit, causes a fall in private spending. In the classical model, this fall is exactly equal to the increase in the deficit; in essence, government deficit spending ''crowds out'' an equal amount of private spending.

Currency: The value of coins and paper money.

Currency appreciation: A situation in which it now takes more foreign currency to purchase a unit of domestic currency.

Currency depreciation: A situation in which it now takes less foreign currency to purchase a unit of domestic currency.

Currency leakage: Withdrawal of currency from depository institutions by the nonbank public.

Current account: Account that tracks ongoing international trades and transfers of goods and services; also called the open account.

Current account balance: The value of a country's exports (including military receipts and income on investments abroad) and transfer payments (private and government) relative to the value of that country's imports of goods and services (including military payments) and transfer payments (private and government).

Current account deficit: A situation in which the value of a nation's exports of goods and services (and public and private transfers from the rest of the world) is less than the value of its imports of goods and services (and public and private transfers to the rest of the world).

Current account surplus: A situation in which the value of a nation's exports of goods and services (and public and private transfers from the rest of the world) exceeds the value of its imports of goods and services (and public and private transfers to the rest of the world).

Current yield: The annual coupon rate of interest divided by the current market price of a bond.

Custodian of the financial system: A central bank function under which the bank supervises a nation's payments system to ensure that the financial system operates smoothly.

Daylight overdrafts: Depository institutions' overdrawals of their Federal Reserve or CHIPS accounts for terms of a few minutes or a few hours.

Deadweight loss due to bank monopoly: A portion of consumer surplus that would have existed under competition but that is no longer ob-tained by consumers in a monopoly banking market and also is not redistributed to owners of banks.

Debasement: A reduction in the quantity of precious metal in a metal coin that the government issues as money.

Debt instrument: Direct debt obligations of the issuing individual or firm.

Defensive open-market operations: Fed purchases or sales of government securities in which it uses RPs and reverse RPs to maintain the current level of depository institution reserves.

Deficit spending: Spending financed by borrowing.

Deflation: A decline in the weighted average of all prices through time.

Delivery risk: The risk that a party in a funds transaction may fulfill its end of a credit agreement but that the other party completely fails to follow through on its obligation.

Demand deposits: Deposits placed in a depository institution, payable on demand and transferable by check.

Demand management: The use of monetary and fiscal policies to vary the level of aggregate desired expenditures in pursuit of socially desired levels of real income, employment, and prices.

Demand-pull theory of stagflation: Simultaneous rising short-run inflation and unemployment rates stemming from a long-run adjustment of the economy following a sustained increase in aggregate demand.

Deposit expansion multiplier: The number by which a change in reserves is multiplied to calculate the ultimate change in total deposits in the banking system.

Depository institution capital: Most narrowly defined as equity shares in a bank, but more broadly defined by bank regulators as composed of all items, including equity, that help shield insured deposits from losses in the event of a failure by a bank.

Depository institutions: Financial institutions that accept debt instruments called deposits for savers and lend those deposits out at interest.

Depreciate: Decrease in value.

Desired investment schedule: Combinations of real interest rates and corresponding levels of desired real investment spending.

Direct assistance: The term applied to the FDIC practice of making direct loans to a failed depository institution that it classifies as one that provides ''essential'' services to its community.

Direct deposit payoff: A situation in which the FDIC declares a depository institution insolvent, pays off its depositors, and sells the depository institution's assets.

Dirty float: Managed floating-exchange-rate system that occurs when governments intervene in a floating-exchange-rate system in order to keep their own currencies from appreciating or depreciating.

Discount rate: The rate of interest the Fed charges on its loans to depository institutions.

Discount window policy: The terms and conditions under which the Fed lends to depository institutions.

Discounted present value: The value today of funds to be received in the future.

Diseconomies of scale or **scale diseconomies:** Rises in the average cost as the scale size of a bank increases.

Divisia aggregate: A monetary aggregate that is constructed by converting a conventional monetary aggregate into a weighted average of its individual components; those components that mostly provide a

transactions service are weighted more heavily than those components that provide more of a store-of-value service.

Double coincidence of wants: A situation in which a person who has good A to trade and wants good B finds someone who has good B to trade and wants good A.

Dynamic open-market operations: Open-market operations in which the Fed intends for outright purchases and sales to change the level of depository institution reserves.

Economic costs: Both the *explicit costs,* including interest expenses and explicit real resource costs, that a bank must incur in its day-to-day operations and the *implicit opportunity costs* a bank incurs because its owners could be devoting factors of production to alternative uses.

Economic good: A scarce commodity.

Economic profits: Total revenues less economic costs.

Economies of scale or **scale economies:** Declines in the average cost as the scale size of a bank increases.

Economies of scope or **scope economies:** A situation in which a bank achieves cost savings by diversifying its product offerings and services.

Edge Act: Law that allows deposits to be accepted across state lines if they are used to finance the production of goods that are primarily to be exported.

Effective *LM* schedule: The horizontal *LM* schedule that effectively is produced when the Fed uses an interest rate target.

Efficiency loss due to bank monopoly: The nonattainment of allocative efficiency that arises from monopolistic banking, in which the last dollar of lending by banks does not reflect properly the true cost of producing that last dollar of loans;

implies that resources used for lending by banks are not allocated in the least costly way.

Efficiency wage theory: The hypothesis that the productivity of workers depends on the level of the real wage rate.

Efficient structure theory: The theory that proposes that banks that are more efficient gain a larger market share and are more profitable than other banks.

Electronic benefits transfer (EBT): A government-operated network that disburses cash payments to individuals who qualify for government benefits such as Aid to Families with Dependent Children or food stamps.

Equation of exchange: An accounting identity that states that the nominal value of all monetary transactions for final goods and services is equal to the nominal value of the output of goods and services purchased; discussed most fully by the American economist Irving Fisher.

Equity capital: Owners' share in a depository institution.

Equity instruments: Shares of ownership, such as stock, in a company.

Eurocurrency market: An asset market in which banks raise deposit funds and make loans denominated in currencies of various nations, but located *outside* the countries that issued those currencies.

Excess reserves: Reserves that a depository institution, or the whole banking system, holds above required reserves; total reserves minus required reserves.

Exchange rate: The price of foreign currency in terms of a unit of domestic currency.

Explicit contracts: Contractual arrangements in which the terms of relationships between workers and firms, especially concerning wage payments, are written and legally binding upon both parties.

Export: Sell goods and services to other countries.

Externality: The term for a situation in which the economic transactions between one set of individuals or firms affects the well-being of other individuals or firms that are not involved in those transactions.

Fed: The Federal Reserve System; the central banking system of the United States.

Federal Deposit Insurance Corporation (FDIC): A government agency that insures the deposits held in all federally insured depository institutions. Under the provisions of 1989 legislation, the FDIC maintains separate insurance funds for commercial banks and savings institutions.

Federal financial safety net: The various federal government safeguards against widespread financial failures and panics, including the Fed's custodial role in the financial system, the Fed's function as lender of last resort, and the federal deposit insurance system.

Federal funds: Loans of reserve deposits by one depository institution to another.

Federal funds market: A market in which very short term (usually overnight) funds are exchanged between financial institutions; the funds borrowed and lent are usually reserves on deposit with a Federal Reserve district bank.

Federal funds rate: The interest rate at which federal funds, or interbank loans of reserves, are traded.

Federal funds rate targeting: A monetary policy operating procedure under which the New York Fed's Trading Desk conducts sufficient open-market purchases and sales to keep the federal funds rate at or very near a target level that the FOMC judges to be consistent with achieving an intermediate monetary target;

used by the Fed throughout the 1970s until October 1979 and again since 1989.

Federal Home Loan Bank Board (FHLBB): A committee of three appointed by the President to regulate members of the Federal Home Loan Bank System. It also regulated the FSLIC and the Federal Home Loan Mortgage Corporation. This board was disbanded in 1989.

Federal Open Market Committee (FOMC): A major policy-making unit of the Federal Reserve System that directs its open-market operations.

Federal Reserve Act: Act passed in 1913 that established a central banking system. Control was to be divided between central authorities in Washington, D.C., and twelve regional banks. The federal government, business sector, and member banks were to share in control.

Federal Reserve Board: Seven-member board, created by the original Federal Reserve Act and composed of the secretary of the Treasury, the comptroller of the currency, and five other members; the five members were to represent separate geographical, commercial, and industrial interests.

Federal Reserve float: The difference between the Fed's cash items in process of collection and its deferred availability cash items.

Federal Savings and Loan Insurance Corporation (FSLIC): A government agency that insured deposits held in member savings and loan associations. It was eliminated in 1989.

Fedwire: A large-dollar electronic payments network that is owned and operated by the Federal Reserve System.

Fiat money: Money whose face value is more than its market value; paper money not backed by anything but faith in its universal acceptance,

e.g., paper bills and transaction account balances.

Fiduciary monetary standard: A monetary standard under which the currency is not backed by anything except the public's confidence, or faith, that the currency can be exchanged for goods and services.

Field examinations: On-site visits to depository institutions by staff accountants and auditors of bank regulators.

Financial disintermediation: The process by which ultimate lenders remove funds from financial intermediaries and lend funds directly to ultimate borrowers.

Financial institutions: Institutions, such as commercial banks, savings and loan associations, insurance companies, and pension funds, that receive funds from households and lend them to businesses and others.

Financial Institutions Reform, Recovery, and Enforcement Act (FIRREA): 1989 Act with fourteen provisions that made major changes in regulations affecting depository institutions.

Financial instruments: Financial assets such as money and securities.

Financial intermediation: The process by which financial institutions accept savings from households and lend these savings to businesses.

Fiscal agent: A central bank's role as a depository for government funds raised from taxes and borrowings and as a coordinator of the mechanisms and procedures by which the government issues debt instruments when it borrows.

Fiscal policy: A shorthand term for intentional variations in expenditures and/or net taxes by governmental policy makers to stabilize national income.

Fixed exchange rate: A currency price that a central bank pegs at a particular value over a period of time.

Fixed-exchange-rate system: An international payments system in which exchange rates are pegged at some official level and only minor fluctuations are permitted.

Floating exchange rate: A currency price that is determined by the forces of supply and demand in the foreign exchange market, with little or no governmental interference.

Floating-exchange-rate system: An international payments system under which exchange rates are allowed to rise or to fall as supply and demand conditions dictate.

FOMC directive: Federal Open Market Committee instructions to account managers that include (1) a qualitative stabilization goal; (2) specific target ranges in terms of credit conditions, interest rates, and monetary aggregates; and (3) targets that take into account special calendar events.

Foreign exchange futures: Standardized forward exchange contracts used for a few widely traded currencies in highly developed market locations.

Foreign exchange options: Financial contracts giving the holder the right to buy or sell a fixed amount of a currency at a predetermined exchange rate.

Foreign exchange risk: The risk an individual or firm incurs by holding and trading foreign currencies; also called currency risk.

Foreign official deposits: Deposit accounts that foreign governments or official financial institutions hold with the Fed, usually as checking accounts that they use to make dollar-denominated payments in the United States.

Forty-five-degree line: A schedule of points for which an amount measured on the horizontal axis is equal to the corresponding amount measured on the vertical axis; in the traditional Keynesian model, a schedule of combinations of aggregate desired expenditures and real national income for which the economy is in equilibrium.

Forward contract: A financial contract in which people agree to exchange a specific commodity for a specified price on some specific future date.

Forward discount: The amount by which the current spot exchange rate for a currency exceeds the current forward exchange rate.

Forward exchange markets: Markets for currency trades in which deliveries of currencies exchanged occur at designated future times following agreements on terms of transactions.

Forward exchange rate: The current price of a currency to be delivered at a future time.

Forward premium: The amount by which the current forward exchange rate for a currency exceeds the current spot exchange rate.

Fractional reserve banking: A system in which depository institutions hold reserves equal to less than 100 percent of total deposits.

Free-banking laws: Laws during the 1800s that facilitated the formation of banks; businesses could obtain banking charters by complying with a general incorporation law; an act of government legislation was not necessary to create a bank.

Free reserves: Excess reserves minus borrowed reserves.

Free silver: A term in the late nineteenth century that referred broadly to a proposal to permit unlimited coinage of silver as dictated by the monetary needs of the economy.

Full-bodied money: Money whose face value is equal to its market value, such as pure gold or silver coins.

Full-capacity output level: The amount of goods and services that the economy could employ if all resources were employed to their utmost.

Future: A forward contract executed in a formal commodities exchange market.

Futures price: The price specified in a futures contract.

General equilibrium analysis: Analysis of the effects on equilibrium in the loan or deposit market caused by changes in conditions in one of the markets that takes into account the interdependence of that market with the other.

General-obligation bonds: Municipal bonds that are secured by the taxing power of the issuing municipality.

Generally accepted accounting principles (GAAP): A network of concepts, principles, and procedures developed by the accounting profession to develop and report financial information.

Geographic market: The land area that includes nearly all the buyers and sellers of a good or service.

Glass-Steagall Act: Also known as the Banking Act of 1933. The act created the FDIC, prohibited deposit-taking banks from underwriting "ineligible" securities, prohibited commercial banks from paying interest on checking accounts, and authorized the Federal Reserve to regulate interest rates on time and savings deposits.

Gold bullion: In a gold standard, the amount of gold used as money.

Gold certificates: Titles to stocks of gold issued by the United States Treasury to the Federal Reserve System and held by the Fed as an asset.

Gold reserve ratio: In a gold standard, the ratio of gold bullion to the total quantity of money including bullion and other media of exchange such as currency notes.

Goodwill: The accounting value of a firm's "going concern" or "franchise" value.

Greenbacks: A fiduciary, nonredeemable paper money issued by the United States (the Union) during the Civil War.

Gross domestic product (GDP): The value of goods and services actually produced using factors of production owned by citizens of the country in which production takes place.

Group of Five (G5): A set of nations—France, Germany, Japan, the United Kingdom, and the United States—that periodically cooperates in economic policy making.

Group of Seven (G7): The G5 nations plus Canada and Italy.

Group of Ten (G10): The G7 nations plus Belgium, the Netherlands, and Sweden.

Hedging instrument: A financial instrument that permits an individual or firm to ensure against asset price fluctuations.

Implementation (or response) lag: The interval between the recognition of a need for a countercyclical policy action and actual implementation of the policy action.

Implicit contracts: Unwritten agreements between workers and firms concerning terms like wage payments that may or may not be legally binding.

Import: Purchase goods and services from other countries.

Import quotas: Restrictions on the quantity of imports.

Income-induced consumption: The amount of household consumption spending induced by real income that households receive.

Income price deflator: A measure of the level of prices of goods and services in terms of prices in a base year; by definition, P is equal to Y/y, where Y is the current output valued in current prices and y is real output produced.

Indifference curve: A schedule of combinations of consumption alternatives that yield the same level of utility.

Indirect payoff: A situation in which the FDIC arranges for another depository institution to assume only the insured deposits of a failed institution and makes a direct payment for the estimated recoverable portion of the claims of the failed institution's uninsured depositors.

Inflation: A sustained rise in the weighted average of all prices over time.

Inflation bias: A tendency for the economy to experience continuing inflation as a result of discretionary monetary policy that takes place because of the time inconsistency problem of monetary policy.

Inflationary gap: The amount by which aggregate desired expenditures exceed real output at the full-employment level of real national income.

Input-output table: A tabulation of all elements that figure into the production and pricing decisions of all workers and firms in the economy.

Inside money: Money held in the form of bank deposits.

Insider-outsider theory: The idea that "insider" employees, by virtue of the costs involved in replacing them, are able to keep potential "outsiders" from being hired at a lower real wage rate than the insiders earn.

Instruments: Policy tools used by the Fed, such as open-market operations.

Interest: A payment for obtaining credit.

Interest-elastic demand for money: Demand for money that is relatively sensitive to changes in the interest rate.

Interest-elastic desired investment: Desired investment that is relatively sensitive to changes in the interest rate.

Interest elasticity of desired investment: A measure of the relative responsiveness of desired investment spending to changes in the interest rate.

Interest elasticity of money demand: A measure of the relative responsiveness of desired holdings of money balances to changes in the interest rate.

Interest expenses: Costs incurred by a bank through payment of interest in exchange for funds, obtained by issuing deposits, to use in its lending activities.

Interest-inelastic demand for money: Demand for money that is relatively insensitive to changes in the interest rate.

Interest-inelastic desired investment: Desired investment that is relatively insensitive to changes in the interest rate.

Interest rate: The percentage rate of return received from lending or saving funds.

Interest Rate Adjustment Act of 1966: Act that placed interest rate ceilings on thrift institutions.

Intermediate target: An economic variable whose value the Fed chooses to control only because it feels that doing so is consistent with its ultimate objectives.

International Banking Facilities (IBFs): Legal mechanisms under which banks maintain separate accounting ledgers for recording international loans and deposits.

International integration: The development of strong ties, linkages, and interactions among individuals, firms, markets, and governments of different nations.

International Lending Supervision Act: 1983 act that authorized the Federal Reserve, the FDIC, and the Office of the Comptroller of the Currency to set and enforce capital requirements.

International Monetary Fund (IMF): An international agency, created by the Bretton Woods Agreement, that helps nations that have temporary liquidity problems.

International policy cooperation: The sharing of information about national policy objectives, procedures, and data.

International policy coordination: Actions taken by the governments of nations for the mutual benefit of those nations.

International policy externalities: Policy spillover effects from one nation to another that occur when the nations are structurally interdependent and nations do not consider the implications of their own policies for the well-being of citizens in other nations.

Investment: An addition to the amount of capital goods.

IS schedule: A locus of all combinations of real income levels and interest rates that are consistent with the attainment of equilibrium real income.

IS-LM equilibrium: The single point where the *IS* and *LM* schedules intersect; at this point, the economy attains equilibrium real income and simultaneously achieves money market equilibrium.

Jumbo certificate of deposit (jumbo CD): A large (face value over $100,000) time deposit, usually issued to businesses, that matures at a specific date; the interest rate depends on market conditions at the time of issuance.

Keynesian monetary policy transmission mechanism: Essential Keynesian theory of how changes in the quantity of money are transmitted to other variables in the economy. A constant-price increase in the nominal money supply reduces the nominal interest rate via a liquidity effect, and this fall in the interest rate stimulates a rise in desired investment spending and aggregate desired expenditures that causes equilibrium real income to increase.

L: M3 plus other liquid assets (such as Treasury bills and U.S. savings bonds).

Lagged reserve accounting (LRA) system: A method of calculating a depository institution's current required reserves at the Fed based on the institution's average daily net deposits for the week that was two weeks earlier.

Large-denomination time deposits: Savings deposits with set maturities that have denominations greater than or equal to $100,000.

Large-dollar payments systems: Payments networks that specialize in processing payments that typically have very large dollar values.

Law of diminishing marginal returns: The law that states that each successive addition of a unit of a factor of production, such as labor, eventually produces a smaller gain in output produced.

Law of diminishing marginal utility: As more of a good or service is consumed, utility rises, and so marginal utility, the gain in utility, is positive; nevertheless, as more is consumed, the gain in utility for each extra unit declines, so that marginal utility diminishes.

Lender of last resort: An institution that stands ready to make a loan to any and all illiquid but solvent depository institutions in the face of an impending bank run or analogous crisis.

Liability: An obligation to make a payment at some future date.

Liquidity: The ease with which an individual can, at an unknown future time, sell an asset, at a known nominal dollar price, on short notice, and with minimum costs.

Liquidity approach: An approach to measuring money that stresses the role of money as a temporary store of value.

Liquidity effect: A reduction in the nominal rate of interest that results from an increase in the nominal quantity of money supplied, holding the level of prices unchanged.

Liquidity risk: The risk that arises from the possibility that a payment, even if made in full, may not be made when due.

Liquidity trap: The very shallow ranges of the money demand and *LM* schedules along which virtually everyone agrees that market interest rates are likely to rise in the future and that money is an asset far superior to bonds; in a liquidity trap, the demand for real money balances is nearly completely interest-elastic.

LM schedule: A locus of all combinations of real income levels and interest rates that are consistent with the attainment of equilibrium in the market for money.

Loan commitment: A bank promise to make a loan, up to some specified maximum limit, within a given period at predetermined interest rate terms.

Loan loss provision: Additions to loan loss reserves by depository institutions within a given interval, such as a year.

Loan loss reserve: Cash assets that depository institutions hold as contingencies against anticipated loan defaults by borrowers.

Loan participations: Lending arrangements in which banks own shares in large loans to businesses and may in many circumstances sell these loan shares to other banks.

Loanable funds: The term that classical economists use to refer to the amount of real income that households save, representing titles to real output.

London Interbank Offer Rate (LIBOR): The interest rate at which six large London banks would lend funds to or deposit funds with each other each morning when market trading opens.

Long position: An agreement to buy a specific quantity of some commodity in the future at a stated price.

Long-run average total cost (LRATC) schedule: A schedule that shows the average costs incurred by a bank in producing various output levels if all factors of production are permitted to vary.

M1: The value of currency and transactions deposits owned by the nonbank public.

M2: M1 plus (1) savings and small-denomination time deposits at all depository institutions, (2) overnight repurchase agreements at commercial banks, (3) overnight Eurodollars held by U.S. residents (other than banks) at Caribbean branches of member banks, and (4) balances of money market mutual funds.

M3: M2 plus (1) large-denomination (over $100,000) time deposits at all depository institutions, (2) term repurchase agreements at commercial banks and savings and loan associations, and (3) institution-only money market mutual fund balances.

Macroeconomic variables: Quantities, such as national income or the price level, that are economywide measures of economic performance.

Management consignment program: FHLBB program that re-

moved incumbent managers of insolvent thrifts and replaced them with a consigned group of managers from other thrifts in the same region.

Margin requirement: The percentage of the purchase price of stocks or bonds that a customer must pay when funds are borrowed to finance the purchase.

Marginal cost: The increase in total production cost resulting from a 1-unit increase in production of a good or service.

Marginal product of capital: The gain in production of goods and services that may be consumed in the future yielded by the use of an additional unit of a capital good in the present.

Marginal product of labor: The change in total output resulting from a 1-unit increase in the quantity of labor employed in production.

Marginal propensity to consume (MPC): The additional consumption caused by an increase in disposable income; a change in consumption spending divided by a corresponding change in disposable income; the slope of the consumption function as graphed against disposable income.

Marginal propensity to save (MPS): The additional saving caused by an increase in disposable income; a change in saving divided by a corresponding change in disposable income; the slope of the saving function as graphed against disposable income.

Marginal revenue: The gain in total revenues resulting from a 1-unit increase in production of a good or service.

Market: A group of buyers and sellers whose actions significantly influence the production, quality, and price of specific goods or services.

Market concentration: The extent to which the few largest banks dom-

inate the shares of loans or deposits in banking markets.

Market failure: A situation that occurs when a private market benefits only those who participate in the market but fails to meet the needs of other members of society whose welfare is affected by that market.

Market for bank reserves: The nationwide market in which the Federal Reserve System supplies reserves through its open-market operations and via the discount window; depository institutions demand these reserves for use in meeting reserve requirements and in holding prudential, excess reserves.

Market performance: The degree to which both allocative and technical efficiencies are attained in banking markets.

Market rate of interest: The actual interest rate at which parties agree to exchange a loan for a promise to repay the loan in the future.

Market risk: The risk that a creditor may not receive full payment on a debt because the borrower defaults on the original transaction, requiring both parties to strike a new agreement.

Maturity: The termination or due date of a debt.

Medium of exchange: Whatever is accepted as payment for purchases of goods or services; a necessary property of money.

Minimum efficient scale: The bank size that yields the minimum long-run average total cost for the bank.

Monetarists: Economists who believe that monetary policy actions have pronounced effects on the economy—but that fiscal policy actions do not.

Monetary base: A "base" amount of money that serves as the foundation for a nation's monetary system. Under a gold standard, this is the amount of gold bullion. At present this is government-supplied money consisting of currency held by the public and in vaults of depository institutions, plus reserves of depository institutions. Also called the reserve base, or high-powered money.

Monetary policy discretion: Monetary policy actions that the Fed makes in response to economic events as they occur, rather than in ways it might previously have planned in the absence of those events.

Monetary policy rule: A policy strategy to which a central bank commits, meaning that it will follow that strategy no matter what happens to other economic variables.

Money: A medium that is universally acceptable in an economy both by sellers of goods and services as payment for the goods and services and by creditors as payment for debts.

Money center banks: Very large banks that engage in national and international lending and deposit businesses.

Money illusion: The state that exists when economic agents change their behavior in response to changes in nominal values, even if there are no changes in real (price-level-adjusted) values.

Money market: A market in which securities with a maturity of less than one year (short term) are exchanged.

Money market mutual funds: Funds from the public that an investment company accepts and uses to acquire credit instruments. The funds can usually be withdrawn by checks written on the fund.

Money multiplier: A number by which a reserve measure, such as the monetary base, is multiplied to obtain the total quantity of money in the economy.

Money orders: Titles to currency

that sometimes are used in exchange for goods and services.

Moral hazard problem: A problem that results from the government insuring bank deposits. The government puts its faith in the ''moral characters'' of the managers of the depository institutions it insures, thereby exposing itself to a hazard that the depository institution managers will undertake risky, or even fraudulent, actions.

Moral suasion: A monetary policy tool of the Fed in which it uses its power of persuasion to induce financial institutions to behave in the public interest.

Mortgage-backed securities: Mortgages that are collateralized by pools of real estate mortgages.

Multi-bank holding companies: Corporations that own and control two or more independently incorporated banks; also called group banking.

Multiplier effect: The ratio of a change in the equilibrium level of national income to an increase in autonomous aggregate expenditures. In the basic Keynesian model, when the aggregate expenditure schedule shifts vertically, the equilibrium level of national income changes by a multiple of the amount of the shift.

Multisector economies: Economies that are composed of sectors within which economic behavior is best represented by different economic theories, making no single theory the best single description of the economy as a whole.

National Banking Act: Act passed in 1864 that, among other things, prohibited branch banking, imposed required reserves, taxed state banks out of existence, and required national banks to deposit $100 of special 2 percent government bonds for every $90 of bank notes.

National Credit Union Adminis-

tration (NCUA): A federal agency that insures credit union deposits.

National income identity: An identity that states that real national income equals real household consumption plus real household saving plus real taxes plus real imports, or $y \equiv c + s + t + m$.

National product identity: An identity stating that real national product equals household consumption plus real realized investment plus government spending plus real export spending, or $y \equiv c + i_r + g + x$.

Natural level of employment: As predicted by the classical model, the level of employment toward which the economy tends when workers have perfect information about price level movements and, thus, about the real wage they earn and how it is changing over time. At the natural level of employment, the natural level of output is produced.

Natural level of output: Level of output that occurs when there is full information.

Natural monopoly: A situation in which the technology of producing a particular good or service implies economies of scale at any output level for a firm, so that the most technically efficient market structure is one large firm.

Natural rate of unemployment: An average amount of unemployment around the natural level of employment.

Near monies: Assets that are highly liquid but are not considered M1 money, such as U.S. Treasury bills and savings deposits in banks and in savings and loan associations; only slight capital gains or losses are possible on near monies.

Negative externality: A market transaction that, without compensating them, reduces the economic well-being of other individuals or firms not involved in the transaction.

Negative funds gap: The situation in which a bank's ratio of variable-rate assets to total assets is less than its ratio of variable-rate liabilities to total liabilities.

Net aggregate expenditures: Expenditures equal to autonomous consumption, net of the consumption-reducing effect of taxes, plus autonomous desired investment and autonomous government spending.

Net autonomous consumption: Autonomous consumption, net of the consumption-reducing effect of taxes.

Net loan losses: Net reductions in income incurred by depository institutions when borrowers default on their loans.

Net worth certificates: Certificates authorized by the Garn–St Germain Act of 1982 and issued by distressed thrifts to the FSLIC in exchange for promissory notes. The thrift may use promissory notes in computing net worth; therefore, the FSLIC intended for these certificates to help a thrift buy time to strengthen its financial base.

Neutrality of money: The idea that money is neutral if changes in its quantity affect only nominal values, and if real variables like employment, national output, and the composition of national output do not change when the quantity of money varies.

New Keynesian theorists: Economists who have developed economic models based on the idea that "demand creates its own supply" as a result of various possible coordination failures.

Nominal interest rate: The rate of exchange between a dollar today and a dollar at some future date.

Nominal yield: The annual coupon rate of interest divided by the face amount of a bond.

Nonbank public: Households and firms.

Nonborrowed base: The monetary base minus borrowed reserves.

Nonborrowed reserves: Total reserves minus borrowed reserves.

Nonborrowed reserves targeting: A monetary policy operating procedure under which the New York Fed's Trading Desk bought and sold securities in sufficient quantities to keep the level of nonborrowed reserves on or near a target growth path; adopted because of its automatic stabilizing properties in the face of money demand variability that cause the money stock to deviate from the Fed's target, this procedure was used from October 1979 until roughly October 1982.

Noncontrollable liabilities: Liabilities whose quantities primarily are controlled by bank customers instead of the bank.

Nonperforming loans: Loans that a depository anticipates will experience partial or complete default of interest and/or principal payments.

Note issuance: The creation of paper money by a government or a central or commercial bank.

NOW accounts: Negotiable order of withdrawal accounts; interest-bearing savings accounts on which checks can be written.

Observational equivalence problem: The difficulty that occurs when two theories have the same predictions about the economy, in testing whether one theory is better than the other.

Office of the Comptroller of the Currency: The office in the U.S. Treasury Department that supervises the regulation and examination of national banks.

Office of Thrift Supervision (OTS): A regulatory authority created in 1989; it is based in the De-partment of the Treasury and has primary responsibility for regulating savings and loan associations and savings banks.

Official settlements balance: The sum of the current account balance and the capital account balance, plus errors and omissions.

One-bank holding company: A business organization that owns one bank and is involved in other commercial activities.

Open-market operations: The purchase or sale of U.S. Treasury securities or federal agency securities by the Fed; a method of monetary control.

Operating procedure: The manner in which the Fed conducts monetary policy on a day-to-day basis.

Opportunity cost: The economic cost of any activity, measured by the highest-valued alternative activity; the cost of a forgone alternative.

Optimal currency area: A geographical region within which fixed exchange rates may be maintained without hindering international adjustments and, under some circumstances, in which it may be least costly to have a single, common currency.

Option pricing models: Financial models that can be used to assign dollar values to parties involved in financial transactions, such as the exchange of deposit insurance guarantees, that entail different contingencies for the interested parties.

Options: Financial contracts that grant the holder the right to buy and/or sell specified securities or goods in specific amounts and at specific prices for a specific period of time.

Outside money: Money in the form of currency and bank reserves; the monetary base.

Partial equilibrium analysis: An analysis of the effects on equilibrium in the loan or deposit market caused by changes in conditions in only that market, abstracting from the interdependence of that market with the other.

Passbook savings accounts: Savings accounts in which a ''passbook'' contains all records of account balances and activity; the accounts have no set maturities, and the passbook must be presented for withdrawals and deposits.

Payments system: The institutional structure through which households, firms, and financial institutions exchange funds.

Peg: Fix a rate, such as a nominal interest rate, at a certain level. When a rate is pegged, policy actions are implemented to keep that rate constant (pegged).

Penalty rates: Interest rates, such as the Fed's discount rate, that are set above market interest rates and that thereby penalize the borrowing institution.

Phillips curve: A curve that shows an inverse relationship between inflation and unemployment.

Pledged assets: Assets, usually in the form of Treasury securities or municipal bonds, that depository institutions must hold as collateral against deposits made by federal, state, and local governments.

Point-of-sale (POS) networks: Payments systems that permit consumers to pay for purchases through direct deductions from their deposit accounts at financial institutions.

Point-of-sale transfers: Transfers of funds made directly, using wire networks, from an individual's account to the firm from which a good or service is purchased at the location where the sale is made.

Policy coordination: The joint determination of policy actions by separate policy authorities, such as different governmental agencies within a country or between countries, in pursuit of common economic goals.

Policy indicator: An economic variable whose changes imply possible future movements in an ultimate objective of monetary policy.

Policy ineffectiveness proposition: The new classical conclusion that policy actions have no real effects in the short run if the policy actions were anticipated, and not in the long run even if the policy actions were unanticipated.

Policy time lags: Time intervals between the need for a countercyclical monetary policy action and the ultimate effects of that action on an economic variable.

Pool-of-funds approach: A portfolio management technique that emphasizes safety over short-term profitability; on the basis of a desired level of liquidity, funds are allocated first to primary reserves and then to secondary reserves, loan requests, and finally purchase of long-term securities.

Populism: A political movement of the late nineteenth century that became aligned with the free-silver movement.

Portfolio demand for money: Term for a simplified version of Keynes's model of the speculative demand for money. In the simplified model, individuals hold both money and bonds but adjust the composition of their wealth portfolios in light of their speculations about interest rate movements.

Portfolio deregulation: The process by which regulatory agencies permit financial institutions more discretion over the types of assets they can acquire.

Positive externality: A market transaction that increases the economic well-being of other individuals or firms not involved in the transaction without charging them.

Positive funds gap: The situation in which a bank's ratio of variable-rate assets to total assets exceeds its ratio of variable-rate liabilities to total liabilities.

Precautionary motive: Rationale for people to hold money as a contingency in case a need should arise to make unplanned expenditures.

Preferred stock: A share of ownership in a firm that entitles the holder to first claim on the assets of the firm but affords less control than a common-stock holder over the firm's direction and management.

Present value: The value of a future quantity from the perspective of the present.

Price inertia: A tendency for the level of prices to resist change with the passage of time.

Primary market: A market in which the purchases and sales of a newly issued security are made.

Primary service area: A geographical area that includes a certain percentage of the identifiable buyers and sellers of all banking services.

Prime rate: The interest rate charged by banks on short-term loans to the most creditworthy corporations.

Principal: The amount of a loan.

Procyclical monetary policy: Monetary policy actions that reinforce movements in economic variables such as real income and that thereby add to real income variability.

Producer surplus: The amount by which the interest that a lender receives for a loan exceeds the market interest that the lender would have been willing to accept for making the loan.

Production function: A relationship between possible quantities of factors of production and the amount of output of goods and services that firms can produce with current technology.

Production possibilities set: All possible production possibilities that an individual or firm faces over a given time interval.

Profitability risk: The risk that a firm's underlying profitability may be affected by its foreign currency transactions.

Protectionism: The use of national policies to restrict imports of goods or services to improve the prospects of domestic industries that produce those goods or services.

Prudent (or **prudential**) **reserves:** Reserves that depository institutions voluntarily hold above required reserves in order to remain liquid as a precaution in case of troubled times.

Public-choice theory: A theory of regulation that proposes that regulators set rules that permit firms to earn profits above perfectly competitive levels but below those they could earn if they could set their prices at purely monopolistic levels.

Public-interest theory: A theory of regulation that proposes that regulators choose policies that maximize the welfare of society as a whole.

Purchase and assumption: A situation in which the FDIC arranges for a failed depository institution to be merged with a healthy institution, which purchases most of the failed institution's assets and assumes responsibility for most of its outstanding liabilities.

Purchasing power of money: A measure of the amount of goods and services that a unit of money can be used to purchase.

Pure barter economy: An economy in which an individual who wishes to obtain goods and services must search for a second individual who is willing to provide those goods and services in exchange for goods and services the first individual is willing to provide.

Pure gold standard: A monetary standard in which only gold bullion is used as money, and so the nation's gold reserve ratio is equal to 1.

Quantity theory of money: The theory that people hold money for transactions purposes.

Rate of exchange: The amount of one good or service that must be given up to obtain another good or service.

Rate of return from saving: The ratio of a total return from saving to the initial amount saved.

Rational expectations hypothesis: The idea that individuals form expectations based on all available past and current information and on a basic understanding of how the economy works.

Real balance effect: An increase in the nominal rate of interest that results from an increase in the level of prices of goods and services, holding the nominal quantity of money supplied unchanged.

Real business cycle theorists: Economists who have developed economics based on the idea that "supply creates its own demand."

Real business cycle theory: An extension and modification of the theories of the new classical economists of the 1970s and 1980s, in which money is neutral and only real, supply-side factors matter in influencing labor employment and real output.

Real disposable income: A household's after-tax income.

Real estate loans: Bank loans for construction and purchases of buildings.

Real export spending: The real value of goods and services produced by domestic firms and exported to other countries.

Real household consumption: The real flow of spending by households on goods and services.

Real household saving: The amount of income that households save through financial markets.

Real imports: The flow of spending by households for the purchase of goods and services from other countries.

Real interest rate: The rate of exchange between real things (goods and services) today and real things at some future period; an interest rate that has been adjusted for expected changes in the price level.

Real money balances: The price-level-adjusted value of the nominal, current-dollar quantity of money, defined as the ratio of the nominal money stock to the price level; the real purchasing power of the nominal quantity of money.

Real national income: The total amount of price-level-adjusted factor payments (wages and salaries, interest and dividends, rents, and profits).

Real net taxes: The amount of real taxes paid to the government by households, net of any transfer payments (such as Social Security benefits) to households by the government.

Real realized investment: Actual real firm expenditures in the product markets.

Real resource expenses: Expenses that a bank must incur in its day-to-day operations in the forms of explicit payments of wages and salaries to employees and payments to owners of other factors of production and, in addition, in the form of implicit opportunity costs arising from the fact that the bank could be devoting its factors of production to alternative uses.

Recessionary gap: The amount by which equilibrium real income exceeds aggregate desired expenditures at the full-employment level of real income.

Recognition lag: The interval that passes between the need for a countercyclical policy action and the recognition of this need by a policy maker.

Rediscounting: The process of discounting by central banks to private banks that borrow reserves on the basis of collateral that already has been discounted once.

Redistribution effect due to bank monopoly: The transfer of some portion of the consumer surplus that would have arisen under competition to the owners of banks that arises in a monopolistic banking system.

Regional banks: Banks that primarily participate in loan and deposit markets across state lines in the regions around their headquarters locations.

Regulatory accounting principles (RAP): Accounting definitions applied to depository institutions that define "income" and "assets" more liberally than GAAP; that is, RAP includes some items in income and assets that generally accepted accounting practices do not.

Regulatory arbitrage: A process by which financial institutions seek to limit the effects of regulatory differences across nations by shifting funds from highly regulated nations to nations whose authorities impose weaker restrictions on banking and financial activities.

Regulatory risk: The risk that regulators may make decisions that, after the fact, turn out to have been poor ones.

Representative full-bodied money: Money that is of negligible value as a commodity but is "backed by" (can be converted into, at a fixed nominal price) a valuable commodity, such as gold or silver.

Repurchase agreement at a commercial bank (REPO or RP): An agreement made by a bank to sell Treasury or federal agency securities to its customers, coupled with an agreement to repurchase them at a price that includes accumulated interest.

Required reserve ratio: The percentage of total deposits that the Fed requires depository institutions to hold in the form of vault cash or in a reserve account with the Fed.

Required reserves: The value of reserves that a depository institution must hold in the form of vault cash or in a reserve account with the Fed; required reserves are equal to some percentage of total deposits.

Reserve deposits: Deposits that depository institutions hold at the Federal Reserve System.

Reserves: The portion of total deposits held by depository institutions that is not lent; instead these funds are held to meet day-to-day withdrawals or reserve requirements.

Resolution: The act of closing a failed thrift or otherwise disposing of its assets.

Resource transfer: A transfer of title to resources.

Resumption Act of 1875: Act that authorized a full resumption of the gold standard in 1879.

Return on assets: The ratio of a depository institution's net income relative to the depository institution's assets.

Return on equity: The ratio of a depository institution's net income relative to the depository institution's equity capital.

Revenue bonds: Municipal bonds that are secured by the earnings of the project financed by the bond sales.

Revolving credit commitment: A bank loan commitment in which the borrower may borrow and/or repay repeatedly, much like a credit card account.

Risk-adjusted assets: A measure of a bank's actual assets and its off-bal-

ance-sheet loan guarantees that accounts for regulators' perceptions of risk and that is used by regulators to compute a bank's capital requirements.

Risk premium: A differential between interest rates on different securities with the same maturity that arises from perceptions of lenders that the securities have differing risks of default.

Risk structure of interest rates: The relationship among yields for bonds that have the same term to maturity but have differing default risks, liquidity, and tax treatment.

Safety and soundness regulation: The regulatory task of auditing and otherwise supervising the activities of depository institutions to help prevent these institutions from becoming insolvent.

Saving: Forgone consumption.

Savings and loan association: An institution that traditionally has specialized in mortgage-related activities.

Savings Association Insurance Fund (SAIF): The FDIC's insurance funds for savings and loan associations and savings banks, established in 1989 to replace the FSLIC.

Savings bank: An institution that originally was intended to be primarily a savings institution for small savers; like savings and loan associations, these institutions have tended to specialize in mortgage financing.

Say's law: J. B. Say's dictum that supply creates its own demand.

Scale: A measure of the overall size a bank chooses when it may vary all factors of production.

Scope: The overall range of operations of a business, in terms of the different types of goods and services it produces.

Secondary market: A market in

which previously issued securities are bought and sold.

Secondary reserves: Highly liquid short-term assets that can be used to supplement reserves during times of liquidity strains.

Securities: Documents attesting to ownership or creditorship in a business organization or public body such as local, state, or federal government.

Securitization: The process of pooling similar loans and selling the loan package as a tradable security, an asset-backed obligation, or a form of CMO.

Seigniorage: The process whereby governments gain ''profit'' by placing a face value on a coin or other monetary token that exceeds its inherent market value.

Shiftability theory: The theory that banks can solve their liquidity problem by purchasing assets that are highly liquid.

Short position: An agreement to deliver a specific quantity of some commodity in the future at a stated price.

Short run: According to the monetarists, a period of time short enough that economic agents do not have complete information about aggregate prices and inflation, so that expected prices and inflation may differ from actual prices and inflation.

Simple-sum monetary aggregates: Measures of money that are constructed by directly summing together different components.

Small-denomination time deposits: Savings deposits with set maturities for which the amount of the deposit is less than $100,000.

Small menu costs: The costs firms incur when they make price changes, which include both the costs of changing prices in menus or catalogs and the costs of renegotiating agreements with customers.

Special drawing rights (SDRs): A reserve asset created by the IMF, which countries can use to settle international payments.

Special drawing rights certificates: Assets held by the Fed that are Treasury obligations to the Fed for its share of financing of special drawing rights; these, in turn, are a type of international currency (established in the 1970s).

Specie Circular Act of 1836: A law that required most federal land purchases to be paid for in gold.

Speculative demand for money: Keynes's theoretical motivation for an inverse relationship between the nominal interest rate and desired money holdings.

Spot exchange market: The market for transactions in currencies that take place immediately after traders reach agreement on the rate of exchange.

Spot exchange rate: The price of a currency to be delivered immediately.

Spot price: The price at which a commodity can be purchased right now; today's cash price.

Spread: The difference between the interest rate on a long-term security and the interest rate on a short-term security with otherwise similar characteristics.

Stagflation: The simultaneous existence of high rates of inflation and unemployment.

Standard of deferred payment: A property of an asset that makes it desirable for use as a means of settling debts maturing in the future; an essential property of money.

Statement savings accounts: Savings accounts in which the holder receives periodic written statements of balances and account activity; accounts have no set maturities, and withdrawals and deposits may be made by mail.

Sterilization: Actions by central banks to offset international currency flows with domestic open-market operations.

Store of value: The ability of an item to hold value over time; a necessary property of money.

Strategy: The approach one takes to accomplishing an objective, such as winning a game.

Structural interdependence: A situation in which the economic systems of two or more nations are interlinked, and so economic events and policy actions in one of the nations have effects on economic performance in the others.

Structure-conduct-performance (SCP) model: The theory that proposes that market structure (which includes the number and size distribution of firms) influences the conduct of banks in the market, and, in turn, bank conduct determines the performance of the market.

Subordinated debt: A bank liability issued with the provision that all other liability holders have priority in the event of failure of the institution, which often is issued in the form of subordinated debentures.

Subscription: An offering of new issues of U.S. Treasury notes or bonds at announced coupon rates.

Supplementary capital: Capital that includes a portion of the bank's loan loss reserves and subordinated debt; called Tier Two capital.

Swap: A foreign exchange transaction that combines elements of both spot and forward exchanges into a single trade.

Syndicated loan: A common type of loan in Eurocurrency markets, in which the terms of the loan are negotiated by a small group of banks that later sell shares of the loan to other banks that they recruit into the ''syndicate'' of banks participating in the loan agreement.

Systemic risk: The risk that some institutions in a payments system, because their transactions are interlinked with those of other institutions, may be unable to honor credit agreements as a result of failures in otherwise unrelated transactions between the other institutions; a form of negative externality in a payments system.

T-account: A simplified balance sheet that includes only the assets and liabilities (or their changes) under discussion.

Target zones: Bands within which central banks permit their nations' exchange rates to vary; the central banks intervene in foreign exchange markets to stabilize their exchange rates only if the exchange rates move outside the upper or lower limit of the target zone.

Tariffs: Taxes imposed on imports.

Technical efficiency: The production of a good or service at minimum long-run average cost. In banking, the efficiency gained when bank services are provided at the lowest possible cost in terms of the social resources that the banks expend in the process.

Technical inefficiency: The production of a good or service at more than the minimum long-run average total cost.

Term premium: A yield differential that securities investors and issuers demand for differing maturities.

Term structure of interest rates: The relationship on a specific date between short-term and long-term interest rates for credit instruments that have similar risks.

Thrift institution: At present, any depository institution that is not a commercial bank, including savings and loan associations, savings banks, and credit unions.

Time inconsistency problem: A monetary policy problem that can re-sult from the existence of wage contracts. Although a monetary rule that achieves zero inflation is consistent with the desires and strategies of both private agents and the Fed, it becomes inconsistent with those strategies if the Fed can change the money stock at a later time, after contract wages are set.

Total capital: The sum of core (Tier One) and supplementary (Tier Two) capital.

Total credit: The total amount of lending that all banks do.

Total reserves: The sum of a bank's required and excess reserves.

Trading Desk: The term that refers to the office in the New York Federal Reserve Bank that conducts securities trading for the Fed.

Trading-post economy: A system of organized barter in which individuals continue to trade goods and services for other goods and services.

Transaction costs: The explicit costs an individual incurs in making a trade for a good or service.

Transaction risk: The risk a party to a long-term currency credit contract incurs that the currency's exchange rate could change during the time of the credit agreement.

Transactions accounts: NOW accounts, ATS accounts, CUSD accounts, and demand deposits at mutual savings banks.

Transactions approach: An approach to measuring money that stresses the role of money as a medium of exchange.

Transactions motive: Rationale for people to hold money because they want to make planned purchases of goods and services.

Transmission lag: The interval that elapses between the implementation of an intended countercyclical policy and its ultimate effects on an economic variable.

Treasury bill: A short-term (15 days to 1 year) promissory note issued by the U.S. Treasury and secured by the ''full faith and credit of the United States.''

Treasury bill rate: The percentage discounted from the par value of a T-bill, calculated on a 360-day year.

Treasury bond: A long-term (10 years or more) promissory note issued by the U.S. Treasury and secured by the ''full faith and credit of the United States.''

Treasury note: A medium-term (1 to 10 years) promissory note issued by the U.S. Treasury and secured by the ''full faith and credit of the United States.''

Treasury Note Act of 1890: Also known as the Sherman Silver Purchase Act. The act required the Treasury to purchase silver annually and to issue U.S. notes backed by the silver.

Ultimate objectives: The end economic goals that the Fed seeks to achieve through its monetary policies.

Underground, or **subterranean, economy:** That economy that consists of illegal activities and otherwise legal activities that are unreported to the Internal Revenue Service.

Unit banking: A restriction preventing banks from operating at more than one location; a prohibition against branch banking.

Unit of account: A measure by which prices and values are expressed; the common denominator of the price system; an essential property of money.

Universal banking: The ability of banks to offer an almost unlimited array of financial services.

User-cost approach: An approach

to measuring bank output that classifies a financial product as output if its net contribution to profits is greater than zero and as an input if its net contribution to profits is negative.

Utility: Satisfaction derived from consuming a good or service.

Value-added approach: An approach to measuring bank output that considers outputs to be those categories of financial products that contribute the most value to the bank's operations.

Value of the marginal product of labor: The valuation of labor's marginal product at current market prices, measured as the marginal product of labor times the selling price of output per unit.

Variable-rate assets (VRAs): Assets that can be rolled over (or renewed), and therefore repriced, during the bank's planning horizon.

Variable-rate liabilities (VRLs): Liabilities that can be renewed, and therefore repriced, during the bank's planning period.

Vault cash: Currency held by a depository institution.

Wage indexation: The pegging of wages to prices, so that wages automatically adjust to changes in prices.

Waiting costs: The costs that an individual incurs while waiting to make an exchange for a desired good or service.

Wealth: Net worth; the value of assets minus liabilities (debt) at a given moment in time.

Wire transfers: Transfers of funds between individuals or firms accomplished through electronic transmissions over wire or cable networks or telephone lines.

World index funds: Groupings of financial assets of different national origin whose variations in returns tend to offset one another.

Yield curve: The relationship that exists on a specific date between nominal interest rates earned by different bonds with similar characteristics but with different maturities.

Yield to maturity: The rate of return that would be earned by holding a bond to maturity. It reflects the bond price, coupon interest earnings, and any capital gain or loss resulting from holding the bond to maturity.

Zero-coupon bond: A security that pays interest in the form of an agreed-upon price appreciation, rather than through regular coupon payments.

Zero funds gap: The situation in which a bank's ratio of variable-rate assets to total assets equals its ratio of variable-rate liabilities to total liabilities.

Zombie thrifts: S&Ls that technically are insolvent but that, because of regulatory inaction, continue to operate.

Name Index

Subject Index